ספר טהרת הקדש

THE LAWS AND CONCEPTS OF NIDDAH

Rabbi Zvi Sobolofsky

THE LAWS
AND CONCEPTS OF
NIDDAH

•

ספר טהרת הקדש

The Michael Scharf Publication Trust of
Yeshiva University Press
Rabbi Isaac Elchanan Theological Seminary

The RIETS Practical Halakhah Series

Rabbi Daniel Z. Feldman, Series Editor

Maggid Books

The Laws and Concepts of Niddah

First Edition 2010

The Michael Scharf Publication Trust
of Yeshiva University Press

Maggid Books
An Imprint of Koren Publishers Jerusalem Ltd.

POB 8531, New Milford, CT 06776-8531, USA
& POB 2455, London W1A 5WY, England
& POB 4044, Jerusalem 91040, Israel
www.korenpub.com

ISBN 978 1 59264 325 7, *hardcover*

A CIP catalogue record for this title is
available from the British Library.

אשר זעליג וייס
כגן 8
פעיה"ק ירושלם ת"ו

בס"ד

ה' תשרי תשע"א

הן ראיתי את ספרו החשוב על הלכות נדה של ידי"נ המאור הגדול מעוז ומגדול הרה"ג המצויין, המופלג בתורה ובכל מדה נכונה ר' צבי סבלפסקי שליט"א, ראש ישיבה בישיבת רבנו יצחק אלחנן ורב קהילת אור תורה טינעק. ראיתי ושמחתי בלבי כי זה שנים שמכיר אני את מחבר ספר זה, ורב גובריה עד למאד גם בהרבצת תורה לתלמידים וגם בהוראה למעשה, ע"כ שמחתי בראותי מעשה ידיו להתפאר בספר מצויין זה.

על אף שמרוב טרדות המועדים בלימוד ובהוראה לא עלה בידי לעיין הרבה בגוף הספר, בטוחני שספר זה יהיה לתועלת גדולה, בין ללומדים הלכות אלה, ובין לאלה שעוסקים בהוראה למעשה.

ברכתי להרה"ג המחבר היקר שליט"א שהוא סמל ודמות באהבת תורה ובמידותיו התרומיות, שרבים יהנו לאורו שיזרח ויאיר עד לביאת גואל צדק במהרה בימינו.

באהבה רבה
וברכת גמח"ט
אשר וייס

הרב צבי שכטר
ראש ישיבה וראש כולל
ישיבת רבינו יצחק אלחנן

Rabbi Hershel Schachter
24 Bennett Avenue
New York, New York 10033
(212) 795-0630

מכתב ברכה

המפורסמות א"צ ראי', ודבר ידוע
ומפורסם הוא שהב' ידידנו ויקירנו הרה"ר צבי
סובולופסקי נ"י, המשמש כבר כמה שנים כר"מ
אצלנו בישיבה, מאוד מצליח בשיעוריו, בין
בשיעורי פלפול ובין בשיעורי הלכה, בין בישיבה
ובין אצל הבעה"ב, וכבוד מלכים - חקר דבר,
ויפה עשה שסידר להדפיס את שיעוריו לשו"ע
הל' נדה, שיועילו אל אלו שמחוץ לכתלי הישיבה
ליהנות מתורתו. ויה"ר שימשיך הקב"ה להרבות
את גבולו בתלמידים, ויפוצו מעיינותיו חוצה.

בברכה,
צבי שכטר
אלול שנת תש"ע.

Tel: 548-4765

YOUNG ISRAEL OF RIVERDALE

4502 HENRY HUDSON PARKWAY EAST
RIVERDALE, NEW YORK 10471

תשרי תשע"א

Mordechai Willig, Rabbi

שחורות כעורב, פרשיות של תורה, אף על פי שנראות
כאילו הן כעורות ושחורות לאמרן ברבים, כגון הלכות נדה,
הרי הן ערבות עלי (ויקרא רבה יט, ג).

באתי ומחזיק טובה לכב' הרה"ג ר' צבי סרלופסקי שליט"א,
שמלמד הלכות נדה ברבים שנים רבות, באופן ברור
וצנוע, בקהלות בטינק, בישיבתנו, ועוד. וזכיתי לשמוע
סידרת שיעורים במקוה זה שהוקלטו וזכו לתפוצה רבה.
ועכשיו סגנון הרצאתו הערבה והבהירה יוצא לאור
בדפוס לתועלת הרבים מטעם ישיבתנו ומכון להוצאת
ספרים של ישה, בעריכת מפורסמנו, רב ומחבר מוכשר,
הר"ר דניאל פלדמן. ומאד נהניתי לעבור על הספר,
והגם שזכינו לספרים רבים בלשון המדוברת בהלכות נדה,
יש בו תרומה חדשה למי שמבקש ללמוד בדרך של המחבר
שליט"א, מן המקורות בגמרא וראשונים, דרך השלחן ערוך
ונושאי כליו ועד לפוסקי זמננו. זכות מיוחדת יש לקהלתנו
שגדל בו הגאון המחבר שליט"א ודנין בו, מקצת ידיעתו. ויהי
רצון שיקויים הר"ר דר' שליט"א ימשיך ללמוד וללמד ולהורות
לתלמידיו ולמעריציו הרבים שנים רבות מתוך נחת בריאות והרחבה.
בברכה ועתירה מרדכי ווילג

Contents

SECTION II: *KETAMIM*

SECTION III: EVALUATION AND *P'SAK*

SECTION IV: SPECIAL *GEZEIROT* AND UNIQUE SITUATIONS

SECTION V: THE PROCESS OF BECOMING *TEHORAH*

SECTION VI: *HARCHAKOT*

SECTION VII: *VESTOT*

SECTION VIII: *TEVILAH*

Foreword

It is with particular pride that we inaugurate the English language *halakhah le-ma'aseh* series of the RIETS division of the Michael Scharf Publication Trust of Yeshiva University Press with this timely and practical volume focused on the intricacies surrounding the laws of family purity.

The Talmud notes that the terminology employed for marriage – *kiddushin* – derives from the word *hekdesh* (see *Kiddushin* 2b), indicating that marriage is a sacred institution in the Jewish tradition. Our hope is that through diligent study of the laws contained in this volume, the sublime sanctity of the marital relationship will be further appreciated.

Approximately one year ago, we appointed Rabbi Daniel Feldman to the position of coordinator of the RIETS division of the Michael Scharf Publication Trust of Yeshiva University Press. Since that time he has spearheaded the publication of several scholarly volumes under this new banner, all providing illuminating Torah insights and commentary in the classical tradition. Rabbi Feldman is a gifted editor, accomplished author and true *mentsch* who has labored to ensure that these treasures of Torah be packaged and presented decorously.

Many *talmidim* have had the privilege of learning the laws of family purity from Rabbi Zvi Sobolofsky, a long-time friend, and brilliant *Rosh Yeshiva* at *Yeshivat Rabbenu Yitzchak Elchanan*. Rabbi Sobolofsky's lucid style comes across in this volume with the gentle spirit that epitomizes his refined character.

Finally, we acknowledge the encouragement and support of our *Nasi HaYeshiva,* President Richard Joel, our *Rosh HaYeshiva* Rabbi Dr. Norman Lamm, and our Dean Emeritus Rabbi Zevulun Charlop, in supporting the Torah scholarship that fills our *batei midrashot* daily and in fostering a sense of commitment among our *Rashei Yeshiva* to share this scholarship with the broader community. It should be remembered that the name of the original yeshiva entity that eventually merged into our Yeshiva was *Etz Chaim,* epitomizing that Torah is meant not only to be learned, but to be lived. With the publication of this volume, we continue that sacred legacy.

Rabbi Yona Reiss
Max and Marion Grill Dean of RIETS

Introduction

"והזרתם את בני ישראל מטומאתם"

'You should separate the Jewish People from their impurities.' (Vayikra 15:31)

The literal meaning of this *pasuk* refers to the *halakhot* concerning purity and impurity that pertain to the *Mishkan*. One must be exceedingly careful not to defile the sanctity of the *Mishkan* by entering in a state of impurity. Nevertheless, Chazal saw in this *pasuk* an additional meaning. We are taught (*Niddah* 63b) that this *pasuk* serves as the source for certain additional safeguards the *halakhah* requires in the realm of *Hilkhot Niddah* to prevent violations of the *halakhah* proper. Although there is a halakhic dispute concerning the status of the *halakhot* derived from this *pasuk*, as to whether they are actually *MiD'Orayta* or *MiD'Rabanan* (see Chapter 31 in the *sefer*), Chazal saw some connection between the literal interpretation of this *pasuk* concerning the *Mishkan* and the additional level referring to *Hilkhot Niddah*. What is the connection between these two seemingly unrelated areas of *halakhah*?

Chazal teach us that *"Ish ve-ishah, zakhu, Shekhinah beineihem"*. If a man and woman merit it, the Divine Presence dwells in their midst. The term *Shekhinah* is an obvious reference to the *Mishkan* and the area in which Hashem's Presence dwells. If a couple has the ability to create a place for the dwelling of the *Shekhinah*, then, in a certain sense, the *halakhot* of the *Mishkan* apply to that couple. Halakhic standards of purity are absolutely essential in maintaining the sanctity of the actual *Mishkan*. Similarly, the *halakhot* of *Taharat HaMishpachah* are indispensable to the creation of a dwelling place for Hashem in each Jewish home. Purity necessary for the Presence of Hashem must be preserved with the utmost care. We are granted the awesome responsibility and privilege of hosting Hashem's Presence in our midst both in the actual *Mishkan* and in our homes. An absolute commitment to and knowledge of the *halakhot* of *taharah* are necessary to enable the *Shekhinah* to be present.

It is with these thoughts that I thank *HaKadosh Barukh Hu* for enabling me to publish this *sefer, Taharat HaKodesh,* about *Hilkhot Niddah*. As the title indicates, the subject matter focuses on the preservation of purity within the household. I can only hope and pray that this *sefer* will help others in their study and observance of these *halakhot*, thereby enhancing the Presence of *HaKadosh Barukh Hu* in all of our homes. This *sefer* endeavors to present these *halakhot*, beginning with the *sugyot* in the *Gemara* through the *Rishonim*, the *Shulchan Arukh* and the later *poskim*. Modern day applications and new issues are raised, quoting the opinions of the *Gedolei HaPoskim* of our generation. As in all areas of *halakhah*, there are many issues that have different valid halakhic opinions. One should consult one's own *rav* for guidance in these areas.

For the past twenty-eight years I have had the privilege to learn and teach Torah in Yeshivat Rabbenu Yitzchak Elchanan. I originally learned many of the *sugyot* covered in this *sefer* as a *talmid* in the Yeshiva. I want to express a personal *hakarat ha-tov* to President Richard Joel for his tireless work on behalf of the Yeshiva. His vision to spread Torah in so many ways has enabled me to teach Torah through the publishing of this *sefer* by the Yeshiva under the auspices of RIETS Press, through the generosity of the Michael Scharf Publication Trust. I also want to thank Rabbi Dr. Norman Lamm, *Rosh Yeshiva* and Chancellor of our Yeshiva, who has guided us and continues to guide us as our Yeshiva spreads Torah throughout the world. Rabbi Zevulun Charlop, dean emeritus of

RIETS, has been a mentor to me personally, as well as to so many others who have benefited from his advice and encouragement throughout his years at Yeshiva. May Hashem continue to bless him to be a source of inspiration for all of us. I have had the pleasure of teaching Torah over the past two years under the guidance of Rabbi Yona Reiss, the present dean of RIETS. May we both merit to continue working together teaching Torah in our Yeshiva and beyond.

I can never adequately express my appreciation to my *rebbeim* who have taught me Torah and guided me throughout the years. I originally learned *Massekhet Niddah* as a *talmid* in the Marcos and Adina Katz Kollel of RIETS under the leadership of Rabbi Hershel Schachter. I had the *zekhut* to be in Rabbi Schachter's kollel and *shiur* for four years. Rabbi Schachter is a world renowned *posek* with whom I still have the honor of discussing halakhic issues.

As a *talmid* in Yeshiva and through growing up in his shul in Riverdale, NY, I have been a *talmid* of Rabbi Mordechai Willig for close to thirty years. He has not only been my formal *rebbe*, but I have been able to observe him as a *posek* and to spend countless hours discussing with him halakhic issues in so many areas. This *sefer* would never have come to fruition if not for the *shimush* in *Hilkhot Niddah* that I was able to have with him. Rabbi Schachter and Rabbi Willig are my links to our *Mesorah*, and for this I am eternally indebted to them.

In addition to my *shiurim* at Yeshiva, I am blessed to be the *rav* of Congregation Ohr HaTorah in Bergenfield, New Jersey. It is a true pleasure to teach Torah both in my shul and in the greater Bergenfield-Teaneck community. As a *rav*, I have had the opportunity to work together with many other *rabbanim* to enhance the observance of Torah in our community. Particularly in the realm of *Hilkhot Niddah*, I have had many opportunities to consult with Rabbi Yaakov Neuburger and Rabbi Michael Taubes, both experienced *rabbonim* and *poskim* in this field.

There are several individuals who are directly responsible for my ability to spread Torah in our community. Dr. Yitchak Belizon has been the force behind much of the Torah I have been privileged to teach in Teaneck and Bergenfield over the past twelve years. From printing *marei mekomot* to organizing *shiurim*, he has been a real partner in the spreading of Torah. The Congregation Bnai Yeshurun Beis Medrash Program, in which I have participated for twelve years, continues to inspire the entire Bergen County community because of the dedication of Jackie Feigenbaum and Henry Orlinsky.

Henry Orlinsky has been a true friend and supporter of so many of my Torah projects. May Hashem continue to bless Henry, his wife Mindy, their children and grandchildren, Henry's parents and Mindy's mother with many happy and healthy years.

The writing of this *sefer* could never have taken place without the work of my esteemed colleague, friend and *chavruta*, Rabbi Daniel Feldman. Rabbi Feldman worked tirelessly to present my *shiurim* on *Hilkhot Niddah* in a book form. His prolific ability to present Torah material in English in a clear and concise manner has enabled him to become an accomplished author and editor of contemporary Torah literature. May Hashem continue to grant him the opportunities to advance Torah at our Yeshiva, in Etz Chaim of Teaneck, and worldwide.

In the realm of *Hilkhot Niddah*, it is often critical for a *rav* to consult with a physician. Rabbi Dr. Zalman Levine, a reproductive endocrinologist, has made himself available to me on many occasions to explain the pertinent medical information necessary to *pasken* in the area of *Hilkhot Niddah*. Rabbi Dr. Levine, an accomplished *talmid chakham* and an expert in his medical field, has graciously agreed to review this entire *sefer* and has offered many suggestions that have been incorporated into this work. His kindness and sensitivity in assisting couples are well known in our community and beyond. May he continue to serve as a loyal *shaliach* of Hashem in this capacity.

As this *sefer* is about to be published, I look back to all those people in my life who enabled me to reach this wonderful occasion. I can never adequately thank my loving parents, Stanley and Bella Sobolofsky. The love and devotion they have given, and continue to give, to me and my family knows no bounds. It is their encouragement and assistance that is ultimately responsible for this *sefer*. Their steadfast commitment to Torah and *Mitzvot* that they received from their parents has been my link to a *mesorah* of countless generations of *shomrei Torah U'Mitzvot*. May Hashem continue to bless them to reap the *nachat* they so surely deserve.

I was welcomed into the home and hearts of my dear in-laws, Michael and Bracha Samet. Their love and assistance have enabled me to continue to learn and teach Torah over these past sixteen years. I can never thank them enough for raising my wife and her brothers in the spirit of *kedushah* and *taharah* they received from their parents. May Hashem grant them continued *nachat* from their children and grandchildren.

I cannot even begin to express my feelings of gratitude to my wife, Efrat. She has whole-heartedly encouraged me in all of my endeavors to learn and teach Torah. Rabbi Akiva's legendary words to his students about his wife, that "*sheli ve-shelachem shelah hi* – my Torah and your Torah are hers" can truly be applied here as well. Besides her otherwise full time roles as wife, mother, rebbetzin and social worker, she has taken upon herself with indescribable devotion to help facilitate *shiddukhim*. In this role, and as a *kallah* teacher, she has personally enabled many couples to build their homes on the pillars of *kedushah* and *taharah*. I can only ask *HaKadosh Barukh Hu* to continue to bless us as we raise our children Tova Gittel, Meir Yakov, Avraham Zev, and Blima. May each of them have the *zekhut* to serve Hashem for many happy and healthy years.

Chazal quote the *tefillot* of Rabbi Nechunia Ben Hakana that were recited before entering the *Beit HaMidrash* and upon leaving. Both of these *tefillot* are appropriate at this point. May Hashem assist me in my learning and teaching of His Torah. May I be able to guide His people to observe the Torah properly. "*Modeh ani li-fanekha she-samta chelki mi-yoshvei Beit HaMidrash* – Thank you Hashem for granting me the opportunity to be among those who dwell in the *Beit HaMidrash*." Chazal teach us that since the destruction of the *Beit HaMikdash*, Hashem's Presence can only be found in the four *amot* of *halakhah*. It has been my greatest privilege to be in these four *amot*. May the merit of the study and observance of *Hilkhot Niddah* enable Hashem's Presence to dwell in all of our homes.

May we all merit seeing the rebuilding of the *Beit HaMikdash* so we can truly serve Hashem in holiness and purity.

Zvi Sobolofsky
21st of Elul, 5770

Editor's Preface

With gratitude tendered to the *Ribbono Shel Olam,* we present before the learning public the first volume of the RIETS Series of Practical Halakhah.

It is a particular honor that this first volume, on the laws and concepts of *Niddah* and *Tevilah,* is authored by one of our distinguished *Rashei Yeshiva,* Rav Zvi Sobolofsky. Rav Sobolofsky has met with great success as a *rebbe,* a *rav,* a *posek halakhah,* and a *marbitz Torah* in many venues, and it is an auspicious start to the series to be able to bring his Torah to print.

This series is one of many initiatives currently being undertaken at Rabbi Isaac Elchanan Theological Seminary (RIETS), an affiliate of Yeshiva University, as a new stage in our yeshiva's efforts to extend the teaching of Torah at a level that is both deep and wide: advanced and uncompromised in its content and substance, and broad in its accessibility and availability. In recent years, we have seen the release of a growing number of volumes of this initiative, both works written in the classical Hebrew style of the *beit ha-medrash* and in the modern English idiom that allows for an expanded range of communication.

This series, the RIETS Series of Practical Halakhah, endeavors to publish volumes, authored by the *Rashei Yeshiva* of RIETS, which will present the fundamentals of Jewish law together with their conceptual underpinnings. The goal is to convey the halakhic rulings together with an exploration of the process that brought about the conclusions, and to convey the experience of *Talmud Torah* in the sense of textual study, conceptual analysis, and practical application. In order to clarify this process for the reader, when a section of the text is focused more on conceptual analysis or explaining argumentation, rather than on halakhic practice, it is often set apart in a boxed section.

It is also our ideal that the volumes of this series, in addition to presenting the views of the individual author, will provide a perspective on the opinions of the broader RIETS faculty. To that end, we have invited commentary from additional RIETS *rebbeim* who have extensive involvement in teaching the subject matter of this *sefer*, and we are pleased to be able to present notes and rulings from Rav Hershel Schachter, Rav Mordechai Willig, and Rav Yaakov Neuburger.

In order to ensure the accuracy of the medical information in this volume, we have consulted with Rabbi Dr. Zalman Levine, a distinguished reproductive endocrinologist who is himself a RIETS *musmach*. The combination of medical expertise, Torah scholarship, and communal commitment that is the hallmark of his service to his patients and beyond is similarly reflected in his enthusiastic and gracious willingness to assist on this project. The portions of the text and of the footnotes that draw upon medical background were made possible because of his contribution.

We are profoundly grateful to the administration of RIETS for their stalwart guidance of our Yeshiva, and for their dedication in making Yeshivat Rabbenu Yitzchak Elchanan the magnificent center of Torah study and rabbinic training that it is. We are the fortunate beneficiaries of the tireless efforts of President Richard Joel; Rosh Hayeshiva and Chancellor Rav Norman Lamm; RIETS Dean Rav Yona Reiss, Dean Emeritus Rav Zevulun Charlop, and Rav Chaim Bronstein.

This volume is being published through the generosity of the Michael Scharf Publication Trust of Yeshiva University Press, and we express gratitude to Michael and Fiona Scharf for all of their work in bringing Torah literature to print under the auspices of Yeshiva University.

This volume began as a series of *shiurim* given at the RIETS Summer Kollel in Los Angeles, and benefited greatly from the meticulous notes of Rabbi David Berger. Further elucidation was added by Rabbi Ephraim Meth, with the assistance of Rabbis David Nachbar, Meshulam Twersky and Yaakov Werblowsky, and the manuscript was ehanced by the careful review of Rabbis Menachem Aryeh Geilchinsky, Simon Basallely, and Jonathan Feldman.

In order to aid the reader in studying the sources cited in the original, we have appended to the back of this volume a section containing many of the primary sources that are cited in the text. This section does not include every reference, and for considerations of space generally does not repeat sources that are brought earlier in the text. Nonetheless, it is hoped that is will prove a helpful supplement that will bring the reader closer to the direct experience of personally studying and analyzing the discussed topics. Thanks are extended to Rabbis Nosson Rich and Rafi Rosenblum for their work in compiling this section, and to the Bar Ilan Responsa Project for allowing their materials to be utilized in its composition. Finally, a tremendous thank you to Matthew Miller and the wonderful staff at Koren for all of their work in ensuring that the volume is brought to print in the most beautiful way possible.

It is our fervent wish that this volume and those that follow it will add to the realization of our yeshiva's mission, to study, teach, clarify and spread *HaKadosh Barukh Hu*'s holy Torah, *le-hagdilah u-le-ha'adirah.*

Daniel Z. Feldman
9th Tishrei, 5771

Section 1: Establishing The Status of *Niddah*

1.

Determining the Status of *Niddah*

Any study of the laws of *niddah* must determine from the outset a most basic question: what, in *halakhah,* gives a woman the status of *niddah.* This status has two consequences. The first, that the woman becomes ritually impure, is less practical in the current era. The second, that she becomes forbidden to her husband, is the main practical issue in this realm.

The status of *niddah* is, at least in theory, a result of "seeing blood" (*re'iyat dam*). Interpreting the verse,[1] "When a woman has a discharge – her discharge from her flesh being blood", the Talmud[2] derives the principle of *hargashah* (lit. feeling, sensation) from the word "from her flesh," which teaches that a woman is considered by the Torah to be a *niddah* only when she experiences both *hargashah* and the sight of blood. Any blood seen without a *hargashah* is termed a *ketem* (stain), which confers *niddah* status on a Rabbinical level, but not on a Biblical level.

1. *Vayikra* 15:19.
2. *Niddah* 57b.

However, the notion of *hargashah* requires clarification. Halakhic authorities offer at least three definitions of *hargashah*:

a) The Rambam[3] writes that *hargashah* is a form of shaking.

Later authorities discussed how to interpret this position. R. Moshe (Maharam) Shick[4] understood this broadly, writing that the Rambam is referring to any symptom that usually *precedes* a period, such as cramps or soreness in the legs. Most authorities, however, assume that the Rambam is referring to symptoms that usually occur *at the time* of menstruation, not hours or days beforehand. In practice, the Maharam Shick's broader definition has not gained acceptance.

b) The *Terumat HaDeshen*[5] defines *hargashah* as the sensation a woman feels when *niftach pi ha-mekor,* "the mouth of the uterus is opened."

c) The *Noda BiYehudah*[6] defines *hargashah* as "*zivat davar lach*", or the sensation of moisture emerging from the body.

> In support of his position, he brings a proof from the Talmud,[7] which derives from the word "in her flesh" that a woman can become a *niddah* while the blood is still inside of her, without knowing it. Specifically, a woman becomes a *niddah* when blood flows from the uterus to the vaginal area.[8] At the same time, "in her flesh" teaches that *hargashah* is a prerequisite for *niddut*. Just as "her flesh" refers to the vaginal area in the first *halakhah,* that even blood in that area makes her *teme'ah* (lit., impure), it refers to that area in the second *halakhah,* that she must experience *hargashah* in the vaginal area. Neither cramps nor muscular movement occur in that area; *hargashah* must therefore be the feeling of moisture flowing from one place to another.

3. *Hilkhot Issurei Bi'ah* 5:17.
4. *Responsa Maharam Shick,* YD 182.
5. *Responsa* 246, cited in *Shulchan Arukh* YD 190:1.
6. *Responsa* YD, *Mahadura Kama,* 55; cited in *Pitchei Teshuvah,* YD 183:1.
7. *Niddah* 57b.
8. In this, the requirements for *niddah* status differ from the requirements for "*ba'al keri*" status (one who becomes unclean due to a bodily emission); a *niddah* need not see blood leaving her body to attain the status of *niddah.* but a *ba'al keri* must see an emission leave his body to become impure.

R. Ya'akov Loerbaum, in his *Chavot Da'at,*[9] modifies the *Noda BiYehudah*'s opinion. Whereas the *Noda BiYehudah* maintains that *hargashah* is the sensation of blood flowing into the vaginal area of the body, the *Chavot Da'at* asserts that *hargashah* is the sensation of blood flowing out of the uterine area.

The following is his analysis: The Talmud concludes that a woman becomes a *niddah* when blood flows from the *bayit ha-penimi* (lit. inner house, fig. the uterine area) to the *bayit ha-chitzon* (lit. outer house, fig. vaginal area).[10] The *Noda BiYehudah,* however, claims that *hargashah* may occur in the *bayit ha-chitzon.* This presents a chronological problem: how is she considered a *niddah* on a Biblical level before *hargashah* occurs? In other words, since only sight of blood with *hargashah* creates a *niddah,* and the *Noda BiYehudah* places the *hargashah* after the woman is already said to be a *niddah,* how can his placement of the *hargashah* be correct? In view of this question, the *Chavot Da'at* concludes that although the *hargashah* of a flow of moisture is a valid *hargashah,* that is only true when it is felt inside the *bayit ha-penimi* or on the way out.

While the *Chavot Da'at* modifies the *Noda BiYehudah*'s opinion, the *Chatam Sofer*[11] rejects it altogether, asserting that no authority prior to the *Noda BiYehudah* ever suggested moisture flow as a valid *hargashah.* R. Ovadiah Yosef[12] concurred and advocated following the *Chatam Sofer* in rejecting the *Noda BiYehudah.* However, R. Moshe Feinstein[13] took a stringent position, and wrote that that practice should be in accordance with the *Noda BiYehudah.*

In practice, all of the above positions cause some difficulty, as it is commonly the case that women experience none of the above indicators. This reality would seem to call into question whether a contemporary woman is ever given the status of *niddah* on a Biblical level, in the absence of the required *hargashah.*

9. 190:1.
10. The status of the cervix will be discussed.
11. *Responsa,* YD 145, 153.
12. *Taharat HaBayit* 1:4.
13. *Responsa Iggerot Moshe,* YD IV, 17.

However, this is an untenable conclusion. Contemporary rabbinic consensus is to assume that a period is accompanied by a *hargashah,* but that it is either not perceived or it is misperceived. This notion is based on a Talmudic statement that indicates that *hargashot* are not in fact always perceived by the women experiencing them.[14]

As such, the practice has developed to adopt the following guidelines in evaluating the status of a woman who has experienced bleeding:

1. Whenever a woman has a regular period, it is assumed that a *hargashah* has taken place, and she is a *niddah* on a Biblical level.
2. Whenever there is a "significant *flow* of blood," it is also assumed that a *hargashah* has taken place, and she is a *niddah* on a Biblical level.
3. Whenever the blood is not a stream or flow, but rather just a *stain* or a *spot,* it is considered a *ketem.*

The distinction between a flow and a stain or spot is difficult to define, and the terminology is not described in the classical halakhic sources. As such, intuition, experience, and common sense play a large role in the evaluation. A normal period clearly creates the status of *niddah,* and a small spot or stain clearly does not. However, when a woman is on medication, or nursing, or stopping her medication, she might have experiences which are equally describable as a "light flow," or as "heavy staining." A related question concerns a woman who sees a very small amount of blood without classic *hargashah* – usually considered a *ketem* – in a context which makes it likely to be a biological period, either as indicated by timing or by a doctor's assessment. This case is subject to a debate among *poskim* as to whether this constitutes a question on *niddah* on a Biblical level. These situations require individual judgment. In these matters, an inclination toward stringency is appropriate, because this is an uncertainty regarding a Biblical status, which generally demands stringency (*safek D'Orayta le-chumra*).

14. *Niddah* 57b. See *Arukh HaShulchan,* YD 183:61, and see also R. Mordechai Willig, in *Beit Yitzchak.* XXXIX, pp. 323–333.

2.

The Status of a *Hargashah* without Blood

I. INTRODUCTION

The inverse case of that described above would be a situation in which a woman has a *hargashah*, but does not see blood. As explained above, both *hargashah* and seeing of blood are necessary for *niddah* status; accordingly, it would seem that the woman is *tehorah* (lit., pure). However, one of the *Rishonim*, the *Terumat HaDeshen*,[1] maintained otherwise, and ruled that a *hargashah* by itself is sufficient to render the woman *teme'ah*.

His position is based on a ruling of the Talmud:[2]

> If a couple had intercourse and the woman saw blood later, and there was *hargashah* at the time of intercourse, they must bring a *korban chattat* (a sacrifice brought in the event of an inadvertent, definite transgression).

1. *Responsa*, 246.
2. *Niddah* 57b.

The *Terumat HaDeshen* understands this ruling as follows: if blood was found later without a *hargashah,* they would not need a *korban,* because one cannot be sure if that blood was there at the time of intercourse or if it appeared afterward. However, if there was *hargashah* at the time of intercourse, we assume that blood must have come out at that point, and therefore even if they find that blood later, they must bring a *korban.*

It seems from here that the experience of *hargashah* indicates that blood was present. Ordinarily, however, *hargashah* serves a different function: to indicate that blood that was sighted is indeed *niddah* blood. In this case, however, the *hargashah* is being taken as an indication of the very presence of the blood at the time in question.

In other words, the *Terumat HaDeshen* concludes that there are two laws of *hargashah*: 1) *hargashah* classifies blood sighted as *niddah* blood, and not merely a *ketem*; 2) *hargashah* creates a presumption that blood was sighted in the first place.[3]

There is, however, a problem with this proof. In the above case, the woman felt a *hargashah* and later, she indeed found blood. This cannot be sufficient to teach us anything about a case where there she felt a *hargashah* without seeing blood at all.

The *Terumat HaDeshen* cites another proof:

The Talmud[4] rules that a woman must check herself at the *veset* time, the point in her cycle when she commonly finds blood. If she did not check herself at the *veset* time, and later performs a *bedikah* (internal examination) that shows her to be *tehorah,* her status before the *bedikah* requires determination. The Talmud rules that since *vestot* are only Rabbinic (i.e., the Torah does not mandate that the arrival of *veset* time is taken as definite proof that the woman saw blood), failure to perform the *bedikah* does not render her *teme'ah.*

3. As the Talmud mandates the bringing of a *korban,* it is clear that this presumption is effective on the level of Torah law.
4. *Niddah* 16a.

Had *vestot* been of Biblical command (i.e., that the Torah would deem the arrival of a woman's *veset* sufficient indication that she saw blood), she would be *teme'ah* even though she did not find that blood. Similarly, since the Torah mandates that *hargashah* creates a presumption that she saw blood, she is *teme'ah* even though she did not find that blood.

II. PRACTICAL RULING AND CONTEMPORARY APPLICATION

In determining the practical *halakhah,* it is noteworthy that the Rama, in his *Darkhei Moshe,*[5] and the *Radbaz*[6] argue on the proof from *veset,* asserting that the assumption that blood appeared at the *veset* time (had it been Biblically mandated), would certainly have been stronger than the assumption that blood accompanied a *hargashah.* Moreover, they note that the Talmud itself never deems *hargashah* without the sight of blood problematic.

However, the *Shulchan Arukh*[7] cites the *Terumat HaDeshen,* and the Rama[8] does not argue, even though in the *Darkhei Moshe* he questions that position. Therefore, it is assumed, in practice, that the *Terumat HaDeshen* is correct; if a woman feels a *hargashah,* does a *bedikah,* but does not find blood, she is nonetheless a *niddah.*

In determining the type of *hargashah* that would create this presumption that blood was present, we return to our earlier discussion as to the definition of *hargashah.* It would be logical to assume that the *Terumat HaDeshen*'s and Rambam's definitions of *hargashah,* as shaking or as the uterus' mouth's opening, create this presumption.[9] The *Noda BiYehudah*'s definition of *hargashah,* as the feeling of moisture leaving the body, is more open to question. The *Chatam Sofer*[10] argues that even if one believes that the feeling of moisture is a valid *hargashah* to deem

5. *Yoreh De'ah* 188:2.
6. *Responsa* I, 149.
7. *Yoreh De'ah* 190:1.
8. Ibid.; also see Rama 188:1.
9. There are conflicting implications within the *Pitchei Teshuvah* as to whether the Rambam's opinion is included within this assumption; compare YD 190:1 and 190:4.
10. *Responsa,* YD 150; cited in *Pitchei Teshuvah,* YD 190:6.

blood that has been seen as Biblically *tamei,* it is not a valid *hargashah* to create the presumption that blood was present.

Practically, whenever a woman has a *hargashah* of shaking or uterine "mouth-opening", she is a *niddah,* even if she finds no blood. The *Pitchei Teshuvah*[11] rules, as the *Terumat HaDeshen* himself does, that if she checks and finds liquid of a color that is considered *tahor,* we attribute the *hargashah* to that liquid emerging, and she is therefore *tehorah.*[12] Contemporary women never feel the "mouth-opening", and rarely feel shaking; and the *Chatam Sofer* has asserted that the feeling of moisture cannot create the presumption of blood's presence. Therefore, the *Terumat HaDeshen*'s ruling is rarely applicable today.

Some *poskim* recommend that when a woman has some kind of a feeling of moisture, even though this is not really included in the *Terumat HaDeshen*'s *hargashah,* she should do a *bedikah.* In light of the fact that the *Terumat HaDeshen*'s ruling has only tenuous support from the Talmud, and in light of the fact that the case described by the *Terumat HaDeshen* rarely occurs in modern times, it is questionable whether contemporary women who feel *hargashot* have to check at all. There are three opinions on this matter:

1) The *Chokhmat Adam*[13] writes that if a woman knows she often gets *hargashot* and she checks and finds either no blood or clear discharges, she should not have to check anymore. Hence, all a woman must do is check herself after a *hargashah* on three separate occasions. If she finds nothing, it is assumed that all her *hargashot* do not render her *teme'ah.* She is therefore never again obligated to do a *bedikah* after *hargashah.*

2) R. Moshe Feinstein[14] maintains that the *Chokhmat Adam*'s ruling is too easy to subvert. If women check themselves three times during pregnancy, they will certainly not find blood, but this should not exempt them from checking after *hargashot* at other points in their cycle. Similarly, if a women checks for blood during the middle of her cycle, this

11. *Yoreh De'ah* 190:6.
12. See also *Shulchan Arukh* 188:1.
13. 113:3.
14. *Responsa Iggerot Moshe* YD IV, 17:9.

should not be sufficient to prove that a *hargashah* later in her cycle does not indicate the presence of blood. Accordingly, R. Feinstein suggests that women should do *bedikot* three times at each point in their cycle.

3) Some *poskim* argue that women are not required to perform *bedikot* under these circumstances at all. In earlier times, it was possible for a woman to bleed and not know about it, because the blood may have been wiped away or may have fallen to the ground. In contemporary times, however, a woman's underwear will indicate any bleeding, and is a sufficient, standing *bedikah*.

3.

The "Uterus Opening" and its Ramifications: Childbirth, Gynecological Exams, and Related Questions

I. INTRODUCTION

Beyond the issue of *hargashah,* the question must be considered as to the effect of the "opening of the uterus", a reality that may be created by events such as the initiation of childbirth, or the performance of certain gynecological procedures. The possibility exists that these 'openings", even without evident bleeding, may create a status of *niddah.*

This possibility emerges from a discussion in the Talmud[1] as follows:

1. *Niddah* 21a–b.

A dispute is recorded concerning a woman who discharges a piece of flesh. The *Chakhamim* rule that if there was blood together with the discharge, she is a *niddah*; if there was no blood, she is not a *niddah*. R. Yehudah maintains that she is a *niddah* even if she does not find blood, because "*ei efshar li-petichat ha-kever bi-lo dam*", it is impossible for the uterus to open without bleeding. *Halakhah* normally follows the *Chakhamim*, as the Rambam[2] does in this case; but since there is a universally accepted Talmudic discussion[3] that assumes R. Yehudah's position, most *Rishonim* rule like R. Yehudah. Practically, the *Rama*[4] rules stringently, like R. Yehudah, as well.

II. DEFINING "OPENING OF THE UTERUS"

However, defining "opening of the uterus" remains a question. Elsewhere, the Talmud[5] rules that one may desecrate *Shabbat* to help a pregnant woman after she experiences "opening of the uterus", and thus establishes herself as one in need of medical care. The Talmud defines this term vis-à-vis *Shabbat*; it remains to be determined whether those definitions can be applied to the laws of *niddah*.

Three definitions are offered in the Talmud for this term:

1. The "opening" occurs when blood begins to gush. This definition is irrelevant to the laws of *niddah*, because once blood begins to gush, the woman is a *niddah* even without the uterus' opening.
2. The "opening" occurs when the woman sits on the birthing stool.
3. The "opening" occurs when the woman's friends have to help her walk.

Both of these last two definitions are unclear as to their relevance, since in contemporary times birthing stools and friends helping to walk are not

2. *Hilkhot Issurei Bi'ah* 5:13.
3. *Niddah* 66a.
4. *Yoreh De'ah* 194:2.
5. *Shabbat* 129a.

part of the childbirth process. As such, the practical application of this concept is the subject of at least three different interpretations, as follows:

1) The *Nachalat Shivah*[6] quotes a tradition from "the women of Poland" that whenever a woman goes into labor and has difficulty walking on her own, even if she does not deliver her baby for a few weeks, she is forbidden to her husband until she waits *shivah nekiyim* (seven clean days) and immerses in the *mikveh*. This tradition is a combination of the latter two opinions mentioned above about "opening of the uterus" regarding *Shabbat,* as applied to the laws of *niddah*. Most *poskim* do not accept this tradition, for two independent reasons, which form the bases for the other two opinions.

2) The *Sidrei Taharah*[7] accepts the premise that one may derive the laws of *niddah* from the laws of Shabbat. He rejects, however, the supposition that a woman can experience "opening of the uterus" without soon giving birth. In the *Nachalat Shivah*'s case, the woman must not have experienced "opening of the uterus," since she did not deliver until weeks later. Hence, if a woman goes into labor and has difficulty walking, she is forbidden to her husband lest she soon deliver. If she does indeed deliver, it would be the case that she is a *niddah,* acquiring that status from the beginning of the process, at a point comparable to the "birthing stool" stage. Only if she does not give birth do we determine retroactively that she was not a *niddah,* as she has not actually experienced opening of the uterus.

3) The *Chavot Da'at*[8] questions the comparison between the *Shabbat* and *niddah*. He argues that the "opening of the uterus" means different things in different places. One may desecrate the Shabbat for a woman who experiences "opening of the uterus" even if nothing has yet emerged, since such a woman is classified as one in need of medical care. This definition is consistent with the case presented by the Talmud in *Shabbat,* where "opening of the uterus" occurs without anything emerging. In contrast, a woman is only a *niddah* if her uterus opens and something emerges. This definition is consistent with the case presented

6. II, #9, cited in *Pitchei Teshuvah* 194:8.
7. 194:25.
8. 194:1.

by the Talmud in *Massekhet Niddah,* in which a piece of flesh was discharged when the uterus opened. In effect, the *Chavot Da'at* maintains that it is entirely meaningless, for the purposes of *niddah,* that a woman is in the process of giving birth; if the child comes out, then she is a *niddah,* but if the child does not come out at that time, she is not a *niddah.*

Even if the *Nachalat Shivah*'s ruling is accepted, it is nonetheless difficult to pinpoint when the stage of "going into labor" begins. Similarly, we cannot identify the point when the woman has difficulty walking independently, since contemporary women often receive epidural anesthesia that takes away the pain of labor. In such cases, the woman cannot walk because she is on the epidural, and this time need not correlate with any stage of labor.

In light of this reality, many authorities feel that one may treat this law leniently, for a combination of reasons:

1. The Rambam's ruling that "opening of the uterus" alone does not make women *niddot;*
2. The *Chavot Da'at*'s belief that uterine opening, when nothing emerges, does not suffice to render women *niddot;*
3. The reality that even if the opinions of these two eminent *poskim* are rejected, it can never be certain that the woman has reached a stage of labor equivalent to "opening of the uterus";
4. The fact that potential transgressions of *hilkhot niddah* involved during childbirth are often not those of a Biblical nature (or are of lesser severity); generally, they only impact on whether or not the couple must observe *harchakot.*

When the woman's water breaks, blood is often present, rendering the woman a *niddah.* It is important to note that blood seen during childbirth is only considered to be *niddah* blood if it is produced during the process of childbirth itself. Often, a day or two before the woman gives birth, she will excrete some mildly bloody mucous. *Poskim* assume that this mucous is treated as blood from a wound and not *niddah* blood, because this blood comes from capillaries in the cervix as it readies itself for childbirth, and not from the uterus.

R. Moshe Feinstein[9] ruled that if a pregnant woman goes to the doctor at the beginning of her ninth month, and is told that her cervix is one centimeter dilated, she has not experienced "opening of the uterus" and she remains permitted to her husband. This ruling appears to be based on the fact that women are often somewhat dilated a month before delivery, yet no halakhic authority ever required them to check for such dilation, out of fear that it renders them forbidden to their husbands.

III. OPENING FROM WITHIN AND FROM WITHOUT

The *Noda BiYehudah*[10] notes that the Talmud only discussed a case when a discharge of flesh causes an "opening of the uterus" from within; it remains to be determined, however, what the status would be if something from outside comes in and causes an "opening of the uterus". The *Noda BiYehudah* took a stringent view on this question, because the Talmud does not differentiate between causes for uterine openings. This opinion is supported by a comment of the *Beit Yosef*:

The Talmud records that when blood emerged from the uterus via a tube, without touching the woman's flesh, the woman is *tehorah.*[11] The *Beit Yosef*[12] asks: notwithstanding the status of that blood, why should the insertion of a tube itself not cause an "opening of the uterus" and render the woman a *niddah*? He answers his question by asserting that "opening of the uterus" refers only to a large opening, while tubes only creates a minor opening. It is, however, clear from the *Beit Yosef* that if something akin to a tube, which causes an opening from without, causes a significant opening, it would render the woman a *niddah.*

Some *Acharonim,* including the *Chazon Ish,*[13] question the *Noda BiYehudah*'s premise. They note that it is possible to argue that when the uterus is opened from without, it does not render the woman a *niddah,* and thus to claim, in opposition to the *Beit Yosef* and the *Noda BiYehudah,*

9. YD II,76. See also *Shiurei Shevet HaLevi* 192, 2, 4.
10. *Tinyana,* YD 120; cited in *Pitchei Teshuvah* YD 194:4.
11. *Niddah* 21b; see below, Chap. 4.
12. YD 188:3, s.v. *ve-davka.* See also *Tosafot, Niddah* 22b, s.v. *liflog.*
13. YD 83:1.

that a tube inserted into the uterus does not render the woman a *niddah* because it does not cause the uterus to open from within.

The *Noda BiYehudah* suggests that when a doctor inserts his finger into the vaginal area, this may cause a halakhically significant "opening of the uterus." Later *poskim*[14] argue that this is no different than a standard *bedikah,* where the woman wraps a cloth around her finger and inserts it into the vaginal area. Just as a *bedikah* does not induce *niddut,* as it does not go far enough towards the uterus to cause a uterine opening, a doctor's finger does not induce *niddut* either.

However, if a medical instrument longer than a finger is inserted into the vaginal area, it may render the woman a *niddah,* if it is large enough and if it reaches far enough.

Regarding size, we have seen the *Beit Yosef* who argues that a tube is too thin to create "opening of the uterus." The Vilna Gaon,[15] basing his opinion on a *Mishnah,*[16] rules that an "opening of the uterus" is a measurement that can be understood as approximately 15 mm in diameter. The instruments most commonly used currently are smaller than 15 mm, so even if the *Noda BiYehudah* is correct that a doctor's checking the vaginal area renders women *niddot,* many contemporary medical procedures do not reach the necessary threshold to do so.

Regarding the instrument's reach, the uterus halakhically begins at the point between the *bayit ha-penimi* ("inner house") and the *bayit ha-chitzon* ("outer house"), between the place where blood found does not render women *niddot* and the place where blood does render them *niddot.* The uterus is part of the *bayit ha-penimi.* For the purposes of *halakhah,* the cervix might be treated as an independent organ that stretches from the vaginal area to well inside the uterus.[17] The blood from the uterus

14. See *Pitchei Teshuvah* 194:4.
15. *Bi'ur HaGra,* YD 188:23.
16. *Ohalot* 7:4, where the phrase "*petichat ha-kever*" also appears.
17. From a medical and anatomical perspective, however, the cervix is actually part of the uterus, and is in fact the long entryway of the uterus that protrudes into the vaginal canal. The uterus is comprised of two parts, termed in Latin the "cervix uteri" (uterine neck), and the "corpus uteri" (uterine body). While the cervical portion of the uterus is functionally distinct from the body of the uterus, anatomically it is part of the same organ.

travels through the cervix to the vaginal area and eventually leaves the body. It is unclear whether the cervix is part of the *bayit ha-penimi* or not. This question is important, because many gynecological procedures enter the cervix but do not enter the uterus. If the cervix is not part of the *bayit ha-penimi,* then these procedures do not create "opening of the uterus," and even use of an instrument wider than 15mm in that area will not be a problem. If the cervix is part of the *bayit ha-penimi,* then use of a 15 mm instrument there renders the woman a *niddah.* (R. Shlomo Zalman Auerbach ruled that the cervix is part of the *bayit ha-penimi.*[18])

In practice, every gynecological procedure must be analyzed independently to determine the size of the instrument being used, and how far into the body the instrument is inserted.

In sum, there are a few reasons to be lenient regarding the impact of medical procedures on a woman's *niddah* status: 1) the Rambam's ruling that the uterus can open without blood leaving; 2) the *Chazon Ish*'s observation that when the uterus is opened from outside, blood does not necessarily leave; 3) most gynecological instruments are less than 15mm in diameter; 4) even if the instrument is 15mm or larger in diameter, some procedures do not reach the area defined by many *poskim* as the uterine opening. In reality, the combination of the last two reasons results in most procedures being unproblematic, particularly as the more invasive the procedure, the more likely it is that a smaller instrument will be used. It is thus rare, although still possible, that a gynecological procedure will render a woman a *niddah* due to considerations of "opening of the uterus". When actual bleeding occurs, the question is more complex, as will be discussed later.

18. See p. 22.

4.

Blood That Emerges through a Tube

The Talmud[1] rules that if blood were to emerge from a woman's body through a tube, she is *tehorah*. This ruling is derived from the core verse discussed above: blood seen "in her flesh" renders her *teme'ah*, but blood seen not "in her flesh," but rather through a tube, does not. *Acharonim* debate the scope and the nature of this law, and, by extension, whether or not it has contemporary relevance.

The *Shulchan Arukh HaRav*[2] asserts that the Talmud only deems a woman *tehorah* when the insertion of the tube itself causes the sighting of blood; since the blood is not emerging on it is own, but rather is induced, it is not considered to be *niddah* blood. According to this, the exclusion only applies if the tube reaches all the way into the uterus, where it provokes the bleeding. Blood that emerges on its own from the uterus, and only later flows through a tube, would be *tamei*. Furthermore, this exclusion applies only when the blood was certainly caused by the

1. *Niddah* 21b.
2. YD 188:8.

tube's insertion; when the blood can be attributed to a woman's natural period, it would not be deemed *tahor.*

However, R. Shlomo Zalman Auerbach[3] understood the ruling of the Talmud differently. He argues that any blood that does not touch the woman's flesh as it exits the uterus and the body is *tahor*, regardless of whether the bleeding results from a natural period or from a wound created by the tube's insertion. R. Auerbach also writes that the tube need not extend into the cervix-uterus area; it needs only to reach the threshold between the cervix and vaginal area. Most authorities maintain that the cervix should be classified as part of the vaginal area, not as part of the uterus. Hence, for the blood to be considered *tahor*, the tube must be extended to the threshold between the cervix and the uterus. R. Auerbach is further innovative in arguing that the cervix is classified as part of the uterus, and that the tube therefore need only be extended to the threshold between the cervix and the vaginal area.[4]

(This position may contain a stringency as well. R. Auerbach's conflation of the uterus and cervix means that not only uterine openings, but even cervical openings, are assumed to produce blood that renders a woman *teme'ah*. Hence, when the cervix opens more than 15mm, even not by natural processes but as a result of intrusive medical procedures, it may render the woman *teme'ah*.[5])

3. *Responsa Minchat Shlomo* II, 72.
4. Although R. Auerbach considers the uterus and the cervix one area, only blood that emerges from the uterus renders a woman *teme'ah*; blood from the cervix does not do so. Blood only renders a woman *teme'ah* if it results from the deterioration of the endometrial lining, which occurs only in the uterus. Any blood from the cervix cannot be a product of the endometrial lining, and is therefore considered *tahor* blood from a wound, rather than *tamei niddah* blood.
5. It is, however, also possible that this stringency would necessarily not follow from R. Auerbach's position. The term "cervical openings," requires clarification, as the cervix has significant length to it, such that there is a distinct difference between what is called the "external cervical os" and the "internal cervical os" (colloquially referred to as external os and internal os). The external os is the opening of the cervix into the vaginal canal, and is visible on internal vaginal examination. An instrument passing through the external os will then pass through a few centimeters of the endocervix, or cervical canal, and will then encounter the internal os, which is the internal junction of the cervix uteri and corpus uteri – the internal point at which the cervix opens into the uterus proper. The endocervix, cervical canal, between the external

R. Auerbach's explanation could, theoretically, help to address situations where a woman is forbidden to her husband by *halakhah* at the most fertile time of the cycle. Ordinarily, women see blood once every 30 days; this renders them *teme'ah* for approximately 14 days, and *tehorah* for a similar amount of time. If a woman has a very short cycle she may ovulate before she goes to the *mikveh*, thereby preventing her from becoming pregnant. Today, this problem is usually overcome by adjusting the woman's cycle through medication. Prior to the utilization of this approach, Rabbi Auerbach suggested a novel solution to this problem. According to R. Auerbach, a woman in these circumstances may insert a tube into her body when she anticipates her period's arrival, and allow the blood to travel through the tube. Since the tube prevents the blood from touching her flesh, she never becomes a *niddah*. Practically, however, R. Auerbach's innovative lenient ruling is generally not followed, as the concurrence of other great *poskim* has for the most part not been forthcoming, which led R. Auerbach himself to retract his recommendation.[6]

os and internal os, is not lined by endometrium. The endometrial lining consists of a certain architecture of cells which is found only in the corpus of the uterus beyond the internal os of the cervix. The cervical canal is lined by an endocervical lining, which is functionally and microscopically distinct from endometrium. Thus, if R. Auerbach agrees that blood would only render a woman *teme'ah* if it results from the deterioration of the endometrial lining, then it can be argued that in any event there is no halakhic impact: if it is the external os that is opened (dilated), but no instrument goes through the internal os, then any bleeding would be coming only from the endocervix, and should not be *teme'ah*; and if the internal os is also dilated, then that would be defined as an opening of the uterus according to all opinions.

6. R. Auerbach's initial proposal was also printed in the journal *Noam* (VII, pp. 134–175). In the following installment of that journal (VIII, p. 275) R. Auerbach writes that in consideration of the fact that other leading Torah authorities have not agreed with him, he is categorizing his words as a suggestion not meant for practical purposes (*"bi-tur hatza'ah, vi-lo chas ve-chalilah le-ma'aseh"*). (In that same volume, R. Menachem M. Kasher published a lengthy essay [pp. 293–349] in which he posits that the suggestion of the tube may be valuable for other purposes.)

From a medical perspective, it should also be noted that there are significant practical issues in the construction and placement of such a tube: there would have to be a watertight seal of the tube against the external cervical os, which would require the engineering of an adhesive which would connect the tube to the external os, and remain dry in the moist environment of the cervix within a watertight seal. Otherwise, it is not feasible that no blood would leak around the tube and contact the flesh.

5.

The "Stringency of Jewish Women"

I. THE BIBLICAL LAWS OF *NIDDAH, ZAVAH KETANAH,* & *ZAVAH GEDOLAH*

In order to properly understand how the laws of *niddah* are practiced today, it is important to have a perspective on the development of this area of *halakhah* from the presentation in the Torah and through the Rabbinic enactments and practices that followed.

The Torah states that the sight of blood can create varying levels of impurity in a woman, depending on when it occurs (i.e. during the days of *niddut* or days of *zivah,* to be defined below). If a woman sees blood during her "days of *niddut*" she becomes a *niddah* for seven days. As long as the bleeding ceases before the end of the seven days, even if she sees blood all seven days, she may go to the *mikveh* after the seventh day and thus becomes *tehorah.*

If a woman sees blood during the "days of *zivah*" she becomes a "*zavah ketanah*". She must wait until the next day, check herself, and purify herself in the *mikveh* if she sees no more blood. If she sees blood on the second day, she must check herself the following day, and purify herself in the *mikveh* if she sees no more blood. A *zavah ketanah* is also called a "*shomeret yom keneged yom*", one who watches "a day for a day", i.e. one who must observe one clean day for the previous day on which she saw blood.

If a woman sees blood for three days in a row during her days of *zivah,* she is called a *zavah gedolah.* R. Saadiah Gaon[1] wrote that a woman can be a *zavah gedolah* even if she sees blood on three non-consecutive days, but the authors of the *Tosafot*[2] and most other authorities maintain that this is inconsistent with the Talmud's rulings. Having been established as a *zavah gedolah,* she must wait seven clean days before purifying herself in the *mikveh.*

In some ways the status of *niddah* is the most stringent, because even the tiniest drop of blood makes one a *niddah* for an entire week. However, in other ways the status of *zavah gedolah* is more stringent, because the *zavah* must wait seven *clean* days, while a *niddah* need not wait seven *clean* days.

In determining which days are the "days of *niddut,*" and which days are "days of *zivah*", the Talmud[3] states that women have a cycle of seven days of *niddut,* and then eleven days of *zivah.* The source for these numbers could either be a completely unwritten tradition originating at Sinai, or a hermeneutic derivation from scripture. Either way, the seven-eleven cycle is of Biblical, not Rabbinic origin.

There is a significant debate among the *Rishonim* as to when the "seven-eleven" cycle starts. The Rambam[4] maintains that the first day of a woman's first period is considered the first day of her days of *niddut,* and the six following days complete her days of *niddut.* The next eleven days are her days of *zivah,* and the next seven days are days of *niddut,* and so on forever. According to the Rambam, only two things can change this perpetual cycle: 1) the woman becoming pregnant; or 2) the woman developing a set cycle of her own, in which case the seven days begin at the beginning of her cycle.[5]

1. Cited in *Tosafot, Niddah* 52a s.v. *vi-arba'ah leilot.*
2. *Tosafot,* ibid. See also Ramban, *Chiddushim, Niddah* 54a.
3. Ibid. 72b.
4. *Hilkhot Issurei Bi'ah* 6:4–6.
5. See *Chiddushei R. Chaim HaLevi, Hilkhot Niddah* 4:14.

The other *Rishonim*[6] argue that it is impossible to have a perpetual cycle of seven and eleven days. Such a cycle would not match a woman's biological cycle; the woman might end up counting her seven clean days during the days of *niddut*, and get her normal period during the days of *zivah*. Rather, writes the Ramban, the days of *niddut* begin when a woman gets her period, the eleven days that follow are the days of *zivah*, and the days of *niddut* only begin again when she gets her next period. The time between the eleventh day of the days of *zivah* and her next period is neutral. Moreover, if a woman became a *zavah gedolah* and had to count seven clean days, the days of *niddut* would only begin when the seven clean days were completed.

II. R. YEHUDAH HANASI'S DECREE

Whichever system was followed, that of the Ramban or of the Rambam, it was exceedingly difficult for women to keep track of whether they were a *niddah*, a *zavah ketanah*, or a *zavah gedolah*. Therefore, R. Yehudah HaNasi decreed that we treat each bleeding as if it were the more extreme scenario.[7] This means that if a woman bleeds for one day, we must assume she is a *niddah* and not a *zavah ketanah*, and she will have to wait the remaining six days, rather than one clean day. If she sees blood for two days in a row, we assume that the first day was the last of the "days of *zivah*," making the second day the first of the "days of *niddut*." Hence, the woman must wait six more days, rather than one clean day. If she sees blood for three days in a row, we assume she is a *zavah gedolah*, not a *niddah*, and require her to wait seven clean days after she stops bleeding, rather than seven days from the first time she saw blood.

III. THE "JEWISH WOMEN'S STRINGENCY"

The Talmud adds that "Jewish women were stringent on themselves, that even if they see a spot of blood like a mustard seed, they sit for it seven clean days." *Rishonim* ask: why were the Jewish women more stringent than R. Yehudah HaNasi? Moreover, why did they adopt such an apparently self-contradictory stringency: if a woman sees a drop of

6. See Ramban, *Chiddushim, Niddah* 54a; *Hilkhot Niddah* 1:11.
7. *Niddah* 66a.

blood during the days of *niddut,* then she is a *niddah* and must wait exactly seven days; if she sees a drop of blood during the days of *zivah,* then she is a *zavah ketanah* and has to wait only one clean day. Either way, it would seem to make no sense to wait seven clean days for less than three days of seeing blood.

The Ran[8] explains that a little drop of blood could theoretically make a woman sit seven clean days, if she sees it when she is already observing her seven clean days. The drop of blood makes the days unclean, so that she has to start counting seven clean days again. Technically, the drop of blood does not cause her to sit seven clean days; it merely breaks up the seven clean days she is already counting and forces her to start again. The Jewish women knew that sometimes a small drop of blood could obligate them to count seven clean days. Therefore, to get into the habit of counting seven clean days, they decided to do so for any and every sight of blood.

Rabbenu Yonah[9] offers a different explanation, noting that one need not literally "see" blood to become *teme'ah*; as long as blood leaves the "inner house," the woman is *teme'ah.*[10] The Jewish women reasoned that a flow from the "inner house" could take place without blood leaving the body. Therefore, when a woman sees a little blood on Wednesday, it is possible that blood left the "inner house" on Monday and Tuesday as well. If that did occur, and it took place during the days of *zivah,* then woman would become a *zavah gedolah* and thus require seven clean days.[11]

IV. EXEMPTIONS FROM THE STRINGENCY

The *Rishonim* give two explanations as to the nature of this stringency. The Rashba[12] writes that since, in later generations, this stringency has become universally accepted, it is binding. The Ritva[13] agrees that the stringency is now obligatory; however, he understands the process differently. He states that even though this started out as a grass-roots

8. *Shevu'ot* 4a, s.v. *ve-af al gav.*
9. *Berakhot* 22a, s.v. *she-afilu.*
10. See 1:1.
11. See also Rashi, *Megillah* 28b, s.v. *she-hichmiru.*
12. See Ra'avad in *Ba'alei HaNefesh,* introduction to *Sha'ar Ha-Ketamim.*
13. *Niddah* 66a, p. 409 in Mossad HaRav Kook edition.

practice (*minhag*), Chazal later realized its value and enacted it into law. The practical difference between these two opinions is whether or not there is some case, some difficult circumstance, in which this stringency can be sidestepped.[14]

For instance, some women have short cycles, and have extreme difficulty completing their seven clean days. One of the European *gedolim*, R. David of Novardok, in his *Galya Massekhet*,[15] followed the view of the Rashba and ruled leniently on this issue. He argued that always waiting seven clean days is only a *minhag*, and one can override a *minhag* to fulfill the mitzvah of procreation. However, most *poskim*, including R. Moshe Feinstein and R. Shlomo Zalman Auerbach, rule that women must observe what they deem a Rabbinic law of counting seven clean days. In most cases, the question doesn't arise, as most women see blood for three days in a row, and must wait seven clean days on account of R. Yehudah HaNasi's decree, which is inviolable even in difficult situations.

Some commentaries[16] suggest that the "stringency of Jewish women" (*Chumrat Benot Yisrael*) will fall by the wayside when the third Temple is built, because the statuses of a *niddah* and a *zavah* differ regarding *korbanot* (sacrifices). The Rambam,[17] however, may imply that women will have to keep track of their halakhic status (i.e. *niddah, zavah ketanah* or *zavah gedolah*) for *korbanot*, but will still observe the "stringency of Jewish women" for purposes of *taharot* (the laws of purity and impurity) and the prohibition to their husbands.

V. SCOPE OF THE STRINGENCY

Some *Rishonim* argue that the Jewish women intended to adopt this stringency only for blood that renders them *teme'ah*. Rabbenu Yonah,[18] however, asserts that the Jewish women were stringent for yellow "blood",

14. To compare, Ashkenazim could eat *kitniyot* on Pesach, in cases where there is no other food available, since abstaining from *kitniyot* is only a *minhag*, not an actual Rabbinic law, it could be overridden in circumstances of great difficulty. See *Mishnah Berurah, Orach Chaim* 453:7.
15. I, YD #4.
16. See *Meshekh Chokhmah, Shemot* 12:22.
17. *Hilkhot Issurei Bi'ah* 11:10.
18. *Berakhot* ibid.

even though it does not render them *teme'ah*. Similarly, Ra'avad[19] and Ramban hold that although blood attributable to a wound is *tahor*, the Jewish women were stringent and waited seven clean days after it. Moreover, Ramban argues that the Jewish women were stringent with regard to blood that a woman sees in the weeks after childbirth, which is *tahor* according to Torah law. Practically, we do not accept any of these stringencies, and we do not require women to wait seven clean days after seeing blood that is *tahor*. Blood following childbirth will be discussed later, as its status today is different than in Talmudic times.

19. Cited by the Rosh (*Niddah* 10:3).

Section II: *Ketamim*

6.

The Decree of *Ketamim*

I. INTRODUCTION

As we have seen, in order for a woman to be considered a *niddah* on a Biblical level, she must experience the *hargashah* of a flow of blood, rather than simply see a stain on her clothing. Nonetheless, the Rabbis decreed that such a stain, known as a *ketem,* does render the woman a *niddah* on a Rabbinical level.[1]

The *Rishonim* offer various explanations for this enactment. Rashi[2] asserts that *Chazal* were concerned that a *hargashah* had taken place, but the woman failed to perceive it. The authors of the *Tosafot*[3] argue that even in instances that it is certain that there was no *hargashah,* Chazal decreed Rabbinic *niddah* status on women who see *ketamim.* However, *Tosafot* do not explain why they made this decree.

Since this law is Rabbinic in nature, it is subject to a lenient approach, and indeed certain general leniencies are built into its structure.

One such leniency is called *teliyah* (lit. "hanging"), the ability to be *toleh* (lit. "hang") the spot of blood on a source other than the one

1. *Niddah* 57b.
2. 58a, s.v. *MiD'Rabanan.*
3. 58a, s.v. *modeh Shmuel.*

that would make a woman *teme'ah*. If there is good reason to think the blood may have come from someplace other than from the woman's body, or that the blood came from a part of her body that does not make her *teme'ah* (e.g. she has a cut on some part of her leg), we are lenient and rule that the woman is *tehorah*.

> The Talmud relates the following incident: A woman once came to R. Akiva to show him a *ketem*. He asked if she had a wound, and she responded that indeed she had a cut that had since healed, but it could have once caused blood to get to the spot where the *ketem* was found. R. Akiva ruled leniently. His students looked at him incredulously, but he felt it valid to be "*toleh*" a *ketem* on such a wound, and was therefore lenient.[4]

One common contemporary example of *teliyah* would be a situation of hemorrhoids that sometimes bleed; it is reasonable to assume that the blood came from the hemorrhoids, and is not *niddah* blood. However, if a woman has no such condition, this *teliyah* would not be valid.

II. THE MINIMUM SIZE OF A *KETEM*

In the Mishnaic and Talmudic eras, houses were bug-infested, and bed sheets were often stained with the blood of squashed bugs. Women commonly found bug blood on their sheets. The Talmud rules that it is valid to be "*toleh*" *ketamim* on squashed bugs.[5]

However, this *teliyah* is only valid if the spot was small enough to reasonably have come from a bug. If the spot is larger than a "*gris*", or a bean (about the size of a penny), it could not have come from a bug, and that possibility does not provide a valid *teliyah*. Only if the spot is smaller than a *gris* do we assume it came from a bug.

The conceptual nature of this leniency regarding *ketamim* smaller than a *gris* is the subject of debate. Some *poskim* understood that it is a standard *teliyah*, subject to the same restrictions of ordinary *teliyot*. For example, according to this view, this *teliyah*, like other *teliyot*, may only

4. *Niddah* 58b.
5. *Niddah* 58b.

be utilized where it is reasonable to assume that the *ketem* came from a bug; the *teliyah* may not be utilized where the probability is very low that this *ketem* came from a bug.

Others suggest that since this type of *teliyah* applied to everybody worldwide, Chazal decided that a *ketem* would only be considered a *ketem* when it is the size of a *gris*; in other words, the law of *ketem* took on a standardized minimum size as a result of this widespread *teliyah*. Hence, any *ketem* smaller than a *gris* is *tahor*, even when it very likely did not come from a bug.

This issue is manifestly practical for the contemporary woman who finds a stain on her sheets or underwear, and has no *teliyah* other than that this *ketem* is smaller than a *gris*. If the first interpretation is correct, then, since our homes are not bug-infested, the *teliyah* on bug blood is inapplicable, and she is *teme'ah*. If, however, the second interpretation is correct, then the size of a *ketem* was irrevocably set to be a *gris*, and we can be lenient in the modern era as well.

The *Chatam Sofer*[6] provides a second reason to be lenient in contemporary times. As noted above, the *Tosafot* leave unexplained the question as to why Chazal decreed the Rabbinic status of *niddah* on women who saw *ketamim*. Perhaps, suggests the *Chatam Sofer*, the reason is primarily relevant to the laws of ritual purity, and only secondarily relevant to the laws of forbidden intercourse. Biblically, for ritual purposes relevant when the Temple is standing, *niddah* blood is *tamei*. In the present era, we are all considered *tamei*, and the *tumah* of *niddah* blood cannot add to our *tumah*. In the times of the *Beit HaMikdash*, *niddah* blood was *tamei*, and would render *terumah* and *korbanot* inedible. The Torah says that the blood of a *ketem* carries the *tumah* of *niddah* but does not confer impurity or prohibition on the woman. To avoid confusion, which would result if the blood was *tamei* but the woman was *tehorah*, Chazal decreed that the woman was also *teme'ah*, and also forbidden to her husband. When *Tosafot* say that Chazal decreed Rabbinic *niddah* status on a woman who saw a *ketem* without *hargashah*, they meant that Chazal forbade her to her husband and made her *teme'ah* so

6. *Responsa*, YD 182. See also *Chiddushei HaRan*, *Niddah* 57b.

that the apparent paradox of "*tamei*" blood coming from a woman who is *tehorah* should not lead to error and confusion.

As a result of its origins in the rules of purity and impurity, the Ra'avad[7] quotes an opinion, which he rejects, that since the *tumah* of *ketamim* is irrelevant in contemporary times, the subsidiary part of the decree – that one who sees a *ketem* is forbidden to her husband – is also null and void. Similarly, the Rif does not quote any laws of *ketamim,* perhaps because he agrees with the view cited in the Ra'avad that *ketamim* are inapplicable today.[8] Although in practice we do not rule like the Rif or the view in the Ra'avad (the decree was a legislated by a great Sanhedrin, and we can only nullify it if we convene an even greater Sanhedrin, as the *Chatam Sofer* emphasizes) in theory, the laws of *ketamim* should no longer apply.

Hence, we keep the laws of *ketamim* primarily to maintain fealty to the law as it was historically practiced. Consequently, our application of *ketamim* should not be any more stringent than it was in years past. Since, historically, women were "*toleh*" a spot smaller than a *gris* on bugs, we may continue to use this leniency. Logically, the leniency should be inapplicable; however, since *ketamim* laws as a whole are observed as a continuation of past practice, we may be as lenient as they were in the past.

To summarize, if the size requirement is derived from the standard rules of *teliyah,* it would be necessary to have a circumstance where the blood originating from a bug is a reasonable possibility. Alternatively, there are reasons to rule that a *ketem* smaller than a *gris* is not problematic, even in contemporary times when it is unlikely to be the blood of a bug: Chazal may have decided that the classification of *ketem* is applied only to a spot larger than a *gris,* perhaps because our concern for *ketamim* stems from the legitimate conformity to historical norms, and since those norms exclude spots smaller than a *gris,* we need not be concerned for such spots.

The initial question mentioned above, whether a *ketem* smaller than a *gris* is *tahor* because it is not classified as a *ketem,* or whether it is

7. *Ba'alei HaNefesh, Sha'ar Ha-Ketamim,* citing the *Eshkol.*
8. See *Arukh LeNer, Niddah* 58b, s.v. *od.*

tahor because it probably came from a bug, likely affects the resolution of at least four other issues:

1. **A *Ketem* Found during the *Shivah Nekiyim*:** Normally, a woman must wait seven clean days (*shivah nekiyim*) before she can immerse and become pure. The Rama[9] quotes a traditional practice not to rely on any *teliyot* during the first three days of the *shivah nekiyim*. We know that the woman just concluded her period, and she probably has some residual blood; we therefore assume that the blood she sees during the first three days is *niddah* blood. Nonetheless, the Rama cites an opinion from the *Terumat HaDeshen*,[10] who rules that a *ketem* smaller than a *gris* is not a problem, even during the first three days of *shivah nekiyim*. This is because a *ketem* smaller than a *gris* is not classified as a *ketem*, a principle that remains true even when *teliyot* in general are not relied upon.[11]
2. **Non-Red Blood:** The Ra'avad[12] writes that if a woman finds a black spot[13] smaller than a *gris*, she is *teme'ah*, because bugs do not have black blood. It would seem that the Ra'avad is working within a system where *ketamim* smaller than a *gris* are classified as actual *ketamim*, and are only *tahor* when they probably originated from a bug. By contrast, those who think a *ketem* smaller than a *gris* is not classified as a *ketem* would permit a woman who sees even black blood under such circumstances.
3. ***Safek Shiur*:** The *Badei HaShulchan*[14] discusses a case in which a woman saw a *ketem*, but washed it away, and was not sure if the *ketem* was the size of a *gris* or not. If the understanding is

9. *Yoreh De'ah* 196:10.
10. *Responsa*, 249.
11. Further, another reason (which is actually given by the *Terumat HaDeshen*) to differentiate between the *teliyah* of less than a *gris* and other *teliyot* is that it otherwise would become almost impossible to become *tehorah*, as bugs were prevalent.
12. *Sha'ar Ha-Ketamim*, #5, s.v. *vi-ha-din ha-chamishi*; cited in *Pitchei Teshuvah*, YD 190:12 and R. Akiva Eiger, *Chiddushim* to *Yoreh De'ah* 190:5.
13. Black blood is also *tamei*; see Chap. 10.
14. 190:5, *Bi'urim*, s.v. *yesh*.

that *ketamim* smaller than a gris are *tahor* because they probably came from a bug, a stringent approach would have to apply, as uncertainty negates the efficacy of all *teliyot*. This is because a *ketem* is *tamei* by default, unless there is a clear reason for it to be *tahor*. However, if a *ketem* smaller than a *gris* is not classified as a *ketem*, then there is no default status. Hence, the uncertainty would result in a permissive ruling.

4. **A *Ketem* Found on the Body:** The Rambam[15] writes that a *ketem* found on a woman's body is always *tamei*, regardless of size. Only a *ketem* found on a cloth can be considered *tahor* due to size. Presumably, the Rambam is working within the system of probability; thus, he is assuming that if a *ketem* is on the body, even though it is less than a *gris*, the likelihood that it came from the woman cannot be ignored, even if a theoretical *teliyah* is present (while a *ketem* found somewhere other than on the woman's body can be attributed to a *teliyah* such as a bug). The other position, that a blood spot smaller than a *gris* is not classified as a *ketem*, would not distinguish between *ketamim* found on flesh or on cloth. While the *Shakh*[16] does rule like the Rambam, the *halakhah* has nonetheless not followed this position.

It appears that this remains a valid approach, and likewise a *ketem* smaller than a *gris* may be considered *tahor* independently, without need for the rules of *teliyah*. Accordingly, one may assume leniently in the cases of the four contingent situations listed above.

III. DIFFERENCES BETWEEN *KETAMIM* ON FLESH AND ON CLOTH

Even if it is assumed, against the Rambam's view, that a *ketem* smaller than a *gris* is *tahor* even on a woman's body, there are nevertheless stringencies to that situation when compared to that of a *ketem* found on a cloth.[17]

One such difference can be seen in a view cited in the *Shulchan*

15. *Hilkhot Issurei Bi'ah* 9:6.
16. YD 190:10.
17. See *Niddah* 57b.

Arukh.[18] This position concerns the question of a grouping of little spots ("*tippei tippin*") that collectively add up to more than the size of a *gris*, while each spot on its own is too small. The ruling in *Shulchan Arukh* is that the spots are combined when they are found on the woman's body, but they are not combined if they are found on a cloth. The Rashba[19] maintains that *tippei tippin* on the woman's body are combined only if they are in the general vicinity of one another.[20]

Although spots on a cloth, each smaller than a *gris*, do not combine to equal a *gris*, there is a dispute among the *poskim* as to the parameters of this *halakhah*. If each spot that is of a problematic color is less than a *gris* but connected to another spot by a non-problematic color, the stain is subject to a dispute as to its status. Although the *Chavot Da'at* argues that we must include all the colors in calculating a *gris*, the *Me'il Tzedakah* (#62) maintains that although we view this as one stain, the permissible colors are not counted to reach the amount of a *gris*.[21] Many *poskim* are lenient and follow this view.

18. *Yoreh De'ah* 190:8.
19. *Torat HaBayit HaKatzar, Sha'ar Ha-Ketamim*, p. 291 in Mossad HaRav Kook edition, s.v. *lo*.
20. See also R. Ovadiah Yosef, *Taharat HaBayit*, 1, 8:4, 379–380.
21. The *Me'il Tzedakah* is discussing a stain that is on clothing that is both white and colored, while the *Chavot Da'at* is discussing both that case and the case of a stain that is itself both red and another color.

7.

Ketamim Found on an Object That Cannot Become Ritually Impure

I. ORIGIN OF THE LAW

Another significant limitation on the *ketamim* rule concerns the type of material upon which the stain is found. An object which is not subject to ritual impurity is similarly unable to bear a *ketem* that is *tamei*. This rule emerges from a discussion beginning in the *Mishnah*[1] and analyzed by the *Rishonim*:

> The opinion of R. Nechemiah is that the Rabbis did not decree *niddah* status on women who find *ketamim* on objects that cannot become ritually impure. The Talmud seems to rule in accordance with R. Nechemiah's view,[2] even though other *Tannaim* reject his position.

1. *Niddah* 59b.
2. Ibid. 60b.

Surprisingly, however, the Talmud[3] deliberates about the status of a woman who found a *ketem* on a loom, which, as a flat wooden tool, should not be subject to impurity. If, indeed, a loom cannot become ritually impure, the possible eligibility for *ketamim* presents a serious problem for those who rule like R. Nechemiah.

There are three basic approaches to this contradiction between R. Nechemiah and the case of the loom:

1. The Ra'avad[4] writes that a loom indeed cannot become ritually impure, just like all flat wooden vessels cannot become ritually impure. This is proof that the *halakhah* is against R. Nechemiah.
2. The *Ba'al HaMa'or*[5] argues that the loom in the Talmud's case was indeed capable of becoming ritually impure, since it was not flat and had a receptacle.[6] Hence, the case is atypical and poses no problem to R. Nechemiah's position.
3. The authors of the *Tosafot*[7] suggest that the operative element in this issue is different categories in the laws of *tumah*. They write that even though the loom could not become impure via contact with *niddah* blood, it was capable of becoming impure by contracting *tzara'at*. *Tosafot*'s approach is innovative, since they expand the definition of "objects capable of becoming ritually impure" to include additional categories of impurity, and thereby limit the scope of R. Nechemiah's leniency.

The *Shakh*[8] rules in accordance with *Tosafot*'s version of R. Nechemiah.

3. Ibid. 58a.
4. *Ba'alei HaNefesh, Sha'ar Ha-Ketamim* 11, 12.
5. *Sela HaMachloket* to *Ba'alei HaNefesh, Sha'ar Ha-Ketamim*, gloss #2.
6. A wooden utensil is susceptible to impurity if it has a receptacle; see *Keilim* 2:1 and 15:1.
7. 58a. s.v. *keRebbe*.
8. YD 190:16.

II. RATIONALE BEHIND THE LAW

The standard explanation for R. Nechemiah's law is given by the *Noda BiYehudah*,[9] based on the understanding that the law of *ketamim* was instituted as a stringency for women who came in contact with objects that must remain ritually pure.[10] To avoid treating a woman as *teme'ah* for *taharot* and at the same time as *tehorah* for her husband, Chazal decreed that *ketamim* should make a woman *teme'ah* to her husband too. This is consistent with the idea mentioned earlier in the name of the *Chatam Sofer*, that to render a woman's clothing as *tamei* while she remained *tehorah* was a source of potential confusion, and accordingly she had to be ruled *teme'ah* as well. Therefore, it makes sense that Chazal only decreed *ketamim* impure when they are found on something that is susceptible to ritual impurity.

This position does not explain all the details of the law, as compared to some of the complex points of the laws of purity and impurity:

For instance, if we strictly followed this rationale, then *ketamim* on objects that cannot become *tamei* through *niddah* blood should always be *tahor*, even if they can become *tamei* through *tzara'at*. Yet, as noted above, the *Tosafot* explicitly reject this. The *Noda BiYehudah* explains that Chazal did not want to make the law too intricate, presumably because the law was created to decrease confusion. Therefore, they made their decree comprehensive: whenever blood is found on an object capable of contracting any form of *tumah*, it is *tamei*, even though logically that should not be so.

There is another issue with the *Noda BiYehudah*'s explanation. The *Sidrei Taharah*[11] notes that *niddah* blood renders *tamei* anything that carries it, as well as anything that touches it. Hence, if a *ketem* is found on something that cannot become impure, and that object is resting on something which can become impure, the *ketem* should be *tamei*.

9. Responsa, *Mahadura Kama*, YD 52.
10. See p. 19; *Responsa Chatam Sofer*, YD 182.
11. 190:93, s.v. *mi-zeh*.

For example, if a woman finds a *ketem* on a piece of plastic she is holding, although the plastic cannot become *tamei* via touching, the woman herself can become *teme'ah* through the act of carrying. Practically, a *ketem* found in such situations is *tahor*, and this poses a challenge to the explanation of the *Noda BiYehudah*.

In defense of the *Noda BiYehudah*'s position, it could be postulated that as Chazal wanted to avoid complications, they only decreed that *ketamim* were *tamei* when found on objects that can become *tamei*, and not on objects that cannot, even if the *ketamim* were found in situations where they could potentially convey *tumah* to something other than the object upon which they were found.

III. CONTEMPORARY APPLICATIONS: TOILET BOWLS & PAPER:

While this notion is rooted in the classical laws of purity and impurity, it has a significant impact on contemporary practice. This leniency is invoked, for example, in cases where a *ketem* is found on the ground, which cannot become impure. This would extend even to a *ketem* found on a toilet; since a toilet is considered to be connected to the ground, its status is like the ground itself, and it cannot become ritually impure. A *ketem* found on a standard toilet is therefore not a problem; however, a toilet bowl on an airplane is not connected to the ground, and is therefore potentially subject to impurity, and, by extension, the rules of *ketamim*.

A significant percentage of *ketamim* are found on toilet paper or tissues, posing the critical question of whether or not paper is subject to ritually impurity. Some *Acharonim*[12] assert that since paper is made out of rags, it may have come from a cloth, which would be subject to *tumah*. Paper itself would therefore be capable of becoming *tamei*, and this leniency would not apply. Others describe paper as coming from trees, and thus not susceptible to impurity. There have been different ways of producing paper throughout history, thereby contributing to the different approaches to this question.

12. See *Pitchei Teshuvah* 190:18.

R. Moshe Feinstein[13] writes that this whole debate is inapplicable to the contemporary situation, because disposable items cannot become ritually impure. Although paper was once reusable, tissues and toilet paper nowadays are certainly disposable and therefore cannot become *tamei.* Similarly, if a woman finds a *ketem* on a sanitary pad, she remains *tehorah* according to this reasoning.[14] However, a woman who finds a significant amount of blood on a pad or on toilet paper may have to be concerned that this flow was the equivalent of *hargashah,* which would pose a problem on a Biblical level, regardless of the issue of ritual impurity.

Although some *poskim* are less inclined to be lenient regarding toilet paper, a lenient attitude toward this issue is legitimate and consistent with the Rabbinical character of the decree of *ketamim,* which indicates a lenient approach to most issues in this area.

IV. SYNTHETIC MATERIALS

Modern synthetic materials present another question as to the possibility of *tumah,* and, with that, of problematic *ketamim.* Only certain materials, such as earthenware and wood, are listed by the Torah as capable of becoming *tamei.* It is assumed that plastic and other synthetic materials, not being included in this list, therefore cannot become *tamei.*

However, this assumption only applies to non-clothing items. Clothing composed of materials not discussed by the Torah can become *tamei.* Therefore, if a *ketem* appears on a plastic raincoat or some other synthetic cloth, that could be a serious problem.

The *Chazon Ish,*[15] though, ruled that plastic clothing is not susceptible to *tumah,* because only items that are sewn together are classified by *halakhah* as clothing. Sheets of plastic that are not sewn together are not clothing. This is evident from the laws of *tzitzit.* One is only obligated to fasten *tzitzit* to "clothing". The Talmud[16] exempts leather from

13. *Responsa Iggerot Moshe, Yoreh De'ah* III, 53, and IV, 17:14.
14. Although women generally discover *ketamim* on toilet paper or pads while holding the object, the assumption is that our practice does not follow the above-cited position of the *Sidrei Taharah* who rules that *ketamim* in such cases are *tamei.*
15. See *Chazon Ish, Hilkhot Mikva'ot* 126:7.
16. *Menachot* 40b.

this rule, since the leather need not be sewn together, and is therefore not considered clothing.

According to the view of the *Chazon Ish*, it would emerge that polyester clothing can become *tamei*, since polyester is sewn or woven. Other *Acharonim*,[17] however, argued against this conclusion, invoking a combination of principles: a) the statement of the *Mishnah*[18] that *kol she-ba-yam tahor*, "anything that comes entirely from water is *tahor*," together with b) the assumption that the rule governing water can be extended to other liquids such as oil or petroleum. Accordingly, it can be concluded that oil or petroleum products such as polyester, like water products, are by nature *tahor*.

Even according to the *poskim* of the latter view, the principle that "anything that comes entirely from water is *tahor*," applies only if the entire cloth is made out of that material. Hence, a *ketem* found on any polyester blend (i.e. with cotton or wool) would still be *tamei*. R. Ovadiah Yosef[19] rules that even items labeled "100% polyester" are subject to *ketamim*, because they almost certainly have some cotton threads in them, as manufacturers are permitted by law to include small amounts of cotton thread as stitching in polyester garments and to omit them on the label. Therefore, one must be careful regarding such products and assume that the laws of *ketamim* apply.

17. See *Responsa Iggerot Moshe*, YD III, 53.
18. *Keilim* 17:13.
19. *Taharat HaBayit* 8:11.

8.

Ketamim on Colored Clothing

I. ORIGIN OF THE LAW:

Another exception to the laws of *ketamim* pertains to stains found on colored (non-white) clothing. The existence of this leniency is the subject of a dispute among the *Tannaim* of the *Mishnah,*[1] and the Talmud gives no clear indication of how to rule. Indeed, the Ramban[2] ruled stringently in this area. However, most *Rishonim,* as well as the *Shulchan Arukh* and *Rama,*[3] rule leniently. Although the *Noda BiYehudah*[4] suggested that a stringent approach would be appropriate, that is not the general consensus.

The consensus to accept this exclusion is despite a contrary approach asserted by one of the *Rishonim*:

The *Hagahot Maimoniyot*[5] quotes *Rabbenu Simchah* who radically

1. *Niddah* 61b.
2. *Hilkhot Niddah* 4:6.
3. *Yoreh De'ah* 190:10.
4. *Dagul MeRevavah,* YD, ibid. s.v. *al beged.*
5. *Hilkhot Issurei Bi'ah* 9:6.

limits the leniency of colored clothing, in a manner that would eliminate its contemporary practical value. According to *Rabbenu Simchah*, it is the clothing itself that does not become *tamei*, but the woman is still forbidden to her husband. Nonetheless, the *halakhah* is ruled against the view of *Rabbenu Simchah*, and the leniency of *ketamim* on colored clothing is used to permit couples to be together.[6]

II. RATIONALE AND SCOPE OF THIS LENIENCY

Rashi[7] explains the permitting of a *ketem* found on colored clothing by noting that it is hard to tell exactly what color the *ketem* is under those circumstances. Since certain colors of blood are *tahor*, a lenient ruling is appropriate if the color of the stain cannot be discerned. However, if this is the rationale behind the leniency, a distinction should be made between different colors of clothing; for example, blood can be easily perceived on yellow clothing, but difficult to see on black clothing. As the *halakhah* makes no such distinction, we must assume, within Rashi's understanding, that for the sake of simplicity, Chazal decreed that a *ketem* on any colored clothing is not a problem. The *Chatam Sofer*[8] maintained that the leniency of colored clothing does not apply to undergarments; however, this ruling has not been accepted, as the *Chazon Ish* notes.[9]

III. THE WEARING OF COLORED CLOTHING, AND WHITE CLOTHING DURING *SHIVAH NEKIYIM*

In light of the above, the practice is that women generally wear colored clothing and thus minimize the possibility of seeing a problematic *ketem*. The Rambam[10] wrote that Chazal "instituted" (*tiknu*) that women should wear colored clothing. The Talmud, however, implies otherwise, that doing so is a woman's option, and not a mandatory institution or decree. The Rama[11] appears to adopt a middle position, that this practice is not

6. This position is also emphasized by the *Noda BiYehudah*, cited above, in his advocacy for stringency.
7. *Niddah* 61b s.v. *le-hakel*.
8. *Responsa Chatam Sofer*, YD 161.
9. *Chazon Ish*, YD 89:4.
10. *Hilkhot Issurei Bi'ah* 9:7.
11. *Yoreh De'ah* 190:10.

a Rabbinic law, but it is still a very good idea, and women should be encouraged to always wear colored clothing.

This encouragement should begin even before marriage, before the woman goes to the *mikveh* for the first time. Women who wear white clothing during the days preceding their wedding run the risk of finding *ketamim* during that time and becoming prohibited to their grooms. Accordingly, brides should be instructed to wear colored clothing as soon as they finish counting their seven clean days.

By contrast, white clothing is worn during the "seven clean days", the *shivah nekiyim,* a period that is also known as *yemei libbun,* lit. "days of whitening". Some *Rishonim*[12] understood from this phrase that women must wear white and check for *ketamim* during that week. It is not assumed practically that women are actually obligated to wear white, but the Rama[13] writes that this was indeed the traditional custom, as is also the case in contemporary practice.

However, because the wearing of white is only a traditional practice, and not an actual law, it can be suspended in extraordinary circumstances. For example, R. Akiva Eiger[14] allows a woman who stains constantly to wear colored clothing during the *shivah nekiyim* and thereby prevent indefinite prohibited status due to *ketamim.* Similarly, even in the absence of a medical condition, the leniency of permitting *ketamim* found on colored clothing still applies if colored clothing was worn inadvertently, or due to the unavailability of white clothing. While some *poskim* are stringent concerning *ketamim* found during the first three days, which are treated more stringently than the remaining days of *shivah nekiyim,* this approach has not been accepted. Presumably, for the sake of simplicity, the leniency of colored clothing applies universally, as with the leniency of *ketamim* less than the size of a *gris,* and is not based on statistical probabilities, as would be the case with a regular *teliyah.*

12. See *Torat HaBayit HaArukh, bayit 7 sha'ar* 2, and *Sefer HaManhig, Hilkhot Niddah* p. 546.
13. *Yoreh De'ah* 196:3.
14. *Responsa R. Akiva Eiger, Tinyana* #34.

9.

Ketamim Found after Intercourse or after Urination

I. THE QUESTION OF "MASKED *HARGASHOT*"

We have seen that a woman is *teme'ah* on the level of Biblical law in only two circumstances: if she sees a flow of blood, or if she sees a spot accompanied by a *hargashah*. There are some cases, however, where we may be concerned that a spot of blood without *hargashah* still renders her a *niddah* on a Biblical level. If a *ketem* appears just after a woman went to the bathroom or had intercourse, and she had no *hargashah*, an issue of debate presents itself: on the one hand, the normal rules of *ketamim* should apply; however, there may also be the possibility that a *hargashah* was present, and the sensations of these other activities masked the *hargashah* and prevented it from being perceived.

One of the *Rishonim*, the *Maharam*,[1] displayed his view on this subject in the context of a rebuke he issued to a woman who performed too many *bedikot*. In the course of this rebuke, he writes that any *ketamim*

1. Cited by *Hagahot Maimoniyot, Hilkhot Issurei Bi'ah* 4:20.

that appear after intercourse are only a function of Rabbinic law. The implication given is thus that there is no concern for masked *hargashah* at the time of intercourse. By contrast, others disagree,[2] and understand the Talmudic perspective to be that there is a concern for masked *hargashah*.

The final ruling on this issue is unclear. The *Chavot Da'at*[3] and *Sidrei Taharah*[4] are stringent on the matter, while others are not. Still, this concern is limited; if, for example, a woman finds a *ketem* a full day after intercourse, it is not assumed that the *ketem* appeared during intercourse and that she had a *hargashah* that was misperceived.

II. THEORETICAL GUIDELINES

The *Mishnah*[5] discusses whether or not it is assumed that blood found after intercourse was present during intercourse. If the blood was present during intercourse, that act was thus an inadvertent transgression, and, accordingly, both the man and woman must bring a "*chattat*" offering. Concerning this offering, the Talmud[6] makes three rulings, depending on the applicable circumstances. First, at times the couple must bring a "*chattat*" (an offering brought when one is certain he or she committed a sin), since we presume with certainty that she became a *niddah* during intercourse. Second, at times they must bring an "*asham talui*" (an offering brought when one is uncertain if he or she committed a sin), since we are not sure if blood was present at that time. Third, at times we assume the blood was not there, and no *korban* is brought.

The criteria that are used by the Talmud to determine when each ruling applies are as follows. First, we must determine where the blood was found. If it was found on the man, it must have been there at the time of intercourse, and they are to bring a *chattat*. If blood is found on her, it must then be determined *when* the blood was found.

2. See *Pitchei Teshuvah* YD 183:1.
3. *Chiddushim*, 183:2.
4. 190:36.
5. *Niddah* 14b.
6. Ibid.

If it is found immediately after intercourse, it was there during intercourse, and they each bring a *chattat*.

If it was found a few moments after intercourse, then it is deemed uncertain whether or not it was there during intercourse, and they are each to bring an *asham talui*. If it is found hours after intercourse, it is assumed the bleeding began after intercourse, and the couple need not bring any *korban*.

The definitions of these three time scenarios – immediately after, moments after, and hours after intercourse – apply differently to the following law, known as "*ro'ah dam machamat tashmish*". This case, as it appears in the Talmud, is not referring to a stain found after intercourse, but rather to actual bleeding. If, on three consecutive occasions, intercourse causes a woman to bleed, the couple may never again have intercourse and must divorce, if the blood cannot be attributed to a wound which wouldn't render the woman a *niddah*.[7] The issue is then presented as to how it is determined whether or not it was intercourse that causes her to bleed. If the blood is found on the husband, or by the wife upon her immediately checking herself, it certainly was caused by intercourse with the resulting subsequent prohibition of ever having intercourse. If it was found by the wife soon after, it is suspected to be caused by intercourse, and out of doubt would also result in the prohibition against further intercourse. If the blood was found much later, it can be safely assumed to not have been caused by intercourse, with no halakhic significance for the future.

These two laws operate under the same guidelines: at the point when it is no longer assumed that intercourse causes bleeding, hours after intercourse, is also the earliest point there would be no concern for a masked *hargashah*.

III. PRACTICAL GUIDELINES

These terms – immediately, moments, and hours after intercourse – clearly require more precise definitions. The ruling in the Talmud[8] is that the couple must bring a *chattat* only if the woman has a *bedikah*

7. See *Niddah* 65b.
8. *Niddah* 14a.

cloth in her hand before the couple disengages, and she checks at the moment of disengagement. By contrast, they bring an *asham talui* if she delays checking herself for the time it takes to reach beneath the bed or beside the bed for a *bedikah* cloth.

The Rama[9] quotes Ra'avad, who writes that we do not know exactly how long it takes a woman to reach for a *bedikah* cloth and check herself; we are not experts in quantifying the Talmud's measurements. Therefore, it should be assumed that intercourse caused any blood found "soon after" (*samukh*) intercourse. That term, however, is open to a wide range of interpretation. Some *Acharonim* adduce proof from the Talmud's usage in *Massekhet Pesachim,* where "soon after" means approximately half an hour;[10] while other *Acharonim* adduce proof from the law that one should recite a *berakhah* "soon after" he washes *netilat yadayim,*[11] which is understood as approximately fifteen seconds.[12]

Despite the conceptually stringent approach taken in assuming masked *hargashah* is a concern, in practical terms, one may adopt a lenient position on this issue, and any blood found more than fifteen seconds after intercourse is treated as a *ketem*. The reasons for this position are as follows: 1) the *Maharam*'s view that there is never a concern for masked *hargashah*; 2) the Talmud's lenient stance on blood found after the time it takes a woman to reach a cloth and do a *bedikah,* which is probably less than fifteen seconds; 3) the *Badei HaShulchan* asserts that the only concern is that the most active part of intercourse will mask a *hargashah,* and the fifteen seconds are counted from that point. Clearly, such a standard makes it exceedingly unlikely that blood will be seen that will qualify. This last leniency applies only to the concern for masked *hargashah* during intercourse, not during urination; however, it is noteworthy that the *Chazon Ish*[13] maintained that there is less of a concern for masked *hargashot* during urination than there is during intercourse.

9. *Yoreh De'ah* 187:1.
10. See *Pesachim* 99b and Rashbam, s.v. *arvei*. *Taharat HaBayit,* 1:5, p. 202 cites this view in the name of *Mekor Mayim Chayim*.
11. See *Tosafot, Sotah* 39a, s.v. *kol kohen*.
12. See the *Acharonim* cited in *Badei HaShulchan,* 187, as well as *Taharat HaBayit,* ibid, citing *Shiyarei Taharah*.
13. YD, *Hilkhot Niddah* 90:1; See *Badei HaShulchan* ibid.

IV. BLOOD FOUND IN URINE

The Talmud[14] rules that if a woman finds blood in her urine, it is assumed it is not *niddah* blood, since *niddah* blood rarely emerges together with urine. Some *Rishonim* understand this to mean that blood in urine is not even a considered a *ketem*, while *Rabbenu Chananel*[15] limits the ruling to meaning that this blood does not render the woman a *niddah* on a Biblical level, but it is still considered a *ketem*. The *Shulchan Arukh*[16] rules leniently in accordance with the first view, but the Rama[17] rules like *Rabbenu Chananel* and considers the blood a *ketem*.[18] Accordingly, Ashkenazim are stringent, following the Rama, while Sefardim are lenient, following the *Shulchan Arukh*. Some *poskim* accept the view that the blood is a *ketem*, but are nonetheless lenient in practice: they argue that the *ketem* is deemed *tahor*, as such *ketamim* are usually found in the water of the toilet bowl, and this water may not be susceptible to impurity, thereby being exempt from the laws of *ketamim*.

14. *Niddah* 59b.
15. See *Beit Yosef, Yoreh De'ah* 191, s.v. *katvu*.
16. *Yoreh De'ah* 191:1.
17. Ibid.
18. Note, as well, the understanding of the *Shakh*, 191:3 and 4.

Section III: Evaluation and *P'sak*

10.

The Different Colors of "Blood"

The *Mishnah*[1] cites a tradition that there will always be cases of *niddah* blood that cannot be easily classified as *tahor* or *tamei*. This is indicated by a verse in the Torah: "When something is too awesome for you, for judgment, between blood and blood."[2] In such cases, rabbinic leadership should be consulted: "Get up and go to the place that *Hashem* has chosen…to the judge of your days, seek, and he will tell you the word of the law." Accordingly, the identification and distinguishing of the various colors that appear in this context is a major subject of halakhic attention.

It should be noted that many of the substances discussed here are not actually "blood", but as Chazal used the word *dam* in considering all of the questionable emissions, the word "blood" will be used here as a general term.

1. *Niddah* 19a.
2. *Devarim* 17:8.

I. RED AND BLACK

The *Mishnah* states that *niddah* blood that is deemed *tamei* can take four different shades of red. Black blood is also *tamei*, because it is assumed that the blood began as red, and turned black later. The Talmud describes, by comparison, each shade of red; one is similar to certain wines, another to certain leaves, etc. It is clear is that emissions that are not red are not problematic. Moreover, even if an emission is red, if it is not one of the four shades, it is not problematic.

The Talmud[3] records that some early *Amoraim* had trouble discerning between *tahor* and *tamei* shades of red. If the *Amoraim* could not tell the difference, this is certainly the case in later generations. Consequently, the Rosh[4] writes that the post-Talmudic practice is to deem *tamei* every shade of red, and thus any shade may render the woman a *niddah* on a Biblical level, which demands a stringent approach. Practically, it is assumed that anything red is *niddah* blood, while anything not red is *tahor.* It must still be determined, however, which colors belong to the red "family" and which do not.

II. GREEN AND YELLOW

The *Mishnah*[5] records a dispute about "*yarok*" blood, and ultimately rules that it is *tahor. Tosafot*[6] claim that "*yarok*" means yellow. Despite its usage in modern Hebrew, it would seem "*yarok*" cannot mean green in this instance, because it would appear indisputable that green blood is *tahor.* Hence, both yellow and green blood are *tahor.* The Meiri,[7] however, writes that "*yarok*" really does mean green. He explains that green could be *tamei* just as black is *tamei,* because dark green could be confused with black. Therefore, in his view, since there is no discussion about yellow in the Mishnah, yellow blood may be *tamei.* All contemporary issues regarding yellow blood or mucous revolve around this dispute between *Tosafot* and the Meiri about how to translate the word "*yarok*".

3. *Niddah* 20b.
4. *Niddah* 2:4.
5. *Niddah* 19a.
6. *Niddah* 19b s.v. *ha-yarok.* See also Rosh, ibid.
7. Commentary to the *Mishnah,* 19a.

Even if *Tosafot*'s explanation that "*yarok*" means yellow is accepted, some *Rishonim* still argue a stringent approach is called for. The Ritva[8] refers to the tradition to not trust human eyesight on this issue, and to not distinguish between red and colors that seem far removed from red. If this tradition is accepted, then even if Chazal had ruled leniently regarding yellow, stringency would still be required practically.

As discussed earlier, The Talmud teaches that Jewish women were stringent on themselves, and conducted themselves as *tamei* even if they saw only a "drop of blood like mustard." Most *Rishonim* interpret this to mean that they were stringent even for drops the *size* of a mustard seed; however, Rabbenu Yonah[9] claims that they were stringent on drops the *color* of mustard, which is yellow. This is similar to the Ritva's position, as it maintains that yellow blood was once deemed *tahor*, but is now treated as *tamei*. According to the Ritva, this change was instituted after the time of the Talmud; while according to Rabbenu Yonah, Jewish women adopted this change in the Amoraic era.

In terms of practice, the *Shulchan Arukh,*[10] followed by Rama, *Shakh,* and *Taz,* is lenient, in accordance with *Tosafot* and the Rosh. The *Shulchan Arukh* does not accept the Ritva's Geonic tradition regarding other colors, and favors the standard interpretation of "a drop of blood like mustard" over Rabbenu Yonah's interpretation. Despite this, R. Ovadiah Bartenura[11] wrote that nobody deems yellow blood *tahor.*

The *Chokhmat Adam*[12] suggests that the status of yellow blood should depend on the circumstances, as follows: If a woman finds yellow blood in the middle of her cycle, she should be ruled as *tehorah*. Since she has not recently seen blood, and her previous status was *tehorah,* this creates a "*chezkat taharah*", an assumption that her previous status of *taharah* continues even when there is a chance that it changed. However, if she finds yellow blood while performing her *hefsek taharah,* it should be ruled that she is *teme'ah,* since she has just recently seen

8. *Chiddushim* to *Niddah* 19a, s.v. *ha-yarok*.
9. *Talmidei Rabbenu Yonah, Berakhot* 22a in pages of the Rif.
10. *Yoreh De'ah* 188:1.
11. Commentary to the Mishnah, *Niddah* 2:7.
12. *Sha'ar Beit Ha-Nashim,* 117.

blood, and her previous status was *teme'ah*. This is a "*chezkat tumah*", an assumption that her previous status of *teme'ah* continues even when there is a chance that it changed. The *Chokhmat Adam* is unsure how to rule if she finds yellow blood during the *shivah nekiyim*; he concludes that since the *hefsek taharah* was successful, the decisive factor is her new status of not seeing blood, not her previous status of *teme'ah*. The Ramban[13] is also stringent when there is uncertainty about the validity of a *hefsek taharah*, but lenient on questions that arise during the *shivah nekiyim*.[14] Although some authorities follow this view of the *Chokhmat Adam*, many other authorities reject it, since it is against the ruling of the *Shulchan Arukh*, *Rama*, *Shakh*, and *Taz*.

III. BROWN

Unlike yellow and green blood, the status of brown blood is not discussed by *Rishonim*. The earliest source that discusses brown blood is the *Sidrei Taharah*,[15] who quotes R. Yaakov Emden's decision[16] that brown blood is deemed *tahor*. However, there are two reasons to question this ruling:

1) Dark brown is similar to black, and perhaps should therefore be treated stringently. However, this argument is problematic, since the Talmud clearly states that only really dark, jet black is *tamei*, and dark brown is usually not confusable with black of this type. Yet, some nonetheless argue that brown belongs to the black family, and just as contemporary practice is to forbid anything in the red family, this approach should be applied as well to everything in the black family.

2) Some *poskim* claim that brown actually belongs to the red family, and if that is so it should certainly be deemed *tamei*.

Even those who are lenient with regard to brown blood must be stringent on brown blood that has a rusty, maroon, or reddish hue. Similarly, if any small part of a brown stain has a reddish tint, it renders

13. *Chiddushim, Niddah* 5a.
14. See ch. 21.
15. 188:1.
16. *She'ailat Ya'avetz*, I, 44.

the woman *teme'ah,* in light of the ruling of the *Shulchan Arukh*[17] that even the tiniest amount of red on a *bedikah* cloth is enough to render the woman a *niddah.* Therefore, one who is lenient on brown blood must be extremely careful to make sure there is no red at all in the stain. Rendering a lenient ruling on brown stains is best done by one who has spent a significant amount of time with an experienced *posek* to get a sense for what is considered brown and what is considered red or black.

Sometimes, a streak of red can be found running across a brown stain. As stated above, this may cause the woman to be ruled *teme'ah;* however, it is important to be aware that it may also be dirt or a string, thus leaving the woman *tehorah.*

In terms of the practical approach to be taken with regard to brown stains, the *Arukh HaShulchan* and the *Badei HaShulchan*[18] are lenient on this issue, and there are various traditions amongst contemporary *rabbanim.*

IV. PINK

Poskim assume that pink belongs to the red family, and is therefore *tamei.* However, R. Shmuel Wosner[19] writes that although pink blood is *tamei,* sometimes blood that is pink when moist turns brown, tan, or white when dry. This pink blood is *tahor;* the *poskim* who render pink blood *tamei* do so only for blood that is still pink when it dries.

17. *Yoreh De'ah* 190:33.
18. 188:6.
19. *Shiurei Shevet HaLevi,* p. 93, s.v. *vi-od.*

11.

Determining the Color of Blood Stains

I. STAINS THAT ARE STILL WET OR MAY HAVE CHANGED COLOR

The Talmud[1] rules that if a rabbi sees a *bedikah* cloth the day after it was used, and the colors look dry and faint, he should not speculate as to how it may have looked when it was still wet, but must rule based on the present appearance of the colors. This rule is known as *ein la-dayan ela mah she-einav ro'ot,* "the judge has only [to consider] what his eyes see."

The *Bach*[2] writes that although the rabbi should not consider how the color may have changed between the past and the present, he should be conscious of how it may change between the present and future. Thus, if a rabbi is presented with a wet *bedikah* cloth, he should wait until it dries and give his ruling at that time. In his view, one cannot rule leniently on a stain while it is still wet. The *Shakh,*[3] however, disagrees and

1. *Niddah* 20b.
2. *Yoreh De'ah* 188:1 s.v. *ve-ishah.*
3. *Yoreh De'ah* 188:3.

argues that a rabbi may issue a ruling based on the appearance of a stain while it is still wet.

Practically, women should be advised to contact a rabbi as soon as possible rather than collecting a week's worth of *bedikah* cloths and bringing them to the rabbi all at once. Ideally, the ruling should be based on the stain's color immediately after it dries. If the stain is not shown for a week, that initial color could change from red to brown. Although one may be lenient when presented with old stains, because "the judge has only [to consider] what his eyes see," it is not ideal to rely on this principle unnecessarily.

If a woman brings a stain that appears brown, but insists that it was bright red when she first saw it, *poskim* write that the rabbi should rule based on the woman's report, not based on what his eyes see. However, in cases where the rabbi suspects the woman's report is inaccurate, he should not rule based on the woman's report, but rather based on what his eyes see. Each rabbi must evaluate on a case by case basis whether or not the woman's claim is reliable.

The Talmud[4] discusses the various circumstances under which a rabbi should look at the blood stains, such as by candlelight, sunlight, strong light, or weak light. The conclusion in that discussion is that one should not look at the blood at night, or when the sun is obstructed by clouds, but rather in moderate daylight. However, the *Torat HaShelamim*[5] notes that contemporary discussion does not focus on these requirements; in fact, the *Shulchan Arukh* did not even cite the ruling that stains should not be examined at night. The *Torat HaShelamim* therefore concludes that these laws no longer apply. Perfect lighting was only needed to distinguish between *tahor* red and *tamei* red, not to distinguish between red and other colors. Since contemporary practice is to deem everything in the red family *tamei*, perfect lighting is not required. Other *poskim* add that electric lights are comparable to sunlight, not to candlelight, so stains may be checked by electric lights even at night.

Practically, rabbis may examine *bedikah* cloths at night with electric lights. However, different lights can distort the true appearance of the

4. *Niddah* 20b.

5. YD 188:1.

stain. Incandescent bulbs give the stain a more reddish tint than sunlight, while fluorescent lights give less of a reddish tint than sunlight. Therefore, the best kind of light for checking stains is still sunlight. If someone comes with a *bedikah* cloth at night, one should preferably wait until morning and then look at it in sunlight. Only if the stain is obviously yellow, and does not appear red even under an incandescent bulb, is it appropriate to issue a lenient ruling at night. If there is any uncertainty about the stain's color, one should not rule decisively at night, but should examine it in the morning and then give a ruling.

Women should be urged to show any stains to her rabbi immediately, rather than waiting to show them until the night of immersion, which risks delaying the immersion. If a stain looked red under electric light, but the next morning looked *tahor* under sunlight, it is possible to be lenient. This is because the appearance of stains viewed at night is usually distorted, and one cannot trust that it reflects the stain's true color. Some *poskim* say that if one was certain that it was red at night, he should not be lenient even if it looks *tahor* by day. However, R. Moshe Feinstein[6] was lenient even in such a case, because any conclusion drawn while viewing a stain under electric light is considered not as reliable as a conclusion reached using sunlight.

II. A HUSBAND RULING ON HIS WIFE'S STATUS

The Talmud[7] records that R. Nachman's wife, Yalta, showed her blood stains to a number of rabbis, but, apparently, did not show them to her husband. The *Tosafot*[8] offer several theories as to why she did not consult her husband: perhaps her husband was not an expert at determining the color of blood; or perhaps she was afraid he would be too stringent, since the ruling affected him personally. The simplest explanation would have been that it is improper for a husband to rule on his own wife's status; by not providing that explanation, the authors of the *Tosafot* show that they clearly hold that she was halakhically permitted to show the stains to her husband. Further support for *Tosafot*'s implied

6. *Responsa Iggerot Moshe*, YD IV, 17:5.
7. *Niddah* 20b.
8. Ibid. s.v. *kol yoma*.

ruling can be adduced from the generally accepted fact that rabbis may issue halakhic rulings, without suspicion of bias, in other matters that affect themselves and their families.

In contrast, R. Shimshon of Senz[9] does suggest the simpler approach, that R. Nachman's wife did not show these stains to her husband because a husband cannot rule for his wife. While it may be true that rabbis can rule for themselves, after proper research and consideration, that objects of questionable status are permitted; that is because these objects have no "*chezkat issur*", or previously established prohibited status. However, according to R. Shimshon of Senz's suggestion, rabbis cannot rule for themselves that objects previously forbidden have become permitted, and similarly cannot rule on their wives' status if it involves changing a "*chezkat issur*" such as ruling on the validity of a *hefsek taharah*.

In practice, the custom is that a husband may answer his wife's questions, even if she was previously certainly forbidden to him, and the ruling would reverse that status.

9. Commentary to *Negaim* 2:5.

12.

Blood from a Wound

1. One basis for leniency toward the sighting of blood is the possibility that the blood is from a wound, rather than menstrual blood. This possibility is noted in the Talmud,[1] where it is stated that if a woman has a wound and sees blood, she may assume that the blood came from the wound, and she need not be concerned that the blood is *niddah* blood.

The notion of assuming blood to come from a wound extends to the possibility of a wound in the "*mekor*", or "source" of *niddah* blood. For this question, two types of wounds must be considered: those found in the uterus, and those found in other parts of the reproductive system. It is readily understood that it is possible to be lenient toward blood from a non-uterine wound, because that blood probably did not originate from the endometrial lining.

Moreover, it emerges from the Talmudic discussion that is also possible to be lenient regarding blood that is from a wound in the uterus itself. This attitude could be based on one of two possible perspectives:

1. Perhaps even blood from the endometrial lining that is discharged

1. *Niddah* 65b–66a.

as a result of a wound, not as a result of the lining's natural deterioration, is *tahor.*

2. Alternatively, perhaps blood from a uterine wound is *tahor* only when it does not come from the endometrial lining. If this explanation is correct, it would mean that blood from the endometrial lining is always *tamei,* whether it emerges as a result of a wound or as a result of natural deterioration.

Most medical procedures that take place inside the uterus, such as endometrial biopsies, cause the endometrial lining to bleed. According to the first explanation, any blood that results from such procedures is *tahor;* while according to the second explanation, such blood would render the woman a *niddah.*

Contemporary *poskim* have taken varied views in terms of the practical stance on this issue. The *Chazon Ish,*[2] in his halakhic commentaries, appears to adopt the first, lenient position; however, in a published letter written to a doctor,[3] his expressed opinion is more ambiguous, leading some interpreters to claim that he took the second, stringent position. R. Shlomo Zalman Auerbach[4] took the lenient position, while many *poskim* question this position.

In contrast with the lenient explanation, the stringent opinion requires the assumption that the uterus can bleed independently of the lining, in order to explain how uterine bleeding can ever be *tahor.* However, scientific evidence suggests that the uterus cannot bleed independently, under normal circumstances, thus providing support for the lenient explanation. However, the stringent explanation can be defended by noting that the cervix can bleed independently of the endometrial lining, taken together with the previously cited view of R. Shlomo Zalman Auerbach[5] in classifying the uterus and cervix as one area. Hence, blood from the uterine part of that shared area renders the woman a *niddah,* while blood from the cervical part of that area does not.

2. *Chazon Ish Yoreh De'ah* 81.
3. *Pe'er Ha-Dor,* vol. 4, p. 131.
4. Cited in *Nishmat Avraham,* 187 p. 81 in old editions.
5. See p. 12 and fn 4 there.

11. For the purposes of assuming a wound to be the cause of bleeding, the *Rishonim* distinguish between wounds known to bleed and wounds not known to bleed. Only in the instance of the former type can it undisputedly be assumed that any blood she finds came from that wound.

However, that term itself, "wounds known to bleed", is subject to interpretation, with at least two theories possible:

1. It may refer only to a situation where it is known there is a wound, and it is known specifically that it is bleeding, either because a doctor made the incision and saw it bleed, or the doctor examined the area and discovered a bleeding wound.
2. Alternatively, the *Shakh*[6] writes that it is sufficient to know that such wounds normally bleed, even if this wound has not been actively observed bleeding.

In the instance of wounds not known to bleed, *Rishonim* dispute whether the woman may assume that any blood found came from these wounds. The *Mordechai*[7] seems to be of the opinion that women cannot assume that blood came from wounds of this type, while the Rashba[8] maintains that she can assume that blood came from such wounds.

Simply put, "wounds not known to bleed" refers to wounds that generally do not produce blood. This definition is propounded by the *Beit Yosef*[9] and the Vilna Gaon.[10] The *Shakh,*[11] however, defines wounds not known to bleed as wounds that generally produce blood, but that have not in this case been actively observed to produce blood. His logic appears to be as follows:

6. YD 187:21.
7. *Niddah* # 735.
8. *Torat HaBayit* 7:4, p. 276 in Mossad HaRav Kook edition; and *Chiddushim, Niddah* 66a, s.v. *vi-ne'emenet ishah.*
9. YD 187:5.
10. *Bi'ur HaGra,* YD 187:14.
11. YD 187:24.

> The *Shakh* could not believe that the Rashba would allow women to assume that blood came from a wound not generally known to bleed. When a woman with such a wound finds blood, the *Shakh* claimed, she cannot assume with certainty that the wound produced this blood. Since certainty is lacking, and the matter has Biblical significance, one must be stringent and assume the blood came from the endometrial lining, since halakhic practice always rules stringently when uncertain about matters affecting Biblical laws.

In his view, the Rashba meant what the *Mordechai* explicitly said, that wounds need not be actively observed to bleed; the two *Rishonim* simply used different phrases to describe the same phenomenon.

The *Chakham Tzvi*[12] brings a further proof for the *Shakh*: The *Mishnah*[13] relates that R. Akiva was lenient concerning *ketamim,* and deemed *tahor* the *ketem* of a woman who had once had a wound that produced blood. Apparently, only a *ketem* is *tahor* in such situations; real flows of blood, or blood on a *bedikah* cloth, would be *tamei.* The *Chakham Tzvi* assumes that this case of a wound that healed is comparable to a wound not known to bleed.

The *Chazon Ish*[14] and others[15] reject this proof because in the *Mishnah*'s case, the wound already healed and the probability that the wound caused this blood is low. By contrast, where there is an existing wound, there is greater probability that the stain did not come from the endometrial lining, and one may be lenient even when non-*ketem* blood is found. For the purposes of this discussion, the simple reading of the Rashba, against the *Shakh*'s stringent interpretation, will be assumed.

In practice, the *Shulchan Arukh*[16] rules like the Rashba's lenient opinion. For those who follow the *Shulchan Arukh,* if a woman finds blood on her *bedikah* cloth but has an established wound either in or out

12. *Responsa,* #46.
13. *Niddah* 58b.
14. *Chazon Ish* ibid.
15. See *Taharat HaBayit,* p. 233, fn s.v. *hineh b'ikar.*
16. *Yoreh De'ah* 187:5.

of the uterine area, she is not a *niddah*. The Rama,[17] however, rules like the *Mordechai* that only wounds known to bleed save women from *niddut*.

Nonetheless, even the Rama is lenient, like the opinion of the Rashba, under certain circumstances. These circumstances are complex, and draw upon involved discussions of the *Rishonim* and the *poskim*.

For example:

a) When blood is found not at the woman's *veset* time: The Talmud[18] teaches that blood seen after intercourse can, theoretically, permanently forbid a woman to her husband, because it is assumed that the experience of intercourse will always cause her to become a *niddah*, unless she has either a wound or a *veset* (an established pattern as to when she is likely to see blood). *Rishonim* offer three explanations of why blood after intercourse is not problematic if the woman has a *veset*.

1. Rashi[19] explains that if the woman occasionally, cyclically sees blood after intercourse, she is permitted to her husband. For instance, she is permitted if she sees blood after every intercourse that takes place on the month's first day. In such a situation, she may conclude that the blood is a result of her regular period, not of a period caused by intercourse.
2. Rambam[20] explains that if the couple had intercourse close to the woman's normal period, it may be assumed that the blood resulted from her normal period, and it need not be assumed it resulted from the intercourse.[21] This explanation is very similar to Rashi's. The *Shulchan Arukh*'s ruling[22] follows the Rambam.
3. The *Mordechai*[23] notes that when a woman bleeds after intercourse,

17. Ibid.
18. *Niddah* 65b–66a.
19. 66a, s.v. *ve-im*.
20. *Hilkhot Issurei Bi'ah* 4:20.
21. This interpretation is problematic, as intercourse at the time of the *veset* is generally prohibited; the commentaries to the Rambam and later authorities address this issue.
22. *Yoreh De'ah* 187:4.
23. *Hilkhot Niddah,* 735.

> there are two consequences: she becomes a *niddah*, and she has potential to become permanently forbidden to her husband, if she bleeds two further times after intercourse. Rashi and the Rambam both explained that the sight of blood sometimes does not create potential to permanently forbid the woman to her husband. The *Mordechai*, in contrast, addresses the other consequence, and claims that the sight of blood sometimes does not render the woman a *niddah*. If a woman has a *veset kavu'a*, and sees blood not during the time of her *veset*, it is assumed the blood is from a wound. This blood does not render her a *niddah*, nor does it create potential to forbid her to her husband.

The *Mordechai*'s statement is extremely innovative. Accordingly, the Rama[24] qualifies it by adding that only women with wounds, albeit wounds not known to bleed, can assume that blood seen not at their *veset* times is *tahor*. Women without wounds who see blood not at their *veset* time must assume that the blood came from the endometrial lining, and that they are *tamei*. Essentially, the Rama is combining the leniency of the *Mordechai* with that of the Rashba; when both conditions – a wound and non-*veset* bleeding – are met, one may be lenient.

The *Shakh*[25] further qualifies the *Mordechai*'s statement by adding that if the woman sees the blood after intercourse not at her *veset* time, it is assumed that intercourse caused a wound and produced blood. However, without intercourse, blood seen not during a woman's *veset* still renders her a *niddah*.

At first glance, the *Mordechai*'s ruling has little contemporary relevance; the *Mordechai* deals with women who have *vestot kevu'ot*, established *vestot*, while most contemporary women have no *vestot kevu'ot*. However, upon further consideration, the *Mordechai*'s ruling is indeed relevant to contemporary women. The *Terumat HaDeshen*[26] rules that if a woman never sees blood before a certain day in the cycle, e.g. she never sees blood less than 27 days after her period, she may sometimes

24. *Yoreh De'ah* 187:5.
25. YD 187:20.
26. *Responsa*, 247; cited in *Shulchan Arukh*, YD 186:3.

act leniently during those 27 days as if she has a *veset kavu'a*. In other words, the *Terumat HaDeshen* is acknowledging a semi-*veset*, one that is effective in delineating days when a period will *not* happen. Hence, if a contemporary woman never before saw blood in the 27 days following her period, and sees blood during these days for the first time, she may assume the blood came from a wound, if she has a wound not known to bleed or if she had intercourse. The *Pitchei Teshuvah*[27] applies this type of *veset* to this discussion.

Even with the Rama's qualification, the Mordechai's ruling remains extremely innovative. As such, the *Shakh*[28] argues that it is only assumed that intercourse caused the wound to prevent the dissolution of marriages. Ordinarily, if a woman sees blood after intercourse on three consecutive occasions, she must be divorced. Hence, the Rama rules that if this blood appears during the time preceding her *veset kavu'a*, we assume that it came from a wound and do not require them to divorce. However, we do not assume that blood came from a wound to exempt women from *niddah* status; hence, even if blood appears after intercourse, before the *veset kavu'a*'s time, the woman is deemed a *niddah*. Most *poskim* accept this ruling of the *Shakh* and in practice, Ashkenazim do not rely on this Rama to be lenient on issues of *niddah* blood.

b) A Situation of "*Sfek Sfeika*" (double uncertainty): The Rama's second circumstance of leniency applies when it is uncertain whether blood came from the endometrial lining or from a wound not known to produce blood, and it is also uncertain whether it came from the uterus or from other areas of the reproductive system. Here, the principle of "*sfek sfeika*" is invoked, which allows a lenient position to be assumed when two separate variables are both undetermined. In this case, there are indeed two open questions: maybe the blood is from the other areas; and even if it is from the uterus, maybe it comes from a wound in the uterus.

In this case, in contrast with the *Shakh*'s understanding of the first leniency, *Acharonim* maintain that the Rama meant to be lenient

27. YD 187:26.
28. YD 187:20.

not only vis-à-vis not classifying blood as a result of intercourse, but also for not deeming the woman a *niddah*.

In analyzing this ruling of the Rama, one must note and evaluate the assumptions that he makes to reach this ruling:

1) One questionable assumption is that *sfek sfeika* is a valid halakhic tool when dealing with the laws of *niddah*. *Sfek sfeika* is effective in most areas of the Torah; the laws of *niddah* may differ, however, because the severe "*kareit*" penalty that accompanies intercourse with a *niddah* may require greater hesitancy in cases of uncertainty.

In fact, the utilization of *sfek sfeika* in other areas of *halakhah* requires explanation. In general, in Biblical laws, stringency is required when the facts are undetermined (*safek D'Orayta le-chumra*). However, the Rambam suggests that this rule is itself a Rabbinic innovation. On the level of Biblical law, one may actually be lenient in any situation of uncertainty. Chazal decreed, however, that one must be stringent when uncertain about any area of Biblical law. As many *Acharonim* explain, a *sfek sfeika* would mean, in effect, that the need to follow that Rabbinic law is itself unclear. Thus, leniency would be allowed, because it is essentially a Rabbinic requirement that is at question.

Many *Rishonim* questioned the Rambam's view that acting stringently in cases of uncertainty is only by dint of a Rabbinic decree. They note that the Torah requires an *asham talui*, a sacrifice, when one is not sure if he or she committed certain sins. If the Rambam is right, and one may be lenient in cases of uncertainty, why would the Torah obligate somebody to bring a sacrifice for doing something permitted? The Rambam could respond to this challenge in two ways.[29] First, one must distinguish between ordinary prohibitions and *kareit* prohibitions. An *asham talui*, he could explain, is only brought for *kareit* prohibitions, such as the consumption of forbidden animal fats. Regarding such prohibitions, the Torah is indeed stringent even in cases of uncertainty. As such, a *sfek sfeika* regarding a *kareit* prohibition is invested with Biblical strength, and the Rabbis ruled that one must therefore be stringent.

29. In actuality, there are two versions of the Rambam's text, each presenting one possible answer.

Accordingly, since *niddah* is a *kareit* prohibition, the leniency of *sfek sfeika* cannot apply to it.

The Rambam's second possible answer is based on one understanding of *asham talui* found in the Talmud.[30] According to this understanding, one only brings an *asham talui* when he has two fats in front of him, one kosher and one not kosher, and then eats one of them without knowing which he ate. This case is called "*ikba issura*", a case of established prohibition, since the presence of a forbidden item is established, and the uncertainty only relates to whether the item he took was the forbidden one or the permitted one. By contrast, an *asham talui* is not brought when one ate a single piece of fat and was not sure if that piece was permitted or forbidden. This case is called "*lo ikba issura*", a case where no prohibition is established, where the very presence of a forbidden item is uncertain.

According to the Rambam, one is Biblically permitted to eat a single piece of meat if he is uncertain about its *kashrut* status; this is *lo ikba issura*. Hence, no *asham* offering is brought for eating such meat. However, if a Biblically prohibited item is certainly present in a group, one is forbidden to eat the entire group; this is *ikba issura*. Hence, an *asham* offering is brought when one ate from such a forbidden group. According to this, there is no distinction between *kareit* prohibitions and general prohibitions. Therefore, the Rama could safely rule that *sfek sfeika* works even for *kareit* prohibitions such as *niddah*.

Alternatively, the Rama may reject the Rambam's approach, and instead favor the understanding of *sfek sfeika* adopted by many other *Rishonim*. The Rashba, for instance, argues that *sfek sfeika* derives its lenient status by acting as a "*rov*", a majority. In a *sfek sfeika*, three of the four possibilities militate for leniency. In our case, the possibility that blood came either from a wound in the uterus or from other parts of the reproductive system is greater than the possibility that the blood came from the endometrial lining. The Torah commands that one should usually follow the majority; if the majority of possibilities combine in the direction of leniency, one may be lenient.[31]

30. *Keritot* 17a–18a.

31. The concept of *rov*, following the majority, as applied by Chazal, at least in this usage,

In sum, the Rama writes explicitly that *sfek sfeika* works for *niddah,* perhaps based on one explanation of the Rambam, and perhaps based on the Rashba.

2) A second novel principle emerges from the Rama's application of *sfek sfeika* to the laws of *niddah.* Usually, the regular rules of uncertainty do not apply to questions of ritual purity and impurity. The Talmud[32] teaches that if a married woman is credibly accused of committing a sin with another man in a "private domain", but there is uncertainty about the accusation's truth, she is stringently deemed a *sotah,* a wayward woman, and forbidden to her husband. The Talmud derives from here that an uncertainty regarding ritual purity that originates in a "private domain" is stringently deemed impure, while uncertainty originating in a "public domain" is deemed pure. The *Mishnah*[33] states that we are stringent on uncertainties that originate in a "private domain" even if there is a *sfek sfeika*; clearly, the regular leniency of *sfek sfeika* does not apply to uncertainties regarding ritual impurity.

Thus, a second question demands consideration: Are the laws of *niddah* to be categorized as laws regarding ritual impurity? When a woman becomes a *niddah,* there are two ramifications: first, she becomes ritually impure, and second, she becomes forbidden to her husband. To categorize the laws of *niddah,* it would be necessary to determine which element is dominant. If the laws of *niddah* belong with those of ritual impurity, since uncertainties regarding *niddut* generally arise in "private domains," one cannot be lenient even in cases of *sfek sfeika.* However, if the laws of *niddah* do not belong with those of ritual impurity, one may be lenient in cases of *sfek sfeika.* The Rama, by ruling leniently when *sfek sfeika* occurs in the laws of *niddah,* clearly does not consider the laws of *niddah* to be, at their core, laws of ritual impurity.

There are two ways to explain this. The authors of the *Tosafot*[34] argue that each consequence of a woman's *niddut* status is classified with

is not the same as the concept of majority applied by statisticians. The evidence used to determine *rov* for this purpose is not gathered empirically, nor is majority determined by percentage.

32. *Sotah* 28b.

33. *Taharot* 6:4.

34. *Bava Kama* 11a, s.v. *de-ein.*

a different set of laws. Her status regarding ritual impurity is unaffected by the existence of a *sfek sfeika,* while her permissibility to her husband is affected by the *sfek sfeika.* Needless to say, this approach of *Tosafot* is extremely innovative.

Tosafot[35] elsewhere argue that there are two types of ritual impurity: impurity that originates outside the body, and impurity that originates inside the body. The laws of *sotah,* from whence we derive that *sfek sfeika* does not apply to impurity, deal with impurity that originates outside the body. In contrast, the laws of *niddah* deal with impurity that originates inside the body. Since these two types of impurity are fundamentally different, we cannot derive the principle of stringency in *sfek sfeika* from *sotah* to *niddah.* According to this opinion of *Tosafot* as well, *sfek sfeika* is grounds for leniency in the laws of *niddah,* even though they involve ritual impurity.

The most potent challenge to the Rama, however, is raised by the *Shakh.*[36] The *Shakh* writes that the *sfek sfeika* presented by the Rama would violate the rule that one cannot combine two uncertainties to form a valid *sfek sfeika* when those uncertainties are too similar to one another, i.e. when they are essentially the same uncertainty reworded in different terms. The Rama's *sfek sfeika* – that maybe the blood is not *niddah* blood because it is from the other parts of the reproductive system, and even if it is from the uterus, maybe it is not *niddah* blood because it came from a wound – is really only one uncertainty: is this blood from a wound, or is it *niddah* blood? A comparable case would be where a woman came to a rabbi and said that she had two wounds that are each not known to produce blood, and the rabbi says that it is a *sfek sfeika* because blood could be from the first wound, and even if it is not, it could still be from the second wound. This is clearly not a *sfek sfeika;* it is merely two supports for one side of a single uncertainty. By contrast, a real *sfek sfeika* involves two separate halakhic uncertainties.

The *Noda BiYehudah*[37] answers this question by asserting that two uncertainties are only considered too similar if each leads to exactly the

35. *Niddah* 2a, s.v. *me-eit.*
36. YD 187:22.
37. *Kama,* YD 47.

same conclusion. Two uncertainties are considered sufficiently different if they have different halakhic outcomes. Since there is a difference between blood from a non-uterine wound and blood from a uterine wound, the Rama's *sfek sfeika* is valid. This difference is based on a passage in the Talmud[38] which records a dispute about whether blood from a wound in the uterus is *tahor* or *tamei*. The *Noda BiYehudah* assumes that we rule that blood from a uterine wound is *tamei*; although it doesn't cause the woman to be a *niddah*, the blood itself is *tamei* and imparts *tumah* to items it comes in contact with. In contrast, everyone agrees that blood from a non-uterine wound is *tahor*: not only is the woman not rendered a *niddah*, the blood does not impart *tumah* to anything. Hence, since bloods from these two types of wounds have different halakhic statuses, they are sufficiently dissimilar to combine for a *sfek sfeika*.

c) ***Ketamim*:** The third situation in which the Rama relies on the Rashba's definition of wounds not known to bleed is with regard to *ketamim*.[39] Thus, if a woman finds a large *ketem*, and has a wound generally known to bleed but not actively observed to bleed in this case, she may assume the *ketem* came from that wound. This is one of the many leniencies that *halakhah* provides for cases of *ketamim*.

The *poskim* also discuss a situation less blatant than even a wound not known to bleed: a "*ke'aiv*", an experience of discomfort or irritation, not clearly the result of a known wound. A dispute exists as to whether a *ketem* can be assumed to come from this unverified wound. The best advice for women in such situations is to go to a doctor and have the source of their irritation examined; often, the doctor will find a wound, which one may then assume was the source of the *ketem*.

38. *Niddah* 66a.
39. *Yoreh De'ah* 187:5.

13.

Halakhic Reliance upon Medical Opinion

As we have seen, a number of issues in the laws of *niddah* draw upon medical expertise (e.g. the status of a wound, the details of a procedure that may cause the uterus to open). Accordingly, it becomes critical to know if information gained from doctors is generally deemed reliable by *halakhah*.

In at least one instance, the Talmud[1] indicates that one may issue a halakhic ruling based on information gained from a doctor. This passage deals with a case where doctors declare that a person will die if he does not eat; such a person may, based on the doctors' pronouncement, eat on the fast of Yom Kippur. However, the potential application from this case is limited. It is possible to understand, as many *poskim* do, that the doctor's pronouncement does not necessarily create a definitive halakhic reality; rather, it is sufficient to render the situation one of a "*safek sakkanah*", where there is significant basis to be concerned for a risk to life, which is sufficient cause to permit the patient to eat. It would

1. *Yoma* 83a.

remain unclear, from this source alone, if the doctor's ruling suffices to establish a reliable halakhic certainty.

The questions in the area of *niddah* and a physician's reliability can be put as two separate issues: 1) Can medical expertise be relied upon as halakhic fact; 2) As a general rule, is it automatically assumed that the doctor is always telling the truth?

Of relevance is a story related in the Talmud,[2] concerning a woman who discharged an unidentified substance from her uterus. The Talmud records that in such circumstances, in order to determine what the substance was, Chazal, after consulting with doctors, would put the substance in water. If it dissolved, they concluded it was blood, and if not, they concluded it was not blood. It is somewhat unclear what to glean from this passage: on the one hand, doctors were consulted; on the other, a halakhic ruling was not issued until the Rabbis performed a particular test.

The Rosh[3] explains that the doctors only recommended their test because the doctors could not definitively say there was a wound, and therefore advocated that the test be done. It emerges, according to the Rosh, that doctors are relied upon when they say they know something with certainty.

However, other *Rishonim* argue with the Rosh. The *Tur*[4] cites the *Sefer HaTerumah*[5] as noting that it might be the case that doctors' views are accepted as reliable only in certain cases, such as situations in which there is no previously established status of "forbidden". For example: As discussed above, in the extremely rare instance that a woman sees blood as a result of intercourse three times in a row, she and her husband become forbidden to one another and they must divorce. If a doctor were to perform a procedure on her, and consequently claim that she is forever cured, and that she will never see blood as a result of intercourse again, could they remain together? The *Sefer HaTerumah* is unsure if this testimony would be accepted in such a case, because the

2. *Niddah* 22b.
3. *Tosfei HaRosh,* ibid.
4. *Yoreh De'ah* 187:8.
5. # 107.

woman has already been established as forbidden to her husband. The doctor's view would be relied upon, however, had she not yet become forbidden to her husband.

This distinction has its roots in the Talmudic debate about whether or not one witness is deemed reliable.[6] The emerging conclusion of this debate is that a single witness is believed to clarify matters where no previous status has been established, but not to remove someone or something from an established status. For example: if it is unclear whether or not an item of food is kosher, a single witness is believed to say that it is kosher. However, if it is known that the food was not kosher at one time, the witness is not believed to testify that its status has changed and it is now kosher.

The Ritzba[7] further extends this link between a lone witness and doctors. Observant Jews in good standing are always trusted in halakhic matters; hence, observant doctors may be relied upon. However, if the witness is non-Jewish or non-observant, his testimony is only relied upon if it is revealed without foreknowledge of its halakhic implications (*meisiach le-fi tumo*). Consequently, the testimony of non-Jewish or non-observant doctors would only be accepted if they are unaware of their testimony's halakhic ramifications. Contemporary practice is to only rely on non-observant or non-Jewish witnesses in certain limited areas of *halakhah* (such matters that are only Rabbinic in nature, and also matters relating to permitting *agunot*, which has unique urgency), and as such, according to the Ritzba's premise, such doctors would not be relied upon for *niddah* questions.

However, an additional basis to accept such testimony can be constructed on the words of the authors of the *Tosafot*.[8] They explain the premise that a non-Jewish professional connoisseur is believed to declare a piece of food kosher based on its taste. This occurs in a situation in which non-kosher food was mixed with kosher food and the status of the mixture depends on whether the non-kosher food can still be

6. See *Yevamot* 88a and *Gittin* 2b.
7. Cited in *Hagahot Maimoniyot* (*Kushta*) *Hilkhot Issurei Bi'ah* 4:20 and in *Beit Yosef* to YD 187:8.
8. *Chullin* 97a, s.v. *samchinan*.

tasted. Since he is a professional connoisseur, his culinary expertise can be trusted, as we assume that professionals will never act in a way that imperils their reputation (known elsewhere as "*uman lo mari nafshei*"). Presumably, this principle applies to contemporary doctors. Doctors will tell patients the truth, if for no other reason than otherwise they will harm their professional reputation. Therefore, if their medical expertise is trusted, it can likewise be assumed they are telling the truth.

In practice, the majority of modern day *poskim* assume that one may rely on the testimony of doctors in halakhic matters. In the matter of *niddah*, they base this decision, in addition to the above factors, on the fact that contemporary medicine is not the same as in previous era, when medical assessment would need to be based more heavily on theory. In the Talmudic era, doctors could not perform internal examinations as they can now. Today, each doctor can look and describe what he or she sees. Doctors are believed to say that a woman has a wound, not only because of their professional reputation, but because the presence of the wound is something objectively verifiable. The Talmud assumes that nobody will lie about something that many others can independently verify[9] (*milta di-avidi li-igluyei*). Consequently, it is accepted that one can rely upon all doctors, Jewish and non-Jewish, observant and non-observant alike.

9. *Bekhorot* 36a.

Section IV: Special *Gezeirot* and Unique Situations

14.

Dam Betulim – Hymenal Blood

The blood that emerges when a couple has intercourse for the first time, known as *dam betulim,* is subject to a distinct status in the laws of *niddah.* Initially, the Rabbis assume that this "hymenal blood" is not a problem on a Biblical level; since it clearly does not come from the uterus, it should be *tahor,* like all blood known to come from a wound. The *Mishnah*[1] discusses at what point, after the first intercourse, it must be assumed that the blood present is no longer hymenal blood, and is instead *niddah* blood. The *Mishnah* concludes that each case must be judged independently, and provides various guidelines based on the age and history of the woman involved. However, the Talmud[2] rules that all of the *Mishnah's* time spans are no longer relevant, and it is ruled that any blood seen after the first intercourse is considered *niddah* blood, even if it is known for certain that it is hymenal blood. This indicates that Chazal eliminated the presumed leniency of hymenal blood altogether;

1. *Niddah* 64b.
2. *Niddah* 65b.

for practical purposes, they equated such blood to *niddah* blood completely. Accordingly, under most circumstances, a newly-married couple is required to separate and initiate *niddah* observance immediately after their first act of intercourse.

There are a number of explanations given by the *Rishonim* as to what prompted this ruling, including:

1. Ramban[3] maintains that blood from a wound, including hymenal blood, is only *tahor* if one is able to discern between such blood and *niddah* blood. In the Talmudic era, many rabbis were indeed able to differentiate between these types of blood.[4]
2. Nowadays, however, we are not able discern between them, and we must forbid everything of this type. Other *Rishonim* disagree and argue that as long as one does not know for certain that the blood is *niddah* blood, if the woman has a condition or an abrasion that is bleeding, we can assume it is blood from a wound. In practice, the majority view in the *Rishonim* against the Ramban has been accepted, and blood from a wound is deemed *tahor*.
3. Rashba[5] explains that hymenal blood and blood from a wound are actually permitted, by both Biblical and Rabbinic law. However, since the laws of blood from a wound are so confusing and difficult, Chazal were inclined to abolish them altogether, lest people make grievous errors. They refrained from unilaterally declaring blood from a wound forbidden, because this would have been an overbearing hardship. Instead, they made the following compromise: if a woman had a chronic condition or a wound that causes ongoing bleeding, they were lenient, because otherwise that woman would never be permitted to her husband. However, in cases where a woman has merely a passing or temporary wound, they declared blood from a wound *tamei*. The classic example of a temporary wound is hymenal blood, where the woman bleeds for a few days at most. According to the Rashba's position, any

3. *Hilkhot Niddah* 3:7–9.
4. *Niddah* 20b.
5. *Responsa*, VII, 161.

type of temporary wound would be subject to Chazal's stringency, and any blood from such a wound is considered *niddah* blood.[6] In practice this implied ruling of the Rashba has not been accepted.

4. The Rashba also notes that it is possible that the couple had intercourse in a way that did not break the hymenal ring,[7] and thus Chazal deemed as insufficient the probability that blood resulting from the first intercourse came from the hymenal ring, and therefore forbade it. It seems that his understanding is that it is only assumed that blood came from a wound if the probability of this being the case rises above a certain threshold. The *Sidrei Taharah*[8] asserts that this is a difficult argument to accept; it is patently obvious, he argues, that blood that emerges after the first intercourse is hymenal blood, and indeed the Rashba[9] himself notes that this is generally the case.
5. As the above explanations are all subject to dispute, the most accepted approach is that of the Rosh.[10] In his view, the stringency on hymenal blood is based on the concern that *niddah* blood is mixed in with the hymenal blood. However, he notes, this is not enough to explain why the concern applies even in situations where this is unlikely; the stringency is applied universally because of the difficulty in ascertaining when the concern is relevant and when it is not. As such, the Rabbis instituted the policy in all cases.

This concern applies uniquely to hymenal blood, but not to blood from an ordinary wound, for various reasons. The Ra'avad[11] writes that the concern is that the pain associated with the experience of the first intercourse will cause *niddah* blood to emerge with the hymenal blood; similarly, the *Sefer HaEshkol*[12] maintains that the concern is that

6. See *Sidrei Taharah* YD 193:1.
7. See *Niddah* 64b.
8. 193:1.
9. *Torat HaBayit* p. 50 in Mossad HaRav Kook edition.
10. *Niddah* 10:1.
11. *Ba'alei HaNefesh, Sha'ar HaPerishah* 3:5, p. 29 in Mossad HaRav Kook edition.
12. *Birkhot Chatanim* 47.

the state of arousal engendered by intercourse will cause some *niddah* blood to emerge.

The *Rishonim* debate the contemporary application of this law. The Ra'avad writes that if the first intercourse does not result in bleeding, the couple need not separate.[13] Other *Rishonim* argue, based on the Talmud phraseology that "she participates in the first intercourse and separates herself from her husband"; the implication is that she is forbidden by Rabbinic law, even if there is no blood at all.

The necessity for this policy is explained by most *Rishonim* as based on the assumption that there indeed was blood, but that something happened to it. One possibility is that it was covered by semen; if this is the issue, if the intercourse does not reach the stage where semen is discharged, there is no concern. Another possibility is that the blood was mistakenly wiped off; if that is the issue, even without a discharge there is basis for concern.

The *Shulchan Arukh*[14] rules that the relevant assumption is that the semen covered up the blood, in which case one could be lenient when there was no semen. Many *Acharonim*, however, are concerned that there was blood that was wiped away; indeed, the standard contemporary ruling is that the woman is forbidden to her husband even if no blood is seen, and even if the husband did not discharge semen.

If that is the case, application of this rule requires determining when intercourse has taken place. Generally, the halakhic definition of intercourse does not require full penetration of the vaginal area. Nevertheless, the Rama[15] writes that the concern of blood that has been wiped off is present only when there has been full penetration, but not when there has been only partial penetration.

Due to their inexperience, newlyweds are often not sure if there was full or only partial penetration. In practice, different *rabbanim* take different approaches to this issue. R. Shmuel Wosner[16] maintains that once the couple feels that most of the male organ has penetrated, they

13. *Ba'alei HaNefesh* ibid; also cited in *Hagahot Maimoniyot, Issurei Bi'ah* 11:3.
14. *Yoreh De'ah* 193:1.
15. Ibid.
16. *Shiurei Shevet HaLevi,* 193:7.

may not have intercourse again, because there may have been full penetration despite their lack of awareness. Others argue that if the couple felt only an incomplete penetration, they may follow the Rama's leniency and have intercourse again.

Often, however, the couple cannot report anything. Since hymenal blood probably is not *niddah* blood, and we assume it to be *niddah* blood only due to layers of stringency, one may be lenient in this case, for several reasons: 1) hymenal blood is Biblically *tahor*; 2) The Ra'avad is completely lenient when there is no blood; 3) Although the *halakhah* in this case generally does not follow the Ra'avad, many cases where the couple is unsure about the depth of penetration do not involve semen, in which case even the *Shulchan Arukh* is lenient. Only the situation in which the couple felt a total penetration requires stringency. These issues must be dealt with on a case by case basis; nevertheless, if blood is seen then these deliberations are irrelevant, and the woman is definitely a *niddah*.

With the exception of unusual circumstances, the practice of having a doctor break the hymen is generally not recommended. However, if the doctor does break the hymen, the status of blood that comes out is the subject of debate. As noted above, the Ra'avad maintained that hymenal blood is *tamei* because the pain of intercourse may have caused *niddah* blood to also emerge, while the *Sefer HaEshkol* was of the opinion that the arousal may have caused *niddah* blood to emerge. According to the view of the *Sefer HaEshkol*, the woman is clearly not a *niddah* in this case because there is no arousal when the doctor breaks her hymen. However, the view of the Ra'avad would indicate stringency, because there is pain involved in the procedure (although the usual practice today is to use either local or general anesthesia, which would presumably neutralize that factor). In practice, R. Moshe Feinstein[17] is lenient on this issue. R. Ovadiah Yosef[18] is lenient as well, while the *Minchat Yitzchak*[19] takes a stringent stance.

R. Moshe Feinstein also discusses the case of a woman who no

17. *Responsa Iggerot Moshe, Yoreh De'ah* I, 87.
18. *Taharat HaBayit*, 10:9, p. 519.
19. *Responsa Minchat Yitzchak*, IV, 58.

longer has a hymenal ring because it was removed during childhood through a medical procedure. Some *poskim* maintain that just as we do not make exceptions even when there is no blood, we do not make exceptions when there is no hymen. Others argue that there is no reason for the couple to separate after intercourse if we know for certain that she has no hymenal blood. In fact the Maharsha[20] is lenient, but *Acharonim* debate whether or not one may follow his ruling. In practice, R. Moshe Feinstein was lenient in a case where a doctor tells her with certainty that she will not bleed. In general, one has a right to rule leniently on these matters, because it is a Rabbinic prohibition that is involved.

20. *Ketubot* 4a.

15.

Dam Chimud

I. THE ENACTMENT OF *DAM CHIMUD*

The Talmud[1] states that when one proposes marriage to a woman, the woman must count *shivah nekiyim* and go to the *mikveh*. This is the case even if she was never a *niddah*, or she has already gone through menopause.[2] Chazal assume that the excitement, or arousal, related to the marriage proposal will likely trigger the release of blood, which they call *dam chimud*, lit. "blood of anticipation." The Talmud in this context assumes that *dam chimud* is *niddah* blood.

In contrast, the Talmud elsewhere[3] relates that Ifra Hurmiz, a non-Jew who kept the laws of family purity, once sent her *bedikah* cloth to Rava, who said that the blood on that cloth was *dam chimud*. This passage implies that *dam chimud* is perceivably distinct from *niddah* blood. The *Rishonim* quotes three possible answers to this apparent contradiction:

1. *Niddah* 66a.
2. This second detail is not recorded in the Talmud but is found in *Pitchei Teshuvah*, YD 192:2.
3. *Niddah* 20b.

1. The Ran[4] writes that in actuality, there is no halakhic difference between *dam chimud* and *niddah* blood; when Rava said that Ifra Hurmiz' cloth was stained with *dam chimud,* he was not ruling the blood as *tahor,* but merely stating the distinction in order to impress Ifra Hurmiz with his skills in discerning different types of blood, to prove that Chazal were wise.
2. Alternatively, the Ran also suggests that *dam chimud* is indeed distinct from *niddah* blood, and should be *tahor* even on the Rabbinical level; nonetheless, Chazal assume that some *niddah* blood got mixed with the *dam chimud,* and therefore were stringent.
3. The *Or Zarua*[5] writes that *dam chimud* is *tahor* on a Biblical level, but Chazal forbade it, without the concern that *niddah* blood was mixed with it. Further, we are concerned for *dam chimud* even when no blood is found.

In the modern era, there is no way to know what is *dam chimud* and what is not, and thus any blood from the uterus is deemed *niddah* blood, assuming there is no wound that may have caused it.

There is some debate as to when the enactment concerning *dam chimud* was instituted. The *Taz*[6] raises the question that in the story related in *Megillat Rut,* there is no concern displayed for *dam chimud.* In that text, it is related that Rut came to Boaz at night, and she is told that he will marry her in the morning. The *Taz* notes that these circumstances should require a wait of *shivah nekiyim,* followed by immersion in the *mikveh.*

To answer this question, he provides two suggestions:

1. *Dam chimud* is not *tamei* when the marriage proposal will be closely followed by the marriage. When everything happens at a rapid pace, there may be no time for the woman to become excited or aroused, and accordingly there is no concern that *dam chimud* will be seen.

4. *Chiddushei HaRan, Niddah* 20b, s.v. *hai.*
5. Section 341.
6. YD 192:1.

2. Alternatively, *tumah* was only decreed on *dam chimud* at a later point in history. The *Taz* reasons that this decree could only have been made once the notion of Rabbinically-ordained *niddut* without *hargashah* was created, and this notion was only instituted after the time of Boaz.

The Rambam[7] presents the chronology differently. He places the decree regarding *dam chimud* at the time that the Jewish women adopted the stringency of treating all blood as *niddah* blood. This was during the era of R. Zeira, which would place it at the beginning of the period of the *Amoraim.*

II. DEFINING THE POINT OF "MARRIAGE PROPOSAL" IN CONTEMPORARY PRACTICE

In any event, the current existence of this enactment of *dam chimud* requires defining the contemporary equivalent of the Talmudic era's "marriage proposal". One might initially assume that it is what is colloquially called "engagement"; However, many *poskim* believe that the relevant stage is reached only when the *tenaim*, the financial obligations of the couple and their families to each other, are signed, because at that point it is clear that the couple is serious about getting married. This is difficult to accept in terms of contemporary practice, since in many communities the *tenaim* are written and signed just hours before the *chuppah*, and some couples do not have *tenaim* altogether.

Later *poskim* understood that the *tenaim* were viewed as significant because they indicated a binding monetary commitment made by both parties. Therefore, in the modern era, the "marriage proposal" takes place when the couple's parents put down non-refundable deposits on the wedding hall, the flowers, the photographer, and the like.

It is important to note that the Rosh[8] believes that the "marriage proposal" takes place much closer to the wedding. In fact, he feels that the degree of arousal grows as the wedding approaches.

7. *Hilkhot Issurei Bi'ah* 11:9–10.
8. *Niddah* 10:4.

The Rashba[9] writes that as soon as there is a "marriage proposal," the woman must wait *shivah nekiyim* and go to the *mikveh* in order to become *tehorah*. If so, then a woman who gets her period twenty days before the wedding could begin counting *shivah nekiyim* fifteen days before the wedding, and those *shivah nekiyim* would suffice for her ordinary period and for any *dam chimud* she might have seen. However, as noted above, the Rosh argues. He writes that the time of arousal is not only when the money is laid out, but rather is the entire time between the proposal and the wedding. Accordingly, in his view, the *shivah nekiyim* and the *mikveh* immersion should be as close to the wedding as possible.

The Rama[10] rules that brides must go to the *mikveh* no more than four days prior to their weddings. The basis for the number "four" in this case is somewhat complex:

The *Mishnah*[11] states that virgins, historically, would get married on Wednesdays, and presumably they went to the *mikveh* on Tuesday nights. In the era of the Rama, in the European Jewish communities, weddings were often held on a Friday afternoon, because the people were so poor that they could not afford both a wedding feast and a Shabbat meal, and thus they combined the two. The couple would not have the first intercourse until Shabbat ended, because some were of the opinion that it is forbidden to have the first intercourse on Shabbat. Even though the couple got married on Friday, European women still went to the *mikveh* on Tuesday night, because that was the traditional practice. Since the end of Shabbat is four nights after Tuesday night, the Rama, inferring from the accepted practice of his time, concluded that going to the *mikveh* four nights before the first act of intercourse is close enough to satisfy the Rosh's opinion.

In practice, this ruling of the Rama is followed, and accordingly women who are getting married on Sunday may go to the *mikveh* as early as Wednesday night.

9. *Torat HaBayit* p. 63.
10. *Yoreh De'ah* 192:2.
11. *Ketubot* 2a.

III. *BEDIKOT* FOLLOWING THE IMMERSION

The Rama rules that if the woman cannot go to the *mikveh* within four days before the wedding, she may go earlier, but with the proviso that she check herself with a *bedikah* cloth between her immersion and the wedding. If she did not check herself, however, she is still considered *tehorah*. Some *Acharonim* are stringent and require her to check herself even if she goes within four days of her wedding, but the Rama makes no mention of such *bedikot*. Further, some *poskim* are strongly opposed to performing these *bedikot* because a woman may irritate herself and cause blood to come out. Those *Acharonim* who do require such *bedikot* do not suspend this requirement until either after the wedding or after the first intercourse.

The Rama also writes that, *bediavad*, if she checks herself once within seven days, it is sufficient. The practical implications of this statement are unclear. Some *Acharonim* believe the Rama is, all told, presenting three scenarios: a) If the bride goes to the *mikveh* within four days of the wedding, no *bedikah* is necessary. b) If she immerses more than four days before the wedding, but within a week, a *bedikah* is required, but its absence does not change her status. c) If she immerses more than a week before the wedding, a *bedikah* is required, and when omitted, she is presumed to be a *niddah*.

Other *Acharonim* argue that the Rama's statement is regarding *bedikot* during the *shivah nekiyim*. They maintain that the Rama means that when a woman becomes a *niddah* because of *dam chimud*, then one *bedikah* is enough, even though it is generally ruled that a minimum of two *bedikot* are required during *shivah nekiyim*. According to these *Acharonim*, the Rama is lenient on the number of *bedikot* during *shivah nekiyim* because the law of *dam chimud* is only Rabbinic in nature.

In contemporary times, brides go to the *mikveh* before their weddings because they are *niddot* on a Biblical level.[12] However, the positions of the Rosh and the Rama concerning *dam chimud* continue to impact on the details of this immersion. Accordingly, women should not go to

12. Accordingly, the *Shulchan Arukh*'s statement (192:1) that a *hefsek taharah* is not required following *dam chimud* is not practically relevant; see *Shakh*, 192:2.

the *mikveh* immediately after they get their periods, but should instead wait until near the time of the wedding, ideally immersing within four days of the wedding, as discussed above.

16.

The Prohibition of *Yichud* Prior to *Bi'ah Rishonah*

I. THE ORIGIN OF THE LAW

The prohibition forbidding a man and woman from being in *yichud*, seclusion, with one another is generally only relevant to men and women who are not married to each other. However, there are potential applications of this prohibition even in the context of marriage. One such situation involves a woman who has the status of a *niddah* on either a Biblical or Rabbinic level at the time of marriage.

The Rabbinic status of *niddah* could potentially result from the bride's failure to wait *shivah nekiyim* following the point of concern for *dam chimud* (the possibility that anticipation for the wedding might trigger a sighting of blood, as discussed in the previous section). A scenario involving Biblical *niddah* status would be when the woman was a *niddah* at the time of the *chuppah*.

These situations are addressed by the Talmudic statement[1] that the prohibition forbidding *yichud* is inapplicable to a husband and wife while the wife is a *niddah*. However, the Talmud qualifies its principle

1. *Ketubot* 4a.

and limits the allowance to a couple who have previously had relations. A couple, though, which has not yet consummated their marriage, is still governed by the prohibition of *yichud*.

II. THE PROHIBITION OF *YICHUD*: BIBLICAL OR RABBINIC

It is generally assumed that the prohibition of *yichud* is Biblical in nature deriving from the verse:[2] "If your brother, the son of your mother, or your son, or your daughter, or the wife of your bosom, or your friend, that is as your own soul, entice you secretly, saying: 'Let us go and serve other gods,' which you have not known, you, nor your fathers". On the surface, the verse is discussing the secretive enticement to worship *avodah zarah*; however, the Rabbis[3] highlighted an additional layer of understanding which relates the verse to a man and woman who interact in seclusion. The Biblical prohibition, however, would be limited to women who are halakhically classified as "*arayot*", a category whose definition will be discussed below. Later, King David introduced a Rabbinic enactment forbidding seclusion with all Jewish women, whether *halakhah* deems them "*arayot*" or not, in the aftermath of the incident of Amnon and Tamar.[4] King David's enactment focused exclusively on Jewish men and women; however, a later decree instituted in the days of the students of Shammai and Hillel extended the Rabbinic prohibition to include non-Jews as well.

With this framework in the background, the nature of the prohibition of *yichud* as it applies to one's wife while she is a *niddah* should hinge upon the halakhic classification of the prohibition of *niddah,* more specifically whether it is regarded as a type of "*arayot*". To address that issue, two central questions must be considered: what are the defining features of the category of *arayot*; and, given that definition, does *niddah* qualify to be incorporated within that category. *Rishonim* and *Acharonim* develop three possibilities:

1. Some *Acharonim* adopt a broad interpretation of the term *arayot*

2. *Devarim* 13:7.
3. *Avodah Zarah* 36b.
4. Ibid.

for the purposes of *yichud,* and include within this category any relationship that is Biblically forbidden. Accordingly, since it is Biblically forbidden to have relations with a *niddah,* it would follow that the prohibition of *yichud* possesses Biblical standing.

Others interpret the term *arayot* more narrowly, and, consequently, open up more of a question as to whether the prohibition of *niddah* fits the specific qualifications of the category of *arayot*:

2. The Rambam[5] defines the category of *arayot* as consisting of any forbidden relationship that entails the punishment of "*kareit*" (excision). According to this definition, the category of *arayot* would incorporate the prohibition of *niddah,* and the resulting prohibition of *yichud* would be Biblical in nature.
3. Rabbenu Tam[6] offers an alternate, narrower definition of the category of *arayot,* one which results in the exclusion of a *niddah* from this category. The term *arayot,* in his view, is reserved for a woman who is permissible to one category of people, yet prohibited to a second category. Since a *niddah* is prohibited to everyone, that prohibition is not within the classification of *arayot.* Consequently, the prohibition of *yichud* with a woman who is a *niddah* would only have a Rabbinic foundation.

An additional consideration that must be addressed in this context is whether the level of prohibition forbidding *yichud* with a *niddah* applies equally when the woman is one's own wife. Even if the prohibition of *yichud* is Biblically mandated in the general case, perhaps the prohibition would be Rabbinic in nature with respect to one's wife. *Tosafot*'s rationale for the prohibition of *niddah* provides potential grounds for such a distinction. The authors of the *Tosafot*[7] wonder how a husband and wife are permitted to live in *yichud* if the prohibition of *yichud* is Biblically forbidden. They explain that specific parameters naturally limit

5. *Hilkhot Ishut* 1:5 and *Hilkhot Issurei Bi'ah* 4:1.
6. *Sefer HaYashar, Responsa* 80:1.
7. *Sotah* 7a, s.v. *niddah*; *Sanhedrin* 37a, s.v. *haTorah.*

the application of the prohibition, even if it is Biblically mandated. For example, a father and daughter or a mother and son are not governed by the laws of *yichud* since there is little concern that their seclusion might devolve into forbidden interaction. This structured limitation also applies to a husband and wife while the wife is a *niddah*. The imminent restoration of permissibility, coupled with the current reality of her forbidden status, serve as reliable deterrents from any forbidden interaction. In these specific cases, when the concern that seclusion might lead to forbidden interactions is alleviated, the prohibition of *yichud* is suspended.

In light of *Tosafot*'s perspective, the prohibition of *yichud*, as it applies to a husband and wife prior to the consummation of their marriage, is entirely understandable. Since the couple's yearning for one another is overwhelmingly powerful, the imminent restoration of permissibility and the wife's current status of being a *niddah* fail to serve as a sufficient deterrent. At the same time, it is not clear whether this consideration, and its distinction from the general exception regarding a husband and wife, exists within the Biblical framework of the prohibition of *yichud* or whether it is an additional consideration that enters on the Rabbinic plane. Clarification of this uncertainty is of paramount importance, as it determines whether the prohibition of *yichud* under question is Biblical or Rabbinic in nature. The application of certain leniencies concerning this matter might hinge upon this determination.

III. THE UNIQUE PARAMETERS OF *YICHUD* PRIOR TO *BI'AH RISHONAH*

The Talmud,[8] in its description of the prohibition of *yichud* prior to the consummation of the marriage, uses a peculiar phrase, describing the situation as: "The husband sleeps amongst the men, while the wife sleeps amongst the women." It would have been simpler to state plainly that there is a prohibition of *yichud*. The Ra'avad[9] infers from the Talmud's characterization that unique parameters govern this instance of the prohibition of *yichud*. The Talmud's focus on the sleeping arrangements of the husband and wife indicates that the prohibition of *yichud* is limited

8. *Ketubot* 4a.
9. *Ba'alei HaNefesh, Sha'ar HaPerishah* 1:22, p. 26 in Mossad HaRav Kook edition.

to the nighttime, and is inapplicable during the daytime. Furthermore, the leniency regarding the daytime can then be extended even into the evening, until the time one begins to ready oneself for going to sleep. The *Chazon Ish*[10] reasoned that the Ra'avad endorsed the viewpoint that views this application of *yichud* as being Rabbinic in nature; otherwise, the Ra'avad would not have ruled so leniently. This assertion regarding the Rabbinic character of the prohibition might be significant, irrespective of one's acceptance of the Ra'avad's specific conclusion.

Based on the Talmud's unusual formulation, the Ra'avad derived a second anomalous feature concerning this specific application of *yichud*, although this parameter contains a stringent bent. Generally, the presence of one additional man together with a couple is sufficient to remove any violation of *yichud*. The Ra'avad claims that the Talmud's dual focus on the husband and the wife indicates that the standards are elevated prior to the consummation of the marriage. A dual "protection" is required; not only must the husband be accompanied by another male, the wife must be accompanied by an additional female. Some *Acharonim* develop this point even further and require two additional men and women, due to the Talmud's plural formulation of "men" and "women." Others explain, however, that the plural form includes the husband and wife, and, as a result, they only require one additional male and female.

The Rosh[11] disputes the Ra'avad on both counts, arguing instead that the Talmud's linguistic formulation is insignificant. The Rosh is, therefore, stringent regarding the application of the prohibition by day as well as by night; however, at the same time, he is lenient with regard to the sufficiency of a single, additional male to disrupt the seclusion of husband and wife.[12]

IV. PRACTICAL APPLICATIONS

The Rama[13] rules that the *halakhah* is in accordance with the stringencies of both opinions. As such, the prohibition of *yichud* applies during the

10. *Yoreh De'ah* 91:3.
11. *Moed Katan* 3:36.
12. Note, in the Makhon Yerushalayim edition of the Tur, YD 192, fn 38.
13. *Yoreh De'ah* 192:4.

daytime in accordance with the opinion of the Rosh, and the presence of an additional male and female are required at nighttime in accordance with the perspective of the Ra'avad. During the daytime, however, only a single, additional person needs to be present, since the Ra'avad's stringency of "dual protection" will not apply during a time period in which he denied the existence of any prohibition.

The Rama adds that a child may serve the role of additional male presence if he understands the general concepts of male/female relations.[14] *Poskim* debate the precise level of maturity necessary in order to qualify. Some *poskim* argue that the standard for maturity is established by a child's self awareness not to appear in public spaces of the house without clothes on. At that stage, the child will understand that the couple is acting inappropriately and might report what he witnessed to others. This fear will serve as a deterrent to the couple.

With these principles and definitions in mind, the *Badei HaShulchan*[15] presents the standard practice of having a child in the "*yichud* room" together with the newlywed couple in a situation in which the bride is a *niddah* at the time of the wedding. If the wedding is being conducted at an exceptionally late hour, one that would be regarded as a time for sleep, then a boy and girl should be present together with the couple.

V. CONSUMMATION OF THE MARRIAGE: A PRACTICAL DEFINITION

Still to be determined is the question of at what stage does *halakhah* consider the marriage to be consummated, thereby eliminating the prohibition of *yichud* between a husband and wife. With respect to most *halakhot*, the stage of *ha'ara'ah*, contact and initial penetration, is halakhically deemed to be an act of intercourse. With respect to the *halakhah* of *yichud*, there is an additional psychological consideration that must be factored in beyond the strict halakhic definition. The question, in this context, is whether the relative likelihood of the couple engaging in forbidden behavior increases, decreases, or remains constant after *ha'ara'ah* occurs. Some *poskim*, including Rav Moshe Feinstein, argue that once

14. See *Shakh*, 192:14.

15. 192:55.

ha'ara'ah occurs the couple can be trusted to successfully overcome their desires and wait until the wife's permissibility is restored. As a result, the prohibition of *yichud* is already suspended after *ha'ara'ah.* Other *poskim,* including the *Badei HaShulchan,*[16] contend that until the marriage is fully consummated the overwhelmingly powerful yearnings remain as potent as they were beforehand, if not stronger. This situation can potentially extend for some time, and circumstances of great need can become a basis for leniency. The *Chazon Ish* raises the Rabbinic nature of the prohibition of *yichud,* as was mentioned before, as an additional consideration to be lenient.

Occasionally, the bride becomes a *niddah* before the couple is able to reach even the stage of *ha'ara'ah.* Some *poskim* rule that in such a case the prohibition of *yichud* would apply. However, a surprising ruling of the *Terumat HaDeshen*[17] might provide a foundation for leniency. The *Terumat HaDeshen* discusses a case in which a couple (ill-advisedly) deliberately delayed consummating their marriage for several evenings prior to the bride becoming a *niddah.* In such a situation, the *Terumat HaDeshen* rules that the prohibition of *yichud* is uprooted. The couple's display of restraint until this point earns confidence in their ability to overcome their desires. As a result, despite their failure to consummate their marriage, they are permitted to have *yichud* with one another.

The Rama[18] does cite the position of the *Terumat HaDeshen* as an opinion, but the application of this ruling of the *Terumat HaDeshen* to the current discussion, of a couple that is unsuccessful in consummating their marriage over an extended period of a time, is subject to debate amongst the *poskim.* The *Chazon Ish* ruled stringently on this matter, unwilling to extend his aforementioned leniency to a situation where even *ha'ara'ah* has not taken place. In the situation discussed by the *Terumat HaDeshen,* the couple exhibited restraint for several nights, demonstrating that their yearnings were not overpowering. However, in the present discussion, the couple has tried on multiple occasions, albeit unsuccessfully, to consummate their marriage. As such, the prohibition

16. 192, *Bi'urim,* s.v. *kodem,* p. 238.
17. *Responsa,* 253.
18. *Yoreh De'ah* 192:4.

of *yichud* is appropriate and necessary. R. Ovadiah Yosef,[19] however, quotes the opinion of the *Cheishev HaEifod* who issues a lenient ruling provided that the couple has at least experienced *kiruv basar*, physical contact. R. Ovadiah Yosef's own perspective is that a *rav* should judge each situation individually, independently assessing each couple's capacity to overcome temptation, and evaluating if the likelihood of sin is small enough to allow for leniency. Although reaching such a decision is complex and challenging, the guidelines set forth by R. Ovadiah Yosef should be followed to the best of one's ability.

19. *Taharat HaBayit* p. 494.

17.

A Woman Who Gives Birth

I. THE ELIMINATED LENIENCY OF *DAM KOSHI*

The rules regulating the *niddah* status of a woman who has given birth have been significantly enhanced by Rabbinic legislation. By Torah law, when a woman gives birth, she becomes *teme'ah* for a period of time: seven days after the birth of a boy, and fourteen days after the birth of a girl (even though she continues to bleed long after that time).[1] This is called *tumat yoledet*. In addition to this status, the woman also becomes a *niddah* because of the blood that emerged during the birth process. The *niddah* status does not have consequences on the Biblical level, because the seven days that a *niddah* must wait is matched or exceeded by the time period of *yoledet*.

However, if the woman is not only a *yoledet* but also a *zavah gedolah* (i.e. she bleeds for three days during the "*yemei zivah*" before going into labor), then, in theory, even the Torah would obligate her to count *shivah nekiyim*. Nonetheless, the *Mishnah*[2] teaches that it is also an aspect of Torah law that any blood related to the birthing process is called "*dam koshi*" and is completely *tahor*. Accordingly, the blood the

1. *Vayikra* 12:2.
2. *Niddah* 36b.

woman saw three days before birth would not make her a *zavah gedolah*. There are three opinions listed as to as to how close to birth the blood must be seen in order to be labeled *dam koshi*: a) within 40–50 days (R. Meir); b) during the ninth month (R. Yehudah); c) within two weeks (R. Yose and R. Shimon).

The Talmud, in its discussion on the *Mishnah*, proceeds to narrow the definition of "close to childbirth" even further. The Talmud notes that it is possible for a woman to experience labor pains and give birth ten days later. In such a case, it would be difficult to maintain that blood that she saw a week before those labor pains is considered *dam koshi*. The Talmud further states that if a woman has a break (*shofi*) in the labor, then the blood she sees during or before the first instance of labor cannot be considered *dam koshi*. If so, then it is possible for a woman to be considered a *yoledet* and a *zavah gedolah* at the same time, if the following occurs: If the bleeding was considerably earlier than the labor, or even if it was within a few days of labor but there was a break in the labor, then the blood that she sees is *tamei*, and she is considered to be a *zavah gedolah*. However, the *Rishonim* assert that we no longer try to determine whether or not there was a break in the labor. Instead, we treat each and every woman as a *zavah*, and, in view of the "stringency of Jewish women", every woman who gives birth in modern times also has to count *shivah nekiyim*. In effect, the Talmud and *Rishonim* combine to eliminate the leniency of *dam koshi*.

II. THE ELIMINATED LENIENCY OF *DAM TOHAR*

The Torah also states explicitly that a woman is *teme'ah* for seven days after the birth of a boy and fourteen days after the birth of a girl, and then she goes to the *mikveh*. Any blood she sees after that is labeled "*dam tohar*" and is *tahor* on a Biblical level. The Ramban[3] maintained that this leniency was eliminated as part of the "stringency of Jewish women". The Rambam[4] records that, although some communities were still lenient with regard to *dam tohar*, the *Geonim* essentially eliminated the leniency. The difference between the assessments of the Ramban and the Rambam

3. *Hilkhot Niddah* 7:20.
4. *Hilkhot Issurei Bi'ah* 11:5–7.

would be whether or not every single community in the world has to be stringent on this matter; in fact, the Rambam writes that some communities never accepted upon themselves the stringency of forbidding *dam tohar*, and were not obligated to do so. Nevertheless, in contemporary times, every community world-wide has come to accept this stringency.

Thus far, it has been established that in practice, a woman who has given birth is obligated to wait *shivah nekiyim*, and cannot start that count until all bleeding stops, as *dam tohar* is now treated as *tamei*. Accordingly, in keeping with this understanding, if a woman stops seeing blood twenty five days after giving birth, she can wait *shivah nekiyim* and then become permitted to her husband again.

III. THE PRACTICE TO WAIT 40 OR 80 DAYS BEFORE IMMERSION:

The Rambam[5] writes that, in some locations, the women were considered prohibited throughout the period of *dam tohar* – forty days after the birth of a boy, and eighty days after the birth of a girl – and would only immerse after that time. The Rambam claims that this practice came from the Karaites, and that to follow it is therefore tainted by heresy. Others, however, tried to justify this practice:

1. The Rama[6] notes that there is a Talmudic debate about whether or not a woman who stops bleeding during her *yemei leidah* (the first seven or fourteen days after birth) can count those days toward her *shivah nekiyim*, which Rava allowed and Abaye did not. All the *Rishonim* followed Rava, except for Rabbenu Tam, who followed Abaye.[7] Additionally, the opinion of *Beit Hillel*, which the *halakhah* follows, is that *yemei leidah* are only terminated when the fourteen days (or seven days) are completed

5. *Hilkhot Issurei Bi'ah* 11:15.
6. *Yoreh De'ah* 194, *Darkhei Moshe HaArukh*, 3.
7. The *Shulchan Arukh* (YD 194:3) follows the majority view of the *Rishonim* in this case, and this is relevant in the event of a miscarriage. The woman must count fourteen *yemei leidah*, out of concern that the child was a girl. However, if the bleeding stops, according to this ruling, she may count those days toward her *shivah nekiyim*.

and when the woman goes to the *mikveh*. Thus, notes the Rama, if one wishes to take into account the view of Rabbenu Tam, then every woman who gives birth must actually go to the *mikveh* twice, once after the *yemei leidah* (to officially begin the *yemei tohar*), and again after the *shivah nekiyim* (to become permitted to her husband). The Rama adds that even *Beit Hillel* would have to agree that if a woman did not go to the *mikveh* after her *yemei leidah,* she would still become eligible to count her *shivah nekiyim* after the entire forty or eighty days had been completed. Thus, the Rama suggests, the practice of waiting forty or eighty days comes from a desire to accommodate the view of Rabbenu Tam, but to only go to the *mikveh* once (immersion in the time and place of the Rama often meant utilizing freezing lakes during the harsh Polish winters). Later *Acharonim* challenge this theory on two grounds: a) following Rabbenu Tam's view on this matter has not been the practice in any community; and b) actually doing so would require waiting 87 days (eighty to end the *yemei leidah,* and then *shivah nekiyim* afterward) instead of just eighty days.

2. The *Sefer Aguddah*[8] suggests that the source for this practice is based on a statement in the Talmud[9] that on the last night of the *yemei tohar,* the couple is prohibited to one another. Some communities followed the practice to refrain the entire period of *yemei tohar* as a safeguard lest the couple forget to refrain on this last night. According to this approach, this practice would apparently not be relevant today. The prohibition of the last night of *yemei tohar* is because we are concerned that since until now, the woman has been disregarding any blood because it has been *dam tohar,* she may mistakenly continue doing so even after *yemei tohar* are over.

8. *Pesachim* ch. 10, 96, cited in Darkhei *Moshe* 194:2*.
9. *Pesachim* 113b.

Chazal instituted this prohibition as a demarcation to avoid this error. We no longer permit *dam tohar,* and therefore this entire concern is irrelevant. If the 40th night is permissible today, there is no need to refrain during the entire *yemei tohar* according to the reason mentioned by the *Sefer Aguddah.*

IV. CONTEMPORARY APPLICATION:

In practice, the Rama[10] rules that whatever the origin of this position, it is rejected. However, the notion that every woman who gives birth is a treated as a *zavah gedolah* is followed, as is the practice to forbid *dam tohar.* Further, although it is permissible for a woman to count her seven or fourteen *yemei leidah* as a part of the *shivah nekiyim,* that is usually only possible in the unfortunate event that a woman miscarries. Generally, a woman will continue to bleed for several weeks following childbirth, and become *tehorah* a full week after that stops.

10. *Yoreh De'ah* 194:1.

Section v: The Process of Becoming *Tehorah*

18.

Waiting before *Shivah Nekiyim*: the Rule of "*Poletet*"

Before the status of *niddah* can be removed, a woman must count *shivah nekiyim,* seven clean days. It remains to be determined, though, at what point that count can be permitted to begin.

The Talmudic discussion of *shivah nekiyim* is with regard to a man who is declared a *zav* (one who sees an unnatural emission, in contrast with a *ba'al keri,* which is one who sees an emission of semen). The Talmud[1] derives from a verse[2] that any contraction of ritual impurity during a *zav's shivah nekiyim* breaks up the count, and forces him to begin the count anew. A question is posed as to what happens if a *zav* sees semen, or *tumat keri,* during his *shivah nekiyim*: is it assumed that just as impurity resulting from seeing *zivah* fluids breaks up the *shivah*

1. *Niddah* 22a.
2. *Vayikra* 15:28.

nekiyim, so does impurity resulting from *keri*; or is impurity resulting from the *keri* weaker than impurity resulting from the sight of *zivah* fluids? The Talmud concludes that impurity resulting from *keri* only partially affects the *shivah nekiyim*. The day on which semen was seen cannot count as one of the *shivah nekiyim*, but on the following day the count picks up where it left off. In other words, *keri* merely cancels out the day on which it was seen.

The Talmud[3] further on debates whether this law of discounting one day on account of *keri* has any bearing on the law of *shivah nekiyim* regarding a *zavah* (a status shared with the contemporary *niddah*). *Keri* generally makes a woman *teme'ah*, but it is unclear if the impact of this *tumah* is the same as the impact of blood or not. On the one hand, this discharge, like blood, is a form of ritual impurity that results from a bodily emission. On the other hand, this discharge, unlike blood, has its origins outside the woman's body. The Talmud concludes that discharged semen is similar to blood, since it results from an emission, and therefore any day on which a woman discharged semen cannot count toward her *shivah nekiyim*. Therefore, if a woman had intercourse on Sunday, became a *niddah* on Monday, and then stopped bleeding, if she discharged semen on Tuesday, the *shivah nekiyim* cannot begin until Wednesday.

Further, as the *Rishonim* note, the concern is not only that semen will be discharged with the woman's knowledge; there is a concern as well that there will be a discharge and the woman will not be aware. Accordingly, women cannot begin to count the *shivah nekiyim* until they can be sure that they will no longer discharge semen.

In contradistinction to the above, the Talmud[4] allows women (on a Biblical level) to immerse in the *mikveh* at the beginning of the seventh day of *shivah nekiyim*, because *halakhah* treats counting a partial day as counting a whole clean day (*miktzat ha-yom ki-kulo*). However, if they see blood before the end of that day, the whole count is retroactively invalidated. Therefore, the Talmud cautions couples against having intercourse on the seventh day, even after the woman has gone to the

3. *Niddah* 33a–b.
4. *Niddah* 67b.

mikveh, lest there be bleeding, which would invalidate the whole count, and the couple would incur a penalty of *kareit.* The Talmud implies that only the possibility of seeing blood makes intercourse on the seventh day problematic; the certainty that the woman will discharge semen after the intercourse does not render intercourse problematic. In view of the above, however, the discharge should strike the seventh day from *shivah nekiyim,* leaving the woman a *zavah gedolah* even if she does not see blood.

Rishonim offer three main approaches to explain why the Talmud is not concerned that the woman will certainly discharge semen on the seventh day if she has intercourse:

1. Rabbenu Tam[5] writes that semen only interrupts the *shivah nekiyim* if it comes from a *zav,* not if it comes from a healthy person. By extension, the *shivah nekiyim* of a woman is interrupted only if she discharged semen of a *zav,* a very uncommon occurrence. The Talmud is not concerned about discharges on the seventh day, since most men are not *zavim.* Hence, according to Rabbenu Tam, a woman need not be concerned about unnoticed discharges if her husband is known to not be a *zav.*
2. The Ra'avad[6] explains that discharges impact differently on a woman's status vis-à-vis ritual impurity and her status vis-à-vis her husband. Discharges only affect the *shivah nekiyim* with regard to ritual impurity, but do not affect the time for her to become permitted to her husband. The Rosh notes that according to the Ra'avad, a woman must keep two counts, and go to the *mikveh* twice;[7] once to become permitted to her husband, and later to become ritually pure.[8]

5. Cited in Rosh, *Niddah* 4:1.
6. Ibid.
7. See *Ma'adanei Yom Tov* to Rosh, #9.
8. This comment touches upon a fundamental dispute among the *Rishonim* as to whether or not one can separate a woman's ritual impurity from her relationship with her husband. The core issue at stake is what precisely makes the woman forbidden to her husband: the blood, or the status of ritual impurity caused by the blood. If one believes that the blood first causes ritual impurity, and the ritual impurity

3. The Rosh[9] notes that semen does not cancel the *zavah*'s seven clean days in the same manner that blood cancels the *zavah*'s *shivah nekiyim*. Semen merely postpones the *zav* or *zavah*'s count by one day, but does not require her to begin counting anew. There are two possible ways to explain this: a) semen completely negates the day on which it was seen; b) semen merely prevents that day from being called a "clean day," but does not render that day unclean. The practical difference between these approaches concerns semen seen by a woman on the seventh day after she has gone to the *mikveh*. If semen renders the day unclean, there is no difference whether it is seen before or after immersion. However, if it merely prevents the day from being counted as clean, it does not affect the seventh day. On the seventh day, since part of the day is akin to a whole day, the sight of semen is not powerful enough to retroactively revoke this status. If the Talmud adopts this latter approach, it needs not be concerned about semen discharged after the woman immerses on the seventh day.

In sum, we have three approaches regarding the law of *poletet*. According to Rabbenu Tam, this law only applies to semen of a *zav*, and will therefore arise very infrequently, especially in contemporary times. According

makes her forbidden to her husband, then it is impossible for her to be ritually impure but not forbidden to her husband. Permission for intercourse is a subcategory of the laws of purity. If, however, one believes that blood directly generates both statuses independently, then a woman can be ritually impure but not forbidden to her husband. Permission for intercourse is a subcategory of the laws of permitted and forbidden things.

Interestingly, the Vilna Gaon sees the laws of *niddah* as the paradigm for all laws governing permitted and forbidden things. The verse (*Devarim* 17:8) divides all *halakhah* into three categories: "between blood and blood, between law and law, and between affliction and affliction." The Gaon writes that "blood and blood" refers to *niddah*, where rabbis must distinguish between blood that renders a woman forbidden and blood that does not. This is the paradigm for all *halakhot* governing forbidden and permitted items. "Law and law" refers to monetary cases, and "affliction and affliction" refers to cases of ritual impurity that result from *tzara'at* afflictions. This is the paradigm for laws of ritual impurity.

9. *Niddah* 4:1

to the Ra'avad, this law only relates to ritual impurity, so there is certainly no problem today. Only according to the Rosh is there an issue in the modern era; yet even the Rosh accepts that the law does not apply on the seventh day of *shivah nekiyim* after the woman has gone to the *mikveh*. The majority of *Rishonim* follow the view of the Rosh, as does the *Shulchan Arukh*.[10] Therefore, the law of *poletet* applies today. This means not only that the sight of semen interrupts *shivah nekiyim*, but that women cannot begin counting the *shivah nekiyim* until the concern of discharged semen has passed.

In determining how long the concern of *poletet* applies, it is important to note that only viable semen, that can actually fertilize an egg, cancels *shivah nekiyim*. The Talmud[11] and *Rishonim* debate how long semen remains viable, as do contemporary physicians. The Rambam[12] maintains that semen cancels *shivah nekiyim* for three twelve-hour periods after being deposited in the woman. Most *Rishonim*, as well as the *Shulchan Arukh*,[13] maintain that semen cancels *shivah nekiyim* for six twelve-hour periods. According to this view, women must wait 72 hours, or three days, before beginning *shivah nekiyim*. We have yet to explain, though, how the waiting period has been extended from 72 hours to five days.

10. *Yoreh De'ah* 196:10.
11. *Shabbat* 86b.
12. *Hilkhot Sh'ar Avot HaTumah* 5:11.
13. *Yoreh De'ah* 196:11.

19.

Waiting Five Days prior to Beginning *Shivah Nekiyim*

I. THE DISPUTE BETWEEN THE *SHULCHAN ARUKH* AND RAMA

As a result of the concern of the Rosh, that *poletet* applies today, a woman is required to wait seventy-two hours prior to beginning her observance of *shivah nekiyim*. Since each of the days of *shivah nekiyim* must be entirely clean, if the seventy-two hours terminate in the middle of a particular day, the remainder of that day is also disqualified from counting as the first day of *shivah nekiyim*. For example, if a couple had relations on Sunday evening, the seventy-two hours would conclude on Wednesday evening; however, since part of Wednesday evening was consumed by the concern for an emission of semen, the woman would have to wait until Thursday evening to begin counting *shivah nekiyim*. It is due to this consideration that many *Rishonim* express the *halakhah* as requiring a woman to wait four days prior to beginning her *shivah nekiyim*. The *Shulchan Arukh*[1] rules in accordance with these *Rishonim*, and requires all women to delay their observance of *shivah nekiyim* until

1. *Yoreh De'ah* 196:11.

after four days have passed. It should be noted that the measure of four days is a minimum waiting period. If a woman continues to bleed, the onset of her *shivah nekiyim* will be prolonged accordingly.

The Rama,[2] however, adds an additional day to the minimum waiting period required prior to allowing the woman to perform a *hefsek taharah* (the *bedikah* that allows the *shivah nekiyim* to begin, as discussed below). The Rama introduces a concern for an extenuating circumstance should the couple have relations during the period of *bein ha-shemashot* (twilight). For example, if a couple had relations during the *bein ha-shemashot* period on Sunday night, the seventy-two hours may conclude on Wednesday evening prior to nightfall or following nightfall. The difference between the two calculations is whether the couple may count Thursday as the first day of *shivah nekiyim,* or would the couple instead be required to wait until Friday. The Rama was concerned that a couple might calculate the seventy-two hours according to the more lenient method, when in truth their relations really occurred during the evening, leading to the more stringent calculation. In order to alleviate this concern, the Rama added an additional day to the waiting period preceding *shivah nekiyim*. Moreover, even though the concern only exists in a situation in which the couple actually had relations during *bein ha-shemashot,* the Rama, nevertheless, required all women to wait five days prior to performing a *hefsek taharah*. If a woman, for example, sees blood on Sunday evening, the couple would be required to wait five days, and would only be able to start counting *shivah nekiyim* on Friday night.

In many instances, the concern for the emission of semen and the additional day introduced by the Rama will not bear any practical ramifications since it might anyway take four or five days for a woman's bleeding to subside. However, in a case in which a woman has a short period and in a situation of a *ketem,* the enactment will bear great relevance. The Rama strengthens the force of this enactment by issuing a condemnation against anyone who fails to observe the additional day.

2. Ibid.

II. THE UNQUALIFIED NATURE OF THE CONCERN

Presumably, the concern for the emission of semen, in its various forms, should only apply in cases in which the couple had relations immediately prior to the wife becoming a *niddah*. In a situation, though, where the couple could not or did not have relations, a woman should be permitted to start counting *shivah nekiyim* immediately following the cessation of bleeding. In fact, the *Shulchan Arukh*[3] rules that a couple who refrained from having relations during the four days prior to the start of bleeding may, indeed, start counting *shivah nekiyim* immediately. If they had relations three days beforehand, they only need to wait one day before beginning *shivah nekiyim*. On the surface, the *Shulchan Arukh*'s limitation is quite sensible since the entire concern is driven by the consideration for an emission of semen. If the couple has abstained from relations, the entire concern dissipates.

Despite the evident logic underlying the *Shulchan Arukh*'s position, the Rama[4] rules that all women must wait five days prior to beginning *shivah nekiyim*. In order to avoid confusing calculations and unique circumstances, the *halakhah* equates all situations, irrespective of whether or not the couple had relations in actuality, or was even capable of engaging in relations, prior to the onset of bleeding. Even if the husband was in the hospital or otherwise unavailable, and was thus incapable of having relations with his wife, his wife must still wait five days following the initial sighting of blood in order to begin counting *shivah nekiyim*.

III. EXCEPTIONS TO THE RULE

Despite the unqualified, absolute nature of a *lo pelug* (an across-the-board policy of no exceptions), *poskim*, nonetheless, sought to establish several logical exceptions to the ruling of the Rama.

An overarching principle that encompasses many of the specific exceptions is the ability to be lenient if the couple not only abstained from relations or could not have relations, but were prevented from

3. Ibid.
4. Ibid.

having relations due to a halakhic impediment. These exceptions may include:

1. A Sighting of Blood During *Shivah Nekiyim*: If a woman discovers a *ketem* or sees blood during *shivah nekiyim*, she is not required to wait five days prior to re-starting her count of *shivah nekiyim*.[5] The Rama's unqualified enactment that applies irrespective of circumstance assumes that the couple, in theory, could have had relations. In that case, the exact location of the husband is inconsequential. However, if it was halakhically impossible for them to have had relations since the wife has already been a *niddah*, minimally, for five days, then there would be no requirement to wait an additional five days.
2. A Woman Who Has Not Gone to the *Mikveh*: In the event that a woman has not gone to the *mikveh* while her husband has been away, the ruling would be analogous to the previous one. The woman is forbidden to her husband anyway due to her status as a *niddah*, and, as a result, she need not wait five days prior to beginning her observance of *shivah nekiyim*.
3. A Bride Prior to Her Wedding: The situation of an engaged woman who has had the Biblical status of being a *niddah* since her first period is analogous to the previous situation in which a woman possessed the status of a *niddah* even prior to her most recent period. Since it was halakhically prohibited for her to have had relations with anyone, the concern for the emission of semen should be inapplicable. As a result, she should not be required to wait five days prior to observing *shivah nekiyim* before her wedding. The *Shakh*[6] is uncertain as to whether or not this assertion is correct; however, the *Dagul MeRevavah*[7] asserts that this is indeed the case. In practice, a bride is not required to wait five days prior to observing her *shivah nekiyim*.
4. When Relations are Prohibited Due to *Aveilut* or a *Veset*: An

5. See *Shakh*, YD 196:22.
6. YD 196:20.
7. To *Shakh* ibid.

additional scenario which may qualify as an exception involves the prohibition on having relations due to the husband's or wife's observance of *aveilut.* Some *poskim*[8] believe that the Rama's unqualified enactment would apply even in this scenario. Others,[9] though, argue that the enactment is inapplicable in any situation in which the couple was halakhically forbidden from having relations. This is true whether the halakhic impediment is due to the prohibition of *niddah, aveilut,* or any other prohibition. In the area of *niddah,* a common situation included under this category involves the prohibition resulting from the time of the *veset* (the time when *halakhah* is concerned that the period is imminent, as discussed further on). Often, the *veset* will coincide with the days preceding a woman's period, and thus the question becomes whether the day of the *veset* can count as one of the five days, since it entails a prohibition on having relations. One has the right to be lenient in these situations since the entire enactment is a compilation of stringencies.

5. A Doctor's Instructions: R. Moshe Feinstein[10] discusses a situation in which a doctor instructs a couple to abstain from relations for a given period of time, and immediately subsequent to that period of time the wife has her period. Since the couple was forbidden from having relations, it would seem possible to waive the requirement to wait five days. Nonetheless, R. Feinstein rules that in such a situation the ruling of the Rama must be adhered to, since it is not a given that all couples will listen to the doctor.[11]

IV. ASCERTAINING THE PRESENCE OF *SHICHVAT ZERA*

The main issue behind the requirement to wait four or five days is the concern that a woman might emit semen during the interim period. This fact raises the question of whether it is possible to physically remove the

8. See *Badei HaShulchan* in *Bi'urim* to *Shakh,* ibid.
9. See *Responsa Iggerot Moshe,* YD IV, 17:21.
10. Ibid.
11. R. Feinstein also considers the question of whether the doctor's instruction can be considered equivalent to a prohibition, regardless of whether the couple will comply.

semen from a woman's body, and if so, would such a step eliminate the requirement to wait five days prior to observing *shivah nekiyim*. Some *Rishonim*[12] were of the opinion, based on a statement in the Talmud,[13] that if a woman lay on her stomach she could successfully remove the semen in her body. Other *Rishonim*, though, challenge the effectiveness of this measure, and, as a result, it cannot be relied upon. *Rishonim* note, though, that a woman can manually remove the semen from her body in an effective manner.[14] If she does so, they suggest, she would not have to wait before beginning *shivah nekiyim*. The Rama[15] does not endorse this solution, since it is impossible to ascertain that all traces of semen have been removed. In addition, even if a woman could verify her successful removal of the semen, it would not be in any way superior to abstention from having relations to begin with. As a result, the Rama's unqualified enactment would apply to this case as well.

In this instance as well, the Rama insists that all Ashkenazim follow his ruling, and he reinforces its strength with an admonition issued to all those who fail to adhere to it. Practically, *Ashkenazim* rule stringently like the Rama, whereas *Sephardim*, including R. Ovadiah Yosef, rule leniently like the *Shulchan Arukh*.

V. RARE OR UNUSUAL APPLICATIONS OF THE RAMA'S ENACTMENT:

There are a number of exceptional cases which call into question the potential application of the Rama's enactment, and the unqualified nature of its implementation:

1. Following the Consummation of Marriage: The Maharal of

12. See *Beit Yosef* YD 196.
13. *Niddah* 42a.
14. Some question why it would be permissible for a woman to remove the semen in light of the general prohibition forbidding the wanton destruction of semen (see *Torat HaShelamim* 196:23). The allowance may be due to the fact that any semen within her reach would be incapable of fertilizing an egg; or, alternatively, the possibility that women are not subject to that general prohibition.
15. *Yoreh De'ah* 196:13.

Prague[16] argues that since the treatment of hymenal blood as if it is menstrual blood, as well as the requirement to wait five days, are both stringencies, we do not pair the two stringencies with one another. As a result, a newlywed bride is only required to wait four days, not the ordinary five days. In some cases, this leniency will be inconsequential, as the bride may receive her regular period shortly after the wedding.

2. The Discovery of Blood Following Immersion, Prior to Relations: *Poskim* debate concerning the situation of a woman who sees blood immediately following her immersion in the *mikveh*, before she has the chance to have relations with her husband. The *Noda BiYehudah*[17] cites conflicting opinions whether this case would constitute an exception to the absolute nature of the Rama's enactment, exempting her from the requirement to wait five days prior to re-counting *shivah nekiyim*. A couple has a right to be lenient in this exceptional case, especially due to the stringent nature of the enactment to begin with.
3. Issues of Conception: Earlier, we noted the problem of a woman whose cycle does not allow her to become permitted to her husband at the times when conception is possible, together with the suggestions of R. Shlomo Zalman Auerbach and the *Galya Massekhet*.[18] Although neither of these two opinions have found acceptance, other measures may ease some of the difficulty. A partial measure entails eliminating the couple's observance of the fifth day prior to *shivah nekiyim*. Since the fifth day was an additional stringency, it is likely that even the Rama would not have required its universal observance if the *mitzvah* of *peru u-rvu* was at stake. If the woman ovulates earlier in her cycle, however, it is likely that the elimination of a single day will not alleviate the problem. An additional measure can be suggested if her period is shorter than four days. If the couple abstains from having relations several days prior to the expected arrival of her period, then

16. Cited in *Taz*, YD 196:5.
17. *Responsa, Tinyana*, YD 125.
18. See p. 16–17.

the couple may rely on the *Rishonim* and the *Shulchan Arukh* who allow her, in such a case, to begin counting *shivah nekiyim* immediately following the cessation of bleeding. Many rabbis advise couples facing this challenge to attempt this potential solution,[19] or to try removing all of the semen following relations.

4. An Error in Calculating *Shivah Nekiyim*: *Poskim* also consider the situation of a woman who unintentionally immersed in the *mikveh* on the wrong night; for example, she erroneously immersed on the night of the seventh day, and subsequently had relations with her husband before realizing her mistake. She would certainly be required to wait seventy-two hours, the equivalent of four halakhic days, due to the concern that she might emit semen over the course of that time. The *Semak*[20] argues, though, that she does not need to wait the fifth day since her situation is a *milta de-lo shekhicha,* an infrequent occurrence, not covered by the enactment. If, in the described situation, the couple did not have relations until the daytime of the seventh day, then, while the woman would be required to immerse in the *mikveh* a second time, she would nonetheless not be delayed in doing so. This ruling is in accordance with the *Rosh*'s perspective that the emission of semen during the daytime of the seventh day of *shivah nekiyim* is inconsequential. The *Shakh*[21] notes that the *Semak* did not distinguish between different points of time on the seventh day, and may not agree with the *Rosh*'s conclusion. According to the *Semak*, even if the couple did not have relations until the daytime of the seventh day, she should have to wait before going to the *mikveh*.
5. An Invalid Immersion: A more common scenario involves a woman who immersed in the *mikveh* on the correct evening, proceeds to have relations with her husband, and only realizes subsequently that her immersion was invalidated by the presence of a *chatzitzah,* an obstruction between her body and the water.

19. See *Responsa Iggerot Moshe,* YD IV, 17:22.
20. 293, cited in *Beit Yosef* 196:12, s.v. *vi-katav.*
21. YD 196:24.

The *Semak*[22] rules that in this situation the woman is required to immerse a second time, but she is not required to wait at all since, essentially, the *shivah nekiyim* were already completed.

22. Ibid.

20.

Hefsek Taharah

I. THE REQUIREMENT OF *HEFSEK TAHARAH*

The requirement of *hefsek taharah* first appears in the *Mishnah*.[1] On the Biblical level, a woman does not require *shivah nekiyim* after becoming a *niddah*. She can bleed for seven consecutive days, and as long as she stops seeing blood before the end of the seventh day, she may go to the *mikveh* that night and become *tehorah*. However, she must know for sure that the bleeding has completely stopped. A *niddah* cannot simply go to the *mikveh* after seven days, and assume the bleeding has stopped; since she has been established as one who is bleeding, there must be an active observation that her bleeding has stopped, which has come to be known as a *hefsek taharah*. Similarly, a *zavah gedolah* has been established to bleed, and must actively observe that her bleeding stopped to begin counting *shivah nekiyim*.[2] The *hefsek taharah* involves what is known as a *bedikah*, the insertion of a cloth into the vaginal area; the cloth is used to check that there is no more blood present.

In contemporary practice, every woman waits *shivah nekiyim*, because of the concern that she may be a *zavah gedolah*. Accordingly,

1. *Niddah* 68a.
2. See Rosh 10:5, per *Niddah* 69a.

the *Shulchan Arukh*[3] rules that women need a *hefsek taharah* well before they go to the *mikveh*; they must check themselves before the *shivah nekiyim*, because it must be established that they are genuinely clean before they start counting.

Since the *hefsek taharah* must be completed before the *shivah nekiyim* begin, and since the *shivah nekiyim* begin at nighttime, the *hefsek taharah* must be performed during the day. It is assumed that *sheki'at ha-chamah* (lit. sunset) is the beginning of nightfall, so a valid *hefsek taharah* must be performed before *sheki'at ha-chamah*.[4] In view of what we have seen about the mandatory four or five day wait, every woman must wait five days from the beginning of her bleeding and then perform a *hefsek taharah* before she begins counting the *shivah nekiyim*.

The *Mishnah* assumes that once a woman sees blood, her established status as a *niddah* can only be broken by a *hefsek taharah*. This question of whether the obligation of *hefsek taharah* is Biblical or Rabbinic is the subject of a debate amongst the *Rishonim*.

One could argue that, according to Biblical law, it is assumed that the *status quo ante* (*chazakah*) of bleeding remains in force until it is proven that she has stopped bleeding. Alternatively, one could also argue that the Torah does not make this assumption, and *hefsek taharah* is something Chazal created to ensure that the bleeding has stopped.

The *Tosafot HaRosh*[5] mentions both possibilities. The Rambam[6] apparently believes that *hefsek taharah* is Biblically necessary, based on the following analysis:[7]

3. *Yoreh De'ah* 196:1.
4. Actually, the period between *sheki'at ha-chamah* and *tzeit ha-kokhavim* (the emergence of the stars), known as *bein ha-shemashot*, has indeterminate status in *halakhah*; as such, the *hefsek taharah* must be done before *sheki'at ha-chamah* to guarantee that it precedes the beginning of a new day.
5. *Niddah* 69a, s.v. *v'ei*.
6. *Hilkhot Issurei Bi'ah* 6:22–23.
7. See *Badei HaShulchan* 196:1, *Bi'urim*, s.v. *bodeket*, p. 287.

The *Mishnah*[8] states that if a woman becomes a *niddah,* and passes through the seven days of *niddut* and the first three days of *zivah* without checking herself, it is uncertain if she became or did not become a *zavah gedolah.* The woman was established as seeing blood, and she never proved that she had stopped bleeding. As such, *halakhah* is concerned that she may have continued to bleed through the first three days of *zivah,* and may therefore be a *zavah gedolah.* The Rambam adds that when this woman concludes her *shivah nekiyim,* she brings the bird-offering ordinarily brought by people who are uncertain whether or not they are obligated in an offering. To understand the implication of this extra line in the Rambam, we must briefly consider the background of sacrificial offerings.

Many sacrificial offerings may be brought either because the Torah demands them or because someone volunteers to bring them, with the exception of a *chattat* offering. One can only bring a *chattat* offering when the Torah obligates him to bring it, and one may not bring a voluntary *chattat* offering. Therefore, when one is uncertain whether or not he must bring an ordinary offering, he may stipulate that his offering is either a fulfillment of his obligation, or a voluntary donation. However, when one is uncertain if he must bring a *chattat* offering, the *chattat* offering may not be brought. If one attempts to bring the offering voluntarily, he may transgress the prohibition of sacrificing unconsecrated or improperly consecrated animals in the *Beit HaMikdash.* However, there is one instance when a *chattat* may be brought when one is uncertain whether or not he sinned. For some situations, the Torah only requires one to bring a bird-offering as *chattat,* not an animal-offering. In these cases, the *chattat* bird-offering is brought even when there is uncertainty.

A *zavah gedolah,* according to Biblical law, must bring a *chattat* bird-offering. This being the case, if a woman is possibly a *zavah gedolah* on the Biblical level, she must bring the bird-offering brought when one is uncertain whether or not he sinned. In the case of a woman who has not done a *hefsek taharah* after the days of *niddah,*

8. *Niddah* 68a.

and has allowed three days of *zivah* to pass, the Talmud rules that one must be stringent, but mentions nothing about her bringing this *chattat* offering. The Rambam, however, adds that she must bring this offering. *Acharonim* note that if the *hefsek taharah* is only Rabbinic in nature, at the Biblical level this woman's bleeding is assumed to have stopped, and there is not even a possibility that she is a *zavah gedolah*. Hence, at the Biblical level she should not bring a bird-offering, even though this offering is brought when one is uncertain about his or her status.

The Rambam's ruling, then, indicates that on the Biblical level, the woman's bleeding is assumed to possibly continue. Hence, she is possibly a *zavah gedolah,* and brings the corresponding *chattat* offering. Similarly, since it is assumed that her bleeding continues, she needs a *hefsek taharah* by Biblical law to establish that her bleeding stopped.

Thus, according to the Rambam, *hefsek taharah* is required by Biblical law, while the *Tosafot HaRosh* argues that it is likely only required by Rabbinical law.[9] According to the Rambam, there would be a tendency toward stringency in questions relating to *hefsek taharah,* while according to that view in the Rosh there can be a tendency toward leniency. In any case, the *Shulchan Arukh* rules that a *hefsek taharah* is required in order to begin the *shivah nekiyim.*

II. THE IMPACT OF NON-*NIDDAH* BLEEDING ON *HEFSEK TAHARAH*

It has previously been established that a woman who sees blood known to be from a wound remains completely *tehorah.* However, the situation is significantly more complicated if this wound is present at the time of a *hefsek taharah,* as it may interfere with the possibility of establishing that the *niddah* bleeding has stopped. The *Chavot Da'at*[10] writes that in such a situation, it cannot be said for certain that she has stopped bleeding *niddah* blood; even if the doctors say her blood is coming from the

9. The *Arukh HaShulchan,* YD 196:1, cites *Vayikra* 15:25 as the Biblical source for *hefsek taharah.*
10. YD 196:3, *Bi'urim,* s.v. *u-ve-hachi.*

wound, it remains uncertain, leaving the status of "prohibited" in place. This ruling would seem to pose a great difficulty in a situation in which a woman has a condition that causes there to always be blood on her *bedikah* cloth.

It may be that solutions exist to these problems. The *Zikhron Yosef*,[11] quoted by R. Akiva Eiger[12] and the *Chazon Ish*,[13] argued that another halakhically acceptable form of *hefsek taharah* exists. Generally, the process of *hefsek taharah* involves a *bedikah* cloth being inserted into the vaginal area. Yet, there may be another option. The Talmud[14] discusses the case of a man who comes home from a trip late at night and finds his wife asleep, and poses the question of whether he can assume she is *tehorah*. The Talmud states that if he knows her cycle, and knows that her days of *niddut* are over, then perhaps he can assume she is *tehorah*; however, the issue is raised, she may not have gone to the *mikveh*.

The *Zikhron Yosef* points out that the only potential problem raised by the Talmud is that the woman may not have gone to the *mikveh*; it is never brought up that she may not have performed a *hefsek taharah*. Thus, he derives that if a woman has a set cycle, and she never bleeds for more than a set number of days, then once those days are up there is no need for a *bedikah* cloth. Instead, the fact that we know she never bleeds past a certain point functions as her *hefsek taharah*. If this type of *hefsek taharah* is valid, it could save numerous women from the situation that emerges from the ruling of the *Chavot Da'at*; as long as the woman has never bled *niddah* blood for more than a certain number of days, the passing of those days would function as her *hefsek taharah* and it would be able to be assumed that any blood found after that originated from her wound.

However, in addressing this notion, R. Akiva Eiger cites the dispute regarding whether *vestot* (the times when *halakhah* is concerned that the period is imminent, and mandates acting accordingly) are significant on a Biblical or Rabbinical level, i.e. is a woman obligated Biblically

11. YD #10.
12. *Responsa*, YD #60, s.v. *gam mah she-dan.*
13. YD 92:22.
14. *Niddah* 15b.

or only Rabbinically to check herself during her *veset*. He points out that there are clear indications that the Talmudic passage quoted by the *Zikhron Yosef* assumes that *vestot* are Biblically significant. According to this opinion, *vestot* are taken very seriously, and it is assumed that just as she will probably bleed when the *veset* begins, and therefore there is a requirement of a *bedikah* on the *veset*, she will probably not bleed when the *veset* ends, and thus does not require a *bedikah* for the *hefsek taharah*.

If, however, it is ruled that *vestot* are only Rabbinically significant, then just as the concern that she will bleed at the beginning of the *veset* is only Rabbinic in nature, the assumption that she will stop bleeding at the end of her *veset* is also Rabbinic, and perhaps this Rabbinic-level presumption is not enough to exempt her from doing a *bedikah*. Accordingly, R. Akiva Eiger concludes that *vestot* are Rabbinic, and therefore *veset* alone cannot be relied upon as a *hefsek taharah*, and a *bedikah* would be required as well. Based on this analysis, R. Akiva Eiger rejects the *Zikhron Yosef*, and writes that only the standard *hefsek taharah* is effective, and, in view of *Chavot Da'at*, a woman with a wound that bleeds is in a difficult situation in terms of becoming *tehorah*.

However, many *Acharonim* write to defend the *Zikhron Yosef*. The general trend among these *Acharonim* is to argue that even though *vestot* are only Rabbinic, in this case, *vestot* have Biblical significance. First, they point out that it is of sound logic to rely on *vestot* on a Biblical level. If a woman has stopped seeing blood after five days for the last 20 years, then there is a very strong probability that the same will happen now. As such, it actually requires explanation as to why *vestot* are generally understood as Rabbinic, and *Acharonim* offer three opinions about why this should be:

1. The *Noda BiYehudah*[15] writes that *vestot* are only Rabbinic because every *veset* involves a conflict between two established statuses: first, that she is established to see blood every set number of days, and second, that she is established to be *tehorah* and permitted before the *veset* time arrives. It is decided that these statuses cancel each other out, and it is ruled that she is permitted until proven

15. *Responsa, Mahadura Kama Yoreh De'ah* 55.

forbidden. In view of this explanation, the view of the *Zikhron Yosef* can be revived. If *bedikot* at the beginning of *vestot* are Rabbinic because the presumption that the woman saw blood is cancelled out by the established status of being permitted to her husband, then at the end of the cycle the opposite happens – the woman's established status of not bleeding after a certain number of days should cancel out the established status of being forbidden to her husband, and she should be permitted until proven forbidden. If the *Noda BiYehudah* is accepted, then the *Zikhron Yosef*'s brand of *hefsek taharah* stands, and it can be relied upon when a woman has a wound known to bleed.

2. The *Melo Ha-Ro'im*[16] maintains that *vestot* are not a proof Biblically that she has bled, because counteracting this "proof" is the fact that she hasn't felt anything. The fact that she doesn't feel anything "proves" she didn't see and as such, according to the Torah, she is permitted. In determining whether her regular cycle should be an indicator that her bleeding has ended, there is nothing counteracting that indication and as such, Biblically, it can be declared that her bleeding ended, notwithstanding the lack of an actual check with a *bedikah* cloth.
3. The *Chazon Ish*[17] argues that *vestot* are Rabbinic because there is no license to rely on past history. There are many factors that can affect a woman's period (stress, travel, eating patterns, sleep patterns, etc.), so much so that even if she has followed a pattern the last twenty years, anything happening in her internal or external environment can affect her *veset*. Past events cannot predict what will happen in the future. According to his explanation, *vestot* are Rabbinic because they are unreliable, and they certainly cannot be relied upon as a *hefsek taharah*. If the *Chazon Ish* is right, then the *Zikhron Yosef*'s view would not be acceptable.

It would seem, then, that the viability of the *Zikhron Yosef*'s ruling depends on which explanation is accepted about why *vestot* are only

16. *Ma'arekhet Vestot, ot* 13; see *Taharat HaBayit*, I, p. 91.
17. *Chazon Ish* YD 80:19.

Rabbinic. According to the *Chavot Da'at* and *Noda BiYehudah*, the *Zikhron Yosef* can be accepted, while according to the *Chazon Ish*, it would not appear to be acceptable.

Interestingly, however, even the *Chazon Ish* may agree with the *Zikhron Yosef*. It is possible to maintain that only the beginning of a *veset* is unreliable, subject to all kinds of environmental influences, but the duration of the *veset* remains constant despite travel, stress, or diet. If this is true, *vestot* can be reliable to indicate when the bleeding stops and to act as a valid *hefsek taharah*. In view of this explanation, all three opinions in the *Acharonim* indicate that the *Zikhron Yosef* is followed.

The *Sidrei Taharah*,[18] however, notes a *Mishnah*[19] that stresses how women must do an actual *bedikah* as a *hefsek taharah*, without mentioning that the *veset*'s end counts as a *hefsek taharah*. Accordingly, the *Sidrei Taharah* writes that the *Zikhron Yosef*'s opinion is completely incorrect. The *Chazon Ish*[20] defends the *Zikhron Yosef*, and argues that the *Mishnah* is dealing with women who cannot rely on his type of *hefsek taharah*, i.e. they have no set time at which they stop seeing *niddah* blood, and must therefore resort to doing *bedikot*.

In practice, some *poskim* say we may rely on the *Zikhron Yosef* since the majority of *Acharonim* seem to support it, but others are hesitant to rule against R. Akiva Eiger and the *Sidrei Taharah*. It is important to note that this leniency of the *Zikhron Yosef* would not apply in a case where a woman past menopause becomes a *niddah* due to a medical procedure, since the bleeding in such a case is not related to *vestot* at all.

Even if the *Zikhron Yosef* is rejected, there may be another reason for leniency. The *Noda BiYehudah*[21] and *Chatam Sofer*[22] claim, based on their reading of a statement of the Ra'avad,[23] that there is another way to do a *hefsek taharah*. He invokes a case where on day five of her period

18. 196:23, s.v. *ela*.
19. *Niddah* 68a. The *Mishnah* is referring to a *niddah*, not a *zavah*, but presumably the *halakhah* is the same.
20. YD 92:22.
21. *Kama*, YD 46 and 49.
22. *Responsa*, YD 177.
23. A similar idea can be found in the Rashba's *Torat HaBayit*, 7:5, p. 322, s.v. *vi'atah niva'er*.

a woman has a feeling she is clean, but cannot find a *bedikah* cloth. The *Noda BiYehudah* believes that there is a solution to allow this woman to begin *shivah nekiyim*: the woman should concentrate closely on the sensations of her body; if she does not experience a *hargashah,* she is considered no longer an active *niddah.* Even those who do not accept the *Zikhron Yosef* alone may be willing to combine his position with the *Noda BiYehudah*'s version of a *hefsek taharah.* This means that a woman would wait until the point in her period when she has never seen *niddah* blood, and concentrate on her sensations, and if she does not experience any *hargashah,* then she may begin *shivah nekiyim.* Of course, this combination of innovative kinds of *hefsek taharah* should only be utilized in extenuating circumstance where it is permissible to be lenient. This is particularly so as the *Noda BiYehudah*'s position is additionally difficult to apply in contemporary times when women generally do not experience *hargashah.*

In the event that a woman cannot perform a standard *bedikah* with a *bedikah* cloth (e.g. she has undergone a medical procedure and the doctors say that nothing may enter the vaginal area for a certain amount of time), some *poskim* suggest that she can still do a *hefsek taharah* by having a doctor look inside and see if there is any blood. The whole point of inserting a *bedikah* cloth is to see if there is any blood left, and certainly looking inside is just as effective, if not more so. Therefore, if a woman does not do a *bedikah* but the doctor finds no blood, she has in effect performed a valid *hefsek taharah.*

III. THE USE OF MULTIPLE CLOTHS TO OBTAIN A CLEAN *HEFSEK TAHARAH*

As discussed, the purpose of *hefsek taharah* is to prove that the bleeding has actually stopped. The above discussion addressed situations where the bleeding was believed to have stopped, but a clean *hefsek taharah* could not be obtained. What must be considered next is the inverse situation: a woman who does produce a clean cloth at the *hefsek taharah,* despite the fact that there is reason to believe the blood is still present.

The *Chazon Ish*[24] discusses a case where a woman has a medical

24. YD 81.

condition and continues to stain after her period has concluded. If such a woman washes herself out and then produces a clean *bedikah,* it would seem to be illogical, maintains the *Chazon Ish,* to allow her to start *shivah nekiyim* based on that clean *bedikah* cloth. It would appear that the *Chazon Ish* agrees with the *Zikhron Yosef* that the point of *bedikah* cloths is to prove that there is no more blood, not just to produce a clean cloth.

It is frequently the case that women take a number of *bedikah* cloths, and use a few of them until they produce a clean one. Later *poskim* considered the permissibility of this practice, particularly in light of the *Chazon Ish*'s statement. Some *poskim* argued that since this stringency has not been mentioned prior to the *Chazon Ish,* the practice is permissible. *Poskim* split into roughly two camps to reconcile the *Chazon Ish* with this apparent argument against him:

1. The *Badei HaShulchan* points to the fact that a woman is ideally supposed to insert a cloth into the vaginal area before sunset and leave it there until after three stars become visible (*mokh dachuk*). If she does not find blood on that cloth, then she has indeed fulfilled the *Chazon Ish*'s requirement of proving that there is no more blood there. No earlier *posek* mentioned the *Chazon Ish*'s stringency because women in previous generations used to insert a single cloth in the vaginal area for an extended period of time,[25] and thus this omission is not a challenge to the *Chazon Ish*'s position.
2. R. Ovadiah Yosef[26] writes that the *Chazon Ish* was only opposed to repeating *bedikot* in a case where the woman has a condition and we know she has not stopped bleeding. Only in such cases would it be inappropriate to allow the use of multiple *bedikah* cloths. In a standard situation where a woman has almost certainly stopped bleeding, even the *Chazon Ish* would allow her to do multiple *bedikot* to wipe off any residue dried blood.

25. See *Badei HaShulchan,* 196:1, *Bi'urim,* s.v. *She-tifsok bi-taharah,* who raises objections to this approach.
26. *Taharat HaBayit,* II, 262–263.

It emerges that the *Badei HaShulchan* and R. Ovadiah Yosef stand on opposite extremes with regard to using multiple *bedikah* cloths. In practice, even if one follows the *Badei HaShulchan,* it stands to reason that there must be some acceptable time span between *bedikot.* If a woman does a *bedikah* and finds blood, but another *bedikah* cloth is clean three hours later, presumably even the *Badei HaShulchan* must be lenient. Unfortunately, the *Chazon Ish* does not give any indication of how long there should be between *bedikot.* However, R. Moshe Feinstein[27] writes that a woman who washes herself should wait at least fifteen minutes before performing her *bedikah,* as that is enough time for blood to appear again if she really is bleeding.[28] Here, too, it seems that waiting fifteen minutes between *bedikot* would be acceptable to the *Chazon Ish* and the *Badei HaShulchan.* Even less than fifteen minutes might very well suffice, as it is unclear from the *Chazon Ish* how much waiting is necessary. If a *mokh* is done, this would circumvent the issue.

27. *Responsa Iggerot Moshe,* YD II, 71.
28. Although the context R. Feinstein's responsum was concerning *bedikot* during *shivah nekiyim,* it would seem reasonable to extrapolate to a *hefsek taharah.*

21.

Bedikot Chorin U-Sedakin – Thorough Internal Checking

I. THE PERFORMANCE OF *BEDIKOT* FOR THE PURPOSES OF RITUAL PURITY

A woman is required to perform several "*bedikot*", internal checks, throughout the process of becoming *tehorah*. The background for defining a "*bedikah*" in the Talmud begins in the context of what is, on the surface, a discussion of the laws of ritual purity and impurity. The opening *Mishnah* in *Massekhet Niddah*[1] records a three way debate regarding the extent that a woman who sees blood can be defined as *teme'ah* retroactively. According to Shammai, any item the woman touched prior to the actual sighting of blood remains *tahor*. Her status of ritual impurity begins from the moment she see blood and onward, and it does not affect her presumptive status until that point. Hillel maintains she receives the status of ritual impurity retroactively from the last time she checked herself and established with certainty that she was pure.

1. *Niddah* 2a.

The position of the *Chakhamim* in the *Mishnah* reflects a compromise between the two viewpoints. On the one hand, they adopt the Rabbinic measure establishing her ritual impurity retroactively; at the same time, they limit the maximum extent of her impurity to the previous twenty four hours. If the woman performed a *bedikah* within that timeframe and verified her ritual purity, such a *bedikah* would further limit the extent of her retroactive impurity. The Rambam[2] follows this last view.

The *Mishnah*[3] establishes, in the context of the observance of the laws of purity and impurity, that all women would perform two *bedikot* daily, and in addition they must check themselves before and after marital relations. The *bedikot* performed on a daily basis were an extra precaution due to the women's involvement in touching *taharot*. Performing additional *bedikot* would ensure that anything she touched previously would remain ritually pure even if she eventually becomes a *niddah*. The *bedikah* performed prior to marital relations was required only secondarily, once they were already engaging in frequent *bedikot* for the sake of ritual purity.[4] This system of *bedikot*, then, is limited to the era of the *Beit HaMikdash* when individuals were scrupulously aware of their status of ritual purity and impurity.

As mentioned above, the *Mishnah* states that a *bedikah* performed within the twenty-four hours preceding a sighting of blood has the capacity to minimize the extent of a woman's retroactive impurity. The Talmud[5] qualifies the *Mishnah*'s ruling, and excludes the *bedikah* performed prior to marital relations from possessing that capability. In anxious anticipation to have relations with her husband, a woman may haphazardly and improperly perform a *bedikah* in an unexacting manner, and as a result such a *bedikah* fails to assert with certainty the woman's purity.

2. *Hilkhot Metame Mishkav U-Moshav* 3:4; see also *Hilkhot Issurei Bi'ah* 9:3.
3. *Niddah* 11a.
4. *Niddah* 11b.
5. *Niddah* 5a.

II. THE DEFINITION OF *BEDIKOT* REGARDING *HILKHOT NIDDAH*

Despite the context of the Talmud's discussion, the area of ritual purity and impurity, this passage provides the foundation for the *Rishonim*'s definition of a *bedikah* for contemporary purposes as well. Three prevailing opinions debate the extent and quality of the *bedikah* required in contemporary times.

1. The Ra'avad[6] distinguishes between the quality of *bedikot* required to ensure one's status as being ritually pure as opposed to the type of *bedikot* necessary to permit a woman to her husband. The quality of *bedikot* demanded by the *halakhah* differs in varying contexts. With respect to the domain of ritual purity, *bedikot chorin u-sedakin,* demanding, exacting *bedikot* which investigate every corner and fold in the vaginal area, are required. However, with respect to permitting a woman to her husband, the realm of *issur ve-heter,* a more basic *bedikah* suffices. The Ra'avad believes that the lower standard suffices not only for the derivative *bedikot* required prior to marital relations on account of the multiple *bedikot* already performed for the purposes of ritual purity, it even suffices for the *bedikot* of *hefsek taharah* and *shivah nekiyim.*
2. The Ramban[7] draws a distinction between the standards required for *hefsek taharah* as opposed to the measures needed for *shivah nekiyim.* Prior to the *bedikah* of *hefsek taharah,* a woman has the presumptive status that she will continue to see blood. As such, the *bedikah* of *hefsek taharah,* which overturns the previous presumptive status and creates a new one, must be a rigorous *bedikah* of *bedikot chorin u-sedakin.* During the *shivah nekiyim,* when she no longer possesses the presumptive status of seeing blood, the *bedikot* performed are of a less rigorous standard.[8]

6. *Ba'alei HaNefesh, Sha'ar HaSefirah* 3.
7. Ramban 5a, s.v. *mi-tokh* and *Hilkhot Niddah* 9:22. (However, note also 2:6 and 9:23, and see also *Makhon Yerushalayim* edition of the *Tur,* YD 196, *hagahot ve-ha'arot* 18.).
8. For more on this distinction, see Chapter 8, section 2.

3. The Rashba[9] rejects the entire distinction between the realm of ritual purity and impurity, on the one hand, and the domain of *issur ve-heter*, on the other. According to the Rashba, a single definition characterizes all *bedikot*, namely *bedikot chorin u-sedakin*. The term '*bedikah*' is oftentimes juxtaposed to the alternative expression '*kinuach*,' indicating that the term '*bedikah*' connotes a more rigorous style of checking. With that in mind, the *Mishnah*'s[10] requirement to perform *bedikot* for *hefsek taharah* and *shivah nekiyim*, must demand a thorough *bedikah* of *chorin u-sedakin*.

III. CONTEMPORARY APPLICATIONS

The *Shulchan Arukh*[11] rules in accordance with the stringent viewpoint expressed by the Rashba. The *Noda BiYehudah*[12] wonders, in light of the *Shulchan Arukh*'s ruling, what a woman should do if she is incapable of performing the more exacting *bedikot* of *chorin u-sedakin*. In such less than optimal cases, he suggests relying on the less demanding perspective of the Ra'avad, especially in light of the *Tosafot HaRosh*'s[13] understanding that the *bedikah* of *hefsek taharah* is only required Rabbinically.

An important application of the previous discussion arises in a situation in which a woman exhausts the *bedikah* cloths at her disposal, and must resort to using tissue paper instead. Some *poskim*[14] discourage the use of tissue paper since a thorough *bedikah* cannot be performed without tearing the paper. As a result, a *bedikah* performed with tissue paper would be tantamount to a *bedikah* which does not investigate the *chorin u-sedakin*. A *bedikah* of that type would most probably not be allowed according to the *Shulchan Arukh*, but might be accepted in less than optimal cases according to the *Noda BiYehudah*.

An additional practical consideration relates to the extent to which the *bedikah* cloth must penetrate internally. Many *Rishonim*[15] sup-

9. Rashba 5a, s.v. *mi-tokh* and *Torat HaBayit HaArukh* 7:5.
10. *Niddah* 10:3.
11. *Yoreh De'ah* 196:6.
12. *Responsa* YD, *kama*, 46 and *Tinyana*, 129.
13. *Niddah* 69a.
14. See *Shiurei Shevet HaLevi*, 196:6 and *Responsa Be'er Moshe*, II, 62.
15. See Rosh, *Niddah* 10:5.

plied the measure of *ad makom she-ha-shamash dash,* the extent to which the man's organ reaches during relations. The *Beit Yosef*[16] was uncertain what the origin was for this measure, and claims that many women conveyed their difficulties to him regarding the implementation of such a requirement. In fact, an attempt to reach that far carries the danger of causing irritation and actually causing blood to appear. In the *Shulchan Arukh,*[17] he rules that the woman should insert the cloth *ad makom she-ha-shamash dash* on each day, and if this is too difficult, at least for the *hefsek taharah* and the first day. The Rama[18] rules leniently in this regard; instead, he encourages women to insert the *bedikah* cloth to the best of their ability and to try to move it around to all of the *chorin u-sedakin.*

In light of some reported difficulties in performing an effective *bedikah,* some *poskim* discuss whether women should be advised to lubricate the *bedikah* cloth, thereby easing its entrance and maneuverability. On the one hand, a lubricant will assist the performance of the *bedikah,* at the same time it may distort the color of the blood which may appear on the *bedikah* cloth. Many *poskim*[19] adopt a lenient stance and permit a woman to dampen the *bedikah* cloth with water, or to apply a completely transparent lubricant, such as KY jelly, which will not affect the color adversely, if she is experiencing difficulty performing *bedikot.*

It is important to be mindful of the nature of the various requirements surrounding *bedikot.* Despite the *Shulchan Arukh*'s hesitation concerning the insertion of a *bedikah* cloth *ad makom she-ha-shamash dash,* it is certainly not required on a Biblical level. In fact, the *Sidrei Taharah*[20] attempts to prove that it is a Rabbinic requirement at best, based on the case of a *betulah* who must perform *bedikot* prior to getting married. Clearly, says the *Sidrei Taharah,* the requirement of *ad makom she-ha-shamash dash* cannot be mandated on a Biblical level, as it would puncture the bride's *betulim* in this case.[21] Furthermore, it is conceivable that the condition of *chorin u-sedakin* is also only a Rabbinic demand.

16. *Yoreh De'ah* 196, s.v. *vi-yesh lish'ol.*
17. *Yoreh De'ah* 196:6.
18. Ibid.
19. See *Responsa Maharsham,* 1, 146.
20. YD 196:23.
21. However, from a medical perspective, this proof is questionable, as it is inconsistent

Finally, the *Chazon Ish*[22] goes so far as to assert that wiping around the area externally several times and ascertaining that no blood is emerging satisfies the Biblical requirement to perform a *bedikah*. While being ever mindful of the background of the requirements of *bedikot*, women should attempt to insert the *bedikah* cloth as far as they can and attempt to check all of the *chorin u-sedakin*, while simultaneously being exceedingly careful not to hurt themselves or cause any additional bleeding.

with the reality of female anatomy, which generally does allow for such an examination without damage to the *betulim*. Nonetheless, the *Sidrei Taharah* may have been referencing the difficulty, rather than impossibility, of doing so.

22. *Chazon Ish*, YD, *Hilkhot Niddah* 92:21.

22.

The Requirements for *Hefsek Taharah* for an Initial Sighting of Blood

I. THE APPROPRIATE TIME FOR A *HEFSEK TAHARAH*

A *hefsek taharah* must be performed before the beginning of the seven clean days. Since sunset may be halakhically considered the beginning of the next day, a *hefsek taharah* should be performed prior to sunset. Although there are different opinions as to whether a *hefsek taharah* performed shortly after sunset may still be valid, based on different understandings of precisely when the next day begins, one should be extremely careful to perform one before sunset, as many *poskim* invalidate a *hefsek taharah* performed even immediately after sunset.

The *Mishnah*[1] records a debate with respect to the appropriate time for performing a *hefsek taharah* for a *niddah*. The *Tanna kama* (the first opinion in the *Mishnah*) believes that the *hefsek taharah* is acceptable (at least after the fact), at any point during the seventh day; however, R. Yehudah invalidates the *hefsek taharah* done early on that day.

1. *Niddah* 68a.

R. Yehudah is concerned that some blood may still emerge prior to the evening, and, as a result, he requires the *hefsek taharah* to be performed after the time for *minchah*. *Rishonim* dispute which time of *minchah* R. Yehudah requires a woman to wait for: The *Ra'ah*[2] believes that it suffices to wait for the time of *minchah gedolah,* six and a half halakhic hours into the day. The *Beit Yosef,*[3] however, argues that R. Yehudah is referring to the time of *minchah ketanah,* the equivalent of nine and a half halakhic hours into the day. The *Mishnah* then cites the view of the *Chakhamim,* that a *hefsek taharah* may theoretically be done even on the day after the initial sighting of blood.

II. A SIGHTING OF BLOOD FOR A SINGLE DAY

The Talmud[4] proceeds to describe a scenario in which the *Tanna kama* and *Chakhamim* may adopt R. Yehudah's perspective, forbidding a woman from performing a *hefsek taharah* prior to the time for *minchah*. If a woman bleeds initially for several hours one morning, what the Talmud refers to as *ra'atah yom rishon,* and subsequently seeks to perform a *hefsek taharah* on the same day, R. Yehudah HaNasi is uncertain as to whether or not the *Chakhamim* would permit her to do so prior to the time for *minchah*. In this case, the *Chakhamim* might agree that she must wait until later in the day prior to performing a *hefsek taharah* since, at the given moment, her "source of blood" is apparently open and producing her current flow of blood and thus there is a greater concern that she is still issuing blood.

As a consequence of R. Yehudah HaNasi's uncertainty, *Rishonim* debate how to rule on this matter. The Rashba[5] rules leniently on this point, based on the conclusion of the discussion in the Talmud. Most *Rishonim,* however, argue that in a scenario of *ra'atah yom rishon,* a *hefsek taharah* performed earlier in the day is at least a topic of concern.

On the surface, if we adopt the perspective of most *Rishonim,* the *Chakhamim* would adopt the standard of R. Yehudah in a situation

2. *Bedek HaBayit,* 7:5, s.v. *katav ha-chakham.*
3. *Yoreh De'ah* 196:1, s.v. *u-bein ha-shemashot.*
4. *Niddah* 68b.
5. *Torat HaBayit* 7:5, s.v.*vi-af al gav.*

of *ra'atah yom rishon*. As such, a woman would be allowed to perform a *hefsek taharah* following the time for *minchah*. The Rama,[6] basing himself on the opinion of *Tosafot*,[7] does, indeed, rule this way, requiring the woman to wait until close to *bein ha-shemashot*. Other *poskim*, including the *Shulchan Arukh*[8] and the Vilna Gaon,[9] argue that a situation of *ra'atah yom rishon* is more severe than a standard instance of R. Yehudah's opinion. In a scenario of *ra'atah yom rishon*, the *hefsek taharah* should be delayed until moments before *bein ha-shemashot*, and the *bedikah* cloth should remain inserted inside a woman's body for some time. This is known as a *mokh*, and will be elaborated upon in a later discussion.

In summary, three perspectives debate the *Chakhamim*'s opinion in a case of *ra'atah yom rishon*. According to the Rashba, a woman may still perform the *hefsek taharah* at any point after the bleeding stops. According to the Rama, she is required to wait until close to *bein ha-shemashot*; whereas the *Shulchan Arukh* and Vilna Gaon insist on a *mokh dachuk*.

III. CONTEMPORARY PRACTICAL APPLICATIONS OF *RA'ATAH YOM RISHON*

At first glance, while the scenario of *ra'atah yom rishon* was relevant in the time of the Talmud, it seems to be a theoretical issue with little contemporary relevance, for both practical and halakhic reasons. On a practical plane, most women do not bleed for only a single day, making the current discussion seemingly moot. Moreover, in terms of halakhic considerations, even if it were to happen, due to the concern of *poletet shichvat zera*, a woman would still be required to wait until the fourth or fifth day before beginning to count *shivah nekiyim*. Consequentially, this discussion of *halakhah* seems to be highly theoretical without actual application. However, *Acharonim* present numerous situations, both common and unlikely scenarios, in which the *halakhah* may find practical application.

6. *Yoreh De'ah* 196:2.
7. *Niddah* 68b, s.v. *amru*. See *Bi'ur HaGra*, 196:8, and *Sidrei Taharah* 196:9.
8. *Yoreh De'ah* ibid.
9. *Bi'ur HaGra* 196:7 and 8.

The *Chazon Ish*[10] addresses a case in which a woman is interested in performing a *hefsek taharah* well in advance of the beginning of *shivah nekiyim*. A woman who had a brief period, for only one morning, is permitted to perform an immediate *hefsek taharah* even though it will precede her observance of *shivah nekiyim* by several days. In such a situation, the *halakhah* of *ra'atah yom rishon* will determine when on the first day she is permitted to perform her *hefsek taharah*.

The *Chavot Da'at*[11] offers a significantly more common example of *ra'atah yom rishon*'s practical application. In principle, only certain shades of red should render a woman a *niddah*; however, in the modern era, since we are not as adept at distinguishing one shade from another, we are stringent concerning all shades of red. This stringency, which is due to uncertainty, represents the fact that it cannot be fully ascertained whether a specific specimen of blood is *tahor* or *tamei*. As a result, in a standard situation of *niddah*, it is conceivable that the blood which emerged on the first four days was actually *tahor*, and only the fifth day's blood is *tamei*. It is possible, then, that every situation in which a woman is a *niddah* should really be treated as a case of *ra'atah yom rishon*, since only the fifth day's blood, the morning of her pending *hefsek taharah*, is *tamei*. The *Chavot Da'at*, therefore, requires every woman to regard herself as a possible *ra'atah yom rishon*, demanding that she use a *mokh* in accordance with the aforementioned stringent position of the *Shulchan Arukh* and Vilna Gaon. Most *poskim* disregard the concern of the *Chavot Da'at*, claiming that a regularly scheduled period is not categorized as one of doubt as to whether all of the blood is truly *tamei*.

The *Shakh*[12] argues that any sighting of blood during the *shivah nekiyim* is analogous to a case of *ra'atah yom rishon*. However, the *Shakh* writes that *ketamim* are an exception to that rule. Whether a *ketem* is the cause of the original onset of *niddah* status, or is responsible for undoing a woman's current observance of *shivah nekiyim*, a *ketem* is not subject to the rules of *ra'atah yom rishon*. The entire concern of R. Yehudah HaNasi, prompting him to reconsider the *Chakhamim*'s position in this case, was

10. YD 92:45.
11. YD 196:1.
12. YD 196:6.

due to the possibility that the woman's uterus was still issuing blood. In the case of a *ketem*, this concern is neutralized.[13] Very often, it is a *ketem* that is responsible for disrupting the observance of *shivah nekiyim*, which would limit the applicability of the *Shakh*'s previous assertion.

IV. A SIGHTING OF BLOOD ON A *BEDIKAH* CLOTH

The *Shakh* has asserted that a sighting of blood during *shivah nekiyim* would be regarded as the halakhic equivalent of *ra'atah yom rishon*, whereas the appearance of a *ketem* would not. An in-between situation which must be addressed is the halakhic standing of blood which is found on a *bedikah* cloth. On the one hand, many of the leniencies that apply to *ketamim* do not apply to a *bedikah* cloth; at the same time, without a *hargashah*, it is questionable whether to equate, on a Biblical level, a *bedikah* cloth with a real sighting of blood. The halakhic assessment of blood found on a *bedikah* cloth with regard to the status of *ra'atah yom rishon* is critical, especially considering the prevalence of this event.

The *Badei HaShulchan* assumes that blood found on a *bedikah* cloth during *shivah nekiyim* is treated in accordance with the laws of *ra'atah yom rishon*. Accordingly, a woman who sees blood on a *bedikah* cloth during *shivah nekiyim* would not be permitted to perform a *hefsek taharah* on that morning. In fact, according to the opinions of the *Shulchan Arukh* and the Vilna Gaon, such a woman would even be required to use a *mokh*. R. Ovadiah Yosef[14] disagrees, arguing that blood found on a *bedikah* cloth should be treated like a *ketem*. As such, in his view, a woman who finds blood on her *bedikah* cloth may perform her *hefsek taharah* in the morning.

The stringency of the *Badei HaShulchan*'s ruling is somewhat mitigated by his own qualification.[15] The driving force behind the rule of *ra'atah yom rishon* is the concern that a woman's uterus was just opened, thereby creating a concern that it is still issuing forth blood. This concern would only apply if the present sighting of blood is viewed as a new occurrence, and not the continuation of a previous incident of seeing

13. See *Machatzit HaShekel*, YD 196, s.v. *efshar le-hakel.*
14. *Taharat HaBayit* II, 288–289.
15. *Badei HaShulchan* 196:2, *Bi'urim*, s.v. *livdok*, 293–294.

blood. In light of this qualification, the *Badei HaShulchan* distinguishes between the earlier part of *shivah nekiyim,* during which time blood on a *bedikah* cloth may be viewed as a continuation of her previous sighting, as opposed to the latter half of *shivah nekiyim,* in which the appearance of blood would be regarded as a new sighting. The *Shakh*'s contention, that a sighting of blood during *shivah nekiyim* has the halakhic status of *ra'atah yom rishon,* is only during the latter half of *shivah nekiyim.* The *Badei HaShulchan* draws the line between the first day of *shivah nekiyim* and the remainder of the seven days. On the first day, any blood found on a *bedikah* cloth is considered to be an extension of the previous five days, and is not treated with the stringencies of *ra'atah yom rishon.* Subsequent to the first day, however, one is required to be stringent out of uncertainty. Whether the *Shakh* would agree to this distinction is questionable, since he does not qualify his assertion.

R. Shmuel Wosner[16] adopts the viewpoint of the *Badei HaShulchan* without the suggested leniency on the first day of *shivah nekiyim.* However, there is one scenario in which R. Wosner is lenient during the initial stages of *shivah nekiyim*: If a woman performs a *hefsek taharah* during the afternoon of the fifth day, and subsequently finds blood on the *mokh* she inserts shortly afterward during the *bein hashemashot* between the fifth day and the first day of *shivah nekiyim,* she is not required to treat the blood discovered on the *mokh* like a case of *ra'atah yom rishon.* As a result, she is permitted to do a *hefsek taharah* the following morning, and is not required to delay the *hefsek taharah* until later on. Presumably, R. Wosner's lenient ruling is due to the unlikelihood that blood found on a *mokh* shortly after a *hefsek taharah* would be regarded as a new sighting of blood which would generate the concern that the source of blood was freshly opened.

V. SUMMARY

The following conclusions may be reached in light of the background discussion developed above:

1. A *Mokh* Following a Regular Period: The *Rishonim* and *Shulchan*

16. *Shiurei Shevet HaLevi,* 196:2:1.

Arukh indicate that a woman should generally try to insert a *mokh* along with every *hefsek taharah,* even though it is only required, in principle, according to the *Chavot Da'at*. Failure to do so, however, does not invalidate the *hefsek taharah*.

2. A Status of *Niddah* Due to a *Ketem*: In accordance with the *Shakh*'s perspective, a status of *niddah* which results from the discovery of a *ketem* does not necessitate the insertion of a *mokh*. In fact, the rabbi will often discourage a woman from using a *mokh,* since doing so may cause further irritation and bleeding.
3. A Sighting of Blood on a *Bedikah* Cloth: There is a range of issues to be considered in addressing whether a *mokh* is ever required by the letter of the law. The Rashba is of the opinion that the *Chakhamim* never require the usage of a *mokh,* and always permits a woman to perform a *hefsek taharah* in the morning. In addition, the Rama, who does accept the distinction between *ra'atah yom rishon* and other scenarios of *hefsek taharah,* only insisted on delaying the *hefsek taharah* until the time for *minchah,* but never required the use of a *mokh*. Furthermore, R. Ovadiah Yosef believes that blood found on a *bedikah* cloth shares the same halakhic status as a *ketem* with respect to this issue. As a result, for all of the above considerations there is certainly room to be lenient. Nevertheless, a woman should still try to insert a *mokh* if she finds a stain on her *bedikah* cloth, just as she should ideally use a *mokh* along with every *hefsek taharah*. If, for specific reasons, this poses a difficulty, she should at least delay her *hefsek taharah* until after the time of *minchah ketanah,* nine and a half halakhic hours into the day, in order to at least fulfill the perspectives of the Rama and *Beit Yosef*. In most cases, the use of a *mokh* will be a recommended practice, and not an activity that is required, strictly speaking.

23.

The *Mokh Dachuk*

In theory, the *mokh dachuk* is supposed to be the best possible *bedikah*, a foolproof indicator that the uterus is no longer producing blood. As to how the *mokh* is performed, the *Chavot Da'at*[1] maintains that the woman must fill the vaginal area with cloth, so that any blood whatsoever will show up on the *mokh*. R. Akiva Eiger[2] writes that this is accomplished by inserting the cloth so far inward that any blood coming out of the uterus will appear on the *mokh*.

In truth, what it is called a *mokh* today fulfills neither of these definitions. Women generally insert a regular sized *bedikah* cloth as far as such a cloth usually goes, and leave it there from before sunset until after dark. This practice is halakhically questionable as to whether it truly suffices for a *mokh*; however, the *poskim* do not object to this practice, because there is in any event no actual need for a *mokh*.

The *mokh* does not need to be inserted right after the *hefsek taharah*; it can be inserted a minute or two before sunset, and it can be taken out at nightfall. There are different opinions as to how long this

1. YD 191:8.
2. *Responsa*, #60.

time is. This period also changes depending on the time of year, and it is also affected by the distance one is from the equator. Based on these factors, in the New York area, for example, a *mokh* that is inserted until 25 minutes after sunset should suffice.

24.

Bedikot during *Shivah Nekiyim*

I. INTRODUCTION

The period of *shivah nekiyim* has two unique characteristics. First, any sight of blood breaks the *shivah nekiyim* and the count must begin anew; second, women regularly perform *bedikot* during this time to check for blood.[1] Regarding the necessity of seven clean days, the Torah[2] teaches that for a *zavah gedolah* to become *tehorah*, seven days must pass without any sight of blood. The Talmud[3] derives that these seven days must be consecutive. Regarding the practice of *bedikot*, however, there seems to be no source in the Torah. It is possible, therefore, that *bedikot* were instituted by Chazal.

However, several *Acharonim* believe that *bedikot* may be Biblically required. These *Acharonim* base their position on a cryptic comment of the *Beit Yosef*. In reference to a dispute about the minimum required

1. See *Niddah* 68a.
2. *Vayikra* 15:28.
3. *Niddah* 67b.

number of *bedikot*, the *Beit Yosef*[4] writes that he is stringent, because there may be a "*kareit*" penalty involved. The *Acharonim* understood that if there is a risk of a *kareit* prohibition, then the obligation for *bedikot* must be Biblical. Assuming this is correct, it is left to be determined how this law is derived from the Torah.

The *Chavot Da'at,*[5] assuming that *bedikot* are Biblical, raises the following problem. A *hargashah* is required for a woman to be Biblically deemed a *niddah*. If so, what is the point of *bedikot*? If the woman had *hargashah* and then discovered blood, such blood certainly cancels the *shivah nekiyim*; if there was no *hargashah,* the blood is not Biblically considered *niddah* blood, and should not cancel the *shivah nekiyim* on that level. Either way, it is unclear why a *bedikah* is necessary.

The *Chavot Da'at* concludes that although blood without *hargashah* is not *tamei* on the Biblical level, it still cancels *shivah nekiyim* on that level. If this opinion is accepted, then all the leniencies for *ketamim* should not apply during that period. The usual leniency for *ketamim* is because the required *hargashah* is lacking; where no *hargashah* is required, *ketamim* should demand stringency.

In resolution of this issue, the *Chavot Da'at* claims that there are two laws regarding *ketamim,* based on two parts of a Biblical verse.[6] The first part of the verse, "the flow will be blood," teaches that only blood that is flowing and not *ketamim* renders women Biblically *niddot.*[7] The second part of the verse, "in her flesh," also teaches that only flows perceptible while still in the woman's flesh render women *niddot,* and not flows that are only perceptible when they leave the body.[8] Many *Acharonim* are bothered by this apparent redundancy in the verse's messages, which leads the *Chavot Da'at* to assert that the first part of the verse deals with a woman who finds blood but does not know where it came from. One would think to be stringent, because this blood possibly came from the endometrial lining, and uncertainty in Biblical areas must be treated

4. *Yoreh De'ah* 196:4 (1), s.v. *katav haAgur.*
5. YD 196:3.
6. *Vayikra* 15:19.
7. *Niddah* 58b.
8. *Niddah* 57b.

stringently. The verse teaches that in this situation of uncertainty, however, the *halakhah* rules leniently. This rule applies at all points of the menstrual cycle. The second part of the verse deals with a case where it is certain that the blood is coming from the uterus, but the woman is Biblically *tehorah,* since there was no *hargashah.* This rule, which is more lenient than the previous rule, does not apply during *shivah nekiyim,* since the *hargashah* that generated the *niddah* status attaches to all subsequent sightings of blood until the woman becomes permitted.

In sum, according to this view, only some types of *ketamim* are problematic during *shivah nekiyim.* If a woman finds a *ketem* and does not know where it came from, the leniencies of *ketamim* can be applied. Therefore, if a woman has a wound that sometimes bleeds, her *shivah nekiyim* will not be cancelled by a *ketem.* However, if a woman with no wound finds a *ketem,* the *shivah nekiyim* is cancelled on a Biblical level even if there was no *hargashah.* This stringency has far reaching ramifications, as it would eliminate the leniencies of *ketamim* smaller than a *gris* and *ketamim* on objects that cannot become ritually impure.

R. Shlomo Zalman Auerbach[9] writes that this view of the *Chavot Da'at* is not accepted in practice. He proves this based on the Rama's ruling[10] that one is lenient regarding *ketamim* smaller than a *gris* during the entire *shivah nekiyim,* which the *Chavot Da'at* would never allow.

The *Sidrei Taharah*[11] writes that there is a difference between a cancellation of *shivah nekiyim,* and a halt in the count of *shivah nekiyim. Ketamim* do not cancel the count, but they prevent the day of their appearance from being counted. This is similar to the *halakhah* concerning *poletet,* discussed earlier. Although the entire count is not cancelled, that day cannot be counted. The suggestion of the *Sidrei Taharah* that such a distinction exists within specific sighting of blood is subject to a dispute between the *Rishonim*:

The Talmud[12] rules that blood resulting from contractions neither makes women *zavot* nor cancels their *shivah nekiyim.* The Rambam and

9. *Responsa Minchat Shlomo, Tinyana* 72:24, s.v. *akh.*
10. *Yoreh De'ah* 196:10.
11. YD 192:4.
12. *Niddah* 37a.

Ra'avad argue about whether or not a day when contraction blood was seen can count for the *shivah nekiyim*. The Rambam[13] writes that it can, but the Ra'avad[14] maintains that it cannot. The *Sidrei Taharah* asserts that just as the Ra'avad believes that contraction blood does not cancel, but does halt the *shivah nekiyim*, *ketamim* halt the *shivah nekiyim* without canceling them. This, he claims, is why *bedikot* must be performed on a Biblical level: to ensure that no *ketamim* are present and that the *shivah nekiyim* were not halted for that day. According to the *Sidrei Taharah*, blood without *hargashah* Biblically interferes with *shivah nekiyim*, and therefore no leniencies of *ketamim* can be applied during *shivah nekiyim*.

The *Sidrei Taharah*'s position, like that of the *Chavot Da'at*, is vulnerable to R. Auerbach's critique. It ignores the Rama's ruling that the leniencies of *ketamim* are applied to maintain the *shivah nekiyim*. In addition, the *Chazon Ish*[15] argues that it is not logical to compare *ketamim* with contraction blood. *Ketamim* have no Biblical significance whatsoever; in contrast, contraction blood does have Biblical significance. As he explains, blood without *hargashah* is simply not considered a "sight of blood" on the level of Biblical law at all, and therefore it is never significant in affecting Biblical law. Contraction blood, however, really is a "sight of blood", but the Torah nonetheless provided a leniency that blood associated with childbirth does not make a woman a *zavah* (although she does become a *niddah* if it is during her days of *niddah*). Therefore, the fact that the Ra'avad rules that contraction blood halts *shivah nekiyim* does not prove that *ketamim* halt the *shivah nekiyim*.

At this point, the views of both the *Chavot Da'at* and *Sidrei Taharah* have been rejected, so the question stands as to why, according to Biblical law, women are required to perform *bedikot* during *shivah nekiyim*. One possible suggestion may be that *bedikot* are not actually required for the purpose of searching for blood, but rather as a prerequisite for actively counting each day as "clean", in keeping with the Torah's statement: "she should count for herself."[16] This would then parallel the

13. *Hilkhot Issurei Bi'ah* 7:10.

14. Ibid.

15. YD 121:15.

16. *Vayikra* 15:28.

affirmative counting required to fulfill the *mitzvah* of *Sefirat HaOmer*. The *bedikah* would serve as the confirmation that the day can indeed be counted, and thus be a realization of that Biblical requirement.

Alternatively, the *Chazon Ish*[17] suggests that *bedikot* are actually not Biblically required; apparently, when the *Beit Yosef* mentioned the *kareit* prohibition as relevant to *bedikot,* he only meant that we should treat *bedikot* strictly as part of the broader realm of *hilkhot niddah,* which is subject to *kareit.*

In sum, there are three opinions about the nature of *bedikot* during *shivah nekiyim*: a) the *Chavot Da'at* and *Sidrei Taharah* believe *bedikot* are required Biblically, because *ketamim* can Biblically affect the count of *shivah nekiyim;* b) *bedikot* may be required Biblically as a fulfillment for proper counting; c) the *Chazon Ish* believes *bedikot* are only required Rabbinically.

II. THE NUMBER OF REQUIRED *BEDIKOT*

It remains to be determined just how many *bedikot* are required. The *Mishnah*[18] records an argument about a woman who only performed *bedikot* on the first and seventh day of *shivah nekiyim.* Most *Rishonim* assume that ideally, women should do *bedikot* on all seven days, and the argument in the *Mishnah* is about what is sufficient post facto. The *Ba'al HaMa'or,*[19] however, explains the dispute as pertaining to how women should act in an ideal situation. The *Shulchan Arukh*[20] follows the majority view of *Rishonim* and rules that women must do *bedikot* every day of the *shivah nekiyim.*

The Ramban[21] writes that one *bedikah* a day is sufficient, while the *Hagahot Maimoniyot*[22] quotes other authorities[23] who require two *bedikot* every day, one in the morning and one before sunset. The *Beit*

17. YD 92:10.
18. *Niddah* 68b.
19. *Sela HaMachloket, Sha'ar HaSefirah vi-ha-bedikah, hasagah* 2.
20. *Yoreh De'ah* 196:4.
21. *Hilkhot Niddah* 2:3.
22. *Hilkhot Issurei Bi'ah* 6:4.
23. See *Semag, lavin* 111; cited in *Beit Yosef, Yoreh De'ah* 196, s.v. *vi-ha-Semag.*

Yosef[24] assumes that the concept of two *bedikot,* and the significance of sunrise and sunset, are imported from the laws of ritual purity, as such *bedikot* are prescribed for women who deal with items that must remain ritually pure.[25] The contemporary laws of *niddah* relate only to a woman's permission to be with her husband, not to the laws of ritual purity. Hence, the Ramban maintains that two *bedikot* are not required.

The *Shulchan Arukh* rules in accordance with the *Hagahot Maimoniyot,* and none of the early *Acharonim* disagree. Later *poskim,* however, add that if *bedikot* cause irritation or bleeding, then one may follow the Ramban and perform only one *bedikah.* Some *rabbanim* instruct women under ordinary circumstances to follow the Ramban, since many contemporary women cause themselves to bleed while performing *bedikot.* All authorities agree that if one *bedikah* a day was performed, the *shivah nekiyim* are valid.

It remains to be clarified, though, what the bare minimum of *bedikot* is that can be deemed sufficient. The aforementioned *Mishnah* records three opinions about the status of a woman who did *bedikot* only on the first and seventh days: a) R. Akiva maintains that the first day's *bedikah* was worthless, and the seventh day counts as the first day of a new *shivah nekiyim;* b) R. Yehoshua argues that every day on which she does a *bedikah* counts towards *shivah nekiyim,* while days without *bedikot* do not count; hence, she has accrued two of the seven clean days after the seventh day's *bedikah;*[26] c) R. Eliezer is of the opinion that these *shivah nekiyim* are acceptable post facto even though no *bedikot* were performed on the interim days.

The Talmud[27] concludes that although the *halakhah* generally follows R. Yehoshua against R. Eliezer, in this case the *halakhah* follows R. Eliezer. The Talmud also asks: when R. Eliezer ruled that *bedikot* on the first and last days work post facto, is this the absolute minimum, or can one be lenient for even one *bedikah* either at the beginning or the end of

24. *Yoreh De'ah* 196, s.v. *u-mah she-katav Rabbenu she-ba-sefer.*
25. See the *Mishnah, Niddah* 11a.
26. This supports the *Sidrei Taharah*'s view that occurrences other than sighting semen can halt, but not cancel, the *shivah nekiyim.*
27. *Niddah* 68b and 7b.

the *shivah nekiyim*? Rav and R. Chanina debate this issue: According to Rav, R. Eliezer allows even one *bedikah* on either day one or day seven, while R. Chanina believes that R. Eliezer requires at least two *bedikot*, one on the first and one on the seventh day.

The Ra'ah and the Rashba debate whether or not Rav would be lenient if a woman did her single *bedikah* on any day other than one and seven. The Rashba,[28] quoting the Ra'avad, writes that even one *bedikah* in the middle of the *shivah nekiyim* is sufficient according to Rav, while the Ra'ah[29] writes that one *bedikah* is only sufficient if performed on the first or seventh day.

This debate appears to reflect a fundamental dispute regarding the purpose of *bedikot*. The Ra'ah believes that *bedikot* are a prerequisite for proper counting, for *sefirah*. This ordinarily requires *bedikot* on all seven days; however, R. Eliezer believes that the first and last days act as framing markers, and support the remainder of days that lack *bedikot*. Hence, only the first and last days, which have unique significance as the commencement or conclusion of the count, will suffice. *Bedikot* on any other day are meaningless, since they in no way contribute to *sefirah*. In contrast, the Rashba[30] understands that the purpose of *shivah nekiyim* is to prove that bleeding has stopped. There is no formal dimension of counting necessary during these days. One *bedikah* on any day proves that the woman has ceased to see blood.

In practice, most *Rishonim* follow the view of Rav, that a single *bedikah* is sufficient. However, the *Sefer Mitzvot Katan* rules in accordance with R. Chanina, that two *bedikot* are necessary, and the *Beit Yosef*[31] similarly rules that two *bedikot* should be required, reflecting stringency, since a "*kareit*" prohibition is involved. Thus, according to the *Shulchan Arukh*,[32] if the first or seventh day's *bedikah* was omitted, the *shivah nekiyim* are not valid. However, since most *Rishonim* agree with Rav, leniency is possible under certain circumstances. The *Chatam Sofer*[33]

28. *Torat HaBayit Arukh*, 7:5, s.v. *vi-od*.
29. *Bedek HaBayit*, 7:5, s.v. *bi-inyan*.
30. *Mishmeret HaBayit* 3:5, s.v. *amar ha-koteiv*.
31. *Yoreh De'ah* 196:4(1) s.v. *katav haAgur*.
32. *Yoreh De'ah* 196:4.
33. *Responsa*, YD 178, cited in *Pitchei Teshuvah*, YD 196:7.

discusses a woman who did a *bedikah* on day one, but forgot the *bedikah* on day seven, and subsequently immersed and had intercourse with her husband. According to the *Shulchan Arukh*'s strict ruling, she is still a *niddah*, and the immersion was ineffective. However, the *Chatam Sofer* writes that since she already immersed and had intercourse, one may rely on the majority opinion in *Rishonim*. The *Chatam Sofer* would not be lenient if this woman had performed only one *bedikah* in the middle of the *shivah nekiyim*, since in that case the Ra'ah would also still deem her a *niddah*. R. Ovadiah Yosef[34] cites *Acharonim* who rule, against the *Chatam Sofer*, that one may follow the Rashba's ruling against the Ra'ah. Therefore, one may be lenient even when a lone *bedikah* was performed in the middle of the *shivah nekiyim*, provided the couple already had intercourse. If the couple has not been together after immersion, the *Acharonim* agree that they are forbidden to one another until a proper *shivah nekiyim* have been counted.

If a woman performs the *bedikah* of the seventh day during *bein ha-shemashot*, the period that may be day and may be night between the seventh and eighth day, one can be lenient on account of a double uncertainty: the *bedikah* may have taken place during daytime, and even if it did not, most *Rishonim* rule that a *bedikah* on the first day alone is sufficient.

If a woman did *bedikot* on the first six days but missed the seventh day, the *Noda BiYehudah*[35] suggests that she perform a *bedikah* on the eighth day and essentially act as if that the first day never existed; hence, in replacing the first day with the second, the second with the third, etc. she has counted the first and seventh days and only missed the sixth.

If a woman did a *bedikah* on the first day and on some other day, but forgot to do it on the seventh day, the *Noda BiYehudah* suggests that she perform a *bedikah* on the eighth day. This is more difficult to understand than his previous solution: if she counts day eight and acts as if that day one never existed, then it would turn out that she counted day seven and some earlier day, but either way she did not count both the first and seventh days. The *Noda BiYehudah* explains that a *bedikah* in

34. *Taharat HaBayit*, II, 312–313.

35. *Responsa, Tinyana*, YD 128; cited in *Pitchei Teshuvah*, YD 196:6.

the middle of *shivah nekiyim* links the first and eighth days' *bedikot* and creates a valid *shivah nekiyim*. In his commentary to the *Shulchan Arukh*, *Dagul MeRevavah*,[36] he is lenient even when *bedikot* were performed on the second and fifth days; however, in his responsa he adopts the stringent stance. In practice, a stringent view is followed in such cases. Although *bedikot* of day one and day eight can be linked by a middle day *bedikah*, two other days cannot suffice to fulfill the obligation to check at the beginning and the conclusion of the *shivah nekiyim*.

36. YD 196:6.

25.

The Performance of *Bedikot* at Nighttime

I. THE PROPER TIME FOR *BEDIKOT*

The question must now be considered as to whether a *bedikah* may be performed at nighttime, or if it is at least acceptable on a less than optimal level if it has already been done.

The *Mishnah*[1] addresses a seemingly unrelated issue; however, the underlying principles may be related to this case. The *Mishnah* states that a woman who prematurely goes to the *mikveh* on the seventh night of *shivah nekiyim,* instead of waiting until the daytime of the seventh day, invalidates her *tevilah* (immersion). This is true even though she is not required to wait until the completion of the seventh day, due to the principle of "*miktzat ha-yom ki-kulo*", which teaches that a part of the day sometimes qualifies as the halakhic equivalent of a complete day. Nonetheless, her *tevilah* on the previous night is invalid. The reasoning behind the *Mishnah*'s invalidation in this case is due to the limitation of the principle of *miktzat ha-yom ki-kulo* only to the daytime.

1. See *Niddah* 71b, and the Talmud's discussion on 72a.

Tosafot[2] assume that the *halakhah* is in accordance with this *Mishnah,* and conclude on its basis that a *bedikah* performed at night would, likewise, be invalid. Just as the nighttime fails to qualify as the day of the seventh with respect to *tevilah,* it is not regarded as the seventh day in connection to *bedikot* either. On the surface, *Tosafot*'s invalidation would seem to be on a Biblical level. To reject *Tosafot*'s viewpoint, one would have to reject one of the two assumptions their conclusion rests upon: a) *Tosafot* affirms the assertion of the *Mishnah* that the principle of *miktzat ha-yom ki-kulo* is inapplicable to the evening; b) *Tosafot* equates the timeframe for *tevilah* with the timeframe for *bedikot,* and extrapolates from one to the other. A rejection of either assumption would undermine *Tosafot*'s conclusion.

II. THE APPLICATION OF *MIKTZAT HA-YOM KI-KULO* TO THE EVENING

Tosafot's first assumption, ruling in accordance with the *Mishnah,* seems to be founded on solid grounding since no dissenting opinion appears in the *Mishnah*. In truth, however, the matter is not as self-evident as it would appear to be. An intricate debate between R. Shimon and R. Yose elsewhere in the Talmud[3] concerning a sighting of blood following an immersion on the seventh day reopens the issue.

According to R. Shimon, if a woman sees blood following her immersion on the seventh day of *shivah nekiyim,* the sighting would undermine her immersion and render her a *niddah* retroactively. R. Yose, however, disagrees, claiming that the sighting of blood following the woman's immersion creates a new status of *niddah* from that point and onward; however, it does not alter her previous status of *taharah* which resulted from her immersion. A practical ramification of the dispute between R. Shimon and R. Yose relates to a ruling concerning a *zavah ketanah*. A *zavah ketanah,* who sees blood on one day, is required to wait one clean day in order to restore her status of purity. On a Biblical level, she is permitted to immerse in a *mikveh* following daybreak of the first clean day. If she witnesses an additional sighting of blood subsequent

2. *Niddah* 69a, s.v. *shivah,* and 71b, s.v. *ha-ro'eh.*
3. *Pesachim* 80b.

to her immersion, R. Shimon would now render her a *zavah gedolah* if this occurs on three consecutive days, since, retroactively, she never experienced a clean day, whereas R. Yose would argue that she obtains the status of *zavah ketanah* anew for the following day.

The Talmud[4] challenges R. Yose's perspective, since, according to his opinion, it is seemingly impossible to attain the status of *zavah gedolah*. The initial moment of daybreak on the clean day should disrupt any potential combination between the previous day's sighting of blood and a subsequent sighting of blood on the clean day. Even if a woman sees blood for three consecutive days, R. Yose should only render her a *zavah ketanah* due to each sighting of blood being independent of the others. The Talmud justifies R. Yose's opinion, claiming that the status of *zavah gedolah* would be obtained if a woman bleeds unabatedly for three consecutive days.

Rashi[5] questions the Talmud's resolution, claiming that a far simpler scenario ought to have been suggested. If a woman sees blood for three consecutive days at nighttime, even R. Yose should concur to her status as a *zavah gedolah*. Since the principle of *miktzat ha-yom ki-kulo* does not apply during the evening, the previous day's sighting of blood remains in effect, enabling it to combine with the subsequent evening's sighting. The Talmud's decision to ignore this resolution leads Rashi to conclude that R. Yose must apply the principle of *miktzat ha-yom ki-kulo* even to the nighttime. For this reason, the only potential scenario in which the status of *zavah gedolah* would materialize is in a case in which a woman bleeds continuously for three consecutive days. According to Rashi, R. Yose's view may be accepted, thereby rejecting the view of the *Mishnah* that an immersion on the night preceding the seventh day is invalid.

R. Tam[6] offers a different interpretation to the Talmud's resolution. In truth, R. Yose would deem a woman a *zavah gedolah* if she saw blood for three consecutive evenings, since the principle of *miktzat ha-yom ki-kulo* is indeed inapplicable to the nighttime; nonetheless, the

4. *Pesachim* 81a.
5. Quoted in *Tosafot, Niddah* 71b, s.v. *ha-ro'eh*.
6. *Tosafot* ibid.

Talmud still suggested an alternative scenario of seeing blood continuously for three consecutive days. The Talmud prefers a scenario in which the sighting of blood occurred during the daytime since it conforms to the literal understanding of the verse which describes a *zavah gedolah*, stating "*ki yazuv zov damah yamim rabbim*", using the word "*yamim*", meaning days. Since the verse focuses on the sighting of blood during the daytime, the Talmud avoids the alternative explanation which entails the sighting of blood at nighttime. According to R. Tam, the unanimous character of the *Mishnah* is upheld, thereby denying the application of *miktzat ha-yom ki-kulo* to the evening.

The dispute between Rashi and R. Tam regarding the application of *miktzat ha-yom ki-kulo* at nighttime has broader ramifications than the specific context of *hilkhot niddah*. R. Meir of Rothenberg[7] raises a potential application of *miktzat ha-yom ki-kulo* at nighttime within the context of *aveilut*. Generally speaking, there are two circumstances in which *miktzat ha-yom ki-kulo* may affect the area of *aveilut*. On the one hand, the principle determines that on the seventh day of *shivah* the mourner need not sit for the entire day; rather, it suffices for the mourner to observe only a portion of the day. In addition, the principle affects the observance of *aveilut* in a circumstance of *shemu'ah rechokah*, a scenario in which an individual becomes aware of the passing of a close relative thirty days after the burial. Under such circumstances, the mourner only observes a single day of *aveilut*. Due to the principle of *miktzat ha-yom ki-kulo*, however, the mourner only observes the laws of mourning for a component of the day.

R. Meir of Rothenberg notes that the two applications of *miktzat ha-yom ki-kulo* differ in nature. The first application seeks to incorporate a small component of the day as part of an ongoing count, whereas the second application of the principle seeks to establish the minimum for a single day's integrity. R. Meir of Rothenberg distinguishes between the two applications with respect to the principle's application at nighttime. A component of a day may only be incorporated within an ongoing count if one has observed part of the daytime; however, with respect to the integrity of a single day even a nighttime observance qualifies for

7. Quoted in *Tur, Yoreh De'ah* 395.

the principle of *miktzat ha-yom ki-kulo*. The notion of *sefirah,* counting, is reserved for the daytime hours of a day. The *Radbaz,* cited in *Pitchei Teshuvah,*[8] advances this argument one step further and relies on the application of *miktzat ha-yom ki-kulo* at nighttime, in certain pressing circumstances, even within the context of the last day of *shivah*. The current discussion would have great bearing on the application of the laws of mourning observed during *Sefirat HaOmer* during the nighttime of *Lag BaOmer.*

In *Hilkhot Aveilut,* the *Shulchan Arukh*[9] rules in accordance with the viewpoint of R. Meir of Rothenberg; as a result, the principle of *miktzat ha-yom ki-kulo* should not be applicable to the nighttime with respect to any laws pertaining to *shivah nekiyim.*

III. PRACTICAL SCENARIOS OF NIGHTTIME *BEDIKOT*

There are a couple of situations in which the halakhic standing of a nighttime *bedikah* becomes highly relevant. One such scenario relates to the ability for a *mokh,* if it remains in a woman's body for a portion of the evening of the first day of *shivah nekiyim,* to also satisfy the need for a *bedikah* on the first day. In general, the *Rishonim* dispute the degree of thoroughness required for a *bedikah*. Regarding this point, the *Shulchan Arukh*[10] ruled stringently whereas the *Noda BiYehudah*[11] is willing to adopt a lenient viewpoint in certain exceptionally extenuating circumstances. The *Noda BiYehudah* was unwilling to be lenient regarding the *hefsek taharah*; however, he believes that the lenient ruling could potentially apply to the *bedikot* of *shivah nekiyim*. As a result, a *mokh* which was left in a woman's body for a portion of the evening could, in theory, count as the first *bedikah* of *shivah nekiyim,* and would also meet the standard of a thorough internal check. The foundation for the *Noda BiYehudah*'s leniency is his reliance on the aforementioned position of R. Yose. Just as R. Yose permits a woman to immerse at night, based on the principle of *miktzat ha-yom ki-kulo,* he would allow her to perform

8. *Yoreh De'ah* 395:1.
9. *Yoreh De'ah* 395:1; see also Rama.
10. *Yoreh De'ah* 196:6.
11. *Responsa* 46, cited in *Pitchei Teshuvah* 196:9.

a *bedikah* at night as well. The *Noda BiYehudah* notes, however, that this ruling would be limited to Rashi's understanding of R. Yose's position. The *Noda BiYehudah*'s ruling is surprising on two levels: his willingness to accept the unique position of Rashi and, secondly, his reliance on R. Yose's position, a position the Talmud seemingly rejected in a different passage.

A more prevalent example of a nighttime *bedikah*'s practicality relates to a *bedikah* performed in the early morning, before sunrise. The *Mishnah*[12] teaches that any *mitzvah* whose timeframe is the daytime hours should ideally be performed after *netz ha-chamah* (sunrise), despite the technical onset of halakhic day occurring at *alot ha-shachar* (dawn). The immersion of a *zavah ketanah* is one example mentioned by the *Mishnah* as belonging to this category. If *Tosafot*'s perspective is correct, and the performance of *bedikot* must be done during the day, a woman would be required to wait until after *netz ha-chamah* in order to engage in a *bedikah*. This stipulation becomes increasingly difficult to adhere to during the winter months when *netz ha-chamah* might be delayed until well after seven o' clock. Many *poskim* are of the opinion that despite the attendant challenge in waiting until after *netz ha-chamah*, a *bedikah* should still not be performed until after that point in time. One exception to this overwhelming majority is the opinion of R. Avraham David Rabinowitz Teomim, known as the *Aderet*. The *Aderet*[13] believed that the stringency requiring one to wait until after *netz ha-chamah* despite the halakhic definition of day resulting from *alot ha-shachar* is no longer applicable nowadays. The stringency was motivated by potential miscalculation and confusion regarding the precise moment of daybreak; however, with the advent of clocks the concern is no longer relevant. All other *poskim*, though, still require a woman to wait until after *netz ha-chamah* in order to perform a *bedikah*. It is important to note that a *bedikah* that is performed before *netz ha-chamah* but after *alot ha-shachar* would still be acceptable on a less than

12. *Megillah* 20a.
13. See *Sedei Chemed*, vol. 3, p. 347.

optimal level. The *Badei HaShulchan*[14] notes that the Rambam[15] might dispute this point; however, the standard understanding of the matter would validate such a *bedikah* after the fact.

IV. COMPARING THE TIMEFRAME FOR *TEVILAH* WITH THE TIMEFRAME FOR *BEDIKOT*

As was mentioned earlier, *Tosafot*'s ruling which invalidated nighttime *bedikot* was based on two premises, the second of which extrapolated from the timeframe for *tevilah* to the ideal timeframe for *bedikot*. The *Chazon Ish*[16] challenges *Tosafot*'s assumption, and claims that the other *Rishonim* did not accept such an equation.[17]

The underlying point of dispute between *Tosafot* and the *Chazon Ish* may relate to the nature of *bedikot* during *shivah nekiyim* and their relationship to the *sefirah*, the count, of *shivah nekiyim*. Immersion at night is invalid, according to the *Mishnah*, since it depends on the completion of the count of seven days, and the unit of seven days can only be completed during the daytime of the seventh day. Thus, it is necessary to determine whether the *bedikot* are associated with the counting of the *shivah nekiyim*.

If the *bedikot* are essentially the manner in which a woman counts the days of *shivah nekiyim*, a viewpoint subscribed to by the *Ra'ah*,[18] then the concepts of *bedikot* and *sefirah* are naturally intertwined. It would follow that the *bedikot* should also be performed during the daytime. If the *bedikot*, however, are not associated with the count of *shivah nekiyim*, rather with the pragmatic investigation as to the presence of blood, then the laws pertaining to *sefirah* should not necessarily govern the performance of *bedikot*. The *Chazon Ish* reasons that if a sighting of blood at night will undermine a woman's observance of *shivah nekiyim*, then a

14. 196:79, *tziyunim* 156.
15. *Hilkhot Issurei Bi'ah* 6:9; see also 6:12.
16. YD 92:12.
17. See also Rama, 196:4, who expresses concern for proper lighting at night, implying that only a technical problem exists for nighttime *bedikot*, not a legal exclusion. See *Sidrei Taharah* 196:19.
18. See earlier p. 165.

bedikah at night, aimed at ascertaining that very appearance of blood, should be equally valid at night.

Seemingly, this issue concerning the relationship between *bedikot* and *sefirah* hinges upon the differing viewpoints of the Rashba and the Ra'ah as to whether *bedikot* are for the purposes of counting, or to establish that the day is clean. As a result, it should follow that since the *halakhah* is in accordance with the Rashba's perspective, the *Chazon Ish*'s conclusion validating nighttime *bedikot* should be adopted. In addition, the *Noda BiYehudah* challenges *Tosafot*'s opening assumption on the basis of Rashi's understanding of R. Yose's opinion, thereby allowing for a lenient assessment of nighttime *bedikot* in extenuating circumstances. Yet, no *Rishon* explicitly disputes *Tosafot*, and, as a result, the generally accepted opinion is to refrain from performing *bedikot* at nighttime, at least ideally.

26.

Counting the "*Shivah Nekiyim*"

I. VERBAL COUNTING:

The authors of the *Tosafot*[1] note a critical distinction between the counting of *Sefirat HaOmer* and the counting of the *shivah nekiyim*: while our Sages instituted the recitation of a *berakhah* when counting *Sefirat HaOmer*, no such blessing is recited over the counting of the *shivah nekiyim*. *Tosafot* explain this discrepancy as a function of the certainty with which each count is performed. *Sefirat HaOmer* warrants a blessing because completion of the counting is entirely in the control of the individual: as long as one remembers to count forty nine consecutive nights, one will certainly complete the count. *Shivah nekiyim*, however, is quite different. Even if a woman remembers to count each day, the possibility remains that she will observe blood during one of the days, thereby cancelling the count until that point. Because of such a possibility, one never recites a blessing on the counting of *shivah nekiyim*.

The *Acharonim* debate the exact intention and application of this

1. *Ketubot* 72a, s.v. *vi-safrah*.

comment of *Tosafot*. The *Shelah HaKadosh*[2] understands *Tosafot* to be teaching that the counting of *shivah nekiyim* constitutes an active *mitzvah*. As such, a woman would likely be required to verbally count in a manner similar to *Sefirat HaOmer*: "*ha-yom yom rishon*, etc – Today is the first day of the *shivah nekiyim*." The *Noda BiYehudah*,[3] however, disagrees. Unlike *Sefirat HaOmer*, *shivah nekiyim*, in his view, do not demand a formal verbal articulation; rather, the requirement of *shivah nekiyim* is simply to know that seven clean days have passed. The practice is in accordance with the view of the *Noda BiYehudah*.

II. MISTAKES IN THE COUNT

The *Responsa Me'il Tzedakah*[4] discusses a situation[5] relevant to the following case: a woman performed a proper *hefsek taharah* and began counting the *shivah nekiyim*. In the middle of her count, she observes some spotting, and therefore performs a new *hefsek taharah* and restarts her count. After she does this, however, the spots that she observed were subsequently determined to be *tahor*, presenting a halakhic question. On one hand, the subsequent determination reveals that her original *shivah nekiyim* were, in reality, never cancelled. On the other hand, perhaps her conscious rejection of the original *shivah nekiyim*, albeit on the basis of mistaken information, effectively cancels the original count. Favoring the latter analysis, the *Me'il Tzedakah* rules that the woman's "*heseich ha-da'at*", or lapse in intent, cancels her count, and she may only rely on the days counted since her second *hefsek taharah*. The *Me'il Tzedakah* offers two reasons for this stringency, one practical and one conceptual in nature:

Once the woman believes that the spotting has cancelled the *shivah nekiyim*, she will no longer be vigilant to detect new stains until she performs the next *hefsek taharah*. As such, she may have experienced an unnoticed blood flow in between her original despair and her sub-

2. *Shnei Luchot HaBrit, Sha'ar HaOtiyot, Hilkhot Bi'ah/Niddah/Kedushat HaZivug*, #57, p. 452 (Jerusalem 5753 ed.); see *Pitchei Teshuvah* YD 196:4.
3. *Responsa, Tinyana*, YD 123; see *Pitchei Teshuvah*, ibid.
4. *Responsa*, #63; see *Pitchei Teshuvah*, 196:3 and *Sidrei Taharah* 196:18.
5. The actual situation he considers is somewhat different from what is described here, but the case presented here is a more common scenario.

sequent *hefsek taharah*. The nature of this concern is purely pragmatic: because the woman has despaired of her original *shivah nekiyim*, we suspect that she may have missed additional *tamei* blood which would actually invalidate her original count.

Alternatively, perhaps *halakhah* demands a conscious counting of the *shivah nekiyim*. Any "lapse in intent" will therefore cancel the counting which has already been performed. In contrast to the pragmatic focus of the first reason, this reason appears more formal and fundamental in nature. Regardless of whether or not blood actually appeared, the count is inherently invalid if it was not accompanied by appropriate intent throughout. Indeed, this answer is somewhat reminiscent of the opinion of the *Shelah HaKadosh*, assuming the existence of a formal mitzvah of "*sefirah*" as opposed to mere knowledge of the days which have passed. While the *Shelah* understood this *mitzvah* to necessitate verbal articulation, the *Me'il Tzedakah* understands it as requiring, at least, conscious intent throughout the seven days.

The validity of the *Me'il Tzedakah*'s stringency may relate to the aforementioned dispute between the Rashba and the Ra'ah.[6] According to the Ra'ah, the performance of *bedikot* serves as a form of counting the "*sefirah*". As such, the stringency of the *Me'il Tzedakah* is quite reasonable. According to the Rashba, however, the *bedikot* serve as a pragmatic means of detecting *niddah* blood, and the second reason of the *Me'il Tzedakah* would be inapplicable. One is left to decide whether or not to accept the *Me'il Tzedakah*'s first concern.

III. EVALUATING THE STRINGENCY OF THE *ME'IL TZEDAKAH*:

A group of *Acharonim*, including the *Lechem Ve-Simlah*[7] and others,[8] categorically reject the *Me'il Tzedakah*, noting the lack of Talmudic support for his position. In fact, several *Acharonim* note that the Talmud appears

6. See earlier p. 96.
7. 196:13, in *Simlah*.
8. For example, this position is implicit in *Responsa Iggerot Moshe*, EH IV, 14.

to expressly contradict the view of the *Me'il Tzedakah*. The *Mishnah*[9] rules that a woman who is mentally disabled and low-functioning, can fulfill the requirement of *shivah nekiyim* if a competent woman keeps track of the days and regularly performs *bedikot* on her behalf. Although the assisting woman can only perform *bedikot* at limited times and the woman in *shivah nekiyim* lacks legal awareness, the Talmud appears unconcerned about potential undetected *niddah* blood. Accordingly, the *Me'il Tzedakah*'s first concern, that a woman who loses sight of her count may fail to notice blood in the interim, is unfounded. Despite these objections, however, some *Acharonim* defend the *Me'il Tzedakah* and actually accept his stringency.

IV. RAMIFICATIONS WITHIN THE *ME'IL TZEDAKAH*:

The two reasons provided for the stringency of the *Me'il Tzedakah* may result in various legal ramifications. One affected situation would be that of a woman who mistakenly interrupts her count, but recognizes her error on the same day. If the problem with an interruption is the "*heseich ha-da'at*", or formal lapse in intent, then perhaps a lapse which lasts for less than a day may be deemed insignificant, because she still "counts" that day. If, however, the problem is more practical in nature – namely, that a lapse in concentration may result in unobserved blood, then even a slight lapse in vigilance would be problematic. Some authorities rule that even if one generally accepts the ruling of the *Me'il Tzedakah*, one could justifiably rule leniently in this case, since one of the *Me'il Tzedakah's* two reasons does not apply.

A second practical ramification of this dispute pertains to how a woman who has erroneously interrupted her count should proceed after recognizing her error. Although the days of her mental lapse certainly cannot count towards the *shivah nekiyim*, many authorities rule that she may continue her original count. These authorities must perceive the *Me'il Tzedakah*'s stringency as stemming primarily from a formal lapse in intent from the *shivah nekiyim*. While days which pass without proper intent cannot possibly count towards the *shivah nekiyim*

9. *Niddah* 13b.

themselves, the lack of intent alone does not undermine the original counting which was performed (similar to the rule of *poletet*). Accordingly, such a woman would be allowed to resume her count from where she left. Other authorities, however, maintain that she must start anew. Such authorities apparently perceive the stringency as a function of a pragmatic concern for unobserved *niddah* blood. In terms of the final *halakhah*, one may justifiably opt for a lenient approach to this issue as well, since, as noted earlier, stringency would require several questionable assumptions.

V. CONTEMPORARY APPLICATION:

Ideally, the scenario of the *Me'il Tzedakah* should be irrelevant in practice: any woman who is unsure about a possible interruption to her *shivah nekiyim* should immediately contact a rabbi, and in the meantime assume that her *shivah nekiyim* is still intact. If a woman is unable to contact a rabbi immediately, she should attempt to satisfy both possibilities: on one hand, she should perform another *hefsek taharah*, but on the other hand, she should not relinquish her focus on her original *shivah nekiyim* (in light of the ruling of the *Me'il Tzedakah*). Practically, she should perform a *bedikah* on the following day, with the intention that it should serve as either "day one" of the new count or "day x" of the old count, and she should continue to perform such *bedikot* until contacting a rabbi. Indeed, it is preferable to maintain two simultaneous counts than to simply start over without further investigation. A rabbi must then analyze each situation individually, in order to determine the appropriate course of action.

The above suggestion, that a woman should maintain two simultaneous hypothetical counts, assumes the validity of a "double" or "uncertain" counting. This assumption, however, is possibly challenged by the opinion associated with the *Devar Avraham*[10] in regards to *Sefirat HaOmer*. This opinion suggests that a count done without certainty is not considered a halakhically valid "counting". This view, however, is

10. *Responsa*, I, 34.

not applied in practice;[11] as such, women are permitted to maintain simultaneous counts of *shivah nekiyim* as a result of uncertainty, keeping track both of their original count and what the count would be if the original *shivah* nekiyim was broken up.

This issue may also be relevant to a ruling of R. Moshe Feinstein[12] regarding the requirement of *hefsek taharah*. R. Feinstein rules that a woman should not count the same act as both a *hefsek taharah* and a *mokh*. In other words, a woman should not insert a *bedikah* cloth at the time of her *hefsek taharah*, and then simply leave it there until dark to fulfill the *mokh* requirement. R. Feinstein explains his rationale: the *hefsek taharah* should occur before sunset, so that a woman may begin counting the *Shivah Nekiyim* from that night. However, if a woman leaves the *bedikah* cloth inserted and only inspected the results of her *hefsek taharah* after sunset, then she will only know retroactively – i.e., after sunset – if her *shivah nekiyim* have actually commenced. In demanding absolute knowledge and awareness on the part of the woman, R. Feinstein's reasoning somewhat resembles that of the *Me'il Tzedakah*. In practice, a lenient approach is usually followed regarding women who are unsure about the viability of their current *shivah nekiyim*, as long as they do not believe for certain that the count has been broken. Therefore, R. Feinstein's stringent ruling in this case is somewhat surprising.

Nevertheless, R. Feinstein's suggestion not to do the *hefsek taharah* and the *mokh* together remains valuable for the following practical reason. If a woman uses the *hefsek taharah* cloth as the *mokh* and finds blood on the cloth, the *hefsek taharah* is disregarded and she must wait another day to commence her count. If, however, she uses a separate

11. In truth, the *Devar Avraham* retracts his stringency in light of a ruling of the *Ba'al HaMa'or* (*Pesachim* 28a in *dappei HaRif*), but the *Devar Avraham* is nonetheless often mistakenly identified as categorically rejecting the possibility of an "uncertain" counting. Regarding *Sefirat HaOmer*, the *Ba'al HaMa'or* rules that a Jew in the Diaspora should not count a double counting (due to the uncertainty of the festival dates), as such a double counting would result in counting the 49th night of the *omer* on *Shavuot* itself, thereby denigrating the sanctity of the festival. The *Devar Avraham* infers from the *Ba'al HaMa'or* that the only reason not to perform an "uncertain" counting is the technical problem of disrespecting *Shavuot*. Intrinsically, though, such a counting would be technically valid.

12. *Responsa Iggerot Moshe*, YD II, 79.

bedikah cloth for the *hefsek taharah,* then even if it the cloth displays a problematic color, she still has time to perform one or two more attempts before sunset to salvage that day. Indeed, sometimes the blood that appears on the first *bedikah* cloth is just residue from prior days, and doing an early *bedikah* can clear that away to allow for a successful *hefsek taharah.*[13]

13. For more on the recommended time and procedure for the *hefsek taharah* see Ch. 20 , sec. 1.

27.

Defining a "Day" For the Purpose of *Shivah Nekiyim*

I. BEGINNING A "DAY" BEFORE SUNDOWN

There are a few important issues that arise with regard to the definition of a "day" for the purposes of *shivah nekiyim*. The *Rishonim* discuss the law in the following case: A man recites *ma'ariv* before *sheki'ah*, following the Talmudic view[1] that one may do so after *plag ha-minchah*. His wife, however, is interested in performing a *hefsek taharah* at that time, as it is not yet *sheki'ah*. The question is then raised as to whether the husband's recitation of *ma'ariv* has officially declared the halakhic day to be over. Some *poskim* felt that the woman must wait until the following afternoon, while other *poskim* claim that it does not officially become night for her simply because the local community has already recited *ma'ariv*, and thus a *hefsek taharah* would still be possible. However, if this situation occurs several minutes before *sheki'ah* on a Friday night, an additional issue would have to be considered. At that point, the woman will have already lit candles, invoking the principle of *Tosefet Shabbat* (adding on to Shabbat), and effectively welcoming in the next

1. This is the implication of the position of R. Yehudah found in *Berakhot* 27a.

day. This distinction between weekdays and Friday night is suggested by the Rama.[2] He rules that women should be careful to perform the *hefsek taharah* before lighting candles on Friday night, although after the fact they may do so even after lighting candles.

II. THE NATURE OF *TOSEFET SHABBAT* AND *YOM TOV*

The acceptability of performing a *hefsek taharah* for Friday after accepting the sanctity of Shabbat early may relate to a fundamental rabbinic dispute regarding the nature of the time period colloquially referred to as "Early Shabbat." The *Tosafot*[3] record a debate regarding whether or not one can fulfill the obligatory Friday night meal during the period of "Early Shabbat." It seems apparent that one could understand the nature of the "Early Shabbat" institution in one of two possible ways:

1. When one accepts "Early Shabbat," one transforms the weekday Friday afternoon into a sanctified Shabbat evening. The sanctity of Shabbat actually commences before nightfall, and one can fulfill all of the *mitzvot* of Shabbat during this time period.
2. Shabbat always begins at nightfall, regardless of one's acceptance of the day. When one accepts "Early Shabbat," one merely opts to observe the prohibitions of Shabbat on Friday afternoon. Although referred to as "Early Shabbat," the period is *not* actually "Shabbat." Rather, it is still a weekday, but with a prohibition of labor; in which case one could not fulfill *mitzvot* specific to Shabbat.

This question is also the focus of a dispute between the Maharshal and the *Taz*[4] with regard to eating in the *sukkah* on the night of *Shemini Atzeret*. For those outside of the land of Israel, the Talmud rules that one eats in the *sukkah* without reciting a *berakhah* of *"leishev ba-sukkah."* The Maharshal rules that one who accepts the sanctity of *Shemini Atzeret* early should not eat the yom tov meal during that time, as doing

2. *Yoreh De'ah* 196:1.
3. *Pesachim* 99b, s.v. *samukh*.
4. *Orach Chaim* 668:1.

so would present an uncertainty regarding whether or not one should still recite the blessing of "*leishev ba-sukkah*." The *Taz*, however, argues that once the yom tov of *Shemini Atzeret* has been accepted, one would absolutely *not* recite a blessing of "*leishev ba-sukkah*," since the holiday of *Sukkot* has formally ended. Apparently, the Maharshal and the *Taz* are arguing about the fundamental nature of "Early Shabbat" and "Early Yom Tov." According to the Maharshal, early acceptance of yom tov does not "transform" the day. As such, uncertainty remains as to whether one should recite the blessing that pertains to *Sukkot*. According to the *Taz*, however, early acceptance of yom tov absolutely "transforms" the day. Therefore, *Sukkot* has formally ended, and no blessing would be recited.

The acceptability of performing Friday's *hefsek taharah* during the period of "Early Shabbat" may relate to this analysis as well. If the early acceptance of Shabbat merely superimposes the prohibitions of Shabbat onto the weekday afternoon of Friday, a woman should seemingly still be able to perform the *hefsek taharah* of Friday. If, however, the acceptance marks the transformation of Friday afternoon into Shabbat night, the day has come to an end, and Friday's *hefsek taharah* can no longer be completed. Given that the *Mishnah Berurah* technically permits the fulfillment of the Friday night Shabbat meal during "Early Shabbat," it appears that normative halakhah views "Early Shabbat" as a transformation or an extension of Shabbat itself. Accordingly, a woman would not be able to fulfill Friday's *hefsek taharah* during "Early Shabbat."

However, differentiations may be made between the laws of Shabbat and the laws of *niddah*. That is to say, even if the acceptance of "Early Shabbat" transforms the day in regards to the laws of Shabbat, it is still possible that the obligations of *niddah* may still be fulfilled. Indeed, most *poskim* permit the performance of a *hefsek taharah*, even after candle lighting if one forgot to do so previously.[5]

III. TRAVELING BETWEEN TIME ZONES:

A further application of these laws pertains to the contemporary issue of time zones. If, for example, a woman flies from Los Angeles to New York (losing three hours) on the seventh day of her *shivah nekiyim*, the

5. see Ch. 23.

question arises as to whether she may immerse in the *mikveh* at sunset in New York, and be with her husband, even though she has not really waited a complete seven days. There are a number of opinions on the matter:

1. Some opinions[6] assert that the Torah's phraseology of "*vi-safrah lah* – she shall count *for her*" – hints that the reckoning of the *shivah nekiyim* always follows the woman's perspective, as opposed to the objective time zone in which she is located. As such, she must personally experience seven sets of twenty four complete hours, and would have to wait an additional three hours after landing in New York.
2. Some opinions suggest a compromise. Because the Torah permitted a *zavah* to immerse in the *mikveh* during the daytime of day seven, and the requirement to wait until nightfall is only Rabbinic,[7] a woman in this situation would be allowed to go to the *mikveh* in New York while it is still open, and then wait however long she has to wait to complete the hours of a standard *shivah nekiyim* before being with her husband.
3. Most opinions,[8] however, maintain that the conclusion of *shivah nekiyim* is entirely dependent upon the current time zone: a woman who flies from Los Angeles to New York could immerse and be with her husband immediately upon nightfall in New York. In general, *halakhah* accords primary significance to the time zone in which a person is presently situated. For example, a person from New York who visits Los Angeles does not need to be concerned to observe Shabbat according to New York time. The *Radbaz*[9] already noted that different places in the world have different times, and he ruled that one follows his or her present time zone.

6. See *Responsa Kinyan Torah*, II, 52, and *Responsa Divrei Shalom, Tinyana*, 79.
7. See chapter 33, p. 255.
8. See *Responsa Minchat Yitzchak*, VI, 84, and *Responsa Shevet HaLevi* II, 93, and VI, 129.
9. *Responsa*, I, 76.

In practice, the lenient approach is followed, in accordance with the third opinion.

IV. TRAVELING ACROSS THE INTERNATIONAL DATELINE:

The issue becomes more complicated, however, when a woman crosses the international dateline. In such a situation, she loses a sunset. The question emerges whether *shivah nekiyim* follows the number of *hours* since the *hefsek taharah,* or the number of complete *days* (i.e. sunrises and sunsets) that have passed since that time.

The issue is further complicated by the fact that there are three major opinions regarding the precise location of the halakhic dateline:

1. The *Chazon Ish*[10] maintains that the dateline is 90° east of Jerusalem, leaving Japan on the western side of the dateline. According to the *Chazon Ish,* Shabbat in Japan is on the day the world calls Sunday.
2. R. Yechiel Michel Tukachinsky[11] argues that the dateline is 180° east of Jerusalem, leaving Japan on Israel's side of the dateline, and Hawaii on the western side. According to this opinion, Shabbat in Hawaii is on the day the world calls Friday.
3. R. Tzvi Pesach Frank[12] denies the concept of an objective halakhic international dateline; rather, one simply follows whatever day of the week the natives say it is. According to R. Tzvi Pesach Frank, Shabbat is always on the day the world calls Saturday.

A woman crossing any of these datelines during *shivah nekiyim* should present an inquiry as to how to properly count *shivah nekiyim.*

10. *Kuntres 18 Sha'ot,* printed in *Sefer Chazon Ish* on *Orach Chaim-Moed,* #64.
11. *Kuntres HaYomam BiKadur Ha'aretz.*
12. *Responsa Har Tzvi* OC I, 138.

28.

Ketamim during *Shivah Nekiyim*

If a woman finds a *ketem* during her *shivah nekiyim,* she must begin counting anew. However, *ketamim* found during *shivah nekiyim* are subject to all the leniencies of *ketamim* found at other points in the menstrual cycle. This means that a *ketem* smaller than a *gris,* a *ketem* on objects that cannot become ritually impure, or a *ketem* on colored cloth do not undo the clean days of *shivah nekiyim.* These three leniencies are not functions of probability; rather, they were never included in the Rabbinic decree to treat *ketamim* as genuine sightings of blood.[1] Leniencies that are based on probability, however, might not apply during parts of the *shivah nekiyim.*

The *Mordechai,*[2] *Terumat HaDeshen,*[3] and the Rama[4] believe that

1. See Ch. 2.
2. *Niddah* 735, s.v. *ne'emenet.*
3. *Responsa,* #249.
4. *Yoreh De'ah* 196:10.

the first three days of *shivah nekiyim* differ from the remaining days. During the first three days, one must be concerned that the endometrial lining is still shedding. Generally, leniencies are applied to *ketamim* because there is good probability that the blood did not come from the endometrial lining; during the first three days of the *shivah nekiyim*, this probability is weak and cannot be relied upon. Hence, in practice, there is a reluctance to assume that *ketamim* larger than a *gris* came from a wound, or any source other than the endometrial lining.

Despite the concern that the endometrial lining is still shedding, even Ashkenazim accept certain probabilistic assumptions during the first three days of *shivah nekiyim*. The Rama rules that we are lenient on *ketamim* that come from a woman with a wound known to bleed, because such *ketamim* clearly do not come from the endometrial lining's blood. In contrast, the *Shakh*[5] argues that even a wound known to bleed is not good enough, and only if a woman has a chronic problem that causes her to constantly see *ketamim* is she permitted to assume that a *ketem* came from her wound. Accordingly, if a woman has a wound known to bleed that will heal in a few days, the Rama would be lenient, and the *Shakh* would be stringent.

Some *poskim* believe that the Rama's stringency does not apply to a woman who became a *niddah* due to a *ketem*, because the concern that the endometrial lining is shedding does not exist. Assuming this is true, some authorities suggest that one may be lenient in the following case: If a woman gets her regular period, and then her *shivah nekiyim* is broken up by a *ketem*, and then she sees another *ketem* during the first three days of her new *shivah nekiyim*, one can be lenient, as long as the new *ketem* did not appear within three days of the first *hefsek taharah*. They reason that regardless of the appearance of *ketamim*, it is not assumed that the endometrial lining is still shedding once three days following the original *hefsek taharah* have passed. Hence, the second *ketem* likely did not come from the endometrial lining.

Many *poskim* are lenient concerning this practice of not relying on probabilities that the blood emanated from a different source during the first three days of *shivah nekiyim*. This practice is not recorded

5. YD 196:13.

in the Talmud and is not accepted by Sefardic authorities. Even the Ashkenazic authorities who accept it view it as a stringency, not as an absolute *halakhah,* and thus are lenient when questions occur concerning its applicability.

29.

White Clothes during *Shivah Nekiyim*

The Talmud[1] refers to *shivah nekiyim* as "*yemei libun*," "days of whiteness." Some *poskim* interpret this to mean that women are supposed to wear white clothing during this time,[2] but others maintain that the description indicates simply that the days are meant to certify that the women are clean of blood, in other words, white meaning not red. It is the accepted ruling that it is not strictly necessary to wear white clothes during this time,[3] but it is a long standing traditional practice among both Sefardim and Ashkenazim to do so (at least in terms of undergarments).

Because wearing white clothing is only a traditional practice, and not an absolute law, there are exceptions. If a woman begins her *shivah nekiyim* and realizes that she has no white clothes, she may wear colored clothing. If a woman has serious problems with spotting during *shivah nekiyim*, she may also wear colored clothes. This is consistent with the

1. *Shabbat* 13b.
2. See Rashi, *Shabbat* 13b, s.v. *libunayikh*, and *Bi'ur HaGra*, YD 196:10.
3. See Rama, *Yoreh De'ah* 196:3.

policy that serious spotting problems are governed by post facto halakhic rules, not by the rules that apply to ideal situations. Hence, for example, women with serious bleeding problems may perform only two *bedikot* during the entire *shivah nekiyim*, as this is acceptable post facto.

Poskim dispute when to apply these leniencies of allowing fewer *bedikot* and wearing colored clothing. The *Badei HaShulchan*[4] writes that earlier *poskim* were only willing to reduce the number of *bedikot* when it is certain that the bleeding problem results from a wound, but if the woman is bleeding from the uterus it is not possible to be lenient for her. However, R. Moshe Feinstein[5] feels that one can be lenient even on blood from the uterus, since blood found without *hargashah* is only Rabbinically problematic. Many rabbis are lenient in accordance with this view.

In terms of when the practice of wearing white is implemented, some *poskim* say to start wearing the white clothing only after the woman removes the *mokh dachuk*, since there is no need to wear white clothes while the *mokh* is in because the *mokh* will catch any blood that comes out. It is rare for a woman to find blood on underwear but not on the *mokh*. Others argue that she must start wearing white clothes immediately after the *hefsek taharah*, before the *mokh*.

Traditionally, women sleep on white sheets during the *shivah nekiyim*. Some maintain, however, that it is enough for women to wear white underwear to bed, claiming there is no need for white sheets when blood can be detected by white underwear. Others maintain the traditional practice, even though it would seem to be unnecessary.

R. Moshe Feinstein[6] was asked if women must wear a white bathing suit when swimming. He rules leniently, because women obviously do not need to wear white while showering, so presumably they need not wear white while swimming.

4. YD 196:4, *biurim*, s.v. *ve-yesh omrim*, p. 302.
5. *Responsa Iggerot Moshe*, YD, II, 78.
6. *Responsa Iggerot Moshe*, YD, IV, 17:29.

Section VI: *Harchakot*

30.

Harchakot: Separation between the Husband and Wife during the Time of *Niddah*

I. ORIGIN OF THE PROHIBITION OF PHYSICAL CONTACT:

The Talmud[1] relates that a great scholar died at a young age. His wife came to the *beit midrash* and asked why he died so young. Ultimately, the conclusion given is that his death was a punishment for failure to observe *harchakot,* rules of separation, during *shivah nekiyim*. One of the *harchakot* mentioned is abstaining from touching in any way.

The Rambam[2] derives the prohibition of physical contact from the verse,[3] "*lo tikrivu li-galot ervah* – do not come close to revealing an

1. *Shabbat* 13a.
2. *Sefer HaMitzvot,* prohibition 353; *Hilkhot Issurei Bi'ah* 21:1. The Rambam bases his position on the Sifra, cited by the Rosh (*Niddah* 7:2); see also *Avot D'Rav Natan,* beginning of Chapter 2.
3. *Vayikra* 18:6.

ervah." Whereas the Torah could have written "do not reveal," it wrote "do not come close" to teach that anything leading to *ervah* is also Biblically prohibited.

The Ramban[4] argues that the cited verse, "do not come close," is only relevant as an *asmachta*, and that even touching is only Rabbinically prohibited. He furthermore argues that touching a *niddah* is perhaps comparable to *chatzi shiur* ("a fraction of the minimum measurement"; for example, having nonkosher food, in a quantity smaller than that which incurs liability), where intercourse is comparable to a full *shiur*. According to this, touching would be Biblically prohibited even according to the Ramban, but not to the degree the Rambam maintains. This argument is extremely innovative, since the term *chatzi shiur* usually refers to quantitative differences (i.e. half a *ke-zayit*, where a whole *zayit* is a full *shiur*), while the Ramban uses it here to refer to a qualitative difference.

In the end, the Ramban appears to reject this notion, and seems to conclude that touching is only Rabbinically prohibited.

The Scope of the Prohibition

The Rambam describes the prohibition of physical contact as applying to hugging, kissing, or "*kiruv basar*". The *Beit Yosef*[5] writes that the Rambam would include any touching in this Biblical prohibition, but the *Shakh*[6] argues that only touching in an affectionate way is Biblically prohibited, whereas other touching is Rabbinically prohibited.

If the *Shakh* is correct, one could argue that the prohibition against unaffectionate contact applies only to one's wife when she is a *niddah*, and not to other *arayot*, since these *harchakot* were only instituted for spouses. Based on this, the *Shakh* defends the practice for women to have male doctors. Since the doctor's contact is unaffectionate, it is permitted. Moreover, R. Moshe Feinstein[7] rules that one may travel by

4. *Hasagot* to *Sefer HaMitzvot*.
5. *Yoreh De'ah* 195:17, s.v. *vi-katav*.
6. YD 195:20.
7. *Responsa Iggerot Moshe*, EH II, 14.

subway even if he will be pushed against a woman, since his contact would be unaffectionate.

The *Noda BiYehudah*[8] was asked whether a husband may physically help his wife immerse in the *mikveh,* when no attendant is available. While the *Beit Yosef* would definitely prohibit this, the *Shakh* would likely permit it, since practically there is no concern that the couple will have intercourse in the brief moment before the woman becomes *tehorah,* and the contact itself is not affectionate. The *Noda BiYehudah* himself inclines towards permitting in this situation.

II. NOT PASSING THINGS TO ONE ANOTHER

One of the most well-known *harchakot* is for spouses to not hand things to each other, even without touching. Despite the prominence of this *harchakah,* there are no explicit Talmudic sources for this. The first explicit source is the *Machzor Vitri,*[9] who reports that Rashi was stringent to not hand things or receive things directly from his wife while she was a *niddah.*

There are two potential foundations for Rashi's stringency, both disputed by *Tosafot*:

1) In some versions of the Talmudic story about the scholar who died young,[10] one error the couple made was that the woman brought her husband a pitcher. This implies that spouses may not hand things to one another. The authors of the *Tosafot*[11] write that this may not prove the existence of the *harchakah* of passing objects; perhaps bringing the pitcher was specifically problematic because the couple might touch while transferring the object, whereas passing objects without touching is permitted.

2) The Talmud[12] writes that a woman in a state of *niddah* cannot pour a cup of wine for her husband. Some say that this includes pouring *and handing* him the cup. *Tosafot*[13] write that this is not a sufficient proof,

8. *Responsa, Tinyana,* YD 122; cited in *Pitchei Teshuvah* 195:2.
9. #499, p. 608 in Hurwitz edition; *Tosafot, Ketubot* 61a, s.v. *michlifa.*
10. See *Rosh, Ketubot* 5:24.
11. *Shabbat* 13b, s.v. *bi-yemei, Ketubot* 61a, s.v. *michlifa.*
12. *Ketubot* 61a.
13. To *Ketubot,* ibid.

because handing a cup of a wine is more affectionate than passing, for example, keys or salt. *Tosafot*[14] also claim that the prohibition is only pouring wine, and not handing it. Hence, according to *Tosafot*, there is no known source for Rashi's conduct in this matter.

The *Maggid Mishnah*[15] notes that the Rambam seems to not accept the prohibition of passing things, as he only records the prohibition of passing things regarding cups of wine, not regarding anything else.

In practice, the *Shulchan Arukh*[16] accepts Rashi's stringency. Therefore, even though there appears to be no compelling Talmudic source for this *harchakah*, it is nonetheless binding.

Explaining the *Harchakah* of Not Passing Things to One Another

There are two known rationales for the *harchakah* of not passing objects:

1) The Rashba[17] writes that this *harchakah* is a Rabbinic decree, lest the couple ultimately touch one another.

2) The Rashba[18] also writes that this *harchakah* is to keep the couple from becoming too intimate with one another (*hergel davar*), which itself is forbidden, lest it result in intercourse.

There may be some practical differences between these two rationales. For example, the Rama[19] prohibits couples from throwing things to one another, while others question whether this is correct. The resolution of this dispute likely depends on which rationale of the Rashba we adopt: if the first reason is correct, that passing things is prohibited because of the concern of touching, then throwing and catching is more likely permitted since the spouses are standing far away from each other and are not likely to touch. However, if the *harchakah* is based on *hergel davar*, throwing and catching is more likely to be prohibited since it may still lead to frivolity and ultimately intercourse.

Another question affected by the difference between the two rationales is that of passing things with a "*shinnui*", in an unnatural man-

14. To *Shabbat*, ibid.
15. *Hilkhot Ishut*, 21:8.
16. *Yoreh De'ah* 195:2.
17. *Torat HaBayit Katzar*, 7:2.
18. *Responsa*, 1, 1188; see *Beit Yosef*, *Even HaEzer* 21.
19. *Yoreh De'ah* 195:2.

ner. The Ritva[20] implies that handing things with a *shinnui* is permitted. He derives this from the Talmudic ruling that a woman may hand her husband a cup with her less-used hand. This makes little sense according to the first rationale, that passing may lead to touching, since passing with the less-used hand will actually be more likely to lead to touching. The license to do so only makes sense according to the second rationale, that passing will lead to *hergel davar* and ultimately transgression, because handing things with a *shinnui* will remind them of her *niddut* and prevent *hergel davar.*

In practice, as noted, the Rama rules that spouses should not throw things to one another during the time of *niddah,* and the Ritva's leniency regarding *shinnui* has not been accepted. The *halakhah* appears to take into account, stringently, both rationales of the Rashba.

Some common scenarios where the *harchakah* of passing things is relevant and must be clarified include the following:

1) Passing a Baby: The *Pitchei Teshuvah*[21] quotes the Tashbetz[22] who permits passing a baby due to the rule, grounded in the laws of carrying on *Shabbat,* that "*chai nosei et atzmo* – a living thing is considered to be carrying itself",[23] and therefore carrying a baby on Shabbat would only be prohibited Rabbinically. The *Arukh HaShulchan*[24] objects to this, because while this principle may mitigate the act of carrying as a labor prohibited on Shabbat, there remains a concern that the couple will touch while passing a baby, or that passing the baby may lead to *hergel davar.* As such, the principle that "a living thing is considered to be carrying itself" is used by the Talmud to Biblically permit carrying live things on Shabbat, but may not be true in *hilkhot niddah.* Moreover, some *Rishonim* maintain that "a living thing is considered to be carrying itself" only applies to things that can walk under their own power, but not to babies who cannot walk alone. Therefore, most *poskim* do not rely on this view of the Tashbetz. Rabbi Mordechai Willig, however, permits

20. *Ketubot* 61a, s.v. *Shmuel.*
21. YD 195:3.
22. III, 58:5 and 230.
23. *Shabbat* 94a and 141b; *Yoma* 9a.
24. YD 195:5.

passing a baby, because the *halakhah* is generally lenient on *harchakot* when a *choleh she-ein bo sakkanah* (a sick individual, even in a non-life-threatening situation) is involved.[25] Although this leniency usually is applied when one of the spouses is a *choleh*, Rabbi Willig feels that it applies here since all babies are considered *cholim*.[26]

2) Giving the Wedding Ring at a *Chuppat Niddah*: Some *poskim* rule that when the bride is a *niddah*, the groom should drop the ring into her hand rather than place it on her finger in a normal fashion. The *Badei HaShulchan*[27] and others say that he may place the ring on her finger, because *harchakot* only apply between spouses, and the groom and bride are not really married until he puts the ring on her finger. However, this leniency might not apply to handing her the *ketubah* after they have been married. Therefore, the groom should hand his bride her *ketubah* via a third party. This can usually be done with minimal awkwardness.

3) Carrying Heavy Objects: R. Ovadiah Yosef[28] writes that it is permissible for spouses to carry a heavy object together, since the prohibition against passing things is merely a stringency that is kept whenever possible, but is not absolute. Other *poskim* agree, based on the assumption that there is no romance in lifting heavy objects. Although some *poskim* argue, one has the right to rely on R. Ovadiah Yosef.

In general, one should use common sense in applying this *harchakah*, and one should try not to embarrass one's spouse when applying it.[29]

III. THE *HARCHAKAH* OF NOT EATING TOGETHER

There is a *harchakah* based on a *Mishnah*,[30] that a married couple should not eat together when the wife is a *niddah*, because that may lead to intercourse. As this *harchakah* does have a mishnaic source, it is applied more stringently.

25. See below pp. 214–215.
26. It should be noted that this applies only to the baby, and not to items needed for the care of the baby.
27. YD 195:18.
28. *Taharat HaBayit*, II, 12:3, p. 91.
29. See also *Shakh* YD 195:17 and *Responsa Iggerot Moshe*, YD II, 77.
30. *Shabbat* 11a; see *Gemara* on 13a.

There are three opinions as to the scope of this prohibition:

1. The Rambam[31] only records a problem to eat out of the same plate or bowl, like eating popcorn out of one bowl.
2. The Rosh[32] writes that the couple may not share a little tray or table that two people generally would not share. However, they may sit across from each other at a regular sized table.[33]
3. Other *Rishonim* argue that it is prohibited to sit at the same table, regardless of size.[34]

The *Shulchan Arukh*[35] rules against the Rambam, and does not quote the Rosh, consequently leaving in place the most stringent view, prohibiting even eating at the same regular sized table.

Exceptions to This Rule

Two people, one eating meat and one eating milk, may eat at one table if there is an indicating *siman* or *hekker* between them, such as if they eat on separate tablecloths or placemats. Presumably, this leniency can be applied to this *harchakah* as well.[36] Just as one will remember not to take food from the plate on the other tablecloth because it is dairy, one will remember not to take food from his wife's plate because she is a *niddah*. However, this leniency may not work if the couple always uses placemats, and they may require one of the other solutions listed below.

A couple may eat together if they place something out of the ordinary on the table as a *hekker*. The *Pitchei Teshuvah*[37] writes that couples may eat together if other people, presumably those who qualify as

31. *Hilkhot Issurei Bi'ah* 11:18.
32. *Shabbat* 1:32.
33. The Rosh suggests this approach as explanation of the reality he observed of couples eating at the same table. *Mishmeret HaBayit* 7:2, p. 32, makes the same observation, and the Ritva (*Shabbat* 13a, s.v. *Vi-ha di-t'nan*) makes the same suggestion as the Rosh.
34. See Ra'avad, *Ba'alei HaNefesh*, beginning of *Sha'ar HaPerishah*.
35. *Yoreh De'ah* 195:3.
36. See *Yoreh De'ah* 195:3.
37. YD 195:5.

shomrim in the laws of *yichud* (i.e. people whose presence inhibits intimacy), are present and eating with them.[38] This leniency only applies to the prohibition against eating at the same table, not to that of sharing a plate.

IV. NOT EATING ONE'S WIFE'S LEFTOVERS

In the Talmudic story about the scholar who died young, the wife described one *harchakah* that he violated as, "he ate with me and drank with me." This phrasing conveys the impression that they ate together at the same table, reflecting the previously discussed *harchakah*. However, the *Hagahot Maimoniyot*[39] quote R. Eliezer of Metz, who writes that in actuality, the husband drank his wife's leftovers. Hence, he rules that husbands may not drink their wife's leftovers when she is a *niddah*. Interestingly, he seems to permit wives to drink their husband's leftovers. Even more interesting is the fact that the *Shulchan Arukh*[40] rules that he may not *drink* her leftovers, but does not explicitly rule that he may not *eat* her leftovers. If this prohibition is derived from the Talmudic story, it should include eating and drinking,[41] which is indeed a position cited by the Rama.[42]

In practice, although many *Rishonim* did not agree with R. Eliezer's reading of the Talmud,[43] the rule is accepted, as reflected by the fact that the *Shulchan Arukh* quotes it.

Scope of the *Harchakah*

There are a number of exceptions to this *harchakah*. The Rama[44] writes that if a wife is drinking from one vessel and pours her leftovers into another vessel, her husband may drink from the second vessel. Further, husbands may drink their wife's leftovers if she is no longer in the room.

38. See also *Bedek HaBayit* 7:2, p. 31.
39. *Hilkhot Issurei Bi'ah* 11:30.
40. *Yoreh De'ah* 195:4.
41. This issue is raised by the *Shakh*, YD 195:8.
42. *Yoreh De'ah* 195:3.
43. The *Sidrei Taharah* (YD 195:8) offers two suggestions.
44. *Yoreh De'ah* 195:4.

If another person ate some of the food after the wife, then her husband may eat these leftovers, as that will presumably not lead to *hergel davar.*

Had the Talmud used the phrase "we drank together," or "I drank with him," it would have implied that her eating his leftovers is also forbidden. The language of the Talmud, "he drank with me," implies that only his eating her leftovers is forbidden. Hence, a woman may drink her husband's leftovers. Therefore, for example, if a couple wants to share a can of soda, the husband should drink first and the wife second. It is not clear why this *harchakah* should only apply to men.[45]

If the husband does not realize that he is about to drink from his wife's leftovers, he may drink them, and his wife does not have to stop him; if he is unaware, then his drinking is not *derekh chibbah.* Some later *poskim*[46] discuss whether it is a problem to take from the same salt shaker or serving dish; however, it would appear that these activities should be permitted.

Due to this *harchakah,* the custom at *Sheva Berakhot* is to pour separate cups for the husband and wife. We assume that the woman became a *niddah* soon after the wedding, and giving them separate cups will avoid potential problems.

V. *HARCHAKOT* RELATING TO BEDS:

The Talmudic story mentioned above implies that couples may not sleep in the same bed, apparently even if they are fully clothed, while the wife is a *niddah.* This prohibition applies even in a large, king size bed; indeed, the Mordechai[47] writes that it applies even with two separate beds that are touching. The reason for this is either *hergel davar,* since sleeping on touching beds may lead to intercourse, or *mar'it ayin,* out of the concern that two touching beds appear like one bed. Contemporary *poskim* consider the rules regulating unconventional arrangements such as trundle beds and bunk beds.[48]

In view of this law, many *poskim* feel there is a problem to share a

45. See *Arukh HaShulchan,* YD 195:11.
46. See *Shiurei Shevet HaLevi,* 195:8.
47. *Shabbat* 238.
48. See *Badei HaShulchan,* 195:105, 195:6, *Bi'urim,* s.v. *afilu.*

headboard. They also say that there should be some space between the beds, so the sheets and covers do not touch, or so that one cannot roll from one bed directly onto the other. If one cannot roll from one bed onto the other without falling on the floor, there is no need to place a nightstand in between the beds.

The Ra'avad[49] writes that a husband may not sleep on a bed that is "reserved" for his wife, even if she is not there. The Rashba[50] derives this from the Talmudic ruling[51] that neither a husband nor wife can make their spouse's bed while the spouse is standing there. Apparently, spouses should try to stay away from each other's bed during the time of *niddah*. If so, it would seem to be all the more so the case that spouses should not sleep in each other's bed.

While a sleeper sofa that anybody can use, for example, is not considered "reserved for her", the exact definition of what bed is or is not "reserved" for her is unclear. It is also unclear whether the designation can be switched from spouse to spouse. *Poskim* discuss whether or not one may sit on his or her spouse's bed. It is possible that greater grounds exist for leniency for her to sit on his bed.

VI. THE MOVING BENCH:

The Mordechai[52] writes that a couple should not sit on a bench together, and the *Terumat HaDeshen*[53] modifies this by noting that a bench that is connected to the ground is permissible; hence, the problem is with a "*safsal ha-mitnadned*", or a "moving bench". The Rama[54] quotes this stringency, but the Beit Yosef writes that it is unheard of amongst the Sefardim, and in the *Shulchan Arukh* he does not quote it. The *Taz*[55] understands this stringency as falling under the category of sitting on her bed, but the *Shakh*[56] argues that this relates to the prohibition of

49. *Ba'alei HaNefesh*, end of *Sha'ar HaPerishah*, p. 29 s.v. *vi-raiti*.
50. *Torat HaBayit* 7:2 s.v. *katav*.
51. *Ketubot* 61a.
52. *Shabbat*, 238.
53. *Responsa*, 251.
54. *Yoreh De'ah* 195:5.
55. YD 195:6.
56. *Nekuddat HaKesef*, YD 195:1.

physical contact, because his movement will make her move and vice-versa. Ashkenazim are stringent on this matter, following the view of the Rama. The *poskim* say that it is only forbidden to sit together on a moving bench when one can feel the weight of the other person when he or she moves around. Hence, R. Moshe Feinstein[57] allowed sitting together in the back seat of a car, even though it is technically a bench and it does move.

VII. GOING ON TRIPS TOGETHER:

After recording the concept of *safsal ha-mitnadned*, the Rama writes that a couple should not travel in the same horse and buggy together. This prohibition applies if they are going for a leisure ride, but not if they are traveling for business. There are two ways to understand the Rama's reasoning:

1. Some *Acharonim* feel that riding in a buggy for pleasure is forbidden, since buggies are like a moving bench. If so, the Rama's statement is actually a leniency, removing business trips from the category of *safsal ha-mitnadned*.
2. Others believe that moving benches are forbidden even on business trips. They explain that riding in a buggy is forbidden because it is romantic, and thus involves *hergel davar*. Business trips, in contrast with the buggy ride, are permitted because they are not romantic. This latter opinion contains two stringencies: first, moving benches are prohibited even on business trips; second, one cannot go on a vacation or leisure trip with one's wife while she is a *niddah*.

Although it is unclear what the Rama really meant, *poskim* say it is best to avoid such vacations or trips with one's wife while she is a *niddah*. Even if the Rama did not prohibit this, avoidance of such trips will minimize frivolity and *hergel davar*. Therefore, it is assumed that going on a romantic trip or vacation with one's wife while she is a *niddah* is forbidden.

Defining precisely what constitutes an inappropriate trip is

57. *Responsa Iggerot Moshe*, YD II, 77.

difficult. Trips and activities one would only do with one's wife and not with friends would fall into such a category.

The *Shulchan Arukh*[58] rules that frivolous or romantic[59] speech is forbidden when one's wife is a *niddah*. The definition of such speech often depends on the situation. One must be careful to avoid activity or even words that are associated with physical contact.

VIII. NOT TO LOOK AT PARTS NORMALLY COVERED:

The Talmud[60] is inconclusive concerning what areas of the wife's person the husband may look at while she is a *niddah*. The Rambam[61] writes that the only problematic part is the *makom ervah*, but the Ra'avad believes that one cannot look at "her covered places." The *Shulchan Arukh* in *Hilkhot Niddah*[62] follows the Ra'avad, but in *Even HaEzer*[63] he follows the Rambam.[64] The practice is to be stringent, since this law has a direct source in the Talmud.

R. Moshe Feinstein[65] defines "her covered places" as the parts of a woman that she usually covers in her house even when no men other than her husband are present. This would not necessarily include her hair, if she usually does not cover her hair in the house. If she wears short sleeves in the house, she can continue to wear short sleeves while she is a *niddah*. However, if she does not normally wear short sleeves in the house, then she could not do so while she is a *niddah*. In brief, she can continue to wear in her house whatever she normally wears in her house.

This issue is relevant to men who want to be with their wives during childbirth. A husband cannot hold his wife's hand during childbirth, because at a certain point she becomes a *niddah*. In view of what we have just learned, he must also be careful to not look at certain parts

58. As explained by Rama, 195:1.
59. See *Shakh*, YD 195:2.
60. *Nedarim* 20a.
61. *Hilkhot Issurei Bi'ah* 21:4, as understood by the *Maggid Mishnah*.
62. *Yoreh De'ah* 195:7.
63. *Even HaEzer* 21:4.
64. Consistent with that view, he cites the *Maggid Mishnah*'s comments in *Beit Yosef* (EH 21:4, s.v. *vi-khein mutar*).
65. *Responsa Iggerot Moshe*, YD II, 75.

of her body while in the delivery room. R. Moshe Feinstein[66] permits husbands to be present in the delivery room, provided they are careful to look away. Other *poskim*, however, say that husbands should not be present at all because their wives will be uncovered.

Just as the *Noda BiYehudah* suggested permitting physically helping one's wife down to the *mikveh*, he permits the husband, when necessary for that purpose, to look at his wife and ensure she goes completely under the water. These rulings are based on the assumption that since she will be permissible immediately after *tevilah*, there is no concern that they will violate the *halakhah* now. The *Noda BiYehudah* supports his rulings with a practice of the Sar MiKutzi, one of the Tosafists. The Sar MiKutzi felt that scabs may be *chatzitzot* and invalidate an immersion,[67] and he therefore would check his wife to make sure she had picked off her scabs. Clearly, in certain situations one can look at his wife right before she goes to the *mikveh*. The *Noda BiYehudah* acknowledges that this may not be a perfect proof, since the Sar MiKutzi may have assumed, like the Rambam's view, that one may look at his wife in every place except the *makom ervah*. Moreover, the *Noda BiYehudah*'s son suggests that perhaps the Sar MiKutzi checked his wife after she came out of the *mikveh* and was no longer a *niddah*, and not before she went. Either way, one can rely on the *Noda BiYehudah*'s leniency in a *she'at ha-dechak*, when there is nobody else available to supervise his wife's *tevilah*.

IX. LISTENING TO ONE'S WIFE SING:

The Talmud[68] derives a connection linking that which one is prohibited from doing with a married woman to that which one is prohibited to do with his own wife when she is a *niddah*. As such, some *poskim* rule that just as one may not listen to a married woman singing, a husband may not listen to his wife sing while she is a *niddah*.[69] It is clear, however, that this derivation has limitations, because even though one may not gaze at a married woman, one may certainly gaze at his own wife.

66. *Responsa Iggerot Moshe* ibid.
67. See Ch. 35, Sec. VI.
68. *Shabbat* 13a.
69. See *Pitchei Teshuvah*, YD 195:10.

R. Ovadiah Yosef[70] therefore allows husbands to listen to their wife's singing. A further support for this leniency could emerge from R. Moshe Feinstein's position about "her covered places." Just as he may look at any normally uncovered part of her, he may listen to her singing if she normally sings. Although R. Moshe Feinstein himself rejects this parallel,[71] and forbids husbands to listen to their wives singing when she is a *niddah*, other *poskim* are lenient.

X. DILUTING WINE, MAKING BEDS, AND WASHING FACE, HANDS, AND FEET

The Talmud[72] rules that a *niddah* cannot dilute wine or make the bed for her husband, nor may she wash his face, hands, or feet. The Rashba[73] writes that the prohibition of diluting only applies to wine, and the *Hagahot Maimoniyot*[74] maintains that it only applies if she mixes the wine in his presence and then brings it to him. If either of these positions were accepted, this *harchakah* would rarely be an issue in contemporary settings. However, the *Shakh*[75] quotes an opinion that it is prohibited for a *niddah* to place any kind of food or drink before her husband, when it is meant specifically for him personally. The *Shakh* finds support for his position from the *Tanna D'Bei Eliyahu Rabbah* (ch. 15), where it states that Elijah chastised a wife for bringing a pitcher to her husband when she was a *niddah*. Although there are others ways to explain why bringing a pitcher is problematic, the *Shakh* believes the wife was setting food before her husband. In practice, the *Shakh*'s view is followed.[76]

The Talmud allows a woman to bring the cup with a *shinnui*, or to place it a short distance away from the husband; also, she may bring serving plates to the table.

The *Shulchan Arukh*[77] writes that a man should not pass a cup of

70. *Taharat HaBayit* 12:29.
71. *Responsa Iggerot Moshe*, YD II, 75.
72. *Ketubot* 61a.
73. *Torat HaBayit Katzar* 7:2, 4a.
74. *Hilkhot Issurei Bi'ah* 11:50.
75. YD 195:13.
76. However, see *Sidrei Taharah*, 195:18 and *Taharat HaBayit* 12:33, II, p. 187.
77. *Yoreh De'ah* 195:13.

wine to his wife while she is a *niddah,* even via a third party, and even if it is a cup upon which special *berakhot* (i.e. *Birkat haMazon*) were recited. This prohibition is most relevant regarding *Kiddush* on Shabbat. Several points are important in balancing this *harchakah* with fulfilling the obligation of *Kiddush* on Shabbat: First, women need not drink from the cup in order to fulfill their Kiddush obligation, although it is preferable to partake of the *Kiddush* wine. Second, the husband can put the cup down and she can pick it up later and drink a bit. Some *poskim* maintain that if there are many guests at the table, or if one has many children, it is permitted to pour many cups and pass them around until one's wife receives a cup. Other *poskim* question this leniency.

In terms of the prohibition of "making beds", the *Shulchan Arukh*[78] writes that she may not make the bed in a comfortable manner. Merely moving mattresses is permissible. Further, it is only a problem if the husband is watching at the time.

In terms of the prohibition of "washing face, hands, and feet", the Rashba[79] writes that this prohibition cannot be literal, i.e. washing one another, because a couple is not even allowed to touch one another. Women used to pour water over their husbands without touching, while the husband washed himself; this would be prohibited while she is a *niddah.* Based on this Rashba, the *Taz*[80] writes that preparing the water for him to wash is permitted. The *Shakh,*[81] citing Rabbenu Yonah, writes that the additional prohibition of washing must refer to preparing the bath. In practice, the *Shakh*'s view is followed. Some *poskim* forbid filling up a washing cup for one another, but others are lenient about this, because that is something one would do for his friend as well, and involves no intimacy.

78. *Yoreh De'ah* 195:11.
79. *Torat HaBayit Arukh* 7:2, 4a.
80. YD 195:8.
81. YD 195:16.

XI. *HARCHAKOT* DURING THE *NIDDAH* PERIOD VS. *SHIVAH NEKIYIM*

Rashi[82] indicates that there may be differences between *harchakot* during the *niddah* days and during the *shivah nekiyim*. Rabbenu Tam[83] records that, in previous centuries, women used to go to the *mikveh* twice, once after the Biblical *niddah* days and once after the *shivah nekiyim*. There are a number of possibilities raised as to why such an immersion would be done, as the women would nonetheless be prohibited to their husbands until after the second immersion. Perhaps they felt that immersion *be-z'man*, on time, is a *mitzvah*. Alternatively, perhaps they immersed to remove the Biblical *niddah* status, to permit them to touch *taharot* even though they remain prohibited to their husbands. Women who abided by this practice of a double immersion were Biblically forbidden to their husbands during the *niddah* days, and only Rabbinically forbidden to their husbands during the *shivah nekiyim*. For them, it made sense to be more stringent during the *niddah* days, and lenient on *harchakot* during *shivah nekiyim*. In the modern era, women do not immerse until the conclusion of *shivah nekiyim*, because it is assumed that there is no *mitzvah* to immerse "on time", and because there are no *taharot*. Accordingly, there is no reason to distinguish between the *niddah* days and *shivah nekiyim*, since the woman is Biblically forbidden to her husband during both.

The Rama[84] quotes a practice to eat with one's wife from the same plate during *shivah nekiyim*, but adds that one should not follow this practice. Once, husband and wife would eat together on the last day of *shivah nekiyim* before the woman immersed, presumably to do something in anticipation of their imminent permission to be together.[85] The basis for this liberty is unclear: perhaps those who adhered to this practice followed the Rambam, who only forbids eating from the same plate; or the Rosh, who permits sharing a big table; or perhaps they subscribe to the *Noda BiYehudah*'s suggestion, that the immediate moments

82. *Ketubot* 61a, s.v. *michlifa leih*.
83. Cited in *Tosafot, Shabbat* 13b, s.v. *bi-yemei*.
84. *Yoreh De'ah* 195:14.
85. See *Darkhei Moshe* YD 195:8 and *Shakh* YD 195:17.

before immersion are more lenient than earlier parts of *shivah nekiyim*. Whatever the rationale once was, today this practice is frowned upon.

XII. *HARCHAKOT* DURING ILLNESS

With regard to *harchakot* when one spouse is ill, the *Shulchan Arukh* draws a distinction between cases where the husband is sick and where the wife is sick. If the wife is sick, then the tendency is to be stringent out of concern that the husband will pressure her to be with him. If the husband is sick, there is less of a concern.

As cited by the *Beit Yosef*,[86] the Ramban is lenient on all *harchakot* if the woman is mortally ill; her husband may touch her, carry her, etc.[87] The *Beit Yosef*, however, notes that the Ramban thinks the *harchakah* of hugging and kissing is only Rabbinic. According to the Rambam, who believes that hugging and kissing are Biblically forbidden, stringency may be required even when a woman is mortally ill. If even unromantic *negi'ah* is Biblically forbidden, it might be forbidden under all circumstances. In practice, although some *harchakot* are Biblical, this view of the *Beit Yosef* is rejected. The *Shakh* argues that touching in a non-affectionate way is only prohibited Rabbinically and would therefore be permissible in situations of illness, when there is no other option available.

86. *Yoreh De'ah* 195:17, s.v. *vi-katav od.*
87. *Responsa HaMeyuchasot Li-haRamban*, 127.

Section VII: *Vestot*

31.

Vestot

I. THE *VESET:* BIBLICAL LAW OR RABBINIC LAW?

The topic of *vestot* is a challenging and complicated one, encompassing much detail and analysis. The discussion here will focus on the most relevant aspects.

The "*veset*", as identified by the Talmud, is the point at which a woman expects to have her period, as indicated by various criteria that will be explained below. On the day of the *veset*, a *bedikah* must be performed. The Talmud[1] considers the consequences of a failure to do so. In the Talmud's analysis, the determinant issue is the origin of the *veset* rule, which may be either Biblical or Rabbinic in nature. If the concern is Biblical, it follows that the role of the *bedikah* is to negate that concern; consequently, when one is not done, a status of "*niddah*" must be assumed. However, if there is no Biblical presumption of *niddut*, omitting the *bedikah* may be less consequential, and one performed later can clarify her status.

The possibility of Biblical origin requires explanation, as there are no obvious Torah passages addressing *vestot*. Rashi[2] explains the

1. *Niddah* 16a.
2. *Niddah* 15a, s.v. *D'Orayta*.

potential source as being *halakhah leMoshe miSinai*, and additional possibilities are suggested by other *Rishonim*. In any event, the Talmud's conclusion is apparently that the *veset* rule is Rabbinical in nature, and consequently omitting the *bedikah* does not create a presumption of *niddah* status, once the *veset* passes. This is the ruling recorded in *Shulchan Arukh*.[3]

II. "*PERISHAH*" – MARITAL SEPARATION AT THE TIME OF THE *VESET*

The *veset* rule contains another component, however. The husband and wife are obligated to separate from each other at the time of the *veset*, out of concern that the period is either imminent or in process.[4]

This aspect is connected by the Talmud to a Biblical verse,[5] which states "*Vi-hizartem et Bnai Yisrael mi-tumatam* – and you shall separate Bnai Yisrael from their impurity". The *Rishonim* address the unusual implications of this statement: apparently, the *veset* is a Rabbinically ordained concept, and yet has ramifications in Biblical law. Several approaches are offered to explain this apparent paradox:

1. One possibility is to conclude that the rule of separation is actually not of Biblical origin, and that the verse cited in connection with the concept is actually an *asmakhta*. This is the view of the *Ra'avad*[6] (cited by the *Rosh*[7]).
2. Several later authorities, however, maintained the position that separation is a Biblical mandate, and offered various theories to explain how that could be the case if the *veset* itself is of Rabbinic origin. These theories include the following:
   a. The *Noda BiYehudah*[8] maintains that the existence of the

3. YD 184:9.
4. *Niddah* 63b, as well as *Yevamot* 62b and *Pesachim* 72b.
5. *Vayikra* 15:31.
6. *Ba'alei Ha-Nefesh, Sha'ar Tikun Vestot.*
7. *Niddah*, 9:2.
8. *Responsa, Mahadura Kama, Yoreh De'ah* 55, and *Tinyana*, 103; see *Pitchei Teshuvah*, YD 184:3.

veset creates a presumption, a *chazakah,* that the woman will become a *niddah.* As is often the case, this *chazakah* is authoritative on a Biblical level, thus effectively granting the *veset* the status of Biblical law. Nonetheless, the obligation to perform a *bedikah* is of Rabbinic origin, and accordingly, failure to do so is of lesser consequence.

This is because the *chazakah* of the impending period – essentially a statistical reality – is countered by another *chazakah,* a "*chazakah m'ikara*" – the presumption of the *status quo ante.* In this case, the woman is presently not a *niddah,* and that fact is recognized as a *chazakah* of equal weight.

In the *Noda BiYehudah*'s understanding, this second *chazakah,* that the woman maintains her permitted status, interacts differently with the two rules of *veset,* the *bedikah* requirement and the obligation of separation. The *bedikah* requirement reflects a concern that the period has already begun; the *chazakah* of permitted status is sufficiently authoritative to overwhelm that concern, rendering the *bedikah* necessary only on a Rabbinic level.

Vis-à-vis the separation requirement, however, the concern is not only that the period has begun, but also that it may begin imminently. To negate this concern the *chazakah* of permitted status would have to assert not only a statement about the present, but about the near future as well. Apparently, the permission *chazakah* is less effective in asserting the second part of that statement,[9] and the *veset chazakah* – the pattern that the onset of the period is immediately forthcoming – is dominant. Accordingly, the requirement of separation reflects Biblical law, as dictated by the rules of *chazakah.*

9. The *Noda BiYehudah*'s source for this position is a passage in the Talmud (*Gittin* 28a–b), where a distinction is made concerning the assumption that a missing husband is alive, on the basis of the *status quo ante* that he was alive when last seen. The Talmud states that this presumption is effective to establish that he is alive at this point, but not that he will continue to be in the future.

b. The *Chavot Da'at* agrees with the above premises that the *veset* represents a *chazakah* effective on a Biblical level, and mandates separation, and yet that a woman who fails to perform a *bedikah* at that point maintains her permitted status. His explanation diverges, however, in that he focuses on the lack of *hargashah*. This missing element effectively counters the presumption of the *veset* that *niddut* has begun. However, as with the above approach, this addresses only the present, and not the future, as a *hargashah* may be forthcoming; thus, again explaining a distinction between a Biblical requirement of separation and a Rabbinic obligation of *bedikah*.

c. The *Chazon Ish*[10] maintains that the Talmudic debate about the authority of the *veset* reflects the quality of the *chazakah*. The view that a *veset* is Biblically binding presumes that the pattern is a reliable one. The dominant view, however, assigns Rabbinic status to the *veset* because of the numerous variables that exist to affect the onset of the period: sleep patterns, change in diet, travel, weather, etc. These factors collectively impact the pattern to such a degree that it is no longer reliable and predictable, and thus cannot establish reality on a Biblical level. However, there continues to exist a significant risk that the period may begin imminently; this risk is sufficient to forbid marital intimacy on a Biblical level.

Thus far, it appears that the view that separation is a Biblical obligation is mainly held by later authorities (the *Noda Bi-Yehudah, Chavot Da'at,* and *Chazon Ish*); *Rishonim* apparently are represented by the Ra'avad, maintaining *vestot* are Rabbinical, who is cited by the *Shakh*[11] as practical *halakhah*.

However, there are *Rishonim* who did feel that separation was obligated on a *D'Orayta* level, although, these *Rishonim* – the Ra'ah[12]

10. *Yoreh De'ah* 80:7–8.
11. YD 184:5.
12. *Bedek HaBayit* 7:2, 4a.

and the Ritva[13] – are focused on a more specific timeframe, the actual part of the day when the pattern has shown the onset of the period to be immediately forthcoming.

III. WHEN THE *VESET* IS AT THE TIME OF THE HUSBAND LEAVING ON A TRIP

Assuming separation at the time of the *veset* to be a *D'Orayta* obligation prompts the reevaluation of a Talmudic ruling: the obligation of a man to engage in marital relations (literally, to "visit his wife") before embarking on an extended trip.[14] As R. Moshe Feinstein explains,[15] this rule is a function of the spousal responsibility a man has toward his wife, which entails his being available to her at the times and with the frequency that can be presumed to be within her expectations.[16]

The Talmud continues to state that this obligation maintains even at the time approaching (*s'mukhah*) the *veset*. If the assumption is that separation at that time is obligatory by dint of Rabbinic law, this can be understood; the Rabbis have the right to adjust their own enactments and declare exceptions. However, if the rule is *MiD'Orayta*, this becomes more difficult; how would such a rule be suspended because the husband is going on a trip? [17]

A number of possible approaches can be found to this question:

1. The *Ritva*[18] offers a unique understanding of the Talmud's statement, noting that there is a verse[19] cited, "And you shall know that your tent is in peace; and you shall visit your habitation, and shall miss nothing". The passage, advocating proper treatment

13. *Sh'vuot* 18a, s.v. *li-olam*.
14. *Yevamot* 62b.
15. *Responsa Iggerot Moshe*, EH III, 28.
16. See Rashi, *Bereishit* 32:15.
17. Similarly, some *Acharonim* debated the question of whether relations at the time approaching the *veset* can be permitted at other times when the relations are considered a *mitzvah*, such as the wedding night and the night of *tevilah*. From a practical standpoint, it does not appear that leniencies in this area are allowed.
18. *Sh'vuot* 18b, s.v. *tanu Rabbanan*.
19. *Iyov* 5:24.

of one's wife, can perhaps be read as a promise: if one treats his wife with consideration, and attends to her before his voyage, God will assure that she will not be a *niddah* at that time, thus eliminating any need for separation. This understanding is not shared by other commentaries.

2. One could suggest a simpler approach according to the *Rishonim* cited above, who maintain that separation is *MiD'Orayta* only during certain parts of the day. If so, the ruling concerning travel can be interpreted as referring to instances when this is not the case.
3. The above assumes that the Talmud is mandating actual marital relations at this time. However, there is a variant text – that of Rabbenu Tam – which leads to the conclusion that this is not the case; rather, the Talmud is only requiring the husband to spend quality time with wife, but not actual relations.[20] If this is the case, the statement poses no challenge to the assumption that separation is required *MiD'Orayta*.

This ambiguity makes it difficult to use this passage to derive any conclusions about the status of the separation requirement, and continues into recorded *halakhah:* The *Shulchan Arukh*[21] cites the ruling as mandating actual relations, apparently assuming that the *veset* separation is Rabbinic in nature;[22] the *Rama,* however, equivocates, and praises stringency, that would limit the contact to other forms of affection.

IV. AFFECTIONATE PHYSICAL CONTACT AT THE TIME OF THE *VESET*

The above discussion raises the issue of the permissibility of affectionate physical contact, short of actual relations, during the time of the *veset*. The Ramban[23] asserts that the prohibition of relations at this time does not extend to the *harchakot* that are in effect during the time of *niddah*.

20. *Tosafot, Yevamot* 62b, s.v. *chayav adam,* and *Sefer HaYashar, Chiddushim,* 45.
21. *Yoreh De'ah* 184:10.
22. This explanation is stated by the *Taz* (#14). The *Shulchan Arukh*'s interpretation of the Talmudic statement is also consistent with his words in *Orach Chaim* 240:1, where he also equates "visiting" with marital relations.
23. *Hilkhot Niddah* 8:10.

Presumably, this reference is to all of the *harchakot*; nonetheless, there is analysis in the *Rishonim* and later *poskim* concerning the permissibility of affectionate physical contact, known as "*chibbuk vi-nishuk*" (literally, hugging and kissing).

From an analytical perspective, it is important to note that this question involves the intersection of two rules that have debatable status as far as whether they are *MiD'Orayta*: The rule of separation, and the general prohibition of *chibbuk ve-nishuk* with a woman who is a *niddah*. If either rule is *MiD'Rabanan*, it is feasible that the Ramban's intent would be to allow even *chibbuk ve-nishuk* during the time of the *veset*. On the matter of *chibbuk ve-nishuk* with a *niddah*, the Ramban is indeed on record as believing that the prohibition is Rabbinic in origin.[24]

However, the ruling of the *Chatam Sofer*[25] differs from this analysis, in that he believes both rules are *MiD'Orayta*, and nonetheless rules leniently on the above question. He provides two reasons why actual relations are to be forbidden, but not any activity short of that: a) perhaps the concern is actually that the period will be provoked by the act itself; b) the concern is not actually the act of relations in general will be the cause, but that it will be simultaneous with the period; if this fact is discovered in the middle of the act, it will be very difficult to avoid a transgression, as even withdrawal in a state of arousal constitutes a violation. This issue, however, would not affect other forms of affectionate contact.

For practical purposes, the *halakhah* is generally in accord with the lenient view that allows *chibbuk ve-nishuk*. However, there are some *poskim* who maintain that a "*ba'al nefesh*" should act stringently in this area, although even these are lenient on the other *harchakot*. Further, the *Badei HaShulchan* maintains that *chibbuk ve-nishuk* would be permitted during those *vestot* that are less universally observed; these will be identified below.

24. *Hasagot* to *Sefer HaMitzvot*, prohibition 353.
25. *Responsa, Yoreh De'ah* 170.

V. A *VESET KAVU'A* VS. A *VESET SHE-EINO KAVU'A*

Once rules that pertain to the *veset* have been established, it then remains necessary to determine what day or days are considered the *veset,* and to what extent the above rules will apply.

The Talmud[26] distinguishes between a situation where a set pattern has been established as to the onset of the period, a "*veset kavu'a*", and one where there has not been a pattern, a "*veset she-eino kavu'a*" which is simply the time when the previous period occurred. There is a dispute among the *Tannaim* as to what constitutes a pattern, and the established *halakhah* is that a pattern is set when the woman has her period at that time on three consecutive occasions.

The Talmud enumerates several practical differences between the two categories of *veset*:

1. The *bedikah*: The obligation to perform a *bedikah* applies in both instances, according to most opinions. However, the obligation is viewed more leniently in the case of a "*veset she-eino kavu'a*", with some contemporary *poskim* not requiring one at all, and failure to do the *bedikah* does not affect the permitted status of the woman. In the case of the "*veset kavu'a*", however, the woman is not permitted to her husband until there has been a clean *bedikah*.[27]
2. Changing the *veset*: Another difference between them is how easily the *veset* is undone. The accepted *halakhah* is that a "*veset she-eino kavu'a*" is undone (and reestablished on the new day) by just one instance of deviation, while a "*veset kavu'a*" is undone only through three consecutive deviations from the *veset.*

VI. FIVE TYPES OF *VESTOT:*

The term *veset* actually refers to a number of different indicia for the onset of the period that are recognized by *halakhah.*[28] Included in this list are:

1. *Veset Haflagah*: This is the term some *Rishonim* use for what is also

26. *Niddah* 63b–64a.
27. See *Shulchan Arukh, Yoreh De'ah* 189:4.
28. See *Beit Yosef,* YD 189, s.v. *vi-da.*

called *veset ha-yamim*, an interval *veset*. This *veset* is determined simply by calculating the number of days between a woman's last original sighting of blood and her current one. The expectation is that she will again see blood that same number of days after her current sighting. If this same interval occurred for three months in a row, a "*veset kavu'a*" would be created, while if her most recent interval was different than the previous one, then the most recent interval would be a "*veset she-eino kavu'a*".

2. *Veset LeYom HaChodesh*. This term is used by the Talmud apparently to denote a *veset* reflecting the day of the month when the last period began. For example, if a woman's period falls out on a certain day of the month (e.g. the 15th of Av), the same date in the next month (the 15th of Elul) would be considered the *veset le-yom ha-chodesh*; this may fall out on the same day as the *veset haflagah*.

   The existence of this *veset* is subject to a disagreement among the *Rishonim*. The authors of the *Tosafot*[29] assert that that this type of *veset* exists, while the Ramban[30] argues that the Talmudic texts referenced by *Tosafot* are referring to something else, and there is no *veset* of this type. Nonetheless, the Ramban recommends taking this *veset* into consideration notwithstanding, and the *Shulchan Arukh*[31] rules without reservation that there is a *veset le-yom ha-chodesh*.

   There is a dispute between Ra'ah and the Rashba[32] as to which calendar this *veset* follows:

   The Ra'ah maintains that it follows the lunar calendar (the *molad* and the *chalakim*, etc).

   The Rashba argues that it follows the halakhic calendar, even though the halakhic calendar can fall out of synch with the lunar calendar. He adduces a proof from a statement in the Talmud Yerushalmi that indicates that the temporal events of this world

29. *Niddah* 64a, s.v. *itmar*.
30. *Chiddushim, Niddah* 64a.
31. *Yoreh De'ah* 189:6.
32. *Bedek HaBayit* and *Mishmeret HaBayit* 7:3, p. 9a.

fall in line with the ruling of *Beit Din*. The *Shulchan Arukh* rules in accordance with this view, which is the accepted *halakhah*.[33]

3. *Veset HaDilug*: The *veset ha-dilug* is a variation on the two previously described *vestot*. An example of this type would be if a woman begins her period on the 15th of one month, the 16th of the next month and the 17th of the next month, or she has an interval of 28 days, then 29 days, and then 30 days. The *veset ha-dilug* would be the next link in the sequence: in the first case, it would be the 18th of the following month; in the second case it would be 31 days after the last period.

   The Talmud[34] indicates that a pattern such as this is recognized as a *veset*. However, there is a dispute recorded there as to how many links in the sequence are required to create a *veset ha-dilug*, four (the opinion of Shmuel) or three (the opinion of Rav). *Rishonim* argue as to which view is authoritative, and the *Shulchan Arukh*[35] rules that in a situation where Rav's version of *veset ha-dilug* has displayed itself, the stringencies of both *veset kavu'a* and *veset she-eino kavu'a* must be followed. Both versions of *veset ha-dilug* are rarely seen in contemporary times.

The three *vestot* described above all address the time when the onset of a period originally took place. In this context, it is important to observe that in order to create a pattern, the occurrences all must be within the same part of the day, defined in halakhic terms; either halakhic day or halakhic night. This limitation further reduces the possibility of a *veset kavu'a* being established.

The next two types are of a different nature, focusing on aspects not connected to the clock or the calendar:

1. *Veset HaGuf*: The *veset ha-guf*, also described in the Talmud,[36] refers to bodily indications that a woman consistently experiences

33. See *Shakh*, YD 189:13.
34. *Niddah* 64a.
35. *Yoreh De'ah* 189:7.
36. *Niddah* 63a–b.

before beginning her period, such as a headache or cramping in the legs; when these symptoms present themselves, the woman must separate from her husband. Staining may also be one such symptom. Even though, due to the rules of *ketamim,* there are times when staining will not create a *niddah* status, under the relevant circumstances it may constitute a *veset ha-guf,* requiring separation.

2. *Veset HaKefitzah*: The *veset ha-kefitzah* describes a circumstance when a physical action causes the period, as opposed to the *veset ha-guf,* where it is the period that causes the symptoms. The Talmud discusses this issue in two places, once focusing on *kefitzah,* jumping,[37] and another on eating.[38] There is some ambiguity both in the Talmud as well as in the *Rishonim*[39] and the *Shulchan Arukh*[40] as to whether either or both of these types create a recognized *veset.* This topic takes on significant relevance in a contemporary context, in that contemporary *poskim* have considered extensively whether the pattern established by taking birth control pills constitutes the modern day form of this *veset.*[41] It is accepted by the *poskim* that a couple must separate if her period is imminent due to the cycle being controlled by pills.

VII. DETERMINING THE TIME OF SEPARATION DURING A *VESET*

Having determined a woman's *vestot,* the question then becomes pinpointing the time when separation is obligatory. The *Mishnah*[42] states that a couple must separate for the entire time of the *veset,* known as the *onat ha-veset.* Therefore, if she began her previous period during the daytime, the separation will be during the daytime, and likewise during the nighttime if she began her previous period during the nighttime.

Defining "daytime" and "nighttime" in halakhic terminology is

37. *Niddah* 11a.
38. *Niddah* 63b.
39. See, for example, *Tosafot, Niddah* 63b, s.v. *akhlah.*
40. *Yoreh De'ah* 189:23.
41. For more on birth control pills, see p. 241.
42. *Niddah* 63b.

somewhat complex. For some purposes, these times begin, respectively, with *alot ha-shachar* (dawn) and *tzeit ha-kokhavim* (the emergence of three stars). However, for the purposes of determining the *veset,* this is likely not the case. Most authorities follow the view of the *Chavot Da'at*[43] that the relevant times in this case are *netz ha-chamah* (sunrise) and *sheki'ah* (sunset). This is important, and can affect the *halakhah* in many instances. For example, in the winter months in many locations *netz ha-chamah* can be later than 7:00 AM. In such a case, a woman may wake up in the morning and begin her period, believing that it is the daytime, unaware that it may still be halakhic night. As a result, in the following month she will be required to separate from her husband at night, the halakhic timeframe for the *veset,* not during the day. Due to the frequent discrepancy between halakhic categorization of night and day from conventional classification, women must adopt a conscientious awareness regarding the onset of *netz ha-chamah* and *sheki'ah.*

There is an additional complication regarding the definition of "daytime" and "nighttime" that needs to be considered. The *Shakh*[44] cites the position of the *Avi'asaf* that the definition of "daytime" and "nighttime" is not determined by the makeup of the particular day of the *veset;* rather, it is determined by sunrise and sunset on the equinox, namely from 6:00 AM until 6:00 PM. This new definition successfully preserves, on a constant basis, the measurement of twelve hours for the *onat ha-veset,* irrespective of the season. Most *Rishonim* disagree and claim that "daytime" and "nighttime" are determined by sunrise and sunset of the day of the *veset.* If, for example, a woman has her period during the daytime at the beginning of the winter, most *Rishonim* would argue that she observes the *veset* during the daytime of the following month, even though the day will be shorter. The *Shakh*'s presentation of the *Avi'asaf,* however, would argue that she must observe the *veset* from 6:00 am until 6:00 pm even if that timeframe may extend into the evening. The *Shakh* also applies this principle as a leniency in a scenario in which the woman had her period at "nighttime" during the winter. In theory, the "nighttime" may exceed twelve hours; however, the couple need

43. YD 184:5; see *Pitchei Teshuvah* 189:10.

44. YD 184:7.

not separate for more than twelve hours.[45] The accepted practice is not in accordance with the *Shakh,* and a couple should separate during the *onat ha-veset* spanning from *sheki'ah* until *netz* or from *netz* until *sheki'ah.*

The *Or Zarua*[46] extended the timeframe during which a couple must separate around the time of the *veset.* A couple must separate during the *onah* in which the *veset* occurs, and, in addition, they must also separate during the previous *onah.* For example, if a woman had her period in the afternoon of the fifteenth of Av, she and her husband would have to separate during the daytime of the fifteenth of Elul, and, as well, during the previous night. The motivation for the *Or Zarua*'s stringency is debated. Some argue that the additional period of time is an extra precautionary measure; however, the *Shakh*[47] offers a principled explanation. The *Shakh* argues that the time of the *veset* possesses a focused and pinpointed definition, and is, therefore, determined by the specific time of day. If, for example, a woman always has her period at 3:00 pm, that specific time of day represents her *onat ha-veset.* In addition, the couple must separate during the *onah ha-samukh le-veset,* during the entire timeframe which encompasses the *onat ha-veset.* In a situation, however, wherein a woman consistently sees at random points during the day, there is no fixed moment that can be defined as the *onat ha-veset.* As a result, the entire twelve hour period would then be defined as the *onat ha-veset.* Consequently, the additional separation that is required during the *onah ha-samukh le-veset,* during the time period juxtaposed to the *onat ha-veset,* would then take the form of the previous time period, as well, yielding the stringency of the *Or Zarua.* To help demonstrate this principle, if a woman received her period at 7:00 am, 9:00 am, and 11:45 am, the entire day, spanning from *netz ha-chamah* until *sheki'ah* would be defined as the *onat ha-veset.* As a result, the previous evening would constitute the *onah ha-samukh le-veset.* This observance of two entire *onot* of separation, each one comprised of a twelve hour separation, represents the stringency of the *Or Zarua.*

45. See *Drishah,* YD 184:2, for a discussion of the exact starting and ending times of the separation.
46. I, 358, quoted in *Beit Yosef,* 184:2(1), s.v. *u-mah she-katav.*
47. YD 184:7.

In addition to the *Shakh*'s acceptance of the *Or Zarua*'s position, outlined in the previous paragraph, the *Chatam Sofer*[48] likewise defended the *Or Zarua*'s perspective. In all likelihood, the *Chatam Sofer*'s support resulted from his perspective that the separation of a couple during the time of the *veset* is Biblically required. Many *Acharonim,* however, reject the *Or Zarua*'s stringency either by omission, like the *Shulchan Arukh* and the Rama, or through explicit argumentation. Rav Akiva Eiger[49] dismisses the *Shakh*'s justification of the stringency, questioning whether *Chazal* ever prohibited more than the day itself, regardless of at what part or parts of the day blood was seen. Perhaps, there remains a limited, precise *onat ha-veset,* one, however, which cannot be predetermined. The *Chazon Ish*[50] concurs that the common practice is not in accordance with the *Or Zarua.*

From a practical standpoint, a couple is not required to follow the stringency of the *Or Zarua,* and there are different customs concerning this stringency. The *Badei HaShulchan*[51] notes that most people are lenient regarding affectionate physical contact even during the actual *onat ha-veset*; as a result, one should certainly refrain from adopting strict measures on this point during the *Or Zarua*'s extension. If a couple chooses not to adopt the stringency of the *Or Zarua* and does engage in affectionate physical contact even during the *onat ha-veset,* the manifestation of separation during the *onat ha-veset* will be greatly reduced. Since most women have their period during the day, a time during which marital relations are generally deemed inappropriate anyway, their separation will hardly differ from their general daily interaction.

VIII. UNCERTAINTY REGARDING THE ONSET OF A SIGHTING OF BLOOD

A halakhic ramification of the primary question discussed earlier, whether *vestot* are Biblically mandated or Rabbinic in nature, is the reso-

48. *Responsa* II, YD 179.
49. *Hagahot* to *Shulchan Arukh,* YD 184:2–3.
50. See *Badei HaShulchan,* 184, *tziyunim,* 28.
51. YD 184:17.

lution of situations of uncertainty. The Ra'avad[52] discusses a scenario in which a woman sees blood sometime around *netz ha-chamah,* but she is not positive whether the onset of the occurrence of blood preceded or followed *netz.* He argues that the woman is permitted to adopt a lenient stance and assume that the blood initially appeared after *netz,* thereby limiting her observance of the *veset* to a single time period after *netz.* The foundation for his ruling is the *veset*'s Rabbinic nature. As we noted earlier, the *Chatam Sofer,*[53] among others, believes that a couple's separation during the time of the *veset* is Biblically mandated, and he, therefore, rules in a stringent manner, requiring the couple to observe both the nighttime and daytime as the *veset* due to the uncertainty. Another common situation which resembles the case of the Ra'avad involves a woman who immediately realizes upon awakening in the morning that she had her period. In such a case, despite the woman's uncertainty as to when the blood initially appeared, the *Badei HaShulchan*[54] maintains her presumptive status of purity until the last possible moment, thus assigning it to a time following *netz.*

An additional scenario of uncertainty might develop if a woman loses track of her *veset* for one reason or another. Here again, like in the previous situation, the *halakhah*'s navigation of the uncertainty will depend on the source of *vestot,* if they are Biblically mandated or Rabbinic in nature. If the couple's separation is required on a Biblical level, then they must be stringent throughout the entire period of uncertainty. If, however, the source of *vestot* is Rabbinic in nature, then there exists greater leeway to rule leniently due to the principle of *safek D'Rabbanan le-kula.* In fact, R. Ovadiah Yosef rules leniently in these scenarios of uncertainty due to the reality that the number of days which are not subsumed under the *veset* constitute a majority relative to days that are part of the *veset,* thus making the default position outside of the *veset.* Due to the complexity of these scenarios of uncertainty, *poskim* strongly suggest that women maintain a *veset* calendar, either electronically or

52. *Ba'alei HaNefesh, Sha'ar Tikun HaVestot* 1:4; see Rosh, *Niddah* 9:2.

53. *Responsa* II, YD ibid.

54. YD 184:31.

on paper, in order to keep careful track of their *vestot*. A woman's reliance on her own memory or that of her husband should be discouraged.

IX. DOES A *KETEM* CREATE A *VESET* FOR SEEING BLOOD?

Although many *Rishonim* believed that the entire duration of seeing blood comprised the *veset,* even if, for example, it lasts for five days, practically we adopt the viewpoint that limits the *veset* to the initial sighting of blood. The Talmud stipulates that only a sighting of blood accompanied by a *hargashah* can create a *veset* whereas the appearance of a *ketem* fails to establish a *veset,* and this is the *halakhah* recorded in the *Tur* and the *Shulchan Arukh,*[55] that "*ein bi-ketamim mishum veset*".

The exception to the previous rule is the appearance of a *ketem* on a *bedikah* cloth. In such a scenario, the *ketem* takes on the character of an actual sighting of blood, and is capable of establishing a *veset.* Many limit this ruling, however, to the appearance of a *ketem* on a *bedikah* cloth for three consecutive months on the same day of the month, thereby establishing a *veset kavu'a.*[56] If the *ketem,* though, was found only on one occasion it would fail to mark the day as a *veset.* As a result, this *halakhah* is not generally relevant nowadays since most women do not establish a *veset kavu'a.*

An additional situation in which a *ketem* may potentially establish a *veset* is when initial spotting occurs in the late afternoon, serving as a precursor for a sighting of blood that commences after *sheki'ah.* R. Moshe Feinstein[57] rules that in this scenario the *ketem* is evaluated as the initiation of the subsequent sighting of blood. As such, the appearance of the *ketem* will determine the time of the *veset,* and not the subsequent sighting of blood later that evening. Many other *poskim* debate R. Feinstein's assertion, maintaining that the Talmudic dictum disqualifying *ketamim* from establishing a *veset* is an absolute rule.[58]

55. *Yoreh De'ah* 190:54.
56. See *Perishah,* YD 190:91 and *Hagahot R. Akiva Eiger* 190:54.
57. See *Responsa Iggerot Moshe,* YD III, 46:2 and 51.
58. See *Badei HaShulchan,* 190:504.

X. THE QUASI *VESET KAVU'A* OF THE *NODA BIYEHUDAH*

The Rama[59] discusses a case in which a woman does not have a *veset kavu'a,* yet she consistently sees over the course of a certain number of days since her last period. An example of this phenomenon would be a woman who consistently sees at random points between twenty eight and thirty two days from the time of her previous period; however, she never sees blood before twenty eight days or after thirty two days. Although the Talmud (by omission) implies that such a woman has the status of a *veset she-eino kavu'a,* the Rama makes a cryptic comment whose interpretation is subject to debate. The *Shakh*[60] argues that the Rama was not saying anything innovative, whereas the *Noda BiYehudah*[61] claims that the Rama treats the entire span of days between twenty eight and thirty two days as a quasi *veset kavu'a.* As a result, the obligation to separate that is incumbent on the couple would apply for the entire span of four days.

The *Noda BiYehudah*'s perspective yields a great stringency, and, to some degree, one's receptiveness of his position will be influenced by the source for *vestot,* whether they are Biblically mandated or Rabbinic in nature. In practice, many *poskim* are lenient concerning this matter, and one has the right to rely upon them. Some rabbis suggest, however, to perform a *bedikah* prior to marital relations in order to avoid any concern of "seeing blood on account of relations" since the sighting of blood during that span of days is inevitable. Other rabbis, who are more hesitant to engage in unnecessary *bedikot,* encourage a woman to wipe around the external area to check if any blood is present in order to alleviate the stated concern. It is important to note that these additional measures are merely precautionary, as many *poskim* do not accept the *Noda BiYehudah*'s opinion.

59. *Yoreh De'ah* 189:13; see also 184:2.
60. YD 189:39.
61. *Responsa, kama,* YD 46, s.v. *ubazeh*; see *Pitchei Teshuvah* YD 184:8.

XI. THE ORIGIN OF THE *ONAH BEINONIT*

The *Mishnah*[62] discusses a case in which a man returns home from a trip, and his return coincides with his wife being (as the Talmud explains) "*be-tokh yemei onatah* – in the midst of the days of her *onah*." Rashi[63] defines this ambiguous phrase as referring to the *onah beinonit,* the time at which an average woman has her period. Other *Rishonim,* including the Rambam[64] and Ra'ah,[65] claim that the Talmud is not introducing a new concept; rather, the Talmud is discussing already known *vestot* like *veset ha-chodesh* and *veset haflagah.* Rashi's interpretation is supported by other *Rishonim* such as the Ramban[66] and the Rashba,[67] and is later codified in the *Shulchan Arukh.*[68] An important distinction, though, differentiates Rashi's interpretation from the manner in which the *Shulchan Arukh* codifies the *halakhah.* Rashi applied the notion of *onah beinonit* even to a woman who has established a *veset kavu'a,* whereas the *Shulchan Arukh* limits the *halakhah* of *onah beinonit* to a woman who has a *veset she-eino kavu'a.*

Some *Rishonim* ascribe to the *onah beinonit* the equivalent severity that pertains to a *veset kavu'a.* In other words, a woman must perform a *bedikah* at the time of the *onah beinonit,* and failure to do so results in a prohibition to engage in marital relations until the requisite *bedikah* is performed.[69]

XII. DETERMINING THE DATE OF THE *ONAH BEINONIT*

The determination of the *onah beinonit* is subject to a three way dispute amongst the *Acharonim.* The *Beit Yosef*[70] and the *Bach*[71] advance the conventional understanding that the *onah beinonit* is calculated as the

62. *Niddah* 15a.
63. s.v. *be-tokh.* Concerning the source of Rashi's interpretation, see *Niddah* 9b and *Yerushalmi Niddah,* 2:4.
64. *Hilkhot Issurei Bi'ah* 4:9, with *Maggid Mishnah.*
65. *Bedek HaBayit* 7:2.
66. *Hilkhot Niddah* 5:5.
67. *Torat HaBayit* 7:2.
68. *Yoreh De'ah* 189:1.
69. See *Yoreh De'ah* 184:9 and 189:4.
70. *Yoreh De'ah* 189:1.
71. YD 189:1 and 15.

thirtieth day following the initial sighting of blood from the woman's previous period, with the initial sighting counting as the first day. The *Chavot Da'at*[72] objects, and argues that the thirty-first day subsequent to the previous initial sighting of blood serves as the *onah beinonit*. The *Shakh*[73] disputes both opinions not only regarding the specific numeric calculation of days, but with regard to the entire method of calculation. The *Shakh* argues that the *onah beinonit* is rooted in the presumption that a woman will have her period one calendar month after the previous sighting of blood. As a result, the *onah beinonit* will occasionally coincide with the thirtieth day, but, at times, it will fall out on the thirty-first day.

On the surface, according to the *Shakh*, the *onah beinonit* will always overlap with the *veset ha-chodesh*, yet they are distinguished by the *onah beinonit*'s added severity of containing the status of a type of *veset kavu'a*. Later *Acharonim* note that, in truth, the two calculations will not necessarily coincide in all scenarios even according to the *Shakh*. The *Sidrei Taharah*[74] constructs a representative scenario in which a woman initially has her period on *Rosh Chodesh Nissan*, and subsequently sees again on the twentieth day of *Nissan*. In this scheme, *Rosh Chodesh Iyyar* represents the *veset ha-chodesh*, yet it does not serve as the *onah beinonit*. The underlying reason for this distinction is that a *veset she-eino kavu'a* can be established as a result of one sighting of blood, and is not uprooted until that same date passes without any occurrence. Hence, until *Rosh Chodesh Cheshvan* passes without any sighting of blood, it serves as the *veset she-eino kavu'a*. The *onah beinonit*, however, is defined as the identical calendar date of the month corresponding to the last sighting of blood. In this scenario, once the woman has her period on the twentieth day of *Nissan*, the *onah beinonit* is recalculated to be the twentieth day of *Iyyar*, the corresponding calendar date to the last sighting of blood on the twentieth day of *Nissan*. Evidently, even the *Shakh* will admit that the *onah beinonit* and the *veset ha-chodesh* will not always coincide with one another.

Most of the early *Acharonim* adopted the conventional viewpoint

72. *Bi'urim*, 189:12 and *Chiddushim*, 189:2; see *Pitchei Teshuvah* 189:10.
73. YD 189:30.
74. YD 189:12.

of the *Beit Yosef* and the *Bach,* calculating the *onah beinonit* as the thirtieth day following the previous initial sighting of blood. Later *Acharonim,* though, accounted for the *Chavot Da'at's* perspective as well, and argued to observe both the thirtieth and thirty-first days as the *onah beinonit.* Although the opinion that the 30th day is the basic *halakhah,* there are some who adopt both the 30th and the 31st as the *onah beinonit.*

XIII. THE *VESET* OF THE *TERUMAT HADESHEN* AND ITS IMPLICATIONS FOR THE *ONAH BEINONIT*

The *Terumat HaDeshen*[75] innovated a new type of *veset* which not only foresees when a woman is expected to see blood, but which days are precluded from that possibility. For example, if a woman never has her period prior to the thirty-third day, she establishes a *veset* to not see prior to that point in time. The significance of the *Terumat HaDeshen's* novel assertion, which does not appear in the Talmud, is the eradication of the observance of the *onah beinonit* for such a woman. Many *poskim* were hesitant to accept the *Terumat HaDeshen's* assertion, and the *Chavot Da'at*[76] reasons that the absence of sources supporting his position indicates his error in reasoning. As a result, such a woman would be required to continue observing the laws of the *onah beinonit.*

In truth, though, *poskim* are divided in their receptiveness to the *Terumat HaDeshen's* opinion. Some later *poskim* garner support for the *Terumat HaDeshen* from a position of the Ritva, and conclude that such a woman may ignore the laws of the *onah beinonit.* In accordance with this viewpoint, R. Moshe Feinstein[77] and R. Ovadiah Yosef rule leniently on this matter. Other *poskim* like R. Ya'akov Kaminetzky and the *Badei HaShulchan,*[78] however, uphold earlier reservations, and dismiss the leniency of the *Terumat HaDeshen.*

75. *Responsa,* 247.
76. YD 186:3.
77. *Responsa Iggerot Moshe,* YD, II, 72.
78. YD 186:25.

XIV. PRACTICAL GUIDELINES FOR OBSERVING *HILKHOT VESTOT*

In summary, in order for a woman to properly keep track of and observe the various times of her *veset,* she should carefully record when she had her period. This includes the day of the month and the time of day of her period, namely whether the initial sighting occurred between *sheki'ah* and *netz* or between *netz* and *sheki'ah.* Afterward, she should calculate three things:

1. *Onah Beinonit*: this date is the most essential to be aware of since she is required to perform a *bedikah* as a prerequisite before engaging in marital relations. One point of uncertainty, as was noted above, is whether to observe the thirtieth or the thirty-first day as the *onah beinonit.*
2. *Veset LeYom HaChodesh*: the calculation of this date may overlap with the *onah beinonit,* although not necessarily so, even according to the *Shakh,* as was noted by the aforementioned analysis of the *Sidrei Taharah.*
3. *Veset Haflagah*: the calculation of this *veset* requires a woman to know the date of her last two periods and to calculate the interval between them.

Being mindful of these three factors will suffice in order to accurately calculate the *vestot* for most women. Those women with exceptional circumstances should consult a rav regarding their particular situation.

XV. PREGNANT & NURSING WOMEN

The Talmud[79] addresses the situations of pregnant and nursing women and assumes that the observance of *vestot* is halted during these times due to the reality that a woman ceases to bleed on these occasions. *Rishonim* and *Acharonim* engage in elaborate discussions concerning the underlying assumptions of the Talmud and their related concepts. We will focus primarily on the practical *halakhot* that emerge from these discussions.

79. *Niddah* 9a.

The *Shulchan Arukh*[80] records that the laws of *vestot* are suspended after the pregnancy becomes noticeable, which occurs after the third month. On the surface, the basis for this ruling is due to the reality that women, in Talmudic times, continued to bleed until after the third month of pregnancy. There is considerable debate whether this ruling continues to apply in an age in which women stop bleeding in the beginning stages of pregnancy.[81] R. Akiva Eiger,[82] in light of changed circumstances already in his day, had a related question posed to him, and responded that the law, as codified by the *Shulchan Arukh,* should be retained. In other words, the laws of *vestot* continue to apply until after the first three months of pregnancy. R. Moshe Feinstein,[83] however, believed that women's menstrual cycles had changed biologically since the times of the Talmud; as a result, women are no longer required to observe the laws of *vestot* once it is determined that they are indeed pregnant. R. Feinstein felt that this determination must be made by a doctor; however, contemporary home pregnancy tests are overwhelmingly accurate, and perhaps one has the right to rely on their positive indication. It is important to note that even R. Feinstein felt that a couple should preferably be stringent to follow the view of R. Akiva Eiger, although technically this is not required.

The above debate is nearly inconsequential from a practical standpoint. Most women, nowadays, are only concerned with observing a *veset she-eino kavu'a*. As such, the *veset* is effectively eradicated with a single passing of itself without any occurrence of seeing blood. In most instances, a woman will not realize that she is pregnant until she misses her first period which happens to coincide with the timing of her *veset she-eino kavu'a*. Hence, the cognizance of her pregnancy will almost always follow the prior undoing of her *veset she-eino kavu'a,* making the debate between R. Akiva Eiger and R. Feinstein a moot issue. The one

80. *Yoreh De'ah* 189:33.
81. Some women experience staining at the beginning of pregnancy, and this may present both a halakhic and medical issue. In such a situation, a doctor and rav should be notified immediately.
82. *Responsa, kama,* 128.
83. *Responsa Iggerot Moshe,* YD III, 52. Compare, however, YD IV, 17:1.

scenario in which their debate will have practical relevance is in a situation in which the woman discovers that she is pregnant prior to the arrival of one of her various *vestot*.

The application of *vestot* following childbirth also raises an interesting discrepancy between the biological reality during the times of the Talmud compared with contemporary circumstances. The Talmud[84] rules that a woman need not observe the laws of *vestot* for up to two years following childbirth. The assumption of the Talmud is that her body will not return to its previous cycle until after two years have passed. In contemporary times, it is evident that a woman's body resumes its regular menstrual cycle in less than two years. As a result, many *poskim* believe that the laws of *vestot* resume immediately after her regular menstrual cycle returns.

XVI. A CYCLE REGULATED BY BIRTH CONTROL PILLS

The application of *vestot* concerning a woman whose cycle is regulated by birth control pills raises an interesting question particularly with regard to her continued observance of the *onah beinonit*. Interestingly, the Radbaz[85] was asked a related question involving an analogous situation in which a woman's cycle was regulated by her ingestion of a specific drink. The Radbaz ruled that if the drink effectively regulated the woman's cycle then she is considered to have a *veset kavu'a* in all respects. As a result, since women whose cycles are regulated by birth control bleed every twenty-eight days like clockwork, it is regarded as a *veset kavu'a*. A woman who is taking birth control pills will usually bleed about forty-eight hours subsequent to beginning the placebo pill, and should begin observing the halakhic equivalent of a *veset kavu'a* twenty-four hours after taking this pill. On the opposite end, when a woman stops taking birth control pills, the artificially constructed *veset kavu'a* immediately ceases to be observed.

84. *Niddah* 9a.
85. *Responsa*, VIII, 136.

XVII. A WOMAN WHO LACKS A *VESET KAVU'A*

A woman who lacks a *veset kavu'a* could, theoretically, see blood at any given moment given the haphazard nature of the arrival of her period. On the surface, this lack of expectancy might produce a perpetual element of concern that she might momentarily see blood. The *beraita*[86] records a debate amongst the *Tannaim* how to account for this element of uncertainty. According to Rabbi Meir, a husband must divorce his wife if she possesses a *veset she-eino kavu'a* due to the perpetual concern that she will have her period simultaneous with having marital relations. Normative practice, however, follows the opinion of Rabbi Chanina who maintains that as long as a *bedikah* is performed the couple may remain married. There is considerable debate among the *Rishonim* as to how to understand Rabbi Chanina's opinion.

Rashi[87] believes that, in general, a woman without a *veset kavu'a* is not required to perform any *bedikot* in order to remain permissible to her husband. The Talmud is discussing an isolated instance in which a woman would often do *bedikot* anyway for the purpose of retaining her purity to touch *taharot*. In such a scenario, she should additionally perform *bedikot* prior to engaging in marital relations. In the modern era, however, when the laws of ritual purity are no longer observed, a woman without a *veset kavu'a* would not be required to perform any *bedikot*.

Rabbenu Chananel[88] disagrees and maintains the simple understanding of the Talmud. According to Rabbi Chanina, a woman who lacks a *veset kavu'a* is permitted to remain married to her husband; however, she must consistently perform a *bedikah* prior to engaging in marital relations.

The Rif[89] explains the position of Rabbi Chanina in a different manner, although the interpretation of his explanation is subject to dispute. The Rif explains that Rabbi Chanina is particularly addressing the concern of "*re'iyat dam machamat tashmish*," the sighting of blood

86. *Niddah* 12b.
87. *Niddah* 12b s.v. *mahn*.
88. Cited in Rosh, *Niddah* 1:5.
89. *Ketubot* 60b in *dappei HaRif*.

caused and brought about by marital relations. When must a woman without a *veset kavu'a* dispel this concern by performing a *bedikah*? The Ran[90] explains the intent of the Rif as relating to the first three times a woman of this type engages in marital relations. Since this woman lacks a *veset kavu'a*, any event or occurrence, in theory, may trigger her sighting of blood. As a result, she needs to create a presumption on account of three *bedikot* ruling out marital relations as a potential cause. Once she has dispelled that possibility, she no longer needs to perform any *bedikot* of this kind for the rest of her marriage. According to the Ran, the initial concern was not set off by any specific event; rather, the fear of "*re'iyat dam machamat tashmish*" is a general fear that must be quieted. Most *Rishonim* share the Ran's interpretation of the Rif, and, at face value, this interpretation is codified in the *Shulchan Arukh*.[91] The Ra'avad,[92] though, limited the concern of the Rif to the specific instance in which some prior occurrence produces the fear of "*re'iyat dam machamat tashmish*." The concern for a sighting of blood and the resulting need to check three times only applies if the woman without a *veset* actually saw blood following marital relations on one occasion. In general, though, even a woman who lacks a *veset kavu'a* does not need to perform any *bedikot*. The *Shakh*[93] further limits the application of Rabbi Chanina's position, arguing that the *bedikah* discussed in the Talmud is never imposed as a requirement. The *Shakh* notes that the Rif cites Rabbi Chanina's ruling in *Massekhet Ketubot* and not in *Hilkhot Niddah*. Due to this anomaly, the *Shakh* interprets that the Rif understood Rabbi Chanina to be relating to a very specific incident. A husband is permitted to divorce his wife without paying her the sum of money contained in the *ketubah* if she sees blood following marital relations on three occasions. In order to determine the veracity of his claim, his wife must perform a *bedikah* and find blood on three occasions. According to the *Shakh*'s understanding,

90. *Niddah* 12b.
91. *Yoreh De'ah* 186:2.
92. *Ba'alei HaNefesh, Sha'ar HaSefirah vi-HaBedikah*, 3, p. 70 in Mossad HaRav Kook ed.
93. YD 186:1.

there never exists an imperative for a woman without a *veset kavu'a* to perform a *bedikah* prior to marital relations.

In summary, Rashi believes that during a time in which we are no longer meticulous concerning ritual impurity no woman ever has to perform *bedikot* before relations. Rabbenu Chananel disagrees and claims, on the contrary, all women who lack a *veset kavu'a* must engage in *bedikot* prior to marital relations. The Rif, though, limits the need for *bedikot* to the concern of "*re'iyat dam machamat tashmish*." Three interpretations are advanced on behalf of the Rif. According to the Ran, all women must perform these *bedikot*, but only during the first three times they engage in marital relations in order to rule out relations as a cause of seeing blood. According to the Ra'avad, the concern is limited to a situation in which the woman actually saw blood following relations on one occasion. The opinion of the *Shakh* limits the *bedikot* even further to a context of a husband attempting to divorce his wife without payment of *ketubah*. In general, though, there is no need to perform any *bedikot* to dispel this fear.

Many *poskim* adopt the *Shulchan Arukh*'s ruling in accordance with the Ran's classic interpretation of the Rif. As such, any woman who lacks a *veset kavu'a* would be required to perform *bedikot* following the first three occasions that she engages in marital relations. The *Shakh*, though, claims that the common practice in his day was in accordance with his interpretation. There are different customs today concerning these initial three *bedikot*.

If a woman is interested in following the more stringent view of the *Shulchan Arukh* it is important to be wary, in this context, of the aforementioned position of the *Terumat HaDeshen*. The *Terumat HaDeshen* adopted the viewpoint that if a woman never sees prior to a certain day, it is regarded as if she has a *veset kavu'a* regarding all of the days prior to that point in time. As a result, during the days leading up to the given point in time a woman is permitted to engage in marital relations without performing any *bedikot*. This is due to the woman's interim status as having a *veset kavu'a*. After the demarcating day has passed, however, the woman now is deemed to have a *veset she-eino kavu'a*, and would subsequently need to do a *bedikah* in order to permit herself to her husband. It is important to note, then, that a woman, who wishes to adopt the stringent reading of the *Shulchan Arukh* and perform three *bedikot,* must do so following the passage of the day which distinguishes her *veset* from being *kavu'a* to *eino kavu'a.* Only after her *veset* obtains the status of a *veset she-eino kavu'a,* should her *bedikot* be effective in precluding marital relations as a potential cause of her seeing blood. Some *poskim* are lenient on this matter and permit a woman to perform *bedikot* even earlier in the month; however, logically, the *bedikot* should only be effective after she gains the status of having a *veset she-eino kavu'a.*

Section VIII: *Tevilah*

32.

Tevilah BeZmanah Mitzvah

I. INTRODUCTION

Immersion in the *mikveh,* or *tevilah,* is indispensable in the *taharah* process by all accounts; and yet, surprisingly enough, the exact source of the requirement is a matter of debate amongst the *Rishonim.*

Tosafot[1] cites three suggestions:

1. Rav Yehudah Gaon[2] suggests that the requisite *tevilah* can be derived through a *kal v'chomer* (a fortiori reasoning): if an object which became *tamei* through the touch of a *niddah* must be purified through *tevilah,* then certainly a *niddah* herself is subject to the same requirement.
2. Rabbenu Tam believes that this question is implicitly addressed in a statement in the Talmud.[3] The Talmud derives the obligation of *tevilat keilim* from how the Jews were instructed to handle the vessels they had obtained in the course of their victory over Midyan. There, concerning those vessels, the Torah commanded

1. *Yevamot* 47b, s.v. *bi-makom.*
2. See *Teshuvot HaGeonim* (Musafiah), 45.
3. *Avodah Zarah* 75b.

"*akh bi-mei niddah yitchatta* – rather they shall be purified with the sprinkling waters", which the Talmud interprets to mean that they must be immersed in waters which potentially could purify a *niddah*. Here, argues Rabbenu Tam, the notion of *tevilah* for a *niddah* is clearly referenced.[4]

3. Rabbenu Yitzchak points to a different statement in the Talmud,[5] which quotes a difference of opinion between the *Chakhamim* and Rabbi Akiva as to how the phrase "*vi-ha-davah bi-nidatah*"[6] which, in its simple sense, means "she who is separate in her separateness" and is seemingly redundant, should be interpreted. The *Chakhamim* take the verse to mean that a *niddah* has to behave as one who is set apart, or "*niddui*". Rabbi Akiva, however, maintains that the verse means to say that a woman remains in her *niddah* status until something occurs to change her status, namely *tevilah*. In truth, it is difficult to understand why the other authors of the *Tosafot* offer alternative sources for *tevilah* than that of Rabbi Akiva.
4. The Rambam[7] maintains that there is no direct link between *tevilah* and *niddah*; however, since others who are *tamei* must go to the *mikveh* to become *tahor*, we understand that this is a general principle applicable to *niddah* as well.

What everyone does agree on is that a *niddah*, by Torah law, must go to the *mikveh* before she can become *tehorah*, and, by extension, resume normal marital relations; if a couple were to engage in such relations before she would do *tevilah*, they would incur the *kareit* penalty.

R. Elchanan Wasserman[8] points out that all of the sources brought in the *Rishonim* only prove that a woman is not *tehorah* until she

4. Apparently, Rabbenu Tam is of the opinion that *tevilat keilim* is a Biblical obligation, a topic of debate among *Rishonim* and *Acharonim*.
5. *Shabbat* 64b.
6. *Vayikra* 15:33. This is the verse cited in standard texts of the Talmud. However, the text in *Tosafot* cites a different verse (*Vayikra* 15:19); see *Beit Yosef*, YD 197:15, s.v. *katav girsat Tosafot*, and fn 3.
7. *Hilkhot Issurei Bi'ah* 4:3.
8. *Kovetz Ha'arot*, 39.

goes to the *mikveh,* though none of them tells us directly that a woman is forbidden to her husband until that point. He concludes, based on the fact that the *Rishonim* assume they are connected, that the purity element of *niddah* and the prohibition of marital relations are inseparable, and that the latter is an extension of the former. As has been discussed above, this is not universally agreed upon. [9]

II. IS *TEVILAH* "ON TIME" A *MITZVAH*?

The Talmud[10] discusses whether or not it is assumed that "*tevilah be-zmanah mitzvah*", that is, whether or not there is an affirmative *mitzvah* for a *niddah* to go to the *mikveh* at the earliest possible time or not. What underlies this question is whether or not there is a broader *mitzvah* of achieving *taharah* at the earliest possible time. Most *Rishonim*[11] rule that *tevilah be-zmanah* is not a *mitzvah.*

On the other hand, the *Shulchan Arukh*[12] does record the phrase "*tevilah be-zmanah mitzvah*" and this is, understandably, a source of some confusion. However, a careful reading of the *Shulchan Arukh* makes it apparent that he does not mean this phrase in the sense that the discussions of the *Mishnah* meant it; rather, he means that it is a *mitzvah* to go to the *mikveh* and become *tehorah* in order to have relations and fulfill the *mitzvah* of *peru u-rvu.* The *poskim* point out that this *mitzvah* of *tevilah* remains even when the couple has technically fulfilled *peru u-rvu* (i.e., they have at least one son and one daughter), because the verse[13] of "*la-erev al tanach yadekha* – in the evening do not withhold your hand" is understood by the Talmud to indicate that a couple should try to have as many children as they can. However, if the couple knows for a fact that she will not conceive (i.e. she is on birth control, under permissible circumstances), there would not be a *mitzvah* to go to the *mikveh* at the earliest possible time. While the *mitzvah* of "*onah*", mandating regular intimacy, is still a consideration for a couple in such a situation, in a

9. See Ch. 18, fn 8.
10. *Niddah* 30a; *Yoma* 8a and 88a; *Shabbat* 121a.
11. For example, *Tosafot, Yoma* 8a, s.v. *di-kulei.*
12. *Yoreh De'ah,* 197:2.
13. *Kohelet* 11:6.

case where there is a mutual agreement to forgo their *onah* privilege, the woman wouldn't have to strain herself to go to the *mikveh* on time.

As such, if the husband is not in town when the wife finishes her *shivah nekiyim*, the woman has no obligation to go the *mikveh* right away. If she prefers to go the *mikveh* before her husband joins her, there is no apparent halakhic problem involved; however, Kabbalistic sources indicate that a woman should not go to the *mikveh* while her husband is away. The *Shulchan Arukh* writes that a woman whose husband is out of town doesn't have to go to the *mikveh*; however, some observe, there is no mention of any reason to specifically refrain from going to the *mikveh*. Therefore, women are not obligated to go to the *mikveh*, but they certainly may immerse if they so wish. Some communities follow the custom for women not to immerse if the husband is out of town, but this is not based on halakhic considerations.

III. THE PROHIBITION OF *TEVILAH* ON YOM KIPPUR AND TISHAH B'AV

The Talmud[14] considers whether one who immerses in a *mikveh* on Yom Kippur is in violation of the prohibition of *rechitzah*, bathing for pleasure. From the ensuing discussion, two potentially ameliorating factors seem to emerge: if one holds *tevilah be-zmanah* as a *mitzvah*, or if there is a legitimate necessity,[15] then one who immersed would not be in violation of the prohibition against *rechitzah*.

The authors of *Tosafot*[16] maintain that neither of these two considerations are relevant today. Since the contemporary custom is to treat all *niddot* as *zavot*, there is never a true situation of *tevilah be-zmanah*. Moreover, since there are no longer any foods which must be kept *tahor*, the only practical necessity of *tevilah* would be to resume marital relations, which is clearly not an extenuating factor on Yom Kippur or Tishah B'Av, as marital relations are proscribed on those days. The *halakhah* follows *Tosafot*, and the *mikva'ot* are indeed closed on the nights of Yom Kippur and Tishah B'Av.

14. *Yoma* 88a; *Beitzah* 18b.
15. In the Talmud's discussion, it is the *tevilah* of a *ba'al keri*.
16. *Beitzah* 18b, s.v. *kol*.

IV. *TEVILAH* ON THE NIGHT OF SHABBAT OR YOM TOV

As noted above, the *Shulchan Arukh* deems *tevilah be-zmanah* a *mitzvah* in a different sense than the matter was considered in the Talmud; namely, while it is not a *mitzvah* unto itself, if the *tevilah* is facilitating *peru u-rvu* it is indeed a *mitzvah* and should be done punctually. This notion also plays a role in a ruling of the Rama, albeit one which is not followed today.

The Talmud[17] relates that the *Chakhamim* forbade *tevilah* of utensils on Shabbat; one of the concerns mentioned is that *tevilah* might be misunderstood as a violation of the forbidden *melakhah* of *metaken*, or fixing something which is broken. Similarly, a utensil which is impure is halakhically "broken", and immersing it would be a form of fixing. The Talmud further explains that *tevilah* of a person was exempted from this enactment because the act of *tevilah* by a person could be construed as an attempt to cool off, and not necessarily to attain *taharah*, which would have resembled *metaken*.

This explanation of the permissibility of *tevilah* of a person on Shabbat led some to question if, in a time and place where the alternate "cooling off" explanation was not likely, the exemption would still apply. Some maintained that since *tevilah* of a person had not been included in the enactment, it is always permissible, even if the alternative explanation is not credible. There were those, however, who maintained that *tevilah* of a person is in fact prohibited on Shabbat under those circumstances.

Against this backdrop, the Rama[18] made the following ruling: considering that *tevilah* on Shabbat entails relying on the lenient opinion above, as well as on several dispensations vis-à-vis the obligation of *chafifah* (which will be discussed below), one should only be permitted to rely on these opinions if they are motivated by the desire to fulfill the *mitzvah* of *peru u-rvu*. As such, a woman who delays her *tevilah* to Friday night should not be allowed to go to the *mikveh*.

The ruling of the Rama is not the common custom, and contemporary *poskim*[19] have written that the Rama is not followed in this regard.

17. *Beitzah* 18a.
18. *Yoreh De'ah*, 197:2.
19. *Responsa Shevet HaLevi*, IV, 107.

33.

Immersion during the Daytime

I. IMMERSION DURING THE DAYTIME OF DAY SEVEN AND DAY EIGHT

On a Biblical level, a woman is required to wait seven days from the time of her period before she is permitted to immerse in the *mikveh*.[1] For example, if a woman initially sees blood on Monday afternoon, she is only permitted to perform *tevilah* on the following Sunday evening, the night after the seventh day. Premature immersion on Sunday afternoon is devoid of any halakhic effect, and would result in the punishment of *kareit* should the couple engage in marital relations.

Although a woman's premature immersion during the daytime of the seventh day is invalid on a Biblical level, her immersion on the eighth day, even during the daytime, would be effective on a Biblical plane. The Talmud[2] cites a dispute regarding the halakhic standing of a daytime immersion on the eighth day on a Rabbinic level. According to one perspective, such an immersion is perfectly acceptable; however,

1. See *Pesachim* 4b.
2. *Niddah* 67b.

a second opinion forbids such activity due to the concern of misimpression. The fear of *serakh bitah,* a misinterpretation by the woman's daughter thinking that her mother went to the *mikveh* on the seventh day as opposed to the eighth day, impels this opinion to legislate against a daytime immersion even on the eighth day. The *Rishonim* rule in accordance with this Rabbinic enactment and forbid any immersion during the daytime, even when the concern is seemingly inapplicable. As a result, a woman would be unable to immerse during the eighth day even if she has no daughters.

II. APPLICATION OF THE ENACTMENT TO *SHIVAH NEKIYIM*

The above analysis is relevant to the Biblical phenomenon of a *niddah* who is only required to wait seven days prior to immersion. In contemporary times, however, women observe the laws of *niddah* in accordance with the timeframe of a *zavah gedolah.* As such, they are no longer capable of going to the *mikveh* following the passage of seven days from the time of the period; rather, they must observe *shivah nekiyim,* seven clean days, before immersing in the *mikveh.* According to the opinion of R. Shimon,[3] the principle of *"miktzat ha-yom ki-kulo",* considering part of the day as the entire day, applies to the seventh and final day of *shivah nekiyim,* permitting a woman to immerse in the *mikveh* on the seventh day (provided, as the *Chakhamim* note, that she abstains from marital relations until the evening). The underlying rationale for this restriction is a lingering concern that she might still see blood before nightfall thereby undoing her observance of *shivah nekiyim.* Apparently, a subsequent sighting of blood is the sole potential problem, but it is entirely permissible for the *zavah gedolah* to immerse in the *mikveh* even during the day.

Rishonim express differing perspectives as to how these concerns are addressed in practical *halakhah*:

1. The *Ba'al HaMa'or*[4] argues that there is no intrinsic problem with a woman immersing during the daytime of the seventh day of

3. *Niddah* 67b.
4. *Ba'alei HaNefesh, Sha'ar HaTevilah,* 41, *hasagah* 1.

shivah nekiyim. Not only is the immersion during the daytime effective on a Biblical plane, the Rabbinic concern of *serakh bitah* is not fully applicable. Even if a woman's daughter reaches the mistaken conclusion that her mother immersed on the seventh day as opposed to the eighth day, the result would not be catastrophic, as her error would not lead to the potential punishment of *kareit*. Due to these considerations, the *Ba'al HaMa'or* rules that, today, all women are permitted to immerse in the *mikveh* during the daytime of the final day of *shivah nekiyim*. At the same time, it is important to note that marital relations remain forbidden until after nightfall.

2. The *Hagahot Maimoniyot*[5] presents a tempered version of the *Ba'al HaMa'or*'s ruling, one that permits women to immerse in the *mikveh* by day on the eighth day, but not on the seventh. The *Hagahot Maimoniyot* assumes that a daytime immersion on the seventh day is outlawed not only due to the concern of *serakh bitah*, but, in addition, the restriction stems from the fear for a subsequent sighting of blood. The latter concern is responsible for barring immersion on the seventh day, in addition to forbidding relations until the evening. For this reason, even though the concern for *serakh bitah* might not be relevant on the seventh day of *shivah nekiyim*, the apprehension regarding a subsequent sighting of blood would still apply. As a result, contemporary women may immerse in the *mikveh* during the day, but only on the eighth day.
3. *Tosafot*[6] reject both perspectives, and argue that daytime immersion is prohibited even in contemporary circumstances for a dual reason. On one level, the concern for a subsequent sighting of blood, which would retroactively undo the observance of *shivah nekiyim*, forbids not only marital relations but immersion itself. Furthermore, the Rabbinic enactment due to *serakh bitah* applies to *shivah nekiyim* just as it applies to the eighth day of a Biblical *niddah*.

5. *Hilkhot Issurei Bi'ah* 11:1, citing Ra'avyah, *Niddah*, 190.
6. *Tosafot, Niddah* 67b, s.v. *aval* and s.v. *mishum*.

The *Shulchan Arukh*[7] rules in accordance with the position of *Tosafot*, and forbids women from immersing during the daytime; however, it is important to bear in mind that the prohibition following the completion of *shivah nekiyim*, due to the concern of *serakh bitah*, is far less severe than the prohibition on the seventh day, which is the result of a concern that the *shivah nekiyim* might be overturned retroactively.

III. POTENTIAL LENIENCIES ON DAY SEVEN AND DAY EIGHT

The Talmud[8] establishes a precedent for ruling leniently as a result of pressing circumstances. In a situation in which travelling to a *mikveh* at nighttime poses a dangerous threat, a woman is permitted to immerse by day on the eighth day. In the Talmud's context, the foreboding threat of wild animals or thieves is responsible for allowing a woman to travel and immerse in the *mikveh* on the eighth day, despite the concern for a potential Biblical violation by a woman's daughter.[9]

A more challenging application involves the possibility of permitting a daytime immersion even on the seventh day of *shivah nekiyim*. Although the *Ba'al HaMa'or* consistently permitted an immersion at that time, his perspective is omitted entirely from the *Shulchan Arukh*. The *Bach*[10] implicitly suggests that a foundation for leniency exists in the principle of "*she'at ha-dechak ke-bediavad dami*". This principle asserts that *mitzvah* performance that is, at least, acceptable on a basic level after the fact (*bediavad*), can be accepted straight out in situations of duress. In truth, the *bediavad* acceptance of an immersion performed on the seventh day is subject to a dispute amongst the *Rishonim*. The *Shulchan Arukh*[11] rules leniently on this point, and validates an immersion on the seventh day, should it be done, whereas the *Shakh*[12] cites opinions who are stringent concerning this matter. Basing himself on the perspective

7. *Yoreh De'ah* 197:3.
8. *Niddah* 67b.
9. In unsafe neighborhoods this leniency has been followed if travel at night is not a safe option.
10. YD 197:8, s.v. *u-ba'al*.
11. *Yoreh De'ah* 197:5.
12. YD 197:11.

of the *Shulchan Arukh,* the *Bach* cites the Ra'avyah as arguing that one may act leniently, even on the seventh day, under severely pressing circumstances (although the *Bach* himself disagrees).

An example of a severe pressing circumstance involves a woman who lives beyond walking distance from the *mikveh.* If, for example, the night after *shivah nekiyim* ushers in a three day *yom tov,* preventing a woman from immersing on the seventh day would be tantamount to delaying her immersion for three days. Under such conditions, some *poskim* rule leniently.

An additional leniency, which is subject to debate amongst the *Rishonim,* might exist if a woman immerses on the seventh day but waits until after nightfall before returning home. R. Tam[13] argues that since the restriction preventing a woman from immersing on the seventh day of *shivah nekiyim* is only due to the rabbinic concerns of *serakh bitah* and the cancellation of the observance of *shivah nekiyim* due to a subsequent sighting of blood, delaying a woman's return home until after *tzeit ha-kokhavim* should alleviate both concerns. On the one hand, the potential undoing of *shivah nekiyim* will be determined by that point in time, and, in addition, a daughter will not receive any misimpression if her mother returns home after nightfall. The *Rashbam*[14] disagrees, and his argument is formulated in two variant ways. One version of the *Rashbam*'s objection insists that a woman always immerse after nightfall. A second representation of the *Rashbam*'s viewpoint goes one step further, demanding that a woman not even leave her home before *tzeit.* In truth, the second concern would only be pertinent if a woman performs all of her preparations at home. The *Shulchan Arukh*[15] rules in accordance with the first version of the *Rashbam*'s viewpoint, and, as a result, women may not immerse prior to *tzeit,* however, they may leave their homes before that point in time.

Although the *Shulchan Arukh* absolutely rejects the position of R. Tam, a group of *Acharonim* reconsidered his opinion within normative halakhah by qualifying the nature of the rejection. The *Avodat*

13. Cited in Rosh, *Mikva'ot,* 36.
14. Cited in Rosh, ibid.
15. *Yoreh De'ah* 197:3; see *Shakh,* 197:6.

HaGershuni,[16] cited in the *Sidrei Taharah*,[17] explains that, in truth, R. Tam is correct in believing that the concern for *shivah nekiyim*'s cancellation due to a subsequent sighting of blood is solved by delaying her return until after *tzeit*. The rejection of R. Tam rests upon the conviction that *serakh bitah* is not alleviated by her delayed return if she leaves and immerses during the daytime. By isolating the rejection of R. Tam to the single point of *serakh bitah*, the *Avodat HaGershuni* opens the door to a potential leniency in pressing circumstances, as was evident in the *Talmud*. In the example provided above, a woman who lives beyond walking distance from the *mikveh* and whose *shivah nekiyim* conclude on *erev yom tov* of a three day *yom tov*, would be permitted to immerse during the seventh day. The solution of immersing by day and returning after nightfall, however, will not benefit her in this situation since she will be incapable of making the return walk home on *yom tov*. A number of suggestions are provided by the *Acharonim* in order to help facilitate the leniency's relevance.

The *Chatam Sofer*[18] suggests, at first, that the woman immerse during the day and then circle in the streets until after *tzeit*. He also raises an additional possibility of arranging for the wife to remain at a friend's house until after nightfall. He finds fault with this possibility, though, since attending a friend's house does not adequately preclude the possibility of her seeing her husband before nightfall. R. Moshe Feinstein[19] argues that the woman's return to her own home prior to nightfall is permitted provided that the husband leaves the house beforehand. The husband may go to shul early, thereby allowing his wife to return home. Although R. Feinstein rules leniently in this situation, some *poskim*[20] reject this possibility since the permission utilizes the *Avodat HaGershuni*'s novel interpretation of the rejection of R. Tam as its foundation.

This question is prevalent in many cities which do not have a

16. *Responsa*, 20.
17. YD 197:9.
18. *Responsa*, YD 197.
19. *Responsa Iggerot Moshe*, YD, III, 60.
20. *Shi'urei Shevet HaLevi*, 197:3[2].

centrally located *mikveh* and applies to couples who might be spending Shabbat in a place which does not have a *mikveh*. There are different contemporary opinions as to whether to rely on the opinion of those who are lenient. Even those who rely on this opinion should only do so in extraordinary circumstances; this should not become a precedent for immersing Friday afternoon for mere convenience.

IV. A BRIDE'S IMMERSION ON THE SEVENTH DAY

The case of a bride prior to her wedding offers an additional exception to the general prohibition against immersing during the daytime of the seventh day. If the wedding will be conducted at night, a bride may immerse on the seventh day since the results of the *shivah nekiyim* possibly becoming undone does not apply to her. Since it is forbidden for the couple to engage in marital relations until after they are married, there is no potential danger in the cancellation of the *shivah nekiyim* subsequent to the immersion. The Rama[21] codifies this viewpoint of the *Maharil*; however, the extent of the *Maharil*'s leniency is subject to debate. The *Shakh*[22] believes that the Rama is only lenient during the daytime of the eighth day, whereas the *Noda BiYehudah,* in his *Dagul MeRevavah*[23] thinks that a bride may immerse even on the seventh day. The general practice is to follow the opinion of the *Dagul MeRevavah.*

As was mentioned previously, the leniency concerning a bride is conditioned on the wedding transpiring at night. If, however, the wedding will be conducted during the day, then the possibility of the couple having relations prior to nightfall returns. In a case in which the seventh day of *shivah nekiyim* coincides with a daytime wedding, the *Noda BiYehudah* insists that the couple delay the wedding until after nightfall. If that is not feasible, although the *Noda BiYehudah* forbids it, R. Akiva Eiger[24] does permit the couple to get married during the daytime (as long as they do not have *yichud* prior to nightfall).

21. *Yoreh De'ah* 197:3.
22. YD 197:9.
23. YD 197:3.
24. *Responsa, Tinyana,* 71.

34.

Cleansing before Immersion: *Chafifah*

The Talmud[1] writes that a *chatzitzah* (in this case, a substance separating any part of the flesh from the *mikveh* water)[2] can invalidate the immersion, either Biblically or Rabbinically. Accordingly, a woman is required to make sure she has no *chatzitzot* prior to the *tevilah*. On a Biblical level, this is accomplished by checking her body to make sure there is nothing on her; this is called *iyun*, checking. However, Ezra the Scribe made a Rabbinical decree that women must also perform *chafifah*, thorough cleansing, to be even more certain that there are no *chatzitzot*. *Chafifah* involves cleaning, scrubbing, and similar activities. *Rishonim* note that since *chafifah* is Rabbinically mandated as an obligation, its omission invalidates the immersion on the Rabbinical level, so a woman who immersed without first performing *chafifah* must immerse a second time.

Acharonim debate whether or not women must check themselves

1. *Bava Kama* 82a.
2. See ch. 35.

as they did before Ezra required *chafifah*. The *Taz*[3] argues that checking is no longer necessary now that women perform *chafifah*. In theory, then, a woman may do *chafifah* with her eyes closed. The *Shiyurei Taharah*,[4] however, argues that *chafifah* is only a supplement to checking, so a woman must still look at herself, although she may do this while she is scrubbing. The traditional practice follows the view of the *Shiyurei Taharah*.

Rishonim discuss exactly what the *chafifah* entails. Rabbenu Tam,[5] in response to a contradiction between Talmudic passages,[6] writes that the essence of *chafifah* is to clean, wash, scrub, and comb the hair; for the rest of the body, neither *chafifah* nor bathing are required, as checking suffices in those areas. It is assumed that Rabbenu Tam requires women to scrape every place on their bodies where there is a gathering of hair. The *Shakh*[7] notes that the purpose of *chafifah* is to remove all knots from the hair. Women generally use a brush to comb out knots in the hair on their heads, while they use their hands to remove any knots in pubic hair. This led many *poskim* to conclude that using one's hands is sufficient for *chafifah*, so if a woman lacks a brush for her head then she may still remove the knots with her hands.

The *Tosafot*[8] cite Rabbenu Shemarya, a student of Rashi, who writes in Rashi's name that the view later taken by Rabbenu Tam is incorrect, and that *chafifah* applies not only to hair, but to the entire body. In practice, even Rabbenu Tam acknowledges that the traditional practice is for all women to bathe thoroughly before immersing. Indeed, women traditionally take a bath followed by a shower, as this certainly gets rid of all *chatzitzot*. *Poskim*[9] instruct women to take a bath for 30 minutes and then shower. If a woman has medical conditions that prevent her from taking a bath, she must still shower and can then subsequently immerse.

The Talmud[10] states that women should not wash their hair with

3. YD 199:4.
4. YD 199:5, s.v. *u-baTaz*.
5. *Tosafot*, *Niddah* 66b, s.v. *im samukh*.
6. *Niddah* ibid, and *Chullin* 10a.
7. YD 199:1.
8. *Niddah*, ibid.
9. See, for example, *Shi'urei Shevet HaLevi*, 199:6.
10. *Niddah* 66b.

products that make the hair stick together; in the modern era, shampoos are not considered problematic. The Talmud also rules that women not wash in cold water because it may cause their hair to become entangled.

The Talmud gives two possible ideal times for *chafifah*, along with two supporting rationales: a) *chafifah* at night is better, because it is closer to the immersion and allows less time for a *chatzitzah* to develop; b) *chafifah* during the daytime is better, because women will do a more thorough *chafifah* during the day, when they are not in a rush to get home to their husbands. It is unclear which rationale the Talmud accepts. Hence, R. Achai Gaon,[11] in his *She'iltot*, rules that *chafifah* at night is preferable, while Rashi[12] rules that *chafifah* during the daytime is better.

In regard to practice, the *Tosafot*[13] write that we try to satisfy both opinions, and women should therefore try to begin *chafifah* during the daytime and continue into the nighttime. However, if one has difficulty timing the *chafifah* properly, *poskim* conclude that *chafifah* either during daytime or nighttime is acceptable. If a woman has a choice between one or the other, the preferable option is a matter of debate: The *Shulchan Arukh*[14] rules that nighttime is better, while the *Shakh*[15] feels that daytime is preferred.

When a woman immerses on Shabbat or Yom Tov, she must perform *chafifah* during the daytime preceding Shabbat or Yom Tov (as the *chafifah* involves combing hair, which is prohibited on those days); even R. Achai Gaon certainly agrees that *chafifah* during the day is ideal in such cases. In the case of a woman who will immerse on the night after Shabbat or Yom Tov, *Tosafot*[16] and the *Shulchan Arukh*[17] assume that Rashi agrees that she should perform *chafifah* at night. The *Shakh*,[18] however, writes that Rashi was so concerned that women would overlook a

11. *Parashat Acharei Mot*, 96; cited in *Tosafot, Niddah* 68a, s.v. *kakh*
12. *Niddah* 68a s.v. *ha d'efshar*; see *Tosafot*, ibid.
13. *Niddah* 68a, s.v. *kakh*.
14. *Yoreh De'ah* 199:3.
15. YD 199:6; see also 199:9.
16. *Niddah* 68a, s.v. *kakh*.
17. *Yoreh De'ah* 199:4.
18. YD 199:6.

chatzitzah in their rush to return to their husbands that he felt it better for them to perform *chafifah* on the day before Shabbat, despite the fact that this creates a 24 hour gap between *chafifah* and immersion. Indeed, the *Shakh* rules that if Yom Tov extends for two days, women should perform *chafifah* before the first day of Yom Tov, despite the 48 hour gap between *chafifah* and immersion. Only when two days of Yom Tov are preceded or followed by Shabbat should women do *chafifah* at night, after Yom Tov or Shabbat conclude. However, this nighttime *chafifah* alone is not sufficient, and women must also do a *chafifah* on the afternoon before the three day Yom Tov begins.

The Rama[19] records a traditional practice among Ashkenazim to do *chafifah* both on Friday afternoon and after Shabbat, and this practice is followed. There are two possible ways to explain this practice:

1. The Rama believes that it is best to do *chafifah* right before immersion. The *chafifah* on Friday afternoon is added so that most of the work will be completed before nighttime, thus shortening the necessary time required for *chafifah* at night. According to this explanation, *chafifah* on Friday afternoon may at times be dispensed with. Moreover, according to this explanation, women should not bathe during the nine days, when bathing is proscribed, if their *tevilah* will take place after Tishah B'Av.
2. Perhaps the Rama believes (like the *Shakh*) that *chafifah* by day on Friday afternoon is critical, but a *chafifah* is added at night as an extra precaution. According to this, women may bathe on the day preceding Tishah B'Av in anticipation of immersing on the night after Tishah B'Av, since bathing during the daytime is critical. However, the Rama[20] rules that women may bathe before Tishah B'Av only when it is not feasible to do so afterward, thus casting doubt on this second explanation.

In practice, women should try to take a long bath on Friday afternoon, because the *Shakh* believes that *chafifah* must be performed by day. Even

19. *Yoreh De'ah* 199:4.
20. *Orach Chaim*, 551:16; see *Dagul MeRevavah* ibid., as cited by *Bi'ur Halakhah*, s.v. *im*.

the *Shulchan Arukh* acknowledges that women might rush their baths at night after Shabbat, so ideally they should also bathe on Friday afternoon.

When Tishah B'Av falls out on Sunday, women should do *chafifah* on Friday afternoon, to satisfy the view of the *Shakh* who felt that *chafifah* by day, even 48 hours before immersion and during the nine days, is necessary and therefore permitted. However, women should still shower before immersion on the night after Tishah B'Av.

35.

Chatzitzot

Before beginning the laws of *chatzitzah,* it is important to note the statement of the Ramban,[1] which is quoted by the *Badei HaShulchan.*[2] The Ramban observes that efforts to eliminate all *chatzitzot* can easily become overwhelming. Therefore, he maintains, the proper approach is to simply do *chafifah* in a thorough but reasonable manner, follow the halakhic guidelines as to what is a *chatzitzah* and what is not. After *tevilah,* one should not start second-guessing oneself that maybe one didn't do a sufficient job removing *chatzitzot.*

I. BIBLICAL *CHATZITZOT* – "*ROV*" AND "*MAKPID*"

The Talmud says that there are two defining elements of a *chatzitzah,* which have the status of *halakhah leMoshe miSinai*:

1. "*rov*" – the *chatzitzah* has to appear on the majority of her body.
2. "*makpid*" – the *chatzitzah* has to be something that people care enough about to remove.

1. *Hilkhot Niddah,* 9:25.
2. YD 198:207.

The Talmud[3] also derives that the laws of *chatzitzot* apply both to a woman's body and her hair,[4] and a *chatzitzah* in either area can invalidate a *tevilah* on the Biblical level.

Chazal, however, decreed that even matter on the body which fits only one of the criteria of *rov* or *makpid* alone would be considered a *chatzitzah* and invalidate the *tevilah*. A *chatzitzah* which fits neither, strictly speaking, is not a problem, yet the Rama[5] writes that the custom is to remove those as well, as a precautionary measure.

As one would assume, the vast majority of the cases that come up today are regarding *chatzitzot* about which people are *makpid* but do not cover *rov* of the body (*mi'ut ha-makpid*), because it is very rare to find a *chatzitzah* that covers the majority of the body. It is left, then, to define the standards of *rov* and *makpid* for the purposes of determining what qualifies as a *chatzitzah* and what does not.

II. DEFINING *ROV*:

Rashi[6] writes that the standards of *rov* and *makpid* relate to the woman's hair. This statement is somewhat difficult to understand, as it is generally assumed that those standards apply to *chatzitzot* on the woman's body as well. *Rishonim* offer two possible interpretations of Rashi:

a) According to *Tosafot*,[7] Rashi is propounding a startling stringency: namely, everything we assumed to be true of *chatzitzah* on a Biblical level – that it must be *rov* and *makpid* – is only true regarding *chatzitzah* on hair. As far as the body, however, a *chatzitzah* can invalidate the *tevilah* on a Biblical level even if it is not *rov* or *makpid*.

Tosafot notes that this would seem to be contradicted by an explicit statement in the Talmud,[8] which struggles how to understand the *halakhah* that the immersion of a pregnant convert will be effective

3. *Sukkah* 6a, *Bava Kama* 82a.
4. The hair is included based on a derivation of the seemingly extraneous word "*et*" in "*vi-rachatz et besaro ba-mayim*" (*Vayikra* 14:9). Note, however, *Eiruvin* 4b, where the Talmud seems to be using a different verse.
5. *Yoreh De'ah* 198:1.
6. *Niddah* 67b, s.v. *rubo*; *Sukkah* 6b *rubo*; *Eiruvin* 4b, s.v. *rubo*.
7. *Sukkah* 6b, s.v. *devar Torah*; *Eiruvin* 4b, s.v. *devar Torah*.
8. *Yevamot* 78a.

for her unborn child as well. At one point in the ensuing discussion, the Talmud attempts to answer that the fetus can hardly be considered to be *makpid* on his mother's presence. (The Talmud rejects this by pointing out that a *chatzitzah* which encompasses the whole body doesn't need to be considered *makpid* to invalidate the *tevilah,* and finally concludes that the mother's body isn't foreign to the fetus, and therefore the issue of *chatzitzah* isn't relevant at all.) Clearly, *Tosafot* point out, the standards of *rov* and *makpid* are relevant to *chatzitzot* of the body as well.

b) The Ritva[9] understands Rashi differently. According to the Ritva's interpretation, Rashi thought the Gemara was merely saying that *chatzitzot* on both the hair and the body have to be *rov* and *makpid.*

At the heart of the Ritva's understanding of Rashi is a very controversial assumption; namely, that the hair and the rest of the body comprise two distinct areas in terms of *chatzitzah.* Thus, if a *chatzitzah* covers a majority of the hair alone, it is a *chatzitzah* on a Biblical level.

This question is debated by the Rambam and the Ra'avad. The Rambam[10] felt that the Talmud's derivation merely meant that the hair should be reckoned as part of the body surface when determining if a *chatzitzah* covers a majority of the body. The Ra'avad,[11] however, agrees with the opinion of the *Geonim* that the Talmud's derivation is meant to single out the hair as a distinct area with regards to *chatzitzah.*[12]

In terms of the practical *halakhah,* it is assumed that the standards of *rov* and *makpid* do apply to *chatzitzot* of the body. Moreover, the *Shulchan Arukh*[13] rules like the *Geonim* that a *chatzitzah* on the majority of the hair alone is indeed a *chatzitzah* on a Biblical level (assuming, of course, that it is also *makpid*).

The later *poskim* raise two issues surrounding this opinion of the *Geonim*:

9. *Eiruvin* 4b, s.v. *ki*; compare his comments to *Sukkah* 6b, s.v. *vi-ha.*
10. *Hilkhot Mikva'ot* 2:15.
11. *Hasagot HaRa'avad* ibid.
12. The Me'iri (*Eiruvin* 4b) is of the opinion that the principle of the *Geonim* is not limited to hair alone; rather, a *chatzitzah* which covers the majority of *any* discrete limb (and is *makpid*) is a *chatzitzah* on a Biblical level. This opinion is not represented in *Shulchan Arukh.*
13. *Yoreh De'ah* 198:5.

1. Is every grouping of hair on the body to be considered distinct areas, or is all the hair considered to be part of one body of hair? The practical difference, of course, is a *chatzitzah* which covers the majority of one area of hair.[14]
2. Is *rov* calculated with the number of hairs in mind, or with the area of the hair? If more than 50% of the hairs have a *chatzitzah* covering a minority of their area, is this to be considered a *chatzitzah* on a Biblical level?[15]

As it is difficult to give conclusive answers to these questions, women should take care to be very thorough when cleaning their hair.

III. DEFINING *MAKPID*

It appears to have been a matter of dispute amongst the *Rishonim* as to whether the definition of "*makpid*" follows what the majority of the population consider objectionable, or each individual's standard. The Rashba[16] is clearly of the opinion that the standard of *chatzitzah* is a standardized one, while the Rambam,[17] who mentions a personal standard, may also have agreed with the notion of a standardized *makpid*.[18]

The later *poskim*, such as the *Taz*[19] and the *Shakh*,[20] assume that we are concerned about both standards; thus, both a *chatzitzah* which people are generally concerned about, as well as a *chatzitzah* which the individual woman objects to, would constitute a *chatzitzah*.

The *Mishnah*[21] states that a ring is a *chatzitzah*, and the Ra'avad[22] examines this ruling; seemingly, the ring (in addition to only covering a minority of the body) is usually on the finger because the wearer desires

14. See *Badei HaShulchan*, 198:39.
15. Ibid, 198:38, and *Bi'urim*, s.v. *rov sa'arah*.
16. *Torat HaBayit HaKatzar* 7:7.
17. *Hilkhot Mikva'ot*, 1:12 and 2:15; see *Sidrei Taharah* 198:5.
18. As to whether or not the Rashba and the Rambam are in agreement, compare *Beit Yosef* and *Sidrei Taharah*.
19. YD 198:2, 3.
20. YD 198:2.
21. *Mikva'ot* 9:1.
22. *Sha'ar HaTevilah* 2:6; see Rosh, *Hilkhot Mikva'ot*, 26.

it to be there, and therefore should not be problematic as *makpid*. The Ra'avad explains that if one is careful to remove the ring at certain points, e.g. kneading or showering, he is considered to be *makpid* on the ring, and thus its presence could invalidate the *tevilah*. This opinion of the Ra'avad is codified in *Shulchan Arukh*,[23] and, while the Ran[24] may disagree, is considered normative.

The *Pitchei Teshuvah*[25] cites, in the name of the *Zikhron Yosef*,[26] an important explanation of the Ra'avad's intention: only things which will be removed in the near future, says the *Zikhron Yosef*, fit the Ra'avad's criterion of *makpid*. R. Moshe Feinstein[27] understood this as follows: something which one could become *makpid* about at any moment in time is problematic; an object which one will not be *makpid* about will not be problematic according to the Ra'avad. To put this in concrete examples, one may become *makpid* about a ring at any time – a woman may very well decide to bake bread tomorrow and, consequently, be *makpid* on the ring; by contrast, a dental filling, which is actually the subject of R. Feinstein's discussion, even if one were to know that it would be removed at a later date, is not considered to be subject to being *makpid* because the woman wants it there until a specific time that has not yet arrived. It should be noted that R. Feinstein's understanding of the *Zikhron Yosef* is not universally agreed upon.

In the case of the filling, R. Feinstein felt there was another reason to be lenient,[28] and that was the fact that the temporary filling would be replaced with a permanent filling; since that area of the body would always be covered, the woman could not considered to be *makpid* on it. R. Feinstein's fundamental assertion is that *makpid* is not a function of the substance on the body, but the area of the body itself. Thus, since the woman doesn't object to her tooth being permanently covered, she is not considered *makpid*. R. Tzvi Pesach Frank and others adopt this line of reasoning as well.

23. *Yoreh De'ah* 198:23.
24. Cited by *Badei HaShulchan* in *Bi'urim*.
25. YD 198:1, 16.
26. *Responsa*, YD 10, s.v. *vi-li-inyan*.
27. *Responsa Iggerot Moshe*, YD I, 97:1.
28. *Iggerot Moshe* ibid, part 2.

There are, however, some who rule differently than R. Feinstein. As such, some contemporary *poskim* are only willing to be lenient if the filling will be in for some time, thus satisfying all interpretations of the *Zikhron Yosef*. The exact amount of time is subject to a variety of opinions: R. Yosef Sholom Elyashiv[29] and R. Feivel Cohen[30] require a month.

If the filling were scheduled to come out the same day as the *tevilah*, one of R. Feinstein's considerations in ruling leniently, namely his reading of the *Zikhron Yosef*, would be irrelevant. However, his understanding that *chatzitzah* relates to the area of the body covered, rather than the covering substance, would still be germane, and R. Feinstein indicates that the latter would be sufficient grounds for leniency.[31]

IV. *CHATZITZOT* IN THE *BEIT HASETARIM*: THEORY

The Talmud[32] discusses the status of the *beit ha-setarim*, the areas of the body which are concealed e.g. inside the mouth, ears, nose, etc. The Talmud states that while the presence of a *chatzitzah* in those areas can invalidate *tevilah*, the *mikveh* water need not actually reach those areas. This may sound paradoxical, but the Talmud references an analogous *halakhah* to explain the rationale:

When bringing a *minchah*, a flour offering, there are set ratios of flour to oil; these ratios are those needed to ensure that the offering be mixed (*bilah*) properly. The Talmud[33] raises the following question: what if an offering which contained the proper ratio was not actually mixed? Rav Zeira answers with the following statement: *kol ha-ra'ui li-bilah – ein bilah mi'akevet bo*. As long as the offering had the potential to be mixed properly, the actual mixing is immaterial.

The Talmud in turn relates that principle to *beit ha-setarim*: as

29. *Chok U-Zeman* ch. 6, *Chok U-Mishpat* n4.
30. *Badei HaShulchan* 198:179.
31. It should be noted that the *Chokhmat Adam* (119:18) did rule that a permanent filling is a *chatzitzah*; however, his view was not accepted, and R. Feinstein (*Iggerot Moshe* ibid, part 6) states that contemporary fillings are different than they once were, and the *Chokhmat Adam* would agree that they are no longer a *chatzitzah*.
32. *Niddah* 66b.
33. *Menachot* 103b.

long as the water could have reached the concealed areas of the body, then there is no concern with what actually transpired.

This analogy would seem to indicate that the *beit ha-setarim* can invalidate a *tevilah* on a Biblical level. Indeed, the *Rishonim* discuss whether this analogy is to be taken literally, or if the requirement is of Rabbinic origin. The *Tosafot*[34] maintain that a *chatzitzah* in the *beit ha-setarim* is problematic on a Biblical level. The primary issue the authors of *Tosafot* have to deal with is the seeming lack of any source for such a requirement, and they offer the following resolution: There is a requirement of *vi-rachatz et kol besaro bamayim,*[35] mandating immersion of the entire body in water; and yet, the Talmud derives from the verse (regarding the *tevilah* of a *ẓav*) "*vi-yadav lo shataf bamayim*"[36] that only areas of the body which are usually exposed need come in contact with the water. It must be, conclude the *Tosafot,* that while the *beit ha-setarim* need not come in actual contact with the waters of the *mikveh,* they must, in potential, be suitable to come in contact with the *mikveh* waters.

The problem with *Tosafot*'s answer is that this example of "*kol ha-ra'ui li-bilah*" seems to be anomalous. Normally, *kol ha-ra'ui li-bilah* is a post facto justification; to take the case of the *korban minchah* as an example, to explain why even though the *minchah* was not actually mixed, it still constitutes a valid offering. Other applications of *kol ha-ra'ui li-bilah* follow this pattern. According to *Tosafot,* however, *kol ha-ra'ui li-bilah* dictates how *tevilah* is to be done ideally. It is difficult to understand why there should be no obligation to have water enter the *beit ha-setarim* at least *le-khatchilah.*

The *Tosafot* answer[37] by distinguishing the case of *tevilah* from other cases. The other applications of *kol ha-ra'ui li-bilah* dealt with specific actions required by the Torah as affirmative obligations; any application of *kol ha-ra'ui li-bilah,* allowing those actions to go unperformed, is perforce subpar. By *tevilah,* however, the Torah prescribed the result, rather than a specific action, and therefore *kol ha-ra'ui li-bilah* can tell

34. *Kiddushin* 25b, s.v. *kol.*
35. *Vayikra* 15:16.
36. *Vayikra* 15:11.
37. *Niddah* 66b, s.v. *kol.*

us how *tevilah* is to be carried out ideally. In other words, *kol ha-ra'ui li-bilah* in the context of an affirmative *mitzvah* will necessarily be post facto, while as it relates to a "*mattir*" – meaning, an action that creates a status, in this case permissibility – it may very well be the standard.

According to *Tosafot*'s understanding, the *beit ha-setarim* would count towards calculating whether a *chatzitzah* covers the majority of the body, according to Torah law.

Many *Rishonim* disagree with *Tosafot*'s interpretation; they believe that if there is no Biblical obligation for the water to reach the *beit ha-setarim,* then it is impossible that the requirement that the water potentially be able to reach that area is of Biblical origin. If so, it still must be explained why the Rabbis decreed that the *beit ha-setarim* be free of *chatzitzot.*

Different rationales are suggested:

1. The Ramban[38] (cited as well by the Ritva[39]) proposes that Chazal decreed that a *chatzitzah* in the *beit ha-setarim* is significant in terms of *taharah* since *tamei* objects carried in the *beit ha-setarim* do render the carrier *tamei.* In order to forestall confusion, Chazal said that *beit ha-setarim* is uniformly significant.
2. The Rashba[40] explains that areas of the body such as the tongue and teeth, when exposed, must be immersed as well. Chazal were concerned that if one of those areas was not cleaned, and subsequently exposed during the *tevilah,* the *tevilah* would be invalidated.

In short, it emerges that the requirement that the *beit ha-setarim* be free of *chatzitzah* has been classified in three ways: as a Biblical obligation (*Tosafot*); as a Rabbinic enactment to make sure the Biblical standards are met (Rashba); and as essentially Rabbinic in nature, a measure taken to prevent confusion with the *halakhot* of *tumah* in the *beit ha-setarim* (Ramban).

38. *Chiddushim, Kiddushin* 25a, s.v. *nehi.*
39. *Kiddushin* 25a, s.v. *makom ha-ra'ui.*
40. *Kiddushin* 25a, s.v. *ha d'amrinan.*

V. *CHATZITZOT* IN THE *BEIT HASETARIM*: PRACTICE

This discussion among the *Rishonim* may have a practical effect in the following case: the Rama[41] rules that, as part of her *mikveh* preparation, a woman must clean her nose. The *Acharonim,* in turn, discuss how much of the inner nose must be cleaned. Some *Acharonim* write that only the tip of the nose must be cleaned; this would seem to follow the Rashba, who felt that the whole concern of *chatzitzah* in the *beit ha-setarim* was only in the areas which could be exposed. Others, however, explain that even according to the Ramban and *Tosafot,* one might limit it to the tip of the nose for the simple reason that any deeper may not be an area that she is *makpid* on.

In any event, it is clear that those who disagree with the Rashba's qualification of the *beit ha-setarim* must delineate the *beit ha-setarim* in some shape or form. The *Noda BiYehudah*[42] posits that any object which is embedded in the body has the status of *beluah,* or absorbed, and would not be considered an external *chatzitzah.*

As the teeth are part of the *beit ha-setarim,* they must be cleaned before *tevilah.* Some *poskim* insist that the woman floss on the day of *tevilah,* while some maintain that a woman who is not used to flossing should not, as the floss can get stuck in the teeth and create a *chatzitzah.*

The *Shulchan Arukh*[43] relates a custom for women not to eat meat on the day they are going to the *mikveh,* as it can be difficult to get the meat out of her teeth, and a *chatzitzah* may be created.[44] This custom is not practiced when it would prevent the woman from partaking in a *seudat mitzvah* such as the meal of Shabbat.[45]

R. Moshe Feinstein[46] advanced a significant *chiddush* on this topic by suggesting that there are two types of *chatzitzot*: one which is stuck to the body, and one which is otherwise impeding the water from reaching part of the body. The first type is an objective problem in and

41. *Yoreh De'ah* 198:43.
42. *Responsa, Kama,* YD 64; cited in *Pitchei Teshuvah,* YD 198:16.
43. *Yoreh De'ah* 198:24.
44. The *Be'er HaGolah* 198:48 identifies this citation with the Rosh; however, see *Beit Yosef* 198:24 where this custom is invoked independently.
45. See *Taz,* YD 198:25.
46. *Responsa Iggerot Moshe,* YD I, 98.

of itself, says R. Feinstein; while the second type is only a concern to the extent that it prevents a valid *tevilah* from taking place.

This *chiddush* is particularly significant as it pertains to *chatzitzot* in the *beit ha-setarim*. Since the *beit ha-setarim* must only be fit for *tevilah* theoretically, the only type of *chatzitzah* which is halakhically significant is that which is stuck to the body. R. Feinstein believes this is indicated by the fact a woman can immerse with her mouth closed: if there were a concern about those *chatzitzot* which merely impede the water flow, assuming that lips can indeed constitute a *chatzitzah*, this would invalidate the *tevilah*.

The *Badei HaShulchan*,[47] among others, takes issue with R. Feinstein's line of reasoning. Firstly, it is not clear that one's body can ever be considered a *chatzitzah* in any form; hence, R. Feinstein's invoking of immersing with the mouth closed as an illustration of his principle is questionable. Moreover, the Talmud[48] says an example of a *chatzitzah* in the *beit ha-setarim* is a bone stuck in between the woman's teeth. This, according to R. Feinstein's classification, is only a *chatzitzah* which impedes water flow, and, as such, shouldn't invalidate the *tevilah*. Presumably, R. Feinstein felt that in such a case, the bone would be considered stuck to the body.

The ramifications of this disagreement are not merely theoretical. One example is the case that R. Feinstein himself dealt with: a woman with an inner ear infection wanted to go to the *mikveh*, but her doctor had instructed her to avoid any contact with water whatsoever. R. Feinstein ruled that she could insert cotton in her inner ear and immerse, reasoning that cotton is a *chatzitzah* only by virtue of its impeding the water, and thus not a problem in the *beit ha-setarim*. According to the *Badei HaShulchan*, however, this would not be an acceptable solution. Another practical difference which results from this disagreement would be the status of contact lenses. R. Feinstein suggested[49] one could be lenient because the lens merely lies on, and does not adhere to, the eyeball.

47. See *Bi'urim* to *Yoreh De'ah* ibid.
48. *Kiddushin* 25a, *Niddah* 66b.
49. *Responsa Iggerot Moshe*, YD I, 104, s.v. *ha-ta'am*.

Using the same line of reasoning, R. Feinstein was lenient regarding a glass eye as well.

In terms of practice, women should remove their contact lenses before going to the *mikveh*; in the case, however, of a woman who has an inner ear condition such as the one mentioned previously, there are different opinions whether to accept R. Feinstein's leniency.

VI. SCABS

The question of whether or not scabs constitute a *chatzitzah* is a discussion which dates back to the Talmud;[50] while the conclusion seems to be that scabs can constitute a *chatzitzah*, the *Rishonim* offer differing parameters of which scabs can affect a *tevilah*.

1. The Mordechai[51] maintains that only a scab which has almost completely healed and can be removed without causing too much discomfort can be considered a *chatzitzah*; if removing the scab will be painful, then the scab wouldn't be considered a *chatzitzah*.
2. The Sar MiKutzi[52] insisted his wife remove all scabs, and even examined her to make sure she had properly removed all her scabs. He assumed that even scabs which are painful to remove constitute a *chatzitzah*.

This disagreement, particularly the Mordechai's contention that a scab which would be painful to remove qualifies as a *davar she-eino makpid*, requires some elucidation. To wit, the Mordechai's stance seemingly is contradicted by a *Mishnah*.[53] The *Mishnah* states that a splinter protruding from the skin is a *chatzitzah*; one which is completely inside the body is not. The *Rishonim* have already noted that the woman presumably isn't removing the protruding splinter precisely because of the pain removing it would cause; accordingly, this *Mishnah* is a challenge to the Mordechai's position.

50. *Niddah* 67a.
51. *Hilkhot Mikva'ot, remez* 748.
52. Quoted in *Taz*, YD 198:14.
53. *Mikva'ot* 10:8.

3. The *Sidrei Taharah*[54] suggests that the Mordechai was only willing to employ this leniency when the potential *chatzitzah* is part of the body. It is not entirely clear, however, why this factor should affect the status of *chatzitzah*.
4. The *Shulchan Arukh HaRav*[55] asserts that pain is a way of classifying the scab; if a scab is painful to remove, then it is not viewed as problematic by dint of its impending removal, for only dried out scabs are classified as such. If a scab is painful, then, it is a *davar she-eino makpid*. This is similar to the Ra'avad's position vis-à-vis a ring which a woman will ultimately want to remove.

In practice, one should try to soak the scabs for a long enough period so that they fall off. If they don't fall off, one has a right to rely on the Mordechai's lenient opinion, especially as scabs normally are only problematic on a Rabbinic level.

VII. BANDAGES

The *Mishnah*[56] states that a bandage[57] is considered a *chatzitzah*. It must be considered, however, why this is so, considering that a bandage doesn't cover most of the body, and the person certainly prefers it to be protecting the wound. Several possible explanations exist:

1. This may be explained by invoking the understanding of Ra'avad that something whose removal will be desired in the future is considered a *davar hamakpid*. This is the view of the *Tzemach Tzedek*.[58]
2. The *Ketav Sofer*[59] explains that bandages are problematic because

54. YD 198:26.
55. *Orach Chaim* 161:6.
56. *Mikva'ot* 9:2.
57. In this context, the reference is to a tight bandage; the *Mishnah* uses the term *ritiyah*, which means plaster. In the case of a loose cloth bandage, the *Shulchan Arukh* (YD 198:23) states that there is no concern of *chatzitzah*.
58. 158:5.
59. *Responsa*, YD 91.

they are periodically removed to inspect the wound or to put on another bandage.

3. The *Badei HaShulchan*[60] points out that the *Ketav Sofer* may have been compelled to offer this alternate explanation, as he agrees with the position of the *Zikhron Yosef* that a temporary *chatzitzah* which is not to be removed until a later, fixed date is not considered a *chatzitzah* until the time of its removal. Were there to be a bandage which was not to be removed until a certain time, the *Zikhron Yosef* would probably not deem it a *chatzitzah.*

Whatever the preferred explanation, all agree that a bandage can constitute a *chatzitzah.*[61]

VIII. STITCHES

The *Badei HaShulchan*[62] considers the question of whether stitches constitute a *chatzitzah.* One consideration is whether the position of the *Zikhron Yosef* is accepted. If the stitches are scheduled to be removed at a later date, then, according to the *Zikhron Yosef,* they do not constitute a *chatzitzah.* Even those who don't accept the *Zikhron Yosef,* however, also have grounds to be lenient. The *Badei HaShulchan* points to the position of the Ramban,[63] who maintains that anything on the body which is not actively removed, but falls away by itself, is considered a *davar she-eino makpid.* Accordingly, the *Badei HaShulchan* rules that there is room to be lenient regarding stitches which will dissolve, but not those which need to be removed by a doctor.

The *Badei HaShulchan* further points out that even according to the *Zikhron Yosef* one could not be lenient if the stitches were no longer serving a function. If the stitches are medically ready to be removed, presumably according to all opinions they would constitute a *chatzitzah.*

60. YD 198:87.
61. See *Sidrei Taharah* YD 198:24.
62. YD 198:23, *Bi'urim,* s.v. *bi-eged,* and 198:173.
63. *Chiddushim, Niddah* 67a.

IX. DIRT BENEATH THE FINGERNAILS AS A *CHATZITZAH*

Both a *Mishnah* and a *tosefta* speak about potential *chatzitzot* beneath the fingernails, and they may or may not be saying the same thing. The *Mishnah*[64] says that dirt under the fingernails is not a problem, but the *tosefta*[65] says that it depends on where the dirt is: if one has a short fingernail that does not extend past the end of the finger, then any dirt beneath the fingernail would actually be on the skin. Since that does not have such a disturbing appearance, it is assumed that one is not *makpid* about it. But, if one has long fingernails such that the dirt beneath them is not touching the skin, then that would be a *chatzitzah* because it looks filthy and one would probably be *makpid* to clean it. The *Rishonim* try to reconcile the *Mishnah* with the *tosefta*:

1. The Rambam[66] simply quotes the *Mishnah* and not the *tosefta*; the *Beit Yosef*[67] explains that the Rambam assumed it was a dispute, and ruled like the *Mishnah*.
2. The Rosh[68] indicates that the *halakhah* is like the *tosefta*, and when the *Mishnah* said that dirt beneath the fingernails is not a problem it was referring to the case of dirt on the skin because that is the most commonly found situation.
3. Rabbenu Tam, quoted in the *Semak*,[69] attempts to reconcile the two by drawing a distinction between dirt that is adhesive (that is thick and stuck in place) and that which is not. Rabbenu Tam believes that the *tosefta* is dealing with the former, which is potentially more of a problem, and distinguishes between that which is touching the skin and that which is not. When the *Mishnah* rules that there is no problem at all, it is dealing with dirt that is not adhesive.

64. *Mikva'ot* 9:2.
65. *Mikva'ot* 6:10.
66. *Hilkhot Mikva'ot* 2:1 and 14.
67. *Yoreh De'ah* 198:18 (1).
68. *Hilkhot Mikva'ot* 26; see commentary of Rosh to *Mikva'ot* 9:2 and 4.
69. *Sefer Mitzvot Katan*, #293, p. 323; also cited in *Beit Yosef*, YD 198:18, s.v. *tzo'ah*.

The *Shulchan Arukh*[70] rules in accordance with the view of the Rosh that dirt that is not opposite the skin is a problem, but it is not clear if he accepts Rabbenu Tam's distinction between that which adheres and that which does not. The *Taz*[71] suggests that Rabbenu Tam's view is accepted only with regard to *netilat yadayim,* where the *halakhah* is quite lenient with regard to *chatzitzot,* but Rabbenu Tam's leniency should not be accepted when it comes to *tevilah.* In practice, the *Taz*'s view is followed, and Rabbenu Tam's position is not accepted regarding *tevilah,* so any dirt that is not opposite the skin is deemed a *chatzitzah.* Further, it is reasonable to maintain that contemporary women are likely more *makpid* about dirt under their fingernails than were women in centuries past. Accordingly, it is possible that the basic law requires that a woman must make sure that all dirt is cleaned out from under her nails before *tevilah,* including dirt that is opposite the skin.

The *Rishonim* mention a custom, which was later quoted in the *Shulchan Arukh,*[72] for women to cut their nails before *tevilah* in order to avoid these problems. The nails need only be cut so that they are completely parallel to the skin; while this is only a custom, and strictly speaking it is enough for the fingernails to be clean, women should be encouraged to follow this very old *minhag Yisrael.* Nevertheless, women who choose merely to clean their nails but leave them long should not be prevented from using the *mikveh,* as was expressed in a ruling of R. Chaim Ozer Grodzinski.[73]

However, if a woman comes to the *mikveh* with a real Rabbinic-level *chatzitzah* (Biblical-level *chatzitzot* are rare in the modern era) and wishes to use the *mikveh* anyway, a very serious question is presented as to whether she should be allowed to do so. On the one hand, the *tevilah* will remove the Biblical prohibition and the accompanying risk of a *kareit* transgression; on the other, allowing such usage will appear to endorse a *tevilah* that is actually invalid by Rabbinic law. Some contemporary

70. *Yoreh De'ah* 198:18.
71. YD 198:19.
72. *Yoreh De'ah* ibid; see *Be'er HaGolah,* 41.
73. *Responsa Achiezer,* III, 33.

poskim suggest the following compromise: Generally, the *mikveh* attendant watches a woman do *tevilah,* and when the woman comes up the attendant tells her that the *tevilah* was *kasher*. In this situation, even if the woman is allowed to use the *mikveh,* it would be inappropriate and misleading for the attendant to declare "*kasher*".

X. THE FINGERNAILS THEMSELVES AS A *CHATZITZAH*

The Rama[74] makes a surprising statement with regard to fingernails: According to some opinions, if a woman only cleans her nails and does not cut them, the nails themselves become *chatzitzot* and invalidate the *tevilah*. In explanation of this, the *Shakh,*[75] citing the Ra'avan,[76] applies the principle of "*kol ha-omed likatzetz ki-katzutz dami*" meaning, everything that is to be cut imminently is considered to have already been cut. With this principle in mind, it can be argued that since a long fingernail will eventually be cut, it is considered as if it has already been cut, in which case now that it is on top of the finger it is equated with a foreign object covering a part of the body.

Although many *poskim,* including the *Taz,*[77] reject this view of the Ra'avan, believing that it is difficult to apply this principle to *chatzitzot,* both the Rama and the *Shakh* seem to accept the Ra'avan's position. The *Shakh* maintains that even if a woman has already done *tevilah* with long nails, she should be told to cut her nails and immerse again. The later *poskim* discuss how far one must take this concern, and whether a woman who has already returned home should really be told to go back and do *tevilah* again. In sum, there are two reasons for a woman to cut her fingernails before *tevilah*: the general *minhag Yisrael* mentioned in the *Rishonim,* and out of concern for the view of the Ra'avan.

74. *Yoreh De'ah* 198:20.

75. YD 198:25.

76. In earlier editions of the *Shulchan Arukh,* the printed *Shakh* cites the Ra'avad on this point, but in later editions it is corrected to Ra'avan.

77. YD 198:21.

XI. SHAVING AND WAXING

If one accepts this view of the Ra'avan, then further problems present themselves. The *Pitchei Teshuvah*[78] cites the *Chatam Sofer*[79] regarding women in Europe who used to shave their heads after getting married. It had been suggested that since these women are scheduled to have their hair cut the day after the consummation of the marriage, then the hair is "*omed likatzetz*" when the women do *tevilah* the day before the wedding, and the *tevilah* should be invalid according to the Ra'avan. The *Chatam Sofer* examines the Talmudic discussion of "*kol ha-omed*" and concludes that the principle only applies when the cutting is supposed to have been done at that time without an action interrupting between now and the cutting; however, since these women only plan to get their hair cut after the consummation of the marriage, it is not considered *omed likatzetz* when they do *tevilah*.[80]

This issue is a very relevant one with regard to women shaving their legs or removing other hair on their bodies. Many *poskim* point out that women who are planning to shave their legs close to the time they go to the *mikveh* should make a point to do so before *tevilah*, because otherwise the Ra'avan's view could pose a problem. While it should be noted that the *Sefer HaTerumah*[81] writes that women used to remove hair after they returned from the *mikveh*, he may have rejected the Ra'avan's view altogether, and thus his report would not be relevant to those who wish to take the Ra'avan's view into account as a stringency.

Some women prefer to use wax to remove their hair, and are told to do so before *tevilah*, out of concern for the view of the Ra'avan. One must be careful to remove any wax left on the skin, because if one is *makpid* on wax that remains, the wax itself would be a *chatzitzah*.

78. YD 198:12.
79. *Responsa*, YD, 195.
80. See *Badei HaShulchan*, YD 198:148, *Bi'urim* s.v. *d'kevar nahagu*, who considers whether hair and fingernails are treated the same way concerning this issue.
81. #104; cited in *Badei HaShulchan*, ibid.

XII. CUTTING FINGERNAILS ON *SHABBAT* FOR *TEVILAH*

If a woman forgot to cut her nails on Friday afternoon or before Yom Tov, and she arrives at the *mikveh* with clean but long nails, the question arises as to whether she can do *tevilah*. The *Taz*[82] maintains that she can immerse, but, as was noted above, the *Taz* did not accept the Ra'avan's position; while the *minhag* of cutting the nails presumably should not be sufficient reason to delay *tevilah* for a night. However, the *Shakh*[83] asserts that the woman must have her nails cut by a non-Jew.

The *Shakh* allows this on the basis of the assumption that the relevant issue is a "*shevut de-shevut be-makom mitzvah*" – a Rabbinic prohibition (asking a non-Jew to perform a *melakhah* on Shabbat) applied to a situation that is itself a Rabbinic prohibition, under the circumstances of performing a *mitzvah*. He assumes this based on the following reasoning:

The *Shakh* cites a *Tosafot*[84] who say that the *halakhah* follows the opinion of R. Shimon, who believes that cutting nails is a "*melakhah she-einah tzerikhah le-gufah*" (a *melakhah* performed for a purpose other than its defining one), which is only a Rabbinic prohibition. However, the *Bi'ur Halakhah*[85] points out that most authorities disagree with this *Tosafot*, and the *Shulchan Arukh*[86] rules, following the view of the Rivash,[87] that cutting nails on Shabbat is Biblically prohibited.

The *Tosafot* assume that during the construction of the *Mishkan* (which provides the paradigm for the various *melakhot* of Shabbat), sheep would be sheared specifically for the wool, in which case cutting hair and fingernails merely to get rid of them (as opposed to desiring the hair or nails themselves) would be a *melakhah she-einah tzerikhah le-gufah*. The Rivash, however, maintains that the hair was also cut off of some animals to make the animal skins look nicer. Similarly, asserts

82. YD 198:21.
83. *Nekuddat HaKesef*, YD ibid.
84. *Shabbat* 94b, s.v. *aval*.
85. *Orach Chaim* 340, s.v. *vi-chayav*.
86. *Orach Chaim* 328:31.
87. *Responsa*, 395.

the Rivash, when people cut their hair and nails to make themselves look nicer, that would be just like the *melakhah* in the times of the *Mishkan* and therefore be Biblically prohibited on Shabbat. Nonetheless, the *Bi'ur Halakhah* points out that even though the Rivash's view is accepted on this matter, even the Rivash would agree that cutting nails before going to the *mikveh* is not *"tzerikhah le-gufah"*, because women in this case are not doing it to make themselves look nicer; quite the contrary, they are doing it despite the fact that they prefer longer nails. Therefore, the *Bi'ur Halakhah* concludes, the *Shakh* may be correct even according to the Rivash.

However, the *Taz* feels that having a non-Jew cut one's nails may be worse than the mere Rabbinic prohibition normally involved with *melakhah* done through a non-Jew, and may even be Biblically prohibited. This is because the woman who has her nails cut may be viewed as *"mesaye'a"*, as facilitating or helping the performance of the transgression, and it may be prohibited by the Torah to do so. The *Shakh*, by contrast, must argue that simply aiding the performance of the transgression is not tantamount to performing the act itself. This debate stems from two seemingly contradictory passages in the Talmud.

The first passage[88] states that one who is ill may ask a non-Jew to apply some sort of treatment to his eye on Yom Tov, and even though the Jew opens his eyes to allow this to happen; the Talmud concludes that *mesaye'a "ein bo mamash"*, is essentially insignificant. In the second passage,[89] however, the Talmud rules that one who sits in the barber shop and has his sideburns completely cut off is liable for punishment for violating the prohibition of *"bal takif"*, the Torah prohibition against cutting sideburns. The Talmud explains this liability by noting that he was following the barber's instructions and moving his head around to facilitate the performance of the transgression, implying that *mesaye'a* is indeed significant.

The Ritva[90] reconciles this contradiction in two ways:

88. *Beitzah* 22a.
89. *Makkot* 20b.
90. *Makkot* 20b, s.v. *bi-mesaye'a.*

1. The act that the patient receiving treatment performed is a common act; people open and close their eyes all day long. Therefore, the fact that one happened to open his eyes specifically when the non-Jew told him to is not a problem – that is insignificant *mesaye'a*. However, the man receiving the prohibited haircut moves his head around to all kinds of abnormal positions to allow the cutting of his sideburns.
2. The difference between the two situations is that the haircut is itself prohibited, while in the case of the treatment, it is only the act of application, the physical action, that is prohibited. Thus, in the former even *mesaye'a* is prohibited, as it makes an active transgression out of what is already a forbidden result; while in the latter case, *mesaye'a* is insignificant, as it is merely facilitating an activity that is not inherently prohibited as far as the result in brings about.

The *Taz* essentially accepts the first explanation of the Ritva, and assumes that it is prohibited by Torah law for a person to perform an abnormal act in order to facilitate a prohibition, and lifting one's hands in the air to have the nails cut qualifies as abnormal. The *Shakh* follows the second explanation of the Ritva (although he does not cite him), and believes that since there is no pre-existing prohibition to have one's nails cut on Shabbat it cannot be Biblically prohibited to facilitate the nail-cutting.

The *halakhah* follows the *Shakh*; therefore, if a woman arrives at the *mikveh* on Shabbat and Yom Tov and has forgotten to cut her nails, the *mikveh* attendant should contact a non-Jew to cut the nails.

XIII. LOOSE OBJECTS

There is a general rule in the laws of *chatzitzah* that a *davar rafui,* a loose object, is not a *chatzitzah* if water can seep in around it.[91] The Talmud[92] says that if a woman has knots in her hair that are loose enough for water to reach all the hairs, then, strictly speaking, her *tevilah* is valid.

The concept of a *davar rafui* appears in other contexts, notably a passage in the Talmud[93] which states that a woman can do *tevilah* even if she is clothed, provided that the clothes are loose fitting and would allow water to reach the skin. Also, a *Mishnah*[94] teaches that if certain types of jewelry are worn loosely, such that water can get beneath, that would also not be a *chatzitzah.*

However, the Rama[95] says that one should try to avoid relying on this rule and thus immersing with foreign objects that are not a *chatzitzah,* out of concern that one will come to immerse with objects that do pose a problem. However, since it is only a custom not to rely on this rule, there is room for leniency in some situations, as noted by the *Badei HaShulchan.*[96] One such case is that of a woman who, when she becomes pregnant, swells in various parts of her body, including her fingers. As a result of this swelling, she will at times be unable to remove her wedding ring, and that may still be the case by the time she is scheduled to do *tevilah* post-childbirth. Some *poskim* say that the ring has to be cut off before *tevilah* can be performed, while others maintain that one can forgo this custom not to rely on a *davar rafui,* assuming the ring is loose enough. Presumably, one determines if the ring is loose enough by giving it a test run and dipping her hand in a cup of water to see if the water gets beneath the ring.

91. This is the view of Rashi, *Shabbat* 57a, s.v. *ha nami.* However, Rashi quotes the view of his *rebbeim* that loose objects also cause a *chatzitzah.* The *Shulchan Arukh* (YD 198:3–4) adopts Rashi's view, while the *Tur* (and possibly the Rama (198:4) as well), follows his *rebbeim.* See *Beit Yosef* and *Pitchei Teshuvah* 198:4.
92. *Niddah* 67a, with Rashi s.v. *nima achat*; see also *Shabbat* 57a.
93. *Beitzah* 18a.
94. *Mikva'ot* 6:5.
95. *Yoreh De'ah* 198:1.
96. YD 198:170, *Bi'urim* s.v. *refuyim.*

XIV LIQUIDS

A *Mishnah*[97] teaches that liquids are not considered to be *chatzitzot,* and the *Rishonim* argue about why that should be:

1. *Tosafot*[98] assumes that this *Mishnah* relates to the rule discussed above; since water can touch the skin despite the liquid covering it, the liquid is not a *chatzitzah.*
2. The *Sefer Yereim,*[99] however, argues that liquid is not considered to be a *chatzitzah* because one is generally not *makpid* about a little bit of liquid on her body.

The important practical ramification between these two opinions is in a case when the liquid substance is a *davar ha-makpid;* since the standards of *makpid* can be subjective, it is possible that a little bit of wet blood would be a *chatzitzah* according to the *Yereim* but not according to *Tosafot.* This is rarely an issue, however, because any liquids on the body should be cleaned off during *chafifah.* If a woman's hands are bleeding, she should try to wipe off any excess blood immediately before *tevilah.* It is assumed that she is not *makpid* about whatever she cannot wipe off. As a rule, the subjective standards of *makpid* and *eino makpid* should be determined based on what the woman would want to clean off if she was not concerned about the laws of *niddah.*

XV. COSMETICS, HAIR DYE & INK

The *Rishonim* discuss the status of different cosmetics such as nail polish or lipstick, and whether or not they should constitute *chatzitzot.* Presumably, if the nail polish or hair-dye is dried, then they should be *chatzitzot.* However, the Rashba[100] maintains that all of these cosmetics are not *chatzitzot* even if they are dried.

He bases this view on a combination of factors.

97. *Mikva'ot* 9:2.
98. *Chullin* 26b, s.v. *hakha.*
99. See Mordechai, *Hilkhot Mikva'ot,* 748.
100. *Torat HaBayit HaKatzar* 7:7, and in *Teshuvot HaMeyuchasot LihaRamban* #124.

1. It may be that anything applied to the body to make it more beautiful may not be a *chatzitzah,* because it is considered part of the body. This is a stronger argument than simply asserting that she is not *makpid* about the make-up being on her body because, as has been noted, even a *davar she-eino makpid* is a *chatzitzah* if it covers everything. Since the *halakhah* follows the view of the Ra'avad and the Geonim that the hair is counted independently, hair-dye which covers all of the hair would be a *chatzitzah* even if she prefers to have it there. However, according to the Rashba's explanation, it would still not be a *chatzitzah.*
2. The Rashba also suggests that dyes which can only be seen but not felt may have no halakhic significance as a *chatzitzah.*

Based on these two reasons, the Rashba rules that dyes and cosmetics are not problematic, and the *Shulchan Arukh*[101] quotes this ruling. The Gaon of Vilna[102] writes that the Rashba's position is indisputable, because it is supported by a passage in the Mishnah[103] which says that the *kohanim* used to immerse the *parokhet* whenever it became *tamei.* The Gaon says that the fact that the *parokhet* could be purified through *tevilah,* even though it was dyed, proves the correctness of the Rashba's view.

In the same ruling as the above, the *Shulchan Arukh* also discusses one who has dyes on their body, albeit not for cosmetic purposes. He makes the following distinction: if the person is a painter, and is not *makpid* about dyes or paints being on her skin, then the dyes are not a *chatzitzah,* but if the person does not work with dyes and is normally *makpid,* then the dyes are a *chatzitzah.* The *Acharonim* point out that this seems to contradict what, until now, had been the operating assumption; namely, that there are certain general standards of "*makpid*" that are not subjective, and subjective versions are only recognized in the direction of stringency. Some[104] resolve this difficulty by positing that painters compose a separate category that, as a group, is not *makpid* about paint

101. *Yoreh De'ah,* 198:17.
102. *Bi'ur HaGra,* YD 198:18 (This proof is cited by the Rashba himself).
103. *Shekalim* 8:4.
104. See *Beit Yosef,* YD 198:17, s.v. *tzeva.*

on their bodies, as opposed to an atypical individual who does not mind being covered in mud.

The *Shulchan Arukh*'s ruling appears difficult for another reason. Considering that the *Shulchan Arukh* just earlier ruled in accordance with the view of the Rashba that cosmetics are not a problem, the subsequent statement that paint can be problematic seems inconsistent with the Rashba's position, particularly his second rationale that that dyes which can only be seen but not felt may have no halakhic significance.

In resolution of this issue, various suggestions have been made:

1. Some suggest that the *Shulchan Arukh* was only willing to rely on the Rashba's opinion on the strength of both reasons, but not on the second reason alone.
2. Other *Acharonim* say that the *Shulchan Arukh* would be lenient even on the strength of only one of the Rashba's reasons, but was not lenient here because he is dealing with a case when there is enough paint for the second reason not to apply either, i.e., when there is so much paint that it really is palpable on the skin.

The practical difference between these two explanations of the *Shulchan Arukh* is a case where someone has a non-cosmetic type of dye on their hands but very little of it: according to the first set of *Acharonim,* since only the second reason of the Rashba applies here, and the *Shulchan Arukh* is not willing to be lenient solely based on that reason, the dye is a *chatzitzah*. According to the second group, the *Shulchan Arukh* is willing to be lenient in such a case where the Rashba's second reason applies. The common application of this rule is the case of a woman who has some iodine on her hands or some ink from a ball point pen: according to the first group it would be a problem, while according to the second group it would not. In practice, the *poskim* say that one should try to scrub off the ink as best as possible, but in exigent circumstances *tevilah* is permitted with such stains.

However, contemporary *poskim* have decided that women cannot go into the *mikveh* with their modern day cosmetics on because the make-up will start to run and will not look pretty, knocking out the Rashba's first reason. Further, sometimes women put on so much lipstick or blush that it is thick enough to cancel out the Rashba's second reason as well. In practice, women are not permitted to do *tevilah* with their make-up on. The same applies to nail polish, because women become *makpid* when it starts to chip, which can happen at any time.

XVI. THE BODY AS A *CHATZITZAH* ON ITSELF – PROPER POSITIONING DURING *TEVILAH*

The Talmud[105] also discusses in what position a woman should perform *tevilah* in order to prevent her body from being a *chatzitzah* on itself. R. Yochanan maintains that a woman should keep her eyes closed but relaxed, so as not to create wrinkles in the eyelids into which the water cannot enter. Reish Lakish adds that a woman should do *tevilah* in a normal fashion, which the Talmud explains as not stretching too much and not bending too much.

There is a dispute regarding how to explain the connection between these two statements:

1. Rashi[106] quotes an older text of the Geonim which reads as follows: R. Yochanan's statement, then the Talmud's statement that the *halakhah* does not follow R. Yochanan because his stringency is only required for the realm of purity and impurity, and instead the *halakhah* follows the lenient view of Reish Lakish. According to this text, Reish Lakish is maintaining that women can just perform *tevilah* normally and not worry about *chatzitzot* of the body. Rabbenu Tam[107] accepts this text.
2. However, Rashi rejects this text, and instead concludes that R. Yochanan and Reish Lakish are making two independent statements. According to Rashi, whereas R. Yochanan was only worried about wrinkles in the eyelids, Reish Lakish was also worried about wrinkles throughout the body.

This dispute about the text impacts two issues: whether R. Yochanan's

105. *Niddah* 67a.
106. Cited in *Tosafot, Niddah* 67a, s.v. *patchah* and in *Machzor Vitri,* 499.
107. In *Tosafot,* ibid.

stringency about the eyes is accepted, and whether Reish Lakish is being lenient or stringent. According to Rashi, Reish Lakish is expressing stringency, and the *halakhah* follows Reish Lakish; thus, there is a concern for *chatzitzot* all over the body. According to Rabbenu Tam, Reish Lakish simply meant that women should do *tevilah* normally, and do not have to be concerned about *chatzitzot* created by the body.

The *Shulchan Arukh*[108] quotes both opinions in different places, and the *poskim* instruct women to be careful not to create any wrinkles in their bodies while doing *tevilah*; nonetheless, after the fact; it would be hard to send a woman back to the *mikveh* for not being so careful.

There is a debate among *Acharonim* regarding how to explain this concern for wrinkles according to those who believe it exists. The difficulty is that clearly women are allowed to have their feet on the ground during *tevilah,* because there is *mikveh* water on their feet from when they originally stepped into the water. That principle is called "*mayim makdimim*". Accordingly, the Taz[109] questions why the rule should be any different with regard to the wrinkles on a woman's body, as water presumably gets in those places the moment a woman steps into the water, before she curls herself up. In fact, the *Taz* concludes that if indeed a woman stood straight up in the water and only curled up when dunking underneath, then the *tevilah* would be valid. There remains only the concern that the woman will curl up even before she goes under the water, preventing the water from reaching every part of her body. Therefore, the *Taz* recommends that women first stand up straight in the *mikveh,* to allow the water to reach every part of their bodies, and then curl up and bring their heads beneath the surface of the water. The *Badei HaShulchan*[110] quotes the Maharsham that women used to do *tevilah* multiple times, to ensure that the water will reach every part of her body at least one of those times, and thereby fulfill the *Taz*'s recommendation. The Maharsham is essentially saying that if the *Taz* is right, then this stringency is not much of an issue at all.

108. *Yoreh De'ah* 198:35 and 39.

109. YD 198:38.

110. YD 198:35, *Bi'urim* s.v. *vi-yesh mi she-omer.*

However, the *Shakh* argues[111] that the *Taz* misunderstood the rule of "*mayim makdimim*". He explains that not only is it the case that the feet originally did come into contact with *mikveh* water, but it is also assumed that there is still a connection between the *mikveh* water and the water beneath her feet. The concern about the wrinkles is that even if the *mikveh* water did originally touch those areas, the wrinkle will be so deep that the original water will not remain in contact with the rest of the *mikveh* water, and therefore the skin inside that wrinkle will not be in contact with the main body of *mikveh* water and the *tevilah* will not be valid. In practice, women are instructed to avoid creating these wrinkles, but after the fact there are many grounds for leniency.

The *Shakh*[112] points out that a *Mishnah*[113] teaches that tightening the lips is problematic. Some argue that the problem is that sealing off the lips prevents water from entering the mouth and creates a situation where the *beit ha-setarim* are not even potentially able to receive water. Others claim that if one tightens her mouth too much it will make part of the lips inaccessible to water. Either way, women have to be more careful about not tightening their lips too much because that could disqualify the *tevilah*.

Although it would appear that the issues involved are matters of concern on a Rabbinic level (because they involve a *mi'ut ha-makpid*, or even *eino makpid*), *Acharonim* take two different tracks in claiming that issues of Torah law may be involved:

1. The *Sidrei Taharah*[114] suggests that a *chatzitzah* which is not *rov* is inconsequential on the Biblical level, based on the general principles of *rov, mi'ut*, and *bitul* (negation by the majority). In other words, the Torah does not recognize a *chatzitzah* that only covers a minority of the body, because by Torah law, the minority is nullified by the majority. If that is the case, then perhaps the Torah is only lenient in cases of *mi'ut* when an external thing is

111. *Nekuddat HaKesef* to *Taz*, 198:38.
112. YD 198:51.
113. *Mikva'ot* 8:5.
114. YD 198:1.

blocking an otherwise accessible part of the body, but not when some part of the body makes another part of body inaccessible, such as when the lips are pursed. This is because, although the Torah views a small piece of dirt as negated, it will not view a small portion of the body (the portion that is interfering) as negated. In other words, the *Sidrei Taharah* understands *bitul* to be effective by equating the object with a part of the body. If, however, even once considered a part of the body it is still an interfering element, *bitul* does not accomplish anything.

2. The *Kiryat Sefer*[115] writes that the *mi'ut* is only inconsequential on a Torah level when it is not placed there specifically to keep out water, but is rather there incidentally. However, if there was a *chatzitzah*, even a *mi'ut*, which was placed there specifically to keep out water, that would be a *chatzitzah* on a Biblical level. The *Badei HaShulchan* notes that, according to this *Kiryat Sefer*, if a woman tightens her lips specifically to keep water out of her mouth that would be a *chatzitzah* on a Biblical level. Nonetheless, he questions if this opinion of the *Kiryat Sefer* is actually considered normative, in light of the fact that other major *poskim* are lenient to allow women to put cotton in their ears, as has been noted above. In practice, the view of the *Kiryat Sefer* does not appear to be accepted.[116]

115. *Mikva'ot*, ch. 2.

116. As an aside, this rule of *mi'ut* not posing a problem on a Biblical level seems comparable to the rule in the realm of *Eiruvin* that a gap that comprises a minority of a wall does not invalidate the *eiruv* on a Biblical level. However, R. Moshe Feinstein (*Responsa Iggerot Moshe*, v, 28) maintains that this only holds true if one builds the walls of the *eiruv* with no gaps, and then a part of the wall falls; however, if the wall was built intentionally with a gap then it would be invalid even by Torah law. The *Chazon Ish* (*Hilkhot Eiruvin* 107:5) asserts that since some streets may have rows of apartment buildings lining an entire side and the only breaks are for intersecting streets, then those breaks may not invalidate the *eiruv* on a Biblical level because they are only a *mi'ut* of the entire wall of buildings. R. Feinstein might argue that those breaks do invalidate the *eiruv* because they are there specifically for people to be able to walk through. The *Kiryat Sefer*'s claim in regard to *chatzitzah* seems

XVII. A WOMAN WHO REQUIRES ASSISTANCE DURING *TEVILAH*

A woman who is handicapped or injured will often need assistance with *tevilah,* requiring someone to escort her into the *mikveh* and even support her while she is in the *mikveh.* However, that reality is faced with two possible halakhic challenges:

1. As the *Badei HaShulchan*[117] notes, many *poskim* feel that there is potentially an issue of *chatzitzah,* presumably on a Rabbinic level (if the helper is only touching a minority of her body).
2. Some *Rishonim* claim that there is possibly a problem on a Biblical level. According to these *Rishonim,* it is possible that *halakhah* views it as part of the woman is outside the *mikveh* during *tevilah,* and the *tevilah* is invalid on a Biblical level.

In considering this situation, the *Mishnah*[118] suggests that the helper first wash her hands in water; then, when she touches the handicapped or injured woman under the water, there is no problem of *chatzitzah,* because the areas in which they are touching are being exposed to the water on the helper's hands (essentially a form of *mayim makdimim*). R. Shimon suggests that the helper simply not hold on very tightly; it would then be as if she is a *davar rafui,* which is not a *chatzitzah,* as was discussed earlier. Although it could be understood that these two suggestions complement one another, the *Rishonim* assume that they are mutually exclusive, and that there is a dispute being recorded. Further, *Rishonim* argue regarding what this dispute is:

1. The Rambam[119] feels that the first solution works according to all opinions, while R. Shimon was even more lenient than the first opinion. According to the Rambam, the author of the first

very similar to R. Feinstein's position in regard to *Eiruvin,* in that they both feel the leniency only applies when the problematic *mi'ut* is not created intentionally. However, in practice, it seems that neither view is followed.

117. YD 198:28, *Bi'urim,* s.v. *lo ta'achoz.*

118. *Mikva'ot* 8:5.

119. *Hilkhot Mikva'ot,* 2:11.

opinion would not accept R. Shimon's leniency, because it is too difficult to guarantee that the grasp will indeed be loose. This causes a problem in both directions: on one hand, if the helper holds on too tight, she could create a *chatzitzah*; but if she holds on too loosely, then that defeats the whole purpose of her being there to support the injured woman.

2. The Rashba,[120] however, assumes that R. Shimon's opinion is undisputed; R. Shimon, however, rejects the first suggestion. This is because even if the helper washes her hands in water beforehand, her hands are still *chatzitzot* if she holds on too tight.[121]

According to the Rashba, then, there are three levels:

1. if she holds on very loosely, this is acceptable to all opinions;
2. if she holds on very tightly, this is unacceptable to all opinions, even if the helper rinses her hands before;
3. if she holds on with "medium looseness", the first opinion would maintain that washing her hands before will help, while R. Shimon believes this will not help.

The *Shulchan Arukh*[122] follows the view of the Rashba that levels a) and c) are valid. However, the *Shakh*[123] quotes the *Bach*[124] who argues that this dispute among the *Rishonim* was never really resolved, and thus suggests that the Rashba's views should not be followed against that of the *Rambam*. Rather, he suggests that the helper indeed wash her hands as the *Rambam* advocates. The *Badei HaShulchan*[125] points out that even this leniency can only be relied upon when the woman is really physically incapable of doing *tevilah* without someone helping her.

In the context of *tevilat keilim*, the Mordechai[126] states that the

120. *Torat HaBayit HaArukh* 7:7.
121. See *Mishmeret HaBayit*, ibid.
122. *Yoreh De'ah* 198:28.
123. YD 198:35, 36.
124. YD 198:27, s.v. *vi-haRashba.*
125. YD 198:213.
126. *Avodah Zarah* 859–860.

individual holding the utensil has to dip his hand in *mikveh* water to avoid *chatzitzah* problems; regular water will not suffice. The Rama[127] quotes this view; however, this seems to contradict a fundamental principle of the laws of *mikva'ot*, namely, that any water that touches the *mikveh* water automatically becomes *mikveh* water, regardless of its previous halakhic status. Accordingly, it would seem there should be no distinction between *mikveh* water and other water. R. Yonatan Eibshutz[128] explains the Mordechai's position as follows: even if one sticks his hand in *mikveh* water, if he takes his hand out of the *mikveh*, then the water on his hand is no longer considered *mikveh* water. Although most assumed that the Mordechai was instructing one to dip his hand in the water and then take it out, grab the utensil and then immerse it, R. Eibshutz maintains that this would actually not be effective according to the Mordechai. Rather, one would be required to stick one hand in the water and leave it there, pick up the utensil with the dry hand and pass the utensil into the submerged hand for it to perform the *tevilah*. To be sure, *tevilat keilim* done without this stringency is clearly valid, particularly as it is questionable as to whether the Mordechai's view is accepted, and, as some point out, the Rama in his citation of the Mordechai does not appear consistent with R. Eibshutz's approach.

Nonetheless, R. Eibshutz's instructions should still be followed to the degree possible. Therefore, the helper should try to have her hand under the water before she touches the woman, and it is possible to maneuver in such a way that this can be done safely and securely. However, if this approach cannot be followed for whatever reason, there are valid positions upon which to rely.

XVIII. NOT PUBLICIZING *MIKVEH* ATTENDANCE

The Rama[129] states that a woman should be discreet about going to *mikveh*, as the details of a woman's status are a private matter. However, in case of need, a woman may tell a third party; the Rama's intention

127. YD 120:2.
128. *Matteh Yehonatan* to YD ibid.
129. *Yoreh De'ah* 198:48.

is that those whom have no reason to tell others shouldn't be sharing intimate information purposelessly.

The *Badei HaShulchan*[130] adds that the Rama limited publicizing the actual *tevilah*; however, if observing certain customs, such as not eating meat on that day, will be conspicuous, there is no need to relax these observances even if it will be apparent that she will go to the *mikveh* that night. R. Moshe Feinstein notes[131] similarly that historically, there was a custom for a woman to wear specific clothes during her time of *niddah*, in which case, reasons R. Moshe, everyone would surely know that she went to *mikveh* when she resumed wearing her regular clothes. The observance of such a custom would not be limited by the Rama's proscription. R. Moshe further ruled that that woman who is due to go to the *mikveh* Friday night may go to shul even though her lack of make-up will clearly indicate that she will be going to the *mikveh* later that night.

XIX. SITUATIONS WHEN A *BERAKHAH* ON *TEVILAH* MAY NOT BE REQUIRED

A woman is generally required to make a *berakhah* prior to her *tevilah*, reciting *"asher kid'shanu bi-mitzvotav vi-tzivanu al ha-tevilah"*. However, there is some uncertainty surrounding a case where the very need for immersion is a dispute amongst the *poskim*, and is thus considered a *safek*. While many *poskim* write that in such a case the woman immersing should not make a *berakhah*, the *Arukh HaShulchan*[132] writes that the woman should indeed make the *berakhah*.

A related discussion revolves around a woman who is going to the *mikveh* as a result of a *ketem*. Some argue that since the original rationale for *ketamim* was a *safek*, the consequent *tevilah* should be treated as one characterized by *safek*; however, others maintain that the original rationale notwithstanding, *ketamim* are a bona fide Rabbinic-level *tumah*, and any resultant immersion would warrant a *berakhah*.

The *Chatam Sofer*[133] discusses the question of what a woman

130. YD 198:24, *Bi'urim*, s.v. *vi-minhag*.
131. *Responsa Iggerot Moshe*, YD II, 77.
132. *Yoreh De'ah* 200:1.
133. *Responsa*, II, YD, 191.

should do with regards to the *berakhah* when her immersion is a function of *minhag,* such as *dam tohar,* and not unequivocal *halakhah* or *safek.* This question is related to a broader discussion about the propriety of reciting *berakhot* on a *minhag.* The general practice seems to be that women do make the *berakhah* in this situation. In fact, there is a widespread approach that women generally make a *berakhah* on all *tevilot,* even for a *safek.* It is likely that *rabbanim* who advocate thusly are concerned that if people are told not to make the *berakhah,* they will treat the *tevilah* lightly.

XX. AT WHICH POINT THE *BERAKHAH* IS RECITED

The *Tosafot* present a dispute as to whether the *berakhah* should be made prior to *tevilah* or afterwards. As a rule, *berakhot* which accompany the performance of *mitzvot* are recited prior to their performance; however, the Talmud[134] states that this is not possible for *tevilah,* because the person immersing cannot make the *berakhah* beforehand. *Tosafot*[135] explain this statement in two ways:

1. This statement of the Talmud refers exclusively to a convert who, prior to his *tevilah,* isn't in a position to make a *berakhah,* because the prospective convert is not Jewish until after the *tevilah;* a *niddah,* by contrast, can and should make the *berakhah* before her *tevilah.*
2. The Ri maintains that Chazal, for the sake of uniformity, required all *berakhot* on *tevilah* to be recited after, similar to the *tevilah* of a convert.

The *Shulchan Arukh*[136] rules that the *berakhah* should be recited beforehand, while the Rama[137] records that the *minhag* is to make the *berakhah* after the *tevilah.* Therefore, Sefardim, following the ruling of the *Shulchan*

134. *Pesachim* 7b.
135. Ibid, s.v. *al ha-tevilah.*
136. *Yoreh De'ah* 200:1.
137. Ibid.

Arukh, should make the *berakhah* before *tevilah*, and Ashkenazim, in accordance with the Rama's ruling, should make the *berakhah* afterwards.

There is a *minhag* amongst Ashkenazim to immerse twice, that is, to dip, make the *berakhah*, and dip again. In this way, women can be conducting themselves in accordance with the opinion of both the *Shulchan Arukh* and the Rama, although it is not clear what the second *tevilah* accomplishes.[138] Some instruct the women to stipulate that if the *halakhah* is really in accordance with the view of the Rama, the second *tevilah* is unnecessary; if the *halakhah* is really in agreement with the *Shulchan Arukh*'s ruling, then only the second *tevilah* should count. However, it is preferable to immerse without getting involved with such calculations, as they may prove to be more detrimental than helpful.[139] Additionally, women have the *minhag* to immerse a third time, and this is the standard *minhag*.

XXI. CONCEALING THE *MAKOM HAERVAH* DURING THE *BERAKHAH*

It is generally assumed that one reciting *berakhot* must be clothed. For those who follow the *Shulchan Arukh* and make the *berakhah* before the *tevilah*, the procedure is straightforward: one could make the *berakhah*, disrobe, and then immerse themselves. However, for those who follow the Rama and make the *berakhah* after the *tevilah*, the question arises as to whether the woman may make the *berakhah* while she is still unclothed in the water.

Strictly speaking, there are technically two points that must be satisfied to make a *berakhah*: 1) the *makom ha-ervah* must be covered, and 2) there should not be a direct line between the heart and the *makom ha-ervah*.

While the woman is in the water, the first condition is fulfilled. Furthermore, the *Shakh*[140] and *Taz*[141] both rule that, for physiological reasons, the second condition is not applicable to women. Accordingly,

138. Possibly, the additional *tevilah* is to satisfy the view of the *Maharsham* mentioned above.

139. See *Badei HaShulchan*, 200:13, *Bi'urim*, s.v. *she-li-achar ha-tevilah*, and *tziyunim* 47 and 48.

140. YD 200:1.

141. YD 200:3.

the *Shakh* and *Taz* write that if the water is up to the woman's neck, she may recite the *berakhah*. Others recommend that women be more stringent and wrap their arms around themselves, but, in terms of the basic *halakhah*, the view of the *Shakh* and the *Taz* may be relied upon.

XXII. FIRST ENCOUNTER UPON LEAVING THE *MIKVEH*

The Rama[142] writes that a woman should first encounter something *tahor* when she emerges from the *mikveh*, and if she encounters something *tamei*, such as a pig or a dog, she should repeat the *tevilah*. This usually does not occur, as a woman typically encounters the *mikveh* attendants or another woman in the waiting room upon emerging from the *mikveh*.

XXIII. INDICATING THAT THE *TEVILAH* HAS BEEN PERFORMED

The Talmud[143] states that a husband should not be with his wife until she tells him that she has immersed[144] and assures him that her *niddah* status has been removed. Accordingly, the *Shulchan Arukh*[145] rules that a woman must indicate verbally that she has in fact immersed in a *mikveh*. However, the *Chavot Da'at*[146] writes that any indication on her part, e.g. lying down next to her husband, is sufficient, maintaining that such assurances need not be verbal.[147] Even according to the *Chavot Da'at*, if a husband comes home on what was supposed to be the *tevilah* night and finds his wife asleep, he wouldn't be permitted to touch her before she confirms that she indeed went to the *mikveh*.

The *Arukh HaShulchan*[148] asserts that even according to those who require a verbal indication, the word "*tavalti*" need not be used. Moreover, if a husband and wife have a standard, non-verbal communication,

142. *Yoreh De'ah* 198:48.
143. *Niddah* 11b.
144. The Talmud uses the phrase "*tehorah ani*" ("I am pure") while the *Shulchan Arukh* has "*tavalti*" ("I have immersed").
145. *Yoreh De'ah* 185:1.
146. YD 195, *Chiddushim*, 1.
147. There is a similar, possibly related dispute whether a woman must verbally assure her husband that she has done a *bedikah* on a day which is a *veset*.
148. YD 185:4.

e.g. the wife handing her husband the car keys when she returns home, that is sufficient as well.

XXIV. NOT TO BATHE OR SHOWER IMMEDIATELY AFTER *TEVILAH*

The Talmud[149] notes that two thousand years ago people had to go to caves and all sorts of dirty places for *tevilah,* and they used to run to the bathhouses when they emerged. Unfortunately, the less knowledgeable people began to assume that it was the bathhouse water that was making them clean and *tehorah,* and stopped going to the actual places of valid *tevilah* caves altogether. Therefore, Chazal decided that whoever went to the bathhouse after *tevilah* continued to have a status of *tamei.*

The Rama[150]quotes from the Mordechai[151] that just as people in the times of the Talmud could not, for example, eat *terumah* under those circumstances, so too women who rush to the shower or bath after *tevilah* are acting inappropriately. The Rama quotes a *minhag* among Ashkenazim for women not to shower or bathe after *tevilah* for this reason. However, most of the *Rishonim,* including the *Shulchan Arukh,* do not say anything at all about not rushing to shower, presumably because that was only a stringency that was instituted for *terumah,* and it is not necessary in the contemporary era to create new stringencies. Nonetheless, the Rama quotes this *minhag* and women do follow it.[152]

Poskim have suggested various guidelines regarding this practice. Some *poskim*[153] maintain that the woman should not go straight from the *mikveh* into one of the baths or showers within the *mikveh* building itself, but can shower once she gets home. Others feel that women should not bathe for the rest of that night. It is difficult to set definite parameters on this point, as the practice is a *minhag* that most *Rishonim* likely did not observe.

149. *Shabbat* 14a.
150. *Yoreh De'ah* 201:75.
151. *Shevuot, remez* 750.
152. The Vilna Gaon (*Bi'ur HaGra,* YD 201:127), however, disagrees.
153. See *Mareh Kohen,* p. 108, n109, citing R. Shlomo Zalman Auerbach, and *Responsa Shevet HaLevi,* V, 125, who writes that the woman can shower once the couple has touched each other.

Notes and Halakhic Rulings by Rabbi Hershel Schachter

Nathan and Vivian Fink
Distinguished Professor of Talmud, RIETS
Rosh Kollel, Adina and Marcos Katz Kollel, RIETS

Chap. 3: The "Uterus Opening" and its Ramifications

The husband should be stringent to not touch his wife once she is on the delivery table because she may be at the point where she cannot walk on her own any more.

Water breaking is not an indication that the woman is *teme'ah.*

If the doctor checks the dilation of the woman and he finds blood on the glove, then the woman is forbidden to her husband.

Chap. 10: The Different Colors of "Blood"

If one could inject a substance into the woman's system which would cause a discoloration of the *dam niddah* then it could be considered *tahor*. Blood is only deemed as *tamei* if it emerges from the body as red and changes color when it comes into the *bayit ha-chitzon*; however, if the color was not red when it left the *bayit ha-penimi,* then the blood would not be *tamei.* (See *Ta Chazi,* #2).

Chap. 11: Determining the Color of Blood Stains

Even in contemporary times, a *rav* may not decide the status of a *mareh dam* at night. The Talmud requires sunlight because of the characteristics that sunlight applies to the *dam*. A very powerful or clear light will not allow the blood to be as clear as the Talmud intends the blood to appear.

If a woman loses the *bedikah* cloth, and she had a *safek* regarding the status of the cloth, then she becomes forbidden to her husband, since we must assume that the color was a *mareh teme'ah*. Therefore, she must begin to count *shivah nekiyim* over again. Even if the woman performed a clean *hefsek taharah*, this new *bedikah* creates a new *safek* and she may be *teme'ah*.

A ruling regarding a *mareh* is considered a *hora'at talmid chakham*, and therefore the woman is not allowed to ask another *rav* to examine her *bedikah* cloth. (See *Responsa Divrei Chaim*, 81.)

There are some who maintain that the only color which is *teme'ah* is "fire-engine red", however, this is not the generally accepted opinion and there are other shades of red which would make a woman *teme'ah*.

Chap. 13: Halakhic Reliance Upon Medical Opinion

The *Mishnah* (*Niddah* 61b) states that we pass seven ingredients over a *ketem* in order to determine if it is *dam niddah*. This would indicate that one is allowed to rely on science to determine if blood is *dam min ha-mekor* or *dam makkah*; in practice, this is acceptable (see *Responsa Shevet HaLevi*, X, 141).

Chap. 14: *Dam Betulim* – Hymenal Blood

A *kallah* may go to the doctor before or after the wedding and have the *betulim* removed so that she does not become *teme'ah* after *bi'ah rishonah*.

Chap. 15: *Dam Chimud*

The *Pitchei Teshuvah* (YD 192:6) notes that a new issue of *dam chimud* arises if a wedding is canceled and not rescheduled immediately. However, if the wedding is simply rescheduled to another day, even if it is a few days before the set wedding date, this does not create a new issue of *dam chimud*.

Chap. 20: *Hefsek Taharah*

We are not stringent regarding a *kallah* waiting five days before her *hefsek taharah*; as soon as she stops bleeding she can begin to count *shivah nekiyim*.

Chap. 23: The *Mokh Dachuk*

R. Moshe Feinstein ruled (see *Halachos of Niddah* page 77 note 168) that the stringency of a *mokh* for all of *bein ha-shemashot* is only applicable if the woman knows there was blood earlier on the fifth day. Therefore, R. Moshe rules that if the woman is undergoing discomfort, and she did not bleed on the day of the *hefsek taharah*, she can forgo the *mokh kol bein ha-shemashot*.

Chap. 30: *Harchakot*

Mei-ikkar ha-din, shaking hands with an *ervah* is not prohibited because it is not *derekh chibbah*, and *negi'ah* that is not *derekh chibbah* is permitted with general *arayot* (see *Peri De'ah* in *Siftei Levi*, 195:20). However, it is always prohibited to touch one's wife who is a *niddah*, even when not *derekh chibbah*.

The leniency to pass babies to each other (see *Tashbetz*, 230) is very difficult to rely on. Regarding carrying a baby carriage, one should only be carried by the husband and wife together if there is a great necessity to do so.

The *Pitchei Teshuvah* (195:10) is uncertain about a man listening to the singing voice of his wife who is a *niddah*, out of concern that it may be categorized as "areas that are normally covered". In practice, one should be stringent on this matter.

When the wife is a *niddah*, the husband and wife should be stringent not to light the *havdalah* candle which the other spouse is holding, and not to smell the *besamim* which the other spouse is holding.

The wife should not turn the shower on for her husband, and she should not fill up a bath tub for her husband, or fill up a cup for *netilat yadayim* for her husband.

The *Pitchei Teshuvah* (195:19) quotes the *Chamudei Daniel*, who says that a woman should not go to shul during her days of *niddah*. This custom of the *Chamudei Daniel* is generally not followed nowadays.

Chap. 31: *Vestot*

The *Chazon Ish,* quoted in *Taharat Bat Yisrael* 9:1, maintains there is no need to observe the *onah* of the *Or Zarua,* because his view is based on a different text of the Talmud.

It is proper to be stringent for the *onah beinonit* of the *Chokhmat Adam* (112:5), and therefore the couple should separate on both the 30th and 31st days.

If a woman takes a pill which removes her period, then we can rely on the doctors and can assume that she is *mesuleket damim* (not subject to bleeding). The husband and wife do not have to be concerned for previous *vestot* regarding *bedikot* and relations. (See *Responsa Minchat Yitzchak* I, 127).

In contemporary times, there are pregnancy tests which can confirm that the woman is pregnant even within the first three months. Nevertheless, a woman should still be stringent for the previous *vestot* from before she took the test. This is in accordance with the view of R. Akiva Eiger (*Responsa,* 128) against that of R. Moshe Feinstein (*Responsa Iggerot Moshe,* YD II, 52). This is also the opinion of the *Sidrei Taharah* (194:7).

Chap. 33: Immersion during the Daytime

The Talmud (*Niddah* 67b) states that women immerse on the eighth day, on account of danger present at night due to lions and thieves, or the cold, or if there was danger of falling on the way to the *mikveh,* or if the gatekeepers closed the gates to the city at night. It would appear from the Talmud that the only type of need that can justify daytime immersion is a communal need, but not a private need. This is also brought by the *Pitchei Teshuvah* (197:11) in the name of the *Chamudei Daniel.* This is, however, against the understanding of the Rambam (*Hilkhot Issurei Bi'ah* 4:8), who maintains that personal issues can be enough to justify daytime immersion; this view is followed by the *Sedei Chemed.*

Chap. 35: *Chatzizot*

If the woman comes to the *mikveh* on *Shabbat* without having cut her nails, a non-Jewish woman should be asked to cut her nails. If that option is not available, she must wait to go to the *mikveh* until *motza'ei Shabbat.*

The *Pitchei Teshuvah* (YD 184:27 and 185:1) asserts that a man must always ask his wife if she is a *niddah* before the first time after the *mikveh,* even if she is lying with him in bed. This is difficult, as the self evident indication (*umdena*) of lying in bed with her husband should be enough to convey to him her permissible status.

It is proper to be stringent for the view of the Rama who rules that a woman should not shower after the *mikveh* until the following nightfall (See *Ginat Egoz,* #21).

Notes and Halakhic Rulings by Rabbi Mordechai Willig

Rabbi Dr. Sol Roth Professor of Talmud and Contemporary Halachah, RIETS
Rosh Kollel, Bella and Harry Wexner Kollel Elyon, RIETS
Rav, Young Israel of Riverdale, NY

Chap 1. Determining the Status of *Niddah*

The *Arukh HaShulchan* assumes that women today are distracted and therefore unaware of the sensation that must accompany *niddah* blood, similar to urination. Nothing has changed since the times of the *Gemara* except for this lack of awareness.

This position is difficult. The *Gemara* (*Niddah* 3a) states that a woman awakens from her sleep when the sensation of *niddah* blood occurs. Women today generally do not awaken. This change cannot be attributed to distraction.

If the views of the Maharam Shick and *Noda BiYehudah* are not accepted, and the sensations mentioned by the Rambam and the *Terumat HaDeshen* are no longer felt, why is there a *niddah* by Torah law today?

The Rashba (*Niddah* 57b) writes that it is the normal way of women to feel sensation when *niddah* blood appears. One can suggest that if, nowadays, it is normal to have a period without the sensation of earlier generations, the woman is a *niddah* by Torah law since she sees blood normally.

Nonetheless, a stain is only rabbinic and the classic leniencies apply. A normal woman has a monthly flow which is a normal period. Stains are generally not the normal way of a woman's period, and do not create *niddah* by Torah law.

What if the normal way of a particular woman is to see a small amount? In *Kovetz Teshuvot* (1, 84), Rav Elyashiv cites the Rambam (*Hilkhot Issurei Bi'ah* 4:1), that a newborn can be a *niddah* by Torah law, if a small amount of blood is found. Since this is the normal way that newborns bleed (and 7% do, according to medical sources), the newborn is a *niddah* by Torah law.

A typical woman, who does experience a monthly flow, is a *niddah* by Torah law at that point. Pre-menstrual or mid-cycle staining are not her normal way of *niddah* blood.

Recently developed contraceptive methods, pills or IUDs, eliminate bleeding almost entirely. Often there is a "monthly drop" of blood. This cyclical drop is her normal way of bleeding, and may constitute *niddah* by Torah law. As such, the leniencies of stains may not apply.

Rav Elyashiv goes further. He rules that even though the sensations of the Maharam Shick and the *Noda BiYehudah,* namely, premenstrual cramps and a liquid flow, respectively, are not accepted as such, they are indicators of a normal way of *niddah* blood. Therefore, the blood makes her a *niddah* by Torah law, and the leniencies of stains do not apply (see *Mishmeret HaTaharah,* Ch. 1, end of fns 12, 14, 15).

Most authorities apply these leniencies even if the woman experienced cramps or felt a liquid flow. Apparently, if she has a significant monthly flow, the stains are not included in her normal way of bleeding which makes her a *niddah* by Torah law.

A tiny drop of blood on a *bedikah* cloth may create a Torah law of *niddah* as we are concerned that the woman perhaps confused the sensation of *niddah* blood with the pressure of the cloth.

This confusion is possible for the sensations of the Rambam and, possibly, the *Terumat HaDeshen*. If, today, sensation means the normal significant flow, this confusion is no longer possible.

Nonetheless, a drop on a *bedikah* cloth renders a woman a *niddah,* since the Rabbis of the Talmud were strict. Even though the reason, confusion with sensation, no longer applies, the Rabbinic edict is in full force. However, since there is no possibility of being a *niddah* by Torah law, there may be room for leniency when additional factors apply, as determined by a *rav*.

Chap. 3: The "Uterus Opening" and its Ramifications

In determining when the *niddah* status starts at childbirth, it is generally the case that when blood is seen, the status is in effect; however, it is possible that the observed blood is from the mucous plug, and that would be considered external, non-*niddah* blood. The doctor's judgment will determine which is the case.

Chap. 12: Blood from a Wound

The *sfek sfeika* of the Rama (YD 187:5) may be relied on for practical purposes.

Chap. 15: *Dam Chimud*

Regarding a *kallah* performing *bedikot* after the *tevilah* before the wedding, the Rama's view is that if the *tevilah* was done within four days of the consummation of the wedding, there is no need for any *bedikot*; if the *tevilah* was done more than four days prior, there may be a need.

Chap. 20: *Hefsek Taharah*

Regarding multiple *bedikot* before a *hefsek taharah,* and cleaning oneself out first: *le-khatchilah* one should wait five minutes in between *bedikot*; *bediavad,* there is room to be lenient without waiting significantly at all.

Chap. 24: *Bedikot* during *Shivah Nekiyim*

During *shivah nekiyim,* it is sufficient to do one *bedikah* a day *le-khatchilah,* in accordance with the view of the Ramban, the Rashba, and the Rosh that the *Mishnah* (*Niddah* 11a) that mentions two daily *bedikot* is referring to the observance of the laws of *tumah* and *taharah*. The position of the *Shulchan Arukh* (196:4) that requires two daily *bedikot le-khatchilah* is based on the Mordechai (*Hilkhot Niddah* #735). From the words of the Mordechai, it is evident that he is referencing a different social reality, in which the women were mostly found at home and had additional assistance in raising the children; thus, they were able to perform additional *bedikot* in an unpressured environment. In the contemporary setting, however, women are more likely to be found outside the house, or in other less conducive situations, and the risk of irritation from a pressurized *bedikah* is greater. Accordingly, the standard of one daily *bedikah* is appropriate even *le-khatchilah*. (See the journal *Kol Tzvi*, vol. X–XI, pp. 409–410)

If one finds blood on a *bedikah* cloth during the *shivah nekiyim*, and thus must restart the count, a *mokh* is not required, as there is no "initial bleeding" as is the case before the *shivah nekiyim* begin.

Chap. 26: Counting the "*Shivah Nekiyim*"

Regarding the stringency of the *Me'il Tzedakah*, one need only take this view into account if the woman completely was *meisiach da'at* (removed her attention from the matter) and did so for more than a full 24 hours.

Chap. 30: *Harchakot*

A couple may be lenient to pass a baby to one another during *niddah*, as the baby is considered a *choleh* whose needs justify such leniency. This is particularly indicated in light of the reality that couples that take a stringent stand on this matter may actually endanger the baby by placing it on the floor, on top of a car, etc, in ways that are unsafe.

Chap. 31: *Vestot*

1. Regarding the possibility of pre-period staining being considered a *veset ha-guf*, if indeed the woman always has stains before, it may be significant in both directions, *le-kula* and *le-chumra*.
2. A *bedikah* is not required for a *veset she-eino kavu'a*, as indicated by the *Beit Yosef* (YD 184). (See *Kol Tzvi*, ibid, p. 403–405).

3. It seems that the rule that a *ketem* does not have the status of a *techilat re'iyat dam* is an absolute one.
4. Concerning the question of when *onah beinonit* is, and the dispute between the *Chavot Da'at* and the *Shakh,* the *perishah* should take place on day 30, while the *bedikah* should be done on day 31 (see *Kol Tzvi,* ibid, pp. 405–406).
5. It is not necessary to perform *bedikot* to establish that the woman is not *ro'ah dam machamat tashmish,* in accordance with the view of the *Shakh* and R. Moshe Feinstein.

Chap. 33: Immersion during the Daytime

Regarding *tevilah* during the day on the seventh day, one should only be lenient to allow this if otherwise one will be unable to immerse for three days in a row afterward (e.g. a three day yom tov follows).

Chap. 34: Cleansing before Immersion: *Chafifah*

It is proper to floss prior to *tevilah* if the woman is accustomed to flossing. If, however, there is reason to fear that the floss will get stuck in the teeth, it is better not to.

Chap. 35: *Chatzitzot*

1. If a woman wishes to immerse with a rabbinic-level *chatzitzah,* the attendant should allow her to, but not declare the *tevilah* kosher.
2. A woman may shower following her *tevilah* once she has done some action to indicate that she is *tehorah.*

Notes and Halakhic Rulings by Rabbi Yaakov Neuburger

Rosh Yeshiva, RIETS
Rav, Cong. Beth Abraham, Bergenfield, NJ

סימן ט״ו אות ב. בקשר לדין יחוד אצל כלה שפרסה נדה קודם שטבלה אי אסור מדין תורה או מדין דרבנן, שמשמע מלשון הרמב״ם (הל׳ איסורי ביאה כב:א–ב) שסו׳ שאסור מדאו׳ מדברי קבלה, ומאידך מלשון התוס׳ (סוטה ז., ד״ה נדה שהיא בכרת) שאיסורו גזירת חז״ל. ועי׳ בשו״ת ציץ אליעזר (ח״ו סי׳ מ פרק כה אות ג–ד) שהראה כדרכו בקודש שרוב הפוסקים סו׳ שרוב הראשונים סו׳ שהיא גזרה דרבנן. ועי׳ בחזו״א (אהע״ז סי׳ לד, סוף אות ג) שסו׳ שהיא גזרה מדרבנן וראיתו ממה שאל״כ לא היינו מקילין ביום לדעת הראב״ד ועוד הביא ראי׳ שכן סו׳ הרמ״א ממה שמביא הרמ״א דברי תה״ד שיש להקל במי שהי׳ יכול לבעול ולא בעל.

ולפ״ז סו׳ הגראי״ו (צ״א שם) שיש מקום להקל במי שהערה או פחות ומותר להם לבעול שנית ופרסה נדה קודם לזה שמותרים ביחוד אע״ג שמה שבאה עלי׳ אינה נחשבת כביאה גמורה לגבי דין דם בתולים.

סימן ט״ו אות ד. כלה שפרסה נדה או שעוד לא טבלה שנוהגים ע״פ מנהגו של הרמ״א להחמיר כרא״ש וכראב״ד. שמעתי מא׳ מגדולי הפוסקים שיש קבלה מהחזו״א שיש להורות לנהוג כרא״ש בין ביום ובין בלילה, וחד מש״ב שאל הגרשז״א ואישר אמתת הקבלה.

ונראה שביאר הוראתו בחזו״א אהע״ז סי׳ לד, אות ג. שלא בא לחלוק על מנהגו של הרמ״א אלא שביאר שמה שהרמ״א מסיים ״והמנהג ליקח קטן אצל החתן וקטנה אצל הכלה ואין

מתיחדין ביום בלא קטן או קטנה" שאין כוונתו להחמיר כראב"ד וכרא"ש אלא להורות שנוהגים כשיטת הרא"ש ולמה שצריכים עוד שמירה בלילה לכל חשש יחוד. ומה שיש איש ואשה או קטן וקטנה יש ב' שמירות בלילה לכאו"א (והיינו אפי' לשומרים, שהרי הבעל שומר שאשתו עמו ואשה שומרת שאימת בעלה עלי') ועוד שנחלקו הראשונים כמה בעינן לכל שמירה ולמרדכי, מו"ד בד"מ, סגי באחד עם הבעל אפי' לדעת הראב"ד. וא"כ ע"י מנהגו של הרמ"א יוצאים דעתו של הראב"ד אליבא דמרדכי ודעתו של הרא"ש לכל הדעות וסו' שלא צריכים להחמיר לדעתו לראב"ד אליבא דמ"ד שבעינן שנים לכל שמירה שכולי האי ל"צ להחמיר.

ואמנם לא מצאתי לו חבר בין מו"ר וגדולי הפוסקים שמורים למעשה להקל כדברי הרא"ש בלילה, הלא כדי הוא החזו"א וכו' ובפרט בדין שלרוב הפוסקים הוא גזרה דרבנן (עי' צ"א ח"ו סי' מ, כה:ג), ובמיוחד אליבא דראב"ד (שאליבי' סו' להחמיר) הוי לכו"ע דין דרבנן ומלשון הרמ"א בד"מ משמע שסו' כחשבון של החזו"א, ובדבר שמאד קשה על חתן וכלה ובתקופה מאד עדינה לזוג צעיר.

סימן י"ט אות ה. בענין אלו שקשים להן להגיע להכשר טבילה בזמן שיכולות להתעבר, עי' בשו"ת הר צבי (יו"ד סי' קנז) שכדי שתבוא לידי הריון יש להקל ולהתחיל השבעה נקיים ביום ה' מכיון שהשל"ה (מו"ד בפתח"ת) התיר להתחיל למנות ז' נקיים מיום ה' למי שבא ליל טבילתה בליל שבת שלאחר יו"ט, ואם היא תתחיל למנות מיום ה' תקרב הטבילה לחפיפה. וסו' הגרצ"פ שבודאי יסכים השל"ה להקל נגד חומרת הרמ"א ולהתחיל למנות ביום ה' כדי ששתבוא להריון.

שוב העלה הגרצ"פ (שם, וכן במנח"י ח"ג סי' פה) שאשה שראייתה יום או יומים וקשה לה ליכנס להריון מטעם שהיא עוד לא טבלה קודם הביוץ, אמנם א"א להתחיל למנות קודם יום ה' מטעם חשש פליטת ש"ז ואפי' אם נמנעו מלשמש עדין גוזרים לא שמש אטו שמש כדביאר הש"ך (סי' קצו), והציע בזה שהיא תטבול לסירוגין כלו' שלא תטבול לחודש שלם וע"ז אין לגזור לא שימש אטו שימש, ע"ש.

וכשזכיתי לשמוע שיעורי הגר"ש וואזנר שליט"א העלה אחד אם כדי להחמיר למי שצרך להקדים יום אחד כדי שהביוץ יבוא יום קודם הטבילה ויכולה להתחיל למנות ביום ה' כנ"ל אם להחמיר לטבול בסירוגין כדי להקל על חומרת התרה"ד, ודחה הגר"ש ההצעה בב' ידיו.

סימן יט אות ה. והנה יש להעלות על שולחן מלכים אם יש מקום להקל בזוג שמאיזו סיבות כשתטבול תהי' מותרת רק ליום או יומים וקשה עליהן ויש לחוש לשלום בית ולחוש שאולי יבואו להיות נכשלים ח"ו ואם יהיו מותרים לעוד יום אולי יעזור להם, ולכאורה יותר יש לדחוק מחשש שיכשלו או שלום ביתם שניהם יותר מחשש הרחקת חפיפה לטבילה.

סימן יט אות ה. ועוד יש להעלות על שולחן מלכים לזוג שאין להם מקוה קרובה לבית, וליל טבילתם בליל ששי ושבת ה"ה ערב יו"ט וידחו ליל טבילתם ליומים או שלוש אם להחמיר ולדחות אם להקל כשיטת הגרמ"פ ולטבול ביום ששי כחידושו של החת"ס או אם להקל כשאפשר שלא להחמיר כחומרת החמשה ימים של התרוה"ד ולהתחיל למנות יום קודם. וממו"ר ראיתי להקל לזה כשיטת הגרמ"פ כלו' שבזה יש מקום להקל נגד תקנת חז"ל ע"פ שיטת הר"ת והגאונים.

ולכאורה יותר קל להקל נגד הוראת הרמ"א להחמיר לחומרתו של התרה"ד שכבר סלל לנו השל"ה הדרך בזה ומו"ד בפת"ח ובנו עליו הפוסקים כנ"ל.

סימן יט אות ה. בהזרעה מלאכותית קודם יום שביעי לשבעה ימי נקיים נחלקו מו"ר אם להחמיר ולחוש לפליטת ש"ז ולא למנות ד' ימים לאחר ההזרעה. המקילים סו' שכשמזריעים ע"י הזרעה מלאכותית מכניסים הזרע ע"י שפופרת לתוך הרחם ושונה מביאה שמכניסים הזרע לתוך הפרוזדור ואח"כ נמשך הזרע לתוך הרחם. וכשדנתי בדבר עם הרופא המומחה ובר חכים, ידידי הדגול דר. טשאדנאף נ"י הוסיף עוד לחלק שמכניסים כמויות קטנות לתוך הרחם, שמוציאים הזרע מכל מה שמלוה אותן ושונה מזרע לאחר ביאה שנכנס ע"י עוד נוזלים מהגוף.

ומאידך יש מקום להחמיר שלא למנות יום אחד, מכיון שכשמכניסים הזרע לתוך השפופרת, מכניסים השפופרת לתוך מין כוס מלאה זרע וקצת זרע נדבק בשפופרת מבחוץ, ושוב כשמוציאים הזרע לתוך הרחם ג"כ נדבק קצת זרע בעובי השפופרת. וא"כ כשמוציאיים השפופרת מהאשה מוציאים עם השפופרת קצת שכ"ז, ולמה לא נחוש לפליטת שכ"ז שיוצא ע"י השפופרת. ומה שדם היוצא ע"י שפופרת אינה מטמאה היינו מגזה"כ אצל דם (עי' רמב"ם הל' איסורי ביאה) ואינו שייך לכאורה לפליטת ש"ז.

וע"ע בשיעורי שבה"ל (קצו:יב:ג) שהכריע שיש לבדוק בימים אלו לכתחילה מטעם שיטת המעיל צדקה שהיסח הדעת מבטל הנקיים שספרה.

סימן מראות דמים: הוראות לאשה: לענ"ד יש להורות לכלה שלא להחמיר מטעם מראה כתם או עד בדיקה מבלי להראות למו"צ (אלא אם אדום כרמזור או כאגבניה באמצע העד ונמצא בהתחלת ז' נקיים), מכיון שיש שלומדות או שהבינו שעדי בדיקה צריכים להיות נקיים לגמרי מכל צבע וזו טעות. עוד סבה להראות קודם שמחמירות מכיון שלפעמים יש לכלוך ושערות אדומות ומו"צ יבחין ויורה כפי דרכו ולפעמים יחוש למראה הבאה ממכה ומו"צ יכול להדריך השואלת לבדוק יותר.

גם מו"צ שמקיל על מראה חום פשוט, יש לו להורות לכלה לשאול על כל מראה חום שמן הנסיון יש שלא מבחינים בין חום פשוט וחום שמעורב בה מראה אדמומית וצריכים שיורו בה מו"צ. וגם ידוע שאם מסתכלים במראה חום מעורב אדום ע"י אור פלורסינט יבואו להקל במקום שהרבה סו' להחמיר.

ובמשך הזמן יש להדריך לאשה כפי רצונה ודרכה, שמי שרוצה לשאול על כל מראה ומראה, לעודדה אם נוח לה וזו רצונה, ואם רוצה להיות יותר עצמאי וטירחא לה לשאול על כל צבע, לתת לה הוראות על מיני חום כגון קפה עם חלב ועל צבע כלימון וכיו"ב.

סימן מראות דם: מיני אור: יש שסו' שלא צריכים להקפיד להסתכל לאור היום וגם יש לא חשים בכלל להסתכל מתוך הצל. וחילי' דבריהם מדברי התוה"ש (קפח:א) שביאר שמה שהשמיט המחבר כיצד ינהג החכם עצמו לראות ולא העתיק מה שמפורש בש"ס וברמב"ם לראות לאור היום לכתחילה, משום עכשיו שאנו לא מבחינים כמו שהיו מבחינים ובקל יכול לבחין מה לטהר ולה לטמא.

וממו"ר ראיתי שבמקום שאין צורך להורות בלילה, מקפידים להסתכל לאור החמה. ולכאורה יסודם בדעתו של הרמ"א (קצו:ד) "והבדיקה תהיה לאור היום ולא לאור הנר (תא"ו נכ"ו והרשב"א בת"ה), ובדיעבד מהני אפילו לאור הנר (כן משמע בב"י)." וגם התוה"ש בעצמו העיר על הרמ"א (ס"ק ט) שצבע הכתם נראה יותר ברור ביום. ועי' בביאור הגר"א ולכאורה ביאור דבריו שמה שמחמיר לכתחילה ומקיל בדיעבד אינו מטעם שבדיעבד סו' על מה שהצביע התוה"ש בשיטת המחבר אלא שסו' שכן יש להסיק מהסוגיא.

ולכאורה בנקודה זו אם לכתחילה יש לברר צבע הבדיקה לאור הנר נחלקו הרמב"ם והראב"ד והמחבר והרמ"א. עי' ברמב"ם (איסו"ב ה:יב) שהביא שבודקים לאור החמה לכתחילה ומוסיף שחכם יש לו טביעות עין מתי צריך לפסוק על ידי כל הכללים של ראית צבעים ומתי אינו צריך לכל הפרטים. והרמב"ם כתב (שם, יא:ג, יג) שמטמאים בכל מראה דמים אבל לא כתב בהדיא שלכן נשתנה הדין ומורים בכל אור ואור. והראב"ד (שם, ה:יב) סו' שאין להחמיר בפרטי בדיקת הצבע מכיון שכל מראה אדמומית טמאה. ואמנם שהס"ט הקשה על התוה"ש שאולי הראב"ד חולק על פרט אחר של הקפה, סוף כל סוף כתב "**כל** מה שכתב בזה אין בו הלכה למעשה שאין לנו עכשיו דם טהור אלא כל מראה אדמומית טמא." ומלשון התוה"ש משמע שגם הוא סו' שנחלקו המחבר והרמ"א בזה.

ונוסף למה שאנו נוהגים כרמ"א, עוד יש לדקדק בלשון התוה"ש בדעת המחבר ובלשון הערוה"ש שכתבו כן להקל מכיון שאנו מחמירים כפי פשטות לשון המחבר בכל מראה שאינו לבן וירוק. אמנם עי' בפתח"ת (ס"ק א,ב) שאנו דנים במראות חום ושעווה וצריכים עיון ודקדוק וא"כ לכאורה אפי' התוה"ש יודה לפי מנהגנו להחמיר.

ולענ"ד יש להוסיף מן הנסיון שמראה חום מעורב אדמומית לפעמים נראה האדמומית רק לאור החמה, ולכאורה לזה כיונו חז"ל להחמיר.

וז"ב דברי הרמ"א שאמנם שאנו מחמירים בכל צבע אדמומית אבל עדין צריכים לקבוע לאיזו אור קובעים אנו הצבעים.

וע"ע בערוה"ש (קפח:יא,טז) שכן כתב לדינא, "ודע דבמגילה [י"ד א] איתא בפשיטות דאין רואין דם בלילה ובנדה ספ"ב איתא דרואין הדם דווקא בין חמה לצל ידו כלומר נותן ידו כנגד החמה על הדם ועושה צל דבאופן זה המראה ברור בלי טעות וכל הפוסקים לא הזכירו זה כלל והטעם דדווקא בימיהם שהיו מבחינים בין דם לדם א"א לראות בלילה אבל האידנא דכל מראה אדום אסור ורק לבן וירוק כשר אין חילוק בין לילה ליום [ס"ט סק"א] וראיה לזה מרש"י במגילה שם שכתב וכי מראין דם בלילה אם טמא או טהור הלא צריך להבחין מראיתו אם מחמשה דמים הטמאים באשה עכ"ל הרי מפורש דדווקא בין הבחנה אדום לאדום צריך יום דווקא" ולמרות ראיתו לשיטת הס"ט שוב כתב בס"ק טז, "ובוודאי גם עתה נכון לראות דווקא ביום דכמה פעמים ראיתי בחוש דאינו דומה המראה ביום להמראה בלילה אך במקום ההכרח יכול לראות בלילה ולהורות כמו שעיניו רואות."

סימן מראות דם: הדרכה לנשים מתי להביא ספקות למו"צ: מה שמציעים הרבה לזרז לנשים להביא השאלות מיד, לענ"ד מרבה לחץ על נשי דידן שכבר יומן מלאה עבוה"ק וטירדות

ואין להעמיס עליהן עוד למהר לביתו של המו"צ, דבר שא"א להרבה נשים שעבודתם מחוץ לשכונתם. ועוד קשה על המו"צ לענות על כל השאלות בישוב דעת ומיד. ומאידך נכון שלא להניח השאלות לכמה ימים עד שלפעמים הצבע משתנה במקצת.

והלא נוהגים שהבדיקה השניה תהי' סמוכה לשקיעה ועוד כתב הרמ"א לכתחילה לראות העד ביום, וא"כ בע"כ שלכתחילה נוהגים להשהות המראות בחורף רוב היום. וגם ברור מהסוגיא בדף כ: שדנים על מראות לאחר שעבר הלילה. ואולי אם משתנה בשעות פעוטות סימן שלא היה מראה טמאה מאחר שחז"ל לא תקנו זמן מסוים ומוגבל לראית הבדיקות. וא"כ יש להורות לנשים שלא להתעצל ולא לשכוח ובעוד יום להביא וללמדן שתמשיכו למנות בספק לחוש לדעתו של המעיל צדקה. והמו"צ יזדרז כפי מה שאפשר לראות ולפסוק על המראה.

סימן כו, בסוף. כשזכיתי לשמוע שיעוריו של הגר"ש וואזנר שליט"א סיפר שהשאלה הראשונה ששאל לחזו"א מאחר שמינוהו להיות רב בשכונת זכרון מאיר, אם לנהוג כחומרת הרמ"א בענין יולדת והורה לו החזו"א שלא להורות להחמיר כן.

כשזכיתי לשמש הגר"ש אייזען זצ"ל ונכנס אצלו מי שנולד לו ילד לפני כמה שבועות ועדי בדיקת אשתו בידו, לא התיחס לשאלתו והורה לו בתקיפות שלא לדחוק לאשתו ולמהר אותה לטבול, אלא להתיחס לה בעדינות יתירא ולעודדה לנוח הרבה.

יולדת שבא להפסיק בטהרה ולעשות בדיקות ימי שבעה נקיים, תתיעץ עם הרופא שמטעם הבריאות אין לחוש לעשות בדיקות וסביר להקל לה שלא לעשות מוך דחוק מטעם מכה או פצע שיש לה באותו מקום לאחר הלידה. וגם שמעתי מהגרמ"ד טענדלר שליט"א שבמשך ההנקה מאד יבש באותו המקום וכדי להקל ולא לעשות מוך דחוק בעת ההנקה.

גם הרבה פעמים קשה בדיקות ז' ימים ליולדת ואם כבר עברו זמן רב ולא הצליחה למנות שבעה נקיים יש להקל במספר הבדיקות הן ממה שיש פצעים באותו מקום והן ממה שתגרום שתבואו פצעים לאותו מקום. ונראה שאם לא עבר זמן רב, הכל לפי עיני הדיין, אין להקל שהרי כבר נוהגים לחכות לפחות חמשה שבועות מטעם הבריאות ומטעם הדימום ועוד מטעם הדרכת מורי הגר"ש אייזען הנ"ל, ומכל זה אין להחשיבו כשעת הדחק.

עכשיו נראה שהרבה מורי הלכה מורים שמותר לנשים למנוע עוד הריון בעת התחלת ההנקה ע"י לקיחת כדורים. וידוע שהרבה מדממים על ידי כדורים אלו שלוקחים בעת ההנקה. ומצד אחד כדי שיהי' לתועלת צריכה היולדת להתחיל לקיחת הכדורים קודם שתטבול. ומאד אפשר שע"י זה תדמם בימי שבעה נקיים ולא תצליח ליטהר. ולכן נראה שתתחיל לקיחת הכדורים לאחר שהיא תטבול ומניעת הריון תבוא בא"א, והכל כל מתי להתחיל הכדורים בדיוק ואיך למנוע – ע"י עצת הרופא והוראת חכם, שאין הדברים פשוטים.

סימן ל,I: צריכים להזכיר איסור שחוק וקלות ראש ואיסור דברים בטלים הנזכרים בשו"ע (קצה:א) ומקורן באבות דר"נ (ב:א) כן ביאר הגר"א ששחוק וקלות ראש כולם כלולים בדברים בטלים במ"ש "יכול יחבקנה וינשקנה וידבר עמה דברים בטלים ת"ל לא תקרב", וא"כ מה שביאר הראב"ד בבעלי הנפש ומו"ד בטור ובש"ך (ס"ק ב) שדברים בטלים היינו דברי הרגל דברים

שמרגילין לערוה לכאורה זה ביאור בשחוק וקלות ראש ג"כ. ונראה שיש להרחיב הדבר לכל מצב של שחוק וקלות ראש שמרגיש בעצמו שמתחיל לחלל הגדרים שיש לו בדיבור ובהנהגות בפני אחרים, ומחללם מטעם רגשי קלות ראש.

והראוני תלמידי שיש שאוסרים לשחק משחקים כמו שחמט וסביבון וכיו"ב, ובעיוני בספרים מצאתי שהגרמ"מ קארפ (משמרת הטהרה פ"ח אות ו) מביא כן בשם הגרש"י אלישיב שליט"א, וכתב הגר"ש וואזנר שליט"א שיש מקום להחמיר, ולכאורה אם הלכה רפויה וכו' פוק מאי עמא דבר, והי' נראה לי שבאמעריקא אצל תלמידים שלנו אין להחמיר שכאן אינו נחשב כדברי הרגל שירגילו לערוה. והאריך הגרמ"מ לבאר דבריו "שעצם המשחק המתמשך ואוירה הניצות יוצר קירוב גדול והרגל דבר ביניהם" ואפי' אם הדברים נכונים למעשה הרי לא אסרוהו חז"ל וכנראה לא אסרו כל דבר שעלול בכל מקרה מקרה לכל אחד ואחד להביא לנסיונות, וסמכו על ההרחקות שכבר הרבה בהם להזכיר ולהדריך וסמכו על גדרים שכל זוג יראי שמים יעשו לעצמם כפי צורכם.

גם אמרו לי תלמידי שיש שאוסרים להביע אהבה אחד לשני באופו ישיר ופשוט ולענ"ד מה שנחשב כדברים בטלים לכאורה תלויה על כל חוג וחוג, וכנ"ל דברים שמרגילין לערוה. ובהרבה הרבה חוגים להביע אהבה בין איש לאשתו אינם מדברי הרגל ומותרים בעת נדתה.

והענין נחוץ מכיון שבמשך ימי איסורה לבעלה הרבה נשים מרגישות מרוחקות לגמרי ונזופות מבעליהן ואמנם הכוונה טובה אבל מרבה הלחץ על זוג צעיר וגם לאח"כ, ובפרט לאשה שבעת נדותה מרגישה מטבעה קצת עצבות. ומשמע מלשון הרמב"ם (אישות טו:יט) שלעודד אשתו היא מחיובי דרבנן על כל בעל וכן קיום הוא במצות עונה, ששמעתי ממו"ר הגר"צ שכטר שליט"א בשם אביו זצ"ל שלבלות זמן עם אשתו, בפרט בעת נדתה ה"ה קיום בעצם מצות עונה שכמו כן היא.

שם. בקשר למה שהתיר הנו"ב (יו"ד סי' קכב) רק התיר באופן שא"א למצוא דרך אחרת שתטבול תחת פיקוחו של אחר הן לגבי מה שצריכים לעיוני בה והן לגבי מה שצריכים להיות בטוח שטבלה כל גופה לגמרי. והי' נוטה להקל גם רק במקרה זה שהי' ממש בדרך לטבול וליטהר. ומה שמצא מקום להקל אפי' אליבא דש"ך ומכיון שהי' מעשה רב מהמהרי"ק שבדק אשתו קודם טבילה (וע' בהערת בנו שהי' ספק אצלו אם כן הי' המעשה) ממה שלמדנו שמי שבדרך לבטל חמצו האם יש לחוש שיאכלנו. וספקו אם אומרים כן לגבי חשש שכחה בלבד או גם לגבי חשש התגברות היצר דאיסור נדה. אבל ברור שסו' שכל הני הרחקות כולל נגיעה וכולל הסתכלות נאמרו בלא פלוג ובחששות הנ"ל, ורק בדרך ממש להיות מותר מצא מקום להתיר בשעת הדחק.

סימן ל. בקשר למי שמתביש אם יתפרסם שהיא עכשיו בעת נדתה. עי' בשו"ת אגרות משה (יורה דעה חלק ב סימן עז) וז"ל, "ומטעם שהוא כבזיון לה ויש בזה משום כבוד הבריות לא חששו, משום שאין בזה בזיון כ"כ דידוע לכל שהנשים הן נדות י"ב יום בכל חדש כשאינן זקנות ולא מעוברות וצריכין להתרחק מבעליהן באיזה דברים, ואדרבה הא הרבה היו לובשות בגדים מיוחדים לימי הנדות ומזה היו יודעות השכנות שהיא נדה אלמא שלא היו מתביישות בזה." אמנם מה יעשה מי שאשתו כן מתביישת אם חברות שלה ידעו מצבה, ולכאורה מרגישה כן

מרוב צניעותה, ועוד עי׳ בסוף מס׳ ברכות (סב:) מעשה דרב ספרא ודרב רבא שהנהיגו בצניעות ובקפידת בזיונם אפי׳ בדברים ידועים וטבעיים, ואמנם יש לחלק אבל למעשה אין להקל בדיני דרבנן מטעם זה, אבל אולי אפשר להקל בהעברת דבר מידו לידה בפני אחרים לאשה צעירה שמתביישת אם יתפרסם שהיא בנדתה. הרי מכל אסורי הרחקות, הרי העברה מיד ליד ה״ה הכי עלול לפרסם שהיא אסורה, ובאיסור זה יש להעלות על שולחן מלכים אם יש מקום להקל מאחר שיש פוסקים שהקלו בזה בשעת הדחק, עי׳ בספר טהרת הבית להגר״ע יוסף שליט״א, (ח״ב סי׳ יב אות ג), ומה שהקיל שם בהעלת עגלה לקומה גבוה או לאוטובוס, הלא אם אשה מרוב צניעותה מרגשת שהיא מתביש הלא צורכה יותר גדולה מלהטריח אחר לעזור להעלות העגלה. ועוד יש לנמק ממה שראיתי שהרי איסור העברה מיד ליד מביהמ״ד של רש״י ונפסקה בשו״ע ממה שכן נהגו וחיובה מטעם שכן נוהגים ע״פ השו״ע. ולכאורה אצל מנהגים י״ל שלא קבלו בנ״י במקום הדחק והצער. וכן שמעתי בשם א׳ מגדולי ר״י.

סימן ל אות ה. בקשר למטות: הורה לי הגר״נ אלפרט זצ״ל בקשר למטות עם מזרונות נפרדות על קופסא אחת שלא כדאי להקל בזה.

סימן ל אות ה. מטות נפרדות לגמרי עד שלא נוגעות אפי׳ הסמיכות זב״ז עם ״העדבארד״ אחד שמעתי שהיו אוסרים מטעם מראית עין שע״פ רוב לא היו עושים העדבארד אחד למטות נפרדות, נראה שעכשיו מאד מקובל לעשות העדבארד אחד לשתי מטות ועוד ש״שובכו ממש מוכיח עליו״ שאפשר לראות מצורת המטה שהם נפרדים.

סימן ל אות ז. בקשר לטיולים: הנה בודאי שחכם עיניו בראשו ואינו נכון ולא כדאי לתכנן טיול בעת נדתה שהרי כל שינוי מהתעסקות הרגיל ובודאי כשמבלים הרבה זמן ביחד מקרב הדעות והלבבות ביותר ובעת איסורה מגרה היצר ומביא לנסיונות. אמנם בזוג צעיר הרבה פעמים אינן בידן לתכנן מתי יהי׳ להם חופש מעבודה והרבה פעמים צריכים לתכנן כל חופש כמה חדשים בהקדם, ולהחמיר שלא יטיילו בכלל הרי זה קשה על הרבה שעובדים קשה מבלי הזדמנויות לנוח ולטייל ובפרט בצעירים שעמוסים בברכת פרנסה ובברכת ילדים. ולכן לדינא הרי בשו״ת רב פעלים (ח״ג יו״ד סי׳ יז) שהחמיר בזה וסו׳ שכוונת התרומת הדשן לאסור טיולים הרי הוא בעצמו סו׳ שרק טיול בעלמא בהרים אסור אבל לבקר קרובים או בעיר מותר ובערוה״ש שהוא ממקורות האיסור טיולים לדינא אסר טיול בגנות ובפרדסים בעגלה ע״י ספסל המתנדנד והוסיף ״אפי׳ לילך לטייל ביחד אינו נכון״ וע״ז כתב הגרמ״פ (יו״ד ח״ב סי׳ פג) ״ובדבר ללכת יחד לבקר אצל חברים או לטיול איני רואה בזה שיהיה איסור״ שאין לחוש לנגיעה במצב שאינן טרודין וכן כתב לאלו שנוסעים לטיול במכונה שאין לחוש שיתקרבו זל״ז. וגם הגר״ש וואזנר (שיעורי שבה״ל קצה:ה:י) כתב שמסתבר להחמיר לא ללכת להרים לבד בלי עוד אנשים. (והוסיף שכשהיו הרכבות עם קרונות נפרדים שישבו לבד בקרון כתבו הגדולים להחמיר כשנוסעים לטיול). ולכן אם מתוכנן טיול בעת נדתה יש לארגן שיהי׳ טיול עם התעסקות הרבה ולא טיולי נוף בעלמא במנוחה, ויעשו גדרים בעצמם שלא יבואו לנסיונות ויזהרו בכל ההרחקות שלשם זה תיקנו ולא להחמיר יותר מהם.

סימן ל אות ח: בענין כיסוי ראש בעת נדתה: קודם החתונה שאלתי הגר"נ אלפרט זצ"ל והורה שתכסה ראשה בעת נדתה בבית מטעם ההיקש בין אישה נדה וא"א כדמובא בפסק תשובה. ופעם הורה לי הגר"ד ליפשיץ זצ"ל שתכסה ראשה אלא כדרכו הוסיף שלא להטריח על האשה יותר מדי ואם לאחר שכבר שהתחילה ליפול לשנה ונפל כיסוי ראשה לא להטריח לה עוד.

ונחלקו פוסקי זמננו במש"כ בשו"ע שאסור להסתכל במקומות המכוסים שהגרמ"פ זצ"ל (אגרו"מ יו"ד ח"ב סי' עה) והגרע"י שליט"א (טהרת הבית ח"ב) סו' שאסור להסתכל במקומות שרגילה לכסות בבית והגר"ש וואזנר שליט"א מביא שנוהגים לכסות ראשה בעת נדתה וכתב הגר"נ קרליץ שליט"א (חוט השני) שכוונת השו"ע שמקומות המכוסים כפי מה שכתב באו"ח סי' עה אסור להסתכל בהם. עוד כתב הגר"פ כהן שליט"א (בדי השולחן קצה:ז) לשאול על מה שפירשו הגרמ"פ זצ"ל והגרע"י שליט"א ממה שאסור להסתכל בעקבה והשו"ע פסק עקבה ממש, והרבה להוכיח מכמה מקורות שעקבת אנשים בזמניהם לא היו מכוסים בבית.

והאוסרים סו' שכן מוכרח לפרש השו"ע מאחר שלמדנו בסוגיא (שבת יג.) להקיש איסור אשתו נדה לאיסור א"א. ונראה שהגרמ"פ סו' שמההיקש לומדים לאסור אצל אשתו נדה כל מה שיכול להביא לידי איסור מטעם חוסר הרגל אצלו. שכן יש לישב מה שחושש לספקו של הפתחי תשובה לגבי קול אשתו נדה ומה שמיקל אצל שער אשתו נדה. ולכאורה כן יש לישב מה שכתב הרמ"א שמותר להסתכל במקומות הגלוים אע"פ שנהנה בראייתה, למרות שלפי פשטות לשון ההיקש יש לאסור.

ולפי לשון הרמב"ן נראה לאסור, וז"ל (שבת יג.) "והדר פשטינן לאיסורא דקריבה גופא אסירא מהיקישא דאשת איש דהתם ודאי כל קריבה אסורה ואפי' בלא יחוד דלא אתי השתא לידי ביאה דהא אפי' להסתכל בה אסור בערוה אף אשתו נדה בכל ענין אסור". ואולי נחלקו הראשונים בדבר זה, והרמ"א קי"ל כראשונים שחולקים על הרמב"ן.

סימן ל"א: בקשר לבדיקות שעושים לאחר ביאה בג' פעמים ראשונים לאחר הנישואין לאשה שאין לה וסת. הגר"ד ליפשיץ זצ"ל הורה לי למעשה שלא לבדוק ג"פ הראשונים לאחר הנישואין לאשה שאין לה וסת, ולא שאלתי ממנו נימוקי הוראתו. ובפשטות הורה לנהוג כמסקנת הש"ך (ס"ק א). והגר"ש וואזנר שליט"א (שיעורי שבט הלוי) כתב שמעיקר הדין אין צריך לבדוק, "אבל כדאי להחמיר". ומה שכתב התוה"ש וכמה אחרונים שקשה להקל נגד פסק המחבר ומור"ם ומסיים "דבמקום שנהגו להקל אין להחמיר כי יש להם גדולי פוסקים שיסמכו עליהם" אפשר שאנן כמקום שלא נוהגים להחמיר מכיון שרוב הנשים שבודקות לאחר הנישואין ג"פ, בודקות מיד ועושות שלא כהוגן ודלא ככוונת המחבר ורמ"א מב' סיבות. א' שבודקות קודם שכלו בתוליה, וב' כדביאר החת"ס (הגהות מו"ד בשיעורי שבט הלוי קפו:ב:ד) "שאשה שיש לה קביעות שלא לראות עד כ"ה יום ומכ"ה יום אין לה קביעות צריכה לבדוק ג' בדיקות אלו אחר שעברו כ"ה יום דעד כ"ה יום הוי כוסת קבוע ואין כאן הוכחה לזמן שדינה כאין לה וסת, ואם בדקה בהם לא עלו לה וצריכה לבדוק שוב לאחר כ"ה יום", ע"ש בהמשך דבריו.

ומה שמלמדים לכלות לבדוק בג' הפעמים הראשונים קודם שברור שבודאי כלו לה כל בתוליה, לכאורה טעות הוא שגורם לזוג צעיר צער שאם ימצאו דם בתולים על הבדיקה שמאד

מאד עלול שימצאו, יצטרכו לפרוש מדין דם בתולים. והרי אין שום מצוה לבדוק לדם בתולים. אלא הנוהגים להחמיר לחכות ולא לבדוק עד שברור שכלו כל בתוליה. וב"ה מצאתי שכן העיר בס' גופי הלכות (קפד: ס"ק יג) וכן ראיתי בשם הגר"ש וואזנר שליט"א.

Sources

.1

תלמוד בבלי מסכת נדה דף נז עמוד ב – אמר שמואל: בדקה קרקע עולם וישבה עליה, ומצאה דם עליה – טהורה, שנאמר (ויקרא טו) בבשרה – עד שתרגיש בבשרה.

רמב"ם הלכות איסורי ביאה פרק ה הלכה יז – האשה שהשתינה מים ויצא דם עם מי רגלים, בין שהשתינה והיא עומדת בין שהשתינה והיא יושבת הרי זו טהורה, ואפילו הרגיש גופה ונזדעזעה אינה חוששת שהרגשת מי רגלים היא זו שאין מי רגלים מן החדר ודם זה דם מכה הוא בחלחולת או בכוליא.

שו"ת מהר"ם שיק יו"ד סימן קפב – ומטעם זה נראה דמ"ש הרמב"ם בפ"ה מה' איסו"ב הלכה י"ז דהרגשה מקרי אם האברים מזדעים דזה לאו דווקא דוודאי ה"ה אף שאר שינוי בגוף ולכן אני חוששב אשה שיש לה חולי וכאבים דאפשר דהם הרגשת דמי המקום או אפשר דהרגשת דם המכה ולכך אין ברור לי שדם ההוא הוא רק דם בלא הרגשה שיהא טהור מן התורה.

תרומת הדשן סימן רמו – מ"מ בנ"ד הואיל ומצאת ליחלוחית דלובן על העד אמרינן דההיא טיפת לובן היא דארגשה דלובן וירוק נמי מן המקור קאתי, כדמוכח בפשיטות בכמה דוכתא פ' כל היד. וכ"כ הרמב"ן וז"ל: לא כל משקה החדר טמא אלא הדם בלבד לפיכך אם שתת מן הרחם לובן או ירוק אע"פ שסמיכתה כדם טהור ע"כ. וכיון דנוכל למיתלי ההרגשה במידי תלינן כדאמרינן פ' הרואה כתם(/נדה נז ע"ב) אימור הרגשת עד אימור הרגשת השמש, כל שכן דפתיחת המקור גופא כך נראה לפי התלמוד ומתוך ההלכה.

שולחן ערוך יורה דעה הלכות נדה סימן קצ סעיף א – דבר תורה אין האשה מטמאה ולא אסורה לבעלה עד שתרגיש שיצא דם מבשרה, וחכמים גזרו על כתם שנמצא בגופה או בבגדיה, שהיא טמאה, ואסורה לבעלה אפילו לא הרגישה ואפילו בדקה עצמה ומצאה טהורה. וצריכה הפסק טהרה, שתבדוק עצמה ותמצא טהורה, ואח"כ תמנה שבעה נקיים חוץ מיום המציאה כאילו ראתה ודאי, וכמו שיתבאר לקמן סימן קצ"ו). א ואם הרגישה שנפתח מקורה להוציא דם ובדקה אחר כך ולא מצאה כלום, יש מי שאומר שהיא טמאה.

שו"ת נודע ביהודה מהדורה קמא – יורה דעה סימן נה – ומעתה נוכל לומר לכל הפוסקים בעינן הרגשה מן התורה. ומאי ניהו הרגשה שירגישו אם הרגשת פתיחת המקור או אף הרגשת זיבת דבר לח בבשרה. נלע"ד דאף הרגשת זיבת דבר לח חשיב הרגשה ולא בעינן הרגשת פתיחת המקור דוקא והרי עיקר ההרגשה יליף שמואל מבשרה שתרגיש בבשרה והרי האי בשר לאו על בשר המקור קאי שהרי מזה ילפינן שמטמאה בפנים כבחוץ והרי אינה מטמאה אלא מן השינים ולחוץ וא"כ האי בשרה היינו בשרה שמן השינים ולחוץ וא"כ גם שתרגיש בשרה היינו בשר זה והרי זה כבר הוא חוץ לפתח המקור ואיך נימא שבעינן שתרגיש פתיחת המקור. אע"כ לא בעינן רק שבשרה ירגיש זיבת הדם ואם מרגשת זיבת דבר לח הרי כבר הרגישה והרגשת המקור לא נזכר בפסוק אלא הרגשת הבשר. ואם זה הדבר מלתא דמסתבר הוא אמינא עוד גם הוכחה לזה שהרי בכל הסוגיא דף נ"ז ע"ב שמפלפל להקשות כמה קושיות על דברי שמואל דבעי הרגשה מכמה משניות וברייתות ולמה לא מקשה ממשנה קדומה בפרק שני דף י"ז ע"ב דם הנמצא בפרוזדור ספיקו טמא היכי דמי אי דארגשה פתיחת המקור א"כ אין זה ספק אלא ודאי מן המקור ואי דלא ארגשה א"כ אפילו הוא מן המקור טהור הוא לגמרי בלא הרגשה א"ו דלא בעינן כלל הרגשת המקור אלא הרגשת זיבת דבר לח בבשרה. ובזה אי אפשר להבחין אם מן המקור או מן העליה.

תלמוד בבלי מסכת נדה דף נז עמוד ב – אמר שמואל: בדקה קרקע עולם וישבה עליה, ומצאה דם עליה – טהורה, שנאמר (ויקרא טו) בבשרה – עד שתרגיש בבשרה.

חוות דעת סימן קצ סעיף א' – אמנם נראה דבעינן שתרגיש שזב ממקורה דאם לא הרגישה שזב ממקורה רק שמרגשת שזב בפרוזדור נראה דטהורה כיון שבשעה שנפל מהמקור לפרוזדור לא הרגישה ורחמנא טהרי' להדם שבא בלא הרגשה מאין יתחיל הטומאה בפרוזדור.

שו"ת חתם סופר חלק ב (יורה דעה) סימן קמה – אני אומר בודאי אם האשה מרגשת ממש קשה לי להתיר אך כפי הנראה מכותלי שאלתך שאין ההרגשה שלה אלא זיבת דבר לח והנה בתשו' שב יעקב מוכיח דע"כ זיבת דבר לח לאו הרגשה היא מדאמרינן ר"פ הרואה כתם גבי מי רגלים אי דארגש' יושבת אמאי טהורה אי דלא ארגשה כו' וקשה מה ספק יש כאן הא בודאי ארגשה זיבת דבר לח שהרי הטילה מי רגלים אע"כ שאין זה הרגשה הגם שמוז"ה מהרשש"כ דחה זה שם בתשובה דה"ק אי ארגשה הרגשה גמורה יושבת אמאי טהורה ע"ש ודבריו תמוהי' עכ"פ איך אמר אי דלא ארגשה עומדת אמאי טמאה אמאי לא תהיה טמאה נהי דלא הרגישה

הרגשה גמורה מ"מ זיבת דבר לח מיהא ארגשה ויש לדחוק בזה עוד הארכתי בתשוב' א' והבאתי ראיה ממ"ש ריש נדה ישנה נמי אגב צערה מתערה משמע דכל הרגשה הוא מחמת צער ולא זיבת דבר לח בעלמא דפשוט דע"י דבר לח לא מתערא וכן משמע נמי מלשון התוס' נדה דף ע"א ד"ה והא אשה מכוסה היא כו' יע"ש שמבואר שפתיחת פי המקור הוא ההרגשה או צער כעין עקיצת מי רגלים וכה"ג ולא זיבת דבר לח והנה בתשו' נב"י סי' נ"ה כ' סתם דלא נ"ל ככת הקודמים אלא דזיבת דבר לח הוא הרגשה דאוריי' ולא שת לבו לסתור ראי' א' מאלו הנאמרים לעיל אך רק הוא הבי' ראי' מדנפקא לן הרגשה מבשרה שתרגיש בבשרה והאי קרא נמי אתי שמטמא בביה"ח והיינו חוץ לפה"מ שם מתטמא זה הוא הבשר דמיירי בי' קרא דשם הוא ג"כ מקום ההרגש והוא בביה"ח ש"מ דזיבת דבר לח הוא הרגשה דאוריי' ודבריו תמוהים אדרבא דוק מיני' לאידך גיסא הא ממעטי' נמי בבשרה ולא בשפופרת והיינו אם תכניס השפופרת לפי המקור ותקבל הדם דאלו לא תכניסנה אלא לביה"ח א"כ כבר היא טמאה משעה שיצא הדם חוץ לפי המקור אע"כ אתא למעוטי בבשרה של עצמה ר"ל שיעבור הדם בפי מקורה ולא שיהי' שם שפופרת לקבלו וא"כ הרי מבואר דהך בשר היינו פי המקור ושם צריכה שתרגיש ומ"ש מדרשא בבשרה בפנים כבחוץ הוא מבואר בנדה מ"א ע"ב דהיינו מקום שהשמש דש והיינו פי המקור למעיי' בלשון הרמב"ם פ"ה מא"ב ה"ד ובפי' המשנה ועוד הארכתי בזה בתשו' אחרת מ"מ בהא מסקינן דעיקור הרגשה דאוריי' היא לפע"ד הרגשת פתיחת פה"מ או צער כעקיצת מי רגלים אבל לא זיבת דבר לח.

פרטי דינים היוצאים מכל מ"ש הוא כך:

א אם האשה הזאת מוצאת כל אלו גם כשהמקור למעלה במקומו אזי ידי מסולקת הימנה ורק אם כשהמקור במקומו לא תמצא בכמו אלו רק כשהוא חוץ למקומו אז יש להתיר כאשר יתבאר אי"ה.

ב אם תרגיש האשה בראיות אלו הרגשת פתיחת פה"מ או כעקיצת מי רגלים ג"כ אין לי עסק בזה ורק כשההרגש הוא רק זיבת דבר לח ומוצאת בכל פעם כנ"ל אז אם אפי' גם ע"י בדיקה תמצא אעפ"י שאז י"ל הרגשה ממש היה לה וקסברה הרגשת עד הוא מ"מ כיון דבלא"ה בפלתי שדא נרגא בהרגשת עד גם כי אינו נכון לפע"ד כמו שמבואר אצלינו במקומו מכל מקום הכא כיון דבלא"ה רוב ראייתה שע"י זיבת דבר לח הם באותו אופן ממש שע"י בדיקת העד אמרי' היינו הך ממש ותלינן להקל.

שו"ת חתם סופר חלק ב (יורה דעה) סימן קנג – ואע"ג דבתשובה אחרת בררתי שהעיקר דזיבת דבר לח לא הוה הרגשה וכדעת מורי זקני הגאון מהרשש"ך בתשו' שב יעקב וראי' ברורה שלו מר"פ בנות כותים בשקלא וטרי' דהרגשת מי רגלים הוא ואי ס"ד דבר לח הוה הרגשה אין לך דבר לח יותר ממ"ר ומאי פריך מעיקרא אי דלא ארגשה וכו' ואני הוספתי כמה ראיות ודחיתי דברי נב"י וכן אני מורה הלכה למעשה וכן קבלתי ממורי זצ"ל מ"מ הכא לא דיינינן אהרגשת זיבת דבר לח אלא שעי"ז שהיא מרגשת כך ואומרת להבעל ע"כ צריך הוא לפרוש באבר מת שמא הך זיבה הוא דם וארגשה פתיחת המקור ג"כ אלא שחשבה הרגשת שמש הוא כתי' ש"ס ר"פ בנות כותים נמצא לפ"ז קשה עלי קצת לסמוך בנידון שלפנינו על התירים דלמעלה.

שו"ת אגרות משה יורה דעה חלק ד סימן יז – בעניין סילוק דמים בזה"ז במעוברת ובמינקת, בכמה ענייני מראות, בעניין הרגשה דזיבת דבר לח, ובכמה ענייני כתמים: ז. הרגישה שיצא דם מגופה, אבל לא שזב מהמקור: במחלוקת החו"ד (סימן ק"צ ס"ק א') עם הנו"ב (מהדו"ק יו"ד סימן נ"ה ד"ה ומעתה נוכל לומר) בהרגישה שיצא מגופה אבל לא הרגישה שזב מהמקור אלא מהפרוזדור, דהחו"ד סובר דאינה הרגשה, וכתב דהוא דלא כדמשמע מהנו"ב, עיי"ש. הנה לא ידוע לנשי שלנו אם הרגשתה כשזב הדם מגופה אם הוא רק מפרוזדור או מן המקור, וכ"ש שאין יודעות בהרגשתן אם מהמקור או מן העליה. ועיין במ"מ פ"ה אי"ב ה"ה בסופו, שכתב בשם הרמב"ן שבזה"ז אין בקיאות בדבר, שלכן כל דם שתרגיש האשה ביציאתן טמאה (במ"מ איתא בשם הרמב"ן, בזמן הזה שאין בקיאות בדבר כל שהאשה מוצאה דם בעד שלה טמאה, וכן הוא בהלכות נדה לרמב"ן פרק ג', אבל הן הן הדברים, שאין נפ"מ בידיעת האשה ובהרגשתה מהיכן בא הדם) כיוון שהרגשת זיבת דבר לח נחשבה הרגשה, ואין לזה דין כתם אלא דין ראייה שהוא אף במשהו, הוא לדינא בכל הרגשה בשעת יציאה מהגוף. ואף שהחו"ד והנו"ב דנו בזה אנן גריעי טובא מינייהו.

אבל כל זה בהרגישה יציאה מהגוף. אבל מה שהרגישה שנעשה בין רגליה לח מאיזה משקה, אין להחשיב זה להרגשה. דהלחות שנעשה אחר שכבר יצא, לא שייך שלא להרגיש, דבכל אופן שבא לשם דבר הלח איכא הרגשה לכל. והרגשה, אף להנו"ב ולחו"ד, הוא בהרגשה בשעת היציאה שמרגשת איך שיצא מהגוף. אבל זה לבדו סגי לדידן, שלא בקיאי הנשי לידע מאין הם – אם ממקור או מעליה או מפרוזדור – שאם הרגישה שיצאו מהגוף טמאה אף בפחות מכשיעור. ואם לא הרגישה אלא רק אחר שיצאו, מצד לחות הדם, שזה הא הוא הרגש מוכרח מאחר שכבר יצאו, אין זה בחשיבות הרגשה ויש ע"ז דין כתם שהוא דווקא בכשיעור כגריס ועוד – אפילו על בשרה – לשיטה ראשונה בסימן ק"צ סעיף ו'. ואם מונח שם מוך ומטלית וכדומה שהדם ירד רק לשם ולא נגע בבשרה, תהיה טהורה, אף לשיטה שניה שהוא שיטת הרמב"ם, בפחות מכשיעור דכגריס ועוד. וכמדומני שנוהגין להקל כשיטה הראשונה שהוא כרוב הראשונים, אף שהש"ך ס"ק י' פוסק להחמיר, עיין בתוה"ש ס"ק ט' ובסד"ט ס"ק י"ב שדחו דבריו, ולכן אין להחמיר בכתמים. ח. הרגישה זיבת דבר לח שיוצא מגופה ולא בדקה מיד, וכשבדקה לא מצאה כלום: ובהרגישה זיבת דבר לח שיוצא מגופה ולא בדקה מיד, ואח"כ בדקה ולא מצאה כלום, שכתר"ה נסתפק אם יש לדמות זה להרגישה שנפתח מקורה להוציא דם, ובדקה אח"כ ולא מצאה כלום. דיש מי שאומר דהיא טמאה (שו"ע סי' ק"צ סעיף א') ולית מאן דפליג על זה כדאיתא בתוה"ש סק"ב, ומה שנקט המחבר לשון יש מי שאומר הוא משום שמצא זה רק בתרומת הדשן. או שזיבת דבר לח, אף להסוברין שנחשבה הרגשה, הא הביא בפ"ת סק"ו בשם החת"ס (יו"ד סי' ק"נ) שאינה בדין הרגשה אלא בראתה דם – להחשיבה רואה בהרגשה שהיא טמאה גם מדאורייתא. אבל אם לא ראתה אינה מוציאה מחזקת טהרתה. שלכן מכיוון שלא מצאה כלום, יש לטהר. הנה לע"ד לעניין לא מצאה כלום על בדיקתה יש להחמיר, דהרי כיוון שהרגישה זיבת דבר לח, הרי ודאי היה איזו לחלוחית והי"ל לימצא על הבדיקה. אך בהכרח שנפל ממנה קודם שבדקה כיוון ששהתה מלבדוק, שזה לכאורה יש לאסור. ט. נשים שרגילות להרגיש זיבת דבר לח, וכשבודקות מוצאות מראות טהורות: אלו נשים שרגילות להרגיש זיבת

דבר לח יוצא מגופן וכשבודקות מוצאות מראות טהורות, אם ידוע זה להן עי"ז שכל הפעמים שהרגישה היה זה מראה טהור – ולא שייך להחשיב זה ידיעה ברורה אלא כשהיה זה בזמנים שונים, היינו כגון ביום ובלילה בשעת עבודתה ובשעת מנוחה וכדומה. אם בכל זמן ובכל אופן בדקה והיו מראות טהורות, יש לסמוך אם בדקה ג' פעמים. ואם היו הג' בדיקות בזמן אחד ובאופן אחד, ואפילו יותר מג', אינו מועיל אלא לאותו הזמן ואותו האופן. ומהני זה רק לימי טהרה ממש שלה, וליום הוסת לא מהני בשום אופן. ולשבעת ימי ספירת נקיים שלה צריכה בדיקה ג"פ ביחוד לימי ספירה – אם יהיו ג"פ אף בימי ספירה של הרבה פעמים שבדקה והיו זה מראות טהורות, תוכל לסמוך ע"ז, כן נראה לע"ד. י. אשה שהרגישה שנפתח מקורה, ובדקה ולא מצאה כלום: הנה אשה שהרגישה שנפתח מקורה, הא איתא בש"ע סימן ק"צ סוף סעיף א', אף בבדקה ולא מצאה כלום יש מי שאומר שהיא טמאה. ואיתא בתוה"ש שלא מצינו בב"י מי שחולק עליו, רק שדרך המחבר לכתוב בלשון יש מי שאומר כשלא ראה זה אלא בפוסק אחד. אבל פשוט שבמצאה מראות טהורות טהורה, ומפורש כן בלשון המחבר סימן קפ"ח סוף סעיף א', והרמ"א כתב ע"ז וכן עיקר. וא"כ גם בלבושה מכנסים ואפילו מהודקים לגופה ובדקה תיכף ולא מצאה עלייהו כלום, נמי אין טעם לטהרה. דיש לחוש שמא יצא רק מעט דם, ונתקנח על בשרה שם, או אף נפל באופן רחוק. ולפ"מ שכתבתי לעיל (סעיף ח') אף בהרגשת זיבת דבר לח, נמי יש לאוסרה. וא"כ כ"ש כשלא בדקה תיכף אלא אח"כ, שאינו כלום. אך שייך לשאול זה באשה שלא הרגישה כלום, אלא המחוייבת לבדוק מאיזה טעם, ולא בדקה עד אחר שהשתינה, אם מועיל בבדיקת המכנסים. אבל הא פשוט שבדיקת המכנסים לבד לא יועיל, דאשה המחוייבת לבדוק צריכה גם לבדוק גופה, וכיוון שהשתינה הא א"א שוב לבדוק גופה, ואין לטהרה כשמחוייבת בדיקה. אבל ציור למעשה ע"ז שצריכה לבדוק דווקא ברגע מסויים, הוא דבר רחוק. יא. אשה שיש לה מכה שמוציאה דם, והרגישה זיבת דבר לח ומצאה דם, אם תולה הדם במכתה. ובאשה שיש לה מכה באותו מקום שמוציאה דם, והרגישה זיבת דבר לח ומצאה דם, אם יש לתלות במכה. הנה אם הרגישה שיצא מגופה דבר הלח באופן שהרגשה כזו לא שייך ביציאת דם ממכה, הוא ודאי הרגשת דם נדה. ואם הרגשתה הוא רק בזה שהרגישה שנעשה לח בגופה בין רגליה, אין זה בחשיבות הרגשה דדם נדה כלל (לעיל אות ז') והוי רק כראיית דם בעלמא, שכיוון שיש לה מכה יש לה לתלות במכה. וגם בימי ספירת הז' נקיים יש לה לתלות במכה, אם כבר היה לה הפסק טהרה וגם היתה בדיקה נקיה ביום הראשון פעם אחת. אבל בשעת הוסת, או מל' יום לל' יום, אין תולין במכתה, כמפורש ברמ"א סימן קפ"ז סעיף ה'. ואם לא ראתה דם אלא כתמים תולה במכתה אפילו בשעת וסתה, כדאיתא שם ברמ"א וכתמים תולה בכל עניין, ופי' הש"ך בס"ק כ"ז שהוא אפילו בשעת וסתה, וכנראה שלא פליגי עליו שלכן יש להורות כן.

תלמוד בבלי מסכת נדה דף נז עמוד ב – תא שמע, האשה שהיא עושה צרכיה וראתה דם, רבי מאיר אומר: אם עומדת – טמאה, ואם יושבת – טהורה. היכי דמי? אי דארגשה – יושבת אמאי טהורה? אלא לאו – דלא ארגשה, וקתני עומדת – טמאה! לעולם – דארגשה, ואימור הרגשת מי רגלים הואי. עומדת – הדור מי רגלים למקור ואייתי דם, ויושבת טהורה. ת"ש: עד שהיה

נתון תחת הכר ונמצא עליו דם, אם עגול – טהור, ואם משוך – טמא. היכי דמי? אי דארגישה – עגול אמאי טהור? אלא לאו – דלא ארגישה וקתני משוך – טמא! לא, לעולם – דארגישה, ואימור הרגשת עד הואי, משוך – ודאי מגופה אתא, עגול – טהור. תא שמע: נמצא על שלו – טמאין וחייבין בקרבן, נמצא על שלה אתיום – טמאין וחייבין בקרבן, נמצא על שלה לאחר זמן – טמאים מספק, ופטורין מן הקרבן. היכי דמי? אי דארגישה – לאחר זמן אמאי פטורין מן הקרבן? אלא לאו – דלא ארגישה, וקתני נמצא על שלה אתיום – טמאין וחייבין בקרבן! לא, לעולם – דארגישה, ואימא הרגשת שמש הוה. תא שמע, נמצאת אתה אומר, ג׳ ספקות באשה: על בשרה, ספק טמא ספק טהור – טמא; על חלוקה, ספק טמא ספק טהור – טהור; ובמגעות ובהיסטות – הלך אחר הרוב, מאי הלך אחר הרוב? לאו אם רוב ימיה טמאין – טמאה, ואע״ג דלא ארגשה! לא, אם רוב ימיה בהרגשה חזיא – טמאה, דאימור: ארגשה ולאו אדעתה.

ערוך השולחן יורה דעה הלכות נדה סימן קפג:סא – ודע שנמצא בתשו׳ לאחד מהגדולים [ש״י סי׳ ט׳ בשם מהרשש״ך] שחקר על זה לנשים בקיאות ואמרו לו שטבעית טבעית יש יש מהן שמרגישות בפתיחות פי המקור ויש מהן שאינן מרגישות בהרגשה זו רק בהרגשות דזיבת דם נדה כולן מרגישות עכ״ל והבל יפצה פי הנשים האלה ולא ידעי מאי קאמרי ורבותינו נאמנים עלינו יותר מהן וגם אינן משקרות בדבריהן אלא שאינן מבינות ודע דכל דבר מותרות שבגוף שהגוף צריך לדחותם הטביע הקב״ה בטבע הגוף שכשיגיע זמן דחיפתם לחוץ שיפתחו אז נקבי הפליטה שעד כה היו סתומים ולצורך דחיית המותרות נתפתחו ויוצאים לחוץ כמו יציאה לגדולים ולקטנים וצואת החוטם ובאשה נתוסף גם הדמים מהמקור לדחיפת המותרות וזהו שהש״ס מדמה להרגשת מי רגלים מפני שסמוכים זל״ז וכזה כן זה וזהו הכרח שיפתח המקור דא״א כלל באופן אחר ובשעת הפתיחה יש הרגשה וקצת צער עד שמפני זה גם יקיץ משנתו כדברי רבותינו ז״ל.

.2

תרומת הדשן סימן רמו – שאלה: אשה שהרגישה בעצמה שנפתח מקורה להוציא דם, והלכה ובדקה את עצמה מיד ומצאתה על העד לחלוחית לבן ולא לבן לגמרי אלא כמראית בגד לבן שנפל עליו אבק שהוכהה לבנונית יש לטהר האשה או לאו? תשובה: יראה דצריך להתיישב בדבר, ...וא״ת בנ״ד יש לטמאות טפי מטעם אחר שהרי הרגישה, ונראה דאשה דהרגישה ובדקה אח״כ ולא מצאתה כלום יש לטמאה, דודאי יצא טיפת דם כחרדל ונתקנח או נימוק. דהרגשה סברא דאורייתא היא, היכא דליכא למיתלי ההרגשה במידי אחריני, כדמוכח בפרק הרואה כתם (נדה נ״ז ע״ב) דפריך אנמצא לאחר זמן פטורין מן הקרבן אי דארגישה אמאי פטורין, אלמא דסברא דאורייתא היא מדחייב עלה קרבן, וכיון דסברא דאורייתא היא הוי כלמ״ד וסתות דאורייתא, דאפילו בדקה ומצאתה טהורה טמאה כדאיתא פ׳ כל היד (נדה טז ע״א). מ״מ בנ״ד הואיל ומצאת ליחלוחית דלובן על העד אמרינן דההיא טיפת לובן היא דארגשה דלובן וירוק נמי מן המקור קאתי, כדמוכח בפשיטות בכמה דוכתא פ׳ כל היד. וכ״כ הרמב״ן וז״ל: לא כל משקה החדר טמא אלא הדם בלבד לפיכך אם שתת מן הרחם לובן או ירוק אע״פ שסמיכתה כדם טהור ע״כ. וכיון דנוכל למיתלי ההרגשה במידי תלינן כדאמרינן פ׳ הרואה כתם (נדה נז ע״ב) אימור

הרגשת עד אימור הרגשת השמש, כל שכן דפתיחת המקור גופא כך נראה לפי התלמוד ומתוך ההלכה. אמנם ירא אנכי להקל אם נמצא על העד ליחלוחית דסמיך ושיש בו משום קצת, אע"ג דלובן הוא מפני הטועים שאינם יודעים להפליא בין דם לדם, אבל אם אינו אלא מראה וכמו צבע בעלמא וגם לא ארגישה, דלפעמים כה"ג בא מלכלוך זוהמות בית החיצון הואיל ומראה טהור בודאי כגוון לובן יש לטהר.

תלמוד בבלי מסכת נדה דף נז עמוד ב – תא שמע: נמצא על שלו – טמאין וחייבין בקרבן, נמצא על שלה אתיום – טמאין וחייבין בקרבן, נמצא על שלה לאחר זמן – טמאים מספק, ופטורין מן הקרבן. היכי דמי? אי דארגישה – לאחר זמן אמאי פטורין מן הקרבן? אלא לאו – דלא ארגישה, וקתני נמצא על שלה אתיום – טמאין וחייבין בקרבן! לא, לעולם – דארגישה, ואימא הרגשת שמש הוה.

תלמוד בבלי מסכת נדה דף טז עמוד א – בעו מיניה מרב נחמן: וסתות דאורייתא או דרבנן? אמר להו: מדאמר הונא חברין משמיה דרב, אשה שיש לה וסת, והגיע שעת וסתה ולא בדקה, ולבסוף ראתה – חוששת לוסתה וחוששת לראייתה אלמא – וסתות דאורייתא. איכא דאמרי, הכי קא"ל: טעמא – דראתה, הא לא ראתה – אין חוששין, אלמא – וסתות דרבנן.

דרכי משה יו"ד קפח:ב – וכ"ה בדברי הטור דיש להכשיר אפילו בסמיך ועב הרבה ולכן נראה דיש לסמוך עלייהו להכשיר. גם מה שכתב מהרא"י דהרגשה דאורייתא כדמשמע פרק הרואה כתם צ"ע דבגמ' ריש הרואה כתם לא קאמר דהרגשה דאורייתא אלא במצאה כתם עם הרגשה או שמצאה דם במי רגלים אבל בלאו הכי לא משמע שם דטמא גם לא ראיתי לאחד מן הפוסקים שכתבו לטמאותה בהרגשה בלא ראיה כלל ולכן דבריו צ"ע.

שו"ת רדב"ז חלק א סימן קמט – שאלת על אשה שהרגישה בשעת וסתה ובדקה עצמה ולא מצאה או שמצאה לבן עב קצת אם היא טמאה או טהורה. תשובה דבר זה תמצא מבואר למה"רר ישראל ז"ל סי' רמ"ו והוא ז"ל העלה דאם לא מצאה כלום טמאה דהרגשה סברא דאורייתא היא היכא דליכא למיתלי ההרגשה במידי כדמוכח בפרק הרואה כתם דפריך אנמצא לאחר זמן פטורים מן הקרבן אי דארגישא אמאי פטורים אלמא סברא דאורייתא היא מדמחייב עליה קרבן וכיון דסברא דאורייתא היא הוי כלמ"ד וסתות דאורייתא דאפי' בדקה ומצאה טהורה טמאה כדאיתא בפרק כל היד והיכא דאיכא למיתלי להרגשה כגון שמצאה לבן או כל מראה טהור העלה ז"ל להלכה טהורה היא אבל למעשה כתב אמנם ירא אנכי להקל אם נמצא על העד לחלוחית דסמיך ויש בו מישוש קצת אע"ג דלובן הוא מפני הטועים שאינם יודעים להפליא בין דם לדם ע"כ. ואני אומר כי המקיים חומרא זו עובר משום נשי עמי תגרשון מבית תענגוהו ומבטל מצות עונה: גם מה שכתב דאם הרגישה ובדקה אחר כך ולא מצאה כלום יש לטמאה דודאי יצא טיפת דם כחרדל ונתקנח או נימוח דהרגשה סברא דאורייתא היא וכו' כדלעיל. אינו נכון אצלי כלל דמשמע מדבריו שטמאה מן התורה והא ודאי ליתא דהא כלל גדול אמרו אין האשה מטמאה מן התורה עד שתרגיש ותראה. וז"ל הרמב"ם ז"ל ראש פרק תשיעי אין האשה מתטמאה מן

התורה בנדה או בזיבה עד שתרגיש ותראה דם יוצא בבשרה וכו׳ ואם ראיית דם בלא הרגשה אינה טמאה מן התורה איך היא טמאה בהרגשה בלא ראיית דם. וכי תימא דאומדן דעתא דודאי טפת דם כחרדל יצא ונימוח וכי מאומדן דעת תביא קרבן ונמצאת מביאה חולין לעזרה. והא דמוכח לה מפרק הרואה דפריך תלמודא אנמצא לאחר זמן פטורין מן הקרבן אי דארגישה אמאי פטורין אלמא סברא דאורייתא היא מדמחייב קרבן עליה לאו הוכחה הוא דהתם בנמצא דם על השמש עסקינן ומשום הכי פריך כיון דאיכא דם והרגישה ודאי משעת ההרגשה יצא ואמאי פטורים מקרבן אבל הרגשה בלא דם לא אמרו שיהיו חייבין. ומרוב פשיטות הדבר אני אומר שלא היתה כוונת הרב לומר שהרגשה בלא דם הוי טמאה מן התורה אלא כך היתה כוונתו כיון דהרגשה אם נמצא הדם לאחר זמן תלינן דבזמן ההרגשה יצא והיא טמאה מן התורה. אלמא הרגשה סברא דאורייתא היא הילכך אית לן למיחש מדרבנן אפי׳ היכא דבדקה ולא מצאת דם וגם זה אינו מחוור אצלי שאין לנו לחדש גזרות מדעתינו מה שלא גזרו הראשונים דבשלמא דם בלא הרגשה יש לגזור אבל הרגשה בלא דם לא גזרו וכן בדין שלא יגזרו על ההרגשה שיש כמה מיני מאורעות שמהם תבוא הרגשה לאשה ואינה פתיחת הקבר הילכך לא חששו לה כלל דהא אפי׳ היכא דאיכא דם אמרינן בגמרא דתלינן בהרגשת מי רגלים ובהרגשת עד ובהרגשת שמש וכ״ש היכא דליכא דם דתליא בכל דהוא לא מטמאינן לה אפי׳ מדרבנן.

כללא דמלתא דאם הרגישה בשעת וסתה בלאו הכי אסורה לשמש כל עונת הוסת ואם הרגישה שלא בשעת וסתה יש לחוש כל זמן שלא בדקה אבל אם בדקה עצמה יפה אינה חוששת כלל ודי להן לבנות ישראל שהחמירו על עצמן שאפי׳ רואות טיפת דם כחרדל יושבות עליה שבעת ימים נקיים אבל בלא טיפת דם לא מצינו שהחמירו כלל מתוך ההלכה ומתוך דברי הפוסקים: ואיפשר שבזמנו של הרב ובמקומו היו הנשים מחמירות על עצמן גם בהרגשה בלא דם ומצא להם סמך כל דהוא מהך סוגיא דפרק הרואה כתם. אבל בזמנינו ובמקומינו לא ראיתי ולא שמעתי מי שנוהג חומרא זו.

שולחן ערוך יורה דעה סימן קפח סעיף א ברמ״א – ואם הרגישה שנפתח מקורה, ובדקה מיד ולא מצאה כלום, וע״ל סימן ק״ץ.

שו״ת חתם סופר חלק ב (יורה דעה) סימן קנ – אמנם בהרגשת פתיחת פי המקור וזיעזוע כל הגוף וכדומה או עקוצה כמו עקוצת מי רגלים שהם הרגשת גמורות מה״ת בזה לבי חוכך להחמיר אפי׳ בכתונת מכ״ש בעד שאינו בדוק דעדיף מכתונת והטעם דמשום דמיד שהרגשה אבדה לה חזקת טהרה שלה עד שתבדוק מפני שרוב הזמנים אינה מרגשת באופן זה ואעפ״י שגם על ידי מראות כשרות מרגשת כמ״ש תה״ד מ״מ רוב הנשים אין מרגשת ברוב הזמנים כ״א בהגיע תור דם לצאת וא״כ כ״ז שלא בדקה עצמה הרי היא בספק טמאה ספק הרגשה ממראה טמאה ספק ממראה טהורה ואם בדקה ונאבד העד בטמאה מחזקי׳ לה והה״נ בדקה בעד שאינו בדוק לה ויש לי להבי׳ ראי׳ לזה מש״ס פ״ק דנדה י״ד ע״ב דקאמר והא רבי משום נדה מטמאה לה משו״ה מגיה׳ הברייתא ההיא משום נדה אתמר ואם איתא לימא הא דמטמא משום נדה מיירי בבדקה עצמה ע״י שהרגישה והא דטמא משום כתם היינו שלא הרגשה ורק חשש שמא הרגשת עד והוה כמו הרגשת מ״ר דר״מ ור״י ומשו״ה מדמה לי׳ לפלוגתת ר״מ ור״י דהאשה שעושה צרכי׳

ומנ"ל להגי' הבריי' ודוחק לומר דפשיטא לי' שאין לחלק כלל בין בדיקה שע"י הרגשה לבדיקת שחרית וערבית דודאי סברא גדולה יש לחלק ביניהם אע"כ פשיטא להש"ס דע"י הרגשה אבדה חזקתה וטמאה אפי' בפחו' מכגריס ועוד ואיך אמר רבי בעי כגריס ועוד לאפוקי מדם מאכולות וע"כ דמיירי בבדיקת שחרי' וערבי' בעלמא ולא בבדיקה שע"י הרגשה ואפ"ה מטמא משום נדה משו"ה הוצרך להגיה הבריי' ההיא משום נדה אתמר.

מיהו כל זה בהרגשת פה"מ וכדומה דלא שכיחי הני הרגשות אלא על ידי שום מראה תהיה טהורה או טמאה ואבדה חזקתה עד שתבדוק אבל הרגשת זיבת דבר לח אפי' יהיבנא ליה להגאון נב"י ז"ל שהוא הרגשה דאוריי' (מה שאינני מודה לו) מ"מ היינו שאם ראתה דם ע"י הרגשה כזו חייבים עלי' כרת שהרי הרגישה בבשרה וקורא אני בה בבשרה שתרגיש בבשרה אבל שיהיה הרגשה כזו מוציאה מחזקת טהרה שלה עד שנאמר שאם נאבד העד או שאינו בדוק תהיה בספק טומאה זה לא אמרי' וא"א לאומרו כלל דכיון דהני נשי דידן רוב ימיהם מרגישים זיבת דבר לח ואיננו דבר חידוש אצלה כמו פתיחת פה"מ והרי אשה בחזקת טהרה עומדת בין וסת לוסת ואיה חזקת טהרתה ודוקא הרגשת פה"מ שהוא דבר רחוק ולא יארע לה כן על הרוב אלא בשעת וסתה וכדומה א"כ אבדה חזקתה משא"כ בזיבת דבר לח ופשיטא שאינה טמאה יותר אלא כשאר בדיקות עד שאינו בדוק.

פתחי תשובה יורה דעה סימן קצ ס"ק ו – ולא מצאה כלום – אבל אם מצאה מראות כשרות כגון ליחה לבנה או ירוקה או כמראה גע"ל טהורה ותולה הרגשתה בזו כמבואר לעיל ר"ס קפ"ח.

שולחן ערוך יורה דעה סימן קפח סעיף א – כל מראה אדום, בין אם היא כהה הרבה, או עמוק, טמאים. וכן כל מראה שחור. ואין טהור אלא מראה לבן וכן מראה ג ירוק, אפילו כמראה השעוה או הזהב, וכ"ש הירוק ככרתי או כעשבים. (מרדכי). וכן מראה שקורין בל"א בלו"א בכלל ירוק הוא), ואפילו יש בו סמיכות דם והוא עב הרבה, ואפילו הרגישה שנפתח מקורה, ובדקה מיד ומצאה מראות הללו, טהורה.

חכמת אדם כלל קיג ס"ק ג – ונ"ל דה"ה נשים שרגיל בהם ליחה לבנה ומוחזקות בזה אפי' הרגישה זיבת דבר לח ולא בדקה טהורה כיון שמוחזקת בכך ורגילה בכך תלינן במצוי.

3.

תלמוד בבלי מסכת נדה דף כא עמוד א – גמ'. אמר רב יהודה אמר שמואל: לא טימא רבי יהודה אלא בחתיכה של ארבעת מיני דמים, אבל של שאר מיני דמים – טהורה. ור' יוחנן אמר: של ארבעת מיני דמים – דברי הכל טמאה, של שאר מיני דמים – דברי הכל טהורה, לא נחלקו אלא שהפילה ואינה יודעת מה הפילה; רבי יהודה סבר: זיל בתר רוב חתיכות, ורוב חתיכות של (מיני) ארבעת מיני דמים הויין. ורבנן סברי: לא אמרינן רוב חתיכות של ארבעת מיני דמים. איני, והא כי אתא רב הושעיא מנהרדעא, אתא ואייתי מתניתא בידיה: המפלת חתיכה אדומה, שחורה, ירוקה, ולבנה, אם יש עמה דם – טמאה, ואם לאו – טהורה. רבי יהודה אומר בין כך ובין כך טמאה – קשיא לשמואל בחדא, ולרבי יוחנן בתרתי! לשמואל בחדא – דאמר שמואל: לא טימא

רבי יהודה אלא בחתיכה של ארבעת מיני דמים, והא קתני ירוקה ולבנה, ופליג רבי יהודה! וכי תימא: כי פליג רבי יהודה – אאדומה ושחורה, ואירוקה ולבנה – לא, אלא ירוקה ולבנה למאן קתני לה? אילימא רבנן – השתא אדומה ושחורה מטהרי רבנן, ירוקה ולבנה מיבעיא? אלא לאו – לרבי יהודה, ופליג! ותו, לרבי יוחנן דאמר: של ארבעת מיני דמים – דברי הכל טמאה, הא קתני אדומה ושחורה ופליגי רבנן! וכי תימא: כי פליגי רבנן – אירוקה ולבנה, אבל אאדומה ושחורה – לא, אלא אדומה ושחורה למאן קתני לה? אילימא רבי יהודה – השתא ירוקה ולבנה טמאה, אדומה ושחורה מיבעיא? אלא לאו – רבנן, ופליגי! אלא אמר רב נחמן בר יצחק: באפשר לפתיחת הקבר בלא דם קמיפלגי, ובפלוגתא דהני תנאי, דתניא: קשתה שנים ולשלישי הפילה, ואינה יודעת מה הפילה – הרי זו ספק לידה ספק זיבה, מביאה קרבן ואינו נאכל. רבי יהושע אומר: מביאה קרבן ונאכל, שאי אפשר לפתיחת הקבר בלא דם.

רמב"ם הלכות איסורי ביאה פרק ה הלכה י – המפלת חתיכה אע"פ שהיא אדומה אם יש עמה דם טמאה ואם לאו טהורה ואפילו נקרעה החתיכה ונמצאת מליאה דם הרי זו טהורה שאין זה דם נדה אלא דם חתיכה.

תלמוד בבלי מסכת נדה דף סו עמוד א – אדבריה רבא לרב שמואל ודרש: קשתה שני ימים ולשלישי הפילה – תשב שבעה נקיים. קסבר: אין קשוי לנפלים, ואי אפשר לפתיחת הקבר בלא דם. א"ל רב פפא לרבא: מאי אריא, קשתה שני ימים – אפילו משהו בעלמא! דהא א"ר זירא: בנות ישראל החמירו על עצמן, שאפילו רואות טפת דם כחרדל – יושבות עליה שבעה נקיים! א"ל: אמינא לך איסורא, ואת אמרת מנהגא? היכא דאחמור – אחמור, היכא דלא אחמור – לא אחמור.

שולחן ערוך יורה דעה הלכות נדה סימן קצד סעיף ב – המפלת בתוך מ' ב אינה חוששת לולד אבל חוששת משום נדה, אפילו לא ראתה. הגה: מפני שא"א לפתיחת הקבר בלא דם, ונפקא מינה דמיד לאחר שספרה ז' נקיים מותרת ואינה חוששת לולד (ד"ע).

תלמוד בבלי מסכת שבת דף קכט עמוד א – מאימתי פתיחת הקבר? אמר אביי: משעה שתשב על המשבר. רב הונא בריה דרב יהושע אמר: משעה שהדם שותת ויורד. ואמרי לה: משעה שחברותיה נושאות אותה באגפיה.

פתחי תשובה יורה דעה סימן קצד:ח – רובו – עבה"ט של הרב מהרי"ט ז"ל שהביא בשם תשובת נחלת שבעה סי' ט' באשה שישבה על המשבר ופסקו החבלין וצירין דצריכה שבעה נקיים משום דאמרינן בשבת מאימתי מחללין עליה שבת משעת פתיחת הקבר וקתני עלה מאימתי פתיחת הקבר משעה שישבה על המשבר וא"א לפתיחת הקבר בלא דם ע"ש ועיין ח"ד שחלק על דברי נ"ש אלו ופסק להתיר ע"ש (וכן הסכימו בספר כרתי ופלתי וס"ט אלא דבמקום שנהגו איסור לא ישנו [גם בשאלות ותשובות תשובה מאהבה חלק א' סי' קי"ד השיג על הנ"ש והורה להתיר והסכים עמו רבו הגאון בעל נו"ב ז"ל [וכן הסכים בתשו' חתם סופר סי' קע"ט והוסיף עוד לומר

דאף המנהג שהעידו נשי פולין לפני בעל נ"ש אינו אלא בסתם אבל אם בדקוה המילדות ומצאו הפתח סגור אפילו מנהג ליכא ע"ש]. ועי' בספר בינת אדם ועמש"ל סק"ד.

סדרי טהרה סימן קצד ס"ק כה – ומ"ש בס' כו"פ דבאותה שעה צריך הבעל להזהר בה נ"ל דלאו דוקא באותה שעה שישבה על המשבר אלא מיד שאחזוה צירים וחבלי לידה ומבקשת להביא לה חכמה צריך הבעל להזהר בה דודאי לאו ישיבת המשבר גורם פה"ק אלא כל שהיא קרובה ללידה כ"כ שצריכה לישב על המשבר ואיכא למיחש אלו היתה המילדת מזומנת אצלה היתה מושיבה מיד על המשבר לכן צריך להיות ניזהר בה ואם אח"כ נתגלה שטעות היה אצלה אין כאן שום מיחוש דהא חזינן דטעות היה ואין לחוש דנפתח הקבר ואח"כ נסתם דזה לא שכיח וטפי מיסתבר למיתלי בטעות.

חוות דעת סימן קצד ס"ק א – ולענ"ד לא נראה כן הא דאמרינן בסוף הסימן ביוצא דופן דטהורה מנדה וכי מיירי בלא ישבה על המשבר כלל אלא ודאי נראה דהא דאמרינן דא"א לפתיחת הקבר בלא דם היינו דוקא כשהפילה איזה דבר דנפתח הקבר כ"כ עד שיצא ממנה אז אמרינן דא"א בלא דם אבל כשנפתח הקבר ולא יצא ממנה אף דם אינו יוצא ואין ראיה ממה שחשובה חולה לומר שיצא גם כן ממנה דם.

שו"ת נודע ביהודה מהדורה תנינא – יורה דעה סימן קכ – ושאלה שניה אשר שאל האריכות ללא צורך ופשוט הא שמה שאמרו אי אפשר לפה"ק בלא דם אין חילוק בין גרם הפתיחה הוא מבפנים ובין גרם הפתיחה הוא מבחוץ שהרופא הכניס אצבעו או איזה כלי ופתח פי המקור, גם אין חילוק בין היא ילדה או זקינה המסולקת מדמים או מעוברת ומניקה תמיד אין פתיחת הקבר בלא דם. ולרוב הטרדה אקצר. דברי הד"ש.

בית יוסף יורה דעה סימן קפח – ודוקא חתיכות קטנות דומיא דשפופרת אבל חתיכה גדולה טמאה אפילו לא ראתה כלום שאי אפשר לפתיחת קבר בלא דם. בריש פרק המפלת (שם) תנן המפלת חתיכה אם יש עמה דם טמאה ואם לאו טהורה רבי יהודה אומר בין כך ובין כך טמאה ואוקימנא בגמרא דבשביל החתיכה עצמה אינה טמאה אפילו היא מארבע מראות דמים אלא בהא הוא דפליגי דרבנן סברי אפשר לפתיחת הקבר בלא דם ורבי יהודה סבר אי אפשר לפתיחת הקבר בלא דם ופסק הרא"ש (פ"ג סי' א) דהלכה כרבי יהודה וקשה שהרי הוא ז"ל כתב (סוף סי' ב) דאיפשיטא בעיין דרואה דם בשפופרת טהורה ומשמע נמי מדבריו דסבר דהלכה כרבנן דסברי דאין דרכה של אשה לראות דם בחתיכה ולפי מה שפסק כרבי יהודה דאמר אי אפשר לפתיחת הקבר בלא דם רואה בשפופרת או בחתיכה אמאי מטהר לה הרי נפתח הקבר על ידם ואי אפשר בלא דם ולכך חילק רבינו בין חתיכה קטנה לגדולה דקטנה אין בה פתיחת הקבר שנאמר שאי אפשר לה בלא דם ותדע דהא דאמרינן דרבנן סברי אין דרכה של אשה לראות דם בחתיכה בחתיכה קטנה קאמרי ולא בגדולה דהא כיון דמייתי לה בגמרא (איבעיא) [אאיבעיא] דשפופרת משמע בחתיכה קטנה דומיא דשפופרת קאמרי וכן כתבו התוספות (כב: ד"ה ליפלוג) והרשב"א (ת"ה ב"ז סוף ש"א ארוך וקצר ג:, ש"ו ארוך כז. וקצר כו:) והרא"ש (פ"ג סי' ג) ז"ל גבי

רואה כמין קליפות כמין שערות כמין עפר כמין יבחושים אדומים תטיל למים אם נימוחו טמאה ואם לאו טהורה דאפילו רבי יהודה דסבר דאי אפשר לפתיחת הקבר בלא דם בהא מודה דאם לא נימוחו טהורה משום דאין פתיחת הקבר לדברים קטנים כאלו.

תוספות מסכת נדה דף כב עמוד ב – ליפלוג נמי רבי יהודה בהא – אשערה וקליפה לא פריך דליפלוג רבי יהודה דמועטין נינהו ולא שייך בהו פתיחת קבר.

חזון איש יו"ד סימן פג סעיף א' – בפ"ת סי' קצ"ד סק"ד הביא בשם הנו"ב דמה שאמרו א"א לפה"ק בלא דם אין חילוק בין גרם הפתיחה מבפנים ובין מבחוץ, צ"ע דהא איכא מ"ד אפשר לפה"ק בלא דם וא"כ למעוטי בפלוגתא עדיף ופתה"ק המוזכר בגמ' היינו ישבה על המשבר או חברותיה נושאות אותה על אגפיה כדאמר שבת קכ"ט א', וכו' אבל מ"מ שמעינן דפתה"ק דבגמרא הוא אתערותא דלידה ומנ"ל לחדש בפתיחה מבחוץ דאינו ענין לאתערותא דלידה שפועל על כל גופה וחשיבא בסכנה לחלל השבת.

שו"ת אגרות משה יורה דעה חלק ב סימן עו – הנה בדבר אשה שישבה על המשבר ואח"כ נפסקו הצירין והחבלים שבעל הנ"ש הובא בפ"ת יו"ד סימן קצ"ד סק"ח סובר שצריכה ז' נקיים משום דמחשיב זה פתיחת הקבר מהא דבשבת דף קכ"ט אמר אביי דפה"ק הוא משעה שתשב על המשבר ופה"ק א"א בלא דם והאחרונים חולקים ומתירין ושואל כתר"ה אם הוא גם בלא בדיקה או שצריכה לכל הפחות בדיקה, הנה יש חלוק בין טעם החו"ד שפליג ומתיר ובין טעם הסד"ט, דהחו"ד בסק"א משמע דג"כ מודה להנ"ש דהיה פה"ק מאחר שהיו לה צירים וחבלים אך שמחדש דפה"ק כשלא יצא ממנה שום דבר אמרינן דגם דם לא יצא ממנה ואין ראיה ממה שחשובה חולה בפה"ק לחלל שבת אף בלא יצא ע"ז כלום לומר שיצא ממנה דם, עיי"ש שזהו כוונתו, דלכן מסתבר שיש להצריך בדיקה דכיון שעכ"פ היתה פה"ק שהוא להוציא איזה דבר דאין דרכו להפתח לפי רובא דרובא פעמים בלא הוצאת איזה דבר עב אבל מאחר שעכ"פ לא יצא כלום מוכרחין לומר שהיא מהמיעוט שנפתח גם בלא הוצאת שום דבר אלא ענין חולי הוא או מקרה בעלמא שגם לא מצד מחלה, וממילא לא על פה"ק כזה נאמר א"א לפה"ק בלא דם שזה נאמר על רובא פה"ק שמפילות איזה דבר, ולא על פה"ק דלא מצוי כלל דאולי גם דם אינו יוצא, אבל אין לומר בשביל זה שודאי לא יצא דם דהא גם זה לא נמצא בגמ' שלכן מסתבר שהוא ספק שמא יצא דם ותועיל בדיקה, אבל עכ"פ יש להצריך בדיקה. אבל הסד"ט סי' קצ"ד בס"ק כ"ה בשם ספר סולת למנחה סובר דאיגלאי מלתא דלא הי' פה"ק כלל וחבלי שוא היו וכן הביא מכו"פ דלפ"ז אין להצריך בדיקה מאחר דאיגלאי שלא היה לה פה"ק כלל דלדידהו משמע שליכא כלל פה"ק בלא הפלת איזה דבר ולשון הכו"פ דלא שכיח שיהיה נפתח ויחזור ויסתום כוונתו דליכא כלל דבר כזה ולכן בהכרח שהיה טעות וכאבא בעלמא הוא דכאיב לה, ואולי יש לפרש כפשוטו דלא שכיח כלל היינו מכיון שלא מצוי כלל לא אמרינן דמה שראינו שלא יצא כלום שבאשה זו אירע מה שלא מצוי אלא אמרינן שהיה טעות וממילא ג"כ אין להצריך בדיקה כיון דאין חוששין כלל לזה. ומשמע שרוב האחרונים סברי דאיגלאי שהיה טעות ולא נפתח הקבר כלל וכן הוא

בחת"ס חיו"ד סימן קע"ט דלכן אין להצריך בדיקה אך אולי מהראוי להחמיר לכתחלה לחוש להחו"ד להצריכה לבדוק אבל כשלא עשתה בדיקה שהוא לאסור אין להחמיר כלל.

והנה לכאורה יצא עוד מחלוקת בנפתח הקבר בשביל שצריכה לילד אבל עברו איזה שעות ולפעמים גם יום שלם שלא ילדה דבסד"ט מסיק דצריך הבעל ליזהר ממנה תיכף כשישבה על המשבר דאיכא כבר פה"ק פורתא אף שעדיין יכולה להלך, דהוא רק מחמת שסובר כהסולת למנחה דאם אך איכא פה"ק היתה נאסרת מצד איסור נדה אך שפליג עליו דהסולת למנחה סובר דכל זמן שיכולה להלך ליכא פה"ק והסד"ט סובר דאיכא פה"ק לחשש איסור נדה אף בפחות מעיגול הראש כפיקה שעדיין יכולה להלך ומתני' דאהלות פ"ז מ"ד מפרש דהוא דוקא לענין שלא יתחשב טומאה בלועה עיי"ש, דלכן כיון שישבה על המשבר דליכא טעות ומה שיכולה להלך הוא משום שהוא פה"ק פורתא נמי טמאה לבעלה משום נדה, אבל להחו"ד דסובר דפה"ק ממש כשלא יצא ממנה שום דבר אמרינן דגם דם אפשר לא יצא אין לאוסרה לבעלה כשבדקה ולא מצאה דם ולא צריך ליזהר מליגע בה, ולדינא בזה צריך להחמיר כהסד"ט.

ועל החו"ד למה שכתבתי שסובר דפתיחת הקבר אך כיון שלא יצא ממנה שום דבר אמרינן שגם דם לא יצא ממנה, לכאורה יקשה דהא בהרגישה שנפתח מקורה ובדקה ולא מצאה כלום מפורש בסימן ק"צ סעיף א' יש מי שאומר שהיא טמאה, ועיין במשנה אחרונה בנדה פ"ג מ"א שכתב בשביל זה דאפילו להפוסקים דאפשר לפתה"ק בלא דם היינו במפלת חתיכה או שום דבר אבל נפתח הקבר ולא יצא ממנה שום דבר א"א שלא יצא ממנה כל שהו דם ונאבד במיעוטו, והוא לכאורה ההיפוך מהחו"ד. וצריך לומר דיש חלוק בין פה"ק דחשבה מזה שצריכה להוליד הולד שפה"ק זה אינו להוציא דם אלא הולד וכיון שלא יצא הולד ולא נפילת חתיכות אמרינן להחו"ד שאף להפוסקים שא"א לפה"ק בלא דם מכיון שלא יצא שום דבר לא יצא גם דם, אבל פתיחת המקור שהרגישה שכתב המחבר שהיא טמאה מפורש שם שנפתח מקורה להוציא דם, שהיא הרגשה אחרת, ופלא שהמשנ"א השמיט מלשון הש"ע תיבות להוציא דם. אבל אפשר שהמשנ"א סובר דאין לנשים לידע זה ויאסור מצד זה בכל הרגשת פתיחת הקבר אך מ"מ אפשר גם לומר דבמעוברת שיש לה צירים וחבלים שהרגשה זו הוא רק להולדה דפה"ק זה אין לחוש לדם נדה כשלא יצא ממנה דבר כהחו"ד, אבל המשנ"א משמע שאינו סובר כהחו"ד.

ובדבר מה שראה באיזה ספר רפואה שבשבועות האחרונות החלק של הרחם אצל פתח הרחם נעשם דק מכח התכווצות ומתחיל לפתוח מעט ושמע שלפעמים נפתח כמטבע הנקרא ניקל וגם כמטבע הנקרא קוואדער, הנה אם היה האמת דנפתח כמטבע ניקל וכ"ש קוואדער היה זה פה"ק והיה תלוי במחלוקת החו"ד והסד"ט שהיה לן להחמיר, אבל האמת שאינו כן ועד סמוך להלידה אינו נפתח והנידון של הנ"ש הוא מצד הצירים והחבלים שישבה כבר על המשבר סובר הנ"ש דהיתה פה"ק ללידה ואח"כ עבר זה וחזר ונסתם וע"ז כתבו דלא שכיח דיחזור ויסתום שלכן אמרינן שודאי טעו מלומר שנסתם ולדברי מה ששמע כתר"ה הרי נשאר פתוח שלכן אין לחוש לדבריהם ואין לאסור כדלעיל.

פתחי תשובה יורה דעה סימן קצד – לפתיחת הקבר – עי' בנודע ביהודה תניינא חיו"ד ס"ס ק"כ דמה שאמרו א"א לפה"ק בלא דם אין חילוק בין גרם הפתיחה מבפנים ובין מבחוץ כגון שהרופא

הכניס אצבעו או איזה כלי ופתח פי המקור גם אין חילוק בין אם היא ילדה או זקנה מעוברת או מניקה תמיד אין פה"ק בלא דם ע"ש. [ועי' בספר בינת אדם סי' כ"ג דכתב עליו דמ"ש כגון שהרופא הכניס אצבעו אגב שיטפיה כ"כ ולא דק שהרי עיקר הבדיקה בהפסק טהרה שתכניס אצבעה בעומק א"ו דאין זה ענין לפה"ק שהרי אפילו האבר כשהוא גדול הרבה אינו מגיע רק עד הפרוזדור ולא לחדר כמ"ש התוי"ט בשם רמב"ם פ"ב דנדה מ"ה ע"ש. גם בתשו' ח"ס סי' קע"ט כתב דהן אשה הבודקת עצמה בחו"ס והן המילדת שבדקה לעולם לא יגעו בפה"ק שהוא המקור אלא בבה"ח ובשום אופן אינה יכולה להכניס אצבעה לפנים עד שתפתח בטבע וזה נקרא פה"ק שא"א בלא דם ע"ש]. ועי' בשו"ת תשובה מאהבה ח"א סי' קט"ז בתשובת הגאון בעל נו"ב ז"ל שם שכתב דמה שאמרו אין פה"ק בלא דם היינו אם הקבר נפתח ויצא ממנו דבר גוש כמו ולד או חתיכה כל שאינו דק כשפופרת דק של קש או שילדה רוח אבל כשלא יצא דבר או שיצא דבר דק מאד משקה לא אמרינן אין פה"ק בלא דם דאל"כ היכא משכחת כלל דם טהור הרי עכ"פ נפתח הקבר ע"ש עוד.

ביאור הגר"א יורה דעה סימן קפח [כג] – אם היא כו'. הרא"ש שם ולפתיחת הקבר לא חיישינן לדברים קטנים כאלו וכ"כ בת"ה והביאו ראיה מדפריך שם בגמ' וליפליג נמי ר"י כו' ולא פריך ארישא כמין קליפה כו' ועתוס' שם ד"ה ליפליג כו' וכ' ב"י דשיעור חתיכה קטנה לא ידעינן ומיהו כיון דבשפופרת חזינן דטהור ה"נ בחתיכות כעין שפופרת וכ"כ הטור וכ' ב"י דשפופרת עצמה לא ידעינן לכן משערינן קנה דק כו' (ליקוט) אם היא חתיכה כו'. שאינו מפורש שיעור החתיכה לפתיחת הקבר אבל בפ"ז דאהלות אמרינן אין לנפלים כו' (ע"כ).

משנה מסכת אהלות פרק ז משנה ד – האשה שהיא מקשה לילד והוציאוה מבית לבית הראשון טמא בספק והשני בודאי אמר רבי יהודה אימתי בזמן שהיא ניטלת בגפים אבל אם היתה מהלכת הראשון טהור שמשנפתח הקבר אין פנאי להלך אין לנפלים פתיחת הקבר עד שיעגילו ראש כפיקה.

.4

תלמוד בבלי מסכת נדה דף כא עמוד ב – בעא מיניה רבי ירמיה מרבי זירא: הרואה דם בשפופרת מהו? (ויקרא ט"ו) בבשרה אמר רחמנא ולא בשפופרת או דלמא – האי בבשרה מיבעי ליה – שמטמאה מבפנים כבחוץ? אמר ליה: בבשרה אמר רחמנא ולא בשפופרת; דאי בבשרה מבעי ליה שמטמאה מבפנים כבחוץ – א"כ נימא קרא (בבשר), מאי בבשרה – שמע מינה תרתי. והא"ר יוחנן משום רבי שמעון בן יוחי: המפלת חתיכה – קורעה, אם יש בה דם אגור – טמאה, ואם לאו – טהורה! הכי השתא? התם – דרכה של אשה לראות דם בחתיכה, הכא – אין דרכה של אשה לראות דם בשפופרת. לימא שפופרת תנאי היא; דתניא, המפלת חתיכה, אף על פי שמלאה דם, אם יש עמה דם – טמאה, ואם לאו – טהורה. רבי אליעזר אומר: בבשרה – ולא בשפיר, ולא בחתיכה. ר' אליעזר היינו תנא קמא! אימא: שרבי אליעזר אומר בבשרה ולא בשפיר ולא בחתיכה, וחכמים אומרים: אין זה דם נדה אלא דם חתיכה תנא קמא נמי טהורי מטהר! אלא דפלי פלויי איכא בינייהו, תנא קמא סבר: בבשרה – ולא בשפיר ולא בחתיכה, והוא הדין

לשפופרת; והני מילי – היכא דשיעא, אבל פלי פלויי – טמאה, מאי טעמיה – בבשרה קרינא ביה. ואתו רבנן למימר: אף על גב דפלי פלויי – אין זה דם נדה אלא דם חתיכה, הא דם נדה ודאי טמא, ואפילו בשפופרת נמי.

שולחן ערוך הרב יורה דעה הלכות נדה סימן קפח סעיף ח – הכניסה שפופרת. עד המקור (רא"ש) פירוש ועד בכלל שהכניסתו לתוך מקור דמיה ונכנס הדם בשפופרת והוציאתו לחוץ ואין דרך נשים לראות כן ומשום הכי טהורה שנאמר דם יהיה זובה בבשרה בבשרה ולא בשפופרת וטעמא דקרא לאו משום חציצה הוא שהשפופרת מפסקת בין דם לבשר בית החיצון אלא טעמא דקרא משום שאין דרך נשים לראות דם בזה הענין ולא טמא הכתוב אלא בשרואה כדרך שהנשים רגילות לראות. ואף על פי שהכניסה השפופרת לתוך המקור ואין פתיחת הקבר בלא דם כדלקמן ודם שעל ידי פתיחת הקבר דרך נשים הוא (בכל עת לידתן) הכא מיירי בשפופרת של קנה שהוא דק ולא נפתח הקבר על ידו (ב"י) כדלקמן סוף סי' זה (אבל בשפופרת עבה שהקבר נפתח על ידו כיון שאי אפשר לפתיחת הקבר בלא דם ודרך נשים הוא לראות דם על ידי פתיחת הקבר אין השפופרת מועלת לטהר הדם שיוצא על ידי פתיחת הקבר כדרך הנשים דמה לי שנפתח הקבר על ידי ולד שלם או מחותך או חתיכות בשר או שפופרת שכבר ריבה הכתוב זוב דמה לרבות רואה מחמת אונס כל שהיא רואה כדרך הנשים דהיינו שזב הדם מעצמו על ידי פתיחת הקבר או אונס אחר ולא שהוציאתו השפופרת בעצמה בכניסתה למקור שלא על ידי פתיחת הקבר כגון של קנה דק שלא נפתח הקבר על ידו). כן דעת הטור ושו"ע לפי דעת הרא"ש. ועיין לקמן דעת התוס' והרמב"ם.

שו"ת מנחת שלמה תנינא (ב–ג) סימן עב – ענף ב'. בענין ראתה דם בשפופרת ה) הצעת תקנה של לבישת שפופרת, ולהקדים בכך זמן הטבילה. ו) דעת רוב הראשונים דהא דראתה בשפופרת טהורה הוא משום חציצה בין הדם והבשר, ואפי' אם השפופרת רק בפרוזדור ג"כ טהורה. ז) מבאר דעת המאירי בענין ראתה בשפופרת. ח) ראתה בשפופרת טהורה גם מדרבנן אפי' אם הדם יצא כרגיל ולא מחמת השפופרת, ואם יש חילוק בין אם הדם "תוך" השפופרת או "על" השפופרת. ט) דעת הר"ן דטעמא דראתה בשפופרת טהורה הוא משום דליכא הרגשה, ודעת החולקים עליו. י) שטת הר"ש והרא"ש רטעמא דראתה בשפופרת טהורה הוא משום דאין דרך לראות בענין זה, וכתב בשו"ע הרב ז"ל דלדידהו אינה טהורה אא"כ יציאת הדם היתה מחמת השפופרת, וגם דוקא שלא בשעת וסתה. יא) אפשר שגם הר"ש סובר טעמא דחציצה, כן פירש בדבריו רבנו ירוחם ז"ל. יב) מביא מגדולי אחרונים שלא פירשו בדעת הר"ש כהרב ז"ל. יג) מוכיח מהב"י כהרב ז"ל, מבאר דברי החוו"ד בענין שפופרת דקה ועבה, ומעיר על פירוש הרב בדעת הר"ש. יד) ביאור דברי הב"י הנ"ל, בענין יצא ממנה דם דרך האויר, גם הצ"צ נוטה דבחציצה תליא מלתא, הערה על שטת הרב ז"ל, ודעת המהרש"א בענין זה. טו) בע"ס פרדס רמונים מפרש בדעת הטור ושו"ע שאף אם יש חציצה טמאה עכ"פ מדרבנן, ומבאר שאין דבריו מוכרחים. טז) מסתפק בנוגע לההצעה של שפופרת אם צריכים לחשוש שראתה דם תיכף עם סילוק השפופרת, ואם חייבת לבדוק תיכף. יז) מסיק שצריכים לחשוש לדעת הרב ז"ל ולצאת מחשש איסור תורה, ובענין ספק שנולד בדאורייתא ונתגלגל לדרבנן. יח) דעת מרן הגרצ"פ ז"ל בענין שפופרת קצרה. יט) מבאר דברי

הנצי״ב ז״ל בענין אשה שעשו לה נתוח והדם יוצא דרך צנור השתן. כ) אשה שראתה ג׳ פעמים מ״ת, או ראתה פעם אחת בליל טבילה, אם יש לה תקנה ע״י לבישת שפופרת. כא) בענין לבישת שפופרת, או בדיקה ע״י מוך דחוק, בנוגע לחששא דדם חימוד.

ה) ברם נראה דאע״ג שכתבנו שגם בשעת הדחק גדול א״א להקל ולעבור אחומרא דר׳ זירא, מ״מ נלענ״ד תקנה אחרת לאותן נשים אשר נפשן בשאלתן להקדים טבילתן, והוא שתלבש האשה יום או יומים לפני הוסת שפופרת של גומי דק על פי המקור ויהי׳ סגור ומהודק היטב על פי המקור באופן שאפי׳ טפת דם פחות מכחרדל לא תוכל לצאת מחוץ לשפופרת, והקצה השני של השפופרת יהי׳ פתוח ונמשך עד חוץ לגופה ממש באופן שכל הדם היוצא מן האשה לא יגע כלל בבשרה שבפנים ושבבית החיצון אלא יצא כולו מהמקור עד חוץ לגופה אך ורק דרך השפופרת, ולאחר שתרגיש ותדע ברור שכבר פסקה לראות דם תנגב היטב בזהירות רבה את תוך השפופרת עיין לקמן אות ט״ז, ואח״כ תסיר את השפופרת ותוציאנה מגופה באופן שלא יהי׳ שום צל של ספק שמא יצאה טפת דם מהשפופרת לתוך הגוף, וכאשר יעברו ז׳ ימים מתחלת ראיתה תפסיק בטהרה כנדה דאורייתא ותטבול מספק בלי ברכה בליל יום ח׳ ותהי׳ טהורה מיד. ועתה הנני לנמק ולבאר בע״ה דבר זה מהגמ׳ והפוסקים, והנני תפלה שלא אכשל ח״ו לומר על טמא טהור ויהי ד׳ בעזרי לומר על טהור טהור.

במס׳ נדה דף כ״א ע״ב בעא מיניה ר׳ ירמיה מר׳ זירא הרואה דם בשפופרת מהו [הכניסה קנה חלול באותו מקום ונמצא בתוכו דם] בבשרה אמר רחמנא ולא בשפופרת [דם יהי׳ זובה בבשרה שיצא דרך כותלי בית הרחם ואין מפסיק] או דלמא האי בבשרה מיבעי ליה שמטמאה מבפנים כבחוץ [מאחר שיצא מן המקור לפרוזדור והעמידו כותליה מיד היא מטמאה משא״כ בזב ובעל קרי דאין מטמאין עד שתצא טומאתן לחוץ] אמר לי׳ בבשרה אמר רחמנא ולא בשפופרת דאי בבשרה מיבעי לי׳ שמטמאה מבפנים כבחוץ נימא קרא בשרה מאי בבשרה ש״מ תרתי, והא א״ר יוחנן משום רשב״י המפלת חתיכה קורעה אם יש בה דם אגור טמאה ואם לאו טהורה [ומאי שנא משפופרת] הכי השתא התם דרכה של אשה לראות דם בחתיכה [הלכך בבשרה קרינא ביה דמין במינו לא חייץ] הכא אין דרכה של אשה לראות דם בשפופרת. לימא שפופרת תנאי היא דתניא המפלת חתיכה אע״פ שמלאה דם אם יש עמה דם טמאה ואם לאו טהורה – שר׳ אליעזר אומר בבשרה ולא בשפיר ולא בחתיכה וחכמים אומרים אין זה דם נדה אלא דם חתיכה, תנא קמא נמי טהורי מטהר אלא דפלי פלויי [שיש בה שורות שורות ביקועים והדם שם] איכא בינייהו ת״ק סבר בבשרה ולא בשפיר ולא בחתיכה וה״ה לשפופרת [דת״ק לא מטהר לה אלא מגזיה״כ סבר האי דם טמא הוא ומשום חציצה היא טהורה ומשום גזיה״כ וה״ה לשפופרת כיון דטעמא משום חציצה הוא] והני מילי היכא דשיעא [חתיכה והדם בתוכה לא נגע] אבל פלי פלויי [והדם שם ונוגע ברחם] טמאה מ״ט בבשרה קרינא ביה, ואתו רבנן למימר אע״ג דפלי פלויי אין זה דם נדה אלא דם חתיכה הא דם נדה ודאי טמא ואפי׳ בשפופרת נמי [רבנן בתראי לא דייקי לישנא דקרא והא דמטהרי משום דלאו דם נדה הוא הלכך לא שנא בתוכה כי שיעא ולא שנא פלי פלויי דנגע ברחם טהורה אבל שפופרת דם נדה היא טמאה דלא דרשינן בבשרה אלא לטמא בפנים כבחוץ] אמר אביי בשפופרת כו״ע לא פליגי דטהורה [דאין דרך הרואה בכך והרש״ל מחק דברים אלה והגיה דדייקינן לישנא דקרא] כי פליגי בחתיכה מר סבר

דרכה של אשה לראות דם בחתיכה ומר סבר אין דרכה של אשה לראות דם בחתיכה [כי פליגי בחתיכה ודפלי פלויי דת"ק סבר בבשרה למעוטי תוך חתיכה אבל דם הנראה בבקעים טמא דהאי בבשרה קרינן ביה ורבנן בתראי סברי אפי' פלי פלויי טהורה דאין זה דם נדה דאין דרכה של אשה לראות דם בחתיכה] עכ"ל הגמ' עם פירוש רש"י ז"ל.

ו) הרי מבואר דעת רש"י דאף שלפי הס"ד רק ר"א ממעט שפופרת משום חציצה מדרשא דבבשרה ואילו רבנן לא דרשי כלל בבשרה למעט חציצה, מ"מ לפי תירוצו של אביי דקיי"ל כוותיה מודו כו"ע דבשפופרת טהורה משום דדרשינן מקרא למעט חציצה ולא נחלקו אלא בחתיכה ובפלי פלויי דלא שייך כלל טעמא דחציצה וטעמייהו דרבנן דמטהרי הוא משום דסברי דאין זה דם נדה. אולם התוס' בד"ה כי הקשו על רש"י "דא"כ השתא אין דרך לראות דם בחתיכה לא הוי כההיא דאין דרכה לראות בשפופרת דהתם הוי דם נדות אלא שאין דרכה לראות באותו ענין", ולכן פירשו דלאביי לא נחלקו ר"א ורבנן אלא בחתיכה העשויה כמין שפופרת שחוצץ בין הדם והבשר דר"א מטמא משום דרק שפיר וחתיכה שמקיפים את הדם מכל הצדדים חייצי וכן שפופרת חייץ נמי מפני שאינו מינו אבל חתיכה כעין שפופרת אינה חוצצת ואילו רבנן סברי דכיון שאין דרכה לראות בענין זה גם חתיכה חוצצת, אבל בפלי פלויי כיון שהדם נוגע בבשר גם רבנן מטמאים, ועיי"ש בריטב"א ובחדושי הר"ן דנראה שסוברים כרש"י ומיישבים קושית התוס', אבל עכ"פ מבואר שגם להתוס' בשפופרת טהורה לכו"ע משום דחוצץ בין הדם והבשר, אולם הרמב"ן ז"ל ג"כ מקשה על רש"י כהתוס' ופירש משום כך דרבנן פליגי אר"א וסברי דדרכה של אשה לראות דם בחתיכה ולא טיהרו אלא מפני שאין זה דם נדה אלא דם חתיכה אבל היכא דהוי ודאי דם נדה כגון שמצאה בתוך החתיכה דם אגור טמאה, ואילו ר"א סובר אין דרכה של אשה לראות דם בחתיכה ולכן אף אם דם ממש כנוס בתוך החתיכה ג"כ טהורה משום דגם חתיכה הו"ל כשפופרת, ונמצא דאף שהרמב"ן מפרש בדיוק להיפך מפירוש התוס' מ"מ בראתה דם בשפופרת שאינו מין בשר גם להרמב"ן ז"ל מודו כו"ע דטהורה. והרשב"א ז"ל דוחה פירוש הרמב"ן ומפרש כעין שטת התוס' דפליגי בחתיכה העשויה כמין מרזב דלר"א גם חתיכה חוצצת ואילו לרבנן חתיכה אינה חוצצת דמין במינו אינו חוצץ אלא היינו טעמא דטהורה משום דאין זה דם נדה, ונ"מ היכא דהכניסה ידה בפנים והוציאה דם מן המקור דלר"א טהורה מפני שידה ג"כ חוצצת אע"ג דהוי בשר ואילו לרבנן כיון שהוא ודאי דם נדה אין בשר חוצץ דמין במינו הוא עיי"ש. גם בע"ס האשכול פירש בהל' נדה כהרשב"א וכתב נמי דאם הוציאה דם בידה דטמאה דמין במינו אינו חוצץ, וגם הוסיף דה"ה נמי אם יש בתוך החתיכה דם אגור שהחתיכה נראית ככלי המחזיק דם שהוא ודאי דם נדה דאין החתיכה חוצצת מפני שהוא מין במינו עיי"ש, אבל מ"מ גם האשכול והרשב"א שפיר סברי דאם ראתה דם בשפופרת טהורה לכו"ע משום טעמא דשפופרת שאינו מינו ודאי חייץ, גם הרמב"ם ז"ל פסק בפ"ה מאיסורי ביאה הט"ז "האשה שהכניסה שפופרת בפרוזדור וראתה הדם בתוך שפופרת טהורה שנאמר דם יהיה זובה בבשרה עד שתראה בבשרה כדרך שהנשים רואות ואין דרך האשה לראות בשפופרת", ומבואר שאפי' אם השפופרת רק בפרוזדור ג"כ טהורה הואיל ואין הדם נוגע בבשר שבבית החיצון.

אך צ"ע דבתר הכי אמר התם רבא דר"א ורבנן פליגי אם מקור מקומו טהור או טמא, ולפי המבואר לעיל דהא דראתה בשפופרת טהורה היינו אפי' השפופרת מונחת רק בבית החיצון כיון

שלא נגע הדם בבשר שבביה״ח אשר על מקום זה אמרה תורה בבשרה ודרשינן מיניה למעט שפופרת, וממילא נראה שאף אם השפופרת ארוכה יותר מ״מ מה שהיא חוצצת מבין השינים ולפנים לא מעלה ולא מוריד, וכיון שכן נראה דמוכח מהכא דלמ״ד מקור מקומו טהור גם אם ראתה האשה דם נדה ממש ויצא ממקורה, מ״מ כל זמן שאותו דם לא נגע עדיין בבשר שבביה״ח אמרינן דכמו שהאשה עצמה אינה נטמאת כך גם הדם עדיין טהור הוא ולא חל עליו שם דם נדה כי אם בשעה שעובר את הגבול מבית הפנימי לביה״ח. דאל״כ איך אפשר לומר דלאחר שיצא מהמקור וכבר חל עליו שם של דם נדה ומטמא במגע ובמשא יהי׳ טהור אח״כ אם בבואו לביה״ח הוא נכנס לשפופרת, וע״כ כדאמרן דלא רק שאין האשה נקראת בשם ״רואה״ אלא גם הדם עצמו אינו קרוי דם נדה אלא בשעה שעובר את הגבול של בין השיניים. ומ״ש דאם הרגישה שנפתח מקורה טמאה היינו לא שבאותו רגע כבר חשיב דם נדה רק אח״כ כשהדם נוגע בביה״ח, וכיון שכן צ״ע דבדף מ״ב ע״א אמר רב יולדת שירדה לטבול מטומאה לטהרה ונעקר ממנה דם בירידה טמאה, ועיי״ש בתוס׳ וברמב״ן וכו׳ דפליגי ארש״י וסברי שרק נעקר מן המקור אבל לא יצא עדיין לביה״ח ואפי״ה נקרא דם טמא אע״פ שהיציאה לביה״ח כבר היתה בימי טוהר וסוגיא דהתם אזלי גם למ״ד מקור מקומו טהור, ואפי׳ לרש״י ג״כ אפשר שהדם טמא אלא דכיון שהוא עדיין בפנים סובר דמהני ליה טבילה כמו דמהני לדם שבמקור למ״ד שמקומו טמא אבל אפשר שגם לרש״י שפיר קרוי דם יולדת גם בהיותו בבית הפנימי, וכיון שכן קשה דכמו שחל על הדם שם של דם יולדת וטמא גם לפני שיצא לביה״ח ה״נ בדם נדה נהי דאין האשה נטמאת אלא לאחר שהדם נוגע בביה״ח אבל הדם עצמו שפיר טמא גם קודם, ברם נראה דשאני יולדת שהדם יצא ממנה בהיותה טמאה וה״נ בנדה וזבה שיצא מהם דם לאחר שכבר נטמאו שפיר אמרינן דקרוי בשם דם נדה גם לפני שיצא לביה״ח, אבל בתחלת נדתה שפיר נראה דלא חל על הדם שם דם נדה אלא לאחר שנוגע בבשר שבביה״ח ומטמא את האשה אבל לא לפני זה, דהא טעמא דדם נדה טמא ילפינן בר״פ דם הנדה מהא דאמר קרא ״והדוה בנדתה מדוה כמותה״ וכיון שכן נראה דבתחלת נדתה כמו שהאשה אינה נטמאת אלא בביה״ח כך גם הדם לא חל עליו שם דם נדה אלא בביה״ח, אך צ״ע קצת ממה שהקשו שם התוס׳ בר״פ דם הנדה דאמאי איצטריך קרא לטמא דם הנדה ותפ״ל שאם לאחרים גורם טומאה לעצמו לא כ״ש, ואם כדברינו הרי אין הדם גורם טומאה אלא בביה״ח והפסוק בא להודיענו דלאחר שהיא כבר נדה שפיר טמא גם לפני זה, ואפשר דלא משמע להו שהלמוד בא רק לענין זה וצ״ע, ומיהו למ״ד מקור מקומו טמא ודאי טמא גם בשעה שהדם הוא עדיין בתוך המקור ולא נעקר ממנו וכמו״ש הרמב״ן בדף מ״א ע״ב ״דבמקומו הוא נעשה דם הנדה״ אך צ״ע דהא דתנן בסוף מס׳ נדה האשה שמתה ויצא ממנה דם שמטמא משום כתם, כתב המאירי ״ואפילו מתה כשיצא שהרי מ״מ עבר דרך מקור והמקור מקומו טמא ואף לאחר מיתה״, ולא ידעתי מה דחקו לחדש שגם לאחר מיתה נקרא עדיין בשם מקור ותפ״ל שהדם כבר היה בתוך המקור בחיותה, ומוכח שסובר דרק בשעת יציאה מהמקור הוא נטמא ועיין בנוב״ת חיו״ד סי׳ צ״ז וצ״ע.

ז) אולם המאירי הוא היחידי שחולק על כל הפוסקים הנ״ל ופירש או גרס בגמ׳ דבשפופרת כו״ע לא פליגי דטמאה ולא בעינן דוקא בבשרה, אך כיון שדבריו הם נגד כל הפוסקים נראה דלהלכה אין לחוש כלל לשטה זו, אולם גם כתב שם עוד חדוש גדול בפירוש דברי הגמ׳ וז״ל

״הרואה דם בשפופרת, והיא שהכניסה שפופרת לפנים, אם הוציא ראש השפופרת לחוץ עד שיצא הדם דרך השפופרת שלא בראית פני כותלי הרחם הואיל ויצא מ״מ טמאה, אבל אם לא יצא הדם מן השפופרת אלא שעדיין הוא בתוכו כנגד בית החיצון, שאילו היה כן באשה עצמה אע״פ שלא יצא לחוץ טמאה בנדה וזבה מדכתיב דם יהיה זובה בבשרה, ובזב ובעל קרי אינו טמא עד שיצא לחוץ, שאלוה כאן אם בנדה ובתוך השפופרת טמאה אם לאו״ עכ״ל, ומשמע מדבריו דגם מי שסובר דבשפופרת טהורה היינו דוקא כל זמן שהדם הוא עדיין בתוך השפופרת כנגד בית החיצון אבל לאחר שהדם יצא לגמרי מגופה שפיר טמאה לכו״ע גם בשפופרת, וביאור דבריו נראה דכיון דמהך קרא דבבשרה דרשינן שמטמאה בפנים כבחוץ משא״כ בזב ובקרי, לכן אמרינן נמי דלא חידשה תורה להחמיר באשה יותר מבזב ובעל קרי אלא כשראתה ממש בבשרה ולא בשפופרת משא״כ לאחר שיצא הדם לגמרי לחוץ שפיר טמאה נדה אפי׳ עבר דרך שפופרת ולא נגע כלל בבשר, [בגמ׳ נדה מ״א ע״ב סובר ר״ל דגם אם יצא דם ממקורה דרך הדופן הרי היא טמאה נדה לכו״ע ולא בעינן דוקא דרך ערותה ומוכח דאע״ג דגזיה״כ הוא דמטמאת בפנים כבחוץ מיד כשהדם נוגע בבשר שבבית החיצון אפי״ה כשיצא לגמרי מהגוף כ״ש דטמאה ונמצא דלר״ל אם נטמאת דרך דופן כ״ש שנטמאת דרך שפופרת לאחר שיצא לגמרי מגופה והיינו ממש כהמאירי וצ״ע] אך כיון שדברי תימה הם שהרי להדיא מבואר שם בכל הסוגיא דמיירי שהדם יצא אח״כ לגמרי לחוץ ואפי״ה היא טהורה ואי אפשר כלל לפרש כדבריו שכל הדיון הוא רק על אותו זמן מועט שהדם נמצא עדיין בתוך השפופרת כנגד בית החיצון, גם בהערות של המו״ל הרה״ג ר׳ אברהם סופר שליט״א כתב שלא מצא לו חבר בין כל הפוסקים שלפנינו, ולכן כדי שלא יהיו דבריו תמוהים וחתומים נלענ״ד לדחוק שנתכוין לומר דלא אמרינן שהיא טהורה אא״כ ראש השפופרת שלצד חוץ מגיע עד לבית החיצון שהוא מבין השינים ולחוץ אשר אילו הדם היה יוצא מגופה כרגיל ומגיע עד לאותו מקום היתה נטמאת בכך משום דחשיב כאילו הדם כבר יצא ממנה, רק אז הוא דאמרינן שאם הגיע עד למקום זה דרך שפופרת הרי היא טהורה אפי׳ אם אח״כ יצא ממש הדם לחוץ, וכמו דאמרינן גבי מעשרות שאם הגיעו לעונת החיוב בפטור הרי הן פטורין לעולם. משא״כ אם השפופרת קצרה וראשה מגעת רק עד למקום שהוא עדיין מבין השניים ולפנים, אע״פ שיציאת הדם מהמקור היתה דרך שפופרת אפי״ה טמאה, כיון דלאחר שהדם יצא מהשפופרת ונגע בבשרה הרי הוא עדיין מבין השיניים ולפנים אשר גם אם היה הדם יוצא מגופה כרגיל לא היתה עדיין נטמאת בכך, בכה״ג שפיר אמרינן דבשעה שהדם עובר אח״כ את הגבול שמבין השיניים ולפנים ויוצא לבית החיצון שפיר טמאה, וזה לא כהחת״ס בחיו״ד סי׳ קע״א שכתב דשפופרת לאו דוקא אלא הוא הדין אם הכניסה טבעת קצרה לפי המקור באופן שתחוץ בין פי המקור לדם לא תיטמא, וטעמו הוא משום דסובר ששפתי פי המקור הוא המקום שגורם טומאה, ואילו המאירי סובר שבין השיניים לאו היינו שפתי פי המקור, ולכן סובר דבכה״ג שהשפופרת קצרה הרי היא טמאה. גם אפשר לומר שרצה המאירי לפרש את הגמ׳ גם לר״ל דפליג אר׳ יוחנן וסובר בדף מ״א ע״ב שאף אם יצא הדם דרך דופן ג״כ טמאה, ולדידיה פשוט הוא דה״ה נמי שגם בשפופרת טמאה כיון דלא בעינן כלל שיצא דרך ערותה וכך לי דרך שפופרת או דרך דופן, אולם כל זה דוקא לאחר שהדם יצא ממש לחוץ משא״כ לענין זה דדרשינן מבשרה שמטמאת מבפנים כבחוץ והיא טמאה גם

בשעה שהדם הוא עדיין בבית החיצון לענין זה מצינן שפיר למידרש גם לר״ל דבעינן דוקא בבשרה ולא בשפופרת.

ח) המורם מכל האמור דאשה שראתה דם בשפופרת טהורה וכן פסק השו״ע בסי׳ קפ״ח סעיף ג׳ ״הכניסה שפופרת והוציאה בה דם טהורה״ ומפשטות דברי השו״ע וגם מפורש כתב כן בעל סדרי טהרה והחכמת אדם בכלל קי״ב בבינת אדם אות ז׳ ועוד גדולי אחרונים דפשוט הדבר בלי שום חולק שטהורה האשה גם מדרבנן ואע״ג שגזרו חכמים טומאה גם על דם שהאשה לא הרגישה כלל ביציאתו אשר גם זה נלמד בריש פ״ח דנדה מקרא דבבשרה עד שתרגיש בבשרה ואפי״ה גזרו טומאה גם על כתמים, מ״מ בראתה דרך שפופרת לא גזרו שום טומאה והיא טהורה ודאי גם מדרבנן. והרבה טעמים וסברות נאמרו באחרונים אהא דלא החמירו רבנן בשפופרת [בס׳ פרדס רמונים בחקירתו השניה שבפתיחת הספר בענין כתמים הקשה דבכה״ג שהשפופרת סתומה מצד אחד ומקבלת טומאה הרי הו״ל ככתם שנמצא ע״ג דבר המקבל טומאה עיי״ש, ולענ״ד פשוט הוא דהרי זה דומה לכתם שנמצא על סדין שיודעים ברור שיצא מהמקור דרך דופן דלא כלום הוא וה״נ בשפופרת] וכמו כן נראה דלדעת כל הפוסקים הנ״ל שהזכרנו פשוט הוא דאפי׳ בכה״ג שלא יצא הדם מגופה מחמת השפופרת אלא הדם יצא ממנה כרגיל מפני שהגיע שעת וסתה אפי״ה אם אין הדם נוגע בבשרה רק יוצא דרך שפופרת הרי היא טהורה, ולרווחא דמלתא אעתיק מ״ש בשו״ע הרב ז״ל בסי׳ קפ״ח בסק״ט וז״ל ״ולדבריהם [של רש״י ותוס׳ והרמב״ם] בשפופרת שהכניסתה בפרוזדור עד מקום שהשמש דש שהוא תחלת בית החיצון ויצא הדם עצמו מהמקור ונכנס בשפופרת כגון שהיתה שעת וסתה טהורה אע״ג שלא הוציאתו השפופרת [כלומר אע״פ שיציאת הדם לא היתה מחמת השפופרת] כיון שלא נגע בבשר בית החיצון וכן הוא ברמב״ם בהדיא״ עכ״ל, ואין לומר דמיעוטא דשפופרת הוא משום דכיון שהדם יוצא משפופרת ולא מהבשר שבמקור אין זה חשיב כדם מקור אלא כדם שפופרת כעין מה שאמרו אין זה דם נדה אלא דם חתיכה, ונמצא לפי״ז דהמיעוט הוא רק כשהשפופרת היא ממש בתוך המקור ולא כשלבשתו על המקור, דלהדיא כתב רש״י דבעינן שיצא דרך כותלי בית הרחם דלאו היינו מקור וגם מפורש כתב הרמב״ם שהכניסה שפופרת בפרוזדור, וכן מוכח מהאשכול והרשב״א שדברו מהכנסת ידה דאי אפשר כלל להכניס בתוך המקור, וכמו״ש החת״ס בסי׳ קע״ט ״כי לעולם לא תגיע אצבע הנשים בפתח הקבר אלא בבית החיצון״ וגם החכ״א כתב על הנו״ב דמה שכתב ״כגון שהרופא הכניס אצבעו אגב שיטפיה כתב כך ולא דק״, ועיין גם בשו״ע הרב ז״ל שכתב שם בסק״י וז״ל ״לפי שטתם אם הכניסה שפופרת לפרוזדור לבד בעת ראית וסתה ויצא דם וסתה לתוך השפופרת טהורה הואיל ואין דרך נשים לראות כן בהפסק בין דם לבין החיצון אע״פ שעיקר הראיה שהיא עקירת הדם מהמקור הוא כדרך הנשים״ עכ״ל, ועיין גם בפירוש על הרמב״ם מר״ד עראמה ז״ל שפירש שהכניסה השפופרת עד בין השינים ולא לתוך המקור, ולפי״ז פשוט הוא דלדעת כל הפוסקים הנ״ל שהזכרנו אין שום מקום לחלק בין תחבה האשה את השפופרת תוך המקור או רק הלבישה אותו על פי המקור והדם שיצא מהמקור כדרכו עבר דרך השפופרת ולא ראה ולא נגע כלל בבשר שהיא ג״כ טהורה כיון דגזיה״כ הוא דאינה טמאה אא״כ הדם נוגע ממש בבשרה ולא כשיש שפופרת החוצץ בין הדם והבשר. ומוכח נמי כדברינו ממ״ש הרמב״ן בהל׳ נדה פ״ג ה״ב ״האשה מטמאה בין באונס בין ברצון

ואפילו לא יצא הדם לחוץ ולא נעקר מן המקור ועדיין הוא בבית החיצון טמאה, וביה"ח זו בין השינים מקום שמגיע אליו האצבע בשעת גמר ביאה ובין השינים עצמו כלפנים, ובזה"ז שאין בקיאות בדבר כל שהאשה מוציאה דם בעד שלה טמאה", והרבו לתמוה ע"ז הסד"ט בסי' קפ"ג סק"ג ועוד גדולי אחרונים דכיון שהוציאה את הדם לחוץ הרי יצא ממש לחוץ וטמאה וא"כ מאי נ"מ אם בקיאין בזה"ז או לא, ותירצו ע"ז הרבה גדולי אחרונים דהוצאת הדם מבפנים ע"י עד דומה להוציאה דם ע"י שפופרת ולכן רק מפני שאין אנו בקיאין אנו מטמאין בכל ענין אבל אם היינו יודעים ברור שהעד הוציא את הדם מבין השינים ולפנים לא היתה נטמאת אע"פ שהדם יצא ממש לחוץ, אך נפישי רבוואתי דלא ניחא להו בהך תירוצא וסברי שרק אם הדם יצא "תוך" שפופרת אז הוא דחייץ משא"כ אם הוא "על" עד או על שפופרת כיון שרואה את פני הבשר לא חייץ עיין בזה בשו"ע הרב בסוף הקו"א לסי' קפ"ג ובשו"ת ברית אברהם שהאריך בזה הרבה בפתחי נדה, ובטעמא דמלתא נלענ"ד דטעמא דחציצה הוא מפני שאין דרך לראות בכך ולכן סברי דדוקא תוך שפופרת הוא דלא רגיל משא"כ ע"י עד או קיסם או אפי' "על" שפופרת שפיר טמאה, אולם לענ"ד צ"ע ממ"ש לעיל מהאשכול והרשב"א שכתבו דאם הכניסה אצבעה והוציא דם שהיא טהורה אי לאו מפני שהאצבע מין אחד עם הבשר עיי"ש אע"ג דאצבע דומה ממש לעד, ודוחק גדול לומר דמיירי שהכניסה ב' אצבעות והדם הי' כל הזמן תוך ב' האצבעות, אבל עכ"פ חזינן מכולהו הני רבוואתי דסברי בפשיטות בדעת הרמב"ן שאם הכניסה שפופרת מבין השינים ולפנים אע"פ שלא הכניסתו ממש לתוך המקור ג"כ טהורה וכדאמרן.

ט) ברם צ"ע טובא דבריש פ"ח דנדה פריך הגמ' אהא דיליף שמואל מקרא דבבשרה שאין אשה טמאה עד שתרגיש בבשרה דהאי בבשרה מיבעי ליה בבשרה ולא בשפיר ולא בחתיכה ומשני "תרתי שמע מיניה" וכתב ע"ז הר"ן בחדושיו "דכיון דדרשינן מבבשרה עד שתרגיש בבשרה ממילא משמע ולא בשפיר ולא בהרגשה שאין בכיוצא בזה הרגשת דם אלא הרגשת שפיר וחתיכה" עכ"ל, הרי מבואר שסובר דטעמא דממעטינן שפיר וחתיכה הוא משום דליכא הרגשה, ופשוט הוא דה"ה נמי בשפופרת דהרי חד טעמא לכולהו, וכיון שכן משמע דרק אם הכניסה את השפופרת לתוך המקור אז היא טהורה משא"כ אם הלבישה שפופרת על פי המקור ומרגשת בפתיחת פי המקור כדרכה תמיד בשעת וסתה שפיר טמאה, וכ"ש דקשה טפי לפי המבואר לעיל שגם הר"ן פירש בסוגית הגמ' כרש"י דהטעם הוא משום חציצה, ונלענ"ד דצריכים ע"כ לומר שהר"ן סובר דהרגשה לאו היינו הרגשת פתיחת פי המקור אלא הרגשת זיבת דבר לח מהבשר שמבין השינים ולפנים עד להבשר שבבית החיצון וכידוע שרבות האריכו בזה גדולי האחרונים, וגם אפשר שסובר דבעינן הרגשת פתיחת המקור למען דעת שהדם בא מן המקור אבל גם צריכים שתרגיש אח"כ שהדם עובר את הגבול של בין השינים ונוגע בבשר שבבית החיצון וכמו"ש בנוב"ת סי' קי"ט בהג"ה עיי"ש. ואף אם ננקוט כמו שנראה מפשטות הדברים דסגי בפתיחת פי המקור גרידא יתכן לומר דהוא משום דתלינן שמסתמא היא גם מרגשת בזיבת דבר לח משא"כ כשיש שפופרת ואינה יכולה בשום אופן להרגיש אין זה קרוי כלל הרגשה, ואף אם השפופרת הוא של גומי דק אשר אינו מונע את הרגשת הזיבה מ"מ אין זה חשיב הרגשה מעליא וטהורה כיון שיש עכ"פ דבר החוצץ [ועיין במאירי דף כ"ד ע"א שכתב לענין שפיר מלא דם שיש בה טומאת נדה מפני שאין זה דומה לחתיכה שהיא עבה ביותר ואין

זה ענין לכאן] ורבות נהניתי כאשר ראיתי בקו"א שבשו"ע הרב ז"ל שכתב בריש הל' נדה "ולהר"ן סבירא ליה דהרגשת בית החיצון דייקא בעינן דהא הרגשת יציאתו מהמקור יכול להיות גם ברואה בשפופרת" והיינו כדברינו, ובר מן דין יש לדעת דאף שהר"ן כתב דטעם אחד לשניהם אולם הרשב"א והריטב"א לא סברי הכי וכתבו בריש פ"ח דנדה דכיון דשקולין נינהו שמעינן שפיר תרתי מחדא דרשא וגם בתוספי הרא"ש בסוגיין דף כ"א פירש דשתי דרשות חלוקות הן עיי"ש. ואף גם לטעמו של הר"ן נלענ"ד שאפי' אם היא רואה ויודעת ברור שהדם יוצא ממקורה מ"מ אין זה קרוי הרגשה ואף שהמאירי כתב בדף ס"ג ע"א "עד שתראה או שתרגיש שכבר יצא הדם לבית החיצון" דמשמע שסגי בראיה גרידא נלענ"ד דאין זה בדוקא, ועיין ברמב"ם ריש פ"ט מאיסורי ביאה ובשו"ע הרב סי' קפ"ג בקו"א במהדו"ב דהרגשה וראיה חדא מלתא, וגם יבואר בע"ה להלן שגם להר"ן אין האשה נטמאת אא"כ נגע הדם באותו חלק מהבשר שהיא צריכה להרגיש שם אבל אם זה בשפופרת ה"ז חשיב גם להר"ן כאילו נשאר בפנים או יצא דרך דופן ולא נגע כלל במקום שהתורה אמרה ששם היא נטמאת, המורם מהאמור עד כה דלכולהו הני רבוואתי אית לן למימר דבכה"ג דנד"ד הרי היא טהורה, ונראה דאף לאחר שהרגילה עצמה בכך ללבוש שפופרת מדי חדש בחדשו למטרה זו שזיבת הדם תהא דרך השפופרת אפי"ה חוצצת ולא אמרינן דהיינו רביתייהו, אלא אדרבה כל שהלבישה הוא כדי לחצוץ עדיף טפי וכמו"ש החכמת אדם בכלל קכ"ח לענין כלי בתוך כלי, דאף שאם הכלים מיוחדים לכך אפי' מאה חשובים כאחד מ"מ אם תחלת עשיית ב' הכלים היה כדי שיחשב ככלי בתוך כלי עדיף טפי וחוצצים אע"פ שייחדן כך לעולם.

י) אך יש עוד שטה אחרת והיא שטת הרא"ש שתמה על פירוש רש"י ותוס' ופירש משום כך כהר"ש מקוצי שכתב "דרבנן ור' אליעזר פליגי בטעמא דקרא דדרשינן בבשרה ולא בשפופרת, ר"א סבר דממעטינן שפופרת מטעם הפסקה וכן חתיכה היכא דאין הדם נוגע בבשרה אבל אי פלי פלויי קרינן שפיר בבשרה, ורבנן סברי טעמא דממעטינן שפופרת משום דאין דרכה של אשה לראות דם כך וכן חתיכה נמי אפי' אי פלי פלויי לפי שאין דרך הנשים לראות כך" עכ"ל, ומעתה אע"ג שגם הרא"ש פסק שם להדיא דרואה דם בשפופרת טהורה אבל כיון דקיי"ל כחכמים דר"א שאין הטעם משום חציצה אלא מפני שאין דרך נשים לראות כך, יתכן דכל זה דוקא אם תחבה השפופרת "תוך" המקור וגורמת בכך להוצאת הדם דרק אז היא טהורה משום דחשיב ראיה שלא כדרכה משא"כ אם לבשה שפופרת "על" פי המקור והדם יוצא ממנה כדרכו אלא שאין נוגע בבשר שבבית החיצון מנלן שהיא טהורה כיון דלרבנן כל הענין של חציצה לא מעלה ולא מוריד, וגם נראה דלדעת הר"ש והרא"ש מסתבר דכל זה דוקא שלא בשעת וסתה דאז תלינן שהשפופרת גרמה ליציאת הדם משא"כ בשעת וסתה דאורח בזמנו בא ולא קשור כלל עם השפופרת אפשר דשפיר טמאה לרבנן גם אם הכניסה את השפופרת לתוך המקור ממש, וגם נלענ"ד דכיון שהרא"ש סובר דלרבנן אין הטעם משום חציצה הוצרך שפיר לומר דמ"ש בריש פ"ח דנדה "תרתי שמע מיניה" היינו שבאמת ב' דרשות חלוקות הן ולא כהר"ן שכתב מפני שטעם אחד לשניהם דליכא הרגשה כיון שלהרא"ש אין זה קשור כלל עם חציצה, וגם הר"ש מטהר שם משום כך באשה שנעקר המקור שלה והדם יוצא ממנה בלי שום חציצה דאפי"ה טהורה הואיל ואין דרך נשים לראות כך עיי"ש, ומפורש כתב כן בשו"ע הרב ז"ל בסי' קפ"ח

סק״ח וגם נדחק לומר משום כך דמה שכתב הרא״ש שהכניסה את השפופרת עד המקור פירושו ועד בכלל שהכניסתו ממש לתוך מקור דמיה ותולין שהדם יצא מפני שהשפופרת הוציאתו משם, ומה שהבאנו לעיל משו״ע הרב דמטהר גם בשעת וסתה אפילו כשהשפופרת מגעת רק עד השיניים והדם יוצא כדרכו תמיד הוא רק לשאר הראשונים אבל לא להר״ש והרא״ש עיי״ש [ועיין בחת״ס חיו״ד סוף סי׳ קע״א שכתב גם בדעת הר״ן דטעמא דמטהרינן בשפופרת הוא מפני שלא יצא הדם מעצמו אלא מחמת השפופרת שעורר את הדם לצאת, ולענ״ד צ״ע דלדעת הר״ן שפירש בגמ׳ כרש״י ותוס׳ נמצא שאף אם הכניסה השפופרת עד המקור ולא עד בכלל ג״כ טהורה] ומעתה כיון דמפשטות דברי השו״ע שפסק בסי׳ קפ״ח לקולא באשה שנעקר מקור שלה משמע דפסק כהר״ש גם להקל, וכן לענין שפופרת כתב רק בהאי לישנא ״הכניסה שפופרת והוציאה בה דם״ דמשמע קצת שהגורם ליציאת הדם היה השפופרת, נמצא דאין שום מקום להקל אם הרכיבה האשה את השפופרת על פי המקור והדם יוצא מגופה כדרכה תמיד אפי׳ שלא בשעת וסתה וכ״ש בשעת וסתה.

יא) אולם טרם שאבאר דמוכח מכמה מחברים שהבינו בדעת הר״ש דלא כהרב ז״ל הנני לבאר דפירושו של הרב ז״ל בדעת הר״ש לענ״ד אינו מוכרח שהרי אפשר לומר דהא גופא שאין הדם נוגע בבשרה אלא על דבר החוצץ חשיב שלא כדרך ראיה וטהורה שפיר גם לרבנן כי התורה אמרה שאין אשה נטמאת אלא א״כ הדם זב ויוצא ממנה כדרכו תמיד דרך בשרה ולא כשהוא זב ע״ג דבר החוצץ, וכמו שלענין מאכלות אסורות אם בלע איסור שהוא כרוך ומכוסה בדבר החוצץ בין המאכל והפה מיקרי שלא כדרך אכילתן ה״נ חשיב כאן שלא כדרך ראיה, וכן מצינו גבי לידת בכור שאם כרכו בסיב או בטליתו והוציאו באופן שלא נגע ברחם הסתפקו בגמ׳ דלא יהא קדוש בבכורה מפני שלא נגע ברחם כך גם כאן דוקא אם הדם יוצא מהמקור ונוגע ממש בבשרה רק אז חל על הדם ועל האשה טומאת נדה ולא כשהוא זב ע״ג דבר החוצץ [ועיין גם במס׳ סוטה י״ח ע״א ״השקה בסיב מהו בשפופרת מהו דרך שתיה בכך או אין דרך שתיה בכך תיקו״] ולפי״ז פירוש דברי הר״ש כך הוא דבין ר״א ובין רבנן סברי שאם ראתה דרך שפופרת כיון שאין דרך האשה לראות דם בכך הרי היא טהורה אלא שר״א סובר דדרכה של אשה לראות גם בחתיכה ולכן אי פלי פלויי טמאה ורק אם הדם הוא תוך החתיכה ואינו נוגע כלל בבשר אין זה חשיב דרך ראיה כיון דהוי ע״י הפסקה ורבנן סברי דכמו שממעטינן ע״ג דבר החוצץ משום טעמא דלאו דרך ראיה בכך כמו כן ממעטינן נמי דם חתיכה אפי׳ אם פלי פלויי משום דכיון שאין דרך דם נדה לבוא בזה הענין הרי היא טהורה, ומיהו שפופרת לא דמי לחתיכה ובכה״ג דפלי פלויי כגון שיש נקב בתוך שפופרת ומקצת מהדם נוגע בבשר שפיר טמאה משום דאע״ג דאין דרך אשה לראות דרך שפופרת אבל כיון דבזה הטעם הוא רק משום חציצה לכן לא דמי לחתיכה ואם כלשהו מהדם נוגע בבשר שפיר חשיב כדרכה בכך וטמאה. וגם רחש לבי לומר דמה שפסק הר״ש לטהר באשה שנעקר מקורה משום טעמא דאין דרך נשים לראות כך אין זה דוקא לרבנן כי אפשר דבכה״ג גם ר״א מודה דאין דרך דם לבוא בזה הענין וטהורה כיון דמפורש אמר ר״א דטעמא דמטמא בפלי פלויי הוא רק משום דסובר שדרכה של אשה לראות דם בחתיכה, ולעומת זה יתכן לומר דמ״ש בטור ובשו״ע באשה שנעקר מקור שלה דטהורה אשר רבים תמהו איך סמכו להקל באיסור כרת לסמוך לקולא על הר״ש נגד כל הראשונים, ולדברינו נראה דיתכן

שגם הרמב"ם ועוד מהראשונים הנ"ל ג"כ מצי סברי הכי דכמו שמטהרינן אם יש דבר המפסיק משום טעמא דאין דרך לראות בכך ה"נ בנעקר המקור ג"כ לאו אורחא בכך ולא רק בהפסקה לחוד תליא מלתא, והא דבחתיכה מטמאינן אי פלי פלויי היינו משום דלא ס"ל דאין דרכה בכך.

ומסתבר כדברינו שהרי גם לרש"י ותוס' ושאר הראשונים עיקר הטעם דמטהרינן בשפופרת מפורש אמרו מפני שאין דרך לראות בכך וכן מבואר בגמ' בכל הסוגיא דאין דרך לראות דם בשפופרת, ומפורש כתב כן הרמב"ם בפ"ה מאיסורי ביאה וז"ל, האשה שהכניסה שפופרת בפרוזדור וראתה הדם בתוך השפופרת טהורה שנאמר דם יהי' זובה בבשרה עד שתראה בבשרה כדרך שהנשים רואות ואין דרך האשה לראות בשפופרת עכ"ל, הרי להדיא דאע"ג שמטהר אפי' אם רק הכניסה שפופרת בפרוזדור והיציאה מן המקור היתה כדרכה אפי"ה כל שיש דבר המפסיק מטהרינן לה משום טעמא דאין דרך אשה לראות בכך, ופשוט הוא דלדידהו אפילו אם יצא הדם כדרכו מפני שהגיע שעת וסתה ולא היתה כלל ראיתה מחמת השפופרת דאפי"ה אמרינן דאין דרך ראיה בכך וטהורה וא"כ מהיכ"ת לא נאמר כן גם אליבא דהר"ש [ולולא דברי התוס' הי' נראה לפרש גם בדעת רש"י דסובר כהר"ש ולגרוס שפיר ברש"י דטעמא דבשפופרת לכו"ע טהורה הוא משום דאין דרך הרואה בכך ולא כהרש"ל שהגיה "דדייקינן לישנא דקרא" וצ"ע] הן אמנם ידעתי דלכל הראשונים יכולים לומר דמה שאמרו אין דרך לראות בכך כוונתם דחשיב משום כך כאינו מינו וחוצץ ואף גם בחתיכה שהיא מין אחד עם הבשר מ"מ אי הוה אמרינן שאין דרך לראות בכך היתה חוצצת אע"ג דהוי מין במינו ורק מפני שדרכה לראות בכך לא מיקרי דבר החוצץ, משא"כ להר"ש צריכים שיהי' ממש שלא כדרך ראיה, אבל מ"מ מנלן לחדש מחלוקת גדולה זו בין הר"ש ושאר פוסקים שלא נזכר כלל בשום מקום, ואדרבה חושבני שגם בדעת רש"י יותר מסתבר לומר דכיון שהוא אינו מינו וחוצץ הרי זה חשיב כאין דרך לראות בכך ולפיכך טהורה, וגם משמע קצת כדברינו ממה שהזכיר הר"ש גם בדעת רבנן "ודם נוגע בבשרה" וכן הוא גם בקיצור פסקי הרא"ש פ"ג ה"ב "הרואה דם בשפופרת טהורה וכן בחתיכה אפילו פלי פלויי ונגע בבשרה טהורה" דמשמע דטעמא דטהורה בשפופרת הוא מפני שאין הדם נוגע בבשרה ומוכח דגם לרבנן אם יש דבר המפסיק בין הדם והבשר אין זה דרך ראיה וטהורה.

גם ראיתי ברבנו ירוחם חלק חוה נתיב כ"ו חלק א' שכתב "הרואה דם בשפופרת ולא נגע בבשרה טהורה, וכן בחתיכה שיוצאה מן המקור לבית החיצון ואפי' פלי פלויי ונגע בבשרה טהורה, וכן פירש הר"ש מקוצי שאין דרכה של אשה לראות דם בחתיכה וכיון שלא ראתה כדרך שהנשים רגילות טהורה אע"ג דהוי דם וגם נוגע בבשרה וכן עשה הוא מעשה באשה שנעקר מקור שלה – וטהר אותה לבעלה כיון שאין דרך כל הנשים לראות כך" עכ"ל, ורואים בעליל דאף שרבנו ירוחם ז"ל הוא תלמיד הרא"ש "וידוע שכל דבריו הם בנויים עפ"י הרא"ש" כמו"ש המג"א בסי' תקנ"ט סק"ח אפי"ה מפורש כתב בדעת הר"ש דהא דראתה בשפופרת טהורה היינו דוקא בכה"ג שלא נגע הדם בבשרה, ואם כהרב ז"ל צריכים רק שהיציאה תהי' מחמת שפופרת אבל כמו שבחתיכה היא טהורה אע"ג דפלי פלויי והדם נוגע בבשר כך גם בשפופרת, ואף אם השפופרת קצרה וכשהדם יוצא ממנה הוא נכנס ונוגע בבשר שבביה"פ ויוצא משם לביה"ח אף גם בזה טהורה היא לדעת הרב ז"ל, ועיין גם באבנ"ז סי' רכ"ה אות מ"ז דלפי מה דאזיל התם בשטת הרב ז"ל מפורש כתב דבשפופרת היא טהורה גם בפלי פלויי וכתב נמי שכן פסק השו"ע

וזה נגד דברי רבנו ירוחם ז"ל. גם נלענ"ד דחוץ ממה שדוחק גדול הוא לפרש בדברי הרא"ש כהרב ז"ל דמה שכתב "עד" המקור כוונתו דוקא "תוך" המקור, גם נראה דכיון שהכנסת שפופרת לתוך המקור ממש הוא דבר קשה מאד ולא שכיח כלל כמו"ש בשו"ת משאת בנימין המובא להלן, וכיון שכן בפסקי הרא"ש וברבנו ירוחם לא הי' להם לסתום אלא היו צריכים להדגיש בפירוש דמיירי דוקא באשה שהכניסה שפופרת ממש לתוך המקור, גם יש לדעת דלפירוש הרב ז"ל בדעת הר"ש והרא"ש נמצא דשפופרת דר' אליעזר חלוק טובא משפופרת דרבנן שהרי לר"א דמטהר משום חציצה צריכים שתהא השפופרת מונחת בכל בית החיצון או עכ"פ בתחלתו אבל אם היא קצרה ומונחת רק בתוך המקור לאו כלום הוא ואילו לרבנן לא מטהרינן אא"כ השפופרת מונחת ממש בתוך המקור וגם מוציאה משם את הדם ובכה"ג שפיר מטהרינן אף אם השפופרת קצרה והדם נוגע בבשר שבבית החיצון, וא"כ להלכה דקיי"ל כרבנן היו צריכים הפוסקים להדגיש דלא מטהרינן בסוג שפופרת של ר"א אלא צריכים דוקא כעין שפופרת דרבנן, אולם לדברינו ניחא. ונראה שגם הלבוש סובר כן וז"ל "הכניסה שפופרת באותו מקום ונמצא בתוכו דם טהורה שלא טמאתה התורה אלא בדם היוצא כדרך יציאתו מרוב הנשים דהיינו דם שיוצא דרך כותלי בית הרחם דכתיב דם יהי' זובה בבשרה והיינו שיהי' זב דרך בשרה בכותלי בית הרחם כדרכו בסתם נשים", ומשמע שרק הנגיעה בבשר עושה את הדם לדם נדה.

יב) ועיין בשו"ת דברי חיים מצאנז יו"ד ח"ב סי' ס"ג דמפורש כתב גם אליבא דהר"ש והרא"ש דלית מאן דפליג שאין האשה נטמאת אא"כ הדם נוגע בבשרה שבבית החיצון ולא ע"ג דבר החוצץ בין הדם והבשר, וראיתי בשו"ת אמרי יושר להגאון ר"מ אריק ז"ל בח"ב סוף סי' ע"א שהביא את הדברי חיים הנ"ל וכתב, וצ"ע דהא להר"ש הא דרואה דם בשפופרת אינו מדין חציצה שאינו נוגע בבשרה רק משום שאין דרך לראות בענין זה כמבואר להדיא ברא"ש וא"כ מנ"ל לומר היתר זה דאינו נוגע בבשרה להר"ש, ואפשר דגם הר"ש מודה דכל היכא דהוי חציצה כגון דם בתוך השפופרת ואינו נוגע בבשרה טהור מטעם חציצה כרש"י אך דהר"ש מפרש הא דדם שבשפופרת טהור היינו גם כשרואה הדם "על" השפופרת א"כ בכה"ג נוגע בבשרה ואין שום חציצה אפי"ה טהור דאין דרכה לראות בזה האופן וכמ"ש בשו"ע הרב ז"ל סי' קפ"ח בקו"א אבל כשהדם בתוך השפופרת דהוי חציצה גם להר"ש טהורה אף אם היה דרכה לראות מטעם חציצה דבבשרה כתיב עכ"ל. ולענ"ד צ"ע דא"כ איך כתב הר"ש ופליגי רבנן ור"א בטעמא דקרא דדרשינן בבשרה ולא בשפופרת – "ורבנן סברי טעמא דממעטינן שפופרת משום דאין דרכה של אשה לראות דם כך" ותפ"ל שגם רבנן מודים לר"א דדרשינן מהך קרא למעט הפסקה בין הדם והבשר כי זה ודאי לא ניתן להאמר שגם מצד הסברא יודעים למעט חציצה דמהיכ"ת נימא הכי, וכיון שכן מנלן למידרש תרתי מהך קרא דבבשרה, ולכן יותר נראה שהדברי חיים הבין בדעת הרא"ש כדאמרן דהא גופא שהדם יוצא ממנה ע"ג דבר המפסיק חשיב שלא כדרך ראיה וטהורה שפיר גם לרבנן משום הך טעמא דאין דרכה של אשה לראות דם כך, אבל עכ"פ חזינן שגם הדברי חיים סובר ברור בדעת הר"ש והרא"ש דאם ראתה בשפופרת טהורה אפי' בכה"ג שאין לתלות כלל שיציאת הדם מן המקור היתה מחמת השפופרת רק גזיה"כ הוא דבכל ענין טהורה מחמת חציצה דמיקרי נמי שלא כדרכה.

גם ראיתי בשו"ת ברית אברהם בפתחי נדה סי' מ' אות א' שכתב בפשיטות בכוונת דברי הר"ש כדברינו ולא כהרב ז"ל וז"ל "ואין הפירוש בדברי הר"ש דפליגי בטעמא דקרא דמר לא

ס"ל האי טעמא ומר לא ס"ל האי טעמא אך כיון דפליגי אי דרכה לראות בחתיכה ממילא לר"א ליכא נ"מ בטעמא דאין דרך ראיה לענין שפופרת או חתיכה דבלא"ה טהור משום חציצה דהא גם בחתיכה דהוי דרך ראיה מ"מ היכי דלא אפלי אימעוט משום חציצה ולרבנן בתראי דס"ל אין דרכה וכו' ממילא ליכא נ"מ בטעמא דחציצה דבין שפופרת ובין חתיכה גם היכי דפלויי אימעוט משום דאין דרך ראיה בכך אבל כו"ע ס"ל דתיבת בבשרה ממעט דכל היכי דלא הוי דרך ראיה או היכי דהוי חציצה לא הוי בבשרה ולא הוי תרתי דרשות אך דכל זה לא הוי בבשרה וזה ברור בכוונת הר"ש" עכ"ל, וכן כתב שם בתשובותיו כמה פעמים שגם לפירוש הר"ש אין דרך אשה לראות דם תוך איזה דבר אחר וטהורה היא משום כך, גם ראיתי בעונג יו"ט סי' פ"ד דלהדיא כתב גם אליבא דהר"ש שאם ראתה דם בשפופרת אפי' אם הגיע שעת וסתה והכניסה שפופרת ויצא הדם דרך השפופרת דאף בכה"ג שלא נכנס כלל השפופרת תוך הרחם אלא אדרבה הכניסה את פי הרחם לתוך השפופרת והדם יוצא ממנה כדרכה תמיד אפי"ה טהורה משום טעמא דחציצה, ופוסק משום כך הלכה למעשה דאם פי המקור היה תוך שפופרת והכניסה לתוכו ספוג וראתה דם דיש להקל ממטעם חציצה כדדרשינן בבשרה ולא בשפופרת עיי"ש, אך עיקר יסודו שם הוא משום דקשיא לי' דכיון שאין דרך לראות דם בשפופרת א"כ מאי בעי ר' ירמי' מר' זירא ראתה דם בשפופרת מהו אי דרשינן בבשרה ולא בשפופרת ומטהרינן משום חציצה ותפ"ל שטהורה מפני שאין דרך לראות דם בשפופרת, וגם עיי"ש שכתב דלהכי מיבעי ליה ברואה דם בשפופרת ולא ברואה דם בקיסם כדמיבעי לי' גבי קרי משום דגבי אשה בקיסם טהורה בלאו האי טעמא דחציצה משום שאין דרכה של אשה לראות בקיסם עיי"ש, ולענ"ד דבריו תמוהים דאי לאו משום דרשא דקרא מהיכ"ת נימא דבכה"ג שראתה שלא כדרכה שהיא טהורה והרי להדיא פירש הר"ש דר"א ורבנן פליגי בהך דרשא של בבשרה ולא בשפופרת דר"א סובר משום חציצה ואילו לרבנן לא דרשינן מהך קרא אלא למעט ראתה שלא כדרכה. גם נלענ"ד ראי' ברורה מהנו"ב שפירש ג"כ כדברינו בדעת הר"ש והרא"ש דכתב להוכיח בחיוד"ק סי' נ"ה דהרגשת זיבת דבר לח בביה"ח מיקרי הרגשה מהא דמבבשרה ילפינן דבעינן עד שתרגיש בבשרה ומהך קרא גופא ילפינן נמי שמטמאת בפנים כבחוץ דהיינו בבית החיצון א"כ מוכח שגם ההרגשה צריכה להיות באותו בשר שבביה"ח עיי"ש, ולכאורה קשה טובא כיון דלדעת הר"ש והרא"ש דקיי"ל כוותייהו הא דדרשינן מבבשרה למעט שפופרת היינו משום דיציאת הדם מהמקור לא היתה כדרכה א"כ מוכח דאע"ג דבבשרה קאי על בית החיצון אפי"ה דרשינן מיניה נמי לענין יציאת דם מהמקור וכיון שכן מ"ט לא נאמר דהרגשה היינו דוקא פתיחת הקבר, וראיתי שהחת"ס בחיו"ד סי' קס"ז הקשה כן על הנו"ב, אולם לדברינו ניחא דשפיר דרשינן מבבשרה למעט גם אם הכניסה שפופרת בפרוזדור עד המקור או עד בין השיניים משום טעמא דאין דרך לראות דם ע"ג דבר החוצץ אלא דרבנן סברי דממילא שמעינן נמי דכל שהוא שלא כדרכו טהור ומטהרינן משום כך גם אם עיקר יציאת הדם מהמקור לא היתה כדרכה אף בכה"ג שלא שייך כלל טעמא דחציצה, ועיין גם בחזו"א חיו"ד סי' ק"ט אות ד' שכתב "כיון דבשעת יציאת בין השיניים הוי דרך שפופרת לא חשיב ראיה דנהי דהוי יציאה מן המקור אבל הוי כיצא דרך דופן ולא דרך הפתח" ועיי"ש שכתב דברים הללו אליבא דהר"ש והרא"ש.

יג) אלא שלכאורה מוכח מהטור והב״י שהבינו בדעת הר״ש כפירושו של בעל שו״ע הרב ז״ל, דהטור כתב בסי׳ קפ״ח אהא דראתה דם בחתיכה טהורה דהיינו דוקא בחתיכה קטנה ״דומיא דשפופרת״ אבל חתיכה גדולה טמאה אפי׳ לא ראתה כלום משום דא״א לפתיה״ק בלא דם, ופירש הב״י דהא דראתה בשפופרת טהורה צריכים לומר דמיירי דוקא בשפופרת דקה דאיל״ה תפ״ל שהיא טמאה משום טעמא דפתיחת הקבר שאי אפשר בלא דם, ותמהו ע״ז התפל״מ והחוו״ד בסק״ג וז״ל ״ולבי מגמגם בה דמה בכך דא״א בלא דם הא דם לפנינו ותלינן שהדם ירד דרך השפופרת וכיון שדם זה טיהרה רחמנא מהיכ״ת ניחוש לדם אחר – ונראה דאף המחבר חזר בו שלא כתב [בשו״ע] דבעינן שיהא השפופרת דק שבדקים אלא ודאי דגם בשפופרת גדול תלינן שהדם שיצא בפתיחת המקור יצא דרך השפופרת״ עכ״ל, אך הרבו לתמוה עליו דנעלם מהחוו״ד שבסוף סי׳ קפ״ח מפורש כתב הב״י בשו״ע ״כשיעור שפופרת קנה דק שבדקים״ אולם הרב ז״ל מבאר יפה עפ״י שטתו את דברי הב״י וכתב ״דאם השפופרת עבה שהקבר נפתח על ידה כיון שא״א לפתיה״ק בלא דם ודרך נשים לראות דם ע״י פתיה״ק אין השפופרת מועלת לטהר הדם שיוצא ע״י פתיה״ק כדרך הנשים דמה לי שנפתח הקבר ע״י ולד שלם או ע״י שפופרת שכבר ריבה הכתוב זוב דמה לרבות רואה מחמת אונס כל שהיא רואה כדרך הנשים דהיינו שזב הדם מעצמו ע״י פתיה״ק או אונס אחר ולא ממעטינן אלא כשהוציאתו השפופרת בעצמה בכניסתה למקור שלא ע״י פתיה״ק כגון של קנה דק שלא נפתח הקבר על ידו כן דעת הטור ושו״ע לפ״ד הרא״ש עכ״ל, ונמצא דלכאורה א״א כלל להבין דברי הטור והשו״ע אא״כ נפרש בדברי הר״ש והרא״ש כהרב ז״ל, וכיון שכן בכה״ג שלבישת השפופרת היתה על פי המקור ופתיחת הקבר היא כדרכה שפיר טמאה וזה לא כדברינו, ברם נלענ״ד דלא טעה ח״ו החוו״ד בדבר משנה ולא נעלם ממנו הלכה מפורשת בשו״ע רק סובר דמ״ש הטור ״דוקא חתיכות קטנות דומיא דשפופרת״ היינו משום דסתמא דמלתא אין רגילים להכניס לאותו מקום כי אם דבר דק ודומיא דהכי מיירי גם בחתיכה שהיא קטנה, אבל אין ה״נ שאף אם תכניס שפופרת עבה לתוך המקור ג״כ לא קשה מהא דא״א לפתיה״ק בלא דם כיון שהדם יוצא דרך השפופרת ולא נוגע בבשרה, ובפרט דאם ננקוט כהסוברים דהא דא״א לפתיה״ק בלא דם הוא רק כשנפתח מאליו מבפנים ולא ע״י דבר הבא מן החוץ הרי בלא״ה לא קשה מידי גבי שפופרת, ונמצא דמ״ש דמיירי בשפופרת דקה הוא רק משום דסתמא דמלתא הכי הוה אבל עיקר כוונתם הוא לומר דדומיא דהכי גבי ראתה דם בחתיכה לא אמרינן דטהורה אלא בחתיכה קטנה ולא בגדולה כיון שא״א לפתיה״ק בלא דם, ובאמת הי׳ אפשר לפרש כן גם בדברי הב״י שבטור אלא שמפורש כתב שם ״רואה בשפופרת או בחתיכה אמאי מטהר לה הרי נפתח הקבר על ידם וא״א בלא דם״ וגם ממ״ש שם בסוף הסימן ״ומיהו שיעורא דשפופרת גופיה לא איתפרש לן אם עבה אם דק״ [גם האשכול בסי׳ מ׳ כתב ״בחתיכה קטנה ס״ל לרבא אפשר שתצא בלא דם וכן נראה מהא דאבעי מיניה ר׳ ירמי׳ מר׳ זירא״ ומשמע דגם בשפופרת קשיא לי׳ מהא דא״א לפתיה״ק בלא דם] מכל זה רואים בעליל שסובר דבשפופרת עבה טמאה מפני שא״א בלא דם וכן סובר גם הגר״א ז״ל בס״ק כ״ג, אבל מ״מ מדברי הטור והשו״ע לא שמעינן מידי ויכולים שפיר לומר כהחוו״ד שהב״י חזר בו. הלום ראיתי בתשו׳ בית יצחק יו״ד ח״ב סי׳ י״ד אות ח׳ שהביא מס׳ באר יעקב סי׳ קפ״ז משמי׳ דהגאון ר׳ ישעי׳ פיק

ז"ל שכתב דגם הב"י לא כוון רק בחתיכה ולא בשפופרת אולם הגאון ר' יוסף איטיגען ז"ל כתב שם דאין להוציא את דברי הב"י מפשטן דקיימי שפיר גם אשפופרת.

אך גם לדעת הב"י שבטור נלענ"ד דפירושו של הרב ז"ל צ"ע טובא הלא פשוט הוא דטעמא דהחמירו רבנן וגזרו טומאה גם אם ראתה דם בלא שום הרגשה או אפי' מצאה כתם על סדין היינו משום גזירה אטו הרגישה משא"כ בשפופרת שפיר טהורה גם מדרבנן כיון דגזיה"כ הוא דטהורה אין שום טעם לגזור ולהחמיר, ואפי' להר"ן בריש פ"ח דנדה שהבאנו לעיל שכתב דטעמא דראתה דם בשפופרת טהורה הוי נמי משום דלא ארגשה זיבת דם בבשרה, מ"מ כיון שיש דבר החוצץ ולא משכחת כלל שתרגיש וגם כיון דלא שכיח כ"כ מצינן שפיר לומר דבכה"ג לא גזרו רבנן, אבל אי אמרינן דבשעת וסתה לעולם טמאה וגם שלא בשעת וסתה יש נ"מ בין אם השפופרת הוציאה את הדם או שהדם הי' יוצא מאליו גם מבלעדי השפופרת, וכן אם השפופרת עבה ג"כ טמאה מה"ת אע"פ שרק השפופרת גרמה לפתיה"ק, וא"כ איך אפשר לומר דבזה השאירו רבנן את דין התורה ולא החמירו לגזור הא אטו הא והיא טהורה לגמרי גם מדרבנן, ובפרט שקרוב הדבר להיות ספק גמור דאורייתא דמה טעם לא נחשוש דשמא הי' יוצא הדם מאליו גם בלי השפופרת, וגם קשה דנהי דחזקה ודאית של א"א לפתיה"ק בלא דם לא אמרינן אלא בשפופרת עבה מ"מ גם בשפופרת דקה כיון שבאמת ראתה דם מ"ט לא נחשוש דשמא גם פתיחה מועטה זו גרמה ליציאת הדם ואיך מטהרינן לה ודאי גם מדרבנן, גם צ"ע דאיך סתם הב"י ומקשה בפשיטות מהא דא"א לפתיה"ק בלא דם והרי אין מקום לקושיתו אלא לשטת הר"ש בלבד ולא לרש"י ותוס' ושאר הראשונים שהזכרנו קודם דלדידהו לא מיירי כלל שהכניסה השפופרת תוך המקור כי אם לתוך הפרוזדור בלבד דלא שייך כלל פתיה"ק, ואף גם בדעת הר"ש אין זה כ"כ פשוט מ"ש הרב ז"ל לחלק דהוצאת דם ע"י שפופרת חשיב שלא כדרכה ואילו פתיחת הקבר הבאה מחמת השפופרת שפיר מיקרי כדרכה והרי אפשר שפיר לומר דכיון שהגורם ליציאת הדם היה מפני פתיה"ק שבאה ע"י שפופרת דגם זה חשיב שלא כדרכה [וכמו שלהדיא כתב כן הברית אברהם אשר יובא בע"ה להלן] ואיך סתמו וכתבו דבריהם בפשיטות גמורה.

יד) ולכן נראה כהאחרונים שכתבו בכוונת הטור והב"י דסברי דכיון שא"א לפתיה"ק בלא דם לכן בשפופרת עבה יש לחשוש דשמא בשעה שתחבה השפופרת לתוך המקור יצאה ממנה טפת דם לתוך בשרה או נדבק על השפופרת מבחוץ וכיון שהדם רואה את פני הבשר סברי דבכה"ג טמאה, וגם נלענ"ד דוגמא לחשש זה ממ"ש בנדה ל"ח ע"א לאפוקי ממ"ד שא"א לפתיה"ק בלא דם ולכאורה קשה דהרי שפיר ראתה דם לאחר הלידה ומהיכ"ת נימא שגם ראתה לפני הלידה ומוכח מזה דלמ"ד שא"א בלא דם חיישינן שתיכף עם הפתיחה מיד יוצא ממנה דם עיי"ש. [גם יש ספק ביצא הדם ממקורה דרך האויר ולא נגע כלל בבשרה אשר הגאון מוהרש"ק ז"ל מסתפק בזה בספרו מי נדה סי' קפ"ח בקו"א סעיף ג' וגם הרב ז"ל בקו"א סוף סי' קפ"ג מסתפק בכך, וחושבני דלדעת האשכול והרשב"א דלר' אליעזר אע"ג דדרכה של אשה לראות דם בחתיכה ואע"ג דמין במינו הוא אפי"ה שפיר חוצץ ומטהר גם אם הכניסה ידה והוציאה דם היינו משום דסובר דבעינן דוקא נגיעה בבשר וה"נ דרך האויר ג"כ טהורה דסו"ס לא נגע בבשר, משא"כ לחכמים דאם יש דם אגור בתוך חתיכה טמאה אע"ג דסברי שאין דרך לראות דם בחתיכה ואפי"ה כיון דמין במינו הוא לא חייץ ה"ה נמי דרך האויר דהא סברא הוא דאע"ג

שהחתיכה הוי מין אחד עם בשר האשה מ"מ נגיעה מיהא ליתא ולא עדיף מאויר] וגם אפשר דבשעה שמוציאה אח"כ את השפופרת מגופה אף גם אז יש להסתפק דשמא יצאה ממנה טפת דם כחרדל לתוך בשרה שבפנים ויעבור אח"כ לבית החיצון, ולכן נראה דאין שום הכרח מהב"י שפירש בדעת הר"ש והרא"ש כהרב ז"ל. גם ראיתי בצ"צ החדש חיו"ד סי' קכ"ח שכתב דלולא דברי הטור והשו"ע הי' יותר נראה לומר שגם לדעת הר"ש כל שיש הפסקה בין הדם והבשר מודים רבנן לר"א שהיא טהורה ורק משום קושית החוו"ד בדבריהם כתב דמסתבר כדעת זקנו הרב ז"ל ואעפ"י כן כתב שם דאפשר גם לומר דבשפופרת גסה ס"ל להטור והשו"ע דאם המקור נפתח יש לחשוש דיוצא דם גם שלא דרך השפופרת אלא בדופנו מבחוץ ודם זה טמא, אלא שחושב פירוש זה לדוחק כי מנין לו להטור לחדש דבר זה ועיי"ש דאעפי"כ מסיים שם הצ"צ וכתב "והדבר צ"ע כי בסוגיא נראה עיקר כמו"ש החוו"ד דבחציצה תליא מלתא", גם יפה העיר לי בזה בני הרב ר' אברהם דב שליט"א דלדעת הרב ז"ל בדעת הר"ש קשה טובא במה שאמרו בגמ'"בשפופרת כו"ע לא פליגי דטהורה כי פליגי בחתיכה" דהרי תרי גווני שפופרת הם לר"א מונח בבית החיצון שאין לו קשר עם פי המקור ולרבנן להיפך ולא ראי זה כראי זה ומה שייך לומר דלא פליגי בשפופרת, וכמו כן קשה איך אפשר לומר דלא פליגי והא איכא נ"מ בראתה דרך שפופרת בשעת וסתה דלר"א טהורה ולרבנן טמאה, גם ראיתי בברית אברהם הנ"ל שכתב בסי' ל"ט אות א' דלא איכפת לן כלל אם הדם יוצא מחמת עצמו או שהובא מהמקור ע"י דבר אחר שנכנס לתוכו והוציא משם את הדם כההיא דהדר מי רגלים ואייתי דם או יצא ע"י עד או שמש וכדומה אלא העיקר הוא שלא יעבור הדם דרך קנה חלול דכיון שהוא תוך דבר אחר אין דרך לראות בכך, ובכוונת דברי הטור והב"י הנ"ל כתב נמי דלפיכך הצריכו שהשפופרת תהא דקה דבעבה חיישינן דשמא ע"י פתיה"ק נדבק מעט דם מבחוץ ע"ג כותלי השפופרת דחשיב שפיר דרך ראיה כיון שאין זה "תוך" דבר אחר עיי"ש.

אך צ"ע דהנה בדף כ"ב ע"א הק' המהרש"א בתוד"ה כי פליגי דכיון שלפי פי' התוס' לא נחלקו אלא בחתיכה כעין מרזב ולא פליגי כלל רבנן אהא דקאמר ר' אליעזר בהדיא למעט שפיר וחתיכה "א"כ אמאי לא שביק המתרץ סברת המקשה דפליגי בפלי פלויי ולא פליגי חכמים אדרשא דבבשרה" ונדחק לתרץ "אע"ג דחכמים אית להו דרשא דבבשרה מ"מ שפיר פליגי חכמים אדרשא דבבשרה דקאמר ר"א בהדיא והיינו דלר"א לא אימעוט מבבשרה אלא שפיר וחתיכה אבל חתיכה כעין שפופרת לא אימעט ופליגי חכמים עלי' דכעין שפופרת נמי אימעט מבבשרה ועיין בהרא"ש בזה בשם ר"ש מקוצי ובפירושו יתישב טפי דפליגי חכמים אמאי דקאמר ר"א בהדיא" עכ"ל, ומעתה בשלמא אם נפרש בדעת הרא"ש כהרב ז"ל ניחא דר"א ממעט הפסקה ואילו רבנן פליגי עלי' ולא ס"ל כלל טעמא דהפסקה אלא מפני שאין דרך לראות, אבל אי אמרינן דרבנן מודו נמי לר"א דאין דרך לראות ע"י הפסקה רק הוסיפו לטהר גם בפלי פלויי משום דגם בזה אין דרך לראות נמצא שגם להר"ש לא פליגי כלל רבנן אמאי דקאמר ר"א בהדיא, אך אפשר שגם המהרש"א סובר שפיר כמו שאמרנו אלא שהוא סובר דר"א מטהר משום חציצה ולכן דוקא כשהדבר החוצץ הוא אינו מינו ואילו רבנן פליגי עלי' וסברי דכל שלא ראתה כדרך שרגילים לראות טהורה, ונמצא דבכה"ג שראתה דרך שפופרת של גומי וכדומה שפיר מודים רבנן גם אליבא דהמהרש"א דלאו דרך ראי' בכך והיא טהורה.

טו) גם הגאון בעל פרדס רמונים כתב בפתחי נדה בחקירה ששית אות ט"ז אליבא דהר"ש והרא"ש "דלרבנן דמטהרי אפי' בחתיכה דפלי פלויי מה"ט דאין דרכה לראות בחתיכה מכ"ש דמטהרי היכי דאיכא הפסקה בין דם לבשר דבהא אפילו ר' אליעזר מודה" וכן כתב מפורש בסי' קפ"ח אות י"ב וז"ל "ובשפופרת לדעת הר"ש והרא"ש איירי בש"ס שלא הכניסה השפופרת למקור – ומטהרינן לה אפי' ארגשה בפתיחת פי המקור דמ"מ היה הפסקה בין דם לבשר והתורה אמרה דם יהיה זובה בבשרה דוקא וגם חז"ל לא גזרו על זה – ואע"ג שהדם יוצא כדרכו מהמקור אפי"ה טהורה" עכ"ל, אלא שבדעת הטור והמחבר סובר הגאון הנ"ל דהן אמנם שמן התורה היא טהורה כיון שאין הדם נוגע בבשרה וכמבואר בש"ס אבל מ"מ לאחר שגזרו חז"ל טומאה אפי' אם ראתה בלא הרגשה כלל ה"נ יש לטמא גם אם ראתה בשפופרת ולכן סברי דלענין זה שתהא טהורה גם מדרבנן צריכים דוקא שתכניס השפופרת לתוך המקור ממש דבכה"ג שפיר אמרינן דכיון שהדם יוצא שלא כדרכו מחמת השפופרת לא גזרו רבנן, ומכיון שכן סברי נמי דאינה טהורה אלא בשפופרת דקה דאם היא עבה אע"ג שפתיה"ק היתה מחמת השפופרת שהכניסה לשם מ"מ אין זה מועיל לטהרה כיון דלאחר שהקבר כבר נפתח ה"ז חשיב כאילו עיקר ראיתה הוא לפי טבעו משום דדמי לראתה מחמת אונס של קפיצה וכדומה דמיקרי נמי דרך ראיה עיי"ש בפתיחה אות י"ד, ונמצא שבדעת הטור והמחבר שפיר סובר במקצת כהרב ז"ל כלומר דלענין זה שתהא טהורה גם מדרבנן צריכים דוקא שיהי' שינוי בעיקר הוצאת הדם מהמקור, אך היות ולהדיא מבואר שם דלפי פירושו נמצא שדברי הטור והמחבר הם נגד כל הראשונים, וגם תמוה מאד איך לא הזכירו כלל דלדעת כל הראשונים טהורה שפיר גם מדרבנן משום טעמא דחציצה בלבד, וכיון שזה תמוה ואיכא נמי לפרושי בדעת הטור דמיירי בשפופרת קצרה באופן שרק מהמקור יוצא הדם שלא כדרכו ואח"כ הדם נוגע שפיר בבשרה דבכה"ג שפיר אמרינן דאינה טהורה אלא א"כ הי' שינוי בעיקר יציאת הדם מהמקור שלא יצא כלל כדרכו מחמת עצמו אלא מחמת השפופרת, משא"כ בכה"ג דמאי דחשיב שלא כדרכו הוא רק משום חציצה שפיר מסתבר דכיון שמחמת השפופרת נפתח הקבר והדם יוצא אח"כ כדרכו מבין השיניים ונוגע בבשר שבבית החיצון שהיא ודאי טמאה מדאורייתא, וגם אפשר לפרש בדעת הטור כמו"ש קודם דבכה"ג שהכניסה השפופרת לתוך המקור שפיר סברי דבשפופרת עבה יש לחשוש דשמא בשעת פתיה"ק יצא מעט דם ונדבק בדופני השפופרת מבחוץ, וכיון שכן נראה דאין לזוז מכל דברי הראשונים להחמיר בדרבנן ואית לן למינקט להלכה דבכה"ג שמתחלת יציאתו מהמקור ועד סופו לא נגע כלל הדם בבשר דהרי היא טהורה גם מדרבנן אע"פ שהדם עצמו שפיר יצא כדרכו בלא שום שינוי, אך יש להדגיש דאף שראתה בשפופרת טהורה מ"מ לענין קביעות וסת אין דינה חלוק משאר נשים והוא פשוט וא"צ לפנים.

טז) אולם לכאורה צ"ע הרי גם נדה אינה טובלת מה"ת אלא א"כ הפסיקה קודם בטהרה, וכיון דכללא הוא דכל שנפתח מקורה הרי הוא בחזקת פתוח ועומד אפילו עברו כמה ימים ואינה מרגשת כלום, נמצא דבנד"ד אף אם תסיר את השפופרת ותראה שהוא נקי מדם מ"מ כיון שמעינה פתוח יש לחשוש שתיכף עם הוצאת השפופרת מהגוף ראתה טפת דם בבשרה, וכיון שכן תו לא מהני מה שתפסיק אחר כך בטהרה ותבדוק בחורין ובסדקין כיון דחיישינן שתיכף עם סילוק השפופרת ראתה טיפת דם בבשרה בלא שפופרת, ואין לסמוך כלל על זה שהאשה תתן את

לבה להרגיש דכיון שהיא טרודה בסילוק השפופרת אפשר שהרגישה ותלתה בהוצאת השפופרת כדאמרינן הכי גבי עד וכדומה, אולם גם באשה שהרגישה ממש שנפתח מקורה ובדקה אח"כ ולא מצאה כלום דקיי"ל שהיא טמאה רבו החולקים על החוו"ד וסוברים דכל זה דוקא בשבדקה לאחר שיעור וסת אבל אם בדקה תוך שיעור וסת הרי היא טהורה עיי"ש בפת"ש סי' ק"צ סק"ה ובדרכ"ת, ונמצא שאם תזדרז לבדוק עצמה תיכף עם סילוק השפופרת אין לחשוש כלל לשמא ראתה דם ונאבד, אך גם נראה שאף להחוו"ד דוקא התם הוא דמטמאינן לה משום דכיון שהרגישה שנפתח מקורה הרי ודאי ראתה ולכן חיישינן אע"פ שאינה מוצאת כלום, משא"כ הכא שהאשה יודעת ומרגישה שכבר עברו הימים שהיא רגילה לראות בהם לכן הן אמנם דלא קיי"ל כהזכרון יוסף (הובא בתשו' רע"א סי' ס') שסובר דכיון שרוב נשים פוסקות מלראות ביום ה' או ביום ו' תו לא מוקמינן לה בחזקת רואה, מ"מ בנד"ד כיון דמה שראתה מקודם בשפופרת אמרינן שהיא טהורה אפשר דמוקמינן לה אחזקת טהרה ואמרינן שלאחר הוצאת השפופרת תו לא ראתה כלום, ועיין גם באבנ"ז סי' רנ"ב שכתב בפשיטות דמה שאין סומכין על הזכרון יוסף הוא רק חומרא דרבנן וכיון שכן אפשר דכל זה דוקא באשה שכבר נטמאה אבל לא בטהורה לחשוש לראיה חדשה.

וסמוכין לכך מגמ' נדה דף ל"ו ע"א ברואה דם טוהר דאמרינן שבתוך מעל"ע דיה שעתה אפילו לרב שסובר דמעין אחד הוא ומפשטות דברי הגמ' והרמב"ם משמע דלא מיירי כלל שהפסיקה בטהרה והיינו משום דכיון שאינה מרגשת כלום לא אמרינן שהיא בחזקת רואה הואיל ומה שראתה קודם היה בימי טוהר, ומצינן נמי הכי בגיורת שנתגיירה דכל זמן שלא הרגישה הרי היא בחזקת טהורה ולא מטמאינן לה מפני זה שלא הפסיקה בטהרה בגיותה ולומר דגם לאחר שנתגיירה עדיין מעינה פתוח ולהצריך תמיד בדיקת חו"ס לפני גירותה עיין במהרש"ל במס' כתובות דף ל"ז ע"א וה"נ גם כאן, גם אפשר דדוקא בזבה דבעינן ספורין ובדוקין לא סמכינן על זה שכבר עברו הימים שהיא רגילה לראות ולומר דמסתמא תו לא ראתה, משא"כ בהפסק טהרה של נדה שהוא רק לדעת דתו לא ראתה דם אפשר דלאחר ה' או ו' ימים סמכינן שפיר על זה שאינה מרגשת כלום ושפיר מהני בדיקה גם לאחר שעור וסת מסילוק השפופרת, וגם אמרו שם בגמ' לענין יולדת בזוב שצריכה ז' נקיים דמ"מ ללוי שסובר ב' מעינות הן סגי במה שתפסוק משהו לאחר הי"ד יום של ימי טומאתה ואע"ג שגם לוי מודה שרק לדינא הוא דחשיב כב' מעינות אבל לא שכך הוא המציאות, ואפי"ה לא נזכר שם שלאחר ימי טהרתה חייבת לבדוק עצמה עוד פעם למען דעת שנסתם מעינה, גם כתבנו לעיל באות ג' מהפת"ש שהביא מהחת"ס שכתב כמה פעמים דבנדה דאורייתא סגי אפי' לא פסקה בטהרה כל שעברו עליה הימים הראויים לזיבת דמי נדתה על הרוב פסקה לה חזקת ראיה, אך ליתר שאת אפשר גם להחמיר ולבדוק היטב בשעה שלובשת עדיין השפופרת וכמו"ש בנוב"ת חיו"ד סוף סי' קל"ה, ואף אם קשה להכניס מוך בתוך השפופרת ולבדוק בדיקה גמורה עד פי המקור ג"כ מהני כמו בבדיקת בתולה דאף שהיא נדה או זבה גמורה אפי"ה סגי במה שבודקת עצמה עד מקום הבתולים וה"נ בנד"ד סגי במה שתבדוק חלק גדול מהשפופרת, גם נראה דמה שאין סומכים על קינוח ומצריכים בדיקת חו"ס גם לבעלה היינו משום דחיישינן שמא לא נסתם כלל המקור והדם מתעכב שם בחו"ס, וכיון שכן בשפופרת של גומי חושבני שאם האשה עומדת ובודקת עצמה עד כמה שידה מגעת מסתבר דאין לחשוש לשמא נתעכב הדם באמצע.

יז) מכל האמור עד כה הי׳ נראה לכאורה באיש ואשה שנמצאים במקום שאין מקוה טהרה לבנות ישראל דאפשר להפקיע ממנה איסור נדה ע״י זה שתלבש שפופרת של גומי לפני שיגיע זמן הוסת כאמור לעיל באות ד׳ כיון דאסקינן דלכו״ע טהורה היא בכך אפי׳ מדרבנן, אך כיון שמפשטות דברי השו״ע משמע דפסקו כהר״ש והרא״ש וכיון שבעל שו״ע הרב ז״ל סובר דלדעת הר״ש והרא״ש הרי היא טמאה נדה בכה״ג מדאורייתא אי אפשר כלל להקל, משא״כ לענין נד״ד כיון שלא ראתה יותר משבעה ימים והיא רק נדה ולא זבה וכשתטבול לאחר ז׳ ימים הרי תצא ודאי מטומאת נדה דאורייתא, חושבני דאין ראוי להחמיר בזה, ואע״ג שאם נולד ספק בדאורייתא ודרבנן יחד נקטינן להחמיר גם בדרבנן כי היכי דלא ליתו לזלזולי בדרבנן וכ״ש בכה״ג דנד״ד שהספק נולד בדאורייתא ונפסק הדין להחמיר ורק לאחר זמן כשטבלה בסוף ז׳ לנדותה נתגלגל הספק לדרבנן, מ״מ נ״ל דכיון שבנד״ד לדעת כל הפוסקים אינה נדה כלל ועיין במשכנ״י חיו״ד סי׳ מ״ב שכתב דלענין דינא קשה מאד לפסוק כהר״ש לקולא כיון דרש״י ותוס׳ והרמב״ם והרמב״ן והרשב״א והר״ן כולם פירשו בסוגית הגמ׳ דטעמא דטהורה הוא רק משום חציצה עיי״ש, וכיון שכן הו״ל רק ספק איסור וכיון שאף גם להר״ש והרא״ש ג״כ נתבאר דנפישי רבוותי דסברי שהיא טהורה ואי לאו שכבר הורה זקן להחמיר היינו צריכים לפסוק גם בזה להקל, לכן די לנו לחשוש לדעת הרב ז״ל ולהחמיר בדאורייתא ממש אבל לא במה שכבר נתגלגל לדרבנן וכ״ש בשעת הדחק שיש לחוש להוצאת אשה מיד בעלה ודאי נלענ״ד להקל. ועיין גם ביו״ד סי׳ נ״ז סעיף כ״א דדבר שאסור משום ספיקא דפלוגתא מותר למכרו לעכו״ם ולא חיישינן שיחזור וימכרנו לישראל ועיי״ש בש״ך שהביא מהתה״ד דכיון שאיסור מכירה לעכו״ם הוא מדרבנן לכן אמרינן דסד״ר לקולא ואע״ג שעיקר הספק נולד בדאורייתא מ״מ בספיקא דדינא שפיר מקילים בדרבנן אף אם נתגלגל מדאורייתא [עיי׳ בתשו׳ רע״א סי׳ ס״ד שהביא חדוש זה משמיה דהגאון ר״מ ווייל ודחאו, וצ״ע שלא הזכירו כלל את דברי הרמ״א והש״ך] ואף שהש״ך מפקפק קצת מ״מ בכה״ג שמעיקר הדין מותר ולא אסור אלא מחמת חומרא כתב גם הש״ך להקל וה״נ גם כאן, גם נלענ״ד דאין זה חשיב כזלזול בדרבנן דמצינן נמי בכה״ג לענין ספק תרומה שאסור מה״ת מפני הספק ופשוט הוא דאינה מתבטלת גם במינה אלא בששים ואפי״ה לענין דימוע תנן בכמה משניות דאינה מדמעת והיינו משום דלענין דימוע שאינו אלא מדרבנן ונוהג רק בתרומה שפיר הקילו חכמים אע״פ שהספק נולד בדאורייתא, וגם נראה פשוט דמה שטובלת לאחר ז׳ לא חשיב כלל כעושה ספק דרבנן לכתחילה, ובפרט שבזמן הש״ס נהגו כולן בטבילה זו.

יח) אך ראיתי בקונט׳ הר צבי שבסוף טור יו״ד הנדפס מחדש שכתב שם מרן הגאון מוהרצ״פ פרנק ז״ל בסי׳ קפ״ח וז״ל "ובאותו ענין נשאלתי מרב אחד ע״ד אשה שיש לה סכנה אם תתעבר ועפ״י הרופאים הניחה מכסה של גומי על פי המקור כדי למנוע ממנה הריון ולדעת הרב הנז׳ הי׳ פוסק שאם תראה דם בתוך המכסה לא תטמא משום דקיי״ל הרואה דם בשפופרת טהורה, ואמרתי לו שזה טעות דמה שהרואה בשפופרת טהורה היינו דהשפופרת גורם לדם שיצא וכמו שהבאתי לעיל מדברי שו״ע הרב ז״ל, וזה שנקטו בלשונם שאין דרכה של אשה לראות כך משא״כ כאן דהמכסה אינו גורם לדם שיצא דראית הדם כדרך ראיתה ובודאי דין טומאה יש כאן", עכ״ל. ותמיהני דלא נחית להא שגם הרב ז״ל לא כתב כן אלא לדעת הרא״ש, ואף גם אליבא דהרא״ש נתבאר לעיל דאין זה מוכרח ונפישי רבוואתי דפליגי עלי׳ גם בהא,

וגם הגאון העצום בעל ברית אברהם אשר הוא עצמו מביאו שם כתב נמי בפשיטות דלא כהרב ז"ל וכמו"ש לעיל. ואיך שהוא נראה דמה שכתב בפשיטות "שזה טעות" היינו מפני שהמכסה שעושים למניעת הריון הוא קטן ולכן אף שהדם היוצא מהמקור עובר תחלה דרך אותו מכסה מ"מ כיון שמשם יוצא הדם לבית הפנימי ונוגע בבשרה פשוט הוא דאין שום מקום לצדד בזה קולא אלא בכה"ג שהשפופרת היא בתוך המקור ממש וגורמת ליציאת הדם [אף גם זה דוקא שלא בשעת וסתה] דאז אע"פ שהשפופרת קצרה והדם נוגע אח"כ בבשרה ויוצא מביה"פ לביה"ח אפי"ה כיון שעיקר יציאת הדם מהמקור הוא מחמת השפופרת אפשר שהיא טהורה וכמו"ש בשו"ע הרב ז"ל משא"כ במכסה קטן וקצר שרק מרכיבים אותו מלמעלה על פי המקור שפיר כתב שהיא ודאי טמאה, עכ"פ נלענ"ד דבכה"ג שיצאנו לגמרי מידי ספק איסור תורה וכל החשש הוא רק בדרבנן מסתבר דאפשר שפיר להקל במקום צער גדול ומצות פו"ר.

יט) והנה גאון ישראל הנצי"ב ז"ל נשאל במשיב דבר סי' ל"ד (הובא בדרכ"ת סי' קפ"ח) לענין אשה שהרופאים עשו לה ניתוח ותפרו את פי הרחם באופן שהוא נכנס לתוך כיס השתן, אלא שאינה יכולה להטהר מפני שנוטף דם תדיר עם השתן והנה דעת נוטה של הגאון השואל הרב הכולל מנויארק ז"ל דכיון שהדם יוצא דרך כיס השתן ה"ז כיוצא דרך דופן, אולם הנצי"ב ז"ל דוחה דבריו וכתב "דאינו ענין ליוצא דופן דהתם לא יצא מפי המקור כלל אלא מכותלי הרחם יצא דם דרך דופן משא"כ בנד"ד יצא מפי המקור אלא שנכנס לכיס ומשם לבית החיצון" עכ"ל, ולענ"ד צ"ע אטו אם יצליח הרופא לכוין את פי המקור כנגד הבטן ולהוציא מהמקור את הולד דרך הבטן וכי לאו יוצא דופן הוא ומנין לנו שאם יוצא מפי המקור דתו לא חשיב יוצא דופן והרי כל הטעם הוא מפני שאין אשה טמאה אא"כ יוצא ממנה מדוה דרך ערותה ודבר זה ברור דגם אשה שאין לה מקור או שהרופאים הוציאו ממנה את מקורה דאפי"ה נשאר על אותו מקום שם ערוה לכל דבר, ולעומת זה הבא על הערוה דרך הדופן לתוך פי המקור יתכן דלאו ביאה היא כלל, ואולי עיקר כוונתו שם דכיון דאחר שהדם יוצא מפי המקור דרך הדופן כלומר דרך שביל השתן הוא חוזר שוב לבית החיצון שפיר חשיב כיוצא דרך ערותה וצ"ע. אולם גם הנצי"ב ז"ל נוטה שם להקל מטעמא אחרינא משום דדמי לאשה שנפל מקור שלה למטה ויוצא דם דטהורה להרא"ש משום שאין דרך לראות כן וה"נ גם כאן אין דרך לראות דם נדה דרך צנורות השתן, ותמה ע"ז שם מרן הגרצ"פ ז"ל "ולענ"ד יש לדון בה טובא דגדר שאינו דרך ראיה היינו שיציאת הדם מהמקור אינו בדרך טבעי אלא ע"י גורם חיצוני כמו שפופרת וכדומה אבל בנד"ד הרי יציאת הדם מהמקור הוא טבעי אלא שפי המקור אינו כנגד בית החיצון ויוצא דרך כיס השתן בזה י"ל דהרי סו"ס כשהדם יוצא מכיס השתן הרי נכנס שוב לביה"ח ועיכוב חציצה דאמרינן שמעכבת הטומאה מנ"ל דצריך שיעבור כל ביה"ח הא שפיר י"ל דסגי אם עובר דרך מקצת ביה"ח. ויש להוסיף דגם כלפי כיס השתן נמי י"ל דמין במינו אינו חוצץ ושוב דינו כאילו עובר כל ביה"ח וכמו"ש רש"י גבי חתיכה דמין במינו לא חייץ", והנה מה שתמה באחרונה דכיס השתן חשיב מין במינו לא הבינותי דבשלמא רואה דם בחתיכת בשר או שהאשה הכניסה ידה והוציאה דם כמו"ש האשכול והרשב"א שפיר אמרינן דכיון שהוא אותו המין לא חייץ וחשיב כאילו הדם יצא כדרכו דרך בשרה אבל אם הדם אינו יוצא כלל דרך שביל הדמים שהוא מקומו הקבוע כי אם דרך שביל אחר שבגופה אשר דרך שם יוצא תמיד שתן ולא דם איך שייך לומר דהואיל וגם השביל הזה של

השתן הוא של בשר דחשיב כמין אחד עם שביל הדמים ולא חייץ והלוא שני השבילים קבועים בגופה ומחולקים לשנים ומה טעם יבטל האחד לגבי השני, וקל וחומר הוא מחציצה ואין זה שייך כלל להא דמין במינו אינו חוצץ, וכמו כן בנוגע לתמיהתו הראשונה צ״ע דהנה דבר זה פשוט הוא דאשה ודאי נטמאת במקצת ביה״ח אלא שהגאון הנצי״ב ז״ל לא אזיל כלל בשטת הרב ז״ל ולפיכך שפיר סובר דהואיל והדם יוצא מפי המקור ועובר כל הזמן ע״ג דבר החוצץ עד לביה״ח אין זו דרך ראיה והרי היא טהורה כיון דבשעה שהטומאה מתחלת דהיינו בשעה שהדם עובר את הגבול מבין השינים ולפנים ונוגע בבית החיצון לא הי׳ כלל הדם בשביל הדמים אלא בשביל השתן והוא פשוט, ומ״מ אין ללמוד מהנצי״ב ז״ל להתיר גם במקום שיש ספק איסור תורה כי נראה דעיקר טעמו הוא משום דאין דרך לראות בזה הענין אבל משום חציצה גרידא יתכן דלא הי׳ מתיר [בדברי הנצי״ב שם מבואר דלרש״י המיעוט של חתיכה הוא משום חציצה ולהתוס׳ מפני שאין דרך לראות כך, ובעניי לא ידעתי חילוק זה וצ״ע] ולפיכך גם אתמה ע״ז שמרן הגרצ״פ ז״ל מקשה עליו מהא דכיס השתן חשיב מין במינו עם שביל הדמים ותפ״ל דמ״מ אין דרך ראיה בכך דהרי גם אשה שנעקר מקורה למטה בתוך הפרוזדור חשיב נמי מין במינו ואפי״ה היא טהורה לשטת הרא״ש, ועיין גם בדברי חיים ח״ב סי׳ ס״ג שכתב לענין מקור שנעקר ונפל עד לביה״ח דרואין את המקור כאילו הוא חוצץ בין הדם והבשר הפנימי ודומה לשפופרת שטהורה וסובר דשפיר חוצץ אע״ג שהוא מין במינו עייש״ה.

כ) וכמו כן נלענ״ד באשה שראתה ג׳ פעמים רצופים מחמת תשמיש דאין לה תקנה ואסור להשהותה, אבל מ״מ מבואר ברמ״א בסי׳ קפ״ז סעיף י׳ שאם עברה ושמשה באיסור ולא ראתה דמותרת משום דתשמיש זה שלא ראתה בו עדיף מבדיקת שפופרת והכריעו האחרונים שגם בפעם אחת סגי, דיש לדון לפי״ז שאם תלבש על פי האם שפופרת דקה של בד לבן לפני תשמיש ומיד לאחר תשמיש תוציא את השפופרת ותבדוק היטב את עצמה ואת הבד שאם לא תמצא שום מראה דם תהי׳ שפיר מותרת לבעלה, שהרי כל האיסור של רואה דם מ״ת הוא מפני שהתשמיש חשיב כשעת וסתה וחיישינן שמא תראה דם בשעת תשמיש, משא״כ אם תלבש שפופרת זו שאמרנו הרי אפילו אם תראה דם בשעת תשמיש מ״מ כיון שאין הדם יכול לצאת מן השיניים ולחוץ שפיר מותרת לבעלה אף אם היינו יודעים ברור שתראה דם בשעת תשמיש ונמצא דבשעה שבא עליה אינו צריך כלל לחוש לאיסור נדה, וממילא שאם יתברר אח״כ שלא ראתה דם דהו״ל נמי בדיקה מעליתא, ומה שלא נזכר כלל בפוסקים עצה זו אפשר דבשעתם לא ידעו עדיין דרך בטוחה לסגור את הרחם שלא תצא ממנו אפילו טפת דם פחות מכחרדל, משא״כ בזמננו דאפשר שפיר להבטיח דבר זה ומה גם בשעה שהאשה שוכבת ואין הדם נדחף כלל כלפי מעלה אפשר דיכולים שפיר לסמוך על בדיקה קלה זו שאמרנו, ואף דחשיב לפי״ז כמשמשת במוך כיון שפי האם סגור ואינה יכולה בשום אופן להתעבר מ״מ מותר כדי שלא להוציא אשה מיד בעלה, והן אמנם דבכה״ג שהשמש ארוך ונוגע בשעת תשמיש בפי הרחם אפשר דאין זה חשיב בדיקה כיון דבאופן זה שאמרנו השפופרת מפסקת ואין האצבע נוגעת במקור, אבל באצבע בינונית אשר בשום פעם אינה נוגעת בפי המקור צע״ג למעשה כיון דנפישי רבוואתי דס״ל דהא דרואה מחמת תשמיש נאסרת הוא רק מטעם וסתות שאינו אלא מדרבנן אפי׳ אם הרגישה בכל הג׳ פעמים [ועיין בחלקת מחוקק סי׳ קי״ט ס״ק כ״ב שסובר דראתה ג׳ פעמים מ״ת

אסורה מה"ת ועיין בזה בהעמק שאלה שאילתא פ"ט מ"מ להלכה נקטינן שהוא רק מדרבנן], ועכ"פ בכה"ג דלא הרגישה מודו כו"ע דאינה אלא מדרבנן, וא"כ אפשר דבדרבנן אין לחוש בזה לאיסור נדה ומותר שפיר לסמוך על בדיקה זו שאמרנו, וגם נראה דאפי' להטעם דחיישינן שיש לה חולי שממלאה ונופצת, מ"מ אם תלבש שפופרת קצרה והבד יהי' דק ורך ומכסה רק את פי המקור בלבד מסתבר דהוי בדיקה גמורה לכל מיני אצבעות, ואע"ג דבזה שבשעת ביאה מונחת שפופרת באותו מקום חלוק הוא מסתם תשמיש, אך לעומת זה חושבני דדמי טפי לתשמיש מבדיקת שפופרת שנזכר בגמ' ובשו"ע דהתם ליכא כלל שום חימוד ולאו שם תשמיש עליו כלל וכלל וגם חלוק הוא מעובי האצבע וכמו שהאריך בזה החוו"ד, משא"כ בבדיקה זו שכתבנו אע"ג דחלוק הוא במקצת מסתם תשמיש מ"מ חשיב טפי דרך תשמיש מבדיקת שפופרת, ועיין בשו"ת שב יעקב שהרחיק עצמו מבדיקת שפופרת שנזכר בשו"ע מפני שצריכים לזה הרבה מבינות וזריזות וחשש לדעת הראב"ד והרמב"ן ועוד דסברי שאין אנו בקיאין בזה"ז לסמוך על בדיקת שפופרת, אולם באופן זה שאמרנו יתכן דכל מורה ודאין יוכל לעשות כן לכתחלה.

גם נרויח בזה שאם רצתה לבדוק עצמה בעודה תחת בעלה הראשון אחר ששימשה ג' פעמים דמבואר במפרשי השו"ע דיש לחוש לדעת רש"י ואין לסמוך על בדיקת שפופרת שבשו"ע אלא היכא דאיכא נמי עוד צד להקל, דמ"מ נראה שאם תעשה כדברינו וגם תעשה אח"כ את הבדיקה שבשו"ע מסתבר דאפשר שפיר להקל, וכמו כן באשה שהתעסקה ברפואות ולדברי הרופאים כבר נתרפאה אלא שאעפ"י כן לא סמכינן בכה"ג על רופאים להתיר אותם בתשמיש, דמ"מ בצירוף עם בדיקה זו שכתבנו נראה דתוכל שפיר אח"כ לשמש כדרכה ואם לא תראה דם תהא מותרת. גם ידוע מ"ש החוו"ד באשה שראתה בליל טבילה אחר תשמיש אפי' במופלג מהתשמיש שאסורה לשמש לעולם בליל טבילה, וגם יש סוברים שאף אם ראתה בליל ב' של טבילה ג"כ אסורה לעולם בליל ב' משום דחיישינן שמא טבילה דאתמול גרם לה עיין בפת"ש סי' קפ"ז ס"ק מ"ג אולם לדידן יש לה תקנה ע"י זה שתלבש שפופרת הנ"ל בליל הטבילה כיון דמה שאסור לבוא עלי' הוא רק מחמת וסתות דרבנן ואם לא תמצא דם ה"ז נעקר ודאי בפעם אחת, ואף אם יתעקש מישהו לומר דלענין רואה מחמת תשמיש דחיישינן שיש לה חולי שממלאה ונופצת לא מהני בדיקה דידן שע"י שפופרת מ"מ לענין ראתה בליל טבילה דהוי רק משום וסתות שפיר מהני בדיקה זו ותחזור להיתירה. ועיין גם בשו"ע סי' קפ"ז לענין רואה מחמת תשמיש דאם שמשה סמוך לוסתה וראתה דם תולין בוסתה ולא חשבינן לה רואה מחמת תשמיש ועיי"ש בפרישה ובש"ך שנדחקו לפרש דמיירי דוקא כשעברה ושמשה בעבירה אולם לדברינו יתכן שלבשה שפופרת דשפיר מותר לבוא עליה בכה"ג סמוך לוסתה, וגם עיי"ש בש"ך סק"ל דלא משכחת עברה וראתה ג' פעמים רצופין בלא טבילה אלא בעבירה אולם לדברינו משכחת ע"י שפופרת דאינה נטמאת ומ"מ הוחזקה להיות רואה מחמת תשמיש. ועיין גם בפת"ש שם ס"ק י"ד דאם עשתה בדיקת שפופרת ונמצא דם על ראשו דשוב אין מועיל לה שום בדיקת שפופרת אפי' אם לא תמצא דם, אולם לדברינו עדיין יש לה תקנה ע"י בדיקה של לבישת שפופרת.

כא) כמו כן נלענ"ד בהא דחוששין לדם חימוד בתבעוה לינשא וצריכה לישב ז' נקיים דמבואר בפוסקים שנוהג דין זה גם בזקינה שהיא כבר מסולקת מדמים, דלפי דברינו אם הם נמצאים במקום שאין מקוה טהרה לבנות ישראל יש לה תקנה ללבוש לפני שעת התביעה

שפופרת ולהיות לבוש בה עד לאחר התביעה ואח"כ תוכל שפיר להסיר את השפופרת ולבדוק עצמה כל יום עד הנשואין ואם כל הזמן לא תמצא דם תהיה מותרת להנשא, דכיון דחששא דחימוד אינו אלא גזירה דרבנן אפשר שפיר לסמוך אהא דראתה דם בשפופרת טהורה גם מדרבנן [גם ידוע מ"ש הר"ן והמאירי בסופ"ב דנדה דדם חימוד לאו דם נדה הוא כלל רק חיישינן דאגב גררא דדם חימוד נמשך גם דם נדות עמו], אולם בלא"ה נ"ל תקנה אחרת שתשים מוך דחוק ברחמה כל שעת התביעה וכמו"ש החוו"ד בריש סימן קצ"ב דאהא שפיר סמכינן משום דאי הוה דם על המוך איבעי ליה לאשתכוחי, ואח"כ תבדוק עצמה כל יום עד שתינשא, כי דוקא בשעת תביעה ממש לא סמכינן אבדיקת עד דמתוך שהוא דם מועט חוששין שמא נאבד אבל אח"כ רק צריכים לבדוק כל יום ותו לא מידי, דהא ברור הדבר שאם תבעה לינשא ביום א' שעה אחת לפני השקיעה הרי היא פוסקת תיכף בטהרה ומתחלת למנות ממחרת וטובלת לאחר ז' באור ליום ב' ומוכח מזה דלא חיישינן שראתה דם מחמת חימוד כי אם ממש בשעת התביעה אבל אח"כ רק צריכה לבדוק את עצמה ולא יותר, דאי הוה חיישינן דשמא נמשך החימוד גם בערב וראתה גם בלילה טפת דם ולא הרגישה בו לא היה מועיל כלל מה שתטבול באור ליום ב' שהרי עדיין היא בתוך ז', ואף להרא"ש בפרק תינוקת סימן ד' שסובר "דיותר שהיא קרובה לזמן החתונה יותר לבה הומה ומשתאה ותדיר חיישינן שמא מחמת חימוד תראה" היינו דצריכים משום כך לבדוק אבל לא יותר, וכיון שכן אם תלבש שפופרת או תשים מוך דחוק כל שעת התביעה שפיר מהני בדיקה ואינה צריכה כלל טבילה וצ"ע, אך יש להזהר לעשות כל זה באופן שהאשה לא תגמור בדעתה דמה שאומרים לה ללבוש שפופרת או להכניס מוך דחוק דחשיב כבר כתביעה לנשואין דאם לא כן יש לחשוש תיכף לחימוד ואפשר שתראה דם רגע אחד לפני הלבישה ותו לא מהני כלל אח"כ שפופרת או מוך דחוק, והוא פשוט.

.5

רמב"ם הלכות איסורי ביאה פרק ו הלכה ד – כל שבעת הימים שנקבעה לה וסת בתחלתן הן הנקראין ימי נדתה, בין ראתה בהן דם בין לא ראתה בהן דם, ומפני מה נקראין ימי נדה מפני שהן ראויין לנדה וכל דם שתראה בהם דם נדה יחשב.

הלכה ה – וכל אחד עשר יום שאחר השבעה הן הנקראין ימי זיבתה, בין ראתה בהן דם בין לא ראתה, ולמה נקראין ימי זיבה מפני שהן ראויין לזיבה, וכל דם שתראה בהן דם זיבה יחשב, והזהר בשני שמות אלו שהן ימי נדתה וימי זיבתה.

הלכה ו – כל ימי האשה מיום שיקבע לה וסת עד שתמות או עד שיעקר הוסת ליום אחר תספור לעולם שבעה מתחלת יום הוסת ואחריהן אחד עשר [ואחריהן] שבעה ואחריהן אחד עשר, ותזהר במנין כדי שתדע בעת שתראה דם אם בימי נדה ראתה או בימי זיבה, שכל ימיה של אשה כך הן שבעה ימי נדה וי"א ימי זיבה, אלא אם כן הפסיקה הלידה כמו שיתבאר.

חידושי הרמב"ן מסכת נדה דף נד עמוד א – ובואו ונצווח על דברי הרמב"ם פאסי ז"ל שכתב בחבורו שהאשה שראתה תחלה מונה שבעה לנידתה וסמוך להן אחד עשר ואח"כ מונה ז'

לנדות אע״פ שאינה רואה בהן ואחריהן אחד עשר ואם ראתה בהן הרי היא זבה וכן כל ימיה, ואם קבעה לה וסת תחלת הוסת הוא יום נדות וממנו מונה שמונה עשר ומונה שבעה לנדותה אע״פ שלא ראתה ואם ראתה אחריהן באחד עשר זבה היא, עוד שבש וכתב שאפילו ראתה תשיעי ועשירי ואחד עשר ושנים עשר הרי זו זבה ותחלת נדה, וכל אלו דברי הבאי שלדבריו לא תמצא לרואה שבעה טמאים ושבעה טהורים שתשמש אלא שבוע שני ולסוף תשעה שבועות משמשת ששה ימים בשבוע העשירי וחמשה ימים משבוע שנים עשר ופתחה של זו לסוף שמונה עשר שבועות ובגמרא אמרו רביע ימיה מתוך עשרים ושמונה יום והוא טרח ונדחק לפרש בחיבורו רביע ימיה ולא קיים אלא בתוך כ״ח הראשון, וכן לדבריו בשמונה ימים טמאים ושמונה טהורים אינה משמשת חמשה עשר יום אלא מתוך מ״ח ראשונים אבל במ״ח שניים אינה משמשת אלא שלשה ימים, וכיון שלא אמרו משמשת ארבעה עשר יום מתוך שלשים ושנים או משמשת שמונה עשר מתוך תשעים וששה וכן כיוצא במנינין הללו ש״מ שפתחה של זו מ״ח ומכאן ואילך חוזרת חלילה, וכן האשה שראתה עשרה ימים טמאים ועשרה ימים טהורים אין זיבתה ושימושה שוים אלא פעם אחת בלבד לפי דברי הרב ז״ל, שהרי כשהיא חוזרת ורואה כן בשניה בשמונה ימים טהורים נשלמו ימי זיבה ראשונה והתחילו ימי נדה, נמצא שבעשרה ימים טמאים השניים חמשה ימים מימי זיבה ואין ימי שמושה בטהורים אלא שלשה, וכן למאה וכן לאלף למה מנו חכמים שבעה לנדה והשאר לזיבות והלא נעשית היא נדה אע״פ שלא ספרה לזיבה.

ועוד לדבריו מצינו אשה רואה יום אחד מסוף ימי נדה ויושבת עליו ששה ימים מימי הזיבה ואין לנדה ספירה אלא בימיה, וכן שנוי בכמה מקומות במסכתא זו שהרואה יום מ״א לזכר ויום פ״א לנקבה הרי היא תחלת נדה ואין מונין לימים שמקודם לכן והטעם לפי שכבר נשלם המניין, והרב ז״ל הודה ביולדת שמפסקת ומתחלת למנות מתחלת ראיה שלאחר מלאת, ולדבריו צריך הוא להביא ראיה מן התורה לשנוי זה שהוא משנה היולדת משאר נשים שאפילו כשאינן רואות הן מונות ימי נדה וזיבה כאלו הן רואות.

ועוד דהא בפ׳ בנות כותים (ל״ט ב׳) אמרינן דלכו״ע נדה ופתחה מכ״ז מנינן ואם היינו מונין משעת ראיה ראשונה כ״ז בימי זיבה קאי לה, ועוד מהא דתנן היתה למודה לראות יום ט״ו ואוקמה שמואל ט״ו לטבילתה שהן כ״ב לראייתה וכו׳ ואם אתה מונה כל ימי נדות וזיבה לתחלת ראיה ראשונה שראתה זו כי הדרי אתו כ״ב תליתאי בימי זיבה קיימי והיאך קבעה וסת בכך שאין האשה קובעת וסת בי״א כדאיתא התם בשלהי בנות כותים, ואין הוסת נקבע אלא בשלשה הפלגות כדבעינן לפרושי לקמן, וכל שכן לרב הונא בריה דרב יהושע דקשיא דאמר אינה חוששת בתוך אחד עשר, וכל זה במסכתא הזאת.

ותמהני עליו אם העביר עיניו בפתחי נדה במס׳ ערכין (ח׳ א׳) דתנו רבנן טועה שאמרה יום אחד טמא ראיתי פתחה שבעה עשר, פי׳ שאפילו היה תחלת ימי נדות הרי השלימה עליו ששה ועמדה י״א אחריהן נמצאת חוזרת לתחלת נדות וכל שכן אם היה בימי זיבה שכבר עברו ימי זיבתה וימים שהיתה ראויה להיות נדה, ואלו לדברי הרב ז״ל אי אפשר דהא איכא למיחש שאותו יום בתוך אחד עשר הי׳ וכשעמדה אחריו שבעה עשר נמצא עומדת בימי הזיבה למנין הראוי, וכן כל השמועה, ומדאמרינן התם נמי ארבעה וחמשה ימים טמאים ראיתי וכן כולם את

שמע בהדיא דמשעה שנעשית זבה גדולה אינה נעשית נדה לעולם עד שתספור שבעה נקיים שלה, ואין לי להאריך.

וכן יש שבושין בחבורי הראשונים בקצתם, כגון רב סעדיה שכתב שכל אחד עשר יום שבין נדה לנדה בשלש ראיות של שלשה ימים נעשית זבה גדולה בין ברצופין בין במפוזרין, וזה טעות מתפרש כאן ובכמה מקומות דרצופין בעינן ולא מפוזרין. ועל כיוצא בדברים הללו ידוו כל הדווים שהתורה משתכחת מלומדיה ואין אדם מוצא הלכה ברורה במקום אחד.

תלמוד בבלי מסכת נדה דף סו עמוד א – אמר רב יוסף אמר רב יהודה אמר רב, התקין רבי בשדות: ראתה יום אחד – תשב ששה והוא, שנים – תשב ששה והן, שלשה – תשב שבעה נקיים.

חידושי הר"ן שבועות ד. ד"ה אף על גב – ואע"ג דהאי תקנתא דרבי בסוודית וכו' מוציאה לכל ספק. תמיה למה הנהיגו חכמים מילתא יתירה כיון דתקנתא דרבי סגי חומר בנות ישראל למה לי ישתתרצו כדי שלא יטעו בדבר שלפעמים תהא זבה גדולה ותהא סבורה שלא ראתה אלא שנים כגון שראתה שתי ראיות ואחת מהן בין השמשות ולא תספור אלא ששה והן וכדי שלא יבא לטעות בכיוצא בזה השוו מדותם שאפילו בדם טפה כחרדל יהו יושבות ז' נקיים ועדיין אין זה מספיק אלא י"ל שכיון שלפעמים בטפה כחרדל יושבת ז' נקיים דהיינו בזיבה הסותרת החמירו בנות ישראל עלע עצמן לעשות כל דם שתראה כאילו היא סותרת ורבותא דטפת דם כחרדל היינו משום דהוה מצי למימר דבדם מרובה דוקא הוא שראוי להחמיר בו דשמא יצא מן המקור בשלשה ימים זה אחר זה ושהה בפרוזדור שהוא כמו שיצא לחוץ כדדרשינן לעיל וצריכה מה"ת שבעת ימים נקיים אם הוא בימי זיבה ולהכי נקט טפה כחרדל אע"ג דודאי אינה אלא ראיה אחת.

תלמידי רבינו יונה ברכות כב. ד"ה שאפילו – אלא פשר הדבר הוא כך שאם היה אומר דם סתם היינו אומרים שאין בזה חומרא כל כך מפני ששלשה בתים הם באשה חדר עליה ופרוזדור וכשהדם מרובה אפשר שמהיום שלשה ימים נעקר ויצא ביום הראשון מעט בבית הפנימי וביום השני נעקר מעט ויצא בבית האמצעי ועכשיו ביום השלישי נתקבץ הכל בבית החיצון ואע"פ שאינו מן הדין שיחוש האדם לדם שבפנים אלא כשבודקת ורואה בבית החיצון אפילו הכי כיון שאפשר שיהיה בזה הענין היינו אומרים שראוי לחוש וא"כ אין בזה חומרא גדולה שהרי אפשר נעקר הדם מהיום ג' ימים ודין הוא שנדון אותה כמו זבה גדולה ותשב ז' ימים נקיים אבל כשהדם הוא מועט רחוק הדבר לומר ששלשה משהויין היו ובכל יום ויום נעקר משהו אחד וקמ"ל שאע"פ שהוא דבר רחוק שדבר מועט כל כך שיהיה נעקר מהיום שלשה ימים אפ"ה החמירו על עצמן ודנו אותו כאילו נעקר לגמרי ויושבת עליו ז' נקיים.

רש"י מסכת מגילה דף כח עמוד ב – שהחמירו על עצמן – דמדאורייתא אין צריכה שבעה נקיים אלא הרואה שלושה ימים רצופים בתוך אחד עשר יום שבין נדה לנדה, אבל בתחלת נדתה – אפילו ראתה כל שבעה ופסקה לערב – טובלת בלילה, והן החמירו על עצמן, לפי שאין הכל בקיאים בפתח נדתה אימתי הן עומדות באחד עשר ימים שבין נדה לנדה ואם תאמר: לא יחמירו

אלא בשלשה רצופין, כדכתיב ימים רבים בלא עת נדתה (ויקרא טו) – פעמים שראיית דם נדה מזקיקתה לשבעה נקיים מן התורה, כיצד התחילה לספור שבעה נקיים לאחר שהיתה זבה גמורה, וספרה שבעה נקיים, ובשביעי ראתה אפילו כחרדל – סתרה הכל, וצריכה לחזור ולספור שבעה נקיים, אי נמי: שמא ראתה שני ימים ולא ידעה, והיום ראתה וידעה, דהוו להו שלשה ימים רצופין, וצריכה שבעה נקיים, ועל כן החמירו.

חידושי הריטב"א מסכת נדה דף סו עמוד א – אמר ר' זירא בנות ישראל הן החמירו על עצמן שאפילו רואות טיפת דם כחרדל יושבות עליה שבעה ימים נקיים. כבר פירשתיה יפה במסכת מגילה בסייעתא דשמיא, ומה שצריך לברר בכאן שאין חומר בנות ישראל מפני שמטמאות על מיעוט הדם דהא מוכחא בכולה מכלתין דמדאוריתא דם כל שהוא מטמא אותה ואפילו פחות מחרדל, אבל החומרא שיושבות שבעה נקיים על ראיה אחת, שאין לנו שבעה נקיים אפילו בטועה אלא בשלש ראיות בשלשה ימים, אבל באחת או שתים סגי לה שתשב ששה והוא אע"פ שהיא טועה וכתקנתיה דרבי, והן החמירו לדון עצמה כזבה הסותרת שמטמאה בדם בכל שהוא וצריכה שבעה וזו חומרא גדולה, ורבי לא רצה להפריז בתקנתו כל כך כיון שאין טומאה סותרת מעצמה אלא שחוזרת לטומאתה וכאילו לא ספרה, ומה שהוצרכו לומר בכאן אפילו רואות טיפת דם כחרדל זהו להודיע גודל החומרא, שאילו היתה ראיה מרובה היה אפשר לומר שראוי הוא לחוש בדרך רחוק שמא שלש ראיות היו בשלשה ימים ונצטרפו בפרוזדור בימי זיבה, אבל עכשיו שהיא כחרדל אף חששא זו אינה כאן, אלא שבנות ישראל קדושות רצו להחמיר ולעשות עצמן כסותרת כדי להשוות כל ראיותיהן ולישב על כולן שבעה נקיים, וכיון דעבדה ר' זירא שמעתא ובפרק אין עומדין (ברכות ל"א א') מנו לה להלכה פסוקה, למדנו כי חכמים קבלו מהם כן ועשו אותה תקנה ופשט איסוריה בכל העולם ואין כח לבטלה ולא להקל בה כלל, וכבר כתבנו (לעיל ל"ח א') שבכלל תקנה זו שלא לישב יולדת על דם טוהר, שכשם שחששנו לטועות בין ימי נדה לימי זיבה, כל שכן שראוי לחוש לטעות בין ימי לידה לימי טוהר, ובקטנה בתולה גזרו וכל שכן ביולדת ושופעת דם.

משך חכמה שמות יב:כב – דוגמא ההלכה פסוקה דרבי זירא שבנות ישראל החמירו על עצמן וכו' ובזמן המקדש על כרחך שיבטל דאי לאו הכי לא תדע אשה מתי להביא קרבן זיבה.

רא"ש מסכת נדה פרק י סימן ג – כתב הראב"ד ז"ל ועכשיו אין אנו בקיאין בבדיקה. ועוד שאפי' ידוע שבא מן הצדדין הרי גזרו בבנות ישראל כל הרואה [טיפת דם] כחרדל שיושבת עליו שבעה נקיים.

6.

תלמוד בבלי מסכת נדה דף נז עמוד ב – אמר שמואל: בדקה קרקע עולם וישבה עליה, ומצאה דם עליה – טהורה, שנאמר (ויקרא טו) בבשרה – עד שתרגיש בבשרה. האי בבשרה – מיבעי ליה שמטמאה בפנים כבחוץ! א"כ לימא קרא בבשר, מאי בבשרה – שמע מינה: עד שתרגיש בבשרה. ואכתי מיבעי ליה: בבשרה – ולא בשפיר, ולא בחתיכה! תרתי שמע מינה.

תא שמע, האשה שהיא עושה צרכיה וראתה דם, רבי מאיר אומר: אם עומדת – טמאה, ואם יושבת – טהורה. היכי דמי? אי דארגשה – יושבת אמאי טהורה? אלא לאו – דלא ארגשה, וקתני עומדת – טמאה! לעולם – דארגשה, ואימור הרגשת מי רגלים הואי. עומדת – הדור מי רגלים למקור ואייתי דם, ויושבת טהורה. ת"ש: עד שהיה נתון תחת הכר ונמצא עליו דם, אם עגול – טהור, ואם משוך – טמא. היכי דמי? אי דארגישה – עגול אמאי טהור? אלא לאו – דלא ארגישה וקתני משוך – טמא! לא, לעולם – דארגישה, ואימור הרגשת עד הואי, משוך – ודאי מגופה אתא, עגול – טהור. תא שמע: נמצא על שלו – טמאין וחייבין בקרבן, נמצא על שלה אתיום – טמאין וחייבין בקרבן, נמצא על שלה לאחר זמן – טמאים מספק, ופטורין מן הקרבן. היכי דמי? אי דארגישה – לאחר זמן אמאי פטורין מן הקרבן? אלא לאו – דלא ארגישה, וקתני נמצא על שלה אתיום – טמאין וחייבין בקרבן! לא, לעולם – דארגישה, ואימא הרגשת שמש הוה. תא שמע, נמצאת אתה אומר, ג' ספקות באשה: על בשרה, ספק טמא ספק טהור – טמא; על חלוקה, ספק טמא ספק טהור – טהור; ובמגעות ובהיסטות – הלך אחר הרוב, מאי הלך אחר הרוב? לאו אם רוב ימיה טמאין – טמאה, ואע"ג דלא ארגשה! לא, אם רוב ימיה בהרגשה חזיא – טמאה, דאימור: ארגשה ולאו אדעתה. אמר מר: על בשרה, ספק טמא ספק טהור – טמא; על חלוקה, ספק טמא ספק טהור – טהור. ה"ד? אי מחגור ולמטה – על חלוקה אמאי טהור? והא תנן מן החגור ולמטה – טמא! ואי מחגור ולמעלה, על בשרה אמאי טמא? והתנן ראתה דם על בשרה שלא כנגד בית התורפה – טהורה אב"א: מחגור ולמטה, ואב"א: מחגור ולמעלה. אי בעית אימא מחגור ולמטה – כגון שעברה בשוק של טבחים, על בשרה – מגופה אתאי, דאי מעלמא אתאי – על חלוקה מיבעי ליה אשתכוחי. על חלוקה – מעלמא אתא דאי מגופה אתא – על בשרה מיבעי ליה אשתכוחי. ואיבעית אימא – מחגור ולמעלה – כגון דאזדקרה; על בשרה – ודאי מגופה אתאי, דאי מעלמא אתאי – על חלוקה איבעי ליה אשתכוחי, על חלוקה – מעלמא אתאי, דאי מגופה אתאי – על בשרה איבעי ליה אשתכוחי. קתני מיהת על בשרה ספק טמא ספק טהור – טמא ואע"ג דלא הרגישה! ועוד, תנן: הרואה כתם על בשרה כנגד בית התורפה – טמאה ואע"ג דלא הרגישה! אמר רב ירמיה מדפתי: מודה שמואל שהיא טמאה מדרבנן.

רש"י מסכת נדה דף נח עמוד א – מדרבנן – דלמא ארגשה ולאו אדעתה.

תוספות מסכת נדה דף נח עמוד א – מודה שמואל שהיא טמאה מדרבנן – פי' הקונטרס דתלינן דלמא ארגשה ולאו אדעתה ואין נראה דאפילו מוחזק לה שלא הרגישה טמאה הואיל וראתה דם נדות ורב אשי נמי מודה דלשמואל היכא דלא הרגישה טהורה מן התורה וטמאה מדרבנן אלא אתי לפרושי דכי נמצא אקרקע דטהורה אפילו מדרבנן.

תלמוד בבלי מסכת נדה דף נח עמוד ב – מעשה באשה אחת שבאת לפני ר"ע, אמרה לו: ראיתי כתם. אמר לה: שמא מכה היתה ביך? אמרה לו: הן, וחיתה. אמר לה: שמא יכולה להגלע ולהוציא דם? אמרה לו: הן. וטהרה ר"ע. ראה תלמידיו מסתכלין זה בזה, אמר להם: מה הדבר קשה בעיניכם? שלא אמרו חכמים הדבר להחמיר – אלא להקל, שנאמר (ויקרא ט"ו) ואשה כי תהיה זבה דם יהיה זובה בבשרה, דם ולא כתם.

תלמוד בבלי מסכת נדה דף נח עמוד ב – הרגה מאכולת – הרי זו תולה בה. הרגה מאכולת. הרגה – אין, לא הרגה – לא. מתני' מני? רשב"ג היא, דתניא, הרגה. תולה, לא הרגה – אינה תולה – דברי רשב"ג, וחכ"א: בין כך ובין כך – תולה. אמר רשב"ג: לדברי אין קץ, ולדברי חברי אין סוף. לדברי אין קץ – שאין לך אשה שטהורה לבעלה, שאין לך כל מטה ומטה שאין בה כמה טיפי דם מאכולת. לדברי חברי אין סוף – שאין לך אשה שאינה טהורה לבעלה, שאין לך כל סדין וסדין שאין בו כמה טיפי דם. אבל נראין דברי ר' חנינא בן אנטיגנוס מדברי ומדבריהם, שהיה אומר: עד כמה היא תולה – עד כגריס של פול, ולדבריו אנו מודים.

שו"ת חתם סופר חלק ב (יורה דעה) סימן קפב – וע"ד שיעור כתם הנה הנכון כפ"מ שהעלה בתשו' מעיל צדקה ודקדקתי אחריו בצמצו' רב וכן הוא בלי פקפוק אך מה שהקש' איך אפשר לתלות שיעור זה במאכול' בזמנינו אעתיק לו מה שכתבתי בחידושי בדף נ"ח ע"א כל דבר שאינו מקבל טומאה וכו' וז"ל עיי' תוס' בטעמא דמלתא וצ"ע ועיי' פלתי ונב"י. והנלע"ד דהנה הכ"מ הקשה לטהר כל הכתמים מטעם ספק ספיקא ותי' הא בשוק של מטבחים לא עברה ובציפור לא נתעסקה והתי' תמוה דמספיקא לא נפקא דלמא עברה ולאו אדעתה וצריך לפרש עפ"י מ"ש ט"ז רסי' ק"ץ מאי ס"ס הוא זה הרי רוב דמים שמן המקור בהרגש' יוצאים ותי' במנחת יעקב אה"נ רוב דמים מן המקור בהרגשה והאי מדלא ארגשה אין כאן רוב מהמקור והא"ש גם קו' שלי ויפה תי' כ"מ דהא לא עברה בשוק של טבחי' ואת"ל עברה ולאו אדעתה א"כ ה"נ נימא ארגש' ולאו אדעתה והדרי' לרוב דמים מן המקור ואין כאן ס"ס וא"ש דברי כ"מ.

אלא אכתי י"ל בשלמא עברה בשוק ולאו אדעתה דהוי מלתא דלא רמי עלי' ומה לה להשגיח אם עברה בשוק של מטבחיים או לא משא"כ הרגשת גופה לטומאה וטהרה בודאי עיני' ולבה שם כל הימים ולא שייך כ"כ ארגשה ולאו אדעתה והדר' קו' לדוכתי' דה"ל ס"ס ולפי זה א"ש בעזה"י דאשה העסוקה בטהרות בבגדים המקבלים טומאה צריכה שפיר לתת לב על מקום עמידתה וישיבתה וכל פסיעה ופסיעה כי חוששים אפי' לספק הרוקים הנמצאים ולדם נבלה ושרץ וכל מילי והוה שפיר מלתא דרמי עלה ואי אפ"ה תימא לאו אדעתה ה"נ נימא ארגשה ולאו אדעתה דתרוייהו מלתא דרמיא עלה הוא וא"כ אזדא לי' ס"ס ושפיר טמאו כתם בבגד המקבל עכ"פ טומאת נגעי' שצריכה לתת לב שלא תבוא לידי נגע לבן אדמדם ועיי' בפלתי וק"ל.

והנה הרב אב"ד הוה ס"ל דלא אמרו כתמים אלא לטהרות ולא לבעלה וראב"ד תמה עליו מלקמן דף נ"ח ע"ב דאמרי' אין לך אשה שטהורה לבעלה אע"כ לבעלה נמי חיישי' לכתמים וכן הלכתא ולפי הנ"ל נראה דעכ"פ צדקו דברי הראב"ד בהא שתחלת גזירת כתמים הי' כשהיה עוסקים בטהרות מטעם הנ"ל וממילא נאסר נמי לבעלה ועכשיו נמי שבטלו טהרות מ"מ דבר שנאסר במנין צריך מנין אחר להתירו ובזה א"ש הא דבעינן שיעור גריס אע"ג דבזמנינו לא אשכחן מאכולת כה"ג מ"מ אין לך אלא מה שנאסר במנין הראשון שהי' מאכולת גדול כגריס הקלקי ואע"ג דליכא עכשיו כהאי גוונא מ"מ עכשיו בלא"ה הי' לנו לטהר כל הכתמים רק שא"א להתיר מה שנאסר במנין הראשון ושיעור קטן לא נאסר מעולם וא"ש הכל בעזה"י עכ"ל בחי'.

בעלי הנפש שער הכתמים פתיחה – והרי אני נזקק תחלה לאותן שאומרים שאין הכתמים נוהגים בזמן הזה, וראייתם כי הכתמים מדרבנן הם כמו שאמרו במשנה (נדה נח ב) דם יהיה זובה

בבשרה ולא הרואה כתם. וכן מעת לעת שבנדה דרבנן, וכשם שאין מעת לעת אלא לטהרות כך אין הכתמים אלא לטהרות, וכשהיא מטמאה את בועלה ועושה משכבות ומושבות הכל לטהרות, כמו שאמר ר׳ עקיבא (יד א) במעת לעת שבנדה שמטמאה את בועלה לטהרות ועושה משכבות ומושבות לטמא טהרות אבל לבעלה אין בה איסור. זהו טעם המתירים. והבל הוא בידם, שהרי אמרו בברייתא (נט א) לא אמרו כתמים להקל על דברי תורה אלא להחמיר על דברי תורה, כלומר לעשות סייג לתורה, אלמא לענין איסור נדה נאמרו. ועוד שהרי אמרו (נב ב) בכתמים פעמים שהם מביאין לידי זיבה, כלומר לידי קרבן, כיצד לבשה שלשה חלוקים הבדוקים לה וכו׳ הן הן הכתמים המביאין לידי זיבה. ואקשינן השתא שלושה חלוקין דלאו מגופא חזיא חיישא שני ימים וחלוק אחד מיבעיא מהו דתימא כל כי האי גוונא מביאה קרבן ונאכל קמ״ל שאינו נאכל, הא קרבן מיהת מתיא. ש״מ דלענין לאיסור נמי נאמרו, דאי לטומאה בלחוד קרבן מאי עבידתיה, ואפילו בשלשה חלוקים. ועוד שהרי אמרו בפרק הרואה כתם (נח ב) לדברי אין קץ לדברי חברי אין סוף, לדברי אין קץ שאין לך אשה שטהורה לבעלה שאין כל מטה ומטה שאין עליה כמה טיפי דמים. מדקאמר שטהורה לבעלה ש״מ דלענין איסור בעלה קאמרינן, דאי לטהרות לימא שאין לך אשה שהיא טהורה. ואין אנו צריכין להרבות דברים על זה שכבר הוחזקו בנות ישראל שהן נוהגות איסור בכתמים, וקיימא לן מנהגא מילתא היא כדרבי זירא דאמר (נדה סו א) בנות ישראל הן החמירו על עצמן שאפילו רואות טפת דם כחרדל יושבות עליה שבעה נקיים. והלכה פסוקה היא זו (ברכות לא א). וכן הדין בכתמים שכבר נהגו בהן איסור.

ערוך לנר מסכת נידה דף נח עמוד ב – בגמרא שטהורה לבעלה. כ׳ הר״ן מכאן השיב הראב״ד ז״ל על הרב אב״ד ז״ל במ״ש עיינתי בכל מילי דרבוותא ולא אשכחא בהון דינא דכתמים אי נהיגי בהון האידנא או לא וכו׳ וזו היא תשובה לדבריו דמדאמרינן אין לך אשה שטהורה לבעלה אלמא כתמים לבעל נאמר עכ״ל ובודאי תימה גדולה היא והנה הר״א אב״ד ז״ל אינו יחיד בשיטה זו דכבר הביא הראב״ד בבעל הנפש שער הכתמים שיטה זו בשם יש אומרים ולא בספק אלא בחלוטין ולודאי אמרו שאין כתמים נוהגים בזה״ז והשיב גם שם עליהם מסוגיא דהכא ולענ״ד יש לומר ביישוב שיטתם דשם הביא הראב״ד שנתנו טעמם כיון דכתמים דרבנן ומעת לעת דרבנן כמו שמעל״ע אינו רק לטהרות כך אין הכתמים אלא לטהרות והנה לפי המבואר לעיל (ד ב) טומאת מל״ע היא משום דתקינו לבדוק ולעיל (יא ב) אמרינן דאשה שאין לה וסת אסורה לשמש עד שתבדוק דמגו דצריכה בדיקה לטהרות צריכה ג״כ בדיקה לבעלה אבל בלא עסוקה בטהרות לא ע״ש ולכן י״ל כמו דלענין בדיקה טמאה לבעלה בלא בדיקה דוקא בעסוקה בטהרות כמו כן י״ל לענין כתם דעיקר נאמר לענין טהרות ומגו דטמאה לטהרות טמאה ג״כ לבעלה אבל בזמן דליכא טהרות אין כאן ג״כ טומאה לבעלה ובזה מדוייק למה כתבו דאין נוהגין בזמן הזה ולא כתבו העיקר דאין נוהג רק לטהרות דבאמת בזמן דאיכא טהרות כגון בימי רשב״ג נוהג גם לבעלה.

עוד כתב הראב״ד שם על שיטה זו דהבל היא בידם שהרי אמרינן לקמן דאמרו חכמים כתמים להחמיר על ד״ת כלומר לעשות סייג לתורה אלמא לענין איסור נדה נאמרו עכ״ד וראי׳ זו לא הבנתי וכי לענין טהרות שלא לבא לאכול תרומה בטומאה שהיא במיתה או קדשים בטומאה

שהיא בכרת לא הוי ג"כ סייג לתורה וביותר תמהתי על מה שכתב הראב"ד עוד ראי' נגד שיטה זו ממה דאמרינן לעיל (נב ב) כתמים פעמים שהם מביאין לידי זיבה כלומר לידי קרבן כיצד לבשה ג' חלוקים וכו' קמ"ל דאינו נאכל הא קרבן מיהא מייתי ש"מ דלענין איסור נאמר ולא לענין טהרות דאי לטומאת טהרות בלבד קרבן מאי עבידתי' ואפילו בג' חלוקים עכ"ל ולא זכיתי להבין שהרי קרבן זו לא משום טהרות ולא משום נדה הוא אלא משום ספק זבה גדולה כדמוכח ממה דנקט ג' חלוקים להיות ג' ראיות ומדמייתי קרבן ואינו נאכל שזה לא שייך רק בחטאת העוף שהיא קרבן זיבה ולא בקרבן בועל נדה וזבה שאינו רק חטאת בהמה ואולי כוונתו מדחיישינן לזיבה א"כ טמאה גם לבעלה אמנם כבר כתבו הרמב"ן והר"ן שם כיון דכתמים דרבנן אי אפשר שתביא קרבן אפילו לא נאכל ולכן פירשו מה דקאמר קא משמע לן דאינה מביאה קרבן וא"כ י"ל דגם בעלי שיטה זו דכתמים אינן טמאים רק לטהרות מפרשים כן ולכן מכל ראיות הראב"ד לענ"ד אין ראי' נגד שיטה זו שכפי הנראה היא גם שיטת הרי"ף שהשמיט כל דיני כתם בהלכותיו.

שולחן ערוך יורה דעה הלכות נדה סימן קצ סעיף ה – לא גזרו על הכתם אלא אם כן יש בו כגריס ועוד, ושיעור הגריס הוא כט' עדשים ג' על ג' (טור), ושיעור עדשה כד' שערות (אגור בשם מהרי"ל) (שהוא ל"ו שערות כמו שהן קבועות בגופו של אדם) (תשובת מהרי"ו סימן כ"ב ס"ב). וכל זמן שאין בו כזה השיעור אנו תולין לומר דם כנה הוא, אף על פי שלא הרגה כנה. אבל כשיש בו כזה השיעור אין תולין בכנה, בין אם הוא מרובע או אם הוא ארוך. ואם נזדמן לה גריס יותר גדול מזה השיעור, משערין בו.

שולחן ערוך יורה דעה הלכות נדה סימן קצ סעיף י – כתם שנמצא על דבר שאינו מקבל טומאה, לא גזרו עליו. כיצד, בדקה קרקע עולם (או בית הכסא שאינו מקבל טומאה), (מרדכי ה"נ בשם סמ"ג וסמ"ק) או כל דבר שאינו מקבל טומאה, וישבה עליו ומצאה בו כתם, וכן כתם שנמצא על בגד צבוע, טהורה. (לפיכך, תלבש האשה בגדי צבעונין, כדי להצילה מכתמים) (הרמב"ם ובגמרא פרק האשה).

תרומת הדשן סימן רמט – שאלה: הא דכתב ס' התרומה ובמרדכי ובהגה"ה במיימון מייתי לה, דשלשה ימים הראשונים של ספירת שבעה נקיים צריכין טהורים לגמרי, ואם מצאתה בהן כתם אע"פ שיכולה לתלות אותה במכה או בחבורה אינה תולה ואם מצאה פחות מכגריס יכולה לתלות בדם מאכולת או לאו?

תשובה: יראה דדוקא אמר ספר התרומה דאינו תולה בחבורה או בדם צפור והיינו כתם שהוא כגריס ועוד דפחות מכאן אינו צריך לתלותו בחבורה וכה"ג אלא תלינן אותו בדם מאכולת, וא"כ סברא לומר דווקא כתם גדול דלא שכיחי כולי האי ואפשר ליזהר בו לא תלינן בשלשה ימים הראשונים, אבל כתם פחות מכגריס ודאי תלינן ליה לעולם, דאל"כ אין שום אשה יכולה לטהר. והכי תניא פ' הרואה כתם (נדה נח ע"ב) אמר רשב"ג לדברי אין קץ דאין לך אשה שהיא טהורה לבעלה לעולם, שאין כל מיטה ומיטה שאין עליה כמה וכמה טיפות דם מאכולת, פי' לדברי שאני אומר דאם לא הרגה מאכולת אינה תולה בה אפילו פחות מכגריס ועוד טמאה, וא"כ אין

לך אשה טהורה. הא קמן דאין אדם יכול ליזהר ממאכולת, וא"כ אי לא תלינן במאכולת בשלשה ימים הראשונים אין אשה יכולה לספור שבעה נקיים.

פתחי תשובה יורה דעה סימן קצ:יב – דם כנה הוא – עי' בתשובת מעיל צדקה סוף סי' כ' שכתב וכן שמעתי מן החברים דהיה מן הראוי לטמא כתם שחור שקטן מגריס מטעם הזה עצמו שא"א לתלות במאכולת שהוא אדום ואילו כן לא ימלט שיזכרהו הפוסקים עכ"ל ועי' בס"ט שתמה עליו דנעלם ממנו דברי הראב"ד בס' בעה"נ שכתב כן בהדיא דאינה תולה במאכולת אלא כתם אדום. וכתב ומ"מ במקומות שמצוין פרעושים שלכלוך שלהם שחור ואין לך סדין וסדין שלא נמצא בו טיפות שחורות מאלו בודאי יש לתלות בהם והכל כפי ראות עיני המורה ע"ש.

רבי עקיבא איגר יורה דעה סימן קצ סעיף ה' – אנו תולין לומר. במראה שחור טמאה אף פחות מגריס. בעל הנפש.

רמב"ם הלכות איסורי ביאה פרק ט הלכה ו – מה בין כתם הנמצא על בשרה לכתם הנמצא על בגדה, שהכתם הנמצא על בשרה אין לו שיעור, והנמצא על הבגד אינו מטמא עד שיהיה כגריס הקילקי שהוא מרובע שיש בו כדי תשע עדשות שלש על שלש היה פחות משיעור זה טהור, נמצא טיפין טיפין אין מצטרפות, היה ארוך הרי זה מצטרף.

ש"ך יורה דעה סימן קצ:י – וי"א כו' – והב"ח ס"ס י"ב פסק כהי"א דלקמן ס"ח ולפע"ד אין להקל כלל דבש"ס (דף נ"ח ע"א) גבי לא דילמא עביד כרצועה משמע כהרמב"ם דאל"כ תקשה מאי איריא התם על בשרו ספק טמא על חלוקו ספק טהור הא על חלוקו נמי כתב ארוך מצטרף כדאיתא בברייתא ובט"ו לעיל סעיף ה' ודוק וכ"נ דעת התוס' והרא"ש וכ"פ בהג"מ בשם רבי שמחה.

תלמוד בבלי מסכת נדה דף נז עמוד ב – מתני'. הרואה כתם על בשרה, כנגד בית התורפה – מטמאה, ושלא כנגד בית התורפה – טהורה. על עקבה ועל ראש גודלה – טמאה. על שוקה ועל פרסותיה, מבפנים – טמאה, מבחוץ – טהורה, ועל הצדדין מכאן ומכאן – טהורה. ראתה על חלוקה, מן החגור ולמטה – טמאה, מן החגור ולמעלה – טהורה. ראתה על בית יד של חלוק, אם מגיע כנגד בית התורפה – טמאה, ואם לאו – טהורה. היתה פושטתו ומתכסה בו בלילה, כל מקום שנמצא בו כתם – טמאה, מפני שהוא חוזר. וכן בפוליוס.

תא שמע, נמצאת אתה אומר, ג' ספקות באשה: על בשרה, ספק טמא ספק טהור – טמא; על חלוקה, ספק טמא ספק טהור – טהור; ובמגעות ובהיסטות – הלך אחר הרוב, מאי הלך אחר הרוב? לאו אם רוב ימיה טמאין – טמאה, ואע"ג דלא ארגשה! לא, אם רוב ימיה בהרגשה חזיא – טמאה, דאימור: ארגשה ולאו אדעתה. אמר מר: על בשרה, ספק טמא ספק טהור – טמא; על חלוקה, ספק טמא ספק טהור – טהור. ה"ד? אי מחגור ולמטה – על חלוקה אמאי טהור? והא תנן מן החגור ולמטה – טמא! ואי מחגור ולמעלה, על בשרה אמאי טמא? והתנן ראתה דם על בשרה שלא כנגד בית התורפה – טהורה אב"א: מחגור ולמטה, ואב"א: מחגור ולמעלה. אי בעית

אימא מחגור ולמטה – כגון שעברה בשוק של טבחים, על בשרה – מגופה אתאי, דאי מעלמא אתאי – על חלוקה מיבעי ליה אשתכוחי. על חלוקה – מעלמא אתא דאי מגופה אתא – על בשרה מיבעי ליה אשתכוחי. ואיבעית אימא – מחגור ולמעלה – כגון דאזדקרה; על בשרה – ודאי מגופה אתאי, דאי מעלמא אתאי – על חלוקה איבעי ליה אשתכוחי, על חלוקה – מעלמא אתאי, דאי מגופה אתאי – על בשרה איבעי ליה אשתכוחי. קתני מיהת על בשרה ספק טמא ספק טהור – טמא ואע"ג דלא הרגישה! ועוד, תנן: הרואה כתם על בשרה כנגד בית התורפה – טמאה ואע"ג דלא הרגישה! אמר רב ירמיה מדפתי: מודה שמואל שהיא טמאה מדרבנן.

שולחן ערוך יורה דעה הלכות נדה סימן קצ סעיף ח – אם אין בכתם במקום אחד כגריס ועוד, אע"פ שיש שם טיפין הרבה סמוכין זה לזה עד שאם נצרפם יש בהם יותר מכגריס, טהורה, שאנו תולין כל טיפה וטיפה בכנה עד שיהא בו כגריס ועוד במקום אחד. וי"א דהני מילי כשנמצאו על חלוקה, אבל אם נמצאו על בשרה, מצטרפין לכגריס ועוד.

תורת הבית הקצר בית ז שער ד – לא נמצא השיעור כולו מצורף ממש במקום אחד אלא שנמצאו טפין טפין סמוכים זה לזה אם על בשרה הם ויש בין כולם כגריס ועוד טמאה שכל שהוא ספק על בשרה ספיקו טמא, אבל נמצאו על חלוקה בעניין זה טהורה עד שיהא בו גריס ועוד מחובר [דף טז עמוד א] ביחד במקום אחד.

רבי עקיבא איגר יורה דעה סימן קצ סעיף י – על בגד צבוע טהורה. אם הוא מנומר צבע על לבן והכתם על הצבע ויוצא על קצותי' על הלבן אם במה שיש על הלבן יש בו כשיעור הצבע מצרפן לכתם א' אבל אם אין בו כשיעור רק בהצטרפות שעל הצבע טהורה. ת' מעיל צדקה (סס"ב) וכן אם ראתה כתם לבן ובשני קצותיו מראה אדום הלבן מצרפן להאדום שיהיה כתם א' ואם יש באדום יחד שיעור כתם טמאה ע"ש.

פתחי תשובה יורה דעה סימן קצ:כ – בגד צבוע – ועי' בתשובת מעיל צדקה סי' ס"ב בדין כתם שנמצא על בגד מנומר גוונים הרבה לבנים ושאר צבעים ולא היה כשיעור כתם על נימור לבן אחד אלא שהיה מחובר ועבר ע"ג חלק הצבוע צבע תכלת ויוצא על גב הלבן שבצדו באופן שבין שני חלקים שע"ג פספס שני הלבנים היה בין שניהם כשיעור ונסתפק השואל אם מצטרפין לטמא הואיל והפסיק ביניהם הצבע וגם אם כל הצבעים מצילין על הכתמים והעלה דגם כל הצבעים מצילין. ואין הכתם שעל הצבע מצטרף. אבל שני הלבנים מצטרפים כיון שהכל הוא כתם אחד ומתחבר ע"י הכתם שעל הצבע דעושה חבור לצרף שני הלבנים אהדדי שאם יש בין שניהם כגריס טמאה ובאם לאו טהורה אע"ג שעם חלק הצבע הוא כגריס דחלק הצבע אינו מצטרף להשלים השיעור ע"ש והעתיקו ג"כ הס"ט ס"ק כ"א ובחכמת אדם שם דין יו"ד (ובבה"ט של הרב מהרי"ט ס"ק ת' לא העתיק יפה) אכן הח"ד כתב דגם מקום הצבוע מצטרף לכשיעור ע"ש ועי' בזה בתשו' תפארת צבי חי"ד סי' כ"ד דעתו ג"כ להחמיר דמצטרף ע"ש גם בשו"ת תשובה מאהבה ח"א סו"ס קס"ג מחמיר בזה וכמ"ש בס"ק שאחר זה.

חוות דעת שם – ואם חצי גריס על מקום צבוע וחצי גריס על מקום הלבן טמאה וכן אם חצי גריס יש לו מראה טהורה והחצי מראה טמאה וניכר שהכל כתם אחד טמאה. ובתשובת האחרונים מקילין עד שיהיה באדום שיעור גריס חוץ מקום הלבן דוקא. אמנם האדום שעל שתי מקומות הלבנים מצטרפין אף שמקום הצבוע מפסיק כיון שגם עליו יש דם.

שו"ת אגרות משה יורה דעה חלק ג סימן נג – כתם הנמצא על ניילאן ונייר ובנמצא מקצתו במקום צבוע בע"ה סיון תשל"ז לידידי הרה"ג אלימלך בלוט שליט"א.

ובדבר כתם שנמצא מקצתו במקום צבוע הנה נחלקו בזה האחרונים באם מצטרף גם מקום הצבוע להשיעור דהמעיל צדקה שהובא בחדושי רעק"א ובפ"ת סק"כ סובר דאינו מצטרף אלא מועיל לחבר שני חצאי השיעור שבלבנים, ובחו"ד סק"ט סובר שמצטרף, נראה שהוא בשיעור כגריס ועוד שלא טימאו בפחות מזה משום תליה במאכולת, שודאי ג"כ לא טימאו בפחות מכשיעור אף במקום שלא מצויים מאכולת דלא פלוג בין המקומות, שלכן סובר המעיל צדקה שלא פלוג בפחות מכשיעור כלל וצריך שיהא השיעור כולו דוקא במקום שמטמא כתם ובמראה שמטמא משום דלא פלוג בדין הטומאה דכתמים שצריכים שיעור, והחו"ד סובר שזה לא שייך למה שלא פלוג בין המקומות דהתם אם היה גם במקום זה מאכולות היה צריך ג"כ שיעור זה, והוי הלא פלוג להחשיב כל המקומות כאיכא שם מאכולות שלכך לא שייך כשהחצי שיעור טהור מצד אחר מחמת שהוא ע"ג בגד צבוע ומחמת שהוא במראה טהור, וכן יפלגו בחצי על דבר שאינו מקבל טומאה והחצי על דבר המקבל טומאה, ולדינא כיון שטעם החו"ד מסתבר מהראוי להחמיר כהחו"ד אף שהוא איסור דרבנן ואף שרוב אחרונים סוברים כהמעיל צדקה, אבל במי שאין לו בנים ובשעת הדחק יש להקל כהמעיל צדקה. ידידו, משה פיינשטיין.

7.

תלמוד בבלי מסכת נדה דף נט עמוד ב – מתני'. השאילה חלוקה לנכרית או לנדה – הרי זו תולה בה. ג' נשים שלבשו חלוק אחד, או שישבו על ספסל אחד ונמצא עליו דם – כולן טמאות. ישבו על ספסל של אבן, או על האיצטבא של מרחץ – רבי נחמיה מטהר, שהיה רבי נחמיה אומר: כל דבר שאינו מקבל טומאה – אינו מקבל כתמים.

תלמוד בבלי מסכת נדה דף ס עמוד ב – שלש שלבשו כו' שהיה ר' נחמיה כו': אמר רב מתנה: מ"ט דר' נחמיה – דכתיב (ישעיהו ג') ונקתה לארץ תשב, כיון שישבה לארץ – נקתה. אמר רב הונא אמר רבי חנינא: מטהר היה רבי נחמיה אפילו באחורי כלי חרס. פשיטא! מהו דתימא: ליגזור גבו אטו תוכו – קמ"ל. אמר אביי: מטהר היה ר' נחמיה במטלניות שאין בהן שלש על שלש, דלא חזיין לא לעניים ולא לעשירים. דרש רב חייא בר רב מתנה משמיה דרב: הלכה כר' נחמיה. אמר ליה רב נחמן: אבא תני מעשה בא לפני חכמים וטמאום, ואת אמרת הלכה כרבי נחמיה? מאי היא? דתניא: שתי נשים שהיו טוחנות ברחיים של יד, ונמצא דם תחת הפנימית – שתיהן טמאות, תחת החיצונה – החיצונה טמאה, והפנימית טהורה, בינתים – שתיהן טמאות. היה מעשה ונמצא דם על שפתה של אמבטי, ועל עלה של זית בשעה שמסיקות את התנור, ובא

מעשה לפני חכמים – וטמאום. תנאי היא, דתניא: ר׳ יעקב מטמא, ורבי נחמיה מטהר, והורו חכמים כרבי נחמיה.

תלמוד בבלי מסכת נדה דף נח עמוד א – ההיא איתתא דאשתכח לה דמא במשתיתא, אתאי לקמיה דרבי ינאי, אמר לה: תיזיל ותיתי. והתניא: אין שונין בטהרות! כי אמרינן אין שונין – לקולא, אבל לחומרא – שונין.

בעלי הנפש שער הכתמים סימן ב – ואפילו בדקה קרקע עולם וישבה עליו ומצאה עליו דם אם אין לה לתלות במאכולת דהיינו יותר מגריס טמאה, כדאמרינן לקמן, דאין הלכה כרבי נחמיה דאמר כל דבר שאינו מקבל טומאה אינו מקבל כתמים מההיא אתתא דהוה משתיא במשתיתא ואשתכח דם תותא במשתיתא וכו׳ (נדה נח א).

בעלי הנפש שער הכתמים – השגות הרז״ה סימן ב – עוד כתב הרב דאין הלכה כרבי נחמיה מההיא דהות משתיא ואזלא ואשתכח דם תותה במשתיתא. ואין זו ראיה לדבריו, כי משתיתא כלי אורג הוא ודבר המקבל טומאה הוא דמתרגמינן עם המסכת (שופטים טז, יג) עם אכסנא במשתיתא. ואדרבא דר׳ נחמיה עדיפא דאוקימתא דרב אשי דאמר שמואל דאמר כר׳ נחמיה, ורב נמי הכי סבירא ליה דדרש ר׳ חייא בר אבא משמיה דרב הלכה כרבי נחמיה (נדה ס ב), ובברייתא תניא (שם) הורו חכמים כר׳ נחמיה. וההיא דתניא (שם) מעשה בא לפני חכמים וטמאום אוקימנא כר׳ יעקב בר פלוגתיה דר׳ נחמיה, מ״מ דר׳ נחמיה עדיפא דתליא באשלי רברבי כרב ושמואל.

משנה מסכת כלים פרק ב – [א] כלי עץ וכלי עור וכלי עצם וכלי זכוכית פשוטיהן טהורים ומקבליהן טמאים נשברו טהרו חזר ועשה מהם כלים מקבלין טומאה מיכן ולהבא כלי חרס וכלי נתר טומאתן שוה מיתטמאין ומטמאין באויר ומיטמאין מאחוריהן ואינן מיטמאין מגביהן ושבירתן היא טהרתן.

משנה מסכת כלים פרק טו – [א] כלי עץ כלי עור כלי עצם כלי זכוכית פשוטיהן טהורין ומקבליהן טמאים נשברו טהרו חזר ועשה מהן כלים מקבלין טומאה מכאן ולהבא השידה והתיבה והמגדל כוורת הקש וכוורת הקנים ובור ספינה אלכסנדרית שיש להם שולים והן מחזיקין ארבעים סאה בלח שהם כורים ביבש הרי אלו טהורין ושאר כל הכלים בין מקבלין בין אינם מקבלין טמאין דברי ר״מ רבי יהודה אומר דרדור עגלה וקוסטות המלכים ועריבת העבדנין ובור ספינה קטנה והארון אע״פ שמקבלין טמאין שאינן עשויין ליטלטל אלא במה שבתוכן ושאר כל הכלים המקבלים טהורין ושאינן מקבלין טמאין אין בין דברי רבי מאיר לדברי רבי יהודה אלא עריבת בעל הבית.

תוספות מסכת נדה דף נח עמוד א – כרבי נחמיה דאמר כל דבר שאינו מקבל טומאה כו׳ – טעמא דרבי נחמיה כיון דדבר שהכתם בו טהור גם על האשה לא גזרו טומאה וההיא משתיתא דבסמוך נהי דלא מקבלה טומאה מ״מ מקבל טומאה בנגעים.

ש"ך יורה דעה סימן קצ:טז – או כל דבר כו' – וכן אפי' מין שהוא מקבל טומאה אלא ששיעורו גרם לו כגון מטלית שאין בו ג' על ג' כדאיתא בש"ס ומביאו ב"י וכ"כ הפוסקים ומבואר מדברי התוס' ריש דף נ"ח ומדברי הרא"ש פרק האשה שכתבו משתיתא נהי דלא מקבל טומאה מ"מ מקבל טומאת נגעים דכלי שמקבל טומא' נגעים אע"פ שאין מקבל שאר טומאה מקבל כתמים וטמאה.

שו"ת נודע ביהודה מהדורה קמא – יורה דעה סימן נב – שאלה: לבאר טעמיה דרבי נחמיה דאמר דבר שאינו מקבל טומאה אינו מקבל כתמים.

תשובה: לע"ד נראה משום דהכ"מ תמה למה כתמים טמאים הא הוי ס"ס ספק מעלמא ואת"ל ממנה שמא מן הצדדים עיין עליו בריש פ"ט מא"ב. ובתשובות האחרונים שדו ביה נרגא דספק מן הצדדים אינו ספק שהרי שנינו דם הנמצא בפרוזדור חייבים עליו על ביאת מקדש שחזקתו מן המקור. ואני אומר שגם משום ספק זה לחוד שמא מעלמא היה לטהר שהרי אין כאן איסור תורה כלל שהרי לא הרגישה ובאיסור דרבנן מהני ספק אחד להקל. ונראה לע"ד שאף שמן התורה בעינן הרגשה היינו לטמא האשה משום נדה טומאת שבעה ולהיות אסורה לבעלה כל שבעה. אבל עכ"פ לדידן דקיי"ל דמקור מקומו טמא א"כ הדם שעכ"פ טמא הוא ומטמא האשה טומאת ערב מן התורה נמצא שע"כ אנו צריכין לטמא האשה טומאת ערב שהוא ספק אחד של תורה שמא ממנה וכיון שכבר טמאוה טומאת ערב עשינו אותו שהוא מן המקור שוב מוכרחין לטמא אותה משום נדה מדרבנן שאמרו שאף בלי הרגשה טמאה. אלא דלכאורה אפילו טומאת ערב לא היה לנו לטמא את האשה שהרי יש ס"ס ספק אינו ממנה כלל ואת"ל ממנה שמא נטף להדיא מאותו מקום לחוץ ולא נגע בבשרה מחוץ ומגע בית הסתרים אינו מטמא וכיון שאינה טמאה נדה א"כ אין טומאתה רק משום מגע ויש ספק שמא לא נגע הדם בבשרה לחוץ. אבל תינח שאין אנו מוכרחים לטמא האשה אבל עכ"פ צריכין אנו לטמא הבגד שנמצא הכתם משום מגע. ונמצא החלטנו לומר שהוא מן האשה שהרי בזה יש ספק תורה ולכך שלא לחלק מוכרחים אנו לטמא גם האשה משום נדה מדרבנן דלא בעי הרגשה (שער ציון: עי' בספר כובע ישועה על מס' ב"ק (דף ל"ח) ד"ה מרקם מה שהעיר ידידי הרב הגאון הגדול ר' משה בצלאל לוריא שליט"א האב"ד דסייני יעויי"ש). וזהו בנמצא בדבר המקבל טומאה אבל בדבר שאינו מקבל טומאה לא שייך סברא הנ"ל. ולכך אינו מקבל כתמים. ואף שאפילו דבר שמקבל רק טומאת נגעים גזרו בו כתמים היינו שלא לחלק בדבר המקבל טומאה גזרו על הכל. ומצאתי מפורש בהגהות מיי' פ"ט מא"ב אות ה' וטעמיה דר' נחמיה כיון דהדבר שהכתם בו טהור גם על האשה לא גזרו והאי משתיתא נהי דלא מקבל טומאת כתם מ"מ מקבל טומאת נגעים עכ"ל. וג"כ צריך לפרש טעמו שלא חלקו בדבר המקבל טומאה. (הגהות שכר טוב: נ"ב עי' תשו' שיבת ציון סי' מ'. הגהות הלכה למשה) כ' לבאר טעמיה דר' נחמי' פ"ט דנדה דאמר כל דבר שאינו מקבל טומאה אינו מקבל כתמים דהכ"מ רפ"ט מהא"ב תמה למה כתמים טמאים הא הוי ס"ס ס' מעלמא ואת"ל ממנה שמא מן הצדדים ובתשובות האחרוני' שדו ביה נרגא דס' מן הצדדים אינו ספק שהרי שנינו דם הנמצא בפרוזדור חייבי' עליו משום ביאת מקדש שחזקתו מן המקור אלא דבאמת משום ספק זה לחוד שמא מעלמא הי' ראוי לטהר שאין כאן איסור תורה כלל שהרי לא

הרגישה ובאיסור דרבנן ספק א׳ להקל ונר׳ שאף מה״ת בעי׳ הרגשה היינו לטמא האשה משום נדה טומאת שבעה ולאסרה לבעלה אבל עכ״פ לדידן דקיי״ל מקור מקומו טמא א״כ הדם טמא ועכ״פ צריכי׳ אנו לטמא הבגד שנמצא הכתם משום מגע ונמצא החלטנו לומר שהוא מן האשה שהרי בזה יש ספק תורה ולכך שלא לחלק מוכרחי׳ אנו לטמא גם האשה מדרבנן דלא בעי׳ הרגשה וזהו בנמצא בדבר המקבל טומאה אבל לא בדבר שאינו מקבל טומאה שאין אנו צריכי׳ לטמא הבגד משום מגע דם נדה ותמוה לי טובא דא״כ גם בגד שכבר טמא במגע נדה או דם נדה לא יקבל כתמים שהרי אין אנו צריכים לטמא הבגד שנמצא בו הכתם משום ס׳ שמא הדם מגופה דבלא״ה טמא הוא מכבר ולפ״ז אנן שאין רגילין בטהרות ואין נוהגי׳ להטביל בגדים לטהרן וכל החלוקות והסדינין טמאין משום מגע נדה לא הי׳ שייך גבי דידן טומאת כתם וישתקע הדבר. ועוד עיין ביו״ד סי׳ ק״ץ סעיף י׳ דקיי״ל כר׳ נחמי׳ ובסעיף מ״ד כ׳ המחבר לבשה חלוק בימי נדתה ולא בדקתו ולבשתה בימי טהרתה ונמצא בו כתם תולה שמימי נדותה היא ומוכח דאם בדקתו שא״י לתלות הרי היא טמאה אע״פ שהחלוק כבר טמא ממה שלבשתו בימי נדתה – והנה בדוחק גדול הי׳ אפ״ל לתרץ דבדבר המקבל טומאה כיון שהוצרכו חכמינו ז״ל לגזור טומאת כתם גזרו ג״כ על בגדי׳ שכבר טמאין כיון דאין ניכר בבגד אם הוא טמא או טהור וכולא חדא גזרה היא משא״כ בדבר שאינו מקבל טומאה דניכר שפיר ואין להחליף בדבר המקבל טומאה לא גזרו – אלא שאני תמה הא אפי׳ בנמצא כתם על דבר שאינו מקבל טומאה יש לנו לדון על הכתם עצמו אם הוא דם טמא או דם טהור לענין אם יגע בו אדם או כלי טהור דאפי׳ נתייבש הדם מטמא דדם נדה מטמא יבש כדאיתא רפ״ז דנדה.

סדרי טהרה קצ:צג – מזה יצא לנו חידוש דין דהא דקיי״ל בנמצא כתם על דבר שאינו מקבל טומאה דלא גזרו בהא וטהורה מ״מ אם אותו דבר שנמצא עליו הכתם מונח ע״ג דבר המקבל טומאה כיון שאותו דבר שאינו מקבל טומאה מונח ע״ד שמקבל טומאה ונטמא משום משא לכך גם האשה טמאה.

פתחי תשובה יורה דעה סימן קצ:י – לא גזרו עליו – עי׳ בתשובת נו״ב חיו״ד סי׳ נ״ב טעם לזה ועי׳ ח״ד שהשיג עליו (ועי׳ מזה בתשו׳ חתם סופר סי׳ קפ״ב) ועי׳ בנודע ביהודה תניינא סי׳ ק״ה שכתב דנייר שלנו מקבל כתמים דלא גרע מלבדים דמקבל טומאה ע״ש ועי׳ בשו״ת שיבת ציון סי׳ ל״ט שגדול אחד הקשה על דברי הנודע ביהודה הנ״ל ממה שכתב הרמב״ם בהדיא פרק ב׳ מהל׳ כלים דהנייר אינו מקבל טומאה והיינו טעמא דלא דמי ללבדים דבנייר פנים חדשות בא לכאן והשיב לו דיש חילוק בין נייר שלנו שנעשה מבלויי סחבות או מעשבים כתושים שהוא מעשה לבדים זה בודאי מקבל טומאה והביא ע״ז ראיה גדולה אבל נייר שהיה להם בדורות הקודמים ועדיין עושים כן במדינות הודו מעלי אילנות וירקות או על קליפת עצים שהחליקו והתקינו אותם לקבל הדין זה אינו מקבל טומאה ומזה מיירי הרמב״ם והשיג על אותו הגדול במ״ש דלא דמו ללבדים כיון דפ״ח בא לכאן. דז״א שהרי אין אנו דנין שיקבל טומאה מפני שהיה ארוג בתחלה אלא ממה שנעשה עתה מעשה לבדים ע״ש. ועי׳ בס״ט שכתב אם נמצא על נייר שלא ע״י בדיקה וקינוח אלא שעברה עליו או ישבה עליו כתב בתוי״ט פ״ב דכלים דאין טומאה שייך בנייר הגם דאיהו מיירי בנייר שהיה בזמן הש״ס שהיה מעשבים מה שאין כן בנייר דידן שהוא נעשה מבגדי

פשתן מ"מ נראה דאין חילוק שהב"פ נטחן ופנים חדשות בא לכאן עכ"ל וכ"כ בחכמת אדם כלל קי"ג דין ח' ואילו ראו דברי הנו"ב ודברי בנו הגאון נר"ו בתשובה הנ"ל לא כתבו כן [עתה נדפס שו"ת ח"ס חלק ששי ושם בסי' פ"א כתב דאפילו נייר דידן אינו מקבל טומאה ולא כתמים דכיון שנכתשו הדק היטב ונמסו במים ונהפכו לפנים אחרות פרחה דין צמר ופשתים מנייהו ועוד נ"ל דלא מקרי צו"פ אלא העומדים לבגד ואריג וחבלים ולבדים וכדומה אבל הני ניירות שמיוחדים לצרכים אחרים א"כ אפילו צו"פ בעינא נימא מעשה עץ שימש כמבואר בחולין קכ"ט ע"א כו' ומסיים ע"כ בכתמים הנמצאים הולכין להקל אך בבדיקת עד שאינו בדוק אם הוא נייר אע"פ שלענין שיעור כגריס ועוד יש לו דין כתם מ"מ לענין זה לא אומר להקל בנייר ע"ש] ועי' בס"ט לקמן סעיף ט"ו סס"ק ל"ו שכ' דצ"ע היכא דשמשה מטתה ואח"כ מצאה כתם ע"ד שאינו מקבל טומאה או על בגד צבוע דבעלמא קי"ל דטהורה אע"ג דודאי מגופה כיון דשלא בהרגשה חזיא אבל כאן דספק דאורייתא הוא די"ל הרגישה וסברה הרגשת שמש הוא טמאה ע"ש. ואם מצאה כתם זה סמוך להטלת מי רגלים יש ג"כ ספק זה עמש"ל ר"ס קפ"ג (ועי' בתשו' חמדת שלמה סי' כ' בד"ה עכ"פ שהביא ראיה דגם בכה"ג טהורה ע"ש) ועי' עוד בס"ט לענין אם גם בשוטה תלינן בנמצא על דבר שאינו מקבל טומאה או ע"ג בגד צבוע ע"ש.

שו"ת אגרות משה יורה דעה חלק ד סימן יז – יד. מראה שנמצא על הניירות הדקות מאד שנעשו לקינוח בבית הכסא ו"הטישוס", אם יש לו דין כתם.

בניירות דקות מאד שנעשו במדינותינו לקינוח בבה"כ, ואף הנייר שקורין "טישוס" יש להקל, גם להורות למעשה, שאין ע"ז דין כתמים. דהא לענין כתמים אף בחת"ס ח"ו סימן פ"א מפורש שהנייר, אף שנעשו מצמר ופשתים, לא מקבלי דין כתמים והובא בפ"ת סימן ק"צ ס"ק י"ח. אבל מש"כ שלעניין בדיקת עד שאינו בדוק אינו רוצה להקל, נראה דהוא דווקא בנייר עב שלא נבטל מכל תשמיש, ולא בניירות דקות דבמקומנו שנבטל מכל תשמיש, וגם לא נעשו מצמר ופשתים, שבהם יש להקל אף בזה בפשיטות. ואף החכ"א לגירסא שלנו (דלא כדכתב החת"ס שלדברי החכ"א נייר אינו מקבל טומאה) שנייר הוא דבר המקבל טומאה, מסתבר שיודה בנייר דק שלנו שאינו מקבל טומאה. לא רק אלו שנעשים מעץ ועשבים וכדומה, אלא אף אם נעשה מצמר ופשתים נמי אין זה דבר המקבל טומאה, שהרי לא נעשה לתשמיש המתקיים, וגם לא ראוי לדבר מתקיים, ולכן ודאי שלכו"ע לא מקבלי דין כתמים.

חזון איש הלכות מקואות קכ"ו אות ז' – ובגומי נראה דגם כלי קיבול טהור [ואפשר שאין מטמאין מדרס כדין גלי גללים כלי אדמה ולא מקרי דיש במינן טהורה דלאו מינה דעץ נינהו] דלאו מינה דעץ נינהו. עוד יש לדון אחרי שנתרבו שאר בגדים אף שיאנו אריג הלא גם לבדים טמאים, ואמנם נראה דלא נתרבו אלא צמר גמלים וצמר גפן וכיו"ב שהן בטוי' ואריגה כצמר ופשתים אבל לא דברים הנמסים ונתכים, וכ"ה לשון הר"מ פ"א מה"כ הי"א י"ב.

תלמוד בבלי מסכת מנחות דף מ עמוד ב – ואמר רבא: הא מילתא אמרי, ואיתמר במערבא משמיה דר' זירא כוותי: היא של בגד וכנפיה של עור – חייבת, היא של עור וכנפיה של בגד – פטורה, מאי טעמא? עיקר בגד בעינן.

משנה מסכת כלים פרק יז – [יג] כל שבים טהור חוץ מכלב המים מפני שהוא בורח ליבשה דברי ר"ע העושה כלים מן הגדל בים וחבר להם מן הגדל בארץ אפי' חוט אפי' משיחה דבר שהוא מקבל טומאה טמא.

8.

תלמוד בבלי מסכת נדה דף סא עמוד ב – ת"ר, בגד צבוע – מטמא משום כתם, רבי נתן בר יוסף אומר: אינו מטמא משום כתם, שלא תקנו בגדי צבעונין לאשה אלא להקל על כתמיהן. תקנו? מאי תקנינהו? אלא שלא הותרו בגדי צבעונין לאשה אלא להקל על כתמיהן. הותרו – מכלל דאסירי? אין, דתנן: בפולמוס של אספסינוס גזרו על עטרות חתנים ועל האירוס. בקשו לגזור על בגדי צבעונין, אמרי: הא עדיפא – כדי להקל על כתמיהן.

הלכות נדה לרמב"ן פרק ד הלכה ו' – מצאה ע"ג בגדים אפילו היו כלי צבעונין מכיון שהדם ניכר בהן טמאה.

דגול מרבבה יורה דעה סימן קצ סעיף י – תמהני שלא הביאו שום חולק ובהגה"מ פ"ט מא"ב אות ו' כ' בשם רבינו שמחה ובשם ראב"ן שלא אמרו בגמ' דבר זה אלא לטהר הבגד שלא יטמא טהורות אבל האשה טמאה לבעלה אפילו נמצא בבגדי צבעונין וכיון שגם הרמב"ן מחמיר כמבואר בב"י קשה להקל נגד שלשה חמורי עולם.

הגהות מיימוניות הלכות איסורי ביאה פרק ט [ו] – כר' יוחנן בן יוסף דמייתי ראיה מדורות הראשונים דתניא בפולמוס של אספסיינוס גזרו כו' עד בקשו לגזור אף על בגדי צבעונים אמרו הא עדיפי להקל על כתמיהם ודלא כתנא קמא דאמר בגד צבוע מטמא משום כתם וכן פסק רבינו שמחה וכתב עוד דההיא קילותא לא נאמרה אלא לבגד שלא לטמא טהרות הנוגעים בו אבל האשה טמאה מדלא קאמר בגד צבוע אין מקבל כתמים כלישנא דתנן במתני' וכן כתב ראב"ן כדבריו שאפילו היו כולן צבעונין מכיון שהכתם ניכר בהן טמא.

רש"י מסכת נדה דף סא עמוד ב – להקל על כתמיהן – שאין הכתם ניכר בו כמראה דם גמור.

שו"ת חתם סופר חלק ב (יורה דעה) סימן קסא – שלום רב לי"נ הרב הגדול החרוץ המופלג כמה"ו נפתלי ני'.

ע"ד שאלתו שאלת חכם באשה שאינה יכולה לטהר מחמ' מציאו' כתמים תמיד אם יש לתקן לה שתלבש על גופה ובשרה כתונת מבגדי צבעונים שאינם מקבלים כתמים וכמ"ש רמ"א בש"ע (יו"ד) סי' ק"צ סעיף י' אלא שהגאון בדגול מרבבה שדי בי' נרגא כיון שרבינו שמחה שבהגה' מיי' פ"ג מא"ב אות ו' כ' שלא נאמר זה בש"ס אלא לטהרות ולא לבעלה וע"ז כ' מעלתו דרבינו שמחה לטעמי' דס"ל ז' סממני' מעבירין על הכתם נמי אינו אלא לטהרות אבל למאי דקי"ל דאפי' לבעלה מהני העברת סממנים אם כן ה"ה תקנת בגדי צבעונים נמי מועיל לבעלה אלו דבריו.

ולא הבנתי זה דל"ד להדדי דהתם רבינו שמחה ה"ק דמתניתין מיירי בודאי דם נדה על הבגד והאשה טמאה ודאי לבעלה ולטהרות וכבסו הבגד והעבירו עליו ז' סממנים לנקות מן הדם

ומה שנשאר רושם אחר העברת ז׳ סממנים אינו אלא טומאה בלועה ואינו מטמא טהרות מכאן ואילך אבל האשה טמאה לבעל׳ ולטהרות כיון דודאי דם נדה הוא וזהו שיטת רבינו שמחה שם וכן דעת ראב״ד ספ״ג מה׳ א״ב ונידון דידן מלתא אחריתי הוא דס״ל כתם הנמצא על בגד צבוע והוא ספק דם נדה לא הקילו בו לבעלה כי אם לטהרות ולא יכולתי להלום ולחבר ב׳ דינים אלו.

ומה שנלע״ד בענין זה הנה מסברא חצונה י״ל דיותר יש להקל בכתם הנמצא בבגד עליון ואינו נמצא בכתונת כלל יותר ממה שמקילין בנמצא בכתונת והוא דבר פשוט והנה בגמר׳ נדה ס״א ע״ב אמרי׳ תקנו בגדי צבעונים לאשה כו׳ ופריך מאי תקנו ומשני לא הותרו אלא משום לטהר כתמים ופריך הותרו מכלל דהיו ראוים לאסור ומשני אין כשגזרו בפולמס של אספאסינוס היה ראוי לגזור גם על בגדי צבעונים של אשה והניחום משום טהרות כתמים והנה פשוט דלא היה ראוי׳ לאסור אלא בגדי צבעונים בבגד עליון אבל למטה תחת הבגדים ככתונת שאינו אלא מלבוש הזיעה בזה אינו ראוי׳ לאסור ולא נמנו עליו כלל לאסור וממילא לא מצינו שנמנו להתיר וכיון שלא מצינו התירו מפורש יש לנו לומר ולחלק מסברא כנ״ל שלא התירו אלא בבגד שעל החלוק אבל ללבוש חלוק צבוע סמוך לגוף ממש לטהר כתמי׳ מנא לן.

ואיברא סברת רבינו שמחה והראב״ן שבהגה׳ מיי׳ הנ״ל צ״ע דבכל דוכתא מצינן דמקלינן לבעלה טפי מטהרות עד דהראב״ד הוי ס״ל למימר דכל חומרות כתמים הוא רק בעסוקה בטהרות ולבעלה כלל לא ואיך יחמירו לבעלה טפי מטהרות ולישב גם לשון שכ׳ תקנו בגדי צבעונים לאשה ובש״ס פריך מאי תקנו והכ״מ כ׳ כשנמנו בפולמס של אספסינוס ועסקו בבגדי צבעונים ולא אסרום ממילא תקנו והוא דוחק והרמ״א שינה לשון הרמב״ם וכ׳ לפיכך תלבש האשה בגדי צבעונים ולא כ׳ תקנו וכ׳ מנחת יעקב ששינה לשון הרמב״ם מפני קו׳ כ״מ ועדיין לא הועיל טוב הי׳ לו לשתוק מזה כלל גם לשון הש״ס אינו מטמא משום כתם קשה כמ״ש הגה׳ מיימ׳ דה״ל למימר אין בו משום כתם דהוה משמע לבעלה אבל האי לישנא אינו מטמא משום כתם משמע דלטהרות מיירי והנלע״ד בכ״ז דודאי ברייתא לטהרות מיירי ומשו״ה פריך הש״ס מאי תקנו בשלמא לבעלה שייך תקנו משום ביטול פריה ורביה וכדומה אבל לטהרות לא שייך תיקון ומשני בפולמס של אספאסינו׳ לא גזרו על בגדי צבעונים משום טהרות וממילא ניחא הא דלא תקנו לבעלה משום הא דר׳ ישמעאל ס״פ חזקת הבתים דאר״י מיום שגזרה מלכות כו׳ ראוי׳ היה שנגזור על עצמינו שלא לישא נשים כו׳ ונמצא זרעו של אברהם אבינו עליו השלום כלה מאיליו אלא שאין גוזרין גזירה על הצבור שאין רוב הצבור יכולין לעמוד בה נמצא באותו פולמס לא היה ראויה שיעשו תקנה משום ביטול פו״ר ודי שלא אסרו לישא נשים וע״כ לא הוו בה אלא משום טהרות וידוע דהמרדכי כ׳ משו״ה אין כופין עתה על פו״ר משום הך דס״פ חזקת הנ״ל ואמנם רוב הפוסקים ורמב״ם בכלל לא ס״ל כן ובש״ע רפיא הלכה הלזו ועיין ב״ש סי׳ א׳ סק״ו ונ״ל טעם החולקים על המרדכי וס״ל לכוף וכדמשמע בהרמב״ם וכמבואר בריב״ש סי׳ ס״ו למעיי׳ בפנים וצ״ל דס״ל ר״י לא אמרו אלא לאנשי דורו קרוב לזמן החורבן אבל אח״כ הקילו עולם מעלינו תלי״ת וכמבואר גם כן פ׳ הניזקין בסוגיא דסקריקון וא״כ חזר הדין למקומו לכוף על פו״ר הנה כי כן נ״ל רבינו שמחה ס״ל כיון דבפולמס של אספסינוס לא הוו בה אלא לטהרות ולא להקל ולתקן לה בגדי צבעונים משום בעלה אותו הטעם בעצמו עדיין במקומו וכדעת המרדכי הנ״ל ורמב״ם לטעמיה ס״ל כיון דהוו בה בפולמס וראויה היה שיתקנו אז תקנה

קבוע שתלבש בגדי צבעונים לבעלה ונהי דלא תקנו כן היינו באותו הדור שהיה דור של שמד אבל בזה"ז כשם שכופין על פו"ר ה"נ תקון קבוע הוא ללבוש בגדי צבעונים ור"מא אחז דרכו להיות הדין רפוי' בידינו לא כ' בלשון תקנה גם לא כרבינו שמחה אלא ברצון האשה תלוי הדבר.

וכעין זה י"ל דברי הראב"ד ז"ל שכתב דבזה"ז שהחמירו בנות ישראל על עצמן בחומרא דר"ז ה"נ נחמיר ברואה מחמת תשמיש שלא לבדוק בשפופרת עב"י סימן קפ"ז והוא תמוה מה ענין זה לזה וי"ל דכל קולא שהקילו בשפופרת הוא לבעלה ומשום שלא תתעגן ותתגרש וכיון שהן החמירו על עצמן בחומרת ר"ז ומי נתן להם רשות להרבות בחומרו' אלו ולבטל הבעל מפ"ור וע"כ משום דבזה"ז הניחו להן להחמיר על עצמם מטעמים הנ"ל א"כ ה"נ לא ניקול להם בבדיקת שפופרת בזה"ז מטעם הזה בעצמו.

היוצא מדברינו לדינא דקיי"ל כרמ"א דאשה הלובשת בגדי צבעונים מצלת על כתמים שלא לחוש לדברי רבינו שמחה נהי דתקוני לא מתקנין כהרמב"ם מכל מקום אין מוחין בידם גם כן וזה דוקא בבגד עליון אבל בגד הסמוך לבשר כחלוק וכתונת לא שמענו.

חזון איש סימן פט סעיף ד – בפ"ת יו"ד סי' ק"צ סקכ"א הביא בשם הח"ס דבגד הסמוך לבשר כמו חלוק וכתנת לא הותרו בהן כתמים בבגדי צבעונים, תמוה מאד דאילו היה חילוק בדבר איך סתמו הדבר כל הפוסקים ונתנו מכשול לרבים וגם בסברא אין חילוק שהרי במקום דליכא למיחוש אין חוששין, וכמש"כ בפ"ת סקכ"ו, ובמקום דאפשר לדם המקור לבוא אין חילוק בין סמוך לבשר לבגד השני, והעיקר דסתימת הראשונים והאחרונים כפירושו שאין בהם דין כתמים כלל, ובר"מ מבואר דאפי' ישבה ערומה על בגד צבוע ואח"כ נמצא עליו כתם טהורה כדין ישבה על דבר שאינו מקבל טומאה.

רמב"ם הלכות איסורי ביאה פרק ט הלכה ז – כתם שנמצא ע"ד שאינו מקבל טומאה טהור ואינה חוששת לו, כיצד ישבה על כלי אבנים כלי אדמה וכלי גללים או על עור הדג או על כלי חרש מגבו או על בגד ד שאין בו ג' אצבעות על ג' אצבעות ונמצא עליהן דם טהורה, אפילו בדקה הקרקע וישבה עליה ונמצא כתם על הקרקע כשעמדה הרי זו טהורה, שכל שאינו מקבל טומאה לא גזרו על כתם שימצא בו, ולא במקבל טומאה אלא א"כ היה לבן אבל כלי צבעונין אין חוששין לכתם הנמצא בהן, לפיכך תקנו חכמים שתלבש האשה בגדי צבעונין כדי להצילה מדין הכתמים.

תורת הבית הארוך בית ז שער ב – פירוש ימי ליבון ימי הספירה שהיא לובשת לבנים לספירת שבעה.

ספר המנהיג הלכות נדה עמוד תקמו – הלכות נידה הצריכות לבל יקלו בהם בני אדם: כתו' במס' שבת פ"ק [י"ג ע"א] מעשה בתלמיד אחד שקרא ושנה ושימש תלמידי חכמי' הרבה ומת בחצי ימיו והיתה אשתו שואלת מה זה ועל מה זה. נזדמן לה אליהו ז"ל, אמ' לה ביתי בימי נידותייך מה היה אצליך אמרה חס ושלו' לא נגע בי, בימי ליבוניך מהו אצליך אמרה אוכל עימי ושותה עימי וישן עימי בקירוב בשר ולא עשה מעשה, אמ' ברוך ה' שהרגו, שנ' ואל אשה בטומאת נידתה.

הגדה זאת בכל ספרי העולם. ויש לתמוה וכי היו מחמירין בימי נידה דאוריית' כימי ליבון דזבה והלא בנידה דאוריית' אף אם תראה כל ז' ופוסקת לערב שביעי טובלת ומשמשת, ואילו בזבה תשב ז' נקיים בלא דם כלל ותטבול ותשמש. על כן הגירסא על הנכון כמות שהיא בפרקי אבות דר' נתן, [פ"ב] בתי בימי זיבותיך מהו אצליך חס ושלו' לא נגע בי, בימי ליבונייך שהיו מחמירין בזיבה ממש מימי ליבון, ואם הגדה בהפך אז אתא שפיר, ימי ליבון הן שסופרות ז' נקיים ולובשות בגדים לבנים שאם תראה בהם תכיר ותסתיר את המנויין.

שולחן ערוך יורה דעה הלכות נדה סימן קצו סעיף ג – ביום שפסקה מלראות ובודקת עצמה כאמור, תלבש חלוק הבדוק לה שאין בו כתם, ובלילה תשים סדינים הבדוקים מכתמים, ומיום המחרת תתחיל לספור שבעה נקיים. הגה: ז ומנהג כשר הוא כשהאשה פוסקת בטהרה שתרחץ ולובשת לבנים; אמנם אם לא רחצה רק פניה של מטה, די בכך (מרדכי בשם רוקח), וכן נוהגין ואין לשנות; אבל בשעת הדחק, כגון אשה ההולכת בדרך ואין לה בגדים, תוכל לספור ז' נקיים רק שהחלוק יהיה נקי ובדוק מדם (אגור והגהות ש"ד ס"ס י"ט).

שו"ת רבי עקיבא איגר מהדורה תניינא סימן לד – לכבוד ידידי הרב ר' שלום נ"י מ"ץ בבוג.

ע"ד שאלתו באשה שמוצאת תמיד בבדיקה דם, ובכל פעם במקום א' ושלא בשעת וסתה, ובלילה בשינה מתחככת בסדין באותו מקום, ולמחקתו מוצאת בסדין כמה טיפי דמים, וא"י לטהר לבעלה:

בעניי איני רואה מקום להקל, מקור הדין בפסקי מהרא"י (סי' מ"ז) וז"ל, אשר כתבת שיש לה הוכחה שיש לה טהרה (היינו מכה) אך שא"י אם מוציאה דם, ודאי חד עד לחוד לא מהני, דלהדיא כתב המרדכי דבעינן שיודעת דמכתה מוציאה דם אז תולית במכתה, אמנם בנ"ד מצאנו ב' צדדים להתיר, א' כמו שכתבת שכ"ז שבודקת בחורין וסדקין אינה מוצאת הכתמים, נראה דר"ל דבמקום אחד מוצאה לעולם, א"כ אם אותו מקום קצת סברא לטהר דמוכח דמצדדים בא ממכה וכ"ש במרגשת בבדיקה כשנוגעת שם דכואב לה קצת, ובשארי חורים וסדקים אינה מרגשת כאב כלל, עוד כתב במרדכי אברייתא אם יש לה וסת תולה בווסתה, פי' דיכולה לומר הדם שרואית טהור שעדיין לא הגיע ווסתה ותולה במכתה, אע"ג דרש"י פי' בדרך אחר, נוכל לצרף דעת המרדכי ג"כ לשאר צדדים, לכן נראה אם איתנהו לכל הני צדדים תוכל לסמוך להחזיקה לטהורה עכ"ל המהרא"י, והוא בקוצר בש"ע (סי קפ"ז).

והנה דעת הט"ז דבעי' דוקא כל הצדדים דיש לה מכה, ויש לה ווסת ושלא בשעת ווסתה, ובכל פעם מוצאת רק במקום א'. ודעת הש"ך בנקה"כ דחד צד מהני אי שלא בשעת ווסתה הקבוע, אי שאינה מוצאת תמיד רק על אותו צד, ונראה דאזלי לשיטתייהו, דהט"ז לשיטתו בסק"ח דהמרדכי דמיקל שלא בשעת ווסתה, היינו רק ביש לה מכה, א"כ ע"כ מה דמסיים המהרא"י דאע"ג דרש"י פי' בענין אחר נוכל וכו' לכן אי איתנהו להנהו הצדדים, היינו במה שהוא שלא בשעת ווסתה, וגם אינה מוצאת רק במקום א', דאל"כ אלא דמיקל בחד צד, א"כ הוא ממש כהמרדכי, והרי המהרא"י לא סמך על המרדכי לחוד, רק בצירוף שאר צדדים, ובש"ך שם דס"ל דהמרדכי מיקל שלא בשעת ווסתה אף בלא מכה, מש"ה י"ל דמהרא"י צירף דעת המרדכי להיכי דיש לה מכה ושלא בשעת ווסתה, או ע"י דמוצאת תמיד בצד אחד, ואך כ"ז אף להש"ך מ"מ

בעינן בירור שיש לה מכה, אלא אף דא"י אם המכה מוצאת דם, בזה מהני חד צד מהצדדים הנ"ל, אבל בנ"ד דלית לה מכה לא מהני ב' הצדדים דשלא בשעת ווסתה ומוצאת דם תמיד במקום אחד, והכאב לחוד לא מקרי מכה, והמהרא"י נקט לה דרך כ"ש שאם גם מרגשת כאב, אבל הכל בנוי על שיש לה הוכחה שיש לה מכה, וגם הט"ז דכתב דכאב במכה, היינו ביש לה מכה ומוצאת תמיד ע"י כאב מורה הכאב דהדם מהמכה, אבל כאב לחוד אינו במכה.

ולדעתי יש מזור ותעלה, שבלילה תאסור ידיה שלא תמשמש מתוך שינה, והספירת ז"נ ההפסק טהרה יהי' בדיקה כראוי. וכן עוד פעם א' ביום הא', ופעם אחת ביום ז' ותבדוק בפשתן דק בכל מקום במתינות ולא תדחוק, כי זה לא מצינו שהחיוב בדיקה יהי' ע"י דחיקת העד, ובשארי הימים שבין יום הא' ליום ז' של ספירת ז"נ תבדוק בכל יום ע"י הכנסת עד בשפת הרחם, דזהו מקרי בדיקה להראב"ד, ותלבוש בגדי צבעונים וכן הסדינים ומכסה הכרים יהיה הכל בבגדי צבעונים שאין מקבלין כתמים, כן נראה לענ"ד: ידידו עקיבא גינז מא"ש.

.9

הגהות מיימוניות הלכות איסורי ביאה פרק ד [כ] – כל הבדיקות האלו לא הוזכרו אלא לענין עסוקה בטהרות אבל לדידן כל לבעלה לא בעי בדיקה וכל הנשים בחזקת טהורות לבעליהם כדלעיל בפרק זה. וכתב רבינו שמחה שאין אשה רשאה להחמיר על עצמה לבדוק אחר תשמיש אבל לבדוק קודם תשמיש רשאי אדם להחמיר על עצמו כדתנן כל היד המרבה לבדוק וכו' וכן משמע מעובדא דאמר רב כהנא שאילתוה לאינשי ביתיה דרב פפא כו' ע"ש וכן מורי רבינו מיחה באשה שהיתה בודקת תמיד אחר תשמיש ואע"פ שאין לה וסת למה תחמיר לקלקל עצמה בדבר שאסרו לה חכמים כיון דמדאורייתא בעינן שתרגיש בבשרה אלא דרבנן אסור רואה בלא הרגשה כמו כתמים והם אמרו דהיכא דאשכחה דם אסרו והם אמרו שלא לבדוק ע"כ וכן פסק רשב"ם בספ"ק וז"ל ושמעינן מהכא בין אשה שיש לה וסת בין שאין לה בזמן הזה דליכא טהרות לא בעיא בדיקה לא שחרית ולא ערבית לא לפני תשמיש ולא אחר כך כדלקמן בסמוך ואפילו רצתה להחמיר על עצמה לא שבקינן לה להחמיר דאם כן לבו נוקפו עכ"ל. וכן כתב ברוקח.

פתחי תשובה יורה דעה סימן קפג:א – שתרגיש – עבה"ט ודע דשלשה מיני הרגשות יש לענין שתהא טמאה מדאורייתא א' שנזדעזע גופה כמ"ש הרמב"ם פ"ה מהלכות א"ב דין י"ד. ב' שנפתח מקורה כמבואר בסי' קפ"ח ובסי' ק"ץ ס"א. והשלישית נמצא בשו"ת האחרונים ז"ל כשמרגשת שדבר לח זב ממנה בפנים וע' בזה בתשובת נודע ביהודה חלק יו"ד סי' נ"ה ובספר ח"ד סי' ק"צ סק"א [אמנם בת' ח"ס חולק ע"ז בכמה תשובות והאריך לבאר דזיבת דבר לח לאו הרגשה הוא ע"ש בסי' קמ"ה וקנ"ג וקס"ז וקע"א וכתב שם שכן הוא מורה ובא הלכה למעשה וכן קיבל ממורו הגאון מוהר"ר נתן אדלער ז"ל] ואם מצאה דם בבדיקה בלא הרגשה או אחר תשמיש בלא הרגשה אי הוי ספק דאורייתא ונימא הא דלא ארגשה משום דסברה הרגש עד או שמש הוא או לא ע' בשו"ת שב יעקב ובתשובת כתר כהונה סי' מ"ח שהאריכו בזה וע' בדברי השל"ה שהבאתי לקמן סי' קפ"ח ס"א אמנם הכו"פ והס"ט וח"ד כתבו דהוא דאורייתא אבל בקינוח או שלא הכניסה העד בעומק אלא מהפרוזדור ולחוץ אינו אלא מדרבנן כשלא הרגישה וכן סמוך להטלת מי רגלים הוא ג"כ דאורייתא ח"ד ע"ש.

חוות דעת חידושים סימן קפג סעיף ב – ואם מצאה דם בבדיקה אפילו בלא הרגשה הוא דאורייתא דאימר טעתה בהרגשת עד.

סדרי טהרה סימן קצ סעיף לו – מיהו צ"ע היכא דשימשה מטתה ואחר כך מצאה כתם על דבר שאינו מקבל טומאה או על בגד צבוע דבעלמא קיי"ל דטהורה אע"ג דוודאי מגיפה אתיא כיון דשלא בהרגשה חזיא אבל כאן דסד"א הוא די"ל ארגשה וסברה הרגשת שמש הוא טמאה.

משנה מסכת נדה דף יד עמוד א – מתני'. דרך בנות ישראל משמשות בשני עדים אחד לו ואחד לה והצנועות מתקנות שלישי לתקן את הבית נמצא על שלו – טמאין וחייבין קרבן. נמצא על שלה, אותיום – טמאין וחייבין בקרבן, נמצא על שלה לאחר זמן – טמאין מספק, ופטורין מן הקרבן. איזהו אחר זמן כדי שתרד מן המטה ותדיח פניה ואח"כ מטמאה מעת לעת ואינה מטמאה את בועלה ר"ע אומר: אף מטמאה את בועלה מודים חכמים לרבי עקיבא ברואה כתם שמטמאה את בועלה.

תלמוד בבלי מסכת נדה דף יד עמוד ב – נמצא על שלה לאחר זמן וכו'. תנא: וחייבין אשם תלוי. ותנא דידן מ"ט? בעינן חתיכה משתי חתיכות.

תלמוד בבלי מסכת נדה דף סה עמוד ב – תנו רבנן: הרואה דם מחמת תשמיש – משמשת פעם ראשונה ושניה ושלישית, מכאן ואילך – לא תשמש, עד שתתגרש ותנשא לאחר. ניסת לאחר וראתה דם מחמת תשמיש – משמשת פעם ראשונה ושניה ושלישית, מכאן ואילך – לא תשמש, עד שתתגרש ותנשא לאחר. ניסת לאחר וראתה דם מחמת תשמיש – משמשת פעם ראשונה ושניה ושלישית, מכאן ואילך לא תשמש עד שתבדוק עצמה.

שולחן ערוך יורה דעה הלכות נדה סימן קפז סעיף א – אשה שראתה דם מחמת תשמיש מיד, בכדי שתושיט ידה לתחת הכר, או לתחת הכסת, ותטול עד לבדוק בו, ותקנח עצמה, משמשת ב ג"פ. אם בכל ג' פעמים רצופים ראתה דם, (וכ"ש אם מצאה ג' פעמים דם ד על עד שלו), (מרדכי וכן כ' ב"י בשם תרומת הדשן וסמ"ג), אסורה לשמש עם בעל זה, אלא תתגרש ותנשא לאחר. נשאת לאחר, וראתה דם מחמת תשמיש ג' פעמים רצופים, אסורה לשמש גם עם אותו בעל, אלא תתגרש ותנשא לשלישי. ואם גם עם השלישי ראתה דם מחמת תשמיש ג"פ רצופים, לא תנשא לאחר אלא אסורה לכל עד שתבדוק. הגה: וי"א שאין אנו בקיאין איזה מקרי מחמת תשמיש, כי אין בקיאין בשיעור הנזכר, ולכן כל שרואה ג"פ סמוך לתשמיש מקרי לדידן מחמת תשמיש, ונאסרה על בעלה. (ב"י בשם הראב"ד שכ"כ בשי"א). ואלו ג"פ צריכים להיות רצופים, אבל אם לא היו רצופים לא נאסרה על בעלה. (ב"י בשם הרמב"ם וכ"כ הרשב"א סימן תתל"ט ומהרי"ו נ"ג) (וכן כתב המחבר בסמוך). ואין חילוק בין אם ראתה ג' פעמים מיד שנשאה, ובין נתקלקלה אח"כ וראתה ג' פעמים. (מרדכי ריש ה"נ ובתשובת הרשב"א סימן תתל"ט ובתוס'). וכל זה לא מיירי אלא בראתה סמוך לתשמיש, אבל אם לא ראתה סמוך לתשמיש, לא נאסרה על בעלה, ומותרת לו לאחר טהרתה תמיד (ב"י בשם סה"ת וסמ"ג) ודינה כמו שאין לה וסת.

תלמוד בבלי מסכת פסחים דף צט עמוד ב – משנה. ערב פסחים סמוך למנחה לא יאכל אדם עד שתחשך. אפילו עני שבישראל לא יאכל עד שיסב. ולא יפחתו לו מארבע כוסות של יין, ואפילו מן התמחוי גמרא. מאי איריא ערבי פסחים? אפילו ערבי שבתות וימים טובים נמי, דתניא: לא יאכל אדם בערבי שבתות וימים טובים מן המנחה ולמעלה, כדי שיכנס לשבת כשהוא תאוה, דברי רבי יהודה. רבי יוסי אומר: אוכל והולך עד שתחשך. אמר רב הונא: לא צריכא אלא לרבי יוסי, דאמר: אוכל והולך עד שתחשך, הני מילי – בערבי שבתות וימים טובים, אבל בערב הפסח, משום חיובא דמצה – מודה. רב פפא אמר: אפילו תימא רבי יהודה, התם בערבי שבתות וימים טובים – מן המנחה ולמעלה הוא דאסיר, סמוך למנחה – שרי. אבל בערב הפסח, אפילו סמוך למנחה – נמי אסור.

רשב"ם מסכת פסחים דף צט עמוד ב – ערבי פסחים סמוך למנחה. מנחה קטנה. קודם למנחה מעט חצי שעה בתחלת שעה עשירית דתנן (לעיל דף נח א) תמיד נשחט בשמנה ומחצה וקרב בתשעה ומחצה נמצאת מנחה קטנה בט' ומחצה וסמוך ליה היינו חצי שעה קודם בסוף שעה תשיעית ותחלת שעה עשירית.

תוספות מסכת סוטה דף לט עמוד א – כל כהן שלא נטל ידיו – פירש רש"י אמר לי רבי אם נטל ידיו שחרית ונטהר כהן אינו צריך ליטול ידיו כשעולה לדוכן וכמדומה שהועתק מהגהת תלמיד שהרי אין לשונו משמע כך דפירש שלא נטל ידיו לפני עלותו לדוכן משמע ממש סמוך ועוד דמייתי גמרא קרא שאו ידיכם קדש וברכו משמע תיכף לנטילת ידים ברכת כהנים דמשמע ליה השתא דבברכת כהנים משתעי קרא דהיא בנשיאות ידים ומשמע בירושלמי פ"ח דברכות דבברכה דמשתעי קרא בעינן נטילת ידים סמוך לה דמייתי לה התם אברכת המזון והכי איתא שלשה תכיפות הן תיכף לסמיכה שחיטה שנאמר וסמך ושחט תיכף לנטילת ידים ברכה שנא' שאו ידיכם וברכו תיכף לגאולה תפלה שנא' יהיו לרצון אמרי פי וגו' וכתיב בתריה יענך ה' ביום צרה ובפ' כיצד מברכין (ברכות מב.) משמע דההיא ברכה איירי בברכת המזון מיהו שמעינן מינה דבעינן תיכף נטילת ידים בברכה דמשתעי ביה קרא והכא מייתי לה אברכת כהנים ועוד אי מיירי הכא בשלא נטל ידיו בשחרית אמאי נקט כהן לנשיאות כפים תיפוק ליה משום דברי תורה שצריך ליטול ידיו כדאמרי' בפ"ק דברכות (דף יא:) ובפ"ב (שם יד:) אמר רבי חייא בר רב אשי זימנין סגיאין הוה קאימנן קמיה דרב לתנויי לן פירקא בסיפרא דבי רב ומקדים וקאי ומשי ידיה ומברך ומנח תפילין והדר אמר לן ואמר נמי התם דבעי לאהדורי בתר מיא לנט"י לק"ש מיל ומה לי ק"ש ומה לי ברכת כהנים אי משום דצריך ברכה לפניה הכא נמי צריך ברכה לפניה כדאמר לקמן להכי מסתבר דהכא בנטילת ידים תיכף לברכה מיירי ושיעור תכיפה איכא למישמע מתכיפת סמיכה לשחיטה דאמרי' בפ' כל הפסולין (זבחים לג.) כל הסמיכות שהיו שם קורא אני בהם תיכף לסמיכה שחיטה חוץ מזו שהיתה בשער נקנור שאין מצורע יכול ליכנס שם אלמא כדי מהלך משער נקנור עד בית המטבחים לא חשיבה תכיפה ובמסכת מדות (פ"ה מ"א) משמע דלא הוי טפי מעשרים ושתים אמה מקום דריסת רגלי ישראל ומקום דריסת רגלי הכהנים שכל אחד היו י"א אמה.

חזון איש יורה דעה הלכות נדה סימן צ אות א – ולמאי דמסקינן דשלא בהרגשה טמאה מדרבנן י"ל דצער מ"ר לא חשיבא כראתה בהרגשה ולא דמי למ"ר דהדור למקור ולשמש דחשיב הדם היוצא מן המקור כראי' בהרגשה וכמ"ש לעיל.

תלמוד בבלי מסכת נדה דף נט עמוד ב – מתני'. האשה שהיא עושה צרכיה, וראתה דם. רבי מאיר אומר: אם עומדת – טמאה, ואם יושבת – טהורה. ר' יוסי אומר: בין כך ובין כך – טהורה. איש ואשה שעשו צרכיהן לתוך הספל, ונמצא דם על המים, רבי יוסי – מטהר, ורבי שמעון – מטמא, שאין דרך האיש להוציא דם, אלא שחזקת דמים מן האשה.

גמ'. מאי שנא עומדת – דאמרינן מי רגלים הדור למקור ואייתי דם, יושבת נמי נימא מי רגלים הדור למקור ואייתי דם! אמר שמואל: במזנקת, מזנקת נמי, דלמא בתר דתמו מיא אתא דם? אמר ר' אבא: ביושבת על שפת הספל, ומזנקת בתוך הספל, ונמצא דם בתוך הספל. דאם איתא דבתר דתמו מיא אתא – על שפת הספל איבעי ליה לאשתכוחי. אמר שמואל, ואמרי לה אמר רב יהודה אמר שמואל: הלכה כר' יוסי. וכן אורי ליה רבי אבא לקלא: הלכה כרבי יוסי.

בית יוסף יורה דעה סימן קצא – כתבו הגהות מיימוניות בפרק ה' (אות ב) בשם הר"ם (שם ושו"ת מהר"ם מרוטנבורג דפוס פראג סי' תרל ודפוס לבוב סי' תג) שרבינו חננאל פירש דאפילו בנמצא דם על המים דמטהר ר' יוסי לא טהורה לגמרי קאמר אלא טהורה משום נדה וטמאה משום כתם וכן כתב המרדכי (שבועות סי' תשלה דף א ע"ד) בשם הר"ם והר"ן כתב בתשובה הנזכרת כלשון הזה מה שכתבת בשם הר"מ בשם רבינו חננאל דכי טיהר רבי יוסי דוקא לטהרות טיהר אבל לבעלה מודה לרבי מאיר אין אלו אלא דברי נביאות ואין להם על מה שיסמוכו ולאו רבינו חננאל ז"ל חתים עלה עכ"ל: ואף על פי שכתב הר"ן כן וגם הרב המגיד כתב בפרק י"א (הי"ג) דמשתנת דם עם מי רגלים הכל מודים שהיא טהורה אין נראה לדחות דברים אלו שאמרו בשם רבינו חננאל בגיליתא דחטתא שהרי הרשב"א כתב כן בשמו בשער הכתמים (תוה"א יט.) גבי בדקה בעד שאינו בדוק והניחתו בקופסא וגם התוספות (ד"ה ור' יוסי) והרא"ש (סי' ב) כתבו כן בשמו בפרק כל היד (יד:) וסמך דבריו נראה לי שהוא מדתנן בסיפא דמתניתין (נט:) איש ואשה שעשו צרכיהם לתוך הספל ונמצא דם על המים ר' יוסי מטהר ומבואר דהאי ספק ספיקא הוא ופריך בגמרא דהא למה לי השתא ברישא דליכא אלא חד ספיקא מטהר ר' יוסי בסיפא דהוי ספק ספיקא לא כל שכן ומשני מהו דתימא הני מילי דיעבד אבל לכתחלה לא קמ"ל כלומר דממשנה יתירה שמעינן דאפילו לכתחלה מטהר והדבר ברור דדיעבד לא שייך אלא לטהרות ולא לבעלה וכן פירש רש"י ז"ל (ד"ה דיעבד) דלטהרות קאמר ומשמע לרבינו חננאל דכיון דגלי לן תלמודא דלטהרות איירי ר' יוסי איכא למימר דלא טיהר אלא לטהרות בלבד ולא לבעלה ואע"ג דלענין בדיקה מחמירינן לטהרות טפי מלבעלה כדמשמע בפ"ק דנדה (יא:) שאני התם דמשום דגזירת מעת לעת לא שייכא אלא בטהרות מפני כך הצריכו בדיקה להן אע"ג דלבעלה לא צריך אבל בענין זה יש להחמיר לבעלה דהוי איסור כרת יותר מלטהרות דלית בהו איסור כרת וראיה לדבר מדגרסינן בפרק כל היד (יד.) בדקה בעד שאינו בדוק לה והניחתו בקופסא ולמחר מצאה עליו דם רבי אומר טמאה משום נדה רבי חייא אומר טמאה משום כתם ואמרינן תו התם (ע"ב) דרבי מטמא ורבי יוסי מטהר ואמר רבי זירא כשטימא רבי כרבי מאיר וכשטיהר ר' יוסי

לעצמו טיהר כלומר דאזיל לטעמיה דתנן האשה שהיא עושה צרכיה וראתה דם וכו׳ הא משמע התם בהדיא דרבי מאיר מטמא משום נדה וא״כ דיינו לומר דרבי יוסי מטהר משום נדה בלבד אבל מודה הוא דטמאה משום כתם דאם לא כן נמצא דמפלגינן בינייהו טובא ועוד דמדחזינן דרבי חייא מפליג על רבי בעד שאינו בדוק ומטמא משום כתם א״כ אף באשה שהיא עושה צרכיה הוא מטמא משום כתם ומסתמא אית לן למימר דרבי חייא כרבי יוסי ס״ל והא עדיפא מלומר דבמתניתין דהאשה שהיא עושה צרכיה איכא שלש מחלוקות ולא הוזכרו לא במשנה ולא בברייתא אלא דברי רבי מאיר ורבי יוסי בלבד ובאמת שסמך זה גדול בעיני עד שהוא ראוי לקרותו ראיה ולפסוק כן אלא שהפוסקים לא סמכו על זה משום דאיכא לדחויי ומכל מקום אין לדחות דבריו לגמרי ולומר דאין להם על מה שיסמוכו ומיהו לענין הלכה כיון שהפוסקים פסקו לטהר אף לבעלה עליהם סומכים.

שולחן ערוך יורה דעה הלכות נדה סימן קצא סעיף א – האשה שהשתינה מים ויצא דם עם מי רגליה, בין שהשתינה והיא עומדת, בין שהשתינה והיא יושבת, הרי זו טהורה. ואפילו הרגישה גופה ונזדעזעה, אינה חוששת, שהרגשת מי רגליה היא זו שאין מי רגלים מן החדר, ודם זה דם מכה הוא בחלחולת או בכוליא. הגה: ב] וי״א דאין להתירה אלא ביושבת והשתינה, אבל בעומדת, אם מקלחת לתוך הספל ונמצא שם דם, טהורה. אבל אם שותתת על שפת הספל ונמצא שם דם, טמאה, דהואיל (והמקום) צר חוזרין למקור ומביאים דם, (הטור בשם הרא״ש). וי״א דאפילו ביושבת אין להתיר אלא במקלחת ונמצא הדם תוך הספל, אבל על שפת הספל, טמאה. ובעומדת, בכל ענין, טמאה. (מרדכי ה״נ וב״י בשם הגהות מיימוני וש״ד וב״ז סימן ק״צ וכן משמע מתשובת הר״ן ומהר״ם בתשובות סימן תר״ל ואגודה והגהת ש״ד בשם מהר״ט), והכי נהוג. ודוקא כשנמצא הדם בספל שהיא משתנת שם לחוד, דידוע שהוא ממנה, אבל אם נמצא בספל שאיש ואשה מטילין שם מים, טהורה בכל ענין (טור ופוסקים מהש״ס). וכל זה אם נמצא דם במקרה, אבל אשה שרגילה לראות דם במי רגלים ומרגשת כאב בשעה שמטלת מים כגון החולי שקורין (הארי״ן וינ״ד), נראה דיש להתיר בכל ענין, דהא איכא ידים מוכיחות שיש לה מכה המכאיב אותה בהטלת מי רגלים וממנו הדם יוצא. ואפילו אם מצאה דם אחר הטלת מי רגלים, כשמקנחת עצמה, טהורה, דמאחר דמרגשת כאב ואינה מוצאה דם רק אחר הטלת מי רגלים, ודאי דם מכה הוא, (בהגהת ש״ד בשם מהרי״ל והוא בתשובת מהרי״ל סימן ר״ג /קע״ג/ שכ״כ בשם מהר״ש וב״י בשם אגור בשם מהר״ש). אך יש מחמירין שלא להתיר רק באשה שיש לה וסת להצריכה בדיקה (דעת מהרי״ל שם), דהיינו קודם שתשתין, תבדוק עצמה היטב בחורין ובסדקין ואם לא תמצא דם תכניס מוך נקי על המקור בפנים, ותשתין ותקנח עצמה יפה ממי רגליה ותוציא המוך, אם נקיה היא הוכחה גדולה דאין הדם מן המקור, (שם ובמהרי״ו), והכי נהוג. ואם בדקה עצמה ג׳ פעמים בכהאי גווני ומצאה המוך נקי, מותרת אחר כך בלא בדיקה שלא בשעת וסתה, דחזקה דדם מכה הוא מאחר שאינה מוצאה אותו רק אחר שהשתינה. וכל זה דוקא שמרגשת כאב עם מי רגליה, אבל אם אינה מרגשת כאב ובודקת עצמה אחר הטלת מים ומוצאה דם, אם לא מצאה דם במי רגליה ודאי טמאה, (כן משמע שם ובהגהות מיימוני ובמרדכי שם). אבל אם מצאה דם תוך מי רגליה וגם על העד שבדקה עצמה בו, יש אומרים דהיא טמאה,

דלא התירו רק דם שנמצא תוך מי רגליה, (מרדכי ה"נ). וי"א שהיא טהורה דדם שנמצא תולין שעדיין נשאר מתמצית מי רגליה, (ב"י ממשמעות הרא"ש והר"ן). ויש להחמיר, מיהו אינה צריכה לבדוק אחר זה. ואפילו אם היתה רגילה לראות אם בדקה עצמה שלש פעמים ומצאה טהורה, שוב אינה צריכה בדיקה, (שם במרדכי). ואם אינה רגילה לראות רק לפרקים, קובעת לה וסת אם הוא בדרך קבע, בין וסת שוה בין וסת דילוגין. ואם אינה מוצאה דם אח"כ כשבודקת עצמה, רק קרטין קרטין כמו חול וחצץ אדום, ונמצא כזה ג"כ במי רגליה ובשעת וסתה, או לפעמים אחרים רואה דם ממש כשאר נשים, ואינה מוצאת אותו חול רק אחר מי רגליה, יא טהורה, דאינו דם רק חול שדרכו להוולד בכליות, (ב"י בשם תשובת הר"ן).

ש"ך יורה דעה סימן קצא:ג – וי"א דאפילו כו' – כן נלפע"ד מוכח מהש"ס והירושלמי כהי"א אלו שהם ר"ח וסייעתו (שכל דבריו דברי קבלה) והוא מהש"ס דפרק כל היד דף י"ד ע"ב משמע דר' יוסי גבי עד שאינו בדוק (דלעיל סי' ק"צ סל"ה) מטמא משום כתם וכן הוא בירושלמי שם להדיא ובש"ס התם מדמה עד שאינו בדוק לאשה שעושה צרכיה וכ"כ הרשב"א בתה"א דף קע"ח והתוס' שם דדמי להדדי אם כן הא דאמרינן בש"ס דרבי יוסי מטהר אף לכתחלה לטהרות קאי דוקא אסיפא ולא ארישא (דברישא מודה ר"י דאסורה לכתחלה לטהרות וכן לבעלה) וכן הוא בתוס' שם ובמרדכי פ"ב דשבועות ואגודה פרק האשה ובהגהת ש"ד סימן ג' וכן מוכח ברש"י במה שפירש קמ"ל דממשנה יתירה דלא אצטריך דאפילו לכתחלה קאמר ע"ש גם הרשב"א בת"ה שם כתב דפשטא דשמעתא דפרק כל היד משמע כר"ח אלא שאח"כ חלק עליו והיינו לפי מה שפי' הוא דאף לכתחלה ארישא נמי קאי וז"א גם בב"י דחק לחלק בין טהרות לבעלה (וע"כ כ' בסוף דבריו שיש לדחות דברי ר"ח ולפמ"ש א"א לדחות כלל) וז"א אלא דכי היכי דלטהרות לכתחלה אסור ה"ה לבעלה ובזה א"ש מה שהקשה הר"ן בתשו' סימן נ"ד ומביאה הב"י דהיכי אפשר ששמואל ורבי אבא תרוויהו ס"ל כרבי יוסי ושקלי וטרי אליבא דר"מ כו' ומה שתירץ הר"ן דמודה ר' יוסי בנמצא על שפת הספל לחוד הוא דוחק דהא אינהו לא מיירי כלל בהכי אלא אע"ג דפסקו כר"י היינו לענין דיעבד במאי דפליג עליה דר"מ אבל לענין לכתחלה דמודה ליה כל מאי דשייך גבי ר"מ בדיעבד שייך גבי ר"י לענין לכתחלה וכל זה ברור ומדברי האחרונים וגם לקמן מדברי הרב וכן משמע בעט"ז דמשום חומרא אין לפסוק נגד ר"ח ולפעד"נ כן בש"ס וירושלמי.

ש"ך יורה דעה סימן קצא:ד – אלא במקלחת – ולא שותתת ויושבת על שפת הספל ונמצא דם תוך הספל לחוד דאם איתא דבתר דתמו מיא אתא על שפת הספל איבעי ליה לאשתכוחי אבל אם נמצא על שפת הספל גם כן טמאה דאמרינן בתר דתמו מיא אתי דם כן משמע בש"ס וכ"כ הר"ן לרבי מאיר ומודה ליה ר"י לטהרות לכתחלה וכן לבעלה וכדפי' בסמוך אבל ביושבת באמצע הספל טמאה והרב קיצר במובן.

.10

תלמוד בבלי מסכת נדה דף יט עמוד א – מתני'. חמשה דמים טמאים באשה: האדום, והשחור, וכקרן כרכום, וכמימי אדמה, וכמזוג. בש"א: אף כמימי תלתן, וכמימי בשר צלי, וב"ה מטהרים. הירוק, עקביא בן מהללאל מטמא, וחכמים מטהרין. אמר רבי מאיר: אם אינו מטמא משום

כתם – מטמא משום משקה. רבי יוסי אומר: לא כך ולא כך. איזהו אדום – כדם המכה, שחור – כחרת, עמוק מכן – טמא, דיהה מכן – טהור. וכקרן כרכום – כברור שבו, וכמימי אדמה – מבקעת בית כרם ומיצף מים, וכמזוג שני חלקים מים ואחד יין, מן היין השרוני.

דברים פרק יז:ח – כי יפלא ממך דבר למשפט בין דם לדם בין דין לדין ובין נגע לנגע דברי ריבת בשעריך וקמת ועלית אל המקום אשר יבחר ה' אלקיך בו.

תלמוד בבלי מסכת נדה דף כ עמוד ב – אמר רבי יוחנן: חכמתא דרבי חנינא גרמא לי דלא אחזי דמא, מטמינא – מטהר, מטהרנא – מטמא. אמר רבי אלעזר: ענוותנותא דרבי חנינא גרמא לי דחזאי דמא, ומה רבי חנינא דענותן הוא – מחית נפשיה לספק וחזי, אנא לא אחזי? אמר רבי זירא: טבעא דבבל גרמא לי דלא חזאי דמא, דאמינא בטבעא לא ידענא, בדמא ידענא? למימרא דבטבעא תליא מלתא, והא רבה הוא דידע בטבעא ולא ידע בדמא! כל שכן קאמר, ומה רבה דידע בטבעא – לא חזא דמא, ואנא אחזי? עולא אקלע לפומבדיתא, אייתו לקמיה דמא ולא חזא, אמר: ומה רבי אלעזר דמרא דארעא דישראל הוה, כי מקלע לאתרא דר' יהודה – לא חזי דמא, אנא אחזי? ואמאי קרו ליה מרא דארעא דישראל? דההיא אתתא דאייתא דמא לקמיה דרבי אלעזר, הוה יתיב רבי אמי קמיה, ארחיה, אמר לה: האי דם חימוד הוא. בתר דנפקה אטפל לה רבי אמי. א"ל: בעלי היה בדרך וחמדתיו, קרי עליה: (תהלים כה) סוד ה' ליראיו. אפרא הורמיז אמיה דשבור מלכא שדרה דמא לקמיה דרבא, הוה יתיב רב עובדיה קמיה, ארחיה אמר לה: האי דם חימוד הוא. אמרה ליה לבריה: תא חזי כמה חכימי יהודאי! א"ל: דלמא כסומא בארובה? הדר שדרה ליה שתין מיני דמא, וכולהו אמרינהו, ההוא בתרא דם כנים הוה, ולא ידע, אסתייע מילתא ושדר לה סריקותא דמקטלא כלמי; אמרה: יהודאי, בתווני דלבא יתביתו! אמר רב יהודה: מרישא הוה חזינא דמא, כיון דאמרה לי אמיה דיצחק ברי: האי טיפתא קמייתא לא מייתינן לה קמייהו דרבנן, משום דזהימא – לא חזינא, בין טמאה לטהורה ודאי חזינא.

רא"ש מסכת נדה פרק ב סימן ד – [דף יט ע"א] מתני' חמשה דמים טמאים באשה האדום והשחור וכקרן כרכום וכמימי אדמה וכמזוג (אדמה) ב"ש אומרים אף כמימי תלתן וכמימי בשר צלי. וב"ה מטהרין הירוק עקביא בן מהללאל מטמא וחכמים מטהרין. פר"י דמכאן משמע דירוק סתם הוא צבע הדומה לחלמון של ביצה או לזהב הנוטה למראה אדמומית וכן משמע בפרק אלו טריפות (דף מז ב) גבי מראות הריאה דקאמר ככשותא וכמוריקא וכביצה טריפה אלא ירוק דכשירה היכי דמי ככרתי ובפרק לולב הגזול (דף לד ב) נמי אמרינן ירוק ככרתי מכלל דסתם ירוק לא הוי ככרתי. ואמר בבראשית רבה וירק את חניכיו מלמד שהוריקן בזהב וכן הוא אומר ואברותיה בירקרק חרוץ. אלמא דסתם ירוק הוא צבע הנוטה לאדמומית כזהב ובדורות הללו אין בקי במראות דמים לישען על חכמתו ולהפריד בין דם לדם ואפילו בימי חכמי הש"ס היו מן החכמים שהיו נמנעים מלראות דמים. כ"ש האידנא שאין לטהר שום דם הנוטה למראה אדמומית אם לא שיהא לבן וירוק כמראה הזהב אע"ג דתנא קמא סבר דדם ירוק תולין עליו. נראה דהלכה כחכמים דמטהרין כי היכי דהלכה כב"ה דמטהרין כמימי תלתן וכמימי בשר צלי ולא כת"ק דאמר תולין. ה"ה בדם ירוק אין הלכה כת"ק.

תוספות מסכת נדה דף יט עמוד ב – הירוק עקביא בן מהללאל מטמא – האי ירוק היינו כאתרוג ולא ירוק ככרתי דאין זה נוטה לאדמומית וסתם ירוק כן הוא כדאמר בלולב הגזול (סוכה דף לד: ושם) ירוק ככרתי מכלל דסתם ירוק לאו הכי הוא.

בית הבחירה למאירי מסכת נדה דף יט עמוד א – וירוק זה שאנו מטהרין אנו רגילין לפרש ירוק כרתי ומ"מ בתוספות פירשוה אפילו בירקרקות הנוטה מעט לאדמימות הקרוי גירוק והביאו ראיה שאלו בירוק ככרתי לא היה עקביא בן מהללאל חולק לאסור שהרי אין לה שיכות עם מראה דם כלל אלא בירוק הקרוי גירוק וכן הביאוה ממה שאמרו במסכת נגעים ירקרק כשעוה ובבראשית רבה אמרו וירק את חניכיו שהוריקן בזהב כדכתוב ואברותיה בירקרק חרוץ אלמא ירקרק זהו מראה הזהב או השעוה ואע"פ שאמרו גם כן וירק את חניכיו שהריקן בתורה וכן שהוריקן באבן טובה ואבנים טובות שבצבע ירוק ירוק ככרתי הוא מ"מ משמע שיש ירוק בצבע הקרוי גירוק ועליו ראוי לומר שהיה עקביא מטמא ומ"מ לדעתי זו ודאי טמאה שהרי לענין ריאה ירוקה כחלמון ביצה וכמוריקה של כרכום טרפה ירוקה ככרתי כשרה אלמא מין זה של ירוקות הנקרא גירוק בכלל צבע הכרכום הוא והרי פירשנו שכל כקרן כרכום טמאה ואין לך בו אלא שתאמר שקרן הכרכום נוטה לאדמימות יותר מן הכרכום הבינוני ואם כך אתה אומר פירצה דחוקה היא ואין לכנס בה בזמן שנתמעט הבקיאות ועקביא שהיה מטמא בירוק ככרתי היה מטמא ואע"פ שאין לירוק שום שיכות עם מראה דמים לא מטעם זה אלא שהיה סבור שאדום היה ולקה מעט וזהו ירקותו וכדאיתא בגמרא ומתוך כך איני מכשיר בזו אלא הירוק הגמור הדומה לכרתי.

חידושי הריטב"א מסכת נדה דף יט עמוד א – הירוק. פירשו בתוספות כי הוא גוון שהוא גרו"ג בלע"ז ולא אותו שקורין וירד"י דההוא לאו ממין דם אדום הוא כלל וסתם דם אדום כדאיתא בגמ', ובמסכת נגעים (תוספתא פ"א ה"ג) קתני ירקרק כשעוה, ועוד שבשום מקום לא הזכירו ירוק סתם אלא על הגרו"ג ואידך ירוק ככרתי אמרו, וכההיא דאמרינן בפרק אלו טרפות (חולין מ"ז ב') ואלא ירוקה כשרה היכי משכחת לה ככרתי, וכן בפרק לולב הגזול (סוכה ל"ד ב') גבי אתרוג, וכן אמרו בבראשית רבה (פמ"ג) וירק את חניכיו שהוריקן בזהב וכן הוא אומר ואברותיה בירקרק חרוץ כלומר כמראה הזהב, אבל בירוק ככרתי טהור הוא לדברי הכל, ואף בירוק זה מצאנו בעדיות (פ"ה מ"ז) שהוא אחד מארבעה דברים שחזר בו עקביא בסוף ימיו ולא לתלות חזר בו אלא לטהר לגמרי כדברי ר' יוסי, דהא לא קתני התם בפלוגתא אלא לר' יוסי, והכי סוגיין בפרק המפלת (לקמן כ"א ב') כר' יוסי, מעתה אף בזמן הזה שאין אנו רואין דם, כל שהוא לבן או ירוק ככרתי טהור הוא ואין חוששין לו, וכן הסכימו רבותינו ז"ל כולם.

רבינו יונה על הרי"ף מסכת ברכות דף כב עמוד א – *שאפילו רואות טפת דם כחרדל וכו'* י"מ שהחומרא היתה מפני שהיתה מראה הדם כעין החרדל ואין זה נראה דמה חומרא היתה זו שזה מן הדין הוא דהא בהדיא קי"ל במס' נדה שדם כמראה החרדל מטמא.

ר' עובדיה מברטנורא מסכת נדה פרק ב – *שני חלקים מים ואחד יין מן היין השרוני* – הבא מארץ השרון, מקום ידוע בארץ ישראל. פירוש אחר, יין העשוי מן הגפנים הנטועים בבקעה ובעמק.

לשון חבצלת השרון. ובזמן הזה, כל מה שתראה באשה מאותו מקום, טמא, חוץ מן הלבן והירוק. ומימינו לא שמענו מי שטיהר שום מראה דם, אלא הלבן והירוק ככרתי בלבד.

חכמת אדם שער בית הנשים כלל קיז – (ט) אחר זה תקח בגד פשתן לבן ישן (כי החדש הוא קשה ויכולה לקלקל עצמה) או צמר גפן ותכניס באותו מקום לחורין ולסדקין עד מקום שהשמש דש ותראה אם יש בו שום מראה אדמומית או שחור ונראה לי אפילו כמראה געל כשעוה ופשיטא כזהב יש להחמיר בבדיקה זו (דאף על גב דקיימא לן בסימן קפ"ח דירוק טהור כיון דשל"ה כתב בשם רש"ל שכתב מהר"ם מינץ בשם הגדולים דאין לטהר במהירות ולכן על כל פנים בבדיקה זו שעדיין היא בחזקת רואה יש להחמיר כן נראה לי) ואם יקשה בעיניה מאד להכניס כל כך בעומק מכל מקום תבדוק היטב בחורין ובסדקים בעומק יפה כפי כוחה אבל אם תכניס רק מעט ומקנחת עצמה אינו מועיל כלום ולא הוי בדיקה כלל (סעיף ו') ואותן הנשים הבודקות באצבע הן נדות גמורות לכל דבריהן (סדרי טהרה בשם הגהות שערי דורא):

חידושי הרמב"ן מסכת נדה דף ה עמוד א – מתוך שמהומה לביתה אין מכניסתו לחורין ולסדקין. מכאן למד הראב"ד ז"ל שכל לבעלה אינו צריך בדיקת חורין וסדקין, שהרי בדיקה זו אינה מועילה לטהרות מפני שאין בה בדיקת חורין וסדקין ואע"פ כן מועלת לגבי בעלה, ועוד הביא ראיה ממה שאמרו (י"ב א') דתביעה הרי היא כבדיקה לגבי בעלה, והוא ז"ל כתב שיש מי שחולק ואמר דבדיקת זבה בין ביום ההפסקה בין בבדיקת השבעה בעינן בדיקה מעולה כשל טהרות, ולא הקלו לגבי בעל אלא בבדיקת המעלות כגון זו שאשה העסוקה בטהרות הצריכו בדיקה זו אף לבעלה מתוך חומר שהחמרת עליה בטהרות, אבל בדיקה מעולה הצריכה להן מחמת הבעל עצמו צריכה להיות בדיקה מעולה, ועוד שיש להחמיר אפילו בבדיקת מעלות, ומה שאמר כאן אינה מכניסתו לא שלא הוצרכה אלא מתוך שמהומה לביתה חוששין לטהרות שמא לא עשתה כהוגן ולא הכניסתו לחורין ולסדקין, והוא כעין מה שאמרו בסמוך ניחוש שמא תראה טפת דם ותחפנו שכבת זרע וכו', וכן נראה מדברי רש"י ז"ל דכל בדיקה היינו לחורין וסדקין בשילהי פירקין (י"ב א' ד"ה לבדיקה), ולפי הסברא יש להכריע שבדיקת ההפסקה שהיא מעלה אותה מטומאה לטהרה ומוציא אותה מחזקה לחזקה צריכה להיות בדיקה מעולה שאין אחריה עליו ספק, אבל בדיקת השבעה כיון שכבר פסקה להעמידה בחזקתה בבדיקה כל דהוא סגיא, דהא אפילו לא בדקה כלל אלא בשעת ההפסקה ובסוף שבעה טהורה לקמן בפרק בתרא (ס"ח ב'), הילכך לקולא כדברי הראב"ד ז"ל, ובעל נפש לא יקל בכך.

סדרי טהרה סימן קפח ס"ק א – מ"כ דם הנוטה לצבע ברוין בל"א שהוא כעין קליפות ערמונים וכמשקה הקאווי שהוא טהור ואצ"ל בכתם לפי שאין נוטה לאדמומית כ"א לשחור וכבר שנינו דיהה מכן טהור.

שו"ת שאילת יעבץ חלק א סימן מד – מראה דם הנוטה לצבע ברוי"ן (חום) בל"א שהוא כעין קליפת הערמונים וכמשקה הקאוי (הקפה) לא נתבאר בש"ע ובאחרונים אם הוא ממראות דמים טמאים. ונ"ל להקל בו. דודאי עדיף ממימי בשר צלי. דידוע שיש בו אדמיתות וכמ"ש גם

הפוסקים. ואפ"ה מטהרי ליה ב"ה וקיי"ל כוותייהו. ואע"ג דאנן מחמרינן ביה. היא גופה חומרא גדולה, דהא שפיר בקיאינן בגוויה, אלא משום דלא ליתי לאחלופי. כיון דאית ביה נטייה לאודם. משא"כ במראה ברוי"ן הנז'. שאין לו נטייה לאדמומית אלא לשחרות. וכבר שנינו משנה שלמה בשחור עצמו דיהה מכן טהור. ולית בה ספקא ולא חומרא מדינא דגמרא, כמו בשאר מראות שנחלקו בהן בדיהה. וכ"ש בירוק ברוי"ן שהרי אינו שחור ולא אפי' דיהה דדיהה שלו. אלא שעמוק שלו נוטה קצת לשחרות הדיהה. ועוד ק"ו מירוק דמקילינן ביה טובא. ואפי' במראה הזהב. שהרי יש בו ודאי נטייה חזקה אל האודם. וכן כתבו התוס'. ויש ממנו שהוא אדום כדם. וכמ"ש רז"ל זהב פרויים שדומה לדם הפרים. וגם הנמצא אצלינו כשהוא יוצא מיד הצורף מבי סילקי, קרוב מאד לגוון אדום ממש. ואפ"ה סמכינן להתירו כשאין לו נטייה לאדום, כ"ש בירוק ברוי"ן שהוא רחוק מאד מן האדום. ואע"פ שיהא עמוק הרבה. אינו אלא כדיהה דשחור. שהוא טהור בלי ספק, ולכן אין להחמיר כלל בברוי"ן הנז', ובכתם פשיטא דלית דחש ליה. כך נלע"ד והשי"ת בחסדו יצילנו משגיאות יעב"ץ ס"ט.

שולחן ערוך יורה דעה הלכות נדה סימן קצ סעיף לג – האשה שבדקה עצמה בעד (פירוש סמרטוט מענין וכבגד עדים כל צדקותינו) (ישעיה סד, ה) הבדוק לה, ונמצא עליו אפילו טיפה כחרדל, בין עגול בין משוך, טמאה. ולא עוד, אלא אפילו נמצא על הכתם מאכולת מעוכה, טמאה. וכן הדין כשבדקה בו והניחתו בקופסא ואחר שעה בדקה אותו ומצאה עליו דם כל שהוא, בין משוך בין עגול, טמאה.

11.

תלמוד בבלי מסכת נדה דף כ עמוד ב – רבי ראה דם בלילה – וטימא, ראה ביום – וטיהר, המתין שעה אחת – חזר וטימא, אמר: אוי לי שמא טעיתי! שמא טעיתי? ודאי טעה! דתניא: לא יאמר חכם אילו היה לח היה ודאי טמא, אלא אמר אין לו לדיין אלא מה שעיניו רואות מעיקרא אחזקיה בטמא כיון דחזא לצפרא דאשתני אמר (ליה) ודאי טהור הוה, ובלילה הוא דלא אתחזי שפיר, כיון דחזא דהדר אשתני אמר: האי – טמא הוא, ומפכח הוא דקא מפכח ואזיל.

ב"ח יורה דעה סימן קפח – ואשה שרואה מראה ירוק ולאחר שנתייבשו הכתמים נעשו קצותיו אדומים מכל סביביו נראה דמדינא טמאה היא וכדאמרינן בפרק כל היד בשחור דכשנעקר מן הגוף הוא לוקה ומשחיר משל לדם מכה לכשנעקרה הוא משחיר ודכוותיה חיישינן בירוק זה דכשנעקר מן הגוף הוא לוקה ונעשה ירוק (ולכשיתייבש) [וכשנתייבש] חזר קצת למראהו שהיה אדום מתחלה ואיכא למימר דעד כאן לא פליגי חכמים אעקביא בן מהללאל דאמר ירוק מילקי לקי אלא בנשאר ירוק מתחלתו ועד סופו התם הוא דלא חיישינן ללקוי אבל כשנשתנה לאחר שנתייבש ונעשה אדום בקצותיו שפיר חיישינן ללקוי אף לרבנן ומדינא היא טמאה ולכן כשיביאו מראה ירוק ולבן לפני המורה בעודו לח לא יורה בו דבר עד שיתייבש.

ש"ך יורה דעה סימן קפח:ג – ירוק כו' – כ' הב"ח דהיינו כשנשאר ירוק מתחלתו ועד סופו אבל כשנשתנה לאחר שנתייבש הכתם ונעשה אדום בקצותיו טמאה דכשנעקר מן הגוף הוא

לקה ונעשה ירוק וכשנתייבש חזר למראהו קצת שהיה אדום מתחלה ולכן כשיבא מראה ירוק ולבן לפני המורה בעודו לח לא יורה בו דבר עד שנתייבש עכ"ל ואין נוהגין כן ונראה דאחזוקי ריעותא לא מחזקינן וכדאמרינן בפרק אלו טרפות גבי מראות הבני מעיים דא"צ לשלקן לראותן אם נשתנה מראיתם דאחזוקי ריעותא לא מחזקינן ונתבאר לעיל סי' (צ"ב) [נ"ב] ס"ק י"א וה"ה הכא כנ"ל.

תלמוד בבלי מסכת נדה דף כ עמוד ב – רבי בדיק לאור הנר, רבי ישמעאל ברבי יוסף בדיק ביום המעונן ביני עמודי. אמר רב אמי בר שמואל: וכולן אין בודקין אותן אלא בין חמה לצל. רב נחמן אמר רבה בר אבוה: בחמה, ובצל ידו.

תורת השלמים סימן קפח ס"ק א – וז"ל הטור דבר תורה ה' דמים טמאים באשה ותו לא והאידנא חזרו לטמאות כל שיש בו מראה אדום וכו' ונ"ל דמטעם זה לא העתיק הטור והמחבר כיצד ינהג החכם עצמו לראות דם נדה דהיינו אם רואין דם בלילה ולעשות צל בידו על הדם כמבואר בסוף פ' כל היד וכ"כ הרמב"ם פ"ה מהא"ב משום דלדידן אינו טהור אלא מראה לבן וירוק וזה א"צ עיון ודקדוק היטב כי בקל יכול להבחין כל זה לכן בכל ענין שירצה החכם יוכל לראות כדי לטהרה או לטמאה וכ"כ הראב"ד בהשגות בפ"ה מהא"ב.

שו"ת אגרות משה יורה דעה חלק ד סימן יז – ה. מראה שנראה בלילה נוטה למראה דם, וביום נראה טהור.

ובמראה שראה הרב המורה לאור החשמל בלילה והיה נראה לו נוטה למראה דם, ומחמת הספק השאירו למחר לעיין לאור היום, וראהו לאור היום כמראה טהור, פשוט שצריך להתירו. לא רק כשלא פסק עדיין משום שהיה גם בעצמו מסופק שמא אין הראייה דלאור החשמל היה בטוב, אלא אף כשהחליט בדעתו בלילה להורות שהיא טמאה ע"פ ראייתו לאור החשמל, אבל נשארה אצלו המראה שנשאל עליה וראה ביום שהוא מראה טהור, יש לו לחזור מהוראתו ולטהר. ואין לחוש לנשתנה, שלא מצוי. דהא אף לרבי לא היה חש מתחילה לשמא נשתנה, וחזר בו כשראהו טהור ביום ממה שאחזקיה בראייתו בלילה לטמא. שמשמע מרש"י שפסק מתחילה בלילה דינו לטומאה, דהא כתב על מעיקרא אחזקיה בטומאה, כלומר אמש לא מספק טימא אלא שפיר חזייה ואחזיק בטומאה דאמרינן לקמן רבי בדיק לאור הנר. ומ"מ לצפרא דאישתני חזר בו וטיהר. ורק אחר שחזא לאחר שעה דהדר אישתני, דהיה מוכח דהוא שינוי שנעשה ביום, הדר למילתיה קמייתא וטימאו. וג"כ לא מדין ודאי, אף שבלילה היה סבור שהיא טמאה ודאי, דהא אמר אוי לי שמא טעיתי – במה שחזרתי וטימאתי. הרי חזינן שאין לנו לחוש לנשתנה מכפי שיצא מגוף האשה. דאף בנשתנה ודאי מכפי שחזא רבי בלילה, הא בלא ההכרח דנשתנה עוד הפעם הא אומר רבי דודאי טעה בלילה, ולא דנשתנה הדם היום מהמראה שיצא מהגוף. אלמא דהוא דבר שלא מצוי ואין לחוש לזה. אף אם היה החליט בלילה שהוא מראה טמא וגם פסק כן, וכ"ש שאין לחוש לזה כשלא החליט לזה אלא שנדמה לו בעלמא וסמך על מה שיראה ביום, שאין לו לחוש לשמא היה מראה טמא ונשתנה, אלא שצריך לטהר ודאי.

תלמוד בבלי מסכת נדה דף כ עמוד ב – תא שמע: דילתא אייתא דמא לקמיה דרבה בר בר חנה – וטמי לה, לקמיה דרב יצחק בריה דרב יהודה – ודכי לה.

תוספות מסכת נדה דף כ עמוד ב – כל יומא הוה מטהר לי כה"ג – משמע שלא היתה רגילה להראות לרב נחמן בעלה ושמא לא היה בקי והא דאמר ר"נ לעיל (דף יט:) בדם הקזה קבלה היתה בידו אי נמי היתה חוששת שמא היה מחמיר על עצמו להיות לבו נוקפו ופורש ולא יסמוך על חכמתו אי נמי שלא תתגנה בפניו אבל אין לומר דאסור לראות דמי אשתו דהא במס' נגעים (פ"ב מ"ה) תנן כל הנגעים אדם רואה חוץ מנגעי עצמו ר"מ אומר אף לא נגעי קרוביו כל הנדרים אדם מתיר חוץ מנדרי עצמו ר' יהושע אומר אף לא נדרי אשתו ואילו כל הדמים אדם רואה חוץ מדמי אשתו לא קתני.

ר"ש מסכת נגעים פרק ב – דהא אשכחן בסוף פרק ב' דנדה (דף כ ב) דילתא אייתאי דמה לקמיה דרבה בר בר חנה ולא היתה מראה לר"נ בעלה אע"פ שהיה בקי בדמים כדקאמר התם (יט ב) אדום כדם הקזה לא משום דאסור אלא כדי שלא תתגנה עליו. ועוד תניא בתוספתא [פ"א] נאמן הכהן לומר נגע זה פשה ונגע זה לא פשע אם בהרת קדמה לשער לבן אם שער לבן קדם לבהרת ונאמן הוא על נגעי עצמו ושמא יש לחלק בין היכא דאיתחזיק איסורא להיכא דלא איתחזיק איסורא כדאשכחן בריש האשה רבה (דף פח.) דמחלק גבי עד אחד נאמן באיסורין דצורבא מרבנן חזי לנפשיה היכא דלא איתחזיק איסורא אבל היכא דאיתחזיק איסורא לא.

.12

תלמוד בבלי מסכת נדה דף סו עמוד א – ואם יש לה מכה באותו מקום – תולה במכתה, ואם יש לה וסת – תולה בוסתה. ואם היה דם מכתה משונה מדם ראייתה – אינה תולה. ונאמנת אשה לומר מכה יש לי במקור שממנה דם יוצא – דברי רבי, רשב"ג אומר: דם מכה הבא מן המקור – טמא. ורבותינו העידו על דם המכה הבא מן המקור שהוא טהור. מאי בינייהו? אמר עולא: מקור מקומו טמא איכא בינייהו.

ש"ך יורה דעה סימן קפז:כא – אם על פי שאינה יודעת שמכתה מוציאה דם – פירוש אפילו אינה יודעת כלל שדרכה של המכה להוציא דם ועי"ל ס"ק כ"ו.

הלכות נדה למרדכי רמז תשל"ה – נאמנת אשה לומר מכה יש לי באותו מקום שממנה יוצא דם [*ס"א משמע] דוקא שיודעת שיצא הדם מן המכה תולה בה אבל מספק אינה תולה אבל בשעת וסתה אפילו יודעת בודאי שהדם יוצא מן המכה אינה תולה בו דאל"כ לא תהיה טמאה לעולם אמנם כתמי' שתמצא בבגדיה טהורה ותולה במכה אפילו אינה יודעת שהמכה מוציאה דם דבכתמים הלכו חכמים להקל משום דכתמים דרבנן ואשה שנמצאת כתם דם בחלוקה או בסדינה אם יודעת שיש לה גרב או חבורה שאם היתה מסירה הגלד והקליפה היתה מוציאה דם טהורה ותולה בו בכתם זה או בבנה או בבעלה ששכבו עמה או אשה אחרת ויודעת שיש להם מכה וגרב ויודעת שהם יכולים להוציא דם ע"י קליפת הגלד טהורה ותולה בהן אע"פ שעתה אין

מוציאין מכל מקום שמא חפפו וגרדו עצמן עד שהוציאו דם ולאו אדעתייהו או אם נתעסקה בצפור או ישבה בצד המתעסקין תולה בהן וטהורה אפילו אם הכתם גדול ואם אין כל אלו בה ואין לה במה לתלות או אם אין גדול הכתם מכגריס של פול ר׳ יוחנן בן אנטיגנוס אומר תולה במאכולת אע״פ שלא הרגה תולה בה וטהורה שאין לך כל מטה ומטה שאין בה כמה טיפי דמים וא״כ לא תמצא אשה שטהורה לבעלה לכן אם הכתם כגריס תולה במאכולת שהוא פרעוש וטהורה כל זה שנינו פרק הרואה כתם וכן הלכה.

תורת הבית הארוך בית ז שער ד – והא דקתני נאמנת לומר מכה יש לה שממנה הדם שותת ויורד לאו נאמנת לומר שממנה שותת ויורד קאמר אלא כלפי שאמר אם יש לה מכה תולה במכתה קא אמר שאין אנו צריכין לדעת בבירור שיש לה מכה אלא היא עצמה מרגשת במכה ונאמנת לומר מכה יש לה שיש שם דם תולה במכתה שאני אומר ממנה הדם שותת ויורד. ובלישנא דתוספתא לא מצאתי שממנה הדם שותת ויורד אלא כך שנויה בתוספתא ונאמנת אשה לומר מכה יש לי מן המקור ע״כ.

חידושי הרשב״א מסכת נדה דף סו עמוד א – ונאמנת אשה לומר מכה יש לה שממנה הדם שותת ויורד. מסתברא דה״פ נאמנת אשה לומר מכה יש לה, וכל שהיא נאמנת במכה מן הסתם היא תולה שממנה הדם שותת ויורד שהרי היא אינה בקיאה בלא בדיקה אם הדם מן המכה או מן המקור, ואם בבדיקה מאי שנא כי אית לה מכה אפי׳ בלא ידיעת מכה טהורה דהא קתני בידוע שהוא מן הצדדין, ועוד דהא קתני בהדיא ואם יש לה מכה תולה במכתה אלמא מן הסתם תולה, ובלישנא דתוספתא לא מצאתי שממנה הדם שותת ויורד אלא כך היא שנויה בתוספתא ונאמנת אשה לומר מכה יש לה מן המקור, ודרך הגמ׳ היא להוסיף בלשון התוספתא דרך פירוש בעלמא וכאלו הוא מגוף התוספתא.

בית יוסף יורה דעה סימן קפז – ה (ב) וכתב הרשב״א ז״ל בסוף שער ד׳ (ארוך שם) אהא דקתני אם יש לה מכה באותו מקום תולה במכתה מסתברא דאפילו אינה מרגשת ממש שהדם שותת ויורד מן המכה חדא דאין עיניה בין מכתה ואי אפשר לה לידע אלא בבדיקת שפופרת והא דקתני נאמנת לומר מכה יש לי שממנה הדם שותת ויורד לאו נאמנת לומר דממנה שותת ויורד קאמר אלא כלפי שאמר אם יש לה מכה תולה במכתה קאמר שאין אנו צריכים לדעת בבירור שיש לה מכה אלא היא עצמה מרגשת במכה ונאמנת לומר מכה יש לי ששם יש דם תולה במכתה שאני אומר ממנה הדם שותת ויורד ובלישנא דתוספתא (נדה פ״ח ה״ב) לא מצאתי שממנה הדם שותת ויורד אלא כך היא שנויה בתוספתא ונאמנת אשה לומר מכה יש לי מן המקור ע״כ ודרך הגמרא (בכל מקום) [בכמה מקומות] להוסיף בלשון התוספתא דרך פירוש בעלמא ושונין כאילו הוא מגוף התוספתא עכ״ל: אבל הגהות מיימוניות כתבו בפרק י״א מהלכות איסורי ביאה (אות ח) בשם ספר התרומה (סי׳ צב ד״ה ודין) דאשה שיש לה מכה באותו מקום ואינה יודעת אם מוציאה דם, אם בודקת עצמה באותו מקום ומוציאה דם או אם מרגשת כשהדם נופל מהרחם טמאה ואינה תולה במכה דתניא נאמנת אשה לומר מכה יש לי באותו מקום שממנה יוצא הדם משמע דוקא כשיודעת שיוצא דם מן המכה תולה בה אבל אם ספק לה אינה תולה

אבל בשעת וסתה אפילו יודעת בודאי שהמכה היא מוציאה דם אינה תולה דאם לא כן לעולם לא תהא טמאה מיהו כתמים תולה בה עכ"ל וכן כתב המרדכי (סי' תשלה דף א ע"ג): ומה שכתבו דבשעת וסתה אינה תולה כן כתב סמ"ג (לאוין קיא לט.) וסמ"ק (סו"ס רצג) והיה נראה לכאורה דליכא מאן דפליג ביה דהא נימוקו עמו הוא אלא שמצאתי להרמב"ם ז"ל שכתב בפרק ח' (הי"ד) אשה שראתה דם מחמת מכה שיש לה באותו מקום אף על פי שראתה בשעת וסתה היא טהורה והדם טהור שהוסתות מדבריהם וכן כתב הרשב"א ז"ל בסוף שער ד' (שם כג.) מפני מה אמרו שתולה במכתה לפי שהאשה בחזקת טהרה עומדת אפילו הגיע שעת וסתה וסתות דרבנן ומספק אל תאסרנה לעולם והביא ראיה (שם כב: כג.) מדתניא בפרק בנות כותים הרואה דם מחמת מכה אפילו בתוך ימי נדתה טהורה דברי רבן שמעון בן גמליאל רבי אומר אם יש לה וסת חוששת לוסתה ואוקמה רבא דכולי עלמא וסתות דרבנן והכא במקור מקומו טמא קמיפלגי וקיי"ל כאוקימתא דרבא דוסתות דרבנן וכיון שכן זו שרואה דם אפילו בשעת תשמיש ואפילו כשהגיע וסתה טהורה דאשה בחזקת טהורה עומדת ותלינן להקל שאני אומר דם זה מן המכה בא ולא נחלקו רשב"ג ורבי בדבר זה וא"ת והלא בנשים דעלמא חיישינן לעונת הוסת כולה ואף על פי שלא ראתה והיאך אתה מתיר את זו שהיא בשעת וסתה ועוד שהרי דם לפניך י"ל ההיא דרבנן היא ומשום דאפשר למיקם עלה דמילתא אבל הכא ליכא למיקם אמילתא ואין דנין אפשר משאי אפשר (יבמות מו.) שאם כן אף אתה אוסרה על בעלה לעולם עכ"ל.

כתב הראב"ד (בעה"נ שעה"ס פג כג. ע) דהאידנא לא סמכינן אהך בדיקה להתירה. כלומר לפי שאין אנו בקיאין בה ועוד שאפילו אם היינו בקיאים וידוע לנו שהוא מן הצדדין הרי בנות ישראל החמירו על עצמן וכו'.

ביאור הגר"א יורה דעה סימן קפז:יד – וכ"ז כו' וכן כו'. עתוס' שם ט"ז א' ד"ה ומ"ס כו' ע"ש דדעת תוס' דבש"פ א"צ שמרגשת שממכה באו אבל כשמרגשת אף בשעת ווסתה טהורה כמש"ש בגמ' לא דכ"ע כו' והרשב"א מיקל אף בשאינה יודעת שמכתה מוציאה דם אף בשעת ווסתה וראיה מתוספתא בברייתא הנ"ל ונאמנת כו' לא הוזכר שממנה מוצא דם זה והגמ' ביאר לפי' בעלמא ומ"מ רוב הפוסקים מסכימין לדעת תוס' ומיהו כ' בש"ד דאף שלא בשעת ווסתה דוקא שידוע שהמכה מוציא דם אף שאינה מרגשת שממנו יוצא דם זה ועפ"ז הכריע הרב כאן וכ"ז כו' ועט"ז וש"ך.

(ליקוט) וכ"ז כו'. ז"ל המרדכי נאמנת אשה לומר כו' דוקא שיודעת שיוצא הדם מן המכה תולה בה אבל מספק אינה תולה אבל בשעת ווסתה אפילו יודעת ודאי שהדם יוצא מן המכה אינה תולה בה דאל"כ לא תהיה טמאה לעולם אמנם כתמיה שתמצא בבגדים טהורה ותולה במכה אפילו אינה יודעת שהמכה מוציא דם דבכתמים הלכו חכמים להקל משום דכתמים דרבנן ומשמע מדבריו אפילו ידוע שדם זה יוצא מהמכה טמאה בשעת ווסתה וכן משמע מדברי הרב וצע"ג שהוא נגד הגמ' ועוד משמע מדברי המרדכי דאף שלא בשעת ווסתה צריך שתדע שדם זה יוצא מהמכה אבל לשון סה"ת סי' צ"ב אשה שי"ל מכה באותו מקום ואינה יודעת אם מוציאה דם אם לאו כו' טמאה ואינה תולה במכה דתניא נאמנת אשה לומר מכה יש לי באותו מקום שממנה יוצא דם משמע דוקא יודעת שיוצא דם מן המכה תולה בה אבל אם ספק לה אינה

תולה אבל בשעתווסתה אפילו יודעת בודאי שדם יוצא מן המכה אינה תולה בה דאל"כ לא תהא טמאה לעולם אמנם כל כתמים שתמצא בבגדיה טהורים ותולה במכה אפילו אינה יודעת שהמכה מוציאה דם דבכתמים הלכו חכמים להקל וסתם מכה לפעמים היא מוציאה דם והעתיקו הג"מ פי"א בקוצר ומשמע מדבריו שכל החילוקים הוא בסתם שהמכה מוציא ולא דם זה ונראה שט"ס הוא במרדכי שהרי כל דבריו הוא דברי סה"ת וכ"ה לשון הרב ומ"ש באשה שי"ל ווסת כו' אע"פ כו' אע"ג שלא משמע כן מדברי הפוסקים סמך בזה על דברי המרדכי שפי' מ"ש בגמ' ואם יש לה ווסת תולה בווסתה דאם י"ל ווסת קבוע תולה שלא בשעת ווסתה במכה אפילו אין לה מכה כלל ואף שאין הלכה כדבריו מ"מ יש להצטרף בזה דעת הרשב"א שאין מצריך כלל לידע שהמכה מוציאה דם אפילו בשעת ווסתה כן י"ל דעת הרב אבל [יש מפרשים] טעמו של הרב שהבין דברי המרדכי כך דשלא בשעת ווסתה א"צ לידע שהמכה מוציא דם וז"ל המרדכי ואם י"ל ווסת זמן קבוע שהיא רואה דם תולה בווסתה שיכולה לומר זה הדם שרואה טהור שעדיין לא הגיע ווסתה ותולה במכתה שיכולה לומר מן מכתה היא וטהורה אם היה דם מכתה משונה כו' ומפרש ותולה במכתה קאי אדלעיל מיניה וכן הבין מהרי"א בסי' מ"ז שכתב עוד כ' במרדכי כו' ואם י"ל ווסת תולה בווסתה פי' כו' דעדיין לא הגיע ווסתה ותולה במכתה כו' אלמא דס"ל דאין אורח בא אלא בזמנו מהני דתולין במכה מה שאין תולין בל"ז והיינו אע"ג שאין ידוע שהמכה מוציא דם וכנ"ל אבל העיקר שתולה במכתה הוא פיסקא בפ"ע ועתשו' מהר"ם סי' תרכ"ה וכ"כ ש"ך. ועיינתי בב"י סד"ה ואם שמשה כו' ובד"מ ס"ק ג' שגם הם הבינו כן שהוא בפ"ע ע"ש ושם וע"כ צ"ל כמ"ש לעיל שצירף דעת הרשב"א עמו.

ש"ך יורה דעה סימן קפז:כד – אא"כ יודעת בודאי שמכתה מוציאה דם – אע"פ שאינה מרגשת עתה שדם זה הוא בא ממכתה (וכן באשה שיש לה וסת ומצאה דם שלא בשעת וסתה אע"ג דלענין רואה מחמת תשמיש סגי אע"פ שאינה יודעת שמכתה מוציאה דם כששמשה שלא בשעת וסתה דסמכינן בהא אהמרדכי וכמו שנתבאר מ"מ שלא בשעת תשמיש אם בדקה עצמה ומצאה דם או כשמרגשת שהדם נופל מהרחם דבעינן שתדע שמכתה מוציאה דם סגי כשיודעת שדרך מכתה להוציא דם אע"פ שלא הרגישה עתה שדם זה הוא ממכתה) כן הוכחתי בספרי מדברי התוספות פרק כל היד (דף ט"ז ע"א) ומדברי האגור פרק כל היד ופ' תינוקת ומדברי הגהמי"י פי"א מה' א"ב בשם ס"ה והמרדכי ומביאם ב"י ומדברי הש"ד ס"ו ומתשובת מהרי"ל סימן ר"ג הועתק בהג"ה ש"ד סימן ז' וכן כתב בדרישה שי"ד והוכחתי שם דגם הרשב"א בת"ה מודה לזה דלא קאמר אלא שא"צ שתדע שמרגשת עתה שהדם הוא בא ממכתה אבל צריכא שתדע שמכתה מוציאה דם והבית יוסף וד"מ וב"ח הבינו שהרשב"א פליג.

שו"ת חכם צבי סימן מו – החכם המרומם הש"י אד"ש אל יירע בעיני כ"ת איחור תשובתי כי הסיבות המטרידות הקיפוני ועתה כאשר נפניתי הנני משיב ככל מצותך אשר היא עלי חובה על דבר האשה שמחמת קושי לידה נולד לה חולי שלא תוכל להתעבר ומן אז והלאה תמיד אחר טבילת' ב' או ג' ימים מוצאה בחלוקה או בבדיקתה כתמי' נוטי' למראה אדמומי' והם כמו חתיכות קטנות כמו חול ולאחר זמן כשמתחילות להתייבש משתנות ממראיהן למרא' שחור בתכלית השחרות וכשממשמשי' בהם נופלים מהבגד כמו חודי מחט ולא נשאר שום רושם כלל

מהאודם רק ככתם לבן ומרגשת כאב וצער בשעת תשמיש והרופאים והמילדת של גוים אומרים שכתמים האלו מהאם כו׳ והב״ח בסי׳ פ״ה בתשו׳ העלה דהיכא דלא אפשר בבדיקה כו׳ דפשיטא דכיון שיש לה מכה תולה במכתה וטהורה לבעלה אע״פ שאינה יודעת דמכתה מוציאה דם כו׳ עכ״ל כו׳ וגם יש לצדד להיתר ממה שהכתם הוא כמו חול ויש לדמותו לתשו׳ הט״ז סי׳ קצ״א אך כמדומה לי שהרב זקנו הגאון זצלל״ה בס׳ שער אפרים העלה בפלפולו דדוקא ברואה דם מחמת תשמיש תולין כו׳ דאל״כ תאסר לעול׳ משא״כ בשאר נשים ובנ״ד שיש לה היתר ב׳ או ג׳ ימים אפשר לומר דמחמירין ע״כ תורף שאלת חכם.

תשובה יידע כת״ר שאף שמפרשי הטור ז״ל ס״ל דלהרשב״א אף שאינה יודעת שמכתה מוציאה דם בשום פעם אפ״ה תולין בה כמבואר בדבריהם: הדבר תמוה מאוד בעיני שהרי אף בכתמי׳ קלים שנינו בסו״פ הרואה כתם דף נ״ח אם יש בה מכה והיא יכול׳ להגלע ולהוציא דם הרי זה תולה בה הרי דלא תלינן אפי׳ כתם אלא במכה שהיא יכולה להגלע וא״כ האיך תיסק אדעתין למימר ברואה ממש שאף בסתם מכה שאין אנו יודעין בה אם יכולה להגלע ולהוציא דם שתולה בה יציבא בארעא וגיורא בשמי שמיא וא״ת שאף שאין אנו צריכין לידע שמכתה מוציא׳ דם מ״מ צריכין אנו לידע שיכולה להגלע ולהוציא דם חדא שלא נזכר זה בדבריהם ז״ל ועוד וכי ידה ועיניה באותו מקום לידע ולהבחין בדבר זה בחדרי בטנה ועוד בפירוש אמר ר׳ עקיבא לתלמידיו כשראה אותן מסתכלין זה בזה מה הדבר קשה בעיניכם שלא אמרו חכמים הדבר להחמיר אלא להקל שנאמר כו׳ דם ולא כתם הרי בפירוש דברואה ממש אין לנו להקל אפילו ביכולה להגלע שהרי אין זה סתם אלא רואה: אלא על כרחך כוונת הרשב״א ז״ל לומר דלא בעינן שתהא צריכה לומר שאותו הדם ממש הוא שותת ויורד מן המכה אלא כיון שמרגשת בעצמה שיש לה מכה שמוציאה דם אף שאינה יודעת באותה פעם שהדם ההוא שותת ויורד מן המכה כיון שמכתה מוציא דם תולה בה אבל באינה יודעת אם מכתה מוציאה דם מהי תיתי לתלות בה דאף שהאשה בחזקת טהרה עומדת ומוקמינן לה אחזקתה מ״מ לא אמרי׳ הכי אלא כשהוא ספק שקול וכיון שיש לה מכה המוציאה דם בודאי הרי הוא ספק שקול ספק מן המקור ספק מן המכה שיש בה דם: אבל כשאינה יודעת בודאי שמכתה מוציאה דם הרי אין כאן ספק שקול שהרי דרך המקור להוציא דם בודאי ודרך המכה ספק ונהי דשלא בשעת וסתה היה אפשר לומר דאין דרך המקור להוציא דם שלא בשעת וסתה ולכך יש לתלות לקולא אבל הרשב״א ז״ל מטהרה אפי׳ בשעת וסתה כמבואר בדבריו בתה״א דקפ״א ע״ב וא״כ היכי אתי ספק דם דמן המכה ומוציא מידי ודאי דם המקור אף דהאשה עומדת בחזקת טהרה אלא ע״כ הרשב״א מיירי בדידעה בודאי שדרך מכתה להוציא דם אלא שאינ׳ יודעת אם דם זה הוא מן המכה והא דדחיק הרשב״א לפרש הלשון שבגמ׳ ונאמנת אשה לומר מכה יש לה שממנה הדם שותת ויורד וז״ל שאני אומר ממנה הדם שותת ויורד עכ״ל ולא קאמר שממנה הדם שותת ויורד בפעם אחרת הוא משום דגירסתו ז״ל היתה שממנה הדם (בה׳ הידיעה) שותת ויורד דמשמע זה הדם שעליו אנו דנין ועוד דסתם מכה שאנו עסיקין בה בדיני נדה וכתמים במכה המוציאה דם מיירי וחידוש הוא שחידשו ופירשו לנו בדני כתמים אם יכולה להגלע ולהוציא דם תולין בה ולולי שפירשו לנו כן בפירוש הו״א דצריכה להוציא דם בפועל כדי שיתלו בה ואם אין המכה כך אין תולין בה ממילא משמע דמכה זו שבמקור במוציאה דם קמיירי וא״כ מה לנו לפרש שממנה הדם שותת ויורד על עיקר המכה שדרכה להוציא דם פשיטא דבהכי איירי והוה סליק אדעתין למימר דעל דם

זה שהוא רואה עתה קאי לכך נדחק לפרש מה שפירש ואין להקשות א״כ האיך כ׳ הרשב״א וא״א לידע אלא בבדיקת שפופרת והלא אף בבדיקת שפופרת א״א לה לידע דבשלמא אם הבדיקה היא לידע אם מכתה מוציאה דם אם לא ניחא דבבדיקת שפופרת אפשר לה לידע אם מכתה מוציא דם אם לא דמגעת במוך שבראש המכחול במכה אם יש בה דם בידוע שמכתה מוציאה דם ואם לאו אין מכתה מוציאה דם אבל אם הבדיקה היא לידע אם זה הדם ששותת ויורד עתה הוא מן המכה האיך אפשר לעמוד על דבר זה כיון שבשעת ירידת הדם היא מכנסת המכחול במקורה אף אם נוגעת במוך שבמכחול במכה ומוצאת עליו דם נימא מן המקור ירד לתוך השפופרת ונפל על המוך שנגע במכה דבלא״ה נמי תיקשי מאי ענין בדיקת שפופרת להכא כיון שהמכה במקור עצמו ואינה טהורה אא״כ ימצא דם בראש המכחול אחר נגיעתו במכה וקודם זה מספקינן לה בספק מן המקור האיך בדיקה זו תוציאנה מידי ספקא אף שימצא דם בראש המכחול נימא דקודם נגיעתו כבר היה עליו דם מן המקור מה תאמר כיון שאינה שופעת ואינה שעת וסתה אין לנו לחוש לדם מן המקור ומסתמא אמרי׳ מן דם המכה הוא א״כ כל עיקר בדיקה זו למה אף בלא בדיקה אמור דם מכה הוא מה שרואה שלא בשעת וסתה דמסתמא אף ארואה שלא בשעת וסתה נמי היה מצריכה בדיקה ואף אם תרצה לחלק בין רואה לאינה רואה דבאינ׳ רואה אמרי׳ אלו הוה דם הוה אתי וכיון שאינו בא אלא ע״י שפופרת במוך הנוגע במקום המכה מסתמא דם מכה הוא עכ״ז כיון דהך בדיקה דנקיט הרשב״א ע״כ איזה באופן בדיקה האמורה בתלמוד דהתם בנמצא בראש המוך טמאה וכאן אדרבה טהרתה תלויי׳ בזה דהא אם אינה מוצאה דם בראש המוך אין לה הוכחה שמכתה מוציאה דם וכיון שכן אף אתה אמור דבדיקת הרשב״א היא באופן שאף ששופעת יכולה לידע אם הוא מן המכה וכגון שסותמת פי השפופרת באיזה דבר עד שמניחתו סמוך למכתה ובהגיעה שמה מוציאה הסתימה ומכנסת מכחול ובראשו מוך שהולך דרך ישרה למקום המכה או שמנחת השפופרת על מקום המכה בלי מכחול ורואה אם מנטפת השפופרת בעודה עומדת ראשה במכה או דלרווחא דמילתא נקיט הרשב״א הך בדיקה דאפילו תימא דבמכה שבצדדין מיירי דאז אפשר לה ע״י בדיקה וכעין בדיקת התלמוד ממש עאפ״כ מוכח בתלמוד דלא בעינן בדיקה כלל ובלא בדיקה א״א לה לידע שזה הדם שותת ויורד מן המכה אבל אפשר לה לידע אם מכתה מוציאה דם אפי׳ בלא בדיקה שהרי הרשב״א כ׳ בפירוש ונאמנת לומר מכה יש לה שיש שם דם הרי שצריכה לומר שיש לה מכה שיש שם דם וא״כ ע״כ יודעת היא להבחין בין מכה שיש שם דם למכה שאין שם דאין לומר דגם זה הוא פירוש וביאור ולא שתהא האשה צריכה לומר כך דעל הראשונים אנו מצטערים על הפי׳ הנאמר בגמ׳ מיותר והוצרך הרשב״א לדחוק ולפרשו ומה לו להרשב״א להרבות דוחק ואם ליישב דברי התלמוד בא יותר מרווח הי״ל לומר בקיצור ונאמנת אשה לומר מכה יש לה ותולה במכתה שאני אומר ממנה הדם שותת ויורד ועוד דאם גם זה מן התוס׳ כך הי״ל לומר מכה יש לה ותולה במכתה שאני אומר יש שם דם וממנה הדם שותת ויורד אלא ע״כ שהאשה צריכה לומר שהמכה שיש לה יש שם דם דאל״ה אינה תולה בה וא״כ כל שלא אמרה כן אף להרשב״א אינה תולה בה ובקשתי לי חבר בפירוש דברי הרשב״א ומצאתי לי רב בעל ש״ך ז״ל בסי׳ קפ״ז ס״ק כ״ד שכתב בקצרה שדעת הרשב״א כדעת כל הפוסקים ושכן הוכיח בספרו ולא זכינו לו ואיך שיהיה חלילה לנו להקל באיסור כרת ודיינו אם נקל כסברת מו״ז הגאון בעל שער אפרים זצלל״ה בשא״א לו בענין אחר אא״כ תתגרש.

תלמוד בבלי מסכת נדה דף נח עמוד ב – מתני'. ותולה בכל דבר שהיא יכולה לתלות; שחטה בהמה חיה ועוף, נתעסקה בכתמים, או שישבה בצד העסוקין בהן, הרגה מאכולת – הרי זו תולה בה. עד כמה תולה? רבי חנינא בן אנטיגנוס אומר: עד כגריס של פול, ואף ע"פ שלא הרגה. ותולה בבנה או בבעלה. אם יש בה מכה, והיא יכולה להגלע ולהוציא דם – הרי זו תולה. מעשה באשה אחת שבאת לפני ר"ע, אמרה לו: ראיתי כתם. אמר לה: שמא מכה היתה ביך? אמרה לו: הן, וחיתה. אמר לה: שמא יכולה להגלע ולהוציא דם? אמרה לו: הן. וטהרה ר"ע. ראה תלמידיו מסתכלין זה בזה, אמר להם: מה הדבר קשה בעיניכם? שלא אמרו חכמים הדבר להחמיר – אלא להקל, שנאמר (ויקרא ט"ו) ואשה כי תהיה זבה דם יהיה זובה בבשרה, דם ולא כתם. עד שהוא נתון תחת הכר ונמצא עליו דם, עגול – טהור, משוך – טמא, דברי ר"א ברבי צדוק.

שולחן ערוך יורה דעה הלכות נדה סימן קפז סעיף ה – אם יש מכה באותו מקום, תולין בדם מכתה. ואם דם מכתה משונה מדם ראייתה, אינה תולה בדם מכתה. הגה: וכל זה באשה שיש לה וסת קבוע, ואז יכולים לתלות שלא בשעת וסתה במכתה, אע"פ שאינה יודעת בודאי שמכתה הוציאה דם. (כך משמע בפסקי מהרא"י סימן מ"ז ובהגהות ש"ד) וכן אם אין לה וסת קבוע, והוא ספק אם הדם בא מן המקור או מן הצדדין, תלינן במכה מכח ספק ספיקא, ספק מן הצדדין או מן המקור, ואת"ל מן המקור, שמא הוא מן המכה. אבל אם ידוע שבא מן המקור, אע"פ שיש לה מכה במקור, אינה תולה במכה, כג אם אין לה וסת קבוע, כד אלא אם כן יודעת בודאי שמכתה מוציאה דם. (כן משמע במרדכי ה"נ ובהג"מ פי"א דא"ב) (ועיין ס"ק כ"ב). ומ"מ בשעת וסתה, או מל' יום לל' יום, כו אינה תולה במכתה, דאל"כ לא תיטמא לעולם. (ג"ז שם ובב"י בשם סמ"ג וסמ"ק). וכתמים, תולה בה (לד) בכל ענין (במרדכי).

תלמוד בבלי מסכת נדה דף סה עמוד ב, דף סו עמוד א – תנו רבנן: הרואה דם מחמת תשמיש – משמשת פעם ראשונה ושניה ושלישית, מכאן ואילך – לא תשמש, עד שתתגרש ותנשא לאחר. ניסת לאחר וראתה דם מחמת תשמיש – משמשת פעם ראשונה ושניה ושלישית, מכאן ואילך – לא תשמש, עד שתתגרש ותנשא לאחר. ניסת לאחר וראתה דם מחמת תשמיש – משמשת פעם ראשונה ושניה ושלישית, מכאן ואילך לא תשמש עד שתבדוק עצמה. כיצד בודקת את עצמה – מביאה שפופרת ובתוכה מכחול, ומוך מונח על ראשו, אם נמצא דם על ראש המוך – בידוע שמן המקור הוא בא, לא נמצא דם על ראשו – בידוע שמן הצדדין הוא בא. ואם יש לה מכה באותו מקום – תולה במכתה, ואם יש לה וסת – תולה בוסתה. ואם היה דם מכתה משונה מדם ראייתה – אינה תולה.

רש"י מסכת נדה דף סו עמוד א – ואם יש לה וסת – לקלקול הזה שאינה רואה כל שעה מחמת תשמיש אלא לפרקים תולה בוסתה ומשמשת בלא בדיקה בין וסת לוסת.

רמב"ם הלכות איסורי ביאה פרק ד הלכה כ – מי שראתה דם בשעת תשמיש הרי זו מותרת לשמש כשתטהר פעם שניה, ראתה דם בפעם שניה משמשת פעם שלישית, ראתה דם בשלישית הרי זו אסורה לשמש עם בעל זה לעולם, בד"א בשלא היה שם דבר לתלות בו אבל אם

שמשה סמוך לוסתה תולה בוסת, היתה בה מכה תולה במכה, ואם היה דם מכתה משונה מדם שתראה בעת התשמיש אינה תולה במכה, ונאמנת אשה לומר מכה יש לי בתוך המקור שממנה הדם יוצא ותהיה מותרת לבעלה, ואע"פ שדם יוצא מן המקור בשעת תשמיש.

שולחן ערוך יורה דעה הלכות נדה סימן קפז סעיף ד – אם שמשה סמוך לוסתה, אנו תולין ראייתה משום וסתה ולא חשבינן לה רואה מחמת תשמיש.

ש"ך יורה דעה סימן קפז כ – וכ"ז כו' – עיין בספרי שהוכחתי דס"ל להמרדכי (ותשו' מהר"ם דפוס פראג סימן תרנ"ה) דאם יש לה וסת זמן קבוע שהיא רואה תולה שלא בשעת וסתה בוסתה אפילו אין לה מכה כלל אמרינן שזהו דם טהור הוא מן הצדדים מחמת מיעוך תשמיש שהרי עדיין לא הגיע וסתה והוכחתי שם שגם מהרא"י בפסקיו סימן מ"ז הבין כן אלא דדייק מהמרדכי מכח כל שכן דכיון דסבירא ליה דמחזקה אין אורח בא אלא בזמנו מהני דתולין דדם טהור הוא מה שלא היו תולין בלא זה מכל שכן דסבירא ליה דהיכא דאיכא מכה אע"פ שאינה מוציאה דם דטהורה ובכהאי גוונא אפשר דאף הפוסקים החולקים אהמרדכי מודים כיון דאיכא עוד צד היתר שיש לה מכה ועל פי הדברים האלה הם דברי הרב והב"ח הבין פשט המרדכי דותולה במכתה כו' נקשר אתולה בוסתה והאריך בקושיות ופירוקים וכבר סתרתי שם כל דבריו בארוכה ע"ש אלא הדבר ברור שהמרדכי מציין הברייתא ותולה במכתה כו' וכן מוכח בבית יוסף וד"מ ובתשו' מהר"מ פדוו"א סימן ט' וי' ושאר אחרונים והוא פשוט ולפ"ז נראה דאין להתיר אלא לבעלה משום דבכמה מקומות חשו חז"ל שלא להוציא אשה מבעלה ומשום עגונה הקילו הלכך אין להחזיקה ברואה מחמת תשמיש אבל מ"מ צריכה לישב ז' נקיים דבכה"ג אין לסמוך אהמרדכי דהא מדברי רש"י נראה שחולק וגם הרמב"ן והרשב"א והרמב"ם והטור ושאר כל הפוסקים שפירשו ואם יש לה וסת ושמשה סמוך לוסתה תולין בוסתה אלמא לא שמשה סמוך לוסתה אפילו יש לה וסת לא תלינן דדם טהור הוא וכ"כ בתשובת מהר"מ פדוואה סי' י' ואשר נסתפק מעלתך אם יש להקל כדברי המרדכי בפי' ואם יש לה וסת תולה בוסתה כו' קולא גדולה היא ומי הוא אשר חיילים יגבר להקל נגד כל הפוסקים האחרים עכ"ל וכן הרב לא הקיל אלא שלא להחזיקה ברואה מחמת תשמיש (וגם זה בשיש לה מכה אע"פ שאינה מוציאה דם) ומדברי הב"ח נראה דמתיר בכל ענין ולפעד"נ כמ"ש.

תרומת הדשן סימן רמז – שאלה: אשה שרגילה לראות בענין זה שלעולם לא בפחות מי"ד ימים אחר טבילתה, אבל לאחר ארבע עשרה ימים אין לה קבע, לפעמים בט"ו או בט"ז או י"ז ולפעמים בכ"א בכ"ג בכ"ד לאחר טבילה אין לה קביעות לדלוגים הללו כלל, אי חשיבי בכה"ג אשה שאין לה ווסת להצריכה בדיקה לבעלה בכל תשמיש או לאו?

תשובה: יראה דזו אינה צריכה בדיקה כלל לכל אשר תשמש קודם ארבע עשרה יום לטבילתה, ואפי' לפי' ר"ח ור"ת דפסקו דאין לה וסת בעי בדיקה לבעלה וכתב א"ז ואשירי שיש להחמיר כדבריהם, מ"מ נראה דהך אשה לאו אין לה וסת מיקרי קודם הארבע עשרה ימים. ואע"ג דבפ"ק דנידה דף ט ע"ב לא משמע תלמודא הכי דקאמר התם עברה עליה ג' עונות וראתה ועוד עברה עליה ג' עונות וראתה ועוד עברה שלשה עונות וראתה מטמא מעת לעת ולא

שכיונה אלא שפיחתה והותירה. ופירש רש"י פיחתה כגון שראתה בתחילה ליום תשעים ושלש ואח"כ לתשעים ושנים ואח"כ לתשעים ואחד, ומפורש התם דבכה"ג הרי היא כאשה שאין לה וסת שמטמאה מעת לעת, והיינו משום דחיישינן דילמא מאתמול ביום תשעים ראתה דם לבית החיצון. והשתא אמאי חיישינן להכי הא אשה זו לא ראתה כלל תוך תשעים יום, ותיהוי כיש לה וסת לענין זה שלא תחוש לראיית דמים תוך תשעים יום, ואמאי מטמאין מעת לעת טפי בפיחתה מבכיונה, דמסיק תלמודא דאם כיונה קבעה לה וסת ודייה שעתה כרבי דוסא. אע"כ הואיל ואין אורח שלה בזמנה בא אע"פ שיש לו זמן שאינו מקדים כלל לבא בו לא חשבינן יש לה ווסת. אמנם נראה דאין ראייה כלל דודאי לענין מעת לעת דטהרות אחמור רבנן טפי, ובעינן טעם וסברא ברורה דלא אתי דם, כגון שיש לה וסת מכוון דודאי אין אורח בא אלא בזמנו, כה"ג דייה שעתה לרבי דוסא, אבל לענין בדיקה לבעלה לא בעינן אלא סברא בעלמא דראוי לומר דלא קאתי דם. ותדע דהא רבנן דר' דוסא מטמאין מעת לעת אפי' באשה שיש לה וסת, ובדיקה לבעלה תנן דכל הנשים בחזקת טהורה לבעליהן, וההיא ע"כ ביש לה וסת לכל הפחות איירי, וליכא מאן דפליג אההיא מתניתין, אע"כ במעת לעת מחמירינן טפי. וה"נ מוכח פ' בנות כותים נדה לט ע"א, דתנן התם כל אחד עשר יום בחזקת טהור הן, וקאמרינן בגמרא למאי הלכתא אמר רב חסדא לא נצרכא אלא לרבי מאיר דאמר אשה שאין לה וסת אסורה לשמש הנ"מ בימי נידה אבל בימי זיבה מותרת, אלמא שאפילו לרבי מאיר דמחמיר טפי באין לה וסת דאסורה לשמש אפילו ע"י בדיקה בימי זיבה לא חייש. ולענין מעת לעת מייתי ברייתא התם תיובתא לרבא דאפילו בימי זיבה מטמא מעת לעת, כל שכן דלרבי חנינא בן אנטיגנוס דמתירה ע"י בדיקה דאית לן לחלק בין לבעלה למעת לעת. ונראה דטעם יפה לחלק דלענין מעת לעת הרי דם לפניך אלא דלא ידעינן אימת קאתי, וכיון דאיכא ריעותא לפנינו מטמאין למפרע, אבל בדיקה לבעלה אינה אלא משום שמא תראה בשעת תשמיש, ואהא ליכא ריעותא לפנינו. והיכא דאיכא סברא בעלמא אמרינן דאינה צריכה בדיקה ואינו נגד הסברא לחלק ולהקל, שהרי רשב"ם והרבה גאונים פסקו דלכל לבעלה לא בעי בדיקה, ואפילו אי בעי לאחמורי לא שבקינן לה משום דלבו נוקפו ופורש, ומהאי טעמא אין דוחק לחלק ולהקל אפילו לאינך גאונים המחמירין. ולענין לפרוש מאשה שדרכה לראות בענין זה עונה אחת סמוך לראייה מבואר שילהי פ' האשה.

שולחן ערוך יורה דעה הלכות נדה סימן קפו סעיף ג – אשה שאינה רואה בפחות מי"ד ימים אחר טבילתה, אבל לאחר י"ד ימים אין לה קבע עד י"ד יום, דינה כדין אשה שיש לה וסת.

פתחי תשובה יורה דעה סימן קפז כו – וסת קבוע – ואם אין לה וסת קבוע רק שאינה רואה עד אחר י"ד יום אחר טבילתה נראה דעד י"ד יום דינה כדין אשה שיש לה וסת גם לענין זה כמו בסי' קפ"ו סעיף ג' וכן כתב הח"ד.

תלמוד בבלי מסכת כריתות דף יז עמוד א, דף יח עמוד א – מתני'. ספק אכל חלב ספק לא אכל, ואפילו אכל, ספק יש בו כשיעור וספק אין בו; שומן וחלב לפניו, ואכל אחד מהן ואינו יודע איזה מהן אכל; אשתו ואחותו עמו בבית, שגג באחת מהן ואינו יודע באיזו מהן שגג; שבת ויום חול,

ועשה מלאכה באחד מהן ואינו יודע באיזו מהן עשה – מביא אשם תלוי. כשם שאם אכל חלב וחלב בהעלם אחת אינו חייב אלא חטאת אחת, כן על לא הודע שלהן אינו מביא אלא אשם תלוי אחד. אם היתה ידיעה בינתים, כשם שהוא מביא חטאת על כל אחת ואחת, כך מביא אשם תלוי על כל אחת ואחת. כשם שאכל חלב ודם ופיגול ונותר בהעלם אחת חייב על כל אחת ואחת, כך על לא הודע שלהן מביא אשם תלוי על כל אחת ואחת.

גמ׳. איתמר, רב אסי אמר: חתיכה אחת שנינו, ספק של חלב ספק של שומן; חייא בר רב אמר: חתיכה משתי חתיכות שנינו. במאי קא מיפלגי? רב אסי סבר: יש אם למסורת, (ויקרא ה׳) מצות כתיב; וחייא בר רב אמר: יש אם למקרא, מצוות קרינן. איתיביה רב הונא לרב אסי, ואמרי לה חייא בר רב לרב אסי: חלב ושומן לפניו ואכל אחת מהן; מאי לאו מדסיפא שתי חתיכות, רישא נמי שתי חתיכות! אמר להו רב: לא תיזלא בתר איפכא, דיכול לשנויי לכו: סיפא בשתי חתיכות, רישא בחתיכה אחת. אי הכי, יש לומר חתיכה אחת מחייב, שתי חתיכות צריכא למימר? זו ואין צריך למימר זו. ולחייא בר רב דאמר: מדסיפא בשתי חתיכות, רישא נמי בשתי חתיכות, מיתנא תרתי למה לי? פרושי קא מפרש: ספק אכל [חלב] ספק לא אכל (חלב) – מביא אשם תלוי, כיצד? כגון שהיה חלב ושומן לפניו. אמר רב יהודה אמר רב: היו לפניו שתי חתיכות, אחת של שומן ואחת של חלב, אכל אחת מהן ואינו יודע איזו מהן אכל – חייב; חתיכה אחת, ספק של חלב ספק של שומן ואכלה – פטור. אמר רבא: מאי טעמא דרב? דאמר קרא: (ויקרא ד׳) ועשה אחת מכל מצות ה׳ בשגגה, עד שישגוג בשתים, מצות כתיב, מצוות קרינן. איתיביה אביי, רבי אליעזר אומר: כוי, חייבין עליו אשם תלוי! אמר לו, ר׳ אליעזר סבר: יש אם למסורת, מצות כתיב. איתיביה: ספק בן תשעה לראשון או בן שבעה לאחרון – יוציא והולד כשר, וחייב באשם תלוי! הא מני? רבי אליעזר היא. איתיביה: נמצא על שלו – טמאין וחייבין בקרבן, על שלה אתיום – טמאין וחייבין בקרבן, נמצא על שלה לאחר זמן – טמאין מספק ופטורין מן הקרבן, ותני עלה: חייב משום אשם תלוי! הא מני? רבי אליעזר היא. א״ר חייא אמר רב: היו לפניו שתי חתיכות, אחת של חלב ואחת של שומן, ואכל אחת מהן ואינו יודע איזה מהן אכל – חייב; חתיכה, ספק של שומן ספק של חלב ואכלה – פטור. א״ר זירא: מ״ט דרב? קסבר: שתי חתיכות אפשר לברר איסורו, חתיכה אחת אי אפשר לברר איסורו. מאי איכא בין טעמא דרבא לטעמא דרבי זירא? איכא בינייהו כזית ומחצה, לרבא – ליכא מצוות ופטור, לרבי זירא – אפשר לברר איסורו. איתיביה רבי ירמיה לרבי זירא, רבי אליעזר אומר: כוי, חייבין על חלבו אשם תלוי! אמר ליה, רבי אליעזר סבר: לא בעינן לברר איסורו. איתיביה: ספק בן תשעה לראשון או בן שבעה לאחרון – יוציא והולד כשר, וחייב באשם תלוי! הא מני? רבי אליעזר היא. איתיביה: נמצא על שלה אתיום – טמאין וחייבין בקרבן, נמצא על שלה לאחר זמן – טמאין מספק ופטורין מן הקרבן, ותני עלה: וחייבין באשם תלוי! הא מני? רבי אליעזר היא. אמר רב נחמן אמר רבה בר אבוה אמר רב: היו לפניו שתי חתיכות, אחת של חלב ואחת של שומן, ואכל אחת מהן ואינו יודע איזו מהן אכל – חייב; חתיכה, ספק של חלב ספק של שומן ואכלה – פטור. אמר רב נחמן: מאי טעמא דרב? קסבר: שתי חתיכות איקבע איסורא, חתיכה אחת לא קבעה איסורא. מאי איכא בין איקבע איסורא לשאי אפשר לברר איסוריה? איכא בינייהו כגון שהיו לפניו שתי חתיכות, אחת של חלב ואחת של שומן, ובא עובד כוכבים ואכל את הראשונה ובא ישראל ואכל את השניה,

לרבא – ליכא מצוות בעידנא דאכל ישראל, לר׳ זירא – אי אפשר לברר איסוריה, לרב נחמן – איקבע איסורא. איתיביה רבא לרב נחמן, רבי אליעזר אומר: כוי, חייבין על חלבו אשם תלוי! ר׳ אליעזר לא בעי קביעותא לאיסורא. איתיביה: ספק בן ט׳ לראשון או בן ז׳ לאחרון – יוציא והולד כשר, וחייבין באשם תלוי! הא מני? ר׳ אליעזר היא. איתיביה: נמצא על שלו – טמאין וחייבין בקרבן, נמצא על שלה אתיום – טמאין וחייבין בקרבן, נמצא על שלה לאחר זמן – טמאים מספק ופטורין מן הקרבן, ותני עלה: וחייבין באשם תלוי! אישתיק. לבתר דנפק, אמר: מאי טעמא לא אמרי ליה דהא מני? רבי מאיר היא, דלא בעי קביעותא לאיסורא, דתניא: השוחט אשם תלוי בחוץ – ר׳ מאיר מחייב, וחכמים פוטרין. ואמאי? לימא ליה דר׳ אליעזר היא! הא קמ״ל, דר״מ בשיטת ר׳ אליעזר קאי.

תלמוד בבלי מסכת סוטה דף כח עמוד ב – מה סוטה רשות היחיד, אף שרץ רשות היחיד, ומה סוטה דבר שיש בו דעת לישאל, אף שרץ דבר שיש בו דעת לישאל; ומכאן אמרו: דבר שיש בו דעת לישאל, ברשות היחיד – ספיקו טמא, ברה״ר – ספיקו טהור, ושאין בו דעת לישאל, בין ברה״י בין ברה״ר – ספיקו טהור.

תוספות מסכת בבא קמא דף יא עמוד א – דאין מקצת שליא בלא ולד – וא״ת לר״א דאמר חוששין משום דאין מקצת שליא בלא ולד אבל אם היה מקצת שליא בלא ולד לא היתה חוששת ה״ד אי ברה״ר אפי׳ בחד ספיקא מטהרי׳ ואי ברה״י אפי׳ בספק ספיקא נמי טמא דהא תנן (טהרות פ״ו מ״ד) כל ספיקות שאתה יכול להרבות ברה״י אפי׳ ספק ספיקא טמא וי״ל דשמעתין איירי לענין לאוסרה לבעלה.

תוספות מסכת נדה דף ב עמוד א – מעת לעת – מפרש בגמ׳ דתולין לא אוכלין ולא שורפין ודוקא לקדשים או לתרומה אבל לחולין לכ״ע דיה שעתה דאוקמא לה בחזקת טהורה וא״ת מאי שנא מכל ספק טומאה דברה״י טמא ודאי אף לחולין ולא מוקמינן בחזקת טהרה משום דילפי׳ (לקמן דף ג.) מסוטה מדפריך בגמרא לר״ש אי מה סוטה טמאה ודאי ברה״י אף הכא טמאה ודאי ומשני שאני סוטה דאיכא רגלים לדבר משמע דלרבנן דאמרי ברה״י טמאות אתי שפיר וטעם דתרתי לריעותא לא הוצרך אלא לטמא אפילו בר״ה וי״ל דלא ילפינן מסוטה לטמאה למפרע ולכך בטומאה דמעת לעת מוקמינן לה אחזקתה וא״ת במעת לעת דקיל טפי משאר טומאות כדפרישית אמאי החמירו בו לטמאה אף בר״ה ובכל שאר טומאות אמרינן בר״ה ספקו טהור כדמוכח בשמעתין דקאמר והלל כי קאמר אוקי מילתא אחזקתה כגון ספק נגע ספק לא נגע אבל במעל״ע כו׳ ולא אמרינן אוקי מילתא אחזקתה אלא בר״ה אלמא במעת לעת אף בר״ה טמא וכן לקמן (דף ה:) מוקי מתני׳ כשנושאין אותה חברותיה במטה א״כ הוו להו תלתא והוי ר״ה כדמוכח בריש שני נזירים (נזיר נז.) ואפ״ה המטה טמאה ואע״ג דיש לדחות כגון שהכילה מפסקת בין נדה לחברותיה אין נראה דבהדיא יש בירושל׳ דמגעה בר״ה מטמא במעת לעת וי״ל דאף בר״ה לא נטהר בקדשים משום חזקת טהרה כיון דאיכא ריעותא מגופה ואע״ג דמסוטה ילפינן לטהר בר״ה אפי׳ היכא דליכא חזקה כמו שאפרש לקמן הכא לא ילפינן מסוטה משום שהאשה שראתה השתא ודאי טמאה היא ולא גמרינן מסוטה לטהר בר״ה אלא כמו ספק נגע ספק לא נגע שגם

עתה בספק דומיא דסוטה ומיהו בדבר שאין בו דעת לישאל טהור במעת לעת דלקמן מקשינן אמתני׳ דבר שאין בו דעת לישאל הוא ומוקמינן בשחברותיה נושאות אותה במטה והיינו משום דדבר שאין בו דעת לישאל לא גמרינן מסוטה וגו׳ אלא גמרינן לטהר מדרב גידל דאמר רב גידל (סוטה דף כט.) כתיב והבשר אשר יגע בכל טמא לא יאכל הא ספק טהור וכתיב כל טהור יאכל בשר הא ספק טמא אלא כאן שאין בו דעת לישאל כאן שיש בו דעת לישאל ובטומאת בשר קדש שייך למפרע כמו להבא ועוד י״ל דלא גמרינן מסוטה אלא טומאת מגע ולא טומאת ראייה לכך מטמא אף ברה״ר אבל דבר שאין בו דעת לישאל טהור דבטומאת בשר קדש שייך טומאה ע״י ראיית הזב או הזבה או הנדה דאסרינן לאכול בשר קדש והוי בכלל כל טהור יאכל בשר (ויקרא ז) וא״ת מאי שנא דבנגע באחד בלילה (לקמן דף ד.) דמטמאין רבנן אף בר״ה כדמוכח בתוספתא היכא דלא ראהו חי מבערב משום דכל הטומאות כשעת מציאתן ואשה נמי אמרינן (לקמן דף ד.) כיון דשכיחי בה דמים כאינה בדוקה דמיא ואמאי מטהרינן לחולין אף ברה״י וי״ל דלקמן [נמי] בנגע באחד בלילה מיירי בקדשים וכן קופה (לקמן דף ג:) דפריך הלל לשמאי איירי בקדשים דאי לאו הכי תקשה ליה לנפשיה וכן פלוגתא דחזקיה ור׳ יוחנן (שם) המדלה י׳ דליים מים מיירי במים שנעשו על טהרת הקדש ללוש בהן עיסת מנחות או להדיח בהן בשר קדש דכקדש דמו וא״ת ומ״ש דאמרינן בנגע באחד לשרוף ובמעת לעת אמרינן תולין דאשה נמי מיקריא במקום מציאתה דכל מקום שהיא טומאתה עמה דאי לאו הכי תקשי אשה לחזקיה דמטהר בקופה ממקום למקום וי״ל משום דלבו נוקפו ויבטל מפריה ורביה דסבור דשכיחא טומאה כיון ששורפין עליה תרומה ופריש דכה״ג אמרינן לקמן (דף ג:) והא דפריך הלל לשמאי היינו משום דלבו נוקפו לא היה לו לטהר לגמרי וגו׳ אך קשה לפ״ז מאי פריך להלל ממקוה נימא משום דלבו נוקפו וא״ת אמאי מטהר שמאי טפי באשה מבקופה ונגע באחד אע״ג דמשני שמאי דאשה אין לה שוליים היינו להאי לישנא דאי הוה דם מעיקרא הוה אתי אבל לשאר לישני לית לן האי טעמא וי״ל דטעמא דשמאי משום דאשה בדוקה היא והא דקאמר כיון דשכיחי בה דמים כאינה בדוקה דמיא היינו להלל וא״ת לר״מ אמאי מטהר בנגע באחד ובאשה תולין וי״ל משום דמוקמה אחזקתה ואשה משום דאיכא ריעותא מגופה.

ש״ך יורה דעה סימן קפז כב – וכן אם אין כו׳ – דין זה הוציא הרב בד״מ מדברי הש״ד סימן ו׳ וז״ל אשה שיש לה מכה באותו מקום ואינה יודעת אם המכה מוציאה דם אם מרגשת בעצמה שהדם בא מן הרחם טמאה ואינה יכולה לתלות במכה ואם יודעת שבא מן המכה טהורה שתולה במכה אבל בשעת וסתה אע״פ שיודעת שבא מן המכה טמאה דאל״כ אשה שיש לה מכה באותו מקום לא תהא טמאה לעולם אך כל כתמיה שנמצאו בבגדיה טהורים שתולים במכה אע״פ שאינה יודעת אם המכה מוציאה דם שבכתמים הולכין להקל עכ״ל וכתב בד״מ שכן משמע מדבריו וכתב אח״כ וכן משמע מהג״ה מיי׳ פי״א מהל׳ א״ב בשם ס״ה והמרדכי דלעיל (שהביא ב״י דבריהם בסימן זה בד״ה אבל הגמי״י כתבו כו׳) עכ״ל ולפענ״ד דמשמע ליה להרב הכי מדכתב הש״ד אם מרגשת בעצמה שהדם בא מן הרחם טמאה כו׳ משמע דוקא כשיודעת שבא מן הרחם דהיינו מן המקור הא לא״ה טהורה אע״פ שאינה יודעת שהמכה מוציאה דם משמע ליה נמי מדכתב סתמא מיירי בין באשה שיש לה וסת קבוע או שאין לה וסת קבוע וע״פ זה כתב וכן

משמע בהג"מ ומרדכי דלעיל שדבריהם כדברי הש"ד אבל באמת לא משמע מידי דלא קאמר אם מרגשת בעצמה שהדם בא מן הרחם כו' אלא לאפוקי סיפא דכל כתמי' תולה במכתה תדע דהרי הגמי"י כתבו בשם ס"ה אשה שיש לה מכה באותו מקום ואינה יודעת אם מכתה מוציאה דם אי לא אם בודקת עצמה באותו מקום ומצאה דם או אם מרגשת כשהדם נופל מהרחם כו' עד מיהו כל כתמיה תולין להקל עכ"ל וכן הוא בסה"ת סימן צ"ב א"כ אדרבה מוכח להדיא מהגמי"י וסה"ת איפכא דאפילו אינה מרגשת כשהדם נופל מהרחם אלא שבדקה באותו מקום מצאה דם טמאה אם אינה יודעת שמכתה מוציאה דם וזה ברור והכי משמע פשט דברי הפוסקים דאפילו בסתמא צריך שתדע שמכתה מוציאה דם ותו קשיא לי על הרב דמאי ספק ספיקא הוא זה הא איכא למימר מיד דלמא דם נדה כה"ג לא מיקרי ס"ס כלל וכמ"ש בדיני ספק ספיקא בדין י"א וי"ג ע"ש שוב מצאתי בתשובת מהר"מ מלובלין סוף סימן קי"א שכתב על הגהות הרב שיש לפקפק על חלוקי דיניו וכולי האי ואולי כוון למה שכתבתי.

שו"ת נודע ביהודה מהדורה קמא – יורה דעה סימן מז – תשובה להאלוף והמרומם הרב מוה' מאיר אריה נר"ו: קבלתי מכתבו. והנה אם ברור שהמכה מוציאה דם אף שאינה יודעת שדם זה עתה שותת מהמכה תולה במכתה ולא ידעתי למה האריך בזה והדבר מבואר בש"ע בסימן קפ"ז בהג"ה סעיף ה' ושם מבואר דבשעת וסתה או מל' יום וכו' טמאה. ואי ס"ד ביודעת שדם זה עתה שותת מן המכה ואיננו דם נדה ולמה תהא טמאה בשעת וסתה או אחת לל' יום אלא הדבר פשוט דסגי ביודעת שהמכה דרכה להוציא וא"צ לידע שדם זה שותת מן המכה. ואף שיש לדחוק דאף ביודעת עתה שדם זה שותת מן המכה מ"מ חיישינן שגם דם המקור דם נדה ממש שותת עמו ולכך בשעת וסתה טמאה. דפשט לשון רמ"א לא משמע כן והש"ך בס"ק כ"ד כתב בהדיא כן. אמנם מה שרצה מעלתו להתיר מטעם ס"ס ורצה לדחות דברי הש"ך בס"ק כ"ח. הנה דברי מעלתו אינם ברורים בזה ולא אאריך כי דברי הש"ך בלא"ה אינם נראים כי כאן אי אפשר להתחיל תיכף שמא דם נדה כי א"א לדם נדה לבוא כ"א מן המקור וא"כ מתחילה צריך לדון אם הוא מן המקור. וכמו בנמצא צפורן של ארי בגבו של אחד וכמבואר הש"ך בכללי ס"ס דין ט"ו. אמנם אין כוונת הש"ך כאן משום ס"ס שאינו מתהפך אלא כוונתו דשני הספיקות הם שם אחד דבין הוא דם מכה ובין הוא דם צדדים הכל שוה שאינו דם נדה וכיון שאין ספק אחד מתיר יותר מחבירו לא מקרי ס"ס וכמבואר בש"ך בכללי הס"ס דין י"א. זהו כוונת הש"ך כאן בהשגתו על רמ"א: אמנם גם בזה דינו של רמ"א אמת והש"ך לא כיון יפה לרוב טרדת עיונו דכאן אין הספיקות שוים כי הספק הראשון מתיר יותר מהשני כי הספק הראשון הוא שמא הוא דם צדדים ואז האשה טהורה והדם טהור. והספק השני ואת"ל מן המקור שמא הוא דם מכה אז אף שהאשה טהורה לבעלה מ"מ הדם טמא לטהרות כי קיי"ל מקור מקומו טמא כמבואר בהרמב"ם הלכות מטמאי משכב פ"ג הלכה ט' ואף שאין לנו עתה טומאה וטהרה מ"מ כיון שהדין דין אמת ואילו היה לנו טהרות היה נפקותא בזה שוב אין הספיקות שוים דבדבר קל שיש חילוק בין הספיקות נדחה כלל זה שב' הספיקות שוב אינם שם אחד ועיין בכללי ס"ס דין י"ב גבי בכורות שחישב הש"ך גם נקבה לס"ס הואיל והיה הנפקותא אילו היה זכר הי' בכור ע"ש. ונשאר משה אמת ותורתו של רמ"א אמת דשפיר הוי ס"ס. אמנם כל זה אם המכה במקור עצמו אבל במכה שחוץ למקור בין אם הדם מן

המכה בין משאר מקומות שבצדדים הדם ג"כ טהור כמו האשה שוב לא מקרי ס"ס כלל. ומעתה שגג מעלתו בנדון דיליה שמכת השבירה היא חוץ להמקור לא מיחשב ס"ס דשני הספיקות הם שם אחד.

גם בלא"ה טעה מעלתו בזה דודאי לא מקרי ס"ס רק אם המכה במקור עצמו אבל אם המכה בצדדים אין כאן ס"ס דאיך תאמר ספק מן הצדדים ספק מן המקור ואת"ל מן המקור א"כ שוב בודאי אינו מן המכה שהרי אין במקור מכה כלל וא"כ שוב בודאי דם נדה הוא ואף אם תתחיל להיפך שמא דם מכה ואת"ל איננו מן המכה שמא דם הצדדים הא ודאי לאו ס"ס דאטו אם תסתפק שמא ממקום זה מהצדדים ואת"ל איננו מן המקום הזה שמא ממקום אחר מהצדדים אטו זה יחשב ס"ס והכא נמי המכה עצמה היא מקום אחד בצדדים ומה לי בדם צדדים אם הוא מן מקום המכה או שאר מקומות שבצדדים. ועוד כשתתחיל שמא דם מכה צריך אתה לומר איזה את"ל הנוטה לאיסור קצת שיהיה שייך לספק הספק השני על האת"ל וזה איננו שייך בזה. וזהו פשוט מאוד דבמכה שבצדדים ליכא ס"ס וטעות נזדקר לפני מר. ועוד דמטעם ס"ס אין להתיר רק באשה העומדת בימי טהרתה אבל נדון דרום מעלתו שעומדת כבר בימי נדותה זה זמן רב ואינה יכולה ליטהר בימי לבונה אין להתירה מטעם ס"ס דהרי אז בחזקת טומאה עומדת קודם שטבלה וס"ס אינו מתיר נגד חזקת איסור וכמבואר בש"ך בכללי ס"ס דין כ"ז וכ"ח וכ"ט ושם מסיק שאף הרמ"א מודה בחזקת איסור בשחיטה ולא פליג רק בגף העוף. ונדון דידן לס"ס בשחיטה דומה ממש דהיינו נגד חזקת טומאה ממש. ובמקום אחר ביארתי ימי ליבונה אם מקרי חזקת איסור תליא בפלוגתא של רש"י ותוס'.

ומה שנסתפק מעלתו שכל מה שמיקל רמ"א הוא רק לענין רואה מחמת תשמיש. הנה לענין מה שמתיר רמ"א ביש לה וסת אף שאינה יודעת כלל שמכתה מוציאה דם זה מבואר בש"ך בהדיא בס"ק כ' שאינו מתירה רק שלא הוחזקה רואה מחמת תשמיש אבל טמאה נדה אמנם בחלוקה שניה ביודעת שמכתה מוציאה דם קצת נראה שמותרת לגמרי אפילו באין לה וסת. אמנם מדברי הש"ך בס"ק כ"ד לא משמע כן דאל"כ למה האריך לענין אשה שיש לה וסת דסגי דיודעת שמכתה מוציאה דם אף באינה יודעת שעתה שותת מן המכה ע"ש והרי כבר כתב בס"ק כ"ג לענין אשה שאין לה וסת שאם רק יודעת שדרך המכה להוציא דם דסגי ואטו יש לה וסת שלא בשעת וסתה גריעה מאין לה וסת כלל. אלא ודאי שהש"ך מפרש דברי רמ"א רק לענין רואה מחמת תשמיש אמנם בהא שיש לה וסת ורואה שלא בשעת וסתה מבואר בש"ך בס"ק כ"ד דאף שלא בשעת תשמיש טהורה אם יודעת שמכתה מוציאה דם. ולדידי חילוקים אחרים בדינים הללו ונתבארו אצלי בארוכה וכבר רמזתי לו שבנדון דידן שהיא בחזקת טומאה יש להחמיר יותר. והנה כתבתי לו ראשי פרקים תשובה על דבריו לקיום הבטחתי בעת יצא לקראתי וקצרתי כל מה דאפשר. ובזה שלום.

תלמוד בבלי מסכת נדה דף סו עמוד א – ונאמנת אשה לומר מכה יש לי במקור שממנה דם יוצא – דברי רבי, רשב"ג אומר: דם מכה הבא מן המקור – טמא. ורבותינו העידו על דם המכה הבא מן המקור שהוא טהור.

13.

תלמוד בבלי מסכת יומא דף פג עמוד א – חולה מאכילין אותו על פי בקיאין. אמר רבי ינאי: חולה אומר צריך, ורופא אומר אינו צריך – שומעין לחולה, מאי טעמא – (משלי יד) לב יודע מרת נפשו. פשיטא! מהו דתימא: רופא קים ליה טפי, קא משמע לן. רופא אומר צריך וחולה אומר אינו צריך – שומעין לרופא. מאי טעמא – תונבא הוא דנקיט ליה. תנן: חולה מאכילין אותו על פי בקיאין. על פי בקיאין – אין, על פי עצמו – לא. על פי בקיאין – אין, על פי בקי אחד – לא! – הכא במאי עסקינן – דאמר לא צריכנא. וליספו ליה על פי בקי! לא צריכא, דאיכא אחרינא בהדיה, דאמר: לא צריך. מאכילין אותו על פי בקיאין. פשיטא! ספק נפשות הוא וספק נפשות להקל! לא צריכא דאיכא תרי אחריני בהדיה, דאמרי: לא צריך. ואף על גב דאמר רב ספרא: תרי כמאה, ומאה כתרי – הני מילי לענין עדות, אבל לענין אומדנא – בתר דעות אזלינן. והני מילי לענין אומדנא דממונא, אבל הכא – ספק נפשות הוא. והא מדקתני סיפא: ואם אין שם בקיאין – מאכילין אותו על פי עצמו, מכלל דרישא דאמר צריך! חסורי מיחסרא והכי קתני: במה דברים אמורים – דאמר לא צריך אני, אבל אמר צריך אני – אין שם בקיאין תרי אלא חד דאמר לא צריך – מאכילין אותו על פי עצמו. מר בר רב אשי אמר: כל היכא דאמר צריך אני אפילו איכא מאה דאמרי לא צריך – לדידיה שמעינן, שנאמר לב יודע מרת נפשו. תנן: אם אין שם בקיאין – מאכילין אותו על פי עצמו. טעמא – דליכא בקיאין, הא איכא בקיאין – לא! הכי קאמר: במה דברים אמורים – דאמר לא צריך אני, אבל אמר צריך אני – אין שם בקיאין כלל מאכילין אותו על פי עצמו, שנאמר לב יודע מרת נפשו.

תלמוד בבלי מסכת נדה דף כב עמוד ב – מעשה באשה שהיתה מפלת כמין קליפות אדומות, ובאו ושאלו את אבא, ואבא שאל לחכמים, וחכמים שאלו לרופאים, ואמרו להם: אשה זו מכה יש לה בתוך מעיה שממנה מפלת כמין קליפות, תטיל למים, אם נמוחו – טמאה. ושוב מעשה באשה שהיתה מפלת כמין שערות אדומות, ובאה ושאלה את אבא, ואבא שאל לחכמים, וחכמים לרופאים, ואמרו להם: שומא יש לה בתוך מעיה, שממנה מפלת כמין שערות אדומות, תטיל למים, אם נמוחו – טמאה.

תוספי הרא"ש נדה כ"ב: – לא שהיה ברור לרופאים שהיה לה מכה בתוך מעיה דא"כ אפילו אם נימוחו טהורה, כדאמרינן לעיל הרואה דם מחמת מכה אפילו בתוך ימי נדתה טהורה. אלא אמרו הרופאים אולי אשה זו מכה יש לה בתוך מעיה ויבדק הדבר ע"י הטלת מים, אם נימוחו דם נדה הוא ולא בא מחמת המכה.

טור יורה דעה סימן קפז – כתוב בספר התרומה שאם תרצה להתרפאות צריכה שתתרפא קודם שתתחזק אבל לאחר שתתחזק צריך עיון אם תוכל לסמוך על רפואה לשמש אח"כ אפילו אם הוא רופא מומחה.

ספר התרומה הלכות נדה סימן קז – והשתא אסיקנא אשה שרואה דם מחמת תשמיש מותרת עוד לשמש עדיי' ראתה מחמת פעם שנייה לאחר שתטהר מחמת תשמיש מותרת עוד פעם

שלישית ואם עדיין ראתה מחמת תשמיש לפי' רבינו שלמה אסורה לשמש עוד לבעל ראשון ואפי' בבדיקת הכנסת מכחול בשפופרת אבר כיון שהוחזקה לו בשלשה פעמים. וגם יכולה למצא היתר לעצמה להתגרש ולינשא לשני בלא בדיקה אבל לפי הפשט כמו שמפרש מורי רבי' מותרת לראשון ע"י בדיקה שתשים שפופרת של אבר באותו מקום ובתוכה מכחול ובראשה מוך אם נמצא דם בראש המוך נתברר הדבר שמן המקור בא ואסורה. ואם לאו נתברר הדבר שמן הצדדין בא ומותרת. אך אם נמצא הדם בראש המכחול שעתה אסורה לראשון אסור' לינשא גם לשני ולא נתירנה מטעם לחוד של כל האצבעות אינם שוות וצריכה להיות עגונה כל הימים כך פירשתי לעיל. והני מילי שרואה מיד לאחר תשמיש או אחר זמן כדי שתרד מן המטה דהוי חיוב אשם תלוי. וכ"ש שנמצא הדם על שלו כשפירש ממנה דכי האי גוונא קרוי רואה מחמת תשמיש. ואסורה לו לאחר ג"פ אבל אחר זמן תשמיש יותר מן הזמן שפי' אינה אסורה לו בכך אפי' פעמים רבות אלא מותר' לו לאחר ז' נקיים ואם יש רופא שסבור לרפאות' לעצור הדם מלבא בתשמיש טוב הדבר לנסות הרפואה לאחר פעם ראשונה או שנייה קודם שהוחזקה אבל לאחר פעם שלישית שכבר הוחזקה צריך עיון אם תוכל לסמוך על הרפואה אפי' הוא רופא מומחה בדבר זה ולשמש אחרי כן פעם רביעית.

תלמוד בבלי מסכת גיטין דף ב עמוד ב – ולרבה, דאמר לפי שאין בקיאין לשמה, ליבעי תרי, מידי דהוה אכל עדיות שבתורה! עד אחד נאמן באיסורין. אימור דאמרינן עד אחד נאמן באיסורין, כגון חתיכה ספק של חלב ספק של שומן, דלא איתחזק איסורא, אבל הכא דאיתחזק איסורא דאשת איש הוי דבר שבערוה, ואין דבר שבערוה פחות משנים! רוב בקיאין הן.

תלמוד בבלי מסכת יבמות דף פז עמוד ב – מדקתני סיפא: נשאת שלא ברשות מותרת לחזור לו, שלא ברשות ב"ד אלא בעדים, מכלל דרישא ברשות ב"ד ובעד אחד, אלמא עד אחד נאמן; ותנן נמי: הוחזקו להיות משיאין עד מפי עד, ואשה מפי אשה, ואשה מפי עבד ומפי שפחה, אלמא עד אחד מהימן; ותנן נמי: עד אחד אומר אכלת חלב, והוא אומר לא אכלתי – פטור, טעמא דאמר לא אכלתי, הא אישתיק מהימן, אלמא עד אחד מהימן מדאורייתא. מנא לן? דתניא: (ויקרא ד') או הודע אליו חטאתו – ולא שיודיעוהו אחרים, יכול אע"פ שאינו מכחישו יהא פטור? תלמוד לומר: או הודע אליו, מ"מ; היכי דמי? אילימא דאתו תרי ולא קא מכחיש להו, קרא למה לי? אלא לאו חד, וכי לא קא מכחיש ליה מהימן, ש"מ: עד אחד נאמן. וממאי דמשום דמהימן? דלמא משום דקא שתיק, ושתיקה כהודאה דמיא! תדע, דקתני סיפא: אמרו שנים אכלת חלב, והוא אומר לא אכלתי – פטור, רבי מאיר מחייב; אמר ר' מאיר, קל וחומר: אם הביאוהו שנים לידי מיתה חמורה, לא יביאוהו לידי קרבן הקל? אמרו לו: מה אם ירצה לומר מזיד הייתי; רישא מ"ט קא מחייבי רבנן? אילימא משום דמהימן, והא תרי בעלמא דאע"ג דקא מכחיש להו אינהו מהימני, וקא פטרי רבנן! אלא לאו משום דאישתיק, ושתיקה כהודאה דמיא! אלא סברא היא, מידי דהוה אחתיכה ספק של חלב ספק של שומן, ואתא עד אחד ואמר ברי לי דשומן הוא, דמהימן. מי דמי? התם לא איתחזק איסורא, הכא איתחזק איסורא דאשת איש, ואין דבר שבערוה פחות משנים! הא לא דמיא אלא לחתיכה דודאי חלב, ואתא עד אחד ואמר ברי לי דשומן הוה, דלא מהימן! מי דמי? התם אפי' אתו בי מאה לא מהימני, הכא כיון דכי אתו בי תרי מהימני, חד נמי להימניה, מידי דהוה

אטבל, הקדש, וקונמות. האי טבל היכי דמי? אי דידיה – משום דבידו לתקנו, אלא דאחר, מאי קסבר? אי קא סבר: תורם משלו על של חברו – אינו צריך דעת בעלים, משום דבידו לתקנו, ואי קסבר: צריך דעת בעלים, ואמר אנא ידענא ביה דמתקן, היא גופה מנלן? הקדש נמי, אי קדושת דמים – משום דבידו לפדותו, אי קדושת הגוף, אי דידיה – משום דבידו לאיתשולי עליה, אלא דאחר, ואמר ידענא ביה דאיתשיל מריה עליה, היא גופה מנלן? קונמות נמי, אי קסבר: יש מעילה בקונמות וקדושת דמים נחתא להו, משום דבידו לפדותו, ואי קסבר: אין מעילה בקונמות, ואיסור בעלמא הוא דרכיב להו אכתפיה, אי דידיה – משום דבידו לאיתשולי עליה, אלא דאחר, ואמר אנא ידענא דאיתשיל מריה עליה, היא גופה מנלן? אמר ר' זירא: מתוך חומר שהחמרת עליה בסופה הקלת עליה בתחלה, לא ליחמיר ולא ליקיל! משום עיגונא אקילו בה רבנן.

בית יוסף יורה דעה סימן קפז – ח: כתב בספר התרומה (סי' קז) שאם תרצה להתרפאות צריכה שתתרפא קודם שתתחזק אבל לאחר שתתחזק צריך עיון אם תוכל לסמוך על רפואה לשמש אח"כ אפילו אם הוא רופא מומחה. כן כתב בסמ"ג (לאוין קיא לט:) גם כן וכן כתב סמ"ק (סו"ס רצג) וזה לשונו צ"ע אם הוא יהודי רופא מומחה אם תוכל לסמוך עליו אם לא וכתבו הגהות מיימוניות בפרק ד' (דפוס קושטא הכ"א) דברי סמ"ג ואחר כך כתבו (שם, ובתשובה סוף איסו"ב סי' ג) בשם ריצב"א שאם אמר הרופא שנתרפאת משמשת על סמך דיבורו אם הוא ישראל כדאמרינן בירושלמי (שבת פ"ו ה"ב) נאמן הרופא לומר קמיע זה מומחה וריפאתי בו שלש פעמים אע"פ שיש לדחות דההוא איירי שידענו שריפא בו פעם ראשונה מ"מ דעתי נוטה להתיר בכל ענין אבל אין בידי להתיר על פי דיבור גוי אפילו ברופא [מומחה לרבים] דלא מרע נפשיה דקרינן בהו אשר פיהם דבר שוא (תהלים קמד ח) ומיהו אם תראה האשה שפסק דם וסתה וראייה שלה ע"י רפואות וניכר שהועילו נראה דיש לסמוך אף על הגוי כי לדבר זה יש רפואה כי ההיא (שם סו.) דהפילה חררת דם ואמר רבי נתרפאה זאת עכ"ל:

תוספות מסכת חולין דף צז עמוד א – סמכינן אקפילא – אע"ג דעובד כוכבים הוא כיון דקפילא הוא לא משקר שלא יפסיד אומנתו.

תלמוד בבלי מסכת בכורות דף לו עמוד א – גמ'. אמר רב יהודה אמר רב: נאמן הכהן לומר בכור זה נתן לי ישראל במומו. מאי טעמא? כל מילתא דעבידא לאיגלויי – לא משקרי בה אינשי.

14.

תלמוד בבלי מסכת נדה דף סד עמוד ב – תינוקת שלא הגיע זמנה לראות, וניסת, ב"ש אומרים: נותנין לה ארבע לילות, וב"ה אומרים: עד שתחיה המכה. הגיע זמנה לראות וניסת, ב"ש אומרים: נותנין לה לילה הראשון, וב"ה אומרים: עד מוצאי שבת, ארבע לילות. ראתה ועודה בבית אביה, ב"ש אומרים: נותנין לה בעילת מצוה, וב"ה אומרים: כל הלילה כולה.

תלמוד בבלי מסכת נדה דף סה עמוד ב – רב ושמואל דאמרי תרוייהו: הלכה – בועל בעילת מצוה ופורש.

הלכות נדה לרמב"ן פרק ג – ז. היה בה מכה תוך אותו מקום והרי הדם שותת, יש מי שהורה שמטהרין אותה אפילו בזמן הזה, ויראה לי שמטמאין אותה שאם היה דם מכתה משונה מדם ראייתה טמאה דין התלמוד, וא"כ פעמים אתה מביא אותנו להקיף ולבדוק בדמים.

ח. אבל האשה שהשתינה מים ויצא דם עם מי רגלים בין מעומד בין מיושב ואפילו הרגישה גופה ונזדעזעה אינה חוששת אפי' בזמן הזה שהרגשת מי רגלים היא זו, ובידוע שאין דם הבא עם מי רגלים אלא דם מכה.

ט. הבועל את הבתולה אפילו היתה קטנה שלא הגיע זמנה לראות בועל בעילת מצוה וגומר ביאתו ופורש, ויושבת שבעה ימים נקיים מאחר שיפסוק הדם כשאר הרואות, מכאן אתה למד שאין תולין במכה שאין לך מכה גדולה מן הקטנה שנבעלה והדם שותת ממנה מחמת הבעילה.

תלמוד בבלי מסכת נדה דף כ עמוד ב – אפרא הורמיז אמיה דשבור מלכא שדרה דמא לקמיה דרבא, הוה יתיב רב עובדיה קמיה, ארחיה אמר לה: האי דם חימוד הוא. אמרה ליה לבריה: תא חזי כמה חכימי יהודאי! א"ל: דלמא כסומא בארובה? הדר שדרה ליה שתין מיני דמא, וכולהו אמרינהו, ההוא בתרא דם כנים הוה, ולא ידע, אסתייע מילתא ושדר לה סריקותא דמקטלא כלמי; אמרה: יהודאי, בתווני דלבא יתביתו!

שו"ת הרשב"א חלק ז סימן קסא – ואע"פ שהבועל את הבתולה ואפי' קטנה חששו להחמיר בדמיה דאסיקנא התם בכולהו בועל בעילת מצוה ופורש ואע"פ שאין לך מכה גדולה מזו התם משום דאיכא למיחש לשמואל דאמר יכולני לבעול כמה בתולות בלא דם אבל כאן דאיכא מכה ממש תלינן. ועוד דבבתולה יש להחמיר לפי שאינה אלא שעה אחת ופעם אחת אבל כאן אם תחוש אף אתה אוסרה על בעלה:

תלמוד בבלי מסכת נדה דף סד עמוד ב – דאמר שמואל: יכולני לבעול כמה בעילות בלא דם.

סדרי טהרה קצג:א – ובאמת על התירוץ הראשון קשה מאד כיון דהא דשמואל לא שכיחא.

תורת הבית עמ' נ' – ובהטיה לא תלינן דמלתא דלא שכיחא הוא.

רא"ש מסכת נדה פרק י סימן א – גמ' אמר רב בוגרת נותנין לה כל לילה הראשונה. וה"מ בלא ראתה. אבל ראתה אין נותנין לה אלא בעילת מצוה ותו לא [דף סה ע"ב] רב ושמואל דאמרי תרווייהו הלכתא בועל בעילת מצוה ופורש סברי כרבותינו דתניא רבותינו חזרו ונמנו שהוא בועל בעילת מצוה ופורש ואע"ג דרב קאמר בוגרת נותנין לה כל לילה הראשונה אליבא דמתני' אמר ואיהו סבר כרבותינו שהסכימו להחמיר בדורות האחרונים. אמר עולא כי הוו רבי יוחנן וריש לקיש בתינוקת לא מסקי בה אלא כדמסיק תעלא מבי כרבא ומסיימי בה הכי בועל בעילת מצוה ופורש ולישנא משמע כי הוו בתינוקת בכל חילוקי בתולות האמורות בפרק תינוקת אפילו בלא הגיע זמנה לראות ולא ראתה בכולן החמירו בשוה ונראה לי דטעם לחומרא זו לא בשביל שנחוש שמא יצא דם מן המקור עם דם בתולים דלמה נחוש בתינוקת שלא הגיע זמנה לראות ואפי'

באשה גדולה למה נחוש הא אמרינן לקמן (סימן ג) דאפי' אשה שהוחזקה להיות רואה מחמת תשמיש אם יש לה מכה תולה במכתה ולא חיישינן שמא יצא דם המקור עם דם מכתה. ואין לך מכה גדולה מזו שנבעלה ויצא ממנה דם בתולים אלא טעם חומרא זו משום דבעילת מצוה לכל מסורה ואין הכל בקיאין בחילוק שיש בין תינוקת שלא הגיע זמנה לראות ובין הגיע זמנה ובין בוגרת ובין ראתה ובין שלא ראתה ועוד משום דחתן יצרו תוקפו הלכך הסכימו רבותינו להשוות כולן וליתן להם דין חומרא שבחומרות.

בעלי הנפש שער הפרישה סימן ג – ואיכא מאן דאמר דהאי דאמרינן בועל בעילת מצוה ופורש לא שנא היכא דבעל ומצא דם ולא שנא היכא דבעל ולא מצא דם, דחיישינן שמא עם צער הבתולים אתא דם החדר שהוא טמא. ואיכא מאן דאמר דוקא היכא דבעל ומצא דם, אבל לא מצא דם אינו צריך לפרוש. ומסתברא לקולא, והוא דבדקה שפיר בבית החיצון ולא חזיא שום אדמימות, מפני שהיא כבדיקת הנדה והזבה כדכתבינן לקמן בשער הבדיקה. ודומה לי כי מפני החומר הזה נהגו מעוכות של בית רבי (יבמות לד ב) שלא יבאו לידי זה הספק בבעילת מצוה.

ספר האשכול (אלבק) הלכות ברכת חתנים דף רטז עמוד א – וההוא דאמ' הרי שהיה טבחו טבוח ויינו מזוג ומת אביו של חתן או אמה של כלה וכו' עד בועל בעילת מצוה ופורש, ואמ' מסייע ליה לר' יוחנן דאמר אע"פ שאמרו אין אבלות במועד אבל דברים שבצנעה נוהג, דמשמע דאי לאו אבלות לא היה פורש והא קי"ל דכל תינוק(ו)ת שנשאת בועל בעילת מצוה ופורש, מפני שדם בתולי' מרגילי' לדם הנדה, שמפני שנרעדת מן הבעילה תחלה היא פורסת נדה דכתיב ותתחלחל המלכה וגו'. ואיכא מאן דמתרץ בהא בריתא דתני בועל בעילת מצוה ופורש משום אבלות, הא לאו אבלות לא פריש. אליבא דמתניתין דתינוק(ו)ת דבית הלל עד שתחיה המכה או ארבע לילות או כל הלילה שלה, דבתר כן החמירו ואמרו בועל בעילת מצוה ופורש [וצריכה] ז' נקיים. ואיכא [מאן] דמתרץ הא דאמרי' הכא פורש משום אבלות הא לאו הכי שרי, באלמנה שהיא בעולה שאינה צריכה לפרוש [אלא] משום אבלות:

שולחן ערוך יורה דעה סימן קצג:א – הכונס את הבתולה, בועל בעילת מצוה וגומר ביאתו ופורש מיד. אפילו היא קטנה שלא הגיע זמנה לראות ולא ראתה, ואפילו בדקה ולא מצאה דם, טמאה שמא ראתה טיפת דם כחרדל וחיפהו שכבת זרע. הגה: ויש מקילין אם לא ראתה דם, (הגהות מיימוני בשם איכא מ"ד). ונהגו להקל אם לא גמר ביאה רק הערה בה ולא ראתה דם; אבל אם בא עליה ביאה ממש, צריך לפרוש ממנה אע"פ שלא ראתה דם (טור וב"י בשם רוב הפוסקים). ובעל נפש יחוש לעצמו שלא לשחוק בתינוקות. וצריכה שתפסוק בטהרה ותבדוק כל שבעה, ולא תתחיל למנות ב עד יום ה' לשימושה. ונוהג עמה ככל דיני נדה לענין הרחקה; אלא שנדה גמורה אסור לו לישן על מטתה אפילו כשאינה במטה, וזו מותר לו לישן באותה מטה, לאחר שעמדה מאצלו, ואפילו בסדין שהדם עליו.

שו"ת אגרות משה יורה דעה חלק א סימן פז – בהוציאו הבתולים ע"י אינסטרומענט אם צריכה לישב ז' נקיים. נשאלתי מאחד כאשר לא היה אפשר לו לבעול ביאה ראשונה מצד שהפתח היה

סתום ביותר והוצרכה לרופא שיפתח את הפתח באינסטרומענט ולהוציא הדם בתולים ואם לא יבעול באותו יום אמר הרופא שיש לחוש שיתדבק עוד הפעם אם יש בזה דין פרישה עד אחר ספירת ז׳ נקיים וטבילה.

והשבתי שמותרת לבעלה ואינה צריכה ז׳ נקיים וטבילה כי הרי דם בתולים הוא בעצם דם מכה ורק במה שיצאו ע״י ביאה אסרו חכמים ולא ע״י הכאת עץ ומאשינקעס (ומכונות). ועיין ברא״ש ר״פ תינוקת ובב״י יו״ד סי׳ קצ״ג בשם הרשב״א מה שתירצו על עצם הגזירה וטעמיהם ליתנהו ביצאו ע״י הכאת עץ וכדומה, ואף טעם ב׳ דהרשב״א דמשום שהיא מכה רק לפי שעה אסרו אין שייך בכאן שיש לחוש שידבקו עוד הפעם וא״כ הוא חשש לעולם שלא יוכל לבעול. אך אף אם לא היה מה לחוש שיתדבקו נמי יש להתיר חדא דטעם זה של הרשב״א אינו להלכה עיין בסד״ט שהקשה ממה שתולין אף במכה שהיא לפי שעה, ועוד דברור דגם הרשב״א יודה שתלינן דלא כסד״ט בדעת הרשב״א ורק הוא טעם נוסף על מה שחששו בביאה לדם חמוד שהוא חשש רחוק משום שהוא לפי שעה אבל ע״י עץ וכדומה שליכא חמוד אין לחוש אף לדידיה. ואף לרמב״ן בהלכותיו סוף ספר בעלי הנפש שסובר שאין תולין במכה כדחזינן שאסרו בבתולים נמי מסתבר שע״י עץ וכדומה מותרת דהרי אין מקום לחוש כלל והוי זה דבר ברור שהוא דם הבתולים ורק ע״י ביאה שקצת ספק יש דלמא היה גם דם מהחמוד רק שיש לתלות אוסר הרמב״ן ויליף מזה גם שאין תולין במכה כיון שיש קצת ספק שמא הוא גם דם נדה אבל לא בידוע שרק מהמכה יצא הדם שבזה לא יפלוג הרמב״ן. ולכן אין לנו אלא מה שמצינו שאסרו חכמים שהוא רק כשיצאו הבתולים ע״י ביאה.

ואם ע״י ביאתו אח״כ ימצא דם עדין יתלה בדם בתולים ויצטרכו לפרוש עד שתספור ז׳ נקיים ועד שתטבול. ואם לא ימצא דם לא יצטרך לפרוש דיש לתלות שכל הדם יצא ע״י מעשה הרופא אף אם יאמר שעשה רק פרצה דחוקה, משה פיינשטין.

שו״ת מנחת יצחק חלק ד סימן נח – בדם בתולים שהוציאו ע״י רופאים. ב״ה יום ב׳ ג׳ דחנוכה תשכ״ג לפ״ק. שוכט״ס לכבוד הרב הגאון המפורסם בכל קצוי תבל סוע״ה וכו׳ כש״ת מוהר״מ פיינשטיין שליט״א, ר״מ מתיבתא תפארת ירושלם בניו – יארק. אחדשת״ה כמשפט לאוהבי שמו, הנני בזה ע״ד מעשה רב אשר בא לידי לפני איזה שבועות, שנשאלתי ע״ז מאברך ת״ח אשר נשא אשה והי׳ פתחה סתום יותר מהרגיל, ולא הי׳ יכול לבעלה בשום אופן, עד שדרשה ברופאים, והוציאו ממנה הדם בתולים ע״י אינסטרומענט (מכשיר), ונתעורר השאלה אם צריכה לישב ז׳ נקיים, משום דם בתולים, וגם אם להאמין לרופאים שלא הגיעו לפי המקור להוציא דם נדות.

(א) והנה באשר שלענ״ד נראה להחמיר, וכן הוראתי להלכה למעשה, ואך אח״ז ראיתי בספרו דמר כהד״ג (חיו״ד סי׳ פ״ז), שהקיל בזה, אבל יש להעיר בכ״ז שכתב כהד״ג, ואבקשו לחזור עוה״פ על פרשתא דא, ולהשמיענו חוו״ד.

ואקדים, שאף שלא מצאתי בפוסקים שידברו בזה להדיא לברר הלכה זו, אבל מכללא דרך אגב, נראה שהי׳ פשוט להם להחמיר, אף בהשרת דם בתולים, שלא ע״י ביאה.

(א) בתשובת נחלת שבעה (סי׳ ס׳), במה שהביא שם דברי הש״ס (נדה י׳ ע״ב), וז״ל ת״ר חזקה בנות ישראל עד שלא הגיעו לפרקן וכו׳ משהגיעו לפרקן וכו׳ ר׳ יהודא אומר אין בודקין

אותן בידם מפני שמעוותות אותם וכו׳ עכ״ל, ופי׳ רש״י שמעוותות אותן, כלומר מסרטין לה בצפורן ומייתי לה לידי ראי׳ עכ״ל, וא״כ ה״ה ומכ״ש דמייתי לה לידי השרת בתולי׳, ואפשר דהיא היא עכ״ל, וש״מ דס״ל לפשיטות דהשרת בתולי׳ ע״י סריטת היד, דינו כמו ראי׳, והיינו כמו משנה אחרונה, הברייתא (ס״ה ע״ב), שגזרו על הבתולים, (ועי׳ בנובי״ת (יו״ד סי׳ צ״ד) דרצונו לומר דעוד בימי רבי נתחדשה גזירה זו, ולפרש כן דברי התוספתא עיי״ש).

(ב) בתשו׳ נוב״י קמא א״ע (סי׳ כ״ב), במה שדן שם, שבזה״ז אין לומר שאינה מתעברת מביאה ראשונה, דאולי הערה בה ולא גמר ביאתו בפעם אחת, ובין כך השיר בתולי׳ ולא הרגיש ולבסוף בעל, וגם שמא מיעך ומשמש בה קודם ביאה ולא הרגיש בהשרת בתולים עיי״ש, דנראה בפירוש דדייק כן, משום דאם הי׳ מרגיש, הי׳ אסור לבוא עלי׳ אח״ז, בין לענין אם הערה בה, ובין לענין מיעך ומשמש בה, דאם כוונתו על המציאות, שהי׳ כן, ואי אפשר לברר לשאול הבעל, הי׳ צ״ל דאינו זוכר ודו״ק (ובנוגע לנידונו שם, הי׳ אפשר להוסיף, עפי״ד מהרי״ל (דף ס׳) שהובא בנחלת שבעה שהחמיר מהר״ש בבדיקות הכלות עד מקום שהשמש דש עיי״ש, והנחלת שבעה כתב דאי אפשר לבתולה לבדוק עצמה באופן הנ״ל, שלא תשיר בתולי׳ באצבע עיי״ש, והביאו בסדרי טהרה (סוסי׳ קצ״ב), ומה״ט כתב באמת בסד״ט (סי׳ קצ״ו ס״ק כ״ג) לחלק בין אפשר ללא אפשר עיי״ש, אבל יתכן דאולי מחמת צניעות החמירה על עצמה, לבדוק יותר, והשירה בתולי׳ בלא ידיעה) וגו׳.

(ט) וכל הנ״ל ליתר שאת, אבל לפי הנראה, שלהלכה למעשה גזרו בדם בתולים, אף אם בודאי אין שם דם נדות, ואף שלא על ידי ביאה, דודאי אם נאמר כסברת כהד״ג, א״כ אף אם יהי׳ כן למשל בספירת ז׳ נקיים, אחר שבא עלי׳ פעם ראשונה ולא הוציא כל הבתולים, ואח״כ ע״י הכאת עץ וכדומה יצאו דם בתולים, יש לתלות במכת בתולים, כמו שתולין בשאר מכה המוציא דם, וא״כ היכא דאנן אומרים דנתגלע המכת בתולים מעצמן, (ולא שייך כ״כ בזה אף סברת החלחול שבא ע״י דחיקה פירצה מבחוץ הנ״ל), ומכ״ש רק בכתם, בודאי הי׳ אפשר לתלות בזה, וכמו שהדין בשאר מכה המוציא דם, לפי המבואר בפוסקים, והרי לפי היוצא מן דברי הטור וש״ע ופוסקים (בסי׳ ק״צ סעי׳ מ״ב), דתולין הכתם בבתולה שדמי׳ טהורין, אפילו בזמן הזה, שאין נותנין לבתולה אלא בעילת מצוה בלבד, אפי״ה תולה בה, לפי שדמים מצויין בה, ועיי״ש בב״ח, שפי׳, דאע״ג דבזמן הזה אם אתה תולה כתם זה בה, אתה מקלקלה לטמאה מחמת כתם זה וכו׳, אפי״ה תולה בה יותר לפי שדמיה מצויין בה עיי״ש, ומוכח שם דאף אם יהי׳ שלא בשעת תשמיש, כגון בזמן ספירת ז׳ נקיים, עי׳ בפרישה שם, ומ״מ היא טמאה, אף דעיקר הטעם שתולין בה יותר מבחברתה, היא מטעם שדמי׳ מצויין בה, היינו דם בתולים, ולא דם נדות שלא ע״י ביאה, ושלא ע״י דחיקת פירצה מבחוץ, ומ״מ גורם לה טומאה, ואמאי לא מטהרינן גם אותה, אף אם יהי׳ ראי׳ ממש, ומכל שכן אם הוי רק כתם, די״ל דמעלמא אתי׳, – ובאמת ראיתי בס׳ טהרת ישראל (סי׳ ק״צ בבאר יצחק אות תק״ה), דהעתיק מספר מלב״ט (בקצר ססק״ד), שכתב בזה״ל, לפי מה שהעלתי (בסימן קפ״ז סק״ט), דכיון דחזינן בקטנה שלא הגיע זמנה לראות ולא ראתה, דנותנין לה עד שתחי׳ המכה אפי׳ זמן רב, אלמא חזינן דמכה זאת יכולה להתגלע זמן רב ולהוציא דם, ואם כן בודאי דחברתה יכולה לתלות במכת בתולים, ואם אמנם, דלכאורה אפשר לומר, דגם היא עצמה יכולה לתלות כתם במכת בתולים, דבשלמא בראתה דם

שייך שפיר לומר דגזרו אבל לא בכתם, באמת זה אינו דהא חזינן, דלדידן אף בקטנה שלא הגיע זמנה לראות ולא ראתה, אעפי"כ צריכה לישב ז' נקיים אחר בעילת מצוה, ולא תלינן במכת בתולים, הרי דלא חלקו חז"ל, ובכל גוונא אם אתה אומר אנו תולין כתם זה במכת בתולים, א"כ שייך שפיר גזירת חז"ל, דברואה דם ממכת בתולים היא טמאה עכ"ל, ועי' שם דמיירי בכתם שראתה בתוך ימי ספירתה, ובראי' כה"ג הי' ניחא לי', ובכתם קשי' לי', ומתרץ שפיר כנ"ל, וא"כ הה"ד ומכ"ש היכא דהוציא הדם ע"י מעשה בפירצה דחוקה, דיש איסור דם בתולים. וכן מוכח להדיא מתשו' פנים מאירות (ח"ג סי' כ"א) וביותר במה שכתב שם, וגדולה מזו נראה לי דאפילו בדקה עצמה בשפופרת וכו', דאז ברור דלאו מן המקור אלא מן הצדדים וכו', אפ"ה טמאה לבעלה, דהא גזרו על דם בתולים שתהי' אסורה לבעלה וכו' עיי"ש, וש"מ דגזרו על דם בתולים, אף בודאי של"ה דם נדות, וגם כתב שם לדחות, דא"א לחלק ולומר, דבמילתא דלא שכיחא לא גזרו עיי"ש.

(י) וכ"ז אף בנודע בודאי, שהרופא לא נגע במקור ע"י האינסטרומענט/המכשיר/, אבל נודע שכמה האריכו האחרונים בבדיקת הרופאי' ע"י אינסטרומענט ונאמנותם, ואף המקילים הקילו רק אם לא נמצא דם, וכתבתי מזה בספרי (ח"ג סי' פ"ד), ובהוציא דם, ואומר שהוא מהצדדים, יש לספק אם הוא נאמן, ואולי כהד"ג לשיטתו בזה במש"כ בספרו (שם סי' פ"ג).

(יא) ובינותי בספרי גדולי האחרונים, ומצאתי שאלתנו בתשו' מהרש"ם (ח"א סי' ר"י), וז"ל וע"ד שאלתו בבתולה שנשאת, והי' רחמה צר מלבוא עלי', והרופא פתח מעט גידי דם בתולים על ידי כלי אינסטרומענט, ויצא דם, אם יש לסמוך ע"ד הרופא, שהוא רק דם בתולים, ולא מן המקור, להקל לענין הפסק טהרה, ומסיק דבנוגע לד' עונות שהקילו ברואה דם בתולים, שהוא רק חומרא בעלמא, יש להאמין להרופא, עיי"ש, הרי, דבנוגע לעיקר טומאת דם בתולים, ע"י מעשה הרופא, פשיטא לי' להחמיר, אם מטעם גזירת חכמים, אם מטעם אי נאמנות הרופא של"ה מן המקור, והקיל רק לענין ד' עונות כנ"ל.

ב אמנם אם ספרה ז' נקיים וטבלה, ואח"כ בעלה ולא מצא דם, בזה שפיר צדקו מאד דברי כהד"ג שם, דלא יצטרך לפרוש, דיש לתלות שכל הדם יצא ע"י מעשה הרופא, – ונראה ראי' לזה, מדברי המהרש"א (כתובות צ"ד ע"א על תוד"ה ובועל), דכתב ויש לדקדק וכו', הא אית בי' משום דם בתולים וכו', ויש מתרצים בזה, דאיירי במוכת עץ וכו' עיי"ש, הרי דבמוכת עץ ליכא משום דם בתולים, וא"כ הה"ד ע"י מעשה הרופא, שוב ראיתי בדרכ"ת (ה' נדה קצ"ה סק"ה), שהביא משו"ת זרע אמת (ח"ב סי' פ"ד) שכתב, דאף במוכה עץ צריך לפרוש בביאה ראשונה, דאף דאין לה טענת בתולים, אבל מ"מ לא כלו בתולי' לגמרי מכל וכל, ואין לה פתח פתוח, כמ"ש התוס' (כתובות ט' ע"א) עיי"ש, ואולי י"ל, דע"י מעשה רופא עדיף וצ"ע.

ג וגם צדקו מאד דברי כהד"ג דאם נמצא לה דם בבעילתו, זה הוכחה שעדיין נשאר לה דם בתולים, ובנדון דפה כן הי', אבל אמרו לי שהרופא אומר שעשה נתוח להרחיב הפתח, והדם הוא מחמת הנתוח.

(א) והנה בנוגע לדם בתולים שיצאו ע"י מעשה הרופאים לשיטתי הנ"ל, דהוי כמו שיצאו ע"י ביאת הבעל, יש לדון, שכמו שהי' הדין בביאת הבעל, דבודאי אף אם חוץ ממכת הבתולים, הי' לה באותו מקום מכה אחרת המוציאה דם, צריכה טהרה, – והי' נראה לפרש בזה, הכוונה,

בחידושי אנשי שם שעה"ג הרי"ף (שבועות פ"ב), שהביא שם הרי"ף, את דברי הירושלמי (והיא שם בברכות פ"ב ה"ו ויש בזה גירסות שונות), בעון קומי ר' יוחנן מהו לתלות בדם המכה ולא אורי, (ועי' בזה במרדכי ובב"ח בתשו' סי' פ"ג), והביא בחא"ש בשם מהר"מ שפי', מהו לתלות ראייתה של בתולה מביאה ראשונה בדם המכה, אם יש לה מכה וכו' עיי"ש, וי"ל כוונתו, דרצונו לומר דלא קאי על נשים דעלמא, שיש להם מכה, ולא על מכת חבורה של הבתולים, כמו שדחקו עצמם המפרשים, וכמבואר בתשו' הב"ח שם, אלא קאי על מכה, אם יש מכה לאשה, (חוץ מכת החבורה), בביאה ראשונה, אם נדון בזה כמו באשה אחרת שיש לה מכה, דתולין הדם בה, או כמו שאין תולין במכת חבורה של הבתולים, כן אין תולין בזה, ואמר דלא אורי להקל, וממילא כן הוא הדין במעשה הוצאת הבתולים ע"י נתוח.

(ב) ואף דיש לדון דשאני ע"י ביאת הבעל, דלכ"פ – וכן הוא לפי ההלכה, – דאפילו לא ראתה צריכה ז' נקיים וטבילה, משום דיש לחוש לשמא חפהו ש"ז [שכבת זרע], עי' (בסי' קצ"ג), וא"כ מכ"ש דלא תלינן בדם המכה, דיש לחוש לתערובת דם בתולים בתוכו, דלא עדיף משמא חפהו ש"ז, משא"כ ע"י מעשה הרופא דבלא ראתה כלל בודאי אין להחמיר, אבל יש לחלק, דבלא ראתה יש הוכחה שלא יצאו הבתולים, ולשמא חפהו, ל"ש במעשה הרופא, ולשמא נאבד, ל"ש רק בחימוד, שהולכת אנה ואנה כמבואר בפוסקים, אבל כאן אין הוכחה שאין כאן תערובת דמים.

(ג) אמנם צ"ע מה יהי' הדין במה שראתה, – אחרי מעשה הנתוח של הרופא – בעת בעילת הבעל, די"ל, דהבתולים כבר כלו במעשה הרופא, ומה שראתה כעת הוא מחמת הנתוח, – ויש להביא לזה, מדברי הפמ"א בתשו' שם, שכתב, ומ"מ יש לצדד להקל באיסור דרבנן, כיון דיש לספק שמא מן הצדדים בא משאר מכה, ולא מדם בתולים עיש"ה. ובנד"ד, הרי נודע דיש לה מכת נתוח, אך לעומת זה שם מיירי אחרי בדיקת שפופרת עיי"ש, וגם מיירי, באופן שאי אפשר לטהר עצמה לבעלה עיי"ש, ע"כ צדד למצוא איזה תקנה, אבל בלתי זאת, כמו בנד"ד, בביאה הראשונה שראתה דם, ומכת הנתוח הוי מכה עוברת, בודאי יש להחמיר, כמו במכת חבורה של בתולים עצמן, אף דכאן לא שייך החילוק של הסד"ט, בטעם ב' של הרשב"א הנ"ל, אבל עדיין שייכים בבעילה הראשונה, איזה מטעמים אחרים, שכתבו הראשונים, שלא לתלות במכת חבורה של הבתולים, וי"ל דהה"ד בצירוף שאר מכה.

(ד) אמנם אח"כ באו הזוג, ואמרו שקשה לה לטהר עצמה, והקלתי ע"י הפסק טהרה ובדיקת יום א' וז' לבד כמבואר בפוסקים, – אבל שוב שאלו, שהרופא אמר להם שבודאי תראה דם עוד בכמה בעילות שאח"ז, מחמת הנתוח, שעדיין לא נתרפאה לגמרי, – ובזה חשבתי, שאולי אפשר למצוא להם תקנה, עפי"ד הפנים מאירות הנ"ל, דמוכח מדבריו, שהחמיר רק מטעם ממ"נ, או דהוי דם בתולים, או דם נדות עייש"ה, אבל בכגון דא, דקרוב לודאי, דאחרי מעשה הרופא, בצירוף בעילה הראשונה, כבר יצא ממנה כל הדם בתולים, ודם זה הוי מחמת הנתוח, אולי י"ל דתולין להקל עייש"ה בפמ"א ודו"ק וצע"ג. ובזה הנני דושת"ה וחותם בכל חותמי ברכות, יצחק יעקב ווייס.

מהרש"א חידושי הלכות מסכת כתובות דף ד עמוד א – תד"ה ובועל כו' קודם שיקבר כו' ודייק לה מדקתני כל אותן הימים כו' מדלא התיר אלא בעילת מצוה כו' עכ"ל פי' לדבריהם דודאי מוכח

לקמן בהדיא בגמ׳ דפורש קודם שיקבר דקאמרינן אילימא דקתני בועל בעילת מצוה ופורש התם משום דלא חל עליו אבילתא כו׳ ומשמע להו דדייק ליה לתלמודא מברייתא מהא דדייק בסמוך דדברים של צנעא נוהג דהיינו מדקתני כל אותן הימים דמשמע דבכל ז׳ ימי המשתה וז׳ ימי אבילות פורש ואוסר אפי׳ בעילת מצוה אלא דבועל בעילת מצוה קודם שיקבר ומרישא הא דבעילת מצוה אסור בימי אבילות לא ה״מ למידק כו׳ ואהא קשיא ליה לרשב״א דמ״מ הך מילתא דדייק לקמן דדברים של צנעא נוהג ברגל דלא שייך ביה בעילת מצוה ה״מ לדיוקא שפיר מרישא מדלא התיר אלא בעילת מצוה ותירץ ר״י דהמ״ל פורש משום דם בתולים כו׳ ויש לדקדק לקמן דקאמר דהוא ישן בין האנשים כו׳ היינו משום דאבילות קילא ליה לעבור הא אית ביה נמי משום דם בתולים דלא קילא ליה לעבור ותהא ישנה עמו כדאמר רב יוסף דמשום נדות לא קילא ליה לעבור ויש מתרצים בזה דאיירי במוכת עץ א״נ באלמנה שנשאת לבחור דעושה שבעת ימי המשתה וליכא דם בתולים והוא דחוק אבל מדברי הרא״ש למדתי בזה לתרץ דאיירי הך ברייתא לפי משנה ראשונה דאין לפרוש משום דם בתולים מיהו ק״ק מאי קא קשיא להו לתוס׳ לקמן דתקשי לרב ושמואל ברייתא דהכא דאימא דרב ושמואל אוקמוה לפי משנה אחרונה ומשום דם בתולים הוא פורש ולית להו הא דרב יוסף דקאמר בפירסה נדה ישנה עמו בבעל ולדברי הר״מ הלוי שכתב הרא״ש בשמו דאפילו לרב יוסף בדם בתולים דקילא ליה כמו אבילות הוא ישן בין האנשים והיא ישינה בין הנשים קשה מאי קאמר מסייע ליה לר״י דאימא משום דם בתולים הוא פורש ולמשנה אחרונה ויש ליישב ודו״ק:

.15

תלמוד בבלי מסכת נדה דף סו עמוד א – דאמר רבא: תבעוה לינשא ונתפייסה – צריכה לישב שבעה נקיים.

פתחי תשובה יורה דעה סימן קצב:ב – בין גדולה בין קטנה – עי׳ בתשובת גבעת שאול סי׳ ס״ה דאף אם היא זקינה ומסולקת דמים צריכה לישב שבעה נקיים ע״ש ועי׳ בתשו׳ מקום שמואל סי׳ ל״ג שנשאל באשה אחת שנתעברה מנואף ואח״כ דברו על לבבו לקחת אותה לאשה וכבר נתעברה ממנו כשבעה חדשים אם צריכה לספור שבעה נקיים או נימא כיון דמעוברת בחזקת מסולקת דמים לא חיישינן שמא מחמת חימוד ראתה והשיב דזה פשוט דצריכה שבעה נקיים וק״ו הוא מקטנה וכ״כ להדיא בספר מנחת יעקב סוף סי׳ זה ע״ש וכמדומה שראיתי כן בתשו׳ הרדב״ז ח״ג.

תלמוד בבלי מסכת נדה דף כ עמוד ב – אפרא הורמיז אמיה דשבור מלכא שדרה דמא לקמיה דרבא, הוה יתיב רב עובדיה קמיה, ארחיה אמר לה: האי דם חימוד הוא. אמרה ליה לבריה: תא חזי כמה חכימי יהודאי!

חידושי הר״ן נדה כ:ד״ה האי – פירשו בו דם חימוד הוא וטהור והקשו על זה מדאמרי׳ בפ׳ בתרא דמכלתין תבעוה לינשא ונתפייסה צריכה לישב ז׳ נקיים כלומר משום דמחמדא אלמא משמע דדם חימוד טמא הוא. אלא ודאי האי דקאמר דם חמוד לא לטהרו אחר כן אלא כדי להראות

חכמתו. ול"נ דאפשר דאי קים לן ודאי דדם חימוד טהור. והאי דצריכה לישב ז' נקיים, משום דאגב חימוד מתעוררים דמיה. ואף על פי שדם חימוד טהור, אפשר שנמשך אף דם נדות עמו.

ספר אור זרוע ח"א – הלכות נדה סימן שמא – אמר רבא תבעוה לינשא ונתפייסה צריכה לישב שבעה נקיים כו' עד אימור דאמר רבא בגדולה דקא חזיא קטנה דלא חזיא מאי א"ל בפירוש אמר רבא בין גדולה בין קטנה גדולה טעמא מאי משום דמחמדא קטנה נמי חמודי מחמדא. פי' רשב"ם ל"ש בתולה שהגיע זמנה ל"ש בתולה שלא הגיע זמנה כדאמר רבא בהדיא בסיפא ל"ש אלמנה ונתפייסה. נתרצית לינשא לבעל וצריכה לישב ז' נקיים קודם חופה שמא מחמת תאוה ראתה דם שכן דרך אשה לחמוד קודם חופה ימים או עשור. ולכלהו אין אנו חוששין אם ראתה דם אם לאו שהרי תוכל לטבול קודם בעילת מצוה. אבל ז' ימים הסמוכין לבעילת מצוה דהיינו ליל ראשון דחופה אנו חוששין שאם תראה בהם דם לא מהני לה טבילה דקודם בעילת מצוה. שהרי צריכה לספור שבעה נקיים. והלכך לובשת בגדים לבנים כל ז' ימים קודם חופה ופורסת סדין לבן במטתה ובודקת פעם אחת או פעמים ביום ואם לא ראתה בהם דם טובלת בליל בעילת מצוה קודם בעילה שמא ראתה דם שנה או שנתים בימי בתולי' ולא טבלה ומיטהרת עכשיו בטבילה זו ואם לא שמרה ז' נקיים קודם לכן לא תיבעל בליל ראשון עד שתשמור ז' נקיים מליל ראשון ואילך שמא ביום שלפני החופה ראתה דם מחמת חימוד עכ"ל. ונראה בעיני דאע"ג דפ' רבינו שמואל דבודקת פעם אחת או פעמים ביום. דהיינו דוק' לכתחלה מיהו אם לא בדקה כ"א ביום ראשון ויום שביעי נמי טהורה כדתנן פ' תינוקת הזב והזבה שבדקו עצמן ביום ראשון ומצאו טהור וביום השביעי ומצאו טהור ובשאר כל הימים לא בדקו ר' אליעזר אומר הרי הן בחזקת טהרה ר' יהושע אומר אין להם אלא יום ראשון ויום שביעי בלבד. וקיי"ל פ"ק דהלכה כר"א אפי' זבה וודאית כש"כ נשי דידן האידנא דספק נדות וספק זיבות נינהו. והיכא שבדקה עצמה יום ראשון ויום השמיני ומצאת טהור' ושאר הימים לא בדקה איפליגו פרק תינוקת ואמר רב היא היא דכמו שהתיר ר' אליעזר כשבדקה בשביעי ה"נ בשמיני. ור' חנינא אמר תחלתן וסופן בעינן והכא תחלתן איכא וסופן ליכא. ונראה בעיני שהלכה כרב. ואפי' תמצא לומר שהלכה כר' חנינא. ה"מ בזבה ודאית. אבל הכא ספק זבה וספק נדה. ואת"ל ספק זבה סתרה ספק [נדה] לא סתרה ותו הואיל דשביעי ושמיני מצאת טהור רגלים לדבר שכולם טהורים הם ושפיר משתרייא לר"א דקיי"ל כוותי' דלא בעי ספורים לפנינו. ומזה הטעם נמי נראה בעיני דהלכה כרב אם לא בדקה כ"א בשביעי ומצאת טהור שטהורה לבעלה דאמר רב ששת אמר ר' ירמי' בר אבא אמר רב נדה שהפרישה בטהרה בשלישי שלה סופרתו למנין שבעה נדה ספורין למה לה. אלא אימא זבה שהפריש' בטהרה בשלישי שלה סופרתו למנין שבעה. א"ל רב ששת לר' ירמי' בר אבא רב ככותאי אמר לשמעתי' דאמרי יום שפסקה בו סופרתו למנין שבעה א"ל כי קאמר רב לבד מיום ג' פשיטא לא צריכא כגון דלא בדקה עד יום שביעי ואשמעינן התם תחלתן אע"פ שאין סופן קמ"ל הכא סופן אע"פ שאין תחלתן דסד"א תחלתן אע"פ שאין סופן הוא דאמרי' דאוקמי' אחזקתי' אבל סופן אע"פ שאין תחלתן לא קמ"ל. ונראה בעיני דהלכה כרב מטעם ספק ספיקא כדפי'. וכן הוא האמת כמו שפירש רשב"ם דגם אלמנה שנתפייסה לינשא צריכה לישב שבעה נקיים. דהא נמי מחמדא אע"פ שהי' נבעלה כבר. וראי' לדבר דאמר בהחולץ רב

כי איקלע לדרשיש אמר מאן הויא ליומא ורב נחמן כי מקלע לשכנציב אמר מאן הויא ליומא. ופריך והאמר רבא תבעוה לינשא צריכה ז׳ נקיים. ואי ס״ד דבאלמנה לא מחמדא שכבר נבעלה לישני לה שהיו מכריזין בעבור האלמנה שאינה מחמדת אלא מדלא שני הכי ש״מ דאלמנה נמי מחמדת. וחזינא בהלכה בשמעתין דדם חימוד טמא הוא. הלכך הא דס״פ כל היד דההיא איתתא דאתאי דם לקמי׳ דר׳ אלעזר הוה יתיב ר׳ אמי קמי׳ א״ל האי דם חימוד הוא וכו׳ אין לפרש דם חימוד וטהור. דא״כ תקשי מהכא אלא חכמתו יתירה אתא לאשמועינן וכן פי׳ רשב״ם התם. ואת״ל דהא דא״ל ר׳ אלעזר לר׳ אמי האי דם חימוד הוא דה״ק דם חימוד וטהור אז יש לך לפרש טהור מדאורייתא וטמא מדרבנן והכא מדרבנן: פ׳ תינוקת רבינא איעסק לי׳ לברי׳ בי רב חביבא א״ל סבר מר למכתב כתובה לארבע׳ א״ל אין כי מטא לארבע׳ א״ל ננטר מר עד ארבעה אחריני א״ל מ״ט עביד מר הכי א״ל לא סבר לה מר להא דרבא דאמר תבעוה לינשא ונתפייסה צריכה לישב ז׳ נקיים. פי׳ רשב״ם כי מטא ההוא יומא שהי׳ להם לכתוב כתובה אמר לי׳ לרבינ׳ לינטר מר עד ארבע׳ אחרינא עד יום רביעי בשבת אחרת מיום רביעי זה עד שבעה ימים וההוא יום רביעי לכתוב כתובה כדין בתול׳ הנשאת ליום הרביעי א״ל רב חביבא לרבינא לא סבר לה מר להא דאמר רבא כו׳ בתמי׳ ובתולה זו שתנשא לבנך שכחה ולא שמרה ז׳ נקיים קודם יום זה ושמא אתמול ראתה ולא מהניא טבילה דהשתא לבעול לאורתא הלכך לינטר מר עד ארבעי אחריני ותתן אל דעתה ותשב ז׳ נקיי׳ ותיבעל בליל ראשון של חופה כמשפט הבתולו׳ להכנס בליל ראשון לחופתן עכ״ל. משמ׳ לכאור׳ מהכא שאין לאדם להכניס נדה וצריך להמתין עד שתטהר כדי שיוכל לכונסה [ואמרי׳ פ״ק דכתובות הגיע זמן בא׳ בשבת מתוך שאינו יכול לכונסה לפיכך כו׳ או שפירסה נדה] אינו מעלה לה מזונות פי׳ שאינו יכול לבוא עליה ומדנקט שאינו יכול לכונסה משמע שלכתחלה לא יכנוס נדה עד שתטהר מפני שצריך לבעול בעילת מצוה בליל חופתה. ואמר פ״ק דכתובות והלכתא דמותר לבעול לכתחלה בשבת. ורבינו משה ב״ר מיימון זצ״ל כתב לא תנשא נדה עד שתטהר ואין מברכין לה ברכת חתנים עד שתטהר. ואם עבר ונשא וברך אינו חוזר ומברך עכ״ל. ואמר בפ׳ האומר בקידושין מה אחות אשה לא תפסי בה קידושין אף כל עריות לא תפסי בה קידושין. ופרכי׳ א״ה אפי׳ נדה נמי אלמה אמר אביי הכל מודים הבא על הנדה ועל הסוטה שאין הולד ממזר אמר חזקיה א״ק ותהי נדתה עליו אפי׳ בשעת נדתה תהא בה הויה והיינו משמע דיעבד תפסי בה קידושין אבל לכתחלה אין לקדשה ולא לכונסה עד שתטהר. מיהו היכא שכבר הכינו צרכי הסעודה ופירסה נדה. ה״ז כונסה לכתחלה ומקדשה ומקבלת הטבעת מידו דכיון דעדיין לא נתקדשה ואינ׳ מותרת לבוא עלי׳ לית לן בה אם יגע בידה. וכמדומה אני שכך הורה מורי רבינו שמחה ועבד עובדא בנפשי׳. וכתב בשאילתות דרב אחאי גאון ובתר דמפיק סדר בתולין מחייבין לברך ברוך א״י אמ״ה אשר צג אגוז בגן עדן שושנת עמקים בל ימשול זר במעין חתום ע״כ אילת אהבים שמרה בטהרה חוק לא הפירה ברוך אתה ה׳ הבוחר בזרעו של אברהם:

ט״ז יורה דעה סימן קצב ס״ק א – (א) שמא מחמת חימוד כו׳. כתב הרב המגיד בפרק (ט׳) [י״א] דהלכות א״ב דזו היא מדרבנן דהם החמירו בגזירה זאת ומן התורה מותרת גמורה שהרי אפילו ראתה בלא הרגשה מן התורה אינה טמאה כ״ש זו שלא מצאה אפילו כתם כו׳ עכ״ל ובזה ניחא

לי הא דאיתא פ"ק דסוטה גבי תמר ותשב בפתח עינים שנתנה עינים לדבריה שאמרה ליהודה טהורה אני מנדה וכן מצינו ברות שנכנסה למטתו של בועז אחר שטבלה וקשה הא צריכים שבעה נקיים אחר שנתפייסו ביחד לישא זה את זו ולפי מה שכתבתי ניחא דעדיין לא היתה גזרה זאת אלא דצ"ע כיון שהיא מדרבנן היכן מצינו שחידשו גזירה זו אי בההיא דרבא דאמר תבעוה לינשא ונתפייסה צריכה לישב שבעה נקיים ורבא הוא שהמציא חומרא זו בימיו קשה מההיא דפרק החולץ רב כי איקלע לדרדשיר אמר מאן בעי' למיהוי איתתא ליומא ופרכינן עליה והא אמר רבא תבעוה לינשא ונתפייסה צריכה לישב כו' מאי פריך הא נתחדשה חומרא זאת בימי רבא ונראה לי דבאותה שעה שגזרו חכמים על הכתמים כדאיתא ריש סימן ק"צ ולא התירו בשביל שלא הרגישה נעשה גם גזירה זאת ואין מועיל לה מה שלא הרגישה כנ"ל: ועוד נראה לתרץ דגבי תמר ורות לא היה חשש שמא תראה מחמת חימוד דמיד שנתפייס יהודה ובועז אז היו עמהם במטה והוי ליה כמי שיש לו פת בסלו מה שאין כן בשאר כלה:

רמב"ם הלכות איסורי ביאה פרק יא הלכה ט והלכה י – יתר על זה כל בת שתבעוה להנשא ורצתה שוהה שבעת ימים נקיים מאחר שרצתה ואחר כך תהיה מותרת להבעל, שמא מחמודה לאיש ראתה דם טיפה אחת ולא הרגישה בה, בין שהיתה האשה גדולה בין שהיתה קטנה צריכה לישב ז' נקיים מאחר שרצתה ואחר כך תטבול ותבעל. השגת הראב"ד: כל בת שתבעוה להנשא וכו'. כתב הראב"ד ז"ל א"א, כל ראתה שהוא מוזכר בכאן טעות גדולה מן הסופר שאפילו בלא הרגשה היא טמאה ודאי והאי ראתה רצתה היא, עכ"ל.

וכל הדברים האלו חומרא יתירה שנהגו בה בנות ישראל מימי חכמי הגמרא ואין לסור ממנה לעולם, לפיכך כל אשה שרצתה כשתבעוה להנשא לא תנשא עד שתספור ותטבול ואם נשאת לתלמיד חכם מותרת להנשא מיד ותספור מאחר שנשאתו ותטבול, שתלמיד חכם יודע שהיא אסורה ונזהר מזה ולא יקרב לה עד שתטבול. השגת הראב"ד:ואם נשאת לת"ח וכו'. כתב הראב"ד ז"ל א"א מה שחילק זה בין ת"ח לשאר בני אדם הוציא אותו ממה שאמרו כי מיקלע רב נחמן לשכנציב הוה אמר מאן הויא ליומא ואקשו עליה מדרבא תבעוה לינשא ונתפייסה ושני דמודע לה מעיקרא והדר אקשי ליה מדראב"י כל הנושא אשה במקומות הרבה על זה נאמר ומלאה הארץ זמה ושני ליה רבנן קלא אית להו ואבע"א רבנן יחודי בעלמא הוא דמייחדי להו והוא סובר שמתייחדין היו עמהן אחר נישואין ולא בועלין, ואני איני אומר כן אלא כיון שהנשים היו מיוחדות להם ולכשירצו ישאום פת בסלו הוא ואתרתי קושייתא קא מתרץ לה והא מעשה דבריה דרבינא בי רב חביבא צורבא מרבנן הוה וחש ליה לדרבנן ועוד חופה דאיסורא היכי הוו עבדי וכלה שפירסה נדה אסור להתייחד עמה עכ"ל.

רא"ש מסכת נדה פרק י סימן ד – אמר רבא תבעוה להנשא ונתפייסה צריכה לישב שבעה נקיים לא שנא גדולה ולא שנא קטנה. דחיישינן שמא מחמת חימוד ראתה טיפת דם כחרדל ולא הרגישה בו. וצריכה לישב ז' נקיים חוץ מן יום התביעה. ויש מן הגדולים שכתבו שאינה צריכה לא הפסק טהרה ולא בדיקה כלל בימי הספירה לא בתחלתן ולא בסופן. אלא כל שהמתינה ז' נקיים בתר התביעה הרי היא טובלת וטהורה. שהרי זו לא ראתה כלום אלא חשש ראייה בעלמא. ולא הוחזקה מעיינה פתוח להצריכה בדיקה. וסעדו את דבריהם מעובדא דרבינא. דאיעסק

לבריה בי רב חביבא ואמר ליום פלוני נכתוב כתובה. ואיעכב שבעה יומי בתר ההוא יומא. ואתא ואמר ליה מאי טעמא עבד מר הכי. ואז אמר לו מאי טעמא עבד מר הכי. ורב חביבא לא צוה לבדוק את בתו כי היה סבור דרבא לא אמר אלא בגדולה אבל בתו שהיתה קטנה לא היתה צריכה לישב ז׳ נקיים ואעפ״כ כנסה. ואינה ראייה כלל דא״כ אפי׳ ישיבת ז׳ אין כאן כלל ומה תועלת יש בהמתנת שבעה ימים. כיון דרב חביבא סבר דבקטנה לא חיישינן לחימוד. אלא ה״ג בסיפרי אשכנז אמר ליה לכתוב כתובה אמר ליה לינטר מר עד ארבע אחרינא. אמר ליה אמאי א״ל לא סבר לה מר להא דרבא תבעוה לינשא וכו׳ והודיעו שאין חילוק בין קטנה לגדולה. ואז הפריש בתו כל שבעה קודם החופה. ויש מן הגדולים שכתבו שאינה צריכה הפסק טהרה אבל בדיקה כל שבעה צריכה. ולדעתם אני מסכים דחיישינן בכל יום שמא תראה. דיותר שהיא קרובה לזמן החופה יותר לבה הומה ומשתאה. ותדיר חיישינן שמא מחמת חימוד תראה. ולכך הזכיר רבא בדבריו ז׳ נקיים לא מחמת חומרא דרבי זירא אלא אפי׳ קודם שנהגו חומרא דרבי זירא. דבימי רבא לא פשטה חומרא דרבי זירא בכל מקום. כדקאמר ליה רבא לרב פפא אמינא לך איסורא ואת אמרת לי מנהגא היכא דאחמור אחמור והיכא דלא אחמור לא אחמור. אלא שבעה נקיים דקא אמר רבא שיהו נקיים בבדיקה. דבכל יום חיישנן שמא מחמת חימוד תראה:

תורת הבית עמ׳ ס״ג – תבועה לינשא ונפייסה כיצד. גרסינן בפרק תינוקת אמר רבא תבעוה לינשא וניפייסה צריכה לישב שבעה נקיים. פירוש שמא חמדה ומחמת חמודה ראתה ואפילו לא הרגישה, ולא עוד אלא אפילו בדקה ומצאה טהורה חוששין שמא ראתה דם טיפה כחרדל ונאבדה. וצריכה לישב שבעה נקיים חוץ מיום התביעה.

שולחן ערוך יורה דעה סימן קצב סעיף ב – שבעת ימים הללו מונים אותה משעה שהיא סומכת בדעתה ומכינה עצמה לחופה, אף על פי שלא נתקדשה עדיין. הגה: ויש לסמוך הטבילה סמוך לבעילת מצוה בכל מה דאפשר, (כך משמע במרדכי בשם רשב״ם ור״מ ורוקח בשם אביו ורבותיו ובהגהת מיימוני פי״א דהלכות א״ב), והמנהג לטבול הכלה ליל ד׳ אף על פי שלא תבעל קודם מוצאי שבת (מרדכי שם), אבל אין להרחיק הטבילה מן הבעילה יותר מזה. ואם לא תבעל במוצאי שבת, יש לה לבדוק עצמה בכל יום עד בעילת מצוה, (שם ובהגה ובתוספות פ״ק דיומא דף י״ח), ודוקא לכתחלה, אבל בדיעבד אין להחמיר אם בדקה רק פעם אחת תוך ז׳ (ב״י). ד וכל חתן ישאל לכלה קודם שיגע בה, אם שמרה ז׳ נקיים, (הג״ה ש״ד).

תלמוד בבלי מסכת כתובות דף ב עמוד א – בתולה נשאת ליום הרביעי, ואלמנה – ליום החמישי; שפעמים בשבת בתי דינין יושבין בעיירות, ביום השני וביום החמישי, שאם היה לו טענת בתולים היה משכים לבית דין.

שולחן ערוך יורה דעה סימן קצב סעיף א – תבעוה לינשא ונתפייסה, צריכה לישב שבעה נקיים, בין גדולה בין קטנה, ואפילו בדקה עצמה בשעת תביעה ומצאה טהורה, שמא מחמת חימוד ראתה טיפת דם כחרדל ולא הרגישה בו. ומונה ז׳ ממחרת יום התביעה ואינה צריכה הפסק טהרה, שאף על פי שלא בדקה ביום התביעה להפסיק בטהרה, מונה מיום המחרת ז׳ נקיים.

ומיהו צריכה בדיקה תוך ז׳ כל יום לכתחלה (ב״י בשם הרא״ש וב״ח שג״כ דעת רמב״ן), מיהו בדיעבד אם לא בדקה עצמה רק פעם אחת תוך ז׳ סגי) (ב״י והאחרונים).

ש״ך על שולחן ערוך יורה דעה סימן קצב סעיף א – ב ומיהו צריכה כו׳ – ז״ל בית יוסף ולדעת הרא״ש לכתחלה מיהא צריכה לבדוק בכל יום מהז׳ ומיהו בדיעבד בפעם אחת שבדקה תוך שבעה סגי דלא עדיפא מרואה ודאית עכ״ל, ונראה דר״ל דלא עדיפא מרואה ודאית דס״ל להרא״ש לקמן סימן קצ״ו דסגי בדיעבד בבדקה פעם אחת תוך ז׳ ולפי זה לדידן דקי״ל התם סעיף ד׳ דלא סגי אלא בבדקה ביום א׳ וביום ז׳ ה״ה הכא אבל אין נראה כן דעת הרב והאחרונים אלא נראה דסבירא ליה דהכא כיון דלא ראתה ודאי עדיף טפי:

.16

תלמוד בבלי מסכת כתובות דף ד עמוד א – דרש רב יוסף בריה דרבא משמיה דרבא: ל״ש אלא שלא בעל, אבל בעל – אשתו ישנה עמו. והא הכא דבבעל עסקינן, וקתני: הוא ישן בין האנשים והיא ישנה בין הנשים! כי קאמר – אפירסה אשתו נדה. הא וכן קתני! הכי קאמר: וכן מי שפירסה אשתו נדה ולא בעל, הוא ישן בין האנשים ואשתו ישנה בין הנשים.

דברים פרק יג פסוק ז – כי יסיתך אחיך בן אמך או בנך או בתך או אשת חיקך או רעך אשר כנפשך בסתר לאמר נלכה ונעבדה אלהים אחרים אשר לא ידעת אתה ואבתיך:

תלמוד בבלי מסכת עבודה זרה דף לו עמוד ב – ייחוד דבת ישראל דאורייתא היא! דאמר ר׳ יוחנן משום ר״ש בן יהוצדק: רמז לייחוד מן התורה מנין? שנאמר: (דברים יג) כי יסיתך אחיך בן אמך, וכי בן אם מסית, בן אב אינו מסית? אלא, בן מתייחד עם אמו, ואין אחר מתייחד עם כל עריות שבתורה! ייחוד דאורייתא דאשת איש, ואתא דוד וגזר אפי׳ אייחוד דפנויה, ואתו תלמידי בית שמאי ובית הלל גזור אפי׳ אייחוד דעובדת כוכבים.

רמב״ם הלכות אישות פרק א הלכה ה – כל שאסר ביאתו בתורה וחייב על ביאתו כרת והן האמורות בִפרשת אחרי מות הן הנקראין עריות וכל אחת מהן נקראת ערוה כגון אם ואחות ובת וכיוצא בהן.

רמב״ם הלכות איסורי ביאה פרק ד הלכה א – הנדה הרי היא כשאר כל העריות המערה בה [בין כדרכה בין שלא כדרכה] חייב כרת ואפילו היתה קטנה בת שלש שנים ויום אחד כשאר עריות שהבת מתטמאה בנדה ואפילו ביום לידתה, ובת עשרה ימים מטמאה בזיבה ודבר זה מפי השמועה למדו שאין הפרש בין גדולה לקטנה לטומאת נדות וזבות.

ספר הישר (חלק התשובות) סימן פ – א. (בענין נדה אי מקרי ערוה). מתוך דבריך אחי ר׳ אפרים למדנו בארבעה אתה עוסק. ואם על ארבעה לא אשיבך על חמש אנו מפרשים, מה אחות אשה מיוחדת שהיא ערוה (יבמות דף ג׳ ע״ב) לאפוקי נדה. אע״ג דכתיב בה אל אשה בנדת דותה לא תקרב לגלות וכו׳ אין התלמוד קורא ערוה אלא דלא תליא ביומי וטבילה. וכן אין דבר שבערוה

פחות משנים אין חזקת נדה בכלל ולא ספירתה תדע דכי יליף בפ' האומר לחברו (קידושין דף ס"ז ע"ב) מאחות אשה במה מצינו מפרש מה אחות אשה מיוחדת שהיא ערוה וכו' וכי יליף מהיקשא דר' יונה אינו מזכיר ערוה דאין משיבין על ההיקש, ואההוא פריך אפילו נדה נמי, אבל על מה מצינו מפרש מה אחות אשה מיוחדת שהיא ערוה וכו' ולא פריך מנדה כלל. ועוד תימא מ"ט יליף ממה מצינו לילף מהיקשא דר' יונה, אלא ע"כ למעוטי נדה דאם כן לכתוב לצרור גבי נדה דקילא דגבי לא תקח דאשה אל אחותה ליכא למימר א"כ יכתב לא יקח אצל נדה כדמקשה אני דתפסי בה קידושי. ותמה אני למה שאלת על דרב יהודה, וכי דרב יהודה עדיפא מדרשא דריש מכילתין. ועוד פריך מהיקשא דר' יונה לדבריך ותיתי נדה. ושגגתו חטאת אגב ריהטא דזדונו כרת, אבל בע"כ במיוחדת שהיא ערוה לא נקט בכדי. וכל היקש דהאומר לחברו הייתי נותן כאן בעל כרחך דלא תפשי בה קידושי ולא תלי ביומי וטבילה אם הייתי צריך, אך איני חושש להזכיר [ממזר מגו] דברי ר' יהושע. ועוד שאני מראה לך שלא דקדקת בריש מכילתין. ודרב יהודה הכי איתא כל יבמה שאין אני קורא בה בשעת נפילה יבמה יבא עליה מחמת איסור הדוחה יבום הרי היא כאשת אח שיש לו בנים, שהוא איסור הדוחה יבום. תדע דבדינא הבא על יבמתו (יבמות דף נ"ד ע"א) דכל עצמו מנדה, לא קאמר מיוחדת שהיא ערוה כדקאמר בהאומר לחברו אע"ג דתלמודא קאמר לתרוויהו והא דמייתינן דרב יהודה בפ' ב"ש (יבמות דף קי"א ע"ב) גבי קטן להקים לאחיו שם בישראל ופריך ואימא ה"נ, דההוא קטן דומה לאיסור אחות אשה שיש לה היתר לאחר זמן ומשעה שנאסרה אין לה היתר, וכן קטן משעה שנולד אין לו היתר באשת אחיו אפילו ימות אחיו ישנו בצרת צרה ודומה לעריות כגון אחות אשה, אבל נדה יש לה היתר כל שעה שטובלת אם היה מת אחיו. ואינה דומה לשום ערוה דאין שום ערוה ליומא אם היתה נופלת לייבום לבו ביום.

תוספות מסכת סוטה דף ז עמוד א – נדה שהיא בכרת בעלה נאמן עליה – תימה דמשמע בפרק אין מעמידין (ע"ז דף לו:) דיחוד דעריות דאורייתא אם כן יחוד דנדה מנלן דשרי ויש לומר דוקא יחוד דעריות דאין להן היתר דומיא דבן עם אמו אסרה תורה אבל נדה לא.

תוספות מסכת סנהדרין דף לז עמוד א – התורה העידה עלינו סוגה בשושנים – לענין דם נדות נדרש כשאומרת דם כשושנה אדומה ראיתי מיד פורש וא"ת והא יחוד דאורייתא היא כדדרשינן (לעיל דף כא:) מכי יסיתך אחיך בן אמך והיכי אתא קרא דדברי קבלה למישרי מאי דכתיב באורייתא וי"ל דלא אסרה תורה אלא כעין אמו דלא עבידא דמשתריא אבל נדה סופה ליטהר ומיהו היכא דלא בעל אפילו נדה אסורה להתייחד כדאמרי' בפ"ק דכתובות (דף ד.) לא בעל הוא ישן בין האנשים ואשתו ישינה בין הנשים וא"ת והא אמרי' בפ"ק דשבת (דף יג.) מקיש אשתו נדה לאשת רעהו מה אשת רעהו הוא בבגדו והיא בבגדה אסור כו' ופי' שם בקונט' משום ייחוד דאשת איש אף אשתו נדה והכא אמר סוגה בשושנים וי"ל דהוא בבגדו והיא בבגדה אסורה באשת איש אפי' בלא ייחוד משום איקרובי דעתה שנהנין ומתחממין זה מזה ויש תימה מ"ש דייחוד דנדה שרייא מסוגה בשושנים והוא בבגדו והיא בבגדה אסרת מהיקש דאשת איש איפוך אנא וי"ל דמסתבר טפי לאסור הוא בבגדו והיא בבגדה לפי שמתקרבין יחד ונהנין זה מזה כדפרישית.

בעלי הנפש שער הפרישה סימן א – אך יש נדה אחרת שהיא צריכה פרישה גדולה מזו והיא הכלה שלא נבעלה ופירסה נדה שהוא אסור להתיחד עמה בלילה, אלא הוא ישן בין האנשים ואשתו ישנה בין הנשים כדאיתא בכתובות בפ׳ ראשון (ד א). ומדקאמר בין האנשים ובין הנשים משמע שצריך להיות בבית אנשים ונשים זולתי החתן והכלה, ומיעוט אנשים שנים ומיעוט נשים שתים. והוא ישן לצד אחד עם האנשים והיא ישנה לצד אחר עם הנשים, נמצא הייחוד הזה חמור יותר מיחוד של אשת איש שהיא מתיחדת עם שני אנשים כשרים, וזו אינה מתיחדת עם בעלה עד שיהו שם אנשים ונשים, והטעם מפני שהיא אשתו והיא כלה והיצר מקטרג עליה.

וי״א דלענין יחוד אשה אחרת נמי בכי האי גוונא בעינן טפי, וכי אמרינן (קדושין פ ב) דאשה אחת מתייחדת עם שני אנשים כשרים הני מילי ביום, אבל בלילה לישן עמה בבית אחד אסור עד שיהיו שם שלשה כשרים, מפני שהוא דומה לדרך, דאמרינן (קדושין פא א) לא שנו אלא בעיר אבל בדרך עד שיהו שלשה שמא יצטרך אחד מהם לנקביו ונמצא זה מתיחד עם הערוה. והכא נמי חיישינן דילמא אדנאים חד מינייהו אזיל חד ועביד איסורא, ומסתברא כוותיה. מיהו שמירת נשים לא בעינן כלל, ממעשה (שבת קכז ב) דר׳ יהושע שהלך הוא ותלמידיו לפדות ריבה אחת ובלילה השכיבה תחת מרגלותיו ה.

ושלשה כשרים נמי דאמרינן לענין יחוד, לאו כשרים כי האידנא, דהא אפילו רב ורב יהודה לא חשבו נפשיהו כשרים כדאיתא בקדושין (פא א). מיהו הכא לענין הוא ישן בין האנשים והיא ישנה בין הנשים לא דייקינן בהו בכשרים כולי האי, מפני שהוא שומר את אשתו מהם והיא נשמרת בהם ממנו, הואיל ואין להם רשות להקל בה את ראשם. כך נראה לי.

חזון איש יו״ד צא:ג – ונראה דהאי יחוד הוא מדרבנן דמן הדין התורה העידה עלינו דאל״כ לא היינו מקילין ביום לדעת הר״א, וכן לא היה מקיל התה״ד בהיה יכול לבעול ולא בעל כמש״כ רמ״א, ולפיכך הנוהגים להקל באמה עמה יש מקום אי ננקוט קולא כרא״ש דסגי בחד שמירה וכהמרדכי דחדא עמה סגי, אלא שיש להחמיר עדיין דבלילה צריך שלשה כדאיתא אה״ע סי׳ כ״ב, ולפ״ז א״א למנקט תרויהו קולי דלדעת הרא״ש ע״כ צריך לפרש אנשים שנים ונשים שתים.

רא״ש מועד קטן ג:ל״ו – הראב״ד ז״ל דתרוייהו דוקא שיהו אנשים ישנים עם החתן ונשים עם הכלה ודוקא בלילה אבל ביום מותר להתייחד עמה כשאר נשים ואינו אסור אלא בתשמיש אבל במיני פרישות כמזיגת הכוס והצעת המטה ורחיצת פניו ידיו ורגליו מותר ולא עוד אלא אפילו בחיבוק ונישוק וכיוצא בו מותר ע״כ. ומאד הפליג החכם להחמיר בלילה להצריך שתי שמירות והפליג להקל ביום להתיר יחוד חיבוק ונישוק.

שולחן ערוך יורה דעה סימן קצב סעיף ד – הגה: יש אומרים אם היתה טהורה כשנשאת ולא בא עליה, ופירסה נדה אחר כך, א״צ שימור עוד, (ת״ה סימן רנ״ג והגהות אלפסי), והמחמיר תע״ב (ת״ה שם). ואין לחלק בזה בין בחור לאלמן או בתולה לאלמנה, (רבינו ירוחם נתיב כ״ו). י״א שאסורה ליחד עמו ביום, כמו בלילה, וא״צ להיות שתי שמירות, רק הוא בין האנשים או היא בין הנשים (טור בשם הרא״ש). ואם אינם ישנים בחדר א׳ אינן צריכים שימור כלל, (ב״י בשם

הרשב"א). וי"א דבלילה צריך שתי שמירות, וביום מותר להתייחד, (הראב"ד). והמנהג ליקח קטן אצל החתן וקטנה אצל הכלה, ואין מתיחדין ביום בלא קטן או קטנה.

ש"ך על שולחן ערוך יורה דעה סימן קצב סעיף ד – והמנהג ליקח קטן כו' – וע"ל סימן שמ"ב כתבתי בשם הב"ח דצ"ל שיודעים טעם ביאה ושאין מוסרין עצמם לביאה:

שו"ת תרומת הדשן סי' רנ"ג – שאלה בחרו כנס בתולה והיתה טהורה בשעת החופה וכמה לילמות אח"כ, ומכל מקום לא בעל אותה עד שחזרה ופירסה נידה אסורים הן עוד להתייחד בלי שומר אצלם או לאו? תשובה, יראה דצריך להתיישב בדבר, דבהוראה זו איכא פלוגתא דרבוותא. אחד מן הגדולים הורה לאסור הואיל ולא בעל עדיין כדמשמע לישנא דתלמודא בסתמא, לא שנו אלא שלא בעל כו'. וחד מרבוותא התיר ואמר דמה שאמר הספר דבלא בעל אסור להיתייחד, היינו דווקא היכא דלא הוות חזיא לבעול בתחילת החופה חיישינן דילמא תקיף עליו יצרו, אבל בנדון דידן דחזינן דלא תקיף ליה יצריה באשה זו אפילו בשעת החופה, ולא בא עליה מעולם וראויה היתה לו לא חיישינן לייחדו דידה דודאי לא יעבור דלא תקיף יצריה. והיה נראה להביא סעד לסברא זו מה דשור המועד חוזר לתמותו כדחיזנן דראה שוורים ג' פעמים ולא נגח, אע"ג דאיהו נמי תקיף יצריה ליגח כדאיתא פ' כיצד הרגל (ב"ק דף י"ט:), מ"מ כי חזינן דנח יצריה דיינינן ליה בתם ואל אמרינן דבהא זימנין הוא דנח יצריה והיום או למחר הדר ליה יצריה. ה"נ בנ"ד אע"ג דקים להו לרבנן דבסתם אדם תקיף ליה יצריה באעשה שלא בא עליה מעולם, היכא דחזינן דהאי גברא לא תקיף ליה יצריה דיינינן ליה כמי שנתייחד עם אשתו נידה שבא עליה כבר, ומ"מ המחמיר תבוא עליו ברכה, הנראה לע"ד כתבתי, עכ"ל.

.17

ויקרא פרק יב פסוק ב – דבר אל בני ישראל לאמר אשה כי תזריע וילדה זכר וטמאה שבעת ימים כימי נדת דותה תטמא:

תלמוד בבלי מסכת נדה דף לו עמוד ב – מתני'. המקשה נדה, קשתה שלשה ימים בתוך י"א יום, ושפתה מעת לעת וילדה – הרי זו יולדת בזוב – דברי רבי אליעזר, רבי יהושע אומר: לילה ויום, כלילי שבת ויומו. ששפתה מן הצער, ולא מן הדם. כמה היא קישויה? ר' מאיר אומר: אפילו ארבעים וחמשים יום, רבי יהודה אומר: דיה חדשה, ר' יוסי ור' שמעון אומרים: אין קישוי יותר משתי שבתות.

הלכות נדה לרמב"ן פרק ז אות כ – כ. לא הפרישו בנות ישראל מדם נדה לדם לידה אפילו בתוך ימי טוהר שיש לחוש לקלקול גדול ולטעות, שהרי רוב המפילות אנו מטמאין אותן לפי שאין בקיאות בדבר, והרבה מהן שיושבות מספק לזכר ולנקבה ולנדה מדין תלמוד, ואם תרגיל את האשה להנהיג טהרה בדם הבא בימי טוהר, יבואו לומר שכל שאנו מטמאין אותה לידה יש לה ימי טוהר, וכן יבואו לטעות בספירת זיבתן ולומר כשם שאין דם זה מטמא וסותר בספירה כך היא עולה, והרי הדברים ק"ו אם החמירו בנות ישראל על עצמן שאפי' רואות דם טפה כחרדל

יושבות ז׳ נקיים ולא רצו להוציא עצמן בתקנת ב״ד שתשב ששה והוא כדי שתהא ספירת כולן שוה כל ימיהן ולא יבא לידי טעות, כ״ש שיהא להן לחוש שלא תהא האשה שופעת ומשמשת, לפיכך כל הרואה דם טפה כחרדל אפילו בתוך ימי טוהר תשב ז׳ נקיים כאלו ראתה קודם שתלד, וה״ז בכלל חומר שהחמירו בנות ישראל על עצמן, אע״פ שמקצת מקומות נוהגין קולא בימי טוהר כבר הסכימו הגאונים ועשו סמיכה והחרימו על כל מי שיעשה כן, אלא הרי האשה שרואה בימי טוהר שלה כמו שהיא בשאר הימים שרואה בהן.

רמב״ם הלכות איסורי ביאה פרק יא הלכה ה–ז – וכן כל היולדת בזמן הזה הרי היא כיולדת בזוב וצריכה שבעת ימים נקיים כמו שביארנו, ומנהג פשוט בשנער ובארץ הצבי ובספרד ובמערב שאם ראתה דם בתוך ימי מלאת אע״פ שראתה אחר שספרה שבעת ימים נקיים וטבלה הרי זו סופרת שבעת ימים נקיים אחר שיפסוק הדם ואין נותנין לה ימי טוהר כלל, אלא כל דם שתראה האשה בין דם קושי בין דם טוהר הכל טמא וסופרת שבעת ימים נקיים אחר שיפסוק הדם.

ודין זה בימי הגאונים נתחדש והם גזרו שלא יהיה שם דם טוהר כלל שזה שהחמירו על עצמן בימי חכמי הגמרא אינו אלא ברואה דם שהוא טמא שיושבת עליו ז׳ נקיים, אבל דם שתראה בימי טוהר אחר ספירה וטבילה אין לחוש לו שאין ימי טוהר ראויין לא לנדה ולא לזיבה כמו שביארנו.

ושמענו שבצרפת בועלים על דם טוהר כדין הגמרא עד היום אחר ספירה וטבילה מטומאת יולדת בזוב ודבר זה תלוי במנהג.

רמב״ם הלכות איסורי ביאה פרק יא הלכה טו – וכן זה שתמצא במקצת מקומות ותמצא תשובות למקצת הגאונים שיולדת זכר לא תשמש מטתה עד סוף ארבעים, ויולדת נקבה אחר שמונים, ואע״פ שלא ראתה דם אלא בתוך השבעה, אין זה מנהג אלא טעות הוא באותן התשובות ודרך אפיקורוסות באותן המקומות ומן הצדוקין למדו דבר זה, ומצוה לכופן כדי להוציא מלבן ולהחזירן לדברי חכמים שתספור ז׳ ימים נקיים בלבד כמו שביארנו.

דרכי משה הארוך יו״ד קצד:ג – וכתבו התוספות והמרדכי דף שלא ע״ב והגהות מיימוניות פרק ז׳ דאיסורי ביאה דרבינו תם סבירא ליה דימי לידה שאינה רואה בהן אינם עולין לימי ספירתה וכתבו דלדברי רבינו תם א״כ היה נראה להצריך לכל יולדת ב׳ טבילות קודם שתהא מותרת לבעלה אחת לאחר ז׳ לזכר ואחר י״ד לנקיבה להשלים ימי לידתה שתוכל לספור אחר כך ז׳ נקיים ואח״כ תטבול ומותרת לבעלה דאם לא טבלה קודם הספירה א״כ הכל קרוי ימי לידה עד שתטבול ואין עולין לסברת רבינו תם עכ״ל.

ואף על פי שכל הגאונים וחכמים אחרים חולקים על רבינו תם ופוסקים דעולין לימי הספירה מ״מ כתבתי דעת רבינו תם ליישב המנהג שנהגו קצת שאין אשה טובלת לאחר לידה אלא אחר אבעים לזכר ושמונים לנקיבה אע״פ שאינה רואה בהן שכתב מהרי״ק בתשובותיו שורש קמ״ד שהמנהג רחוק הרבה בעיניו וגם הרמב״ם ז״ל כתב שהוא מנהג מינות וצדוקות וראוי לכופן להוציא מלבן של צדוקים וכתב שם שאפשר שסמכו על פוסק אחד הנקרא תניא שכתב שאפשר שהראשונים החמירו על שמצאו בקעה וגדרו גדר ועל כיוצא בזה שמע בני מוסר

אביך וכו׳ ולכן אין למחות ביד הנוהגים כן הואיל ויש להן על מי שיסמכו עכ״ל. גם באגודה בערבי פסחים סי׳ צו כתב שהוא מטעם גזירה וגדר ובית יוסף כתב בשם הריב״ש אם נהגו זו לגדר ופרישות אע״פ שהוא מותר או מפני נקיות שבאותן הימים דמים מצויין בהן ראוי להניחן על מנהגן ואין מתירין אותו בפניהם אבל אם נהגו כן בטעות מפני שסבורים שאסור מן הדין ראוי להודיען שטועים הם ושהוא מנהג שיצא להן מן הצדוקים כדרך שכתב הרמב״ם עכ״ל. אמנם לי נראה דמדרבינו תם החמירו על עצמן כך דהסמ״ג והגהות מיימוניות כתבו אע״פ שכל הגאונים חולקים על רבינו תם נהגו בצרפת להחמיר כרבינו תם לומר דאין עולין הואיל והדבר יצא מפיו ע״כ ואם כן הואיל ואין עולין ימי הלידה אף על פי שאינה רואה בהן א״כ לדידן שאין נוהגין בשתי טבילות א״כ פשוט שצריכה להמתין מלספור ז׳ נקיים עד אחר ארבעים יום לזכר ושמונים יום לנקיבה ומזו נשתרבב המנהג ולכן אין למחות כלל ביד הנוהגין להחמיר כדעת רבינו תם ואע״ג דלטעם זו של ב׳ טבילות אין חילוק בהן אם הוא תוך שמונים או אחר כך דלעולם היא בנדתה עד שתבוא במים מ״מ אפשר דאותן שנהגו מנהג זה ראו להחמיר כדברי רבינו תם תוך עיקר ימי לידתה דהיינו תוך ארבעים יום לזכר ושמונים יום לנקבה אבל לא אח״כ וכן פסק מהרי״ל דיש להחמיר להרחיק אחר לידה פ״א יום עכ״ל ונראה דמהרי״ל סבירא ליה גם כן הטעם משום גזירה דלפי הטעם שפירשתי צריכה להמתין לספור ז׳ נקיים אחר שמונים יום שדמונים יום אינן עולין לה בנקיים כן נראה לי ליישב המנהג. ומ״מ פשוט הוא דאין להחמיר במקום שמקילין הואיל וכל הפוסקים חולקים על רבינו תם וכן משמע בתשובת תרומת הדשן סימן רנ״ה דאין להקפיד בדבר.

ספר אגודה פסחים פרק י׳ צ״ו – הישובת על דם טוהר אסורה לשמש עד כמה עונה. נראה לי דמשום הכי רגילות נשים יולדות להמתין לטבול וכו׳ ורואות פן ישכחו העונה.

תלמוד בבלי מסכת פסחים דף קיג עמוד ב – והיושבת על דם טהור – אסורה לשמש. עד כמה? אמר רב: עונה.

בית יוסף יורה דעה סימן קצד – ומ״ש ולאחר ל״ג אסורה אפילו אם שופעת מתוך ל״ג לאחר שלשים ושלשה. אפלוגתא דרב ולוי שכתבתי בסמוך אמרינן בגמרא דאיכא בינייהו תו שופעת מתוך ארבעים לאחר ארבעים לזכר ומתוך שמונים לאחר שמונים לנקבה דבהא רב לחומרא ולוי לקולא ואיפסיקא בגמרא בהא נמי הלכתא כרב:

ומ״ש וצריכה לפרוש מבעלה ליל מ״א אפילו אם אינה רואה. בפרק ערבי פסחים (קיג:) היושבת על דם טוהר אסורה לשמש וכמה אמר רב עונה וכתב הרא״ש בסוף פרק המפלת (סי׳ ה) וז״ל ובמקומות שבועלים על דם טוהר צריכים לפרוש ליל מ״א לזכר וליל פ״א לנקבה אפילו לא ראתה דמתוך שהורגלה לשמש כל ימי טוהר ואפילו תראה חיישינן שמא גם עתה תראה ולאו אדעתה לכן יודיענה בעלה שהוא פורש ממנה לילה זה בשביל שכלו ימי טוהר שלה והכי אמרינן בפרק ערבי פסחים היושבת על דם טוהר אסורה לשמש וכמה אמר רב עונה ופירש רש״י לילה אחת כדפירישית ובשם רבותיו פירש לילה ויום וכתב דאין נראה לו פירוש רבותיו דבכל דוכתא אמרינן כדאיתא בנדה (סג:) דעונה אחת הוי לילה אחת או יום גבי פרישת עונה אחת

סמוך לוסתה וגבי מי שהיו גתיו ובית בדיו טמאים (נדה סה:) עכ"ל והם דברי הראב"ד בספר בעלי הנפש (שער תיקון הוסתות עמ' סב) ודחה דברי בה"ג (סי' מב) שפירש שהטעם משום דכיון דנפקא מימי טהרה לימי טומאה הוי ליה כשעת וסתה וכ"כ סמ"ג (לאוין קיא דף לז ע"ד) וספר התרומה (סי' צז) כדברי הרא"ש ממש וסמ"ק (סי' רפז עמ' שיט) סתם וכתב שיש לפרוש ליל מ"א וליל פ"א לנקבה ולא חילק בין מקום שנוהגים לישב על דם טוהר למקום שאין נוהגים ואפשר שסובר כפירוש בה"ג אי נמי לא איירי אלא למקום שנוהגין לישב על דם טוהר וכדברי הרא"ש וסמ"ג וספר התרומה ולא חשש לפרש כן לפי שסמך על מה שכתב סמ"ג אי נמי דמשום דבמקומו היו יושבים על דם טוהר כתב הדין סתם ולא חשש לחלק בדבר:

שולחן ערוך יורה דעה סימן קצד סעיף א – הגה: ולאחר ז' לזכר וי"ד לנקבה, מותרת לבעלה מיד, מאחר שספרה ז' נקיים ולא חזרה וראתה. מיהו יש מקומות שנוהגין שאין טובלין תוך מ' לזכר ושמונים לנקבה, (בית יוסף בשם מהרי"ק שהביא התניא ובאגודה פרק ע"פ ובמהרי"ל), ואין להתיר במקום שנהגו להחמיר (ריב"ש); אבל במקום שאין מנהג, אין להחמיר כלל רק מיד שלא ראתה דם אחר ז' לזכר וי"ד לנקבה וספרה ז' נקיים, מותרת לבעלה (ת"ה סימן רנ"ה). אבל אם חזרה וראתה, אפילו טפת דם כחרדל, טמאה אע"ג דמדאורייתא דם טהור הוא כבר פשט המנהג בכל ישראל שאין בועלין על דם טהור (ב"י ואגור וטור ופוסקים בשם הגאונים), ודינו כשאר דם לכל דבר.

18.

תלמוד בבלי מסכת נדה דף כב עמוד א – בעא מיניה רבה מרב הונא: הרואה קרי בקיסם מהו? (ויקרא ט"ו) ממנו אמר רחמנא – עד דנפיק מבשרו – ולא בקיסם, או דלמא האי ממנו – עד שתצא טומאתו לחוץ ואפי' בקיסם נמי? אמר ליה: תיפוק ליה דהוא עצמו אינו מטמא אלא בחתימת פי האמה. למימרא דנוגע הוי? אלא מעתה – אל יסתור בזיבה! אלמה תניא: (ויקרא טו) זאת תורת הזב ואשר תצא ממנו שכבת זרע מה זיבה סותרת – אף שכבת זרע נמי סותר? אמר ליה: סתירה, היינו טעמא דסותר – לפי שאי אפשר לה בלא צחצוחי זיבה. אלא מעתה תסתור כל ז'! אלמה תניא: זאת תורת הזב וגו' מה זיבה סותרת – אף שכבת זרע סותר, אי מה זיבה סותרת כל ז' אף שכבת זרע נמי סותר כל ז'? ת"ל (ויקרא ט"ו) לטמאה בה – אין לך בה אלא מה שאמור בה – סותרת יום אחד? אמר ליה: גזירת הכתוב היא, זיבה גמורה דלא ערבה בה שכבת זרע – סותרת כל שבעה, צחצוחי זיבה דערבה בה שכבת זרע – לא סותרת אלא יום אחד.

ויקרא פרק טו פסוק כח – ואם טהרה מזובה וספרה לה שבעת ימים ואחר תטהר:

תלמוד בבלי מסכת נדה דף לג עמוד א – בעי רמי בר חמא: פולטת שכבת זרע מהו שתסתור בזיבה? רואה היתה וסותרת, או דילמא, נוגעת היתה – ולא סתרה? אמר רבא: לפום חורפא שבשתא, נהי נמי דסתרה, כמה תסתור? תסתור שבעה – דיה כבועלה, תסתור יום אחד – (ויקרא טו) ואחר תטהר אמר רחמנא אחר – אחר לכולן, שלא תהא טומאה מפסקת ביניהם. וליטעמיך, זב גופיה היכי סתר? לטהרתו אמר רחמנא, שלא תהא טומאה מפסקת ביניהן! אלא

מאי אית לך למימר – שלא תהא טומאת זיבה מפסקת ביניהן, הכא נמי – שלא תהא טומאת זיבה מפסקת ביניהן.

תלמוד בבלי מסכת נדה דף סז עמוד ב – אמר ליה רב פפא לרבא ולאביי: מכדי האידנא כולהו ספק זבות שוינהו רבנן, ליטבלינהו בימָמא דשביעאה? משום דרבי שמעון, דתניא (ויקרא ט"ו) אחר תטהר – אחר אחר לכולן, שלא תהא טומאה מפסקת ביניהן. ר' שמעון אומר: אחר תטהר – אחר מעשה תטהר. אבל אמרו חכמים: אסור לעשות כן, שמא תבא לידי ספק.

רא"ש מסכת נדה פרק ד סימן א – ור"ת פי' דרמי בר חמא לא מיבעי ליה אלא באשה שבא עליה זב. דהא אמרי' (שם) דיה כבעולה ובועלה לא סתר אלא משום דכתיב ביה זיבה. ולא נהירא דהא מקרא נפקא לן לקמן בפרק יוצא דופן (דף מב ב) דרואה הויא. ולי נראה דקשה לפירושו מהא דמיבעיא לן לקמן (שם א) אי רואה הויא מדאחמור רחמנא אבעלי קריין בסיני. ועוד מדפריך (לקמן ד' מא ב) אמילתיה דר' שמעון מקרא דורחצו במים וטמא עד הערב אלמא בכל פולטת איירי. ועוד דקאמר לקמן (ד' מב ב) אפילו לרבי שמעון לא אמרו דיה כבועלה אלא לטמא בפנים כבחוץ. אבל לסתור ולטמא במשהו רואה הויא אלמא דעדיפא מבועלה לענין סתירה והראב"ד ז"ל כתב בתשובה שלא אמרו פולטת שכבת זרע שסותרת אלא לטהרות בלבד אבל לבעלה אינה סותרת. מדאמר לקמן (ד' לז א) גבי קושי דבר הגורם סותר ושאין גורם אינו סותר. ופולטת אינה גורמת טומאה לבעלה אינה סותרת לבעלה. דבריו תמוהים היאך תסתור לחצאין. שעלו לה ימי ספירתה לבעלה וטהורה לשמש ואסורה לטהרות ולקודש ולמקדש. ועל בעיא (ד' לז א) דקושי מהו שתסתור בזיבה דבר המטמא סותר או דלמא דבר הגורם סותר פירש"י וקרי אע"פ שאינו גורם זיבה גורם מיהא טומאת יום אחד הלכך סותר יום אחד. וכן נמי תני (שם) אבוה דרבי אבין מה גרם לו זובו ז' לפיכך סותר ז'. מה גרם לו קריו יום אחד לפיכך סותר יום אחד. ועוד הביא ראיה מדתני (לקמן ד' סז ב) ר"ש אומר ואחר תטהר אחר מעשה תטהר אבל אמרו חכמים אסור לעשות כן שלא תבוא לידי ספק (נדה) אלמא אי לאו חששא דשמא תראה דם לאחר תשמיש משמשת והולכת ואינה חוששת שמא תפלוט שכבת זרע. ולא מסתבר שלא התירה תורה אלא על מנת שלא תתהפך ולא תלך כלל אחר תשמיש כל היום. ובפ' המפלת (ד' כט ב) גבי טועה אמר בעשרים וחד תשמש. ונ"ל שאינה ראיה דפולטת אינה סותרת יום אחרון. דודאי דם בזבה וזיבה בזב שסותרין כל המנין סותרין עד ערב יום ז' אבל פולטת שכבת זרע שאינה סותרת אלא יום אחד אם פלטה אחר שספרה מקצת היום שוב אינה סותרת. דעיקר סתירת שכבת זרע הוא משום דלא מיקרו נקיים. וכיון שספרה מקצת יום וטהרה לבעלה כבר שלמו הנקיים ושוב אין שכבת זרע סותרת. וכן זב נמי שרואה קרי בשביעי. וסעד לדבר מדתנן בפ"ק דזבים הרואה קרי ביום השלישי לספירת זובו ב"ש אומרים סותר שני ימים שלפניו וב"ה אומרים לא סתר אלא יומו כו'. ומודים ברואה ברביעי שלא סתר אלא יומו ברואה קרי אבל אם רואה זוב אפילו ביום שביעי סותר את שלפניו. מכלל שזה החילוק יש בין זוב לקרי שזוב סותר ביום ז' אבל קרי אינו סותר ביום שביעי. אע"פ שיכולני לפרש דה"ק דזוב אפי' בשביעי סותר הכל וקרי אף ברביעי אינו סותר אלא יומו. ומיהו גם בז' סותר את יומו. מיהו מסתבר טפי כדפרישית דמהו שהזכיר ביום הז' היינו משום שיש חילוק בין זוב לקרי בראיית יום שביעי. ושוב מצאתי כדברי בשם

ה"ר יונה ז"ל והביא ראיה מדם נדה דאינו סותר אף לדברי ב"ש דאית ליה שימור באחד עשר כדאיתא בסוף מכילתין. כ"ש קרי שאינו סותר אחר טהרה. ונכון להחמיר כדברי ר"י וכן נוהגין בצרפת ובאשכנז.

שולחן ערוך יורה דעה סימן קצו סעיף י – השבעה נקיים צריך שיהיו רצופים שלא תראה דם בהם, שאם ראתה דם יב אפילו בסוף יום השביעי סתרה כל הימים וצריכה לפסוק בטהרה ולחזור ולמנות שבעה נקיים.

תלמוד בבלי מסכת שבת דף פו עמוד ב – אמר רבי חייא ברבי אבא אמר רבי יוחנן: זו דברי רבי ישמעאל ורבי עקיבא, אבל חכמים אומרים: שש עונות שלמות בעינן. אמר רב חסדא: מחלוקת – שפירשה מן האשה, אבל פירשה מן האיש – טמאה כל זמן שהיא לחה. מתיב רב ששת: (ויקרא טו) וכל בגד וכל עור אשר יהיה עליו שכבת זרע – פרט לשכבת זרע שהיא סרוחה. מאי לאו, שפירשה מן האיש? – לא, שפירשה מן האשה. בעי רב פפא: שכבת זרע של ישראל במעי נכרית מהו? ישראל דדאיגי במצות – חביל גופייהו, נכרים דלא דאיגי במצות – לא, או דילמא: כיון דאכלין שקצים ורמשים – חביל גופייהו? ואם תמצי לומר כיון דאכלי שקצים ורמשים – חביל גופייהו, במעי בהמה מהו? אשה (היא) דאית לה פרוזדור – מסרחת, אבל בהמה דלית לה פרוזדור – לא, או דילמא: לא שנא? – תיקו.

רמב"ם הלכות שאר אבות הטומאה פרק ה הלכה יא – האשה שפלטה שכבת זרע אם פלטה אותה בתוך שלש עונות הרי היא טמאה כרואה קרי, לפיכך סותרת יום אחד אם היתה זבה כאיש שראה קרי, ומטמאה בכל שהוא אע"פ שלא יצאת לחוץ אלא נעקרה והגיעה לבין השיניים נטמאה שהרי שכבת זרע כדמה מה דמה מטמא בפנים אף שכבת זרע שתפלוט תטמא אותה בפנים.

שולחן ערוך יורה דעה סימן קצו סעיף יא – הפולטת שכבת זרע בימי ספירתה, אם הוא תוך ו' עונות לשמושה סותרת אותו יום. לפיכך המשמשת מטתה וראתה אחר כך ופסקה, אינה מתחלת לספור שבעה נקיים עד שיעברו עליה ו' עונות שלימות טו שמא תפלוט; לפיכך אינה מתחלת לספור טז עד יום ה' לשמושה, כגון אם שמשה במוצאי שבת אינה מתחלת לספור עד יום ה', דקיי"ל אין שכבת זרע מסריח עד שיעברו עליו ששה עונות שלימות יז מעת לעת; ואם שמשה במוצאי שבת ופלטה ליל ד', קודם עת שימושה במוצאי שבת, עדיין היא עומדת בתוך עונה ששית לשמושה סותרת, הילכך יום ה' יהיה ראשון לספירתה. הגה: ותפסוק יום ד' לעת ערב, ויום ה' עולה למניין. ויש שכתבו שיש להמתין עוד יום אחד, דהיינו שלא תתחיל למנות יט עד יום הששי והוא יהיה יום ראשון לספירתה, דחיישינן שמא תשמש ביום הראשון בין השמשות ותסבור שהוא יום, ואפשר שהוא לילה, ואם תתחיל למנות מיום חמישי יהיה תוך ששה עונות לשמושה, על כן יש להוסיף עוד יום אחד דמעתה אי אפשר לבא לידי טעות (ת"ה סימן רמ"ה והאגור בשם ר"י מולין וש"ד וכ"כ מהרא"י ומהרי"ק שורש ל"ה), וכן נוהגין בכל מדינות אלו, ואין לשנות. ויש נשים שנהגו להחמיר עוד להמתין עד שבעה ימים (שם בת"ה),

ואין טעם בדבר והמחמיר יחמיר והמיקל נשכר להקדים עצמו למצוה. ויש שכתבו שעכשיו אין לחלק בין שמשה עם בעלה ללא שמשה, כא וכל אשה שרואה, אפילו כתם, כב צריכה להמתין ה׳ ימים עם יום שראתה בו ותפסוק לעת ערב ותספור ז׳ נקיים (שם בת״ה בשם א״ז ומהרי״ק) וכן נוהגין במדינות אלו ואין לשנות (סה״ת וסמ״ג).

19.

דגול מרבבה על הש״ך קצו כ – אולי כוונתו כשלא היתה נדה קודם לראיה, כגון בתולה שראתה פעם ראשונה ועד עתה היתה בתולת דמים או מניקה שהיתה טהורה בעת מיתת בעלה וראתה עתה פעם ראשון אחר כ״ד חדש. אבל אם היתה כבר נדה לא שייך חומרא זו כלל.

שו״ת אגרות משה יורה דעה חלק ד סימן יז – כא. אשה שכשראתה, היתה פרושה מבעלה מחמת איסור או משום מחלה, אם עולה לה זמן הפרישה להמתנת החמישה שלפני הז׳ נקיים, וביאור המנהגים דהמתנת חמישה ימים ושבעה ימים שהביא הרמ״א.

אשה שפירשה מבעלה מחמת שהיה יום הוסת, ונוהגת לפרוש כל המעל״ע, ובא הוסת מיד בלילה דאחר כך. כיוון דמחמת איסור היתה הפרישה, נחשב יום זה במנין החמישה ימים דנוהגין שלא למנותן בז׳ הנקיים.

וימי אבלות שלו או שלה, דאסורין בתשמיש מצד איסור האבלות שלא מצד איסור נדות, שבס׳ דרכי תשובה סימן קצ״ו ס״ק פ״ו הביא מס׳ תוספת ירושלים דדעתו היתה תחילה שאינה צריכה להמתין מאחר דהיתה אסורה בתשמיש, אף שהוא מצד איסור אחר דאבלות. אבל חזר בו ממה שראה במדרש תנחומא (מצורע פרשה ז׳), דהאשה צריכה שתהא שומרת ט״ו יום ואחרי כן מותרת לבעלה, כיצד היא עושה שומרת ז׳ ימי נדתה ואחרי כן סופרת ז׳ ימי נקיים ונטהרת ביום השמיני וטובלת טבילה חמורה אחר שקיעת החמה. שלפי טעם זה, לא מהני לא אבלות ולא הבתולים.

הנה לע״ד מסתבר שא״צ להמתין מיום הראייה אלא ד׳ ימים שהצריכו להמתין כדכתב הרא״ש (נדה פ״ד סימן א׳) שמא תפלוט ש״ז, ואם פלטה סותרת מעיקר הדין ויש מקום לגזור בלא שמשה אטו שמשה כמבואר לקמן, ויום הראשון שצריכה להמתין רק מחמת חשש דשמא תשמש בין השמשות, נמנה גם מימי האבלות, כיוון שהוא מחמת איסור אף שאינו מחמת איסור נדה, דכל שלא שייך שתשמש אינה צריכה להמתין חמישה ימים, אלא ארבעה בלבד ככלה, עי׳ לעיל אות י״ח. וכן נפטרו מלמנות יום החמישי כשראתה דם תיכף בתחילת מוצאי יו״כ ובתחלת מוצאי ט׳ באב. ומה שחזר בו מחמת שמדרש תנחומא סובר כהמנהג שהביא הרמ״א (שם סעיף י״א) דיש נשים שנהגו להחמיר להמתין עוד ז׳ ימים, וכוונתו להוסיף בזה על דברי הרמ״א – שמצד המנהג שהביא הרמ״א לא איכפת לן אם יהיו שלשה ימים הראשונים נאסרין גם שלא מצד איסור נדה, ומצד מדרש תנחומא הוא דווקא לטהרה מנדותה ולא מצד איסורים אחרים.

אבל דבריו תמוהין מאד לחלוק על כל רבותינו, שליכא כלל מאן דסובר דנדה צריכה אף לחומרא יותר מז׳ נקיים אחר הימים שראתה. אך כדי שלא תסתור המנין דז׳ הנקיים בהפסק דפליטת ש״ז אינה יכולה להתחיל מנין הנקיים קודם ד׳ מעל״ע, ושייך להחמיר אף בלא שמשה כשהיתה מותרת בתשמיש אטו שמשה. ואף שסגי בשביל זה להחמיר רק עד יום חמישי, מ״מ

מביא הרמ"א שיש קצת מחמירין שלא להתחיל למנות הנקיים עד ז' ימים מהראייה, שע"ז כתב הרמ"א שאין טעם בדבר, משום דודאי לא שייך לומר שהוא משום דהצריכו ז' נקיים לנדה אחר שכלו ימי הטומאה ממש, דז' ימים שטימאה התורה בנדה הוא גם ברואה כל ז' הימים. עיין במש"כ בדברות משה ב"ק סימן ט"ז ענף ה' ד"ה והנה בנדה, בביאור הדבר, דנדה נחשבת דבר טמא בעצם, ולא שדם הנדה מטמאה, שהרי היא טמאה גם בימים שלא ראתה דם, וא"כ מסתבר שגם טיפה הראשונה לא טמאה ימים טהורים, רק שטיפה ראשונה עשתה את גוף האשה לעצם אשה נדה שהוא דבר טמא בעצם כל זמן שהיא נדה שהוא משך שבעת ימים, וממילא היא טמאה כל שבעת הימים ואין חילוק בין רואה ללא רואה יותר. ויש לומר לפיכך דלא שייך שישנו מדרבנן גדרי דיני התורה ויאמרו שדין אשה נדה הוא שאינה נטהרת לאחר שבעה ימים, אלא לאחר שתספור עוד שבעה נקיים. אלא מה שהחמירו הוא משום שלא יטעו הנשים השוו להן, שלעולם צריכות ז' נקיים. ומשום שצריך שיהיו רצופין הצריכו גם בנדה לאחר שפסקה מלראות שלא תסתור גם ש"ז שסותר רק יום אחד. דלכן כיוון שהיתה טהורה קודם ראותה דם נדותה, שהיה שייך שתשמש עם בעלה, לא חילקו והצריכו לכל אשה אף שלא שמשה להתחיל לספור ז' הנקיים אחר ד' ימים, אף שראתה רק יום אחד. והרמ"א כתב שלא תתחיל לספור ז' הנקיים עד אחר חמישה ימים, שיש עדיין חשש קטן לשמא שמשה עם בעלה ביה"ש דיום שנעשית נדה.

אבל כתב שיש קצת שאין מתחילות לספור ז' הנקיים עד אחר ז' ימים, וברור לו שג"כ הוא מאיזה חשש ולא מחמת שהחמירו לשנות גדרי טומאת נדה דאורייתא, שלכן כתב שאין טעם בדבר, והמיקל נשכר להקדים עצמו למצוה. ומשמע לענ"ד שידע טעמם, דהא לא ביטל מנהגם לגמרי אלא משום דמקדים עצמו למצוה. וגם כתב והמחמיר יחמיר, שברור שכוונתו שטוב עשה לחוש למנהג, ואינו עובר על ועונתה לא תגרע, אף שהיא היתה רוצית להתחיל לספור מיום הששי והוא אמר לה לעשות כמנהג חומרא זו דהמתנת ז' ימים שנהגו בעירו שם. דאם לא כן, אלא דהרמ"א לא חש כלל למנהג, היה מקצר לכתוב ואין לחוש למנהגם. דלכן מוכרחין לומר דסובר דרק בכוונתו להקדים עצמו למצוה רשאי, אבל אם הוא בשביל הרשות – ראוי יותר שיעשה כהמנהג. וגם הרוצה לעשות כהמנהג שפיר עושה, ואינו עובר בכלום. והטעם דבעצם יש למה שנהגו טעם, שהוא כדי שלא לחלק בין הנשים. דהא יש הרבה נשים שרואות ז' ימים, ואף כי הן עכ"פ מיעוט לגבי כולהו נשי דעלמא, הן הרבה שכדאי להתחשב עמהן לעניין שנחשוש שיראו נשים אלה חילוק ביניהן לשאר נשים, ואולי לא יבינו טעם החילוק ויבואו לידי זלזול שיפסקו בטהרה קודם שיפסקו מלראות. וכמו המנהג דאין מתחילות לספור עד אחר חמישה ימים, שאף שלא מצוי כלל תשמיש בביה"ש מכל מקום ניחא להרמ"א בחומרא זו. ורק שהתם הפעם שמזדמן ששמשה בין השמשות הוא דבר מובן לכל שצריכה להמתין עוד יום, אבל המתנת גם יום ו' ויום ז' לא מובן למי שיודע דיני התורה וטעמיה, אבל הוא בשביל שאין יודעים שגם זה הוא טעם לגזור. וטעם זה אינו חשוב כל כך, משום דיותר טוב להסביר אותם שידעו דיני התורה, מלתקן לפי חסרון ידיעתם. אבל לא מבטל זה הרמ"א לגמרי, דלכן רק לכוונת הקדימה למצוה סובר הרמ"א דשפיר עושה המיקל. אבל בשביל הרשות, היה ראוי יותר שיעשה כהמנהג, וגם סובר שהרוצה להחמיר ולעשות כהמנהג אינו עובר בכלום.

אבל לומר שיסברו דצריכה כל אשה נדה להתחיל לספור ז׳ נקיים אחר שיעברו שבעת ימי נדותה – לא שייך לומר בדעתם, כי למה יתקנו בלא טעם לעקור דיני תורה, ולהצריך ז׳ נקיים אחר ז׳ ימי הנדה. וגם מסתבר שהיה אסור לתקן דבר כזה שהוא עקירת דין תורה. וגם בלא זה כשאיכא מחלוקת בין שאר מדרשי חז״ל לגמ׳ דידן יש לפסוק כגמ׳ דידן, ואין לחוש כלל למה שנמצא באיזה מדרש. והדין ברור ופשוט בכל מדינותינו כהרמ״א, להמתין ה׳ ימים מיום הראייה ולספור אחר כך ז׳ הנקיים. אבל הוא רק כששייך מציאות חשש סתירה שהיו לה ימי היתר לבעלה. אבל כשלא היה יום ראוי לתשמיש, משום שהיה יוה״כ או ט׳ באב או ימי אבלות שלו או שלה, לא שייך זה.

ולשון המדרש תנחומא הוא מוקשה גם בלא זה מדברים ברורים. שאיתא שם שמדינא גם בראתה יום א׳ ויום ב׳ ויום ג׳ מימים די״א שאחר נדותה, תהיה שומרת יום אחד, ורק כשתראה יום ד׳ תהיה זבה, והוא טעות. וגם איתא שם דרק אחר ט״ו תטהר, שג״כ הוא טעות אפילו אם נימא שצריכה להמתין שבעה ימים ורק אז לספור שבעה נקיים. דהא תיכף כשטבלה בלילה אחר שספרה ז׳ הנקיים מותרת לבעלה, דטבול יום הוא רק לטהרות. ועיין כאן בפי׳ עץ יוסף שהביא שהקשה זה המג״א בספר זית רענן על הילקוט.

ובאשה שהיתה אסורה מתשמיש מצד שאסרוה הרופאים מצד איזה מחלה, פשוט שלא מצרפינן הזמן שפירשו בשביל זה לסך חמשת הימים. דלא נחשב זה עניין איסור, אף שבעצם איכא איסור דחבלת הגוף לדברי הרופא, שלא נחשב זה איסור לאינשי.

בית יוסף יורה דעה סימן קצו – ומ״ש רבינו אמנם אם תרצה לספור מיום מחרת ראייתה תקנח יפה באותו מקום במוך או בבגד וכו׳. כ״כ הרא״ש בפרק בנות כותים (ס״א) וז״ל אם תרצה להתחיל ספירתה מיום מחרת ראייתה תקנח יפה במוך או בבגד דק להפליט כל הזרע או תרחץ במים חמים ויפליטו המים חמין כל הזרע וכן תנן בפרק ח׳ דמקואות (מ״ד) האשה ששימשה וירדה וטבלה ולא כיבדה את הבית כאילו לא טבלה ומשמע הא אם כיבדה הבית קודם טבילה לא חיישינן תו לפליטה עד כאן והביא עוד ראיות לדבר וכן כתב גם כן הרשב״א בתורת הבית (הארוך ב״ז ש״ה כו. הקצר כד:):

ומ״ש רבינו שהרמב״ן כתב שהוא הדין אם הלכה ברגליה פלטה כל הזרע. כן כתבו הרשב״א והגהות מיימוניות (איסו״ב פ״ו אות ב) בשמו וכ״כ הרמב״ן בהלכותיו (פ״ב ה״י) וטעמא מדאמרינן בפרק יוצא דופן (מא:) אי דאזלא בכרעה בהדי דאזלא שדיתיה וכתב הרשב״א דההיא דתנן בפרק ח׳ דמקואות דקתני טבלה ולא כיבדה את הבית כאילו לא טבלה תפתר בשלא הלכה אעפ״כ אם כיבדה הבית טהורה דסתמא נתכבד כולו וכיבדה את הבית יש מפרשים לשון נקי ויש מפרשים כיבוד בית ממש שבשעה שהיא שוחה לכבד ומרחבת ירכותיה פולטת הכל א״נ ההיא דמסכת מקואות כשהלכה דפלטתו בבית החיצון וכותלי בית הרחם העמידוהו ומשום הכי צריכה כיבוד לטהרות משום נגיעה דשכבת זרע אלא דלית לה דין פולטת לראייה:

ומ״ש ולא נהירא לאדוני אבי ז״ל. בפרק בנות כותים כתב וז״ל אין להקל מהא דאמרינן בפרק יוצא דופן אי דאזלא בכרעא בהדי דאזלא שדיתיה ויסמכו על זה שהולכות משעת תשמיש עד הלילה כדי שיפליטו דהכי פירושו דילמא בהדי דאזלא שדיתיה ופלטה ואמאי אמר רבא אי אפשר שלא תפלוט חיישינן איבעי ליה למימר ומוקי לה בשהטבילוה במטה ולא הלכה הילכך

לא פלטה אבל אינו ברור שתפלוט הכל על ידי הילוך עכ"ל וכך הם דברי סמ"ג (לאוין קיא דף לז ע"ד) וספר התרומה (סי' צה) ומ"מ בכיבדה הבית או רחצה בחמין כבר נתבאר שדעת הרא"ש להתיר והרשב"א כתב בתורת הבית הקצר (שם) הלכה ברגליה חזקה דרך הילוכה פלטה הכל ויש מי שמורה גם בזו להחמיר עד שתקנח יפה יפה או שתכבד את הבית לעולם ילמד אדם בתוך ביתו שתהא מכבדת בית התורף יפה יפה ורוחצת בחמין כדי שלא תבוא לידי ספיקות הללו עד כאן נראה מדבריו דתרתי בעי כיבוד ורחיצה כדי לצאת ידי כל ספק וכ"כ בספר התרומה (שם) וז"ל אם תרצה להתחיל לספור ממחרת הראייה יכולה בזה הענין שתכניס מוך או בגד רך באותו מקום ותקנח יפה יפה להסיר השכבת זרע ואם דואגת שלא תדע לקנח יפה תרחץ בחמין גם תקנח עצמה ולא חיישינן שתפלוט עוד אח"כ בלא הרגשה ואז תוכל להתחיל ולספור מיום המחרת: אבל סמ"ק (סי' רצג עמ' שכב) כתב יש אומרים שאם רחצה היטב במים חמין אותו מקום שמתחלת למנות למחרתו וליתא דאין אנו בקיאים בזה ע"כ ואין לומר דלא ממעט אלא רחיצת חמין אבל לא הכנסת מוך שהרי בהגהות מיימוניות פרק ו' מהלכות איסורי ביאה (דפוס קושטא הט"ז) כתוב בשם סמ"ק דאין לנו עתה לסמוך על בדיקת מוך שתכניס באותו מקום דאין אנו בקיאין בזה ולעולם צריכות להמתין שש עונות שלימות ע"כ משמע דאפילו בדעביד תרווייהו קינוח ורחיצה לא מהני דכיון דאין אנו בקיאים בהם כי עביד תרווייהו מאי הוי אע"פ שבקצת הגהות מיימוניות לא נמצא לשון זה מ"מ מדברי סמ"ק עצמו נלמוד דכשם שאין אנו בקיאים ברחיצת חמין כך אין אנו בקיאים בקינוח כלומר שאין אנו יודעים עד איזה מקום צריך להגיע המים החמין או הבגד שמקנחת בו כדי שנדע ודאי שנפלט השכבת זרע כולו ומ"מ כיון ששום אחד מהפוסקים לא כתב כן שפיר דמי להתיר על ידי קינוח או רחיצת חמין:

שולחן ערוך יורה דעה סימן קצו סעיף יג – האשה ששמשה מטתה וראתה אחר כך ופסקה, ורוצה לספור מיום מחרת ראייתה, תקנח יפה יפה אותו מקום במוך או בבגד להפליט כל הזרע או תרחוץ במים חמין והם יפליטו כל הזרע. הגה: ויש אומרים דאין אנו בקיאין בזמן הזה ואין לסמוך על זה (הגהות מיימוני פ"ו וסמ"ק), כה והכי נהוג דהרי כבר נתבאר שאנו נוהגין להמתין אפילו לא שמשה כלל, כדי שלא לחלק בין ספירה לספירה, כ"ש בכהאי גוונא; וכל הפורץ גדר בדברים אלו במקום שנהגו להחמיר, ישכנו נחש.

ט"ז יורה דעה סימן קצו ס"ק ה – וכבר כתבתי בסי' קצ"ג בשם מהר"ל מפראג שבכלה אחר בעילת מצוה תוכל למנות מיום ה' לשימושה ורצונו לומר דלא גזרינן בה שמא תשמש באותו יום בסופו דהיינו בין השמשות ונראה טעמו כיון דאין כאן דם נדה רק דם בתולים לא החמירו בו משום תשמיש בין השמשות אבל אם באמת נבעלה בעילת מצוה בין השמשות נראה ודאי דחשבינן לה כאלו נבעלת בלילה שאחר אותו בין השמשות אפילו גבי כלה נמצא שאם נבעלה הכלה ליל מ"ש תמנה מיום חמישי ואם נבעלה בביה"ש של סוף יום א' תמנה מיום ו' כנלע"ד:

שו"ת נודע ביהודה מהדורה תנינא – יורה דעה סימן קכה – תשובה לכבוד אהובי ידידי וחביבי הרב הגדול המופלא ומופלג בתורה ויראה החכם השלם במעלות ומדות כבוד שמו מוהר"ר ליב איגר נ"י מהלברשטאט:

מכתבו מן א״ח סכות העבר קבלתי ואמנם רבו הטרדות מכל צד ובפרט בבוא מכתבו היה עת האסף וזמן קהלה לכל התלמידים ותחלת הזמן גרמא דעציראה והנחתי מכתבו למשמרת ובין כך לא פסקו הטרדות ולא ראיתי במכתבו דבר נחוץ לשעה והרחבתי הדבר ויאמין לי שעד אתמול לא עיינתי במכתבו, ועתה אשיב על שאלותיו על ראשון ראשון לציון. על דבר מורה אחד שהורה הלכה למעשה באשה שטבלה ואחר טבילה קודם ששימשה ראתה דם ובעלה היה בעיר שתמנה תיכף ז׳ נקיים. הנה המורה הזה לא הורה כראוי כי מי הוא זה אשר ירים יד בתורת משה הוא הרב רמ״א סימן קצ״ו ושני האחרונים הש״ך והט״ז הסכימו על ידו וכבר נתפשט המנהג כן בכל מדינות פולין ואשכנז וא״כ איך מלאו לבו של המורה להקל בלי שום צורך ודחק וראוי המורה הזה לגעור בו אבל לענשו באיזה עונש אין אני רואה כי מאוד אני תמה על קדמונינו שהחמירו בדבר זה חומרות יתירות וגוף דין זה שפולטת שכבת זרע ממש תסתור בזיבה אפילו בזבה דאורייתא אינו מוסכם מכל הפוסקים ודעת הראב״ד שלא אמרו דבר זה אלא לטהרות ולא לבעלה. והנה טעמו של הראב״ד הובא בתהה״א בית שביעי שער חמישי מדאמר ר״ש בנדה דף ס״ז ע״ב ואחר תטהר אחר מעשה תטהר אבל אמרו חכמים אסור לעשות כן שמא תבוא לידי ספק נמצא שהתורה התירה לה לשמש ביום השביעי ומסתמא לא אמרה תורה שתשמש ותשאר במטה ולא תתהפך וא״כ הרי תפלוט ושמשה זבה למפרע. א״ו שאין פולטת ש״ז סותרת רק לטהרות ולא לבעלה ורבינו יונה דחה ראייתו לפי שאין ש״ז סותר ביום השביעי דמקצת היום ככלו וכן הובאו דברים הללו ברבינו אשר פ׳ בנות כותים. וטעם הדבר שש״ז אינו סותר ביום השביעי ודם סותר אפילו ביום השביעי הוא משום דדם סותר כל המנין לכן סותר עד הערב של יום שביעי אבל ש״ז שאינו סותר אלא יומו לכך ביום השביעי נשאר מקצת היום:

ואני אומר דראיית הראב״ד נכונה דתינח זה לפי האמת שש״ז אינו סותר כל המנין רק יומו אבל אי הוה ש״ז סותר כל ז׳ ודאי שהיה סותר גם ביום השביעי ולפ״ז קשה הרי בפ׳ בנות כותים דף ל״ג בעי רמי בר חמא פולטת ש״ז מהו שתסתור בזיבה כו׳ אמר רבא לפום חורפא שבשתא נהי נמי דסתרה כמה תסתור תסתור ז׳ די כבועלה כו׳. והנה זה אינו כ״כ ראיה הכרחית למימר שדי כבועלה ויותר ה״ל לרבא למימר תסתור שבעה א״כ גם ביום ז׳ סותרת ורחמנא אמר אחר תטהר אחר מעשה תטהר ולפי הנראה רבנן דדרשו אחר תטהר אחר לכולן שלא תהא טומאה מפסקת ור״ש דדריש אחר מעשה תטהר לא פליגי מר אמר חדא כו׳. אלא ודאי מדלא הוכיח רבא מזה מכלל דכל דין שכבת זרע שסותר אינו רק לטהרות ולא לבעלה וכדברי הראב״ד. ואמנם גוף ראיית הראב״ד אינו אלא למאן דמפרש אחר מעשה תטהר לתשמיש אבל אמרו חכמים אסור לעשות כן לשמש נמצא מדאורייתא מותרת לשמש. אבל לפירש״י ותוס׳ בדף ס״ז ע״ב בד״ה אבל אמרו חכמים כו׳ אחר תטהר היינו הטבילה שמותרת לטבול ביום שביעי אבל אמרו חכמים אסור לעשות כן היינו שאסרו הטבילה א״כ איכא למימר שבאמת התשמיש אסור מן התורה משום פולטת ש״ז ועכ״פ לדעת הראב״ד אין מקום בזמננו לפליטת ש״ז לסתור שאין לנו טהרות. ודעת ר״ת הוא שדוקא במשמשת עם הזב ופלטה ש״ז של זב הוא שסתרה משום צחצוחי זיבה הובאו דבריו ג״כ ברשב״א ובהרא״ש שם ור״י הזקן בעל התוס׳ ורבינו יונה המחמירים בדבר והרשב״א שם כתב שכל הגאונים והרי״ף שלא הזכירו דבר זה משמע דס״ל כהראב״ד וכן הכריע הרשב״א להלכה אלא שמסיק שבעל נפש יחמיר לעצמו כדברי ר״י הזקן

והנה החמיר ר״י הזקן בדבר זה שלא תתחיל עד יום ה׳ לשימושה שמא תפלוט. ואמנם זה בזבה גדולה שראתה ג׳ ימים אבל ברואה רק יום אחד שאין כאן הצרכת ז׳ נקיים מה״ת כלל רק חומרא דר״ז שבנות ישראל החמירו על עצמן שסופרות ז׳ נקיים ושנחמיר גם בזו שלא תמנה עד יום ה׳ לשימושה זה חומרא גדולה. ואמנם הרשב״א שם כתב בפירוש שאם ראתה והפסיקה בו ביום צריכה להמתין כן וכן הוא בטור סימן קצ״ו והוא מפורש בדברי התוס׳ בדף ל״ג ע״א בד״ה רואה הויא שכתבו שגם בדין חומרא דר״ז הדין כן שמסתמא כעין דאורייתא תיקון:

ואני אומר שבדבר זה היה לי לדון שהרי הרשב״א יפה דבר שהגאונים והרי״ף בודאי סברי כהראב״ד מדהשמיטו דין זה ואמנם הרב ב״י בסימן קצ״ו כתב שאין ראיה מדהשמיטו הרי״ף שכמה דינים השמיט הרי״ף כי דרכו להשמיט מה שאינו מצוי וגם זה אינו מצוי שרוב הנשים דרכן להמשיך ראייתן חמשה או ששה ימים ואינן צריכות לדין זה עכ״ל הרב״י. ואני אומר שדבריו דחוקים וכמה נשים רואות יום או יומים ופוסקות. ואמנם אומר אני דהוה ליה להב״י למדרש ביה מרגניתא בכוונת הרי״ף ודריש ביה חספא אחר מחילת כבודו:

והנראה לפענ״ד בכוונת הרי״ף והגאונים שהשמיטו דבר זה דסתירת ש״ז לא משום דס״ל כהראב״ד אלא משום דהתוספות דף ל״ג ע״א בד״ה רואה הויא כתבו אומר ר״י דמשכחת בשמשה בהיתר שתסתור ע״י פליטה אחר ראיית ג״י רצופים דקיימ״ל כרבנן דר״ע דבעינן שש עונות שלימות כו׳ ע״ש בתוספות. ולפי זה לדעת הרמב״ם בפ״ה משאה״ט שאין פולטת מטמאה רק עד שלש עונות לא משכחת דין זה בהיתר כלל כי אם בעברה ושימשה באיסור ודבר זה ודאי לא שכיח. ולכך לא הביאו הרי״ף והגאונים הך דפליטת ש״ז לפי שהם ס״ל כהרמב״ם שאין ש״ז מטמא רק ג׳ עונות ולא משכחת רק באיסור ולא שכיח אבל דברי הרב״י דחוקים ועוד שהרי חזינן שהרי״ף הביא בהלכות נדה הך דתיקן רבי בשדות ושוב הביא חומרא דר״ז שרואה טיפת דם כחרדל יושבת ז״נ ולדברי הב״י למאי הלכתא הביא הך דר״ז הא לא שכיח שתראה פחות מג״י רצופים וכיון שכבר כתב הרי״ף שאין בקיאין בימי נדה וזיבה ממילא צריכה ז״נ. א״ו דשפיר שכיח שרואה יום אחד בלבד ודלא כב״י:

ומעתה לפי תירוצי בדעת הרי״ף שהשמיט הך דפליטה משום דלא משכחת בהיתר ממילא מוכח דהרי״ף גם בהא לא ס״ל כדעת התוספות שכתבו דאפילו בחומרא דר״ז ג״כ אמרו שפולטת ש״ז סותרת דאי ס״ד דהרי״ף ס״ל בזה כהתוספות אכתי היה לו להביא הך דפליטת ש״ז שהרי חומרא דר״ז משכחת לה בשימשה בהיתר קודם שראתה דם ביום ההוא ושוב פולטת ביום שלאחריו וסותר ואם שימשה באחד בשבת שעה קודם הלילה ותיכף אחר התשמיש ראתה דם והפסיקה בטהרה אי אפשר לה למנות ז״נ כי אם מרביעי בשבת ואילך שהרי אם תפלוט ליל שלישי בשבת עדיין הוא תוך ג׳ עונות. א״ו דסובר הרי״ף דבחומרא דר״ז שהנקיים הם מדרבנן לא סתרה בפליטת ש״ז ולהרמב״ם ג״כ בודאי בראתה יום א׳ ומשמרת ז״נ משום חומרא דר״ז לא סתרה שהרי טעמם של התוספות הוא משום כעין דאורייתא תיקון ואם נימא שבחומרא דר״ז לא תסתור תעשה כן בנקיים של זבה ממש וזה שייך לדעת התוספות שפולטת עד שש עונות ומשכחת לה גם בזבה דאורייתא ששימשה בהיתר ותפלוט תוך ימי הספירה אבל להרמב״ם דלא משכחת בזבה דאורייתא שתפלוט בימי נקיים כי אם בשמשה בנדתה ולא שייך לגזור בחומרא דר״ז משום זיבה דאטו חיישינן שתשמש נדה לכתחלה. ומעתה כיון דבראב״ד לא נזכר פליטת

ש״ז לגבי בעלה כלל ולר״ת הוא דוקא ש״ז של זב ולהרי״ף והרמב״ם והגאונים דוקא בזבה שראתה ג״י אבל לא בחומרא דר״ז לא ידעתי למה החמירו הקדמונים כל כך מהרי״ק ומהרא״י לגזור עוד לא שמשה אטו שמשה. אבל כיון שכבר קדמונים אחזו שער והרמ״א והאחרונים הסכימו מי יבוא אחר המנהג ועכ״פ אין לענוש את המורה ודי לגערו בנזיפה שלא יוסיף להבא להקל בדבר. ובפני יהושע ראיתי שמיקל בראתה תיכף אחר הטבילה קודם ששימשה ופשוט שהט״ז בס״ק ד׳ מחמיר גם בזה שהרי לא הקיל רק בראתה תיכף אחר חופתה שלא באה עדיין לכלל תשמיש:

ואני תמה על הפני יהושע שמה בכך שראתה אחר הטבילה ומה בין זו לשאר אשה שלא שימשה כמה ימים שמחמיר רמ״א ולומר שחולק בזה על רמ״א קשה שהרי מתחלה רצה להביא ראיה לדבריו מדברי רמ״א אלא שדחה שאין משם ראיה ע״ש. אבל עכ״פ אנו רואין שעכ״פ בצד האפשר היה אצלו שרמ״א מסכים לדין ההוא וגם סיום דבריו שכתב אבל אין נראה כי ההמתנה עצמה בלא שימשה היא חומרא יתירא כו׳ עיין בפני יהושע בסימן י״ב בסופו. משמע שההמתנה בלא שימשה היא חומרא יתירא ולכן אין להוסיף עכ״פ חומרא בזו שראתה תיכף אחר הטבילה ולא ידעתי מה בין זו לשאר אשה שלא שמשה ואולי כוונתו למ״ש לעיל שההמתנה בלא שמשה אפילו בראתה ג״י שהיא זבה גמורה היא חומרא ואיך נוסיף להחמיר בראיה אחת שהוא רק חומרא שהחמירו בנות ישראל. ואמנם בתה״ד משמע להחמיר אף בראיה אחת ובלא שימשה ואולי לראות לאחר הטבילה תיכף קודם תשמיש הוא מלתא דלא שכיחא ולא גזרו בזה. ולפי שגוף חומרות הללו אין להם על מה שיסמכו ולכן הרוצה לסמוך בזה על בעל פ״י מי ימחה בידו לענשו עבור זה. אבל המנהג הפשוט כדברי הט״ז. דברי הד״ש:

שו״ת אגרות משה יורה דעה חלק ד סימן יז – כב. בדין אשה שאין לה בנים ותוכל להתעבר רק אם תטבול קודם ליל י״ג לראייתה.

אשה שאין לה בנים, ולא מצאו הרופאים חיסרון אלא זה שלפי טבעה והסימנים לא תוכל להתעבר כשתטבול ככל הנשים שהוא בליל י״ג, אלא קודם לזה, דצריכה להתחיל לספור ז׳ נקיים תיכף אחרי ד׳ ימים. שהביא כתר״ה מספרי איזה גדולי דורנו שהחמירו, אלא נתנו לה עצה שלא תטבול בכל פעם אלא לסירוגין. שהוא שלא כדחייב מדינא מי שלא קיים פריה ורביה, לבעול בכל עונה עד שיקיים, כדאיתא בש״ע אה״ע סימן ע״ו סעיף ו׳, אף באופן שפטור מצד מצות עונה דחיוב הבעל להאשה. והוא אף במי שמצד טבעה נקל לה להתעבר, כי הא לא ידוע מתי הוא הרצון מלפני השי״ת שתתעבר ממנו, וא״כ כ״ש שאין זו עצה לפני נשי כאלו למנוע מהן תשמיש של חדש שלם. אבל העיקר כדהביא כתר״ה מדברי מלכיאל ומערוך השלחן (סימן קצ״ו סעיף מ׳) שכשהוא צורך גדול להתיר לה להתחיל לספור ז׳ הנקיים מיום ה׳ לראייתה אם אפשר לה. וגם בפ״ת ס״ק ט״ו הביא בשם השל״ה, להתיר להתחיל לספור ביום ה׳, כדי שלא תטבול בליל שבת שבמוצאי יום טוב, בלא שמשה יום שקודם הראייה, ולהסדרי טהרה (ס״ק מ״ב) אף בשמשה. ולכן אין שום טעם להחמיר בזה במקום צורך גדול כזה. אבל כשידוע מתחילה שתצטרך להמתין רק ד׳ ימים, גם הסדרי טהרה יודה שטוב שלא תשמש עם בעלה כל המעל״ע שקודם זמן ראייתה, כדי שיהיו לה חמישה ימים קודם שתתחיל לספור ז׳ הנקיים. אבל כשלא

עשתה כן, יש לעשות לכתחילה להתחיל לספור מיום ה' לראייתה כהשל"ה – בלא שמשה ביום שקודם הראייה בפשיטות. וכשאיכא צורך יותר כגון שמצטערים טובא, יש להתיר להם אף בשמשה כהסדרי טהרה. כי בעצם צדק הסדרי טהרה שבכל אופן יש להתיר לצורך גדול כזה להתחיל לספור הז' נקיים מיום ה'.

ולכן כשצריכה לטבול בליל י"ב, משום דאז לדעת הרופאים הוא הזמן שראוי לה להתעבר, אף שג"כ היה יותר טוב שלא תשמש עם בעלה בהמעל"ע שקודם הוסת, מ"מ אם שכחה, או שלא היה ברור לה יום הוסת ולא פרשה, יהא לה העצה אם אפשר לה להתחיל לספור הז' נקיים מיום ה' ויגמרו ז' הנקיים ביום י"א. אבל כשזמן שאפשר לה להתעבר הוא בליל עשירי, ואפשר לה ליטהר מצד נדותה משום דאינה רואה יותר משני ימים, הא ליכא עצה אחרת אלא אם תפרוש קודם הוסת. שלכן מאחר שהיא פורשת תחילה, אין להתיר לה אלא כשתפרוש ג' ימים קודם הוסת כדכתבתי.

בית יוסף יורה דעה סימן קצו – וכתב סמ"ק (שם) וכן אם טעתה במנין יום אחד וטבלה ושימשה צריכה להמתין שש עונות שלימות וזהו ד' ימים ואחר תמנה יום אחד נקי ותטבול אך סתירה שלאחר שבעה כגון שלא טבלה כראוי ושימשה הרי זו טובלת בכל עת עכ"ל: ומה שכתב דסתירה שלאחר שבעה כגון שלא טבלה כראוי ושימשה הרי זו טובלת בכל עת זה פשוט ממה שאינה סותרת אלא יום אחד והיינו לומר שאותו יום שפלטה בו אינו עולה לה וזו שכבר ספרה ז' נקיים לא שייך בה סתירה וגדולה מזו מבואר בדברי הרא"ש פרק בנות כותים שאחת מהראיות שהביא הראב"ד שפולטת שכבת זרע כל לבעלה אינה סותרת מדתניא (סז:) רבי שמעון אומר ואחר תטהר אחר מעשה תטהר אבל אמרו חכמים אסור לעשות כן שלא תבוא לידי ספק נדה אלמא אי לאו חששא דשמא תראה דם לאחר תשמיש משמשת והולכת ואינה חוששת שמא תפלוט שכבת זרע והוא ז"ל כתב עליו נראה לי שאינה ראיה דפולטת אינה סותרת יום אחרון דודאי דם בזבה וזיבה בזב שסותרין כל המנין סותרין עד ערב יום שביעי אבל פולטת שכבת זרע שאינה סותרת אלא יום אחד אם פלטה אחר שספרה מקצת היום שוב אינה סותרת דעיקר סתירת שכבת זרע היא משום דלא מיקרי נקיים וכיון שספרה מקצת יום וטהורה לבעלה כבר שלמו הנקיים ושוב אין שכבת זרע סותרת והביא ראיה לדבר ואפשר שלזה נתכוין סמ"ק וסתירה דלאחר שבעה דקאמר ביום שביעי ממש הוא אלא דכיון דאמרינן מקצת היום ככולו הוי כאילו הוא לאחר שבעה: ומה שכתב [סמ"ק] שאם טעתה במנין יום אחד וטבלה ושימשה צריכה להמתין ד' ימים ואחר תמנה יום אחד נקי ותטבול אם באנו להסכים דברים אלו עם דברי הרא"ש כמו שכתבתי בסמוך נראה לכאורה דהיינו לומר שאם טבלה בששי ושימשה בתחלת ליל שביעי דלא עלתה לה טבילה עד שתספור היום השביעי גם כן וכיון שאינה יכולה לספור בארבעה ימים אלו משום דחיישינן בהו שמא תפלוט שכבת זרע ותסתור אותו יום נמצא שכשיעברו ד' ימים אלו צריכה למנות יום אחד שחסר לה ממנין השבעה ואח"כ תטבול דאי בטבלה ליל שביעי למה צריכה להמתין כל כך מלטבול הרי כיון שנכנס כבר השביעי הו"ל פולטת ביום אחרון ואינה סותרתו כמו שקדם ויותר נראה לומר דבטבלה ליל ז' נמי מיירי ולא מיקריא פולטת ביום אחרון

אלא בשפלטה אחר שהאיר היום אבל קודם שהאיר היום לא אמרינן ביה מקצת היום ככולו דהא זבה טובלת ביום ז׳ מן התורה כמו שיבואר בסימן שאחר זה אבל בליל ז׳ ודאי לא עלתה לה טבילה. ומכל מקום איכא למידק היאך יצטרף יום ז׳ עם הששה הראשונים הא בעינן שיהיו כל השבעה נקיים רצופים מדכתיב אחר תטהר אחר אחר לכולן וי״ל דההיא לומר שלא תהא טומאת זיבת מפסקת ביניהם שאם ראתה ביניהם פעם אחת אע״פ שלא היתה צריכה לשמור משום דם זה אלא יום אחד סותרת כל מה שספרה קודם לכן וצריכה לספור מחדש ז׳ נקיים אבל בהפסק פליטת שכבת זרע לא איכפת לן והכי אמרינן בפרק בנות כותים (לג:):

20.

תלמוד בבלי מסכת נדה דף סח עמוד א – מתני׳. נדה שבדקה עצמה יום שביעי שחרית ומצאה טהורה, ובין השמשות לא הפרישה, ולאחר ימים בדקה ומצאה טמאה – הרי היא בחזקת טהורה. בדקה עצמה ביום שביעי שחרית ומצאה טמאה, ובין השמשות לא הפרישה, ולאחר זמן בדקה ומצאה טהורה – הרי זו בחזקת טמאה, ומטמאה מעת לעת ומפקידה לפקידה. ואם יש לה וסת – דיה שעתה. ור׳ יהודה אומר: כל שלא הפרישה בטהרה מן המנחה ולמעלה – הרי זו בחזקת טמאה. וחכמים אומרים: אפילו בשנים לנדתה בדקה ומצאה טהורה, ובין השמשות לא הפרישה, ולאחר זמן בדקה ומצאה טמאה – הרי זו בחזקת טהורה.

שולחן ערוך יורה דעה סימן קצו סעיף א – שבעה ימים שהזבה סופרת מתחילין ממחרת יום שפסקה בו. וכך משפטה, אם תראה ב׳ ימים או ג׳ ופסקה מלראות, בודקת ביום שפסקה כדי שתפסוק בטהרה; ובדיקה זו תהיה סמוך לבין השמשות. (וכן נוהגין לכתחלה; ובדיעבד, אפילו לא בדקה עצמה רק שחרית ומצאה עצמה טהורה, סגי בכך). (טור בשם הרשב״א וב״י אף לפי דברי הרא״ש). ולעולם ילמד אדם (להחמיר לכתחלה) בתוך ביתו שתהא בודקת ביום הפסק טהרתה במוך דחוק ושיהא שם כל בין השמשות, שזו בדיקה מוציאה מידי ספק (רשב״א בתה״ק). הגה: וי״א אם התפללו הקהל ערבית ועוד היום גדול, אינה יכולה לבדוק או ללבוש לבנים ולהתחיל ולמנות מיום המחרת, מאחר דהקהל כבר עשו אותו לילה (ת״ה), י״א דמותר אפילו עשו הקהל שבת (אגור בשם ר״י מולין);ונוהגין לכתחלה ליזהר, ובדיעבד אין לחוש. ומקצת נשים נוהגות שאם פסקה קודם ברכו וחזרה לראות כתם או דם תוך ימי ספירתה, אז מפסיקין אפילו לאחר ברכו אם נתקלקלה סמוך לערב, וחושבים דבר זה לדיעבד; ואין למחות בידם, כי כן קבלו מאיזה חכם שהורה להן, והוא מנהג ותיקין.

תוספות הרא״ש, נדה ס״ט – ואי ס״ד לא בעינן ספורים לפנינו ביממא ליטבלה. ואי משום דבעינן הפסקה בשלישי כדקאמר רבא לעיל נדה שהפרישה בטהרה בשבלישי שלה אלמא בלא הפרשה אינה יכולה לספור. חומרא בעלמא היא ומדרבנן ואינה נמנעת בשביל זה מלטבול כיון שטבילה בזמנה מצוה ואפילו בעיא הפסקה מן התורה טובלת דשמא הפסיקה ולאו אדעתא כיון דבאיזה יום שהפסיקה מועלת הפסקתה אבל אין לחוש ולומר שמא בדקה ביום ראשון של ספירה ואיכא תחלתן וסופן שבאתה שעתה שבדקה לנפנו יום שביעי של יום זה.

רמב"ם הלכות איסורי ביאה פרק ו הלכה כב–כ"ג – וכן אם בדקה ביום ראשון מימי הספירה ומצאה טהור וביום הח' ומצאה טהור הרי זו בחזקת טהרה, בדקה ביום ג' לזיבתה ומצאה שפסק הדם ולא בדקה ביום ראשון מימי הספירה ובשביעי בדקה ומצאה טהור ה"ז בחזקת טהרה, והוא הדין לזב בכל אלו הבדיקות שהוא טהור ועלו לו ימי ספירה.

כל אשה שהיא ספק נדה ספק זבה צריכה לישב שבעת ימים נקיים מספק וטובלת בליל שמיני ואחר כך תהיה מותרת לבעלה, ומביאה קרבן זבה ואינו נאכל כמו שיתבאר במקומו.

חוות דעת יו"ד קצו:ג, ביאורים ד"ה ובהכי – ולפ"ז אשה שראתה דם ממש ואח"כ נולד לה מכה אפילו ידוע שמוציאה דם וא"א לה לבדוק אפילו פעם אחת שלא תמצא דם בספירת ז' נקיים טמאה דהא מאותן הימים שיחדה לנקיים אנן ספורין ובדוקין בעינן וזו לא יהא אלא שלא נבדקה דטמאה.

שו"ת זכרון יוסף יורה דעה סימן י – וכדי להראותו כי דבריו הערבים חביבין עלי עד לאחת ועיינתי בהם היטב אמרתי אשתעשע בהם ואפרש את שיחתי לפניו מה שאין נ"ל מהם אשר אני לא כן אחשוב ולבבי לא כן ידמה ולפלפולא בעלמא. והנה פתח פיו בחכמה להמציא היתר ולומר דהבדיקה בז' ימי הספירה אינה רק מדרבנן דמן התורה בספירה בעלמא מבלי הרגשת פתיחת המקור להוציא דם סגי' אלא דסותר את זה מדברי הרמב"ם ריש פ"ט מה' א"ב שכתב שם ה"ז בחזקת שבא בהרגשה ע"כ וש"מ דחיישינן דילמא ארגשה ולאו אדעתה וא"כ ה"נ איכא למיחש להכי:

ולי נראה דאי משום הא לא איריי' דשאני הכא דאיכ' ס"ס דדילמ' לא יצא ממנה שום דם ואת"ל יצא שמא לא ארגשה והוי דם טהור. ולא מיבעי' לדעת הרשב"א וסיעתו והסכמת הפר"ח בסי' ק"י [ס"ק מ"ט] דאמרי' ס"ס אף נגד חזקה פשיט' דשרי' אלא אפי' לדעת הגאון בעל מחבר ספר פני יהושע שכתב בקו' אחרון לחי' במ' כתובות בד"ה ויאמר יהושע וכ"כ בתשובה הובאה בספר שו"ת שב יעקב בחלק י"ד סי' מ"ח דהיכ' דאיתחזק איסור' לא מהני ס"ס להתיר וה"נ איתחזק איסור' דטומאת נדה מ"מ י"ל דה"מ מדרבנן לא שרינן ע"י ס"ס אבל מן התורה אף הגאון מודה דשרי' כאשר יראה לעיני המעיין שם:

ומכ"ש לפמ"ש מעכ"ת דהכ' איכ' נמי רוב' להתירא דרוב הנשים פוסקות מלראות דם ביום ה' או ו' לתחלת ראייתן והנה מתחלה עמדתי מרעיד ומשתומם דמנלי' למימר הכי עד שמצאתי און לו בב"י סי' קצ"ו ריש הסי' בד"ה ומ"ש רבינו ומלשון א"א הרא"ש כו' וז"ל שם אי אפשר משום דרוב נשים פוסקות קודם יום הז' כו' עכ"ל. וכן נ"ל מוכח מן הש"ס דנדה דף ט"ו ע"ב דקאמר התם מחשב ימי וסתה ובא עלי' שפירושו נמי שמחשב ע"פ רגילתה משך זמן ראייתה הקדום וכדמשמע מפירש"י שם דאל"כ במה יודע לו איפו' משך ימי וסתה. וכן מוכח עוד מהא דאמרינן לקמן דף נ"ז ע"ב אם רוב ימי' טמאין כו' אם רוב ימי' בהרגשה קא חזי' כו' וש"מ מזה דאזלינן בתר רוב ימי אשה זו לענין זה. וא"כ איתת' דנד"ד אם ברוב ימי' פוסקות ביום ו' או ז' פשיטא דראוי לומר כבר פסקה וכנ"ל וגם היתיר' שכיח' השתא טפי מאיסור' והיכא דאיכ' ספיק' חזי לן למיתלי להיתר כמ"ש הש"ך בי"ד סי' נו"ן סק"ג ובסי' נ"א סק"ד וכן משמע נמי בהדי' מדברי התו' במ' גיטין דף ב' ע"ב בד"ה עד א' נאמן באיסורין וביבמות פ"ח ע"א בד"ה ברי לי:

וגם זולת הנ"ל נ"ל דאין מדברי הרמב"ם שום סתירה שהרי יש לדקדק על דבריו דס"ל דחיישינן דילמ' ארגשה ולאו אדעת' מן התורה מדכתב אח"ז ומדברי סופרים כו' א"כ קרא דבבשרה לאשמועי' דבעי' הרגשה מאי אהני לן וכמו שהקשו ה"ה הגאוני' הקדומי' מוה' גבריאל זצ"ל ואמ"ו בעל שב יעקב בסי' ל"ו ובסי' מ"א יע"ש. והנה בשב יעקב בסי' מ"א תי' דדוק' בבדקה בעד ומצאה דם מן הלול ולפנים כתב הרמב"ם דה"ז בחזקת שבא בהרגשה דטעתה וחשבה הרגשת העד הוא אבל בלתי בדיקה בעד לא חיישינן דילמ' ארגשה ולאו אדעת'. ועוד תירץ דהרמב"ם רק משום ספיק' דאסור בכה"ג אף מן התורה קאמר ה"ז בחזקת שבא בהרגשה ע"כ. ולפי זה אין מקום לקושי' מעכ"ת דלתי' הראשון הנ"ל י"ל דשאני הכא שאינה בודקת א"ע בעד ולא שייכ' טעות לגבה ולתי' השני הנ"ל י"ל שאני הכא דהוי ס"ס כדכתיבנא לעיל:

שו"ת רבי עקיבא איגר מהדורה קמא סימן ס – וראיתי לתשו' זכרון יוסף דכייל בקבא רבא להקל די"ל בשעת הדחק מודה להראב"ד, ולדעתי קשה לסמוך על זה דפשטות דברי הרשב"א מורים דאינו בדיקה כלל בלא חורין וסדקין, גם מה שדן שם דרוב נשים פוסקות מלראות ביום ה' או ביום ו' לראייתה ועשה סמוכים לזה מסוגיא דנדה (דף ט"ו) בעלה מחשב ימי ווסתה, היינו דמחשב ע"פ רגילתה מקודם משך זמן ראייתה, ובסדרי טהרה (סי' קצ"ו ס"ק כ"ג) ביאר דבריו, אף דמסקינן דמיירי רק בספק ראתה מ"מ מדאמרינן ודאי ראתה מי קאמינא מי יימר דטבלה משמע דרק מה"ט אסורה ולא מטעם מי יימר דפסקה מלראות גם למ"ד דר"ש בר ייבא דר"י מיירי אפילו ודאי ראתה מכח הסברא דמחשבה כפי רגילתה משך ראייתה, מ"מ יפה סתר הס"ט שם ממה דמבואר (דף ס"ח) להדיא דבלא פסיקת טהרה הוי בספק טומאה לעולם עיי"ש, ונדחק לדחות הראיה הנ"ל, ולענ"ד בפשוטו ניחא דהיכן מצינו דר"ש ב"י הי' סבר דר"י מיירי בודאי ראתה, הא י"ל דהי' ס"ל ג"כ דר"י מיירי בספק דאתה אלא דס"ל ווסתות דאורייתא וס"ל דהוי כמו ודאי ראתה, ובזה שפיר יכול לחשוב משך רגילות ראייתה כיון דמחזקינן לראתה רק מכח רגילות ראייתה ממילא אנו דנין ג"כ דפסקה לזמן הרגילה לפסוק, ולזה שאל רשב"י אפילו ילדה נמי והיינו אם נפרש ילדה דבושה לטבול, בפשוטו ניחא דשאל ג"כ בכה"ג היכי דמחזיקינן בראתה מכח הווסתות, ועלה אמרינן כיון דממילא מיירי רק בספק ראתה אבל לא ודאי, והיינו או דבאמת ס' ר"י ווסתות דרבנן או אף אי ווסתות דאורייתא לא הוי כודאי ממש, מש"ה גם בילדה יש להקל, ואם נפרש ילדה דהיינו יולדת ג"כ ניחא דרצה ללמוד כי היכא דאי ווסתות דאורייתא אף דהוי כודאי ראתה מקילין, ה"נ בילדה דנוכל לחשוב ימי ווסתה, והיינו ז' ימים אחר ימי טומאה דאף אם ראתה בהם הוי דם טוהר, ואף למ"ד דמעיין אחד הוא מ"מ משכחת בידע דפסקה רגע אחד ואח"כ הלך לדרכו, ועלה אמרינן כיון דודאי ראתה לא מקילין היינו אף היכי דליכא חשש שמא לא פסקה מלראות כגון דידע דפסקה ואח"כ הלך לדרכו דומיא דילדה דמיירי כה"ג מ"מ לא מקילינן דאימא לא טבלה, אם כן מעולם לא שמעינן דר' שמעון ב"י היה סבר דר"י מיירי בודאי ראתה, אלא דמכח הווסתות הוי כודאי ראתה ובזה יכול לחשוב הרגל משך ראייתה.

גם אף אם נפרש דהי' סבור דמיירי ר"י בודאי ראתה מ"מ י"ל דהיה סבור דווסתות דאורייתא והוי חזקה ה"נ הוי חזקה דאינה רואה רק עד משך כך וכך ימים אבל לדידן דקיי"ל ווסתות דרבנן כי היכי דלא מחזיקין להרגל ראייתה לודאי ראתה דדרך נשים להשתנות עניני

ראייתן, ה"נ לא חשבינן להרגל פסיקתה דודאי פסקה, עכ"פ אחרי שהדין מפורש (בדף ס"ח) דבלא הפרשת טהרה היא בחזקת טומאה אזדא לדברי תשו' זכרון יוסף בהיתר זה [ובההיא ענינא ראיתי בסדרי טהרה (סי' קפ"ד סט"ו) הקשה דבירושלמי מבואר דר"י דאמר בעלה מחשב ימי וסתה היינו דס"ל טבילה בזמנה מצוה, א"כ לדידן ליתא להאי דינא והניח בקושיא, ובעניי איני רואה סרך קושיא דמ"מ הא מדאמרינן בסוגיא דידן עלה דר"ה דאמר הגיע שעת וסתה אסורה, ס"ל ווסתות דאורייתא ואמאי מוקי דלא כהלכתא, הא י"ל דס"ל ווסתות דרבנן אלא דס"ל דטבילה בזמנה לאו מצוה והוי כהלכתא, וביותר כפי דאמרינן דס"ל ווסתות דאורייתא צריך לדחוק דמה דאמר לקמן (דף ט"ז ע"א) משמיה דרב ווסתות דרבנן דליה לא ס"ל כמ"ש התוס' שם, ואמאי לא אמרינן דס"ל באמת ווסתות דרבנן אלא דטבילה בזמנה לאו מצוה, אע"כ דסוגיא דידן ס"ל דמ"מ מקילין אי ווסתות דרבנן וקיי"ל כסוגיא דידן נגד הירושלמי, גם אפשר דבהא פליגי דהירושלמי ס"ל דר"י מצי סבר ג"כ ווסתות דאורייתא דמ"מ לא הוי כמו ודאי ראתה, אבל סוגיין דאמרי' דרבב"ח דמיקל ס"ל ווסתות דרבנן דמיירי ע"כ בשהתה שיעור שתוכל לטבול כדהוכיחו בתוס' ממילא מוכח דאי ווסתות דאורייתא גם בכה"ג אסורה, ומוכח באמת דר"י ס"ל ווסתות דרבנן ומותר אף אי טבילה בזמנה לאו מצוה ונכון], ולזה לכאורה בנ"ד ליכא צד קולא נגד דעת רבותינו המחמירים דס"ל דמדינא בעי' בדיקת חורין וסדקין.

חזון איש יו"ד צב:כב – וג' דחרשת שלא בדקורה עד אחרי עבור ימים שדרך רוב הנשים שפוסקות, טובלין אותה בחזקת טהורה בלא בדיקה, וכמו שהביא הז"י ראי' ברורה מסוגיא דלעיל ט"ו אשה שיש לה וסת בעלה מחשב ימי וסתה וכו' אע"ג דאין כאן הפסק טהרה, והגרע"א ז"ל בתשובותיו סי' השיב משום שהכא לא ראתה בודאי אלא מכח חזקה של וסתות, וצ"ע דמ"מ מוכרח דרוב גמור הוא ולמה לא נסמוך בודאי ראתה, ומיהו לא שייך סברא זו אלא ביש לה וסת וראתה בשעת וסתה, אבל אשה שאין לה וסת או שראתה שלא בשעת וסתה או שראתה בשעת וסתה והמשיכה ראיתה יותר מהרגיל אז צריך בדיקה, ומסוגיא דלעיל ס"ח א' שהקשו הס"ט והגרע"א לדברי הז"י, דמבואר דצריך הפרשת טהרה, נראה דביה"ש לא הפרישה היינו שלא עמדה על טהרתה הדרוש לה, ומיירי באופן שהיתה צריכה בדיקה כגון שלא בשעת וסת או המשיכה ראיתה יותר מהרגיל, ואפשר דהלכך נקט בדקה בז' ומצאה טמאה, אבל יש לה וסת וסומכת על דרך הוסתות מקרי הפרישה ביה"ש ואין זה בכלל המסופר במתני' עכ"פ למדנו מדברי הגרע"א בחרשת שיש לה וסת ועבר זמן וסתה א"צ הפרשת טהרה לאחר הוסת אפי' למ"ד וסתות דאורייתא.

תלמוד בבלי מסכת נדה דף טו עמוד א–טז עמוד א – מתני'. כל הנשים בחזקת טהרה לבעליהן. הבאין מן הדרך – נשיהן להן בחזקת טהרה.

גמ'. למה ליה למתני הבאין מן הדרך? סד"א: הני מילי – היכא דאיתיה במתא, דרמיא אנפשה ובדקה, אבל היכא דליתא במתא – דלא רמיא אנפשה – לא, קא משמע לן. אמר ריש לקיש משום רבי יהודה נשיאה: והוא שבא ומצאה בתוך ימי עונתה. אמר רב הונא: ל"ש אלא שאין לה וסת. אבל יש לה וסת – אסור לשמש. כלפי לייא? אדרבה, איפכא מסתברא! אין לה

וסת – אימא חזאי, יש לה וסת – וסת קביע לה! אלא, אי איתמר – הכי איתמר, אמר רב הונא: ל"ש אלא שלא הגיע שעת וסתה, אבל הגיע שעת וסתה – אסורה, קסבר: וסתות דאורייתא. רבה בר בר חנה אמר: אפילו הגיע שעת וסתה – נמי מותרת, קסבר: וסתות דרבנן. רב אשי מתני הכי, אמר רב הונא: לא שנו אלא שאין לה וסת לימים אלא יש לה וסת לימים ולקפיצות, כיון דבמעשה תליא מילתא – אימא לא קפיץ ולא חזאי. אבל יש לה וסת לימים – אסורה לשמש, קסבר – וסתות דאורייתא. רבה בר בר חנה אמר: אפילו יש לה וסת לימים – מותרת, קסבר – וסתות דרבנן. אמר רב שמואל משמיה דרבי יוחנן: אשה שיש לה וסת – בעלה מחשב ימי וסתה ובא עליה. אמר ליה רב שמואל בר ייבא לרבי אבא: אמר רבי יוחנן אפילו ילדה דבזיזא למטבל? אמר ליה: אטו ודאי ראתה מי אמר רבי יוחנן? אימר דאמר רבי יוחנן – ספק ראתה ספק לא ראתה, ואם תמצא לומר ראתה – אימא טבלה, אבל ודאי ראתה – מי יימר דטבלה? הוה ליה ספק וודאי, ואין ספק מוציא מידי ודאי. ולא? והתניא: חבר שמת והניח מגורה מלאה פירות, אפילו הן בני יומן – הרי הן בחזקת מתוקנין. והא הכא, ודאי טבל, ספק מעושר ספק אינו מעושר, וקאתי ספק ומוציא מידי ודאי! התם ודאי וודאי הוא – כדרב חנינא חוזאה, דאמר רב חנינא חוזאה: חזקה על חבר שאינו מוציא מתחת ידו דבר שאינו מתוקן. ואיבעית אימא: ספק וספק הוא, וכדרבי אושעיא. דא"ר אושעיא: מערים אדם על תבואתו ומכניסה במוץ שלה, כדי שתהא בהמתו אוכלת ופטורה מן המעשר. ואכתי, אין ספק מוציא מידי ודאי? והתניא: מעשה בשפחתו של מסיק אחד ברימון, שהטילה נפל לבור, ובא כהן והציץ בו לידע אם זכר אם נקבה, ובא מעשה לפני חכמים וטהרוהו, מפני שחולדה וברדלס מצויים שם. והא הכא – דודאי הטילה נפל, ספק גררוהו ספק לא גררוהו, וקאתי ספק ומוציא מידי ודאי! לא תימא הטילה נפל לבור, אלא אימא: כמין נפל. והא לידע אם זכר אם נקבה קתני! ה"ק: ובא כהן והציץ בו לידע אם נפל הפילה אם רוח הפילה, ואת"ל נפל הפילה – לידע אם זכר אם נקבה. ואיבעית אימא: כיון דחולדה וברדלס מצויים שם – ודאי גררוהו. בעו מיניה מרב נחמן: וסתות דאורייתא או דרבנן? אמר להו: מדאמר הונא חברין משמיה דרב, אשה שיש לה וסת, והגיע שעת וסתה ולא בדקה, ולבסוף ראתה – חוששת לוסתה וחוששת לראייתה אלמא – וסתות דאורייתא. איכא דאמרי, הכי קא"ל: טעמא – דראתה, הא לא ראתה – אין חוששין, אלמא – וסתות דרבנן. איתמר; אשה שיש לה וסת, והגיע שעת וסתה ולא בדקה, ולבסוף בדקה, אמר רב: בדקה ומצאת טמאה – טמאה, טהורה – טהורה. ושמואל אמר: אפילו בדקה ומצאת טהורה – נמי טמאה, מפני שאורח בזמנו בא. לימא בוסתות קמיפלגי, דמ"ס – דאורייתא, ומ"ס – דרבנן! אמר ר' זירא – דכ"ע – וסתות דאורייתא, כאן – שבדקה עצמה כשיעור וסת, כאן – שלא בדקה עצמה כשיעור וסת. ר"נ בר יצחק אמר: בוסתות גופייהו קמיפלגי, דמ"ס – וסתות דאורייתא, ומר סבר – וסתות דרבנן. אמר רב ששת: כתנאי, ר' אליעזר אומר טמאה נדה, ורבי יהושע אומר תבדק. והני תנאי כי הני תנאי; דתניא, רבי מאיר אומר: טמאה נדה, וחכ"א: תבדק. אמר אביי: אף אנן נמי תנינא; דתנן, ר"מ אומר: אם היתה במחבא, והגיע שעת וסתה ולא בדקה – טהורה, שחרדה מסלקת את הדמים. טעמא – דאיכא חרדה, הא ליכא חרדה – טמאה, אלמא – וסתות דאורייתא. לימא הני תנאי בהא נמי פליגי, דתניא הרואה דם מחמת מכה – אפילו בתוך ימי נדתה טהורה – דברי רשב"ג, רבי אומר: אם יש לה וסת – חוששת לוסתה. מאי לאו, בהא קמיפלגי, דמר סבר –

וסתות דאורייתא, ומר סבר – וסתות דרבנן! אמר רבינא: לא, דכ"ע – וסתות דרבנן, והכא – במקור מקומו טמא קמיפלגי; רשב"ג סבר: אשה – טהורה, ודם טמא – דקאתי דרך מקור, ואמר ליה רבי: אי חיישת לוסת – אשה נמי טמאה, ואי לא חיישת לוסת – מקור מקומו טהור הוא.

שו"ת נודע ביהודה מהדורה קמא – יורה דעה סימן נה – והנה דבריו טובים למ"ד וסתות דאורייתא אבל למ"ד וסתות דרבנן איך נצרף הוסת לחייב בשבילו חטאת ועיקרו מדרבנן. ואין זה דומה למה דמחייבינן במסכת שבועות חטאת ולא אמרינן אנוס הוא היינו שאפי' וסתות דרבנן מ"מ כיון שעכ"פ מוטל עליו מדרבנן לפרוש הימנה שוב אינו אנוס לשמש עמה וממילא חייב חטאת על שגגתו ששימש עם הטמאה ודאי אבל בזה שאנו מסופקים אם היא טמאה כלל כי שמא דם עליה הוא ואיך נימא דבשעת וסת חזקתו מן המקור והלא וסתות דרבנן ולמימר דמתניתין אתיא כמ"ד וסתות דאורייתא קשה הדבר לאמרו לאוקמי משנתנו שהיא סתם משנה דלא כהלכתא. והנלע"ד בזה על פי מה שחידשתי דבר נפלא דלכאורה להנך דסברי וסתות דרבנן קמה כנגדם כחומה אזהרה דוהזרתם וגו' דילפינן מינה אזהרה לבני ישראל שיפרשו עונה סמוך לוסתן והרי עיקר הוסת דרבנן ואיך הזהירה התורה עליו. והראב"ד באמת רצה לומר שזה אסמכתא וכן כתבו הר"ן והרשב"א הובא בב"י סי' קפ"ד. אמנם התוס' ביבמות דף ס"ב כתבו דסמוך לוסתן דאורייתא וכן שטחת לשון הרמב"ם בפ"ד מא"ב הלכה י"ב משמע שהוא מן התורה ואני אומר ודאי שהוא מן התורה ואעפ"כ וסתות דרבנן. ואומר אני אף שנחלקו תנאים ואמוראים אם וסתות דאורייתא או דרבנן אין טעם פלוגתתם דלמ"ד וסתות דרבנן אז מן התורה לא אמרינן חזקה אורח בזמנו בא ועיקר חזקה זו תהי' לדידי' רק מדרבנן א"ו גם לדידי' חזקה זו היא ככל החזקות שבש"ס וחזקה מן התורה היא כדאמרינן בפ"ק דחולין אלא דנגד חזקה זו היא חזקת האשה שבחזקת טהרה עומדת ולכך מן התורה אוקמינן חזקה להדי חזקה וזהו טעם המ"ד וסתות דרבנן.

חזון איש יו"ד פ:יט – ונראה דהנה כבר נתבאר דטעמא דמ"ד וסתות דרבנן שאין זה חזקה כלל, ואע"ג דרוב יש להן וסת היינו עיקר קיום הוסת אבל מצוי שינוי הסדר לוסת אחר ופעמים מקדמת ופעמים מאחרת, וכדאמרינן כתובות ב' ב' כיון דאיכא נשי דקמשנו וסתיהו כשעת וסתה דמי עי"ש, עד שאם נדון בדרך הארץ בראיות משולשות בסדר קיים אם יקוים ראית יום הזה ברוב הנשים ברוב חייהן אין זה אלא כמחצה על מחצה, ולכן היא בחזקתה הראשונה שלא ראתה, ועפ"ז צריך תלמוד טעמא דמ"ד וסתות דאו', ודוחק לומר דפליגי במציאות הדבר.

שו"ת נודע ביהודה מהדורה קמא – יורה דעה סימן מו – והנה אחר כתבי זה בא לידי ספר בעלי הנפש וראיתי שכמו שהעתיק הרב"י דבריו כן הוא. ואף על פי כן אני יפה כוונתי בדעת הראב"ד שכיון שאמרו כיון שתבעה אין בדיקה גדולה מזו הרי עיקר הבדיקה מה שהיא נותנת דעתה אם היא טהורה ואם איתא דהוי דם בבית החיצון היתה מרגשת בעצמה. והנה לא מבעיא לפי מה שהעתיק הרשב"א לשון הראב"ד כיון שתבעה אין לך בדיקה גדולה מזו כלומר לפי שנותנת דעתה ומרגשת אם יש דם בבית החיצון ואין לך בדיקה כל דהו יותר מתביעה עכ"ל הרשב"א מה שהעתיק בשם הראב"ד הגם שבספר בעלי הנפש אשר לפנינו לא נאמר הלשון הזה ממש

מ"מ הרי כתב הראב"ד שם ומסתברא כלישנא קמא שכיון שהקילו על הבדיקה שאפילו בשנים לנדתה וכו' אלמא בבדיקה כל דהו סגי לה עכ"ל הראב"ד. הרי שגם בנוסחא שלפנינו כתב דסגי בבדיקה כל דהו ואעפ"כ יפה כתב שבדיקת נדה וזבה ליום הפסקה ולבדיקת שבעה הוא בדיקת בית החיצון עד מקום שהשמש דש ולא שיש חילוק בין בדיקה שלפני התשמיש ובין בדיקות נדה וזבה הנ"ל שהרי הראב"ד מסיים ומסתברא כלישנא קמא דהיינו שבדיקת נדה וזבה הוא כמו הבדיקה לתשמיש. ואמנם מה שנותנת דעתה ומרגשת בעצמה הוא עצמו בדיקה כל בה"ח עד מקום שהשמש דש שאלמלי היה באותו פעם שם דם היתה מרגשת בעצמה שכותלי בה"ר לא מוקמי דם והיתה מרגשת בזוב הדם בבשרה לחוץ אבל לטהרות החמירו לחוש לחורין וסדקין שהם הם דמוקמי דם ואינה מרגשת אבל לחולין לא חששו לחורין וסדקין וכל לבעלה חולין הוא. אלא שכלפי מה שחישב הראב"ד שם ג' בדיקות חלוקות זו מזו והראשונה מציאת הכתם לשלש נשים ושם הבדיקה היא דוקא קינוח בעלמא אבל אם הכניסה העד בעומק עד מקום דישת השמש אדרבה שוב אינו מועיל לטהר עצמה ולטמא חברותיה. ואמר אח"כ בדיקה שנית לנדה וזבה וכו' והיא בדיקת בית החיצון לומר שזה עיקר הבדיקה שתדע שכל בית החיצון הוא נקי מדם ונתינת דעתה לזה להרגיש בבשרה הוא עצם הבדיקה אלא שנתינת דעת שייך בפקחת ועומדת או מהלכת שאז מרגשת בזיבת הדם אבל בחרשת ושוטה שחברותיה בודקות אותן לא שייך בהן הרגשה לכך צריכה בדיקת בית החיצון וצריכה חברתה הבודקת אותה להכניס העד עד מקום שהשמש דש. אבל בדיקה הראשונה למציאת הכתם לג' נשים לטהר עצמה ולטמא חברותיה אפילו בחרשת ושוטה לא משכחת דמהני רק קינוח ובפקחת השוכבת אפרקיד כפי שיתבאר לקמן לבעלה צריכה להעמיק עד מקום דישת השמש דבשוכבת אפרקיד אין הדם זב ממנה ולא שייכי מרגשת בעצמה. זה הנראה לפע"ד בכוונת דברי הראב"ד דהרי אי אפשר לסתור דברי עצמו שכתב דתביעה הרי היא כבדיקה לגבי בעלה. ועוד שהרי הראב"ד מסיים שם אבל בדיקת החלוק לא כלום הוא שהרי בדקו את עצמן שנינו ובגמרא אמרינן בדקה עצמה לא בדקה חלוקה הרי שלא מיעט הראב"ד אלא בדיקת החלוק. והטעם באמת דלא מהני בדיקת החלוק משום דלא אמרינן מרגשת בעצמה אלא כשנותנת דעתה על מה שהוא בעת הבדיקה אבל בדיקת החלוק הוא אם לא בא עליה מקודם לכן דם ואין זה כל כך ראיה שנותנת דעתה על עצמה ועל בשרה בעת ההיא ממש. באופן שאני נשאר על עמדי שלהראב"ד סגי בבדיקה כל דהו. והרא"ש בפ' תינוקת החמיר בה שצריכה בדיקת חורין וסדקין ועד מקום שהשמש דש. וכן הרז"ה משיג על הראב"ד וכן הסמ"ג וסמ"ק עיין בב"י סי' קצ"ו כולם מחמירין וכן הטור שמה.

שו"ת נודע ביהודה מהדורה קמא – יורה דעה סימן נט – הן אמת שביארתי בתשובה אחרת שעיקר הבדיקה היא משום שבשעת בדיקה נותנת דעתה להרגיש אם דם יוצא מן המקור וא"כ מה שאינה מרגשת שדם יוצא מן המקור מקרי הפסק טהרה אבל הדברים ארוכים ויתבארו במקומם. ולא עוד אלא שעכ"פ פעם אחת יגיע שתהיה שוב טמאה ודאי בשעת וסתה דאטו לעולם לא תטמא וכיון שהבדיקות שבינתים אזדי להו כמי שאינם הרי זו כמו שבדקה ומצאה טמאה ושוב לא בדקה ואח"כ בדקה ומצאה טמאה דאיפליגו שם במס' נדה דף ס"ח רב ולוי והלכה כרב דאמר זבה ודאי וכמו שפסק הרמב"ם בפ"ו מאיסורי ביאה הלכה כ' וא"כ ננעלו

כל שערי הספיקות כי אין ספק מוציא מידי ודאי ולכן יראה שם לצוות אל האשה אולי יקרה לפעמים שתמצא הבדיקה טהורה ואם תוכל לעשות הבחינה המבואר בש"ע סי' קצ"א בהג"ה תנסה ואיך שיעלה בידה יודיעני מעלתו ואז נחכם לה.

שו"ת חתם סופר חלק ב (יורה דעה) סימן קעז – ואומר אני הדין דין אמת גבי הפסק טהרה וא"צ ראי' אבל הספירות נקיים צריך ראיה ואין ראייתו מכרעת דאיך אפשר לומר אם עמדה בין השמשות ולא הרגישה פפה"מ יעלה לה להפסק טהרה הרי אנו דנין שביום וסתה נפתח מקורה להוציא דם וסתה ואנו חוששי' שעודנה פתוח ומורק דם עד שתפסוק לפנינו ואיך נאמר שכיון שלא הרגישה כל בה"ש שנפתח מקורה הרי פסקה דכי כל שעה נפתח מקורה הלא דלמא פתוח ועומד הוא וע"כ אי אפשר אלא שתבדוק בחורין ובסדקין ותדע שנסתם מקורה אבל שוב אח"כ אפשר לענין ספירת נקיים הוה ספורים לפנינו כל שברור לה שהשגיחה על עצמה שחרית א' מז' ימים ויודעת בודאי שאז לא נפתח מקורה ואמנם יהי' זה בהשגחה פרטיות באופן שלא נחוש דלמא ארגשה ולאו אדעתה אלא שתעמוד שעה א' מסיחת דעתה מכל הרהורים ומחשבות ומשגיחת על עצמה ויודעת שלא נפתח מקורה והוה ספורים לפנינו ואך יען שזה בדיקה ק' מאוד ע"כ עיקר הבדיקה ע"י הכנסת עד בחורין ובסדקין ואם לא תמצא דם הרי יצאנו מכל הספיקות וא"כ לא תיקשי מש"ס דאמרה א"י כמה ספרתי היינו כנ"ל שלא השגיחה על עצמה או שלא בדקה בחורין ובסדקין ורש"י פי' בדיקה פשוטה וכן כל הפוסקים שבב"י שאמרו בדיקת חורין וסדקין הוא ס' כרת בודאי כן הוא דמיירי באשה שאינה אומרת ברי לי אלא סומכת על בדיקה וכשאינה מכנסת לחורין וסדקין הוה ס' כרת ואין ראייתו מכרעת כלל.

חזון איש יו"ד פ"א – נראה דאף אם תרחוץ ויהיה נקי לפי שעה ומיד תבדוק במוך דחוק בחורין וסדקין ותמצא את המוך נקי, אין זה הפסק טהרה דאין הפסק טהרה אלא במוצאה עצמה טהורה בתחלת הבדיקה.

שולחן ערוך יורה דעה סימן קצו סעיף ג – הגה: ומנהג כשר הוא כשהאשה פוסקת בטהרה שתרחץ ולובשת לבנים; אמנם אם לא רחצה רק פניה של מטה, די בכך (מרדכי בשם רוקח), וכן נוהגין ואין לשנות; אבל בשעת הדחק, כגון אשה ההולכת בדרך ואין לה בגדים, תוכל לספור ז' נקיים רק שהחלוק יהיה נקי ובדוק מדם (אגור והגהות ש"ד ס"ס י"ט).

שו"ת אגרות משה יורה דעה חלק ב סימן עא – ובדבר אם רשאה לרחוץ עצמה באותו מקום יפה קודם הבדיקות בסתם אשה ליכא חסרון בזה שהרי היא כבר בחזקה שפסקו דמיה, אך תחכה זמן קצר כרבע שעה בערך ולעשות הבדיקה, אבל באשה זו שדרכה זה איזה חדשים שהיא רואה המראה ברוין אם היה ספק לנו בכשרות המראה אין לה לרחוץ דהרי אם לא תראה כפי הרגילות שלה בחדשים האחרונים אולי היה זה ע"י הרחיצה, אבל לדינא כיון שכבר הורה לכתר"ה חכם שהוא מראה טהור ליכא קפידא.

.21

תלמוד בבלי מסכת נדה דף ב עמוד א – מתני'. שמאי אומר: כל הנשים דיין שעתן, הלל אומר: מפקידה לפקידה, ואפילו לימים הרבה. וחכ"א: לא כדברי זה ולא כדברי זה; אלא: מעת לעת – ממעטת על יד מפקידה לפקידה, ומפקידה לפקידה – ממעטת על יד מעת לעת. כל אשה שיש לה וסת – דיה שעתה והמשמשת בעדים הרי זו כפקידה, וממעטת על יד מעת לעת ועל יד מפקידה לפקידה, כיצד דיה שעתה: היתה יושבת במטה ועסוקה בטהרות, ופרשה וראתה – היא טמאה והן טהורות. אע"פ שאמרו מטמאה מעת לעת – אינה מונה אלא משעה שראתה.

רמב"ם הלכות מטמאי משכב ומושב פרק ג הלכה ב – אין משכב בועל נדה ומרכבו כמשכב נדה ומרכבה שהמשכב או המרכב שדרסה עליו נדה אב מאבות הטומאה ומשכב בועל נדה ומרכבו ולד טומאה ככלים שנוגע בהן שאינן מטמאין אדם ולא כלים אלא אוכלין ומשקין בלבד, ולמה נגרעה טומאת משכבו מטומאת משכבה מפני שנאמר בבועל נדה ותהי נדתה עליו וטמא שבעת ימים ונאמר בו כל המשכב אשר ישכב עליו יטמא מאחר שנאמר ותהי נדתה עליו איני יודע שהוא מטמא משכב ולמה נאמר, מפי השמועה למדו שהכתוב נתקו מטומאה חמורה מלטמא אדם וכלים ותלאו בטומאה קלה שיהיה משכבו ולד ולא יטמא אדם וכלים אלא אוכלין ומשקין בלבד כשאר ולדות הטומאות.

תלמוד בבלי מסכת נדה דף יא עמוד א – מתני'. אע"פ שאמרו דיה שעתה – צריכה להיות בודקת, חוץ מן הנדה והיושבת על דם טוהר. ומשמשת בעדים – חוץ מיושבת על דם טוהר, ובתולה שדמיה טהורים. ופעמים צריכה להיות בודקת – שחרית ובין השמשות, ובשעה שהיא עוברת לשמש את ביתה. יתירות עליהן כהנות – בשעה שהן אוכלות בתרומה, רבי יהודה אומר: אף בשעת עברתן מלאכול בתרומה.

תלמוד בבלי מסכת נדה דף יא עמוד ב – פעמים היא צריכה וכו'. א"ר יהודה אמר שמואל: לא שנו אלא לטהרות, אבל לבעלה – מותרת. פשיטא, שחרית תנן! אלא, אי אתמר – אסיפא אתמר, ובשעה שהיא עוברת לשמש את ביתה א"ר יהודה אמר שמואל: לא שנו אלא באשה עסוקה בטהרות, דמגו דבעיא בדיקה לטהרות – בעיא נמי בדיקה לבעלה, אבל אינה עסוקה בטהרות – לא בעיא בדיקה. מאי קמ"ל? תנינא – כל הנשים בחזקת טהרה לבעליהן! אי ממתני' – הוה אמינא: הני מילי – באשה שיש לה וסת. אבל אשה שאין לה וסת – בעיא בדיקה. והא מתני' באשה שיש לה וסת עסקינן! מתני' – בין שיש לה וסת בין אין לה וסת, והא קמ"ל: דאע"ג דיש לה וסת, מגו דבעיא בדיקה לטהרות – בעיא נמי בדיקה לבעלה. והא אמרה שמואל חדא זימנא! דאמר רבי זירא אמר רבי אבא בר ירמיה אמר שמואל: אשה שאין לה וסת – אסורה לשמש עד שתבדוק. ואוקימנא בעסוקה בטהרות! חדא מכלל חברתה אתמר.

תלמוד בבלי מסכת נדה דף ה עמוד א – והמשמשת בעדים כו'. אמר רב יהודה אמר שמואל עד שלפני תשמיש – אינו ממעט כפקידה. מ"ט? אמר רב קטינא: מתוך שמהומה לביתה. וכי מהומה לביתה מאי הוי? מתוך שמהומה לביתה – אינה מכנסת לחורין ולסדקין.

בעלי הנפש שער הספירה והבדיקה סימן ג – עתה אנו צריכין לפרש ענין הבדיקה היאך הוא:ונאמר, כי מצאנו שלש בדיקות חלוקות זו מזו. הראשונה בדיקת קנוח, והיא בדיקה למציאת הכתם לשלש נשים שהיו ישנות במטה אחת ונמצא עליה דם, שאם בדקה עצמה בשיעור וסת למציאת הכתם אם מצאה טמא טיהרה את חברותיה, ואם מצאה טהור טיהרה את עצמה וטמאה את חברותיה כאשר פירשנו בשערי הכתמים. והשנית בדיקת בית החיצון והוא מקום שהשמש דש, והיא בדיקה לנדה ולזבה ליום ההפסקה ולבדיקת השבעה אשר אמרנו למעלה. והשלישית בדיקת חורין וסדקין בבית החיצון, והיא בדיקת הטהרות כאשר אמרו בגמ' (נדה ה א) עד שלפני התשמיש אינו ממעט כפקידה. מאי טעמא, מפני שהבודקת לביתה אינה מכנסת לחורין ולסדקין. הנה ראינו מכאן כי אע"פ שתקנו חכמים בדיקה לתשמיש ולטהרות, עד שלפני תשמיש בדיקה הוא לתשמיש ואינו בדיקה לטהרות, מפני שאינה מכניסתו לחורין ולסדקין. ועוד אמרו (נדה יב א) דתביעה הרי היא כבדיקה לגבי בעלה. ויש מי שאומר דבדיקת זבה בין בבדיקת יום ההפסקה בין בבדיקת השבעה בעינן בדיקה מעולה כבדיקת הטהרות, ולא הקלו לגבי בעל אלא בבדיקת המעלות כאשה העסוקה בטהרות שהצריכוה בדיקה אף לבעלה. ומסתברא כלישנא קמא, מכיון שהקלו על הבדיקה שאפילו בשנים לנדתה בדקה עצמה ומצאה טהור הרי היא בחזקת טהורה, אלמא בבדיקה כל דהו סגי לה.

אבל בדיקת חלוק לא כלום היא שהרי בדקו את עצמן שנינו (משנה סח ב), ובגמ' אמרינן (נדה נג א) בדקה עצמה ולא בדקה חלוקה, אלמא בדיקת עצמה לחוד ובדיקת חלוקה לחוד.

ובדיקת הוסתות שאמרנו שהיא צריכה בדיקה לטהר את יום הוסת כמו כן בבדיקה קלה סגי לה, ואינה צריכה להכניס לחורין ולסדקין. מיהו בעיא בדיקה בבית החיצון. אלא שאין שעות הבדיקות שוות, כי עקר בדיקת הוסתות הוא בשעת הוסת, ואם לא בדקה בשעת הוסת ובדקה עצמה לבסוף ומצאה טהור טהורה. אבל בדיקת הזבה עיקר בדיקתה בתחלת יום הראשון ובסוף יום השביעי כדי שתהא תחלתן וסופן בטהרה, ואם בדקה באחת מהן כבר אמרנו שהיא טהורה.

והבדיקה המעולה שתהא אשה בודקת עצמה בצמר גפן נקי או בצמר נקי ורך או בשחיקי מאני דכתנא. ומכניסתו לאותו מקום, וכל מראה אדמימות שבו נדון כדם.

עוד יש אחרת שהיא צריכה בדיקה ובדיקתה בדיקה קלה, והיא הרואה דם מחמת תשמיש (נדה סה ב, סו א) שצריכה לבדוק פעם ראשונה ושניה ושלישית, ואם ראתה בכולם אסורה לשמש, והוא שבדקה עצמה כשיעור וסת או כדי שתושיט יד לתחת הכר או תחת הכסת ותטול עד ותבדוק בו שיהא בעלה באשם תלוי. אבל אח"כ הרי הוא כמעת לעת שבנדה שאינה מטמאה את בועלה ואינה מוחזקת ברואה דם מחמת תשמיש ואינה נאסרת על בעלה. וי"א שאין אנו בקיאין עכשיו בשיעורין הללו, הלכך כל סמוך לביאה אם בדקה ומצאה דם נאסרת על בעלה והרי היא בחזקת רואה מחמת תשמיש. ומסתברא כוותיה.

הלכך תתגרש ותנשא לאחר ומותרת לשני לשמש עמה שלש פעמים ובבדיקה. ואם ראתה דם שלשה פעמים סמוך לתשמיש, אסורה לו ותתגרש. ותנשא לשלישי ומותרת לשלישי עד שלש פעמים, ואם ראתה עם השלישי שלש פעמים אסורה לכל אדם עד שתבדוק עצמה בשפופרת של אבר ופיו רצוף לתוכו ובתוכו מכחול ובראשו מוך. אם נמצא דם בראש המכחול

בידוע שהוא מן המקור, ואם לאו בידוע שהוא מן הצדדין. והבדיקה הזאת אין לנו עכשיו שאין אנו בקיאין 1בהכנסת המכחול ואולי יתחלף בו בין ראשו לצדדין.

חידושי הרמב"ן מסכת נדה דף ה עמוד א – מתוך שמהומה לביתה אין מכניסתו לחורין ולסדקין. מכאן למד הראב"ד ז"ל שכל לבעלה אינו צריך בדיקת חורין וסדקין, שהרי בדיקה זו אינה מועילה לטהרות מפני שאין בה בדיקת חורין וסדקין ואע"פ כן מועלת לגבי בעלה, ועוד הביא ראיה ממה שאמרו (י"ב א') דתביעה הרי היא כבדיקה לגבי בעלה, והוא ז"ל כתב שיש מי שחולק ואמר דבדיקת זבה בין ביום ההפסקה בין בבדיקת השבעה בעינן בדיקה מעולה כשל טהרות, ולא הקלו לגבי בעל אלא בבדיקת המעלות כגון זו שאשה העסוקה בטהרות הצריכו בדיקה זו אף לבעלה מתוך חומר שהחמרת עליה בטהרות, אבל בדיקה מעולה הצריכה להן מחמת הבעל עצמו צריכה להיות בדיקה מעולה, ועוד שיש להחמיר אפילו בבדיקת מעלות, ומה שאמר כאן אינה מכניסתו לא שלא הוצרכה אלא מתוך שמהומה לביתה חוששין לטהרות שמא לא עשתה כהוגן ולא הכניסתו לחורין ולסדקין, והוא כעין מה שאמרו בסמוך ניחוש שמא תראה טפת דם ותחפנו שכבת זרע וכו', וכן נראה מדברי רש"י ז"ל דכל בדיקה היינו לחורין וסדקין בשילהי פירקין (י"ב א' ד"ה לבדיקה), ולפי הסברא יש להכריע שבדיקת ההפסקה שהיא מעלה אותה מטומאה לטהרה ומוציא אותה מחזקה לחזקה צריכה להיות בדיקה מעולה שאין אחריה עליו ספק, אבל בדיקת השבעה כיון שכבר פסקה להעמידה בחזקתה בבדיקה כל דהוא סגיא, דהא אפילו לא בדקה כלל אלא בשעת ההפסקה ובסוף שבעה טהורה לקמן בפרק בתרא (ס"ח ב'), הילכך לקולא כדברי הראב"ד ז"ל, ובעל נפש לא יקל בכך.

הלכות נדה לרמב"ן פרק ט – כב. תבדוק ביום ההפסקה מבעוד יום בדיקה יפה בדיקת חורין וסדקין יפה יפה ותחליף חלוקה, וכן (נ"א, ואין) בדיקת יום ראשון מימי הספירה ובדיקת יום השביעי כענין זה בבדיקת חורין וסדקין, ודי לה בבדיקת יום ראשון ושביעי, אך מן המובחר הוא לבדוק בכל יום ויום מז' ימי הספירה. וכן שיום ההפסקה לא יעלה למנין הז', גם ברואה יום אחד בשחרית ופסקה לאלתר כל אותו יום טמא הוא ולא תעשה אותו יום הפסקה, שחזקת יום ראשון מעיין פתוח ודמים חוזרין לה, אלא למחר הוא יהיה יום ההפסקה ומיום ג' ואילך תתחיל למנות ז' ימי הספירה.

חידושי הרשב"א מסכת נדה דף ה עמוד א – מתוך שמהומה לביתה אין מכניסתו לחורין ולסדקין. דקדק מכאן הראב"ד ז"ל דכל לבעלה אינה צריכה בדיקת חורין וסדקין, נראה שהוא ז"ל מפרש מתוך שמהומה לביתה אינה בודקת אלא כמה שצריך לה לשעתה לביתה, וכן סייע דבריו מההיא דאמרי' בשילהי פרקין (י"ב א') כיון שתבעה אין לך בדיקה גדולה מזו כלומר לפי שנותנת דעתה ומרגשת אם יש דם בבית החיצון אם אין ואין לך בדיקת כל דהו [יתר] מתביעה, והוא ז"ל כתב דיש מי שאומר דבדיקת זבה בין בהפסק טהרה בין בבדיקת שבעה נקיים צריכה חורין וסדקין ולא הקלו לגבי בעלה אלא בבדיקת המעלות לפי שאין עיקר הבדיקה לבעל מחמת הבעל אלא מחמת מעלת הטהרות שהיא עסוקה בהן והילכך לא הצריכוה אלא בדיקת כל דהו, והדעת

מכרעת כלשון הזה שהדין נותן דלא יהא בעלה שהוא איסור כרת קל ממעלת עסק טהרות, ועוד דאף בזו יש לי לומר דבבאה לישאל אומרין לה לבדוק חורין וסדקין וכאן חשש פשיעה הוא כלומר מתוך שהיא מהומה לביתה ועוד דבעלמא אין אתה מצריכה בדיקה לבעלה חוששין שמא תפשע ולא תבדוק יפה, והרמב"ן נר"ו הכריע בדבר דבדיקת ההפסקה שהיא להעלותה מטומאה לטהרה צריכה חורין וסדקין אבל בדיקת השבעה דכבר בחזקת טהרה עומדת בבדיקה כל דהו סגי, גם זה אינו מספיק לדעתי דכיון שאף אתה מצריכה בדיקה בימי ספירה או בתחלה או בסופה או שמא בכולן למר כדאית ליה ולמר כדאית ליה בשלהי מכלתין (ס"ח ב') ואם לא בדקה כלל הרי היא בחזקת טומאה אף אתה מצריכה בדיקה בכל מקום שמיטמאה בו דמה הועילה זו בחצי בדיקה אם אתה חושש לה אע"פ שהפסיקה טהרה זיל חוש בחורין וסדקין ואם אין אתה חושש לחורין מפני מה אתה חושש לשאר המקומות, ואדרבה הדעת נותנת שיהו חורין וסדקין צריכין בדיקה יותר מפני שהן המעמידין, ועוד דבדיקת חורין היא שנקראת בדיקה אבל בדיקה אחרת אינה נקראת בדיקה אלא קנוח וכדמשמע לקמן בשלהי פרקין (י"ב א') דאמרי' התם בעא מיניה ר' אבא מרב הונא אשה מהו שתבדוק עצמה בתוך שיעור אותיאום לחיב בעלה חטאת א"ל ומי משכחת לה בדיקה בתוך שיעור אותיאום והתניא איזהו אותיאום וכו' הוי אותיאום שאמרו לקנוח ולא לבדיקה, כלומר דבדיקה אינה אלא בדיקת חורין וסדקין וא"א לה בשיעור אותיאום אלא קינוח בלבד כלומר בדיקה כל דהו חוץ לחורין אלמא בדיקה משמע בדיקת חורין וסדקין ואנן בבדיקת שבעה נקיים בדיקה תנינן בהו דאלמא בדיקת חורין הוא.

תורת הבית הארוך בית ז שער ה – ועתה נבאר בדיקה זו אם היא בדיקת חורין וסדקין או די לה בבדיקה שלא בחורין וסדקין. תנן בפרק קמא דנדה המשמשת בעדים הרי זו כפקידה. ואמרינן עלה בגמרא אמר רב יהודה אמר שמואל עד שלפני תשמיש אינו ממעט מפקידה מאי טעמא אמר רב קטינא מתוך שמהומה לביתה אינה מכניסתו לחורין וסדקין. ודקדק מכאן הרב רבי אברהם ז"ל דכל לבעלה אינה צריכה בדיקת חורין וסדקין. נראה שהוא ז"ל מפרש מתוך שמהומה לביתה אינה בודקת בדיקה יפה הצריכה לטהרות אלא כמה שצריכה עכשיו לביתה. וסייע עוד דבריו מדאמרינן בשילהי פירקין כיון שתבעה אין לך בדיקה גדולה מזו כלומר לפי שנותנת דעתה ומרגשת אם יש דם בבית החיצון ואין לך בדיקה כל דהו יתר מתביעה. והוא ז"ל כתב דיש מי שאומר דבדיקת זבה בין בהפסק טהרה בין בבדיקת שבעה נקיים בעינן חורין וסדקין ולא הקלו כאן לגבי בעלה אלא בבדיקת המעלות לפי שאין עיקר הבדיקה לבעל מחמת הבעל אלא מחמת מעלת הטהרות שהיא עסוקה בהן ולפיכך לא הצריכוה אלא בדיקה כל דהו. ובאמת שהדעת מכרעת כלשון הזה השני דהיאך אפשר שיהא בעלה שהוא איסור כרת קיל ממעלת עסק הטהרות. ועוד דאף כאן יש לי לומר דבבאה לישאל אומרים לה לבדוק חורין וסדקין וכאן חשש פשיעה כלומר מתוך שהיא מהומה לביתה ועוד דבעלמא אין אתה מצריכה בדיקה לבעלה חוששין שמא לא תבדוק אלא קלי. והרמב"ן ז"ל הכריע בדבר דבדיקת ההפסקה שהיא להעלותה מטומאה לטהרה צריכה חורין וסדקין אבל בדיקה השבעה דחזקת טהרה עומדת בבדיקה כל דהו סגי. וגם זה אינו מספיק לדעתי דכיון שאתה מצריכה בדיקה בימי ספירה או בתחילה או בסופה או בכולן למר כדאית ליה ולמר כאית ליה בשילהי מכילתין ואם לא בדקה כלל הרי היא בחזקת

טומאה אף אתה מצריכה בדיקה בכל מקום שמיטמאה בו דמה הועילה זו בחצי בדיקה אם אתה חושש לה אע"פ שהפסיק טהרה ז"ל חוש לה אפילו לחורין וסדקין ואם אי אתה חושש לחורין וסדקין מפני מה אתה מצריך לשאר המקומות ואדרבה הדעת נותנת שיהו חורין וסדקין צריכין בדיקה יותר מפני שהן המעמידין. ועוד דכל בדיקת חורין היא שנקראת בדיקה שלא בחורין אינה נקראת בדיקה אלא קינוח וכדמשמע בשילהי פירקא קמא דנדה דבעי מיניה ר' אבא מרב הונא אשה מהו שתבדוק עצמה בתוך שיעור וסת לחייב את בעלה חטאת א"ל ומי משכחת לה בדיקה בתוך שיעור וסת והתניא אי זהו שיעור וסת משל לשמש ועד שעומדין בצד המשקוף ביציאת השמש נכנס עד הוי וסת שאמרו לקינוח ולא לבדיקה אלמא בדיקה בלא חורין וסדקין אינה נקראת בדיקה אלא קינוח ואנן בדיקת שבעה תניא בהו דאלמא בדיקת חורין היא. וכן הדעת מכרעת. א"ר זירא בנות ישראל החמירו על עצמן שאפילו רואות דם טיפה כחרדל יושבות עליה שבעה ימי נקיים.

משנה מסכת נדה פרק י משנה ג – הזב והזבה שבדקו עצמן ביום ראשון ומצאו טהור וביום הז' ומצאו טהור ושאר ימים שבינתיים לא בדקו ר' אליעזר אומר הרי הן בחזקת טהרה רבי יהושע אומר אין להם אלא יום א' ויום ז' בלבד רע"א אין להם אלא יום ז' בלבד.

שולחן ערוך יורה דעה סימן קצו סעיף ו – כל בדיקות אלו, בין בדיקת הפסק טהרה בין בדיקת כל השבעה, צריכות להיות בבגד פשתן לבן ישן, או בצמר גפן, או בצמר לבן נקי ורך, ותכניסנו באותו מקום בעומק לחורים ולסדקים עד מקום שהשמש דש ותראה אם יש בו שום מראה אדמומית, ולא שתכניסהו מעט לקנח עצמה. ואם יקשה בעיניה מאוד להכניסו כל כך בעומק, לפחות בדיקה של יום הפסק טהרה ובדיקה של יום ראשון מהשבעה תהיינה עד מקום שהשמש דש. הגה: ואם לא עשתה כן בבדיקת יום ראשון, תעשה פעם אחת כן מבדיקות שאר הימים (ב"י); מיהו בדיעבד אם לא עשתה כן כלל רק שבדקה עצמה יפה בחורין ובסדקין בעומק היטב כפי כחה, אע"פ שלא הגיע למקום שהשמש דש, סגי לה (ב"י שכ"ד רוב הפוסקים וכן מהרא"י בפסקיו סימן ע"ז /ע"ח/ וב"ח).

שו"ת נודע ביהודה מהדורה קמא – יורה דעה סימן מו – סיומא דפיסקא דהך איתתא שאם תבדוק ולא תמצא דם כלל מחוץ למוך א"כ אין שום דם בצדדים וכל מה שקרה לה עד עכשיו מן המקור היה א"כ הורע חזקתה ובדיקתה חמורה שצריך שיהיה מוך דחוק אצלה כל ז' ימי נקיים וכפי שביארתי לעיל. אמנם דם שתמצא מחוץ למוך אינו מזיקה רק שהמוך ישאר נקי. ואם תמצא חוץ למוך שאז אנו תולין כל מה שאירע לה עד היום בצדדים ולא הורע חזקתה אזי זה משפטה בהפסק טהרתה קודם הלילה תרחץ אותו המקום היטב היטב ותכניס מוך דחוק למעלה בעומק מאוד תוך גופה כל מה שתוכל להעמיקו טפי טוב לה ואחר שתכניס תקנח הפרוזדור עד שישאר נקי בלי דם ואם תרצה תרחוץ במים מחוץ למוך עד שיהיה הפרוזדור נקי. וכ"ז תעשה קודם בין השמשות ויהיה המוך אצלה עד הלילה ממש ואז שוב תקנח הפרוזדור שאולי יש שם דם שלא ילכלך המוך ושוב תוציא המוך אם הוא נקי עולה לה להפסק טהרה ושוב בכל ז"נ תקנח רק בכל יום פה שלמטה קינוח בעלמא לא בעומק כלל רק מעט לתוך ראשית הפרוזדור ולא

יותר כן נלע"ד להקל בשעת הדחק. ואם יסכימו עמי כבוד מחותני הרב ועוד מופלגי בראד כאשר כתבתי בראשונה הנני נמנה עמהם לדבר מצוה לטהר אשה לבעלה. וה' יראנו מתורתו נפלאות ויצילנו משגיאות. הקטן יחזקאל.

שו"ת נודע ביהודה מהדורה תנינא – יורה דעה סימן קכט – תשובה לכבוד אהובי תלמידי הותיק ומובהק הרב המופלא ומופלג בתורה ויראה כבוד מוה' אברהם נר"ו.

מכתבו קבלתי. וע"ד אשר הורה בהך איתתא שיש לה מכה בכותלי בית הרחם והמכה אינה מוציאה דם ואמנם אם בודקת עצמה כואב לה מאד מחמת הבדיקה ובזמן ימי ליבונה קשה עליה הבדיקה מרוב הכאב. והורה לה מעלתו שתבדוק בהפסקת טהרה כדין וביום הראשון וביום השביעי ג"כ תבדוק כדין ובשאר ימים שבין ראשון לשביעי לא תבדוק כלל כי באשה זו מיחשב דיעבד מחמת צער וכאב. יפה הורה כי אף שלכתחילה צריכה בדיקה כל ז' ימים דבר יום ביומו שר' אלעזר גופא מודה לכתחלה מדלא פליגי רק בדיעבד ואף שאין ראיה גמורה ממה דנקט במשנה דף ס"ח ע"ב פלוגתייהו בדיעבד ולא נקט לכתחלה להודיע כחא דהיתרא לר"א משום דאיכא למימר דרצה למיתני גם פלוגתא דר' יהושע ור"ע ובלכתחלה ליכא פלוגתא בין ר"י ור"ע כלל. וע"ש בתוספות דף ס"ט ע"א בד"ה והכא קמ"ל שכתבו ג"כ כיוצא בזה. ואמנם מצד הסברא ראוי למעט המחלוקת ודי שמצינו שר"א חולק בדיעבד. וכן מפורש הדבר בתוספות דף ז' ע"ב בד"ה ר"א ואף דאיכא למימר שלא כתבו כן אלא בזבה ודאי אבל נשי דידן ספק זבות נינהו אפשר דמותר לכתחלה לסמוך על בדיקת יום ראשון ויום שביעי. אמנם פשוט לשון התוספות שם משמע דלענין נשי דידן כתבו כן וכן פסק הרא"ש ושאר פוסקים וכן מבואר בש"ע בסימן קצ"ו סעיף ז'. אעפ"כ יפה הורה שהרי הצרכת הדבר לכתחלה ודאי שהוא רק חומרא דרבנן בעלמא ובכמה מקומות מצינו שבמקום צער לא גזרו וכיון שלאשה זו כואב הרבה יותר מדאי אין לך מקום צער יותר מזה, ועוד מטעמא אחרינא הייתי מקיל שהרי יש לחוש שעל ידי רוב הבדיקות יגרמו שהמכה תגלע ותוציא דם ונצטרך אח"כ להקל כאשר תמצא דם לתלות במכה יותר עדיף שלא לבוא לידי קולא זו ושפיר הורה. אמנם אם יכולה בשאר ימי הספירה לקנח מבחוץ קינוח כל דהו טוב להצריכה הקינוח אם לא יכאב לה ועיין בנו"ב סי' מ"ו. ולרוב הטרדא אקצר.

תוס' הרא"ש מסכת נדה דף סט עמוד א – ואי משום דבעינן הפסקה בשלישי כדאמר רבא לעיל, נדה שהפרישה בטהרה בשלישי שלה אלמא בלא הפרשה אינה יכולה לספור. חומרא בעלמא היא ומדרבנן.

רא"ש מסכת נדה פרק י סי' ה' – והר"ז הלוי ז"ל כתב שאין ללמוד בדיקת הזבה שצריכה ז' נקיים מבדיקת נדה הקלה שאינה צריכה אלא הפרשת טהרה בין השמשות לבד ואיני רואה כאן ספק דמסתברא דעדיף האמצע יותר מן הסוף דאיתחזק בטהרה כל הימים שאחר הבדיקה ובדיקה שאמרנו היינו שתכניס בגד לבן או צמר גפן לחורין ולסדקין עד מקום שהשמש דש ולא שתכניסנו מעט לקנח את עצמה. דההוא קינוח מיקרי ולא בדיקה כדמשמע לעיל בשילהי פ"ק (דף יב א) בעי מיניה ר' אבא מרב הונא אשה מהו שתבדוק עצמה בתוך שיעור וסת. ומי משכחת בדיקה בתוך שיעור וסת והתניא איזהו שיעור וסת משל לשמש ועד שעומדין בצד המשקוף

ביציאת השמש נכנס עד הוי וסת שאמרו לקינוח ולא לבדיקה אלמא בלא הכנסה לחורין ולסדקין קינוח מיקרי ולא בדיקה.

בית יוסף יורה דעה סימן קצו – ויש לשאול למצריכין לבדוק עד מקום שהשמש מגיע מנין להם כן ואין לומר שלמדו כן ממה שכתב הרמב"ם בפרק ד' מהלכות איסורי ביאה (הכ"ב) גבי בדיקת אשה הרואה דם מחמת תשמיש שצריכה להכניס המכחול עד צואר הרחם דהיינו מקום שהשמש דש דאי מהא לא איריא דשאני התם שאנו חוששין שמא מחמת פגיעת השמש בצואר הרחם בא הדם מן המקור ולפיכך אנו צריכין שהמכחול יכנס עד שם ואם יצא לבן נדע שהדם שהיא רואה בשעת תשמיש אינו מפגיעת האבר בצואר הרחם אלא מן הצדדין הוא בא וטהורה ואין זה ענין לבדיקה דהכא. ואפשר שטעמם משום דכיון דקיי"ל (נדה מ.) דנשים מיטמאות ביציאת הדם לבית החיצון אע"פ שעדיין לא יצא לחוץ כמו שנתבאר בסימן קפ"ג (מ.) צריכה לבדוק כל הבית החיצון ועד מקום שהשמש דש הוא בית החיצון ומפני כך צריכה לבדוק עד שם ואע"פ שכתב הרמב"ם בפרק ה' מהלכות איסורי ביאה (ה"ד) שבשעת גמר ביאה האבר נכנס בפרוזדור ואינו מגיע עד ראשו שמבפנים אלא רחוק ממנו מעט לפי האצבעות ע"כ דלפי זה אפילו תכניס העד עד מקום שהשמש דש עדיין לא יצאה ידי חובת בדיקת הפרוזדור כולו י"ל דסבירא להו דמאי דאפשר למיבדק בבית החיצון בדקינן א"נ שאינם סוברים בזה כהרמב"ם דהא בפרק יוצא דופן (מא:) בעו הי ניהו בית החיצון במתניתא תנא מקום שהשמש דש והרמב"ם מפרש דעד מקום שהשמש דש הוא בית החיצון אבל עדיין נשאר מבית החיצון קצת לצד פנים והם מפרשים ששם נגמר הבית החיצון: והנראה לי לבעל נפש דכיון דהרא"ש ורבינו ירוחם והגהות מיימוניות הצריכו שהבדיקה תהיה בענין זה, שיצא את כולם ויצוה בביתו דבדיקה שבודקת בהפסקה ובדיקה אחת מבדיקות שבתוך השבעה תהיה בענין שיגיע עד מקום שהשמש דש ושאר הבדיקות אף אם לא יגיע שם לית לן בה שמאחר שרוב הפוסקים פשיטא להו דהלכה כרב דסגי ליה בבדיקה אחת תוך שבעה אע"פ שלכתחלה הצריכו לבדוק בכל יום לענין בדיקה בענין זה שהוא דבר קשה וגם כי רוב הפוסקים אין מצריכים לבדוק בענין זה דיינו לעשות כדברי המצריכים לבדוק בענין זה בבדיקות המוכרחים שהם בדיקת יום ההפסקה ובדיקה אחת בתוך שבעה או בתחלתן או בסופן או באמצען ואע"פ שקצת פוסקים סוברים שצריכה לבדוק בכל יום הלא הם סמ"ג וספר התרומה והם לא הצריכו להכניס עד מקום שהשמש דש הילכך בבדיקות שעושה בששת הימים כמו שרגילות שאינן מגיעות עד מקום שהשמש דש סגי לדברי הכל ומטעם זה אע"פ שסמ"ג וספר התרומה והמרדכי בשם הרוקח מצריכים לבדוק פעמיים ביום נראה דבבדיקה זו הקשה סגי בפעם אחת שתבדוק ביום שהיא בודקת בה והפעם השנית תהיה כשאר בדיקות שהרי המצריכים לבדוק פעמיים ביום לא הצריכו בדיקה עד מקום שהשמש דש הילכך בהכי סגי לכולי עלמא ואמנם נראה לי שצריך לייחד יום אחד בתוך השבעה כדי שיהיה יום מיוחד לבדיקה זו שתדע שתמיד צריכה לבדוק באותו יום באותו ענין ונראה לי שהיום היותר ראוי לייחד הוא היום הראשון כדי שאם תשכח באותו יום מלבדוק בענין זה יהיו לפניה ימים הרבה לתשלומין בעודה תוך שבעה.

שו"ת מהרש"ם חלק א סימן קמו – למחו' הרב המאוה"ג וכו' מו"ה פישל פעלדמאן נ"י מביטשקוף בארץ הגר.

מכתבו הגיעני וע"ד שאלתו בדין אשה שקשה לה לעשות בדיקת ז' נקיים בעד יבש כי כואב לה רק אם תלחלח העד מקודם במים נקל לה לבדוק יפה והעיר רו"מ דיש לחוש שמא ראתה טפת דם כחרדל ונימוק בלחלוחית המים וכהא דדם שנתבטל במים או כהא דט"ד כחרדל וחפהו שכבת זרע. והביא מהא דסימן קצ"ו דתרחץ ותלבש לבנים והו"ל להזהיר לקנח א"ע בפנים קודם בדיקה. והביא בשם הג' רש"ק ז"ל דבאשה שהרגישה פתיחת המקור אחר צאתה מהטבילה יש לתלות ההרגשה על ידי מי הטבילה שנכנסו בפנים. ואדרבא אם נחמיר עליה לבדוק בעד יבש יש לחוש שלא תבדוק יפה ע"י הכאב או שמא יעוותנה כמ"ש הרשב"א בטעמא דאין לבדוק בבגד פשתן חדש שמא יעוותנה עכת"ד. והנה רואה אני דבריו טובים ונכוחים ואם באנו לחוש לזה יהיה אסור לבדוק אחר שהשתינה ועל פי רוב המקום לח מן השתן ברוב היום ויתלחלח העד בהכנסתו ובע"כ דאין לחוש לזה. אולם הוראת הג' רש"ק ז"ל צע"ג למעשה ובהרגישה פהמ"ק בודאי א"א להקל בזה כי אין המים נכנסין ברחיצה בעומק כ"כ זולת בהרגישה זיבת דבר לח אולי יש להקל. וע' בשו"ת ב"ש ח"ב סימן ל"ו מ"ש בדין של החכמת אדם באשה שמצוי בה זיבת דבר לח ע"י ליחות לבנות. ולענ"ד יש לקיים ד' החכ"א בהרגשת זיבת דבר לח שלא בשעת ווסתה אבל לא בהרגשת פהמ"ק. ואכמ"ל וע' שו"ת מהר"י אשכנזי הנדמ"ח סימן כ"ח. והנלע"ד כתבתי.

סדרי טהרה סימן קצו סעיף כג – ובהכי ניחא מה שהקשו הראשונים ז"ל על בתולה שתבעוה להנשא דאֵיך יכולה לבדוק א"ע בעוד שפתחה נעול ומה שתירצו בזה הוא דחוק דהדבר ברור שא"א לבתולה שתבדוק א"ע בחורין וסדקין ומכ"ש בבדיקה עד מקום שהשמש דש שהוא מן הנמנע אלא כיון שחומרא זו אינה אלא מדרבנן אף הם לא החמירו אלא היכא דאפשר משא"כ בא"א סגי לה בבדיקה קלה שהיא סגיא מן התורה.

חזו"א הלכות נדה סימן צב סעיף כא – ונראה דגם בנדה וזבה מהני מה"ת קינוח כמה פעמים סמוכות, קצרו של דבר שהתורה לא נתנה בזה גדרים בענין הבדיקה אלא לעמוד על ידיעת הדבר ע"פ המובן.

22.

תלמוד בבלי מסכת נדה דף סח עמוד א – מתני'. נדה שבדקה עצמה יום שביעי שחרית ומצאה טהורה, ובין השמשות לא הפרישה, ולאחר ימים בדקה ומצאה טמאה – הרי היא בחזקת טהורה. בדקה עצמה ביום שביעי שחרית ומצאה טמאה, ובין השמשות לא הפרישה, ולאחר זמן בדקה ומצאה טהורה – הרי זו בחזקת טמאה, ומטמאה מעת לעת ומפקידה לפקידה. ואם יש לה וסת – דיה שעתה. ור' יהודה אומר: כל שלא הפרישה בטהרה מן המנחה ולמעלה – הרי זו בחזקת טמאה. וחכמים אומרים: אפילו בשנים לנדתה בדקה ומצאה טהורה, ובין השמשות לא הפרישה, ולאחר זמן בדקה ומצאה טמאה – הרי זו בחזקת טהורה.

בדק הבית על תורת הבית בית ז שער ה – כתב החכם כל הנשים שראו דם או שטמאות משום כתם צריכות להפסיק בטהרה קודם שתתחיל לספור שבעה נקיים שלה ואעפ"י שהרגישה

שפסקו דמים לעולם היא בחזקת טומאה עד שתבדוק ותמצא טהור. והביא הא דתנן בפרק תינוקת נדה שבדקה עצמה יום שביעי שחרית ומצאה טהור ובין השמשות לא הפרישה כלומר וטבלה אח"כ אחר ימים בדקה ומצאה טמא הרי היא בחזקת טהרה כלומר עד אותו זמן בדקה עצמה ביום שביעי שחרית ומצאה טמא ובין השמשות לא הפרישה פי' והרגישה בעצמה שפסק הדם וטבלה אחר ימים בדקה ומצאה טהור הרי זו בחזקת טומאה כלומר הרי זו בחזקתה לטומאה כלומר מאותה שעה שבדקה שחרית ביום שביעי ומצאה טמא ומטמאה מעת לעת ומפקידה לפקידה פירוש ארישא קאי דקתני אחר ימים בדקה ומצאה טמא ואם יש לה וסת דיה שעתה רבי יהודה אומר כל שלא הפרישה בטהרה מן המנחה ולמעלה הרי זו בחזקת טומאה דסבר ר' יהודה דהפסקת טומאה והפרשתה בטהרה בשחרית לאו מידי הוא ולא מהני כלום דחוששין דשמא תחזור ותראה בו ביום אלא אם כן מן המנחה ולמעלה שיצא רובו של יום בטהרה וחכמים אומרים אפילו בשני לנדתה בדקה בשחרית ומצאה טהור ובין השמשות לא הפרישה הרי זו בחזקת טהרה ואעפ"י שבדקה אחר הימים ומצאה טמא פי' וג' מחלוקות בדבר: דתנא קמא סבר דבדיקתה בשחרית מהניא ביום שביעי דוקא שדרך נשים להפסיק ביום שביעי וטובלות לערב, ורבי יהודה סבר אפילו ביום שביעי לא מהניא אלא מן המנחה ולמעלה, ורבנן בתראי סברי דבדיקת שחרית מהניא ואפילו ביום שני לנדתה. ובגמרא אמרינן תניא אמרו לו לר' יהודה אלמלא ידיה בין עיניה כל בין השמשות יפה אתה אומר כלומר אלו הייתי חושש לכל יום שביעי לומר שלא יהא לה תקנה אלא אם כן ידיה בין עיניה כל בין השמשות יפה אתה אומר שאתה משוה מדותיך עכשיו שמא עם סלוק ידיה ראתה ולהכי אתה פוסל בדיקתה אם כן מה לי הפרישה בטהרה מן המנחה ביום שביעי להפרישה ביום ראשון שהרי מן המנחה ולמעלה עוד היום גדול ואם באת לחוש אף לו ראוי לחוש ואם אין אתה חושש כיון שבדקה ומצאה טהור א"כ אף בדיקת יום ראשון שחרית תועיל ולא תחוש דאין להפריש בענין זה בין זמן מועט לזמן מרובה.

בית יוסף יורה דעה סימן קצו – ומ"ש רבינו ומלשון אדוני אבי ז"ל יראה שצריכה שתפסוק בטהרה בין השמשות שכתב (קיצור פסקי הרא"ש לנדה) וז"ל ואחר שיפסוק הדם תבדוק עצמה יפה יפה ובדיקה זו תהיה בין השמשות וכו'. נראה מדברי רבינו שהרא"ש סובר דבאיזה יום שתפסוק צריכה לבדוק בין השמשות וכרבי יהודה דמתניתין דאמר כל שלא הפרישה בטהרה מן המנחה ולמעלה הרי זו בחזקת טמאה דהא לא חילק הרא"ש בין יום ראשון לשאר הימים וא"כ הוא קשה למה פסק כיחידאה לכן נראה לי דהרא"ש לא כתב כן לפסק הלכה אלא לרווחא דמילתא דאפילו מאן דסבר דבהפסיקה ביום הראשון נמי סגי בבדיקת שחרית מודה דבאיזה יום שתפסוק עדיף טפי לבדוק בין השמשות דמרחקה נפשה מידי נדנוד ספק וכל שכן לסוברים דבהפסיקה ביום הראשון צריכה בדיקה בין השמשות דלכתחלה אית לן לאורויי דכשהפסיקה בשאר ימים נמי תבדוק בין השמשות כי היכי דלא ליחלף להו יום ראשון בשאר ימים ותדע שדברי הרא"ש הם בהלכות נדה בקוצר שסידר בסוף מסכת נדה להורות לבנות ישראל את המעשה אשר יעשון ולכן כתב דבאיזה יום שתפסוק תבדוק בין השמשות לצאת ידי כל ספק מיהו היכא דבדקה שחרית ולא בדקה בין השמשות בהא לא איירי ואפשר דס"ל כחכמים בתראי או כתנא קמא דמתניתין דסבר דוקא כשפסקה ביום שביעי לא בעיא בדיקת בין השמשות אבל

פסקה בשאר ימים בעיא בדיקת בין השמשות וזה נראה יותר דמשום הכי מסתים לה סתומי אי משום דרוב נשים פוסקות קודם השביעי ואי משום דכיון דבפוסקת בכולהו יומי בעיא בדיקת בין השמשות בר מפוסקת ביום השביעי לית לן לאורויי היתרא ביום השביעי כי היכי דלא ליחלפו שאר יומי ביה אבל לומר דסבר דהלכה כרבי יהודה דבאיזה יום שתפסוק מצריך בדיקת בין השמשות ואפילו בדיעבד כדמשמע מדברי רבינו זה דבר שאין להעלותו על הדעת בשום פנים ורבינו ירוחם (נכ"ו ח"ב דף רכא ע"ד) כתב סתם כדברי הרשב"א נראה שסובר שאין חולק בדבר וגם זה סעד לדברי דאם איתא דהוה ס"ד דפליג הרא"ש במילתא לא הוה שתיק מיניה: ובין השמשות דקא אמרן משמע ודאי דלאו דוקא דהא בין השמשות ספק מן היום ספק מן הלילה הוא ואם לא בדקה קודם לכן אין ראוי שתעלה לה דכיון דמספקא לן שמא מן הלילה הוא נמצא שיום שפוסקת בו סופרתו למנין ז' ועוד דהא רבי יהודה דמחמיר לא אמר אלא מן המנחה ולמעלה ומשמע דממנחה קטנה ולמעלה קאמר ומ"מ דבר פשוט הוא דקודם זמן בין השמשות טובא הוא ואף קודם בין השמשות דרבינו תם (תוס' שבת לה. ד"ה תרי ופסחים צד. ד"ה ר' יהודה) דההוא לא הוי אלא קודם הלילה וזמן מנחה קטנה ב' שעות וחצי קודם הלילה הילכך בין השמשות דקאמר הרא"ש היינו בין השמשות דרבינו תם שעדיין הוא יום גמור וא"נ סמוך לבין השמשות האחרון דאע"ג דמן המנחה ולמעלה סגי מ"מ לכתחלה רצה להורות שתבדוק היותר סמוך ללילה שאפשר כדי לצאת מידי ספק ואילו היה אפשר לה להיות ידיה בין עיניה כל בין השמשות כך היה מורה כדי לצאת ידי כל ספק אבל לפי שאי אפשר לה לעשות כן לא הורה כך אבל מ"מ מה שאפשר לתקן דהיינו לבדוק סמוך לבין השמשות הורה שתעשה כן ולי מה יקרו דברי הרשב"א שכתב בתורת הבית הקצר (ב"ז ש"ה כד.) וז"ל לעולם ילמד אדם בתוך ביתו שתהא האשה בודקת יום הפסק טהרתה במוך דחוק ושיהא שם כל בין השמשות שזו הבדיקה מוציאה מידי כל ספק עכ"ל ורבינו שהעתיק דבריו לא ידעתי למה השמיט תיקון זה שהוא כאילו ידיה בין עיניה כל בין השמשות דתו ליכא לספוקי כלל ונראה שלתיקון זה קורא בדברי הרמב"ן שהביא הרב המגיד ידיה בין עיניה כל בין השמשות דאין לומר דידיה בין עיניה ממש כל בין השמשות קאמר דזה דבר שאי אפשר לעשות כן.

תלמוד בבלי מסכת נדה דף סח עמוד ב – רבי יהודה אומר. תניא, אמרו לו לר' יהודה: אלמלי ידיה מונחות בעיניה כל בין השמשות – יפה אתה אומר, עכשיו – אימר עם סלוק ידיה ראתה, מה לי הפרישה בטהרה בז' מן המנחה ולמעלה – מה לי הפרישה בטהרה בראשון. בראשון – מי איכא למאן דאמר? אין, והתניא אמר רבי: שאלתי את רבי יוסי ור' שמעון כשהיו מהלכים בדרך נדה שבדקה עצמה יום ז' שחרית ומצאה טהורה, ובין השמשות לא הפרישה, ולאחר הימים בדקה ומצאה טמאה, מהו? אמרו לו הרי זו בחזקת טהרה. ששי, חמישי, רביעי, שלישי, שני, מאי? א"ל לא שנא. בראשון לא שאלתי, וטעיתי שלא שאלתי. אטו כולהו לאו בחזקת טומאה קיימי? וכיון דפסק – פסק, ראשון נמי, כיון דפסק – פסק. ומעיקרא מאי סבר? הואיל והוחזק מעין פתוח.

תורת הבית הארוך בית ז שער ה – ואע"ג דר' לא שאל בראשון דקסבר דבראשון לא עלתה לה בדיקה אלא אם כן הפרישה טהרה בין השמשות הואיל והוחזק מעין פתוח ולבסוף נמי לא

אשכחן דאיפשיטא ליה לגמרי דהא טעיתי שלא שאלתי קאמר. מכל מקום כיון דאיהו קאמר טעיתי שלא שאלתי וקא יהיב טעמא דמסתבר מטהר בראשון כבשאר הימים ואשכחן בברייתא דמיפשטא בהדיא מה לי הפרישה טהרה מן המנחה ולמעלה בשביעי מה לי הפרישה בראשון שמעינן מינה דראשון כשני דכיון דפסק פסק וכ"ש עכשיו שהורגלו במוך דחוק שאין לך בדיקה גדולה מזו. ולפיכך אעפ"י שכל הנשים ספק נדות ספק זבות ואפשר שהיא נדה ומעינה פתוח אפילו הכי כל שהפרישה טהורה ואפילו ביום ראשון הרי זו בחזקת טהרה. ויש מחמירין בדבר.

שולחן ערוך יורה דעה סימן קצו סעיף ב – ראתה יום אחד בלבד ופסקה בו ביום, צריכה לבדוק עצמה במוך דחוק ושיהא שם כל בין השמשות. הגה: ובדיעבד אם בדקה עצמה סמוך לבין השמשות ומצאה עצמה טהורה, אע"פ שלא היתה המוך אצלה כל בין השמשות, סגי (טור בשם הרשב"א וה"ה בשם רמב"ן וב"י להרמב"ם וכ"מ בש"ס). אבל בדיקת שחרית לא מהני, הואיל ולא ראתה רק יום אחד (רשב"א ורמב"ן בשם י"א וכ"ד רמב"ם פ"ו מהא"ב ובפי' משנה סוף פ"ד וברטנורה שם).

תוספות מסכת נדה דף סח עמוד ב – אמרו ליה הרי זו בחזקת טהרה – וא"ת תקשה דרבי יוסי דהכא דקאמר דסגי לה בהפרשה שחרית אדרבי יוסי דפרק בא סימן (לעיל דף נג.) דקאמר ומה אילו נדה שלא הפרישה בטהרה מן המנחה ולמעלה לא תהא בחזקת טומאה אלמא בעי הפרשה מן המנחה ולמעלה ויש לומר דהתם מיירי כשהפרישה ביום שראתה בו שחרית והכא מיירי בבדקה שחרית ומצאה טהורה וקשה דאם כן כי פרכינן לרבי יהודה אילו ידיה בעיניה כל בין השמשות וכו' לימא ר' יוסי לנפשיה דהא איהו נמי מצריך הפרשה מן המנחה ולמעלה כשהפרישה ביום שראתה ומה מועיל עיכוב זה שמא עם סילוק ידיה ראתה וי"ל דלנפשיה לא קשה דכיון דהוחזקה רואה שחרית דין הוא להצריכה הפרשה מן המנחה ולמעלה בלא חומרא אלא מן הדין ואין לנו להחמיר ולספק שמא עם סילוק ידיה ראתה להצריכה בדיקה בסוף היום אבל רבי יהודה שבא להחמיר ולספק דאפילו בשלא ראתה שחרית אלא בבדקה עצמה ומצאה טהורה הוא מצריך הפרשה גם בסוף היום היה לו להחמיר ולבדוק מספק שמא עם סילוק ידיה ראתה.

ביאור הגר"א יורה דעה סימן קצו:ח – ובדיעבד כו'. דל"פ במתני' אלא בשבדקה בשחרית ובה"ש לא הפרישה אבל בבה"ש ל"פ וכמש"ש אלמלי כו' אלמא ר"י לא איירי כה"ג ואהא קאמרי חכמים בשני ועב"י. וצ"ע דא"כ לימרו רבנן לנפשייהו בראשון וכ"ד הרמב"ן דוקא במוך דחוק כל בה"ש רק מתוס' שם ד"ה אמרו כו' נראה שא"צ שכ' וי"ל דלנפשיה כו' ומיהו דעת הרמב"ם נראה כסברא ראשונה שסתם וכתב דבדיקת יום ראשון לא מהני ועב"י.

סדרי טהרה סימן קצו סעיף ט ד"ה מיהו – מיהו נ"ל דהתוס' לא ניחא להו לתרוצי הכי משום דלפי שיטתם שכתבו דהא דאמר ר"י מן המנחה ולמעלה מיירי בהפרישה בטהרה ביום שראתה בו וכו' א"ו הא דמאמר ר"י מן המנחה ולמעלה מיירי אפי' בשאין ידיה בעיניה כל ביה"ש ובכה"ג הוא דמבעי' ליה לרבי אי מהני נמי ביום הראשון.

ביאור הגר"א יורה דעה סימן קצ"ו:ז – ראתה יום כו' אבל כו'. כחכמים דמתני'. הרמב"ם ויש שפסקו כברייתא ועבת"ה ומ"מ כ' שיש להחמיר.

חזו"א יורה דעה סימן צב אות מה – צ"ע דהא נ"מ כשבדקה בא' שחרית ולא בדקה תו עד יום ו' ומתחלת לספור על סמך הפסק טהרה של יום א' דלא מהני, אבל בבדקה מן המנחה מהני דלא בעינן הפסק טהרה סמוך לספירה.

חוות דעת סימן קצו בביאורים ס"ק א – משמע מדבריו דאפילו ראתה כל הג' ימים וביום השלישי ג"כ ראתה בשחרית ותיכף אח"כ פסקה ובדקה עצמה שחרית ומצאה טהורה ג"כ מהני. והנה מדברי התוס' נדה דף ס"ח ע"ב בד"ה אמרו ליה מוכח בהדיא דבשחרית יום שראתה לא מהני הפרשה רק בין השמשות ע"ש ולכאורה הוכחה ברורה היא וכ"ה בהדיא ברש"י דף נ"ג בד"ה לא תהא בחזקת טומאה ע"ש ומהתימה שלא הביאו סברתם ועוד כיון דאנן לא בקיאינן בדם ולא בימי נדה וזיבה איכא לספוקי שמא הוא יום ראשון דכ"ע מודו דלא מהני בדיקת שחרית כמבואר בסעיף ב'.

ש"ך יורה דעה סימן קצו:ו – רק יום א' – ומעיינה פתוח וכתוב בספר מעדני מלך דף ש' ע"א וז"ל וא"ת ולדידן מאי נ"מ הא אפילו אשה שרואה כתם נוהגין שצריכה להמתין ה' ימים עם יום שראתה בו ואחר כך תפסוק ותספור ז' נקיים (כדלקמן סי"א) ונ"ל דנ"מ להיכא דחזרה וראתה בתוך ימי הספירה דכיון שלא ראתה רק יום א' בימי הספירה בדיקת שחרית לא מהני אפילו בדיעבד אבל לא ראתה רק כתם אפשר להקל בין בימי הספירה בין בתחילה ע"כ.

מחצית השקל סימן קצו ס"ק ו ד"ה אפשר להקל – ר"ל דמהני בדיקת שחרית בדיעבד אפילו לא ראתה כתם רק יום א' בימי הספירה דכתם לאו מעינה פתוח הוא.

23.

חוות דעת סימן קצא ס"ק ח בביאורים – והא דמבואר בסי' קצ"ו כשבודקת במוך דחוק כל בית הרחם שבדיקה זו מוציאה מידי כל ספק שם מיירי שמניחה חוץ לרחם ג"כ מוך הרבה ומבחוץ ודאי דיכולה לכסות כל בית התורפה שבוודאי אם הדם היה נופל אפי' אם היה יורד דרך סדקין מ"מ במוך שבחוץ היה לו להמצא דם וגם מתחילה בודקת עצמה בכל הסדקין והחורין אבל כשהמוך ברחמה והמוך מתכויץ ברחמה כמבואר בש"ס ודאי דלא נסתמו בהמוך כל החורין וסדקין ויכול הדם לירד דרך הסדק שלא יגע בהמוך לכן נראה דאין בדיקה זו מועלת להתיר דם הנמצא בפרוזדור שחייבין עליו כרת.

שו"ת רבי עקיבא איגר מהדורה קמא סימן ס – א"כ יש תקנה לאחותינו לבדוק בשפופרת ומוך בתוכו ולדחוק המוך הרבה עד שיכנס לפנים ממקום שהשמש דש סמוך לפי האם ממש דבזה יש לומר דהוי הוכחה דאם המקור זב הי' נוטף על המוך ולא בעי בדיקת חו"ס, ונראה ראיה לזה ממה דס"ל לכמה פוסקים דביום א' בעינן ידים בין עיניה כל בין השמשות והיינו מוך דחוק כל בה"ש, ולכאורה מה מהני אף דבודקת מקודם בחורים ובסדקים מ"מ מהיכן ידעינן דפסק המקור

כל בה"ש דלמא זב לצדדים ולא נצטבע המוך ומ"ש בחוות דעת (סימן קצ"א ס"ח) שמניח חוץ לרחם גם כן מוך הרבה ולכסות מבחוץ כל בית התורפה דאם הי' הדם נופל הי' לו למצוא במוך שבחוץ עיין שם, אינו מספיק, דמכל מקום דלמא עדיין הדם עצור בסדקי הרחם, ולא מצינו שיהי' חיוב אחרי הסרת המוך לחזור ולבדוק כל בהס"ת בחו"ס, או להשהות המוך בפתח הרחם כשיעור אשם תלוי, גם ע"י שהי' ליכא ראי' כ"כ דא"כ לא נצטרך כלל בדיקת חו"ס אלא להשהות המוך בשפת הרחם כשיעור א"ת, אע"כ דחיישינן דכותלי בית הרחם מעמידים הדם א"כ מאי מהני מוך דחוק בה"ש, אע"כ דאם המוך דחוק הרבה בעומק אין באפשרות שיזוב הדם מהמקור ולא יגע במוך ובעינן באמת דחוק בעומק מבפנים ממקום שהשמש דש, ובזה נסתר ראיית החוות דעת שם נגד בעל תשובת נודע ביהודא מהא דאמרינן מור דחוק וכו' דיש לומר דהיינו היכי דאינו דחוק בעומק דיש חשש דזב לצדדים והמוך עכביה מלצאת ולא נצטבע המוך, אבל בדחוק בעומק יש לומר דאינו במציאות שלא יצבע הדם.

גם בפשוטו יש לדחות ראייתו דיש לומר דמוך דחוק מא"ל היינו אם בתחילה לא בדקה בחו"ס ואחר שהסירה המוך מצאה דם בזה ניחוש שמא רגע א' תוך שיעור אשם תלוי קודם שימת המוך זב המקור לצדדים וע"י שימת המוך אח"כ עכביה להדם, אבל בדיקת הנ"ב דאחר שימת המוך תרחץ מבחוץ לנקות הפרוזדור שמחוץ למוך ואח"כ בודקת ומוצאת שם דם דליכא חשש שהדם היה מקודם שימת המוך, כיון דבדקה אח"כ שם והי' נקי וליכא חשש רק דעתה זב המקור, ובזה שפיר אמרינן דאלו הי' כן הי' המוך מצטבע.

24.

תלמוד בבלי מסכת נדה דף סח עמוד א – מתני'. נדה שבדקה עצמה יום שביעי שחרית ומצאה טהורה, ובין השמשות לא הפרישה, ולאחר ימים בדקה ומצאה טמאה – הרי היא בחזקת טהורה. בדקה עצמה ביום שביעי שחרית ומצאה טמאה, ובין השמשות לא הפרישה, ולאחר זמן בדקה ומצאה טהורה – הרי זו בחזקת טמאה, ומטמאה מעת לעת ומפקידה לפקידה. ואם יש לה וסת – דיה שעתה. ור' יהודה אומר: כל שלא הפרישה בטהרה מן המנחה ולמעלה – הרי זו בחזקת טמאה. וחכמים אומרים: אפילו בשנים לנדתה בדקה ומצאה טהורה, ובין השמשות לא הפרישה, ולאחר זמן בדקה ומצאה טמאה – הרי זו בחזקת טהורה.

ויקרא פרק טו פסוק כח – ואם טהרה מזובה וספרה לה שבעת ימים ואחר תטהר:

תלמוד בבלי מסכת נדה דף סז עמוד ב – משום דרבי שמעון, דתניא (ויקרא ט"ו) אחר תטהר – אחר אחר לכולן, שלא תהא טומאה מפסקת ביניהן.

בית יוסף יורה דעה סימן קצו – כתב האגור (סי' אלף שעו) בשם התוספות פ"ק דביצה בדקה עצמה יום ראשון ויום שביעי ומצאה טהורה חשוב ספירה רק שבדקה עצמה יום שפסקה בו לערב והפסיקה בטהרה ודוקא יום שביעי אבל ליל שביעי לא והגהות מיימוניות (איסו"ב פ"ו אות ו) בשם הרמב"ן ובשם רבינו שמחה כתבו כדברי סמ"ג וכיון דכל הני רבוותא מספקא להו אין להקל בדבר שהוא ספק איסור כרת.

ויקרא פרק טו פסוק יט – ואשה כי תהיה זבה דם יהיה זבה בבשרה שבעת ימים תהיה בנדתה וכל הנגע בה יטמא עד הערב:

תלמוד בבלי מסכת נדה דף נח עמוד ב – ראה תלמידיו מסתכלין זה בזה, אמר להם: מה הדבר קשה בעיניכם? שלא אמרו חכמים הדבר להחמיר - אלא להקל, שנאמר (ויקרא ט"ו) ואשה כי תהיה זבה דם יהיה זובה בבשרה, דם ולא כתם.

תלמוד בבלי מסכת נדה דף נז עמוד ב – אמר שמואל: בדקה קרקע עולם וישבה עליה, ומצאה דם עליה – טהורה, שנאמר (ויקרא טו) בבשרה – עד שתרגיש בבשרה.

שו"ת מנחת שלמה תנינא (ב–ג) סימן עב – שוב ראיתי שהחוו"ד עצמו כתב שם דטעמא דכתם אינו סותר הוא משום דרשא דר' עקיבא "דם ולא כתם", ואף די"א שהוא רק אסמכתא בעלמא מ"מ נפישי רבוואתי דסברי שהיא דרשא גמורה עיין בבינת אדם שאלה ז' או"ט, ועיין גם בשו"ע הרב בסי' ק"צ סעיף א' שכתב דאף אם נאמר דלא בעיא הרגשה כלל "ליכא איסורא דאורייתא בכתמים שנאמר דם יהי' זובה בבשרה דם ולא כתם, וטעמא משום דאיכא למימר אימא מעלמא אתי כתם זה ולאו מגופה הוא – ואת"ל מגופה שמא מן העליה הוא", וגם יש אומרים דכמו דדרשינן ממזר ודאי ולא ספק או עשירי ודאי ולא ספק כך גם דם שלא מצאה בגופה אף אם יש רק ספק אחד אינו מטמא עיין במרומי שדה להנצי"ב בדף נ"ז ע"ב, ועיין גם בסד"ט סי' ק"צ ס"ק צ"ג שהאריך טובא בהא דאיכא כתמים שאינם סותרים תוך ז' נקיים, ואסיק נמי דטעמא דכתמים רק מדרבנן הוא משום דתלינן דמעלמא אתי ואין צריכים כלל לצרף הטעם דשמא לא הרגישה, אך הוא עצמו כתב שם בד"ה נחזור דלדעת הרמב"ן והרשב"א והר"ן טעמא דכתמים רק מדרבנן הוא משום דבעינן דוקא הרגשה, וגם כתב שם בסוף דבריו דהרמ"א ז"ל סובר דהא דכתמים דרבנן הוא משום דלא ארגשה ואפי"ה מקיל גם בתוך ז' נקיים, וגם כתב שם בסיום דבריו וכן ראיתי בכמה תשובות האחרונים ז"ל דס"ל דאין לחלק בזה בין ספירת ז' נקיים ובין תחילת ראיה דלעולם אם לא ארגשה אינה אלא מדברי סופרים עכ"ל, ועיין גם בספר החשוב פרדס רמונים שהאריך בזה בפתיחה כוללת לספרו.

כה) ונלע"ד דמוכח שלמעשה אין נוהגים לחשוש לדעת החוו"ד דראי' בלי הרגשה ג"כ סותרת מה"ת, ממ"ש הפת"ש בסי' קצ"ו ס"ק י"ב מהחמד"ש חיו"ד סי' כ' שכתב בפשיטות דאם מצאה כתם ע"ג דבר שאינו מקבל טומאה כגון שבדקה קרקע עולם וישבה עליה ויודעים ברור שהדם בא מגופה אפי"ה כיון דבלא הרגשה חזיא לא גזרו רבנן ע"ז טומאה וכן הוא להדיא בשו"ע הרב סי' ק"צ ס"ק כ"א, ואפי' בתוך ג' ימים הראשונים אינה סותרת כלל מנינה כיון דדבר שאינו מקבל טומאה לא הוי בכלל גזירת כתמים, וה"ה נמי במצאה כתם על בגד צבוע וכן נהגו כל בעלי הוראה כמובא בספרי האחרונים, ואם כהחוו"ד או אפי' כהסוברים דעכ"פ אותו היום אינו עולה איך אפשר לטהר, ואף לפי מה דדריש ר' עקיבא לטהר כתם משום דכתיב דם ולא כתם היינו רק בכתם אבל הכא משמע אפי' אם מצאה דם להדיא ג"כ טהורה וכמו"ש הס"ט בסי' ק"צ ס"ק נ"ג וראה בבינת אדם שאלה ז' או"ט, ומעתה אף אם נאמר דמספקינן שמא בא מן העליה ומן הצדדים ולא מן החדר אבל מ"מ ספיקא מיהו הוה וצריכים להחמיר. וחושבני דלמ"ד

מקור מקומו טמא שפיר טמאה טומאת ערב כיון דודאי בא מגופה ולא אמרו שהיא טהורה אלא מטומאת נדה אבל שפיר טמאה כנוגעת בשרץ או בדם נדה, וע"כ מוכח מזה דלא רק שאינו סותר אלא אף גם אותו היום עולה וכ"ש בשפופרת, גם נלענ"ד דאע"ג שגם כתמים של חרשת ושוטה הם רק מדרבנן, מ"מ אם בדקו קרקע עולם וישבו עליה ומצאו דם נראה דטמאה מספק, ועכ"פ בתוך ז' סותרת ודאי מנינה כיון דמחזקינן שהדם ודאי בא בהרגשה, וכמו"כ חושבני דלדעת הש"ך בסי' ק"צ סק"ג דבקטנה שאפי' סדינים שלה מלוכלכים בדם טהורה אמרינן דלגמרי אוקמוה אדאורייתא דאפי' אם בודאי ראתה מ"מ סמכינן אדיבורה וכל שלא הרגישה טהורה [עיי"ש בפת"ש סק"ח שהחוו"ד חולק ע"ז] דה"ה נמי שגם בתוך ז' נקיים אמרינן הכי כיון שלא הזכיר שם הש"ך לחלק. [גם משמע שם מהש"ך דכל שהכתם נמצא על גופה לא מספקינן דשמא מעלמא אתי וכמו"ש בגמ' דף נ"ז ע"ב על בשרה ודאי מגופה אתאי ואפי"ה יש לו רק דין כתם הואיל ולא הרגישה, ולפי"ז צ"ע בחרשת ושוטה שאין אנו יודעים אם הרגישו או לא דלפי"ז אם נמצא כתם על בשרן יהיו טמאין גם בפחות מכגריס וגם צ"ע לענין סתירה בתוך ז' נקיים, ואפשר דאיכא עכ"פ קצת ספק דמעלמא אתי וגם ספק שמא לא בא מן החדר וצ"ע] גם ראיתי בהגהות רע"א ז"ל בשו"ע בתחלת סי' קפ"ג שכתב בדעת הש"ך שם ובסי' קצ"ו דבלי הרגשה לא סותר כלל את הנקיים עיי"ש. וכן ראיתי בשו"ת ברית אברהם בהג"ה שבסי' מ"ב דסובר בפשיטות דשלא בהרגשה לא הוה כלל בגדר ראיה ועולה גם לנקיים. גם ראיתי בהגהות הגאון מקוטנא ז"ל שבס' יבין דעת שכתב שם בסי' ק"צ סעיף יוד "משמע אפי' בספירת ז' נקיים דשלא בהרגשה אינו סותר, ונ"ל דבשוטה וקטנה יש להחמיר" עכ"ל. ועיין בסד"ט סי' קצ"ד סק"ד בד"ה ועפ"י שכתב שם ליישב קושית המהר"ם ומפרש את הגמ' בדף ס"ח ע"ב דמה שאמרו שם "דלמא חזאי" היינו דחוששין שמא ראתה בלי הרגשה, והוכיח מזה דנהי דלא סתר כל ז' אבל מ"מ אותו היום אינו עולה לה מה"ת עיי"ש, אולם לענ"ד נראה דאי אפשר לומר שם בכוונת הגמ' דחוששין באמת לשמא ראתה דא"כ מאי מהני בדיקה של פעם אחת או של ב' פעמים להוציא מחשש זה, וגם מהיכ"ת ניחוש להכי כיון שהפסיקה בטהרה וגם בדקה עצמה ביום ראשון הרי קיימא ודאי בחזקת טהרה, אלא כוונת הגמ' שם לומר דבגלל הספק של שמא ראתה לא חל על אותו יום שם ספור ובדוק אבל לא מפני שבאמת חוששין לכך, וכיון שכן יכול להיות שפיר הפירוש בגמ' דשמא ראתה וארגשה ולאו אדעתה, ונהניתי כשראיתי שהס"ט עצמו בסי' קצ"ו סקל"ד ד"ה ועפ"י דברינו ג"כ פירש כן, וגם מוכח הוא כדברינו שהרי אם נאמר דר' יהושע חושש באמת לשמא ראתה אמאי אינה חייבת להפסיק שנית בטהרה ביום ז' ולהתחיל למנות מיום ח', ולהדיא תנן שאפי' ר' עקיבא אומר אין לה אלא יום ז' בלבד ועיי"ש ברש"י דשמא ראו בינתים ואפי"ה גם אותו יום ז' עולה למנין הנקיים וע"כ שהוא רק לענין זה דלא מיקרי ספור ובדוק, גם מיירי התם בין בזב ובין בזבה ואילו זב לא בעי כלל הרגשה וגם בלי הרגשה סותר כל ז' ואפי"ה סובר ר' יהושע דיש לו יום א' וז'.

תלמוד בבלי מסכת נדה דף לז עמוד א – בעי רבא: קושי מהו שתסתור בזיבה? דבר המטמא סותר – והאי נמי מטמא כימי נדה הוא, או דילמא: דבר הגורם – סותר, והאי – לאו גורם הוא? א"ל אביי: אונס בזיבה יוכיח, שאינו גורם – וסותר! אמר ליה: לאיי, האי נמי גורם הוא,

דתנן, ראה ראייה ראשונה – בודקין אותו, שניה – בודקין אותו, שלישית – אין בודקין אותו. ולרבי אליעזר, דאמר אף בשלישי' בודקין אותו, ה"נ – כיון דלא גרים לא סתר? אמר ליה: לרבי אליעזר – ה"נ. ת"ש, רבי אליעזר אומר: אף בשלישית בודקין אותו, ברביעית אין בודקין אותו. מאי לאו – לסתירה? לא, לטמויה לההיא טיפה במשא. ת"ש, בשלישית, רבי אליעזר אומר: בודקין אותו, ברביעית אין בודקין אותו, לקרבן אמרתי ולא לסתירה! אלא: לר"א – תפשוט דדבר שאינו גורם – סותר, לרבנן מאי? ת"ש, דתני אבוה דרבי אבין: מה גרם לו זובו – שבעה, לפיכך – סותר שבעה, מה גרם לו קריו – יום אחד, לפיכך – סותר יום אחד. מאי שבעה? אילימא דמטמא שבעה – האי מה זובו טמא שבעה מבעי ליה, אלא לאו: דבר הגורם – סותר, דבר שאינו גורם – אינו סותר, ש"מ, אמר אביי: נקטינן, אין קושי סותר בזיבה. ואי משכחת תנא דאמר סותר – ההיא ר"א היא.

רמב"ם הלכות איסורי ביאה פרק ז הלכה י – זבה שפסק זובה והתחילה למנות שבעת ימים נקיים ובא לה דם קושי בתוך ימים נקיים אינו סותר וימי הקושי עולים למנין ז', וכן אם ילדה בשבעה ימים נקיים אין הלידה סותרת, וימי הלידה עולין לה למנין שבעה אע"פ שהיא טמאה בהן שנאמר ואם טהרה מזובה כיון שטהרה מזובה אע"פ שהיא טמאה טומאה אחרת כגון טומאת לידה או טומאת נדה או טומאת צרעת הרי זו סופרת בהן, ואין טומאות אלו וכיוצא בהן סותרין הספירה. השגת הראב"ד: זבה שפסק וכו'. כתב הראב"ד ז"ל א"א זה שבוש שדם הקושי אינו סותר ואינו עולה עכ"ל.

ויקרא פרק טו פסוק כח – ואם טהרה מזובה וספרה לה שבעת ימים ואחר תטהר:

בעלי הנפש שער הספירה והבדיקה – השגות הרז"ה סימן ב – ב. עוד כתב הרב מדקתני הזב והזבה שבדקו עצמן ביום הראשון וביום הז' וכו' לא קתני בודקין אלמא לכתחילה מצות בדיקה כל ז'. מיהו אם לא בדקו אלא בתחלתן ובסופן או בתחילתן ולא בסופן או בסופן ולא בתחילתן טהורה. ולדעתי אין ללמוד ממשנתינו הפרש בין לכתחילה ודיעבד. וכבר מצינו שלמדו רבותינו מכגון זה הלשון אפילו לכתחילה, כי ההיא דפשט ליה רבי יוחנן לההוא סבא (נדה ט א) מדתנן ר' מאיר אומר אם היתה במחבא והגיע עת וסתה ולא בדקה טהורה שחרדה מסלקת את הדמים, אלמא כיון דאיכא חרדה דמיה מסולקין ולא בעיא בדיקה הכא נמי דמים מסולקין ולא בעיא בדיקה. קא פשיט ליה לא בעיא בדיקה ואפילו לכתחילה וכן מפורש בחבור זה בכמה מקומות. ואע"ג דקתני במתניתין ולא בדקה, לא משמע ליה דיעבד אלא אפילו לכתחילה. הכא נמי שבדקו אפ' לכתחילה משמע. ואלו לא נשנית במשנתינו בלכתחילה אלא בדיעבד לא הוצרך תנא דמתניתין לשנות ביום הראשון וביום הז' דהא קיימא ליה לרב הזה דבדיעבד ביום א' סגיא בין בתחלתן בין בסופן בין באמצען. הילכך אין לדקדק מלשון משנתינו לשון דיעבד. וכדי שלא ליתן פתחון פה לבעל דבר לחלוק, אמור לו איידי דתנא ומצאו תנא שבדקו.

שולחן ערוך יורה דעה סימן קצו סעיף ד – בכל יום מז' ימי הספירה צריכה להיות בודקת לכתחלה פעמים בכל יום, ואחת שחרית ואחת סמוך לבין השמשות (טור בשם סה"ת וע"פ);

ואם לא בדקה בכל השבעה אלא פעם אחת, לא שנא בדקה ביום ראשון של השבעה או ביום השביעי או באחד מהאמצעים, מאחר שבדקה ביום שקודם השביעי ומצאה טהורה, עלו לה. אבל אם לא בדקה בכל הז׳, וביום השמיני בדקה ומצאה טהורה, אין לה אלא יום ח׳ בלבד ומשלמת עליו. וי״א שצריך שתבדוק ביום ראשון מהשבעה וביום השביעי, ואין להקל. והבדיקה תהיה לאור היום ולא לאור הנר (תא״ו נכ״ו והרשב״א בת״ה), ובדיעבד מהני אפילו לאור הנר (כן משמע בב״י).

הלכות נדה לרמב״ן פרק ב – ג. כל שבעת הימים צריכה בדיקה פעם אחת בכל יום, בדקה ביום הראשון או בשני או בשלישי ושוב לא בדקה בודקת בשעת טבילתה ודיה, אפילו בדקה ביום שביעי בלבד הרי זו בחזקת טהורה שהרי בדקה והפסיקה קודם לכן.

הגהות מיימוניות הלכות איסורי ביאה פרק ו – [ד] דפסיק תלמודא הלכה כר׳ אליעזר לגבי ר׳ יהושע ור׳ עקיבא ע״ש בפ״ק (דף ז׳ ב) ושמא לא אמר ר׳ אליעזר אלא בדיעבד אבל לכתחילה צריכה לבדוק בכל יום מימי ספירה והלכה למעשה שביום שפוסקת בו מלראות בודקת עצמה יפה בצמר גפן נקי ורקך ולבן או בבלאי בגד פשתן נקיים ולבנים ורכין ומכניסה באותו מקום בעומק כל בין השינים דהיינו מקום דישה כדלעיל פ״ה ומקנחה עצמה בפנים יפה בחורין ובסדקין כן פר״י מהא דפ״ק דנדה דמתוך שמהומה לביתה אין מכניסתו לחורין ולסדקין מכלל דבעיא להכניסו לחורין ולסדקין וכשתוציאו אם תוציאו נקי מכל מראה אדמומית או שחור תלבש חלוק נקי מכתמים ומדמים ותתחיל לספור ז׳ נקיים מיום המחרת וכל ז׳ הימים בודקת כן פעמים ביום שחרית כשעומדת ממיטתה וערבית סמוך לשקיעת החמה ובמוצאי ז׳ שהוא יום ח׳ מיום שפסקה בו תטבול משיהיה לילה כדלעיל פ״ד ע״כ:

ספר מצוות גדול לאוין סימן קיא – וכל ז׳ ימי ספירתה צריכה ליקח בגד פשתן נקי ולבן או מוך (ע״פ סה״ת סי׳ פז) ולהכניסו באותו מקום בעומק ולחורין ולסדקין, שכן מוכיח בפ״ק דנדה (ה, א) שאומר שם כשהיא ממהרת אינה מכניסתו לחורין ולסדקין (ע״פ יראים שם דף כו, א), ולהוציאו ולראות אם ניכר בו שום אדמומית וכן עושה שחרית וערבית, בשחר כשעומדת ממטתה וערבית כשהולכת לבית הכנסת קודם שיהא לילה (ע״פ סה״ת שם).

בית יוסף יורה דעה סימן קצו – ומ״ש רבינו שבספר המצות כתב פעמיים וכו׳. כן הוא בסמ״ג (לאוין קיא דף לו ריש ע״ד) וסמ״ק (סי׳ רצג עמ׳ שכא) וספר התרומה (סי׳ פז) והמרדכי (סי׳ תשלז) בשם הרוקח (סי׳ שיז ד״ה בועל וד״ה שכחה) שבודקת פעמיים בכל יום מימי הספירה פעם אחת בשחרית כשעומדת ממטתה ופעם אחת כשהולכת לערבית ונראה לי שלמדו כן מדתנן בפ״ק דנדה (יא.) פעמים צריכה להיות בודקת שחרית ובין השמשות:

תלמוד בבלי מסכת נדה דף יא עמוד א – מתני׳. אע״פ שאמרו דיה שעתה – צריכה להיות בודקת, חוץ מן הנדה והיושבת על דם טוהר. ומשמשת בעדים – חוץ מיושבת על דם טוהר, ובתולה שדמיה טהורים. ופעמים צריכה להיות בודקת – שחרית ובין השמשות, ובשעה שהיא

עוברת לשמש את ביתה. יתירות עליהן כהנות – בשעה שהן אוכלות בתרומה, רבי יהודה אומר: אף בשעת עברתן מלאכול בתרומה.

תלמוד בבלי מסכת נדה דף סח עמוד ב – תני, ר׳ יוסי ור׳ שמעון אמרי: נראין דברי רבי אליעזר מדברי רבי יהושע, ודברי רבי עקיבא מדברי כולן, אבל הלכה כרבי אליעזר.

תורת הבית הארוך ז:ה ד״ה ועוד – ועוד הוסיף בה הוא ז״ל וכתב ואם בדקה באמצע השבעה ולא בדקה לא בתחלתן ולא בסופן לא שמענו ומסתברא לקולא שהרי שנינו בהפסקת הנדה נדה שבדקה עצמה ביום השביעי שחרית ומצאה טהור אחר שבעת הימים בדקה ומצאה טמא הרי זו בחזקת טהרה וכו׳ וחכמים אומרים אפילו בדקה בשנים לנדתה ומצאה טהור הרי היא בחזקת טהרה הכא בעיא בדיקה והכא בעיא בדיקה הכא סגי לה בבדיקת האמצע והכא סגי לה בבדיקת האמצא עכ״ל.

בדק הבית ז:ה ד״ה בענין – ודבריו תמוהים דאנן שבעה נקיים ספורין בעינן בשלמא כי איכא תחלתן או סופן איכא למימר דסליק לז׳ ספורים דכי איכא בתחלתן ז׳ ספורים גרירי בתריה וכי איכא סופן איכא למימר דבז׳ ספורים דלקמיה גרריה בתריה אבל בדיקה דבאמצא זיל הכא ליכא ז׳ ספורים וזיל הכא ליכא ז׳ ספורים ומהאי טעם ליכא למיגמר בדיקת זבה מבדיקת זבה ולעולם בזבה בעינן סופן או תחילתן בר מההיא בדיקה דהפסיקה בטהרה.

משמרת הבית ג:ה ד״ה אמר הכותב – דכל שהפרישה בטהרה ובסוף הז׳ מצאה טהור חזקה שכולן יצאו בטהרה.

בית יוסף יורה דעה סימן קצו – כתב האגור (סי׳ אלף שעו) בשם התוספות פ״ק דביצה בדקה עצמה יום ראשון ויום שביעי ומצאה טהורה חשוב ספירה רק שבדקה עצמה יום שפסקה בו לערב והפסיקה בטהרה ודוקא יום שביעי אבל ליל שביעי לא והגהות מיימוניות (איסו״ב פ״ו אות ו) בשם הרמב״ן ובשם רבינו שמחה כתבו כדברי סמ״ג וכיון דכל הני רבוותא מספקא להו אין להקל בדבר שהוא ספק איסור כרת:

בית יוסף יורה דעה סימן קצו – כתב האגור (סי׳ אלף שעו) בשם התוספות פ״ק דביצה בדקה עצמה יום ראשון ויום שביעי ומצאה טהורה חשוב ספירה רק שבדקה עצמה יום שפסקה בו לערב והפסיקה בטהרה ודוקא יום שביעי אבל ליל שביעי לא והגהות מיימוניות (איסו״ב פ״ו אות ו) בשם הרמב״ן ובשם רבינו שמחה כתבו כדברי סמ״ג וכיון דכל הני רבוותא מספקא להו אין להקל בדבר שהוא ספק איסור כרת:

שו״ת חתם סופר חלק ב (יורה דעה) סימן קעח – שלום לתלמידי חביבי הרבני המופלג מו״ה דוד ני׳.

גי״ה הגיעני אתמול וקראתיו ומיד נעלם ממנו אבל ידעתי קצת מה היה כתוב בו אודות אשה שלא בדקה בז׳ וכבר לנתה אצל בעלה ובעלה מסופק אם לא התרשלה ולא בדקה גם

בראשון ראוי׳ לגעור בזוג זו שניהם כא׳ לא טובים הספק הזה אינינו מבית יראי ה׳ כי שכחה פ״א לבדוק ליבא דאינשי אינשי אבל להיות לב הבעל נוקף על אשתו אולי גם ביום הראשון לא בדקה מחמת התרשלות והאיך ס״ד בכך ואיך יעלה על הדעת.

מ״מ בעיקור הדין רוב הפוסקים היינו רמב״ם וראב״ד ורמב״ן ורז״ה ורשב״א ורא״ה והרא״ש והטור כולם פה א׳ פסקו כרב ראשון או אחרון אך הראב״ן והסמ״ג והתרומות ומטו בי׳ בשם תוס׳ פ״ק דביצה מספקו להו אולי הלכה כר״ח דראשון וז׳ בעי׳ והרב״י כ׳ שאין להקל נגדם באי׳ כרת מ״מ נ״ל בדיעבד שכבר לנתה אצל בעלה לא שבקינן ספיקא דדהו מפני ודאי דרוב פוסקים הנ״ל דפסקו כרב בודאי.

אך כל זה בבדקה בודאי בא׳ או בז׳ אבל בבדיקת האמצעי דהרז״ה והרא״ה מהאוסרים וגם הרשב״א בתה״א מסיק להחמיר עכ״פ בודאי חזי לאצטרופי להראב״ן וסייעתו לחוש אפי׳ בדיעבד.

וראיתך מאריך להסביר ס׳ הרא״ה בבד״ה מה לי א׳ וז׳ ומה לי אמצעיי׳ שמענה ואתה דע לך דכולהי תנאי דמתני׳ נדה ס״ח ע״ב ס״ל דמדפסקה בטהרה בין השמשות שוב היא בחזקת שלא תחזור ותראה ומ״ע דאוריי׳ שתספור דוקא והספירה בזה גז״ה כמו טבילה במים אבל בלי ספירה נמי בחזקת שלא תראה עוד והנה אותה הספירה אנו מקובלים ממרע״ה מפי הקבלה שאינה צריכה ספירה בפה כמ״ש בס׳ החינוך פ׳ בהר גבי ספירת יובל וקיצור מתק לשונו העתיק בסדרי טהרה סי׳ קצ״ו אך עכ״פ הכנה וכונה לספור בעי והנה לר״א דס״ל דחזקה מעלי׳ היא כאלו בדקו לפנינו מ״מ דברים שבלב אינם דברים ומה מועיל כוונה בלב בלי דיבור אך קיי״ל במחשבתו ניכר מתוך מעשיו מהני דברים שבלב ע״כ הבדיקה ביום א׳ הוה הוראה שמכנת עצמה לספור ולשמור הימים האלה ושוב אינה צריכה בדיקה יותר כי הוא כאלו ידענו שהבדיקות טהורות שהרי מוקמי׳ אחזקה ורק בדיקת יומא קמא הוא להורות אדברים שבלב שבתחלת ימי ספירתה וכן אם בודקת בז׳ מורה על מחשבת לבה כאלו היום פסקה כוונת ספירתה ובזה יי״ח ספירה אבל הספורים הם ע״י חזקת פסיקת טהרה וזה שייך בראשון או בז׳ אבל באמצע אין זה שום הוראה על דבר מה ונהי שהיא בחזקת טהרה וגם במחשבתה כיוונה לשמור נקיי׳ מ״מ דברים שבלב אינם דברים זהו ס׳ ר״א שהלכה כמותו אך ר״י ור״ע ס״ל נהי דמדאפסקה בטהרה הרי הוא בחזקת שאינה רואה ולא תסתור אך לא אלים חזקה שלא ראתה לומר הרי יום א׳ נקי והרי ב׳ ימים נקיים ולא ראינו אין ראי׳ למספר נהי דאין הימים מפסיקי׳ שאינה בחזקת ולא בס׳ רואה מ״מ אין חזקה אלים כ״כ כבודקת ממש ומצאה נקי ועיי׳ זבחי׳ כ״ט ע״א פלוגת׳ רש״י ותוס׳ בלשון ר״ע שאמר בחזקת טהרה ולדינא אין כאן מחלוקת בין לרש״י בין לתוס׳ משפסקה בטהרה ומכ״ש אחר ג׳ ימים שאינה שוב בחזקת רואה כלל אך אם יוצדק לשון חזקת טהרה בזה ס״ל לתוס׳ דלא יוצדק לשון זה ואפי׳ נימא לדינא דקיי״ל כר״א דיכולה לספור על סמך חזקתה מ״מ לר״ע לא יוצדק ומשו״ה פליגי שם תוס׳ ארש״י ואפשר ס״ל לרש״י ר״ע לדברי ר״א קאמר אבל עכ״פ לדינא לכ״ע מוחזקת באינה רואה ואינה סותרת ובנב״י ברוב תשו׳ תמצא נגד זה [ועיי׳ בסי׳ קמ״ד] והנלע״ד כתבתי דש״ת א״נ.

שו״ת נודע ביהודה מהדורה תנינא – יורה דעה סימן קכח – שאם בדקה דרך משל בראשון ובשלישי כבר החלטתי למעלה דלא מהני ואינה יכולה לטבול בשביעי ואם אח״כ שוב לא בדקה עד עשירי אין בידה אלא עשירי אבל אם בודקת אח״כ בשמיני או בתשיעי טובלת לערב. והטעם

נלענ"ד דזה פשוט דאם בדקה בתשיעי דמהני דדל בדיקת יום א' מהכא הרי בדיקת שלישי ותשיעי נחשב ראשון ושביעי והשלישי נעשה ראשון והתשיעי נעשה שביעי וביניהם ה' ימים אלא אפילו בדקה בשמיני דהיינו שבדקה בראשון ובשלישי ובשמיני טובלת בשמיני לערב ומצטרף השמיני עם הראשון ונעשה זה תחלה וזה סוף ואף שיש בין שמיני לראשון יותר מה' ימים השלישי מצרפם. ומנא אמינא לה מדברי ר' יהושע שאמר אין להם אלא ראשון ושביעי וסופרת עוד ה' ימים והרי מונה הראשון עם החמשה הללו והרי מודה ר"י בבדקה ראשון ושמיני שאין לה אלא ח' בלבד הרי שאין הראשון יכול להצטרף עם השמיני ואפ"ה בדקה ראשון ושביעי יש בידה ראשון ושביעי וסופרת עוד ה' הרי שהשביעי מצרף הראשון עם הימים שאחר שבעה להדדי להחשב ז' נקיים וה"ה לדידן. באופן שאמרתי לר' חנינא בדקה ראשון ושלישי ושמיני השלישי מצרף יחד את הראשון עם השמיני. וידעתי שיש לדחות ולומר דר"י דאמר אין לה אלא ראשון ושביעי חומרא בעלמא קאמר לחוש שמא ראתה בינתים וכיון שהיא חומרא כשם דלא משגח על סירוגן ה"נ לא משגח על צירוף ימים שאחר שבעה משא"כ בלא בדקה בשביעי דלר"ח ע"פ דין לא מהני לא מצטרף הראשון כלל למה שאחר שבעה ודוק. דברי ידידו הד"ש:

25.

תלמוד בבלי מסכת נדה דף עא עמוד ב – מתני'. הרואה יום אחד עשר, וטבלה לערב ומשמשה, ב"ש אומר: מטמאין משכב ומושב, וחייבין בקרבן. וב"ה אומרים: פטורים מן הקרבן. טבלה ביום של אחריו ושמשה את ביתה, ואח"כ ראתה, ב"ש אומרים: מטמאין משכב ומושב, ופטורין מן הקרבן. וב"ה אומרים: ה"ז גרגרן. ומודים ברואה בתוך י"א יום, וטבלה לערב ושמשה – שמטמאין משכב ומושב. וחייבין בקרבן. טבלה ביום של אחריו ושמשה – ה"ז תרבות רעה, ומגען ובעילתן תלויין.

תוספות מסכת נדה דף סט עמוד א – שבעה לנדה ושנים לזיבה – מכאן אין יכול לדקדק דלא בעינן ספורים בפנינו מדטובלת אע"פ שלא הפסיקה בטהרה ולא בדקה נמי בתחלת ספורים דאע"ג דלא בעינן ספורים בפנינו בזבה קטנה בזבה גדולה בעינן ועוד דסוף סוף סגי לה במה שבדקה ביום הספירה ומצאה טהורה דאי אין בדיקת סוף היום עולה לספירה לא היה תקנה לבנות ישראל אלא אם כן יבדקו בעליית עמוד השחר דספירת לילה אינה ספירה.

תוספות מסכת נדה דף עא עמוד ב – הרואה יום אחד עשר וטבלה לערב כו' – דספירת ערב לאו ספירה היא כדקאמר בגמרא ושוין בטבילת לילה שאינה טבילה מכאן קשה לפירוש רש"י שפירש בפ' ב' דזבחים (דף כג.) ובפסחים פרק כיצד צולין (דף פא.) דקאמר לר' יוסי דקאמר מקצת היום ככולו וזבה שראתה בשביעי שלה אינה סותרת לאחר טבילה ופריך התם אלא זבה גמורה היכי משכחת לה ומשני בשופעת אי נמי ברואה בשני בין השמשות ופי' רש"י הא דלא משני ברואה בלילות משום דלמ"ד מקצת היום ככולו לילה חשיבא ספירה ולא צריך עמוד השחר לטבול והשתא קשה דא"כ מתני' דלא כר' יוסי וכן מתני' דמגילה פ' הקורא (דף כ.) דתנן כולן שעשו משעלה עמוד השחר כשר משמע דבלילה לא הוי ספירה.

תלמוד בבלי מסכת פסחים דף פ עמוד ב – נטמא טומאת התהום וכו'. בעי רמי בר חמא: כהן המרצה בקרבנותיהן הותרה לו טומאת התהום או לא? מי אמרינן כי גמירי טומאת התהום – בבעלים, בכהן לא גמירי. או דילמא: בזבחא גמירי, לא שנא בכהן ולא שנא בבעלים. – אמר רבא: תא שמע, דתני רבי חייא: לא אמרו טומאת התהום אלא למת בלבד. מת למעוטי מאי – לאו למעוטי טומאת התהום דשרץ? ובמאי עסקינן, אי נימא בבעלים, ובמאן? – אי בנזיר – מי מהני ביה (במדבר ו) כי ימות מת עליו אמר רחמנא. אלא בעושה פסח, הניחא למאן דאמר אין שוחטין וזורקין על טמאי שרץ. אלא למאן דאמר שוחטין וזורקין על טמאי שרץ, השתא טומאה ידועה הותרה לו – טומאת התהום לא כל שכן? אלא לאו בכהן, ושמע מינה: הותרה לו טומאת התהום. – אמר רב יוסף: לא, לעולם בבעלים, ובפסח, ולמעוטי טומאת התהום דזיבה. – וטומאת תהום דזיבה לא מרצה? והתניא, רבי יוסי אומר: שומרת יום כנגד יום ששחטו וזרקו עליה בשני שלה ואחר כך ראתה – אינה אוכלת ופטורה מלעשות פסח שני. מאי טעמא – לאו משום דמרצה ציץ? – אמרי: לא, משום דקסבר רבי יוסי מכאן ולהבא היא מטמאה. – והתניא, רבי יוסי אומר: זב בעל שתי ראיות ששחטו וזרקו עליו בשביעי שלו ואחר כך ראה, וכן שומרת יום כנגד יום ששחטו וזרקו עליה בשני שלה ואחר כך ראתה – הרי אלו מטמאין משכב ומושב למפרע, ופטורים מלעשות פסח שני. – אמרי: מאי למפרע – מדרבנן. ואף רבי אושעיא סבר מטמא למפרע מדרבנן. דתניא, רבי אושעיא אומר: אבל זב שראה בשביעי שלו – סותר את שלפניו. ואמר ליה רבי יוחנן: לא יסתור אלא יומו! – ממה נפשך, אי קסבר למפרע הוא מטמא – אפילו כולהו נסתור. אי קסבר מכאן ולהבא הוא מטמא – יומו נמי לא נסתור! – אלא אימא: לא יסתור ולא יומו. – ואמר ליה: רבי יוסי קאי כוותך. והא רבי יוסי אומר מטמאין משכב ומושב למפרע! אלא לאו שמע מינה: מטמא למפרע מדרבנן, שמע מינה. ולרבי יוסי, השתא דאמר מכאן ולהבא הוא מטמא [למת] בלבד למעוטי מאי? נפשוט מינה דבכהן והותרה לו טומאת התהום! – אמרי: לעולם בבעלים ובפסח, וקסבר: אין שוחטין וזורקין על טמאי שרץ, ואיצטריך למעוטי. אלא לרבי יוסי, זבה גמורה היכי משכחת לה? – בשופעת. אי בעית אימא: כגון שראתה כל שני בין השמשות.

תוספות מסכת נדה דף עא עמוד ב – הרואה יום אחד עשר וטבלה לערב כו' – דספירת ערב לאו ספירה היא כדקאמר בגמרא ושוין בטבילת לילה שאינה טבילה מכאן קשה לפירוש רש"י שפירש בפ' ב' דזבחים (דף כג.) ובפסחים פרק כיצד צולין (דף פא.) דקאמר לר' יוסי דקאמר מקצת היום ככולו וזבה שראתה בשביעי שלה אינה סותרת לאחר טבילה ופריך התם אלא זבה גמורה היכי משכחת לה ומשני בשופעת אי נמי ברואה בשני בין השמשות ופי' רש"י הא דלא משני ברואה בלילות משום דלמ"ד מקצת היום ככולו לילה חשיבא ספירה ולא צריך עמוד השחר לטבול והשתא קשה דא"כ מתני' דלא כר' יוסי וכן מתני' דמגילה פ' הקורא (דף כ.) דתנן כולן שעשו משעלה עמוד השחר כשר משמע דבלילה לא הוי ספירה.

טור יורה דעה סימן שצה – אבל כיון שעומדין המנחמין מאצלו ביום ז' מותר ברחיצה דמקצת היום ככולו ל"ש מקצת יום ז' ל"ש מקצת יום ל' י"א דוקא מקצת יום שצריך לנהוג אבילות קצת היום ומה שנהג בלילה לא חשבינן ככל היום וי"א דה"ה נמי מקצת הלילה חשיב ככל היום

והר"מ מרוטנבור"ק כתב דגבי ז' כיון שצריך ספירות ז' לא חשבינן מקצת לילה ככל היום אבל בשמועה רחוקה שאינו נוהגת אלא יום אחד אם שמע בלילה חשיב ככל היום ור"ת התיר בשעת הדחק לרחוץ בליל ז':

פתחי תשובה יורה דעה סימן שצה ס"ק א – דמקצת היום ככולו – עי' בטור מחלוקת הפוסקים אי בעינן דוקא מקצת היום או אפילו מקצת הלילה ודעת המחבר כדעת הר"מ מרוטנבורג דדוקא מקצת היום בעינן ועיין בשו"ת הרדב"ז ח"ג סי' תקנ"ט שהכריע דלענין ת"ת ותשמיש המטה דאית בהו מצוה אית לן למפסק כדברי המקילין דמקצת לילה ככל היום אבל ברחיצה וסיכה ושאר הדברים דלית בהו מצוה פסקינן כדברי המחמירים דבעו מקצת היום דוקא ולא מקצת הלילה ומיהו צריך להמתין מלשמש בלילה יותר מעט ממה שהוא רגיל כדי שיהא נוהג גם בו מקצת אבילות ע"ש ועי' ברדב"ז החדשות סי' רס"ח:

שולחן ערוך יורה דעה סימן שצה – כיון שעמדו מנחמים מאצל האבל ביום שביעי, מותר בכל דברים שאסור בהם תוך שבעה, דמקצת היום ככולו, לא שנא מקצת יום שביעי לא שנא מקצת יום שלשים,כיון שהנץ החמה ביום שלשים, בטלו ממנו גזרת שלשים (רא"ש ורבינו ירוחם). הגה: ובמדינות אלו שאין המנחמין רגילין לבא ביום ז', צריך להמתין עד שעה שרגילין המנחמים לבא בשאר ימים, דהיינו לאחר יציאה מבית הכנסת שרגילין לבא מנחמין, כן נראה לי, ודלא כמו שרגילין להמתין שעה על היום, דאין הדבר תלוי רק בעמידת המנחמין. (וכן משמע באשירי).

תלמוד בבלי מסכת מגילה דף כ עמוד א – משנה. אין קורין את המגילה, ולא מלין, ולא טובלין, ולא מזין, וכן שומרת יום כנגד יום – לא תטבול עד שתנץ החמה. וכולן שעשו משעלה עמוד השחר – כשר.

רמב"ם הלכות איסורי ביאה פרק ו הלכה ט – כיצד ראתה דם בימי זיבתה, בין שראתה בתחלת הלילה בין שראתה בסוף היום הרי אותו היום כולו טמא וכאילו לא פסק הדם מעת שראתה עד ששקעה החמה ומשמרת כל הלילה, ואם לא ראתה כלום בלילה משכמת למחר וטובלת אחר שתנץ החמה ומשמרת כל היום, אם לא ראתה כלום הרי זה יום אחד טהור כנגד היום הטמא והרי היא מותרת לבעלה לערב.

חזון איש צב:יב – ענין ספירת לילה עיקרו בהא דאין טובלין בליל ז' אלא ביום ז' ואע"ג דמקצת היום עולה מ"מ בעינן מקצת היום ולא מקצת המעל"ע וע"כ דפי' הקרא ימים ולא לילות ומזה למדו רבותינו בעלי התו' דענין הבדיקה שהוא פי' הספירה צריך נמי ביום אבל י"ל דענין הבדיקה שהוא לברר הטהרה צריך לידון אחר דין עצם הטהורין שראית לילה סותרת ואין היום עולה שזה נידון לענין מעל"ע וה"ה הבדיקות צריך בכל ז' המעל"ע בין ביום ובין בלילה וכן לר"א במעל"ע הא' והז', ודברי התו' י"ל דנסתפקו בזה ואם הבדיקה צריך ביום דוקא א"כ בדין שיהא בתחלת היום שזהו עיקר הספירה שהרי אין אמצע היום עולה לספירה וכמש"כ תו' פסחים פ"א וכתבו דא"כ אין תקנה וע"כ דלא בעינן בתחלת היום וא"כ י"ל דגם לילה מהני דלענין בדיקה נידון אחר

מעל"ע, אבל פשט דבריהם נראה דהבדיקה צריך ביום דוקא כיון דהבדיקה הוא פי' הספירה וספירה דקרא היינו הימים וכו'. כל הפוסקים לא הזכירו דין בדיקת לילה, ואין סברא לומר דסמכו על שהזכירו לשון יום דבהרבה מקומות פירושו מעל"ע ולא היו סותמין באיסור כרת ומשמע דס"ל דלענין זה נידון במעל"ע, וכש"כ למאי שנתבאר לעיל סק"ז די"ל דלרב א"צ כלל מעיקר הדין בדיקה אלא ידיעה דמהני בדיקת לילה, וצ"ע.

26.

תוספות מסכת כתובות דף עב עמוד א – וספרה לה לעצמה – וא"ת אמאי אין מברכת זבה על ספירתה כמו שמברכין על ספירת העומר דהא כתיב וספרה וי"ל דאין מברכין אלא ביובל שמברכין ב"ד בכל שנה שלעולם יוכל למנות כסדר וכן עומר אבל זבה שאם תראה תסתור אין לה למנות.

שו"ת נודע ביהודה מהדורה תנינא – יורה דעה סימן קכג – תשובה למר ניהו רבא שלום. הוא ניהו כבוד אהובי ידיד נפשי וחביבי. הגאון המובהק רב פעלים כבוד מוה' ישעיה מברעסלי נר"ו:

מכתבו מן אסרו חג העצרת הגיעני בשבוע זה. והנה מ"ש מעלתו להזהיר את הנשים להתנהג כדברי הגאון הקדוש בעל של"ה שבימי ספירת הנקיים תמנה בכל יום ותאמר היום יום אחד כיון דכתיב וספרה לה עיין בס' של"ה ד' ק"א ע"א: אומר אני הגאון הקדוש הזה לרוב קדושת חסידותו נתקיים בו אוהב מצות לא ישבע מצות ורצה למען צדקו להגדיל תורה ולהרבות במצות. אבל אצלי אחר מ"כ של הגאון אין דבריו מתקבלים ואם המקרא הזה מצוה הוא למה לא מנאו הרמב"ם והרמב"ן ובה"ג וכל מוני המצות למצות עשה ואיתוספו לתרי"ג מצות שתי מצות מצוה בזב לספור שהרי גם בזב כתיב וספר לו שבעת ימים ומצוה בזבה וספרה לה ואפילו אם נימא דזב וזבה כחדא נינהו איתוסף עכ"פ מצוה אחת. אלא ודאי שאין זו מצוה רק הכתוב אומר שתשגיח שיהיו שבעה ימים הללו נקיים שלא תסתור ואין זה דומה למה דכתיב בעומר וספרתם לכם ממחרת השבת וגו' שמיותר לגמרי דהוה ליה למכתב וביום החמשים מיום הביאכם את עומר התנופה ממושבותיכם תביאו וגו' ולמה כתב וספרתם א"ו שמצוה לספור וכן וספרת לך שבע שבתות דיובל ג"כ מיותר דהוה ליה למכתב וכאשר יעברו שבע שבתות שנים יהיו לך ימי שבע וגו' ולמה כתב וספרת א"ו שמצוה לספור אבל בזב וזבה אי כתיב בזב וכי יטהר מזובו ישב שבעת ימים לטהרתו הו"א שאין צריכין להיות נקיים ולכן כתיב וספרת שצריך שישגיח עליהם שיהיו נקיים וכן בזבה. וזה כוונת התוספות בכתובות ע"ב ע"א בסוף ד"ה וספרה לה שכתבו דאין מברכין אלא ביובל כו' שלעולם יוכל למנות כסדר וכן עומר אבל זבה שאם תראה תסתור אין לה למנות. ובזה יש לישב מה שמביא המג"א בשם המרדכי בריש סימן תרמ"א טעם שאין מברכין בשעת עשיית שופר ומגילה הואיל ועושין אותן לכמה שנים ע"ש. ואכתי קשה למה אין מברכין בשעת עשיית מצת מצוה אלא י"ל דשמא תחמיץ העיסה ויהיה ברכה לבטלה. ומטעם זה נ"ל ג"כ דלא תקנו ברכה לשמירת המצות אף שהיא מצות עשה ושמרתם את המצות ובפרט לירושלמי שהיא מצוה משעת קצירה עיין בטור א"ח סימן תנ"ג ולמה לא מברכינן אשר קב"ו על שמירת מצות אלא דלא שייך ברכה דשמא תחמיץ כמ"ש בזיבה שמא תראה ותסתור: כוונתן דביובל ועומר שתמיד הזמן נמשך כסדר לא צריך קרא למכתב וספרת שהרי אין צריך בזה

השגחה כלל א"ו מצוה היא אבל בזבה שאם תראה תסתור ואין הזמן עובר ממילא וצריך השגחה על זה ואם כן אין כוונת הפסוק בוספרה לה על הספירה אלא על ההשגחה שיהיו נקיים ולא למצוה לכך אין לה למנות. זהו הנלע"ד לדחות עיקר דברי השל"ה. אבל לדידן אפילו אם יהיבנא ליה להגאון השל"ה סברתו שפסוק זה וספרה לה למצוה הוא אכתי אין לדבריו קיום בנשי דידן דהרי זה פשוט אף אם נימא שהיא מצוה מ"מ מצוה זו שייכא להטבילה דאטו אם לא תטבול כלל ואין רצונה לטבול מי יש מצוה בספירה הזו אתמהה וא"כ מצוה זו היא כדכתיב שתהיה סמוך לטבילה וזמן הטבילה הוא ביום השביעי וכיון דנשי דידן אסורות לטבול ביום השביעי אינן מקיימות מצוה זו כלל. ועוד דאי וספרה מצוה היא א"כ אף לרבנן דפליגי על ר"ע ולא בעי ספורים לפנינו היינו דלא מעכב אבל עכ"פ מי פליגי חכמים אקרא דכתיב וספרה לה ובעינן עכ"פ למצוה שתספור והא ודאי שאם תטבול שוב אי אפשר לקיים מצות הספירה כיון שכבר טבלה וא"כ איך מקשה במסכת נדה דף ל' ע"א שבועתא קמא דאתיא קמן ליטבלה כו'. והרי כל טבילות הללו הם רק מצות טבילה בזמנה מצוה ואם עי"ז נעקר מצות וספרה לה א"כ מאי אולמא דהאיך מצוה מהאיך מצוה א"ו שאין כאן מצות ספירה כלל ואפילו לר"ע דבעי ספורים לפנינו לאו ספירה בפה רק שנדע בודאי שהם נקיים. ועוד שאם היה זה מצוה א"כ מנ"ל דלא מעכבא הטהרה ואיך סברי רבנן דלא בעינן ספורים לפנינו. והיה זה שלום. דברי הד"ש:

תלמוד בבלי מסכת נדה דף יג עמוד ב – מתני'. החרשת והשוטה והסומא ושנטרפה דעתה, אם יש להם פקחות – מתקנות אותן והן אוכלות בתרומה.

ספר דבר אברהם ח"א סי' ל"ד – הנה בפשוטו נראה שאין ענין הספירה שיוציא מלות המספר מפיו אלא עניינה שידע ויוחלט אצלו מדעת ומהחלט המנין שהוא סופר ובלאו הכי לא מיקרי ספירה כלל אלא קריאת מלות הספירה הוא דהויא ולא ספירה עצמה וכו'. ומעתה דכשאינו מבין ויודע את מספרו מדעת לא מקרי מנין וספירה כלל א"כ בנ"ד במסופק בימי הספירה בודאי אינו מונה שני ימים מספקא, דהיאך יאמר היום שלשה ימים היום ארבעה ימים דאיזה מספר הוא שאם אפשר שהוא שלשה ואפשר שהוא ארבעה א"כ לא הוי מספר כלל שהרי אינו מכיר ואינו יודע בהחלט את המספר שהוא מונה בשלמא אי הוה אמרינן דספירה בלא הבנת הלשון מהניא שפיר היה מקום להסתפק בזה, אבל למ"ש דבעינן הבנה דוקא מפני ידיעת המספר הרי מנין זה של ספק אינה ידיעה כלל וכן אני אומר גם במי שהיה מסופק בימי הספירה ומנה רק מספר אחד מספק שמא יתרמי שיכוון למספר האמיתי דאע"ג דאיתרמי שכיוון מ"מ לא יצא משום דבשעת ספירתו לא הוה ידע בבירור ואין זו ספירה.

שו"ת אגרות משה יורה דעה חלק ב סימן עט – בענין זמן שהיית המוך דחוק וזמן הבדיקה דכל יום שלעת ערב ט"ז מנ"א תש"כ. מע"כ ידידי מו"ה רמ"מ גערטנער שליט"א.

הנה בדבר המוך דחוק כמה זמן הוא צריך להיות בגופה אחר השקיעה, הנה מכיון שיש לנו להחמיר בענין שקיעה וצה"כ וביה"ש, יש להניח המוך קודם השקיעה שהוא בעוד שהשמש נראית ויהיה מונח שם עד אחר צה"כ אליבא דר"ת שהוא ד' מילין שהם ע"ב מינוטן אחר השקיעה, אבל במדינה זו כפי שאנו רואין אף ביום היותר גדול אין להסתפק על יותר מחמשים

מינוט אחר השקיעה והוו אלו החמשים מינוט כדין הע"ב מינוט ויהיה מחלוקת הראשונים בדין ביה"ש ויום ולילה לפי החשבון, ולדידן שיש להחמיר כב' השיטות יש להיות המוך דחוק חמשים מינוט אחר השקיעה. אבל להרבה נשים שקשה להן קצת אין להחמיר כן אלא בראתה רק יום אחד שמדינא צריכה לבדוק במוך דחוק ושיהא שם כל ביה"ש להמחבר, ומש"כ הרמ"א בסימן קצ"ו סעיף ב' שבדיעבד אם בדקה סמוך לביה"ש ומצאה טהורה סגי אע"פ שלא היה המוך אצלה כל ביה"ש, הקשה עליו בסד"ט סק"ט סוף ד"ה ונ"ל ונשאר בצע"ג וכן הקשה הגר"א בסק"ח, ולכן אף שלא נבטלה שיטת הרמ"א מצד הקושיא מ"מ יותר נוטה כדעת המחבר ואינו כספק השקול לכן יש להחמיר להיות אצלה כל הספק דצה"כ. אבל בשאר ימים אף שראתה גם בו שא"צ מדינא מוך דחוק כדמשמע מהמחבר ורמ"א, ועיין בסד"ט מה שנתן טעם לזה בד"ה היוצא, ורק לחומרא בעלמא מצריכין שתפסיק במוך דחוק אין להחמיר בנשים שקשה להן אלא שיהיה שם עד אחר ביה"ש של שיטת הגר"א דהוא כרבע שעה אחר השקיעה, שלבד ששיטתו עיקר הרי אף אם הוא ספק השקול הוא ספק בחומרא בעלמא שיש למיזל לקולא. ואם קשה לפניה טובא הוא כבדיעבד ששעת הדחק כדיעבד דמי וא"צ כלל מוך דחוק שתשהא אצלה, אלא תבדוק קודם השקיעה בדיקה יפה בחורין ובסדקין ויסגי אף כשתוציאנו תיכף. ומ"מ באין צורך למהר הטבילה בשביל פו"ר משום דכבר קיימו פו"ר, טוב שלא תפסיק אשה כזו שקשה לה להשהות אצלה המוך דחוק ביום שראתה אלא למחר, שאז ודאי הוא רק חומרא בעלמא שכיון שקשה לה אין להצריך לה. אבל ביש צורך למהר הטבילה אינה צריכה לחכות אלא אף ביום שראתה תפסיק קודם השקיעה בלא שהיה כשקשה לה טובא.

וטוב לכתחלה בכל הנשים שקודם שמנחת המוך דחוק תעשה בדיקה יפה ותוציאנו קודם שקיעה ותבדקנו, ואח"כ תניח המוך דחוק להיות שם עד אחר צה"כ כפי השיעור שכתבתי, כדי שיהיו ספורין בפנינו בידיעה ברורה קודם שהתחילה הספירה, ולא מצד שתתודע בלילה שהיתה בדיקה טובה ע"י שתראה אחר שתוציא את המוך שהוא אחר צה"כ שהוא מימי הספירה.

.27

שולחן ערוך יורה דעה סימן קצו סעיף א ברמ"א – הגה: וי"א אם התפללו הקהל ערבית ועוד היום גדול, אינה יכולה לבדוק או ללבוש לבנים ולהתחיל ולמנות מיום המחרת, מאחר דהקהל כבר עשו אותו לילה (ת"ה), דמותר ד אפילו עשו הקהל שבת (אגור בשם ר"י מולין); ונוהגין לכתחלה ליזהר, ובדיעבד אין לחוש. ומקצת נשים נוהגות שאם פסקה קודם ברכו וחזרה לראות כתם או דם תוך ימי ספירתה, אז מפסיקין אפילו לאחר ברכו אם נתקלקלה סמוך לערב, וחושבים דבר זה לדיעבד; ואין למחות בידם, כי כן קבלו מאיזה חכם שהורה להן, והוא מנהג ותיקין.

תוספות מסכת פסחים דף צט עמוד ב – סמוך למנחה לא יאכל – ואם תאמר והא אמר בכל שעה (לעיל ד' מ.) בציקות של נכרים ממלא אדם כריסו מהם ובלבד שיאכל כזית מצה באחרונה והכא אסר לאכול אפי' מבעוד יום וי"ל דבאותה הסעודה אדם נזהר ואינו אוכל כל שובעו כדי שיאכל מצה לתיאבון אבל מבעוד יום אין אדם נזהר ואוכל כל שובעו וסבר שעד הלילה יתאוה ואדרבה יהיה שבע יותר כי יתברך המאכל במעיו והא דדייק רבא לקמן (ד' קז:) דחמרא גריר דאי אמרת

מיסעד סעיד בין הכוסות הללו אמאי ישתה אף על גב דבאותה סעודה נזהר מלאכול שובעו אבל בשתיה אי אפשר להזהר א"נ מבין ראשון לשני דאיכא אגדתא והלל דייק דדמי לסעודה אחרת.

ט"ז אורח חיים סימן תרסח:א – כתב רש"ל בתשובה סי' ס"ח שראה הג"ה בשם מהר"ר טעביל שלא היה אוכל בכניס' יום ש"ע עד הלילה דא"כ הי' צריך לברך לישב בסוכה כיון דעדיין יום הוא כו' וכתב רש"ל ראיה לזה מחמת ברכ' לישב בסוכה דאם לא יאמר אות' זה אין ראוי דלמה יגרע ברכ' מחוייבת נהי שהברכות אין מעכבות היינו דיעבד אבל לחיובי עצמו בברכה דהיינו לאכול בסוכה מבע"י ולא לאומרו עון גדול הוא וא"ל דכיון דמוסיף מחול על הקדש א"כ עבר היום זה אינו נהי דמוסיפין בתפלה כדאשכחן רב צלי של שבת בע"ש אבל לא לעשות לילה שהרי ק"ש של ערבית היה או' בשעתו ומ"ה אין ראוי לספור עומר בליל שבת אחר קידוש עד לילה כאשר כתבתי בתשו' סימן י"ג ולאומרו ג"כ אין ראוי דסתרי אהדדי שאם אמר לישב בסוכה חול הוא וקידוש למה הוא בא ואם י"ט הוא לישב בסוכה למה היא בא וראיה גדולה מדברי רי"ף ורא"ש סוף לולב וערבה וז"ל ולענין מיתב בסוכה בש"ע הלכתא מיתב יתבינן ברוכי לא מברכינ' כיון דש"ע הוא דלא אפשר לברוכי על הסוכ' דסתרי אהדדי ומשום דמספקא לן בתרווייהו עבדי' לחומרא יתבי' ונהגו ביה מנהג י"ט דהוא ש"ע לחומרא ע"כ אלמא דאי לא דעבדינן לחומרא מכח ספק לא מצאנו ידינו ורגלינו איך יתבי' ולא מברכין וא"כ היכא שהוא עדיין יום ואין כאן ספק איך יתבי' ולא מברכין ולברך א"א דסתרי אהדדי ושוב עיינתי בר"ן שאין לקצר הברכה המחוייבת אפי' אם אתה עושה י"ט חול שכתב וז"ל פי' מיתב יתבי' אע"ג דידעי' בקביעא דירחי משום דשלחו מתם הזהרו במנהג אבותיכם אבל לא מברכין כי היכי דלא לזלזולי בי"ט כ"פ רי"ף ואע"ג די"ט ב' של פסח עבדי' י"ט ועבדי' ספירת עומר שאני התם דה"ט משום דעומר וקידוש לא בהדדי אתיין אלא עביד כל חד באפי' נפשיה אבל כאן ברכת סוכ' היא בכוס א' עם הקידוש ואם מברך ברכת סוכה בש"ע אתי לזלזולי בי"ט ול"נ דא"צ לכך דספיר' א"א לדחות' משום זלזול דידעינן בקביעא דירחי והוי חייב בספירה מדאורייתא אבל סוכה בח' ספק ז' הוא מדרבנן עכ"ל אלמא אם חייב מדאורייתא אין ראוי שתעקר הברכה וכאן אם יום הוא מחויב מן התורה שלא לאכול חוץ לסוכה ואם אכל צריך לברך ואין ראוי לעוקר' ומ"מ בדיעבד אין נראה לברך שהרי הר"ן אינו חולק על טעם הא' אלא שכתב ול"נ שא"צ כו' ולפי טעם האחד מאחר שהוא בחד ענין א"א לזלזולי בי"ט ולכן איסור גדול הוא למי שמקדש קודם הלילה כו' עכ"ל: אלו דברי הרב רש"ל ואף שאין משיבין הארי לאחר מותו וק"ו בשועל כמוני מ"מ אחוה דעתי שדברי הרב מאד תמוהין ואין הדעת של ע"ד סובלן דלמה גזר תענית בחנם משעת כניסת ש"ע שהוא מבע"י והוא הכרח דתוספת מחול על הקודש הוא דאורייתא וע"כ חייב להתענות עד הלילה וזה ודאי הוא מן הנמנע חדא דודאי לא הוו שתקו חכמים מזה והרי חזינן דטרחי למצוא תקנה ליום הש"ע ליתב ולא לברך ולמה לא מצאו תקנה לכניסתו עד הלילה להציל האדם מאיסור גדול שלא יבוא לאכול קודם הלילה ולכל הפחות היה להם להזהיר אותנו בזה בפרט שרוב העולם אינם יודעין ואנו אין להוסיף איסור על מה שנמצא בדברי הגמ' ופוסקי' ותו דלפי חשש שלו יהא אסור לכנוס לסוכה באותה שעה דהא פסקו הרי"ף ורא"ש וטור דיש לברך על כל פעם שיכנס בה כמ"ש סימן תרל"ט אלא שר"ת פירש שעיקר קביעות היא אכילה מברך על האכילה ופוטר כל הדברים וכיון

שזה אסור לאכול בסוכה במה יפטר ממה שחייב בכניסתו בעיקר הדין וכ"ת דמה שבירך ביום פוטרו זה אינו דהא כבר פנה אותו קביעות והופסק בתפלתו תפלה של ש"ע וכשנכנס אח"כ בעוד יום הוא חייב בעד כניסתו ואין מי שיפטרנו ותו לדבריו בכל י"ט בע"ש יהיה אסור באכילה עד הלילה דכיון דאותו יום חייב לברך על המזון שאוכל לקבוע בו יעלה ויבא מחמת שעדיין הוא יום וקדושת י"ט עליו והנה מחמת שקיבל עליו שבת נסתלק ממנו הי"ט והיאך יעשה ביעלה ויבוא והי׳ צריך שלא יאכל עד הלילה וא"ל שכנגד זה הוא אומר רצה ה"נ נגד לישב בסוכה יאמר קידוש. ובאמת סברא שבנה הרב עליו הוא אינו קיום כלל דודאי מי שמוסיף מחול על הקודש הוא עושה ע"פ צווי תורתינו כבר חלף והלך ממנו חובת היום מה שהיה עליו קודם זה והוה כמו בלילה ומחר ממש ומ"ש הרב לסתור זה מההיא דרב צלי של שבת בע"ש והיה ממתין עם ק"ש עד הלילה וכן בעומר תמהתי על גברא רבא דעימיה שרי נהורא מה חשב בזה דלא קרב זא"ז דק"ש ועומר זמנם בלילה ולמה יקדים מבע"י ולעשות שלא כדינם בשביל מה שקיבל שבת עליו ומה יהיה חסר לו באם ימתין בדברים אלו ולא לסמוך על קבלתו שבת מבע"י וכי לא סגי בלא"ה משא"כ בחיוב סוכה שלפנינו הן מצד הכניסה הן מצד האכילה ע"כ היא נמנעת ממנו בשעה שקיבל קדושת י"ט של ש"ע שבו סותר מצות סוכה ויש לו יכולת לעשות כן פשיטא שתכף נכנס לגדר יתובי יתבי׳ ברוכי לא מברכי׳ והוה כמו בלילה דהפה הקדוש יתעלה ב"ה שצוה עליו מצוה סוכה ביום ההוא הוא הפה הקדוש שהתיר לו אחר שקיבל עליו ש"ע נמצא שכל מ"ש רש"ל מרי"ף והר"ן לאו ראייה היא דאין חילוק כלל בין אחר קבלת ש"ע מבע"י ליום המחרת ומאן יהיב לן משופרי שופרי ואכלינן באותו שעה בסוכה רק שאין מברכים לישב בסוכה כנלע"ד ברור:

שו"ת רדב"ז חלק א סימן עו – שאלת ממני אודיעך דעתי בענין השבת כי יש חילוק גדול בין השוכנים במזרח לשוכנים במערב ונמצא שמה שהוא לאלו שבת הוי לאלו חול:

תשובה דע כי שאלה זו נבוכו בה רבים ונכבדים אבל אודיעך דעתי בה דע כי השבת נמסרה לכל אחד מישראל שנאמר כי אות היא ביני וביניכם וכמו שאות הברית הוא לכל א׳ וא׳ כן השבת נמסר לכל א׳ וא׳ וכיון שהשבת נמסר לכל א׳ בכל מקום שהוא מונה ששה ימים ובסוף הששה עושה שבת שהוא זכר למעשה בראשית שנאמר כי ששת ימים עשה ה׳ וגו׳ שאם אין אתה אומר כן אפילו בארץ ישראל יש חילוק קצת: ואפי׳ תרצה לומר שע"י התוספת שאנו מוסיפין בכניסתו וביציאתו מתוקן מ"מ התוספת הזה דאורייתא היא ונמצא שאין כל בני א"י שוין בתוספת זה שהרי יש מהלך קרוב לד׳ ימים בא"י מן המזרח למערב ואפי׳ בעירות הסמוכות יש חילוק בזה בין טבריה לציפורי כדאמר ר׳ יוסי יהא חלקי עם מכניסי שבת בטבריה ועם מוציאי שבת בציפורי אלא מאי אית לך למימר כי השבת ניתן לכל אחד כפי מקומו אשר הוא דר בו לפי שכבר נשלמו במקומו ששה הקפים שלמים ונכנס השביעי לקודם קודם ולמאוחר מאוחר. וגדולה מזו אמרו המהלך במדבר ולא ידע מתי הוא שבת מונה ו׳ ימים מיום שטעה ומקדש שביעי ומברך בו ברכת היום ומבדיל במוצאי שבת ע"כ ואעפ"י שאינו עושה בכל יום אלא כדי חייו ה"מ מפני שהוא ספק שמא הוא שבת לכל בני אותו המחוז אשר הוא בו וחל עליו איסור שבת א"נ משום דאם הוא שבת הרי יש בו איסור שבת לכל בני העולם שאין חילוק בין השוכנים בקצה המזרח לשוכנים בקצה המערב אלא י"ב שעות או פחות ונמצא שזה עושה מלאכה בזמן שהוא שבת

לכל מ״מ למדנו מדחייבוהו לקדש שביעי משמע דלכל אחד נמסר לעשות זכר למעשה בראשית כל חד וחד כי אתריה תדע שאח׳ שהגיע לישוב וידע שטעה ועשה מלאכה בשבת לא חייבוהו להביא קרבן לא חטאת ולא אשם ולא וידוי משמע שקיים מצות שבת. עוד ראיה מהא דאמרינן עכו״ם ששבת חייב מיתה ולאו דוקא יום השבת אלא שקבע לו יום א׳ לשבות בו משמע שכל מי שעושה מלאכה ששה ושובת יום א׳ סוף סוף שובת נקרא. עוד ראיה שהרי השבת ניתן במרה וממרה לא״י יש קצת חילוק שהרי מרה לדרום וא״י לצפון נמצא שלא היה השבת מצומצם בין מרה לא״י אלא שהוא ית׳ צוה את השבת לישראל לכל אחד מהם או לכלם בכל מקום שימצאו שהרי גלוי וידוע לפניו ית׳ שעתידין בניו לגלות לקצוי הארצות ויהיה ביניהם מרחק גדול וטעם זה אנו צריכים לכל המועדות ויום הכפורים לפי שגם בהם תפול השאלה ודע כי נפל מחלוקת בין הראשונים מאי זה מקום מתחיל היום וגם מאי זה מקום מתחיל יום השבת עיין במ״ש בספר הכוזרי ובעל יסוד עולם ולדעת כולם השוכנים בקצה המזרח השבת להם קודם השוכנים במערב ונמצאו אלו מותרים במלאכה בזמן שאלו אסורים אלא צריכים אנו לומר כי השבת נתן לכל א׳ מישראל כפי מקומו שימנה ו׳ ימים שלמים וישבות בשביעי ובזה יש שכר למעשה בראשית:

שו״ת הר צבי אורח חיים א סימן קלח – להרב מנחם כשר קו התאריך לענין שבת ויוה״כ.

זה כעשר שנים נתעוררה השאלה ע״י הפליטים שנתיישבו ביאפאן וסין בדבר קו התאריך של שבת ויוהכ״פ, ונשאלתי כיצד יתנהגו במקומות ההם.

אני השבתי שעליהם להתנהג כפי שמוחזק שם במקומות ההם בלי שינוי מאנשי המקום הנמצאים שם מכבר.

והנה בשנים הללו יצאו אנשים ת״ח וביניהם גם רבנים גדולים, שלפי דעתם צריכין הבאים שמה לשנות את יום השבת וכן יוהכ״פ. והיטיב אשר עשה בזה ידידי שנכנס בעומק הענין לברר את הדבר כדת של תורה, וקיבץ הרבה מדברי גאוני הדורות שדברו בזה, והראשון בזה הוא בת׳ הרדב״ז שפסק הלכה למעשה שכל מי שבא ממרחק צריך לשמור את השבת כאנשי המקום שבא לשם וכן הוא שיטת הראב״ד ויסוד עולם שחולקים על הכוזרי, וזה מקרוב נדפס בפעה״ק ירושלים ספרו של הגאב״ד מביאליסטוק הגאון ר׳ שמואל מוהליבר ז״ל שמרעיש עולמות על מי שרוצה לשנות את יום השבת.

ובהיות שדבר זה מסכן את שמירת השבת בישראל, לכן חוב קדוש הוא על גדולי דורנו שיעמדו על המשמר, להיות מגודרי גדר, שלא יבואו ח״ו לפרוץ בקדושת השבת. ובפרט שכל עיקר הסיבה לשנות את השבת, הוא ע״פ קו התאריך שנקבע בעיקרו ע״י אומות העולם, כי אין לזה שום יסוד בש״ס ופוסקים שיש קו תאריך בעולם, וזה גופא הוא ראיה ברורה שבאמת אין תאריך קובע ע״פ התורה, דכיצד יחסר בתורתנו דבר כזה שנוגע לקביעות השבת, אלא ע״כ כמו שכותב הרדב״ז, דכך היא מצות השבת, שבכל מקום שהוא יעבוד שש ימים וישבות ביום השביעי, וכלשון התורה בכל מקום שהזהירה על השבת ומינה אין לזוז. ומי שבא לשנות בלי הוכחה מן התורה, יחוש לנפשו שלא יהיה ח״ו בכלל מחטיא את הרבים ובפרט בדבר שהוא מיסודי התורה והשומע יתברך בכל טוב.

.28

מרדכי נדה תשל"ה ד"ה נאמנת – ואם סופרת ז' נקיים מסתברא משלשה ימי נקיים ואילך הכתמים טהורים ואם יש במה לתלות במכה או בחבורה או בדם צפור ואינה סותרת אבל צריכה שתדע בודאי שפסק דם המקור לכך צריך שיהיו שלשה ימים הראשונים של ספירת נקיים לגמרי.

תרומת הדשן סימן רמט – שאלה: הא דכתב [ס'] התרומה ובמרדכי ובהגה"ה במיימון מייתי לה, דשלשה ימים הראשונים של ספירת שבעה נקיים צריכין טהורים לגמרי, ואם מצאתה בהן כתם אע"פ שיכולה לתלות אותה במכה או בחבורה אינה תולה ואם מצאה פחות מכגריס יכולה לתלות בדם מאכולת או לאו?

תשובה: יראה דדוקא אמר ספר התרומה דאינו תולה בחבורה או בדם צפור והיינו כתם שהוא כגריס ועוד דפחות מכאן אינו צריך לתלותו בחבורה וכה"ג אלא תלינן אותו בדם מאכולת, וא"כ סברא לומר דווקא כתם גדול דלא שכיחי כולי האי ואפשר ליזהר בו לא תלינן בשלשה ימים הראשונים, אבל כתם פחות מכגריס ודאי תלינן ליה לעולם, דאל"כ אין שום אשה יכולה לטהר. והכי תניא פ' הרואה כתם נדה נח ע"ב אמר רשב"ג לדברי אין קץ דאין לך אשה שהיא טהורה לבעלה לעולם, שאין כל מיטה ומיטה שאין עליה כמה וכמה טיפות דם מאכולת, פי' לדברי שאני אומר דאם לא הרגה מאכולת אינה תולה בה אפילו פחות מכגריס ועוד טמאה, וא"כ אין לך אשה טהורה. הא קמן דאין אדם יכול ליזהר ממאכולת, וא"כ אי לא תלינן במאכולת בשלשה ימים הראשונים אין אשה יכולה לספור שבעה נקיים.

ש"ך על שולחן ערוך יורה דעה סימן קצו סעיף י – י"א דבג' כו' – ז"ל ד"מ במרדכי אם סופרת תוך ז' ימים נקיים מסתברא מג' ימים ואילך הכתמים טהורים אם יש לתלות במכה או בחבורה או בצפור ואינה אוסרת אבל צריכה לידע בודאי שפסק דם המקור לגמרי לכך צריך שיהא ג' ימים הראשונים של ספירת נקיים טהורים לגמרי (ובמרדכי שם איתא מסה"ת קצרתי) עכ"ל וכן הוא בהגמ"י פ"ט מהא"ב ונ"ל דהא דלא תלינן במכה בשלשה ימים הראשונים דוקא במכה שאינה ידוע שמוציאה דם דתלינן בה שאר כתם כדלעיל סי' קפ"ז (ס"ה) וכ"מ מלשון המרדכי דע"ז קאי אבל במכה שידוע שמוציא' דם נ"ל דתלינן בה אף בג' ימים הראשוני' דהא אפי' רואה ממש תלינן לעיל סי' קפ"ז במכה שמוציאה דם כ"ש כתמים דרבנן וא"ל דשאני ברואה ממש דהוא תחלת ראיה ולכך תלינן במכה ואמרי' דמעיינה סתום עדיין ולא ראתה אבל תוך ספירתה שמעיינה פתוח כבר לא תלינן במכה כלל זה אינו דהרי כתבתי לעיל סימן קפ"ז דיש סוברים בשעת וסתה תלינן במכה הואיל ווסתות דרבנן אם כן כתמים נמי שהן מדרבנן תלינן במכה ואפילו למאן דמחמיר בשעת וסתה היינו הואיל ואיכא למאן דאמר וסתות דאורייתא אבל כתמים שהן דרבנן לכ"ע תלינן במכה שידוע שמוציאה דם כנ"ל לצדד להקל משום דלא חילקו שאר הפוסקים בין כתם שרואה בימי הספירה לשאר כתם אם כן משמע דס"ל דאפי' תוך ג' ימים תלינן כתם בכל מקום שיש לתלות וכ"כ לעיל סימן ק"צ (סמ"א) בשם ב"י בשם רשב"א דתלינן כתם אף בימי ספירתה ואפשר דסה"ת והמרדכי לא החמירו אלא לחומרא בעלמא דהרי כתב בת"ה סימן רמ"ט טעמא דלא תלינן בג' ימים הראשונים הואיל ואפשר ליזהר כו' ואם היה אסור

מדינא לא שייך לחלק משום שאפשר ליזהר אלא ודאי לא החמירו אלא משום שאפשר ליזהר אבל במקום דאי אפשר ליזהר אין להחמיר ולכן התיר בכתם בפחות מכגריס ועוד שתלינן בכינה כן נ"ל דאין להחמיר במכה שידוע שמוציאה דם עכ"ל ד"מ וכל דבריו צל"ע מה שכתב ונראה לי דלא תלינן כו' וכ"מ לשון המרדכי כו' אדרבה פשט דברי המרדכי דמסתימים סתים לה משמע דבכל מכה איירי ועוד דהא אפילו בנתעסקה בדם צפור לא תלינן בה אע"פ שיש דם לפנינו כל שכן במכה שמוציאה דם ולהרב צריך לחלק דשאני דם צפור שהוא ממקום אחר מה שאין כן מכה שבגופה שאי אפשר ליזהר וזה אינו משמע ועוד דהא הם דברי סה"ת והג"מ ופשטן של דברי סה"ת והג"מ משמע דאפילו ממכה שידוע שמוציאה דם לא תלינן דכתבו אם יש לה מכה באותו מקום תולה בה כתמה אפילו אינה יודעת אם היא מוציאה דם או לאו כו' ואם סופרת ז' נקיים כו' לכך צריכה שיהיו שלשה ימים הראשונים של ספירה נקיים לגמרי עכ"ל ומדכתבו ברישא אפי' אינה יודעת שמכתה מוציאה דם משמע דכל שכן כשיודעת ואם כן כיון דרישא בכל גווני סיפא נמי בכל גווני מיירי ועוד מדתלו הפוסקים טעמא שצריכה שתדע בודאי שפסק דם המקור משמע דבג' ימים הראשונים שאינה יודעת בודאי שפסק דם מקורה בכל ענין לא תלינן במכה והכי משמע להדיא בב"ה סימן ק"צ בשם הא"ח וז"ל כתב הר"מ אשה מוכת שחין דבר פשוט הוא שכתמיה טהורים דכיון דשיחני וכיבי שבה ודאי מפקי דמא ונצבעים בה סדינים וחלוקה ואפילו בשעת וסתה וכ"ש בימי לבונה תלינן בה והגיה עליו הר"ף וה"מ לאחר שלשה ללבונה אבל תוך שלשה לא תלינן עכ"ל ודברי הר"מ והר"ף אלו הם בתשב"ץ סימן תפ"א אלמא דאע"ג דודאי מפקי דמא לא תלינן תוך שלשה והא א"ל שכתב הרב לחלק בין מעיינה סתום או פתוח ודאי קושטא והכי משמע מדכתבו הפוסקים שצריכה שתדע בודאי שפסק דם מקורה ומ"ש זה אינו דהרי כתבתי לעיל דיש סוברים כו' אינה סתירה דמ"מ התם אינו ידוע שמעיינה פתוח מה שאין כן הכא ותו דהא התם קי"ל דבשעת וסתה לא תלינן במכתה אפילו ידוע שמוציאה דם וכמ"ש שם בס"ק כ"ו ומ"ש הרב היינו הואיל ואיכא למ"ד וסתות דאורייתא כו' ודאי ליתא דהא ודאי רשב"ג דסובר וסתות דרבנן נמי סבר הכי מטעם ההוכחה דאל"כ לעולם לא תהיה טמאה וכמ"ש שם בס"ק הנ"ל ויותר ה"ל להרב' לומר דאפי' מאן דמחמיר התם היינו משום דאם לא כן לעולם לא תהיה טמאה מה שאין כן הכא אבל כל זה אינו במשמע אלא איפכא מסתברא דהכא כיון דמעיינה פתוח לכ"ע צריכה שתדע בודאי שפסק דם מקורה ומ"ש כן נ"ל לצדד להקל משום דשאר הפוסקים לא חילקו כו' אין זה כדאי להקל דהא בכמה מקומות מצינו כה"ג אפי' היכא שמקצת פוסקים מקילין ושאר פוסקים סתמו דבריהם ואמרינן ילמד הסתום מן המפורש כ"ש הכא שהמפרשים מחמירים ועוד מי לנו גדול מסה"ת ומרדכי והג"ה וכ"ש שגם הר"ף והא"ח ות"ה מסכימים לדבריהם וכ"פ האגודה פרק תינוקת סי' ל"ט ומ"ש וכ"כ לעיל סי' ק"צ בשם רשב"א כו' י"ל דהרשב"א מיירי אחר שלשה ולא עדיפי דברי הרשב"א מדברי הר"מ שכ' בימי לבונה תלינן להקל ופירשו הר"ף לאחר ג' ואפילו יחלוק הרשב"א בזה יחיד הוא נגד כל הני רבוותא בפרט שהן מחמירים ומ"ש ואפשר דלא החמירו אלא לחומרא בעלמא דהא כתב בת"ה סימן רמ"ט כו' לא ידענא מאי הוכחה היא זו דת"ה לא כתב שם אלא דפחות מכגריס ועוד תלינן בכינה הואיל ושכיח טובא וא"א ליזהר א"כ אין לך אשה שתוכל לספור שבעה נקיים מה שאין כן במכה אבל ודאי טעמא הוא משום שצריכה בודאי לידע שפסק דם מקורה שוב מצאתי בב"ח

ס"ס ק"ץ שכתב באשה שהיא מוכת שחין כיון שהדם יוצא תמיד מהשחין שבגופה ונכתם בסדיני' וחלוקה יש לתלות אף בשלשה ימים הראשונים דאל"כ לא תוכל לספור שבעה נקיים לעולם ול"ד לחבורה שבגופה שמוציאה דם ואפילו הכי לא תלי' בה ג' ימים הראשונים דשאני חבורה א' שהיה מכוסה באספלנית שאינה מוציאה דם אלא לפעמים דומיא דמכה שבאותו מקום דכתב סה"ת דלפעמים מוציאה דם אבל מוכת שחין דכל שעה יוצא ממנה דם דמיא למאכולת דתלינן בה אף בשלשה ימים הראשונים וכו' ומכל מקום הכל לפי ענין השחין ודוק עכ"ל מבואר מדבריו דאין להקל אלא במלאה שיחני וכיבי ודם יוצא ממנה תמיד הא לאו הכי אפילו ידוע שמכתה מוציאה דם אין להקל וכ"מ בס' אפי רברבי שהעתיק כל הדברים שבסי' זה רק דין זה שכתב הרב דבמכה שמוציאה דם תולין אף בשלשה ימים הראשונים השמיט רק כתב סתמא שאין תולין כתם כגריס ועוד בשום דבר בשלשה ימים הראשונים ע"ש:

29.

רש"י מסכת שבת דף יג עמוד ב – ליבוניך – כגון זבה שסופרת שבעה נקיים משפסקה, וצריכה להיות לובשת לבנים לבדיקה, שמא תראה ותסתור ספירתה.

ביאור הגר"א יורה דעה סימן קצו ס"ק י – ביום כו' ומנהג כו'. וז"ש בפ"ק דשבת (י"ג ב') בימי ליבוניך כו':

שו"ת אגרות משה יורה דעה חלק ב סימן עח – במראות דמים בבדיקות וכתמים בתוך הז' נקיים, ובמחלל שבת שמל תינוק, ובקבר במקום שמצוי מים אם יש לעשות בהקבר דפנות ורצפה מצעמענט ר"ח סיון תשכ"ו. מע"כ ידידי הנכבד מהר"ר שמואל טאקייער שליט"א.

בדבר האשה שאחרי ג' ימים של הנקיים היא רואה כתם של דם, אם הוא בהרגשה והוא מראה דם הרי ודאי סותרת וצריכה להתחיל למנות מחדש השבעה ימים. ואם יש ספק בהמראה אף שקיל מאילו ראתה בתוך ג' ימים ראשונים, מ"מ מאחר שאין אנו בקיאים בהמראות יש לאסור אם נוטה לאדמימות, וצריכה להראות לחכם שבקי להורות לפי הבקיאות של חכמי דורנו שיאמר אם יש לחוש לפי מה שמחמירין, שאם אין זה נוטה לאדמימות של דם אלא כשעוה וזהב או שהוא רק ברוין לא יסתור. ואם ראתה בתוך ג' ימים של פסיקת הדם יש להחמיר גם במראה געל וברוין. והחכם יורה אם דומה לזה דאם הוא פחות מזה אין להחמיר אף בתוך ג' ימים.

ואם היה זה בלא הרגשה אבל ע"י בדיקה שהוא ספק שמא הרגישה יש מקום להקל בשעת הדחק במראה געל וברוין, אף בג' ימים ראשונים כיון שהוא רק ספק הרגשה. ואם הוא ודאי בלא הרגשה שרק נמצא כתם על בגדיה אף שהוא כשיעור גריס שטמאה בכתם, יש להקל במראה געל וברוין אף בתוך ג' ימים ראשונים, אבל במראה הנוטה לאדמימות יש להחמיר אף בכתם. ויש להורות לאשה זו אם אינה מרגשת אלא שמוצאת כתמים על בגדיה שתלבש בגדים צבעונים, שאף בג' ימים ראשונים אין לאסור כדאיתא בפ"ת סימן קצ"ו ס"ק י"ב בסופו. ואם היא מוצאת בהבדיקות שאחר יום השלישי מספירת ז' נקיים, יש להקל לה שתבדוק רק ביום א' של ימי הנקיים וביום השביעי, שסגי זה בדיעבד כדאיתא בסימן קצ"ו סעיף ד', וכיון שהוא שעת הדחק יש להורות לה שתעשה כן לכתחלה, דכיון שכבר הפסיקה בטהרה שהיא בחזקת שפסקה

דמיה, אין לנו לחוש כל זמן שלא הרגישה שמא תראה דם בבדיקה, ואף שאיזה פעמים מצאה על הבדיקות הרי הוא רק ספק שמא הרגישה ולאו אדעתה שלכתחלה אין לחוש שמא תראה על בדיקה, ורק כשבדקה ומצאה דם מספקינן שמא היה זה ע"י הרגשה.

ובראיית דם כיון שהוא מן המקור אף שאיזה סבות גרמו שיצא הדם מכיון שאין שם מכה הוא מטמאה בדין נדה, וכ"ש כשהסבה היא פסיכית ונערוון (עצבים) שודאי הוא דם נדה ואסורה משום נדה.

שו"ת אגרות משה יורה דעה חלק ד סימן יז – כט. הרוחצת בים בז' נקיים אם צריכה לרחוץ בבגד לבן.

הנשים הרוחצות בים ובבריכות בבגדים שנעשו לזה במדינותינו, אם הן בז' הנקיים צריכות שיהיו לבנים לכה"פ בצד שכלפי הגוף – הנה פשוט שאין צריכות, אך ודאי צריך שיהא נקי מכתמים. דהא רשאית לרחוץ גם ערומה בלא בגדים כלל, ולא גרע מה שלבשה איזה בגד אם אך הוא נקי.

30.

תלמוד בבלי מסכת שבת דף יג עמוד א–ב – תני דבי אליהו: מעשה בתלמיד אחד ששנה הרבה וקרא הרבה, ושימש תלמידי חכמים הרבה, ומת בחצי ימיו. והיתה אשתו נוטלת תפיליו ומחזרתם בבתי כנסיות ובבתי מדרשות, ואמרה להם: כתיב בתורה (דברים ל) כי הוא חייך ואורך ימיך, בעלי ששנה הרבה וקרא הרבה ושימש תלמידי חכמים הרבה – מפני מה מת בחצי ימיו? ולא היה אדם מחזירה דבר. פעם אחת נתארחתי אצלה והיתה מסיחה כל אותו מאורע. ואמרתי לה: בתי, בימי נדותך מה הוא אצלך? אמרה לי: חס ושלום, אפילו באצבע קטנה לא נגע בי. – בימי לבוניך מהו אצלך? – אכל עמי, ושתה עמי, וישן עמי בקירוב בשר, ולא עלתה דעתו על דבר אחר. ואמרתי לה: ברוך המקום שהרגו, שלא נשא פנים לתורה, שהרי אמרה תורה +ויקרא יא /יח/+ ואל אשה בנדת טומאתה לא תקרב.

ספר המצוות לרמב"ם מצות לא תעשה שנג – והמצוה השנ"ג היא שהזהירנו מקרוב לאחת מכל אלו העריות ואפילו בלא ביאה. כגון חבוק ונשיקה והדומה להם מפעולות הזנות. והוא אמרו יתעלה באזהרה מזה (אח"מ יח ו) איש איש אל כל שאר בשרו לא תקרבו לגלות ערוה. כאילו יאמר לא תקרבו מהן קירוב יביא לגלות ערוה. ולשון ספרא [פי"ג ה"ב (בד"ח הט"ו)] לא תקרבו לגלות אין לי אלא שלא יגלה מניין שלא יקרב תלמוד לומר ואל אשה בנדת טומאתה לא תקרב אין לי אלא בנדה בל תקרב ובל תגלה ומניין לכל העריות שהן בבל תקרבו ובל תגלו תלמוד לומר לא תקרבו לגלות. ושם (ה"ח ובד"ח הכ"א) אמרו ונכרתו הנפשות העושות מה תלמוד לומר לפי שנאמר לא תקרבו יכול יהו חייבין כרת על הקריבה ת"ל העושות לא הקרבות. וכבר נכפלה האזהרה באיסור אלו הדמיונות ואמר (שם) לבלתי עשות מחוקות התועבות. אולם אמרו (שם) כמעשה ארץ מצרים אשר ישבתם בה לא תעשו וכמעשה ארץ כנען אשר אני מביא אתכם שמה לא תעשו הנה לא יזהיר בשני אלו הלאוין מחקות התועבות לבד אבל אמנם יזהיר בהם מהתועבות עצמן אשר בארם אחר זה. וזה שהוא הביא שני הלאוין האלה כלל על כל העריות.

ובעבור שהזהיר שלא לעשות כמעשה ארץ מצרים וכמעשה ארץ כנען, וזה כולל כל מה שהיו עושין מן הזימה ומן עבודת האדמה ומרעיית המקנה ויישוב הארץ גם כן, שב לבאר כי אותם הפעולות אשר הזהירך מהם הוא כך וכך ערות לא תגלה ערות לא תגלה וכמו שביאר בסוף המאמר ואמר כי את כל התועבות האל עשו אנשי הארץ. ולשון ספרא יכול לא יבנו בתים ולא יטעו כרמים כמותם תלמוד לומר ובחוקותיהם לא תלכו לא אמרתי אלא בחוקים החקוקים להם ולאבותיהם. ושם אמרו מה היו עושים האיש נושא איש ואשה נושאה אשה ואשה נשאת לשני אנשים. הנה כבר התבאר כי אלו הלאוין שהם כמעשה ארץ מצרים וכמעשה ארץ כנען לא תעשו הם אזהרה מבעילת כל העריות על הכלל ואחר כן כפל האזהרה בהם בפרט ערוה ערוה. וכבר ביארנו אנחנו כל משפטי אלו המצות בשביעי מסנהדרין (מ״ד) מחבורנו הגדול וביארנו שלוקין עליהן. וממה שראוי שתדעהו הוא שכל אשה שחייבין על ביאתה כרת שהנולד מן הביאה ההיא שחייבין בה כרת ייקרא ממזר, והוא שקראו האל יתעלה (פ׳ תצא כג) ממזר. בין שהיתה אותה ביאה בזדון או בשגגה הולד ממזר. חוץ מן הנדה לבד שהולד הנולד ממנה אינו ממזר ואמנם נקרא בן הנדה. וכבר התבאר זה ברביעי ממסכת יבמות (מט א):

רמב״ם הלכות איסורי ביאה פרק כא – כל הבא על ערוה מן העריות דרך איברים או שחבק ונשק דרך תאוה ונהנה בקרוב בשר הרי זה לוקה מן התורה, שנאמר לבלתי עשות מחקות התועבות וגו׳ ונאמר לא תקרבו לגלות ערוה, כלומר לא תקרבו לדברים המביאין לידי גילוי ערוה.

ויקרא פרק יח:ו – איש איש אל כל שאר בשרו לא תקרבו לגלות ערוה אני ה׳:

השגות הרמב״ן לספר המצוות מצות לא תעשה שנג – כתב הרב והמצוה שלש מאות וחמשים ושלש שנמנענו מהתעדן באחת מכל אלה העריות ואפילו בלא ביאה כגון חבוק ונשוק והדומה להם מפעולות המעמיקים בזמה והוא אמרו יתע׳ במניעה הזאת איש איש אל כל שאר בשרו לא תקרבו לגלות ערוה ולשון ספרא אילו נאמר ואל אשה בנדת טומאתה לא תקרב לגלות ערותה אין לי אלא שלא יגלה שלא יקרב מניין תלמוד לומר לא תקרב אין לי אלא נדה [בל תקרב ובל תגלה מנין לכל העריות בבל תקרב ובל תגלה ת״ל לא תקרבו לגלות]. והנה הרב מצא הברייתא הזו המפורשת ותלה דבריו באילן גדול. אבל כפי העיון בתלמוד אין הדבר כן שיהיה בקריבה שאין בה גלוי ערוה כגון חבוק ונשוק לאו ומלקות. שהרי בגמר שבת (יג א) שאלו בנדה אם מותר שישכב בעלה עמה במטה אחת היא בבגדה והוא בבגדו והיו מהם מי שאסר והעלו ופליגא דרבי פדת דאמר רבי פדת לא אסרה תורה אלא קריבה שלגלוי ערוה בלבד שנא׳ איש איש אל כל שאר בשרו לא תקרבו לגלות ערוה. והנה אין לא תקרבו לגלות ערוה נדרש להם לאו בפני עצמו כברייתא השנויה בספרא אבל ידרשוהו בקריבה שלגלוי ערוה בלבד. ומן הידוע עוד ממנהגם בתלמוד שאם היתה הברייתא הזו אצלם אמת והיו דבריו שלרבי פדת חלוקין בכך היו בעלי הגמרא מביאים אותה עליו לתיובתא ואומרים מתיבי אילו נאמר ואל אשה וכו׳ ומעלים ממנה תיובתא דרבי פדת תיובתא. וכיון שלא עשו כן נבין מהם כי אצלם זה האיסור מדרבנן, או יהיה מן התורה דכל דמתהני מאיסורא איסורא הוא כענין בחצי שיעור, אבל אין זה עיקר מדרש בלאו הזה אלא קרא אסמכתא בעלמא. והרבה מאד כן בסיפרא ובסיפרי. ודע כי הקריבה לאשה

בכתוב תאמר על הביאה כענין (תצא כב) ואקרב אליה ולא מצאתי לה בתולים וכתיב (ישעי׳ ח) ואקרב אל הנביאה ותהר ותלד בן. וכן היו נכונים לשלשת ימים אל תגשו אל אשה (יתרו) לא מנעם רק מהביאה מפני שהפולטת שכבת זרע בשלישי טמאה כמו שביארו בגמר שבת (פו א). וכן ואשה אשר תקרב אל כל בהמה לרבעה אותה (קדושים כ) אינו אלא קריבה שלרביעה. ואולי תקשה ותאמר לי כי זה החכם רבי פדת הוא הסובר כן אבל שאר החכמים שחלוקים עליו סוברים כי הקריבה אע״פ שאינה שלגלוי עריות אסורה מן התורה שלכך אמרו ופליגא דרבי פדת, דע שאין מחלוקת רבי פדת וחביריו בזה אבל המאמר היה על שאלתם בנדה אם מותרת לשכב עם בעלה במטה אחת היא בבגדה והוא בבגדו ואע״פ שיש בישנים במטה אחת קריבה וחמום זה מזה כענין (קהלת ד) אם ישכבו שנים וחם להם וכל שישנים במטה אחת אי איפשר להם בלא נגיעה וכדאתמר התם (ברכו׳ כד א) והא איכא עגבות ויש בהם עוד חשש ביאה ובא רב יוסף לאסור מטעם חשש הביאה כדרך שאסרו בעוף שלא יעלה עם הגבינה בשלחן אחד ואע״פ שאפילו האכילה מדבריהם וכל שכן בכאן ששכיבתן במטה אחת קרוב לבא לידי ביאה ודחינו זה משום דאיכא שנוי ודעות ואחר כך באנו ואסרנו הדבר מפני שיש בשכיבתן במטה אחת קריבה והנאה זה מזה. ואמרו במדרש הכתוב ביחזקאל (יח) ואת אשת רעהו לא טמא ואל אשה נדה לא יקרב מקיש אשה נדה לאשת רעהו מה אשת רעהו הוא בבגדו והיא בבגדה אסור אף אשתו נדה הוא בבגדו והיא בבגדה אסור. כלומר שהדבר ידוע שבאשת רעהו אסור הוא לעשות כן אפילו ההסתכלות בה אסור וקולה ערוה (ברכו׳ כד א) והכתוב מזהיר ממנה (משלי ה) הרחק מעליה דרכך ואל תקרב אל פתח ביתה שאפילו בלא ייחוד שאינן באין עתה לידי עברה מנעונו הכתובים מזה, ואם כן אף הנדה והעריות שלשאר אסורות לגמרי מטעם הקריבה ואפילו לא יבאו לידי אסורי ביאה משום שינוי ודעות ועל זה אמרו ופליגא דרבי פדת שהוא סובר שאין אסור בעריות שלשאר אלא בגלוי הערוה ואם כן לא הוקשו לאשת איש שהכל מודים בה שהוא אסור שהרי שלמה צווח כן. והזכירו (שבת יג א) בעולא נמי שאין לו ההיקש הזה לפי שהיה מנשק באחיותיו בהפסק ושינוי אבי ידייהו שלא כדרך הנושקין להכרא ואע״פ שהוא אסור באשת איש. והנה כולם אין להם המדרש הזה מלא תקרבו לגלות ערוה והאוסר מביא אותו מהקש הכתוב שביחזקאל ור׳ פדת ועולא מתירין. ומה שאמר ר׳ פדת לא אסרה תורה, ירצה בו שאינו אסור כלל. כאמרם (מגלה כב ב) לא אסרה תורה אלא פשוט ידים ורגלים ואמרם (ר״ה כד ב) לא אסרה תורה אלא דמות ארבע פנים בהדי הדדי. ואמרו עוד (ב״מ סט ב) כל כי האי רביתא ליכול לא אסרה תורה אלא רבית הבאה מלוה למלוה.

והנה לדעתי הברייתא השנויה בספרא אינה אלא לאיסור השכיבה בקירוב בשר כשיהיו שניהם ערומים וקרא אסמכתא בעלמא משום חשש ביאה שהכל מודים בזה כדתנן (קדושין פ ב) הגדילו זה ישן בכסותו וזה ישן בכסותו. ואילו היה מחלוקת שלרבי פדת בשלתורה במדרש הלאו של לא תקרבו היאך אמרו מקיש אשתו נדה לאשת רעהו מה אשת רעהו הוא בבגדו והיא בבגדה אסור אף אשתו נדה הוא בבגדו והיא בבגדה אסור, והלא ענין הקריבה בכל העריות כתוב אל כל שאר בשרו לא תקרבו ובנדה כתוב מפורש לא תקרב ואיננו כתוב באשת איש. וכן הביאו שם (יג א) לאיסור מימרא דעולא שאמר כל קריבה אסור משום לך לך אמרי׳ לנזירא סחור סחור לכרמא לא תקרב. אם כן כל הדברים אינן לאיסור מן הלאו הזה של לא תקרב. ובגמר ע״ז (יז א) הזכירו

עוד מדרש הכתוב הרחק מעליה דרכך זו המינות והרשות ואל תקרב אל פתח ביתה זו זונה וכמה אמר רב חסדא ארבע אמות ואמרו על זה ופליגא דרבי פדת וכו׳. כי הזונה אצלם הנבעלת ממי שאין קדושין תופסין לו בה כגון העריות [ערמב״ן ש׳ ה עמ׳ קטז: וקכ. ול״ת נה] ולא הוזהרנו עליהם לדעת רבי פדת בהרחקה הזו. וכן מאמרם בשבת (יג ב) בתלמיד שאמרה אשתו לאליהו שהיה ישן עמה בקירוב בשר ולא עלתה דעתו לדבר אחר ואמר לה ברוך המקום שהרגו שלא נשא פנים לתורה שהרי אמרה תורה ואל אשה בנדת טומאתה לא תקרב, מפני שעבר על הגזירה שלדבריהם נענש, ופורץ גדר ישכנו נחש [ע״ז כז ב, שבת קי א]. ואם היה עובר בלאו מן התורה היה אומר ברוך המקום שהרגו שעבר על דברי תורה. ואין זה נקרא משוא פנים. אבל הדבר שהוא משוא פנים לתורה הוא הגדר והסייג הנעשין לדבריה כאמרם (ברכו׳ כ א) ולא אשא פנים לישראל שכתבתי להם בתורה ואכלת ושבעת והם דקדקו על עצמן עד כזית ועד כביצה. כלומר שהם נושאים פנים לתורה ואני אשא להם פנים. והנה זה היה ישן עם הנדה במטה בסינר לבדו מפסיק בינו לבינה והיה בהם קצת קרוב בשר וחיבוק ונשוק ולא מצאו באיסורו אלא משוא פנים לתורה. וראיתי לרב בחבורו הגדול שכתב בספר המדע (במנין בקצר) בלאו הזה שלא ליקרב לעריות בדברים המביאים לידי גלוי ערוה כגון חבוק ונשוק ורמיזה וקפיצה שנ׳ לא תקרבו לגלות ערוה מפי השמועה למדו שזו אזהרה לקריבה המביאה לידי גלוי ערוה. הוסיף עליו שם רמיזה וקפיצה שיהיו בכלל הלאו הזה ואם כן אף עליהם הוא לוקה. ושמא הגיעתהו ברייתא אחרת שהיא שנויה באבות דרבי נתן (פ״ב) ועשו סייג לתורה עשה סייג לדבריך כדרך שעשה הקב״ה סייג לדבריו. ואדם הראשון עשה סייג לדבריו תורה עשתה סייג לדבריה משה עשה סייג לדבריו ואף איוב ואף חכמים ונביאים עשו סייג לדבריהם וקא תני אי זהו סייג שעשתה תורה לדבריה ואל אשה בנדת טומאתה יכול יחבקנה וינשקנה וידבר עמה דברים בטלים ת״ל ואל אשה לא תקרב. ומזה הוסיף הרב רמיזה וקפיצה. והם באמת דברים בטלים שיהיה במדבר עם אשתו נדה שיחה בטלה לאו ומלקות מן התורה.

ובאותה ברייתא שנו עוד יכול תישן עמו בבגדיה על המטה תלמוד לומר לא תקרב יכול תרחץ פניה ותכחול עיניה תלמוד לומר והדוה בנדתה כל הימים שבנדתה תהא בנדוי מכאן אמרו כל המנוולת עצמה בימי טומאתה רוח חכמים נוחה הימנה מעשה באדם אחד וכו׳. וכל אלו אינם אלא אסמכתא והרחק מן העבירה. ובתלמוד העלו שהוא מותר. ושם שנו עוד נאמר כאן לא תקרב ונאמר להלן אל תקרב לדבר המביא לידי עבירה לא תקרבו הרחק מן הכעור ומן הדומה לו שכך אמרו חכמים הרחק מחטא קל שמא יביאך לידי חטא חמור. אם כן אינם אלא גדרים וסייגים להתרחק מן העבירות וסמכו אותם למקרא. ושמא רצונם לומר בסייג שעשתה תורה לדבריה שתפשה תורה לשון קריבה בעריות כדי שיהיו החכמים יכולים לעשות סייג בלשונה וישמעו ממנה הצדיקים הנושאים פנים לתורה כל קריבה שבעולם. וזה דרך אגדה. לא שיהיה זה עיקר הלאו.

ובגמר קדושין (פא ב) במעשה שלרב חנן בר רבא שהושיב בת בתו קטנה בחיקו והודיעוהו שהיתה מקודשת, לומר שזה אסור באשת איש ולא אסרו עליו משום ערוה שלשאר ואחר כך אמרו לו שהוא עובר על דברי שמואל שאמר אין משתמשין באשה כלל ואמר אנא כאידך דשמואל סבירא לי דאמר הכל לשום שמים. ואילו היה בקריבה לאו גמור מן התורה לא הותרה

לחסידים לחכמים העושים מעשיהם לשום שמים. אבל הכל גדר וסייג ומותר בקרובות למי שמוחזק שאינו חשוד לעשות כיעור ונמנע משאר הנשים. ובמסכת יבמות בפרק הבא על יבמתו (נה ב, נו א) אמרו העראה זו הכנסת העטרה גמר ביאה ביאה ממש מכאן ואילך אינה אלא נשיקה ופטור. ואמרם פטור ראיה שאין בו מלקות מן הלאו הזה שלקריבה. ושם (נה א) הביאו העראה בחייבי לאוין למלקות מן המדות הנדרשות ולא הביאו אותו משום קריבה ואפילו בפחות מיכן. ואם תאמר שלא אסרה תורה קריבה אלא בעריות שלחייבי כרתות והלא חייבי לאוין מהם נלמדים בגזירה שוה. והעולה מכל זה שלא נמנה ענין הקריבה לאו בפני עצמו. אלא קריבה שלגילוי ערוה אסר הכתוב. וכך אמרו עוד בסנהדרין בגמרא דבני מערבא (פ"ז סה"ז) כתיב ואל אשה בנדת טומאתה לא תקרב לגלות ערותה אמר רבי יוסי בר' בון היא בל תקרב היא בל תגלה:

בית יוסף יורה דעה סימן קצה – וכתב עוד בתרומת הדשן (סי' רנב) בשם גדול אחד דאשה [נדה] חולה ובעלה רופא אסור למשש לה הדפק ונראה מדבריו שאפילו בשאין רופא זולתו אסור וגם בתשובות להרמב"ן סימן קכ"ז אסר לבעל למשש דפק אשתו נדה ואע"פ שלשון השאלה היה בשיש שם רופאים אחרים אלא דבעלה ניחא לה משום דמזומן תדיר נראה דלמאי דאסר לא שני לן בין יש שם רופאים אחרים לאינם ומיהו אם החולי מסוכן ואין שם רופאים משמע קצת מדבריו דשרי משום פיקוח נפש אלא דאיכא למימר דלטעמיה אזיל (בהשגות על סה"מ ל"ת שנג) דסבר דנגיעת נדה אינה אסורה אלא מדרבנן אבל להרמב"ם (סה"מ שם, והל' איסו"ב פכ"א ה"א) דנגיעת ערוה אסורה מן התורה הכא אע"פ שיש בו פיקוח נפש אפשר דאסור משום דהוי אביזרא דגילוי עריות וצ"ע:

ש"ך יורה דעה סימן קצה:כ – ומיהו אם החולה מסוכן ואין שם רופאים משמע קצת מדברי תשובת הרמב"ן סימן קכ"ז דשרי מפני פיקוח נפש אלא די"ל דלטעמיה אזיל דסבירא ליה דנגיעת נדה אינו אלא מדרבנן אבל להרמב"ם דנגיעת ערוה אסורה מן התורה הכא אע"פ שיש פיקוח נפש אפשר דאסור משום אביזרא דג"ע וצ"ע עכ"ל ב"י, וכ"כ העט"ז ואין נראה דודאי אף להרמב"ם ליכא איסור דאורייתא אלא כשעושה כן דרך תאוה וחיבת ביאה כמש"ל סי' קנ"ז ס"ק י' מה שאין כן הכא וכן המנהג פשוט שרופאים ישראלים ממששים הדפק של אשה אפילו אשת איש או עובדת כוכבים אע"פ שיש רופאים אחרים עובדי כוכבים וכן עושים שאר מיני משמושים ע"פ דרכי הרפואה אלא הדבר פשוט כמ"ש וזה נראה דעת הרב דלעיל בסי' קנ"ז משמע מדבריו כהרמב"ם וכמו שכתבתי שם בס"ק י' וכאן התיר מישוש הדפק מ"מ באין סכנה אסור לבעלה למשש הדפק כשהיא נדה וכדאיתא בתשובת הרמב"ן ובדברי הרב.

שו"ת אגרות משה אבן העזר חלק ב סימן יד – בענין הליכה בסאבוויי ובבאסעס בשעה שא"א ליזהר מנגיעה ודחיפה בנשים מצד הדוחק י' מנ"א תש"כ. מע"כ ידידי מו"ה יעקב שאטטען שליט"א.

בדבר הליכה בסאבוויי ובבאסעס בזמן שהולכים בני אדם לעבודתם שנמצאים שם אנשים ונשים דחופים זה בזה, שקשה מליזהר מנגיעה ודחיפה בנשים אם מותר אז ללכת בשעות אלו שם. הנה מצד הנגיעה ודחיפה בנשים אז ליכא שום איסור משום דאין זה דרך תאוה וחבה, וכל

איסור נגיעה בעריות הוא אף להרמב"ם שסובר שהוא בלאו דלא תקרבו דאורייתא דוקא דרך תאוה כמפורש בדבריו ריש פכ"א מאי"ב, ומשמע שבלא דרך תאוה ליכא אף איסור מדרבנן שלא הזכיר זה, ומפורש כן בש"ך יו"ד סימן קנ"ז סק"י שהרי כתב הש"ך ראיה ממה שמצינו שהאמוראים היו מחבקים ומנשקים לבנותיהם ואחיותיהם. ומש"כ הש"ך יו"ד בסימן קצ"ה סק"כ במשמוש הדפק באשתו נדה שכיון דאינו דרך חיבת ביאה שליכא איסור דאורייתא אף להרמב"ם מותר לבעלה רק במקום סכנה ובליכא סכנה אסור לבעלה למשמש הדפק כשהיא נדה אינו מצד איסור קריבה דאיכא בכל העריות אלא מצד דיני התרחקות בין הבעל לאשתו בימי נדותה שאסרו מדרבנן. ומוכרח זה שם גופיה דהרי כתב שם שהמנהג פשוט שרופאים ישראלים ממשמשים הדפק של אשה אפילו אשת איש או נכרית, ואם היה איסור קריבה אף בלא דרך תאוה אף רק מדרבנן היה אסור להם שלא במקום סכנה, ואף שמצינו דברים שאסרו רבנן והתירו במקום חולי אף בלא סכנה כהא כתובות דף ס' דר' מרינוס אומר גונח יונק חלב בשבת משום דיונק מפרק כלאחר יד הוא שאסור רק מדרבנן ובמקום צערא לא גזרו רבנן ואיירי בליכא סכנה כמפורש שם בתוס' עיי"ש, וכן מותר אף חולה שאין בו סכנה לאכול בט' באב משום שבמקום חולי לא גזרו רבנן כדאיתא בש"ע/או"ח/ סימן תקנ"ד סעיף ו' וכתב הט"ז דהוא אף שברור שאין בו סכנה, ועיין בהגר"א סק"ט שהסכים לזה והביא ראיה ממה שהתירו נעילת הסנדל וסיכה ביו"כ לחולה שאין בו סכנה, מ"מ לא כל איסור דרבנן שוין ויש שאסרו אף לחולה כשליכא סכנה. עיין בר"ן ע"ז דף כ"ז באיסורי אכילה מדרבנן כחמץ שעבר עליו הפסח וכלאי הכרם בחו"ל וגבינה של עכו"ם וסתם יינם וכדומה שאסרו בליכא סכנה, ובשולי עכו"ם התירו לחולה אף שליכא סכנה, והר"ן עצמו מסתפק שמא גם ליהנות באה"נ של דבריהם אסרו בלא סכנה ומי"א הביא דמתרפאין בהנאה אף כדרך הנאתן מאה"נ דרבנן, ופסק כן הרמ"א יו"ד בסימן קנ"ה סעיף ג' דלרפאות בהנאה מאה"נ דרבנן מותר ולאכול ולשתות אסור עיי"ש ולכן כ"ש שלא היו מתירין איסור דרבנן דקריבה לעריות בשביל להתרפאות בחולה שאין בה סכנה שאיסורי ערוה חמור מאיסורי אכילה לענין רפואה ולכן צריך לומר שבלא דרך תאוה לא אסרו כלל דלא נחשב זה קריבה לגילוי ערוה כלל משום שהנגיעה שלא לתאוה וחבה לא יביא כלל לגילוי ערוה והאיסור נאמר לא תקרבו לגלות ערוה שפירושו כתב הרמב"ם כלומר לא תקרבו לדברים המביאין לידי גילוי ערוה ולא ראו צורך לאסור זה כלל אף מדרבנן.

ועוד ראיה מעכו"ם שמותר לרופאים ישראלים למשמש בדפק וכל הנגיעות ומיני משמושים כדכתב שם יו"ד סי' קצ"ה סק"כ הש"ך שהוא רק בשביל הרוחת ממון שלא שייך להתיר איסור אף דרבנן אף אלו שהתירו במקום חולי, והא לא איירי ביש חשש איבה דהא כתב הש"ך דאף ביש שם רופאים אחרים נכרים נוהגין היתר, אלא ודאי שסובר הש"ך שליכא איסור קריבה שלא בדרך תאוה אף לא מדרבנן, ורק באשתו נדה אסור מצד דיני התרחקות. וניחא מה שאיתא בפ"ת יו"ד סי' קצ"ה סקי"ז בשם ספר מקור חיים שיניח בעלה בגד על הדפק ויהיה מותר למשמש, דכיון שהאיסור הוא מצד דיני התרחקות מותר בשינוי הנחת בגד שאיכא היכר.

והנה בתורת השלמים יו"ד סי' קצ"ה ס"ק ט"ו דחה דברי הש"ך דלרמב"ם שאסור מדאורייתא כל שנהנה מנגיעתה בקירוב בשר אפשר דאסור למשש לה הדפק דקרוב הדבר לבוא לידי איסור דאורייתא, ומה שרופאים ממשמשים דפק של א"א ונכרית הוא משום דאין לבו גס

באשה אחרת עיי"ש, ומשמע שאוסר מצד איסור קריבה דאם מצד התרחקות לא היה מחלק בין שיטת הרמב"ם דאוסר קריבה מדאורייתא ובין שיטת הרמב"ן דהוא רק מדרבנן דהא גם להרמב"ן איכא איסור התרחקות בנדה לבעלה, ולכן שפיר דחה דבריו בסד"ט יו"ד סי' קצ"ה ס"ק כ"ד וכתב אין בדבריו ממש דרק במה שאסרו משום הרגל דבר וחייבו התרחקות שייך לחלק בין אשתו נדה דלבו גס בה לאשה דעלמא אבל מה שאסור משום קריבות ודאי חמירא א"א מאשתו נדה, וכן הקשה עליו גם בהג"ה מר' שלמה הכהן במחצית השקל עיי"ש. ואף שרהיטת לשונם משמע שאיסור דרבנן מיהא איכא, פשוט שליכא שום איסור מאותה הראיה עצמה שהרופאים ממשמשים בא"א ובנכרית אף בלא סכנה ואף ביש רופאים אחרים שהם נכרים, ואף מרופאים נכרים הרי יש לאסור מצד האשה הישראלית דבלאו דלא תקרבו וכן אם אסרו מדרבנן הוא אסור להאשה כמו להאיש, אלא ודאי שבלא דרך תאוה ליכא איסור אף לא מדרבנן.

וכוונת תוה"ש נראה דבא לתרץ שיטת הב"י דלהרמב"ם אוסר למשמש הדפק באשתו נדה משום אביזרא דג"ע ולהרמב"ן מתיר, משום דבאשתו נדה קרוב הדבר שכיון שלבו גס בה שנהנה מנגיעתה כשימשמש לה הדפק, אף שהתחלתו למשש לא היה לשם תאוה והנאה אבל קרוב שיבוא לזה ולכן יעבור בלאו אבל בנשים דעלמא אף שחמורות לענין איסור דלא תקרבו אבל הא הוא שלא לכוונת הנאה וחבה ולא יבוא מזה לידי כוונת הנאה וחבה כיון שלא גס בה לכן מותר גם לכתחלה, אבל לרמב"ן שאף נגיעה לכוונת הנאה וחבה הוא רק דרבנן שרי משום פ"נ. ואולי זהו כוונת הגהת ר' שלמה הכהן בסופו עיי"ש אבל הוא כתב דאף לתוה"ש הוא רק מדרבנן ואין לאסור במקום סכנה, ולמה שבארתי הוא מדאורייתא לדידיה שבאשתו יש להחשיב גם זה קריבה לג"ע. ונמצא שאף להתוה"ש ליכא לאחרים שום איסור בנגיעה שלא בדרך תאוה וחבה אף לא מדרבנן.

ונראה דהב"ש סימן כ' סק"א שהביא מתשובת הרמב"ן דאף שלא בדרך חבה אסור להרמב"ם מדאו' והוא סובר דאסור מדרבנן ולדבריו הוא מש"כ הב"י/יו"ד סי' קצ"ה/ לענין משמוש הדפק לבעלה כשהיא נדה עיי"ש, נמי הוא רק לבעלה שסובר כדבארתי בכוונת תוה"ש שמתרץ דברי הב"י, ומוכרח כן מהא דלרופאים אחרים מתיר גם הב"י. ואף שלא משמע כן לשון הב"ש דלא הזכיר שם שאיירי בבעל לאשתו נדה ובש"ע הא איירי בכל עריות, מ"מ מוכרחין לומר דמש"כ וכתב בתשובה אפילו אם אינו עושה דרך חבה עד והש"ך השיג עליו בחנם הוא ענין אחר המסתעף מזה, ולא קאי על עריות דש"ע אלא באשתו נדה וסובר כדבארתי לתוה"ש.

עכ"פ לדינא בנשים אחרות אף בא"א ונדות ונכריות ליכא איסור שלא בדרך תאוה לכו"ע, ולכן לא שייך לחוש מללכת בסאבוויי ובאסעס בשעת הליכה לעבודה שדחוקים ודחופים אנשים ונשים אף שלא יוכל ליזהר מנגיעה ודחיפה בנשים, דהנגיעה בלא מתכוין מחמת שא"א לו ליזהר אין זה דרך תאוה וחבה. ובאם הולך שם גם עם אשתו נדה ויהיה באופן שלא יהיה אפשר ליזהר מליגע בה, אף שלא מצוי זה דהא יכולה לעמוד במקום אחר, אבל אם יזדמן כן, תליא לכאורה במחלוקת הש"ך עם הב"י לפי' תוה"ש והב"ש לפ"מ שבארתי, דלהש"ך אין לאסור כיון שאינו דרך תאוה, ומצד התרחקות נמי לא שייך לאסור, שלא נאסרו אלא דברים שעושין כהרגלם שלא ישכחו שהיא נדה ויעשו כהרגלם גם בתשמיש, וזה ליכא בסאבוויי ובאסעס שאין זה כהרגל הוא עם אשתו אלא כהרגלם עם כל בנ"א. ולהב"י יש לכאורה לאסור דמצד שגס בה קרוב שיהנה

מנגיעתו בה אף שתהיה שלא במתכוין. אבל מסתבר שבנגיעה שלא במתכוין אף באשתו לא שייך לחוש שיבוא ליהנות מנגיעה זו, דרק למשש הדפק שבמתכוין נוגע בה אף שהוא לכוונת היתר לידיעתו לרפאותה סובר הב"י שקרוב הדבר שיבוא גם ליהנות מזה. וכ"ש שאין לחוש בנגיעה מחמת דוחק רבוי בנ"א שאין שם המקום לחשוב ליהנות מזה, שלכן אף להב"י אין לחוש אף כשיזדמן כן גם באשתו נדה.

וכן ליכא איסור מהאי טעמא גם לישב אצל אשה כשליכא מקום אחר דג"כ אין זה דרך תאוה וחבה. ועם אשתו נדה כשצריכין לישב דחוקים יש אולי לאסור להב"י, אבל כיון שרוב האחרונים משמע שסברי כהש"ך, וגם להב"י אין ברור לאיסור דאפשר שאף בישיבה סמוכים אין לחוש לכוונת הנאה לכן אין לאסור.

אבל אם יודע שהוא יבוא לידי הרהור יש לו למנוע מללכת אז אם אין נחוץ לו, ואם מוכרח לילך אז ג"כ לעבודתו אין לאסור לו אף בכה"ג, ויתחזק להסיח דעתו מהן ולהרהר בדברי תורה כעצת הרמב"ם שם הי"ט וע"ז יוכל לסמוך ולילך לעבודתו. ואם יודע שטבעו רע ויבוא מזה לידי קישוי אבר אסור לו לילך אז גם לעבודתו. אבל ח"ו לאדם להיות כן דבא זה מבטלה כדאיתא בכתובות דף נ"ט על האשה וה"ה על האיש וצריך לעסוק בתורה ובמלאכה ולא יהיה כך.

שו"ת נודע ביהודה מהדורה תנינא – יורה דעה סימן קכב – תשובה שלום לכבוד אהובי האלוף התורני הרבני המופלא מוה' יוזל נר"ו מו"צ דק"ק ש"ה י"ץ:

מכתבו קבלתי. וע"ד אשר נשאל באיש ואשה הדרים בכפר בין הנכרים ואין שם יהודי או יהודית זולת הזוג הנ"ל לבדם ואפילו משרתת אין להם. ונשאל מעלתו מהם כשהאשה טובלת אם בעלה יכול לעמוד עליה ולראות שתטבול כדי שתהיה כולה תחת המים וגם אם יוכל בעלה לעזור לה לתמוך בידיו לדחפה תחת המים ע"י שידיח ידיו תחלה במי מקוה משום חציצה רק שהספק הוא משום הסתכלות באשתו נדה ערומה ומשום נגיעתו בה. ומעלתו הורה להיתר מטעם כיון שהוא עוסק בעסקי הטבילה א"כ הוא עצמו מחזר לטהרה מנדתה ולא יכשל בה. והנה בדבר ההסתכלות במקומות המכוסים שבה לית דין צרך בשש שיפה הורה שמותר לצורך טבילה שהרי שני גדולי הדור מהרי"ק והשר מקוצי הצריכו נשותיהם לעמוד לפניהם ערומות לראות אם אין בהם גרב וכמ"ש הט"ז בסימן קצ"ח ס"ק י"ד וכמו שהביא מעלתו בעצמו דברי הט"ז וא"כ מי יפקפק ע"ז ומעשה רב:

ואמנם הנגיעה באשתו בעת הטבילה צריכא עיונא. דהנה לדעת הב"י בסימן קצ"ה שאם בעלה רופא ואין רופא זולתו ויש כאן סכנה אפ"ה לדעת הרמב"ם דנגיעה היא דאורייתא יש כאן אביזרא דג"ע ואסור אפילו במקום סכנה. א"כ סובר הב"י דלדעת הרמב"ם הנגיעה מצד עצמה הוא איסור דאורייתא א"כ אין חילוק בין הוא צורך טבילה או לא שהרי אין טעם הנגיעה משום שמא יבוא עליה אלא הנגיעה מצד עצמה קריבה מקרי והיא בכלל לא תקרבו וא"כ כל זמן שלא עלתה מהמים איסור זה חל מן התורה. ואמנם הש"ך בסימן קצ"ה ס"ק כ' שדי נרגא בדברי הב"י דגם להרמב"ם ליכא איסור תורה אלא כשעושה דרך חבת ביאה ותאוה ע"ש. וכבר פשט המנהג כדבריו וא"כ נגיעת אשתו נדה כשאינו דרך חבה אינו אלא מדרבנן וא"כ הטעם משום שמא יבוא לידי הרגל דבר כדרך שאסרו שאר הרחקות ובזה יש לחקור אם נסמוך בזה

על הסברא שהוא עצמו מחזר לטהרה וכדרך שאמרו בחמץ הוא עצמו מחזר עליו לשרפו מיכל קאכיל מיניה אבל עריות נפשו של אדם מחמדתן וחיישינן שיתגבר יצרו ויעבור בזדון וכן משמע בש"ך בסימן קצ"ה ס"ק י"ט בהיא חולה שאסור לבעלה לשמשה מטעם שחיישינן שיתגבר יצרו עליו ויפייסנה א"כ מה מועיל מה שהוא עצמו מחזר לטהרה דזה מועיל דלא חיישינן לשכחה אבל אינו מועיל לזדון. ואף דלענין אכילה עמה מביא הש"ך שם בס"ק י"ז דבכלות ז' נקיים מביא הראב"ן יש מתירים דאין כאן הרגל עבירה דכיון דמציא למטבל לא שביק היתרא ואכיל איסורא מ"מ אולי לענין נגיעה לא סמכינן על זה ותדע שהרי לא מצינו שום דעה דאחר כלות ז' נקיים יהיה מותר ליגע בה:

ואמנם מדברי השר מקוצי ומהרי"ק שהעמידו לפניהם נשותיהם ערומות והרי אסור להסתכל במקומות המכוסים שבה כמבואר בסימן קצ"ה סעיף ז' וא"כ איך הסתכלו הגדולים הללו א"ו שסמכו על סברא זו כיון שהוא מחזר עליה לטהרה שלא יהיה בה חציצה לא יבוא ברגע זו לידי שכחה וגם להתגברות היצר לא חשו דלא שביק היתרא שהרי תיכף תטבול וא"כ הה"ד לנגיעה. ואמנם יש לדחות כי אולי הגדולים הללו סברי כדעת הרב המגיד בפ' כ"א מא"ב הלכה ד' שדעת הרמב"ם שדוקא במקום התורפה אסור להסתכל באשתו נדה אבל בשאר מקומות המכוסים שבה לא אסרו כלל באשתו נדה ולכך לא הקפידו הגדולים הללו בזה אבל הנגיעה בבשרה אסור מדין התלמוד בודאי אולי אפי' לצורך טבילה אסור שחיישינן שיתגבר יצרו לשעתו. והא דמביא בש"ס במסכת שבת דף י"ג ע"א ראיה מעוף דאינו עולה עם הגבינה על השלחן לענין נדה שתישן עם בעלה היא בבגדה ולדידי לא דמיין דבנדה חיישינן אפילו לזדון י"ל דבתורת כ"ש מייתי שאם עוף אינו עולה דחיישינן לשכחה ק"ו דנדה אסורה. ומה שאמר אח"כ הכא איכא דעות ואיכא שינוי ולדידי דחשש נדה הוא אפילו בזדון א"כ מה מועיל שינוי. י"ל שזה עצמו הוא דמספקא ליה אם החשש גם גבי נדה הוא רק לשכחה וא"כ היכא דאיכא שינוי מהני או דלמא חיישינן לזדון ואינו מועיל שינוי וכיון דמסיק התם לחומרא דהוא בבגדו אסור א"כ איכא למימר דבאמת מטעם חשש זדון אסור. באופן שאין לנו ראיה על דבר זה להתיר. ואמנם גם לאיסור לא מצאתי הוכחה ברורה ומצד הסברא יש מקום לומר שאפילו לתגבורת יצרו לא חיישינן ברגע זו שהיא במים ולמה שביק היתרא שתיכף ברגע זו מותרת בעליתה מן המים. ומעתה אם א"א לה לטבול בענין אחר רק שבעלה יסייע לה לכוף ראשה לתוך המים נלע"ד להסכים להוראתו להתיר. ולרוב הטרדא אקצר. דברי הד"ש:

מחזור ויטרי סימן תצט – דין שאסור ליגע לאשתו כל ימי נידתה אפי' באצבע קטנה. ויש נזהרין אפילו להושיט לה שום דבר. ולכל הפחות דבר של מאכל ומשתה טוב ונכון מליזהר שלא יושיט מידו לידה. וכן בימי ליבונה וספירתה עד שתטבול:

תוספות מסכת שבת דף יג עמוד ב – בימי לבוניך מהו אצלך – לא משום שיש לחלק בין נדות לליבון דהא אמר ר"ע בפרק במה אשה יוצאה (לקמן דף סד:) הרי היא בנדתה עד שתבא במים אלא לפי שידע אליהו שכך היה המעשה ור"ח ורש"י פירשו בפרק אע"פ (כתובות דף סא. ושם) גבי שמואל מחלפא ליה דביתהו בידא דשמאלא היינו בימי ליבונה אין נראה כדפירשתי ור"ת פירש שהיו רגילים לטבול שתי טבילות אחת לסוף שבעה לראייתה שהיא טהורה מדאורייתא

בהך טבילה ואחת לסוף ימי ליבון לכך היה מיקל אותו האיש ורש"י היה נוהג איסור להושיט מפתח מידו לידה בימי נדותה ונראה לר"י שיש סמך מסדר אליהו דקתני אמר לה שמא הבאת לו את השמן שמא הבאת לו את הפך ומיהו התם מסיים ונגע ביך באצבע הקטנה ומפרק אע"פ (שם) דאמר אביי מנח' ליה אפומיה דכובא ורבא מנח' ליה אבי סדיא אין ראיה כי שמא דוקא במזיגת הכוס שיש חיבה יותר כדאמר התם אבל שאר דברים לא ומהכא דקאמר אכל עמי ושתה עמי יכול להיות שלא הקפיד אלא על השכיבה.

תוספות מסכת כתובות דף סא עמוד א – מחלפא דביתהו בידא דשמאלא – במחזור ויטרי פי' הרב ר' שמעיה שהיה נזהר רש"י אפי' שלא ליתן מפתח מידו לידה ומכאן אין ראיה דשאני מזיגת כוס שהוא דבר של חיבה ואסורה אפילו להביא לפניו על השולחן אלא למר מנחא ליה אבי סדיא ולמר אפומא דכובא ומסדר אליהו דקתני גבי ההוא עובדא דמייתי בפ"ק דשבת (דף יג: ושם) באדם אחד שקרא הרבה ושנה הרבה כו' ששאל אליהו לאשתו שמא הבאת לו את הפך שמא הבאת לו את השמן ואמרה לו חס ושלום אפי' באצבע קטנה לא נגע בי נמי אין ראיה דמצינן לפרש דשלא על הבאת הפך היה מקפיד אלא הכי קאמר שמא בשעת הבאת הפך לא נזהרת ונגע ביך וכן משמע שהשיבתו אפילו באצבע קטנה לא נגע בי אבל שלא הביאה לו לא קאמרה ומה שפירש דמחלפא ליה בידא דשמאלא בימי לבונה דמשמע שיש להקל בימי לבונה מבימי נדותה וכן מצינו בפרק קמא דשבת (שם) בההוא עובדא שהבאתי לעיל דקאמר בימי נדותיך מהו אצלך בימי לבוניך מהו אצלך נראה דהיו רגילין לטבול אחר שבעה לראיה כשפוסקת דלא אסירא השתא אלא מדרבנן אבל בזמן הזה שאין רגילות לטבול עד אחר שבעה נקיים אין חילוק בין ימי נדות לימי לבון כדאמרינן במסכת שבת (דף סד:) תהיה בנדתה בהווייתה תהא עד שתבא במים.

תלמוד בבלי מסכת כתובות דף סא עמוד א – אמר רב יצחק בר חנניא אמר רב הונא: כל מלאכות שהאשה עושה לבעלה – נדה עושה לבעלה, חוץ ממזיגת הכוס, והצעת המטה, והרחצת פניו ידיו ורגליו.

מגיד משנה הלכות אישות פרק כא:ח – ודע שממה שכתב רבינו ואינה נותנת אותו בידו כדרכה תמיד נראה ששאר הדברים יכולה היא להושיט מידה לידו וכן דעת קצת מפרשים ויש מחמירין בכל דבר.

שולחן ערוך יורה דעה הלכות נדה סימן קצה:ב – לא יגע בה אפילו באצבע קטנה, ולא יושיט מידו לידה שום דבר ולא יקבלנו מידה, שמא יגע בבשרה.

תורת הבית הקצר בית ז שער ב – ולא יושיט מידו לידה שום דבר שמא יגע בבשרה.

שו"ת הרשב"א חלק א סימן אלף קפח – וכן אפילו הושטת כלי מיד אשתו נדה לידו אסור לפי שלבו גס בה. ובקריבות מעט איכא למיחש להרגל עבירה אבל בשאר נשים שאין לבו גס בהן בדברים אלו כגון הושטת כלי וכיוצא בו אין בהם משום הרגל עברה במי שאין לבו גס בה.

רמ"א יורה דעה הלכות נדה סימן קצה:ב – וכן על ידי זריקה מידו לידה או להיפך, אסור.

חידושי הריטב"א מסכת כתובות דף סא עמוד א – שמואל מחלפא ליה בשמאל. פירוש דמזגא ליה כסא ומנחא קמיה בשמאלא דידה.

פתחי תשובה יורה דעה סימן קצה:ג – ועי' בתשב"ץ ח"ג סי' נ"ח ובסי' ר"ל שכתב דמותר ליטול מידה התינוק משום דחי נושא את עצמו והיא אינה עושה כלום אלא התינוק עצמו הוא יוצא מחיק אמו ובא אל אביו ע"ש. ונראה דאם התינוק קטן או חולה או כפות אסור דאז לא שייך לומר חי נושא את עצמו כמ"ש המג"א בסי' ש"ח ס"ק ע' וע"א ע"ש.

שו"ת תשב"ץ חלק ג סימן רל – וכן אנו נוהגין אלא שיש להקל ליטול תינוק מידה משום דהחי נושא את עצמו כדאי' בפ' המצניע (צ"ד ע"א) ובפ' נוטל (קמ"א ע"ב) והיא אינה עושה כלום אלא התינוק עצמו הוא יוצא מחיק אמו ובא לחיק אביו ובכל זה אין חלוק בין ימי נדות לימי ליבון שלעולם היא בטומאתה עד שתטבול במי מקוה.

תלמוד בבלי מסכת שבת דף צד עמוד א – אמר רבא: אפילו תימא רבנן; עד כאן לא פליגי רבנן עליה דרבי נתן – אלא בבהמה חיה ועוף דמשרבטי נפשייהו, אבל אדם חי דנושא את עצמו – אפילו רבנן מודו.

תלמוד בבלי מסכת שבת דף קמא עמוד ב – אמר רבא: הוציא תינוק חי וכיס תלוי בצוארו – חייב משום כיס. תינוק מת וכיס תלוי לו בצוארו – פטור. תינוק חי וכיס תלוי לו בצוארו – חייב משום כיס. וליחייב נמי משום תינוק! – רבא כרבי נתן סבירא ליה, דאמר: חי נושא את עצמו. וליבטל כיס לגבי תינוק, מי לא תנן: את החי במטה פטור אף על המטה, שהמטה טפילה לו! – מטה לגבי חי – מבטלי ליה, כיס לגבי תינוק – לא מבטלי ליה.

ערוך השולחן יורה דעה הלכות נדה סימן קצה:ה – ולא יגע בה אפילו באצבע קטנה ולכן אסור לו ליתן לה דבר מידו לידה אפילו דבר ארוך מפני חשש נגיעה ולא פלוג רבנן וכן לא יקבל מידה שום דבר מטעם זה ואפילו לזרוק דבר מידו לידה או מידה לידו אסור בכל עניין בין שהזריקה הוא במשך שוה בין שהזריקה למעלה או למטה אסור דהרחקה עבוד רבנן מפני שהוא עמה בתדירות לכן צריך זהירות יתירה כדי שלא יכשלו וכן אין לה להחזיק גחלים בכלי בידה והוא יתחמם בהם אלא תעמיד הכלי על הארץ וכן כשאוחזת אש בידה לא יבעיר ממנה שום דבר כמו שפופרת של טאבא"ק וכיוצא בזה דההבל מחבר ויש בזה התקרבות וכן אין ליטול תינוק מידה או היא מידו וכן ליגע בבגדיה כשהיא לבושה בהם אסור [עי' פ"ת סק"ג בשם תשב"ץ ותמיהני איזה עניין הוא לחי נושא את עצמו ומ"ש בסק"ב בשם הנו"ב דבכפר שאין אשה אחרת רשאי הבעל לעמוד בעת טבילתה ולהחזיק בה משום דבזמן מועט לא חיישינן לתקלה ע"ש בוודאי כן הוא דאפילו אי חיישינן גם לזמן מועט י"ל כדאמרי' בפסחים י"א א הוא עצמו מחזר עליו לשורפו מיכל קאכיל מיניה ע"ש וה"נ כן הוא ודו"ק]:

ש"ך יורה דעה סימן קצה:י"ז – וי"א כו' – ז"ל ד"מ בין בימי נדותה בין בימי לבונה וכבר נתבאר ר"ס זה אמנם מצאתי הג"ה במרדכי בשם ראבי"ה וז"ל אחר ימי ליבון ליכא הרגל עבירה וטוב לאכול עמה כדי שתרצה לטבול אם יכולה לטבול ע"כ וע"ז ראיתי מקילים בימי לבונה ואין נ"ל לסמוך ע"ז וראבי"ה הוא יחיד בזה עכ"ל, והב"ח כ' דאף לפי זה טועים המקילים שהרי לא התיר אלא ביום הז' שאחר ימי ליבון כדי שתתרצה לטבול וגם ליכא הרגל עבירה דאין לחוש שמא יבא עליה ביום הז' כיון שהיא טובלת לערב וגם זו סברא קלושה היא ואין שומעין ליחיד להתי' איסור המפורסם בכל החיבורים ולכן יש לדרוש ברבים דאיסורא קא עבדי הני דאוכלים יחד מקערה א' בימי לבונה ומצאתי בהג"ה ואנשים האוכלים עם נשותיהם בימי ליבונה שלא ירגישו בני הבית שבוש הוא ועוברים על דברי חכמים ונתקבצו כל הקהלות ועשו חרם ע"ז דהר"ח ע"כ והג"ה זו היא בהגהת מהרש"ל ומביאו הדרישה וראב"ן כ' בס"ס של"ה ויש נוהגין שלא לאכול עד כלות שבעה נקיים והוא כשר ונאה דשוב ליכא הרגל עבירה אלא הרגל מצוה דכיון דמצי למטבל לא שביק היתרא ואכיל איסורא ועי"ש שהאריך:

שו"ת אגרות משה יורה דעה חלק ב סימן עז – בענין הרחקות שהצריכו באשתו נדה אם ישנם במקום שנמצאים עמם גם אנשים אחרים כ"ג תמוז תש"כ. מע"כ ידידי הרה"ג מוהר"ר אברהם חיים בהגר"א לעווין שליט"א.

הנה במקום שיש אחרים רואין אם יש דיני הרחקות באשתו נדה שמסתפק כתר"ה דאולי יש להתיר משום דאז אין בו רעיון של קירוב, וגם שבא מזה לידי בזיון להאשה ויש בזה משום כבוד הבריות, ...ומטעם שהוא כבזיון לה ויש בזה משום כבוד הבריות לא חששו, משום שאין בזה בזיון כ"כ דידוע לכל שהנשים הן נדות י"ב יום בכל חדש כשאינן זקנות ולא מעוברות וצריכין להתרחק מבעליהן באיזה דברים, ואדרבה הא הרבה היו לובשות בגדים מיוחדים לימי הנדות ומזה היו יודעות השכנות שהיא נדה אלמא שלא היו מתביישות בזה. ומה שמתביישות כשהיא נמצאת עם אלו שאינן שומרות דיני התורה אין להחשיב בושת כזה לכבוד הבריות להתיר איסורים ואף לא מנהג ישראל בשביל זה, כיון דאדרבה טוב שלא תתבייש אף לפניהן בקיום מצות התורה. ומה שמצינו בנדה דף ע"א בראשונה היו מטבילין כלים ע"ג נדות מתות והיו נדות חיות מתביישות והתקינו מחמת זה לב"ש שיהיו מטבילים ע"ג כל הנשים, אינו משום שיש בושת לפרסם שהיא נדה אלא מטעם שפרש"י שם שמתביישין בזה שאפילו במיתתן הן משונים מכל אדם, ואדרבה משמע שלא הוי הבושת גם שם במה שידעו שמתה נדה אלא משום שמתנהגין במיתת נדה שלא כמו שנוהגין עם כל אדם במיתתן.

תלמוד בבלי מסכת שבת דף יא עמוד א – כיוצא בו: לא יאכל הזב עם הזבה, מפני הרגל עבירה.

רמב"ם הלכות איסורי ביאה פרק יא – ואסור לאדם שידבק באשתו בשבעת ימים נקיים אלו ואע"פ שהיא בכסותה והוא בכסותו ולא יקרב לה ולא יגע בה אפילו באצבע קטנה, ולא יאכל עמה בקערה אחת, כללו של דבר ינהוג עמה בימי ספירה כמו שינהוג בימי נדה שעדיין היא בכרת עד שתטבול כמו שביארנו.

רא״ש מסכת שבת פרק א סי׳ ל״ב – ומה שרגילין עכשיו לאכול עם אשתו נדה בשלחן אחד לפי שבימיהם היו רגילים לאכול כל אחד לבדו על שלחן קטן וכשאשתו עמו על אותו קטן נראה דרך חבה ודמי להצעת מטה ומזיגת כוס והרחצת פניו ידיו ורגליו אבל האידנא שכל בני הבית אוכלין על שלחן אחד אינו דרך חבה ויש שעושין היכר ביניהם והוי כמו שנים שאוכלין יחד זה בשר וזה גבינה:

חידושי הריטב״א מסכת שבת דף יג עמוד א – יש אומרים דבקערה אחת הוא דאסור, ונראין [ה] דברים דבשלחן אחד קאמר ואפילו כל אחד בקערה שלו כדריהטא כולה סוגיין וכפשטה דמתני׳, ועכשו נהגו לאכול בשלחן אחד, ויש אומרים דבשלחנות שלהם [שהיו] קטנות הוא דאסרו, וכל היכא דאיכא בניו ובני ביתו ודאי שרי, ובשר וגבינה נמי היכא דאיכא שינוי שרי כדמשמע לעיל קצת, וכן נהגו.

שולחן ערוך יורה דעה הלכות נדה סימן קצה:ג – לא יאכל עמה על השלחן אא״כ יש שום שינוי שיהיה שום דבר מפסיק בין קערה שלו לקערה שלה, לחם או קנקן, או שיאכל כל אחד במפה שלו.

פתחי תשובה יורה דעה סימן קצה – עבה״ט ועי׳ בתשובת משאת בנימין סי׳ קי״ב באמצע התשובה שכתב דאפילו מקערה אחת שרי לאכול אם גם בני הבית אוכלים עמהם מקערה זו דאין לך הפסק גדול מזה ומ״מ רבים הם המחמירים שלא לאכול מקערה א׳ אפילו עם בני הבית ומדינא אין לאסור ולא נמצא איסור זה ברור בשום דוכתא אך המחמירים יפה עושים באיסור חמור כו׳ ע״ש. ולענ״ד דדוקא על שולחן אחד יש מקום להתיר בזה אף אם גם כשהיא טהורה הם אוכלים בקערה בפ״ע מ״מ כשגם בני הבית אוכלים עמהם עדיף מהיכר אבל מקערה אחת מדינא יש לאסור לפמ״ש הרמ״א שאסור לו לאכול משיורי מאכל שלה א״כ כשאוכלים בקערה אחת בודאי אוכל משיורי מאכל שלה ואי אפשר ליזהר ולדקדק בזה שיפסוק אדם אחר בינתיים ועמ״ש לעיל סי׳ פ״ח ס״ק ד׳:

בדק הבית על תורת הבית בית ז שער ב – כתב החכם דאסור לאכול עמה על השלחן, כי הא דתנן לא יאכל הזב עם הזבה ע״כ. ונראין דברי האומר דדוקא בשאוכלין שניהם בפני עצמן או שמסובין סמוכין אבל אם היו שם אחרים אוכלין ומפסיקין ביניהן מותר.

הגהות מיימוניות הלכות איסורי ביאה פרק יא הלכה ל – ואפילו לשתות בכלי ששתתה בו כתב רא״ם שאסור כדמשמע התם גבי עבודא דתנא דבי אליהו אכל עמי ושתה עמי וכו׳ ועל כל דבריה השיב לה ברוך המקום שהרגו משמע שעל הכל נענש דאל״כ מה לו לתלמוד להזכיר אלא ללמדנו שעל כל אלה נענש אבל אם הורק המשקה מכלי אל כלי אחר אפילו אם הוחזר לכלי הראשון מותר לו לשתות ממנה אחרי שנשתנה בהרקה מכלי אל כלי וכן אם שתה הוא תחלה היא מותרת לשתות אחריו דתנן לא יאכל הזב עם הזבה וה״ה דלא ישתה ולא קאמר לא תאכל הזבה עם הזב ע״כ מספר יריאים. וכן נראה מדקאמרינן גבי עובדא אכל ושתה עמי ולא אמרה

אכלתי ושתיתי עמו או אכלנו ושתינו יחד ואם שתתה והוא אינו יודע שמעתי שאינה צריכה להגיד לו אלא מניחתו לשתות שאין כאן חיבה כלל.

שולחן ערוך יורה דעה הלכות נדה סימן קצה:ד – לא ישתה משיורי כוס ששתתה היא.

ש"ך יורה דעה סימן קצה:ח – לפי שהרב בד"מ כתב דין זה בשם הקונטרס שמצא ע"כ כ' דין זה בשם י"א אבל לפעד"נ דהגמי"י בשם רא"ם ומרדכי (ואגודה ורוקח סימן שי"ח) פ"ק דשבת בשם הר"ש שמהם מקור האי דינא דלקמן סעיף ד' דלא ישתה משיורי כוס ששתתה שם מוכח להדיא דכ"ש דלא יאכל משיורי מאכל שלה ואדרבה שתיה נלמד מאכילה ע"ש:

רמ"א יורה דעה הלכות נדה סימן קצה:ג – י"א שאסור לו לאכול משיורי מאכל שלה, כמו שאסור לשתות משיורי כוס שלה, וכמו שיתבאר.

סדרי טהרה סימן קצה:ח – דבשלמא שתיה א"א בענין אחר כ"א בזה אחר זה משא"כ באכילה דאפשר לאכול שניהם בבת אחת מן הקערה מש"ה בזא"ז ליכא משום הרגל דבר...ועוד דבשתיה מראה חבה כשהוא שותה אחריה דאינש דעלמא אין דרך לשתות משיורי כוס ששתה חבירו כדאי' בא"ח סי' ק"ע משו"ה י"ל אם הוא שותה אחריה מראה חבה יתירה משא"כ באכילה.

רמ"א יורה דעה הלכות נדה סימן קצה:ד – אם לא שמפסיק אדם אחר ביניהם (טור בשם סמ"ג), או שהורק מכוס זה אל כוס אחר אפילו הוחזר לכוס ראשון (הגהמי"י בשם רא"ם ורוקח סימן שי"ח ומרדכי ואגודה פ"ק דשבת); ואם שתתה והוא אינו יודע ורוצה לשתות מכוס שלה, אינה צריכה להגיד לו שלא ישתה (שם); והיא מותרת לשתות מכוס ששתה הוא (ג"ז שם). ואם שתתה מכוס והלכה לה, י"א שמותר לו לשתות המותר, דמאחר שכבר הלכה אין כאן חבה. (בקונטרס הנ"ל).

ערוך השולחן יורה דעה הלכות נדה סימן קצה – ודע דדווקא הוא אסור לשתות משיריה אבל היא משירים שלו מותר בכל עניין דהיא לא מרגלה ליה לעבירה כן כתב רבינו הרמ"א בסעי' ד' ע"ש ואיני מבין דבריו דהן אמת דהיא לא מרגלא ליה מ"מ כיון שהיא שותה בפניו משירים שלו ומראה לו חיבה ניחוש שהוא ירגילה לעבירה וצ"ל דזה שהיא שותה אינו דרך חיבה אלא דווקא כשהוא שותה משיריה אבל א"כ א"צ לטעם דלא מרגלא ליה ואולי באמת זהו הכוונה דבכה"ג ליכא חשש הרגל דבר [עי' ט"ז סק"ה שכתב הטעם דלא מרגלא ליה ע"ש ובדברי הרמ"א י"ל כמ"ש]:

מרדכי מסכת שבת רלח – והר"ם כתב דצריך ליזהר דאם יש שתי מטות ורגלי האחת נוגעת בחברתה שלא ישכב הוא באחת ואשתו נדה באחרת אם לא ישימו הפסק בינתים.

בעלי הנפש שער הפרישה סימן ג – וראיתי בתשובה לרבינו האיי ששאלו אותו על הכלה שנבעלה בעילת מצוה אם צריכה נקיים וטבילה כשאר נדות או לא. והשיב, מנהגא דילן אם

בעל וראתה דם אע"פ שראתה דם יגמור ביאתו ופורש. ונוהגת עצמה כל שבעה כנדה דיתבא לה להאי גיסא כשאר נדות כדי שלא יהא הרגל, וצריכא שבעה נקיים וטבילה כעיקר זבה, אלא שאין אנו מטמאין משכב שתחתיה בשעת בעילה משום דלאו נדה ודאי היא אלא ספק. ואיני עומד על בירור דבריו במה שאמר שאין אנו מטמאין משכב שתחתיה בשעת בעילה משום דלאו נדה ודאי היא, ואלו היתה נדה ודאי כלום יש טומאה וטהרה בזמן הזה לטמא משכב שתחתיה. ונראה מדבריו שאסור לישן על מטתה של נדה אפילו בשעה שאינה במטה משום הרגל. ודוקא נדה ודאי, אבל כלה מותר לישן על אותה מטה אחר שעמדה מאצלו ואפילו באותו סדין שהדם עליו. ואע"פ שאין זה מן ההלכה הרי הם דברים שהדעת מכרעת עליהם.

תלמוד בבלי מסכת כתובות דף סא עמוד א – אמר רב יצחק בר חנניא אמר רב הונא: כל מלאכות שהאשה עושה לבעלה – נדה עושה לבעלה, חוץ ממזיגת הכוס, והצעת המטה, והרחצת פניו ידיו ורגליו. והצעת המטה, אמר רבא: לא אמרן אלא בפניו, אבל שלא בפניו לית לן בה.

מרדכי מסכת שבת רלח – ובספר צפנת פענח כתב בשם רש"י שאסור לישב על כסא ארוך אשר אשתו נדה יושבת עליו.

תרומת הדשן סימן רנא – שאלה: אשה נידה מהו שתשב עם בעלה על העגלה ללכת מעיר לעיר, בדרך זה שלא יגע בה כלל כגון הוא לפנים והיא לאחור?

תשובה: יראה דשרי, וכמדומה לי קרוב לודאי שהתיר לי אחד מהגדולים, וכן ראיתי מועתק מספר אגודה דשריא ואע"ג דכתב מרדכי בפ"ק דשבת בשם ספר הפרדס משמו של רש"י שאסור לישב על ספסל אחד שאשתו נידה יושבת עליו, והך נמי דמי להאי. נראה דאין לדמות להוראה זו אלא מילתא דדמיא לה לגמרי שאין בה סברא לחלק, דבהלכות נידה כתב עליה דהוראה זו חומרא בעלמא היא, וא"כ נוכל לחלק דדוקא ישיבה על הספסל ביחד נראה בדרך חיבה דרך אוהבים להתקבץ יחד ולהתוועד בכה"ג. אבל בישיבה בעגלה שדרך בני אדם נכרים להתקבץ כמה פעמים לבא יחד ולהצטרף לשכור עגלה בין כולם ללכת בה מעיר לעיר לאו מילתא דחיבה היא כלל, דאפילו אם עכשיו אין בעגלה אלא האיש ואשתו וגם עגלה שלהם היא מ"מ לאו דרך חיבה הוא. וכן שמעתי שחלק אחד מהגדולים דלעיל והיה נוהג להתיר לישב יחד על הספסל כשהוא מחובר בכותלי הבית כמו שרגילים לעשות באצטבאות בבית החורף ובבתי הקיץ, והיה אומר דאין לאסור אלא כשהספסל תלוש. אמנם ללכת בעגלה עם אשתו נידה דרך טיול לגנות ולכרמים וכה"ג לא ברירנא להתיר.

רמ"א יורה דעה הלכות נדה סימן קצה:ה – ואסור לישב על ספסל ארוך שמתנדנדת ואינה מחוברת לכותל, כשאשתו נדה יושבת עליו, (מרדכי פ"ק דשבת בשם צפנת פענח בשם רש"י). ויש מתירים כשאדם אחר מפסיק ויושב ביניהן (אגודה פרק התינוקת ות"ה סימן רנ"א).

ט"ז יורה דעה סימן קצה:ו – משמע אפילו ישיבה בעלמא בלא שכיבה דבישיבה נמי איכא הרהור ומצד ההרהור יבוא לידי הרגל עבירה כ"כ ב"י וביש ספרים איתא בטור כאן לא ישכב

ומו"ח ז"ל כתב דטעות סופר בגירסא של לא ישב כיון שלעיל סוף סי' קצ"ג כ' בטור וש"ע לא יישן ולא נראה דהתם קמ"ל דבכלה אפי' שינה שם מותר אבל זה ודאי דגם ישיבה שייך בה הרהור דהא כ' המרדכי ורמ"א מביאו בסמוך דאסור לישב על ספסל ארוך כו' וכ"ש ישיבה במטה שלה דאיכא הרהור טפי ונראה דכ"ש הוא שהיא לא תישן במטה שלו דיש טפי הרהור בשכבה ובקומה אבל ישיבה בעלמא מותר לה על מטה שלו דהיא לא מרגלא ליה כן נ"ל ונגיעה שנוגע בסדין שהוא מלוכלך בדם אין איסור אע"פ שקצת נזהרין מזה ושבוש הוא:

נקודת הכסף יורה דעה קצה:א – דהתם לאו משום הרהור הוא אלא כיון דמתנודדת הוי כנגיעה אי נמי כיון דשניהם יושבים עליה ביחד ה"ל כישן עמה במטה אע"פ שאין נוגעים זו בזו.

שו"ת אגרות משה יורה דעה חלק ב סימן עז – ובדבר ליסע במאשין שכתבתי שיש להתיר באופן שלא יגעו זב"ז הוא אף אם יהיה נדנוד מאחר שאין זה מחמתה עיקר הנדנוד כיון דמאשין הוא דבר כבד, ולכן יש להתיר גם אם אירע שיש נדנוד גם מחמתה מצד הספסל שיושבין שהוא רך, שכיון שהספסל הוא קבוע ומחובר להמאשין יש לדונו כמחובר לכותל שמשמע מסעיף ה' סי' קצ"ה שמותר אף שמתנדנדת דאל"כ לא היה חלוק בין מחובר לכותל לאינו מחובר. ועיין בבית לחם יהודה בשם נחלת שבעה שבקורות ארוכות מותרין דכובדן קובעתן וכמחוברין דמיא, ופשוט שהוא אף באירע שמתנדנד דאל"כ לא היה אומר דכמחוברין דמיא דאף בתלוש ליכא איסור בלא זה וכן הוא במאשין, וטעם ההיתר הוא משום שעצם האיסור ישיבה על ספסל הוא רק חומרא יתירא ולא אסרו זה במחובר שיש להיות לו דין המחובר שאינו מתנדנד, ומפני שאולי יש קצת לפקפק כתבתי שעם עוד אנשים שאינה רוצה לפרסם ודאי יש לסמוך על טעם זה להתיר והוא אף ביש גם איזה נדנוד מחמתה.

תלמוד בבלי מסכת נדרים דף כ עמוד א – רבי אחא ברבי יאשיה אומר: כל הצופה בנשים – סופו בא לידי עבירה, וכל המסתכל בעקבה של אשה – הויין לו בנים שאינן מהוגנין. אמר רב יוסף: ובאשתו נדה. אמר רבי שמעון בן לקיש: עקבה דקתני – במקום הטנופת, שהוא מכוון כנגד העקב.

רמב"ם הלכות איסורי ביאה פרק כא:ד וראב"ד – ומותר לאדם להביט באשתו כשהיא נדה ואע"פ שהיא ערוה, ואע"פ שיש לו הנאת לב ממנה בראייה הואיל והיא מותרת לו לאחר זמן אינו בא בזה לדבר מכשול, אבל לא ישחוק ולא יקל ראש עמה שמא ירגיל לעבירה. כתב הראב"ד ז"ל א"א אבל לא במקום הסתר שלה והכי איתא בנדרים עכ"ל.

שולחן ערוך יורה דעה הלכות נדה קצה:ז – לא יסתכל אפילו בעקבה, ולא במקומות המכוסים שבה.

שולחן ערוך אבן העזר הלכות אישות כא:ד – מותר לאדם להביט באשתו, אע"פ שהיא נדה והיא ערוה לו; אע"פ שיש לו הנאה בראייתה, הואיל והיא מותרת לאחר זמן אינו בא בזה לידי מכשול. אבל לא ישחק ולא יקל ראש עמה.

בית יוסף אבן העזר סימן כא – וכן מותר לאדם להביט באשתו אף ע"פ שהיא נדה והיא ערוה לו וכו'. כ"כ הרמב"ם בפכ"א מהא"ב (ה"ד) וכתב הרב המגיד בפרק אלו מותרים (נדרים כ.) המסתכל בעקבה של אשה הויין ליה בנים שאינם מהוגנים אמר רב יוסף ובאשתו נדה אמר ר"ל עקבה דקתני מקום התורף שהוא מכוון כנגד עקבה משמע הא בשאר מקומות מותר וכן אמרו (שבת סד:) שמותר לאשה להתקשט בימי נדתה כדי שלא תתגנה על בעלה אלמא שמותר להסתכל בה:

שו"ת אגרות משה יורה דעה חלק ב סימן עה – ובדבר קול באשתו נדה אם מותר לשמוע כשמזמרת, הנה הפ"ת סימן קצ"ה סק"י נשאר בצ"ע ולכן מהראוי להחמיר, ובדבר שער אשה נדה לבעלה, הנה ודאי עדיף ממקומות המכוסים שבה, דהנשים שאין מחמירות לעשות כקמחית אלא כפי חיובה שבביתה כשליכא שם אינשי אחריני אינה מכסית שערותיה, שהבעל רגיל בהו תמיד הוא טעם גדול שאין לאסור עליו, וגם לשון האיסור הא נאמר בכתובות דף ע"ב אזהרה לבנות ישראל שלא יצאו בפרוע ראש, ולשון הרמב"ם פכ"ד מאישות הי"א יוצאה בשוק ושער ראשה גלוי ולשון הרמב"ם פכ"א מאי"ב הי"ז וכן לשון הש"ע אה"ע סימן כ"א סעיף ב' לא תלכנה בנות ישראל פרועות ראש בשוק, ואם גם בביתה היתה אסורה חלק גדול בשנה יותר מרביעית ולפעמים גם יותר משלישית לא היה שייך לומר לא תלכנה ובשוק, וכן מסתבר לדינא ומ"מ כל המחמיר בענינים אלו משובח ואם אפשר באופן טוב ושלום היה טוב להחמיר. ובכלל מסתבר לדינא שבמקומות המכוסים שבה שאסור לבעל להסתכל הוא רק במקומות המכוסים אף בביתה כשאין שם רק בעלה או כשאין שום איש דג"כ רגילות להיות מלובשות, דלא מסתבר כלל דיהיה הכוונה למקומות המכוסים כשהולכות בשוק ובפני אינשי אחריני שצריכות ללכת בצניעות יותר אך שטוב להחמיר באופן טוב ושלום כי בענינים אלו המחמיר משובח.

...בדבר מה שאשתו רוצה להיות נעורה בשעת לידתה מטעם שאומרים שיהיו החבלי לידה קלים מעט בזה שתסיח דעתה מן הצער הנה אם היתה שואלת אותי לא הייתי מיעץ לעשות דבר זה כי חבלי לידה הם גדולים שלא יועיל היסח הדעת ורק הוא ענין הערמה בעלמא, אך אם האשה רוצה בכך אין בזה דבר איסור. ובדבר אם יהיה כן אם רשאי הבעל ליגע בה משום דכשהיא במטה אין לידע הזמן שאי אפשר לה ללכת, הנה לענין איסור נדה נאסרת משישבה על המשבר דהוא משעה שמשכיבין אותה במטה מצד חבלי הלידה. עיין בסד"ט סימן קצ"ד ס"ק כ"ה, וגם מסיק שלאו דוקא ישבה על המשבר אלא מיד שאחזוה צירים וחבלי לידה ומבקשת להביא לה חכמה צריך הבעל להזהר בה דודאי לאו ישיבת המשבר גורם פתיחת הקבר אלא כל שהיא קרובה ללידה כל כך שצריכה לישב על המשבר ואיכא למיחש אלו היתה המילדת מזומנת אצלה היתה מושיבה מיד על המשבר צריך להיות נזהר בה, וממילא כ"ש כשיש להסתפק שמא אינה יכולה לילך שודאי אסורה.

ובאם הבעל יכול להיות שמה להשגיח שתעשה הדבר בסדר הנכון וגם לחזק אותה ולאמץ לבה, הנה אם יש צורך איני רואה איסור ואף בלא צורך איני רואה איסור, אבל אסור לו להסתכל ביציאת הולד ממש שהרי אסור לו להסתכל במקומות המכוסים שבה בנדתה ובמקום התורפה הא אסור אפילו בטהורה, אך כשיזהר שלא להסתכל ליכא איסור, וע"י מראה נמי אסור להבעל להסתכל.

תלמוד בבלי מסכת שבת דף יג עמוד א – תא שמע: ואל ההרים לא אכל ועיניו לא נשא אל גלולי בית ישראל ואת אשת רעהו לא טמא ואל אשה נדה לא יקרב, מקיש אשה נדה לאשת רעהו. מה אשת רעהו – הוא בבגדו והיא בבגדה אסור, אף אשתו נדה – הוא בבגדו והיא בבגדה אסור. שמע מינה.

פתחי תשובה יורה דעה סימן קצה:י – צ"ע אי מותר לשמוע קול זמר שלה מאחר דבגמרא דשבת דף י"ג אמר מקיש אשה נדה לאשת רעהו רק דיחוד שרי משום דהתורה העידה סוגה בשושנים כדאיתא בסנהדרין דף ל"ז ועי' בתוספות שם ד"ה התורה העידה א"כ נראה דאסור דהא באשת רעהו אסור כמ"ש בברכות דף כ"ד קול באשה ערוה וכתב הרא"ש שם פירוש לשמוע וכ"כ כל הפוסקים וצ"ע:

תלמוד בבלי מסכת כתובות דף סא עמוד א – אמר רב יצחק בר חנניא אמר רב הונא: כל מלאכות שהאשה עושה לבעלה – נדה עושה לבעלה, חוץ ממזיגת הכוס, והצעת המטה, והרחצת פניו ידיו ורגליו.

תורת הבית הקצר בית ז שער ב – וכל המלאכות שאשה עושה לבעלה נדה עושה לבעלה, חוץ ממזיגת הכוס והצעת המטה והרחצת פניו ידיו ורגליו. מזיגת הכוס בכוס של יין שהוא המרגיל לערוה.

הגהות מיימוניות הלכות איסורי ביאה פרק יא נ' – פי' למזוג לו כוס להושיט לו כדרך שהיא עושה כשהיא טהורה שזהו דבר של חיבה אבל על ידי היכר ושינוי מותר כדאמר התם פרק אע"פ שרבא מנחא ליה אבי סדיא רב פפא מנחא ליה אשרשיפא רבי ירמיה מחלפא ליה דביתהו בידא דשמאלא וכל זה אינו אלא להניח לפניו על השולחן אבל ליתן לידו לעולם אסור. וכתב רא"ם דלא בעינן שינוי אלא כששניהם יחד מזיגה והושטה אבל מזיגה בלא הושטה והושטה בלא מזיגה אפילו בלא שינוי מותר ואע"פ שבספר לא הזכיר אלא הושטת כוס של יין שהוא דבר של חיבה היה נזהר רש"י אפילו ליתן מידו לידה מפתח או חפץ אחר ונראה מזיגה האמורה בגמרא היינו דוקא מזיגה במים אבל מזיגה מן הכלי כמו שאנו עושים אין נראה בזה קירוב דעת כההיא דמוזגים לכוס ואח"כ נוטלים לידים ומיהו על השלחן נראה דאסור אם לא ע"י שינוי כשמואל דמחלפא ליה דביתהו ומיהו ר"ח פי' מוזגת ואח"כ מחלפא ליה ולפי זה היה מותר. והצעת המטה פר"ת ורש"י פרישת סדינים אבל הצעת כרים וכסתות מותר ואין להקל כלל יותר בימי לבון מבימי נדות דכתיב בנדתה תהא עד שתבא במים ע"כ:

ש"ך יורה דעה סימן קצה:י"ג – כתב הב"ח מ"כ בדרשות מהר"ש מאוסטרייך דשלא כדין עושין הבעלי בתים שמניחין נשותיהם לישא הקערות וכיוצא בהן על השלחן מידי דהוה אמזיגת הכוס עכ"ל מיהו למ"ש הגמי"י בשם רא"מ דמזיגה בלא הושטה או הושטה בלא מזיגה מותר אפי' בלא שינוי ה"ה בקערה דליכא אלא הושטה דשרי וכן למ"ש הרשב"א (והב"י לדעת ה"ה) דמזיגת יין במים דוקא אסור אבל שאר משקים אי נמי מזיגה מן הכלי כמו שאנו עושים שרי ה"ה

בקערה אין קפידא ועוד נראה דאפי׳ את״ל דנתינת הקערה על השלחן ה״ל כמזיגת הכוס מ״מ אף במזיגת הכוס אין איסור אלא בכוס המיוחד לבעלה בלבד דאיכא חיבה אבל להביא הקער׳ על השלחן שכל בני בית אוכלים ממנה אין קפידא אע״ג שגם בעלה אוכל עם בני ביתה מאותה קערה דליכא הכא חיבה והכי נקטינן אבל להביא קערה המיוחדת לבעלה אסורה וכמוכח מתנא דבי אליהו וממ״ש סה״ת דאף בהושטה בלבד כשאין בו שינוי אסור במאכל ובמשתה ע״כ ולפי זה משמע דמחמיר ג״כ בשאר משקים:

סדרי טהרה סימן קצה יח – ועיין בב״ח ובש״ך הביאו שכתב דה״ה ליתן הקערה על השלחן ודוקא קערה המיוחדת לבעלה אבל לא כשבני בית אוכלים ממנה וכ״כ ב״ש דף קיג ע״ב והט״ז כתב מדלא אמרו רק מזיגת הכוס ולא אמרו ג״כ תיקון המאכל א״ו דחכמים שיערו זה בחכמתם שאין בזה קירוב דעת רק מעשה עבדות וכ״נ לפמ״ש הרמ״א דוקא מזיגה בפניו והנחה לפניו הוא דאסור הא הנחתה לפניו לחודה שרי ה״ה ה״נ דשרי דאפילו אי משוינן דנתינה מן הקדירה לקערה למזיגה מ״מ כיון שהוא שלא בפניו שריא מיהו הב״ח לשיטתיה דס״ל דאע״פ דהמזיגה היה שלא בפניו כיון דהנחה הוא לפניו אסור משו״ה החמיר בזה אבל למ״ש הרמ״א והסכים לזה הש״ך בס״ק ד אין להחמיר כלל בזה.

שולחן ערוך יורה דעה הלכות נדה סימן קצה:י״ג – כשם שאסורה למזוג לו כך הוא אסור למזוג לה; ולא עוד, אלא אפילו לשלוח לה כוס של יין אסור, לא שנא כוס של ברכה לא שנא כוס אחר, אם הוא מיוחד לה; אבל אם שותים הם מאותו הכוס ושתית איהי אבתרייהו, לית לן בה.

שולחן ערוך יורה דעה הלכות נדה סימן קצה:י״א – אסורה להציע מטתו בפניו; ודוקא פריסת סדינים והמכסה שהוא דרך חבה, אבל הצעת הכרים והכסתות שהוא טורח ואינה דרך חבה, שרי. ושלא בפניו, הכל מותר אפילו הוא יודע שהיא מצעת אותם.

תורת הבית הארוך בית ז שער ב – הרחצת פניו ידיו ורגליו אפילו הוא רוחץ והיא מוצקת שאלו לרחוץ היא בידיה אפילו בלא רחיצה אסור דהא איכא קירוב בשר ואסור ליגע בה אפילו באצבע קטנה. ורחיצה זו אפילו בצונן קאמר.

ט״ז יורה דעה סימן קצה:ח – לכאורה משמע מלשון זה שאסורה ליתן מים בכלי והוא ירחץ אח״כ אבל באמת אינו כן דזה לשון רשב״א אפי׳ הוא רוחץ והיא מוצקת שאילו לרחוץ בידיה אפי׳ בלא רחיצה אסור דהא איכא קירוב בשר ואסור ליגע אפי׳ באצבע קטנה עכ״ל משמע דמותרת להכין לו מים בכלי והוא ירחץ משם דמדכתב הוא רוחץ והיא מוצקת משמע דבשעת רחיצה שלו היא יוצקת ולא שהיא מכינה לו תחילה קודם רחיצתו ותו דאם תפרש דגם זה אסור קשה מנ״ל לאסור זה דהא כתב אח״כ הוכחה שאין לפרש הרחיצה בידה מכח קירוב בשר ש״מ דמיירי כאן במידי דלאו קירוב בשר דהיינו שיוצקת בשעת רחיצה וא״ל דהא גם דבר זה שיוצקת בשעה שהוא רוחץ ג״כ אסור בלאו חיבה דרחיצה אלא מטעם דנוגעת בו על ידי המים הנוזלין מידה לידו י״ל דזהו מגע על ידי דבר אחר שהיא נוגעת בכלי והכלי במים והמים בידו סלקא

דעתך דשרי קמ"ל דאסור משום רחיצה שמביאה לידי חיבה וכן נ"ל מלשון התלמוד שאמר בדין זה דהרחצת פניו ידיו ורגליו אסור ודבר זה שנותנת מים לכלי תחלה בלי יציקה עליו לא מקרי רחיצה כלל והיה לו לומר דנתינת מים להרחצה אסור כמ"ש שם מזיגת הכוס הכי נמי היה לו לומר ונתינת מים מה שאין כן אם יוצקת על ידיו מקרי שפיר רחיצה אלא ודאי כדפיר' דאין איסור בנתינת מים לחוד וכ"כ בדרישה ומ"מ פשוט לי דגם זה בכלל האיסור שאם הוא רוחץ מכלי שיש בו נקב למטה ובשעת רחיצתו היא יוצקת מים להכלי דגם זה מקרי הרחצה כנ"ל:

ש"ך יורה דעה סימן קצה:ח – וכ' הר"ר יונה בספר דרשות הנשים דאסור לתת לפני בעלה קיתון של מים וכלים שירחץ בהם רגליו מפני שהוא דרך חיבה:

רש"י מסכת כתובות דף סא עמוד א – מיחלפא ליה – בימי ליבונה.

תוספות מסכת שבת דף יג עמוד ב – ור"ת פירש שהיו רגילים לטבול שתי טבילות אחת לסוף שבעה לראייתה שהיא טהורה מדאורייתא בהך טבילה ואחת לסוף ימי ליבון לכך היה מיקל אותו האיש.

רמ"א יורה דעה הלכות נדה סימן קצה:י"ד – הגה: וי"א דאין להחמיר בימי ליבונה בענין איסור אכילה עמו בקערה (הגה במרדכי בשם ראבי"ה), וכן נוהגין להקל בזה, ויש להחמיר.

דרכי משה יורה דעה סימן קצה:ח – אמנם מצאתי הגהה במרדכי בשם אבי"ה וזה לשונו אחר ימי ליבון ליכא הרגל עבירה וטוב לאכול עמה כדי שתרצה לטבול אם יכולה לטבול עכ"ל ועל זה ראיתי רבים מקילים בימי ליבונה ואין נראה לי לסמוך על זה וראבי"ה יחיד הוא בדבר זה.

ש"ך יורה דעה סימן קצה:י"ז – ז"ל ד"מ בין בימי נדותה בין בימי לבונה וכבר נתבאר ר"ס זה אמנם מצאתי הג"ה במרדכי בשם ראבי"ה וז"ל אחר ימי ליבון ליכא הרגל עבירה וטוב לאכול עמה כדי שתרצה לטבול אם יכולה לטבול ע"כ וע"ז ראיתי מקילים בימי לבונה ואין נ"ל לסמוך ע"ז וראבי"ה הוא יחיד בזה עכ"ל, והב"ח כ' דאף לפי זה טועים המקילים שהרי לא התיר אלא ביום הז' שאחר ימי ליבון כדי שתתרצה לטבול וגם ליכא הרגל עבירה דאין לחוש שמא יבא עליה ביום הז' כיון שהיא טובלת לערב וגם זו סברא קלושה היא ואין שומעין ליחיד להתי' איסור המפורסם בכל החיבורים ולכן יש לדרוש ברבים דאיסורא קא עבדי הני דאוכלים יחד מקערה א' בימי לבונה ומצאתי בהג"ה ואנשים האוכלים עם נשותיהם בימי ליבונה שלא ירגישו בני הבית שבוש הוא ועוברים על דברי חכמים ונתקבצו כל הקהלות ועשו חרם ע"ז דהר"ח ע"כ והג"ה זו היא בהגהת מהרש"ל ומביאו הדרישה וראב"ן כ' בס"ס של"ה ויש נוהגין שלא לאכול עד כלות שבעה נקיים והוא כשר ונאה דשוב ליכא הרגל עבירה אלא הרגל מצוה דכיון דמצי למטבל לא שביק היתרא ואכיל איסורא ועי"ש שהאריך.

שו"ת הרשב"א המיוחסות לרמב"ן סימן קכז – שאלה: בעל המבין ברפואות, ואשתו נדה וחולה, ויש בעיר רופאים מוחזקין שמבינין כמותו, או יותר: היוכל הבעל למשש בדפק שלה, ביחוד

ושלא ביחוד? ואפשר בשביל ההזמנה יועיל לה, שהאחרים אינם יכולים לראותה תמיד. מי אמרינן: כיון דנגיעה בעלמא, אינה אלא משום שבות, ושבות הותרה בחולי שאין בו סכנה; הא נמי דכוותה? א"ד שאני הכא, דיצרו תקפו. ולך; אמרין נזירא: סחור סחור לכרמא, לא תקרב?

תשובה: מסתברא שאסור. חדא, דאפשר דכל קריבה דאורייתא, כדאמר פרק קמא דשבת (דף י"ג): (יחזקאל י"ח: ו') אל ההרים לא אכל, ועיניו לא נשא אל גלולי, בית ישראל, ואת אשת רעהו לא טמא, ואל אשה נדה לא יקרב. מקיש אשתו נדה, לאשת רעהו. מה אשת רעהו, הוא בבגדו והיא בבגדה, אסור: אף אשתו נדה, הוא בבגדו והיא בבגדה, אסור. ופליגא דרבי פדת. דא"ר פדת: לא אסרה תורה, אלא קריבה של ג"ע, שנאמר: לא תקרבו לגלות ערוה. אלא מאן דאסר שום קריבה, משום: לך לך; אמרין נזירא כו'; אפ"ה איסור דרבנן, איסור הוא. דכיון דהוא חולי שאין בו סכנה, לא נתיר בו איסור דרבנן. שלא כל השבותים שוין: בין ביו"ט, בין בשבת, בין בחולי. דהרבה שבותים התירו בשבת וביו"ט, משום מצוה בעלמא, וכותב בעש"ג משום ישוב א"י, וכיוצא בזה. ופעמים, שמעמידים דבריהם במקום כרת. ועל כרחך, אין אנו למדים להתיר שבות משבות, אלא במקום שאמרו להתיר, מתירין; ובמקום שלא אמרו, אין מתירין. ועוד, שהתירו בשבת, לעשות כל צרכי חולה על ידי נכרי, אע"פ שאמירה לנכרי שבות. ואפ"ה, לא מסתברא שנתיר לו סתם יינם, ושמנו של גיד, וגבינה של נכרים, ושאר איסורים דרבנן. ועוד, שהרי יש בעיר כמותו, ואפשר על ידי אותו אחר. ובמקום שיש היתר ואיסור, אין מאכילין האדם דבר איסור, ואפילו בשל דבריהם. דאטו מי שיש לו יין נסך בתוך ביתו, ויין כשר נמכר בעיר, מי נימא: דניתן לו יין נסך, מפני שהוא מזומן לו יותר? הא ודאי לא! ואפילו בחולה שיש בו סכנה בכיוצא בזה, אין מתירין בלא אומדנא. דחולה, אומדנא בעי. אא"כ דבר ברור הוא, שהוא מסוכן לאותו דבר, אם לא נתן לו מיד. וכדאמר פרק חרש (דף קי"ד): פלוגתא דתינוק אוכל נבלות, אם ב"ד מצווין להפרישו. ופרקינן: שאני התם, משום סכנה. ואקשינן: והא אומדנא בעי? ופריק: סתם תינוק, מסוכן הוא אצל חלב.

31.

תלמוד בבלי מסכת נדה דף טז עמוד א – איתמר; אשה שיש לה וסת, והגיע שעת וסתה ולא בדקה, ולבסוף בדקה, אמר רב: בדקה ומצאת טמאה – טמאה, טהורה – טהורה. ושמואל אמר: אפילו בדקה ומצאת טהורה – נמי טמאה, מפני שאורח בזמנו בא. לימא בוסתות קמיפלגי, דמ"ס – דאורייתא, ומ"ס – דרבנן! אמר ר' זירא – דכ"ע – וסתות דאורייתא, כאן – שבדקה עצמה כשיעור וסת, כאן – שלא בדקה עצמה כשיעור וסת. ר"נ בר יצחק אמר: בוסתות גופייהו קמיפלגי, דמ"ס – וסתות דאורייתא, ומר סבר – וסתות דרבנן. אמר רב ששת: כתנאי, ר' אליעזר אומר טמאה נדה, ורבי יהושע אומר תבדק. והני תנאי כי הני תנאי; דתניא, רבי מאיר אומר: טמאה נדה, וחכ"א: תבדק. אמר אביי: אף אנן נמי תנינא; דתנן, ר"מ אומר: אם היתה במחבא, והגיע שעת וסתה ולא בדקה – טהורה, שחרדה מסלקת את הדמים. טעמא – דאיכא חרדה, הא ליכא חרדה – טמאה, אלמא – וסתות דאורייתא. לימא הני תנאי בהא נמי פליגי, דתניא הרואה דם מחמת מכה – אפילו בתוך ימי נדתה טהורה – דברי רשב"ג, רבי אומר: אם יש לה וסת – חוששת לוסתה. מאי לאו, בהא קמיפלגי, דמר סבר – וסתות דאורייתא, ומר סבר –

וסתות דרבנן! אמר רבינא: לא, דכ"ע – וסתות דרבנן, והכא – במקור מקומו טמא קמיפלגי; רשב"ג סבר: אשה – טהורה, ודם טמא – דקאתי דרך מקור, ואמר ליה רבי: אי חיישת לוסת – אשה נמי טמאה, ואי לא חיישת לוסת – מקור מקומו טהור הוא.

רש"י מסכת נדה דף טו עמוד א – דאורייתא – הלמ"מ דמחזקינן לה בטומאת ספק.

שולחן ערוך יורה דעה הלכות נדה סימן קפד סעיף ט – שאר נשים, צריכות בדיקה כשיגיע הוסת. עבר הוסת ולא בדקה ולא הרגישה, טהורה בלא בדיקה. וי"א שאסורה עד שתבדוק, אם יש לה וסת קבוע, או שהוא יום ל' אע"פ שאינו קבוע. (והכי נהוג, כד וכן הוא לקמן סימן קפ"ט).

תלמוד בבלי מסכת נדה דף סג עמוד ב – תנא כיצד א"ר יוסי ימים ושעות וסתות – היתה למודה להיות רואה מיום עשרים ליום עשרים, ומשש שעות לשש שעות, הגיע יום עשרים ולא ראתה – אסורה לשמש כל שש שעות ראשונות – דברי רבי יהודה, ורבי יוסי מתיר עד שש שעות, וחוששת בשש שעות. עברו שש שעות ולא ראתה – אסורה לשמש כל היום כולו – דברי ר' יהודה, ורבי יוסי מתיר מן המנחה ולמעלה.

היתה למודה. והתניא, רבי יהודה אומר: כל הלילה שלה! לא קשיא, הא – דרגילה לראות בתחלת יממא, והא – דרגילה לראות בסוף ליליא. תני חדא: רבי יהודה אוסרה לפני וסתה ומתירה לאחר וסתה. ותניא אידך: אוסרה לאחר וסתה ומתירה לפני וסתה. ולא קשיא, הא – דרגילה למחזי בסוף ליליא, הא – דרגילה למחזי בתחלת יממא. אמר רבא: הלכה כרבי יהודה. ומי אמר רבא הכי? והתניא: (ויקרא ט"ו) והזרתם את בני ישראל מטומאתם, מכאן א"ר ירמיה: אזהרה לבני ישראל שיפרשו מנשותיהן סמוך לוסתן. וכמה? אמר רבא: עונה. מאי לאו – עונה אחריתי? לא, אותה עונה. ותרתי למה לי? צריכא, דאי אשמועינן הא – הוה אמינא: ה"מ – לטהרות, אבל לבעלה – לא, קמ"ל. ואי מההיא – הוה אמינא: סמוך לוסתה עונה אחריתי, קמ"ל אותה עונה.

תלמוד בבלי מסכת יבמות דף סב עמוד ב – ואמר ריב"ל: חייב אדם לפקוד את אשתו בשעה שהוא יוצא לדרך, שנא': וידעת כי שלום אהלך וגו'. הא מהכא נפקא? מהתם נפקא: (בראשית ג) ואל אישך תשוקתך – מלמד, שהאשה משתוקקת על בעלה בשעה שהוא יוצא לדרך! א"ר יוסף. לא נצרכה אלא סמוך לווסתה. וכמה? אמר רבא: עונה. והני מילי לדבר הרשות, אבל לדבר מצוה – מיטרידי.

תלמוד בבלי מסכת פסחים דף עב עמוד ב – ורבי יוחנן אמר: אשתו נדה בעל – חייב, יבמתו נדה בעל – פטור. איכא דאמרי: כל שכן בההיא דמחייב, דלא עשה מצוה. אית דאמרי: בההיא פטור. מאי טעמא? התם הוא דהוה ליה לשיולי, אבל הכא דלא הוה ליה לשיולי – לא. ורבי יוחנן, מאי שנא יבמתו – דקא עביד מצוה, אשתו נמי קא עביד מצוה! – באשתו מעוברת. – והא איכא שמחת עונה! – שלא בשעת עונתה. – והאמר רבא: חייב אדם לשמח אשתו בדבר מצוה! – סמוך לווסתה. – אי הכי, אפילו יבמתו נמי! – יבמתו בזיז מינה, אשתו לא בזיז מינה.

ויקרא פרק טו:לא – והזרתם את בני ישראל מטמאתם ולא ימתו בטמאתם בטמאם את משכני אשר בתוכם.

בעלי הנפש שער תיקון הוסתות סימן א – ותחלה נאמר כי חשש הוסתות דרבנן הוא. דפלוגתא דרב ושמואל היא דאיתמר (נדה טז א) הגיע שעת וסתה ולא בדקה ולא ראתה אמר רב בדקה ומצאה טמא טמא טהור טהור קסבר וסתות דרבנן ושמואל אמר אפילו בדקה ומצאה טהור טמא קסבר וסתות דאורייתא, וקיימא לן כרב באיסורי. ועוד דמוקמינן (שם) לפלוגתייהו כתנאי דתניא הגיע שעת וסתה ולא בדקה ולא ראתה ר' מאיר אומר טמאה נדה וחכמים אומרים תבדק, שמואל קאי כר' מאיר ורב קאי כרבנן. ועוד מדבעיא מיניה רבא מרב נחמן (שם) וסתות דאורייתא או דרבנן ובלישנא בתרא פשט ליה וסתות דרבנן, אלמא הכי הלכתא. ועוד מדאמרינן ביבמות (סב ב) חייב אדם לפקוד את אשתו בשעה שיוצא לדרך ומוקמינן לה אפילו בשעת וסתה, שמע מינה וסתות דרבנן ובמקום מצוה לא גזור, דאי דאורייתא היכי שרינן ליה, ועוד דקא מחייבינן ליה נמי, אלא ש"מ דרבנן היא. והכין פסק רב אחא (פ' מצורע ריש שאילתא פט) וכן פסק בעל ההלכות. ואע"ג דתניא (נדה סג ב) והזרתם את בני ישראל מטומאתם אזהרה לבני ישראל שיפרשו מנשותיהן סמוך לוסתן וכמה עונה. ההיא אסמכתא בעלמא היא.

רא"ש מסכת נדה פרק ט סי' ב' – כתב הראב"ד ז"ל אם רגילה לראות בהנץ החמה ולא קים לה שפיר אי קודם הנץ או לאחר הנץ יש מחמירין ואוסרין כל הלילה וכל היום וי"א כיון דוסתות דרבנן כל שכן סמוך לוסתה הלכך הוה ליה ספק דרבנן ולקולא ולא חיישינן אלא ליום שהוא ודאי בימי נדתה והכריח הוא להקל ואם רגילה לראות ראיה מרובה מקודם הנץ החמה עד אחר הנץ איכא מאן דאמר אסורה בלילה וביום משום דההיא שעתא כולה שעת הוסת הוא. ואפי' ר' יוסי דאמר ימים ושעות וסתות מודה דשעת הוסת מיהת אסורה לשמש בכולה. הלכך לרבי יהודה דאמר כל העונה כולה ומפני שעת הוסת נאסרה כל העונה כל היום וכל הלילה אסורה. שהרי וסתה הוא ביום ובלילה. ואיכא מאן דאמר דכי האי גוונא בתר תחילת הוסת אזלינן ולא מיתסרא אלא בלילה. אע"ג דכל שעת הוסת אסורה לשמש ואפי' לר' יוסי. הני מילי לשעת הוסת עצמה אבל לאסור את שלפניו ושלאחריו לא אסרינן אלא ההיא עונה (אלא) דתחילת הוסת קאי בגוה. ואם בדקה קודם הנץ החמה ולא ראתה כל אותה שעה אסורה אבל כל היום מותרת לפי שעיקר הוסת בתחילתו הוא והכריע הוא כי הך סברא בתרא מהא דתנן היתה למודה להיות רואה עם הנץ החמה אינה אסורה אלא עם הנץ החמה דברי רבי יוסי רבי יהודה אומר כל היום שלה. ואוקימנא להא דרגילה למיחזי בסוף לילה וכל היכא דתני עם לאלתר משמע ואי סלקא דעתך דכי האי גוונא אסורה ביום ובלילה היכי קתני כל היום שלה והא אי אפשר דלא עיילא ראיה בתוך הנץ החמה ותיאסר בימכא ובליליא. ועוד סתמא קתני להיות רואה ולא מפליג בין ראיה מרובה לראיה מועטת הלכך אינה אסורה אלא עונת הלילה ושעת הוסת בלבד. אמר רבא הלכה כר' יהודה. ומי אמר רבא הכי והתניא והזרתם את בני ישראל [מכאן] אמר ר' אושעיא אזהרה לבני ישראל שיפרשו מנשותיהן סמוך לוסתן. וכמה. אמר רבא עונה מאי לאו עונה אחריתי. לא אותה עונה.

שו"ת נודע ביהודה מהדורה תנינא – יורה דעה סימן קג – והנה דומה אני שלא קרא מעלתו דברי בחיבורי או שנתערבו לו הדברים כי ראה אותם בחפזון בלי עיון כלל. כי מה שכתב שאני כתבתי טעמא דר"ת משום שמא יקדש דהוי חזקה שאינה מבוררת. היכן כתבתי זה וגם היכן חייש ר"ת שמא יקדש ואיפכא כתבתי דלהכי לא חייש שמא יקדש משום דהוי חזקה מבוררת בשעתה עיין שם בחיבורי וגבי הרי זה גיטך שעה אחת קודם מותי שאסורה לאכול בתרומה מיד כתבתי דיש לה שתי חזקות להיתר. חדא חזקת חיים של הבעל, ואידך חזקת היתר שהרי עד עתה יש לה חזקת היתר לתרומה וכתבתי אעפ"כ אסורה לאכול בתרומה מיד משום דחזקת חיים אף שהיא מבוררת בשעתה וגם לא איתרע מעולם מ"מ אין חזקה מועיל לפי שהרי פעם אחת בודאי סופו למות ולכך אי אפשר לסמוך על חזקה זו כלל להבא וחיישינן בכל פעם שמא ימות אחר שעה אבל מ"מ אכתי נשאר חזקת היתר שהיה לה עד עתה היתר לאכול תרומה וכאן לא שייך לומר שבודאי יגיע שעה שתאסר בתרומה כשימות דשמא לא תאסר לעולם ובעלה לא ימות בחייה אבל נגד זה חזקה הזאת איתרע בשעה שנתן לה הגט אף שנתן לה הגירושין שיחולו שעה אחת קודם מותו מ"מ שוב יצאה מחזקתה שקודם הגירושין וכמ"ש התוספות בכתובות כ"ג ע"א ד"ה תרווייהו כו' שבשעה שזרק לה קידושין אף דמספקא לן אולי קרוב לו מ"מ כבר יצאה מחזקת פנויה וליכא למימר אוקמה אחזקתה אלא שגם אחר הגירושין יש לה חזקת היתר שהרי אחרי שראינו שעה אחר הגירושין שלא מת הרי חזינן שאחר הגירושין היתה מותרת וממילא ראוי לאוקמה אחזקת היתר שהרי אח"כ לא נעשה שום ריעותא לגרוע חזקתה אבל נגד זה חזקת היתר שלאחר הגירושין מעולם לא נתבררה בשעתה דהרי תיכף אחר הגירושין חיישינן שמא ימות תוך שעה אך אחר שחי כמה שעות אז נודע שהיתה מותרת לפני שעה וזה מקרי חזקה שלא נתבררה בשעתה. כל זה ביארתי בחיבורי שם. ומעתה פשיטא דלר"ת הטעם משום שחל הגט שעה קודם מותו דאל"כ היתה מותרת מטעם חזקת היתר אבל לא מטעם חזקת חיים וכנ"ל אבל בוסתות שאין להאשה רק חזקת טהרה וחזקה זו ודאי עתידה לסתור שהרי עכ"פ פעם אחת תראה הרי זה דומה לחזקת חיים וחיישינן שמא תראה כמו דחיישינן שמא ימות אבל לא חיישינן שמא ראתה כמו דלא חיישינן שמא כבר מת אבל שם בקינין שפיר כתבו התוספות דמותרים להקריב הקינין דהרי בשעה שמקריבין אמרינן שעדיין לא מת ואפילו ימות תיכף לא מזיק לן עתה שבשעת הקרבה חי הוא.

פתחי תשובה יורה דעה סימן קפד:ג – לפרוש ממנה – עי' בתשו' נודע ביהודה חי"ד סי' נ"ה ונ"ו שהעלה דמה שאמרו וסתות דרבנן היינו לענין שלא אמרינן שכבר ראתה בשעת וסתה משום דנגד חזקה אורח בזמנו בא יש חזקת טהרה אבל לענין לפרוש מאשתו סמוך לוסתה הוא מן התורה דחיישינן שמא תראה ולא אמרינן על להבא נוקים לה בחזקת טהרה דאטו לעולם לא תראה. ודמי להא דאמרו שמא מת לא חיישינן ושמא ימות חיישינן ע"ש ועי' בנו"ב תניינא סי' ק"ג מ"ש בזה ועמש"ל סי' קפ"ז ס"ק מ"ו בשמו [ועי' בתשו' חתם סופר סי' ק"ע וס"ס קע"ט שכתב דהנו"ב כוון סברא זו מדעתו ובאמת היא קדומה בבד"ה להרא"ה וכן קיבל ממורו הגאון ז"ל לחלק בכך ולכן חושש מאד לסברא זו ומשוי לה ספק דאורייתא ע"ש. וכ"כ עוד בכמה תשובות שם אמנם בסי' קע"ה שם הביא דברי הרא"ה ז"ל קצת באורך ולפי האמור שם נראה

דרק גוף הסברא לחלק בין ראתה לשמא תראה קדומה בהרא"ה אבל לדינא יש מרחק רב ביניהם. ואלו דבריו שם בשם הרא"ה אע"ג דוסתות לאו דאורייתא כדי שנחזיק אותה בודאי טמאה אחר שעבר רגע הוסת מ"מ מה"ת אסורה לשמש בעונה הסמוך לוסתה אחר רגע הוסת דודאי אם רגילה לראות באמצע היום ואנו אוסרים אותה לשמש מתחלת הנץ קודם שתגיע רגע הוסת משום שמא ע"י חימום התשמיש יקדים האורח זהו דרבנן אבל אחר אמצע היום שכבר עברה רגע הוסת אע"ג דלא מחזקינן לה בודאי ראתה כיון דוסתות דרבנן ולא אמרי' כבר ראתה אבל מה"ת אסורה לשמש חציה של עונה זו מחצי יום ואילך דשמא תראה עתה מחמת חום התשמיש כיון שכבר הגיע הרגע שהיתה ראויה לראות בהם עכ"ד ע"ש].

תלמוד בבלי מסכת גיטין דף כח עמוד א, דף כח עמוד ב – רבא אמר: שמא מת לא חיישינן, שמא ימות חיישינן.

חזון איש יו"ד סימן פ אות ז–ח – והכא בעיקר ענין הוסתות קמפלגי, דמ"ד דאו' סבר חזקה אלימתא היא ויש לחוש לה אף בלי כל ריעותא והיא מוציאה מחזקת טהרה עד שתאמר ברי לי שלא ראיתי ולא תוכל להעיד כי אם בבדיקה, ומ"ד דרבנן סבר כיון שהימים חלוקין במאכל ובמשתה ובשינוי האויר אשר כל אלה עלולין לשנות את זמני הראי' ולכן אין להוציאה מחזקתה. ומיהו סמוך לוסתה י"ל דהוי מה"ת דמידי חששה לא נפקא והלא אסרה תורה את היחוד ואין אוסרין על היחוד ולא מחזקינן לי' לספק איסור וכן אוכא טובא דצריך האדם להרחיק שלא יבוא לידי איסור ידוע.

ש"ך יורה דעה סימן קפד:ה – צריך לפרוש כו' – היינו מדרבנן כן הסכמת רוב הפוסקים והאחרונים דוסתות דרבנן.

בדק הבית על תורת הבית בית ז שער ב – [דף ד עמוד א] עוד כתב פעמים שאדם צריך לפרוש מן האשה ואעפ"י שלא הרגישה בדם. ואלו הן: מי שהגיע עת וסתה, והבועל את הבתולה, ומי שתבעוה לינשא וניפייסה, והרואה דם מחמת תשמיש. הגיע עת וסתה כיצד כל אשה שיש לה וסת בין וסת קבוע בין וסת שאינו קבוע אסורה לבעלה כל אותה עונה שהיא רגילה לראות בה. וכמה עונה או יום או לילה. רגילה לראות ביום אסורה כל אותו היום רגילה לראות בלילה אסורה כל הלילה. דבר זה דרבנן הוא דמדאורייתא אינה אסורה עד שתראה כמו שיתבאר בשער הוסתות ע"כ. ואינו נכון, דבהדיא מוכח בשבועות גבי היה משמש עם הטהורה ואמרה לו נטמאתי דקודם שתראהו אסורה לו דאורייתא אבל עיקרן של דברים כך הם דפלוגתא הוא וסתות אי דאורייתא אי דרבנן למימרא אי מחזיק' לה בשעת וסתה בודאי רואה ואפי' בדקה אחר כך ומצאה טהורה טמאה דאמרינן דודאי חזאי דאי דאורייתא אמרי' דודאי חזאי ואי דרבנן לא אמרינן בהא דודאי חזאי ולא מחזקי' לה בודאי אלא אמרינן דספק הוא ואפשר דלא חזאי ואם בדקה בתוך זמן שרגילה בו שנמשך לה נדתה ומצאה טמאה הרי היא טמאה דאמרינן דמההיא שעתה הואי ואם בדקה ומצאה טהור טהורה ותו נפקא לן מינה דאי מחזיקנן לה בודאי חזאי אסור לו לבעלה לבא עליה עד שידע שכבר טבלה וטהורה היא ואי אמרת דספיקא הוא מותר הוא לבעלה לבא עליה

אחר שהות ספירת שבעה וטבילה דאמרינן דילמא לא חזאי ואם תמצי לומר חזאי שמא טבלה שדרך הנשים לטבול לאלתר שיוכלו לטבול או להשתדל להודיע לבעליהן שלא יכשלו ומכל מקום בין למר בין למר אפילו למ"ד וסתות דרבנן אפי' בריא לה שלא ראתה אסור לה לשמש משהגיע וסתה כל אותה עונה.

חידושי הריטב"א מסכת שבועות דף יח עמוד א – לעולם שלא בסמוך לוסתה ואפרישה. פירוש ואפרישה בלחוד, דאילו חיוב כניסה ליכא בשלא סמוך לוסתה ואנוס הוא, והוי יודע דסמוך לוסתה האמור כאן אינו סמוך לוסתה האמור לקמן שהוא עונה או יום או לילה, דההיא מדרבנן בעלמא הוי דהא קיימא לן (נדה ט"ז א') וסתות דרבנן, אלא ר"ל אחר שהגיע וסתם או קודם מעט בסמוך ממש.

תלמוד בבלי מסכת יבמות דף סב עמוד ב – ואמר ריב"ל: חייב אדם לפקוד את אשתו בשעה שהוא יוצא לדרך, שנא': וידעת כי שלום אהלך וגו'. הא מהכא נפקא? מהתם נפקא: (בראשית ג) ואל אישך תשוקתך – מלמד, שהאשה משתוקקת על בעלה בשעה שהוא יוצא לדרך! א"ר יוסף. לא נצרכה אלא סמוך לווסתה. וכמה? אמר רבא: עונה. והני מילי לדבר הרשות, אבל לדבר מצוה – מיטרידי.

שו"ת אגרות משה אבן העזר חלק ג סימן כח – ולענ"ד היה נראה דעיקר העונה הוא בשעה שרואה הבעל שהיא משתוקקת אל בעלה שלכן אמר רבא בפסחים דף ע"ב חייב אדם לשמח את אשתו בדבר מצוה שפרש"י אפילו שלא בשעת עונתה אם רואה שמתאוית לו ומנא לו לרבא חיוב זה שהוא חיוב גמור מדאורייתא דהא הקשה דליפטור בשביל זה מחטאת כשנמצאת שהיא נדה מצד טריד בדבר מצוה שאם היה זה רק חיוב מדרבנן לא היה שייך להקשות זה, אלמא שמפרש כן הקרא דעונתה לא יגרע על זה שחייב לשמחה בשעה שרואה שמתאוית לו, וכן ביוצא לדרך שאמר ריב"ל ביבמות דף ס"ב דחייב לפוקדה מטעם זה שהאשה משתוקקת שהוא ודאי חיוב מדאורייתא מדא"ר יוסף דאפילו סמוך לוסתה יפקדנה לפרש"י ועוד הרבה ראשונים שהביא הב"י ביו"ד סימן קפ"ד בד"ה ומ"ש שי"א עיי"ש. ואם היה רק מדרבנן לא מסתבר שהיה שייך להתיר בסמוך לוסתה ומה שלכאורה קשה דביוצא לדרך מותר מצד חיוב דמשתוקקת אפילו סמוך לוסתה וברואה שהיא משתוקקת שחייב כדאמר רבא מתרץ הגמ' דהיה סמוך לוסתה שאסור בפסחים שם דף ע"ב, צריך לומר דיש חלוק בין היכא שלא נעשה ענין שמעורר השתוקקות אלא שהאשה בעצמה נתעורר לה תאוה אף שזהו עונתה לתשמיש דחייבתו התורה לא שייך להתיר סמוך לוסתה דהרי יש איסור גם עליה לשמש סמוך לוסתה כמו עליו וא"כ היה אסור לה להתעורר לתאוה ותשוקה זו עתה דהיה נמצא שנחייבהו לסייע לה לעבור על האיסור דסמוך לוסתה, אבל כשצריך הבעל לצאת לדרך שהוא ענין המעורר בהכרח תאוה ותשוקה להאשה כדדריש מקרא ואל אישך תשוקתך דכן קבע השי"ת שייך שיתירו האיסור דסמוך לוסתה כיון שהתאוה והתשוקה היא מוכרחת ליכא חיוב עליה להבליג על תאותה שהוא צער גדול לה וממילא הוא מחוייב מצד מצות העונה שהוא בלאו עליו אף לדחות איסור דסמוך לוסתה דרבנן לרש"י ודעימיה.

רש"י בראשית פרק לב – (טו) עזים מאתים ותישים עשרים – מאתים עזים צריכות עשרים תישים, וכן כולם, הזכרים כדי צורך הנקבות. ובבראשית רבה (עו ז) דורש מכאן לעונה האמורה בתורה, הטיילים בכל יום, הפועלים שתים בשבת, החמרים אחת בשבת, הגמלים אחת לשלשים יום, הספנים אחת לששה חדשים. ואיני יודע לכוין המדרש הזה בכוון. אך נראה בעיני שלמדנו מכאן שאין העונה שוה בכל אדם אלא לפי טורח המוטל עליו, שמצינו כאן שמסר לכל תיש עשרה עזים, וכן לכל איל, לפי שהם פנוים ממלאכה, דרכן להרבות בתשמיש לעבר עשר נקבות, ובהמה משנתעברה אינה מקבלת זכר, ופרים שעוסקין במלאכה לא מסר לזכר אלא ארבע נקבות, ולחמור שהולך בדרך רחוקה שתי נקבות לזכר, ולגמלים שהולכים דרך יותר רחוקה נקבה אחת לזכר.

חידושי הריטב"א מסכת שבועות דף יח עמוד ב – ת"ר והזרתם את בני ישראל מטומאתם מכאן אמר רבי יאשיה אזהרה לבני ישראל שיפרשו מנשותיהם סמוך לוסתן וכמה אמר רבא עונה. ועונה או יום או לילה, שאם רגילה לראות ביום אפילו בסופו אסורה כל היום, ואם רגילה לראות בלילה ואפילו בסופה אסורה כל הלילה, כדמפרש בדוכתה במסכת נדה (ס"ג ב'), ואיכא למידק למאן דסבר לעיל דאכניסה מחייב מדאורייתא בסמוך לוסתה, וכסברא דאביי ורבא ואידך אמוראי דלעיל וקיימא לן נמי כוותיהו, מהא דאמרינן נמי במסכת יבמות (ס"ב ב') חייב אדם לפקוד את אשתו בשעה שיוצא לדרך שנאמר ופקדת נוך ולא תחטא, ואמרינן שלא נצרכה אלא סמוך לוסתה, היכי דחינן איסורא דאורייתא משום פקידת אשתו, ור"ת ז"ל תירץ דפקידה דהתם אינו רוצה לומר תשמיש ממש כדפירש רש"י ז"ל אלא ריצוי בדברים, ולא נהירא לן חדא דלישנא דליפקוד את אשתו לא משמע הכי, ועוד דכיון דתשמיש אסור למה לאלבשה יצר הרע, ויותר היה נראה לומר דלעולם תשמיש ממש, ופקידה דהתם נמי מדאורייתא גמירי לה שהכתוב מבטיחו שלא יבא בכך לידי חטא שתראה בשעת תשמיש, והיינו דקאמר קרא ופקדת נוך ולא תחטא, והכי גמירי לפירושא דההוא קרא.

איוב פרק ה פסוק כד – וידעת כי שלום אהלך ופקדת נוך ולא תחטא.

תוספות מסכת יבמות דף סב עמוד ב – חייב אדם לפקוד את אשתו – אומר ר"ת דפקידה זו אינו תשמיש אלא כשהוא רוצה לצאת בדרך אם הוא רחוק ממנה לא יצא לדרך אא"כ ישוב אליה ויפקדנה או בתשמיש או בשאר דברים וידבר על לבה ופריך מהתם נפקא ליה מלמד שהאשה משתוקקת על בעלה כשיוצא לדרך ומסתמא כיון שמתאוה לו יש לו לפוקדה דהמכבד אשתו עליו הכתוב אומר אז תקרא וגו' ומשני אמר רב יוסף לא נצרכה אלא לאשתו נדה ה"ג בכל הספרים ישנים והכי פי' דחד קרא אתא דאפילו באשתו נדה יש לו לפוקדה וכמה עונה אע"פ שאסור לשמש מ"מ שמחה ותענוג הוא לה הואיל ורוצה לצאת בדרך והכי אמרי' בריש הדר (עירובין סג: ושם) הישן בקילעא שאיש ואשתו ישנים שם עליו הכתוב אומר נשי עמי תגרשון מבית תענוגיה ואמר רב יוסף התם ואפילו אשתו נדה ומה שהגיהו בספרים לא נצרכה אלא סמוך לוסתה אין נראה כלל דהגיהו כן לפי שרוצין לפרש דפקידה היינו תשמיש ובשבועות (דף יח: ושם) מוכיח דסמוך לוסתה מדאורייתא מוהזרתם את בני ישראל וגו' ועוד דמוקי לה ביוצא

לדבר הרשות וא"כ אפילו למאן דאמר (נדה דף טו.) ווסתות דרבנן אם כן סמוך לווסתה נמי דרבנן מכל מקום למה יהא מותר ביוצא לדבר הרשות.

ספר הישר לר"ת (חלק החידושים) סימן מה – יבמות ס"ב ב' (סי' ט', ה' ד') הבא. אמר ר' יהושע חייב אדם לפקוד את אשתו כו'. נר' לי פקידה זו לאו דווקא תשמיש. אלא כשרוצה לצאת לדרך אם הוא רחוק ממנה לא יצא לדרך אלא אם כן ישוב אליה ויפקדנה או בתשמיש או בשאר צרכים. ולא ילך למרחקים בלא דעתה. ופריך הא מהכא נפקא מהתם נפקא ואל אישך תשוקתך מלמד שהאשה משתוקקת על בעלה בשעה שיוצא לדרך. ומסתמא כיון שמתאוה ומשתוקקת עליו יש לו לפוקדה דהמכבד את אשתו כגופו עליו הכתוב אומר אז תקרא וה' יענה. ומשני אמר רב יוסף לא נצרכה אלא לאשתו נידה. ה"ג בכל הספרים ישנים. והכי פי' חד קרא משמע לן שחייב לפקוד את אשתו אם אינה נידה ויבא עליה וידבר אל לבה עונה שלימה. וקרא אחרינא קמ"ל שאפילו אשתו נידה יש [לו] לפוקדה. וכמה אמר רב' עונה. שאפי' שאסורה בתשמיש שמחה היא ותענוג הוא לה הואיל ורוצה לצאת לדרך. כדאמרי' בעירובין הישן בקילעא שאיש ואשתו ישינים עליו הכתו' אומר נשי עמי תגרשון מבית תענוגיה. ואמר רב [יוסף] התם ואפי' באשתו נידה אלמא שמחה הוא לה. הכא נמי צריך לפוקדה אפי' נידה. וכמה אמר רבה עונה. כדאמרי' מניחין תחת צנור ומימיו מקלחין וכמה אמר רבה עונה. וטובא עונה איכא בתלמוד שאינו בתשמיש. ומה שהוגהו בספרים לא נצרכה אלא סמוך לווסתה שיבוש גדול הגיהו לפי שסברו דפקידה היינו תשמיש. חדא דבשבועות מוכיח דסמוך לווסתה דאורייתא. ועוד דקאמרי' הני מילי לדבר הרשות וכי בשביל דבר הרשות עקרינן והזרתם את בני ישראל מטומאתם דמוקמי' בסמוך לווסתה. אדרבה ידחה דבר הרשות ואל יצא לדבר הרשות בסמוך לווסתה ויתקיימו שני מקראות הללו. אבל לפי מה שפירשתי אתיא שפיר. שאם רוצה לצאת לדבר הרשות ישוב לביתו ויפקוד את אשתו אבל דבר מצוה לא ישוב לפקוד את אשתו דילמא מיטרד ומימנע ולא עביד מצוה אלא (למקום) [ממקום] שהוא שם ילך לדבר מצוה ואל יטרח לשוב לביתו לפקוד [אשתו]. ומשום הכי מייתי בסמוך המכבד את אשתו כו'.

שולחן ערוך יורה דעה הלכות נדה סימן קפד סעיף י – הרוצה לצאת לדרך צריך לפקוד אשתו אפילו סמוך לוסתה. הגה: ואפילו בתשמיש שרי. (טור בשם י"א וב"י בשם רש"י וראב"ד ורשב"א ור' ירוחם). כה ומ"מ כו המחמיר שלא לפקדה רק בדברי רצוי, תע"ב (ב"י בשם סמ"ג). וכבר נתבאר דכל מיני קורבה ואהבה שרי, מלבד תשמיש. ואם הולך לדבר מצוה א"צ לפקוד אשתו. (המ"מ פ"ד דא"ב ובהגהות ש"ד). וי"א אם אדם רוצה לילך לדרך, ואשתו נדה ותטבול כח תוך עונה אחת, צריך להמתין.

ט"ז יורה דעה סימן קפד:יד – ואפילו בתשמיש שרי. – כיון דוסתות דרבנן במקום מצוה לא גזור.

שולחן ערוך אורח חיים הלכות ק"ש ותפלה של ערבית סימן רמ סעיף א – אם היה נשוי, לא יהא רגיל ביותר עם אשתו, אלא בעונה האמורה בתורה. הטיילים, שפרנסתן מצויה להם ואין פורעין

מס, עונתן בכל יום; הפועלים שעושים מלאכה בעיר אחרת ולנין בכל לילה בבתיהם, פעם אחת בשבוע; ואם עושים מלאכה בעירם, פעמים בשבוע; החמרים, אחת בשבוע; הגמלים, אחת לל׳ יום; הספנים, אחת לששה חדשים; ועונת ת״ח מליל שבת לליל שבת; וכל אדם צריך לפקוד את אשתו בליל טבילתה, ובשעה שיוצא לדרך אם אינו הולך לדבר מצוה, וכן אם אשתו מניקה והוא מכיר בה שהיא משדלתו ומרצה אותו ומקשטת עצמה לפניו כדי שיתן דעתו עליה, חייב לפקדה. ואף כשהוא מצוי אצלה לא יכוין להנאתו, אלא כאדם שפורע חובו שהוא חייב בעונתה ולקיים מצות בוראו שיהיו לו בנים עוסקים בתורה ומקיימי מצות בישראל; וכן אם מכוין לתיקון הולד, שבששה חדשים אחרונים יפה לו שמתוך כך יצא מלובן ומזורז, שפיר דמי; ואם הוא מכוין לגדור עצמה בה כדי שלא יתאוה לעבירה, כי רואה יצרו גובר ומתאוה אל הדבר ההוא. הגה: גם בזה יש קיבול שכר, אך (טור) יותר טוב היה לו לדחות את יצרו ולכבוש אותו, כי אבר קטן יש באדם: מרעיבו, שבע; משביעו, רעב; אבל מי שאינו צריך לדבר, אלא שמעורר תאותו כדי למלאות תאותו, זו היא עצת יצר הרע, ומן ההיתר יסיתנו אל האיסור, ועל זה אמרו רבותינו ז״ל: המקשה עצמו לדעת יהא בנדוי.

הלכות נדה לרמב״ן פרק ח:י – כשהאשה חוששת לעונת וסתה הורו מקצת בעלי הוראה שאינה אסורה אלא בתשמיש, אבל שאר פרישות לא החמירו עליה שאין כאן אלא חשש של דבריהם.

שו״ת חתם סופר חלק ב (יורה דעה) סימן קע – אודות אשה שהגיע ליל טבילתה ביום יציאת בעלה לדרך והוא בעונה הסמוך לוסתה אם נאמר שבצירוף ב׳ מצות עונה דהיינו ליל טבילה ויום יציאה לדרך לא נחוש כלל למצות פרישת עונה הסמוך לוסתה.

שאלה זו בעינה נשאלה לפני שבוע העבר ואסרתי בפשיטות והעיקור כי מ״ש רמ״א יו״ד בסימן קפ״ד לחומרא בעלמא לפרוש מתשמיש הוא לענ״ד מעיקור הדין דהש״ך כ׳ בזה משום דקיי״ל וסתות לאו דאורייתא וכ״כ ב״י שם וכן משמע מתוס׳ פ׳ הבע״י ואני קבלתי ממ״ו זצ״ל דאפי׳ למ״ד וסתות ל״ד מ״מ עונה הסמוך לוסתה דאורייתא דשמא ראתה כבר לא חיישינן אבל שמא תראה כמו שמא מת ושמא ימות ושוב נדפס כן בס׳ נב״י ושוב מצאתי כן בבד״ה להרא״ה אלא שחילק שם בין עונה שקודם רגע הוסת לעונה שאחר רגע הוסת ע״ש ואמר לי מורי זצ״ל דאפי׳ להסוברי׳ בש״ך סי׳ קצ״ו סק״ט דקריבה דגילוי עריות דהיינו חבוק ונשוק אסור מה״ת בכל העריות מ״מ מותר לפקוד בקריבה בעלמא בעונה הסמוך לוסתה לצורך מצוה ביוצא לדרך אף על גב דהפרישה היא חיוב מה״ת מ״מ הותר הקריבה משום דהבעילה בעצמה אין בה איסור מה״ת אלא משום שמא תראה באמצע התשמיש ואסור לפרוש באבר חי ויצטרך להשהות עליה משו״ה אסור לכנוס בתחלה על מנת כן אבל בשארי קריבות אם ירגיש היא תודיע לו ויפרוש מיד אלו דברי מורי זצ״ל ודפח״ח ואני התלמיד מוסיף על דבריו בשלמא חמום התשמיש גורם להקדים הזלת הדם קודם זמנו ואיכא למיחש טפי משא״כ בשארי קריבו׳ מה״ת לחוש.

יהי׳ איך שיהיה כיון דאיכא ספק דאורייתא בודאי אין להקל בתשמיש בעונה הסמוך לוסתה אך בעונה דאביאסף ודאור זרוע בהאי יש להקל קצת אלא דלא נשאלתי ע״ז.

תלמוד בבלי מסכת נדה דף סג עמוד ב, דף סד עמוד א – מתני׳. היתה למודה להיות רואה יום ט״ו ושינתה להיות רואה ליום כ׳ – זה וזה אסורין. שינתה פעמים ליום כ׳ – זה וזה אסורין. שינתה ג׳ פעמים ליום כ׳ – הותר ט״ו, וקבעה לה יום כ׳, שאין אשה קובעת לה וסת – עד שתקבענה ג׳ פעמים, ואינה מטהרת מן הוסת – עד שתעקר ממנה ג׳ פעמים. גמ׳. איתמר, ראתה יום חמשה עשר לחדש זה, ויום ט״ז לחדש זה, ויום שבעה עשר לחדש זה. רב אמר: קבעה לה וסת לדילוג. ושמואל אמר: עד שתשלש בדילוג. נימא רב ושמואל בפלוגתא דרבי ורשב״ג קמיפלגי, דתניא, ניסת לראשון – ומת, לשני – ומת, לשלישי לא תנשא – דברי רבי. רשב״ג אומר: לג׳ – תנשא, לד׳ לא תנשא. לא, דכ״ע – כרשב״ג, והכא בהא קמיפלגי; רב סבר – חמשה עשר ממנינא, ושמואל סבר – כיון דלאו בדילוג חזיתיה לאו ממנינא הוא. איתיביה: היתה למודה להיות רואה יום ט״ו ושינתה ליום ששה עשר – זה וזה אסורין, שינתה ליום שבעה עשר – הותר ששה עשר ונאסר חמשה עשר ושבעה עשר, שינתה ליום שמונה עשר – הותרו כולן, ואין אסור אלא משמונה עשר ואילך. קשיא לרב! אמר לך רב: למודה שאני. ודקארי לה, מאי קארי לה? למודה אצטריכא ליה. מהו דתימא: כיון דלמודה, ועקרתיה – בתרי זימני עקרה ליה – קמ״ל. מיתיבי: ראתה יום עשרים ואחד בחדש זה, יום עשרים ושנים בחדש זה, יום עשרים ושלשה בחדש זה – קבעה לה וסת. סירגה ליום עשרים וארבעה – לא קבעה לה וסת. תיובתא דשמואל! אמר לך שמואל: הכא במאי עסקינן – כגון דרגילה למחזי ביום עשרים, ושינתה ליום עשרים ואחד. דיקא נמי, דשבקינן ליום עשרים, ונקט ליום עשרים ואחד – ש״מ.

שולחן ערוך יורה דעה הלכות נדה סימן קפט סעיף ד – עוד יש חילוק בין קבעתו ג׳ פעמים ללא קבעתו ג׳ פעמים, שהקבוע אף על פי שעברה עונתה ולא הרגישה, אסורה לשמש עד שתבדוק ותמצא טהורה. ושלא קבעתו ג״פ, אם הגיע זמן הוסת ולא בדקה ולא ראתה, כיון שעברה עונתה, מותרת. ועונה בינונית, שהיא לל׳ יום, דינה כוסת קבוע.

בית יוסף יורה דעה סימן קפט – יט (ב) ודע שזה שכתב רבינו שיש וסת הגוף תלוי בימים ידועים ויש וסת הגוף שאינו תלוי בימים ידועים אלא בעת המקרה באיזה יום שיהיה כתב הרב המגיד (איסו״ב פ״ח ה״א) שכן הסכימו כל המפרשים שראה אבל מדברי הרמב״ם נראה שהוא סובר שאין כאן שני וסתות חלוקים אלא שהמשנה הודיעה שבוסת הקבוע באים מקרים אלו או אחד מהם ונפק״מ שיש למודה לראות תיכף כשבא המקרה ההוא ויש לאחר שעה ואינה חוששת אלא לשעה ההיא שהיא רגילה לטהרות וכדתנן בפרק האשה (סג:) ונזכר בדבריו בהלכות מטמאי משכב ומושב (פ״ג ה״ו). ונראה לי דלדעת הרמב״ם וסת דאכילת שום ובצלים ופלפלין הוי כוסת דקפיצות דזה וזה מחמת מעשה שעושה ראתה ומפני כך לא כתב וסת דאכילת שום ובצלים ופלפלין דמוסת הקפיצות שכתב נשמעיניה.

תוספות מסכת נדה דף סד עמוד א – איתמר ראתה ט״ו בחדש זה וט״ז בחדש זה – פי׳ דווקא בכי האי גוונא אבל ראתה בג׳ חדשים או בב׳ לחדש או באחד לכ״ע אין צריך יותר כדאמר לעיל בסוף בנות כותים (דף לט:) דחזאי ריש ירחא וריש ירחא כו׳ ואפילו שאחד מלא ואחד חסר ואין הימים שבין ראייה לראייה שוין מ״מ קביעות החדש גורם והיכא דבראשונה אין לה שיעור

בחדש שתהא השניה נראת דילוג מן הראשונה דכ"ע דאין הראשונה מן המנין ובעינן שתשלש בדילוג כגון ראתה עכשיו ושניה בעשרים לה ושלישית בכ"א לשניה ומשום הכי נקט ט"ו בחדש זה ולפירוש זה קשה דבפרק שור שנגח ד' וה' (ב"ק לז:) מדמה נגח יום חמשה עשר בחדש זה וששה עשר בחדש זה ושבעה עשר בחדש זה לפלוגתא דהכא ואם כן היכי קאמר התם לעיל גבי ראה שור ונגח שור ולא נגח דהויא ראשונה מן המנין הא בכי האי גוונא אפי' רב מודה דלא הוי ראשונה מן המנין שהרי לא היתה לשום זמן לא לחדש ולא לשבת ויש לחלק בין סירוגין דימים לסירוגין דשוורים ור"ח פי' קבעה לה וסת לדילוג כשעשתה שלש פעמים כסדר הזה כגון שראתה ט"ו בניסן וי"ו באייר וי"ז בסיון וכן ראתה ט"ו בתמוז וי"ו באב וי"ז באלול ועוד ראתה ט"ו בתשרי וי"ו במרחשון וי"ז בכסליו חוששת מכאן ואילך ט"ו לחדש זה וי"ו לשני וי"ז לשלישי ולשמואל צריכה שתשלש בדילוג שתראה בחדש רביעי יום י"ח ובג' חדשים שאחריהם יום י"ו וי"ז וי"ח וכן בשלישי עוד שאחרי כן דראייה של ט"ו יום בחדש הראשון לא היה ממנינא ותימה למה פי' כן דא"כ כששאל הש"ס לימא בדרבי ורשב"ג קמיפלגי לא פליגי בראייה ראשונה לחוד אלא בשלש ראיות של דילוג ראשון ובמסקנא יהיה הפירוש בע"א ואמאי לא סגי בג' חדשים כדפי' בקונטרס.

חידושי הרמב"ן מסכת נדה דף סד עמוד א – ראתה יום ט"ו בחדש זה וכו'. אם באנו לחשב חדשים מלאים בכולן אין כאן דילוג אלא הוסת שוה להפלגת ל"ב, ואם באנו לפרש אותן בכסדרן חסר ומלא אין סדר לדילוג הזה שהראשונה מט"ו בניסן לט"ז באייר להפלגת ל"ב והשנייה שהיא מט"ז באייר לי"ז בסיון להפלגת ל"א הוא נמצא שלא דילגה אלא קרבה ראיתה, וכשהיא משלשת בדילוג מי"ז בסיון לי"ח בתמוז חזרה להפלגה שוה לל"ב ואין כאן דלוג אלא א"כ דילגה עד י"ט בחדש, ולקמן מתרץ שמואל לברייתא כגון דרגילה למחזי ליום כ' וקתני כ"ג בחדש זה ולפי חשבונך הו"ל למיתני כ"ה, לפיכך פי' הראב"ד ז"ל שכשם שהאשה קובעת וסת להפלגות שוות כך קובעת וסת בימי החדש שאם ראתה ריש ירחא וריש ירחא וריש ירחא קבעה לה וסת לראשי חדשים אע"פ שאין ההפלגות שוות שאחד מלא ואחד חסר, הילכך בזו שדילגה כיון שאין בראיותיה צד השוה לה לא בהפלגות ולא בדילוגין אומרים לימי החדש היא קובעת ולא בהשואה אלא בדילוג, ופסק ר"ח ז"ל כרב באיסורי, ומיהו דוקא בזו שהיא קובעת בימי החדש אבל בימים שקבעה להפלגות אין הראשונה מן המנין דהא לאו בהפלגה חזיתה, וכן כתב ה"ר אברהם, וכזה מורין חכמי הצרפתים בתוספות, וראיה נתנו לדבריהם דהא מתניתין דהיתה למודה לראות יום ט"ו ושינתה פעמים ליום כ' הרי לה ג' ראיות ואינה קובעת עד ששינתה ג' פעמים ליום כ' כדי שיהיו לה שלש הפלגות של עשרים, וא"ת למודה שאני א"כ דקארי ליה לפירכיה דרב מברייתא אמאי קא מייתי לה הא מתני' היא דלמודה שאני, ועוד מדקתני עלה שאין האשה קובעת וסת וכו' ומשמע להו שאין חלוק בין קביעותיה של זו לקביעה אחרת שאינה למודה, והיינו פלוגתייהו דרב סבר כיון דזו לימי החדש היא קובעת אף הראשונה מונין לה שהרי היתה ביום ידוע מן החדש ומתחלתה לדילוג כוונה, ושמואל סבר אם השותה ליום החדש מונין לה הראשונה אבל כיון שדילגה צריכה ג' דילוגין, וק"ל לרב דאמר למודה שאני מתני' אמאי קבעה לה וסת בשינוי של ג' פעמים קמייתא דט"ו שדי לה בתר ראיות ראשונות של ט"ו וליכא אלא

שתי הפלגות, ואיכא למימר לרב לא בעינן אלא שוה מחד צד וכיון שנודעו הפלגותיה של זו בג׳ פעמים כבר הוקבע, וכי קאמר רב למודה שאני משום דהתם ליכא למימר כטעמיה דמשעה ראשונה כוונה לדילוג, דהא לשמואל לא אמרינן למודה שאני כדמתריץ כגון דרגילה למיחזי ליום כ׳ וכו׳ אלמא קמייתא ממנינא כיון דאיכא ג׳ דילוגין מ״מ, [ה״נ לרב כיון דאיכא ג׳ הפלגות מ״מ] קבעה לה דהא איכא היכירא דהפלגה בראשונה דהיינו שלש.

והראשונים הקשו על מה שאמרו שהכל מודים דבהפלגות שלש הפלגות שהן ד׳ ראיות בעינן מההיא דתניא בב״ק ראה שור נגח שור לא נגח שור נגח שור לא נגח שור נגח שור לא נגח נעשה מועד לסירוגין לשוורים ואע״ג דקמייתא לאו בסירוגין הוות מצטרפי, ומתרצין שאני הכא דכיון דאין הפלגה ידועה אלא בשתי ראיות ג׳ הפלגות בעינן דהיינו ד׳ ראיות אבל התם האיכא ג׳ נגיחות, ומיהו לדידי קשיא לי הא דאמרינן בפ״ק (י״א א׳) קפצה וראתה קפצה וראתה (ו)קבעה לה וסת לימים ואוקמה רב אשי כגון דקפץ בחד בשבאי וחזאי וקפץ בחד בשבאי וחזאי ולחד בשבאי אחרינא חזאי בלא קפיצה, ובודאי ימי שבוע לא קבעי וסת אלא בהפלגות שוות כגון דקפץ בחד בשבא ולאחר כ״ב קפץ נמי הכי ולאשוויי ראיות בהפלגה נקט חד בשבא, וקא מני ג׳ ראיות וקאמר דקבעה, ואיכא למימר התם לאו לאשמועינן בכמה הוסת נקבע אתא ומשו״ה לא דק ונקט תלת ראיות בלחוד, דאי לדברי רבי קבעה לה וסת אפילו להפלגות ואי לרשב״ג אפיך סדרא מחד בשבא לחד בירחי.

וחכמי הצרפתים מוסיפין שאף היום גורם וסת כדאשכחן בשור המועד שבת ושבת ושבת נעשה מועד לשבתות הלכך חד בשבא וחד בשבא וחד בשבא קבעה וסת לימי השבוע, נמצאו לדבריהם ג׳ דרכים בוסתות של ימים קביעות היום והחדש וההפלגה, ולדברי הרב ר׳ אברהם שנים הן.

וקורא אני על עצמי מקרא זה (תהלים קל״ט) פליאה דעת ממני נשגבה לא אוכל לה, וכי הוסת מזל יום גורם או מזל שעה גורם שיהא תלוי ביום השבוע או ביום החדש, שהרי להפלגות שוות הדין נותן כן שכבר נתמלאת סאתה של זו וכן דרכן של נשים כולן, וכן של אנשים בחלאים של הפסקות שהן באין בהפסקות שוות או בשעת המולד של לבנה ובמלואה אלא שיהא שיפורא גורם תימא הוא, ולפי דעתי בעניותי לא יפה כוונו הראשונים בחלוקי הוסתות שאני אומר אין וסת אלא להפלגה שוה לפי שהאורח בזמנו הוא בא מתמלא ונופצת לזמן הקבוע שכן טבען של בני אדם.

וזו שאמרו בט״ו בחדש זה וי״ו בחדש זה וי״ז בחדש זה בחדשים השוים הוא או במלאים או בחסרים וההפלגה שלה שוה היא ליום ל״ב, והדילוג שהורו בו אינו אלא דילוג הימים לומר שהיא קובעת וסת לדלג לי״ח לי״ט ולכ׳ וכן לעולם.

ולעיקר המחלוקת של רב ושמואל לפי שהוסת הקבוע להפלגה שוה ולימים השוים כגון מט״ו לט״ו בג׳ ראיות הוא נקבע כשור המועד שבשלש נגיחות נעשה מועד, ואלו נגח בט״ו לחדש ג׳ פעמים וכן בהפלגה שאין בה חדש מכ׳ לכ׳ בג׳ נגיחות הוא מתיעד דאפי׳ בסירוגין נעשה מועד בג׳ נגיחות כמו שפרשתי, וכשנגח בט״ו בחדש זה וי״ו בזה וי״ז בזה אינו נעשה מועד לשמואל עד (שהוא) [שישלש] בדילוג, וכן בוסתות בג׳ ראיות קבעה אותו ואע״ג דקמייתא לאו בהפלגה חזיתה, שהרי אף וסת הדילוג וסת של הפלגה הוא לדברינו ואין יום החדש גורמת קביעותו

כלל וטעמא דאיכא דילוג הא לאו הכי קבעה בג' ראיות וכדאמר רב אשי בפ"ק ואע"ג דראיה קמייתא נמי לאו בהפלגה הות אפ"ה מודה שמואל שקובעת אותו בג' ראיות, שהרי מתחלה כיון שראתה בט"ו בחדש זה [וחזרה וראתה בט"ו בחדש זה] נכרת הפלגת וסתה מעתה וכן בכל הפלגה שתפליג בשתי ראיות ראשונות נודע וסתה לפיכך ראשונה מן המנין, אבל וסת הדילוג כשראתה בט"ו בחדש זה וי"ו בחדש זה לא יודע וסתה של זו שהרי הפליגה ולא דילגה כלל ומנין לנו שלדילוג היא מכוונת שמא תראה בחדש הבא בי"ו והוסת שוה, וכשראתה למחרתו והוסת של דילוג הוא היינו שלישית ואינה ראויה לקבוע בתחלתה, והיינו דקאמר קמייתא לא בדילוג חזיתה כלומר בהפלגה ראשונה עדיין לא היה לה כלל וסת של דילוג אבל בהפלגה שוה מתחלתה כשחזרה וראתה (ויודע) [נודע] וסתה, [ואי קשיא לך מתני' דקתני] שינתה ליום עשרים דבעיא ג' פעמים, למודה שאני לכו"ע [דכיון] דלט"ו היתה למודה לראות בקביעות הך ראיה בתרייתא בתר ראשונה שדינן לה ועכשיו ששנתה ליום אחר לגמרי כמי שמתחלת לראות דמיא, וכי קס"ד לרב דלא אמרינן למודה שאני ולשמואל נמי לית ליה, במדלגת בלחוד היא משום דעכשיו נמי אינו שינוי גמור אלא על הוסת הראשון עצמו מדלגת והולכת מט"ו לי"ו ומראיה דוסת ראשון ניכר וסת שני של דילוג לרב כמו שפי'.

וראיה לדבר ההיא דאמרינן בב"ק נגח שור שור שור וחמור וגמל מהו האי שור קמא בתר שוורים שדינן ליה ואכתי לשוורים הוא דאיעד לשאר מיני לא איעד או דילמא בתר חמור וגמל שדינן ליה ואיעד לכולהו מיני, וה"נ אי חזיא ט"ו וט"ו וט"ו תלת זימני והדר דילגה י"ו וי"ז היינו בעיין, אבל למודה לראות ט"ו וט"ו ד' זימני כיון דאי נמי שדית בתרייתא בתר הני דדילוג אכתי קבעה לט"ו שדינן כולהו בתר מעיקרא דסרכא נקט, וכן נמי בשוורים שור שור ושור ושור וחמור וגמל שור בתרייתא בתר שוורים שדינן ליה דהא איעד להו והשתא הוא דקא מיעד נפשיה לשאר מיני, זהו הדרך שנראה לי בדברים הללו.

ועדיין לבי מהסס מה טעם אמרו בשור המועד נגח בט"ו בחדש זה וי"ו בחדש זה וכו' דאלמא מתיעד הוא בדילוג ובהפלגה וכי מזל יום גורם נגיחות, שאפילו בהפלגה שוה אין הטעם מתחוור בכך כמו שהוא מתחוור בוסתות, אלא י"ל שראו חכמים בכל נגיחות שהן לזמן שוה כגון בין בסירוגין בין בדילוג שאין מתיעד אלא לאותו ענין שעשה לנגיחותיו שכך וסתו של זה ליגח ושמא משלשים לשלשים מוסיף כח ונוגח, וכן כיוצא בדבר זה לעולם למה שהשוה הוא מתיעד ולא לדבר אחר.

ומדברי הרב ר' משה הספרדי ז"ל משמע שאין לו קביעות וסת אלא בהפלגה שוה שאם היה סובר כדברי הרב ר' אברהם או כדעת חכמי התוס' ז"ל היה לו לפרש בחיבורו, והוא ה"ר משה ז"ל פסק כשמואל בדילוג משום דאמרינן דיקא נמי וש"מ, ומסתברא כותיה, וה"ר אברהם ז"ל דן בה להחמיר, ובעל נפש יחוש להחמיר בענין הוסתות בין כדברינו בין כדברי הראשונים עד יערה עלינו או על אחרים רוח ממרום להכריע איזו היא הדרך הישרה שיבור לו האדם, ואם ימצא בחבורי הגאונים או בתשובותיהם ענין מורה על אחת מאלו הדרכים בה ראוי ללכת ולצאת בעקבותיהם.

מהא דקתני בברייתא שינתה לי"ז הותר י"ו ונאסר ט"ו וי"ז. ולא מיתסר נמי י"ח דנימא זו כבר דילגה ונחוש בפעם אחת לוסת של דילוג, ש"מ שאין חוששין לוסת של דילוג כלל עד שתקבענו לגמרי, וזה כתוב בתוספות וכן הורה ה"ר אברהם ז"ל.

היתה למודה להיות רואה יום כ׳ ושנתה ליום ל׳. מדקתני האי לישנא ש״מ דוסת הפלגה הוא דקבעה מכ׳ לכ׳, והשתא ק״ל כיון דקי״ל מראיה לראיה מנינן ולא לפי מנין הראוי כדאיתא בשלהי בנות כותים (ל״ט ב׳) כשהגיע יום כ׳ ולא ראתה ומנו עשרה לתשלום [ל׳] ולא ראתה הגיע יום כ׳ וראתה דקתני כי אורח בזמנו בא מאי נינהו הא ליכא הפלגה דעשרים השתא, ואיכא למימר הכא מנינן למנין הראוי ויום מ׳ לראיה אחרונה זו היא יום כ׳ דקתני, שאם ראתה בעונות הראשונות ביום זה תראה, ואפילו הרחיקה יותר מונין לראיה אחרונה שפסקה בו עכשיו (ולא) [וכל] שאלו ראתה מאותה ראיה ואילך בעונות של כ׳ יארע לה ראיתה ביום [זה] אמרינן אורח בזמנו בא דהכא רגלים לדבר שלמנין הראוי חוזרת, אלא שכל זמן שרואה בוסת השינוי מונין לישן מאותה ראיה, אבל מכיון שהפסיקתו וחזרה לראות ביום אחר אם למנין הראוי חזרה מונין לוסת הראשון לפי אותו מנין ואין אומרין הפלגה של מ׳ היא זו שרגלים לדבר, אבל הרב ר׳ אברהם בר דוד ז״ל פי׳ לזו בוסת החדש לפי דעתו ולמודה ליום כ׳ בחדש ושנתה ליום ל׳ בחדש קתני, ולפי פי׳ בוסת של הפלגה אין אומרים חזר הוסת למקומו עד שתראה עכשיו ותחזור ותראה לסוף עשרים שחזר האורח בזמנו.

שולחן ערוך יורה דעה הלכות נדה סימן קפט סעיף ו – כשם שקובעת וסת בהפלגה מימים שוים ושאינם שוים, כך קובעת בימי החדש ובימי השבוע שוים ושאינם שוים. כיצד, ראתה ג״פ באחד בשבת או בה׳ בשבת, או באחד בניסן ובאחד באייר ובאחד בסיון, או בה׳ בניסן ובה׳ באייר ובה׳ בסיון, קבעה לה וסת באחד בשבת או בה׳ בו, ובאחד בחודש או בה׳ בו, אף על פי שאחד מלא ואחד חסר, אין מדקדקין בכך.

תלמוד בבלי מסכת נדה דף סד עמוד א – איתמר, ראתה יום חמשה עשר לחדש זה, ויום ט״ז לחדש זה, ויום שבעה עשר לחדש זה. רב אמר: קבעה לה וסת לדילוג. ושמואל אמר: עד שתשלש בדילוג.

שולחן ערוך יורה דעה הלכות נדה סימן קפט סעיף ז – כיצד קובעת בימי החדש בדילוג, כגון שראתה בט״ו בניסן וט״ז באייר וי״ז בסיון, לא קבעה וסת עד שתראה בי״ח בתמוז, שאין ראיה ראשונה מצטרפת, כיון שאין ההפלגות שוות. ומיהו אם היה לה וסת קודם שהתחילה, ואח״כ שינתה וראתה בדילוג ג׳ פעמים, קבעה וסת בדילוג. לפי שאף הראשונה בדילוג ראתה אותה, שדילגה מוסת הקבוע לה (רמב״ם ורמב״ן כשמואל וטור לדעת רא״ש אבל בפרק שור שנגח ד׳ וה׳ פסק רא״ש כרב וכן הוא ברמזים שם) וי״א שאע״פ שלא ראתה אלא בט״ו בניסן וי״ו באייר וי״ז בסיון, קבעה וסת וחוששת לי״ח בתמוז וי״ט באב, וכן לעולם. ויש לחוש לדבריהם ולהחמיר.

תלמוד בבלי מסכת נדה דף סג עמוד א, דף סג עמוד ב – תנינא חדא זימנא: כל אשה שיש לה וסת – דיה שעתה! התם – בוסתות דיומי, הכא – בוסתות דגופא, כדקתני: אלו הן וסתות – היתה מפהקת, מעטשת, וחוששת בפי כריסה, ובשפולי מעיה, ושופעת, שופעת? הא שפעה ואזלא! אמר עולא בריה דרב עלאי: בשופעת דם טמא מתוך דם טהור.

תלמוד בבלי מסכת נדה דף יא עמוד א – א"ר הונא: קפצה וראתה, קפצה וראתה, קפצה וראתה – קבעה לה וסת. למאי? אילימא לימים – הא כל יומא דלא קפיץ לא חזאי! אלא לקפיצות, והתניא: כל שתקבענה מחמת אונס – אפילו כמה פעמים לא קבעה וסת! מאי לאו – לא קבעה וסת כלל! לא, לא קבעה וסת לימים לחודייהו ולקפיצות לחודייהו, אבל קבעה לה וסת לימים ולקפיצות. לימים לחודייהו פשיטא! אמר רב אשי: כגון דקפיץ בחד בשבת וחזאי, וקפיץ בחד בשבת וחזאי, [ובשבת קפצה ולא חזאי], ולחד בשבת חזאי בלא קפיצה; מהו דתימא: איגלאי מילתא למפרע דיומא הוא דקגרים ולא קפיצה, קמ"ל דקפיצה נמי דאתמול גרמא, והאי דלא חזאי – משום דאכתי לא מטא זמן קפיצה. לישנא אחרינא, א"ר הונא: קפצה וראתה, קפצה וראתה, קפצה וראתה – קבעה לה וסת לימים ולא לקפיצות. היכי דמי? א"ר אשי: דקפיץ בחד בשבת וחזאי, וקפיץ בחד בשבת וחזאי, (ובשבת קפצה ולא חזאי), ולחד בשבת (אחרינא) חזאי בלא קפיצה – דהתם איגלאי מילתא דיומא הוא דקא גרים.

תלמוד בבלי מסכת נדה דף סג עמוד ב – וכן כיוצא בהן לאתויי מאי? אמר רבה בר עולא: לאתויי אשה שראשה כבד עליה, ואבריה כבדים עליה, ורותתת, וגוסה, אמר רב הונא בר חייא אמר שמואל: הרי אמרו לימים – שנים, לוסתות – אחת, למה שלא מנו חכמים – שלשה. למה שלא מנו חכמים – לאתויי מאי? אמר רב יוסף: לאתויי ראשה כבד עליה, ואבריה כבדין עליה, ורותתת, וגוסה. א"ל אביי: מאי קא משמע לן? מתני' היא, דהא פרשה רבה בר עולא! אלא אמר אביי: לאתויי – אכלה שום וראתה, ואכלה בצלים וראתה, כססה פלפלים וראתה. אמר רב יוסף: לא שמיע לי הא שמעתא. אמר ליה אביי: את אמריתה ניהלן, ואהא אמריתה ניהלן: היתה למודה להיות רואה יום חמשה עשר ושינתה ליום עשרים – זה וזה אסורין. שלש פעמים ליום עשרים – הותר יום חמשה עשר, וקבעה לה יום עשרים, שאין אשה קובעת לה וסת – עד שתקבענה שלש פעמים. ואמרת לן עלה אמר רב יהודה אמר שמואל: זו דברי ר"ג בר רבי שאמר משום רשב"ג, אבל חכמים אומרים: ראתה – אינה צריכה לא לשנות ולא לשלש.

תוספות מסכת נדה דף סג עמוד ב – אכלה שום וראתה – הואיל ועל ידי מעשה הם אינו וסת גמור ולא הוה בכלל דמתני' וא"ת ואמאי לא קאמר נמי קפצה וראתה דהוו נמי על ידי מעשה ויש לומר דאינה קובעת וסת לקפיצות לחודיהו כדאמר בפרק קמא (לעיל יא.) דכל שתקבענה מחמת אונס אפי' כמה פעמים לא קבעה אבל אכלה שום לא חשיב אונס כמו טורח של קפיצה שאין הראייה באה על ידי טורח אלא ממילא.

שולחן ערוך יורה דעה הלכות נדה סימן קפט סעיף כג – כל אלו הוסתות שנקבעים על ידי מקרה אין אחד קובע עם חבירו, אלא כל שפיהקה שלש פעמים וראתה, קבעה וסת. אבל אם פיהקה פעם אחד ונתעטשה שתי פעמים, אין מצטרפים. הגה: אכלה שום וראתה, אכלה בצל וראתה, אכלה פלפלין וראתה, יש אומרים שקבעה לה וסת לראיה ע"י כל אכילת דברים חמים. (הרא"ש פרק האשה ומרדכי ריש שבועות). וי"א שכל זה שתראה ע"י מאכל דינו כמו שתראה ע"י קפיצה ושאר מעשה שהיא עושה, שמקרי ראיה ע"י אונס ואינה קובעת וסת אלא עם הימים. (ב"י

לדעת הרשב"א) וי"א שדינו כוסת שתראה על ידי מקרה שבגופה וקובעת אותו אפילו בלא ימים שוים. (ב"י בשם תוספות).

משנה מסכת נדה ס"ג – היתה למודה להיות רואה יום ט"ו ושינתה להיות רואה ליום כ' זה וזה אסורין שינתה פעמים ליום כ' זה וזה אסורין שינתה ג"פ ליום כ' הותר ט"ו וקבעה לה יום כ' שאין אשה קובעת לה וסת עד שתקבענה ג"פ ואינה מטהרת הוסת עד שתעקר ממנה ג"פ.

חוות דעת סימן קפד סעיף ה – ואף שבכל דבר שתלוי ביום ובלילה חשבינן יום משעת עמוד השחר כדמוכח במגילה (ד' כ') ובכל הפוסקים. וכאן חשבינן אותה לילה דאם ראתה קודם הנץ החמה אף שהוא אחר עלות השחר אינה אסורה רק בלילה ולא ביום אפשר דקים להו לחז"ל דלענין וסת תלוי בהילוך החמה והנץ החמה גורם הראייה וא"כ אפשר דאחר שקיעת החמה חשיב לילה לענין זה אף קודם צ"ה.

פתחי תשובה יורה דעה סימן קפט:י – חוששת – עבה"ט בשם ט"ז דגם כאן חוששת גם ליום א' דר"ח. וכבר חלקו עליו הס"ט והח"ד דכאן שראתה בכ' בניסן ליכא חשש עו"ב שהוא מטעם הפלגה וכבר הפסיקה בראיית כ' ולא מיבעיא לדעת הב"ח המובא בבה"ט ס"ק שאח"ז דבכל וסת הפלגה כשהפסיקה בראיה הוי החשבון מהראיה הסמוכה ודאי דאף לענין עו"ב הדין כן אלא אפילו לדעת הט"ז דפליג שם מ"מ בעונה בינונית דהטעם הוא כמ"ש הר"ן משום דכי לעולם לא תראה ודאי דהחשבון מהראיה הסמוכה וצדקו דברי הב"ח ע"ש ובענין הפלוגתא שבין הט"ז והש"ך בעונה בינונית מאי היא דדעת הט"ז דעו"ב לאו היינו וסת החודש והיא יום ל' לראייתה ואם החודש חסר שניהם הם ליום אחד אבל אם החודש מלא חוששת גם ליום הקודם משום עו"ב. ודעת הש"ך דעו"ב לעולם הוא יום החודש ושיעור עו"ב היינו יום ל"א כסתם חודש דהוא מלא. הנה הח"צ בתשובה סי' קי"ד האריך להשיג על הש"ך והסכים עם הט"ז וכן הסכים הכרתי ופלתי ע"ש ועי' ח"ד שהסכים ג"כ עמהם בהא דעו"ב לאו היינו וסת החודש אמנם לא כדבריהם דהוא יום ל' רק בזה עיקר כהש"ך דהוא יום ל"א וא"כ הוא להיפך דאם החודש מלא שניהם ליום אחד הם ואם החודש חסר חוששת גם ליום שאחריו משום עו"ב ע"ש. ודע דאף לדעת הש"ך ע"כ צ"ל דחילוק יש בין עו"ב לוסת החודש דאילו בוסת החודש כל זמן שלא נקבע ועבר זמנו ולא בדקה מותרת בלא בדיקה כדמשמע בסעיף ד' ובעו"ב אסורה עד שתבדוק כמבואר שם ומשכחת לה וסת החודש בלא עו"ב כגון אם ראתה בינתיים או שיש לה וסת אחר קבוע ואח"כ שינתה ליום אחר וכ"כ האחרונים.

ש"ך יורה דעה סימן קפד:ז – אותו היום כו' – כתב הג"מ בשם אביאסף וכמה עונה יום או לילה ביומי ניסן ותשרי וחצי יום וחצי לילה ביומי תמוז וטבת עכ"ל וב"י דחה דבריו מאחר שהפוסקים לא הזכירוה וגם לישנא דש"ס משמע דלא קפיד אלא על היום או על הלילה לא על השעות כו' והמעדני מלך דפ"ק דנדה והב"ח השיגו עליו דדברי האביאסף נכונים ומבוארים בש"ס פרק תינוקת (דף ס"ה ע"ב) עכ"ד וכן מצאתי בראב"ן סימן שי"ח כהאביאסף ומה שלא הזכירוהו הפוסקים אין ראיה דבסתם יום ובסתם לילה מיירי ואה"נ דבתקופת תמוז וטבת יש לחשוב

שעות זמניות וכה״ג מצינו בכמה דוכתי בש״ס ופוסקים כגון לענין ק״ש בא״ח ר״ס נ״ח ולענין חמץ בע״פ בא״ח סימן תמ״ג ס״א בהג״ה ולענין חישוב תקופות וכה״ג טובי ובא״ז כתב וז״ל פורש ממנה כל אותו יום והלילה שלפניו וכן להיפך עכ״ל ועיין בראב״ן סימן שי״ח ובש״ס פרק האשה סוף דף ס״ג ודוק נ״ל דדעת ראב״ן דודאי אם יש לה וסת קבוע ביום כגון שיש לה וסת לראות לעולם בתחילתו או לעולם באמצעיתו או לעולם בסופו א״צ לפרוש אלא אותו היום ולא לפניו ובהכי איירי בש״ס ופוסקים אבל אם רגילה לראות ביום ואין לה שעה קבועה רק לפעמים בתחלתו ולפעמים באמצעיתו ולפעמים בסופו א״כ כל היום וסתה ודמי כאילו היה וסתה כל היום ודאי דאשה שוסתה כל היום צריכה לפרוש כל לילה שלפניו ובהכי מיירי הא״ז ובזה מיושב שפיר מה שהקשה הב״י דהא״ז הוא נגד הש״ס ולפעד״נ להוציא מן הש״ס כמ״ש ודו״ק גם הב״ח כתב שמשמע שהירא דבר ה׳ נוהג כהא״ז וגם בהגהת ש״ד סימן ז׳ הביא דברי הא״ז במסקנא וכ״כ בא״ו של מהרי״ל בשם מהרי״ל.

דרישה יו״ד סימן קפד ס״ק ב – [אם הוא ביום פורש ממנו אותו היום כולו וכתבו הגהות מיימוניות בשם אביאסף וכמה עונה יום או לילה ביומי ניסן ותשרי וחצי יום וחצי לילה בימי תמוז וטבת עכ״ל ובית יוסף הביאו וכתב עליו ז״ל ונראה שטעמו משום דמשמע ליה דשיעור עונה הוי י״ב שעות מהשעות שהן כ״ד ביום ובלילה ומ״מ נ״ל שאין לחוש לכך מאחר שהפוסקים לא הזכירוהו וגם לישנא דהגמרא משמע דלא קפיד אלא על היום או על הלילה לא על השעות ולא הזכירו שעות בפרק האשה אלא משום פלוגתא דר׳ יוסי דאיתא התם עד כאן לשון בית יוסף וכו׳. ולדעת הגהות מיימוניות הנ״ל שמצריך שתים עשרה שעות גמורות היה נראה לי לומר דאם וסתה ביום בתקופת טבת שהיום אינו ארוך אלא תשע שעות כשבאה לחוש פעם שנית אינה חוששת בתחלת היום אלא צריכה לפרוש שעה ומחצה קודם היום עד שעה ומחצה בתחלת הלילה וכו׳.

ספר אור זרוע ח״א – הלכות נדה סימן שנח – סוף פרק האשה תני חדא ר׳ יהודה אוסרה לאחר וסתה ומתירה לפני וסתה ותני׳ אידך ר׳ יהוד׳ אוסרה לפני וסתה ומתירה לאחר ווסתה ל״ק הא דרגילה למחזי בתחלת יממא והא דרגיל׳ למחזי בסוף ליליא פי׳ הא דרגילה למחזי בתחלת יממא אסור כל היום לאחר ווסתה ומותרת כל הלילה לפני ווסתה אמר רבא הלכ׳ כר׳ יהודה. פי׳ רשב״ם דכל י״ב שעות אסורה אם ווסתה בלילה בין בתחלת׳ בין באמצעית׳ בין בסופה כל הלילה כולה אסורה וכן אם ווסתה ביום כל היום אסור. ומי אמר רבא הכי והתניא והזרתם את בני ישראל מטומאתם א״ר יאשיה מכאן אזהרה לבני ישראל שיפרשו מנשותיהם סמוך לווסתם וכמה אמר רבא עונה מאי לאו עונה אחריתי. פי׳ שאם ווסתה ביום אסורה כל היום וכל הלילה שלפניו ור׳ יהודה לא אסר אלא עונת ווסתה וקשי׳ דרבא אדרבא ומשני לא אותה עונה. פי׳ כי אמר רבא נמי ה״ק אותה עונה בין לפניה בין לאחרי׳ דהיינו סמוך לוסתה הלכך אשה שווסתה ביום אסורה כל הלילה ומותרת כל היום. ובה״ג כתב דרגילא דחזיא בסוף ליליא מאורתא אסיר חליף ליליא ולא חזיא בימימא שריא וכן בסוף יממא ותחלת ליליא. וכבר היו שפירשו דדוקא ביושב בביתו צריך לפרוש סמוך לווסתה עונה. אבל ביוצא לדרך לדבר הרשות אינו פורש ומשמש עמה. אבל לדבר מצוה לא מחייב לפוקדה אפי׳ בלא סמוך לווסתה כי היכי דלא ליטריד

וימנע ממצוה. וראייתם דאמר פ׳ הבא על יבמתו אמר ריב״ל חייב אדם לפקוד את אשתו בשעה שיוצא לדרך שנאמ׳ וידעת כי שלום אהלך ופקדת וגו׳. והא מהכא נפקא מהתם נפקא ואל אישך תשוקתך מלמד שהאשה משתוקקת על בעלה בשעה שיוצא לדרך אמר רב יוסף לא נצרכה אלא סמוך לווסתה. פי׳ שאפי׳ הכי פוקדה בתשמיש ואע״ג דאמור רבנן חייב אדם לפרוש מאשתו סמוך לווסתה וכמה אמר רבא עונה. וה״מ לדבר הרשות פי׳ שחייב לפוקדה כשיוצא לדרך אבל לדבר מצוה מטריד ואינו חייב לפוקדה. ופי׳ ר״ת דשיבוש הוא בידם דבכל הספרים הישנים גרסי׳ לא נצרכה אלא לאשתו נדה והם בעבור שמפרשים דהאי פקידה היינו פקידת תשמיש להכי שיבשו הספרים. ומפרש ר״ת דחד קרא משמע שחייב לפקוד את אשתו ויבוא עלי׳ וידבר על לבה עונה שלימה. וקרא אחרינא משמע שאפי׳ באשתו נדה יש לפוקדה. (וכמה אמר רבא עונה) שאע״פ שאסורה בתשמיש שמחה ותענוג הוא לה הואיל ורוצה לצאת לדרך כדאמר בעירובין הישן בקילעא שאיש ואשתו ישנים בה עליו הכתוב אומר ונשי עמי תגרשון מבית תענוגי׳ ואמר רב יוסף התם אפי׳ באשתו נדה. אלמא שמחה היא לה. התם נמי צריך לפוקדה אפי׳ היא נדה. כמה אמר רבא עונה כדקאמר פ׳ תינוקת מניחן תחת צינור שמימיו מקלחין וכמה (אמר רבא) עונה וטובא עונה איכא בתלמוד שאינה תשמיש. ומה שהגיהו בספרים לא נצרכה אלא סמוך לווסתה שיבוש גדול הגיהו לפי שסברו דפקידה היינו תשמיש. חדא דמשבועות מוכח סמוך לווסתה דאורייתא דתניא פ׳ ידיעות הטומאה ומביאין אשם תלוי על עשה ועל ל״ת שבנדה וכו׳ עד הוי בה רבא במאי אילימא סמוך לווסתה וכו׳ הרי משמע דסמוך לווסתה דאורייתא. ועוד דקאמר וה״מ לדבר הרשות וכי בשביל דבר הרשות עקרי׳ והזרתם את בני ישראל ומוקמ׳ סמוך לווסתה אדרבה ידחה דבר הרשות ואל יצא לדבר הרשות סמוך לווסתה ויתקיימו שני המקראות הללו. אבל לפי׳ ר״ת אתי שפיר שאדם רוצה לצאת לדבר הרשות ישוב לביתו ויפקוד את אשתו אבל לדבר מצוה לא ישוב לפקוד את אשתו דילמא מטריד וממנע ולא עביד מצוה אלא ממקום שהוא שם ילך לדבר מצוה ואל ישוב לביתו לפקוד ומשום הכי מייתי בסמוך התם האוהב את אשתו כגופו ומכבדה יותר מגופו כו׳. ומורי אב״י העזר״י אמר לי שרגילים לפרוש סמוך לוסתה כ״ד שעות שאם רגילה לראות ביום פורש ממנה כל הלילה שלפניו ואם רגילה לראות בלילה פורש ממנה כל הלילה והיום שלפניה. והא דע״פ דאמר שלשה דברים צוה רבי ישמעאל ב״ר יוסי את רבי עד אשתך טבלה אל תזקק עמה לילה הראשון ההיא בנדה דאורייתא ומשום חומרא דר׳ זירא כדאמר התם מ״ט אמר רבא הואיל והוחזק מעיינה פתוח דילמא שפעה זיבה והא בזמן הזה ליכא שהרי היא מונה ז׳ לבד מיום ראייתה.

שו״ת חתם סופר חלק ב (יורה דעה) סימן קעט – וע״ד הדין שאם יהי׳ ליל טבילתה בעונה הסמוך לוסתה אם צריך לנהוג כחומרת הא״ז והראב״ן ופ׳ כן הש״ך לפרוש עונה לפני עונת הראי׳ הנה הש״ך כ׳ שיש להוציא כן מש״ס ובנה״כ ביאר דבריו איך הוציא כן וכ׳ עליו מנחת יעקב שדבריו אינם מוכרחים אלא שהי׳ להראב״ן גרסא אחרת בש״ס ולפי גי׳ שלפנינו ליתא לדינו וכ״כ בס״ט שהאחרונים חלקו על הש״ך ומשמע דס״ל להקל כאחרונים החולקים ע״ש.

ועיינתי בראב״ן סי׳ שי״ח וז״ל תני׳ והזהרתם וכו׳ וכמה אמר רבא עונה וכמה עונה אמר ר״י או יום או לילה שאם וסתה ביום יפרוש בלילה שלפניו ואם וסתה בלילה יפרוש ביום שלפני

לילה בזמן תקופת ניסן ותשרי שהיום והלילה שוין אבל תקופת תמוז וטבת שאין יום ולילה שוין חצי יום וחצי לילה לפני הוסת עכ"ל והנה אין כאן גירס' אחרת בגמרא אלא מדנפשי' הוסיף ביאור דעונה שלפני עונות הראי' קאמר ומייתי ג"כ לכאן ש"ס דר"פ התינוקות דחצי יום וחצי לילה קאמר ואין כאן שינוי גי' כלל ואם הוכחות הש"ך אינה מכרחת א"כ ע"כ הי' לראב"ן וא"ז ראי' אחרת ואנחנו לא נדע לדחות גאונים בגילי דחיטתא.

והנה רואה שראב"ן מחמיר תרי חומרא בחדא דוכתא חומרת האביאסף וחומרת הא"ז חצי יום וחצי לילה ועוד עונה שלפניו ונלע"ד לפי מה דס"ל דהאמור בר"פ התינוקות למיחשב חצי יום וחצי לילה שייך גם הכא בפרישת סמוך לוסתה וא"כ חשבינן כל אשה מרגע ראייתה מעת לעת חצי יום וחצי לילה כגון שתראה אום עשר אוהר בשעה עשר ביום תחשב עד אותו שעה בלילה וכן כולם והנה אמרי' ר"פ התינוקות ר"ג מקיל לענין דם בתולה ויהיב לה לילה וחצי יום ולחד שינוי' משום דכתובה מגהי בה טפי ע"כ הקיל בלא פלוג להוסיף חצי יום על ליל בעילת מצוה וס"ל לראב"ן ק"ו להחמיר דנימא לא פלוג וכיון שאין כל הזמנים שווים לפעמים על ד' שעות ויהיה עונתה מד' שעות עד ד' שעות ולפעמים מאוחר ולפעמים מוקדם א"כ לעולם נוסף להחמיר עונה שלפני' משום לא פלוג מק"ו דר"ג הקיל בעונת בתולים זהו י"ל ס' הראב"ן והאביאסף שלא החמיר לפרוש גם עונה שלפניו דס"ל להקל כשינוי קמא דלי' לי' הך סברא מכתובה מגהי בה טפי כן נלע"ד.

וכיון שזכינו לעמוד ע"ד רבותינו ואיננו אלא משום לא פלוג בשגם וסתו' דרבנן ואפי' להרא"ה בבד"ה דס"ל עונה הסמוך לוסתה חמירה מוסת גופי' דשמא תראה חיישי' טפי והגאון נב"י כיון סברא זו מדעתו והנה היא קדומה בהרא"ה מ"מ היינו בוסת קבוע ג"פ אבל וסת שאינו קבוע כגון אתתא דא שמשנית וסתה תמיד וחוששת ליום ראי' שלה הוה עונה סמוך לוסתה דרבנן א"כ יש להקל בלא פלוג דידי' ולהתיר בעונה הסמוכה לעונת ראי' כדי שלא תתגרש ויקיים הבעל פ"ו והרופא לשבורי לב ומחבש לעצבותם יסיר כל חולי ומדוה וירפא שבר בת עמו מהרה הכ"ד א"נ. פ"ב יום ב' ח"י טבת תקצ"א לפ"ק.

רבי עקיבא איגר יורה דעה סימן קפד – (ש"ך סק"ז) כגון לענין ק"ש. זהו תמוה הא אדרבה שם אזלינן בתר היום דתמיד הזמן עד רביע בין בקיץ בין בחורף.

(בא"ד) וסתה כל היום וודאי. לפענ"ד ערבך ערבא צריך דבפשוטו י"ל דגם בזה א"צ לפרוש בלילה שקודם דחכמים לא אסרו רק אותו היום שהיה בו הראיה. הן שהיה הראיה זמן מעט הן שהיה הראיה כל היום.

בעלי הנפש שער תיקון הוסתות סימן א – והיכא דרגילה למיחזי בהנץ החמה גופיה אי נמי דלא קים לה במילתא שפיר ולא ידעה אי קודם הנץ החמה אי לאחר הנץ החמה, ואיכא מאן דאמר דנקיטינן בה לחומרא ואסורה כל הלילה וכל היום ג. ואיכא מאן דאמר כיון דוסתות דרבנן כל שכן סמוך לוסת, הלכך הוה ליה ספיקא דרבנן ולקולא ולא חיישינן אלא ליום שהוא ודאי בימי נדתה. ומסתברא כוותיה. מיהו להההוא גונא מיהת איבעי ליה לאיניש למיחש ד כי היכי דלא ליתי לידי איסור נדה.

והיכא דרגילה למיחזי ראיה מרובה מקודם הנץ החמה עד לאחר הנץ החמה ודאי. איכא מאן דאמר אסורה בלילה וביום. מאי טעמא, כיון דההיא שעתא כולה שעת הוסת היא, ואפילו לר׳ יוסי דאמר (נדה סג ב) אף ימים ושעות וסתות, מודה דשעת הוסת מיהת אסורה לשמש בכולה, הלכך לר׳ יהודה דאמר כל עונה שלה ומפני שעת הוסת כל העונה נאסרת, כל היום וכל הלילה אסורה שהרי וסתה בלילה וביום הוא. ואיכא מאן דאמר דכל כי האי גוונא בתר תחילת הוסת אזלינן ולא מתסרא אלא בלילה. ואע״ג דכולה שעת הוסת אסורה לשמש ואפילו לר׳ יוסי, הני מילי לשעת הוסת בלחוד, אבל לאסור את שלפניו ואת שלאחריו לא אסרינן אלא לההיא עונה דתחלת הוסת קאי בגוה. ואם בדקה קודם הנץ החמה ולא ראתה אסורה לשמש כל אותה שעה אבל כל היום מותרת, לפי שעיקר הוסת בתחלתו הוא כדאמרינן לקמן שאין האשה קובעת לה וסת בתוך ימי נדתה, אלמא כלהו ימי נדה בתר ראיה קמייתא שדינן להו, והכא נמי סוף ראיה בתר תחילתה שדינן להו. ואנא אכרענא בהא מילתא כי הא סברא בתרא מהא דתניא (נדה סג ב) היתה למודה להיות רואה עם הנץ החמה אינה אסורה אלא עם הנץ החמה דברי ר׳ יוסי ורבי יהודה אומר כל הלילה שלה, ואוקימנא להא דרגילה למחזי בסוף לילה. והא ודאי כל היכא דתני עם לאלתר משמע, ואי ס״ד דכה״ג אסורה ביום ובלילה היכי קתני כל הלילה שלה, והא אי אפשר דלא עיילא ראיה בתוך הנץ החמה ותתסר בימָמא ובליליא, ועוד סתמא קתני להיות רואה ולא מפליג בין ראיה מרובה לראיה מועטת. הילכך אינה אסורה אלא עונת הלילה ושעת הוסת בלבד.

רא״ש מסכת נדה פרק ט סימן ב׳ – כתב הראב״ד ז״ל אם רגילה לראות בהנץ החמה ולא קים לה שפיר אי קודם הנץ או לאחר הנץ יש מחמירין ואוסרין כל הלילה וכל היום וי״א כיון דוסתות דרבנן כל שכן סמוך לוסתה הלכך הוה ליה ספק דרבנן ולקולא ולא חיישינן אלא ליום שהוא ודאי בימי נדתה והכריח הוא להקל ואם רגילה לראות ראיה מרובה מקודם הנץ החמה עד אחר הנץ איכא מאן דאמר אסורה בלילה וביום משום דההיא שעתא כולה שעת הוסת הוא. ואפי׳ ר׳ יוסי דאמר ימים ושעות וסתות מודה דשעת הוסת מיהת אסורה לשמש בכולה. הלכך לרבי יהודה דאמר כל העונה כולה ומפני שעת הוסת נאסרה כל העונה כל היום וכל הלילה אסורה. שהרי וסתה הוא ביום ובלילה. ואיכא מאן דאמר דכי האי גוונא בתר תחילת הוסת אזלינן ולא מיתסרא אלא בלילה. אע״ג דכל שעת הוסת אסורה לשמש ואפי׳ לר׳ יוסי. הני מילי לשעת הוסת עצמה אבל לאסור את שלפניו ושלאחריו לא אסרינן אלא ההיא עונה (אלא) דתחילת הוסת קאי בגוה. ואם בדקה קודם הנץ החמה ולא ראתה כל אותה שעה אסורה אבל כל היום מותרת לפי שעיקר הוסת בתחילתו הוא והכריע הוא כי הך סברא בתרא מהא דתנן היתה למודה להיות רואה עם הנץ החמה אינה אסורה אלא עם הנץ החמה דברי רבי יוסי רבי יהודה אומר כל היום שלה. ואוקימנא להא דרגילה למיחזי בסוף לילה וכל היכא דתני עם לאלתר משמע ואי סלקא דעתך דכי האי גוונא אסורה ביום ובלילה היכי קתני כל היום שלה והא אי אפשר דלא עיילא ראיה בתוך הנץ החמה ותיאסר בימָמא ובליליא. ועוד סתמא קתני להיות רואה ולא מפליג בין ראיה מרובה לראיה מועטת הלכך אינה אסורה אלא עונת הלילה ושעת הוסת בלבד. אמר רבא הלכה כר׳ יהודה. ומי אמר רבא הכי והתניא והזרתם את בני ישראל [מכאן] אמר ר׳ אושעיא אזהרה

לבני ישראל שיפרשו מנשותיהן סמוך לוסתן. וכמה. אמר רבא עונה מאי לאו עונה אחריתי. לא אותה עונה.

שולחן ערוך יורה דעה הלכות נדה סימן קצ סעיף נד – אין בכתמים משום וסת. כיצד, מצאה כתם בר"ח, אפילו שלש פעמים, לא קבעתו ולא עוקרתו. חוץ מכתמי עד הבדוק לה, שהם מטמאים עד בכל שהן, והרי הן כראייות לכל דבר.

פרישה סימן קצ ס"ק צא – הכא בראיית שלשה כתמים בשלשה זמנים לא מיחשב לעקירה דאין זה ראיות אלא נחשב שלש עונות דאם חזרה וראתה רק פעם אחת חזרה לקביעותה.

רבי עקיבא איגר יורה דעה סימן קצ – סעיף נ"ד ולא עוקרתו. היינו לענין דהיה לה וסת קבוע בר"ח ואח"כ ג"פ לא ראתה בר"ח וג"פ מצאה בה' בחודש לא אמרינן דנעקר לגמרי הוסת דר"ח אלא הוי כלא קבעה וסת אחר דאם אח"כ ראתה פ"א בר"ח חזרה לוסתה הראשון. פרישה.

שו"ת אגרות משה יורה דעה חלק ג סימן מו – ב' ובדבר שאשה אינה מרגשת אף לא בשעת שפע הדם גם לא זיבת הדם, ודרכה למצא תחלה כתם על בגדיה פעמים פחות מכגריס ופעמים יותר מכגריס ואחר כמה שעות פעמים פחות פעמים יותר מתחיל הדם לזוב ואירע שהכתם מוצאת ביום ואח"כ בלילה זב הדם, הנה שו"ע או"ח בסימן ק"צ סעי' נ"ד מפורש דאין בכתמים משום וסת, אבל עיין בט"ז ס"ק מ"א דמשמע דהוא משום ספק דשמא אינו מגופה, ולא משום דלא היה בהרגשה דהא מדמה כתמי עד שאינו בדוק שהוא ספק שג"כ אין בו משום וסת אף דשם הוי הספק גם להרגשה, והוא משום דראיות דם אף בלא הרגשה שהיא טהורה מן התורה היו קובעין וסת, וכן מסתבר דהוסת הא הוא ענין טבעי שלכן אף שחסר לה ענין ההרגשה דעכ"פ כשבא הזמן שיוצא הדם הדרך שיצא, וא"כ הכתמים שמוצאת תמיד איזה שעות לפני ראיית הדם הרי לא שייך לומר דהוא ממקום אחר ואפילו לא שבא מדם מאכולת, דדם ממקום אחר וממאכולת לא היה שייך שיבואו דוקא איזה שעות קודם לראיית הדם שלה, וא"כ ברור שבא דם הכתם מגופה, אבל הוא בא שלא בהרגשה שטהור מן התורה וכיון שבא מגופה הרי שייך זה לקבוע הוסת כראייה ממש שלא בהרגשה ששייך לקביעות וסת. ואף שהוא רק משהו דם הא ודאי ראיות דמשהו דם כטיפות נמי קובעין וסת. ולכן אם נזדמן שהכתם היה ביום והראיה היתה בלילה שהוא יום אחר נחשב הוסת מיום ראיית הכתם.

שו"ת אגרות משה יורה דעה חלק ג סימן נא – נשים שדרכן לראות כתמים קודם וסתן מתי עיקר הוסת בע"ה איר תשל"ז להנ"ל.

אותן נשים שדרכן לראות כתמים בלא הרגשה כמה ימים קודם וסתה עיקר הוסת מיום שבא שפע הדם בהרגשה, ואם ראתה כן ג' פעמים או אם דרך זיבת הדם לבוא ג"כ בלא הרגשה עיקר הוסת הוא משתראה הכתמים, דאיגלאי מילתא דכן הוא פתיחת המקור שלה טיפין טיפין תחלה ואח"כ בא השפע וכעין מה שפירש רש"י ריש נדה דף ב' ע"ב בד"ה הגס הגס ע"י שיהיה הדם רבה במקור יוצא ממנו מעט מעט כחרדל מה שאין המקור יכול להחזיקה ויוצא מעט לבית

החיצון וזה כמה ימים התחיל וממילא חוששין לחדש הבא כוסת מזמן שראתה הכתמים ואעפ״י שלא באה בהרגשה דאינה טמאה אלא מדרבנן מ״מ מדקבעה וסתה באופן כזה נחשבת כוסתה דסו״ס ראתה דם וחייב לפרוש מאשתו בזמן שרואה דם אפילו אינה נדה מן התורה, ותו אולי ארגשה ולאו אדעתא – אבל אם הפסיקה בין הכתמים ושפע הדם יום או יומיים או בדקה בינתיים ומצאה טהורה אין וסתה אלא מזמן שבא הדם בהרגשה, ואין חוששין לכתמים משום וסתות כסוף סימן ק״צ, ודינה כדין וסת הגוף, אבל לא שייך לחוש לזה אלא כשהיה זה ג״פ – ואם היה כן ג״פ ובזמן שוה בין לימי החדש בין להפלגה צריך לפרוש ממנה כשהתחילה לראות כתמים בזמנן כהרגילה ואפילו כשהן פחות מכגריס כיון שבאין בזמן הוסת ואם לא באו הכתמים עדיין חוששין ליום הוסת בזמנה וכשלא בא האורח בזמנו הרי נתגלה שאינו מהוסת וטהורה אם לא היו הכתמים כגריס. ידידו, משה פיינשטיין.

שולחן ערוך יורה דעה הלכות נדה סימן קפט סעיף יג – אין האשה קובעת לה וסת, אפילו ראתה שלשה ר״ח זה אחר זה, אלא אם כן יהיו כולם בעונה אחת, ביום או בלילה. ואם ראתה שלש פעמים ביום, והרביעית בלילה, או שלש פעמים בלילה והרביעית ביום, חוששת ביום ובלילה מפני חשש הוסת הראשון ומפני חשש השני, שהוא האחרון, ואם ראתה פעמים ביום ופעמים בלילה, שלא על הסדר, (ולא קבעה אחד מהן ג״פ), או שתראה הראשונה ביום, וג׳ האחרונות בלילה, או הראשונה בלילה והג׳ אחרונות ביום, או שלש בזה ושלש בזה, חוששת לאחרונה בלבד. הגה: האשה שראתה, חוששת לוסת החדש ולהפלגה, עד שתקבע וסת החדש בג״פ, או וסת הפלגה בד״פ, או שתעקר א׳ מהן. כיצד, ראתה בא׳ בניסן וכ׳ בו, חוששת לאחד באייר, מפני ר״ח ניסן. לא ראתה באחד באייר או לא ראתה בו, חוששת לט׳ באייר, שהוא יום כ׳ מראיית יום כ׳ שראתה. ראתה בט׳ באייר או לא ראתה, חוששת לעשרים באייר, שמא קבעה לה וסת כ׳ לחדש, שהרי ראתה עשרים לחדש ניסן. וכן היא חוששת לעולם עד שתקבע וסת א׳ כדינו, דאז אינה חוששת לשני שלא נקבע, או עד שאחד מהן נעקר, אז אינה חוששת לו, אעפ״י שלא נקבע השני (הכל בטור בשם רמב״ן). ואינה חוששת לוסת הדילוגין, עד שתקבענו. כיצד, ראתה ט״ו בניסן, חוששת לט״ו באייר. לא ראתה בט״ו באייר, אינה חוששת לט״ז בו. ראתה ט״ז בו, חוששת לט״ז בסיון ואינה חוששת לשבעה עשר בו. ראתה י״ז בו, חוששת לי״ז בתמוז ואינה חוששת לי״ח בו. ראתה י״ח בתמוז, קבעה לה וסת דילוגין לימי החודש וחוששת לי״ט באב. (ג״ז ממשמעות הטור). וכן בדרך זה בהפלגה ודילוגין, כי אין חלוק ביניהן. רק י״א כי בדילוג חדש, הראייה הראשונה מן המנין, כמו שנתבאר. ראתה ט״ו בניסן והמשיכה ראייתה ד׳ ימים, וביום ט״ז באייר ראתה והמשיכה ראייתה ג׳ ימים, ובסיון התחילה לראות בי״ז בו, י״א שחוששת לדילוג ולוסת שוה, שהרי שילשה לראות ג״פ בי״ז לחדש, (הטור והרמב״ן) וי״א שאין כאן וסת שוה כלל, דהולכין תמיד אחר תחלת הראייה, לט וכן עיקר.

שולחן ערוך יורה דעה הלכות נדה סימן קפד סעיף ב – בשעת וסתה, צריך לפרוש ממנה עונה אחת, ולא משאר קריבות אלא מתשמיש (המטה) בלבד. אם הוא ביום, פורש ממנה אותו היום כולו אפילו אם הוסת בסופו, ומותר מיד בלילה שלאחריו, וכן אם הוא בתחלתו, פורש כל היום ומותר כל הלילה שלפניו. וכן הדין אם הוא בלילה, פורש כל הלילה ומותר ביום שלפניו ולאחריו,

בין שקבעה וסת בג"פ או בפ"א. הגה: וכל זה לא מיירי אלא בוסת התלוי בימים אבל לא בוסת התלוי בשינוי הגוף (ב"י בשם הראב"ד), וע"ל סימן קפ"ט. ואשה שמשנית וסתה להקדים ב' או ג' ימים או לאחר, כשמגיע זמן וסתה צריך לפרוש ממנה ב' או ג' ימים קודם או אחריו.

ש"ך יורה דעה סימן קפט:לט – וכן עיקר – כתוב במעדני מלך דף רצ"ו ע"א תימה דלעיל סימן קפ"ד ס"ד כתב דאשה שמשתני' וסתה להקדים ב' או ג' ימים או לאחר כשמגיע זמן וסתה צריך לפרוש ממנה ב' או ג' ימים קודם או אחריו ע"כ ונראה ליישב דלעיל אין ר"ל שצריך לפרוש כל הג' ימים דא"כ מה ענין שמשתני' וסתה לכאן אלא ר"ל דהיה לה וסת ואח"כ משתנית וסתה להקדים ב' או ג' ימים אז צריכה לפרוש גם קודם הוסת כפי מה שרגילה להקדים כגון שרגילה להקדים ג' ימים צריכה לפרוש אותו יום שרגילה להקדים וכדכתב כאן והיינו שכתב לעיל וע"ל סימן קפ"ט.

שו"ת נודע ביהודה מהדורה קמא – יורה דעה סימן מו – ובזה נלע"ד פירוש דברי רמ"א בהג"ה סימן קפ"ד סעיף ב' ואשה שמשנית וסתה להקדים שנים או ג"י או לאחר צריך לפרוש ממנה שנים או ג"י וכו'. נ"ל פירושו שכך הוא קביעת וסתה שבתוך אלו השנים או השלשה ימים תראה ובגוף אלו הימים אין לה זמן קבוע אימת לפעמים בזה ולפעמים בזה רק עכ"פ לא יעברו ג"י הללו בלי ראיה א"כ כל הג"י המה הוסת וצריך לפרוש בכולן. ובזה אין אנו צריכין למה שנדחק הש"ך בסימן קפ"ט ס"ק ל"ט ע"ש וק"ל.

פתחי תשובה יורה דעה סימן קפד:ח – שמשנית וסתה – עש"ך סי' קפ"ט ס"ק ל"ט ועי' בתשובת נו"ב חי"ד סי' מ"ו שפירש דברי הרב דהיינו שכך הוא קביעת וסתה שבתוך אלו הב' וג' ימים תראה ובגוף אלו הימים אין לה זמן קבוע אימת לפעמים בזה ולפעמים בזה ועכ"פ לא יעברו אלו הג' ימים בלא ראיה א"כ כל הג' ימים וסת הן וצריך לפרוש בכולם ומכח זה המציא דין חדש באשה שהוחזקה שאינה מפסקת לספור ז"נ כל ז' וז' הם אצלה כוסת קבוע וצריכה בדיקה כל ז' בבוקר וערב ובאמצע היום כמה פעמים ולמד זה מסי' קפ"ו ס"ג דעד יום י"ד יום דינה כדין אשה שיש לה וסת ואם לקולא אמרינן כן ק"ו לחומרא כו' ע"ש ואיני מבין ראיתו דשם הוחזקה בודאי שלא תראה באותן י"ד ימים משא"כ בנ"ד שלא הוחזק יום א' מאותן הז' ימים שתראה בו בודאי ומצאתי בח"ד שהשיג עליו בזה ופירש הוא ז"ל דברי הרמ"א באופן אחר דמשנית וסתה להקדים היינו כגון שהיה לה וסת בג' לירחא ועתה הקדימה וראתה ג"פ בב' לירחא וג' לירחא וחזרה וראתה ג"פ בריש ירחא ובב' לירחא דאז חוששת לשלשתן דהימים שהיו בתחלת וסת אף שהן עתה באמצע וסת לא אבדו מעלתן וכן במאחרת כגון שהיה לה וסת קבוע בריש ירחא ואחר כך ראתה ב"פ בב' בירחא דלא נעקר הוסת דריש ירחא עדיין דאין הוסת נעקר עד ג"פ ובפעם הג' ראתה בריש ירחא ובב' בירחא דאז נקבעו שני הוסתות. דב' בירחא ג"כ הוקבע כיון שב"פ הראשונים הוחזק ממעין סתום ואח"כ ראתה ב"פ רק בג' בירחא ובפעם הג' ראתה בריש ירחא ובב' בירחא ובג' לירחא דאז הוקבעו שלשתן וכיון שמשנית וסתה פעמים מקדמת ופעמים מאחרת חיישינן שמא היא באופן ששלשתן הוקבעו מש"ה חוששת לשלשתן ע"ש.

תלמוד בבלי מסכת נדה דף טו עמוד א – מתני'. כל הנשים בחזקת טהרה לבעליהן. הבאין מן הדרך – נשיהן להן בחזקת טהרה. גמ' למה ליה למתני הבאין מן הדרך סד"א הני מילי היכא דאיתיה במתא דרמיא אנפשה ובדקה אבל היכא דליתא במתא דלא רמיא אנפשה לא קא משמע לן אמר ריש לקיש משום רבי יהודה נשיאה והא שבא ומצאה בתוך ימי עונתה.

רש"י מסכת נדה דף טו עמוד א – בתוך ימי עונתה – ל' יום לראייה אבל לאחר ל' בעיא בדיקה הואיל וסתם נשים חזיין לסוף עונה.

תלמוד בבלי מסכת נדה דף ט עמוד ב – וכמה עונה? אמר ריש לקיש משום רבי יהודה נשיאה: עונה בינונית, שלשים יום ורבא אמר רב חסדא: עשרים יום. ולא פליגי, מר קחשיב ימי טומאה וימי טהרה, ומר לא חשיב ימי טומאה.

תלמוד ירושלמי מסכת נדה פרק ב דף נ טור א/ה"ג (פרק ב הלכה ד) – כמה עונה נותנין לה רבי שמעון בן לקיש אמר נותנין לה עונה בינונית שלשים יום אמר רבי יוחנן שונה אני אפילו לאחר שלש שנים מותר ובלבד באשה שיש לה ווסת אמר רבי אבהו והיא ששהת אחר ווסתה שבעת ימים וחש לומר שמא לא טבלה אמר רבי חנינה זאת אומרת שאסור לאשה לשהות בטומאתה.

רמב"ם הלכות איסורי ביאה פרק ד הלכה ט – כל הנשים שיש להן וסת בחזקת טהרה לבעליהן עד שתאמר לו טמאה אני או עד שתוחזק נדה בשכנותיה, הלך בעלה למדינה אחרת והניחה טהורה כשיבוא אינו צריך ה לשאול לה אפילו מצאה ישנה הרי זה מותר לבוא עליה שלא בעונת וסתה ואינו חושש שמא נדה היא, ואם הניחה נדה אסורה לו עד שתאמר לו טהורה אני.

מגיד משנה הלכות איסורי ביאה פרק ד הלכה ט – כל הנשים שיש להן וסת. משנה פרק כל היד (דף ט"ז) כל הנשים בחזקת טהרה לבעליהן והבאין מן הדרך נשיהן להן בחזקת טהרה ובגמרא אמר ר"ל משום רבי יהודה נשיאה והוא שבא ומצאה בתוך ימי עונתה ואמר רב הונא לא שנו אלא שאין לה וסת אבל יש לה וסת אסורה לשמש והקשו כלפי לייא איפכא מסתברא אין לה וסת אימא חזאי יש לה וסת וסת קביע לה אלא אי איתמר הכי איתמר אר"ה ל"ש אלא שלא הגיע שעת וסתה אבל הגיע שעת וסתה אסורה קסבר וסתות דאורייתא רבה בר בר חנה אמר אפילו הגיע שעת וסתה מותרת קסבר וסתות דרבנן רב אשי מתני הכי אמר רב הונא ל"ש אלא שאין לה וסת לימים ויש לה וסת לקפיצות אבל יש לה וסת לימים ולקפיצות כיון דבמעשה תליא מילתא אימור לא קפיץ ולא חזאי אבל יש לה וסת לימים אסורה לשמש קסבר וסתות דאורייתא רבה בר בר חנה אמר אפילו יש לה וסת לימים מותרת קסבר וסתות דרבנן. עוד שם אמר ר' יוחנן אשה שיש לה וסת בעלה מחשב ימי וסתה ובא עליה אמר ליה רב שמואל בר ייבא לרבי אבא אמר ר' יוחנן אפילו ילדה דבזיזא למטבל אמר ליה אטו ודאי ראתה מי אמר ר"י אימור דאמר ר"י ספק ראתה ספק לא ראתה ואת"ל ראתה אימור טבלה אבל ודאי ראתה לא מי יימר דטבלה הוי ליה ספיקא וודאי ואין ספק מוציא מידי ודאי ומשמע דמסקנא דגמרא התם דוסתות דרבנן וכן הסכימו המפרשים ז"ל. ועתה אבאר דעת רבינו הוא מפרש משנתנו בשיש לה וסת

בדוקא מדאמרינן בסוגיא אין לה וסת אימור חזאי וכן נראה מסוגיא דפ״ק. וראיתי לרשב״א ז״ל שהקשה למה אמרו אי איתמר הכי איתמר ל״ש אלא שלא הגיע שעת וסתה וכו׳ הל״ל ל״ש אלא שיש לה וסת אבל אין לה וסת אסורה דהיינו הך דהוה קשיא להו ותירץ דמשום דכל הנשים בחזקת טהרה לבעליהן קתני בין שיש לה וסת בין שאין לה וסת לא אמרו כן והא דאמרי׳ איפכא מסתברא ה״ק אם באת לחלק ביניהם בהפך יש לך לומר אבל קושטא דמילתא שכולן בחזקת טהרה וכתב שזו ראיה גדולה שכולן שוות שלא כדברי רבינו שכתב שיש להן וסת בדוקא. ויש לי לדחותה בטעם נכון ולומר דאה״נ דהוי מצי למימר איפכא איתמר דקושטא דמילתא הכין הוא אלא שאם היו מתרצין כן היו מטעים האומר הראשון מהן ללאו ומלאו להן אבל כשתירץ ואמר שלא הגיע שעת וסתה לא הטעה האומר הראשון אלא ששמע שלא הגיע שעת וסתה ואמר אין לה וסת ומשהגיע שעת וסתה אמר יש לה וסת והוא דבר מצוי לטעות א״נ דקים להו דמימרא דרב הונא הכי איתמר ורבה בר בר חנה הוה פליג עליה זה נראה לי בדעת רבינו. והוא סובר דהא דריש לקיש דאמר והוא שבא ומצאה בתוך ימי עונתה הלכתא היא ומאי עונתה וסתה ופי׳ דר״ל אתא לאשמועינן דלא תימא דכיון דווסתות דרבנן בבא מן הדרך הקלו שאפילו ביום וסתה תהיה מותרת אלא אם בא ביום וסתה אסורה היא לו שמא תראה בשעת תשמיש ומן הטעם שאסרו חכמים לשמש בעונה סמוך לוסת כמו שיתבאר בסמוך אבל אם עברה עונת הוסת אפילו לא עברו אחריה ימים שתוכל לספור בהם הרי היא בחזקת טהרה ואין חוששין שמא ראתה בעונת הוסת וכרבה בר בר חנה דאמר אפילו הגיע עונת וסתה מותרת וסתות דרבנן ולא מצריך שיעור לספירה וכן אמר רבה בר בר חנה אפילו יש לה וסת לימים מותרת קסבר וסתות דרבנן וכיון דקי״ל דוסתות דרבנן קי״ל כוותיה ור״י דאמר מחשב ימי וסתה פי׳ אם עברו ימי ספירה ושתוכל לטבול ס״ל וסתות דאורייתא ולא קי״ל כוותיה וזה נראה דעת ההלכות שכתבו הא דתניא בפ׳ קמא חמרין ופועלין והבאין מבית האבל ובית המשתה נשיהן להן בחזקת טהרה באין ושוהין עמהן בין ערות בין ישנות בד״א בשהניחה בחזקת טהרה אבל הניחה בחזקת טומאה לעולם היא בטומאתה עד שתאמר טהורה אני ע״כ בהלכות ולא חלקו בין עברה עונת הוסת ללא עברה. ויש בדברים אלו שיטות חלוקות למפרשים ז״ל ורבים מהם פי׳ דהא דר״ל דאמר והוא שבא ומצאה בתוך ימי עונתה ר״ל לתוך שלשים יום שהיא עונה בינונית לראיית הנשים ואשאין להם וסת קאי. וזה דעת הרמב״ן ז״ל וז״ל בפסקי הלכותיו בין שיש להן וסת בין שאין להם וסת והוחזקו שלא יהו רואות מחמת תשמיש הרי כלן לבעליהן בחזקת טהרה ובאין ומשמשין עמהן בין ערות בין ישנות בד״א בזמן שמניחין אותן בחזקת טהרה אבל אם הניחו אותן טמאות הרי היא אסורה לו עד שתאמר טבלתי וטהורה אני. הבאין מן הדרך נשיהן להן בחזקת טהרה והוא שבא ומצאה תוך ימי עונתה כמה היא עונה שלשים יום מתחלת ראייה לתחלת ראייה אחרת שרוב הנשים כך הם רואות מל׳ לל׳. בד״א באשה שאין לה וסת אבל אשה שיש לה וסת לימים ה״ז מחשב ימי וסתה אם הגיע שעתו הרי היא אצלו בחזקת טומאה היה לה וסת הגוף ולא וסת יום קבוע הרי היא אצלו בחזקת טהרה עד העונה כמי שאין לה וסת חשב בעלה ימי וסתה או ימי עונתה והרי יש לה שהות אח״כ שתספור ותטבול הרי זו בחזקת טהרה ומותרת לו בין ערה בין ישנה שהרי שתי ספיקות הן שמא [ראתה ושמא] לא ראתה [ושמא ראתה וטבלה +נ״א ואפילו ראתה שמא טבלה+] עכ״ל וזה דעת הרשב״א ז״ל.

בדק הבית על תורת הבית בית ז שער ב – [דף ז עמוד א] ובזו אין לו לחוש כלל. ולהוציא מדברי המחבר שכתב שחוששת לעונה בינונית והיינו משלשים יום לשלשים יום ואינו כלום. ונתלו באותה שמועה שבפרק כל היד עלה דמתניתין דכל הנשים בחזקת טהרה דאמר ריש לקיש משום רבי יהודה נשיאה והוא שבא ומצאה בתוך ימי עונתה. ואינו, דהא אנן סתמא קאמרינן דכל לבעלה לא בעיא בדיקה לעולם באשה שאין לה וסת ומה טעם לחששה זו אחר שאין לה וסת כלל ומה מקום בזה לשלשים יום. אלא ענין אחר היא שמועה זו, והריני מפרשה: אמר ריש לקיש והוא שבא ומצאה בתוך ימי עונתה איש לה וסת קאי דמתניתין בין באין [דף ז עמוד ב] לה בין ביש לה וסת וריש לקיש קאי איש לה וסת וקאמר דכי אמרינן בחזקת טהרה דוקא בשהגיע בתוך ימי עונתה אי זו עונה שתהא לה או משלשים יום או עשרים או אי זמן שיש לה שהגיע בתוך אותו זמן וכגון שהלך מכאן אחר שטהרה וחזר בתוך ימי עונתה אי זו זמן שידועה לה ולאפוקי בשחזר בסוף עונה ואפילו קודם וסתה לומר שהיא אסורה היום ואפילו עונה לפני וסתה אסורה לאותו יום בין בוסת קבוע בין בוסת שאינו קבוע דחוששת לו ונוהגת בו לוסת קבוע ומיתסרא באותה עונה אפילו לפני וסתה ואפילו למאן דאמר וסתות דרבנן ואפילו לבא מן הדרך אעפ"י שהתירו ליוצא לדרך לא התירו לבא שהיא משתוקקת ליוצא יותר ואמר רב הונא לא שנו אלא שלא הגיע עת וסתה אבל הגיע עת וסתה קודם שבא ובא אחר כן אסור לו לעולם עד שידע בודאי שספרה וטבלה דוסתות דאורייתא ומחזקינן לה דודאי חזאי ולא סגיא למשרייהו בספיקא ואפילו נשתהא ביותר אלא בידיעה ודאית. רבה בר בר חנה אמר אפילו הגיע עת וסתה מותר פירוש בשנשתהא כדי ספירת שבעה מאי טעמא וסתות דרבנן מספק דילמא חזאי ואם איתא דחזאי אימר ספרה וטבלה דאורחא דנשי הכי ואתיא כאידך דרבי יוחנן דאמר אשה שיש לה וסת בעלה מחשב ימי וסתה ובא עליה וסבר דוסתות דרבנן וכיון דאישתהי כדי ספירה וטבילה שריא ולכולי עלמא הניחה טמאה הרי היא בחזקתה עד שידע בודאי שהיא טהורה. ביארתי דינין אלו, ומקצתן שלא כדברי המחבר.

הלכות נדה לרמב"ן פרק ה – ה. כמה היא עונה שלשים יום מתחלת ראיה לתחלת ראיה אחרת, שרוב נשים כך הן רואות משלשים לשלשים, בד"א באשה שאין לה וסת אבל אשה שיש לה וסת לימים הרי זה מחשב ימי וסתה אם הגיע שעתן הרי היא בחזקת טומאה אצלו.

תורת הבית הארוך בית ז שער ב – הגיע עת וסתה כיצד כל אשה שיש לה וסת בין וסת קבוע בין שאינו קבוע אסורה לבעלה כל אותה עונה שהיא רגילה לראות בה. וכמה עונה יום או לילה. רגילה לראות ביום אסור כל אותו היום רגילה לראות בלילה אסירה כל אותו [דף ד עמוד ב] הלילה. דבר זה מדרבנן הוא דמדאורייתא עד שתראה כמו שיתבאר בשער הוסתות. יש שאינה אסורה עד שיגיע שעת הוסת ממש כוסתות התלויין במקרים כקפיצה ואכילת פלפלין וכיוצא באלו. ויש שאינה אסורה אלא בתוך הוסת. ודיני וסתות אלו כולן יתבארו בשער הווסתות ולא כתבתי כאן אלא דרך כלל שאדם צריך לפרוש מן האשה אעפ"י שלא ראתה עדיין. אעפ"י שאנו חוששין לווסתות נאמנת היא לומר לא ראיתי ואפילו קבוע לה זמן לראייתה שאפילו בזמן שראתה נאמנת לומר טהרתי שהתורה האמינתה שנאמר וספרה לה לעצמה וכל שכן שנאמנת

בווסת. ישבה לה ולא בדקה בשעת וסתה אם יש לה וסת קבוע אסורה עד שתבדק. בדקה לאחר זמן ומצאה טהורה טהורה ואין אומרין שמא אורח בזמנו בא ולא הרגישה לפי שהווסתות אינן דאורייתא אלא דרבנן כמו שיתבאר בשער הוסתות. היה לה וסת שאינו קבוע אם לא בדקה בשיעור וסת ולא ראתה הרי זו טהורה ואינה צריכה בדיקה דכל שלא הרגישה בדם בשעת וסתה אעפ"י שלא בדקה הרי זו בחזקת טהורה כיון שאין לה וסת קבוע שאין איסור עונה זו אלא מדרבנן. במה דברים אמורים בוסת שאינו קבוע בה והוה לה בפחות מעונה בינונית אבל עונה בינונית שהיא לשלשים יום הרי הוא לה כוסת קבוע לדבר זה שאעפ"י שלא הרגישה בדם אסורה עד שתבדק ותמצא טהור. וסתות עצמן אינן דבר תורה אלא מדבריהם כמו שאמרנו לפיכך היקלו בפרישת העונה יתר מפרישת הנדה. שאלו נדה עצמה כל קריבה אסורה כתשמיש כמו שבארנו ואלו בעונה זו לא אסרו אלא תשמיש בלבד. ועוד הקלו בה ליוצא לדרך שאפילו ממש תשמיש מותר משום דמצוה לפקוד את אשתו בשעה שהוא יוצא לדרך ובמקום מצוה לא גזרו. וכן דעת הרב ר"א ז"ל. ויש מי שאומר שלא התירו ביוצא לדרך אלא דברי הרגל אבל תשמיש ממש אסור. ומכלל דברים אלו למי שאינו יוצא לדרך שאסור בעונה זו אפילו בדברים של הרגל כנדה בעלמא. ונראין דברי הרב שאפילו בתשמיש ממש התירו לו [דף ה עמוד א] דהכין מוכחא שמעתא ביבמות פרק הבא על יבמתו דגרסינן התם אמר רבי יהושע בן לוי כל היודע באשתו שהיא יראת שמים ואינו פוקדה נקרא חוטא שנאמר וידעת כי שלום אהלך ופקדת נוך ולא תחטא פירוש פקידה זו תשמיש. ואמר רבי יהושע בן לוי חייב אדם לפקוד את אשתו כשהוא יוצא לדרך שנאמר וידעת כי שלום אהלך. אלמא פקידה זו תשמיש כפקידה שאמר לענין מי שיודע באשתו שהיא יראת שמים. והא דרבי יהושע בן לוי אוקימנא לה התם בסמוך לוסתה. דאקשינן התם והא מהכא נפקא מהתם נפקא ואל אישך תשוקתך מלמד שהאשה משתוקקת לבעלה בשעה שהוא יוצא לדרך ופרקינן התם אמר יוסף לא נצרכה אלא סמוך לוסתה. אלמא יוצא לדרך בפקידה עצמה מותר ואפילו סמוך לוסתה שאם לולי כן היה לו לומר לא נצרכה אלא סמוך לוסתה ומאי פקידה בדברים אלא ודאי פקידת תשמיש קאמר. ואף רש"י ז"ל כן פירש שם וכן עיקר.

שולחן ערוך יורה דעה הלכות נדה סימן קפט סעיף א – כל אשה שאין לה וסת קבוע, חוששת ליום ל' לראייתה, שהוא עונה בינונית לסתם נשים, ואם יש לה וסת קבוע לזמן ידוע מכ' לכ' או מכ"ה לכ"ה, חוששת לזמן הידוע.

שולחן ערוך יורה דעה הלכות נדה סימן קפד סעיף ט – שאר נשים, צריכות בדיקה כשיגיע הוסת. עבר הוסת ולא בדקה ולא הרגישה, טהורה בלא בדיקה. וי"א שאסורה עד שתבדוק, אם יש לה וסת קבוע, או שהוא יום ל' אע"פ שאינו קבוע. (והכי נהוג, כד וכן הוא לקמן סימן קפ"ט).

שולחן ערוך יורה דעה הלכות נדה סימן קפט סעיף ד – עוד יש חילוק בין קבעתו ג' פעמים ללא קבעתו ג' פעמים, שהקבוע אף על פי שעברה עונתה ולא הרגישה, אסורה לשמש עד שתבדוק ותמצא טהורה. ושלא קבעתו ג"פ, אם הגיע זמן הוסת ולא בדקה ולא ראתה, כיון שעברה עונתה, מותרת. ועונה בינונית, שהיא לל' יום, דינה כוסת קבוע.

בית יוסף יורה דעה סימן קפט – א כל אשה שאין לה וסת קבוע חוששת ליום שלשים לראייתה שהיא עונה בינונית לסתם נשים. בפרק כל היד (טו.) אהא דתנן הבאים מן הדרך נשיהם להם בחזקת טהרה אמר ריש לקיש והוא שבא ומצאה בתוך ימי עונתה ופירש רש"י בתוך ימי עונתה שלשים יום לראייה אבל לאחר שלשים יום בעיא בדיקה הואיל וסתם נשים חזיין לסוף עונה וכתב על זה הרשב"א בתורת הבית (ארוך ב"ז ש"ג טו.) שמע מינה אשה שאין לה וסת בעלה מוזהר עליה ביום העונה דהא לא אשכחן מאן דפליג עליה דריש לקיש ואפילו בבא מן הדרך וכל שכן כשהוא עמה בעיר וכן דעת הר"ן בפרק ב' דשבועות (ד: ד"ה וגרסי' בפרק) ונראה מדבריו (ה. ד"ה וגרסי' תו) שגם הראב"ד סובר כן וכתב עוד הר"ן (ד: שם) דמדברי רש"י (ד"ה לא שנו) נראה דאפילו באשה שיש לה וסת צריכה לחוש לעונתה ולא נהירא דכל שיש לה וסת דמיה מסולקין עד זמן וסת והן הן דברי הרשב"א ז"ל. ומה שפירש רש"י דימי עונה הם שלשים יום מבואר בפ"ק דנדה (ט:) כמה עונה אמר ריש לקיש משום רבי יהודה נשיאה עונה בינונית שלשים יום.

ב"ח יורה דעה סימן קפט – א כל אשה וכו'. מימרא דריש לקיש בפרק כל היד (דף ט"ו א) וכפירוש רש"י דכשאין לה וסת שלשים יום לראייתה היא עונת וסתה כסתם נשים דחזיין לסוף שלשים וצריך לפרוש עונה אחת כשהגיע יום שלשים דאפילו בדקה עצמה ומצאה טהורה אסורה לשמש אבל קודם שלשים מותרת לשמש על ידי בדיקה אחת לפני תשמיש ובדיקה אחת לאחר תשמיש כמסקנת הרא"ש לעיל בסימן קפ"ו וגם לאחר שלשים אסורה לשמש עד שתבדוק ותמצא טהורה כמפורש לעיל בסימן קפ"ד.

טו לשון הרמב"ן וכו' נמצאת אומר שהרואה ליום ראש חודש ניסן חוששת לראש חודש אייר. נראה דחוששת לשני הימים דראש חודש, ביום ראשון חוששת לפי שהוא יום שלשים לראייתה שהוא עונה בינונית דחוששת לו כיון שלא קבעה לה וסת וביום שני דראש חודש חוששת משום ראש חודש דכיון דראתה בר"ח ניסן חוששת שמא תקבע לה וסת שלש פעמים באחד בחודש. ראתה בר"ח אייר חוששת לר"ח סיון, פירוש דאם ראתה ביום ראשון דראש חודש פשיטא דחוששת ליום כ"ט באייר שהוא יום שלשים לראייתה ואין צריך לפרש, אלא שאם לא ראתה אלא ביום שני דראש חודש צריך לפרש דחוששת לר"ח סיון משום תרווייהו משום וסת דראש חודש ומשום שהוא יום שלשים לראייתה, ואם ראתה בר"ח סיון קבעה לה וסת לראשי חדשים, שהרי ראתה באחד בניסן ובאחד באייר ובאחד בסיון ולא תלינן ראיית אחד בסיון לפי שהוא יום שלשים לראיית אחד באייר אלא קבעה לה וסת לראש חודש, אבל אם לא ראתה בא' בסיון נעקר וסת דראש חודש ושוב אינה חוששת לר"ח תמוז אלא חוששת לב' סיון אפשר וכו', ומשמע דאם ראתה בר"ח ניסן וביום ראשון דר"ח אייר וביום כ"ט באייר לא ראתה דחוששת לר"ח סיון אע"פ שהוא יום ל"א לראיית יום ראשון דראש חודש שמא יום ראש חודש הוא הגורם ראייתה ואם ראתה בר"ח סיון קבעה לה וסת דראש חודש וחוששת לר"ח תמוז לשני הימים דראש חודש. והיכא דראתה בר"ח ניסן וביום שני דר"ח אייר ובשני בסיון דאיכא שתי הפלגות מל"א לל"א ונעקר וסת דראש חודש מ"מ כשיגיע ר"ח תמוז חוששת ביום שני דראש חודש משום שהוא יום שלשים לראיית ב' בסיון וחוששת נמי לב' בתמוז לפי שהוא יום ל"א שוה לשתי ההפלגות הראשונות.

חוות דעת ביאורים סימן קפט ס"ק יב – אמנם בהא שכתב הש"ך דעונה בינונית היא מיום ל"א נראה עיקר כדבריו.

חוות דעת חידושים סימן קפט ס"ק ב – ואסורה לשמש כל העונה כמ"ש בסי' קפ"ד ואינה צריכה לחוש לעונה בינונית ואם יש לה וסת הגוף קבוע אם הוסת מובלע בסוף הפיסוק מותרת לעונה בינונית ואם הוא בתחלתו או משנמשך ראייתה גם אחר הפיסוק אסורה לעונה בינונית.

ש"ך יורה דעה סימן קפט:ל – האשה שראתה כו' – כתב הטור ל' הרמב"ן וסת החדש חוששת לו בתחלתו פעם א' אבל וסת ההפלגה א"א לחוש לו עד שתראה ראיה שניה שהרי אינה יודעת לאיזה יום היא מפלגת נמצאת אומר שהרואה ליום ר"ח ניסן חוששת לר"ח אייר ראתה בו חוששת לר"ח סיון ראתה בו הוקבע וסתה לר"ח לא ראתה לר"ח סיון נעקר וסת של ר"ח וחוששת לב' בסיון אפשר שתראה ותקבע וסת להפלגה מל"א לל"א שהרי ראיית ר"ח ניסן ואייר שוות בהפלגה לראית ב' בסיון שניסן מלא ואייר חסר ולעולם חוששת חששות הללו לוסת החדש ולהפלגה עד שתקבע אחד מהן ג"פ כדינו כיצד ראתה באחד בניסן וך' בו כו' וכתב ב"י דמ"ש דחיישינן שתקבע מל"א לל"א לאו למימרא שא"צ לחוש ליום אחר שהרי אין לה וסת קבוע וכל שאין לה וסת קבוע חוששת ליום ל' שהיא עונה בינונית אלא ר"ל שאע"פ שיבא ר"ח ביום ל' לראיה אין לו דין וסת קבוע אבל יש לו דין וסת שאינו קבוע לחוש לו מיהא עכ"ל ומביאו ד"מ ר"ל דאם ראתה ביום ב' דסיון או ביום אחר צריכה לחוש ליום ל' מאותו ראיה וכ"כ בפרישה סכ"ה וכ"כ ב"ח ס"ס ט"ז דאם ראתה בב' בסיון כשיגיע ר"ח תמוז חוששת ליום ב' דר"ח תמוז משום עונה בינונית שהיא ל' ולב' בתמוז שהיא להפלגה עכ"ל והעט"ז כתב ג"כ כדברי הב"י והוסיף דצריכה לחוש לעונה בינונית אף על פי שלא תראה היום ויום ל' אינו נעקר בפעם אחת באשה שאין לה וסת קבוע כמו וסת קבוע באשה שיש לה וסת עכ"ל (ואין זה נכון כלל ודוק) ולפ"ז ה"ה דבתחלת ראייתה צריכה לחוש ליום ל' וליום החודש וכן כתוב בפרישה סכ"ג ובב"ח דמ"ש הרואה לר"ח ניסן חוששת לר"ח אייר היינו לב' הימים דר"ח אייר ליום א' דר"ח חוששת לפי שהוא יום ל' לראייתה שהיא עונה בינונית וליום ב' דר"ח חוששת משום ר"ח ע"כ אבל ק"ל ע"ז דאם כן הרמב"ן והרב שבאו לפרש לנו מהו החששות שצריכה לחוש וכתבו שלעולם צריכה לחוש לוסת החדש ולהפלגה למה לא כתבו ופירשו גם כן שצריכה לחוש לעונה בינונית ואדרבה מפשט דבריהם שכתבו האשה חוששת לוסת החודש ולהפלגה כו' וכן ממ"ש בסוף וכן היא חוששת לשניהם עד שתקבע אחד מהם כדינו כו' משמע שאינה צריכה לחוש אלא לב' חששות הללו ותו לא ועוד תימא דודאי הא דאמרינן עונה בינונית היא ל' יום היינו שצריכה לחוש ליום ל"א לראייתה דעונה בינונית היא ל' יום מתחלת ראיה לתחלת ראיה וכ"כ הרשב"א במשמרת הבית דף קס"ז ע"ב וז"ל וסתם נשים חזיין לסוף עונה וכ"כ הרמב"ן ז"ל וז"ל ומצאה אותה בתוך ימי עונתה כמה היא עונה ל' יום מתחלת ראיה לתחלת ראיה אחרת שרוב הנשים כך הן רואות מל' לל' כו' עכ"ל וכן הביאו הכ"מ פ"ד מהל' א"ב ל' הרמב"ן אהא וכן פירש"י פ' כל היד דט"ו ע"א אהא דכל הנשים בחזקת טהרה לבעליהן והוא שבא ומצאה בתוך ימי עונתה וז"ל בתוך ימי ל' לראיה אבל אחר ל' בעיא בדיקה הואיל וסתם נשים חזיין

לסוף עונה עכ״ל אלמא דאפילו ביום ל׳ גופיה שרי משום דעונה בינונית היא ל׳ יום א״כ א״צ לחוש אלא ליום ל׳ מסוף יום הא׳ שראתה בו דהיינו יום ל״א מתחלת ראייתה וכ״כ הטור לעיל סימן קפ״ד אם שהה ל׳ יום חשיב כהגיע וסתה דסתם עונה ל׳ יום ואסור לסוף ל׳ עד שתבדק אלמא דא״צ לחוש אלא ליום ל״א והכי מוכח נמי מדברי הפוסקים והט״ו לקמן סכ״ז שכתבו דג׳ עונות בינוניות הוא צ׳ יום ואי איתא לא ה״ל אלא פ״ח אלא ודאי עונה היא ל׳ יום מתחלת ראיה לתחלת ראיה ודוק וא״כ קשה נמי לאיזה צורך הוצרך הרמב״ן לומר חוששת לר״ח אייר דמשמע משום ר״ח אייר הוא דחוששת הא בלאו הכי חוששת משום עונה בינונית וכמ״ש וכן לאיזה צורך הוצרך לומר חוששת לב׳ בסיון אפשר שתקבע וסת להפלגה תיפוק ליה דהוא עונה בינונית ותו קשיא טובא לדעת הב״י והפרישה והב״ח דס״ל דכל אשה צריכה לחוש ליום החודש וגם לעונה בינונית א״כ היכי אמרינן דצריכה לחוש לעונה בינונית משום דסתם וסת הוא מל׳ לל׳ והרי היא צריכה לחוש ליום החדש שראתה בו והוא יום שאח״כ אע״פ שלא ראתה אלא פעם אחת וע״כ הוא משום דסתם נשים דרכן כך לראות באותו יום החדש ואם כן קשיאן סתמי אהדדי ואיך מתפיס החבל בשתי ראשים שתאמר דמן הסתם צריכה לחוש ליום החדש שמסתמא תראה לאותו יום ותאמר שמן הסתם צריכה לחוש לעונה בינונית וזהו דבר שאין לו שחר כלל אלא נ״ל דהא דאמרינן בש״ס עונה בינונית ל׳ יום היינו מחדש לחדש בין מלא בין חסר וכהאי גוונא אשכחן טובא בש״ס ופוסקים ל׳ יום שהוא חדש וכן גבי בכור קי״ל לק׳ סימן ש״ה דאינו נפדה עד שיעברו עליו ל׳ יום והוא פשוט בש״ס בדוכתי טובי והיינו חדש כדכתב בס׳ יראים סימן שנ״ג וטעמא דכתיב מבן חדש תפדה והיינו ל׳ יום כו׳ והיינו כ״ט י״ב תשצ״ג כו׳ אבל קודם ל׳ אינו פדוי ע״ש (וע״ל סימן ר״כ ס״ק י״ג) וכן מוכח בס׳ בעלי נפש להראב״ד שכתב שהאשה בתחלה צריכה לחוש לוסת החדש ולוסת ההפלגה ולא הזכיר בספרו כלל שצריכה לחוש לעונה בינונית וגם בסוף שער הוסתות מנה בקצרה כל הוסתות הן הקבוע הן שאינו קבוע ולא מנה עונה בינונית כלל וכן הרמב״ם פ״ח מהא״ב ד״ו כתב דכל יום שראתה בו חוששת ליום הבא שלאחריו ולא הזכיר כלל לחוש לעונה בינונית שהוא שלושים יום וכן הרשב״א בת״ה בשער הוסתות כתב כמה פעמים דמי שאין לה וסת קבוע צריכה לחוש לעונה בינונית שהיא ל׳ יום ולא הזכיר כלל שצריכה לחוש לוסת החדש וכן לקמן סימן קצ״ו (ס״ח) כתב הרמב״ן והט״ו דבחרשת כשלא הוקבע לה וסת הרי היא ככל הנשים וחוששת מל׳ לל׳ יום כו׳ ולא כתבו שצריכה לחוש לעונת החדש אלא ודאי עונה בינונית היינו מחדש לחדש דבאותו יום של חדש שראתה בו צריכה לחוש לחדש הבא ותו לא וראיה ברורה לדברי ממאי דכתבו הפוסקים והט״ו לקמן סכ״ז דג׳ עונות הוא צ׳ יום היינו ממאי דאמרינן בש״ס עונה בינונית היא ל׳ יום וכדאיתא בב״י והרמב״ם פ״ד מהל׳ מטמאי משכב ומושב כ׳ דג׳ עונות היינו ג׳ חדשים ומביאו ב״י לקמן סוף ד״ה ומ״ש ראתה ג׳ ראיות מג׳ עונות מכוונות כו׳ אלמא דמאי דאמרי׳ עונה בינונית ל׳ יום היינו חדש ולכך פי׳ הרמב״ן ורש״י דעונה בינונית היא ל׳ יום מתחלת ראיה לתחלת ראיה אחרת והיינו בסתם חדש דהוא מלא ואה״נ אם החדש חסר הוא כ״ט יום מתחלת ראיה לתחלת ראיה אחרת ולא הוצרכו לפ׳ זה משום דסתם חדש מלא הוא ועוד כיון דלעולם אינה צריכה לחוש אלא לאותו יום החדש אם כן א״צ לדקדק בין מלא וחסר אלא לעולם לאותו יום החדש וע״ל ס״ק ל״ג ומ״ג תמצא עוד ראיות לדברי.

סדרי טהרה סימן קפט ס"ק יב – כגון שראתה בא' בניסן ובכ' בו דצריכה לחוש בר"ח אייר משום וסת החדש וכמ"ש כאן בהג"ה אבל משום עונה בינונית א"צ לחוש שהרי ראתה גם בכ' לחדש ואינה אלא י' ימים עד ר"ח.

חוות דעת ביאורים סימן קפו ס"ק ג – מאוד לבי מגמגם בדין זהדאי נימא דמחמת שהוחזקה שלשה פעמים שאינה רואה בימים אלו הוה דינה בימים אלו כאשה שיש לה וסת אם כן אשה שהיה רואה תמיד אחר שלשים יום וכו' לא תחוש לעונה בינונית וכו' והא ודאי ליתא.

שו"ת אגרות משה יורה דעה חלק ב סימן עב – בענין אשה שרואה תמיד אחר שלשים בלא זמן קבוע אם יש לה לחוש לעונה בינונית כ"ב מנחם אב תשכ"ב. מע"כ ידידי הנכבד מוהר"ר אברהם יצחק שיין שליט"א.

ענף א. הנה בדבר אשה שתמיד היא רואה אחר שלשים אבל אחר שלשים אין לה וסת קבוע אם צריכה לחוש לעונה בינונית באשר שעדיין אין לה וסת קבוע והדין באין לה וסת קבוע שחוששת לעונה בינונית כדאיתא בריש סימן קפ"ט. או דכיון שכל ראיותיה היו לאחר שלשים הוקבע לה וסת לענין זה שאינה רואה בעו"ב ואינה צריכה לחוש להעו"ב, וכהא דמצינו שנחשבת יש לה וסת כה"ג בסימן קפ"ו סעיף ג' באשה שאינה רואה בפחות מי"ד יום אחר טבילתה ולאחר י"ד יום אין לה קבע שעד י"ד יום דינה כיש לה וסת. ושמעת שדעתי נוטה שאינה צריכה לחוש כהעו"ב כצד הב' וכתבת איזה קושיות ואבאר הדבר.

והנה פליגי בזה רבותינו האחרונים שבסד"ט סימן קפ"ט סק"כ בסופו כתב על הא דאיתא בש"ך ס"ק מ"ג על ראתה יום ל' ויום ל"ב ויום ל"ד בשם הב"י דחוששת לעונה בינונית, שהוא דוקא בכה"ג שרק שני פעמים היה אחר שלשים אבל ראתה יום ל"א ול"ב ול"ד אף שאין לה וסת קבוע אינה צריכה לחוש לעו"ב דמ"מ הוחזקה שלא תראה עד אחר שלשים, ודימה זה להדין שעד י"ד היא כיש לה וסת. אבל בחו"ד בסימן קפ"ו סק"ג סובר בפשיטות שחוששת לעו"ב עד שבשביל זה נשאר בקושיא על דין דהש"ע שהוא מתה"ד דעד י"ד היא כמו יש לה וסת, שכתב מאד לבי מגמגם בדין זה דאי נימא דמחמת שהוחזקה ג"פ שאינה רואה בימים אלו הוה דינה בימים אלו כיש לה וסת ושלא בשעת וסתה א"כ אשה שרואה תמיד אחר שלשים ואחר שלשים יום אין לה וסת פעמים מקדמת ופעמים מאחרת לא תחוש לעו"ב דהא איתחזקה שלא תראה עד לאחר שלשים יום והא ודאי ליתא כדמוכח מכל הפוסקים עיי"ש. ועיקר טעמו דהביא מרשב"א בתה"א דלענין זה שנאמר שלא תראה שלא בשעת וסת לא אמרינן חזקה דוסתות דלא אמרינן חזקה דוסתות רק לענין שבשעת וסת ודאי תראה משום דאורח בזמנו בא עיי"ש.

אבל הא לכאורה תמוה טובא דהא הוסת עשה שאין חוששין קודם הוסת ומותר לבא עליה אף בישנה כדאיתא בנדה דף י"ב ודף ט"ו ואיפסק ברמב"ם פ"ד מאי"ב ה"ט ובש"ע סימן קפ"ד סעיף א', ולדעת כל הפוסקים אינה צריכה שום בדיקה אף לא לאחר תשמיש, ואף להרמב"ם שם הט"ז שמצריך בדיקה הא אין זה מחשש איסור דהרי הבדיקה שמצריך הוא לאחר תשמיש שכבר נעשה מעשה, אלא הוא תקנה בעלמא לברר מה שאפשר אלהבא ואטו התקנה שהיתה לטהרות, ולקודם תשמיש לא תיקנו משום דהוא כלא אפשר מהחשש שא"כ לבו נוקפו ופורש.

ובאשה שאין לה וסת אסורה לשמש עד שישאלנה ותאמר שהיא טהורה, ולהרמב"ם והרא"ש צריכה בדיקה אף קודם תשמיש, הרי נמצא שהוסת הוא עושה להתיר שלא לחוש קודם הוסת. ויותר מזה תמוה דהא אדרבה לענין החזקה שראתה מצד אורח בזמנו בא, הא איכא דסברי דהוא רק מדרבנן נדה בדף ט"ו ואיפסק כן ברמב"ם פ"ח הי"ד, ואיכא דסברי דגם באין לה וסת כיון שהיא בחזקת טהורה א"צ בדיקה כלל וכן פסק הש"ך סימן קפ"ו סק"א שאף ג"פ הראשונים לא צריכה לבדוק, ולאחר ג"פ לרוב הפוסקים אינה צריכה לבדוק, ואיך נימא איפכא שהוסת הוא רק להחזיק שראתה בזמנו ואינו מועיל להחזיק שלא ראתה קודם הוסת.

וצריך לומר בכוונתו דרק כשנקבע לה וסת לחוש שהיום הוא זמנו דהאורח לבא נעשה ממילא גם שקודם לכן לא יבא, אבל כשאין לו זמן מתי לבא ורק שהוחזקה בג"פ ויותר שבימים אלו דעד י"ד יום מטבילתה אינה רואה, בזה סובר שאינה חזקה מטעם דכיון דאין לו זמן ידוע שיבא שנמצא שכל פעם שבא הוא כעין מקרה אפשר לחוש גם שיארע איזה מקרה שיבא גם קודם משום דעל מקרה לא שייך חזקה. ואף שלפ"ז יקשה דהניחא אם וסתות דאורייתא אבל אם וסתות דרבנן איך יעשה מזה וסת שלא תראה עד הוסת וסומכין לקולא להתיר תשמיש בלא בדיקה ובלא שאלה, אולי נימא דמצד החזקת טהרה כשידע שהיתה טהורה מותרת, ומה שאסורה באין לה וסת שנמי היא בחזקת טהורה, הוא רק מדרבנן שלזה מועיל הוסתות אף שהוא רק מדרבנן.

אבל יקשה אליבא דסברת הנו"ב הובא בפ"ת סימן קפ"ד סק"ב דהאיסור לפרוש סמוך לוסתה הוא מדאורייתא משום דעל להבא ליכא דין חזקה דשמא ימות חיישינן, וכיון שחזקת וסתות ליכא שלא תראה אלא מחמת שנעשה לה חזקה שתראה בזמנו היא ממילא חזקה שלא תראה עד זמן ההוא, ומאחר שחזקה זו היא רק מדרבנן היה לן להחשיב על כל העת מדאורייתא על להבא שמא תראה, וממילא היה לן לאסור בעצם מדאורייתא לעולם אף בבדיקה דשמא תראה בעוד איזה שעה שלכן יש לאסור סמוך לה שאפשר שעתה הוא הסמוך לראייתה, ואף שבהכרח מותר דאל"כ לא היה מציאות היתר להיות עם אשה והתורה הא חייבה בפו"ר ובמצות עונה, ונימא שבכאן נתחדש לסמוך על החזקה אף אלהבא או שלא מצוי שיגרום התשמיש ראיה אף בסמוך לראייתה ולכן לא נאסרו, א"כ גם בסמוך לוסתה אין לאסור אלא רק מדרבנן. וא"כ משמע שוסתות הוא חזקה ודאית על הימים שלא ראתה שלא תראה בהן ולכן ליכא שום חשש, והנידון אם דאורייתא או דרבנן הוא על זמן הוסת שאמרינן שאורח בזמנו בא שזה אפשר הוא רק מדרבנן משום שכנגדו איכא חזקת טהרה כדכתב הנו"ב ולכן בסמוך לוסתה שהוא אלהבא שאיכא חזקת אורח בזמנו יבא וליכא נגדו חזקת טהרה אוסר מדאורייתא. וא"כ הוא דלא כסברת החו"ד אם יסבור כהנו"ב.

ונצטרך לומר להחו"ד דביש לה וסת קבוע הוא חזקה ודאית שלא מקרים גרמו לה אלא הזמן, והנידון דאפשר הוא רק מדרבנן הוא לענין שזמן הזה הוא הכרח, שאפשר שידחה על ימים אחרים ולא תראה ביום הוסת. ולכן כשיש לה וסת קבוע הוא חזקה ודאית שלא תראה עד הוסת וסומכין ע"ז מדאורייתא אף בלא חזקה דטהרה שלה שלכן מותרת לבעלה קודם הוסת אף שחזקת טהרה אין להועיל לה משום דהוא אלהבא, מצד חזקת הוסתות. אבל כשאין לה וסת קבוע שאפשר שמקרים גרמו לה לראות שלכן אין לה קביעות, אף שאפשר שמצד טבעיות

הימים נמי אין לה קביעות דבשביל זה הא איכא דסובר דוסתות הוא רק מדרבנן אף שודאי אשה מוכרחת לראות מצד משך הימים גם בלא שום מקרה, וא"כ מוכרחין לומר דגם בלא שום מקרה וסבה לראות אפשר לאשה שתראה בלא וסת קבוע לזמן מיוחד, מ"מ הא אפשר גם שאשה זו גורמים לה מקרים לראות דם אף קודם הזמן שהיתה רואה ממילא בלא שום מקרה וסבה, ואחרי שכבר יצאו דמיה ע"י המקרים אין לה שוב דם לצאת בהגעת הימים שהיתה רואה בלא מקרים. ולכן אף שיש לה חזקה בי"ד יום אחר טבילתה לא ראתה בהן סובר החו"ד שחזקה כזו שהמקרים מועילים לאשה זו רק אחר י"ד יום ולא קודם אינה חזקה, דעל מקרים לא שייך חזקה אם אך היא אשה שמועילים בה מקרים כדחזינן שאחר י"ד יום מועילין בה מקרים לפי המסתבר, ורק כשיש לה וסת קבוע אמרינן דחזקה דבאשה זו אין מועילין בה מקרים כלל לכן אין חוששין. זהו מה שמוכרחין לפרש בכוונת החו"ד שהזכיר הא דבאין לה וסת כתב הב"י בשם הר"ן שנראה לומר שמקריים גורמים לראייתה, ואין כוונת הר"ן שהוא ודאי שזה א"א דודאי היתה האשה רואה דם גם בלא מקריים דכי לעולם לא תראה כשלא יזדמן לה איזה מקרה, וגם הא וסתות הוא רק מדרבנן. אבל הוא כדבארתי שפירושו שיותר מסתבר שמה שלא נקבע לה וסת הוא משום שהמקרים נמי גורמין לראייתה וכיון שיצאו דמיה ע"י המקרים אין מה לצאת ממנה ע"י משך הימים. ומכיון שיש לחוש באשה זו שע"י מקרים היא נמי רואה סובר החו"ד שע"ז לא שייך חזקה שבימים אלו לא יועילו בה מקריים. ואף שאפשר שרק כשכבר יש במקור שלה הרבה דם שנתקבץ בהי"ד יום מועילין המקריים להוציאם ולא בפחות מזה שעדיין ליכא הרבה דם במקורה, וכדחזינן בסעיף י"ח/סי' קפ"ט/ שאיכא קביעות וסת לימים ולקפיצות שחוששת רק לכל פעם שתקפוץ באותו זמן, שהטעם הוא שאף שכבר הגיע הזמן שיש בה דמים אינה חוששת בלא קפיצה משום שסך דמים שיש בה לא יצאו מעצמן משום שאין בה סך הרב שיצאו מעצמן וכן בקפצה קודם הזמן אינה חוששת משום שבזמן מועט אין לה סך הדמים שיוכלו לצאת ע"י הקפיצה. וגם משמע שם יותר שאף בקפצה אחר הזמן נמי אינה חוששת, שכתב או שקפצה בשני בשבת, והרי איירי שם שהזמן היה באחד בשבת, שלכאורה הא לא שייך טעם זה שבארתי דביום יותר הא יש להיות במקורה יותר דמים. וצריך לומר דכיון דזה דהקפיצה תגרום יציאת הדם אינו טבעי אלא אונס שלכן לא נקבע וסת על קפיצות לבד אלא עם הימים אין לחוש אף כשהוא עם הימים אלא דוקא לאותו יום ממש משום שאפשר שאין הקפיצה שולטת עליה להוציא הדם אלא באחר/באחד/ בשבת ולא אח"כ אף שיש בה יותר דמים משום דאפשר דבאחד בשבת שהוחזקה שמועיל בה הקפיצה הוא משום שאז גופה הוא בשינוי מימים האחרים. ואף שהיא סברא רחוקה אמרינן בקפיצה שג"כ אינו טבעי ואין סברא לזה שיוציא הדם. עכ"פ הא חזינן שגם מקרים כקפיצה קובעים וסת שלא תראה ע"ז אלא אחר הזמן, וא"כ מ"ט לא נימא שעד י"ד הוקבע וסת שלא יועילו מקריים.

אך אפשר לחלק שדוקא בידוע המקרה שעשה יציאת הדם שהיא הקפיצה שבעצם הוא אונס ולא נקבע עליו וסת אמרינן שאפשר שדוקא ביום זה מועילה הקפיצה, ומצד עצם הדמים שבגופה שודאי יש לה לראות גם בלא קפיצה דכי לעולם לא תראה אפשר לא הגיע הזמן דהא לא ראתה בלא קפצה, ואה"נ כשיבא יום שלשים תחוש לעו"ב כאשה שלא קבעה וסת, אבל בלא ידוע איזה מקרה מוציא הדם ורק מזה שאין לה וסת קבוע ניכר שמקריים גורמים לראייתה

אפשר שלא נזדמן אותו המקרה שמוציא הדם בימים ההם אף שהיה זה הרבה פעמים. ומה שכתב שיש לחוש שתשמיש יגרום, לא מבעיא אם לא היה תשמיש באותן הי"ד יום ששייך לחוש לזה אלא אף בהיה תשמיש כאורחא דמלתא נמי כיון שלא ידעינן המקרה, אפשר שבצרוף שני דברים הוא המקרה המוציא הדם וכשיהיה איזה דבר אף שאינו גורם בעצמו יגרום ע"י התשמיש. ואף שלשון החו"ד דחוק לפירוש זה מוכרחין לומר כן כדי שלא יקשה מקפיצות.

ענף ב. אבל הוא ודאי דחוק טובא דיותר משמע דמועילה חזקת הוסת שלא לחוש לראיה קודם הוסת מלדחוק בכל זה. וגם כיון שיש טעם גדול שהמקריים יועילו רק אחר הזמן די"ד יום שיש במקורה כבר הרבה דמים אין לנו לומר דיועילו גם קודם בפרט שהם שלא כטבע הנשים. ומה שהביא החו"ד בשם הרשב"א ראיה מהא דטמאה מעל"ע שלא בשעת וסתה שחזקת הוסת אין מועיל לומר שלא תראה עד הוסת, תמוה דלכאורה לא מובן הראיה דהא פרש"י נדה בדף ד' דכיון דראתה שלא בזמנה איכא למיחש דלמא מקמי הכי הוה דהא ליכא למימר אורח בזמנו בא, שהרי בא תחלה וא"כ אפשר שבא מעל"ע קודם. וצריך לומר דכוונתו דמצד החזקה דלא תראה תחלה היה לן לומר שיהיה דינה כמו דין הד' נשים שמסולקות מדמים שאמרינן דיין שעתן ולא חיישינן שמא כמו שראתה עתה אף שמסולקת מדמים ראתה גם מעל"ע תחלה, מטעם דכיון דהיא מסולקת מדמים והוא שינוי מכפי שהיה צריך להיות אמרינן דרק עתה נעשה השינוי ולא מעל"ע מקודם, א"כ גם ביש לה וסת שהוא חזקה שלא תראה קודם נמי הוא שינוי במה שראתה שיש לנו לומר שרק עתה נעשה השינוי ולא מעל"ע מקודם, אלא הוא משום דליכא חזקה שלא תראה ולכן מטמאה בראתה מעל"ע למפרע. ונצטרך לומר לדידיה שמתחלה שרצה הגמ' לומר דאפילו שלא בשעת וסתה סובר ר' דוסא שדיה שעתה סובר דוסתות הוא חזקה שלא תראה קודם ובמסקנא פליג וסובר שאינה חזקה לענין שלא תראה, והוא דוחק גדול לפרש כן.

ובפשוטו יש לפרש שכיון שעבידי נשי דקא משניא וסתייהו כדאיתא בריש כתובות, אף שמ"מ היא בחזקת שלא תראה ואין לחוש כל זמן שאין אנו רואים שהיה שינוי מ"מ כששינתה וסתה ויצתה מחזקתה הוא ריעותא לחוש גם על מעל"ע מקודם. ואף שבכל חזקה אמרינן דרק עתה איתרע ולא מתחלה כהא דנגע באחד בלילה כשראהו חי בערב שאף רבנן מודו דטהור אף שבשחר מצאו מת כדאיתא בר"ש פ"ה דטהרות מ"ז משום דאמרינן דאוקמינן אחזקת חי עד עתה שראוהו מת, מ"מ לענין טומאה דמעל"ע מקודם הא לא מוקמינן אחזקתה דהא כל אשה היתה בחזקת טהרה ומ"מ טימאוה מעל"ע מקודם, לכן גם מצד חזקה זו דוסתות החמירו מאותו הטעם עצמו דכיון דמגופה קחזיא לא אמרינן אוקמא אחזקה ולא מחלקין בין חזקה אחת לתרי חזקות, ול"ד לארבע נשים שלא מצוי בהן כלל דם ועדיף מחזקה. ומתחלה היה סבור הגמ' לר' דוסא שמחלק בין חדא חזקה לתרתי.

ומה שהביא החו"ד ראיה מהרא"ש שסובר דאשה שאין לה וסת צריכה בדיקה לעולם ולא מועיל מה שבשלש פעמים לא ראתה מחמת תשמיש שאלמא שגם הרא"ש סובר שלענין שלא תראה ליכא חזקה זו, הנה מה שדחה הרא"ש ספ"ק דנדה דברי הרי"ף שמתיר אשה שאין לה וסת בתשמיש ג"פ בבדיקות משום דכיון דאין לה זמן קבוע לראייתה חיישינן שמא תפרוס נדה תחתיו, אינו משום דדלמא תראה מחמת שהתשמיש יגרום הראיה כדמפרש החו"ד, דאם מצד חשש זה היה לו להרא"ש ליתן טעם על מה שבאין לה זמן קבוע איכא יותר החשש מיש לה

זמן קבוע, דאם גם הרא"ש סובר הטעם של הר"ן דבאין לה זמן קבוע נראה שהמקרים גורמים לה הרי היה זה תירוץ הרי"ף, שהר"ן הא מתרץ בסברא זו הקושיא דלכן מועיל בדיקה בתשמיש ג"פ שאם מצאה טהורה יצאה מחשש זה כמפורש בהר"ן והביאו הב"י והמעיו"ט לתרץ קושית הרא"ש, ואם להרא"ש לא נראה התירוץ מטעם שכתב החו"ד דלענין שלא תראה לא אמרינן חזקה זו אין זה דבר פשוט שלא יצטרך להזכיר זה בקושיתו. אלא ברור שקושיתו היא משום דלא סבר כהר"ן שיש לחוש באין לה וסת שמקרים גורמים לה לראות משום שלא מצוי שתראה מצד קפיצה ושאר מקרים דמטעם זה לא נקבעה וסת לקפיצות משום דהוא רק אונס מה שראתה ולא מצד טבע הנשים כדאיתא בט"ז/סי' קפ"ט/ס"ק ל"ב והסכים לו הש"ך, וכפ"מ שאיתא בד"ח דף ס"ג גם הרא"ש/נדה/ סובר כן. אך שסובר הרא"ש דהחשש הוא דמכיון שאין לה זמן קבוע הרי אפשר שעתה תראה כיון שאין לה וסת כדכתב בסוף קושיתו שבלשון הזה ודאי הוי הפירוש רק זה דכיון שאין לה וסת כל יומא יש לחוש שזמנה הוא שבשביל זה יש לחוש אף כשהתשמיש אינו גורם לה לראות אלא הדם בא לה ממילא כדרך הנשים שיוצאין הדמים כשנתמלא מקורה בדם, ובאשה זו ליכא זמן קבוע למלוי הדם במקורה שלכן יש לחוש שעתה הוא זמנה, וממילא יש לאסור מלשמש בלא בדיקה קודם, וא"כ מה מועיל כשתבדוק ג"פ בג' תשמישים ונדע מזה שהתשמיש אינו גורם לה ראייה הא עכ"פ אפשר שעתה הגיע זמן הראיה שלה.

וגם במה שאוסר ר"מ אף בבדיקה נמי אינו להרא"ש מחשש שמא התשמיש יגרום אלא משום שחושש שמא יהיה הזמן ראיה בשעת תשמיש. ור' חנינא בן אנטיגנוס אינו חושש לשמא תפרוס נדה תחתיו לאסור אף בבדיקה כיון דלא מצוי כל כך שתיכף תהיה נדה. ועיין בתוס' גיטין דף כ"ח דאף לר' יהודה דחייש למיתה ולאביי דלא מחלק בין שמא ימות לשמא מת מ"מ לא חייש לשמא מת לאלתר דאל"כ אשת כהן שיצא בעלה מפתח ביתה לא תאכל בתרומה, ולכן הכא נמי כיון שהיא טהורה וכשלא תראה נדה עד אחר התשמיש הרי מותרת לכן כשבדקה והיא טהורה קודם התשמיש אין לחוש על זמן הקצר שמהבדיקה עד התשמיש תיכף ובאמצע התשמיש שראתה נדה כמו שאין חוששין לאוסרה מלאכול התרומה תיכף מחשש שמא מת קודם האכילה ובאמצע האכילה. ור"מ אף דלמיתה לא חייש לזמן מועט אף ליותר מאכילה, חייש הכא משום דיותר מצוי באשה שאין לה וסת אף לראות תיכף. ור"ח בן אנטיגנוס סובר דכיון שהיא בחזקת טהורה אין לחוש לתיכף שתראה אף שיותר מצוי ממיתה כיון דעכ"פ לא מצוי כל כך. ומה שמצריך בדיקה גם אחר תשמיש הוא מכיון דחזינן שצריך לפרוש סמוך לוסתה עונה אחת והוא מטעם דאף דהתשמיש אינו גורם לראות דם בשאר ימים מ"מ סמוך לוסתה חוששין שמא יגרום למהר יציאת הדם, עיין בפ"ת סימן קפ"ד סק"ג שהביא מחת"ס בשם הרא"ה דהאיסור הוא משום שמא ע"י חמום התשמיש יקדים האורח לבא, וא"כ באשה שאין לה וסת קבוע שיש לחוש על כל יום שמא היום זמנה היה לנו לאסור התשמיש מחשש שמא בסוף העונה יהיה זמנה שזה דבר מצוי ויש לחשוש. אך שאין אוסרין זה משום דדין הפרישה סמוך לוסתה הוא רק מדרבנן, ואף להנו"ב דמשוי לה ספק דאורייתא מ"מ באין לה וסת הוא ס"ס דהא אפשר שאינו סמוך לוסתה ואף אם סמוך אפשר לא יוקדם הראיה. אבל מ"מ חשש שמא היה סמוך לוסתה ובתשמיש הקדים הראיה איכא אף שלא אסרו מלשמש בשביל חשש זה, לכן יש לה לבדוק אחר תשמיש לידע העיוות. ואף שלא תאסר מחמת זה משום דהא בפעם אחר נמי בבדיקה שקודם

תשמיש יסולק החשש דשמא עתה הוא זמנה לראות דלא מצוי כל כך לראות תיכף, ומצד שמא סמוך לוסתה הוא רק מדרבנן וגם הוא ס"ס, מ"מ כיון דאיכא חשש יש לידע העיוות.

ענף ג. ומדויק לשון הרא"ש שכתב דלאחר תשמיש לידע העיוות דחייש ליה לדר"מ שמא תפרוס נדה תחתיו ובאותו שלפני תשמיש כתב כי אותו העד מתקנה ומתירה לשמש דלא חיישינן להא דר"מ שלכאורה הוא סתירה. אבל הוא כדבארתי דגם לר"ח בן אנטיגנוס איכא חשש דשמא תפרוס נדה תחתיו כמו לר"מ, אבל משני טעמים דר"מ חושש מצד זמן הראיה שלה דשמא הוא עתה תיכף אחר הבדיקה ובאמצע התשמיש עוד יותר מחשש מיתה לר' יהודה אליבא דאביי. והטעם אולי משום דר"מ חושש למיעוטא. (ומה שלמיתה לא חייש אולי הוא משום החזקה דחיים דאף לשמא ימות לזמן מועט סובר שאיכא החזקה, ונראה שהוא חזקה מכח רובא דרובא דאין מתים פתאם בזמן מועט. ולרבא אליבא דר' יהודה דחושש לשמא ימות הוא משום דאיכא חזקת טבל כנגדה בחשש בקיעת נוד, וגבי ה"ז גיטך שעה אחת קודם למיתתו אסורה לאכול בתרומה מיד אף שאדרבה אית לה חזקת היתר לאכול בתרומה, הוא משום דכיון דהיא בעצם זרה שהוא דבר האוסרה מתרומה היא נחשבת אף כשהיא תחת בעלה הכהן בחזקת אסורה רק שבעלה הוא המתירה מאיסורה, ולכן מצד עצמה יש להחשיבה כאסורה שזה עומד נגד חזקת חיים דהבעל שבא מכח הרוב שאין מתים לאלתר. ול"ד לשמא מת שלא חיישינן שחזקה זו היא על השתא שיש לו מצד עצמו, שלכן אין להחשיב שחזקת האיסור מצד זרות עומד כנגדו משום שחזקה זו עושה שלא יעשה ספק כלל ונידון כמו שאנחנו רואין אותו חי. אבל אלהבא לא שייך שלא יעשה ספק כיון דהוא ענין לעתיד שלא שייך לידיעת וראיית בנ"א ואין להחשיב הנידון מהחזקה שיחיה כהרוב כמו שאנחנו רואין זה אלא הוא רק דין חזקה להכריע הספק שלכן כיון שאיכא חזקת איסור זרות כנגד אינו יכול להכריע ואסורה מספק. ור"מ אולי מחשיב זה שנפרש התו"מ עכ"פ אף שהיה באופן ברירה כאיתרע החזקת טבל, וכן חזקת איסור זרות שלה איתרע ע"י שניסת לבעלה הכהן והחזקת חיים דהבעל ושלימות הנוד אף אלהבא מצד הרוב לא איתרע לכן מכריע להיתר). ור"ח בן אנטיגנוס סובר דמצד חשש זה אין לאוסרה דעל זמן מועט אין לחוש אף להבא כמו לר' יהודה אליבא דאביי בחשש מיתה ולכן מותרת לתשמיש כשבדקה קודם תשמיש. וזהו מש"כ הרא"ש ומתירה לשמש דלא חיישינן להא דר"מ. אבל הוא רק מצד החשש שמא תראה מחמת שהגיע זמנה תיכף אחר הבדיקה ע"ז אינו חושש אבל להחשש שמא תראה מצד שהוא סמוך לוסתה שהוא עד סוף העונה שהוא זמן גדול חושש גם ר"ח בן אנטיגנוס שיש לחוש שמא תראה נדה תחתיו בעת התשמיש כדמצינו שאסורה סמוך לוסתה לשמש מחשש שמא יקדים הראיה, אך שלא נאסרה בשביל חשש זה כיון שהוא רק ספק סמוך לוסתה אבל לכן מצריך מטעם חשש זה בדיקה לאחר תשמיש לידע העיוות. וזהו מש"כ הרא"ש דחייש ליה לדר"מ שמא תפרוס נדה תחתיו אך שלטעמיה נוגע זה רק להצריך בדיקה גם אחר תשמיש.

וניחא למה שבארתי מש"כ הרא"ש אח"כ ובלבד שלא תתחזק לראות ג"פ זו אחר זו מחמת תשמיש דאז היא אסורה לבעל זה שלכאורה קשה טובא לאיזה צורך נקט זה דהוא מלתא דפשיטא דהא בכל הנשים אף באלו שיש להן וסת איכא דין זה דרואתה מחמת תשמיש ומ"ש באין לה וסת שהוצרך למינקט. דהא לפ"מ שבארתי היה לן להתיר אשה שאין לה וסת שמשתמשת

בבדיקות אף כשתראה ג"פ מחמת תשמיש, משום דאולי אין להחזיקה שהתשמיש גורם לה ראיה שאין זה טבע השנים שתשמיש יגרום ראיה, דמחמת זה כתבו התוס'/נדה/ דף ס"ו דאפילו לרבי בעי ג' זימנין לאחזוקה, וגם הא כמה קולות מקילינן ברואה מחמת תשמיש עד שאומרין שהיא אשה הרואה מחמת תשמיש, וגם הא מפורש בסימן קפ"ז סעיף ד' בשמשה סמוך לוסתה תולין ראייתה משום וסתה ולא חשבינן לה רואה מחמת תשמיש ופי' הש"ך שהוא בעברה ושמשה, והפרישה מפרש עוד יותר להקל שאף בשמשה בהיתר שהוא בהיה וסתה בתחלת היום שמותר בלילה שלפניו, שפי' בתוה"ש ס"ק י"ב טעמו דאף שמזה שמותרת בהלילה שלפניו הוא משום דלא חיישינן שתראה מחמת סמיכות הוסת ביום שלאחריה מ"מ כיון שאין דרך דם לבא מן המקור ע"י תשמיש אמרינן דע"י תשמיש אקדמה לוסתה אף באופן זה שלא אסרו חכמים מצד חשש זה רק באותו היום דמ"מ כיון שיש קצת חשש שתקדים ע"י תשמיש את הראיה אף בלילה שלפניו סגי זה לסלק ממנה חשיבות רואה מחמת תשמיש ומתרץ בזה קושית הש"ך דכיון דלא חיישינן להחמיר כ"ש דאין לתלות לקולא עיי"ש, וכן כתב בסד"ט סק"י והוכיח כן גם מחדושי הר"ן שכתב סברת עצמו שתולה בוסתה לומר שמחמת תשמיש הקדים בדם לבא ולא כתב מההוכחה מעצם הדין דכיון דאסרו סמוך לוסתה אלמא דחיישינן לשמא יקדים ע"י התשמיש משמע שמפרש הר"ן כהפרישה שהיה בלילה שלפניו שלא אסרו מצד החשש שיקדים ע"י התשמיש דמ"מ מחדש שקצת חששא איכא שיש לתלות בזה להוציאה מדין רואה מחמת תשמיש עיי"ש. וא"כ היה סברא גדולה לומר שרק באשה שיש לה וסת אסורה הרואה מחמת תשמיש משום שאין במה לתלות שהרי הוסת הוא רחוק ולא שייך שיקדים, אבל באין לה וסת שאפשר שעתה הוא סמוך לוסתה ומחמת זה ראתה בשעת תשמיש משום שהתשמיש עשה רק להקדים לא נאסור. ל"מ לשיטת הפרישה שמקילין בשביל תליה קטנה שלא חששו לה להחמיר, אלא אף להש"ך דאין תולין אלא בסמוך לוסתה שהוא חשש גדול שהרי חששו גם לאסור, אפשר שבזה עדיף כיון דמה שלא אסרו היה משום דהוא ספק דרבנן ואף אם נימא שהוא מצד ס"ס נמי אמאי לא נימא דנתברר ע"י זה שראתה בשעת התשמיש דהיה סמוך לוסתה ולא שהוא מצד שהיא רואה מחמת תשמיש. לכן חידש הרא"ש דאם תראה בג"פ בשעת תשמיש תהיה אסורה כמו באשה שיש לה וסת ולא נתלה לומר שאירע שכל הג"פ היו סמוך לוסתה אלא שכיון שהיו ג"פ זו אחר זו מוכיחין זו על זו שכולן היו משום שהתשמיש גורם באשה זו ראיית דם משום דרחוק לומר שאירע שהיו סמוך לוסתה, ואף דלומר דהיא רואה מחמת תשמיש הוא ג"כ דבר שלא מצוי מ"מ תליה זו הוא יותר רחוק, ואף אם הם שוין יש לאסור מספק. ונמצא שהוא חדוש גדול דהוצרך הרא"ש לאשמועינן.

ענף ד. וא"כ מוכרח שאין טעם הרא"ש משום שסובר דבאשה שאין לה וסת שנראה שהמקרים גרמו לא מהני חזקה דוסתות שלא תראה, שנמצא שבאין לה וסת יותר יש לחוש שתראה מחמת תשמיש, שא"כ לאיזה צורך נקט כאן דין זה שאסורה בג"פ שתראה בשעת תשמיש דהא כ"ש הוא. וגם למה כתב דלאחר תשמיש הוא לידע העיות שמשמע שאין נוגע להיתרה, הא כיון שסובר דלעולם חוששין שמא תראה מחמת תשמיש הא יש לנו להצריך בדיקה בשביל היתרה דאם תראה ג"פ תאסר כיון שחוששין לזה, אלא ודאי דהפירוש ברא"ש אינו משום דלעולם חושש לשמא תראה מחמת תשמיש שליכא דין וסת לזה שלא תראה, דודאי

איכא וסת לזה שאין התשמיש גורם לה ראיה ואפשר שסובר שאין לחוש כלל לשמא מקרים גורמים לה דלא כר"ן, והחשש הוא שמא עתה תראה מצד טבעה לראות ולא משום מקרה התשמיש כדבארתי. ואדרבה בר"ן שהביא החו"ד הא מפורש שזה שמפרש שבאין לה וסת הוא ע"י מקרים הוא תירוץ על קושית הרא"ש כדאיתא בב"י וד"ח. והוא תימה גדולה על החו"ד איך פי' בכוונת הרא"ש פירוש זר כזה שא"א לפרשו כלל. וגם מש"כ החו"ד על תה"ד שלומר אליבא דסברת הר"ן שאיכא חזקה דלא תראה מחמת מקריים בי"ד הימים שאינה רואה בהם שהוא דחוק הא הר"ן שהביא אומר כן לתרץ דברי הרי"ף. וגם הרשב"א עצמו שהביא ממנו שסובר שלא אמרינן חזקה דוסתות שלא תראה מפרש הוא עצמו בחדושיו לנדה ספ"ק בטעם הרי"ף שבהג"פ שלא ראתה בשעת תשמיש נעשית מוחזקת שלא תראה מחמת תשמיש הרי הרשב"א ג"כ סובר דמועיל חזקת וסת גם לענין שלא תראה וכן סובר גם הרמב"ן בחדושיו לנדה שם. וזהו הטעם שאין לחוש לגמגום החו"ד ודין תה"ד שפסק הש"ע אמת שעד הי"ד יום נידונית כיש לה וסת, וגם בד"ח ספ"ק הביאו להלכה ואין בזה שום קושיא.

וממילא יש ראיה שגם בראתה תמיד אחר שלשים שנעקר דין וסת החדש ועונה בינונית אף שלא קבעה וסת לאחר השלשים דפעמים מקדמת ופעמים מאחרת אין לה לחוש לעונה בינונית כדכתב החו"ד עצמו שתלוי בדין זה דהש"ע דנחשבת יש לה וסת עד הי"ד יום אך שהוא פליג על הש"ע גם בדין הי"ד יום מטעם קושיותיו, וכיון שנתברר שדין הש"ע אמת ממילא גם דין זה יש למילף וכדהוכיח כן בסד"ט לדינא. ואף שכתב הסד"ט לבסוף מיהו יש לומר דאיהו לא הקל אלא לענין בדיקה לפני תשמיש דבלא"ה הרבה גאונים סברי דכל לבעלה לא בעי בדיקה אבל בעלמא אפשר דלא סמכינן על זה עיי"ש, הנה למה שבארתי יש להחשיבה בהי"ד יום לכל דבר כיש לה וסת וממילא גם כשהוחזקה שאינה רואה עד אחר שלשים נמי הוא כיש לה וסת שלא תראה עד אחר שלשים כיון דלכל הפוסקים יש חזקת וסת שלא תראה. ואף החו"ד לא מחלק בינייהו אלא דפליג גם על דין די"ד יום. ולכן נראה שהסד"ט כתב המיהו י"ל רק שאין מזה ראיה כל כך אבל לדינא סובר כדכתב תחלה שאין לה לחוש לעונה בינונית. (ובמה שצייר הסד"ט שם ברואה ל"א ל"ב ל"ד לא היתה צריכה לחוש לעו"ב אינו מדויק כ"כ דהא להש"ך סק"ל הרי ביום ל"א הוא העו"ב ונקט הלשון לפי החולקין על הש"ך, אבל כוונתו שהוחזקה שאינה רואה עד אחר שעבר עו"ב לכל חד כדאית ליה). ועתה נבא לקושית כתר"ה.

הנה מה שהקשה כת"ר מתירוץ נקוה"כ על קושית הט"ז סימן קפ"ט סק"ה ע"ז שאיתא בש"ע דבוסת שלא נקבע ג"פ כיון שעברה עונתה מותרת כשלא ראתה אף שלא בדקה, והא בסימן קפ"ו נפסק דבאין לה וסת צריכה בדיקה לעולם לפני תשמיש, דכאן מיירי שיש לה וסת אלא שאינו קבוע, ופי' החו"ד בסק"ב דכוונת הש"ך הוא כהא דסימן קפ"ו סעיף ג' שעד י"ד יום יש לה וסת שאינה רואה בהם ואחר י"ד יום אין לה קבע שעד הי"ד יום היא בדין יש לה וסת שאינה צריכה בדיקה קודם תשמיש ופעם אחת ראתה קודם הי"ד שאף שצריכה בדיקה אותו יום הוא קיל שאם עבר אותו יום מותרת עד הי"ד יום בלא בדיקה, שלתירוץ זה הא גם במש"כ הש"ע סי' קפ"ט ס"ד אחר זה ועונה בינונית שהיא לשלשים יום דינה כוסת קבוע שאסורה בעבר היום אף שלא ראתה עד שתבדוק, דג"כ יקשה קושית הט"ז דבלא"ה הא צריכה בדיקה ונצטרך נמי לאוקמי כהא דסימן קפ"ו דהיה לה וסת שאינה רואה עד אחר עו"ב אבל אינה קבועה למתי

היא רואה אחר העו״ב שבעברה העו״ב ולא ראתה אסורה עד שתבדוק, הרי חזינן דלא נעקר יום עו״ב בזה שלא ראתה בו ג״פ ויותר. הנה לא קשה כלום דבסיפא איירי שפעם אחת ראתה קודם השלשים שכיון שדין עו״ב הוא כוסת קבוע ואיתא בסעיף ט״ו /סי׳ קפ״ט/ באשה שהיה לה וסת ליום עשרים ושינתה ראיותיה ולא השוה אותם שנעקר וסתה הראשון שאם חזרה לראות ביום הוסת הראשון חוזר לקביעותו הראשון, ולכן כשראתה ג״פ אחר שלשים שנעקר דין עו״ב שאם חזרה לראות פעם אחת קודם שלשים חוזר לדין הראשון שיום השלשים הוא כוסת קבוע ואסורה אף בלא ראתה בו עד שתבדוק. (ודע דקושית הט״ז הוא רק לשיטתו שמיקל בעבר הוסת גם בבדיקה אחר זמן הרבה בסימן קפ״ד ס״ק י״ב. ונחמיר באין לה וסת להצריך לראותו לאלתר קודם התשמיש דלא כהמקילין לראותו למחר עיין בפ״ת סימן קפ״ו סק״ג בשם תשובה מאהבה שנסתפק בזה, ובחו״ד סק״ב בסופו כתב שפליגי בזה רש״י ותוס׳ עם הרשב״א והר״ן ורמב״ן עיי״ש. והחו״ד הזכיר דלא קשה כיון שבאין לה וסת לא צריכה לאור הנר וצ״ע על הט״ז שלא הרגיש בזה, ועל נקה״כ שלדידיה ל״ק כלל דהא סובר כהמחמירין שצריך בדיקה תוך שיעור וסתה והי״ל להזכיר זה).

ומהא דנדה דף ט׳ בזקנה שעברו ג׳ עונות וראתה ועוד ג׳ עונות וראתה ועוד ג׳ עונות וראתה שמטמאה מעל״ע בפיחתה והותירה שפרש״י ראשונה לצ״ג ושניה לצ״ב ושלישית לצ״א, לא קשה כלום דכל רואה דם באין לה וסת מספקינן דשמא היתה הראיה מעל״ע תחלה ונמצא שלא היה לה וסת לענין שלא תראה קודם צ״א דהרי ראתה בצ״א שהוא ספק דאפשר שראיה זו היתה מאתמול והעמידו כותלי הרחם. ומה שלא חששו למעל״ע בב׳ פעמים הראשונים היה זה מדין זקנה. וזהו כוונת תה״ד בתירוצו ע״ז דלענין דם הרי דם לפניך פי׳ שבכל דם שלפנינו היום הראשון למעל״ע תחלה ואין כוונתו משום ריעותא. וגם יום השלשים כיון דנעקר ג״פ אינו ריעותא שוב ול״ק כלום אף לדברי כת״ר. אבל בעצם ל״ק כלום ומוכרח שכוונת תה״ד כדכתבתי. ומה שהזכיר תה״ד שהרי הרשב״ם ועוד פסקו דלבעלה לא בעי בדיקה הנה בסד״ט רוצה לפרש דאולי סמיך להתיר בצרוף דעת המתירין לגמרי אבל יותר מסתבר דגם בל״ז מתיר כדבארתי שמוכרח כן. ואני כבר כתבתי לעיל שליכא חשש שתראה מחמת תשמיש באין לה וסת להרא״ש אלא שמא יארע שהוסת יבא אז ורק להרי״ף יש חשש בזה לתירוץ הר״ן ורק עד ג״פ.

ומה שהקש״ה כת״ר על הנו״ב דסובר דאשה הרואה מחמת תשמיש כשלא היה לה וסת ואח״כ איקבע לה וסת שהותרה, לא מובן לי קושיתו שהנו״ב לשיטתו דרואה מחמת תשמיש הוא מדין וסת ושוסת קבוע עוקר וסת שאינו קבוע אף כשעדיין לא ידוע שנעקר האינו קבוע ומחמת תשמיש הוא אינו קבוע אפילו בהרבה פעמים צדק מאד. ידידו, משה פיינשטיין.

תלמוד בבלי מסכת נדה דף ט עמוד א – בעא מיניה ההוא סבא מר׳ יוחנן: הגיע עת וסתה בימי עבורה ולא בדקה, מהו? קא מיבעיא לי אליבא דמ״ד וסתות דאורייתא. מאי! כיון דוסתות דאורייתא – בעיא בדיקה, או דלמא: כיון דדמיה מסולקין, לא בעיא בדיקה? א״ל, תניתוה: רבי מאיר אומר, אם היתה במחבא והגיע שעת וסתה ולא בדקה – טהורה, שחרדה מסלקת את הדמים. טעמא – דאיכא חרדה, הא ליכא חרדה והגיע וסתה ולא בדקה – טמאה, אלמא: וסתות דאורייתא. וכיון דאיכא חרדה – דמיה מסולקין, ולא בעיא בדיקה; הכא נמי – דמיה מסולקין, ולא בעיא בדיקה.

שולחן ערוך יורה דעה הלכות נדה סימן קפט סעיף לג – מעוברת, לאחר שלשה חדשים לעיבורה ומניקה כל כ"ד חודש אחר לידת הולד,אינה קובעת וסת. אפילו מת הולד או גמלתו, דמים מסולקים מהן כל זמן עיבורה וכל כ"ד חודש. ומ"מ חוששת לראיה שתראה כדרך שחוששת לוסת שאינו קבוע.

שו"ת רבי עקיבא איגר מהדורה קמא סימן קכח – לענ"ד הא הסילוק דמים הוא רק משהוכר עוברה, ואף דעינינו רואות בנשי דידן דמיד כשנתעברו מסולקות דמים ונשתנו הטבעים, וכמ"ש תוס' גבי עינוניתא דוורדא, הא חזינן בש"ע יו"ד (סי' קפ"ט סל"ג) וכן (בס' ק"צ סנ"ב) וא' מעוברת שהוכר עוברה. ולא נזכר רמז באחרוני' שלדידן אף בלא הוכר עוברה כן.

גם מנ"ל דטבלה לנדתה ממש דלמא ראתה כתם, והי' באמת מעלמא, או דראתה מעט נוטה לאדמומית, ואנן אין בקיאין וקמי שמיא היא באמת מראה טהורה, דמעוברת אין מסולקת ממראות טהורות כמ"ש הסדרי טהרה (סי' ק"ץ ד"ה עוד כתב המנ"י וכו') אלא דיש לי הרהורי דברים בזה וכתבתי במקום אחר בעזה"י.

שו"ת אגרות משה יורה דעה חלק ג סימן נב – א' הנה בדבר אשה שכבר ברור שהיא מעוברת ע"י הרגשתה בעצמה באופן ברור או ע"י בדיקות הידועות לרופאים אבל עדיין לא עברו ג' חדשים שלא הוכר עוברה, ודאי דמדינא דגמ' דוקא אחר שעברו ג' חדשים היא בחזקת מסולקת דמים כמפורש בגמ' בנדה דף ז' במתני' לענין דיין שעתן שהוא משיודע עוברה ומפורש בברייתא בדף ח' סומכוס אומר משום ר"מ ג' חדשים ומטעמא דאר"ז דהוא משום דראשה ואבריה כבדין עליה, וכן גם איפסק בש"ע /יו"ד/ סימן קפ"ט אבל הוא מהדברים שנשתנו הטבעים זה איזה מאות שנה שתיכף משנתעברה פסקו דמיה, וידיעת רוב הנשים וכמעט כולן שחושבות ירחי עיבורן משעת הפסקת ראיית הדם בזמן וסתן בערך, וגם סומכין ע"ז לדינא להרבה ענינים כדמצינו בתשובות רבותינו קרוב לארבע מאות שנה שהוא בתשובת הב"ח סימן ק' וכתבה בסוף חדש ניסן שפ"ט שכיון שפירסה נדה היה מבטל קול שזינתה ואין הבת מבעלה וגם היתה אשה מעידה על כך והיה גם הוכחה מזה שילדה לז' חדשים משניסת והיתה גדולה כולד בן ט', משום שזה שפירסה נדה הוא ודאי עדיף טפי מהיו שניהם חבושים בבית האסורים דאיכא אפשר רחוק שזינתה גם עם אחר בבית האסורים עיי"ש, ואף הנו"ב בקמא חאה"ע סימן ס"ט באשה שילדה אח"מ [אחר מות] בעלה בט' חדשים וט"ז יום ופירסה נדה שתי שבועות אח"מ בעלה שהעם רינו דכיון דסתם מעוברת בחזקת מסולקת דמים הרי לא היתה מעוברת מבעלה, ומ"מ התירה הוא רק דאף שודאי לא מצוי שתפרוס נדה כשהיא מעוברת אף רק איזה ימים כרינון העם, אין להוציאה מחזקת כשרותה כי אירע גם שרואות דם כשהן מעוברות, ומה שמסיק ושאלתי פה לרופאים ואמרי לי שדבר זה שכיח מאד מאד לרוב בהרבה נשים שבתחלת עיבורן רואות ושופעות דם בשעת וסתן חדש ושני חדשים, הנה ודאי לשון גוזמא גדולה היא דהרי זה גופא דהנו"ב בעצמו לא ידע וכל העם לא ידעו זה והיינו שגם הנשים המילדות לא ידעו מזה הוא הכרח שאינו דבר מצוי כלל דהא רובא דרובא נשי לא היו הולכות לרופאים להוליד הולד, ואף הדורות שאחרי הנו"ב כי גם בילדותי עדיין לא היו הולכות לרופאים וגם לא לאקושארקעס /למיילדות/ שהן נשים שלמדו בבית ספר דהמדינה לזה שכבר היו נמצאות באיזה מקומות אלא לנשים זקנות שמסרו אחת לחברתה

איך להתנהג, ולא הלכו לרופאים אלא נשים מועטות ורק כשהן חולות, שאף כל הנשים שהלכו לרופאים היו מיעוטא דמיעוטא נגד כל הנשים שבעולם וכ"ש המיעוט מאלו שהלכו לרופאים שעלייהו אמרי שהוא שכיח הוא כמעט שאינו כלום נגד כל הנשים ותמוה על לשון זה שמביא מהרופאים דהרי כיון שהוצרך לשאול מרופאים הרי הוא ברור שבלא זה לא היה יודע זה, שא"כ ברור שנשתנו הטבעים בזה זה מאות בשנים שתיכף כשנתעברות פוסקות מלראות דם ושפיר כתב בתורת השלמים שתיכף כשנתעברה רובן דרובן של הנשים פוסקות מלראות דם.

ומה שהביא הנו"ב דברי הרופאים לא מובן כלל דהא מזה חזינן דרק רופאים ידעו זה שא"כ הוא מיעוטא דמיעוטא אך שמ"מ שפיר הורה שאף שהוא מיעוט נמי אין יכולין להוציא האשה מחזקת כשרות, ופסק הב"ח שבשביל שהבעל ידע שפירסה נדה אין לחוש לדברי המשרתת והקול שיצא עפ"י של המשרתת, ואמירת רשע מפורסם לנואף שבא עליה הרבה פעמים אפילו אם היה כאן וכ"ש כשאינו כאן רק אומרים שבעיר רחוקה הוא נמצא דאף כשאומרים שאיכא שם עדים כשרים אינו כלום, ואף מה שהולד היה לפי השערת הרואין גדול כבן ט' חדשים, שודאי אין להוציא מחזקת כשרותה, והא ודאי גם להנו"ב רובא דרובא ולכה"פ רובא אין רואות דם תיכף כשנתעברה ודאי דזה יכול לדחות אמירת המשרתת ואף אם היה עד כשר וכמו שפסקו ב"ד שהיו שם שהמשרתת אינה נאמנת כלל ודינה כמוציאה דבת שקר אפילו בלא ידיעת הבעל שפירסה נדה, דשפיר כתב הב"ח דגם מטעם זה ידע שפירסה נדה יש לדחות כל החששות מצד המשרתת ומצד הקול ומצד מה שאומרים שאיכא נואף שאומר שזינה עמה ומהוכחת הולד שלהשערת הנשים היה גדול כבן ט', ולמה כתב דפליג על הב"ח דסובר שנחשב כודאי שלא היתה מעוברת וצע"ג שלכאורה הוא כדברי טעות.

והנה במניקה הוא להיפוך שמדינא דגמ' עד כ"ד חדש אין לחוש לראיית דם דהלכה כר' יוסי ור"ש בנדה דף ט' שאבריה מתפרקין ואין נפשה חוזרת עד כ"ד אף כשאינה מניקה וכשמניקה בזמן הכ"ד חדש הוא לכו"ע אף לר"מ, ואיפסק כר' יוסי ור"ש בש"ע /יו"ד/ סימן קפ"ט סעי' ל"ג ובזמננו כשאינה מניקה כמעט כל הנשים רואות דם, ולכן עד שלא תראה פעם ראשונה אינה חוששת כלל דעדיין אית לה חזקת מסולקת דמים אבל כשתראה פעם ראשונה שוב חוששת לעו"ב [לעונה בינונית] ואם היתה לה וסת קבוע לוסת הפלגה קודם עיבורה ראויה לחוש לאותה הפלגה אעפ"י שלא ראתה כל ימי עיבורה אבל וסת שאינו קבוע נעקר בפעם אחת. וכשהיא מניקה נמי רק זמן קצר אין רואות שלכן פשוט שקובעות וסת בזמננו בכ"ד חדש כשאינה מניקה ואף במניקה מסתבר שבזמננו קובעת וסת והוא ג"כ מצד שנשתנו הטבעיות לענין זה, וזה אינו נוגע לענינו אבל כתבתי לך זה להראות שינוי הטבעיים בשני הענינים וזה לא קשה כלום דכן הוא בהרבה דברים.

והנה ראיתי בתשובת רעק"א סימן קכ"ח שכתב ואף דעינינו רואות בנשי דידן דמיד כשנתעברו מסולקות דמים ונשתנו הטבעים הא חזינן בש"ע יו"ד סימן קפ"ט ובסימן ק"צ שבעינן הוכר עוברה, הנה נעלם ממנו הב"ח וגם הנו"ב שסברי שסומכין ע"ז למעשה אף לדברים חמורים וכ"ש לענין הגיע הוסת ולא בדקה ולא הרגישה שיש להקל דאינו איסור דאורייתא וגם הא לשיטה ראשונה טהורה, ורק לכתחלה יש לבדוק מאחר דאפשר לברר. וגם וכי יסבור גם להקל במניקה שהוא מדינא בחזקת מסולקת דמים וכי יקל כן גם בזמננו שנשתנו שרואות דם.

שו"ת אגרות משה יורה דעה חלק ד סימן יז - בעניין סילוק דמים בזה"ז במעוברת ובמינקת, בכמה ענייני מראות, בעניין הרגשה דזיבת דבר לח, ובכמה ענייני כתמים.

בע"ה כ' סיון תשמ"א

תשובה זו נכתבה להרה"ג ר' שמעון איידער שליט"א, שבשעה שכתב את ספרו באנגלית על הלכות נדה שאל את מרן זצ"ל כמה שאלות, וזה אשר השיב לו מרן זצ"ל

א. סילוק דמים בזמננו במעוברת קודם שהוכר עוברה

בדבר מעוברת, שידוע שבזמננו תיכף מכיון שמתעברות פוסקות מלראות דם. ובגמ' בנדה דף ח' ע"ב בברייתא, סומכוס אומר משום ר"מ דהוא ג' חדשים, ואיפסק כן בכל הפוסקים ובש"ע סימן קפ"ט סעיף ל"ג. ואף שידוע שעתה נשתנו הטבעים, ותיכף משמתעברות פוסקות מלראות דם, איתא בתשובת רעק"א סימן קכ"ח שכתב לדחות מה שפקפק הרב דפילא בשם בנו, גבי אשה שבעלה טען שבנה אינו ממנו, ואמר שבא לביתו ביום תענית אסתר וירדה לטבול, וכבר כמה שבועות קודם לא קרב אליה, הרי שמה שהיתה מעוברת אח"כ לא היה ממנו, דבמה שירדה לטבול בתענית אסתר ראיה שלא היתה אז מעוברת דדרך המעוברות שמסולקות מדמים. והשיב רע"א בלשון זה, לע"ד הא הסילוק דמים הוא רק משהוכר עוברה, ואף דעינינו רואות בנשי דידן דמיד שנתעברו מסולקות דמים ונשתנו הטבעים, הא חזינן בש"ע סימן קפ"ט וסי' ק"צ (סעיף נ"ב) דגם שם איתא משהוכר עוברה, ולא נזכר רמז באחרונים שלדידן אף בלא הוכר עוברה כן. וכן ראה כתר"ה באבני נזר יורה דעה סימן רל"ח שג"כ כתב שאין לסמוך על מה שעינינו רואות שמעוברת מסתלק דמה בתחילת עיבורה, ואין לנו לסמוך על דמיוננו אלא בנולד למקוטעין דקים להו לחכז"ל בעלי השו"ע שנשתנה (אהע"ז סי' קנ"ו סעיף ד' ברמ"א).

ולשון האב"נ תמוה לכאורה, דהא ודאי בהא דנולד למקוטעין ואמרינן שאף שלא נולד לט' חדשים שלמים אלא נכנסה לחודש הט' אפילו יום אחד הוי ולד קיימא, ואע"ג דאמרינן בגמרא (ר"ה י"א ע"א) יולדת לט' אינה יולדת למקוטעין, כבר תמהו על זה רבים שהחוש מכחיש זה, אלא שאנו צריכין לומר שעכשיו נשתנו הטבעים (רמ"א עפ"י ב"י בשם הרשב"ץ) צריכין אנו דווקא למה שאמרו חכז"ל בעלי השו"ע שנשתנה. משום דהא אפשר שאותן שנולדו לט' מקוטעין היו בעלי ז' שאישתהו ולכן חזינן שנתקיימו, אבל בני תשעה באמת אינם מתקיימים אלא בתשעה שלמים. שלכן לא היה שייך שנסמוך על עצמנו לומר מזה שנשתנו הטבעין, ולהסיק דאף אותן שמתו קודם שלשים ודאי לא היו נפלים מכיון שנכנסו מקצת בתשיעי. אבל הא דרובא דרובן של כולהו נשי דעלמא שתיכף כשמתעברות פוסקות מלראות דם הוא רק ידיעה בעלמא שהמציאות בזמננו הוא כן, שע"ז היה סגי בעדות בעלמא. והרי ע"ז אית לן עדותן דכו"ע, ובתוכן כל מי שיש לו אשה וכל מורי הוראה דעלמא, ואין זה סמך על דמיונות אלא על ידיעה ברורה דכולהו אינשי. ורעק"א לא כתב שלא אמרינן שנשתנה מאחר שלא הוזכר בש"ע, אלא שכתב שלא הוזכר שלדידן נשתנה הדין בשביל זה לומר שאף בלא הוכר עוברה לא חיישינן. משמע דאף שודאי ברור שנשתנה, מ"מ מקשה דמזה שלא הוזכר בש"ע ולא באחרונים שהדין נשתנה, יש לנו לומר דלא נשתנה הדין אף שנשתנו הטבעים. והטעם אולי משום דאפשר דנסתלקו מהראיות דריבוי דם ובהרגשה, אבל עד שהוכר העובר רואות משהו ובהרגשה קלה, ששייך שידמה לה שהוא ענין הרגשה אחרת, שלכן ברוב הפעמים נאבד זה. ומה שחוששין

לזה הוא אולי משום שאם לא כן הויא הפקעה מהטבעיות שהיה ידוע בזמן הגמ' והגאונים ואף אח"כ מאות בשנים שהיו רואות דם. אבל גם מטעם זה י"ל דנימא שאין רואות כלל כיוון שעכ"פ אנחנו יודעין שאין רואות דם בראייה מורגשת וידועה, ואיך שנימא הוא שינוי גדול בהטבעיות, שלכן יש לנו לומר שנשתנה לגמרי שאין רואות כלל. וכן היה מסתבר לרעק"א בעצם לומר כן, ומסתפקא ליה בזה. ומסיק עוד דיחוי להוכחה שלא היתה מעוברת מהא שטבלה, דדילמא טבלה לכתם או דראתה למראה שרק נוטה לאדמימות, שמחמרינן מצד שאין אנחנו בקיאין. ואולי יש לפרש כוונת האב"נ כדבארתי בכוונת רעק"א, שלא ידוע לנו איך הוא השינוי. דאולי אי ידיעה זו היא רק לחוש שמא היא רואה משהו, ורק הרגשה קלה, אף שהוא דוחק גדול. וגם הוא יסבור שהוא רק ספק, דנסתלק חזקת טהרה ממנה כשבא שעת וסתה.

ובכלל ראיית רעק"א לומר שאולי היתה מעוברת אף שראתה דם וטבלה מהא דמעוברת דאינה קובעת וסת הוא דווקא אחר ג"ח שכבר הוכר עוברה, ולא נזכר בפוסקים שהדין נשתנה, וא"כ גם זו היתה עלולה לראות אף שהיתה מעוברת, אינה ראיה. דשם בסימן קפ"ט סעיף ל"ג איירי באשה שראתה בימי עיבורה, והנפ"מ אם תקבע וסת מכוח ראיות אלה, אולי כיוון שראתה דם כשהיא מעוברת, ושניא היא משאר מעוברות בזה"ז, הרי איגלאי שאשה זו יש לה כטבע הנשים שהיו בדורות הקדמונים שהיו רואות דם עד שהוכר עוברה, שלכן דינה כדורות הראשונות. דכיוון שהיה הטבע דעלמא כך אלפים בשנים, אפשר שאף שנשתנו הטבעים איכא נשי כאלו שגם עתה הם בטבעים שהיו. וכבר ראיתי אשה יונקת שלא הניקה הולד כלל, ולא חזרה לראות דם עד שעברו כ"ד חדש מלידתה, אף שבזמננו אף אלו שמניקות יש שרואות דם, וכשאינן מניקות רואות כולן. ואמרתי דכיוון שבדורות הראשונים היה כן, שהלכה כר' יוסי דאומר בברייתא דנדה דף ט' ע"א דאבריה מתפרקין ואין נפשה חוזרת עליה עד כ"ד חדש, ולא היה תלוי בהנקה בפועל כשיטת רבי מאיר שם, אף שעתה נשתנו הטבעים, אירע שגם עתה נמצאו נשים כאלו. ומטעם זה גם בימינו כל שלא ראתה אין לה לחוש כלל, דתלינן דודאי לא ראתה עדיין, כיוון דהיה דרך הנשים שלא יראו דם, ורק כשראתה יש למה לחוש ותקבע וסת בימינו מכוח ראייה זו. ול"ד לראתה אחר שהוכר עוברה שאעפ"כ אינה קובעת וסת דהוא משום שמעולם לא היו ראויות לראות דם.

אך ראייתו איכא מסעיף ל"ד, דגם לזה שאינה חוששת לוסת הראשון, אפילו היה לה וסת קבוע והגיע תוך הזמן הזה אינה צריכה בדיקה ומותרת לבעלה, איתא דהוא רק משהוכר עוברה. אך אולי נקט משהוכר עוברה בשביל הסיפא, דאפילו שופעות ורואות דם באותן עונות שהן למודות לראות בהן אינו אלא כמקרה. שבלא הוכר עוברה, כיוון שחזינן שראתה, הרי טבעה כדורות הראשונים שיש לה לחוש. אבל יקשה עדיין מסימן קפ"ד סעיף ז', שאיתא שם אם הגיע וסתה בימי עיבורה משהוכר עוברה וכו' א"צ לפרוש סמוך לוסתה, הרי שאף שלא ראתה דם עדיין מה שאין צריכה לחוש הוא דווקא בהוכר עוברה, ולא נזכר כאן דין דשופעת בעונות שהיתה למודה לראות. ועי' לעיל סימן י"ד בהערות לשו"ע סימן קפ"ד סעיף ז', שהעיר מרן זצ"ל רק שבימינו נשתנו הטבעים. וכן הוא מסקנת דברי מרן כאן, שהשו"ע נקט דינא דגמ'. ואולי בסי' קפ"ד נזכר הדין רק בדרך כלל שצריך לפרוש בעונה הסמוכה לוסתה, אבל הגדרת הוסת המדוייקת היא בסימן קפ"ט, ולכן בסימן קפ"ד נקט המחבר רק לישנא דגמ'. ובסימן ק"צ סעיף

נ"ב, בהיו ישנות במיטה אחת ונמצא דם, שאיתא אחת מעוברת שהוכר עוברה ואחת שאינה מעוברת מעוברת טהורה ושאינה מעוברת טמאה, שהביא רעק"א נמי ראיה שדווקא בהוכר עוברה לא חיישינן ושם הרי אין ראיה שראתה דם, לכאורה ניכר שחסר שם איזו בבא. דהי"ל למינקט ואחת שלא הוכר עוברה. ועיין בעה"ש שמשמע שעמד בזה, ונקט ואחת אינה מעוברת או לא הוכר עוברה, דג"כ תמוה, הא ואחת אינה מעוברת מיותר לגמרי דהיא בכלל לא הוכר עוברה, דאינה מעוברת כלל הא ודאי לא הוכר עוברה דלא שייכת כלל לזה. אלא מוכח שנחסר בבא שלימה, דצריך להיות אחת מעוברת שהוכר עוברה ואחת שלא הוכר עוברה תולין בלא הוכר עוברה. אחת מעוברת ואחת שאינה מעוברת, תולין באינה מעוברת. והוא מטעם דכתבתי, דהמעוברת אף שלא הוכר עוברה עדיין, היתה פוסקת מלראות דם גם בזמן הב"י כמו בזמננו. אבל מ"מ כיוון שבדורות הראשונים היו רואות דם כ"ז שלא הוכר עוברה, ואירע מעוברות כאלו גם בזמננו שרואות דם, דלכן כשמעוברת שלא הוכר עוברה ישנה במיטה אחת עם מעוברת שהוכר עוברה ונמצא דם, תולין בלא הוכר עוברה. ואם ישנה מעוברת שלא הוכר עוברה עם אינה מעוברת כלל, תולין באינה מעוברת כלל. וא"כ ראיה שגם בזמן הב"י כבר פסקו המעוברות תיכף כשנתעברו מלראות דם, ולא היו חוששות בסתמא אף כשהגיע זמן וסתה כשהיו יודעות בודאי שהן מעוברות. אבל בראתה אף פעם אחת, יש לה לחשוש שמא טבעה כבדורות הראשונים, ויש לה לחשוש לשמא תראה עוד הפעם עד הכרת העובר כדלעיל.

נמצא שבעצם אין טעם להחמיר לחוש לשמא ראתה במעוברת בזמננו, גם קודם הכרת העובר, כי ליכא שום ראיה לזה, ואדרבה איכא ראיה שאין להחמיר אלא בראתה. אבל מ"מ למעשה, כיוון שרעק"א מסתפק בזה ובאב"נ כתב בפשיטות שאסור, אין להקל. אך מה שראיתי בדרכי תשובה סימן קפ"ט ס"ק קל"ב בשם שערי צדק להגה"צ מדעש, שהצריך תשובה לצורבא מדרבנן שלא פי' מאשתו תיכף כשנתעברה ולא ראתה, ואח"כ ראה דבש"ע מצריך דווקא שתהא הוכר עוברה, לא נראה לע"ד. משום שבעצם הא מסתבר שהדין במעוברת בזמננו שמותרת בלא ראתה, ואין לה לחוש לוסתה מצד הידיעה דכו"ע דמעוברות בזמננו פוסקות תיכף לראות דם. והמחבר בש"ע דינא דגמ' נקט. וממה שלא הוזכר באיזה ספר מדורות האחרונים היתר, אין זה הוכחה גדולה. וגם הי"ל לחשוב שאולי הוזכר זה אך הוא לא ראה, מאחר ששייך לומר שהוא ברור שלא ראתה, והוי זה רק כעבר בשוגג על דברי רבותינו רעק"א ואב"נ שלא מסתבר לחייבו כפרה על זה, שלא כל צורבא מדרבנן בקי בכל ספרי רבותינו האחרונים. אך אולי מאחר שהעובדא היתה שהצורבא מדרבנן לא פירש משום שלא ידע גם מלשון המחבר בש"ע, ע"ז חייבו כפרה. ויותר נראה כמו שהביא מס' אבני צדק שלא הצריכו לכפרה, וצ"ע.

ובספרו צריך כתר"ה לכתוב בלשון הזה, מעוברת קודם הכרת העובר צריכה לבדוק כשהגיע זמן וסתה. (מרן זצ"ל הוסיף על – פה, שהטעם שצריך לכתוב כך בספר קיצורי הלכות נדה באנגלית, הוא שהספר נכתב גם עבור בעלי תשובה, שאינם רגילים בדרכי הגמרא והפסק. ועניין שינוי הטבעים – הגורם לשינוי ההלכה – יהיה מוזר ובלתי מובן עבורם. עם זאת פסק מרן תמיד, בבירור, כמו שביאר לעיל, שאין מעוברת צריכה לחשוש לווסת, מן הרגע שנתברר עיבורה על ידי בדיקה רפואית. וע"ע באגרות יורה דעה חלק א' סימן צ"ז ענף ב', ואבן העזר חלק ב' סימן ה') ואח"כ אם לא ראתה תבדוק בכל יום פעם אחת, וקודם תשמיש. ואם שכחה

איזה פעם מלבדוק, מותרת. אבל כשיגיע יום הוסת, או ביום שלשים, כששכחה ולא בדקה תיכף בשעת הוסת אסורה עד שתבדוק. אבל יש מקום להקל אף כשאיחרה מלבדוק בזמן הוסת, כהב"י שהביא הש"ך סימן קפ"ד ס"ק כ"ג. והטעם שאפשר לסמוך על זה הוא דמדאורייתא אין לאסור בזמננו שפוסקות מעוברות תיכף כשנתעברות מלראות דם. אבל כשראתה אף רק פעם אחת, יש לה לחוש עד ג"ח שהוכר עוברה. ואם לא בדקה בזמן הוסת, תהא אסורה כהש"ך שמסיק דלא כהב"י אלא כהב"ח דיש להחמיר כמסקנת המרדכי.

תלמוד בבלי מסכת נדה דף ט עמוד א – מניקה עד שתגמול וכו'. ת"ר: מניקה שמת בנה בתוך עשרים וארבע חדש – הרי היא ככל הנשים, ומטמאה מעת לעת ומפקידה לפקידה. לפיכך, אם היתה מניקתו והולכת ארבע או חמש שנים – דיה שעתה – דברי ר"מ. רבי יהודה ורבי יוסי ורבי שמעון אומרים: דיין שעתן כל עשרים וארבע חדש, לפיכך, אם היתה מניקתו ארבע וחמש שנים – מטמאה מעת לעת ומפקידה לפקידה. כשתמצא לומר, לדברי ר"מ – דם נעכר ונעשה חלב, לדברי רבי יוסי ורבי יהודה ורבי שמעון – אבריה מתפרקין, ואין נפשה חוזרת עד עשרים וארבע חדש. לפיכך דר"מ למה לי? משום לפיכך דרבי יוסי. ולפיכך דרבי יוסי למה לי? מהו דתימא: רבי יוסי תרתי אית ליה – קמ"ל. תניא נמי הכי: דם נעכר ונעשה חלב – דברי ר"מ, רבי יוסי אומר: אבריה מתפרקין, ואין נפשה חוזרת עליה עד עשרים וארבע חדש.

שו"ת רדב"ז מכתב יד – אורח חיים, יורה דעה (חלק ח) סימן קלו – שאלת: ממני אודיעך דעתי, במקצת נשים ששותות משקה או שאר דברים לעכב ווסתן עשרה או עשרים יום, אם אסור לבעלה לבוא עליה אעפ"י שהיא טהורה דהוי כסמוך לוסתה או לא.

תשובה: כבר ידעת דאיכא פלוגתא ביני רבוותא אם חוששת על ימי משך הוסת או לא, שהראב"ד והרמב"ן ז"ל סבירא להו שחוששת, שכל יום ויום וסת בפני עצמו הוא, ואפילו נעקר יום ראשון חוששת לשאר הימים עד שיעקרו כלם, והר"ז הלוי והרא"ש ז"ל סבירא להו שאינה צריכה לפרוש אלא עונה ראשונה של הוסת, וכיון שעברה עונה ראשונה ולא ראתה מותרת וכן נ"ל שהוא דעת הרמב"ם ז"ל שלא חלק [בהלכ' אסורי ביאה פ"ח] משמע בכל גוונא אם עבר וסתה ולא ראתה מותרת, הילכך בנ"ד אם עבר כל זמן הוסת לכולי עלמא מותרת. ואם נסתה זה המשקה תלתי זימני ומעכב את וסתה הוי חזקה והוי כאילו נעקר וסתה ונקבעה על שתיית המשקה, ובהא פשיטא שהוא מותר לבוא עליה, אבל הספק בפעמים הראשונים שעדיין לא הוחזק הענין ובתוך זמן משך וסתה.

ומסתברא לי דמותר לבא עליה. חדא, דעיקר איסור לבוא על אשתו סמוך לוסתה לא הוי מן התורה אלא מדרבנן, ואע"ג דילפינן לה [שבועות י"ח ע"ב] מקרא דוהזרתם את בני ישראל מטומאותם, אסמכתא בעלמא היא וכן הסכימו המפרשים ז"ל, ומזה הטעם לא אסרו אלא הביאה אבל שאר קריבות מותר לקרב אליה סמוך לוסתה ותו דהוי פלוגתא דרבוותא באיסורא דרבנן, ותו דהרמב"ם והרא"ש ז"ל שאנו נגררים אחריהם מקילין, ותו דאפילו המחמירים יודו בנ"ד, דבשלמא כשאורח מתעכב ללא סבה יש לחוש לו כל ימי משך הוסת, אבל במתעכב על ידי משקה שיש בטבעו לפעול פעולה זו יש לסמוך עליו, וכמו שמועיל ליום הראשון יועיל לשאר ימי משך הוסת, ותו שכבר נסו הדבר הזה פעמים רבות שאר נשים והועיל, הילכך יפרוש

ממנה היום הראשון של הוסת ומותרת אחר כך. ומכל מקום צריכה בדיקה קודם תשמיש, ואע״ג דבשאר נשים אני תופס מילתא מציעתא דאי אית לה וסת קבוע אינה צריכה בדיקה ואם אין לה וסת קבוע צריכה בדיקה בנ״ד הוי כאין לה וסת קבוע וצריכה בדיקה, ואם נסתה אשה זו משקה זה ג׳ פעמים שמעכב וסתה, מסתברא דמשמשת בלא בדיקה. והנראה לעניות דעתי כתבתי.

תלמוד בבלי מסכת נדה דף יב עמוד ב – ת״ר, אשה שאין לה וסת – אסורה לשמש, ואין לה לא כתובה ולא פירות ולא מזונות ולא בלאות, ויוציא ולא מחזיר עולמית – דברי ר״מ. רבי חנינא בן אנטיגנוס אומר: משמשת בשני עדים, הן עותוה הן תקנוה.

רש״י מסכת נדה דף יב עמוד ב – מאן דמתני הא לא מתני הא – לעולם בעסוקה ודקשיא לך תרתי למה לי רב יהודה דמתני הא משמיה דשמואל לא מתני הא דר׳ אבא ורבי אבא לא מתני הא דרב יהודה ואי קשיא הא רב יהודה נמי אמרה דאמר רב יהודה לעיל גבי מתני׳ דקתני לעיל ובשעה שהיא עוברת לשמש את ביתה ואמר רב יהודה אמר שמואל לא שנו אלא בעסוקה כו׳ לאו פירכא היא דרב יהודה לא אשמועינן התם בעסוקה מידי דממתני׳ הוה שמעינן בין עסוקה בין אינה עסוקה ואתא רב יהודה למימר ואשמועינן משמיה דשמואל דשאינה עסוקה לא בעיא בדיקה והכא אשמועינן דהלכה כר״ח וכאותה משנה דעסוקה בטהרות בעיא בדיקה והכא עיקר ואית דמפרשי כי האי לישנא והאמר שמואל חדא זימנא לעיל דאוקימנא למתני׳ דקתני משמשת בעדים בעסוקה בטהרות מאן דמתני הא כו׳ לעולם בשאינה עסוקה ודקשיא לך דרבי אבא בר ירמיה אהא דרב יהודה לא תקשי אמוראי נינהו אליבא דשמואל וטועין בדבר דא״כ קשיא דרב יהודה אדרב יהודה דהא איהו גופיה אמר דשאינה עסוקה לא בעיא בדיקה.

רא״ש מסכת נדה פרק א סי׳ ה׳ – ת״ר אשה שאין לה ווסת אסורה לשמש ואין לה לא כתובה ולא פירות ולא מזונות ולא בלאות ויוציא ולא יחזיר עולמית דברי ר״מ. רבי חנינא בן אנטיגנוס אומר משמשת בשני עדים הן הן עיוותיה הן הן תיקוניה. משום אבא חנן אמרו אוי לו לבעלה. אמר רב יהודה אמר שמואל הלכה כרבי חנינא בן אנטיגנוס במאי אי בעסוקה בטהרות הא אמר שמואל חדא זימנא ואי בשאינה עסוקה האמר שמואל כל לבעלה לא בעיא בדיקה דאמר ר׳ זירא אמר ר׳ אבא בר ירמיה אמר שמואל אשה שאין לה ווסת אסורה לשמש עד שתבדוק ואוקימנא בעסוקה בטהרות. מאן דמתני הא לא מתני הא. פרש״י ז״ל לעולם בעסוקה ודקשיא לך תרתי למה לי. רב יהודה דמתני הא משמיה דשמואל לא מתני הא דרבי אבא ורבי אבא לא מתני הא דרב יהודה. ואי קשיא לך ה״נ רב יהודה אמרה דאמר רב יהודה לעיל גבי מתני׳ דקתני ובשעה שהיא עוברת לשמש את ביתה אמר רב יהודה אמר שמואל לא שנו אלא בעסוקה וכו׳ לאו פירכא היא דרב יהודה לא אשמועינן (התם) בעסוקה מידי דממתני׳ הוה שמעינן בין עסוקה בין שאינה עסוקה ואתא רב יהודה ואשמועינן משמיה דשמואל דשאינה עסוקה לא בעיא בדיקה. והכא אשמועינן דהלכה כר׳ חנינא וכאותה משנה דעסוקה בעיא בדיקה והכא עיקר ואית דמפרשי והא אמרה שמואל חדא זימנא דאוקמה למתני׳ דקתני ומשמשת בעדים בעסוקה בטהרות. מאן דמתני הא לא מתני הא לעולם בשאינה עסוקה ודקשיא לך דרבי אבא בר ירמיה אהא דרב יהודה אמוראי נינהו אליבא דשמואל וטועין בדבר דאם כן קשיא דר״י אדר״י דהא איהו גופיה אמר

דשאינה עסוקה לא בעיא בדיקה. ורבינו חננאל ז״ל כתב ואסיקנא מאן דמתני הא דשמואל לא מתני הא. וקיימא לן כי הא דאמר לה והלכתא כר״ח בן אנטיגנוס וזהו כפי׳ השני שסתר רש״י ורב אלפס ז״ל הביא ברייתא זו בכתובות בסוף אלמנה ת״ר אשה שאין לה וסת אסורה לשמש וכו׳ רבי חנינא בן אנטיגנוס אומר משמשת עם שני עדים והן עיוותיה ותיקוניה שאם תשמש פעם ראשונה ושניה ושלישית בעדים וימצא דם בעד שלו או שלה בעל פעם ופעם הן עיוותיה שהוחזקה נדה כל ימיה ותצא בלא כתובה דלאו בת תשמיש היא ואם שימשה בשני עדים אחד לו ואחד לה ולא נמצא דם באחד מהם ג׳ פעמים הן תיקוניה והרי היא ככל הנשים. אמר רב יהודה אמר שמואל הלכה כר״ח בן אנטיגנוס והשתא לדברי רב אלפס ז״ל המשמשת בשני עדים דקאמר ר׳ חנינא היינו לאחר תשמיש אחד לו ואחד לה מאי קא פריך אי בעסוקה בטהרות הא אמר שמואל חדא זימנא מה ענין הא דשמואל לדהכא. שמואל קאי אבשעה שהיא עוברת לשמש את ביתה וקאמר באשה עסוקה בטהרות דמיגו דבעיא בדיקה לטהרות בעיא בדיקה נמי לבעלה לפני תשמיש ור׳ חנינא איירי בבדיקה שלאחר תשמיש ועוד מאי פריך ואי בשאינה עסוקה בטהרות הא אמרינן כל לבעלה לא בעיא בדיקה הא ר׳ חנינא נמי מודה שאין צריכה לבעלה בדיקה תמיד אלא שלש פעמים להתחזק שלא תראה מחמת תשמיש ושמואל הוא דקאמר אין לה וסת לבעלה [לא] בעיא בדיקה תמיד כשאינה עסוקה בטהרות אבל בעסוקה בטהרות בעיא בדיקה תמיד ואפשר דמודה דבעיא בדיקה ג׳ פעמים להתחזק. ועוד תימה הוא מה מועיל אם שמשה ג׳ פעמים בלא דם להיותה ככל הנשים בשלמא אם מצאה דם ג׳ פעמים אחר תשמיש איכא למימר זו האשה הוחזקה להיות רואה ע״י אבר תשמיש ושוב אינה ראויה לשמש אבל הוחזקה לא מהניא להתירה דהא אשה שאין לה וסת שאסוריה לשמש היינו משום דכיון שאין לה זמן קבוע לראייתה חיישינן שמא תפרוס נדה תחתיו ומה מועיל אם שמשה ג׳ פעמים בלא דם לעולם איכא למיחש עתה תראה כיון שאין לה ווסת. ועוד קשיא דעיקר הבדיקה לא הזכיר רבי חנינא דר״מ אוסר אותה לשמש אפילו בבדיקה דלמא מקלקלא ליה ורבי חנינא לא חייש דלמא מקלקלא ליה מ״מ בדיקה דלפני תשמיש שתדע שהיא טהורה היא המתירה לשמש והיה לו להזכירה הלכך היה נראה לפרש משמשת בשני עדים אחד לפני תשמיש ואחד לאחר תשמיש הן עיוותיה אותו דלאחר תשמיש לידע העיוות דחייש ליה לדר״מ שמא תפרוס נדה תחתיו. ותיקוניה אותו שלפני תשמיש כי אותו העד מתקנה ומתירה לשמש דלא חיישינן להא דר״מ. וכן תעשה כל ימיה ובלבד שלא תתחזק לראות ג׳ פעמים זו אחר זו מחמת תשמיש דאז היא אסורה לבעל זה כדתניא לקמן בפרק בתרא (דף סה ב) והא דנקט עד שלאחר תשמיש תחלה לפי שהוא מורה על העיוות דחייש ר״מ. כך היה נראה בעיני צורתא דשמעתא וכפרש״י דאוקי הלכתא בעסוקה בטהרות אלא שלא מלאני לבי להקל כי דברי ר״ח דברי קבלה הן.

רי״ף מסכת כתובות דף ס עמוד ב – גרסינן בנדה ס״פ ראשון אשה שאין לה וסת אסורה לשמש ואין לה כתובה ולא פירות ולא מזונות ולא בלאות ויוציא ולא יחזיר עולמית ד״ר מאיר ר׳ חנינא בן אנטיגנוס אומר משמשת בשני עדים והן הן עוותיה ותקוניה שאם תשמש פעם ראשונה ושניה ושלישית בעדים וימצא דם על עד שלה או שלו בכל פעם ופעם הרי הן עוותיה שהוחזקה נדה כל ימיה ויוציא בלא כתובה ואין לה לא פירות ולא מזונות ולא בלאות דלאו בת תשמיש היא

דלא חזיא לביאה ולא יחזיר עולמית ואע"ג דהדר איתקן דאי אמרת יחזיר זמנין דאזלא ומינסבא ומיתקנה ויאמר אילו הייתי יודע שכן הוא אפילו נותנין לי מאה מנה לא הייתי מגרשה ונמצא גט בטל ובניה ממזרים ואם שמשה בשני עדים אחד לו ואחד לה שלשה פעמים ולא נמצא דם באחד מהן הרי הן תקוניה והרי היא ככל הנשים אמר רב יהודה אמר שמואל הלכה כרבי חנינא בן אנטיגנוס.

ר"ן מסכת נדה דף יב עמוד ב – והרב אלפס נראה שהוא סבר כדברי רש"י ז"ל באשה שיש לה וסת שאינה צריכה בדיקה שלא הזכיר עדים אלא באשה שאין לה וסת וכו' בזו של ר"ח ן' אנטיגנוס יש לו דרך אחרת שהוא מצריך לה בדיקה שלש פעמים עד שתהא מוחזקת שלא תראה מחמת תשמיש.

שולחן ערוך יורה דעה הלכות נדה סימן קפו סעיף ב – אם אין לה וסת קבוע, שלשה פעמים הראשונים צריכין לבדוק קודם תשמיש ואחר תשמיש, הוא בעד שלו והיא בעד שלה, ואם הוחזקה באותם שלשה פעמים שאינה רואה דם מחמת תשמיש, שוב אינה צריכה בדיקה כלל, לא לפני תשמיש ולא לאחר תשמיש. ולהרמב"ם והרא"ש, כל זמן שאין לה וסת צריכה היא בדיקה לעולם, קודם תשמיש ואחר תשמיש, והרמב"ם מצריך שגם הבעל יבדוק עצמו אחר תשמיש. הגה: ואין צריכין לבדוק עצמם אחר כל תשמיש ותשמיש שעושין בלילה אחת, אלא מקנחין עצמן כל הלילה בעד, ולמחר צריכין בדיקה, ואם נמצא דם טמאה. (ב"י בשם הרמב"ם פ"ד). קנחה עצמה בעד, ואבדה, לא תשמש עד שתבדוק עצמה, הואיל ואין לה וסת.

בעלי הנפש שער הספירה והבדיקה סימן ג – והבדיקה הזו שאמרנו לרואה דם מחמת תשמיש היא נזכרת בדברי ר' חנינא בן אנטיגנוס (נדה יב ב) גבי אשה שאין לה וסת שאמר משמשת בשני עדים אחד לה ואחד לו והן הן עוותיה ותקוניה. ופירש הרב ר' יצחק ז"ל בהלכותיו (רי"ף כתובות ס ב) משמשת בשני עדים אחד לו ואחד לה והן עוותיה אם תראה שלש פעמים שהיא מוחזקת ברואה דם מחמת תשמיש ותקוניה אם לא תראה שהיא ככל הנשים. נראה מדברי הרב שאינה צריכה בדיקה אלא לאחר תשמיש ואע"פ שאין לה וסת, כי שני עדים הללו לאחר תשמיש הם. ועוד נראה מדברי הרב שאם בדקה עצמה שלש פעמים ולא ראתה, שאינה צריכה בדיקה עוד לא לפני תשמיש ולא לאחר תשמיש ואע"פ שאין לה וסת. ולהוציא מדברי האומרים דאשה שאין לה וסת אסורה לשמש בלא בדיקה ואפילו בזמן הזה ואע"פ שאין לנו טהרות, ותולין את שבושם בדברי הרב. והרי הוא מכחישם הכחשה ברורה שהרי פירש שני עדים אחד לו ואחד לה דתרוייהו לאחר תשמיש, ועוד פירש תקוניה אם לא תמצא דם על העד בשלש פעמים והרי היא ככל הנשים לומר שאינה צריכה עוד בדיקה. ואם תאמר הלא דברי ר' חנינא בן אנטיגנוס לפני תשמיש ולאחר תשמיש קאמר לפי הסוגיא, ואיך פי' הרב כך. בודאי כן הוא, כי דברי ר' חנינא בן אנטיגנוס לפני תשמיש ולאחר תשמיש קאמר, ובאשה העסוקה בטהרות קא מיירי כדאיתא בשמעתא. מיהו עכשיו אין לנו טהרות, והרב לא פירש הענין על פי הסוגיא אלא על פי הצורך הנוהג עכשיו, וסמך את הענין על הדומה לו. ועוד תבין ותדע כי לא נחוש עליה לרואה דם מחמת תשמיש עד שיולד בה ריעותא על זה, שהרי כך שנינו בברייתא, נשאת וראתה דם מחמת

תשמיש משמשת פעם ראשונה ושניה ושלישית, ומכאן ואילך לא תשמש וכו׳. וקתני סיפא ואם יש לה וסת תולה בוסתה, ש״מ דרישא באשה שאין לה וסת עסקינן, ואפ״ה קתני נשאת וראתה דם מחמת תשמיש משמשת פעם ראשונה ושניה ושלישית, משמע דקמייתא לאו ממנינא היא. אלמא מעיקרא לא בדקה ולא חיישא ואף על פי שאין לה וסת. וש״מ דאשה שאין לה וסת נמי אי לאו דאתיליד בה ריעותא דראתה דם סמוך לתשמיש לא הוה חיישא. והכין משמע מדברי הרב שכתב במסכת נדה (רי״ף שבועות ב ב) ברייתא דרואה דם מחמת תשמיש אצל דברי ר״ח בן אנטיגנוס, לומר שהן ענין אחד שאין חוששין לאשה שאין לה וסת לכל דבר אלא אם כן נולד בה ריעות זה סמוך לתשמיש. וכל זה שפירש הרב, על פי הצורך הנוהג הוא ולא על פי הסוגיא. כי הסוגיא באשה שלא ראתה מחמת תשמיש קא מיירי, ובאשה העסוקה בטהרות, ושני עדים אחד לפני תשמיש ואחד לאחר תשמיש קאמר, והן עוותיה אם תראה ותקוניה אם לא תראה, ולאפוקי מדרבי מאיר אתא דקא אסר לה לגמרי בין ראתה בין לא ראתה. ולפי הסוגיא אינו רוצה לומר שתהא מתוקנת בשלש פעמים ותהא כשאר כל הנשים, אלא לעולם היא צריכה בדיקה לפני תשמיש ולאחר תשמיש כל זמן שתהא עסוקה בטהרות. אלא תקוניה הם לשעה, שאם לא תמצא דם יכולה לשמש, ואם תמצא דם אינה יכולה לשמש, והן עוותיה לשעתה. והרב ר׳ יצחק לא תפס מדברי ר׳ חנינא בן אנטיגנוס אלא הצורך הנוהג ולא פירש אותם אלא לפי צורך השעה. ודברי הרב נכונים הם וצדיקים ילכו בם. והלכה למעשה כסוגיא דשמעתא דכל לבעלה לא בעיא בדיקה ואפילו אשה שאין לה וסת.

ש״ך יורה דעה סימן קפו א – ג״פ הראשונים כו׳ – באמת כן הבינו הפוסקים הלא המה הרמב״ן והרשב״א והרא״ש והר״ן ושאר פוסקים דברי הרי״ף דס״ל כפי׳ השני שסתר רש״י והוא פירוש ר״ח והלכה כרבי חנינא בן אנטיגנוס דצריכה לבעלה בדיקה ומשמשת בעדים ג״פ הראשונים והאריך הרא״ש לסתור דברי הרי״ף והסכים להלכה דלא בעי בדיקה כלל אלא שלא מלאו לבו להקל נגד פי׳ ר״ח וגם הרשב״א והר״ן נדחקו ליישב דברי הרי״ף ולא מלאו לבם להקל נגדו אע״פ שלענין הדין נראה מדבריהם עיקר להלכה דלא בעי בדיקה כלל לבעלה וגם הב״י והב״ח נדחקו ליישב דברי הרי״ף דס״ל דצריכה בדיקה גם לפני תשמיש ע״ש בדברי כל המפרשים הנזכרים מתוך דבריהם בעצמם שדבריהם דחוקים אבל באמת לא ירדתי לסוף דעת כל אלו הגדולים איך עלה על לבם שדעת הרי״ף לפסוק הלכה כר׳ חנינא ב״א דאשה שאין לה וסת צריכה בדיקה לבעלה אם כן איך קבע הרי״ף הלכה זו בכתובות ס״פ אלמנה ניזוני׳ שאין לה שייכות שם כלל והיה לו לקבוע בהל׳ נדה כי שם מקומה ועוד שהפי׳ שפירש הרי״ף בכתובות ס״פ אלמנה ניזונית משמש׳ בעדים ושאם תשמש פעם אחת וב׳ וג׳ בעדים נמצא על עד שלה או על שלו בכל פעם ופעם הרי הן עותיה שהוחזקה נדה כל ימיה ותצא בלא כתובה ואם שמשה בב׳ עדים אחד לו ואחד לה ג״פ ולא נמצא דם באחד מהם הרי הן תקוניה והרי היא ככל הנשי׳ א״ר יודא אמר שמואל הלכה כר״ח ב״א עכ״ל, עיקר הפי׳ הוא שייך לענין איסור נדה וא״כ ה״ל לקובעה בהל׳ נדה ובריש הל׳ נדה כ׳ הרי״ף ת״ר כל אשה שאין לה וסת אסורה לשמש אין לה כתובה ולא פירות כו׳ דברי ר״מ רחב״א אומר משמשת בב׳ עדים והן עותי׳ ותיקוני׳ וכבר פירשנוה בכתובות אמר ר״י אמר שמואל הלכה כרחב״א, ת״ר נישאת וראתה דם מחמת תשמיש

משמשת פעם ראשונה שניה ושלישית כו׳ ואם יש לה וסת תולה בוסתה עכ״ל הרי שבהלכות נדה לא כתב הפי׳ כלל וכתבו בכתובות וכתב וכבר פירשנוה בכתובות ואיפכא ה״ל למיעבד ועוד יש לדקדק קצת למה כתב וכבר פירשנוה בכתובות הל״ל וכבר פירשנוה שלהי פ׳ אלמנה ניזונת וע״ק לפי דבריהם מאין הוציא הרי״ף לפרש משמשת בעדים ג״פ הא פשטא דמילתא משמע לעולם משמשת בעדים מלבד זה יש להקשות לפי שטתם כמה וכמה קושיות על הרי״ף כמו שהאריכו הפוסקים הנ״ל, אבל האמת יורה דרכו דדעת הרי״ף כדעת כל הפוסקי׳ דאפילו אשה שאין לה וסת לא בעיא בדיקה לבעלה כלל לא לפני התשמיש ולא לאחר התשמיש ולהכי לא כתב הרי״ף בשום מקום בפירוש דצריכה בדיקה אדרבה כ׳ בהל׳ נדה החמרין והפועלין כו׳ נשיהן להן בחזקת טהרה וההיא ברייתא דרחב״א בעסוק׳ בטהרות בדוקא היא וכמו שפרש״י וכל הפוסקים אבל לבעלה לא בעיא בדיקה כלל ולכך לא פי׳ הרי״ף דבר בהל׳ נדה על דברי רחב״א משום דכיון דהאידנא דליכא טהרות לא בעינן בדיקה כלל מיהו נ״מ באשה שראתה דם מחמת תשמיש דצריכה בדיקה ג״פ ומשמשת בעדי׳ וכדקתני בברייתא נשאת וראתה דם מחמת תשמיש כו׳ וכתבה הרי״ף מיד בתר הכי אע״פ שהיא ברייתא בסוף נדה סמכה לכאן מפני שהן ענין א׳ וכדפי׳ והיינו דנקט נשאת וראתה דם מחמ׳ תשמיש משמשת פעם א׳ ב׳ ג׳ משמע דקמייתא לאו ממנינא היא וכל שלא ראתה מחמת תשמי׳ א״צ בדיקה כלל (ולשאר הפוסקים דמפרשים ואם יש לה וסת תולה בוסתה בע״א ומביא׳ ב״י לקמן סי׳ קפ״ז אין זה ראיה די״ל רישא נמי באשה שיש לה וסת היא ע״ש ודו״ק) ולכך כ׳ הרי״ף וכבר פירשנוה בכתובות משום דהכא לענין נדה לא נ״מ במאי דהלכה כרחב״א רק לענין כתובה נ״מ דהלכה כרחב״א דלא הפסידה כתובתה עד שתשמש ג״פ לאפוקי מדר״מ ולכך בכתובות פי׳ הרי״ף יפה דברי רחב״א דנ״מ לענין כתובה והא דלא כ׳ הרי״ף בכתובות דמיירי באשה שראתה דם מחמת תשמיש היינו משום דהתם לא מיירי אלא מדין כתובה ואתא לפסוק הלכה כרחב״א אבל ע״כ מיירי ברואה מחמת תשמיש וסמך עצמו בכתובות אמה שקבע ברייתא זו דרחב״א גבי ברייתא דראתה דם מחמת תשמיש כו׳ או אפשר דלענין כתובה שהוא ממון מצי הבעל למימר כיון דאין לך וסת איני רוצה ליתן לך כתובה ולשמש עמך אלא בעדים שמא תהיה רואה דם מחמת תשמיש ומשמש בעדים ג״פ שתהא יוצאת שוב מחשש רואה דם מחמת תשמיש אבל ודאי אי הבעל לא קפיד משום כתובה לענין איסור נמי לא בעי בדיקה כלל כן נ״ל וזהו ברור ואמת בדעת הרי״ף וע׳ מה שכ׳ הב״י בשם הראב״ד בס׳ בעלי נפש מבואר מדברי הראב״ד שהבין כן דעת הרי״ף ממש כמ״ש אלא שהב״י הביא דברי הראב״ד בקצרה אבל כשתעיין בדברי הראב״ד עצמו בס׳ בעלי הנפש דף ס״ב ע״ב תמצא מבואר דעת הרי״ף כמ״ש (רק שהחילוק שבין ממון לאיסור אינו מבואר שם) ומסיק שם להרי״ף הלכה למעשה כסוגיא דשמעתא דכל לבעלה לא בעיא בדיקה ואפילו אשה שאין לה וסת ע״כ ומעתה כיון דדעת כל הפוסקי׳ דאשה שאין לה וסת לא בעיא בדיקה כלל לפני התשמיש ולאחר התשמיש (חוץ מהרמב״ם שמפרש כל הסוגיא באינה עסוקה בטהרות והוא יחיד נגד כל הפוסקים וגם אין הסוגיא מכרעת כדבריו וגם הרמב״ם גופיה בפי׳ המשנה בפ״ק דנדה כתב דבאינה עסוקה בטהרות קי״ל דכל לבעלה אין צריכה בדיקה אפילו אין לה וסת ועיין שם) אלא שלא מלאו לבם להקל נגד דעת הרי״ף וכבר נתבאר דאדרבה נהפוך הוא דדעת הרי״ף דכל לבעלה לא בעי׳ בדיקה כלל וכמו שמוכח הסוגיא פ״ק דנדה וכמה דוכתי א״כ ודאי

דהכי קי"ל וכ"כ הג"מ פ"ד מהל' א"ב והמרדכי בשם רשב"ם ור"י וסה"ת וסמ"ג דכל לבעלה לא בעי' בדיקה אפילו אין לה וסת בין קודם תשמיש בין לאחר תשמיש ואפילו רוצה להחמיר על עצמה ולבדוק קודם תשמיש או לאחר תשמיש לא שבקינן דאם כן לבו נוקפו עכ"ל, וכן כתב הרוקח ומביאו בית יוסף וכ"כ בש"ד הל' נדה סימן ט"ז בהגהת ש"ד וכן כתב האגור בשם מהרי"ל וכמדומה שכן עמא דבר.

32.

תוספות מסכת יבמות דף מז עמוד ב – במקום שהנדה טובלת – טבילת נדה לא כתב קרא בהדיא ופי' רב יהודה גאון דנפקא לן בק"ו ממגעה דטעון טבילה וכ"ש היא עצמה ור"ת מפרש דנפקא לן מהא דדרשינן בע"ז (דף עה:) אך במי נדה יתחטא מים שהנדה טובלת בהם וכמה הם מ' סאה ורבינו יצחק פירש דנפקא מהא דדרשינן בפ' במה אשה (שבת דף סד:) תהיה בנדתה תהא בנדתה עד שתבא במים.

תשובות הגאונים – מוסאפיה (ליק) סימן מה – תוב שמ"ק טבילה לנדה מן התורה מנין. ואמר קל וחומר ממגעה.

תלמוד בבלי מסכת עבודה זרה דף עה עמוד ב – תנא: וכולן צריכין טבילה בארבעים סאה. מנהני מילי? אמר רבא, דאמר קרא: (במדבר לא) כל דבר אשר יבא באש תעבירו באש וטהר, הוסיף לך הכתוב טהרה אחרת. תני בר קפרא: מתוך שנאמר (במדבר לא) במי נדה – שומע אני שצריך הזאה שלישי ושביעי, ת"ל: אך, חלק; א"כ, מה ת"ל במי נדה? מים שנדה טובלת בהן, הוי אומר: ארבעים סאה. איצטריך למיכתב וטהר, ואיצטריך למיכתב במי נדה; אי כתב וטהר, ה"א וטהר כל דהו, כתב רחמנא במי נדה; ואי כתב רחמנא במי נדה, הוה אמינא הערב שמש כנדה, כתב רחמנא וטהר, לאלתר. אמר רב נחמן אמר רבה בר אבוה: אפי' כלים חדשים במשמע, דהא ישנים וליבנן כחדשים דמו, ואפילו הכי בעי טבילה. מתקיף לה רב ששת: אי הכי, אפי' זוזא דסרבלא נמי! א"ל: כלי סעודה אמורין בפרשה. אמר רב נחמן אמר רבה בר אבוה: לא שנו אלא בלקוחין וכמעשה שהיה, אבל שאולין לא. רב יצחק בר יוסף זבן מנא דמרדא מעובד כוכבים, סבר להטבילה, א"ל ההוא מרבנן ורבי יעקב שמיה, לדידי מפרשא ליה מיניה דרבי יוחנן: כלי מתכות אמורין בפרשה. אמר רב אשי: תהני כלי זכוכית, הואיל וכי נשתברו יש להן תקנה, ככלי מתכות דמו. קוניא – פליגי בה רב אחא ורבינא, חד אמר: כתחלתו, וחד אמר: כסופו. והלכתא: כסופו. איבעיא להו: משכנתא, מאי? אמר מר בר רב אשי: אבא משכן ליה עובד כוכבים כסא דכספא, ואטבליה ואישתי ביה, ולא ידענא אי משום דקסבר: משכנתא כזביני דמיא, אי משום דחזי לעובד כוכבים דדעתיה לשקועיה.

תלמוד בבלי מסכת שבת דף סד עמוד ב – אמר רב: כל שאסרו חכמים לצאת בו לרשות הרבים – אסור לצאת בו לחצר, חוץ מכבול ופאה נכרית. רבי ענני בר ששון משמיה דרבי ישמעאל אמר: הכל ככבול. תנן: בכבול ובפאה נכרית לחצר. בשלמא לרב – ניחא, אלא לרבי ענני בר ששון קשיא! – רבי ענני בר ששון משמיה דמאן קאמר ליה – משמיה דרבי ישמעאל בר יוסי, רבי

ישמעאל בר יוסי תנא הוא ופליג. ורב, מאי שנא הני? – אמר עולא: כדי שלא תתגנה על בעלה. כדתניא: (ויקרא טו) והדוה בנדתה, זקנים הראשונים אמרו: שלא תכחול ולא תפקוס ולא תתקשט בבגדי צבעונין, עד שבא רבי עקיבא ולימד: אם כן אתה מגנה על בעלה, ונמצא בעלה מגרשה. אלא מה תלמוד לומר והדוה בנדתה – בנדתה תהא עד שתבא במים.

ויקרא פרק טו פסוק לג – והדוה בנדתה והזב את זובו לזכר ולנקבה ולאיש אשר ישכב עם טמאה:

רמב"ם הלכות איסורי ביאה פרק ד הלכה ג – במה דברים אמורים שהטומאה תלויה בימים בשטבלה במי מקוה אחר הימים הספורים, אבל נדה וזבה ויולדת שלא טבלו במי מקוה הבא על אחת מהן אפילו אחר כמה שנים חייב כרת, שבימים וטבילה תלה הכתוב שנאמר ורחצו במים זה בנין אב לכל טמא שהוא בטומאתו עד שיטבול.

קובץ הערות סי' ל"ט – וקשה דהתינח לענין טהרות אבל אכתי לבעלה מנלן דצריכה טבילה. וצ"ל דא"א שתהא נדה לחצאין, לטהרות ולא לבעלה, וכיון דלענין טהרות טמאה, אסורה גם לבעלה. ואין להקשות מהא דנדה שנאנסה וטבלה, רב אמר טהורה לביתה ואסורה לאכול בתרומה, דהתם טהורה גם לענין טהרות של חולין, ובעלה חולין הוא. ובתוס' פ"ק דב"ק כתבו לחלק בין טהרות לבעלה, לענין ספק וס"ס, דאף דס"ס טמא ברה"י טומאה ודאית, מ"מ מותרת לבעלה, אלא דיש בזה שני פירושים בהא דספק ברה"י ודאי טמא, בסוגיא דצרת סוטה בתוס' שם, דאם נפרש דאפילו קמי שמיא גליא שלא נגע מ"מ טמא, אפשר לומר דהטומאה החדשה הזאת אינה גורמת לאיסור נדה, אבל אי נימא דגזה"כ לדון אותה כאילו ודאי ראתה ראוי שתהא אסורה גם לבעלה, כיון דהאיסור תלוי בטומאה א"א למיפלגינהו מהדדי.

ובספק רה"ר דטהורה, ומ"מ אסורה לבעלה, התם הטהרה אינה בתורת ודאי אלא בתורת ספק, כדמוכח מדברי הרמב"ם דספק רה"ר טהור מפני שכל הספיקות מדבריהן, וזה אינו אלא בתורת ספק כמבואר בר"ן ספ"ק דקדושין דהמאכיל לחבירו ספק איסור עובר בלפ"ע אם הוא ודאי להמאכיל ומ"מ עדיין אינו מיושב, דאי נימא דהאיסור הוא בתולדה מהטומאה כמו בטומאת מקדש וקדשים בספק טומאה ברה"ר מותר בזה.

תלמוד בבלי מסכת נדה דף ל עמוד א – ש"מ תלת, ש"מ: ר"ע היא, דאמר בעינן ספורים בפנינו, וש"מ – ר"ש היא, דאמר אבל אמרו חכמים אסור לעשות כן שמא תבא לידי ספק, וש"מ – טבילה בזמנה מצוה. ורבי יוסי בר' יהודה אומר: דיה לטבילה באחרונה, ולא אמרינן טבילה בזמנה מצוה.

תלמוד בבלי מסכת יומא דף ח עמוד א – נימא הני תנאי כהני תנאי; דתניא: אחד זה ואחד זה מזין עליו כל שבעה מכל חטאות שהיו שם, דברי רבי מאיר. רבי יוסי אומר: אין מזין עליו אלא שלישי ושביעי בלבד. רבי חנינא סגן הכהנים אומר: כהן השורף את הפרה מזין עליו כל שבעה. כהן גדול ביום הכפורים – אין מזין עליו אלא שלישי ושביעי. מאי לאו בהא קא מיפלגי; רבי מאיר סבר: טומאה דחויה היא בציבור, ורבי יוסי סבר: טומאה היתר היא בציבור. – ותסברא?

אי סבר רבי יוסי היתר היא בציבור – הזאה כלל למה לי? אלא, דכולי עלמא הני תנאי סברי טומאה דחויה היא בציבור, והכא בהא קמיפלגי; רבי מאיר סבר: אמרינן טבילה בזמנה מצוה, ורבי יוסי סבר: לא אמרינן טבילה בזמנה מצוה. – וסבר רבי יוסי לא אמרינן טבילה בזמנה מצוה? והתניא: הרי שהיה שם כתוב על בשרו – הרי זה לא ירחץ, ולא יסוך, ולא יעמוד במקום הטנופת. נזדמנה לו טבילה של מצוה – כורך עליו גמי, וטובל. רבי יוסי אומר: יורד וטובל כדרכו, ובלבד שלא ישפשף. וקיימא לן דבטבילה בזמנה מצוה קא מיפלגי, דתנא קמא סבר: לא אמרינן טבילה בזמנה מצוה, ורבי יוסי סבר: אמרינן טבילה בזמנה מצוה! אלא, דכולי עלמא להני תנאי אמרינן טבילה בזמנה מצוה. והכא בהא קמיפלגי; רבי מאיר סבר: מקשינן הזאה לטבילה, ורבי יוסי סבר: לא מקשינן הזאה לטבילה.

תלמוד בבלי מסכת יומא דף פח עמוד א – תנאי היא, דתניא: כל חייבי טבילות טובלין כדרכן ביום הכפורים. נדה ויולדת טובלות כדרכן בלילי יום הכפורים. בעל קרי טובל והולך עד המנחה. רבי יוסי אומר: כל היום כולו. ורמינהו: הזב והזבה המצורע והמצורעת ובועל נדה וטמא מת – טובלין כדרכן ביום הכפורים. נדה ויולדת טובלות כדרכן בלילי יום הכפורים. בעל קרי טובל והולך כל היום כולו. רבי יוסי אומר: מן המנחה ולמעלה אין יכול לטבול. – לא קשיא, הא – דצלי תפלת נעילה, הא – דלא צלי. אי דצלי – מאי טעמייהו דרבנן? – קא סברי רבנן: טבילה בזמנה מצוה. מכלל דרבי יוסי סבר לאו מצוה? והתניא: הרי שהיה שם כתוב על בשרו הרי זה לא ירחץ ולא יסוך ולא יעמוד במקום הטנופת, נזדמנה לו טבילת מצוה – כורך עליו גמי ויורד וטובל. רבי יוסי אומר: יורד וטובל כדרכו, ובלבד שלא ישפשף. וקיימא לן דבטבילה בזמנה מצוה פליגי! – ההיא רבי יוסי בר יהודה היא. דתניא, רבי יוסי בר יהודה אומר: דיה לטבילה שתהא באחרונה. תנו רבנן: הרואה קרי ביום הכפורים – יורד וטובל, ולערב ישפשף. – לערב? מאי דהוה הוה! – אלא אימא: מבערב ישפשף, (קא סבר מצוה לשפשף). תני תנא קמיה דרב נחמן: הרואה קרי ביום הכפורים – עונותיו מחולין לו. והתניא: עונותיו סדורין! – מאי סדורין – סדורין לימחל. תנא דבי רבי ישמעאל: הרואה קרי ביום הכפורים – ידאג כל השנה כולה, ואם עלתה לו שנה – מובטח לו שהוא בן העולם הבא. אמר רב נחמן בר יצחק: תדע, שכל העולם כולו רעב והוא שבע. כי אתא רב דימי אמר: מפיש חיי, סגי ומסגי.

תלמוד בבלי מסכת שבת דף קכ עמוד ב – דתניא: הרי שהיה שם כתוב לו על בשרו – הרי זה לא ירחוץ ולא יסוך ולא יעמוד במקום הטינופת. נזדמנה לו טבילה של מצוה – כורך עליה גמי ויורד וטובל. רבי יוסי אומר: לעולם יורד וטובל כדרכו, ובלבד שלא ישפשף! – שאני התם דאמר קרא (דברים יב) ואבדתם את שמם מן המקום ההוא לא תעשון כן לה' אלהיכם, עשייה הוא דאסור, גרמא – שרי. – אי הכי, הכא נמי: כתיב (שמות כ) לא תעשה [כל] מלאכה – עשייה הוא דאסור, גרמא שרי! – מתוך שאדם בהול על ממונו – אי שרית ליה אתי לכבויי. – אי הכי – קשיא דרבנן אדרבנן: ומה התם דאדם בהול על ממונו – שרי, הכא לא כל שכן? ותסברא, האי גמי היכי דמי? אי דמיהדק – קא הוי חציצה, אי לא מיהדק – עיילי ביה מיא! – חציצה – תיפוק ליה משום דיו! – בלחה, דתניא: הדם והדיו הדבש והחלב יבשין – חוצצין, לחים – אין חוצצין. מכל מקום קשיא! – אלא אמר רבא בר רב שילא: היינו טעמייהו דרבנן, דקסברי: אסור לעמוד בפני השם

ערום. מכלל דרבי יוסי סבר מותר לעמוד בפני השם ערום? – דמנח ידיה עילויה. – לרבנן נמי, דמנח ידיה עילויה! – זימנין דמשתלי, ושקיל ליה. – לרבי יוסי נמי, זימנין דמשתלי ושקיל ליה! אלא: אי דאיכא גמי – הכי נמי, הכא במאי עסקינן – לאהדורי אגמי. רבנן סברי: טבילה בזמנה לאו מצוה – ומהדרינן, ורבי יוסי סבר: טבילה בזמנה מצוה – ולא מהדרינן. וסבר רבי יוסי טבילה בזמנה מצוה? והתניא: הזב והזבה המצורע והמצורעת בועל נדה וטמא מת – טבילתן ביום, נדה ויולדת – טבילתן בלילה. בעל קרי טובל והולך כל היום כולו, רבי יוסי אומר: מן המנחה ולמעלה – אינו צריך לטבול! ההיא רבי יוסי ברבי יהודה היא, דאמר: דייה טבילה באחרונה.

תוספות מסכת יומא דף ח עמוד א – דכולי עלמא להני תנאי אמרינן טבילה בזמנה מצוה – ר"ת פסק דטבילה בזמנה לאו מצוה היא אע"ג דאמר בפרק המפלת (נדה דף ל. ושם) שמע מינה תלת שמע מינה טבילה בזמנה מצוה אין הלכה כן אלא כרבי יוסי בר' יהודה דאמר התם דיה טבילה באחרונה שהרי מעשים בכל יום שאין לך טובלת בזמנה טבילה של נדה ושל זבה ושל שומרת יום ובפרק בתרא דנדה (דף סז: ושם) אמרינן מכדי האידנא כולהו ספק זבות שוינהו רבנן ליטבלינהו בימָמא דשבעה משמע שלא היו טובלות ביום בשום פעם ור"ח פסק כב"ש וב"ה דפרק המפלת (שם דף ל. ושם) דסברי טבילה בזמנה מצוה ולאו ראייה היא מדסברי ב"ש וב"ה הכי שיהא הלכה כן דודאי ר' יוסי בר' יהודה לא פליג עלייהו אלא ס"ל לא נחלקו ב"ש וב"ה בדבר זה א"כ מצי למימר דהלכתא כר' יוסי ברבי יהודה ומה שעשה רבינו אליהו הזקן זכרונו לברכה באזהרות שלו טבילה בזמנה ועל ארבע גדילים יתד על אזנך תכסה הגדולים מנהגן היה שלא היה מקפיד לכתוב כהלכתן כמו שיסד על סתם נסקלים דנתם ונתחייב תסקלוהו ויאמר המלך תלוהו והיינו כר"א דפרק נגמר הדין (סנהדרין דף מה:) כל הנסקלין נתלין ודלא כרבנן דאמרי אין נתלה אלא מגדף ועובד עבודת כוכבים ומהא דאמר בשמעתא דכולי עלמא אמרינן טבילה בזמנה מצוה אין להביא ראיה דלא הוה מצי למימר איפכא דכולי עלמא לא אמרינן טבילה בזמנה מצוה דא"כ מאי טעמא דר"מ ועוד ר' יוסי נמי על כרחך סבר טבילה בזמנה מצוה כדשמעינן ליה גבי מי שהיה שם כתוב על בשרו.

שולחן ערוך יורה דעה סימן קצז סעיף ב – אם בעלה בעיר, מצוה לטבול בזמנה שלא לבטל מפריה ורביה אפילו לילה אחת.

קהלת פרק יא פסוק ו – בבקר זרע את זרעך ולערב אל תנח ידך כי אינך יודע אי זה יכשר הזה או זה ואם שניהם כאחד טובים:

תוספות מסכת ביצה דף יח עמוד ב – כל חייבי טבילות טובלין כדרכן בין בתשעה באב בין ביום הכפורים – היינו דוקא להני שטובלין טבילת מצוה בזמנה אבל השתא שכל טבילות שנשותינו טובלות היינו טבילה שלא בזמנה דהן סופרות ז' נקיים מספק שהן זבות אינן טובלות בט' באב וביוה"כ ומיהו יש לחלק כדאמר ביומא (דף פח.) נדות ויולדות טבילתן בלילה זבין וזבות טבילתן ביום בעל קרי טובל והולך עד המנחה כדי שיתפלל תפלת המנחה בטהרה אבל לאחר המנחה לא יטבול ומפרש התם טעמא דאי משום תפלת נעילה היה יכול להמתין עד הלילה ויטבול ויתפלל

תפלת נעילה בלילה ואמאי אינו טובל ביום כדי שתהא הטבילה בזמנה אלמא ש"מ דקסבר ההוא תנא דטבילה בזמנה לאו מצוה היא ואפילו הכי שריא ביוה"כ ומיהו בתשעה באב אין טובלין כר' חנינא בן אנטיגנוס דאמר כדאי בית אלהינו לאבד טבילה אחת בשנה וקאמר עלה בירושלמי הורה ר' לוי כר' חנינא בן אנטיגנוס ולית הלכתא כהך משנה דקאמר כל חייבי טבילות וכו' ועוד אומר ר"י דבזמן הזה אין טובלין לא ביוה"כ ולא בט' באב דדוקא הם שהיו עוסקין בטהרות היה צריך לטבול מיד כדי שלא יטמאו הטהרות אבל השתא דהטבילה אינה באה אלא לטהרה לבעלה יכולה היא לרחוץ ולחוף ערב יוה"כ כדי שתסרוק שערה וחופפת מעט למוצאי יום הכפורים משום דצריך חפיפה סמוך לטבילה וכן בט' באב דהא אפי' תטבול ביום הכפורים ובט' באב אסורה לבעלה.

תלמוד בבלי מסכת ביצה דף יח עמוד ב – דתניא: אין מטבילין את הכלי על גב מימיו לטהרו, ואין משיקין את המים בכלי אבן לטהרן, דברי רבי. וחכמים אומרים: מטבילין כלי על גב מימיו לטהרו, ומשיקין את המים בכלי אבן לטהרן. מני? אי רבי – קשיא השקה, אי רבנן – קשיא הטבלה! – איבעית אימא רבי, איבעית אימא רבנן. אי בעית אימא רבי: רישא דברייתא ביום טוב, וסיפא בשבת, וכולה מתניתין ביום טוב, ואיבעית אימא רבנן, וכולה מתניתין בשבת.

שולחן ערוך יורה דעה סימן קצז סעיף ב – הגה: ומותרת לטבול ליל שבת (ר"ח ור' אליה וא"ז ובה"ג וסה"ת וסמ"ג בשם ר' שמואל שהנהיג כך בתו) אם לא יכולה לטבול קודם לכן, (ב"י ומרדכי בשם כמה רבוותא ע"ש). ודוקא אם בעלה בעיר, אבל בלאו הכי אסור, (כן משמע בת"ה סימן רצ"ה /רנ"ה/). ואם היה אפשר לה לטבול קודם לכן, כגון שהיה אחר לידה או שלא היה בעלה בעיר ובא בערב שבת, י"א שאסורה לטבול (שם ובמהרי"ו בפסקיו סימן מ"ח כדעת ב"י); וכן נהגו במקצת מקומות, אבל במקום שאין מנהג אין להחמיר; ובמקום שנהגו להחמיר, גם במוצאי שבת לא תטבול דמאחר שהיה אפשר לה לטבול קודם לכן אין מרחיקין הטבילה מן החפיפה (אגור ובמהרי"ל). וכן אלמנה שאסורה לטבול טבילה ראשונה בליל שבת, משום דאסור לבא עליה ביאה ראשונה בשבת, אסורה לטבול ג"כ במוצאי שבת (מהרי"ל). ויש מקילין ומתירין לטבול במ"ש, הואיל שלא טבלה בשבת משום חשש איסור (בית יוסף).

שו"ת שבט הלוי חלק ד סימן קז – ברמ"א ס"ב, אבל במקום שאין המנהג אין להחמיר והט"ז והב"ח החמירו – והש"ך ותוה"ש והרבה גדולי הפוסקים הקלו, ובספר דעת תורה העתיק מספר מקו"ח שבמקום שאין יכולים לברר המנהג צריכים להחמיר לחוש לדעת הב"ח והט"ז כיון שכ"ה הנהג בקהילות אשכנז יע"ש, אבל בעניותי פה אה"ק ובקהילתינו אין להחמיר בכלל בזה, ופשוט לפסוק כהגאון סדרי טהרה בס"ק ד' דהקיל בכל אופן כשבעלה בעיר אפילו פשעה ולא טבלה בימים שלפני השבת ומכ"ש באונס כל דהו אב"א אונס הגוף ואב"א אונס דצניעות, וכן למעשה פשוט להקל באם לא טבלה קודם מחמת איזה חומרא שהחמירה על עצמה כדמשמע בד"מ כאן, ובספר פ"ז כאן הניח בצ"ע ולמעשה יראה להקל כמש"כ, כי בזמן הזה למי שמכיר מצב הדור ותכונותיו אסור לנו לדחות טבילה כיון דע"פ עיקר הדין אין חשש כמש"כ רבינו הרמ"א בד"מ.

ודע דבפת"ש בסימן ר' מביא מתשובת הר הכרמל סי' כ"ה דכתב דאף במקום שאין נוהגין לברך על הטבילה אחרי הטבילה אלא לפניו מ"מ דוקא בחול אבל בשבת כשטובלות יש לאשה לנהוג לברך אחרי הטבילה או לפניו בלחש יע"ש, ובס' פ"ז סי' ר' כתב טעם הדבר ומביאו כן ג"כ בשם עצי לבונה לפי מש"כ המג"א סי' שכ"ג ס"ק י"ג בשם התשב"ץ בדין הרוצה להטביל כלי בשבת ימלאנו מים מהמקוה ועלתה טבילה להכלי, וכתב המג"א דלא יברך על טבילת כלי דאז אינו מוכח דעושה לשם טבילה וא"כ טבילת נדה בשבת דכל ההיתיר משום דנראה כמיקר ואם לאו אסור משום דמתקן א"כ כשתברך לפני הטבילה מוכח דאין הכונה למיקר אלא לתקן, וזה טעם תשובת הר הכרמל הנ"ל.

ובעניותי דאין הדברים דומים, דודאי טבילת כלים דאין לו היתיר ע"פ הדין אם לא דרך הערמת היתר הנ"ל, צריך שיהיה היתרו מוכח כיון דחז"ל באמת לא נתנו היתר בטבילת כלים, אבל טבילת נדה והטמאים שמעיקרא הקילו ולא גזרו כלל, והטעם דלא גזרו משום דנראה כמיקר ומוכח בגמ' דאף במקום דודאי לא נראה כמיקר התירו דהא התירו ביוה"כ למ"ד טבילה בזמנה מצוה עיין ביצה י"ח ע"ב, א"כ במקום שאנו מתירים הטבילה בשבת (ולא ניכנס בחומרת הגאונים בסי' קצ"ז ס"ב) מה לנו אם לא נראה כמיקר, וכי אשה ההולכת לבית טבילת נשים בשבת בחפיפה ובחמין, וכי לא מוכח הדבר שהיא לטבילה מתכונת אלא דבמקום שהיתרנו ע"פ יסוד היתר חז"ל שוב אין נפ"מ אם הדבר נראה כמטהר מן הטומאה. מ"מ מהיות טוב – טוב לחוש לחומרת הפת"ש, ובפרט לדידן אין נפ"מ כיון דאנחנו מברכים תמיד אחריו.

שוב הראו לי במ"ב סי' שכ"ג בביאור הלכה ד"ה ימלאנו כעין דברינו – אלא שפקפק מדהתוס' יבמות מ"ו ע"ב ד"ה תקוני שכ' דמטעם ב' ת"ח עומדים בשעת טבילה שוב לא נראה כמיקר א"כ משמע דאם מוכח דלטבילה מכוון גם באדם אסור, – איברא בביאור הלכה עצמו הרגיש דדעת הרמב"ם ביבמות שם דלא כתוס' כמש"כ ביו"ד סי' רס"ט דלא ס"ל דכה"ג יחשב כמתקן – אלא דבביאור הלכה הצריך צ"ע למעשה מכח דברי מג"א הנ"ל – דלא יברך על טבילת כלים, והתשב"ץ מסייע לי' – וע"פ מש"כ הבדל גדול יש בין טבילת אדם לטבילת כלים – דדוקא בטבילת כלים החמירו התשב"ץ והמג"א, משא"כ טבילת אדם במקום דהתירו לגמרי התירו חז"ל.

שוב זכיתי לראות בתשובת אבני מילואים סי' י"א כ' ממש כדברינו בחלוק שבין אדם לכלים (ועיין ג"כ בס' נהור שרגא ביבמות שם) – וב"ה שהנחני בדרך אמת.

33.

תלמוד בבלי מסכת נדה דף סז עמוד ב – אמר רב: נדה בזמנה – אינה טובלת אלא בלילה, ושלא בזמנה – טובלת בין ביום בין בלילה. רבי יוחנן אמר: בין בזמנה בין שלא בזמנה – אינה טובלת אלא בלילה, משום סרך בתה. ואף רב הדר ביה, דאמר רבי חייא בר אשי אמר רב: נדה, בין בזמנה בין שלא בזמנה – אינה טובלת אלא בלילה, משום סרך בתה.

תלמוד בבלי מסכת נדה דף סז עמוד ב – אמר ליה רב פפא לרבא ולאביי: מכדי האידנא כולהו ספק זבות שוינהו רבנן, ליטבלינהו בימא דשביעאה? משום דרבי שמעון, דתניא (ויקרא ט"ו)

אחר תטהר – אחר אחר לכולן, שלא תהא טומאה מפסקת ביניהן. ר' שמעון אומר: אחר תטהר – אחר מעשה תטהר. אבל אמרו חכמים: אסור לעשות כן, שמא תבא לידי ספק.

בעלי הנפש שער הטבילה – השגות הרז"ה סימן א – א. כתב הרב א"ר יוחנן נדה בין בזמנה בין שלא בזמנה לא תטבול אלא בלילה משום סרך בתה. ואני אומר שלא נאמרה שמועה זו אלא בזמן שהיו בנות ישראל עומדות על דין תורה, אבל בזמן הזה שהן כלן ספק זבות אין לחוש לסרך בתה וטובלת לז' לספירתה שהוא שמיני לראיתה, ואפילו ביום. ואסורה לשמש עד הערב משום דר"ש. והא דא"ל רב פפי לרבא הא ליטבלן ביומא דשבעה, נראה בעיני שהוא לשון נקיה, כלומר ליטבלן ולישמשן וכההיא דאמרינן ההוא יומא יום טבילה הוה. ותמה על עצמך היאך תטיל איסור בטבילה בזמנה שהיא מצוה מפני חשש רחוק ועמוק עמוק, שהרי כמה ספיקות יש בחשש זה, שמא זבה היא ושמא תשמש בו ביום ושמא תסתור ספירתה. וכבר ראיתי דברי ר' יעקב ז"ל (ספר הישר שו"ת סי' מה, ב) שפירש אסור לעשות כן, אסור לעשות אותו מעשה של טבילה. ואין הפירוש נ"ל, ומפרשינן בספרא (מצורע פרק ט ה"ב) ר"ש אומר ואחר תטהר כיון שטבלה מותרת להתעסק בטהרות אבל אמרו חכמים אסור לעשות כן שלא תבא לידי הספק. מזה נראה שאין האיסור אלא עסק הטהרות וכיוצא בו אבל בטבילה שהיא מצוה בזמנה רחוק הוא בעיני לומר עליה אסור לעשות כן. ואל תתמה על מה שאמרנו טבילה בזמנה מצוה, שהרי שנינו בה כמה סתומות בטועה (נדה ל ב) של ט' טבילות ושל י"א ושל ט"ו ושל ל"ה וצ"ה, והגאונים הביאוה בדבריהם בהלכות נדה ומה שאמר רב אחאי הגאון אין שום ראיה, לדברי האוסרים שכך כתב, ולא מישתרא לגברא עד דמנין ז' נקיים דא"ר זירא (סו א) בנות ישראל הן החמירו על עצמן [וכו', ולאורתא דשביעי טבלא ומשתריא לבעלה, ואי טבלא בימָמא דשביעי לא סלקא לה טבילתה דתניא (שבת קכא א) כל חייבי טבילות טבילתן ביום נדה ויולדת טבילתן בלילה. ומנ"ל, דתניא (ספרא מצורע פרשתא ד ה"ח) מנין לנדה שאינה טובלת מבעוד יום ת"ל שבעת ימים תהיה בנדתה תהא בנדתה כל שבעה. אלו דברי הגאון. ודבריו מפורשים לכל מבין שהוא פתח בדרבנן וסיים בדאוריתא. וכי אפשר לומר שתעלה על דעת הגאון שאם טבלה ביום שביעי דספירת נקיים שלא תעלה לה טבילה, הא מהיכא תיתי, אלא בעל כרחך פתח בדרבנן וסיים בדאוריתא. גם מדברי הרב אלפסי בהלכותיו אין להביא ראיה לאיסור, שהוא כתב בהלכות הכל כסדר הגמרא, ולא שיהא הכל נוהג בזמן הזה אלא כדי שיהיו הדברים ברורים ומפורשים, שאם היה כותב העיקר בכל מקום, העיקר הנוהג בלבד, ומניח את שאינו נוהג, היו ברוב המקומות הדברים סתומים ומתערבבים ולא היו מבוארים ומרווחים. ועוד דהא אמר ליה רבא לרב פפא על הא דר' זירא דגמרא בנות ישראל הן החמירו על עצמן] חומרא היא היכא דאחמור אחמור היכא דלא אחמור לא אחמור.

הגהות מיימוניות הלכות איסורי ביאה פרק יא – [א] וכן כתב בספר התרומה והמצוה שחוששים משום סרך בתה אפילו בדורות אחרונים שנוהגים חומרא דר"ז דגרסינן התם בבבא בתרא אתקין רבא במחוזא משום אבולי משמע שלא התיר אלא משום דוחק ובימי רבא היו נוהגים חומרא דר"ז כדאיתא התם אמר ליה רב פפא לרבא מכדי האידנא ספק זבה שווינהו ליטבלינהו בימָמא דשבעה וכו' וכן התוס' אבל ראבי"ה כתב דאין שייך לחוש בדורות אחרונים משום סרך בתה

שהרי אפילו תטעה בתה לטבול ביום ז׳ סלקא לה טבילה כדלקמן בסוף הפרק וכן רבינו שמחה והא דאתקין רבא כאן זה היה בנערותו ועדיין לא פשטא חומרא דר״ז בכ״מ אבל משפשטה מותרת לטבול ביום ח׳ אפילו בלא דוחק ע״כ:

תוספות מסכת נדה דף סז עמוד ב – אבל אמרו חכמים אסור לעשות כן שלא תבוא לידי ספק – צ״ל אסור לעשות כן לטבול דאי אתשמיש מהו שלא תבוא לידי ספק הא כבר באה בשעת תשמיש שמא תראה והוה ליה למימר שלא תבא לידי ודאי ועוד היכי שרו רבנן לשמש הא ודאי אמרי׳ לקמן במתני׳ (דף עב.) הרי זה תרבות רעה גבי שומרת יום כנגד יום שטבלה בשני לראייתה וקאמר מגעה ובעילתה תלויה וכן משמע בשמעתין מדפריך ונטבלינהו בימּמא דז׳ ומשני משום דר״ש אלמא אטבילה קאמר ר״ש דאסור ומיהו זה יש לדחות דלעולם קאי אתשמיש אבל טבילה שריא לר״ש אלא אח״כ החמירו לאסור בה הטבילה גזרה שמא תשמש אבל קשה דלעיל פ׳ המפלת (דף כט:) בשמעתין דטועה פריך בכ״א תשמש ומשני ר״ש היא דאמר אבל אסור לעשות כן אם כן אתשמיש קאי דהא ודאי בימּמא מטבלינן לה משום טבילה בזמנה מצוה וי״ל דה״פ ר״ש היא דאמר גבי ודאי זבה דאסור לעשות כן לטבול ביום שמא תבא לידי ספק לשמש שבעילתה תהא תלויה הילכך בהך טועה אע״ג דאיכא בה כמה ספקות דשמא לא היתה זבה כלל ואם היתה זבה אימר הרחיקה לידתה ושמא לא תראה אסורה לשמש לר׳ שמעון אבל טבילה תהא מותרת אפילו לר״ש דשרי לה לטבול משום טבילה בזמנה מצוה.

שולחן ערוך יורה דעה סימן קצז סעיף ג – אסורה לטבול ביום ז׳; ואפילו אם ממתנת מלטבול עד יום ח׳ ז או ט׳ אינה יכולה לטבול ביום ח משום סרך בתה. (פי׳ דבוק הבת וקורבתה לעשות כמעשה האם שתטבול ביום כמוה ולא תבחין שאמה לאחר שבעה טבלה ולא בשביעי עצמו). הגה: והכלות הטובלות קודם החופה יכולות לטבול ביום דהא לא באין אצל החתן עד הלילה, אבל אחר החופה דינן כשאר נשים (מהרי״ל).

תלמוד בבלי מסכת נדה דף סז עמוד ב – אתקין רב אידי בנרש למטבל ביומא דתמניא, משום אריותא. רב אחא בר יעקב בפפוניא משום גנבי. רב יהודה בפומבדיתא משום צנה. רבא במחוזא משום אבולאי.

ב״ח יו״ד קצז:ח ד״ה ובע״כ – ובע״כ דהגה״ה זו לא מיירי אלא בנשים שטובלות בשביעי ביום דאי בטובלות בשמיני ביום הא ודאי דליכא מאן דפליג דלא עלתה לה טבילה דכיון דאפילו לכתחילה שרי משום צנה כ״ש דבדיעבד עלתה לה טבילה אף בלא שום אונס. וכדכתב הרשב״א וה״ר ירוחם ומביאו ב״י וא״כ היאך כתב בשם מהר״ם והר״י דהצריך לטבול פעם שניה אלא בע״כ דמיירי בנשים שטובלות ביום השביעי קאמר ולאו ברשיעי עסקינן אלא מיירי כגון דח׳ וט׳ ויותר איכא אונס דאפי׳ ביום אינן יכולות לטבול ביום אבל לא בלילה מפני שסוגרים שערי העיר ובזו קאמר בשם ראבי״ה דעלתה לה טבילה אך לא תשמש עד הלילה וקאמר באגור בשם מהר״ש דצריכה להסתיר טבילתה מבעלה שלא ישמשו עמהם ביום ויבואו לידי ספק דאורייתא שמא תראה ביום שביעי אחר התשמיש ותהא סותרת למפרע כל הז׳.

שולחן ערוך יורה דעה סימן קצז סעיף ה – אם עברה וטבלה בח' ביום בלא אונס, אפילו הכי עלתה לה טבילה; וכן אם עברה וטבלה בז' ביום, עלתה לה טבילה. הגה: ומכל מקום לא תשמש אפילו בשמיני עד הלילה, ותסתיר טבילתה מבעלה עד הלילה (ב"י בשם האגור).

ש"ך על שולחן ערוך יורה דעה סימן קצז סעיף ה – יא וכן אם עברה וטבלה בז' כו' – והב"ח פסק להחמיר כמהרי"ל והג"מ והגהת ש"ד בשם מהר"ם דביום ז' לא עלתה לה טבילה וצריכה טבילה שנית בלילה וטוב להחמיר היכא דאפשר כיון שכן גם כן דעת הראב"ד והג"מ והר"א בשם השאילתות:

רא"ש מסכת נדה הלכות מקוואות סימן לו – לו (יומא ד' ו א) תניא כל חייבי טבילות טבילתן ביום. נדה ויולדת טבילתן בלילה (נדה סז ב) אמר רב נדה בזמנה לא תטבול אלא בלילה. שלא בזמנה תטבול בין ביום ובין בלילה. רבי יוחנן אמר בין בזמנה בין שלא בזמנה לא תטבול אלא בלילה משום סרך בתה. ואף רב הדר ביה דא"ר חייא בר אשי אמר רב נדה בין בזמנה בין שלא בזמנה לא תטבול אלא בלילה משום סרך בתה אתקין רב אידי בר אבין בנרש למיטבל ביממא דתמינאה משום אריותא. רב אחא בר יעקב בפפניא משום גנבי. רב יהודה בפומבדיתא משום צנה. רבא במחוזא משום אבולאי. אמר רב פפא לרבא מכדי האידנא כולהו ספק זבות משוינן להו ליטבלי ביממא דשביעאה (אלא) משום ר"ש. דתניא ואחר תטהר אחר אחר לכולן שלא תהא טומאה מפסקת ביניהן ר"ש אומר אחר תטהר אחר מעשה תטהר אבל אמרו חכמים אסור לעשות כן שמא תבא לידי ספק. הלכך האידנא לא טבלי ביום כלל ביום השביעי משום דר' שמעון. בשמיני ובתשיעי משום סרך בתה שהיא סוברת שאמה טובלת ביום השביעי ותעשה גם היא כן ותבא לידי ספק. ואין לומר דלא שייך סרך בתה אלא לדידהו שהיו נוהגין כדין נדה דאורייתא ואיכא למיחש שמא תטבול בתה בשביעי לנדתה ביום וטבילה זו כמאן דליתא דמיא. אבל משום סרך בתה שתטבול בשביעי האידנא דמדרבנן בעלמא הוא לא חיישי הא ליתא הא רבא במחוזא תקין משום אבולאי למיטבל ביממא דתמניא ואי לאו משום אבולאי הוה אסור משום סרך בתה ובימיו כבר פשטה תקנתא דר' זירא. כדאמר ליה רב פפא לרבא מכדי האידנא כולהו ספק זבות וכו'. ורשב"ם היה מחמיר שלא תטבול עד שתחשך. ור"ת היה אומר שאין צריך להחמיר כל כך רק שתטבול סמוך לחשיכה ותבא לביתה משחשיכה ואז ליכא למיחש לסרך בתה:

ש"ך יורה דעה סימן קצז ס"ק ו – ו אסורה לטבול כו' – משמע אפילו שתטבול סמוך לחשכה ותבא לביתה משתחשך אסור כדעת רשב"ם וסייעתו שכתבו הפוסקים שנכון להחמיר כדבריו כתב הב"ח דאפילו ללכת מביתה לבית הטבילה מבע"י אסור והיינו כשהאשה רוחצת וחופפת בביתה והולכת למקום טבילה אבל כשיש מרחץ ובית הטבילה במקום אחד ואשה הולכת מבע"י למרחץ שעה או שתים קודם חשכה ובאה לביתה אחר חשכה אע"פ שהמרחץ ובית הטבילה קרוב וסמוך לביתה אין כאן משום סרך בתה דהבת יודעת שהיא שוהה ברחיצה וחפיפה במרחץ ואינה טובלת אלא משחשכה עכ"ל מיהו באגור כתוב שהמנהג באשכנז סמוך לחשכה עכ"ל ואפשר דס"ל כר"ת וסייעתו דמותר לטבול סמוך לחשכה רק שתבא לביתה משתחשך וכמדומה

לי שכן נוהגים מ"מ יש להחמיר מיהו נראה דהיינו דוקא ביום ח' דאסור משום סרך בתה לחוד ובכה"ג מיקל ר"ת סמוך לחשכה אבל ביום ז' אין לטבול כלל סמוך לחשכה ויש למחות ביד העושות כן:

שו"ת עבודת הגרשוני סימן כ – תשובה הנה באמת אין הזמן מסכים עמדי כלל לטייל בפרדס. ארוכות וקצרות לפלפל בדברי החכם וראיותיו כראוי לכל משיב לחכם כמוהו ירבה ע"כ היה מן הראוי להטמין ידי עד עת מצוא שעת הכושר להשיב באריכות רק מטובו קאמינא להשיב לו מפני הכבוד אף בקצרה מה שנראה לע"ד על פי הדין ודת של תורה וזה החלי. בעזרת ה' חילי. צורי וגואלי. ואען ואומר להיתר שאלה זו צריכין אנו לבאר דעתו של ר"ת שכתב שאין צריך להחמיר כ"כ ולהמתין עד שתחשך רק שתטבול סמוך לחשיכה ותבא לביתה משתחשך (הובא בפוסקים) אם דעתו שאפילו ביום הז' אין להחמיר כ"כ וטעמו ונימוקו עמו דכיון שלא תבא לביתה עד שתחשך תו ליכא למיחש למידי לא לדר"ש שתבא לידי ספק ולא לסרך בתה ודמי' להא דאי' במהרי"ל שהכלות הטובלת בשעת נשואין יכולין לטבול מבע"י מאחר דאינן באות אצל החתן עד הלילה. (ומה שכתוב מהר"ר ש"ך בזה במחילה מכבודו שגה ברואה ולא ראה מ"ש בהגהות ש"ד דף פ"ו ע"ב בשם מהרי"ל ע"ש) או אם דעתו של ר"ת במ"ש שאין להחמיר כ"כ להמתין עד שתחש' אלא דוקא ביום הח' אבל ביום הז' הוא מודה לרשב"ם שאין להאשה לטבול עד שהוא ודאי לילה (ונלע"ד שאין דעת הפוסקי' שוה בזה ויעברון לפנינו כבני מרון א' לא' למצוא חשבון). והנה ראיתי בש"ד סי' ך' שכתב וז"ל יכולה אשה לטבול סמוך לשקיעת החמה קודם שתחשך דליכא למיחש לדר"ש הואיל ומחשיך לבא כו' ע"ש הרי מבואר דס"ל שאפילו ביום השביעי אין להחמיר להמתין עד שתחשך (ממש והחכם המורה הביא ג"כ בתשובתו דברי הש"ד.) מ"מ צריכין אנו למודעי מה דעת ר"ת בזה. והנה התוספות כתבו בפ' התינוקת בד"ה משום סרך בתה וז"ל ומיהו אומר ר"ת שאין קפידא רק כשתשיב לביתה יהי' לילה ואין צריך שתצא מביתה בלילה דשוב לא תבא לידי ספק ליכא למיחש אם תטבול היא ביום סמוך לחשיכה תטבול בתה בעוד היום גדול דמרגשת הבת בכך שתטבול סמוך לחשיכה כאמה עכ"ל:

והנה מלת ליכא בלי הגה' אין לו הבנה ונלע"ד שצ"ל וליכא למיחש כו' וה"פ שר"ת תרתי קאמר שיכולה לטבול ביום הז' סמוך לחשיכה דכיון כשתשיב לביתה הוא לילה שוב לא תבא לידי ספק. וגם ליכא למיחש לסרך בתה שתטעה ותסבור שאמה טבלה בעוד היום גדול דמרגשת הבת בכך כו'. וא"כ הוא כוונת ר"ת הרי מבואר שר"ת ס"ל כדעת הש"ד הנ"ל שאפילו בז' אין להחמיר ולהמתין עד שתחשך ממש:

והנה ראיתי שמו"ח ז"ל בב"ח שלו העתיק דברי התו' והגיה דליכא למיחש כו' ולפי הגהתו ה"פ שר"ת חדא קאמר דשוב לא תבא לידי ספק ר"ל הבת לא תבא לידי ספק דליכא למיחש כו' ולפ"ז לא הוה מוכח שר"ת מקיל גם ביום ז'. אבל לע"ד אין לשון התו' מוכיחים כן דא"כ הל"ל בקצרה דשוב ליכא למיחש כו' (ובאמת כן הוא לשון הרא"ש) ועוד דשוב לא תבא משמע שקאי אההי' דלעיל מיניה. ואין צריך שתצא בלילה דהיינו האשה הטובלת א"צ שתצא בלילה ועלה קאי שלא תבא לידי ספק ולא קאי אהבת שלא נזכרה עדין חדא ועוד קאמינא אף לפי הגהתו של מו"ח ז"ל מוכח שפיר שר"ת ס"ל שגם ביום הז' אין להחמיר ולהמתין עד שתחשך. שהרי

כתב שמרגשת הבת שתטבול סמוך לחשיכה כאמה ר"ל לפי הגהתו אף אם תטעה הבת ותסבור שאמה טבלה בז' מ"מ תרגיש שתטבול גם היא בז' כאמה סמוך לחשיכה. וא"כ משמע אם תטבול בז' סמוך לחשיכה שפיר עבדית:

כללא דמלתא שלעד"נ שמוכח מתוך דברי התו' שר"ת ס"ל שאפי' בז' אין להחמיר להמתין עד הלילה וכש"ד הנ"ל:

שו"ת חתם סופר חלק ב (יורה דעה) סימן קצז – אך על כל פנים נ"ל שתשהה האשה בהליכה ממקוה לביתה עד הלילה אבל אינו מועיל מה שתלך לבית חברתה באותה העיר כי מה לי בית זה או זה ולא ניתנו דברי' לשיעורים כאלה וכן יש להוכיח מפשטיות הסוגי' כמובן ומכל מקום המחמיר תע"ב והמקיל לא הפסיד עד כאן לשוני שכתבתי במק"א וכעת נראה לי עצת מעלתו נכונה לכתחלה על כל פנים שתפסוק בטהרה גם ביום ד' סמוך לבין השמשות הפונה ליום ה' לראי' ומ"מ לא תתחיל לספור אלא מיום ו' ואילך אחר פסיקת טהרה שנית סמוך לבה"ש הפונה ליום ו' לראי' ואז תטבול ביום ז' שחל בעש"ק ולא תבוא לביתה עד הלילה ליל ש"ק ומ"מ ק' הדבר איך תשהה כ"כ סמוך לשבת בדרך כי כבר כתבתי שאין נ"ל שום היתר במה שהיא בבית חברתה באותה העיר והחכם עיניו בראשו כתבתי בנחיצה וחתמתי שמי. פ"ב יום ה' ערב חנוכה פ"ד לפ"ק. משה"ק סופר מפפ"דמ.

שו"ת אגרות משה יורה דעה חלק ג סימן ס – ונראה דאם הבעל ילך לבהכ"נ זמן קטן קודם זמן הדלקת הנר והיא תכנס לביתה תיכף לזמן הדלקת הנר, ואף שכתב החת"ס דאינו מועיל מה שתלך לבית חברתה באותה העיר כי מה לי בית זה או זה ולא ניתנו דברים לשיעורים, נראה דאין כוונת החת"ס אלא באופן שיכול הוא או היא לבוא להפגש משום דהוא יבין באיזה בית נמצאת והיא הרי יודעת שהוא בבית, אבל כשהלך לביהכ"נ שודאי לא יצא משם עד אחר גמר התפלה ועד שיבא הביתה יהיה כבר בלילה אין לחוש לכלום דהרי לא תלך לביהכ"נ. ובלא זה לא מובן מש"כ לא ניתנו דברים לשיעורים כאלה דהרי אין כאן נתינת שיעורים אלא דבר ברור לכל בשוה שאין לה לבא למקום שהוא נמצא דהוא בבית דהא אין חוששין לשמא יעברו במזיד על איסורין אלא דכשתבא לבעלה יש לחוש שכיון שאיסור קל הוא יזלזלו כשהן יחד, אבל ודאי אין לחוש שישתדלו יטריחו למצא זא"ז אפילו כשהוא איסור קל, אבל מ"מ כיון שהחת"ס אסר כשתהיה בבית חברתה יש לחוש לדבריו, אבל כשילך לביהכ"נ והיא תבוא לביתה אין לחוש אף להחת"ס, וגם נראה דאף שתבא לביתה אם א"א להו להיות ביחוד עד הלילה כגון שיש בבית ילדים נמי אין לחוש לכלום, שלכן אולי במדינתנו בזה"ז בימים הקצרים והבינונים ששום איש אינו הולך לישן מצד האור הגדול שיש בכל בית ורגילין שכנים ואף רחוקים לבא עד שלש וארבע שעות בלילה אין לחוש כלל שיכבו הנרות וילכו לישן עוד קודם הלילה דלא כהמקומות והזמנים שלא היה להם אלא נרות קטנים והיה קשה להשתמש שמפני חשכת הלילה רובא דאינשי היו הולכין לישן בתחלת הלילה היו נמנעים אינשי מלכת לבית אחרים אף כשעה קודם הלילה כדי להכין להשינה והיה שייך לחוש לשמא ילכו לישן גם קודם הלילה, ורק בימים הארוכים יש אולי קצת לחוש, ויש לצרף בשעת הדחק גם סברא זו.

ש"ך יורה דעה סימן קצז ס"ק ט – והכלות כו' – נראה דהיינו דוקא לדידן שהכלות אינן טובלות בז' וכמ"ש בסי' קצ"ו ס"ק כ' וכ"מ במהרי"ל שם דמיירי בכהאי גוונא אבל במקום שהכלות טובלות בז' או לדידן אם אירע לה טבילה בז' כגון שנתקלקלה בימי ספירתה דאז טובלת מיד לאחר ז' אינה יכולה לטבול ביום דהא ביו' זו (לאו משום סרך בתה לחוד) מיתסרי (אלא) משום שמא תראה ותסתור כל מה שלמפרע ונמצאת זבה למפרע כדאיתא בש"ס ופוסקים כנ"ל:

דגול מרבבה קצז בש"ך ס"ק ט' – ודבריו צ"ע דהא ההיתר משום שאין מביאין אותה אצל החתן וא"כ אי אפשר לבוא לבעילת זבה ואעפ"כ לא מלאו לבו של המנחת יעקב לחלוק על הש"ך אף שהרגיש ג"כ בהשגה זו ומ"מ בשעת הדחק נלע"ד להקל אבל באופן שלא יעמידו החופה עד צאת הכוכבים ממש אבל להעמיד החופה ביום ולסמך שאין מיחדים אותן עד הלילה לא מהני בזה.

שו"ת רבי עקיבא איגר מהדורה תניינא סימן עא – וע"ד המנהג בכמה מקומות לאחר החופה עד הלילה, ומקדשים בלילה אם נכון לעשות כן:

דבר זה אין לו יסוד לא בראשונים ולא באחרונים, רק בש"ע אה"ע (סי' קכ"ג בהג"ה) כתב ואין לגרש לכתחילה בלילה, מקור הדין מדברי מהר"י מינ"ץ וז"ל בסי' נ"ז, אשה שקבלה גט בלילה אינה מגורשת, וכן אם הוא קדושין אבל קיום שטרות הוי אפילו בלילה עכ"ל, והביא שם הגט פשוט דברי הרא"ם בשו"ת ח"א סי פ"ב, דכתב הטעם בגט הוי כתחילת דין ומדמי לה לחליצה עיי"ש, אולם בקדושין לא ביאר טעם ספיקתו, ובשו"ת הרא"ם ח"ב סי' ל"ו האריך מאד, בדיני גט בלילה, והעלה דמדינא דאורי' אינו גט, וכתב שם ומגמגם אני על הקדושין משום דכתיב ויצאה והיתה ויש צדדים בדבר עכ"ל, נראה אופן ספיקתו, די"ל דלענין זה ל"ש היקישא ויצאה והיתה כיון דבגט עצמו לא כתיב קרא לפסול בו בלילה רק מסברא כיון דגובה כתובתה הוי כתחילת דין, וכיון דהסברא ליתא בקדושין ממילא אין לפוסלו, וסברא כזו כתב הפני יהושע כתובות (דף ע"ג) לענין תנאי דאפשר לקיים ע"י שליח עיי"ש, ונ"ל ראי' דעכ"פ בקדושין מדינא מהני בלילה, מההיא דאמרינן פ"ט דגיטין המגרש וכו' ולנה עמו בפונדק וכו' אא"ע בב"ז ובעל לשם קדושין, והרי לנה משמע רק בלילה ואפ"ה מהני אם בעל לשם קדושין, גם הרשב"א הביא ראי' דפנוי הבא על הפנויה לא אמרינן אין אדם עושה בעילתו ב"ז, וא"כ לא משכחת לה דנושא מפותת אביו עיי"ש, ודלמא מפותת אביו מיירי שאביו בא עליה בלילה דודאי ליכא קדושין, אע"כ מדינא מהני קדושין בלילה, ובודאי בשעת הדחק אם נמשך עד הלילה יש לסמוך להתיר לקדשה כיון דאפילו בגט רבו המקילים, אך שלא בשעת הדחק ראוי ונכון לקדש ביום לחוש לספיקא דהרא"ם הנ"ל, ואם מנהג העיר בשביל טבילת הכלה, כבר הסכימו בשו"ת עבודת הגירשוני סי' כ' ובשו"ת פנים מאירות ח"ב סי' ד' ובתפארת למשה ואורח מישור וסדרי טהרה, דמותרת לטבול ביום ז' אחר הנץ החמה דלא כהש"ך, מ"מ אם מנהג העיר בשביל הטבילה נראה דקבלו עליהם להחמיר כדעת הש"ך, אין לשנות מנהגם, דלא גרע מדברים המותרים וכו' מאחר דהקדושין בלילה אין קפידא כ"כ, וכדנראה דהרמ"א הביא דברי מהר"י מינץ לענין גט, והשמיט דברי הר"י מינץ לענין קדושין, נראה דלא חש לה לענין קדושין, ועי' בגט פשוט (סי' קכ"ג) דתמה על הרא"ם, דהא סוגיא ערוכה בקדושין (דף ח' וי"א) דקדשה בלילה, עיי"ש, ולענ"ד יש

לדחות, דהא עיקר יסודו דהרא"ם בגט כיון דקיי"ל כר"א ביבמות (דף ק"ד) דחלצה בלילה פסול דחליצה כתחילת דין, ה"נ גט הוי כתחילת דין, א"כ י"ל מה דאמרינן בקדושין (דף ח') ל"צ דיהבה נהיליה בלילה ה"נ דאשתכח וכו', היינו דלת"ק דר"א דיבמות דחליצה בלילה כשר דכגמר דין דמי, ממילא גם גט כשר בלילה, דמשכחת לה דיהבה בלילה, ולר"א עכ"פ משכחת דאשתכח ביני זוזי, וכן ההיא דדף י"א דאר"ז כי קאמינא דקדשה בלילה, י"ל דר"ז ס"ל להלכה כת"ק דר"א בחליצה, וכדס"ל ביבמות שם לרבה בר חייא קטוספאה, אח"ז ראיתי בספר שער המלך ריש הל' גירושין כתב לתרץ קושיית הג"פ הנ"ל, די"ל דהרא"ם ס"ל דבקדושי כסף לא מקשינן ליציאה, ומסתפק רב בקדושי שטר, עיי"ש, ולפי הנ"ל אין הכרח, די"ל דגם בקדושי כסף מספקא ליה, אמנם דברי השער המלך מספיקים ליישב ראיה דידן מההיא לנה עמו בפונדק, די"ל דבאמת כסף וביאה מהני בלילה אבל לא לקדושי שטר, עכ"פ זכינו לדון מכח ראי' דידן דלמנהגינו דמקדשים בכסף מותר בלילה, כן נראה לענ"ד:

.34

תלמוד בבלי מסכת בבא קמא דף פב עמוד א – ושתהא אשה חופפת וטובלת – דאורייתא היא! דתניא: (ויקרא י"ד) ורחץ את בשרו במים – שלא יהא דבר חוצץ בין בשרו למים, את בשרו – את הטפל לבשרו, ומאי ניהו? שער! אמרי: דאורייתא לעיוני דלמא מיקטר, אי נמי מאוס מידי משום חציצה, ואתא איהו תיקן חפיפה.

ט"ז יורה דעה סימן קצט ס"ק ד – (ד) ותחוף כל גופה. – מלשונו משמע דבעינן תחילה עיון ובדיקה בכל גופה ואח"כ תעשה חפיפה בכל גופה והוא תמוה דאמאי לא סגי בחפיפת כל הגוף לחוד דהרי אז בודקת ג"כ דאין לך בדיקה גדולה מזו דאע"פ שאינה רואה במקום שחופפת סגי בהכי דאל"כ היאך תעשה בראשה ובמקומות שא"א לה לראות דהא לא הצריכו בזה שתראה לחברתה אלא דוקא בטבילה אמרו שתעמוד עליה אשה אחרת ולא בחפיפה ועיון אלא דבר פשוט שעל ידי המשמוש שפיר הוה עיון דבר תורה ומכ"ש לפי תקנת עזרא בחפיפה ושטיפה. ונראה דסיפא הוה כאן פירושא דרישא דמה שכתב תחילה שצריכה לעיין בעצמה כו' דהיינו דין תורה וע"ז מסיק אחר כך שתחמיר עליה במקום העיון תעשה חפיפה בכל הגוף ודבר פשוט שאם היא מעיינת ובודקת עצמה בשעת החפיפה דיה בכך ואין צריך בדיקה מיוחדת דוקא:

שיורי טהרה קצט:ה – ובט"ז ס"ק ד' תמה על המחבר במה שנראה מדבריו דבעינן בתחלה עיון ובדיקה ואח"כ חפיפה דתרתי ל"ל הא סגי בחפיפה לחודא ודחק עצמו בכונת המחבר דמ"ש דצריכה לעיין וכו' היינו דין תורה ואח"כ מסיק שתחמיר עליה שבמקום העיון תעשה חפיפה ואין זה במשמע אלא נראה כמ"ש דתרתי בעינן חפיפה ועיון וכן משמע מלשון הר"ר שמעיה בשם רש"י שהביא הטור ע"ש וכ"מ עוד בסי' זה וכ"נ מעט"ז מיהו אם היא מעיינה ובודקת גופה בשעת חפיפה ש"ד וא"צ בדיקה מיוחדת לזה כמ"ש הט"ז ואף המחבר כוון לזה וכל עיקר לא אתי אלא לאשמעינן דבחפפה לחודא לא לא סגיא אלא צריך נמי עיון ובדיקה עם החפיפה ואם תרצה יכולה לעשות העיון והבדיקה בשעת חפיפה כנ"ל.

תוספות מסכת נדה דף סו עמוד ב – ושוב פירש ר"ת דחפיפה לא שייכא אלא בראש והך דחולין איירי בשאר הגוף דליכא חפיפה וכן משמע לעיל דקאמר אשה לא תחוף אלא בחמין כו׳ וקאמר טעמא דמשרו מזיא ומדלא קאמר לא תחוף ראשה ש"מ דבכ"מ חפיפה שייך טעמא דמשרו מזיא דבמקום שער הוא.

תלמוד בבלי מסכת נדה דף סו עמוד ב – ואמר רבא: טבלה ועלתה ונמצא עליה דבר חוצץ, אם סמוך לחפיפה טבלה – אינה צריכה לחוף ולטבול, ואם לאו – צריכה לחוף ולטבול. איכא דאמרי: אם באותו יום שחפפה טבלה – אינה צריכה לחוף ולטבול, ואם לאו – צריכה לחוף ולטבול. מאי בינייהו? איכא בינייהו: למסמך לחפיפה טבילה, למיחף ביממא ולמטבל בליליא.

תלמוד בבלי מסכת חולין דף י עמוד א – מתיב רבא לסיועיה לרב הונא: טבל ועלה ונמצא עליו דבר חוצץ, אע"פ שנתעסק באותו המין כל היום כולו – לא עלתה לו טבילה, עד שיאמר ברי לי שלא היה עלי קודם לכן; והא הכא דודאי טבל, ספק הוה עליה ספק לא הוה עליה, וקאתי ספק ומוציא מידי ודאי! שאני התם, דאיכא למימר: העמד טמא על חזקתו; ואימא לא טבל. ה"נ העמד בהמה על חזקתה ואימר לא נשחטה! הרי שחוטה לפניך. ה"נ הרי טבל לפניך! הא איתילידא ביה ריעותא. ה"נ איתילידא בה ריעותא! סכין איתרעאי, בהמה לא איתרעאי.

ש"ך יורה דעה סימן קצט ס"ק א – א ולסרוק שער ראשה כו׳ – לשון הרמב"ם שהביא הטור עזרא ובית דינו תקנו שתהא חופפת בכל מקום שער שבה במים חמים וסורקת אותן או מפספסת אותן בידיה יפה יפה עכ"ל וכ"כ הרשב"א בתה"ק ומביאו ב"י מבואר מדבריהם דהא דתקן עזרא שתהא אשה חופפת היינו בכ"מ שער כגון שער בית השחי ובית הערוה לא שער ראשה בלבד וכ"כ ראב"ן סי׳ שכ"ו דף ס׳ ע"ד וכי חייפת צריכה לחוף כל שער גופה בין דראש בין דשחי בין דבית התורפה ע"כ וכן משמע בר"ן ושאר פוסקים וכ"כ הב"ח סעיף ב׳ ועכשיו נהגו לסרוק שער ראשן במסרק ושאר שער שבה מפספסת אותן בידיה יפה יפה:

תוספות מסכת נדה דף סו עמוד ב – אבל במחזור ה"ר שמריה מפרש בשם רש"י דבכל הגוף שייך חפיפה כדאמרינן בפ׳ כל כתבי (שבת דף קכ:) הרי שהיה שם כתוב על בשרו ה"ז לא יחוף.

תלמוד בבלי מסכת נדה דף סו עמוד ב – לא תחוף לא בנתר ולא בחול. בנתר – משום דמקטף, ובחול – משום דמסריך.

תוספות מסכת נדה דף סח עמוד א – כך אמרו משמיה דרבי יוחנן אשה לא תחוף בערב שבת ותטבול למוצאי שבת ותמה על עצמך היאך אשה חופפת ביום וטובלת בלילה – שהרי בקושי התירו לה להרחיק חפיפתה כל כך אלא משום דאי חופפת בליל טבילתה אימור לא חייפא שפיר מתוך שמהומה לביתה ממהרת לטבילתה ופירש רש"י הא דאפשר לחוף ביום כגון בימי החול חופפת ביום וטובלת בלילה הא דלא אפשר לחוף ביום כגון שאירעה טבילתה במוצאי שבת ואם תחוף בע"ש תרחיק יותר מדאי מטבילתה חופפת בליל טבילתה במוצאי שבת וא"ת הא דפסקינן לעיל הלכתא כרב חסדא וכדמתרץ רב יימר לא קאי דהכא אמרינן דאינה חופפת ע"ש וטובלת

למוצאי שבת וי"ל דאיכא לאוקמי פסק דלעיל שליל טבילתה במוצ"ש והוא יו"ט אז ודאי תחוף מע"ש ולא תפסיד עונתה הואיל ואינה יכולה לחוף בליל טבילתה ולא ביום שלפני טבילה מ"מ לפירוש רש"י נראה דמותר לחוף בליל טבילה אלא שטוב לה יותר לחוף ביום מפני שמהומה לביתה וכן משמע מדקאמר אשה חופפת ביום ולא קאמר אשה לא תחוף אלא ביום כדקאמר אשה לא תחוף אלא בלילה וכן משמע לעיל בעובדא דבי ריש גלותא דמותר לחוף בליל טבילה ולא מסתבר לפלוגי משום דאיקוט מדמייתי מההוא עובדא דנדה חופפת בלילה משמע אף בלא אונס ובשאלות דרב אחאי פרשת אחרי מות [סי' צו] פירשה הא דאפשר לחוף בליל טבילה שהוא חול לא תרחיק חפיפה מטבילה כלל ואפילו אם היום כמו כן חול לא תחוף אלא בלילה והא דלא אפשר כגון שליל טבילה יום טוב או שבת אז תחוף ביום שלפני הטבילה ואפילו אם יום שלפני הטבילה כמו כן יו"ט או שבת אז תחוף מערב שבת או מערב יו"ט כפסק שלמעלה דדריש מרימר דהילכתא כרב חסדא וכדמתרץ רב יימר ולדברי השאלתות כל זמן שתוכל אין לחוף אלא בליל טבילה מיהא לפי מנהג הנשים של עכשיו ששוהות במרחץ עד הלילה מותר לחוף ביום אף לפי השאלתות ואינו אסור אלא לחוף מבעוד יום ולצאת מן המרחץ קודם הלילה אבל בששהתה שם עד הלילה חפיפה אריכתא היא שכל שעה עוסקת בחפיפת גופה ושערה ותבא עליה ברכה ועוד יש שמחמירות אע"פ שחופפת נושאות עמהן מסרק וסורקות עצמן בבית הטבילה ור"ת פירש ותמה על עצמך זהו כפל מלה כלומר היאך אתה אומר דבר זה שאשה חופפת ביום וטובלת בליל מוצאי שבת והא בעינן סמוך לחפיפה טבילה ואומר ר"י דכי האי גוונא איכא בפסחים פרק כל שעה (דף כג.) ותמה על עצמך היאך חמץ אסור בהנאה כל שבעה.

רש"י מסכת נדה דף סח עמוד א – הא דאפשר – לחוף ביום חופפת ביום. הא דלא אפשר – לחוף כגון מוצאי יום טוב לא תחוף אלא בלילה.

שולחן ערוך יורה דעה סימן קצט סעיף ג – חפיפה צריכה להיות לכתחלה סמוך לטבילתה. והמנהג הכשר שתתחיל לחוף מבעוד יום ועוסקת בחפיפה עד שתחשך, ואז תטבול. וכן מנהג כשר שאף על פי שחפפה, תשא עמה מסרק לבית הטבילה ותסרוק שם. הגה: ובשעת הדחק שצריכה לחוף ביום, או שא"א לה לחוף ביום וצריכה לחוף בלילה, יכולה לעשות (בית יוסף בשם הפוסקים ובשם הרמב"ם פ"ב דמקואות). ובלבד שלא תמהר לביתה ותחוף כראוי.

ש"ך על שולחן ערוך יורה דעה סימן קצט סעיף ג – ו חפיפה כו' – ול"נ מכולה סוגיא דש"ס (נדה דף ס"ז וס"ח) כדעת רש"י וסייעתו דיותר טוב שהחפיפה תהיה ביום היכא דאפשר וכמ"ש בספרי עיין שם והלכך אם חל ליל טבילתה במ"ש או אפילו במוצאי יום טוב שחל להיות אחר שבת חופפת בע"ש וטובלת במ"ש או מוצאי יו"ט כיון שאפשר שהחפיפה תהיה ביום בחול אבל היכא דחל ליל טבילתה בליל ג' שאחר יום טוב כגון שחלו להיות שני יו"ט אחר השבת או שחלו להיות שני י"ט של ר"ה או של גליות ביום ה' ו' וחל ליל טבילתה במ"ש דנמצא יש שלשה ימים בין חפיפה לטבילה ובכה"ג לא אפשר שהחפיפה תהיה רחוקה כל כך וכדסבירא להו לרב חסדא ורב יימר דבכה"ג חופפת בליל טבילתה כיון דרחוקה יותר מדאי והיינו דאמרינן בש"ס והלכתא

אשה חופפת ביום והלכתא אשה לא תחוף אלא בלילה קשיא הלכתא אהלכתא לא קשיא הא דאפשר הא דלא אפשר ע״כ וסמך ש״ס אשקלא וטריא דרב חסדא ודרב יימר דלעיל ונ״ל דגם דעת רש״י כן שפי׳ וז״ל הא דאפשר לחוף ביום חופפת ביום הא דלא אפשר לחוף כגון מוצאי יו״ט לא תחוף אלא בלילה עכ״ל (וכ״פ בס׳ יראים ס״ס קצ״ב) ומ״ש כגון מוצאי יו״ט ר״ל של ר״ה וסמך אלעיל דבכה״ג לא אפשר הא לאו הכי אפשר לחוף בעי״ט ובהכי ניחא שפיר דקיימא כולה סוגיא דלעיל משא״כ להתוס׳ והפוסקים דצריכים לדחוק דאזלה לה סוגיא דלעיל ותו קשה לדבריהם דהא משמע התם להדיא מדברי רב הונא ורב חסדא ורב יימר ומרימר שכך היו נוהגות בנות ישראל בזמניהם לחוף ביום בע״ש או עיו״ט ולטבול במ״ש שהרי מביאין ראיה ממנהגם שמותר לחוף באחד בשבת ולטבול בד׳ או בה׳ בשבת אלא דרב חסדא ודעמיה פליגי בחול דאין דנין אפשר משאי אפשר והכי קא פסיק התם מרימר הלכתא אם כן היאך נאמר דסוגיא דלקמן דפסיק הלכתא פליגא אסוגיא והלכתא ומנהג דלעיל אלא ודאי כדפרישית זהו נ״ל בש״ס ורש״י אלא שהפוסקים לא פירשו כן ולא כתבו כן בשם רש״י ולא ידעתי מנין להם זה ולענין דינא נראה דבכל ענין יש לה להשתטף בחמין ביום בע״ש וערב יו״ט וגם לחוף אז ולחזור ולהשתטף ולחוף בליל טבילתה אם הוא חול וכ״כ הפוסקים וכן בחול מנהג כשר שהחפיפה תתחיל מבע״י ותעסוק בחפיפתה עד שתחשך וכמ״ש הפוסקי׳ והט״ו ואע״ג דהיכא דחל ליל טבילתה שלשה ימים רחוק כגון שבת ושני יו״ט בכה״ג מסקינן בש״ס דחופפת בליל טבילתה שהוא חול י״ל דה״ק לא די לה בחפיפת ע״ש ועי״ט כיון דרחוק כ״כ אלא צריכה לחוף ג״כ בליל טבילתה וגם בע״ש ועיו״ט כיון דחפיפת יום עדיף והכי ניחא למיעבד טפי כיון דנשי דידן חופפות בע״ש ועיו״ט וגם בליל טבילתן א״כ אין להקל להן לחלק בין רחוק שני ימים או שלשה ימים שלא יבואו לידי טעות וכ״כ בש״ד סי׳ י׳ דאף בכה״ג תחוף ג׳ ימים מקודם ג״כ ואפשר דהיינו מדאמרי׳ בש״ס דריש מרימר הלכתא כרב חסדא כדמתרץ רב יימר וחומרי חומרי נקט חומרא דרב חסדא בשני י״ט שאחר השבת שחופפת בע״ש דיותר טוב לחוף ביום וחומרא דרב יימר שחופפת בליל טבילתה כיון דרחוק כ״כ והיינו שכתוב במרדכי בשבועות בפ״ב דנדה פסקינן כרב חסדא דאשה חופפת בע״ש וטובלת אפילו בליל ד׳ כשאירעו שני יו״ט אחר השבת וכ״כ הרא״מ בספרו כרש״י דיותר טוב לחוף ביום מבלילה עכ״ל דלכאורה קשיא דהא פסקינן בש״ס כדמתרץ רב יימר אלא ודאי ס״ל כדרב חסדא וכדמתרץ רב יימר היינו כדפי׳ ולא כפירש״י שם ולישנא כדמתרץ רב יימר אתי שפיר לפי׳ זה אבל לפי׳ רש״י הל״ל וכרב יימר דהא פליג ודוק ומטעם זה נראה שלא חילקו הפוסקים בין שני יו״ט שחלו להיות אחר השבת שחופפת במוצאי יו״ט ובין יו״ט א׳ שחל להיות אחר השבת כדמחלקינן בש״ס בהכי דכיון דכתבו אף בשאר יו״ט דנכון להחמיר לחוף מעיו״ט וגם במוצאי יו״ט א״כ אין חילוק ודוק כי כל זה ברור לדעתי שוב מצאתי בתשובת מהרש״ל סי׳ ו׳ שהכריע כהחולקים על רש״י בלא טענה מוכרחת והנלפע״ד כתבתי עוד כתב מהרש״ל שם על מה שנהגו מקדם להתחיל לחוף ביום ועתה תקנו לחוף בלילה ותעסוק בחפיפה דוקא שעה אחת שלא תהא מהומה לביתה שרי אפי׳ לרש״י מאחר דאיכא חשש איסור שלא ירגישו בטבילותיהן וגם לפעמים הצנועות באות לידי ביטול טבילת מצוה וכ״כ הרב בתשובה סימן כ״א ע״ש שהאריכו בזה:

שולחן ערוך יורה דעה סימן קצט סעיף ד – חל טבילתה במוצאי שבת, שא"א לחוף מבעוד יום, תחוף בליל טבילתה. הגה: ומ"מ מנהג יפה הוא שתרחץ היטב בערב שבת, ובמוצ"ש תחזור ותחוף ותסרוק מעט (טור).

שולחן ערוך אורח חיים סימן תקנא סעיף טז – יש נוהגים שלא לרחוץ מראש חדש, ויש שאין נמנעין אלא בשבת זו, ויש מתענים מי"ז בתמוז עד ט"ב. הגה: ולצורך מצוה שרי; ולכן נדה רוחצת וטובלת (מהרי"ל); ואפי' אם טובלת ליל י' באב, מותר לה לרחוץ בערב ט"ב אם א"א לה לרחוץ ליל י' (אגודה). ונראה דה"ה אשה הלובשת לבנים יכולה לרחוץ מעט כדרכה בשאר שנה, הואיל ואינה עושה לתענוג רק לצורך מצוה. ונוהגין שלא לרחוץ, אפילו בצונן, מראש חודש ואילך. (ת"ה סי' ק"ו /ק"נ/)ואפי' בערב שבת של חזון אסור לרחוץ כ"א ראשו ופניו ידיו ורגליו בצונן (מהרי"ל ותשובת מהרי"ל סי' ט"ז וב"י); ויש מקילים בחפיפת מא הראש בחמין למי שרגיל בכך כל שבת.

.35

הלכות נדה לרמב"ן פרק ט – כה. ומדיני החציצה לא טוב היות האדם מחמיר יותר מדאי ומחפש אחר הספיקות לפסול טבילתה בדבר הקל, כי אם כן אין לדבר סוף, אלא אחר שחפפה ראשה וסרקה במסרק וחפפה ורחצה כל גופה בחמין ונזהרה לבלתי תגע בשום דבר חוצץ ותעשה טבילתה בפשיטות איבריה וכל גופה, לא יכניס אדם ראשו בספיקות החמורות אשר אין להן קץ וסוף, כגון עצמה עיניה ביותר קרצה שפתותיה ביותר ומשאר הספיקות, כי מי יוכל להבחין בין עצמה ביותר ובין לא עצמה ביותר.

תלמוד בבלי מסכת בבא קמא דף פב עמוד א – ושתהא אשה חופפת וטובלת – דאורייתא היא! דתניא: (ויקרא י"ד) ורחץ את בשרו במים – שלא יהא דבר חוצץ בין בשרו למים, את בשרו – את הטפל לבשרו, ומאי ניהו? שער.

תלמוד בבלי מסכת סוכה דף ו עמוד א – חציצין דאורייתא נינהו, דכתיב (ויקרא יד) ורחץ (את בשרו) במים – שלא יהא דבר חוצץ בינו לבין המים! – כי אתאי הלכתא לשערו, כדרבה בר בר חנה. דאמר רבה בר בר חנא: נימא אחת קשורה – חוצצת, שלש – אינן חוצצות. שתים איני יודע. – שערו נמי דאורייתא נינהו, דכתיב ורחץ את בשרו במים – את הטפל לבשרו, ומאי ניהו – שערו.

ויקרא פרק יד פסוק ט – והיה ביום השביעי יגלח את כל שערו את ראשו ואת זקנו ואת גבת עיניו ואת כל שערו יגלח וכבס את בגדיו ורחץ את בשרו במים וטהר.

תלמוד בבלי מסכת עירובין דף ד עמוד ב – חציצין – דאורייתא נינהו! דכתיב (ויקרא טו) ורחץ את כל בשרו (במים) מסורת הש"ס: [ורחץ במים את כל בשרו] – שלא יהא דבר חוצץ בין בשרו למים. במים – במי מקוה, כל בשרו – מים שכל גופו עולה בהן. וכמה הן – אמה על אמה ברום שלש אמות. ושיערו חכמים מי מקוה ארבעים סאה. כי איצטריך הילכתא – לשערו, וכדרבה בר

רב הונא. דאמר רבה בר רב הונא: נימא אחת קשורה – חוצצת, שלש – אינן חוצצות, שתים – איני יודע. שערו נמי דאורייתא הוא, דתניא: ורחץ את כל בשרו – את הטפל לבשרו, וזהו שער! – כי אתאי הילכתא – לרובו ולמיעוטו, ולמקפיד ולשאין מקפיד, וכדרבי יצחק. דאמר רבי יצחק: דבר תורה, רובו ומקפיד עליו – חוצץ, ושאינו מקפיד עליו – אינו חוצץ. וגזרו על רובו שאינו מקפיד משום רובו המקפיד, ועל מיעוטו המקפיד משום רובו המקפיד. – וליגזור נמי על מיעוטו שאינו מקפיד משום מיעוטו המקפיד, אי נמי משום רובו שאינו מקפיד! היא גופה גזירה, ואנן ניקום וניגזור גזירה לגזירה.

שולחן ערוך יורה דעה הלכות נדה סימן קצח סעיף א – צריכה שתטבול כל גופה בפעם אחת; לפיכך צריך שלא יהיה עליה שום דבר החוצץ. ואפילו כל שהוא, ואם דרך בני אדם לפעמים להקפיד עליו, חוצץ אפילו אם אינה מקפדת עליו עתה, או אפילו אינה מקפדת עליו לעולם כיון שדרך רוב בני אדם להקפיד עליו, חוצץ; ואם הוא חופה רוב הגוף, אפילו אין דרך בני אדם להקפיד בכך, חוצץ. הגה: ולכתחלה לא תטבול אפילו בדברים שאינם חוצצין, גזרה אטו דברים החוצצים (הגהות ש"ד).

רש"י מסכת נדה דף סז עמוד ב – רובו – רוב שערו קשור אחת אחת.

רש"י מסכת סוכה דף ו עמוד ב – רובו – רוב שערו מטונף בטיט, או קשור אחת אחת, ומקפיד עליו – חוצץ.

רש"י מסכת עירובין דף ד עמוד ב – רובו – רוב שערו, שאם יש בו דבר החוצץ, כגון דם יבש ודיו וטיט יבש וזפת יבש, או שקשור רובו אחת אחת.

תוספות מסכת סוכה דף ו עמוד ב – דבר תורה רובו ומקפיד עליו חוצץ – י"מ דהכא איירי בשער אבל בבשר חוצץ אפילו מיעוטו שאינו מקפיד וקשה לר"ת מהא דאמרינן פרק הערל (יבמות דף עח. ושם) נכרית מעוברת שנתגיירה בנה אין צריך טבילה ופריך אמאי וכי תימא משום דרבי יצחק האמר רב כהנא לא שנו אלא רובו אבל כולו חוצץ והשתא דעדיפא הוה ליה לאקשויי דבבשר אפילו משהו ואפילו אינו מקפיד חוצץ ועוד מדקיהיב שיעורא בחציצה במסכת מקואות (פ"ט מ"ה) ומייתי לה בסוף אלו קשרים (שבת דף קיד.) על המרדעת רשב"ג אומר עד כאיסר האיטלקי עוד מייתי התם של בנאים של תלמידי חכמים מצד אחד חוצץ ושל בור משני צדדין ובזבחים בסוף דם חטאת (דף צח:) דם על בגדו חוצץ ואם טבח הוא אינו חוצץ רבב על בגדו חוצץ ואם מוכר רבב הוא אינו חוצץ וא"ת כיון דאתא הלכתא לרובו ולא למעוטו א"כ קרא למאי אתא דדרשינן בשרו שלא יהא דבר חוצץ בינו לבין המים וי"ל דאצטריך לבית הסתרים כדאיתא בפרק קמא דקדושין (דף כה).

תוספות מסכת עירובין דף ד עמוד ב – דבר תורה רובו ומקפיד עליו חוצץ – פי' בקונטרס בשערו משמע אבל בשרו אפילו מיעוטו שאינו מקפיד חוצץ וקשה לר"ת דבפרק הערל (יבמות ד' עח. ושם) אמרינן נכרית מעוברת שנתגיירה אין בנה צריך טבילה וקאמר אילימא משום דר'

יצחק הא אמר רב כהנא לא שנו אלא רובו אבל כולו חוצץ והשתא אדרבה הוה ליה למימר כי אמר ר' יצחק בשערו בשרו מי אמר ועוד דבפ' דם חטאת (זבחים ד' צח.) מייתי דם שעל בגדו חוצץ ואם טבח הוא אינו חוצץ ועוד אי בשערו דווקא אם כן כשנאמר הלכה למשה מסיני הוצרך לומר שערו רובו ומקפיד עליו חוצץ אם כן שערו הוי הלכה למשה מסיני ואמאי צריך קרא לשערו וכי האי גוונא פריך בכמה דוכתי.

חידושי הריטב"א מסכת עירובין דף ד עמוד ב – כי איצטריך (קרא) [הלכתא] לרובו ולמעוטו כו'. פי' לחלק לנו ההפרשות שיש בין רובו ומעוטו ומקפיד ושאינו מקפיד, והא דפי' רש"י ז"ל רובו רוב שערו יש שנראה להם שרוצה לומר ואלו בגופו אין דקדוקין אלו אלא אפילו מיעוטו שאינו מקפיד חוצץ, והקשו דא"כ אפילו בבגדים נאמר כן שיש להם דין גופו ואנן אשכחן בזבחים (צ"ח ב') בדם או רבב שעל בגדו שאם היה טבח או מוכר רבב שאינו מקפיד אינו חוצץ, ועוד מההיא (יבמות ע"ח א') דנכרית מעוברת שנתגיירה בנה אין צריך טבילה ואתינן למימר טעמא משום דהוה ליה רובו [שאינו מקפיד] שאינו חוצץ מן התורה ועד כאן לא פרכינן עלה אלא משום דכי אמר ר' יצחק הכא ברובו אבל כולו אע"פ שאינו מקפיד חוצץ מן התורה, אלמא אפילו בגופו איתא לדר' יצחק דליכא חציצה מדאורייתא אלא ברובו המקפיד, וכן פי' ר"ת ז"ל וכן עיקר, אבל נראה שלא נתכוין רש"י ז"ל לכך אלא לאשמועינן דבשערו בלבד משערין ברוב ומיעוט ואין צריך לשער ברוב הגוף והשער וכדעת הגאונים ז"ל, ושלא כדברי הרמב"ם ז"ל שכתב שמשערין הגוף והשער ביחד שאין השער גוף בפני עצמו.

חידושי הריטב"א מסכת סוכה דף ו עמוד ב – והא דאמרינן דבר תורה רובו ואין מקפיד עליו אינו חוצץ. לא תימא אבל בגופו אפילו רובו שאין מקפיד עליו חוצץ שזה אינו אלא אף (כ)גופו [כשערו] דמי, וכן מוכח ביבמות גבי נכרית מעוברת שנתגיירה בנה אין צריך טבילה דפרכינן אמאי אילימא מדרבי יצחק הני מילי רובו אבל כולו לא, ולא אקשי דעדיפא מינה דהני מילי שערו אבל [גופו] אפילו ברובו חוצץ, אלא ודאי שרוב גופו ורוב שערו שוין בדין זה, וכן פי' בתוספות, וכן עיקר.

רמב"ם הלכות מקוואות פרק ב הלכה טו – שתי שערות או יתר שהיו קשורין כאחת קשר אחד אינן חוצצין מפני שהמים באין בהן, ושערה אחת שנקשרה חוצצת והוא שיהיה מקפיד עליה, אבל אם אינו מקפיד עליה עלתה לו טבילה עד שתהיה רוב שערו קשור נימא נימא בפ"ע כזה הורו הגאונים, ויראה לי ששערו של אדם כגופו הוא חשוב לענין טבילה ואינו כגוף בפני עצמו כדי שנאמר רוב השיער אלא אע"פ שכל שיער ראשו קשור נימא נימא אם אינו מקפיד עליו עלתה לו טבילה אא"כ נצטרף לחוצץ אחר על גופו ונמצא הכל רוב גופו כמו שביארנו, ואחד הנדה ואחד שאר הטמאין שיש בראשן שיער. השגת הראב"ד: ויראה לי ששערו עד שיש בראשן שיער. א"א כדברי הגאונים הוא העיקר.

בית הבחירה למאירי מסכת עירובין דף ד עמוד ב – היתה נימא אחת קשורה בה הואיל ושערה אחת קשרה מהודק ביותר הרי הוא חוצץ אם היא מקפדת עליו הא שתי שערות נקשרות בקשר

אחד אינן חוצצות מפני שאין קשרן מהודק ונמצאו המים באין בהם ואם אינו מקפיד על קשריהן אף בקשורים אחד אחד עלתה לו טבילה עד שיהו רוב שערות קשורין אחד אחד כך כתבו הגאונים מפני שהם מפרשים רוב רוב שערו וכן בשאר מקומות רוב האבר וגדולי המחברים מכשירין אף ברוב שער וקשר אחד אחד מפני שהשער נידון כגוף ואפי׳ רוב שערות נקשרין אחד אחד הואיל ורוב הגוף בלא חציצה כשר אא״כ מצטרף עמהן חציצה אחרת לרוב הגוף ומחלוקת זו תלויה בביאור הסוגיא והוא שגדולי הרבנים אין גורסין בזו כי אצטריך הלכתא לרובו ומיעוטו אלא כך הם גורסין אלא לרובו ומיעוטו ומפרשים רובו רוב שערו והם מפרשים דבר תורה הלכה למשה מסיני ואע״פ שלמעלה הוא קורא הלכות סיני דרבנן פעמים קורא אותה דבר תורה פעמים דברי סופרים כמו שכתבנו למעלה ונראה לדבריהם שמן התורה לא היה שער חוצץ אלא בכולו ואתאי הלכתא לרוב שער וגזרו על מיעוטו המקפיד והוא שאמרו בפרק הערל ע״ח א׳ לענין גופו שמן התורה אע״פ שברובו שאינו מקפיד אינו חוצץ כולו מיהא חוצץ ובאה הלכה לרובו וי״מ דבר תורה תורה ממש וגזרו אהלכה ואין נראה כן שאין ראוי לומר בהלכה שלא לגזור בה גזרה לגזרה ולא לשון גזרו ואף אלו מפרשין רובו רוב גופו ולא רוב שערו ולא ששערו לבד יחוץ אא״כ בהצטרפות שאר הגוף וכן נראה מפרק הערל במה שאמרו נכרית שנתגיירה והיא מעוברת אין בנה צריך טבילה והקשו שם אמאי לא ואי משום דאמר רב יצחק דבר תורה רובו שאינו מקפיד אינו חוצץ הא אמר רב כהנא לא שנו אלא רובו אבל כולו חוצץ ותירץ שאני עובר דהיינו רביתיה וזו ודאי בכל הגוף נאמרה.

שולחן ערוך יורה דעה הלכות נדה סימן קצח סעיף ה – שתי שערות או יותר שהיו קשורים ביחד קשר אחד, אינם חוצצין. הגה: ואין חלוק בין אם קשר ב׳ שערות עם שתי שערות, או שקשר ב׳ שערות בפני עצמן (ב״י בשם רשב״א ור״ן); ושערה אחת שנקשרה, חוצצת והוא שתהא מקפדת עליה, אבל אם אינה מקפדת עליה עלתה לה טבילה עד שיהא רוב שערה קשור נימא נימא בפני עצמו.

תורת הבית הקצר בית ז שער ז – המלמולין וכן הגרגרים שנעשים על הבשר כשידיו של אדם מלוכלכים בטיט או בבצק או בזיע והוא מוללן אחת על חברתה הרי אלו חוצצין. טיט היוצרין וטיט היון שהוא טיט הבורות (ועץ) [וגיץ] יוני שהוא הטיט העבה והנדבק הרי אלו חוצצין לפי שנדבקין הרבה ועושין חציצה ודרכן של בני אדם להקפיד עליהם. ואפילו היו בבית הסתרים דרכה של אשה להקפיד עליהן כדי שלא תתגנה על בעלה. ובלבד שדרכה להקפיד עליו, חוצץ ואפילו כחרדל. לא הקפידה זו בהן בטלה אצל כל הנשים, וכל שרובן מקפידות חוצץ אפילו במי שאינה מקפדת.

רמב״ם הלכות מקוואות פרק א הלכה יב – אחד האדם או הכלים לא יהיה דבר חוצץ בינם ובין המים, ואם היה דבר חוצץ בינם ובין המים כגון שהיה בצק או טיט מודבק על בשר האדם או על גוף הכלי ה״ז טמא כשהיה ולא עלתה להן טבילה, דבר תורה אם היה דבר החוצץ חופה את רוב האדם או רוב הכלי לא עלתה להן טבילה והוא שיקפיד עליו ורוצה להעבירו, אבל אם אינו מקפיד עליו ולא שם אותו על לב בין עבר בין לא עבר אינו חוצץ ואע״פ שחופה את רובו, וכן

אם היה חופה מיעוטו אינו חוצץ אע"פ שהוא מקפיד עליו, מדברי סופרים שכל דבר החוצץ אם היה מקפיד עליו לא עלתה לו טבילה אע"פ שהוא על מיעוטו גזירה משום רובו, וכל דבר החוצץ אם היה חופה את רובו לא עלתה לו טבילה אע"פ שאינו מקפיד עליו גזירה משום רובו המקפיד עליו, נמצאת אומר שאם היה על בשר האדם או על גוף הכלי דבר מדברים החוצצין כגון בצק וזפת וכיוצא בהן אפילו טיפה כחרדל והוא מקפיד עליו לא עלתה לו טבילה, ואם אינו מקפיד עליו עלתה לו טבילה, אא"כ היה חופה רוב הכלי או רוב האדם כמו שביארנו.

סדרי טהרה סימן קצח אות ה ד"ה אך – א"ו דאף הרמב"ם ס"ל דאזלינן להחמיר בתר רובא דעלמא והא דמפלגינן בין איש לאשה מיירי שהם אין מקפידין כלל ובנשים כיון דשאר נשים מקפידין בטלה דעתה ובאנשים כיון דאין מקפידין ואיהו נמי לא קפיד מש"ה אינו חוצץ אבל מאן דקפיד ס"ל להרמב"ם דלעולם תלינן בקפידתו להחמיר ולא אזלינן בתר רובא דעלמא.

ט"ז יורה דעה סימן קצח – ב) ואם דרך בני אדם כו'. – נראה ביאור לשון זה דרך בני אדם להקפיד על זה אע"פ שאין רוב בני אדם מקפידין רק קצתן וזו האשה רגילה להקפיד ג"כ על זה בפעמים אחרים רק שעכשיו אינה מקפדת או אפילו אינה מקפדת בשום פעם ורוב בני אדם מקפידים על זה חוצץ אבל אם מקצת בני אדם מקפידין וזו אינה מקפדת לעולם לא הוה חציצה ועי' מה שכתבתי בסעיף י"ח.

ג) כיון שדרך רוב בני אדם כו'. – בב"י נסתפק אם שאר בני אדם אינם מקפידים וזו מקפדת וכתב בד"מ דבמרדכי כתב בהדיא שחוצץ וכן כתב מו"ח ז"ל.

ש"ך יורה דעה סימן קצח:ב – כיון שדרך כו' – והיכא דרוב בני אדם אין מקפידים והיא מקפדת כ' ב"י בשם הרמב"ם וטור דחוצץ וכ"פ הב"ח וכ"כ בד"מ ולקמן בסי' זה כתבתי דברי המרדכי שכתב בהדיא דחוצץ עכ"ל, ונראה דהיינו המרדכי דלקמן סי"ד בהג"ה.

משנה מסכת מקוואות פרק ט משנה א – [א] אלו חוצצין באדם חוטי צמר וחוטי פשתן והרצועות שבראשי הבנות רבי יהודה אומר של צמר ושל שער אינם חוצצין מפני שהמים באין בהם.

בעלי הנפש שער הטבילה סימן ב – ואי קשיא לך חוטי צמר וחוטי פשתן ורצועה שבראשי הבנות אמאי חוצצין הלא מיעוטו שאינו מקפיד הוא. לא, מקפדת היא, דלא תימא כל שאינו מקפיד עליו בשעת הטבילה, אלא אם תקפיד עליו שעה אחת דבר המקפיד עליו הוא שאי אפשר שלא תעביר אותם מעל ראשה בשעה שחופפת את ראשה, וכן הטבעת שבידה אי אפשר שלא תעבירנו בשעת הלישה או בשעה שהיא אופה או מבשלת.

רא"ש מסכת נדה הלכות מקוואות סימן כו – הלכך אשה שהיא בעלת חטטין צריכה לחוף במים עד שיתרככו ורטייה היא איספלנית שנותנים למכה ושרף הוא לחלוחית הנוטף מן האילן ולכשמתייבש הוא נדבק. וגלדי צואה לכלוך הזיעה מתיבשת ונדבקת בבשרו כמין גליד. והמלמולין כשאדם לש עיסתו או מגבל טיט משפשף ידיו זו בזו הנופל מידיו נקרא מלמולין מלשון (דברים כ א) וקטפת מלילות.

תוספתא השירים והנזמים והטבעות וקטלאות אוצצין חוצצין רפין אינם חוצצין. אוצצין פירוש מהודקין כמו בתר איצצא בפרק חבית (דף קמד ב) וא"ת טבעת דחוקה אמאי חוצץ והלא מיעוטו שאין מקפיד הוא ופירש הראב"ד ז"ל לפי שמקפדת להסירו בשעת לישה וכיון שמקפדת בשום פעם אע"פ שאינה מקפדת בשעת טבילה הוי חציצה.

שולחן ערוך יורה דעה הלכות נדה סימן קצח סעיף כג – השירים והנזמים והטבעות והקטלאות אם הם רפוים, אינם חוצצים; ואם הם מהודקים, חוצצים. וכן הדין באגד שעל המכה כט וקשקשים שעל השבר.

פתחי תשובה יורה דעה סימן קצח:א – לפעמים – עי' בשו"ת זכרון יוסף חי"ד סי' יו"ד שכתב דמ"מ בעינן דוקא שמקפדת לעתים מזומנות כאותה שכתב הט"ז ס"ק כ"ג דטבעת מהודקת באצבע חוצץ משום דמסירתו בשעת לישה דהרי אם מיקלע לה עיסה ללוש כמה פעמים היום או מחר מסירתו אבל אם אינה מקפדת רק פ"א לזמן מרובה לא ומ"ש בש"ע אפילו אינה מקפדת עליו עתה כו' אין פירושו אלא שמקפדת עליו לבסוף לזמן רחוק אלא פירושו שאינה מקפדת עתה בשעת טבילה מ"מ מקפדת בימים שקודם ושלאחר הטבילה ע"ש ועמש"ל ס"ק י"ב בשמו.

שו"ת זכרון יוסף יורה דעה סימן י – ולענין חציצת טבעת זה נ"ל דאם לאחר החקירה והדרישה היטב יתאמתו דברי האשה שאינה יכולה לקחתו משם מפני סכנת נפשה וע"כ תניחה' תמיד בתוכה זולת בבוא לה חבלי לידה שההכרח לא יגונה לקחתו כדי שלא ימנע יציאת העובר מרחמה נ"ל דעלתה לה טבילה זו ואין הטבעת חוצץ כיון דאינה מקפדת שהרי מניחתו תמיד ברחמה ה"ל מיעוט' שאינה מקפדת שאינו חוצץ כמ"ש גם מעכ"ת וכה"ג כתב הר"ש סוף מס' מקואות על הא דתני' בתוספת' דמייתי התם של ברזל אינו חוצץ. ואע"ג שמקפדת לקחתו בשעת לידתה נ"ל דאין בכך כלום דלא דמי למה שכתב הראב"ד והביא הב"י והט"ז בסי' קצ"ח סעיף קטן ס"ג דטבעת מהודקת באצבע חוצץ משום דמסירתו בשעת לישה דהתם מיקרי מקפדת לפעמים גם עכשיו שהרי אם מיקלע לה עיסה ללוש כמה פעמים היום או מחר מסירתו ממנה משא"כ טבעת זה שאינה מסירתו עכשיו כלל בשום פעם רק בשעת לידה לא מיקרי מקפדת. ודמי' למה שכתב הטור וש"ע בסי' קצ"ח סעיף ו' דשער דאות' המקום שנדבקו שאינה חוצץ בפנוי' אע"ג שלאחר זמן כשתנשא לאיש תהיה מקפדת מ"מ כיון דהשתא אינה מקפדת אינ' חוצץ ה"נ דכוותי'. וכן בסעי' י"ז גבי צובע שידיו צבועות א"ח וכן מי שאומנתו להיות שוחט וקצב אע"פ שידיו מלוכלכים בדם אינו חוצץ וכי ס"ד שלעולם לא יקנח ידיו אפילו בשבת או רגל וכהאי גוונא או יעזוב אומנתו ואפ"ה קי"ל כיון דעכ"פ אינן מקפידין א"ח וכ"ש אשה דנד"ד דהא ודאי אינה מקפדת עד דאשתנ' גופה ותתעבד ותלד.

שו"ת אגרות משה יורה דעה חלק א סימן צז – בענין בלאמבע פילינג זמנית שהוא סתימה בנקב השן לזמן אם הוא חציצה י"ט מרחשון תרפ"ט ליובאן. מע"כ אחי אהובי הגאון הגדול מוהר"ר מרדכי שליט"א הגאב"ד שקלאוו.

ענף א בדבר בלאמבע שמניחין לסתום בנקב השן על משך חדש ויותר לפעמים ואח"כ מחליפין אותה על אחרת שתשאר קבועה, שנסתפקת לענין חציצה וכתבת ג' טעמים להיתר: ואתה רוצה לידע דעתי העניה בזה.

והנה בטעם ראשון שכתבת שכיון שעל זמן שהניחו היא מקפדת שיהיה דוקא מונח לא מיקרי עתה מקפיד עליו להסירו בשביל ההקפדה שאחרי עבור הזמן, יש לפקפק מהא דסי' קצ"ח סעי' א' דאם אינה מקפדת עתה אך איכא זימנא שמקפדת חוצץ לעולם, והוא מהרא"ש בשם הראב"ד בהלכות מקואות סי' כ"ו גבי טבעת שהקפידא להסירו הוא רק בשעת לישה ולכן חוצץ אף שבכל העת אדרבה היא מקפדת דוקא שלא להסירו בשביל יופי. וא"כ גם הכא לכאורה יש לחצוץ מאחר דתקפיד להסירו לאחר הזמן.

אך יש לחלק כדמחלק בעל זכרון יוסף שהובא בפ"ת סק"א דאם מקפדת רק לזמן מרובה לא הויא עתה קפידא עיי"ש ופשוט שאין כוונתו לחלק בין זמן מרובה כגון למשך שנה ובין זמן מועט כלמשך חדש ופחות דמנא ליה ליתן קצבה ושעור לדבר זה מאחר שבגמ' לא מצינו זה. אלא צריך לומר דכוונתו לחלק בין הקפידא להסיר בשעת לישה שאין לזה זמן קצוב דאפשר שיזדמן לה בכל יום וגם בלילה לכן נחשב בכל עת שהיא מקפדת דאינה יכולה לבטלו על משך זמן ובין כשהקפידא להסיר הוא רק לזמן קצוב דעד זמן ההוא ודאי לא תסלקנו הויא אינה מקפדת עד זמן ההוא ואין חלוק אם זמן ההוא רחוק או קרוב דכיון דהוא זמן ידוע לקפידא אין להחשיבה עתה מקפדת וזהו טעם נכון ולא ניתן לשעורין וזהו כוונתו לע"ד ואף אם אין כוונתו כן מ"מ הוא טעם נכון. וא"כ גם בלאמבע זמנית כיון שיש זמן ידוע להסירו אין להחשיבה עתה מקפדת.

והנה תלוי זה בטעם שאינו מקפיד אינו חוצץ דיש לפרש בשני טעמים (א) דהוא מחמת דנבטל לגוף כיון שלא איכפת לה אם ישאר שם ונחשב כבשרה. (ב) דלאו משום בטול לגוף הוא דהא מיעוטו המקפיד אין שייך שיבטל דהא ודאי תסירנו ומ"מ אינו חוצץ. ואין לומר משום דא"צ שתהיה כולה במים אלא רובה, דהא אם לא היתה כולה במים אף שערה אחת אינה טבילה כלל מדאורייתא כמפורש ברמב"ם פ"א ממקואות ה"א וה"ז, ומ"מ מעוטו המקפיד אינו חוצץ אף שודאי תסירנו, וא"כ צריך לומר דאף כשיש על גופה דבר החוצץ נחשבה שהיא במים כיון שעכ"פ היא כולה במים אף שאין המים דבוקים לגופה. ולכן אם לא היה נכתב קרא שלא יהיה דבר חוצץ בין בשרו למים היה נטהר אף שלטבילה הא בעי שיהיה כל גופו במים משום דאף שיש דבר חוצץ נקרא שגופו הוא במים. אבל חדשה תורה עוד דין שגם לא יהיה דבר חוצץ בין בשרו למים וע"ז באה ההלכה שחדוש זה אינו אלא ברובו המקפיד דמעוטו אף במקפיד או אינו מקפיד אף ברובו אינו חוצץ. והוי אינו מקפיד דין בחציצה כמו מעוטו לא מצד בטול לגוף. אך יש גם לומר כטעם א' דאינו מקפיד הוא משום דנבטל לגוף ומעוטו ג"כ אינו דין חדש בעלמא בדיני חציצה אלא הוא מדין רובו ככולו דכיון דלרוב הגוף אין דבר חוצץ נחשב כאין בגופו חציצה כלל ואף דבביאת מים נתחדש דדוקא כולו בעינן מ"מ בחציצה הוא בדין רובו ככולו ככל דיני התורה. והוי דין מעוטו המקפיד ודין רובו שאינו מקפיד משני טעמים. אבל מזה שכולו חוצץ אף באינו מקפיד משמע דאינו מטעם בטול לגוף דאם מטעם בטול לגוף אף כולו מ"ט חוצץ. ולכן מסתבר יותר שהוא דין בחציצה כטעם ב' דחדשה ההלכה דדין חציצה אינה במעוטו ולא באינו מקפיד אף

ברובו ובכולו חוצץ. אבל הכרח ליכא מזה דאפשר דין כולו הוא חדוש שלא יתבטל למה שבפנים כשאינו נראה כלל. ועיין בסד"ט סי' קצ"ח סק"א שכתב מטעם בטול לגוף אף על מעוטו המקפיד וזה תמוה דכיון דודאי תסירנו איך נימא שיתבטל לגופה עכ"פ באינו מקפיד יש לומר כדבריו.

ואם נימא כטעם א' מטעם בטול לגוף אז אף אם תקפיד להסירו בזמן ידוע ואף שהוא לזמן מרובה נמי א"א לבטלו לגופה כיון שתצטרך להסירו כשיגיע הזמן דלא כדבארתי בבאור חלוק ס' זכרון יוסף. אבל אם נימא כטעם ב' דהוא דין בחציצה ודאי יש לחלק כדבארתי בחלוק ס' זכרון יוסף דבעינן שתהיה מקפדת לדבר שאפשר לה להזדמן בכל עת כמו טבעת בלישה אבל כשיש משך זמן שלא תקפיד נחשב אינה מקפדת דמה"ת נימא שצריך שלא תקפיד לעולם. ולכן מאחר שמסתבר יותר כטעם זה יש לומר בבלאמבע זמנית דכיון דעתה אינה מקפדת אינו חוצץ ואולי צריך גם לסברתך שצריך שעד זמן ההוא תקפיד שיהיה דוקא מונח דאם אין לה שום צורך עתה ואחר זמן תקפיד להסירו יש לה להקפיד גם עתה כי אף עתה אין לה לרצות שיהיה על גופה דבר שתצטרך להסירו אף אחר זמן מרובה אבל כיון שיש לה עתה צורך שיהיה על גופה ורוצה שיהיה אין להחשיב לטעם ב' שמסתבר כותיה מקפדת בשביל מה שתצטרך להסיר לאחר זמן.

אבל בנו"ב סי' ס"ד הובא בפ"ת ס"ק ט"ז דהטבעת של שעוה אם הוא בבית הסתרים קרוי מקפיד משום שצריכה להסירו בשעת הפסק טהרה ובשעת הלידה והחת"ס חולק רק אלידה אבל אם צריכה להסירו בשעת הפסק טהרה מודה שנחשב מקפיד, אף שג"כ יש לה זמן קבוע עד שתפסיק בטהרה ועד עת ההיא מקפדת אדרבה שיהיה דוקא מונח שם דלא כס' זכרון יוסף כפ"מ שבארתי. וא"כ גם בלאמבע זמנית תיחוץ. אך יש לומר דהפסק טהרה מיקרי אין לה זמן קבוע דאף שיש לה וסת אפשר שתתקלקל ותיכף אחר הטבילה תראה טפת דם או כתם ותצטרך להפסיק תיכף בטהרה כדאיתא בסד"ט סי' קצ"ו ס"ק ל"ט בשם ס' מעיל צדקה ומנ"י והסכים לזה. וכן מסתבר לע"ד דמה"ת יגרע בזה שטבלה מקודם הטבילה להצריך שתמתין חמשה ימים כיון שלא שמשה עדין דבשלמא אם שמשה כבר רק שעברו ימים הרבה קודם הראיה שלא שמשה גזרו שמא תשכח ששמשה או שלא תדע לחלק אבל מאחר שלא שמשה עדין כלל אחר הטבילה מ"ט נגזור יותר מלא טבלה. ואולי בהספיקה לשמש רק שאירע שלא שמשה אפשר עוד להחמיר כיון שהטבילה הועילה למעשה ושייך לגזור אטו שמשה אבל בלא הספיקה לשמש וכ"ש כשלא באה לבית אין מה לגזור יותר מראתה קודם הטבילה.

אך בנו"ב תנינא סי' קכ"ה פליג ומצריך אף בראתה תיכף אחר הטבילה להמתין ה' ימים ואולי אמנ"י בראתה קודם שבאה לבית לא פליג. והנה זה שהביא ראיה מהט"ז סי' קצ"ו סק"ז אינו ראיה דזה שנקט הדין להיתר בכלה שראתה קודם שנתייחדה עם החתן מטעם דלא שייך למיגזר לא שמשה אטו שמשה כיון דלא באה עדין לכלל תשמיש ולא נקט ההיתר בכל הנשים שראו סמוך לטבילתן, אולי הוא משום דבכלה הוא מלתא דשכיחא שהחופה היתה סמוך לוסתה ואשמועינן דמ"מ לא גזרו ואולי כ"ש באשה שהוא מלתא דלא שכיחא כדאיתא בסד"ט. ויש רק להביא ראיה מהט"ז לאשה שטבלה סמוך לוסתה שעתה הוא שכיח להצריך ה' ימים, וגם זה יש לדחות משום דזה גופה שתטבול סמוך לוסתה הוא לא שכיח באשה. וכן מסתבר ונדחה ראיית הנו"ב מהט"ז. ולע"ד אדרבה יש ראיה מהט"ז להתיר דהא יש להסתפק בטעם הגזרה אם הוא מחמת שלא תדע לחלק ואם נתיר בלא שמשה תתיר גם בשמשה. או שלזה לא חיישינן דיאמרו

לה דיש חלוק בין שמשה ללא שמשה אך חיישינן שמא תשכח ששמשה. ואם נימא כטעם א׳ אף בכלה שפירסה נדה סמוך לחופתה יש לגזור ועוד יותר מאשה שבאשה לא שכיח ובכלה שכיח כדלעיל. ואם נימא כטעם ב׳ אין לגזור כיון דלא באה לכלל תשמיש וא״כ סובר הט״ז שמתיר בכלה כטעם ב׳ א״כ אף באשה שראתה אחר הטבילה קודם שבאה לבית ואף בבאה לבית אבל קודם שהספיקה לשמש יש להתיר דג״כ אין שייך שמא תשכח. ואולי בכזה מודה גם הנו״ב. וא״כ נמצא שאין להפסק טהרה זמן קבוע.

אך אף אם נימא שפליג הנו״ב וסובר שבכל אופן אחר הטבילה צריכה להמתין ה׳ ימים מ״מ הוא רק למנות הז׳ נקיים אבל להפסיק בטהרה יכולה תיכף דכל אשה רשאה להפסיק בטהרה אם תרצה גם קודם השש עונות רק שהז׳ נקיים תתחיל למנות רק אחר הה׳ ימים ולכן אף שממתינות עם ההפסק טהרה עד אחר החמשה ימים מ״מ כיון שאין זה חיוב אפשר שיזדמן לה לעשות ההפסק טהרה מקודם הו׳ עונות משום שאז יהיה לה יותר נקל להוציא הטבעת וכדומה וא״כ אף להנו״ב לא הוי זמן קבוע להסרת הטבעת ושפיר מחשיב לה הנו״ב מקפיד אבל היכא דיש זמן קבוע אפשר יודה דלא נחשב עתה מקפיד וא״כ בנ״ד לא הוי מקפיד אף לדידהו.

ענף ב ויש להביא ראיה מהחת״ס שכתב בסי׳ קצ״ב הובא בפ״ת ס״ק ט״ז דמה שצריכה להסירו בשעת לידה שאינו בשביל הקפדה אלא לפנות מקום להולד לא חשיב מקפיד וא״כ צריך לומר דסובר שאינו מטעם בטול לגוף דהא א״א לה לבטלו לגופה כיון דתצטרך להסירו לפנות מקום להולד, אלא סובר כטעם ב׳ שהוא דין בחציצה שדוקא מקפיד חוצץ ולכן הכא שאינה מקפדת ע״ז בעצם אלא שצריכה לפנות מקום להולד לא מחשיב מקפיד. וכיון שסובר כטעם ב׳ ודאי מסתבר כדכתבתי לדעת הזכרון יוסף שאם יש זמן קבוע להקפידא לא מיקרי מקפיד. וזה שהוצרך החת״ס לטעם דהוא רק לפנות מקום להולד, משום שלידה ג״כ אין להחשיב זמן קבוע דהא גם כשמפלת צריכה להסירו ונמצא שכשהיא מעוברת אין לה זמן קבוע לזה ואף באינה יודעת שהיא מעוברת אפשר היא מעוברת, שמזה שרואה דם אין ראיה כ״כ שאינה מעוברת כמבואר בגמ׳ ובש״ע סי׳ קפ״ט ואף שעתה נשתנה הטבע קצת דפוסקות הנשים לראות תיכף בהתחלת העבור מ״מ אין זה ודאי ומפורש כן בנו״ב קמא אה״ע סי׳ ס״ט עיי״ש וא״כ יש לה לחוש שמא היא מעוברת ואפשר שתפיל ותצטרך להסיר הטבעת בשביל הלידה ולכן היה נחשב זה מקפיד דאין כאן זמן קצוב והוצרך החת״ס להטעם דהוא רק לפנות מקום להולד.

והנו״ב שסובר שגם הקפידא בשביל לפנות מקום להולד הוא קפידא אינו דוקא משום דסובר כטעם א׳ דאף לטעם ב׳ שהוא דין בחציצה אפשר אינו סובר סברא זו דבשביל לפנות מקום לולד לא תחשב מקפיד. דראיית החת״ס מהמג״א שכתב בסי׳ קס״א שטבעת שאין בו אבן אינו חוצץ באיש אף שמסירו לתפילין ולולב לא מובן דגם לתפילין ולולב אם צריך להסירו הוא רק מטעם חציצה דאיזה פנוי מקום צריך תפילין ולולב ואם אינו חציצה א״צ להסירו לתפילין ולולב. ומה שהביא מהמרדכי דקליעת שערות ראיה לזה לא מובן כוונתו כלל. וגם פירוש דבריו מפנה להסירה הוה כגופה ממש לא מובן כוונת הדברים וה׳ יאיר עיני להבין דברי רבותינו. ונמצא שרק מסברא יש לומר כהחת״ס ואין סובר זה הנו״ב.

ולפ״ז מה שהפ״ת הביא גם בשם בעל זכרון יוסף שבשביל לידה לא נחשבה מקפיד הוא מטעם החת״ס דלפנות מקום לולד לא הוי מקפיד ולא מטעם שהוא לאחר זמן דלא כהפ״ת

שציין לסק"א דהא אין כאן זמן קבוע. וא"כ אפשר יודו כו"ע דלזמן קבוע לא נחשב קודם הזמן קפידא וא"כ אין חוצץ בלאמבע זמנית.

אבל אפשר גם לומר דלידה נחשב זמן קבוע משום דלא שכיח שמעוברת תראה דם וגם לא שכיח שתפיל והוו תרי עניני לא שכיח שאין חוששין בנ"א לזה וא"כ הויא אינה מקפדת עד זמן ההוא וזהו סברת הפ"ת שציין לסק"א וא"כ החת"ס שהוצרך לטעם דלפנות מקום לולד אינה קפידא פליג וסובר דלאחר זמן קבוע נמי נחשב מקפיד וכן יסבור גם הנו"ב. ואף שלהחת"ס מסתבר יותר שלא פליג כיון שסובר דלפנות לא נחשב מקפיד א"כ סובר כטעם ב' ונצטרך לומר כדבארתי שלידה לא נחשב שהוא זמן קבוע כדבארתי. אבל להנו"ב אפשר שזה שפליג אחת"ס וסובר דלפנות מקום לולד נחשב מקפיד הוא משום דסובר כטעם א' מטעם בטול לגוף ולכן גם מצד פנוי מקום לא נבטל לגוף וא"כ בזמן קבוע נמי הוא חוצץ דא"א להתבטל לגוף כדלעיל. וא"כ אפשר שלהנו"ב וגם אולי להחת"ס יחשב בלאמבע זמנית מקפיד ויחצוץ ואף שיותר מסתבר שיודו לזה כדלעיל מ"מ יש לחוש קצת.

והנה יש עוד טעם לומר בזה שאינו מקפיד אינו חוצץ דהוא מחמת שמבטל אותו מקום מלהיות מקום גלוי כיון שלא איכפת לו אם הוא מכוסה ונחשב הגוף שתחתיו כמקום בלוע שלא בעי ביאת מים. ולטעם זה יש לומר כהחת"ס דלפנות מקום לולד לא הוי מקפיד וגם יש לומר כס' זכרון יוסף למה שבארתי דלזמן קבוע לא הוי מקפיד, דאף שכתבתי דלטעם א' שהוא מטעם בטול לגוף בעינן שלעולם לא תקפיד הוא משום דכיון דרוצה שבהבטול יחשב כהגוף דבר שאינו מהגוף ממש צריך שיהיה הבטול לעולם אבל לטעם זה שהוא רק לבטל אותו מקום שהוא מכוסה מחשיבות גלוי כיון שבעצם הוא ממש מכוסה רק שאם יקפיד הוא עומד לינטל ולגלות כגלוי דמי לכן אם עד זמן קבוע אין עומד לינטל אין להחשיבו כנטול עתה וממילא אינו כגלוי אלא בדין מכוסה כמו שהוא עתה באמת ובלוע א"צ לביאת מים ולא אף ראוי לביאת מים.

(וא"כ אפשר עוד לומר לפ"ז כהסד"ט שהוא מטעם בטול לגופו כטעם א' אך לא נימא שתלוי בדעתו מחמת שמבטלו אלא דממילא בטל להגוף רק במקפיד שסופו לינטל הוי כנטול. ובמעוט שלא חשוב נבטל לגופו בכל ענין. וא"כ כ"ז שאין סופו ליטלו לא הוי כנטול אף שלאחר זמן יטלנו. וא"כ אף להסד"ט יש מקום לומר כהזכרון יוסף למה שבארתי. אך הוא דחוק ובפרט לומר במעוט המקפיד שנבטל לגוף כיון דודאי יסירנו).

ולפ"ז ניחא מה שכולו חוצץ דכיון דכולו מכוסה וא"צ ביאת מים א"כ לא יהיה לו ביאת מים כלל ואין כאן טבילה ולכן הוצרך לומר ביבמות דף ע"ח בעובר דהיינו ריביתיה דהוי כגופו ממש. אך טעם זה דחוק מאד ויותר מסתבר כדלעיל.

חכמת אדם שער בית הנשים כלל קיט – יח נראה לי דנשים שיש להם שיניים תחובות אין חוצצין אבל מה שסותמין נקבי השן על ידי רופא כדי שלא תכנוס בו רוח חוצץ ועיין בבינת אדם.

תלמוד בבלי מסכת נדה דף סו עמוד ב – ואמר רבא: לעולם ילמד אדם בתוך ביתו שתהא אשה מדיחה בית קמטיה במים. מיתיבי: בית הקמטים ובית הסתרים אינן צריכין לביאת מים! נהי דביאת מים – לא בעינן, מקום הראוי לביאת מים – בעינן, כדר' זירא. דא"ר זירא: כל הראוי לבילה – אין בילה מעכבת בו, ושאין ראוי לבילה – בילה מעכבת בו.

תוספות מסכת קידושין דף כה עמוד ב – וא"ת בטבילה מנ"ל דבעינן ראוי ויש לומר משום דכתיב ורחץ את כל בשרו דמשמע אפי' בית הסתרים וכתיב וידיו ודרשינן מה ידיו מאבראי אף כל מאבראי וממעטים בית הסתרים מ"מ כיון דאיכא כל דמרבינן אפי' בית הסתרים איכא למימר לכל הפחות להכי מרבי דבעינן ראוי לביאת מים.

ויקרא פרק טו:יא – וכל אשר יגע בו הזב וידיו לא שטף במים וכבס בגדיו ורחץ במים וטמא עד הערב.

תוספות מסכת נדה דף סו עמוד ב – א"ת אמאי לא בעינן ביאת מים לכתחילה בבית הסתרים כמו בילה וקריאה בחליצה ובביכורים וי"ל דאין סברא גבי טבילה שלא הקפידה תורה אלא שיטהר האדם ואין לומר דלכתחילה לבעי דכיון דבדיעבד טהור לכתחלה נמי לא בעי ותעלה לו טבילה אבל בילה ומקרא בכורים וחליצה מצות נינהו הלכך לכתחלה ליעבד.

חידושי הרמב"ן מסכת קידושין דף כה עמוד א – נהי דביאת מים לא בעי מקום הראוי לביאת מים בעינן כדר' זירא. איכא למידק בשלמא בדר' זירא ראוי לבילה בעינן דכתיב בלולה, אלא הכא מנא ליה כלל דבעינן ראוי לבא בו מים, ויש מפרשים ראוי לבא בו מים בעינן מדרבנן, שאע"פ שלא הצריכו חכמים שיהא צריך לבא בו מים הצריכו שיהא ראוי לכך, כשם שמצינו בתורה שהחמיר בראוי לבילה יותר מן הבילה עצמה, ותקון רבנן כעין דאורייתא. ואפשר דהואיל ומצינו לענין טומאה שהוא גלוי אף לענין טבילה גלוי הוא שצריך שיהא ראוי לבא בו מים.

חידושי הריטב"א מסכת קידושין דף כה עמוד א – מקום הראוי לבא מים בעינן. אומר רבינו נר"ו דהא מדרבנן בעלמא הואיל ולענין טומאה דינו כגלוי מן התורה שויוה רבנן לענין טהרה נמי כגלוי, מיהו רחיצה וביאת מים לא בעי דהא כתיב ורחץ את כל בשרו מה בשרו מאבראי אף כל מאבראי.

חידושי הרשב"א מסכת קידושין דף כה עמוד א – הא דאמרינן נהי דביאת מים לא בעינן מקום הראוי לבא בו מים בעינן כדר' זירא. קשיא לן והא לא דמיא לדר"ז דבשלמא בדר"ז בעי' ראוי לבילה משום דכתיב בלולה בשמן ולכתחלה בילה צריכה, וגבי אלם ואלמת בפרק מצות חליצה לפי שאינם בואמר ואמרה, ובקריאת בכורים בפרק המוכר את הספינה משום וענית ואמרת, וכן בכל שאר המקומות שהוזכרו דברי ר' זירא כיוצא באלו, אבל כאן שא"צ ביאת מים ואפי' לכתחלה למה הוצרך למקום ראוי לביאת מים, וי"מ דמדרבנן בעלמא לפי שצריך טבילה כל גופו ד"ת התקינו דלשון ושנים שפעמים מגולין יהו צריכין [להיות] ראוין לבוא בו מים, ובתוס' מתרצים דמכל בשרו דרשינן ליה דאע"ג דכל בשרו למעט בית הסתרים מ"מ כיון דכתיב כל מרבי' להו לבית הסתרים לענין זה שיהיו ראוין לביאת מים.

שולחן ערוך יורה דעה הלכות נדה סימן קצח סעיף מג – אספלנית, מלוגמא ורטיה שעל בית הסתרים, חוצצין; אף על פי שאינם צריכים שיכנסו בהם המים, צריכים שיהיו ראוים ולא יהא בהם דבר חוצץ. הגה: יש אומרים שהאשה צריכה להטיל מים קודם טבילה אם היא צריכה

לכך. גם צריכה לבדוק עצמה בגדולים ובקטנים שלא תהא צריכה לעצור עצמה ולא יהיו ראוים לביאת מים. גם צריכה להסיר צואת החוטם (ש"ד ורא"ן סימן שכ"ו דף ס' ע"ג).

שו"ת נודע ביהודה מהדורה קמא – יורה דעה סימן סד – תשובה לכבוד הרב המאור הגדול מוהר"ר שאול אב"ד ור"מ דק"ק פ"פ דאדר. על דבר האשה אשר הושם טבעת של שעוה תוך עומק הפרוזדור לצורך רפואה. ודאי קרי מקפיד שהרי הוא מתלכלך תמיד בימי נדתה וצריכה להסירה בעת שתפסק בטהרה לנקותו וכן בימי לידה ואולי מעכב גם הבדיקה תמיד בז"נ וצריכה להסירה וא"כ הוה דבר שמקפידין וחוצץ. אמנם אף שאמרו בית הסתרים צריך להיות ראוי לביאת מים דוקא בבית הסתרים אמרו כן אבל במקום הנקרא בלוע לא צריך אפילו ראוי לביאת מים. ואף שהתוס' ס"ל דבה"ס בעי מן התורה ראוי לביאת מים כמבואר בדבריהם בקידושין דף כ"ה ובסוכה דף ו' ע"ב מ"מ בהא דבלוע לא בעי אפילו ראוי לביאת מים לא נחלקו. ואף שהוא מלתא דמשתמע ומסתבר ואין צריך ראיה אמינא להביא ראיה שהרי כתב הריטב"א בפ"ק דקידושין דף כ"ה בשם רבותיו שמה שבית הסתרים צריך ראוי לביאת מים היינו מדרבנן בעלמא הואיל ולענין טומאה דינו כגלוי ע"ש. וא"כ בלוע שלא מקרי גלוי לענין שום טומאה אפילו לטומאת משא א"צ ראוי לביאת מים. ובמס' נדה דף מ"ב ע"ב פליגי אביי ורבא אותו מקום באשה אי בלוע הוה או בית הסתרים ובודאי דהלכתא כרבא דבה"ס הוה וכן פסק הרמב"ם בפ"א מטומאת מת. אמנם עד כאן לא נחלקו אלא בבית החיצון אבל בעומק הרחם למעלה מבית החיצון לכ"ע בלוע הוה. ועיין שם בתוס' דף מ"ב ע"ב ד"ה אמאי טומאה בלועה היא. וכן כתב הרמב"ן בחידושיו שם וכתב דהיינו עד בין השיניים ומשמע במס' נדה דף מ"א ע"ב דהיינו עד מקום שהשמש דש וכן מבואר ברמב"ם בפרק ה' מהלכות א"ב הלכה ב'.

ומעתה לפי שכלי זו עיקר רפואתה שתכניס טבעת זה בעומק מאוד לעכב נפילת הרחם וצריכין אנו לחקור אשה זו אם אומרת שהיא כל כך בעומק עד שהוא עמוק במקום שאין השמש דש ומגיע שם אפילו בשעת גמר ביאה אז שוב מקרי בלוע וא"צ לביאת מים ולא איכפת לן בחציצה וא"צ להסירה בשעת טבילה. אבל אם הוא במקום שהשמש דש הן בתחילת ביאה והן בסוף ביאה הוי חציצה. כ"ז נראה לע"ד להלכה אבל למעשה צריך שיסכים עמי רום מעלתו וגם חותנו הגאון נ"י. ואז אם הוא למעלה ממקום שהשמש דש אני מצטרף עמהם להתיר לטבול בעוד הטבעת בתוכה.

והנה דברי הריטב"א הנ"ל שמה שבה"ס צריך להיות ראוי לביאת מים הוא רק מדרבנן הובא במשנה למלך פ"א ממקואות. אבל האחרונים בי"ד לא ראו דברי הריטב"א הנ"ל ולכן נדחקו בי"ד סי' קצ"ח וקצ"ט בכמה דברים שהקיל הש"ע בבה"ס לענין חציצה מבשאר הגוף ולדעת הריטב"א הדבר פשוט שכיון שהוא דרבנן הקילו.

ט"ז יורה דעה סימן קצח:כה – ומנהג יפה הוא. – ופשוט שאם לא נהגה כן א"צ לעכב הטבילה בשביל זה ובשבת ויו"ט המנהג שאוכלים בשר רק שתזהר לנקר ביותר אחרי כן.

שו"ת אגרות משה יורה דעה חלק א סימן צח – ולכן הנכון לע"ד דבר חדש דיש שני מיני חציצות אחד דדבר חוצץ דבוק על הגוף ולא הוי אותו חלק הגוף ראוי כלל שיבא עליו מים כפי מה שהוא

עתה. ושני דכיסה בדבר אחר את הגוף כמו אוחז באדם וקפצה ידה וכדומה שהאדם בעצמו אין בו שום חסרון לביאת מים רק שדבר אחר האוחז בגופו אינו מניח שיבואו המים לגופו. ותרוייהו הוו חציצה שעכ"פ חוצצין המים מהגוף אבל הוא רק במקום הגלוי שבעינן ביאת מים ממש, דבביה"ס שאין צריך לביאת מים אלא שיהא ראוי לביאת מים אין לפסול רק חציצה דמין הראשון שדבוק שם דבר חוצץ שמצד זה לא הוי מקום ההוא ראוי כלל לביאת מים עתה אבל מין הב' דאין שם דבר חוצץ רק דאדם אוחז שם ומחמת זה אין המים יכולין לבא שם ובעצם הגוף אין שום חסרון נחשב ראוי לביאת מים וכשר דאף שהאוחז אין מניח המים לבא שם אינו כלום דהא אין צריך שיבואו ולכן רשאי שלא להניח את המים ליכנס לשם, דדבר אחר המכסה אינו שייך שיחשיב את המקום שאינו ראוי לביאת מים כיון דלא נשתנה הגוף בזה דאינו דבוק ואינו שייך לו. ולכן כשרה חציצה כזו בבית הסתרים שאין צריך שם ביאת מים ממש רק שהמקום יהיה ראוי לביאת מים והרי הוא ראוי בעצם.

ומדויק עתה מה שדין דביה"ס ובית הקמטים אין צריך שיבואו בהן מים תנן לה במתני' תיכף אחר האוחז באדם וכלים והטבילן טמאים עיי"ש בספ"ח דמקואות משום שע"ז קאי דאשמועינן שאם אוחז בביה"ס ובית הקמטים טהור אף בלא הדיח ידיו משום שא"צ שיבואו בהן המים לכן כשרה חציצה כזו והוא דיוק גדול ממתני'.

ולכן ניחא שפיר הא דרשאה לסתום פיה דסתימת פיה הוא רק חציצה דמין הב' דאוחז באדם שבגוף הפה אין שום חסרון דהוא נקי מכל חציצה שאם תפתח פיה יכנסו שם המים רק שאין מניח המים בדבר אחר מליכנס לשם שזה כשר דאין צריך שם ביאת מים. וזהו שיטת הר"ש ורא"ש וראב"ד שאיפסק בש"ע ונהוג כותייהו. וניחא עתה גם לשון הר"ש סוף מקואות דלעיל מזה לענין חציצה דמין א' כתב שבעינן שהמקום יהיה ראוי לביאת מים. ולכן בדיוק הוסיף תיבת מקום דלכאורה הי"ל רק לכתוב דהא ראוי לביאת מים בעינן וכמו שכתב לשון זה לפי' ראשון בקרצה שפתותיה בסוף פ"ח שכתב נהי דביאת מים לא בעינן ראוי לביאת מים בעינן עיי"ש. אבל הוא בדיוק גדול שמסביר בזה החלוק שחציצה דמין א' שהוא חסרון בעצם המקום חוצץ משום דבעינן שיהיה גם ביה"ס מקום הראוי לביאת מים בעצם ואח"כ בקורצת שפתותיה שהוא מין הב' שהמקום הרי ראוי מצד עצמו לביאת מים ואין בו שום חסרון כתב דלא בעי שיהיה ראוי לביאת מים גם מצד אחר ולכן יכולה לסתום פיה אף שבזה אין ראוי לביאת מים והוא נכון ומדויק מאד.

והנה מוך שבאזנה נמי הוא ממין חציצה הב' דדמי לאוחז באדם וקרצה שפתותיה דהא אין המוך דבוק באזנה רק שמונח שם בלי דבוק ואף במהודק אינו דבוק רק מחמת שמונח בתוך האזן מעמידין אותו כותלי האזן שלא יפול אבל בעצם אינו דבוק וא"כ אין כאן חסרון בעצם מקום האזן שבעצם הוא ראוי לביאת מים כיון שהוא נקי ואין דבוק בו כלום רק שהמוך שהוא דבר אחר מכסהו ואינו מניח המים ליכנס לשם וזה כשר בביה"ס שאין צריך ביאת מים כמו שרשאה לסתום פיה ולעצום עיניה. ורק דבר הנדבק חוצץ כטיט וכדומה ולכן צריכה להדיח בית קמטיה במים משום שהזיעה שם תמיד ואבק מתקבץ שם כדאיתא ברמב"ם פ"ב ממקואות ה"ג שהוא דבר הנדבק שם וחוצץ שהרי בלא מים לא יסורו. (ובש"ע סי' קצ"ט סעי' ו' משמע שמצריך בחמין דוקא) וכן עצם ובשר שבין השנים הוו כנדבקים שם מחמת שהן מסובבים במקום דחוק

כזה שבין השנים שדחוקים זה לזה. אבל מוך שבאזן ודאי אינו כדבוק רק כמונח ומכסה בעלמא. ולכן כיון שביה"ס א"צ לביאת מים ממש אינו חוצץ וכדהוכחתי ממשנה דשבת.

תלמוד בבלי מסכת קידושין דף כה עמוד א ונדה דף סו עמוד ב – והאמר רבין אמר רב אדא אמר רבי יצחק: מעשה בשפחה של בית רבי, שטבלה ועלתה ונמצא עצם בין שיניה, והצריכה רבי טבילה אחרת.

שו"ת אגרות משה יורה דעה חלק א סימן קד – אבל הנה בארתי בתשובה אחת בענין מוך באזן לידידי הגאון ר' שמעון טרעבניק שליט"א דבר חדש בחציצה דבית הסתרים, שאינו חוצץ שם אלא חציצה מדברים המתדבקים כמיני דבק וטיט וכדומה שהמקום נעשה מזה אינו ראוי לביאת מים אבל דברים שאין מתדבקין רק מחמת שמונחים שם אין מניחין להכנס שם מים אין חוצצים בביה"ס שא"צ שיבואו שם מים והוכחתי זה מכמה דברים שנתיישבו בזה (והוא נדפס לעיל בסימן צ"ח) ונמצא לפ"ז גם בהא דעין תותב אף אם מהודק יפה ואף במקפדת להסירו לפעמים מצד צערה וחשש קלקול הגוף נמי לא יחצוץ כיון דחציצה כזו אינו חוצץ בבית הסתרים ותוך העין הוא ביה"ס.

ולטעם זה נראה דהמשקפים שנעשו מחדש שקורין קאנטקט שמשימים מתוך להעפעפים ומקיפין את כל העין שהוא מקום בית הסתרים שג"כ כיון שלא נתדבקו שם בדבק שאינם חוצצים ואם שכחה להסירם א"צ טבילה אחרת ורק לכתחלה כיון שיכולה להסירם בעצמה צריכה להסירם משום מהיות טוב. ובזה לא שייכי טעמי השואל ומשיב. והנני ידידו, משה פיינשטיין.

תלמוד בבלי מסכת נדה דף סז עמוד א – אמר רמי בר אבא: הני רבדי דכוסילתא, עד תלתא יומי – לא חייצי, מכאן ואילך – חייצי.

הלכות מקוואות למרדכי (שבועות) רמז תשמח – ריבדא דכוסילתא פירוש קיבוץ דם שעל נקבי היקז והוא כעין חטטין עד תלתא יומי שהקיז לא חייץ דלח הוא הדם שעל גבו ונכנס בו מים כדאמרי' התם הדם הדיו והחלב יבשים חוצצין לחין אין חוצצין מכאן ואילך חייצי שנעשה יבש ונדבק בדוחק על הבשר ואפילו אם יצטער אם יסיר הגלד מעל גבי המכה או אבעבועות שחין דאין דעתו להסיר עתה וקרוי אינו מקפיד מ"מ רגילות הוא להסיר הכל או שתמתין שתתרפא ותוכל להסיר כל זה פירש רש"י בתשובה.

משנה מסכת מקוואות פרק י משנה ח – אכל אוכלים טמאים ושתה משקים טמאים טבל והקיאן טמאים מפני שאינן טהורים בגוף שתה מים טמאים טבל והקיאם טהורים מפני שהם טהורים בגוף בלע טבעת טהורה נכנס לאהל המת הזה ושנה וטבל והקיאה הרי היא כמות שהיתה בלע טבעת טמאה טובל ואוכל בתרומה הקיאה טמאה וטמאתו חץ שהוא תחוב באדם בזמן שהוא נראה חוצץ ואם אינו נראה טובל ואוכל בתרומתו.

סדרי טהרה סימן קצח אות כו ד"ה ומ"מ – ע"כ ס"ל לחלק בין דבר היוצא מן הגוף ובין דבר אחר החוצץ דבהאי ל"מ מצטער.

שולחן ערוך הרב אורח חיים הלכות נטילת ידים סימן קסא סעיף ו – ריר היוצא מן המכה ומתייבש ונעשה גליד אם אינו מקפיד עליו להסירו או שמצטער להסירו שמעתה אין דעתו להסירה כל זמן שיהיה בענין זה קרוי אינו מקפיד ואינו חוצץ לנטילה אף על פי שלטבילה מחמירין.

משנה מסכת מקוואות פרק ט משנה ב – קלקי הלב והזקן ובית הסתרים באשה לפלוף שחוץ לעין וגלד שחוץ למכה והרטיה שעליה ושרף היבש וגלדי צואה שעל בשרו ובצק שתחת הצפורן והמלמולין וטיט היון וטיט היוצרים וגץ יוני איזהו טיט היון זה טיט הבורות שנאמר (תהלים מ') ויעלני מבור שאון מטיט היון טיט היוצרין כמשמעו ר' יוסי מטהר בשל יוצרין ומטמא בשל מרקה וגץ יוני אלו יתדות הדרכים שאין טובלין בהן ולא מטבילין אותן ושאר כל הטיט מטבילין בו כשהוא לח ולא יטבול באבק שעל רגליו לא יטבול את הקומקמוס בפחמין אלא אם כן שפשף.

שו"ת צמח צדק (לובאוויטש) יורה דעה סימן קנח – ה. אך עכ"ז יש לדקדק אם חשיבי אינו מקפיד. דהנה לשון רש"י פ"ק דעירובין דף ד' ב' בפי' ומקפיד עליו שמצטער על לכלוך זה שבראשו. א"כ י"ל גם הקאלטענש א"א להכחיש דהן משא כבד על האדם. ואע"ג דניחא ליה בהו מצד הרפואה אינו דומה לדבר שאינו מקפיד עליו בעצם כלל. מיהו יש ראיה דאינו נקרא חציצה כה"ג כיון דמ"מ רוצה בקיומן מהמשנה פ"ג דפסחים בצק שבסדקי עריבה כו' אם מקפיד עליו חוצץ ואם רוצה בקיומו הרי הוא כעריבה. ופרש"י שם דמ"ה סע"ב ואם רוצה בקיומו שיתקיים בסדקיו לסתום. אלמא הא דרוצה בקיומו זהו ענין אין מקפיד עליו. מיהו קשה ע"ז מדין רטיה דמשנה שלימה פ"ט דמקוואות מ"ב גלד שחוץ למכה. והרטיה שעליה. הרי דגם רטייה שעל המכה ממש חשוב חציצה אע"ג דרוצה בקיומו עתה ואין רצונה להסירה כלל. וצ"ל דאע"ג שכעת אין דעתו להסירו מ"מ כיון שדעתו להסירו אחר שתתרפא המכה נקרא מקפיד עליו. ואע"פ שכעת רוצה בקיומו. ולא דמי לרוצה בקיומו גבי בצק שבסדקי עריבה דרוצה בקיומו לעולם וכל שיעמוד הבצק ויסתום הסדק הכל ניחא ליה. משא"כ הכא גבי רטיה שרוצה בקיומו רק עד שיתרפא המכה ואזי יסירנה א"כ חשוב מקפיד עליה. וראיה לחילוק זה ממשנה ג"ד פרק בתרא דמקוואות דקשרי העני אינם חוצצים לפי שהקשר ההוא אינו עשוי להתיר לעולם. כמ"ש הרע"ב והוא מדברי הרמב"ם פ"ג דהל' מקוואות דין כ"א כ"ב שקשרים ותפרים שאין עתיד להתירם אינם חוצצים אבל קשרים שעתיד להתירם חוצצים ע"ש במ"ש שהוא עתיד לגלותן ולמתחן. א"כ י"ל כל שעתיד להתיר אפילו אחר זמן רב נקרא מקפיד עליו. וכה"ג כ' הראב"ד בספר בעה"נ שער הטבילה דף י"ט ע"ג וז"ל ואי קשיא חוטי צמר וחוטי פשתן ורצועות שבראשי הבנות אמאי חוצצין. והלא מיעוטו שאינו מקפיד הוא לא מקפדת היא דלא תימא כל שאינו מקפיד עליו בשעת טבילה. אלא אם תקפיד עליו שעה אחרת דבר המקפיד עליו הוא. שא"א שלא תעביר אותם מעל ראשה בשעה שחופפת את ראשה. וכן הטבעת שבידה אי אפשר שלא תעבירנו בשעת לישה. או בשעת שהיא אופה ומבשלת עכ"ל. והביא דבריו הרשב"א בתה"א

בעמוד האחרון בסוף התה"א וכן מבואר ברש"י ר"פ במה אשה לפי' רבותיו דרש"י וגם רש"י עצמו לא הקשה עליהם אלא משום דכיון שהם רפויים והמים באים בהם לא שייך חציצה כלל ע"ש.

שו"ת כתב סופר יורה דעה סימן צא – ואחרי דברים הדברים אלו נבוא לנדון שלפנינו דנלפע"ד להקל מתרי טעמא א) דכל שהו' משום רפואה ונתון על מקומו לזמן קצוב בל יסור בנתיי' עד זמן הקצוב נכנס בגדר לא קפדו ושאני רטיה שע"ג המכה ואגד וקשקשים שעל השבר שמסירים לפעמים לתקנו ולראות אם כבר עלה רפואה עליו וכן הוא בכחול שע"ג העין שאם בא לרפואה שמחליפ' הכחול מזמן לזמן וזה נראה שהוא ג"כ דעת תשובת פמ"א ח"ב סי' קמ"ו שכ' בנדון שלו דאם ע"י רופא מומחה רובם אין מקפידים כדי שתעלה להם רפואה אינו חוצץ במיעוט שערות ובסדרי טהרה תמה עליו מ"ש מרטיה ואגד דהם משום רפואה ומ"מ חוצץ וצ"ל כיון שאפשר להסיר ולפמ"ש א"ש דשאני הנהו שמסירים בנתיים משא"כ בנדון של הפמ"א וכן בנדון שלנו, ב) כיון שא"א להסיר עכשיו רק ע"י כאב גדול מרובה ונאמר לי כי כמעט א"א להסירו רק כשידבק ויתלוש מן העור שבמקומו וכבר הארכנו בביאור שיטות סמ"ק ומרדכי וסה"ת דכל דאיכא צער לשעתו לא מקרי מיעוט המקפיד מעיקר הדין וכתבנו טעם שהחמירו להסיר כל גלד וחטטי' וכ"ז ל"ש בנדון שלנו דכל אנפי' שווים דמכאיב טובא לכל אדם וזמנו קבוע לכל עד שיפול מאליו.

סדרי טהרה סימן קצח אות כד – עיין בא"ח סימן קסא לענין נט"י שכתבו האחרונים ז"ל דמיירי דוקא במקפיד עליו ועיין במע"מ פ' כה שכ' ג"כ כן אבל בפ' התינוקת כ' דלענין טבילה נראה מדברי הטור דס"ל דמסתמא קפדי עליו אע"ג דמדברי הטור בהלכות נט"י מבואר דס"ל דמן הסתם לא קפדי על הרטי' מ"מ לענין טבילה החמיר ע"ש.

חידושי הרמב"ן מסכת נדה דף סז עמוד א – וגלד שעל המכה נמי משום האי טעמא הוא דלא עביד איניש לקלף גלד מכתו משום דקשה למכה עד דיביש ומקליף מנפשיה, וקסבר דהוא דוקא של מכה אבל ריבדא דכוסילתא עד תלתא יומין דלא קפיד איניש עלה לא חייצא מכאן ואילך חייצא אי נמי עד תלתא יומין לחה ולא מעכבא (מיהו) [מיא] מכאן ואילך חייצא דיבישה וקפיד עלה.

תוספתא מסכת מקוואות פרק ו הלכה י – צואה שתחת הצפורן שלא כנגד הבשר והטיט והבצק שתחת הצפורן אפילו כנגד הבשר אין חוצצין כתות של גדיל שאינו מקפיד עליה והאבר והבשר המדולדלין באדם הרי אלו אין חוצצין ר' יוחנן בן יוסף אמר צפורן שפירש רובה הרי זה אינה חוצצת.

רמב"ם הלכות מקוואות פרק ב הלכה א והלכה יד – אלו חוצצין באדם: לפלוף שחוץ לעין, וגלד שחוץ למכה, והדם יבש שעל גבי המכה, והרטייה שעליה, וגלדי צואה שעל בשרו, ובצק או טיט שתחת הציפורן, והמלמולין שעל הגוף, וטיט היון וטיט היוצרים וטיט של דרכים הנמצא שם

תמיד אפילו בימות החמה כל אלו חוצצין, ושאר כל הטיט כשהוא לח אינו חוצץ שהרי נמחה במים וכשהוא יבש חוצץ.

ואלו שאין חוצצין באדם: קלקלי הראש ובית השחי ובית הסתרים שבאיש, ולפלוף שבעין, וגלד שהעלתה המכה, ולכלוכי צואה שעל בשרו, וצואה שתחת הציפורן, וציפורן המדולדלת, וכשות הקטן והוא השיער הדק שעל בשרו, כל אלו אינן חוצצין.

בית יוסף יורה דעה סימן קצח – יח (א) צואה שתחת הציפורן שלא כנגד הבשר חוצץ וכו'. בפרק ט' דמסכת מקוואות שם תנן גבי אלו חוצצין בצק שתחת הציפורן וגבי אלו שאינן חוצצין צואה שתחת הציפורן וכתבו ר"ש והרא"ש (מ"ד) דאיתא בתוספתא (פ"ו ה"ה) צואה שתחת הציפורן שלא כנגד הבשר והבצק שתחת הציפורן אפילו כנגד הבשר הרי אלו חוצצין וכן פסקו הרא"ש בפרק תינוקת (הל' מקוואות סי' כו) והרשב"א בתורת הבית (הקצר ב"ז ש"ז לב.) וכן פסק רבינו ירוחם (נכ"ו ח"ה דף רכד ע"ד) אבל הרמב"ם בפרק ב' מהלכות מקוואות (הל' א, יד) כתב גבי אלו חוצצין בצק או טיט שתחת הציפורן וגבי אלו שאין חוצצין צואה שתחת הציפורן ולא חילק בין כנגד הבשר לשלא כנגד הבשר כלל ועיקר וצריך טעם למה דחה תוספתא זו מהלכתא ואפשר שטעמו משום דמשמע ליה דתוספתא זו פליגא אמתניתין דהא מתניתין לא חילקה בין כנגד הבשר לשלא כנגד הבשר אלא בין בצק לצואה בלחוד הוא דמפלגה וכוותה נקטינן ולא חיישינן לתוספתא והפוסקים שפסקוה סוברים דמתניתין סברה דאיכא ליפלוגי בין כנגד הבשר לשלא כנגד הבשר ומאי דשייר מלפרושי במתניתין פירש בתוספתא והמרדכי כתב בשבועות (סי' תשמז) וז"ל לכלוכי צואה שעל בשרו וצואה שתחת הציפורן סיפא מיירי בלח דאי ביבש היינו גלדי צואה ובצק שחוצצין ע"כ והוא מדברי התוספות בפרק תינוקת (סז. ד"ה לפלוף) ואכתוב דבריהם בסמוך וסמ"ק (סי' רצג עמ' שכג) כתב צואה שתחת הציפורן שלא כנגד הבשר שנינו בתוספתא דחוצצין ואע"ג דבמשנה אמרינן אלו שאין חוצצין לכלוכי צואה וצואה שתחת הציפורן מחלק רבינו תם בין הנדבקת לשאינה נדבקת עכ"ל.

רא"ש מסכת נדה הלכות מקוואות – צואה שתחת הצפורן וצפורן המדולדלת. תוספתא צואה שתחת הצפורן שלא כנגד הבשר והבצק שתחת הצפורן אפי' כנגד הבשר הרי אלו חוצצין.

ספר מצוות קטן מצוה רצג – וצואה שתחת הצפורן שלא כנגד הבשר, שנינו בתוספתא (דמקוואות פ"ו) דחוצצין ואע"ג דבמשנה אמרינן (מקוואות פ"ה) ואלו אין חוצצין לכלוכי צואה וצואה שתחת הצפורן מחלק ר"ת בין נדבקת לשאינה נדבקת גם אומר כי אפי' בנדבקת אם אינה מקפדת אין לה לחוש, ולפלוף שבעין לח אינו חוצץ יבש חוצץ ונהגו הנשים לגלח צפרניהם אעפ"י כי מן הדין בניקר סגי, ובחול המועד (מ"ק י"ח וע"ש בתוס') טוב שתגלחם בשנוי או על ידי גויה.

שולחן ערוך יורה דעה הלכות נדה סימן קצח סעיף יח – צואה שתחת הצפורן שלא כנגד הבשר, חוצץ; כנגד הבשר, אינו חוצץ. ובצק שתחת הצפורן, אפילו כנגד הבשר חוצץ. ואיזהו שלא כנגד הבשר, זה שהצפורן עודף על הבשר. ולפי שאינן יכולות לכוין מה נקרא כנגד הבשר או שלא כנגדו, כג נהגו הנשים ליטול צפרניהם בשעת טבילה.

ט"ז יורה דעה סימן קצח:יט – שלא כנגד הבשר חוצץ. – כתב בית יוסף בשם סמ"ג בשם ר"ת שזה דוקא בטיט הדומה לבצק שנדבק מאוד כגון טיט של יוצרים אבל לא בטיט אחר וצואה ותדע שהרי תנן במקוואות אלו שאין חוצצין לכלוכי צואה שעל בשרו וצואה שתחת הצפורן עכ"ל ולא זכר מזה כאן בש"ע להקל כל כך ומ"מ נראה לי לתרץ בזה מה שהוקשה לרמ"י בלבוש למה אין נזהרין מזה בנטילת ידים ולפי מה שכתבתי ניחא דודאי לענין נטילת ידים שפיר סמכינן על ר"ת דאינו חוצץ רק טיט היוצרים וכיוצא בו.

באר הגולה סימן קצח אות מא – הרא"ש שם והרשב"א בת"ה וש"פ.

שו"ת אחיעזר חלק ג סימן לג – תשובות קצרות בענינים שונים.

(א) בדבר שאלתו אודות הנשים הנוהגות לגדל צפרנים (מאניקיר) שנשאל משתי נשים הרוצות לשמור דיני טהרה וטבילה כדת רק שלא יגזזו את הצפרנים, שמבואר ברמ"א יו"ד סי' קצ"ח ס"כ שאחרי שכבר נהגו ליטול הצפרנים (מחשש שמא נמצא תחת הצפורן מעט טיט וממילא מקפדת על הצפורן או כמש"כ הש"ך שם משום ד' הראב"ד דכיון דעתידין ליטלן חייצי השתא) אפי' אם צפורן אחת נשארה בידה וטבלה צריכה טבילה אחרת.

באמת הקשה ידידי כת"ר לשאול וראוי לדבר על לבן לבלי לשנות ממנהג הנשים הנוטלות הצפרנים קודם הטבילה. אולם אם הדבר נמנע ויוכלו לבוא לידי מכשול להמנע עי"ז מטבילה יש לצדד בזה, כי הנשים מנקות היטב את הצפרנים והן מקפידות דוקא לבלי לגזוז, ורק היכא שרוב בני אדם מקפידים אזלינן בתר רובא כמ"ש בריש סי' קצ"ח ובט"ז סק"ב, והכא באמת רוב בני אדם אינם מקפידים על הצפורן וגם הנשים אינן מקפידות רק בשעת טבילה מחשש החומרא ומנ"ל דרוב הנשים מקפידות ע"ז וגם הנשים שאינן טובלות הלא אינן מקפידות, ומה שהחמירו בזה גם בדיעבד היינו לפי שהיא עצמה מקפדת ע"ז אלא ששכחה ובכה"ג שהיא מקפדת גם היכא דרוב בנ"א אינם מקפידים חוצץ, וכ"ה שי' הרמב"ם והטור והמרדכי מובא בש"ך סק"ב, משא"כ היכא שהיא אינה מקפדת כלל ואדרבה רוצה דוקא שלא לגזוז הצפורן ולטבול כך בזה אם אין רוב בנ"א מקפידים רק שרוב הטובלות מקפידות לא הוי רובא ומכיון דהיא אינה מקפדת אינו חוצץ. גם יש לצרף בזה השיטה דאזלינן בתר דידה, ואם דלא קיי"ל כן להלכה מ"מ יש לצרפה לסניף.

ובעיקר הדין הנה מד' המחבר נראה דצפורן אינה חוצצת אף שמנהג הנשים להסירן כמ"ש בב"י ובשו"ע שם וז"ל ולפי שאין יכולת לכוין מה נקרא נגד הבשר או שלא כנגדו נהגו הנשים ליטול הצפרנים בשעת טבילה ע"כ, נראה דאף אחר המנהג אינו לעיכובא אם רק הי' נקי כמ"ש בסעיף כ' דצפורן עצמה אינה חוצצת וכ"כ בהג' שערי דורא, ורק הרמ"א החמיר בזה דאחר שנהגו להסירן משום חשש קצת טיט הוי אצלן כדין גמור להקפיד על הסרת הצפורן. ונראה שמה"ט הקיל הט"ז בס"ק כ"א בשבת ויו"ט וחוה"מ ע"י ניקור היטב, והא לכאו' במיעוט המקפיד גם בדיעבד לא עלתה לה טבילה, אלא משום דהא דחשוב מיעוט המקפיד אין זה רק מצד חומרא ובשעת הדחק יש לסמוך ע"ד המחבר. ומה"ט נמי יש לסמוך להקל היכא שהיא אינה מקפדת שהנה מבעלי המאניקיר שרוצות דוקא להשאיר הצפרנים, ובזה ל"ש גם חומרת הראב"ד המובא בש"ך שם דצפורן עצמה חוצצת משום דעומד לגזוז, דאצלן אינן עומדת לגזוז (ואפ"ל דלהכי

הקילו בשויו"ט וחוה"מ משום דאף שהנשים החמירו על עצמן והקפידו להסיר הצפרנים לא הי' המנהג רק היכא דאפשר, אבל היכא דלא אפשר כמו בשבת ויו"ט לא החמירו על עצמן וממילא לא הוי קפידא, אלא דלד' הש"ך שחושש לדעת הראב"ד הא עומדות לגזוז לאחר השבת).

והנה בשו"ת משיב דבר חיו"ד סי' מ"ג מ"ד האריך אם להתיר טבילה ביום כדי שלא תבוא לידי חמורות יעוי"ש שמסיק שצריך ישוב הדעת בזה וכ' דבחציצה במיעוט המקפיד שהוא מדרבנן אין להתיר משום שלא תבוא לידי חמורות שלא תטבול, נראה דזהו בגזירה דרבנן המבואר בתלמוד דחוצץ דגם בדיעבד לא עלתה לה טבילה, אבל בנ"ד שאין בזה רק משום חומרא שהחמירו על עצמן ומצד עיקר הדין אין לחוש דצפורן עצמה אינה חוצצת וגם היכא דאי אפשר כמו בשויו"ט מקילין ע"י ניקור גרידא בזה בודאי יש להקל כדי למנוע מאיסור כרת ח"ו.

כל זה כתבתי מה שיש לצדד בזה, אולם באשר לא מצאתי היתר מפורש בדברי רבותינו האחרונים וגם ראוי לחוש דלא ליפוק חורבא מזה, וע"כ אין להורות היתר מפורש רק לצוות בבית הטבילה לבלי למחות בהנשים האלו שאינן מתרצות להסיר הצפרנים העשויות במאניקיר.

שולחן ערוך יורה דעה הלכות נדה סימן קצח סעיף כ – דוקא בצק שתחת הצפורן חוצץ, אבל הצפורן עצמה אינה חוצצת. ואפילו אם היתה גדולה ועומדת ליחתך ופורחת ועוברת מכנגד הבשר, אינה חוצצת. הגה: מיהו כל זה דוקא שאין צואה או בצק תחתיו בשעה שטבלה. ומאחר דכבר נהגו ליטול הצפרנים, אפילו אם צפורן אחת נשאר בידה וטבלה, צריכה טבילה אחרת. (הגהות ש"ד) וכן נוהגין.

ש"ך יורה דעה סימן קצח:כה – צריכה טבילה אחרת – באמת חומרא זו לא נמצאת בשום פוסק ואדרבה מהמשנה והרבה פוסקים וט"ו נראה מבואר דכל שהצפורן נקי בודאי אינו חוצץ אלא ההגהת ש"ד כתב דטוב להחמיר ותטבול שנית משום דא"א שלא יהא בתוכו טיט וע"כ כתב הרב דנוהגין להחמיר וכתב מהר"מ מלובלין בתשו' סי' פ"א דכיון שאין זה מדינא אלא מחומרא נ"ל שלא החמירו אלא כשנמצא ששכחה צפורן א' מיד אחר הטבילה קודם שלנה עם בעלה אבל אם לא מצאה כ"א עד למחר אין ראוי להחמי' שלא תוציא לעז על בעילתה ואפי' אם לא נזקקה לבעלה אותו לילה הדבר מכוער וא"צ טבילה אחרת אם לא נמצא שום לכלוך תחתיו עכ"ל מיהו בהראב"ן סימן שכ"ו דף ס' ע"ד מצאתי וז"ל צריכה לחתוך צפרני ידיה ורגליה דכיון דעתידה ליטלן חייצי השתא עכ"ל וזהו כעין מ"ש הרב ומאחר דכבר נהגו ליטול הצפרנים כו' צריכה טבילה אחרת כו' משמע דטעמא לאו משום דא"א שלא נשאר טיט תחת הציפורן אלא משום דהצפורן עצמו חוצצת וכ"כ הב"ח סי"ט דנ"ל דאפילו ברי לה שלא היה שום טיט כלל יש להחמיר שתטבול פעם שנית שהרי איכא למ"ד אם הצפורן עומדת ליקצץ חוצץ עכ"ל וא"כ צ"ע בפסק זה שפסק מהר"מ מלובלין ע"כ נראה דהיכא דאפשר לה לחזור ולטבול אפילו לא מצאה עד למחר יש לה לחזור ולטבול וכמדומה לי שכן נוהגים להורות אבל היכא דלא אפשר אין להחמיר כיון שעבר הלילה וע"ל סימן קצ"ז ס"ק א'.

ט"ז יורה דעה סימן קצח:כא – ומאחר דכבר נהגו ליטול וכו'. – בהגה' שערי דורא כתב בלשון זה ואם שכחה ולא נטלה צפרניה קודם טבילה אינה חוצצת ובלבד שלא יהא בתוכם טיט ומ"מ

טוב להחמיר ותטבול פעם ב׳ משום דא״א שלא תהא בתוכם טיט עכ״ל ורש״ל העתיק מתשובת מהר״מ בזה דעלתה לה טבילה כל שבודקת תחת צפרניה קודם טבילה ואין שם טיט וצואה ומו״ח ז״ל כתב שנראה לו אפילו אם ברי לה שלא היה שם צואה תטבול פעם שנית שהרי איכא למאן דס״ל דאם הצפורן עומד ליקצץ הוא חוצץ כו׳ ולא דמי לשערו׳ הראש דרוב הנשים אין דרכן ליקצץ משא״כ בצפרנים דכולם קוצצים והוה חציצה אם לא תקצץ עכ״ל ודבריו תמוהים דהא כל הפוסקים כתבו כאן דאינו אלא מנהג בעלמא ליטול הצפרנים ואינו מן הדין ונ״ל דכל מה שמצינו שצריכה לטבול שנית בשכחה ליטול צפורן היינו כל זמן שלא שמשה עם בעלה קודם שנזכר׳ לדבר אבל אם אחר ששמשה נזכרת אין להחמיר עליה ולהצריכה טבילה שנית כיון שאין זה אלא חומרא בעלמא ואפילו אם אין ידוע לה שלא היה שם טיט וצואה דמשמע מהגה׳ ש״ד ותשובת מהר״ם דלעיל שצריכה מדינא טבילה שנית היינו כל זמן שלא שמשה עם בעלה אבל לא אח״כ דהא אפילו אם היה שם צואה מדאוריי׳ אינו חוצץ דרובו ומקפיד בעינן אלא דגזירה דרבנן היא במיעוט המקפיד כדאיתא ריש הסימן אם כן הוה כאן ספיקא דרבנן וכ״ש למ״ש בסעיף י״ח בשם סמ״ג ור״ת דדוקא טיט הנדבק בעינן אע״פ שלא פסקו בש״ע להלכה מ״מ כאן שכבר שמשה ואפשר שהיא נתעברה אם באת להחמיר עליה בטבילה שנית אתה מוציא לעז על אותו הולד וכמו שמצינו בפ״ק דגיטין בלשון זה ואם באת להחמיר עליה אתה מוצא לעז על בניה כן נראה לע״ד ברור ושוב הוגד לי שגדול אחד השיב בתשובה כמו שכתבתי.

פתחי תשובה יורה דעה סימן קצח:י״ב – מיעוטה חוצצת – [עי׳ בתשו׳ חתם סופר סי׳ קצ״ה אודות כלות שטובלות ושערותיהן ארוכות ועתידין לקוץ אחר בעילת מצוה ופקפק רב אחד לחוש שיחוצו כיון שסופן להתגלח והוא ז״ל כתב דאין כאן בית מיחוש ומנהג ישראל תורה היא משם דהא דאמרי׳ בכ״מ כל העומד כו׳ היינו כשעומד להעשות מיד בלי הפסק דבר אחר ביניהם כמ״ש התוס׳ ב״ק דף ע״ו והכא אין השערות עומדות להתגלח עד אחר בעילת מצוה והבעילה מפסקת בין הטבילה לגילוח לא שייך עומד לקוץ כקצוץ ועוד ראיה ברורה מנזיר דמ״ד ע״ב ע״ש].

שו״ת חתם סופר חלק ב (יורה דעה) סימן קצה – שלום וכל טוב לי״נ הרב המאה״ג המופלג החו״ש המפורסם מו״ה יצחק ני׳ אבדק״ק פ״ש.

ע״ד כלות שטובלת ושערותיהן ארוכות ועתידין לקוץ אחר בעילת מצוה א״כ חשש פר״מ שיחוצו כיון שסופן להתגלח ולענ״ד אין כאן בית מיחוש ומנהג ישראל תורה היא ואם אינם נביאים וכו׳.

הנה הא דחוצץ העתיד לקוץ כתב הרב״י סי׳ קצ״ח גבי צפורן ובשר הפורש שהוא מתוספתא וכ׳ טעם נכון דכל העומד לקוץ כקוץ דמי והו״ל חציצה בבית הסתרים מקום חיבור היתר עם חלק הצריך והוא ש״ס ערוך ותוספתא פ׳ בהמה המקשה ע״ג ע״א תוס׳ ד״ה מטביל וכו׳ וב״י לא מייתי מהתוס׳ ע״ש והנה בכל מקום דאמרינן כל העומד לכך כאלו כבר נעשה המעשה היינו כשעומד להעשות מיד בלי הפסק דבר אחר ביניהם כמ״ש תוס׳ בב״ק ע״ו ע״ב ד״ה כל העומד כיון דבין שחיטה וזריקה בעינן מצות קבלת דם בכוס לא אמרינן תו בשעת שחיטה כל העומד לזרוק כזרוק דמי הנה כי כן הכא נהיגי נשי שלא לקוץ השערות עד אחר בעילות

מצוה ממש ומקפדת שתבוא אל החתן בשערות ארוכות אולי יצא להם זה מיצאה בהינומא וראשה פרוע יהי׳ איך שיהי׳ אין השערות עומדת להתגלח בשעת טבילה עד אחר בעילת מצוה והבעילה מפסק׳ בין טבילה לגילוח לא שייך עומד לקוץ כקצוץ ובפרט דטעמ׳ משום מיעוט׳ ומקפיד והכא אדרבה מקפדת שיהי׳ לה אותן השערות ועוד ראי׳ ברורה דאלת״ה נזיר טמא שטבל בשביעי וגילח בשמיני לא עלתה לו טבילה משום שער העומד לקצוץ ומבואר בהדי׳ בנזיר מ״ד ע״ב דיצא ידי טבילה א״כ אין קפידא בשערות אפילו עומד לקצוץ כנלפע״ד אלא שעל טעם האחרון יש לפקפק דאפשר ששער הנקצצים הם רובא ורוב אפי׳ אינו מקפיד חוצץ אבל טעם הראשון נראה ברור ואמת הכ״ד א״נ דש״ת. פ״ב יום ה׳ י״ד טבת קצ״ז לפ״ק. משה״ק סופר מפפ״דמ.

ספר התרומה סימן קד – וצריכה לחתוך צפרניה וכן הוא מנהג ונראה דהיינו טעמא משום הטיט שתחת הצפרנים אבל משום הצפורן שהוא גדול יותר מדאי חוץ לבשר ועתיד לקוצצו בלאו הכי וחוצץ אין נראה טעם זה. שהרי שערות ראשו שגדולין יותר מדאי ועומדין ליקצץ והלא אין רגילות לגלחן בשעת טבילה.

נקודת הכסף סימן קצח על הט״ז קצח ס״ק כא – גם מה שפסק דבשבת תטבול שנית ואסורה לחתוך הצפורן וסיים וראיתי מי ששגג בזה וצוה לחתוך ביום טוב על ידי עובדת כוכבים כו׳ זה שהורה טוב הורה וכמו שאבאר.

תוספות מסכת שבת דף צד עמוד ב – אבל בכלי ד״ה חייב – היינו כרבי יהודה דמחייב במלאכה שאינה צריכה לגופה וא״ת ודילמא רבנן כר״ש סבירא להו ומנא ליה דמחייב בכלי ויש לומר דא״כ ליפלגי בכלי להודיעך כחן דרבנן והא דקאמר מהו דתימא רבנן בכלי נמי פטרי היינו פירושו דס״ל כר״ש וכדפרישית אבל רש״י פירש דפטרי משום דלא שייכא גזיזה אלא בצמר ואין נראה לר״י דבהא ליכא למיטעי דבכל בעלי חיים שייכא גזיזה כדאמר לעיל התולש כנף חייב משום גוזז.

ביאור הלכה סימן שמ – וחייב וכו׳ – הנה התוס׳ כתבו דזהו דוקא לר״י דמלאכה שאין צריך לגופה חייב אבל לר״ש פטור אף בכלי ומשום זה תמהו האחרונים על הרא״ש והטור שהעתיקו הדין הלא הם פסקו כר״ש וגם המחבר האיך סתם הדין בזה בסתמא ובסי׳ שט״ז ס״ח מצדד בדעה הראשונה לפטור והמ״א בסק״א כתב דלמ״ד דמשאצ״ל פטור מיירי בשצריך לשערן אלא דקשה על דבריו דלפ״ז אמאי פסק דבמלקט לבנות מתוך שחורות אפילו באחת חייב הא מ״מ א״צ להשער גופא דאף אם נימא דמיירי שצריך להשערה האחת שליקט הא בעצמה בלבד לית בה שיעורא לחיוב וכי משום דעושה תועלת היפוי בליקוט השערה האחת יושלם בזה השיעור של ב׳ שערות הצריך לגופן אח״כ מצאתי לאחד שהקשה כן ונראה דמטעם קושיא זו נייד הגר״א מדברי המ״א וציין על הדין דמלקט שחורות וכו׳ סתם כדעת הרמב״ם דהלכה כר״י במלאכה שאצ״ל עכ״ל וכן במכות כ׳ ע״ב ציינו דבריהם בשם רשב״ם ג״כ על מימרא זו דמלקט וכו׳ (ואולי י״ל בדוחק דברי המ״א דכיון דחשיבא מלאכת גזיזה בזה אפילו בשערה אחת משום שמתיפה

עי"ז ממילא חשיב אח"כ צריך לגופה ג"כ במה שצריך לשערה זו בלבד) וגם לפי דברי המ"א יהיה מוכרח לבאר ההיא דלעיל בסימן שכ"ח סל"א גבי ציצין וצפורן ע"ש ג"כ בשצריך להן וזהו דוחק גדול מאד וכן בתשו' ח"צ סימן פ"ב דחה בב' ידים מחמת קושיא זו. והנה הגר"א כתב דהשו"ע סתם פה להלכה כדעת הרמב"ם במשאצ"ל דחייב אך מה נעשה בקושית כל האחרונים שהטוש"ע סותרים את עצמן וכנ"ל והנה הריב"ש בסימן שצ"ד [והובא לעיל בסימן ש"ג וגם בסימן זה] כתב דמלאכת הגזיזה חשיבא מלאכה לכו"ע אפילו אין צריך להשער דגזיזה היתה במשכן שלא לצורך הצמר והשער רק לצורך העור כגון בעורות תחשים וע"כ חייב כל שהוא לצורך גופן אע"פ שאינו צריך לשער ומלאכה הצריכה לגופה היא עכ"ל וכיוצא בזה ממש כתב מורו הר"ן בחידושיו על שבת וז"ל מחלוקת ביד פרש"י משום גוזז שאע"פ שאינו צריך לגיזה הואיל והוא צריך ליפות עצמו בגיזה זו אף בזה חייב משום גוזז דומיא דגוזז את השלח שהוא חייב משום גוזז ואף במקום שאינו צריך לגיזה אלא שישאר העור בלא שער כדי שיהא ראוי לאיבוד עכ"ל ואפשר לומר שזהו דעת הטוש"ע ושלא כדעת התוס' ומצאתי בת' ח"צ שהוא הסכים ג"כ דדעת הטוש"ע הוא כדעת הריב"ש ושלא כדעת התוס' והנה ראיתי בספר סדרי טהרה שתמה על הח"צ בזה שהסכים לדעת הריב"ש וכתב דהלא הרא"ש כתב בהדיא בבכורות כ"ה וגם הביא שם כן בשם הרמב"ן דתלישת הצמר מן הבהמה קודם שחיטה וכן הנוצות מן העוף הוא מלאכה שאצ"ל וע"כ דהם ס"ל ג"כ כדעת התוס' ובאמת לאו ראיה הוא כלל כמו שדחה הוא בעצמו אח"כ דשאני התם דהאי תלישה לאו לצורך העור אלא לצורך השחיטה אבל היכא דהוא לצורך העור אע"פ שאין צריך לגיזה ס"ל דחייב וכמ"ש בגוזז מן השלח וכן נמי בעניננו כיון שהוא נוטל הצפרנים או השער להתיפות את עצמו מקרי זה לצורך גופו וכנ"ל בשם הר"ן. והנה השתא שבררנו דסוגיא זו דשבת צ"ד ע"ב ע"כ מיירי בשאינו צריך להשער והצפרנים ע"כ אנו מוכרחין לומר מעוד כמה גדולי הראשונים דס"ל ג"כ כדעת הריב"ש והר"ן הנ"ל הלא המה הר"ח והרמב"ן והסמ"ג והרא"ש ונבארם אחד לאחד. הר"ח דהוא בעצמו פסק כר"ש והוא ג"כ פסק בעניננו בהדיא דבכלי חייב חטאת וגם הרמב"ן דהוא בעצמו הביא בפרק כל כתבי והוכיח שהרי"ף פוסק כר"ש והכא הרי"ף בעצמו העתיק כל הסוגיא דציצין וצפורן וגם הרא"ש והסמ"ג דהם הסכימו בהדיא דהלכה כר"ש דמשאצ"ל פטור ואפ"ה העתיקו שניהם כל הסוגיא דציצין וצפורן ודמלקט שחורות מתוך לבנות דיש בהן חיוב חטאת וע"כ אנו צריכין לומר דכל אלו הפוסקים ס"ל כהר"ן וריב"ש הנ"ל דזה מקרי צורך גופן ולפיכך סתם השו"ע להלכה כן. והנה ראה ראיתי שהגר"א בסימן זה כתב דמסוגיא זו ראיה לפסק הרמב"ם דמשאצ"ל חייב אבל לפי דברי כל הגאונים הנ"ל שס"ל דמשאצ"ל פטור ואעפ"כ העתיקו כולם הסוגיא ע"כ דס"ל כר"ן וריב"ש הנ"ל ועיין בסימן שט"ז סוף סעיף חי"ת בבאור הגר"א שמצדד שם דהלכה דמשאצ"ל פטור וע"כ דהוא מראה פנים לכל שיטה שיש לה מקור גדול בתלמוד. והנה באשה ששכחה ליטול צפרנים בע"ש ואירע ליל טבילתה בשבת בודאי לכתחלה נכון לה ליזהר שתאמר לעו"ג ליטלם ביד ולא בכלי דהוא מלאכה גמורה לדעת הרמב"ם אך בא"א לה ביד מצדד המ"א להקל ע"י עו"ג אף בכלי וכדעת נקודות הכסף ביו"ד סימן קצ"ח וכמ"ש למעלה דבזה מקרי מלאכה שאצ"ל שאין כונה שלה להתנאות בזה רק לצורך טבילה ונ"ל דבצפרני רגליה בודאי טוב יותר להתיר ע"י נקור מלהתיר ע"י עו"ג עיין בפ"ת שם בשם מהר"ר דניאל זצ"ל. ואגב נברר מה שכתבתי במ"ב בפשיטות

דתולש שער מן המתה חייב כ"כ הט"ז והוא מהירושלמי דפרק כלל גדול ואף שהביא הבה"ט שהשיגו היד אהרן באמת הדין עם הט"ז דדברי הט"ז לאו יחידאה הוא כי כן משמע מהרא"ש בבכורות בשם הרמב"ן וכן איתא בהדיא ברא"ש בפרק כלל גדול סימן ו' ובפירוש ר"ח בדף ע"ד ע"ב ובדברי רבינו ירוחם ומה שהביא היד אהרן ראיה מהרמב"ם דפליג ע"ז מדכתב הגוזז וכו' ולא נקט התולש לאו ראיה היא דנקט גוזז משום דרצה לסיים בין מן החי בין מן המת ובתולש אין חייב כ"א לאחר מיתה דאז אורחה בתלישה כמו בגיזה משא"כ מחיים פטור בתלישה דלאו אורחא היא משום דכאיב לה וכן מה שהביא ראיה מדנקט הרמב"ם התולש כנף מן העוף ולא נקט התולש צמר מן הבהמה לאו ראיה היא כלל דדין תולש כנף העוף הוא אפילו מחיים וכדמוכח שם בבכורות ובבהמה מחיים אינו חייב בתולש כ"א בגוזז וכנ"ל וממילא מה שכתב עוד היד אהרן דהירושלמי דלא כהלכתא משום דמגמרא דילן משמע להיפך מדמסקינן שם בבכורות שאני כנף דהיינו אורחיה משמע דהתולש מן הבהמה לאו אורחיה לאו ראיה היא כלל ופליאה עליו דהגמרא שם איירי בתולש מן החי וזה דוקא בעוף חייב ולא בבהמה משא"כ בתולש מן המת גם בבהמה אורחה בתלישה כמו בגיזה וכדאמר בירושלמי תלישתה זו היא גיזתה ולפיכך אין לנו לזוז מדברי הירושלמי שהביאוהו הפוסקים הראשונים.

שולחן ערוך אורח חיים הלכות שבת סימן שכח סעיף לא – צפורן שפרשה וציצין, שהן כמין רצועות דקות שפרשו מעור האצבע, סביב הצפורן, אם פרשו רובן כלפי מעלה ומצערות אותו, להסירן ביד, מותר; בכלי, פטור אבל אסור.לא פרשו רובן, ביד, פטור אבל אסור; בכלי, לה חייב חטאת. ופירש"י: כלפי מעלה, כלפי ראשי אצבעותיו; ור"ת פ' דהיינו כלפי הגוף; וצריך לחוש לשני הפרושים.

תלמוד בבלי מסכת ביצה דף כב עמוד א – בעא מיניה רב אשי מאמימר: מהו לכחול את העין ביום טוב? היכא דאיכא סכנה, כגון רירא, דיצא, דמא, דמעתא, וקדחתא, ותחלת אוכלא – לא מבעיא לי, דאפילו בשבת שרי. כי קמבעיא לי – סוף אוכלא, ופצוחי עינא, מאי? – אמר ליה: אסור. – איתיביה: אין מכבין את הבקעת! ושני ליה כדשנין. אמימר שרי למכחל עינא מנכרי בשבתא. איכא דאמרי: אמימר גופיה כחל עינא מנכרי בשבתא. אמר ליה רב אשי לאמימר, מאי דעתיך – דאמר עולא בריה דרב עילאי: כל צרכי חולה עושין על ידי נכרי בשבת, ואמר רב המנונא: כל דבר שאין בו סכנה – אומר לנכרי ועושה. הני מילי – היכא דלא מסייע בהדיה, אבל מר – קא מסייע בהדיה, דקא עמיץ ופתח! – אמר ליה: איכא רב זביד דקאי כותן, ושניי ליה: מסייע אין בו ממש.

תלמוד בבלי מסכת מכות דף כ עמוד ב – והמקיף פאת ראשו וכו'. ת"ר: פאת ראשו – סוף ראשו, ואיזהו סוף ראשו? זה המשוה צדעיו לאחורי אזנו ולפדחתו. תני תנא קמיה דרב חסדא: אחד המקיף ואחד הניקף לוקה. אמר ליה: מאן דאכיל תמרי בארבילא לקי? דאמר לך: מני? רבי יהודה היא, דאמר: לאו שאין בו מעשה לוקין עליו. רבא אומר: במקיף לעצמו ודברי הכל. רב אשי אומר: במסייע ודברי הכל.

חידושי הריטב"א מסכת מכות דף כ עמוד ב – במססייע ודברי הכל. פירש"י ז"ל שמזמין לו השערות, ואיכא דקשיא ליה הא דאמרינן במס' יו"ט (ביצה כ"ב א') לענין מיכחל כותי לישראל ביו"ט וישראל עמיץ ופתח דמסייע דהתם אין בו ממש שדרך העין למעמץ ומפתח קצת אבל הכא סיוע גדול הוא כשמזמין לו עצמו בשערו, וכש"כ לפירוש רבינו מאיר ז"ל שכתבנו לעיל דבלאו מסייע יש בו לאו ולא בענין סיוע אלא כדי שיהא בו מעשה ללקות עליו, דבמעשה כל דהוא סגי להא, כדאמרינן בעלמא עקימת פיו או עקימת קומה הוי מעשה, וכן פירש הוא ז"ל.

תלמוד בבלי מסכת ביצה דף יח עמוד א – תא שמע, דאמר רב חייא בר אשי אמר רב: נדה שאין לה בגדים – מערמת וטובלת בבגדיה. ואם איתא, – נגזור דלמא אתי לאטבולי בעינייהו! – שאני התם, מתוך שלא הותרה לה אלא על ידי מלבוש – זכורה היא.

משנה מסכת מקוואות פרק ו משנה ה – [ה] השידה והתיבה שבים אין מטבילין בהם אלא אם כן היו נקובין כשפופרת הנוד ר' יהודה אומר בכלי גדול ארבעה טפחים ובקטן רובו אם היה שק או קופה מטבילין בהן כמה שהם מפני שהמים מעורבין היו נתונים תחת הצינור אינם פוסלים את המקוה אלא מטבילין אותן ומעלין אותן כדרכן.

תוספות מסכת חולין דף כו עמוד ב – הכא נמי מבלבלי – ורבא סלקא דעתך דכי נטמאו מעיקרא בפני עצמן אינו מועיל להן השקה אלא בפני עצמן הקשה ה"ר אליעזר ממיץ למה לי טעמא דמבלבלי כי נמי קפי פרי מלעיל סלקא להו השקה כדאשכחן בפרק התערובת (זבחים עח:) גבי יין וחלב לחין אין חוצצין שדרך היין עוברים המים אל גוף האדם ועלתה לו טבילה ונראה דלא קשה מידי דלא דמי דודאי אגבא דגברא או אגבא דמנא מחלחלי בהו מיא אבל דרך השקה לא.

הלכות מקוואות למרדכי (שבועות) רמז תשמח – א"ר יצחק דבר תורה רובו ומקפיד עליו חוצץ דכתיב ורחץ את [*כל] בשרו במים את לרבות את הטפל לבשרו דהיינו השיער אם רובו של שיער נקשר כל נימא ונימא בפני עצמה דרובו ככולו אם מקפיד עליו חוצץ איכא דאמרי אם רוב שערו נתלכלך בטיט או בשאר דבר חוצץ וגזרו על מיעוטו המקפיד כו' כתב הרא"ם בספרו הא דתנן הדם והדיו והחלב יבשים חוצצים לחין אין חוצצין מטעם הקפדה הוא שעל יבש דרך בני אדם להקפיד ועל לחין אין מקפידין אבל אי מקפיד אפי' לח חוצץ (*ואם) [*וכן אם] היא טובלת בטיט צלול שפרה שוחה ושותה אע"פ שהטיט דבוק בבשרה [במיעוטה] והיא אינה מקפדת אינו חוצץ [אבל] אם היא מקפדת חוצץ אף במיעוט וכן מצאתי בתשובת ה"ר אליעזר מורדון והוא ברוקח והמפרש טעמא דברייתא משום שהמים נכנסין בלח טועה שאין לך לח יותר מיין ואמרינן סוף פ"ק דחולין [*כ"ו] מיא יקירי ושכני תתאי ופירי קפי מלעיל ולא קא סלקא להו השקת מים ואין לתת חילוק בין השקה לטבילה דתנן בזבחים פרק התערובות דלי מלא רוקין והטבילו כאילו לא טבל ורוק לח הוא.

תורת הבית הקצר בית ז שער ז – צבעים שעל ידי הנשים או שעל השער לנוי, יראה לי שאין חוצצין לפי שאינן מקפידות בהן לעולם אדרבה חוזרות בהן ומ(ת)חדשות אותם תמיד לנוי.

אע"פ שצבע זה פושט בכל השער ורובו, אע"פ שאינו מקפיד עליו חוצץ, כאן מקפדת ורוצה להיותו [דף לב עמוד ב] והרי זו כאלו הוא מגופו של שער, וכבגד צבוע שאין הצבע כדבר הנוסף וחוצץ אלא כעיקרו של בגד ואינו חוצץ, שהרי מצינו טבילה לפרוכת אע"פ שיש בה(ן) תכלת וארגמן ותולעת שני. ועוד יראה לי שאין ממשו של צבע בשער ועל הידים אלא מראות של צבע ולפיכך אינו חוצץ. ואינו דומה לכתב שחוצץ, שממש הן בכתב.

שולחן ערוך יורה דעה הלכות נדה סימן קצח סעיף יז – צבע שצובעות הנשים על פניהן וידיהן ושער ראשן, אינו חוצץ. וכן מי שהוא צבע וידיו צבועות, אינו חוצץ. הגה: וכן מי שאומנתו להיות שוחט או קצב וידיו תמיד מלוכלכות בדם, אינו חוצץ, שרוב בני אומנות זו אינן מקפידים (ב"י בשם ר"י).

ביאור הגר"א יורה דעה סימן קצח – [יח] צבע כו'. וראיה מפרכת שהיה צבוע תכלת וארגמן כו' ומטבילין אותו כמ"ש בסוף שקלים ועבה"ג.

משנה מסכת שקלים פרק ח משנה ד – פרוכת שנטמאת בולד הטומאה מטבילין אותה בפנים ומכניסין אותה מיד ואת שנטמאת באב הטומאה מטבילין אותה בחוץ ושוטחין אותה בחיל ואם היתה חדשה שוטחין אותה על גג האיצטבא כדי שיראו העם את מלאכתן שהיא נאה.

בית יוסף יורה דעה סימן קצח – יז צבע שצובעות הנשים על פניהן ושער ראשן אינו חוצץ וכן מי שאומנותו צבע וידיו צבועות אינו חוצץ. כ"כ הרא"ש בפרק תינוקת (הל' מקוואות סי' כז) וז"ל נשים הצובעות עצמן נראה שאינו חוצץ כי הוא נוי להן ואינן מקפידות אלא עשאוהו במתכוין ועוד שאין בו ממש אלא חזותא בעלמא וכל אשה שאומנותה לצבוע כיון שדרכה בכך אינה מקפדת כדאמרינן בזבחים פרק דם החטאת (צח:) רבב על בגדו חוצץ ואם מוכר רבב הוא אינו חוצץ עכ"ל וכן כתב הרשב"א בתורת הבית (הקצר ב"ז ש"ז לב.) וז"ל צבעים שעל ידי הנשים או שעל השער לנוי יראה לי שאינן חוצצין לפי שאינן מקפידות בהן לעולם אדרבא חוזרות הן ומחדשות אותן תמיד לנוי אע"פ שצבע זה פושט בכל השער ורובו אף על פי שאינו מקפיד עליו חוצץ כאן אינה מקפדת ורוצה להיותו שם והרי הוא כאילו הוא מגופו של שער וכבגד צבוע שאין הצבע כדבר נוסף וחוצץ אלא כעיקרו של בגד ואינו חוצץ שהרי מצינו (שקלים פ"ח מ"ד, מ"ה) טבילה לפרוכת אע"פ שיש בו תכלת וארגמן ותולעת שני ועוד יראה שאין ממשו של צבע בשער ועל הידים אלא מראיתו של צבע ולפיכך אינו חוצץ ואינו דומה לכתב שחוצץ שממש הדיו בכתב וכן הנשים שמלאכתן לצבוע יראה לי שאין אותו צבע שעל ידיהן חוצץ מן הטעם הזה שאין ממשו של צבע אלא מראיתו ועוד שכל שמלאכתה בכך אינה מקפדת למה הדבר דומה לדם שעל בגדיו של טבח ורבב שעל בגדי רבב שאינו חוצץ שכל הדברים בהקפדה הם תלויין ע"כ כלומר כדרבי יצחק (נדה סז:) דאמר גזרו רבנן על מיעוטו המקפיד ועל רובו שאינו מקפיד אבל על מיעוטו שאינו מקפיד לא גזרו ואע"ג דבשאר נשים דאינן צבעות דרכן להקפיד ולעיל (פג: ד"ה ומ"ש או אפילו) כתבתי דכל שדרך הנשים להקפיד בו אע"פ שזו אינה מקפדת חוצץ י"ל דשאני הכא דגם שאר נשים שהן בני אותה אומנות אינן מקפידות והוא הדין והוא הטעם לטבח ורבב

דאע"ג דשאר אנשים קפדי אדם וארבב כיון שכל בני אותה אומנות לא קפדי לא חייץ ודבריו אלה שכתב בתורת הבית העתיק בתשובת שאלה וכתב אחר כן וזכור אני שדנתי בזה לפני מורי הרב הגדול הרמב"ן ז"ל והודה לדברי הלכה למעשה ע"כ ובתשובות להרמב"ן סימן קכ"ד תמצא בתשובה זו: וכן פסק רבינו ירוחם (נכ"ו ח"ה רכה.) וז"ל צבע שעל ידי הנשים או שעל השער לנוי אינו חוצץ דאינן מקפידות אדרבא חוזרות לצבוע אותן תמיד אע"פ שחופה רוב השער או כולו והרי הוא כגופו של שער שאינו חוצץ והשער הוא כגופו של אדם ועוד שהמראה מן הצבע אין בו ממש ואינו דומה לכתב שחוצץ שהתם ממשות הדיו וכן הנשים שצובעות שמלאכתן בכך ויש מהצבע על ידיהן או על בשרן אינו חוצץ וכן אשה ששוחטת תמיד כמו טבח ויש עליה דם וכן כל שמלאכתה בכך אינה מקפדת כך הסכימו המפרשים ע"כ.

תלמוד בבלי מסכת נדה דף סז עמוד א – א"ר יוחנן: פתחה עיניה ביותר, או עצמה עיניה ביותר – לא עלתה לה טבילה. אמר ריש לקיש: האשה לא תטבול אלא דרך גדילתה. כדתנן: האיש נראה כעודר ומוסק זיתים, אשה נראת כאורגת וכמניקה את בנה.

תוספות מסכת נדה דף סז עמוד א – פתחה עיניה ביותר או עצמה עיניה ביותר – לכך יש ללמוד לכל אשה הטובלת שלא תטבול ותפתח עיניה ולא תעצים עיניה ביותר לפירש"י דלא גרסינן בסמוך דהני שמעתא לטהרות ולכל הפירושים צריך ללמדה לפתוח פיה שיהא ראוי לביאת מים כדאמרינן לעיל דכל בית הסתרים בעינן שיהא ראוי לביאת מים ומייתי נמי משפחתו של רבי שטבלה ונמצא עצם בין שיניה והצריכה רבי טבילה אחרת ותנן נמי בהדיא במס' מקוואות בפ"ח (מ"ה) נדה שנתנה מעות בפיה ירדה וטבלה טהרה מטומאתה אבל טמאה אגב רוקה נתנה שער בפיה קפצה ידיה קמצה שפתותיה כאילו לא טבלה וגם צריך ללמדה להרחיק ירכותיה קצת כדאמרינן בסמוך כאורגת וכמניקה את בנה לענין הגבהת הדד קצת מעל החזה.

מחזור ויטרי סימן תצט – לעולם ילמד אדם בתוך ביתו שתהא אשה מדיחה קמטיה במים. ואע"ג שאינה צריכה לפתוח פיה ולהכניס מים לתוכה. דהא בית הסתרים היא. ולא בעיא טבילה אפי' הכי חציצה פסלה בה כדר' זירא. דכל הראוי לבילה אין בילה מעכבת בו. הכא נמי מקום הראוי לבא מים בעינן וליכא למימר כי איתמר הנהו שמעתתא דחציצה במסכת נדה לטהרות. אבל לבעלה לא. כדמוכח ביבמות בהחולץ. דתניא כל דבר שחוצץ בטבילה חוצץ בגר ובעבד משוחרר ובנידה. והא נידה בנידה לבעלה קמיירי. להתירה קאמרי. דומיא דגר ועבד משוחרר. דאי בנידה לטהרות לטהר את הטומאה צריכא למימר דחציצה מיפסלא לטבילה. והא גבי חציצה לטהר את האדם לטהרות. כת' ורחץ את בשרו במים. וגבי נידה לא כתיבא לא חציצה ולא טבילה. אלא כולהו טבילות מהתם ילפי' להו דחציצה פסלא להו. ועוד אי בטהרות מיירי מאי שנא דנקט נידה טפי מטמא מת וטמא שרץ. אלא ודאי בנידה לבעלה מיירי. ואע"ג דאית ספרים דגרסי במסקנא דההיא שמעתתא דלית הילכתא ככל הני שמעתתא. כי איתמר ההיא לטהרות. אבל לבעלה לא. שיבוש גמור הוא. ול"ג ליה. דהא מייתי סייעתא ממילתא דריש לקיש. והא מילתא לא דמיא מידי לכל שמעתתא דאמרי' לעיל. והכי גרס' לקמן. א"ר שמעון בר לקיש אשה לא תטבול אלא דרך גדילתה. ול"ג כי הא דריש לקיש. ובסיפרו של רבינו יצחק בר' מנחם

לא גרסי' ליה. וכן הנהיגה אחותו מרת בילא משמו את בנות עירה. לחטוט את שיניהם קודם טבילה דאע"ג דבית הסתרים אין צריכין ביאת מים מקום הראוי לבא מים בעינן. כדר' זירא כל הראוי לבילה אין בילה מעכבת. ושאין ראוי לבילה בילה מעכבת. והבא לומר לא אמרו חכמים כן אלא לעיניין טהרות אבל לעיניין אשה לבעלה לא. שנינו בברייתא בגמרא דהחולץ כל דבר שחוצץ בטבילה חוצץ בגר ובעבד משוחרר ובנידה. והכא בנידה לבעלה עסיקינן. דאי לטהרות פשיטא. מאי שנא משאר טהרות ועוד דומייא דגר ועבד משוחרר. שאין טובלים לשם טהרות. אלא לאיסור והיתר. אבל אין להורות כן. שלא להוציא לעז על הראשונות. ועוד דההיא מעשה בשפחה של בית ר' שטבלה ונמצא לה עצם בין שיניה והצריכה ר' טבילה אחרת. ואם תאמר יחידאה היא ויחיד ורבים הלכה כרבים. חדא דמימרא הוא וליכא דפליג עלה. ועוד דרבנן בתראי סמכו עלה וקבעוה. דאמרי' דרש רבא לעולם ילמד אדם בתוך ביתו שתהא אשה מדיחה קמטיה במים כו'. עד מסקנא וכולה ההוא שמעתתא לעיניין אשה לבעלה. ובימי רבא לא היו טהרות. שמיום שפסקו מי חטאת כולנו טמאי מתים. ואין לנו לטהרה עד שיבא מקוה ישר' לזרוק עלינו מים טהורים לטהרנו: שלמה בר' יצחק ז"ל: ועוד צריכה אשה שתסיר מעליה כל גלד וחבורה וגרב שלא יחצוץ על בשרה. ומכה של הקזה עד שלשה ימים לא תחצוץ לפי שעדיין המכה לחה ופתוחה מיכן ואילך חוצצת: חולי שבעין שקורין קצידא. אם לח אינו חוצץ. אם יבש חוצץ. דאמר מר לפלוף שבעין לח אינו חוצץ יבש חוצץ. ואימתי נקרא יבש כשמתחיל לירק. אם פותחת עיניה ביותר גב העין חוצץ למעלה. דא"ר יוחנן פתחה עיניה ביותר או שעצמה עיניה ביותר לא עלתה לה טבילה: כשטובלת פושטת זרועותיה לכאן ולכאן. ופורסת כפיה. ומרחקת אצבעותיה זה מזה כדי שיכנסו המים ביניהם. דאמר ריש לקיש לא תטבול אלא דרך גדילתה. שכן דרכה של אשה כשהיא אורגת פושטות זרועותיה לכאן ולכאן.

שולחן ערוך יורה דעה הלכות נדה סימן קצח סעיף לה – לא תטבול בקומה זקופה, מפני שיש מקומות שמסתתרים בה; ואל תשחה הרבה עד שידבקו סתריה זה בזה, מח אלא שוחה מעט עד שיהיו סתרי בית הערוה נראים כדרך שנראית בשעה שהיא עורכת; ויהיה תחת דדיה נרא' כדרך שנראה בשעה שמניקה את בנה; ויהיה תחת בית השחי נראה כדרך שנראה כשאורגת בעומדין, ואינה צריכה להרחיק ירכותיה זו מזו יותר מדאי וגם לא להרחיק זרועותיה מהגוף יותר מדאי, אלא כדרך שהם בעת הילוכה; ואם שינתה, כגון ששחתה ביותר או זקפה ביותר, מט עלתה לה טבילה (ערוך וסמ"ג ורשב"ץ ורמב"ם); ויש מי שאומר שלא עלתה.

שולחן ערוך יורה דעה הלכות נדה סימן קצח סעיף לט – לא תעצים עיניה ביותר ואל תפתחם ביותר, ואם עשתה כן יש אומרים שלא עלתה לה טבילה (ב' דעות בטור ופוסקים עב"י).

ט"ז יורה דעה סימן קצח – (לח) ויש מי שאומר שלא עלתה לה טבילה. – ק"ל למה יפסול בדיעבד מאי שנא מסעיף ל' דאמרינן מפני שהמים מקדימין ה"נ נימא הכי דהא הקדימו המים לאותן קמטין קודם שנדבקו על ידי הזקיפה או השחיה הרבה ויותר קשה לפי דעת הטור שאפילו בטיט שברגליה אינו חושש כמו שזכרתי לעיל סעיף ל"ג וי"ל דהכא יש חשש שידבקו הקמטים שהם בגוף למעלה מן המים נמצא שבביאתם למים כבר הם מדובקים ולפ"ז אם הכניסה עצמה

עד צוארה במים תחילה הוה טבילה בדיעבד בכל גוונא ונ"ל שנכון לכל אשה שתעשה כן שעכ"פ יש בזה צד מעליותא אם תשחה הרבה ולאו אדעתה.

נקודת הכסף סימן קצח על הט"ז ס"ק לח – לא קשה מידי דהתם פירושו כמו שכתב הרא"ש ומביאו בית יוסף וזה לשונו מפני שהמים מקדמים כלומר דכשתחבה רגליה בטיט כבר קדמו המים ונגעו ברגליה קודם שהגיע לטיט ואותן המים מחוברים למקוה כו'. והלכך לא הוי חציצה דמכל מקום המים שברגליה מחוברים למקוה שהרי רגליה נוגעות בקרקעית המקוה אבל הכא ע"י הקמטין לא יהיו המים שבתוך הקמטין מחוברים למקוה כלל.

ש"ך יורה דעה סימן קצח נא – י"א כו' – במעדני מלך דף שי"ח ע"א תמה מ"ש מקפצה פיה דסתם וכתב דלא עלתה לה טבילה ולא קשה מידי דאפי' מאן דפליג כאן מודה בקרצה שפתותיה דמתני' היא וכדאיתא בכל הפוסקים והחילוק כתב הר"ן וז"ל מ"ש מקרצה שפתותיה דתנן כאילו לא טבלה י"ל דכי עצמה עיניה לא מעכבי קמטים כולי האי שיהיו מעכבים מלבא בהן מים עכ"ל ומביאו ב"י לעיל גבי דין דגלד שעל המכה דף רכ"א ע"ב וכ"כ הרא"ה בספר בדק הבית דף קכ"ט ע"א ועצמה עיניה ביותר או פתחה ביותר אין לחוש לה אלא בקריצת שפתיה לבד עכ"ל וכן מבואר בשאר פוסקים.

משנה מסכת מקוואות פרק ח משנה ה – נדה שנתנה מעות בפיה וירדה וטבלה טהורה מטומאתה אבל טמאה היא על גב רוקה נתנה שערה בפיה קפצה ידה קרצה שפתותיה כאילו לא טבלה האוחז באדם ובכלים ומטבילן טמאין ואם הדיח את ידו במים טהורים רבי שמעון אומר ירפה כדי שיבואו בהם מים בית הסתרים בית הקמטים אינן צריכין שיבואו בהן מים.

סדרי טהרה סימן קצח אות א – ולא דמי להא דקיי"ל דמדאורייתא מעוטו ומקפיד עליו אינו חוצץ דשאני התם דמ"מ הכל מכוסה במי מקוה אלא שיש על מעוטו דבר החוצץ וכיון דלא הוי על רובו בטל לגבי הגוף ולא חייץ מן התורה וכן ברוב ואין מקפיד עליו אבל כשאין כל הגוף וכל השערות מכוסים במי מקוה כאחד ואפי' כ"ש שהיה חוץ למים בשעת הטבילה מעכב והוי כאלו לא טבל.

קרית ספר הלכות מקוואות פרק ב – דברים החוצצין באדם ובכלים אינם אלא ברוב הגוף מדאוריתא ובמקפיד כדאמרינן דכיון דכתיב כל בשרו רובו ככולו וכשאינו מקפיד שיהיה בו דבר החוצץ או לא הוי נמי כבשרו ולא הויא חציצה מדאוריתא כדאמרינן רובו המקפיד ואף על גב דבעינן ראוי לביאת מים מדאוריתא בבית הסתרים כדילפינן לעיל אף על גב דהוי מיעוטו המקפיד איפשר דבית הסתרים כקרצה שפתותיה דאינו ראוי ליכנס מים בפיה הויא חציצה טפי שמכוונת לקרוץ ושלא יכנסו המים וכדתנן פרק ח' כאלו לא טבלה ממעוטו המקפיד שלא היה רוצה בקיומו אי נמי שרוחקת שפתותיה ביותר ומתכסה הבשר החיצון אי נמי איפשר דהא דבעינן בית הסתרים ראוי לביאת מים מדאוריתא היינו כשיש דבר חוצץ בגופו ובהאי חציצה דבית הסתרים מצטרף לרוב ואין חציצה בשיעור אא"כ היה רוב שערו כל נימא קשורה בפני

עצמה לדעת הגאונים ז"ל ולדעת הרב ז"ל אפילו כל שערותיו קשורות אחד אחד לא הויא חציצה אלא א"כ מצטרף לדבר אחר החוצץ בגופו והוי רוב ואם הוא מקפיד הוי דאוריתא וכדאמרינן ושער דאית ביה חציצה ילפינן לה פרקא קמא דעירובין דכתיב את כל בשרו את הטפל לבשרו וזהו שיער וכי אתאי הלכתא דאמרינן חציצין הלכה למשה מסיני היינו לרובו ולמיעוטו למקפיד ושאינו מקפיד דגלי אקרא דחציצת בשר ושיער לא הויא אלא ברובו המקפיד וכדאמרינן.

שו"ת אגרות משה אורח חיים חלק ה סימן כח – ג. בדברי החזון איש שרחובות החוצים זה את זה נחשבים כרשות היחיד מן התורה, משום שנידונים בעומד מרובה על הפרוץ.

וטעם השני שהחזון איש בהלכות עירובין סימן ק"ז אות ה' סובר דעומד מרובה על הפרוץ לית לו שיעורא, שלכן כרכים הגדולים הן בדין רה"י מדאורייתא. שכיון שאיכא רחובות הולכין לאורך העיר ולרוחב העיר, שחלק הבנוי הוא יותר מרוחב הרחוב אף ברחובות היותר רחבים, הרי גם מקום הפרוץ שהוא רוחב הרחוב כעומד דמי, שא"כ הוא מוקף מחיצות מכל ד' הרוחות לכו"ע אף לאלו שלא מצריכין ס' ריבוא עוברין. הוא דבר תמוה, שנמצא שהכרכים היותר גדולים הם רה"י, ורק הכפרים ועיירות הקטנים ביותר שאין להם אלא רחוב מפולש אחד הוא בדין רה"ר. להיפוך מכפי שכל ישראל סבורין שהכרכין שייכין להיות יותר רה"ר. וכדכתב הוא בעצמו שבמשנה ברורה (סימן שמ"ה סעיף ח' ביאור הלכה ד"ה שאין ששים) כתב שלא כדבריו, ודברי המ"ב הוא שיטת כל ישראל בפשיטות.

ועוד הא וודאי גם במדבר שהיו ישראל שרויין במשך י"ב מיל על י"ב מיל, הרי ודאי היו רחובות רחבים ט"ז אמה בין ממזרח למערב בין מדרום לצפון, ומקום האוהלים היו יותר מט"ז אמה רוחב. דהא אין לומר כלל שהיו הרחובות המפולשין כולן עוברים רק בכיוון אחד, דלא היה שייך להגיע למשכן ולמקום משה רק מהרחוב הסמוך למשכן. דהא וודאי לא הלכו דרך החצרות דהיו החצרות מתבטלות מתשמישי הצניעות שלהן, שבלעם היה משבחן בזה, כיון שהרבה אינשי היו עוברין דרך החצרות. ואף שהרה"ר היה רק אצל משה, אבל כיון שמקום מחנה ישראל היה נחשב כמוקף מחיצות, והמחנה דישראל הא היה לארבע רוחות המשכן, שאם זה שהבנוי היה מרובה על מדת הרחוב היה כמחיצה גם במקום הרחוב, הרי היה נמצא שמחנה לויה שהיה באמצע נמי היתה מוקפת במחיצות, ולא שייך שיהיה אף מחנה לויה רה"ר (ולכאורה תמוה, שהרי החזון איש עצמו שם, שלל אפשרות זו, וכתב שבשני רחובות החוצים זה את זה, לא שייך עומד מרובה, כיון דאין כאן מחיצות, ולא שייך עומד אלא אי העומד יעשה רשות היחיד לעצמו – היינו שיש לאחד הרחובות שלוש מחיצות מצד עצמו, על ידי עומד מרובה – אבל אם אינו עושה לעצמו, אינו עושה לאחרים, עיי"ש. ולפי זה אם בדגלי מדבר היו כל הרחובות חוצים זה את זה, אבל פתוחים בקצותיהם, הרי אינם ניתרים בעומד מרובה, ושפיר חשיבי רשות הרבים. ולכאורה אין הוכחה שבדגלי מדבר היו רחובות שלא היו מפולשים כלל, אלא בעלי שלוש מחיצות. ואולי גם זה אינו מסתבר, שלא היו בדגלי מדבר מבואות שכל ייעודם היה לחבר שתי דרכים ראשיות מקבילות, ואז יש למבואות אלו אפילו ארבע מחיצות מצד עומד מרובה, כיוון שלא היו מפולשים מצד אחד של המחנה לצידו השני, וממילא שוב הוו דגלי מדבר רשות היחיד. והקשה זה החזון איש עצמו לגבי ירושלים, עיי"ש בס"ק ח').

אלא מוכרחין לומר שמקום הרחובות שנעשו דווקא לדריסת הרבים מפולש מקצה אל הקצה, לא נחשב שהוא ג"כ נחשב כגדור מצד שהוא מועט נגד העומד דמקום הבנוי, ורק בפרצה בעלמא שלא נעשתה לדריסת הרבים נחשב כגדור מהא דעומד מרובה, דלא כהחזו"א אלא כהמ"ב, ופשיטותא דכל ישראל.

חזון איש הלכות עירובין סימן קז אות ה – ונראה דכל שיש ג' מחיצות של עומ"ר לא אמרינן תו דאתו רבים ומבטלי מחיצתא וכו' ולפ"ז בצורה הזאת לא תמצא רה"ר אף בחוצות רחבות טז אמה וס' רבוא בוקעים בהם שרחוב ב' היא רה"י גמורה מה"ת שיש לה ג' מחיצות עומ"ר אף שרחוב א' וג' עוברות בפרצותיה ורבים בוקעין בהן לא מבטלי מחיצתא.

רמב"ם הלכות מקוואות פרק ב הלכה יא – האוחז באדם ובכלים והטבילן הרי הן בטומאתן, ואע"פ שרפה ידיו עד שבאו בהן המים גזירה שמא לא ירפה, ואם הדיח ידיו במים עלתה להן טבילה.

תורת הבית הארוך בית ז שער ז – האוחז באדם וכלים ומטבילן טמאים. ואם הדיח ידיו במים טהורין. ר' שמעון אומר ירפה שיבואו בהן המים. פירוש לתנא קמא די אם הדיחה ידה במים מפני שמשקה שעל ידיו טופח להטפיח ומתחבר במי המקוה ואין כאן חציצה ור"ש מחמיר ומצריך שירפה ידיו שיבואו בהן המים. כנ"ל.

משמרת הבית על תורת הבית בית ז שער ז – עוד שם שנינו במקוואות האוחז באדם וכלים ומטבילן וכו' אמר הכותב: משענתו משענת הקנה הרצוץ דמאי שנא אוחז באדם דגזרינן רפוי אטו מהודק ומאי שנא באריסא דעל צואר העבד דלא גזרינן, וכן השירים והנזמים והטבעות והקטלאות. דתניא בתוספתא אוצין חוצצין רפויין אין חוצצין דאלמא לא גזרינן. ובאמת דקאמר כחולם חלום דאריסא לא חיישינן אבל באדם שחברו נשען על ידו איכא שפיר למגזר קול דברים שמענו טעם לא שמענו. ועוד דאי באדם משום נשען על ידו, מה נעשה לכלים ששנו במשנה מקוואות ומאן אדם חברו נשען על ידו איכא. ולפיכך פירש המחבר דתנא קמא לקולא ור' שמעון לחומרא עד שירפה את ידו ויעלו שם מים להדיא דאי לאו הכי כיון שהוא עשוי לדחוק את ידיו על האדם והכלים שהוא מטביל הוה ליה כטבעת אוצין וליכא חבור אפילו במשקה טופח ואינו דומה לרגלי הטובל שע"ג קרקע המקוה דהתם כיון שהמים קדמו ועדיין איכא משקה טופח מחובר למקוה לא הוי חציצה אבל כאן סבר רבי שמעון שדרך האוחז בכלים להטבילן שדוחק ידיו עליהן כדי שלא יפלו מידו וכן אוחז בחבירו כדי שלא יפחד להשתקע במים דרכו לדחוק ידיו עליו וימנע מהיות המשקה שעל ידו חבור כלל למקוה ותנא קמא לא חייש להכי ואיכא משקה טופח מחובר ואין כאן חציצה. והוא שכתב שהמים מקדימים ומבטלי לחציצה, לשון נערות הוא דלא שייך כאן ביטול חציצה אלא שאין [דף לג עמוד א] כאן חציצה דמשקה טופח הוי חבור. וקיימא לן כתנא קמא דאין צריך לרפות, אלא אפילו מרפה את ידיו כל שהדיח ידיו תחילה ואינו דוחק הרבה עלתה להן טבילה וטהורין.

שולחן ערוך יורה דעה הלכות נדה סימן קצח סעיף כח – לא תאחוז בה חבירתה בידיה בשעת טבילה לה אלא אם כן רפתה ידה, כדי שיבואו המים במקום אחיזת ידיה; ואם הדיחה ידיה במים תחלה, שרי, שמשקה לח טופח שעל ידיה חבור למי המקוה.

ש"ך יורה דעה סימן קצח: לה–לו – אא"כ רפתה כו' – והב"ח פסק כהרמב"ם והרמב"ן דאפי' ברפתה לא עלתה לה טבילה גזרה אטו לא רפתה ואע"ג דבעלמא לא גזרינן ברפוי הכא שאני דמתוך שהוא בהול ומתפחד פן ישמט מידיו הוא דוחק את ידיו עליו שלא במתכוין ע"כ וכ"כ הרא"ה בס' ב"ה דף ק"ן ע"ב דהכא באוחז בחבירו שחבירו נשען עליו עשוי הוא ומצוי שלא ירפה ושפיר שייך למגזר עכ"ל מיהו בה"ג דפ"ה ע"ב גורס ר"ש אומר עד שירפה כו' והיינו כפי' הרשב"א דאסיפא פליג ודוק.

ואם הדיחה כו' – כתב הדרישה מכאן יש היתר גמור שבשעה שהאשה טובלת וחברתה דחפה במים שיכולה לאחזה בידה בשעת דחיפה אם הדיחה ידיה במים תחלה וא"צ להפריד ידיה ממנה ולא כמו שנוהגין נשי דידן שמפרידין ידיהם ממנה בשעת דחיפה עכ"ל ולפע"ד אין להורות קולא בדברים שנהגו איסור דהלא במשנה ופוסקים אינו אלא דבדיעבד שרי אבל לכתחלה מאן לימא לן ועוד דבכמה וכמה דברים מחמירים לענין נדה שלא מן הדין ואפילו דיעבד כ"ש הכא ועוד שהרי מהר"ר ישראל ברי"ן חולק ואוסר הכא אף בהדיחה ידיה ואף המשאת בנימין שחולק עליו י"ל דמודה לכתחלה מיהו באשה שאינה יכולה לעמוד על רגליה פסק בתשובת משאת בנימין שם סימן פ"א דיש לטובלה ע"י שתאחזנה שתי נשים בזרועותיה וידיחו ידיהם תחילה במים עד שיהא טופח על מנת להטפיח אבל אין לה תקנה שישכיבוה על הסדין ויטבילוה דסדין מקבל טומאה ואסור (כדלקמן סעיף ל"א) עכ"ד ע"ש.

מרדכי מסכת עבודה זרה פרק השוכר את הפועל – ורבינו מאיר [רמז תתס] היה מורה להטביל כלי בתוך כלי [בבאר] ובלבד שיהו המים צפין ע"פ החיצון ושיהא פי החיצון כשפופרת הנוד כדמשמע מתני' דפ"ו דמקוואות השידה והתיבה שבים והכי אמרינן פרק חומר בקדש מטבילין כלי בתוך כלי לתרומה אבל לא לקדש גם הורו שיש לאדם ליזהר אם יטביל לזכוכית מלא מים ויתנהו בדלי מלא מים והדלי שקוע בבור שלא יושיבוהו על שוליו פן יהיה חציצה מחמת כובדו של כלי וחוצץ כדאמרינן פרק חומר בקדש אלא יטהו על צדו ויתגלגל הנה והנה בתוך הכלי בבור ואין להקשות מ"ש מפרסת רגל אדם העומד בקרקע במקוה ואין חוצץ משום דאמרינן שהמים באין לשם טרם יתן רגלו בארץ כדתנן פ"ז הטביל בו את המטה אע"פ שרגליה שוקעות בטיט העבה כשרה מפני שהמים מקדימין דיש לומר דוקא במקוה שלם שהם מחוברים אבל *כשנותן הזכוכית בדלי אפילו מלא מים אינו מועיל כי הם תלושין וגם יש ליזהר בהא דתנן פ"ק דמקוואות האוחז באדם ובכלים ומטבילן טמאים.

שולחן ערוך יורה דעה הלכות הכשר וטבילת כלים סימן קכ סעיף ב – צריך שיהא הכלי רפוי בידו בשעת טבילה, שאם מהדקו בידו הוי חציצה. ואם לחלח ידו במים תחלה, אין לחוש. ודוקא שלחלח ידיו במי מקוה, אבל לא במים תלושים). (כ"מ ממרדכי פרק השוכר).

שולחן ערוך יורה דעה הלכות נדה סימן קצח סעיף מח – נדה שטבלה בלא כוונה, כגון שנפלה לתוך המים או שירדה להקר, הרי זו מותרת לבעלה. הגה: ויש מחמירין ומצריכין אותה טבילה אחרת (ב"י בשם רשב"א ור' ירוחם ורוקח והגהות אשיר"י); ויש להחמיר לכתחלה. יש שכתבו שיש לאשה להיות צנועה בליל טבילתה, וכן נהגו הנשים להסתיר ליל טבילתן שלא לילך במהומה או בפני הבריות, שלא ירגישו בהן בני אדם; ומי שאינה עושה כן, נאמר עליה: ארור שוכב עם בהמה (דברים כז, כא). ויש לנשים ליזהר כשיוצאות מן הטבילה שיפגע בה חברתה, שלא יפגע בה תחילה דבר טמא או חיה ובהמה; סא ואם פגעו בה דברים אלו, אם היא יראת שמים תחזור ותטבול (ש"ד וכל בו ורוקח). ועיין לקמן סוף סימן ר"א אם מותר להטיל חמין למקוה או אם מותר לרחוץ אחר הטבילה.

שו"ת אגרות משה יורה דעה חלק ב סימן עז – ומטעם שהוא כבזיון לה ויש בזה משום כבוד הבריות לא חששו, משום שאין בזה בזיון כ"כ דידוע לכל שהנשים הן נדות י"ב יום בכל חדש כשאינן זקנות ולא מעוברות וצריכין להתרחק מבעליהן באיזה דברים, ואדרבה הא הרבה היו לובשות בגדים מיוחדים לימי הנדות ומזה היו יודעות השכנות שהיא נדה אלמא שלא היו מתביישות בזה.

ערוך השולחן יורה דעה הלכות נדה סימן ר סעיף א – כל אשה חייבת לברך בעת טבילתה ואפילו היושבת על הכתם דהוא מדרבנן מברכת אשר קדשנו במצותיו וצונו על הטבילה דגם על דרבנן שייך וצונו כדכתיב לא תסור מן הדבר אשר יגידו לך וגו' [שבת כ"ג א] ואפילו היושבת על דם טוהר דאינו אלא מנהגא בעלמא מברכת כיון דכל ישראל קבלו עליהם חומרא זו ולא גרע מהלל דר"ח מברכין [עי' תוס' ברכות י"ד ד"ה ימים] ואפי' על ספק כתם מברכת ואין טבילה בלא ברכה לבד כשטבלה ואח"כ חוזרת וטובלת מפני איזה חומרא כגון ששכחה ליטול צפורן וכיוצא בזה טובלת בלא ברכה.

שו"ת חתם סופר חלק ב (יורה דעה) סימן קצא – שלום להרב המופלג בתורה וביראה כבוד מוהר"ר דוד כ"ץ ני' אבדק"ק רעטע יע"א.

אשר אמר שנשאל רבו הגאון בנב"י זצ"ל אם לברך על הטבילה שטובלת היולדת תוך מלאות דהיינו מ' לזכר ופ' לנקבה כיון שאינה אלא ממנהג שנהגו להחמיר שלא לבעול על דם טוהר ולא השיב דבר ברור נחזי אנן התוס' דברכות פ' הי' קורא י"ד ע"ב כ' בשם ר"ת דמברך על הלל דר"ח אע"ג דהוא מנהגא וכן כתב הרא"ש שם ותר"י וחי' רשב"א וכ"כ תוס' בסוכה נ"ד ע"ב ור"ן שם ובתעני' פ' בתרא בתוס' ע"ש וכ' דלא דמי לחביט חביט ולא בריך משום דהוה מנהג נביאים ואמנהגא לא מברכי' והתם היינו טעמא משום דחבטא בעלמא הוא ואמנהג כי האי לא מברכי' ומיהו בתוס' דסוכה כתבו דהלל שייך וציונו טפי כיון שהוא כקורא בתורה רצו לומר דשייך עכ"פ וציונו שהרי ציוה הקב"ה ללמוד תורה וגם הלל בכלל נראה דלרווחא אמלתא כתבו כן אפי' נימא קריאת הלל נמי דמי לחבטא דמעשה זוטא הוא מ"מ שפיר דמי לברך וציונו משום שהוא כקורא בתורה אבל לעולם יודו התוס' דאמנהגא דמעשה רבא מברכי'.

ומ"ש התוס' דמי"ט שני של גליות דמקדשי' ומזכירי' בתפלה אע"ג שאינו אלא מנהגא אין ראי' משום שאינו אומר וציונו ע"ש לא זכיתי להבין מה לי אם אומר וציונו וה' לא ציוה או אם אומר את יום חג פלוני הזה ואינינו אותו היום ותרויי' מחזי כשיקרא וע"כ יפה כח המנהג א"כ ה"נ ותו אף על גב דכ' תוס' דמציונו דתקיעת שופר אין ראי' משום דר"ה לאו ממנהגא הוא אלא מעיקור התקנה מ"מ מציונו דאכילת מרור דליל שני של פסח לא תירצו כלום האמת כי הרא"ש דברכות והר"ן דסוכה מייתי ראי' מציונו דאכילת מצה דליל שני של פסח ולזה י"ל קצת דס"ל כשיטת החזקוני על התורה דמצוה איכא באכילת מצה כל שבעה אע"ג דהיא רשות ואי בעי לא אכיל כלל ומש"ה אין מברכי' כל ז' על מצה מ"מ אי אכיל מצוה קעביד וכבר עשיתי לו סמוכי' בחידושי וא"כ נהי דבעלמא אין מברך על מצה מ"מ בליל י"ט שני שייך לומר וציונו דלא גרע מקריאת הלל שכ' תוס' דשייך וציונו כיון דאיכא מצוה כקורא בתורה אף ע"ג דאי לאו מנהגא דר"ח לא הי' מברך על מצות קריאת הלל אף עפ"י שהוא כקורא בתורה וק"ל.

וכן צ"ע שלא זכרו מברכת וציונו להדליק נר של י"ט מיהו לזה י"ל דאפשר ס"ל להחולקי' על ר"ת כדעת הסוברים דאפי' בי"ט ראשון ובשבת נמי אין מברכי' על הדלקת נר עיי' בתוס' דמס' שבת כ"ה ע"ב ד"ה חובה וכו' ע"ש אך ממרור צע"ג.

איברא מהא דכ' בד"מ והגה' ש"ע א"ח סס"י ת"ץ שלא לברך על קריאת המגילות כיון שאינם רק מנהגא ע"ש עיינתי בגוף שו"ת רמ"א סי' ל"ה ובכל אריכות דבריו לא מצאתי דבר ראוי לסמוך עליו וכבר האריך הלבוש לחלוק ובאליה רבה העלה לברך עכ"פ בלי שם ומלכות וכן הסכים בפרי מגדים ומה שנלע"ד בזה לחלק בין קריאת הלל למגילו' הללו לפמ"ש לעיל דמשמע מתוס' דסוכה דלא ברירה להו שיהי' קריאת הלל מעשה רבא לברך עליו אם לא משום שהוא כקריא' התורה והנה בשלמא הלל שעיקור קריאתו לשיר לא איכפת לן במה שאינו כתוב על הספר ובדיו על הגליון דאפי' אם נימא דפוס הוי ככתיב' מ"מ גליון בעי עמג"א סי' רפ"ד ולע"ד נראה דכל שירי תהילות נאמרים בעל פה דמעיקרא הכי נתקנו דלא נראה שהיו הלוים משוררים בבהמ"ק מתוך הספר או שיהי' עושי הפסח קוראים הלל מתוך הספר וא"כ מעיקרא הכי אתקין ושפיר מברכי' על ההלל כקורא בתורה ובתשוב' חו"י לא עמד בזה משא"כ המגלות הללו אלו הי' מברכי' עליהם הי' צריכים לכותבו בגליון ומעיקרא לא הנהיגו כך שלא להטריח על הציבור וחלוק זה רמוז בתוך דברי רמ"א בתשובה הנ"ל אלא שלא ביאר כל צרכו.

והנה הרא"ש ספיה"כ שהגאון כ' לברך על הטבילה עיה"כ ודחי דבריו דלא עדיף מערבה שהוא מנהג נביאי' וחביט חביט ולא בריך דאין מברכין על מנהגא וכ"ש האי שאינו אלא משום נקיות וטהרה בעלמא להיות כמלאכי השרת ע"ש וצ"ל דס"ל דהאי טבילה לא עדיף מחביטא דערבה דהוה טלטול בעלמא ולא מינכר מצותו כמו הלל שהרי הרא"ש פסק לברך על הלל כר"ת ולא הזכיר כלל טעם דקורא בתורה ולית ליה אלא האי חלוקא דחביטת ערבה ליכא אלא טלטול בעלמא מה שאין כן הלל וצריך לומר דהך טבילה להא דמי' ועיין טור א"ח סי' תר"ו וצ"ע ממ"ש הרא"ש שם להלן דמקום שנהגו להדליק נר ביה"כ מברכי' עליו כמו בשבת ועיין טור וב"י / או"ח/ סי' תר"ו דהחולקים ס"ל שאין לברך אמנהגא וא"כ צריך לומר דהדלקת נר ביה"כ עדיף מטבילה זו דעיה"כ וצריך טעם לחלק ולא ראיתי מי שיתעורר בזה.

היוצא מזה לפי מה דקיי"ל לברך על הלל ועל י"ט ב' דגליות ובפרט על אכילת מרור ועל הדלקת נר בי"ט ב' וביה"כ א"כ יש לברך ג"כ על טבילת הטובלת על דם טוהר דלידה דאין לך מעשה רב מזה דאפי' אי טבילה עיה"כ מעשה זוטא הוא מ"מ הך מנהגא לספור ז' נקיים ולבדוק ולנהוג כל דיני נדה בודאי מעשה רב הוא ומברכי' על הטבילה וכעין ראי' לזה ממה דאר"ז בנות ישראל הן החמירו על עצמן שאפילו רואות טפת דם כחרדל יושבת עליו ז' נקיים וכו' ת"ר יונה בברכות דיש מפורשים כחרדל ר"ל כמראה החרדל וס"ל דמראה טהורה היא בודאי ואפ"ה החמירו על עצמו ור' יונה השיב עליהם ועיי' ר"ן הלכו' נדה ופ' בני העיר נמצא לפי הי"מ הללו הנהיגו עצמן לספור שבעה נקיים על מראה טהורה שהי' ברי להם שהיא טהורה ובלי ספק שברכו על טבילתם דלא לשתמיט שום פוסק לומר שלא יברכו אע"כ כנ"ל דמעשה רבא כהאי מנהגא צריך ברכה לכולי עלמא.

עוד לאלוה מילין דצריך חקירה מ"ש דבמצוה דרבנן שייך לברך וציונו ואמרי' פ' במה מדליקי' היכן ציונו שאל אביך ויגדך או לא תסור ומ"ש מנהגא דקיי"ל דחיובא איכא לקיים מנהגא מדברי קבלה דכתי' אל תטוש תורת אמך כמבואר ר"פ מקום שנהגו דאמר ר' יוחנן לבני בישן אל תטוש תורת אמך ואסר להו למיזל מצור לצידן בע"ש מהאי טעמא א"כ אמאי לא יברך עליהם ויאמר וציונו לקיים אל תטוש תורת אמך והרי מנדין על העובר על מנהגא ועושה מלאכה בי"ט ב' וא"כ אמאי תמהו באומר וציונו.

תו קשי' לי ר"פ מקום שנהגו דנהגו להפריש חלה מארוזא ואמר רב יוסף ליכול זר באפיהו דלמא אתי לאפרושי מן החיוב על הפטור וכ' תוס' דמיירי שלא היה מנהג בטעות דהמנהיגים ידעו שהוא פטור ורק הנהיגו כן להחמיר על עצמם ואפ"ה שייך דלמא אתי לאיפרושי מפטור על החיוב דאיכא אינשי דלא ידעי' וסברי דאורז חייב בחלה מן התורה וצ"ע לדעת החולקים על רבנו תם וס"ל דעל שום מנהג אין מברכי' א"כ הכא ע"כ לא ברכו על חלת האורז להפריש חלה שהרי ידעו שפטור מן התורה רק הם הנהיגו כן מעצמם א"כ איך יבואו לטעות להפריש מפטור על החיוב הא יש להם היכר שאין מברכי' אע"כ צריך לומר שהם ברכו להפריש חלה ואי ס"ד שלא כדין עשו בזה לברך אמנהגא א"כ יפה אמר ר' יוסף ליכול זר באפיהו ומה פריך עליו הא דברים מותרים ואחרים נהגו בהן אי אתה רשאי להתירן בפניהם הא ע"כ היה צריך דתיכלינהו זר באפיהו משום שברכו ברכ' לבטל' וצ"ע.

והנלע"ד בישוב ק' זו דודאי מנהגא בשב ואל תעשה לאסור דבר מה כגון שלא ללכת מצור לצידן בע"ש ושלא לעשות מלאכה בערב פסח ובי"ט שני העובר על זה וקם ועשה מה שנאסר במנהגא ה"ז עובר על לאו דדברי קבלה אל תטוש תורת אמך וכן האוכל חלב דאייתרא וכן במקום שנהגו להפריש חלה מארוזא הם נהגו לאסור העיסה ולעשותו טבל טבול לחלה והאוכלו בטבלו עובר על לא תטוש תורת אמך א"כ ממילא המפריש חלה מארוזא מקיים מצות אל תטוש הנ"ל ומברך וציונו בלי פקפוק וכן נמי י"ט שני שהעושה בו מלאכה מנדין אותו משום שעובר אהנ"ל א"כ ממילא מחייב מדין גמור גם בכל העשין התלוין בו להדליק נר ולאכול מצה ומרור ושייך וציונו וגם לומר את חג פלוני הזה כיון שמנהיגיו מחוייבי' בו מדינא ולא צריך למה שנדחקו בתוס' מציונו דשופר וכל זה בל"ת אבל בקיום עשה כגון מנהג נביאים דערב' אי שב

ולא עשה ולא חביט ערבה אפשר דלא מיקרי עבריין ואין מנדין אותו ולא נאמר על זה אל תטוש תורת אמך משו"ה המקיימו אינו מברך וציונו דהיכן ציונו ואולי בהא פליגי ר"ת והגאוני' דאינהו ס"ל בכל קום ועשה לא שייך אל תטוש וליכא וציונו ור"ת ס"ל מה דלא מינכר מצותו כולי האי הוא דליכא משום אל תטוש כגון טלטול דערבה אבל מצוה דמינכר מצוותו ואיכא מעשה רבה אית בי' משום בל תטוש ומברכים וצונו ואתי' הכל על נכון בעזה"י.

וראיתי בחי' ריטב"א לסוכה מ"ד ע"ש שכ' וז"ל קסבר מנהג נביאים פי' וכיון שאין למנהג עיקור ותקנת חכמי' לנהוג בו אין מברכי' עליו אבל מנהג מצות דרבנן מברכי' עליהם כמו שאנו מברכי' ומקדשי' בי"ט ב' בזה"ז שחייבונו חכמים לנהוג בו מנהג אבותינו ובהכי מפרק לן שפיר מאי דקשיא לרבנן בהא דרב איקלע לבבל וחזי דקרו להלל בר"ח וכו' שמעינן מינה שמברכין על הלל דר"ח אע"פ שהוא ממנהגא ומחוורתא כדפרישנא דשאני התם דאיכ' תקנתא דרבנן למקרי הלל בר"ח במקו' שנהגו בו ע"ש ולא זכיתי להבין דברי' אלו היכן תקנו חכמי' הלל בר"ח הא רב לא ידע מזה מאומ' ואולי כיוון למה שכתבתי אני ועדיין צ"ע ומ"מ מה שכתבתי נראה לי נכון בעז"הי וא"כ בנדון דידן נמי כיון שהנהיגו איסור לבעול על דם טוהר והעובר על זה עובר על בל תטוש תורת אמך בלי ספק א"כ הטבילה היא מדינא ובעי' ברכה באמת והכי נהוג הנלע"ד כתבתי. משה"ק סופר מפפ"דמ.

תוספות מסכת פסחים דף ז עמוד ב – על הטבילה – אומר ר"ח בשם הגאון דוקא בטבילת גר דלא חזי קודם טבילה דלא מצי למימר וצונו דאכתי נכרי הוא אבל שאר חייבי טבילה כגון בעל קרי וכיוצא בו מותר לברך כדאמרינן בפ' מי שמתו (ד' כב.) נהוג עלמא כתלתא סבי כר' יהודה בבעל קרי שיכול להתפלל ולברך וללמוד קודם טבילה אעפ"כ אומר ר"י דאין לגעור בנשים שמברכות אחר הטבילה כיון דאיכא טבילת גר דלא מצי לברך לא חילקו וכן בנטילת ידים לא חילקו בין נטילה של אחר בית הכסא דלא מצי לברך קודם מיהו בנטילה יש טעם אחר לברך אחר נטילה קודם ניגוב כדאמרינן (סוטה ד' ד:) האוכל לחם בלא ניגוב ידים כאילו אוכל לחם טמא וי"מ דבכל טבילות קאמר דגברא לא חזי דקודם שירד למים אינו צריך לברך דילמא משום ביעתותא דמיא מימנע ולא טביל ואחר שיורד אז הוא ערום ואסור לברך משום דלבו רואה את הערוה.

שולחן ערוך יורה דעה הלכות נדה סימן ר סעיף א – כשפושטת מלבושיה, כשעומדת בחלוקה, תברך: אשר קדשנו במצותיו וצונו על הטבילה, ותפשוט חלוקה ותטבול; ואם לא ברכה אז, תברך לאחר שתכנס עד צוארה במים; ואם הם צלולים, עוכרתן ברגליה ומברכת. הגה: ויש אומרים שלא תברך עד אחר הטבילה (טור בשם בעל הלכות גדולות והוא בה"ג דף פ"ה ע"ב ורש"י ורמב"ן סימן שכ"ח וש"ד), וכן נוהגים שלאחר הטבילה, בעודה עומדת תוך המים, מכסית עצמה בבגדה או בחלוקה, ומברכת.

ש"ך יורה דעה סימן ר:א – מכסית עצמה בבגדה כו' – ועכשיו נהגו שלא לכסות עצמה כלל ולברך וקרא עליהם תגר הדרישה דאפי' חיבוק זרועותיה לא מהני אלא להפסיק שלא יהא לבן רואה

את הערוה אבל באשה לא שייך לבן רואה את הערוה כמ״ש הא״ח וז״ל נראה שהנשים יכולות לברך ולהתפלל כשהן לבושות בחלוקן אע״פ שאינן מפסיקות למטה מן החזה לפי שערותן למטה מאד ואין לבן רואה ערוה ולא בעי טוחות בקרקע אלא כשהן ערומות כדי שתתכסה ערותן עכ״ל ומביאו ב״י בא״ח סי׳ ע״ד ופסקו בש״ע שם סעיף ד׳ (וכ״נ דעת הרב שם וכ״כ העט״ז שם בסתם) ואם כן צריך שיהיו המים עכורים דמים צלולים כמי שאינם דמי עכ״ד וגם הב״ח בקונטרס אחרון השיג על הא״ח מהש״ס דפ׳ מי שמתו (דף כ״ד ע״א) גבי עגבות והעלה דבאשה שייך נמי טעמא דלבן רואה ערוה וה״ט דהפוסקים דכתבו הכא דצריך שיהיו המים עכורים וחבוק זרועותיה לא הוי הפסק כלל ואם כן צריך שיהיו המים עכורים או שתלבש חלוקה ולשים ישה על החלוק למטה מלבה דאז הוי הפסק ושארי ליה מאריה להדרישה שנסמך להקל על מ״ש הא״ח דמשמעות הש״ס וכל הפוסקים דלא כוותיה עכ״ד ואענה אני חלקי דודאי נשי דידן נשים חכמניות הן וצדקניות הן דמה שדחה הב״ח דברי הא״ח מהש״ס דפ׳ מי שמתו וכתב על הדרישה שארי ליה מאריה כו׳ התפלל על אחרים והוא צריך לאותו דבר כי איך יעלה על הדעת דהך דהאשה יושבת וקוצה לה חלתה ערומה (אבל עומדת לא וכן האיש לא משום דאף ביושב אין ערותו מכוסה) טעמא משום לבה רואה את הערו׳ וליכ׳ טעמא אחרינא במלתא א״כ בסוף מי שמתו הביאו בתוס׳ והפוסקי׳ מחלוקת אי קי״ל לבו רואה את הערוה אסור או מותר וכתבו דרש״י וקצת פוסקים פסקו דמותר כת״ק די״א בברייתא והא תנן בפ״ב דחלה דאסור לברך ערום משום לבו רואה את הערוה וכן בפ״ק דתרומות דתנן הערום לא יתרום ומפרש טעמא בירושלמי מפני שאינו יכול לברך ערום ואי ס״ד דטעמא משום לבו רואה את הערוה כמו שעלה על דעת הב״ח היכן יתכן לפסוק לבו רואה את הערוה מותר והלא תרתי סתמי דמתני דאסור אע״ג דבברייתא ס״ל לת״ק דמותר ה״ל סתם מתני׳ ומחלוקת דברייתא דהלכה כסתם מתני׳ וכ״ש הכא דאיכא תרי סתמא אלא ודאי הך דחלה ותרומה טעמא לאו משום לבו רואה את הערוה אלא דאפי׳ לבו מכוסה אסור משום גילוי ערוה כדאמרי׳ בס״פ מי שמתו ולא יראה בך ערות דבר אמר רחמנא ונ״ל דבמים צלולים ליכא משום גילוי ערוה והכי מוכח בש״ס ס״פ מי שמתו דפריך אהא דתנן בידר לטבול יתכסה במים ויקרא והרי לבו רואה את הערוה אמר רבי אליעזר במים עכורים שנו דדמיא כארעא סמיכתא ע״כ והשתא אי ס״ד דמים צלולים לא חשיבי כיסוי ערוה למה ליה לאהדורי אפירכא אחריני ולאקשויי והרי לבו רואה את הערוה דלאו קושיא מעליותא היא דאיכא לשנויי קסבר לבו רואה את הערוה מותר וכתנא דברייתא תקשי ליה בפשיטות מיניה וביה דקתני יתכסה במים ויקרא ומאי מהני כיסוי אלא פשיטא ליה דכסוי מהני אפי׳ במים צלולים דמכל מקום ליכא משום ולא יראה בך ערות דבר כיון שעיניו חוץ למים אבל משום לבו רואה את הערוה פריך שפיר כיון דלבו ברשות א׳ עם הערוה ונ״ל ראי׳ לדברי ממ״ש הרשב״א בחידושיו וז״ל והלא לבו רואה את הערוה כלומר שהוא עם הערוה בתוך המים אבל לעיניו רואות את הערוה ליכא למיחש דכיון שעיניו חוץ למים ומסתכל בחוץ אינו רואה את הערוה ואוקימנא בעכורים הראב״ד ז״ל עכ״ל וכ״כ הר״ר יונה ז״ל ומביאם ב״י בא״ח סי׳ ע״ד והכי מוכח נמי התם בש״ס דגרסינן ת״ר מים צלולים ישב בהן עד צוארו וקורא וי״א עוכרן ברגליו ות״ק והרי לבו רואה את הערוה קסבר לבו רואה את הערוה מותר ע״כ הרי דלת״ק אע״ג דלבו רואה את הערוה

מותר ישב בהן עד צוארו ויקרא משום ולא יראה בך ערות דבר ואפ"ה מהני צלולים ניחא השתא דתנא ברא לא פליג אתרתי סתמא דתרומה וחלה וניחא נמי השתא הא דכתב רבי' יונה בשם רבני צרפת אירד לטבול דחיבוק זרועותיו מהני דהקשה בדרישה דסוף סוף הערוה מגולה ועוד אמאי לא משני ש"ס הכי וע"כ הוצרך לדחוק דרבי' יונה קאי ארוחץ בכלי ועם כל זה לפירושו מאי דפריך והלא לבו רואה את הערוה לאו קושיא היא דחיבוק מהני אלא דעיקר קושיתו דהערוה מגולה ועומדת והאי קושיא אחריתא וס"ס לא קשיא והרי לבו רואה את הערוה ולפי מ"ש ניחא דבמים צלולים ליכא משום גילוי ערוה והא דלא משני ש"ס הכי היינו משום דש"ס פריך אתנא דמתניתין דקתני יתכסה במים ויקרא דמשמע דכסוי דמים הוי תקנתא ותו לא צריך תקנתא אחריתא והרי לבו רואה את הערוה וליכא תקנתא בהא וליכא לשנויא בחובק זרועותיו דאם כן ה"ל להתנא לפרושי דמיירי בהכי ומדנקט סתמא יתכסה במים משמע דבא לומר דבמים בלחוד סגי ואין להקשות על התנא גופיה אמאי לא נקיט תקנתא דחיבוק יש לומר דחדא מנייהו נקיט אי נמי דבמים נמי הוי תקנתא לגלוי ערוה מה שאין כן בחיבוק והלכך נקט תקנתא דשוה לתרווייהו ודוק והשתא אתי שפיר הא דכתב הרב בא"ח סי' ע"ד סעיף ב' ואם אין לבו תוך המים רק למעלה מן המים אף בצלולים שרי ע"כ הוצרך הדרישה לדחוק עצמו ולפרש דמיירי שרוחץ בכלי דליכא גלוי ערוה וז"א במשמע ועוד דהא הרשב"א והראב"ד והר"ר יונה (והרב הוציא דין זה מהם כמ"ש הדרישה גופיה) מיירי להדיא בירד לטבול אלא ודאי כדפרישית דכיון שעיניו חוץ למים ומסתכל בחוץ ליכא משום גלוי ערוה (ואע"ג דבערוה בעששית אמרינן התם בס"פ מי שמתו שאסור לקרות ק"ש כנגדה הא מפרש התם טעמא ולא יראה בך ערות דבר אמר רחמנא והא קמתחזיא) והשתא בע"כ מ"ש הראב"ד כאן דעוכרתן ברגליה לאו טעמא הוא משום גלוי ערותה וכמ"ש הדרישה דהא כיון שעיניה חוץ למים אף במים צלולים שרי וכמ"ש הראב"ד גופיה אלא טעמא כמ"ש העט"ז והנ"י והב"ח משום לבה רואה את הערוה והיינו דכתב הראב"ד סתמא דתעכור המים דאי ס"ל טעמא אחרינא ה"ל לפרושי אלא ס"ל הך טעמא דס"פ מי שמתו דעוכרן משום לבו רואה את הערוה ומעתה נסתלקה תלונת הדרישה שהתרעם על המחבר והרב שקצרו כאן ובא"ח דבריהם ונתנו טעות ומכשול למעיינים בקיצור דבריהם אם כוונו למ"ש עכ"ל דודאי אם כוונו למ"ש הם קצרו דבריהם אבל למ"ש כל הדברים פשוטים וברורים וסלקא לן השתא דהראב"ד (וסייעתו) דהכא דכתב דצריך שתעכור המים חולק אהא"ח והיינו דכתב המחבר בא"ח דברי הא"ח בשם יש מי שאומר וא"כ הני נשי דידן אם אינן נביאות הן בנות נביאות הן דס"ל כהא"ח והלכך מברכות במים צלולים שעיניהם חוץ למים ומנהגן תורה היא.

ט"ז יורה דעה סימן ר (ג) – מכסית עצמה כו'. – בדרישה האריך בדין זה וכ' שהנשי' שלנו המברכות על הטביל' בעודם במים ערומות ולא מעכרי המים דלאו שפיר עבדי אף שהן מחבקים זרועותם על גופן דלפי מ"ש מהרמ"י הטעם שצריכים להיות עכורין כדי שלא יהיו לבן רואין את ערותן הי' מהני חבוק זרועותן להפסיק בין לב לערוה אבל באשה אין משום לבן רואה ערותן כיון שערותן למטה מאד וכמ"ש ב"י בשם א"ח בסי' ע"ד וז"ל נראה שהנשים יכולות לברך ולהתפלל כשהן לבושות בחלוקן אע"פ שאין מפסיקות למטה מהחזה לפי שערותן למטה מאד ולא בעי טוחות בקרקע אלא כשהן ערומות כדי שתתכסה ערותן עכ"ל משמע דבנשים האיסור

משום שעומדות ערום בלא כיסוי ערותן ולאו אורח ארעא לעשות כן מפני כבוד השכינה ואם כן מאי מהני חיבוק ידים דאי משום לבן רואות ערותן הא אין צריך באשה הפסקה וע"כ משום כבוד השכינה שלא תעמוד ערום מאי מהני בזה הפסקה בין לב לערוה. זהו תכלית דבריו שם ולעד"נ דהנשים העושות כן בחיבוק ידים הם עושות יפה אפי' לכתחלה ואפי' בלא חיבוק ידים יש להם על מה לסמוך דמ"ש שיש איסור בעמידתה ערומה משום כבוד השכינה הוא תמוה מה לו לבקש טעמים מפני כבוד השכינה והלא איסור דאורייתא מפורש הוא משום לא יראה בך ערות דבר וכמ"ש בקציצת חלה בסי' שכ"ח בי"ד שהאיש אסור לו לקצות חלה ולומר הברכה משום גילוי ערוה ובכל המקומות שאסרו להתפלל כנגד ערות חבירו וה"ה כנגד ערוה שלו אם היא מגולה אע"פ שלבו מכוסה וזהו דבר פשוט אפי' לתינוקות של בית רבן אלא דנראה פשוט ומוכח דאם האדם עומד תוך המים אפי' הם צלולים אין בזה משום גילוי ערוה ולא כדעת בעל הדרישה שס"ל כל שהמים צלולים הוה כאלו עומדת ערום וראיה מפורשת מס"פ מי שמתו במה דתנן יתכסה במים ויקרא ק"ש פרכינן והא לבו רואה את הערוה ומשנינן במים עכורים דכארעא סמיכתא הם ואי אמרת דצלולין הוה משום גילוי ערוה מאי שנא לבו דנקט המקשן דהא פלוגת' בההוא פירקא אם אסור או מותר ה"ל למפרך והא עובר משום לא ירא' בך ערות דבר דהיינו משום גילוי ערוה ואפי' אם לבו מכוסה אלא פשוט דכל שערותו מכוסה במים אע"פ שהם צלולים מכל מקום אין שם גילוי עליהם אע"ג דכשמכוין לראות במים נגד ערותו יכול לראותה מ"מ כיון דבלא מתכוין על אותו מקום לראות דרך המים אין בזה משום גילוי ערוה דומה לזה ממש מצינו בתוס' דנדרים (דף ל') העתקתי' בסי' רי"ז סעיף ל"ו דהדגים שבמים רואין החמה אלא דהחמה לא מקרי רואה אותם כיון שהם מכוסים במים וכן הוא כאן וכ"כ ב"י בא"ח סי' ע"ד בשם הרשב"א וז"ל והלא לבו רואה את הערוה כלומר שלבו עם הערוה בתוך המים אבל לעיניו רוואת את הערוה ליכא למיחש דכיון שעיניו חוץ למים ומסתכל בחוץ אינו רואה את הערוה כו' עכ"ל. הא לך דאפילו ללב רואה אין חשש אא"כ הוא עם הערוה תוך המים וכמשמעות המשנה יתכסה במים אבל אם הלב חוץ למים אין בו חשש. וכן מוכח מדברי ר"ת שהביא ב"י בא"ח סי' ע"ד כשהיה רוחץ בחמין צלולין והיה רוצה לשתות היה מכסה בבגד ממטה ללבו כדי שלא יהא לבו רואה את הערוה עכ"ל ואי הוויין צלולין (בעומד) [כעומד] ערום מה תיקן במה שכיסה לבו ובדרישה כתב דר"ת היה יושב בתוך כלי וע"כ אין בו משום גילוי ערוה ואינו נכון כלל דאף ביושב בכלי בגלוי ערוה ודאי איסור גמור הוא כל שאין שם מים דהא הוא עצמו רואה ערותו וראי' מדאמרינן פ"ק דסוכה סוף דף י' אמר שמואל הישן בכילה ערום והוא [אינו] גבוה י' יוציא ראשו חוץ לכילה ויקרא ק"ש דסבר לבו רואה הערוה מותר כ"כ התוס' נמצא לדידן אסור והוא ממש ככלי שרחץ בו ר"ת אלא ברור דאין שייכות איסור לא יראה בך ערות דבר אלא בשערותו מגולה באינו במים אז אסור כל שקורא כנגדה אא"כ במהפך פניו כמבואר בש"ע בא"ח סי' ע"ה אבל אם הוא תוך המים אין בו משום גלוי ערוה והוה כמו מהפך פנים רק שיש איסור משום לבו רואה הערוה ודמיא למי שכיסה עצמו בלבוש ולא הפסיק בין לבו לערותו וא"כ אשה הטובלת ועומדת במים אחר הטבילה ודאי מהני ההפסק שהיא עושה בידיה בין לבה לערותה כמ"ש בש"ע בא"ח סי' ע"ד היתר גמור ולכאורה היה יותר טוב שלא יכנוס לבה במים כדי שלא יהיו לבה וערותה בתוך המים וכעין שזכרתי בשם מרשב"א אלא דיותר יש צניעות שתהא כולה מכוסה

עד צואר׳ במים כמ״ש בש״ד בהל׳ נדה ואח״כ תחבק בידיה להפסיק שכבר פסק בש״ע בא״ח סי׳ ע״ד סעיף (ל״ו) [ג׳] דהוה הפסקה ואותן שעומדות במים בשעת ברכה ואינן מפסיקין בידיהם בין לב לערוה ג״כ יש להם על מי לסמוך דהיינו על הא״ח שהביא ב״י זכרתיו לעיל דבאשה אין שייך כלל לבה רואה ערותה כיון שהיא למטה מאד וע״כ תוכל לברך בשיש לה לבוש המכסה אף כשאין הפסקה בין לב לערוה תחת הלבוש ומוקי לה לההיא שאמרו בגמרא דבעינן בשעת הפרשת חלה שיהיו פניה טוחות בקרקע היינו משום גלוי ערוה כשהיא ערומה דדבר פשוט אע״פ שאין באשה משום לבה רואה ערוה אפילו כשהיא עומדת מ״מ יש גלוי ערוה בעומדת כדאיתא בפ״ק דסוטה (דף ח׳) האשה נסקלת כשהיא מכוסה מלפניה ואחריה לרבי יהודה מפני שכולה ערוה ופרש״י שבית הבושת שלה נראית מלפניה ומאחריה ועל כן בעינן בגמרא ס״פ מי שמתו לענין חלה שתהא יושבת ואפי׳ ביושבת לא סגי מפני העגבות שלה שמגולות על כן הצריכו שפניה טוחות בקרקע פי׳ דבוקות מאד בקרקע שאפי׳ עגבותיה יהיו מכוסות וא״כ באשה העומדת ויש לה לבוש המכסה ערותה ועגבותיה אף שאין הפסק בין לבה לערותה אין איסור לדעה זאת של א״ח שהביא ב״י ומו״ח ז״ל ס״ל דבעומדת אין שום איסור משום גלוי ערוה לדעת הא״ח הנ״ל וא״צ לפניה טוחות בקרקע אלא לכסות עגבותיה ועל כן הוקשה לו למאי דס״ד בגמרא שם פרק מי שמתו דבעגבות אין בהם משום ערוה למה צריכה להיות יושבת הלא בעומדת ג״כ אין איסור כיון שאין לבה רואה ערותה וע״כ דחה דעת הא״ח מן ההלכה ולא דק בזה דודאי איסור גלוי ערוה יש בה אף בעומדת וכמו שזכרנו אלא קמ״ל בעל א״ח דכל שנתכסה הערוה ועגבות ע״י לבוש אע״פ שאין הפסק בין לב לערוה אפ״ה שרי כמו ביושבת ופניה טוחות בקרקע כיון שערותה למטה מאד אין כאן איסור משום לבה רואה את הערוה ונראה ברור דגם הרא״ש ס״ל כמו הא״ח שהרי כתב הטור סימן זה משמו וז״ל וכ״כ א״א הרא״ש ז״ל כשפושטת מלבושיה כשעומדת בחלוקה תברך ותפשוט חלוקה ותטבל עכ״ל הרי שלא חש אלא לגלוי ערוה לחוד אבל כשלובשת חלוק די בכך אע״פ שאין הפסק בין לבה לערוה שכן דרך ההולכים בחלוק שהרי לא הצריך שיהיה אזור להפסיק אלא ברור דסבירא ליה כא״ח דלעיל שאין באשה משום לבה רואה ערוה ובזה מיושב לשון הטור שהאריך בדברי הרא״ש ולא כתב בקיצור וכ״כ א״א הרא״ש ז״ל כדרכו אלא דבר ברור כיון דלעיל מיניה כתב דברי הראב״ד דס״ל שתברך קודם טבילה ואם לא ברכה קודם טבילה צריכה לעכר המים והיינו ע״כ משום לבה רואה ערותה דלא ס״ל כא״ח דלעיל וכתב הטור שכ״כ הרא״ש לענין שתברך קודם טבילה סבירא ליה כהראב״ד דלא כר״י ובה״ג שכתבו שתברך אחר הטבילה אבל במה שכתב הראב״ד שצריכה לעכר המים בזה לא ס״ל להרא״ש כן אלא די בכך שבעוד חלוקה עליה תברך ולא חיישינן ללבה רואה ערותה וא״כ כיון שהא״ח והרא״ש ס״ל כן דבאשה אין שייך לבה רואה ערותה וכבר פסק כן בש״ע בא״ח סי׳ ע״ד מי ימחה ביד שום אשה שתסמוך על זה וכל שהיא במים אפילו [הם צלולים] ממילא נתכסה ערותה ועגבותיה כאילו היה עליה לבוש מלפניה ומאחריה ואין בה משום גילוי ערוה כמו שהוכחנו לעיל לא אכפת לן בלבה רואה ערותה אבל מ״מ ע״צ היותר טוב תעשה בחבוק ידים להפסיק בין לבה לערותה והיא בתוך המים יצאה ידי חובתה לד״ה ואע״ג שרמ״א כתב כאן שנוהגים לכסות בבגדה או בחלוקה אפשר שבימיו נהגו כן אבל עכשיו לא נהגו כן כמו שהעיד

בעל הדרישה אלא שכתב שלא יפה הם עושים וגם אנו שמענו שהנשים אינן נזהרין אפי' בחיבוק ידים בהפסק בין לב לערוה ונראה שגם זה אליבא דהלכתא אלא שלכתחלה יש לעשות חבוק ידים כמו שאמרנו דאין פקפוק על זה כנלע"ד.

תלמוד בבלי מסכת נדה דף יא עמוד ב – תניא נמי הכי: בד"א – לטהרות, אבל לבעלה – מותרת. בד"א – שהניחה בחזקת טהורה, אבל הניחה בחזקת טמאה – לעולם היא בטומאתה, עד שתאמר לו טהורה אני.

שולחן ערוך יורה דעה הלכות נדה סימן קפה סעיף א – האשה שהיא בחזקת טמאה, אסור לו לבא עליה עד שתאמר לו: טבלתי. הגה: ומאחר שעברו ימים שאפשר לה למנות ולטבול, נאמנת. אפילו רואה בגדים מלוכלכים בדם, נאמנת לומר, בשוק טבחים עברתי, או נתעסקתי בצפור וכדומה לזה.

ערוך השולחן יורה דעה הלכות נדה סימן קפה סעיף ד – בסי' הקודם נתבאר דכשהיה הבעל בדרך ובא מן הדרך כשהניחה טהורה אם יש זמן שהיתה יכולה ליטהר אחרי ימי טומאתה מותר לו לבא עליה בלא שאלה לדעת הטור והש"ע וזהו כשהניחה בחזקת טהורה אבל כשהניחה טמאה אפילו עברו ימים רבים אסור לו לבא עליה עד שתאמר לו טבלתי דהטומאה הוי וודאי והטהרה ספק ואין ספק מוציא מידי וודאי ויראה לי דלאו דווקא באומרת בפיה טבלתי אלא אפילו היא עושה דבר שמרמזת לו טבילתה כגון שנותנת לו חפץ מידה לידו דכשהיא טמאה אסור לעשות כן כמ"ש בסי' קצ"ה ג"כ מותר לו לבא עליה וראיתי מי שאומר דהאמירה מעכבת דאפילו באה ושוכבת אצלו לא מהני [ח"ד סק"ה] ולא ידעתי למה אטו האמירה מעכבת הלא העיקר רק לדעת אם נטהרה וכשהיא מרמזת לו דיו דכמדומני שבנות ישראל בושות לומר בפיהן טבלתי.

תלמוד בבלי מסכת שבת דף יד עמוד א – והבא ראשו ורובו במים שאובין, מאי טעמא גזרו ביה רבנן טומאה? אמר רב ביבי אמר רב אסי: שבתחלה היו טובלין במי מערות מכונסין וסרוחין, והיו נותנין עליהן מים שאובין, התחילו ועשאום קבע – גזרו עליהם טומאה. מאי קבע? – אמר אביי: שהיו אומרים: לא אלו מטהרין – אלא אלו ואלו מטהרין. אמר ליה רבא: מאי נפקא מינה? הא קא טבלי בהנך! אלא אמר רבא: שהיו אומרים לא אלו מטהרין – אלא אלו מטהרין.

שולחן ערוך יורה דעה הלכות מקואות סימן רא סעיף עה – יש מי שאוסר להטיל יורה מלאה מים חמין לתוך המקוה לחממו, וכן למלאת מקוה מים חמין ולחברו לנהר בשפופרת הנוד. הגה: ויש מקילין ומתירין להטיל חמין למקוה כדי לחממו (הגהות מרדכי דהל' נדה בשם ראבי"ה וריב"א). ומכל מקום יש להחמיר אם לא במקום שנהגו להקל, אז אין למחות בידן (בנימין זאב); ובחמי טבריא מותר לכולי עלמא (מרדכי בסוף שבועות). ולאחר הטבילה במי מקוה כשרים, מותרת ליכנס למרחץ כדי שתחמם עצמה (מרדכי); אבל לחזור ולרחוץ אח"כ, קנא יש אוסרים (מרדכי בשם ר' שבט), וכן נהגו.

הלכות מקוואות למרדכי (שבועות) רמז תשנ – שמעתי קורא תגר ומליזין על בנות ישראל הטובלות אם נכנסו אחר הטבילה במרחץ וכן כתב נמי רבינו שב"ט דלא עלתה לה טבילה וראייתם מי"ח דברים שגזרו על הבא ראשו ורובו במים שאובים לאחר טבילה משום שהיו אומרים לא אלו מטהרין אלא אלו מטהרין ורש"י ז"ל פי' התם הבא ראשו ורובו במים שאובים בו ביום של טבילה ובעניותי נראה לי דלא נפסלה הטבילה וקרוב הדבר בעיני דאפי' לכתחלה יכולה לרחוץ בתר טבילה לאלתר דההיא גזירה ליתא אלא דגזרו טומאה על המים שפוסלים (*אדם) [*האדם] שטבל כבר ונטהר וכן פי' רש"י ז"ל משמע מכאן [שאדם] דעלתה לו טבילה דכי גזרו על אדם שקבל טומאה אע"פ שאין משקה מטמא אדם והני מילי לענין לפסול התרומה [*כדתנן ואלו פוסלין את התרומה כו' אבל לחולין לא גזרו ובעלה כו' מ"י] ובעלה חולין הוא כדאמרינן פ' שני דשחיטת חולין גבי נדה שנאנסה וטבלה ע"כ לשון הרב והוא האריך וכן שמעתי ממהר"ם להתיר ולי הדיוט נראה דבמרחצאות שלנו של זיעה ליכא מאן דפליג דשרי אפי' לכתחלה ואפילו לתרומה לא גזור וזאת אשר השיב רבינו שמשון משנץ לר"י אחיו וז"ל אמרו לי שהיית רוצה להתיר למלא מקוה מים חמים ולחברו אל הנהר בשפופרת הנוד ודבר זה ראוי לאסור יותר משום גזירת מרחצאות דאמרינן פ"ב דנדה אמר רבא אשה לא תעמוד על גבי כלי חרס ותטבול סבר רב הונא למימר טעמא משום גזירת מרחצאות הא ע"ג סילתא [*פי' רש"י בקעת עץ] שפיר דמי וכ"ש שראוי כאן לגזור ולאסור.

ביאור הגר"א יורה דעה סימן רא – [קכז] ולאחר כו' אבל כו'. מפ"ק דשבת י"ד א' והבא ראשו כו' שבתחלה כו' לא אלו מטהרין אלא כו' משא"כ להזיע אבל כבר חלקו עליו דגזירה דשם אינו אלא לתרומה שיהא טמא לתרומה מד"ס אבל טבילתו עלתה לו אף לתרומה שאם שהה כמה ימים א"צ הערב שמש וכן טהור כו' וכ"ש לבעלה דבעלה חולין הוא כמ"ש בפ"ב דחולין (ל"א א') לענין כוונה שהוא מהמעלות שגזרו רבנן לתרומה כמ"ש בפ"ב דחגיגה ע"ש.

שו"ת שבט הלוי חלק ה סימן קכה – יקרתו קבלתי ואשיב בקצור, א. עמד בין המבואר סו"ס ר"א ביו"ד דיש אוסרים שהאשה אחרי טבילתה תרחוץ במים וכן נהגו ע"כ, וכב' נשאל כמה זמן אחרי הטבילה אסורה לרחוץ אם רק סמוך לטבילה או כל הלילה אפילו בביתה, וגזירה זו נובעת מדמיון אשה לבעלה לתרומה בשבת י"ד דגזרו ע"ז שלא יאמרו לא אלו מטהרין אלא אלו מטהרין, ושמה פרש"י דגזרו שלא תרחוץ כל היום וכן הביא ממה דאיתא באו"ז הגדול בסי' תשמ"ה וסי' תשל"ח דדעת רבינו האו"ז דאשה שטבלה כל היום אסורה ליכנס למרחץ, ואמנם מרש"י כ' כב' אין ראי' דטבלו ביום סמוך לערב ע"כ אסורה עד שתטהר בלילה, אבל באשה שטובלת בלילה קשה לומר כן, וכי לדעת האו"ז נאסור אותה כל היום, את"ד מע"כ.

אמנם לדידי יראה בעניי דאינה אסורה רק סמוך לטבילה בלבד דכשנכנסה כבר לביתה אע"פ שאינה משמשת עד מאוחר בלילה מכ"מ כיון שבעלה נוגע בה א"כ כבר הואילה הטבילה, וא"כ גם אם תרחץ אח"כ בביתה איך אפשר לומר לא אלו מטהרין אלא אלו מטהרין הלא כבר עשתה הטבילה את שלה, וכן בשאר ראשונים במרדכי נזכר רק אחרי טבילתה, ולשון זה באו"ז אם הוא דוקא משכחת לה באשה הטובלת ביום כגון ביום הח' לצורך או באופנים רחוקים שהתירו

הפוסקים גם ביום ז׳ כמבואר סו״ס קצ״ז בב״ח וקס״ט באופן זה שאסורה לבעלה עד הלילה יש דמיון שלם לתרומה, וכן פשוט לי דאם אחרי שהיתה כבר בביתה עסקה בתוך הבית בדברים שיכולים ללכלך אותה ורחצה אח״כ דלא שייך גזרה זו אלא כשנכנסת למרחץ בלי סבה, ואמנם גם את״ל דרבינו האו״ז מחמיר בכל אופן כיון דשאר הראשונים לית להו בכלל איסור זה, וגם אלו שאית להו לא הזכירו בדבריהם רק סמוך לטבילה, אין לנו להחמיר בדבר זה, ועיין בברכי יוסף דנטה ג״כ להקל.

Bibliography

List of Sources Cited

Dates and cities listed refer to one edition, not necessarily the first or the most recent. Some dates are approximated from the Hebrew dates. An indented listing is a commentary to the work listed immediately before it.

A. THE TALMUD AND COMMENTARIES – *RISHONIM, ACHARONIM,* AND CODES OF MITZVOT AND HALAKHIC CODES OF *RISHONIM*

Arukh Li-Ner. R. Ya'akov Etlinger. Novellae to several tractates, Jerusalem, 1962. Author of *Responsa Binyan Tziyyon.*

Bartenura. R. Ovadiah of Bartenura (ca. 1450–1510). Commentary to the *Mishnah,* printed in standard editions of the *Mishnah.*

Kovetz He'arot. R. Elchanan Bunim Wasserman (1875–1941). Talmudical lectures on *Massekhet Yevamot.* A student of R. Yisrael Meir Kagan and *Rosh Yeshiva* of the Yeshiva of Baranovitz.

Maharsha, Chiddushei Aggadot, and *Chiddushei Halakhot.* R Shmuel Eidels (1555–1631).

Meiri. R. Menachem ben Shlomo HaMeiri (1249–1316), of Provence,

France. Talmudic comments in *Chiddushei HaMeiri* and *Beit HaBechirah*.

Mordechai. R. Mordechai ben Hillel HaKohen (1240–1298) of Germany. In Vilna editions.

Or Zarua. R. Yitzchak ben Moshe (d. 1260) of Vienna. Also known as Riaz.

Ra'avad. R. Avraham ben David (see Section B). Commentary to the *Rif* and to *Torat Kohanim*.

Ramban. R. Moshe ben Nachman (Nachmanides, 1194–1270) of Verona, Italy. Also authored *Chiddushim* to the Torah and many other works.

Ran. Rabbeinu Nissim Gerondi (1290–1375) of Barcelona. Also authored *Derashot HaRan*. His comments are written directly to the Talmud as well as to the code of the *Rif*. In Vilna editions.

Rash. R. Shimshon ben Avraham of Sens (c. 1150–1230). Commentary to *mishnayot* in *Zeraim* and *Taharot*.

Rashba. R. Shlomo ben Aderet (1235–1310) of Barcelona. Also authored many volumes of responsa.

Rashbam. R. Shmuel ben Meir (c. 1085–1158). Grandson of Rashi, Also authored commentary to the Torah. Printed in standard editions of the Talmud, tractates *Bava Batra* and *Pesachim*.

Rashi. R. Shlomo ben Yitzchak (Yitzchaki) (1040–1105) of Troyes, France. Preeminent Biblical and talmudical commentator; also authored responsa.

Rif. R. Yitzchak Al Fasi (1013–1103) of Fez, Morocco. Authored a code of the halakhically relevant portions of the Talmud.

Ritva. R. Yom Tov ben Ishbilli (1250–1330). Also authored responsa.

Rosh. Rabbeinu Asher ben Yechiel (1250–1327), Germany. Code to halakhically relevant sections of the Talmud, and running commentary to *Massekhet Nedarim*.

Ma'adanei Yom Tov. R. Yom Tov Lipman Heller (1578–1654), author of *Tosafot Yom Tov* to the *mishnayot*.

Sefer HaAguddah. R. Alexander Suslin HaKohen. 14th century, Germany. Halakhic commentary to the Talmud.

Sefer HaEshkol. R. Avraham ben Yitzchak (c. 1110–1179) of Narbonne.

Sefer HaManhig, R. Avraham ben Natan HaYarchi (12th century).

Sefer HaMitzvot Le-HaRambam. R. Moshe ben Maimon; printed with most editions of the Mishneh Torah.

Ramban. R. Moshe ben Nachman (Nachmanides; see above). In standard editions. Includes additional mitzvot the Rambam omits.

Sefer HaTerumah. R. Baruch ben Yitzchak (11th–12th century) of Worms and Regensburg.

Sefer Mitzvot Katan. R. Yitzchak ben Yosef (d. 1280) of Corbell. Also known as the *Smak* and *Amudei HaGolah.*

Sefer Yereim. R. Eliezer of Metz (ca 1115–1198). A discussion of the *mitzvot* following the listings of R. Yehudai Gaon and the *Ba'al Halakhot Gedolot,* divided into seven *amudim* (pillars). A French tosafist and student of Rabbenu Tam.

She'iltot D'Rav Achai Gaon. R. Achai MiShabcha (680–760).

Talmidei Rabbenu Yonah. R. Yonah of Gerondi, d. 1263, author of *Sha'arei Teshuvah.* Commentary to *Massekhet Berakhot,* written in his name by students.

Tosafot. Talmudic comments of eleventh- and twelfth-century French and German scholars, printed alongside the text in the Vilna Talmud.

B. THE RAMBAM (MAIMONIDES)'S MISHNEH TORAH AND COMMENTARIES

R. Moshe ben Maimon (1135–1284), known as the Rambam or as Maimonides, authored a codification of the laws in the Talmud, entitled *Mishneh Torah,* or *Yad HaChazakah.* The latter name is a reference to the organization of the work, which is arranged in fourteen volumes (the numerical value of the word *Yad* is fourteen). The following works are commentaries to the Rambam's code.

Chiddushei Rabbenu Chaim HaLevi. R. Chaim Soloveichik (1853–1918) of Brisk. Innovator of the "Brisker" style of analysis. Brisk, 1936.

Hagahot Maimoniyot. R. Moshe HaKohen (d. 1298). Notes citing earlier authorities.

Hasagot HaRa'avad. R. Avraham ben David (1120–1197) of Posquieres. Also authored commentaries to the *Rif* and the *Sifra,* and the *Ba'alei HaNefesh* to the laws of *Niddah.* In standard editions of the *Mishneh Torah.*

Kiryat Sefer. R. Moshe MiTrani. New York, 1966.
Maggid Mishnah. R. Vidal Yom Tov (d. 1370) of Tolosa. In standard editions.

C. THE TUR AND SHULCHAN ARUKH AND COMMENTARIES

R Ya'akov ben Asher (ca. 1270–1340; son of the Rosh; see Section B) of Germany and Toledo, Spain, authored a codification of Jewish law entitled the *Arba'ah Turim* (the "four rows"; see Exodus 28:17), so named as it is divided into four sections: *Orach Chayim,* covering daily life, prayer, and festivals; *Even HaEzer,* on marital law; *Choshen Mishpat,* on civil law; and *Yoreh Deah,* covering the remaining areas of Jewish law, such as *kashrut, niddah,* mourning, vows, and other topics. Two centuries later, R. Yosef Karo (1488–1575), who authored the commentary *Beit Yosef* to the *Turim* (as well as *Kessef Mishneh* to *Mishneh Torah*), earned the title "the *Mechaber*" ("the Author") with his *Shulchan Arukh* ("set table"), which followed the organization of the *Turim* and took into account the rulings of the Rif, the Rosh, and the Rambam. However, the rulings are reflective primarily of the Sephardic background of their author, a fact rectified by R. Moshe Isserles (1520–1572), known as the Rama and author of *Darkhei Moshe* to the *Turim,* who wrote glosses, known as *Mappah* ("tablecloth"), to the *Shulchan Arukh,* representing Ashkenazic practice. Together with the Rama's glosses, the *Shulchan Arukh* has become accepted as the standard text of Jewish law, and the titles listed below are commentaries to that work (or the *Turim,* when indicated as such).

Arukh HaShulchan. R. Yechiel Michel Epstein (1829–1908), comprehensive code on all sections of the *Shulchan Arukh,* adding *Arukh HaShulchan HeAtid* to those areas not covered (ritual impurity, laws of agriculture relevant only in the land of Israel, sacrificial order, etc.). Warsaw, 1900–1912. Rav of Novardok and father of *Torah Temimah* (see *Responsa Benei Banim* II, 8, for a citation of the halakhic authority R. Yosef Eliyahu Henkin concerning the special qualities of this code).

Badei HaShulchan. R. Feivel Cohen (contemporary). Commentary to sections of *Shulchan Arukh Yoreh Deah.* Brooklyn, NY :Rabbi Jacob Joseph School Press, 1999.

Bayit Chadash (*Bach*). R. Yoel Sirkes (1561–1640), Poland. Commentary to the *Tur*; also author of responsa (see later entries) and Talmudic emendations. Rav of Belz, Brest-Litovsk, and Krakow, and father-in-law of *Turei Zahav*.

Be'er Ha-Golah. R. Moshe Rivkes of Vilna. In standard editions.

Biur HaGra. R. Eliyahu ben Shlomo Zalman (1720–1797). Towering scholar known as the *Gaon* of Vilna, or *Gra* (an acronym for *Gaon R. Eliyahu*). Author of more than eighty works.

Chavot Da'at. R. Ya'akov Loerbaum (1760–1832) of Lisa, Poland; author of *Netivot HaMishpat* and many other works. To *Shulchan Arukh Yoreh Deah*,

Chazon Ish. R. Avraham Yeshayah Karelitz (1878–1953), Bnei Brak, Israel. This seven-volume halakhic work actually combines the sections of the Talmud and the *Shulchan Arukh* and defies easy categorization. Bnei Brak, 1958. Also authored *Emunah UBitachon*.

Chiddushei R. Akiva Eiger (see section G). Compiled in several editions, printed in various editions of the *Shulchan Arukh*.

Dagul MeRevavah. R. Yechezkel Landau (1713–1793) Rav of Prague and a leading authority of his time, he also authored *Responsa Noda Bi-Yehudah* and *Tziyyun LeNefesh Chayyah* (*Tzlach*) to the Talmud.

Derishah and *Perishah*. R. Yehoshua Falk (1555–1614), of Lublin, Poland, and Lemberg, Germany. Commentaries to *Tur*. Also author of *Meirat Einayim* to *Shulchan Arukh*.

Machatzit HaShekel. R. Shmuel HaLevi of Kellin. To *Hilkhot Niddah* and *Melichah*. In standard editions.

Matteh Yehonatan. R. Yonatan Eibshutz (1690–1764) of Krakow and Altona, author of *Kereiti U'Pleiti, Urim VeTumim, Ya'arot Devash* and other works. Commentary to *Yoreh Deah*.

Mishnah Berurah. R. Yisrael Meir Kagan (1838–1933) of Radin. Commentary to the *Orach Chaim* section of the *Shulchan Arukh*, evaluating the positions of earlier authorities and arriving at conclusions. Includes the more in-depth *Biur Halakhah* and the *Sha'ar HaTziyyun*, listing sources. One of the preeminent ethical authorities of the late eighteenth and early nineteenth centuries, he authored *Chafetz Chaim* (a name he came himself to be identified with) and *Ahavat Chesed* (see individual listings) as well as many other works, including *Likkutei Halakhot,* a three-part commentary to the talmudical order *Kodoshim,* written in the style of *Mishnah Berurah.*

Pitchei Teshuvah. R. Avraham Zvi Eisenstadt (1813–1868), of Kovno. Summary of responsa arranged according to the order of *Shulchan Arukh.*

Peri Megadim. R. Yosef Teomim (1727–1792). Supercommentary to *Shulchan Arukh* commentaries, including *Aishel Avraham* to *Magen Avraham* and *Mishbetzot Zahav* to *Turei Zahav.* Author of several other works, such as *Teivat Gomeh, Petichah HaKollelet, Shoshannat HaAmakim,* and *Matan Sekharan Shel Mitzvot* (see individual listings), and *Responsa Megadim.*

Shulchan Arukh HaRav. R. Shneur Zalman of Liadi (1745–1833). First Rebbe of Lubavitch (Chabad) and author of the *Tania.*

Sidrei Taharah (*Hilkhot Niddah*) and *Shiyurei Taharah* (*Hilkhot Tevilah*). R. Elchanan Ashkenazi (18th Cent.) Commentary to *Shulchan Arukh* printed in standard editions.

Siftei Kohen (*Shakh*). R. Shabtai HaKohen (1621–1662) In standard editions. Also authored a commentary to the Torah.

Torat HaShelamim. R. Ya'akov Reisher (1670–1733). Lemberg: Salant, 1897. Rav of Prague and other cities, author of *Responsa Shevut Ya'akov.* Commentary to *Yoreh Deah.* In standard editions.

Turei Zahav (*Taz*). R. David ben Shmuel HaLevi (1586–1667) of Krakow, Poland. Also authored a commentary to the Torah.

Nekudat HaKesef. Critiques of the *Shakh* to *Turei Zahav.*

D. COLLECTIONS OF RESPONSA AND HALAKHIC AND TALMUDIC ESSAYS

The following works are either responsa, written to answer halakhic inquiries, or collections of essays on topics of halakhic and Talmudic analysis. The titles of the works of responsa are generally preceded by the term *She'alot U'Teshuvot* ("Questions and Answers"), translated in the text as Responsa and omitted in this listing.

Achiezer. R. Chaim Ozer Grodzenski (1863–1940). Three volumes. Vol. 1, Vilna, 1922; vol. 3, New York, 1946. Chief Rabbi of Vilna and leading halakhic authority of the pre-World War II era.

R. Akiva Eiger. R. Akiva Eiger (1761–1837) of Eisenstadt, Austria, and Posen, Poland. Two volumes of responsa. New York, 1945. One of the leading halakhic authorities of his time, he also authored glosses to *Shulchan Arukh,* as well as the talmudic works *Chiddushim, Derush V'Chiddush,* and *Gilyon HaShas.*

Avodat HaGershuni. R. Gershon Ashkenazi (d. 1693) of Czechoslavakia. Lvov, 1861.

Be'er Moshe. R. Moshe Stern of Debretzin. Brooklyn: Balshon, 1973.

Chacham Tzvi. R. Tzvi Ashkenazi (1660–1718). Rav of Amsterdam, Netherlands, and other cities. Father of R. Ya'akov Emden.

Chatam Sofer. R. Moshe Sofer (1763–1830). Responsa to the four sections of *Shulchan Arukh* and additional volumes. Vienna, 1855. Rav of Pressburg and one of the leading halakhic authorities of his time, he became the son-in-law of R. Akiva Eiger and ancestor to a long line of rabbinic scholars, beginning with his son *Ketav Sofer.* Also authored *chiddushim* to the Talmud and *Shulchan Arukh,* and *Torat Moshe* to the Torah.

Devar Avraham. R. Avraham Dov Ber Cahana Shapiro (1870–1943) of Kovno. Jerusalem, 1968.

Galya Massekhet. R. David ben Moshe (1796–1836) of Novardok , Vilna, Defus Menachem Man V'Simchah Zemel, 1844.

Ginat Egoz. R. Hershel Schachter. Essays on Talmudic Topics. Flatbush Beth Hamedrash, NY, NY, 2007. *Rosh Yeshiva* and *Rosh Kollel* at Yeshivat Rabbenu Yitzchak Elchanan, and author of *Eretz HaTzvi* and *Bi-Ikvei HaTzon.*

Har Tzvi. R. Tzvi Pesach Frank (1873–1960). Responsa to *Orach Chaim* and *Yoreh Deah,* with a section on *Z'raim* (agricultural law). Chief Rabbi of Jerusalem; his ideas appear as well in the multivolumed *Mikraei Kodesh,* and other works, such as *Haderat Kodesh* and *Mikdash Melekh,* and glosses to later works such as *Minchat Chinnukh* and *Or Sameach.*

Iggerot Moshe. R. Moshe Feinstein (1895–1986) of Luban, Poland, and New York, NY. Eight volumes of responsa, beginning in 1961, New York. Considered one of the leading authorities of the late twentieth century, he was *Rosh Yeshiva* of Mesivta Tiferet Yerushalayim in the Lower East Side of Manhattan and also authored *Dibrot Moshe* to several volumes of the Talmud.

Ketav Sofer. R. Avraham Shmuel Binyamin Sofer (1815–1871). Pressburg, 1873. Son of the *Chatam Sofer,* he also authored *chiddushim* to the Torah and to the tractate *Chullin.*

Kinyan Torah Ba-Halakhah. R. Avraham David Horowitz of Strassburg, France, and later a rabbinical court judge in Jerusalem. Eight volumes.

Kovetz Teshuvot. R. Yosef Shalom Elyashiv (contemporary) Collected writings. 3 volumes. Jerusalem, 2000.

Maharam Shick. R. Moshe Shick (1807–1879). Muncacz, 1881. Rav of Chust and student of *Chatam Sofer.*

Maharil. R. Ya'akov Molin (d. 1427) Brooklyn: Unger, 1965.

Maharshal. R. Shlomo Luria (1510–1574) Prague, 1715. Known as *Maharshal,* he also authored the talmudic commentary *Yam Shel Shelomo* and *Chokhemat Shelomo.*

Maharsham. R. Shalom Mordechai Shwadron (1835–1911), Galicia. Also authored *Da'at Torah.*

Me'il Tzedakah. R. Yehudah Lansdorfer (1678–1712). Sedilkov, 1835.

Minchat Shelomoh. R. Shlomo Zalman Auerbach (1910–1995). Jerusalem: Sha'arei Ziv, 1986. *Rosh Yeshiva* of *Yeshivat Kol Torah* of Jerusalem and considered one of the leading authorities of his time. Also authored *Meorei Esh* to the laws of electricity on *Shabbat,* and *Ma'adanei Aretz.*

Minchat Yitzchak. R. Yitzchak Weiss (1902–1989). Ten volumes of responsa. London, 1955. Rabbinical court judge in Manchester, England, and later Rav of *Edah HaChareidis* in Jerusalem.

Nachlat Shivah. R. Shmuel ben David Moshe Halevi (ca. 1625–1681). Amsterdam, 1667.

Noda BiYehudah. R. Yechezkel Landau. Responsa according to the four sections of the *Shulchan Arukh,* in two editions, *Mahadura Kama* and *Tinyana.* Vilna, 1904. See *Dagul MeRevavah,* Section D.

Radbaz. R. David ben Zimra (1479–1573), Chief Rabbi of Egypt. Warsaw, 1862. Also authored commentary to *Mishneh Torah.*

Rashba. R. Shlomo ben Aderet (see Section B).

Rosh. R. Ashen ben Yechiel.

Sefer HaYashar. Responsa of Rabbenu Tam (R. Ya'akov ben Meir, ca. 1100-1171), one of the foremost Tosafists.

She'eilat Ya'avetz. R. Ya'akov Emden (1697–1776) of Altona. Altona, 1739.

Also authored *chiddushim* to the Talmud and *Mor U'Ketziah* to *Shulchan Arukh*.

Shevet HaLevi. R. Shmuel HaLevi Vosner (1913–). Bnei Brak, 1969.

Tashbetz. R. Shimon ben Tzemach Duran. Amsterdam, 1739. See *Zohar HaRakia*, Section C.

Terumat HaDeshen. R. Yisrael Isserlein (1390–1460) of Germany.

Tzemach Tzedek. Responsa of R. Menachem Mendel Schneerson (1784–1866), third *rebbe* of Lubavitch and grandson of the *Ba'al HaTania*. New York: Otzar HaChasidim, 1994

Tzitz Eliezer. R. Eliezer Yehudah Waldenberg (1917–2006). Twenty-one volumes, beginning Jerusalem, 1944. Includes dedicated sections such as "*Ramat Rachel*" and "*Even Yaakov*" on the laws of visiting the sick and of mourning.

Zikhron Yosef. R. Yosef Steinhard (1720–1776) of Germany. Fuerth , 1773.

E. WORKS OF *HALAKHAH*

Ba'alei HaNefesh. R. Avraham ben David of Posquieres, author of *Hasagot HaRa'avad* on the *Mishneh Torah*. Printed with glosses of R. Zerachiah HaLevi, and *Hilkhot Niddah* of the Ramban (See Section regarding all of the above). Jerusalem, 1960.

Chayyei Adam and *Chokhmat Adam*. R. Avraham Danzig (1748–1820), Vilna. Work of *halakhah* relevant to *Orach Chaim* and *Yoreh Deah* sections, respectively, of *Shulchan Arukh*.

Chok U-Zeman. R. Avraham Yehoshua Heshel Bleich. To the laws of *Niddah* and *Tevilah*. With sources and elucidations in the section entitled *Chok U-Mishpat*. Kiryat Sefer: 2002.

Lechem Ve-Simlah. R. Shlomo Gantzfried (1804–1886), Author of *Kitzur Shulchan Arukh*. Commentary to *Shulchan Arukh, Hilkhot Niddah*. Jerusalem: Wagshal, 1980.

Mishmeret HaTaharah. R. Moshe Mordechai Karp (contemporary). To *Hilkhot Niddah*. Kiryat Sefer, 2003.

Nishmat Avraham. Rabbi Abraham S. Abraham. Multi-volume work on medical *halakhah*. Jerusalem, 2007.

Sedei Chemed. R Chaim Chizkiyahu Medini (1832–1904) of Constantinople. Extensive ten-volume collection of halakhic essays, including citations of many contemporaries of the author.

Shiurei Shevet HaLevi. Commentary and lectures to *Hilkhot Niddah* from R. Shmuel HaLevi Wosner, author of *Responsa Shevet HaLevi.* Bnei Brak, 1998.

Ta Chazi. R. David Chazan (contemporary). Compendium on the laws of evaluating the colors of blood. Israel, 1995.

Taharat Bat Yisrael. R. Kalman Kahane (b. 1910). To *Hilkhot Niddah.* Tel Aviv, 1954.

Taharat HaBayit. R. Ovadiah Yosef, former Sefardic Chief Rabbi of Israel and author of *Responsa Yabbia Omer* and *Yechave Da'at.* Two volume work on *Hilkhot Niddah.* Jerusalem, 1987.

Torat HaBayit. Rashba (see Section A.) on parts of Jewish law including *Hilkhot Niddah*; including *Bedek HaBayit,* critiques by the Ra'ah (R. 'Aharon HaLevi of Barcelona); and *Mishmeret HaBayit.* Responses of the Rashba to the *Bedek HaBayit.*

F. JOURNALS AND OTHER WORKS

Much halakhic discussion is found in periodical journals, often published by *yeshivot* or rabbinical organizations. For journals, years listed represent the inititiation of the publication.

Beit Yitzchak. A Publication Devoted to Studies in *Halakhah* by the *Rebbeim* and *Talmidim* [Faculty and Students] of Yeshiva University. Published by the Rabbi Isaac Elchanan Theological Seminary and Student Organization of Yeshiva, 1952.

Kol Tzvi. A Compendium of Essays in Talmudic Studies published by the Bella and Harry Wexner Kollel Elyon and Semikhah Honors Program, Rabbi Isaac Elchanan Theological Seminary, 1999.

Melo Ha-Ro'im. R. Ya'akov Tzvi ben Naftali Jolles (ca. 1778–1825). Collection of halakhic rulings, disputations, and principles. Warsaw, 1854

Meshekh Chokhmah. R. Meir Simchah HaKohen (1843–1926). of Dvinsk. Jerusalem, 1974. Author of *Or Sameach* on the Rambam's *Mishneh Torah.* Commentary to the Torah.

Machzor Vitri. R Simchah ben Shmuel of Vitri (d. 1105). Compilation of liturgy and halakhic rulings, including responsa and rulings of Rashi.

Noam. A Forum for the Clarification of Contemporary Halakhic Problems. Makhon Torah Shelemah, 1958.

Pe'er HaDor. Biographical notes regarding R. Avraham Yesahya Karelitz, the *Chazon Ish*. Bnei Brak, 1966.

Shnei Luchot HaBrit. R. Yeshayahu Horowitz (1565–1630). Jerusalem: *Zikhron Yehudah*, 1993. Work of *halakhah* and Jewish thought.

Glossary

Acharonim: Later Rabbinic authorities, understood as those coming after the publication of the *Shulchan Arukh* of R. Yosef Karo (d. 1575)
Agunot: (lit. chained) women whose unresolved marital status prevents them from remarrying
Arayot: forbidden sexual relationships
Asham talui: a guilt offering specifically for situations when the occurrence of a sin is in doubt
Aveilut: period of mourning

Ba'al keri: one who experienced a nocturnal emission
Bayit ha-chitzon: (lit. outer house) the vaginal area
Bayit ha-penimi: (lit. inner house) the uterine area
Bediavad: after the fact
Bedikah: internal examination
Bein ha-shemashot: twilight, the period after sunset and before nightfall
Beit HaMikdash: The Holy Temple in Jerusalem

Chatzitzah: an intervening object
Chazal: "our Sages of blessed memory", the Rabbis of the Talmudic era

Dam chimud: (lit. blood of desire) uterine bleeding presumed to accompany the finalization of marriage plans

Dam koshi : bleeding related to the birthing process

Gris: a bean (approximately the size of a penny)

Halakhah: Jewish law
Harchakot: lit. "separations", precautionary measures taken during the time of *niddut* to prevent forbidden intercourse
Hargashah: physical sensation
Ha'ara'ah: the initial stage of intercourse

Kareit: Divine capital punishment
Kiruv basar: physical contact
Korban: sacrificial offering
Ke'aiv: an experience of discomfort or irritation
Keri: nocturnal emission
Ketem: blood stain; possible indication of *niddut*

Lo ikba issura: a case where no prohibition is established, where the very presence of a forbidden item is uncertain.
Lo pelug: (lit. no distinction) an across-the-board policy of no exceptions

Miktzat ha-yom ki-kulo: the principle by which any significant component of a day can count as the full day
Mikveh: a ritual bath
Milta de-lo shekhicha: an uncommon occurrence, typically not included in precautionary enactments

Niddah: menstruant, in halakhic terms
Niddut: menstrual state, in halakhic terms
Niftach pi ha-mekor: the mouth of the uterus is opened

Peru u-rvu: the Biblical commandment to populate the world through procreation
Poskim: decisors of Jewish law

Re'iyat dam: a sighting of blood

Ro'ah dam machamat tashmish: one who sees blood as a result of intercourse

Rov: a majority

Safek D'Orayta le-chumra: the principle which states that any uncertain situations must be handled stringently when dealing with matters of Biblical origin

Sfek sfeika: (lit. a double uncertainty) a situation where there are two unknown factors, either of which is capable of providing basis for leniency, and thus there is room for leniency even in matters of Biblical origin

Shivah nekiyim: seven clean days with no sighting of blood; Biblically mandated for a *zavah gedolah,* and in practice observed for a *niddah*

Shomeret yom keneged yom: one who watches "a day for a day", i.e. one who must observe one clean day for the previous day on which she saw blood

Sotah: a wayward (i.e. adulterous) woman

Tahor: pure; in this usage, not a cause of *niddah* status

Tehorah: ritually pure; in this usage, not a *niddah*

Teliyah (lit. "hanging"), the ability to be *toleh* (lit. "hang") the spot of blood on a source other than the one that would make a woman *teme'ah*

Tamei: impure; in this usage, a cause of *niddah* status

Teme'ah: ritually impure; in this usage, having the status of a *niddah*

Terumah: portion of produce given to the *kohanim*; may only be eaten by members of a *kohen*'s household, and may only be eaten in a state of ritual purity

Tzara'at: a physical affliction that causes a state of ritual impurity

Veset: a time when one's period is expected based on a previously established pattern

Yichud: seclusion

Yoledet: new mother

Zavah gedolah: a woman who experiences a flow of blood not associated with her menstrual cycle for three or more consecutive days; *shivah nekiyim* are Biblically required

Zavah ketanah: a woman who experiences a flow of blood not associated with her menstrual cycle for one or two days; *shivah nekiyim* are not Biblically required

Zivah: flow

Zivat davar lach: the sensation of moisture emerging from the body

Index

Y

Z

About the Author

Rabbi Zvi Sobolofsky is a *Rosh Yeshiva* at Yeshiva University. After studying at Yeshivat Kerem B'Yavneh and Yeshiva University, he attended RIETS and then the Azrieli Graduate School of Jewish Education and Administration where he obtained a master's degree in 1996. He was appointed to his current position in the spring of 2002. In addition to teaching Talmud, Jewish law, Jewish thought and ethics, Rabbi Sobolofsky serves as the spiritual leader of Congregation Ohr HaTorah in Bergenfield, NJ and is a lecturer at the Bnai Yeshurun Beis Medrash Program in Teaneck, NJ. He is the author of the book *Reishit Koach,* on *Massekhet Bekhorot* as well as many journal articles.

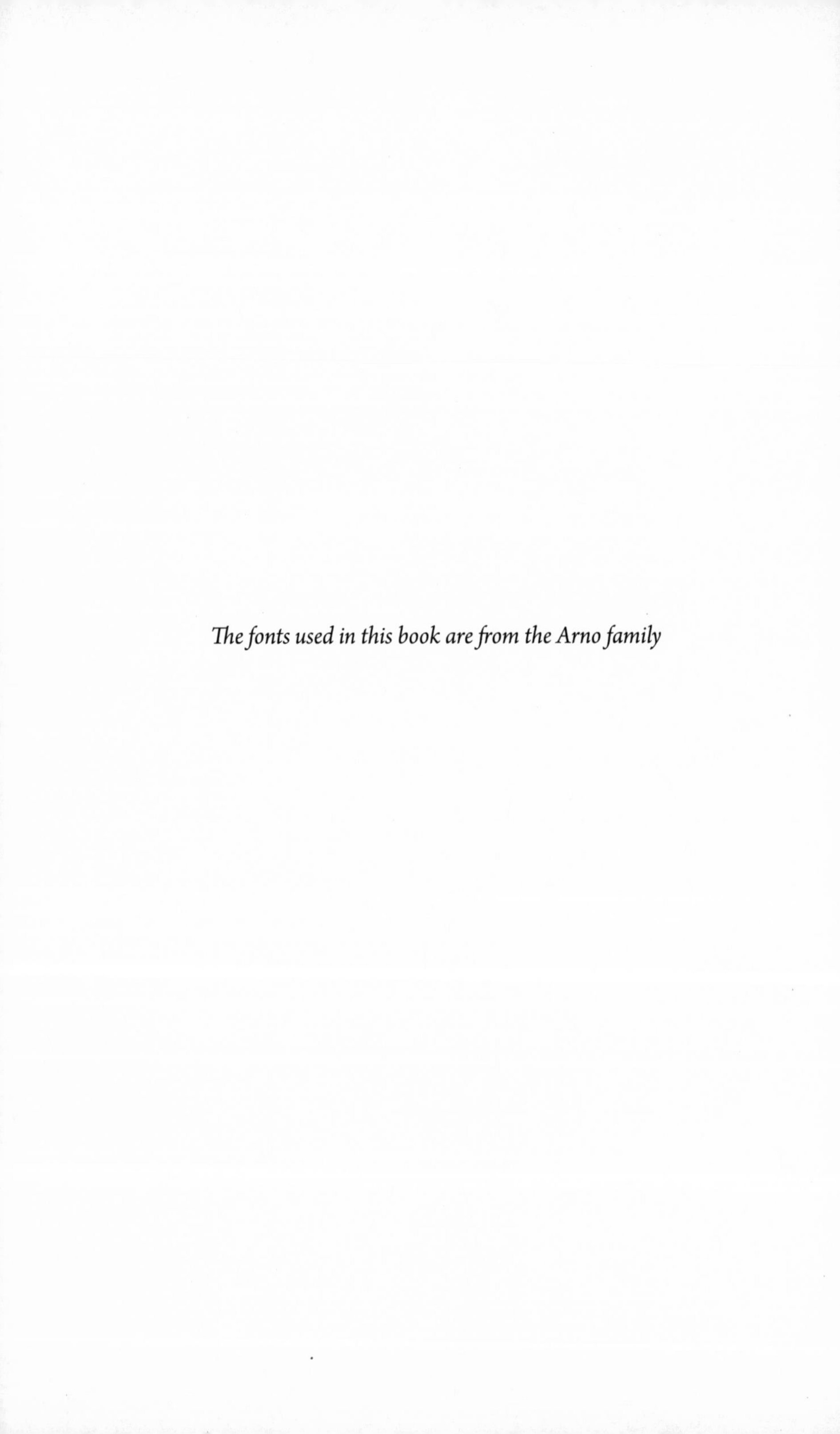

The fonts used in this book are from the Arno family

Maggid Books
The best of contemporary Jewish thought from
Koren Publishers Jerusalem Ltd.